Southern Elections
County and Precinct Data, 1950–1972

Southern Elections

County and Precinct Data, 1950–1972

NUMAN V. BARTLEY and
HUGH D. GRAHAM

Louisiana State University Press

Baton Rouge and London

Library of Congress Cataloging in Publication Data

Bartley, Numan V
    Southern elections.

    1. Elections--Southern States. I. Graham, Hugh
Davis, joint author. II. Title.
JK1967.B37   329'.023'7504   78-5525
ISBN 0-8071-0278-4

CONTENTS

Preface and Acknowledgments   vii

Introduction   ix

I   COUNTY ELECTION DATA

    Alabama   3

    Arkansas   29

    Florida   59

    Georgia   93

    Louisiana   121

    Mississippi   141

    North Carolina   169

    South Carolina   201

    Tennessee   217

    Texas   241

    Virginia   325

II PRECINCT ELECTION DATA

    Alabama   345

    Arkansas   351

    Florida   354

    Georgia   361

    Louisiana   366

    Mississippi   374

    North Carolina   377

    South Carolina   383

    Tennessee   389

    Texas   393

    Virginia   403

MAPS

Alabama	2
Arkansas	28
Florida	58
Georgia	92
Louisiana	120
Mississippi	140
North Carolina	168
South Carolina	200
Tennessee	216
Texas	240
Virginia	324

PREFACE AND ACKNOWLEDGMENTS

When we began this project we thought it would be a relatively simple undertaking. We already had in machine-readable form the bulk of the data reproduced on the following pages, and all that seemed to remain was filling in a limited number of missing elections, preparing an appropriate format, checking the data for errors, and writing introductory material. We soon learned once again, however, that manipulating masses of data is not a simple chore. If nothing else, this project vastly increased our respect for Walter Dean Burnham, Paul T. David, Alexander Heard, Donald S. Strong, Richard M. Scammon, and other compilers who have cataloged and presented election data often more difficult to acquire than the data reported here and who in some cases had access to less sophisticated hardware than was available to us.

In preparing this volume we accumulated a number of debts. We wish to express our thanks to Bernard Wess, Associate Director of Data Processing at UMBC; to Charles Bowen, the long-suffering programmer/analyst, who designed the programs for producing the data; to Irene DuMais, who cleaned the data; and to Jimmy Kilgore, a University of Georgia graduate student, who performed in good spirits the onerous task of checking the data for errors. We, of course, accept the responsibility for those mistakes that remain.

INTRODUCTION

This volume is designed to accomplish a dual purpose. The first is to make available in a convenient form election statistics not collected elsewhere. In this regard we have designed the book to fit into the existing literature. A quarter of a century ago, Alexander Heard and Donald S. Strong compiled Southern Primaries and Elections, 1920-1949 (University: University of Alabama Press, 1950). Both Heard and Strong were associated with V. O. Key, Jr., and the research project that led to the publication of Southern Politics in State and Nation by Alfred A. Knopf in 1949; and their data book contained the election statistics accumulated as the analytical base for Key's modern classic.

Our book begins with the 1950 primary elections and is conceived as a continuation of Southern Primaries and Elections, 1920-1949. These two volumes contain the county-level results of major primary elections and pertinent referenda for the eleven states of the former Confederacy from 1920 to 1972. General election returns by county are not included in this volume, since these are available for the post-World War II years in Richard M. Scammon (comp.), America Votes: A Handbook of Contemporary American Election Statistics (11 vols.; Washington, D.C.: Governmental Affairs Institute, 1956-1975). Scammon has also compiled America at the Polls: A Handbook of American Presidential Election Statistics, 1920-1964 (Pittsburgh: University of Pittsburgh Press, 1965).

The second purpose of this book is a broader one. Unlike the other collections mentioned above, this volume includes basic demographic and geographic analysis. The returns are, of course, reported by county, with the number and percentage of votes received by each candidate and the statewide totals and percentages. But they are additionally aggregated into categories. Demographically, there are metropolitan, town, and rural categories for each state. Specifically, metropolitan counties are those that contained in 1960 all or part of a city of more than 50,000 population, as well as suburban Jefferson Parish in Louisiana and Chesterfield County in Virginia. Town counties contained a city of 20,000 to 50,000 people in 1960. Rural counties are those with no urban community of 20,000 population.

Geographically, the counties in each state are grouped into recognized sectional divisions. The general groupings are mountain, piedmont, black belt, and lowland. The mountain category includes the southern Appalachian counties, the Arkansas Ozark and Ouachita counties, and a number of "traditionally Republican" highland counties. The piedmont counties are those located between the Appalachian Mountains and the fall line, excluding any county containing a 1960 black population of 40 percent or more. The black belt classification includes all counties in which blacks made up 40 percent or more of the population according to the 1960 census. The lowland category contains the tidewater, coastal plains, wire grass, and delta--the predominantly white lowland counties generally.

Alabama, Georgia, North Carolina, and Virginia are divided into these four categories. Mississippi and South Carolina contained no mountain counties, and votes are reported as piedmont, black belt, and lowland. Arkansas counties are grouped as mountain, black belt, and lowland. Florida is divided between the predominantly metropolitan, tourist-oriented southern portion of the state and the northern section that borders Alabama and Georgia, with a separate category for those few counties containing a 1960 black population of more than 40 percent. Louisiana is split between black belt, Catholic Louisiana (those counties in the southern portion of the state in which Catholics were estimated to be in the majority in 1960), and predominantly Protestant northern Louisiana. Texas returns are grouped into eastern Texas, western Texas, Mexican-American Texas (those south Texas counties estimated to contain a Chicano population of 40 percent or more in 1950), and black belt. Finally, Tennessee counties are categorized as east (mountain), middle (Nashville Basin), west (lowland), and black belt (only Fayette and Haywood counties). For a more detailed explanation of these classification procedures, see our Southern Politics and the Second Reconstruction (Baltimore, Md.: Johns Hopkins University Press, 1975). The demographic and sectional totals for each state present a general overview of each election and provide a basis of comparison for the political behavior of any individual county.

Additionally, the latter part of this volume contains a socioeconomic analysis of precinct returns from 24 southern cities: Birmingham and Montgomery in Alabama; Little Rock in Arkansas; Jacksonville and Miami in Florida; Atlanta and Macon in Georgia; Baton Rouge, New Orleans, and Shreveport in Louisiana; Jackson in Mississippi; Charlotte, Greensboro, and Raleigh in North Carolina; Charleston and Columbia in South Carolina; Memphis and Nashville in Tennessee; Fort Worth, Houston, and Waco in Texas; and Norfolk, Richmond, and Roanoke in Virginia. In each city we divided precincts on the basis of census data into five categories that reflected distinctions of race and economic class: 1) black, 2) lower-class white, 3) lower middle-class white, 4) upper middle-class white, and 5) upper-class white.

Precincts were first divided along racial lines, with predominantly black precincts so designated and racially mixed precincts eliminated from the analysis. Predominantly white precincts were then quartiled by assigning equal weight to median family income, median house value, and median years of education. Precincts too heterogeneous to be classified were excluded. Prior to the mid-1960s so few blacks voted in a few Deep South cities-- notably those in Alabama and Mississippi-- that all-black precincts were difficult to isolate. The precinct data suggest the voting tendencies of socioeconomic groups, and they are included for the purpose of fleshing out the individual and categorically aggregated data. It does not necessarily follow, of course, that because the black or lower-class white precincts in a particular city voted in a certain manner, the blacks or lower-class whites throughout the state also did so. But the precinct analysis does indicate the patterns in the 24 cities included and is strongly suggestive as to the socioeconomic voting patterns in other cities and towns. The precinct data include both general and primary election results. Preceding the election data for each state is a separate introduction that summarizes some of the peculiarities of that state's politics, and a county map. The figures on turnout in presidential elections in the state introductions include an estimate of the percentage of citizens of voting age who voted, which is slightly different from voting-age population, since aliens are excluded.

In addition to the analytical material, this work also contains limitations with which users should be aware. Both to conserve space and to make the data more usable, we have in many cases combined the votes for minor candidates under the heading "other" and have in some instances excluded from the printed returns candidates who received a negligible number of votes. The list of elections in each state introduction summarizes the elections and provides total votes and percentages for the candidates. Southern Democratic primary elections often attracted crowded fields of contestants (though rarely as many as the 71 candidates whose names appeared on the ballot in the 1961 special senate election in Texas); to have listed the county returns for all contenders would have made this work much longer and, in our opinion, considerably less useful. Additionally, relatively uncontested primary elections (mainly Senate races in which veteran incumbents brushed aside light opposition or were unopposed altogether) have been excluded. These elections are listed in the state introductions and are marked by asterisks.

This volume grew out of _Southern Politics and the Second Reconstruction,_ our analysis of the main tendencies in southern politics during the post-World War II era. That work contains an extensive bibliography, but it might be worth noting that V. O. Key's pathbreaking _Southern Politics in State and Nation,_ the state-by-state diagnosis in William C. Havard (ed.), _The Changing Politics of the South_ (Baton Rouge: Louisiana State University Press, 1972), and the

regional analysis in _Southern Politics and the Second Reconstruction_ provide the background material that is important in interpreting the data in this volume.

I County Election Data

ALABAMA

COUNTIES

LAUDERDALE
LIMESTONE
MADISON
JACKSON
COLBERT
FRANKLIN
LAWRENCE
MORGAN
MARSHALL
DE KALB
MARION
WINSTON
CULLMAN
CHEROKEE
ETOWAH
BLOUNT
LAMAR
FAYETTE
WALKER
ST CLAIR
CALHOUN
CLEBURNE
JEFFERSON
PICKENS
TUSCALOOSA
SHELBY
TALLADEGA
CLAY
RANDOLPH
GREENE
BIBB
COOSA
CHAMBERS
HALE
CHILTON
TALLAPOOSA
LEE
PERRY
ELMORE
SUMTER
AUTAUGA
MACON
RUSSELL
DALLAS
MONTGOMERY
CHOCTAW
MARENGO
LOWNDES
BULLOCK
WILCOX
BARBOUR
BUTLER
CRENSHAW
PIKE
CLARKE
MONROE
HENRY
WASHINGTON
CONECUH
COVINGTON
COFFEE
DALE
ESCAMBIA
GENEVA
HOUSTON
MOBILE
BALDWIN

SCALE IN MILES

0   50   100   150

STUDY AREA

ALABAMA

Potential voters faced formidable obstacles in Alabama until the mid-1960s. During the early post-World War II years, the $1.50 poll tax was cumulative, though a voter who paid poll taxes through age 45 was exempt thereafter. In 1953 a constitutional amendment limited the cumulative features to two years, and the state attorney general ruled that the amendment thus granted registrants 47 years of age and older a free vote whether they had previously paid the tax or not. Military veterans were also exempt. Other voters 21 to 46 years of age still had to remember to pay the levy by February 1 in election years. Registration also required two years' residency in the state, one year in the county, and three months in the voting district. The most difficult hurdle of all was the voter qualifications amendment of 1951 (ratification election results are reprinted below), which required that a registrant be literate, of good character, and able to answer unassisted a lengthy written questionnaire.

These conditions, in addition to a twentieth-century tradition of limited citizen participation, insured low registration and turnout, especially among black citizens. In 1952 scarcely more than 25,000 blacks were registered, a figure that by 1960 had grown to an estimated 66,000, or 13.7 percent of the black voting-age population. During the mid-1960s, federal intervention in defense of voting rights opened the way to a broader franchise. By 1970 an estimated 315,000 blacks, or 66 percent of the voting-age population, were registered. White voter registration also grew sharply, increasing from approximately 860,000 in 1960 to 1,311,000 in 1970. Blacks comprised an estimated 7.1 percent of the total number of registered voters in 1960 and 19.4 percent in 1970.

The votes cast in presidential elections from 1948 to 1972 illustrate some of the changing themes of Alabama politics. Turnout, expressed both in the number of ballots cast and in the percentage of citizens of voting age who did vote (the figure in parentheses), and the dramatic shifts in partisan preferences of the voters are evident in the following table of returns from presidential elections.

This volume contains 20 Alabama elections, including 9 Democratic gubernatorial primaries, 8 Democratic senatorial primaries, and 3 referenda.

Gubernatorial Primaries

1. May 2, 1950: Elbert Boozer 48,021 (11.9%), Phillip J. Hamm 56,395 (14.0%), J. Bruce Henderson 38,867 (9.7%), Gordon Persons 137,155 (34.1%), Chauncey Sparks 27,404 (6.8%), other 10 candidates 94,444 (23.5%). Total vote was 402,286; turnout of voting-age citizens was 23.1%. (No runoff was held; Phillip J. Hamm conceded.)
2. May 4, 1954: James B. Allen 61,680 (10.4%), Jimmy Faulkner 152,925 (25.7%), James E. Folsom 305,394 (51.2%), J. Bruce Henderson 47,969 (8.1%), C. C. Owen 23,123 (3.9%), other 2 candidates 4,950 (0.8%). Total vote was 596,041; turnout was 33.5%.
3. May 6, 1958: John Patterson 196,859 (31.8%), George C. Wallace 162,435 (26.3%), Jimmy Faulkner 91,512 (14.8%), A. W. Todd 59,240 (9.6%), Laurie C. Battle

38,955 (6.3%), other 9 candidates 69,642 (11.3%). Total vote was 618,643; turnout was 34.1%.

4. June 3, 1958: John Patterson 315,353 (55.7%), George C. Wallace 250,451 (44.3%). Total vote was 565,804; turnout was 31.2%.

5. May 1, 1962: Eugene "Bull" Connor 23,019 (3.6%), Ryan deGraffenried 160,704 (25.3%), James E. Folsom 159,640 (25.1%), MacDonald Gallion 80,374 (12.6%), George C. Wallace 207,062 (32.5%), other 2 candidates 5,606 (0.9%). Total vote was 636,405; turnout was 34.0%.

6. May 29, 1962: Ryan deGraffenried 269,122 (44.1%), George C. Wallace 340,730 (55.9%). Total vote was 609,852; turnout was 32.6%.

7. May 3, 1966: Carl Elliott 71,972 (8.1%), Richmond M. Flowers 172,386 (19.4%), Bob Gilchrist 49,502 (5.6%), Lurleen Wallace 480,841 (54.1%), other 6 candidates 114,137 (12.8%). Total vote was 888,838; turnout was 45.7%.

8. May 5, 1970: Albert Brewer 428,146 (42.0%), George C. Wallace 416,443 (40.8%), Charles Woods 149,887 (14.7%), Asa Carter 15,441 (1.5%), other 3 candidates 9,763 (1.0%). Total vote was 1,019,680; turnout was 50.5%.

9. June 2, 1970: Albert Brewer 525,951 (48.4%), George C. Wallace 559,832 (51.6%). Total vote was 1,085,783; turnout was 53.7%.

Senatorial Primaries

1. May 2, 1950: Lister Hill 228,524 (67.0%), Lawrence McNeil 112,615 (33.0%). Total

vote was 341,139.

2. May 4, 1954: Laurie C. Battle 208,166 (37.5%), John G. Crommelin 19,579 (3.5%), John J. Sparkman 323,807 (58.2%), William C. Irby 4,320 (0.8%). Total vote was 555,872.

3. May 1, 1956: John G. Crommelin 114,635 (31.5%), Lister Hill 249,270 (68.5%). Total vote was 363,905.

* (May 3, 1960: John J. Sparkman won 83.1% against 2 opponents. Total vote was 404,085.)

4. May 1, 1962: John G. Crommelin 56,822 (11.5%), Donald G. Hallmark 72,855 (14.8%), Lister Hill 363,613 (73.7%). Total vote was 493,290.

5. May 3, 1966: John G. Crommelin 114,622 (17.3%), Frank E. Dixon 133,139 (20.1%), John J. Sparkman 378,295 (57.0%), Mrs. Frank R. Stewart 37,889 (5.7%). Total vote was 663,945.

6. May 7, 1968: James B. Allen 224,483 (41.9%), Armistead I. Selden 190,283 (35.5%), Robert Smith 72,928 (13.6%), James E. Folsom 32,004 (6.0%), other 2 candidates 16,294 (3.0%). Total vote was 535,992.

7. June 4, 1968: James B. Allen 196,511 (50.5%), Armistead I. Selden 192,448 (49.5%). Total vote was 388,959.

8. May 2, 1972: Melba Till Allen 194,690 (29.5%), Robert Edington 22,145 (3.4%), Lambert C. Mims 87,461 (13.2%), John J. Sparkman 331,838 (50.3%), other 3 candidates 24,206 (3.7%). Total vote was 660,340.

Special Elections

1. December 11, 1951: Civil Service amendment making "appointments and promotions in the Civil Service" dependent on "merit, fitness and efficiency." For 78,230 (63.5%), Against 44,879 (36.5%). Total vote was 123,109.
2. December 11, 1951: Voter qualifications amendment. For 60,357 (50.15%), Against 59,988 (49.85%). Total vote was 120,345.
3. August 28, 1956: Freedom-of-choice amendment abrogating "any right to education or training at public expense" and empowering the legislature to "authorize the parents or guardians of minors, who desire that such minors shall attend schools provided for their own race, to make election to that end." For 128,586 (61.3%), Against 81,066 (38.7%). Total vote was 209,652.

RETURNS FROM PRESIDENTIAL ELECTIONS

Year	Turnout		Partisan Vote*
1948	214,980	(12.6%)[+]	Dixiecrat 81.0%, Republican 19.0% (Democrats were not on the ballot)
1952	426,120	(24.2%)	Democrat 64.6%, Republican 35.0%
1956	496,861	(27.6%)	Democrat 56.5%, Republican 39.4%, States' Rights 4.1%
1960	570,225	(31.1%)	Democrat (5 electors pledged to the national Democratic ticket, 6 pledged to Harry F. Byrd) 56.8%, Republican 41.7%
1964	698,818	(36.1%)	Republican 69.5%, Unpledged Democrat 30.5%
1968	1,049,922	(52.9%)	American Independent 65.9%, Democrat 18.7%, Republican 14.0%
1972	1,006,111	(44.6%)	Republican 72.4%, Democrat 25.5%

*Totals do not necessarily equal 100%, since minor party percentages are excluded.

[+]Percentage of citizens of voting age who voted is calculated on the basis of a straight-line interpolation of citizen population between census years.

| | DEMOC. GOVERNOR 1950 | | | | | | * DEMOC. SENATOR 1950 | |
| COUNTY | BOOZER | HAMM | HENDERSON | PERSONS | SPARKS | OTHER | HILL | MCNEIL |
	# %	# %	# %	# %	# %	# %*	# %	# %
AUTAUGA	107 4.3	176 7.0	314 12.5	1162 46.4	111 4.4	633 25.3*	1453 65.2	774 34.8
BALDWIN	300 5.5	734 13.4	930 16.9	2432 44.2	559 10.2	542 9.9*	2950 58.7	2079 41.3
BARBOUR	52 1.5	413 11.8	133 3.8	951 27.1	1816 51.7	149 4.2*	2086 69.3	925 30.7
BIBB	117 3.6	638 19.8	370 11.5	1355 42.0	176 5.5	572 17.7*	1730 60.6	1124 39.4
BLOUNT	541 10.3	758 14.4	131 2.5	647 12.3	66 1.3	3116 59.3*	3213 77.6	925 22.4
BULLOCK	100 6.0	261 15.7	268 16.1	702 42.2	176 10.6	157 9.4*	705 49.0	735 51.0
BUTLER	371 9.3	767 19.3	731 18.4	1526 38.3	370 9.3	218 5.5*	2520 71.1	1023 28.9
CALHOUN	7449 67.1	462 4.2	421 3.8	1626 14.7	346 3.1	794 7.2*	6344 73.5	2293 26.5
CHAMBERS	905 16.3	287 5.2	699 12.6	2341 42.1	575 10.3	756 13.6*	3003 82.5	635 17.5
CHEROKEE	1681 47.2	365 10.3	83 2.3	578 16.2	91 2.6	760 21.4*	2551 88.0	349 12.0
CHILTON	121 3.2	221 5.8	350 9.3	1770 46.9	235 6.2	1081 28.6*	2102 65.2	1122 34.8
CHOCTAW	201 6.4	316 10.1	768 24.5	968 30.9	152 4.9	727 23.2*	1355 52.8	1213 47.2
CLARKE	274 5.8	907 19.1	1347 28.3	1319 27.8	98 2.1	807 17.0*	1835 42.5	2481 57.5
CLAY	1116 29.9	517 13.8	171 4.5	1303 34.9	166 4.5	456 12.2*	1951 73.7	697 26.3
CLEBURNE	1714 59.2	121 4.2	67 2.3	514 17.8	88 3.0	389 13.4*	1417 74.8	478 25.2
COFFEE	119 2.5	2873 61.4	198 4.2	1116 23.9	244 5.2	129 2.8*	3073 75.3	1008 24.7
COLBERT	681 10.1	965 14.4	319 4.7	1798 26.7	428 6.4	2533 37.7*	5041 84.3	937 15.7
CONECUH	245 8.5	471 16.3	384 13.3	1156 40.1	330 11.4	299 10.4*	1181 46.8	1344 53.2
COOSA	507 18.4	314 11.4	174 6.3	1269 45.9	150 5.4	348 12.6*	1582 63.9	895 36.1
COVINGTON	252 4.1	1589 25.7	628 10.2	2846 46.0	324 5.2	547 8.8*	3238 62.3	1959 37.7
CRENSHAW	338 8.5	898 22.6	236 5.9	2074 52.2	215 5.4	209 5.3*	2660 77.3	783 22.7
CULLMAN	1475 19.4	1780 23.4	371 4.9	1409 18.5	480 6.3	2106 27.6*	4979 81.5	1130 18.5
DALE	199 4.9	821 20.4	319 7.9	2001 49.7	215 5.3	473 11.7*	1935 55.7	1537 44.3
DALLAS	84 2.0	153 3.6	1356 32.1	1302 30.8	933 22.1	393 9.3*	2012 51.0	1936 49.0
DEKALB	1254 15.1	986 11.9	84 1.0	868 10.4	58 .7	5064 60.9*	5459 89.0	674 11.0
ELMORE	469 7.6	642 10.4	447 7.2	3793 61.4	448 7.3	374 6.1*	3648 66.3	1852 33.7
ESCAMBIA	608 11.6	857 16.4	327 6.3	2533 48.5	429 8.2	473 9.0*	2377 57.8	1739 42.2
ETOWAH	3340 28.1	1090 9.2	444 3.7	4808 40.5	324 2.7	1864 15.7*	7704 74.9	2577 25.1
FAYETTE	121 3.1	349 8.8	103 2.6	994 25.1	87 2.2	2309 58.3*	2272 74.4	783 25.6
FRANKLIN	429 7.8	836 15.1	206 3.7	1910 34.5	252 4.6	1898 34.3*	3821 85.0	673 15.0
GENEVA	62 1.5	1945 46.5	351 8.4	1237 29.6	181 4.3	408 9.8*	2081 57.0	1571 43.0
GREENE	26 2.6	80 8.0	131 13.1	411 41.1	86 8.6	266 26.6*	477 50.6	465 49.4
HALE	29 1.3	160 7.0	427 18.8	997 43.9	272 12.0	388 17.1*	1328 61.7	826 38.3
HENRY	134 5.0	351 13.1	355 13.2	1352 50.4	193 7.2	295 11.0*	1390 59.2	956 40.8
HOUSTON	165 2.5	1351 20.6	988 15.1	2976 45.4	370 5.6	706 10.8*	2065 40.8	2998 59.2
JACKSON	537 9.6	1389 24.9	70 1.3	390 7.0	98 1.8	3105 55.6*	3795 85.1	665 14.9
JEFFERSON	2824 5.1	4516 8.1	7397 13.3	21109 38.0	3732 6.7	15927 28.7*	32004 59.3	21973 40.7
LAMAR	347 8.1	1008 23.5	128 3.0	1381 32.2	110 2.6	1315 30.7*	2153 74.5	737 25.5
LAUDERDALE	924 12.0	887 11.6	332 4.3	2165 28.2	694 9.0	2675 34.8*	5961 87.3	870 12.7
LAWRENCE	1007 21.9	728 15.9	331 7.2	700 15.2	314 6.8	1512 32.9*	2628 76.7	799 23.3
LEE	233 5.0	373 8.1	468 10.1	2750 59.5	466 10.1	333 7.2*	3056 71.0	1251 29.0
LIMESTONE	208 4.3	265 5.5	310 6.4	914 19.0	507 10.5	2609 54.2*	3318 78.4	913 21.6
LOWNDES	52 3.3	128 8.0	514 32.3	576 36.2	187 11.7	135 8.5*	677 44.2	855 55.8
MACON	102 4.1	580 23.4	379 15.3	933 37.6	301 12.1	185 7.5*	1432 62.9	845 37.1
MADISON	714 8.5	1122 13.4	165 2.0	572 6.8	221 2.6	5565 66.6*	4240 87.0	635 13.0
MARENGO	264 7.4	177 4.9	961 26.8	1454 40.5	204 5.7	526 14.7*	1742 52.7	1562 47.3

DEMOC. GOVERNOR 1950   * DEMOC. SENATOR 1950

COUNTY	BOOZER #	%	HAMM #	%	HENDERSON #	%	PERSONS #	%	SPARKS #	%	OTHER #	%*	HILL #	%	MCNEIL #	%
MARION	516	8.4	1319	21.5	186	3.0	1594	26.0	186	3.0	2333	38.0*	3351	77.6	969	22.4
MARSHALL	2205	23.8	2535	27.4	167	1.8	1081	11.7	181	2.0	3079	33.3*	5334	82.6	1121	17.4
MOBILE	2079	9.4	2734	12.4	2370	10.7	9785	44.2	2130	9.6	3022	13.7*	9583	51.1	9178	48.9
MONROE	96	2.9	802	24.0	658	19.7	1227	36.7	251	7.5	310	9.3*	1987	67.0	977	33.0
MONTGOMERY	643	4.2	1725	11.2	1563	10.1	8371	54.1	2005	13.0	1154	7.5*	9203	69.2	4092	30.8
MORGAN	1691	18.8	1121	12.4	806	8.9	1646	18.3	874	9.7	2871	31.9*	5159	64.5	2835	35.5
PERRY	164	7.4	152	6.8	408	18.4	965	43.5	293	13.2	238	10.7*	1233	58.8	864	41.2
PICKENS	171	6.2	96	3.5	369	13.4	611	22.3	67	2.4	1432	52.1*	1377	59.1	952	40.9
PIKE	282	6.5	1004	23.1	257	5.9	1932	44.5	600	13.8	271	6.2*	3091	77.7	886	22.3
RANDOLF	2241	43.9	769	15.1	161	3.2	1267	24.8	196	3.8	470	9.2*	2693	79.9	676	20.1
RUSSELL	9	.3	1768	59.4	145	4.9	667	22.4	194	6.5	193	6.5*	2331	83.8	450	16.2
SHELBY	154	3.4	283	6.3	487	10.8	2395	53.2	180	4.0	1001	22.2*	2229	57.3	1658	42.7
ST. CLAIR	808	26.4	232	7.6	253	8.3	1232	40.2	65	2.1	474	15.5*	1840	69.3	816	30.7
SUMTER	55	3.0	45	2.4	425	23.1	634	34.5	178	9.7	502	27.3*	935	60.3	616	39.7
TALLADEGA	2056	25.7	747	9.3	1202	15.0	2141	26.7	343	4.3	1520	19.0*	3565	53.7	3076	46.3
TALLAPOOSA	592	8.6	1766	25.5	353	5.1	3125	45.2	461	6.7	624	9.0*	4308	75.1	1425	24.9
TUSCALOOSA	629	6.4	1037	10.6	592	6.0	4889	49.9	762	7.8	1897	19.3*	5429	72.1	2100	27.9
WALKER	386	3.7	877	8.4	433	4.1	2784	26.6	288	2.8	5701	54.5*	7045	73.3	2561	26.7
WASHINGTON	264	8.0	458	13.8	825	24.9	993	29.9	145	4.4	634	19.1*	1352	48.5	1438	51.5
WILCOX	31	1.5	73	3.5	1487	71.3	325	15.6	44	2.1	127	6.1*	822	41.6	1154	58.4
WINSTON	151	10.3	225	15.4	34	2.3	503	34.4	83	5.7	465	31.8*	1113	86.7	170	13.3
TOTALS	48021		56395		38867		137155		27404		94444	*	228524		112615	
% OF VOTE	11.9		14.0		9.7		34.1		6.8		23.5	*	67.0		33.0	

GEOGRAPHIC CLASS

	BOOZER		HAMM		HENDERSON		PERSONS		SPARKS		OTHER		HILL		MCNEIL	
LOWLANDS	4386	7.	14260	22.	7172	11.	27993	43.	4812	7.	7143	11.*	31314	56.	24290	44.
BLACK BELT	3492	5.	10605	14.	13380	18.	29541	39.	8861	12.	9405	12.*	41172	61.	25931	39.
PIEDMONT	30968	16.	20460	10.	16550	8.	67857	34.	11948	6.	50269	25.*	115377	68.	53157	32.
MOUNTAIN	9175	15.	11070	18.	1765	3.	11764	19.	1763	3.	27627	44.*	40661	81.	9237	19.

DEMOGRAPHIC CLASS

	BOOZER		HAMM		HENDERSON		PERSONS		SPARKS		OTHER		HILL		MCNEIL	
METRO	10229	8.	12224	10.	12531	10.	49534	40.	9174	7.	29429	24.*	68163	63.	40555	37.
TOWN	10322	25.	5742	14.	4048	10.	10382	25.	3411	8.	7632	18.*	23872	68.	11382	32.
RURAL	27470	12.	38429	16.	22288	9.	77239	33.	14819	6.	57383	24.*	136489	69.	60678	31.

COUNTY	ALLEN #	ALLEN %	FAULKNER #	FAULKNER %	FOLSOM #	FOLSOM %	HENDERSON #	HENDERSON %	OWEN #	OWEN %	BATTLE #	BATTLE %	CROMMELIN #	CROMMELIN %	SPARKMAN #	SPARKMAN %
AUTAUGA	196	5.9	842	25.2	1724	51.6	439	13.1	141	4.2*	1624	49.8	166	5.1	1473	45.1
BALDWIN	339	3.4	4957	49.0	4065	40.2	669	6.6	83	.8*	4396	45.4	948	9.8	4347	44.9
BARBOUR	255	4.9	1018	19.4	3332	63.6	600	11.5	34	.6*	2135	39.5	150	2.8	3121	57.7
BIBB	99	2.1	381	8.0	2263	47.6	138	2.9	1873	39.4*	1966	46.0	52	1.2	2253	52.8
BLOUNT	630	7.6	1140	13.8	6135	74.3	198	2.4	152	1.8*	630	11.4	67	1.2	4840	87.4
BULLOCK	302	14.1	199	9.3	1036	48.2	594	27.6	18	.8*	1377	65.3	97	4.6	634	30.1
BUTLER	377	6.3	1072	18.0	3422	57.3	1041	17.4	55	.9*	2684	46.4	219	3.8	2876	49.8
CALHOUN	3117	19.3	4333	26.9	6581	40.8	679	4.2	1402	8.7*	4204	27.5	316	2.1	10774	70.4
CHAMBERS	850	10.7	2632	33.1	3198	40.2	1110	13.9	172	2.2*	2708	40.5	157	2.3	3825	57.2
CHEROKEE	789	14.0	756	13.4	3457	61.3	396	7.0	242	4.3*	1220	24.4	72	1.4	3712	74.2
CHILTON	476	7.1	1854	27.8	3519	52.8	477	7.2	335	5.0*	3280	52.2	187	3.0	2821	44.9
CHOCTAW	231	5.7	555	13.8	2637	65.6	400	10.0	195	4.9*	2109	61.4	52	1.5	1275	37.1
CLARKE	306	5.0	1058	17.2	3557	57.8	1028	16.7	206	3.3*	3257	56.8	394	6.9	2079	36.3
CLAY	530	10.1	1164	22.1	3057	58.0	172	3.3	346	6.6*	2254	45.7	62	1.3	2614	53.0
CLEBURNE	416	9.6	764	17.6	2742	63.2	106	2.4	309	7.1*	1128	33.3	71	2.1	2189	64.6
COFFEE	161	2.3	768	10.8	5732	80.4	434	6.1	30	.4*	2150	31.9	208	3.1	4378	65.0
COLBERT	694	7.2	2927	30.2	5234	54.1	309	3.2	515	5.3*	1156	14.1	209	2.5	6851	83.4
CONECUH	192	4.1	912	19.6	2957	63.6	457	9.8	133	2.9*	2036	47.1	222	5.1	2069	47.8
COOSA	226	5.6	985	24.6	2411	60.2	249	6.2	134	3.3*	1888	47.6	113	2.8	1965	49.5
COVINGTON	385	3.5	3166	28.7	6179	55.9	1161	10.5	153	1.4*	4533	47.5	200	2.1	4819	50.5
CRENSHAW	189	3.2	899	15.4	4160	71.3	536	9.2	50	.9*	2187	42.0	131	2.5	2890	55.5
CULLMAN	526	4.5	2237	19.2	8465	72.6	289	2.5	135	1.2*	3244	28.0	131	1.1	8192	70.8
DALE	336	5.6	1288	21.4	3699	61.3	649	10.8	60	1.0*	3140	58.2	175	3.2	2078	38.5
DALLAS	1015	15.7	1823	28.1	1685	26.0	1767	27.3	189	2.9*	4124	63.8	176	2.7	2164	33.5
DEKALB	1091	12.2	1196	13.4	6293	70.3	129	1.4	237	2.6*	1689	20.2	94	1.1	6599	78.7
ELMORE	488	5.7	2089	24.4	5058	59.1	844	9.9	81	.9*	3178	38.3	1413	17.0	3717	44.7
ESCAMBIA	374	4.8	1760	22.4	4619	58.8	1015	12.9	82	1.0*	3107	43.4	643	9.0	3410	47.6
ETOWAH	6449	26.1	4199	17.2	13029	52.7	392	1.6	665	2.7*	5924	26.0	488	2.1	16372	71.9
FAYETTE	360	7.0	1398	27.1	3131	60.7	60	1.2	211	4.1*	2173	45.4	68	1.4	2541	53.1
FRANKLIN	389	5.1	2141	28.0	4588	59.9	166	2.2	372	4.9*	1719	23.7	157	2.2	5378	74.1
GENEVA	175	2.9	722	12.1	4541	76.4	478	8.0	29	.5*	2424	43.9	139	2.5	2954	53.5
GREENE	202	13.6	151	10.1	526	35.3	181	12.2	428	28.8*	642	43.5	40	2.7	794	53.8
HALE	475	16.0	610	20.5	1048	35.2	514	17.3	330	11.1*	1250	42.2	47	1.6	1668	56.3
HENRY	172	4.3	605	15.2	2579	64.8	469	11.8	155	3.9*	1523	39.9	104	2.7	2192	57.4
HOUSTON	747	9.5	1230	15.7	4692	59.9	1047	13.4	115	1.5*	3750	53.3	287	4.1	3004	42.7
JACKSON	500	5.6	2050	22.9	5345	59.6	332	3.7	741	8.3*	2003	23.5	55	.6	6456	75.8
JEFFERSON	11938	17.1	25556	36.7	24250	34.8	5853	8.4	2041	2.9*	31608	47.8	1994	3.0	32519	49.2
LAMAR	92	1.5	3291	52.4	2756	43.9	51	.8	85	1.4*	1948	34.5	80	1.4	3619	64.1
LAUDERDALE	918	7.2	4932	38.5	5872	45.9	309	2.4	770	6.0*	1448	11.6	113	.9	10965	87.5
LAWRENCE	832	12.6	1173	17.7	3623	54.8	265	4.0	721	10.9*	1229	19.0	71	1.1	5159	79.9
LEE	1057	16.4	2182	33.9	2354	36.6	693	10.8	147	2.3*	2855	43.6	206	3.1	3488	53.3
LIMESTONE	675	10.4	1453	22.5	2739	42.4	478	7.4	1117	17.3*	897	13.9	75	1.2	5477	84.9
LOWNDES	84	4.5	343	18.3	829	44.3	590	31.5	26	1.4*	1205	64.0	103	5.5	576	30.6
MACON	247	7.7	622	19.5	1647	51.6	652	20.4	26	.8*	1462	47.3	138	4.5	1488	48.2
MADISON	2258	18.2	3502	28.2	5175	41.7	1121	9.0	359	2.9*	953	8.3	277	2.4	10301	89.3
MARENGO	444	9.7	885	19.3	1839	40.2	1003	21.9	408	8.9*	2480	54.9	146	3.2	1888	41.8

	DEMOC. GOVERNOR 1954					DEMOC. SENATOR 1954		
COUNTY	ALLEN	FAULKNER	FOLSOM	HENDERSON	OWEN	BATTLE	CROMMELIN	SPARKMAN
	# %	# %	# %	# %	# %	# %	# %	# %
MARION	292 3.2	1958 21.6	6431 71.1	82 .9	284 3.1*	3375 41.6	88 1.1	4656 57.3
MARSHALL	935 6.9	2335 17.2	9807 72.4	205 1.5	259 1.9*	3197 25.2	146 1.2	9332 73.6
MOBILE	4654 13.7	12129 35.7	13539 39.8	2798 8.2	859 2.5*	13637 47.4	2806 9.8	12319 42.8
MONROE	158 3.5	1429 31.8	2236 49.8	623 13.9	47 1.0*	1920 45.3	212 5.0	2108 49.7
MONTGOMERY	2216 10.9	6697 33.0	8790 43.3	2324 11.4	273 1.3*	8714 46.7	1519 8.1	8443 45.2
MORGAN	2362 17.3	2869 21.1	6613 48.6	854 6.3	921 6.8*	2298 16.8	233 1.7	11170 81.5
PERRY	350 12.1	661 22.8	1142 39.4	489 16.9	260 9.0*	1395 49.1	75 2.6	1370 48.2
PICKENS	249 5.1	1353 27.8	2212 45.4	823 16.9	235 4.8*	1988 42.5	94 2.0	2596 55.5
PIKE	378 6.1	1683 27.3	3437 55.8	605 9.8	61 1.0*	2720 45.7	172 2.9	3060 51.4
RANDOLF	599 8.2	1453 20.0	4568 62.8	320 4.4	329 4.5*	1803 24.6	1007 13.7	4523 61.7
RUSSELL	283 4.6	664 10.8	4020 65.3	1091 17.7	95 1.5*	2115 38.2	117 2.1	3307 59.7
SHELBY	511 7.0	2079 28.4	3856 52.6	617 8.4	265 3.6*	3069 43.7	128 1.8	3823 54.5
ST. CLAIR	422 7.0	1407 23.4	3771 62.8	212 3.5	189 3.1*	2343 40.6	69 1.2	3364 58.2
SUMTER	188 7.5	759 30.2	613 24.4	617 24.6	334 13.3*	1333 53.1	62 2.5	1117 44.5
TALLADEGA	1418 10.4	4256 31.2	6704 49.2	782 5.7	465 3.4*	5625 42.4	382 2.9	7254 54.7
TALLAPOOSA	533 5.0	2355 22.2	6346 59.9	1151 10.9	214 2.0*	3877 37.1	223 2.1	6343 60.7
TUSCALOOSA	2503 14.3	4387 25.0	8412 48.0	1142 6.5	1094 6.2*	5200 32.7	394 2.5	10301 64.8
WALKER	656 4.4	3277 22.0	10171 68.1	393 2.6	430 2.9*	4566 31.6	172 1.2	9703 67.2
WASHINGTON	133 2.8	641 13.5	2910 61.3	836 17.6	231 4.9*	2136 49.8	285 6.6	1871 43.6
WILCOX	82 3.3	165 6.6	777 30.9	1438 57.2	53 2.1*	1644 69.8	69 2.9	642 27.3
WINSTON	154 7.3	548 26.0	1259 59.8	27 1.3	117 5.6*	314 15.5	13 .6	1701 83.9
TOTALS	61680	152925	305394	47969	23123	208166	19579	323807
% OF VOTE	10.4	25.9	51.7	8.1	3.9	37.7	3.5	58.7
GEOGRAPHIC CLASS								
LOWLANDS	7493 7.	27560 27.	54136 54.	9623 10.	1692 2.*	41460 46.	5822 7.	42070 47.
BLACK BELT	8402 8.	24106 23.	52045 49.	17745 17.	3702 3.*	49737 49.	4374 4.	46940 46.
PIEDMONT	39823 14.	83621 28.	137262 47.	18384 6.	14760 5.*	95012 34.	8388 3.	174228 63.
MOUNTAIN	5962 7.	17638 19.	61951 68.	2217 2.	2969 3.*	21957 26.	995 1.	60569 73.
DEMOGRAPHIC CLASS								
METRO	30018 17.	56470 32.	73195 41.	13630 8.	5291 3.*	66036 40.	7478 5.	90255 55.
TOWN	8442 13.	15851 25.	29463 47.	5747 9.	3492 6.*	17939 30.	1242 2.	41384 68.
RURAL	23220 7.	80604 23.	202736 58.	28592 8.	14340 4.*	124191 38.	10859 3.	192168 59.

COUNTY	CROMMELIN #	%	HILL #	%*	BATTLE #	%	FAULKNER #	%	PATTERSON #	%	TODD #	%	WALLACE #	%	OTHER #	%
AUTAUGA	1182	38.6	1877	61.4*	90	2.5	428	11.9	1587	44.2	60	1.7	1110	30.9	314	8.7
BALDWIN	3145	48.1	3395	51.9*	151	1.3	5485	48.5	2888	25.5	575	5.1	1917	16.9	304	2.7
BARBOUR	849	23.4	2774	76.6*	13	.2	194	3.6	348	6.4	40	.7	4736	87.8	66	1.2
BIBB	1028	39.1	1602	60.9*	45	1.1	280	7.1	1978	50.4	56	1.4	387	9.9	1181	30.1
BLOUNT	1116	26.8	3054	73.2*	404	5.6	586	8.1	2757	38.0	1402	19.3	1409	19.4	699	9.6
BULLOCK	778	55.3	630	44.7*	53	2.9	55	3.0	408	22.1	7	.4	1271	68.8	54	2.9
BUTLER	1647	40.1	2462	59.9*	104	1.7	638	10.7	2824	47.3	302	5.1	1783	29.9	315	5.3
CALHOUN	1672	25.7	4828	74.3*	716	4.6	2109	13.5	6111	39.1	931	6.0	4095	26.2	1682	10.8
CHAMBERS	627	16.5	3171	83.5*	445	5.4	1050	12.7	4480	54.3	187	2.3	1663	20.2	422	5.1
CHEROKEE	380	13.8	2376	86.2*	53	.9	685	11.6	2186	37.3	823	14.0	1344	22.9	776	13.2
CHILTON	1314	36.0	2333	64.0*	185	2.9	818	12.6	2943	45.4	263	4.1	1614	24.9	659	10.2
CHOCTAW	824	37.0	1404	63.0*	103	2.4	563	13.3	1812	42.7	198	4.7	1288	30.3	284	6.7
CLARKE	2405	49.0	2502	51.0*	112	1.8	663	10.4	3245	50.9	122	1.9	1821	28.6	407	6.4
CLAY	768	24.2	2409	75.8*	204	3.9	572	10.9	3033	57.6	256	4.9	847	16.1	354	6.7
CLEBURNE	298	17.2	1438	82.8*	39	.9	442	10.1	2498	57.0	382	8.7	748	17.1	274	6.3
COFFEE	1395	24.0	4429	76.0*	47	.7	861	12.2	1086	15.3	271	3.8	4389	61.9	431	6.1
COLBERT	651	10.1	5773	89.9*	427	4.1	2012	19.1	1885	17.9	1921	18.2	2435	23.1	1863	17.7
CONECUH	1600	44.0	2037	56.0*	44	1.0	568	13.1	2062	47.5	263	6.1	1272	29.3	131	3.0
COOSA	957	33.0	1940	67.0*	110	3.1	337	9.4	1746	48.9	271	7.6	817	22.9	288	8.1
COVINGTON	2904	38.9	4552	61.1*	145	1.3	1930	17.9	4943	45.8	242	2.2	3180	29.5	343	3.2
CRENSHAW	87	3.8	2178	96.2*	28	.5	770	13.8	2185	39.2	153	2.7	2216	39.7	227	4.1
CULLMAN	991	17.1	4818	82.9*	354	3.1	1292	11.2	2233	19.4	2877	25.0	3605	31.3	1157	10.0
DALE	908	23.3	2981	76.7*	34	.6	823	13.5	625	10.2	65	1.1	4218	69.1	338	5.5
DALLAS	2357	55.8	1867	44.2*	776	12.4	652	10.4	2199	35.2	104	1.7	2221	35.6	291	4.7
DEKALB	369	8.0	4231	92.0*	81	.8	1362	12.8	4043	37.9	1805	16.9	2181	20.4	1200	11.2
ELMORE	3740	54.6	3106	45.4*	133	1.7	859	10.7	3014	37.7	280	3.5	2935	36.7	770	9.6
ESCAMBIA	2524	45.2	3063	54.8*	107	1.3	1618	19.4	4051	48.7	272	3.3	1895	22.8	383	4.6
ETOWAH	2687	27.4	7125	72.6*	706	3.1	1988	8.6	4899	21.3	950	4.1	3105	13.5	11405	49.5
FAYETTE	656	25.2	1946	74.8*	140	2.4	1192	20.1	2197	37.0	391	6.6	1587	26.7	438	7.4
FRANKLIN	637	11.7	4797	88.3*	50	.6	826	10.4	1092	13.7	4974	62.4	677	8.5	346	4.3
GENEVA	761	23.1	2531	76.9*	28	.4	842	13.0	1366	21.1	273	4.2	3047	47.1	910	14.1
GREENE	216	25.8	621	74.2*	115	7.3	102	6.5	547	34.9	114	7.3	504	32.2	185	11.8
HALE	741	35.1	1371	64.9*	354	12.7	253	9.1	1103	39.6	119	4.3	853	30.6	104	3.7
HENRY	1259	48.4	1341	51.6*	14	.4	430	11.1	630	16.3	200	5.2	2308	59.6	291	7.5
HOUSTON	948	34.3	1815	65.7*	95	.9	1425	13.8	1737	16.9	318	3.1	4933	47.9	1785	17.3
JACKSON	338	7.0	4509	93.0*	164	1.8	1683	18.6	3255	36.0	1647	18.2	1552	17.2	731	8.1
JEFFERSON	20899	38.3	33727	61.7*	23461	26.2	10785	12.1	21603	24.2	7546	8.4	16595	18.6	9461	10.6
LAMAR	754	23.3	2483	76.7*	32	.5	2263	36.9	1897	30.9	882	14.4	838	13.6	229	3.7
LAUDERDALE	420	9.1	4173	90.9*	214	1.7	3210	25.1	2521	19.7	1489	11.6	3503	27.4	1850	14.5
LAWRENCE	711	16.1	3703	83.9*	107	1.5	818	11.8	1712	24.8	1751	25.3	1464	21.2	1058	15.3
LEE	763	19.6	3132	80.4*	185	2.8	995	15.2	2726	41.5	191	2.9	1958	29.8	511	7.8
LIMESTONE	636	12.9	4293	87.1*	220	3.3	932	14.1	1932	29.3	1352	20.5	1092	16.6	1069	16.2
LOWNDES	862	48.2	925	51.8*	93	4.9	170	8.9	620	32.4	14	.7	929	48.6	87	4.5
MACON	544	30.5	1240	69.5*	62	2.0	250	8.0	888	28.5	697	22.3	1028	33.0	188	6.0
MADISON	773	9.8	7155	90.2*	320	2.5	2266	17.4	4737	36.5	1514	11.7	2521	19.4	1633	12.6
MARENGO	1929	47.7	2118	52.3*	123	2.9	385	9.2	1756	41.8	85	2.0	1536	36.5	318	7.6

DEMOC. SENATOR 1956*   DEMOC. GOVERNOR 1958

COUNTY	CROMMELIN #	%	HILL #	%*	BATTLE #	%	FAULKNER #	%	PATTERSON #	%	TODD #	%	WALLACE #	%	OTHER #	%
MARION	588	25.2	1747	74.8*	142	1.7	1278	14.9	2616	30.5	1993	23.2	1949	22.7	608	7.1
MARSHALL	734	17.8	3381	82.2*	434	3.3	1352	10.2	4101	30.9	3419	25.8	2261	17.1	1691	12.8
MOBILE	10716	48.9	11209	51.1*	1347	3.4	9367	23.9	11482	29.4	3453	8.8	10211	26.1	3253	8.3
MONROE	1125	38.0	1832	62.0*	125	2.8	638	14.3	2239	50.2	116	2.6	1250	28.0	94	2.1
MONTGOMERY	4747	30.1	11012	69.9*	974	4.2	4009	17.5	5785	25.2	1641	7.2	8763	38.2	1779	7.8
MORGAN	1334	16.5	6744	83.5*	537	4.0	1849	13.8	3464	25.9	2438	18.2	3281	24.5	1813	13.5
PERRY	800	37.5	1332	62.5*	235	8.5	333	12.0	1398	50.4	43	1.6	622	22.4	143	5.2
PICKENS	1513	59.5	1030	40.5*	318	6.6	536	11.2	2205	45.9	323	6.7	1016	21.2	401	8.4
PIKE	1084	26.8	2968	73.2*	58	.9	736	12.0	1190	19.4	241	3.9	3720	60.7	186	3.0
RANDOLF	564	13.9	3480	86.1*	88	1.1	942	12.2	4221	54.6	745	9.6	1385	17.9	352	4.6
RUSSELL	934	21.3	3454	78.7*	69	1.1	684	10.7	2750	43.2	275	4.3	2449	38.5	139	2.2
SHELBY	1582	41.8	2207	58.2*	243	3.7	739	11.3	2669	40.8	557	8.5	1300	19.9	1032	15.8
ST. CLAIR	966	28.9	2375	71.1*	233	3.0	549	7.0	2290	29.1	273	3.5	926	11.8	3588	45.7
SUMTER	415	35.2	763	64.8*	84	4.0	418	19.8	888	42.1	61	2.9	466	22.1	191	9.1
TALLADEGA	3234	33.0	6571	67.0*	917	7.2	2032	15.9	4542	35.6	1168	9.2	2409	18.9	1681	13.2
TALLAPOOSA	1583	24.5	4869	75.5*	370	3.9	1027	10.9	4848	51.4	224	2.4	2454	26.0	514	5.4
TUSCALOOSA	4098	36.0	7271	64.0*	674	4.3	2201	14.0	6272	39.8	533	3.4	3482	22.1	2582	16.4
WALKER	2781	27.6	7297	72.4*	379	2.5	3070	20.4	3147	20.9	2432	16.2	4722	31.4	1273	8.5
WASHINGTON	1496	46.2	1744	53.8*	52	1.0	778	15.7	2705	54.5	215	4.3	955	19.2	258	5.2
WILCOX	1180	55.1	960	44.9*	142	5.7	197	7.9	1132	45.3	21	.8	888	35.5	121	4.8
WINSTON	111	12.3	789	87.7*	48	2.5	310	15.9	527	27.0	434	22.3	499	25.6	131	6.7
TOTALS	114635		249270		38955		91512		196859		59240		162435		69642	
% OF VOTE	31.5		68.5		6.3		14.8		31.8		9.6		26.3		11.3	

GEOGRAPHIC CLASS

	CROMMELIN #	%	HILL #	%*	BATTLE #	%	FAULKNER #	%	PATTERSON #	%	TODD #	%	WALLACE #	%	OTHER #	%
LOWLANDS	24884	40.	37897	60.*	2034	2.	23899	22.	33068	30.	5837	5.	36961	34.	8232	7.
BLACK BELT	28991	38.	46520	62.*	4061	4.	12902	12.	37616	35.	5046	5.	41834	39.	6089	6.
PIEDMONT	51961	29.	125371	71.*	30751	10.	42267	14.	100218	32.	26551	9.	63441	20.	46709	15.
MOUNTAIN	8799	18.	39482	82.*	2109	2.	12444	14.	25957	28.	21806	24.	20199	22.	8612	9.

DEMOGRAPHIC CLASS

	CROMMELIN #	%	HILL #	%*	BATTLE #	%	FAULKNER #	%	PATTERSON #	%	TODD #	%	WALLACE #	%	OTHER #	%
METRO	43920	36.	77499	64.*	27482	14.	30616	15.	54778	27.	15637	8.	44677	22.	30113	15.
TOWN	7665	25.	22881	75.*	2407	4.	9929	15.	18782	29.	5555	9.	20482	32.	7560	12.
RURAL	63050	30.	148890	70.*	9066	3.	50967	15.	123299	35.	38048	11.	97276	28.	31969	9.

COUNTY	PATTERSON #	%	WALLACE #	%*	CONNOR #	%	GRAFFNRD #	%	FOLSOM #	%	GALLION #	%	WALLACE #	%
AUTAUGA	1897	57.8	1383	42.2*	64	1.9	592	17.3	410	12.0	772	22.5	1590	46.4
BALDWIN	4968	55.6	3967	44.4*	80	.7	3008	26.4	2217	19.5	2345	20.6	3741	32.8
BARBOUR	426	8.5	4586	91.5*	39	.7	124	2.3	461	8.5	205	3.8	4593	84.7
BIBB	2693	77.5	780	22.5*	279	7.8	448	12.5	711	19.8	1211	33.8	936	26.1
BLOUNT	4384	62.2	2659	37.8*	258	3.8	1718	25.1	2479	36.3	675	9.9	1706	25.0
BULLOCK	588	31.6	1275	68.4*	58	2.4	232	9.7	572	24.0	72	3.0	1450	60.8
BUTLER	2921	61.6	1818	38.4*	39	.8	782	15.6	1003	20.1	944	18.9	2232	44.6
CALHOUN	8183	60.7	5306	39.3*	541	3.7	4123	28.1	2478	16.9	2652	18.1	4889	33.3
CHAMBERS	6129	76.0	1934	24.0*	102	1.3	3282	40.7	1171	14.5	1167	14.5	2335	29.0
CHEROKEE	3287	62.4	1979	37.6*	53	.9	959	16.8	2486	43.5	246	4.3	1965	34.4
CHILTON	3825	61.9	2353	38.1*	393	6.0	718	11.0	1317	20.2	966	14.8	3130	48.0
CHOCTAW	1884	54.2	1589	45.8*	36	1.0	275	7.3	915	24.2	331	8.8	2219	58.8
CLARKE	3892	64.4	2153	35.6*	100	1.8	831	15.3	979	18.0	1224	22.5	2296	42.3
CLAY	4100	79.8	1040	20.2*	276	5.7	904	18.6	999	20.5	1179	24.2	1514	31.1
CLEBURNE	3169	78.4	872	21.6*	71	1.8	513	12.9	1146	28.8	664	16.7	1592	39.9
COFFEE	1678	27.1	4521	72.9*	35	.5	547	7.6	2474	34.6	620	8.7	3475	48.6
COLBERT	4283	42.9	5709	57.1*	319	2.8	3234	28.2	3896	34.0	501	4.4	3505	30.6
CONECUH	2110	54.6	1754	45.4*	26	.7	399	10.5	952	25.0	519	13.6	1913	50.2
COOSA	2312	68.2	1077	31.8*	145	4.1	759	21.4	1019	28.7	642	18.1	982	27.7
COVINGTON	6400	59.1	4422	40.9*	94	.9	1382	13.5	1908	18.6	1482	14.5	5372	52.5
CRENSHAW	2744	53.6	2375	46.4*	27	.5	594	11.9	1370	27.5	722	14.5	2266	45.5
CULLMAN	4671	45.3	5664	54.7*	194	1.8	1748	15.8	6661	60.2	817	7.4	1636	14.8
DALE	1294	23.3	4269	76.7*	56	1.0	389	6.9	851	15.2	366	6.5	3952	70.4
DALLAS	3570	58.7	2511	41.3*	167	2.6	1207	19.1	825	13.0	1234	19.5	2901	45.8
DEKALB	6766	66.4	3429	33.6*	72	.7	2005	20.4	4662	47.4	728	7.4	2377	24.1
ELMORE	3954	55.1	3224	44.9*	115	1.5	1297	16.9	1068	13.9	1392	18.1	3816	49.6
ESCAMBIA	5222	64.5	2872	35.5*	72	.8	1206	13.6	2442	27.6	1644	18.6	3486	39.4
ETOWAH	12268	58.1	8848	41.9*	1126	5.1	8599	39.1	5645	25.7	2292	10.4	4312	19.6
FAYETTE	2986	51.6	2803	48.4*	205	3.9	1087	20.5	1658	31.3	504	9.5	1841	34.8
FRANKLIN	3477	48.6	3671	51.4*	141	1.8	1743	22.1	3031	38.4	253	3.2	2721	34.5
GENEVA	2526	43.3	3307	56.7*	65	1.1	615	10.2	1477	24.6	442	7.3	3416	56.8
GREENE	878	55.9	692	44.1*	50	3.2	470	29.8	372	23.6	154	9.8	530	33.6
HALE	1475	59.3	1013	40.7*	149	5.8	594	23.3	337	13.2	305	12.0	1164	45.7
HENRY	1021	28.7	2533	71.3*	34	.9	200	5.3	583	15.5	393	10.4	2557	67.9
HOUSTON	3146	34.7	5918	65.3*	151	1.6	1090	11.4	1936	20.3	799	8.4	5554	58.3
JACKSON	4250	60.9	2725	39.1*	73	.9	1997	23.8	3277	39.0	476	5.7	2579	30.7
JEFFERSON	49993	61.3	31627	38.7*	8997	9.4	36497	38.0	16730	17.4	13001	13.5	20786	21.6
LAMAR	3654	58.0	2651	42.0*	161	2.8	1208	21.4	1831	32.4	243	4.3	2207	39.1
LAUDERDALE	4443	37.8	7309	62.2*	234	1.8	3843	29.3	4647	35.4	495	3.8	3902	29.7
LAWRENCE	3425	56.4	2649	43.6*	184	2.7	1422	20.9	2602	38.2	403	5.9	2193	32.2
LEE	3483	59.3	2393	40.7*	44	.6	2423	35.6	1046	15.4	701	10.3	2596	38.1
LIMESTONE	3720	60.2	2459	39.8*	140	2.0	2151	30.8	2260	32.3	629	9.0	1807	25.9
LOWNDES	820	52.8	734	47.2*	9	.5	235	12.7	504	27.3	240	13.0	857	46.4
MACON	1217	44.6	1512	55.4*	66	1.5	449	10.5	2242	52.4	430	10.1	1089	25.5
MADISON	6046	54.6	5028	45.4*	391	2.3	7724	44.7	4803	27.8	1364	7.9	3004	17.4
MARENGO	2404	58.5	1704	41.5*	79	2.1	606	16.2	487	13.0	571	15.3	1992	53.3

COUNTY	PATTERSON #	%	WALLACE #	%*	CONNOR #	%	GRAFFNRD #	%	FOLSOM #	%	GALLION #	%	WALLACE #	%
MARION	4174	53.8	3589	46.2*	226	2.7	1330	15.7	4072	48.2	292	3.5	2527	29.9
MARSHALL	7495	60.1	4986	39.9*	322	2.4	3140	23.4	6588	49.1	658	4.9	2719	20.3
MOBILE	17629	48.9	18445	51.1*	681	1.4	12454	26.4	11184	23.7	9828	20.9	12974	27.5
MONROE	2284	59.4	1559	40.6*	30	.7	619	14.8	822	19.6	854	20.4	1863	44.5
MONTGOMERY	9997	47.1	11215	52.9*	180	.7	4840	19.2	4703	18.6	4074	16.2	11421	45.3
MORGAN	6498	57.4	4821	42.6*	465	3.1	4839	32.7	4346	29.4	1481	10.0	3653	24.7
PERRY	1571	68.4	726	31.6*	92	3.6	312	12.1	403	15.6	540	20.9	1237	47.9
PICKENS	3020	64.5	1660	35.5*	345	7.4	972	21.0	788	17.0	544	11.7	1982	42.8
PIKE	1873	33.7	3685	66.3*	68	1.2	879	15.7	850	15.2	541	9.7	3268	58.3
RANDOLF	3628	66.4	1832	33.6*	173	2.6	1037	15.8	2656	40.5	640	9.8	2045	31.2
RUSSELL	3214	51.1	3080	48.9*	41	.7	883	14.6	1376	22.8	847	14.0	2889	47.9
SHELBY	4974	64.5	2740	35.5*	589	7.6	1727	22.3	1289	16.7	1519	19.6	2612	33.8
ST. CLAIR	4046	65.9	2092	34.1*	427	6.7	1339	21.1	1620	25.6	818	12.9	2129	33.6
SUMTER	1277	72.2	492	27.8*	61	2.8	566	25.9	353	16.2	334	15.3	868	39.8
TALLADEGA	7354	63.2	4289	36.8*	1166	9.0	3199	24.6	2737	21.0	2582	19.8	3343	25.7
TALLAPOOSA	6418	68.3	2979	31.7*	333	3.3	2565	25.1	2415	23.7	1903	18.6	2990	29.3
TUSCALOOSA	8349	57.2	6242	42.8*	638	3.5	9895	54.6	2808	15.5	1493	8.2	3279	18.1
WALKER	6805	47.2	7599	52.8*	899	6.2	2738	18.9	5240	36.1	916	6.3	4721	32.5
WASHINGTON	3195	66.1	1638	33.9*	201	3.9	404	7.8	1278	24.8	1082	21.0	2188	42.5
WILCOX	1353	67.1	664	32.9*	26	1.4	304	16.8	281	15.6	336	18.6	859	47.6
WINSTON	1617	60.8	1041	39.2*	46	2.3	433	22.0	891	45.3	77	3.9	519	26.4

	PATTERSON	WALLACE	*	CONNOR	GRAFFNRD	FOLSOM	GALLION	WALLACE
TOTALS	315353	250451	*	23019	160704	159640	80374	207062
% OF VOTE	55.7	44.3	*	3.6	25.5	25.3	12.7	32.8

GEOGRAPHIC CLASS

	PATTERSON #	%	WALLACE #	%*	CONNOR #	%	GRAFFNRD #	%	FOLSOM #	%	GALLION #	%	WALLACE #	%
LOWLANDS	48802	49.	51734	51.*	1462	1.	21689	19.	27137	23.	19330	17.	46424	40.
BLACK BELT	49692	51.	48338	49.*	1759	2.	16371	16.	20218	19.	15464	15.	51770	49.
PIEDMONT	169933	60.	113057	40.*	17514	5.	104833	33.	72898	23.	40442	13.	85398	27.
MOUNTAIN	46926	56.	37322	44.*	2284	3.	17811	20.	39387	45.	5138	6.	23470	27.

DEMOGRAPHIC CLASS

	PATTERSON #	%	WALLACE #	%*	CONNOR #	%	GRAFFNRD #	%	FOLSOM #	%	GALLION #	%	WALLACE #	%
METRO	104282	56.	81405	44.*	12013	5.	80009	35.	45873	20.	32052	14.	55776	25.
TOWN	29054	50.	28945	50.*	1599	2.	15985	25.	15608	24.	7508	12.	23788	37.
RURAL	182017	57.	140101	43.*	9407	3.	64710	19.	98159	29.	40814	12.	127498	37.

```
            DEMOC.  RUNOFF    1962*    DEMOC.  SENATOR    1962
                                     *
COUNTY      GRAFFNRD     WALLACE     CROMMELIN    HALLMARK     HILL
             #    %      #     %*     #     %     #     %      #     %
------------------------------------------------*------------------------------------------------------------------------
AUTAUGA      751 25.5   2192 74.5*  1063 32.1    718 21.7   1528 46.2
BALDWIN     4392 42.4   5956 57.6*  1392 12.9   2558 23.7   6865 63.5
BARBOUR      503  8.9   5156 91.1*   347 10.3    617 18.4   2394 71.3
BIBB         716 23.2   2372 76.8*   636 18.9    433 12.9   2294 68.2
BLOUNT      2966 45.7   3524 54.3*   524  9.2    716 12.6   4447 78.2
                                     *
BULLOCK      783 31.5   1700 68.5*   319 18.9    376 22.2    997 58.9
BUTLER      1291 28.1   3306 71.9*  1189 25.4   1137 24.3   2349 50.2
CALHOUN     6781 44.6   8408 55.4*  1065  8.6   1546 12.5   9746 78.9
CHAMBERS    4304 52.5   3899 47.5*   307  6.3    359  7.3   4246 86.4
CHEROKEE    2731 47.2   3053 52.8*   279  6.0    254  5.5   4105 88.5
                                     *
CHILTON     1451 23.6   4686 76.4*   932 16.9    569 10.3   4025 72.8
CHOCTAW      883 24.3   2757 75.7*   313 10.4    238  7.9   2449 81.6
CLARKE      1611 29.9   3771 70.1*   442 14.0    878 27.8   1837 58.2
CLAY        1895 40.4   2800 59.6*   546 14.1    384  9.9   2951 76.0
CLEBURNE    1209 30.4   2774 69.6*   238  8.9    249  9.3   2194 81.8
                                     *
COFFEE      1549 24.0   4902 76.0*   888 13.9    927 14.5   4561 71.5
COLBERT     6584 56.4   5090 43.6*   385  5.4    556  7.8   6184 86.8
CONECUH      667 21.2   2486 78.8*   732 21.9    535 16.0   2072 62.1
COOSA       1624 46.8   1848 53.2*   655 20.9    436 13.9   2037 65.1
COVINGTON   2814 27.9   7284 72.1*  2309 24.6   2073 22.1   5016 53.4
                                     *
CRENSHAW     994 23.6   3221 76.4*   975 22.5    606 14.0   2758 63.6
CULLMAN     4104 43.0   5450 57.0*   608  6.3    781  8.2   8193 85.5
DALE         967 16.7   4832 83.3*   554 14.4    736 17.9   2832 68.7
DALLAS      1602 26.8   4380 73.2*   718 11.5   1562 24.9   3982 63.6
DEKALB      4545 46.6   5198 53.4*   458  5.6    531  6.5   7172 87.9
                                     *
ELMORE      1882 26.3   5273 73.7*  2810 49.2   1009 17.7   1897 33.2
ESCAMBIA    2392 31.0   5327 69.0*  1120 14.9   1352 18.0   5044 67.1
ETOWAH     12051 58.8   8448 41.2*  1042  5.9   1517  8.6  15003 85.4
FAYETTE     2003 36.6   3471 63.4*   352  8.4    454 10.9   3369 80.7
FRANKLIN    2648 43.5   3439 56.5*   387  6.2    463  7.4   5377 86.3
                                     *
GENEVA      1306 24.0   4126 76.0*   735 14.8    675 13.6   3560 71.6
GREENE       629 42.9    836 57.1*    78  5.1    132  8.6   1320 86.3
HALE         682 27.1   1830 72.9*   168  8.0    243 11.6   1677 80.3
HENRY        584 16.2   3028 83.8*   520 15.8    617 18.7   2161 65.5
HOUSTON     2048 22.1   7203 77.9*   835 12.5   1777 26.5   4084 61.0
                                     *
JACKSON     3241 39.0   5067 61.0*   376  5.3    338  4.7   6408 90.0
JEFFERSON  56000 58.0  40472 42.0*  6461  8.9  13615 18.7  52924 72.5
LAMAR       2008 36.1   3560 63.9*   247  6.4    313  8.1   3326 85.6
LAUDERDALE  6478 52.5   5855 47.5*   297  6.2    645  8.8   6404 87.2
LAWRENCE    2976 47.4   3305 52.6*   312  5.6    595 10.7   4634 83.6
                                     *
LEE         2761 43.0   3659 57.0*   306  5.9    545 10.6   4298 83.5
LIMESTONE   3887 54.6   3238 45.4*   431  6.6    680 10.4   5456 83.1
LOWNDES      422 23.0   1415 77.0*   569 30.8    468 25.3    811 43.9
MACON       2361 60.3   1555 39.7*   388 11.6    418 12.5   2528 75.8
MADISON    11844 65.1   6357 34.9*   366  3.4    811  7.5   9636 89.1
                                     *
MARENGO      740 21.3   2740 78.7*   338 12.5    394 14.5   1981 73.0
```

```
        DEMOC.  RUNOFF    1962*    DEMOC.  SENATOR    1962
                            *
COUNTY    GRAFFNRD    WALLACE    CROMMELIN   HALLMARK    HILL
          #     %     #     %*   #     %     #     %     #     %
----------------------------------*----------------------------------------------------------------------
MARION    2259 28.9  5569 71.1*  486  7.3   596  9.0   5553 83.7
MARSHALL  6780 51.8  6310 48.2*  589  7.1   670  8.1   6987 84.7
MOBILE   23622 48.7 24919 51.3* 4218 12.6  7476 22.4  21651 64.9
MONROE     892 24.3  2780 75.7*  500 12.6   595 15.0   2867 72.4
MONTGOMERY 8080 33.6 16000 66.4* 4128 20.5  4763 23.7  11212 55.8
                            *
MORGAN    8705 62.2  5292 37.8*  745  5.5  1361 10.1  11427 84.4
PERRY      620 24.1  1951 75.9*  338 13.4   342 13.6   1839 73.0
PICKENS   1484 32.8  3042 67.2*  488 11.8   423 10.2   3217 77.9
PIKE      1234 21.6  4473 78.4*  654 15.4   659 15.5   2942 69.1
RANDOLF   2261 33.8  4426 66.2*  220  8.0   300 11.0   2219 81.0
                            *
RUSSELL   1483 29.6  3524 70.4*  348  9.6   387 10.7   2875 79.6
SHELBY    2558 38.9  4011 61.1*  743 10.6   673  9.6   5617 79.9
ST. CLAIR 2564 42.7  3446 57.3*  631 11.0   629 10.9   4492 78.1
SUMTER     825 39.9  1243 60.1*  184  8.7   231 11.0   1691 80.3
TALLADEGA 5325 43.9  6797 56.1* 1622 13.1  1462 11.8   9259 75.0
                            *
TALLAPOOSA 3911 42.2  5364 57.8* 1292 21.2   439  7.2   4372 71.6
TUSCALOOSA 11625 64.9  6282 35.1* 1403 10.0  1659 11.8  10944 78.1
WALKER    5867 41.6  8252 58.4* 1168  9.2  1709 13.4   9876 77.4
WASHINGTON 1170 25.5  3427 74.5*  511 11.8  1019 23.5   2814 64.8
WILCOX     479 25.3  1412 74.7*  475 21.8   518 23.7   1189 54.5
                            *                -
WINSTON    718 42.8   961 57.2*   67  4.2   108  6.7   1438 89.2
----------------------------------*----------------------------------------------------------------------
                            *
TOTALS  269122      340730      * 56822      72855      363613
% OF VOTE  44.1       55.9      * 11.5       14.8        73.7
                            *
                            *
GEOGRAPHIC CLASS            *
                            *
LOWLANDS  41254 37.  71197 63.* 13537 15.  19199 21.   59185 64.
BLACK BELT 28606 29.  71577 71.* 14299 17.  16251 19.   55918 65.
PIEDMONT 163403 52. 151133 48.* 24044 10.  31239 13.  188954 77.
MOUNTAIN  35859 43.  46823 57.*  4942  7.   6166  9.   59556 84.
                            *
                            *
DEMOGRAPHIC CLASS           *
                            *
METRO   123222 55. 102478 45.* 17618 10.  29841 18.  121370 72.
TOWN     27097 44.  34662 56.*  4008  8.   7278 15.   38518 77.
RURAL   118803 37. 203590 63.* 35196 13.  35736 13.  203725 74.
```

	DEMOC. SENATOR 1966					DEMOC. GOVERNOR 1966								
COUNTY	CROMMELIN #	%	DIXON #	%	SPARKMAN #	%	STEWART #	%	WALLACE #	%	FLOWERS #	%	ELLIOTT #	%	GILCHRIST #	%	OTHER #	%
AUTAUGA	1663	37.9	819	18.7	1606	36.6	296	6.8	4041	59.4	1683	24.7	131	1.9	245	3.6	706	10.4
BALDWIN	1462	16.2	1887	21.0	5183	57.6	474	5.3	9533	69.1	1251	9.1	664	4.8	605	4.4	1742	12.6
BARBOUR	503	10.0	581	11.5	3602	71.3	368	7.3	5272	61.4	2536	29.5	101	1.2	83	1.0	594	6.9
BIBB	1666	32.9	581	11.5	2519	49.7	303	6.0	3652	68.8	609	11.5	158	3.0	123	2.3	766	14.4
BLOUNT	893	13.6	762	11.6	4590	69.8	328	5.0	3633	50.5	115	1.6	1880	26.1	278	3.9	1291	17.9
BULLOCK	386	17.1	348	15.4	1399	62.0	124	5.5	1857	42.4	2161	49.4	47	1.1	69	1.6	243	5.6
BUTLER	1446	22.3	1151	17.8	3373	52.1	503	7.8	4911	66.7	1419	19.3	101	1.4	279	3.8	652	8.9
CALHOUN	1971	10.2	3417	17.7	11975	62.1	1918	9.9	14094	61.5	2882	12.6	2201	9.6	1344	5.9	2382	10.4
CHAMBERS	452	7.8	1201	20.6	3878	66.5	301	5.2	5965	62.5	1055	11.0	367	3.8	314	3.3	1849	19.4
CHEROKEE	247	5.0	437	8.9	3050	61.9	1191	24.2	4219	66.7	279	4.4	311	4.9	239	3.8	1277	20.2
CHILTON	952	21.8	593	13.6	2523	57.9	289	6.6	4577	75.8	371	6.1	289	4.8	176	2.9	622	10.3
CHOCTAW	641	13.6	490	10.4	3264	69.3	312	6.6	3952	56.6	2337	33.5	110	1.6	128	1.8	453	6.5
CLARKE	892	16.6	1675	31.2	2485	46.2	322	6.0	5422	63.8	2043	24.0	189	2.2	169	2.0	676	8.0
CLAY	553	12.4	760	17.0	2841	63.5	318	7.1	3102	61.2	259	5.1	396	7.8	194	3.8	1115	22.0
CLEBURNE	301	7.9	458	12.0	2752	72.3	295	7.8	3374	73.0	106	2.3	215	4.7	155	3.4	771	16.7
COFFEE	641	11.0	1065	18.2	3644	62.4	490	8.4	6196	71.3	724	8.3	329	3.8	200	2.3	1237	14.2
COLBERT	1507	14.8	2720	26.6	5475	53.6	509	5.0	8149	56.8	1678	11.7	2121	14.8	704	4.9	1701	11.9
CONECUH	702	13.3	1712	32.5	2460	46.8	387	7.4	3748	63.6	1531	26.0	123	2.1	88	1.5	399	6.8
COOSA	861	20.9	1062	25.8	1909	46.3	287	7.0	2506	57.9	659	15.2	173	4.0	180	4.2	812	18.8
COVINGTON	1958	17.5	1976	17.7	6369	57.0	867	7.8	9584	75.9	853	6.8	331	2.6	409	3.2	1452	11.5
CRENSHAW	969	19.7	1362	27.6	2235	45.4	360	7.3	4239	68.6	896	14.5	91	1.5	192	3.1	762	12.3
CULLMAN	912	8.3	1287	11.7	8421	76.6	373	3.4	3967	33.6	140	1.2	2012	17.1	548	4.6	5127	43.5
DALE	594	11.0	1000	18.5	3543	65.7	254	4.7	6309	74.6	1014	12.0	159	1.9	172	2.0	801	9.5
DALLAS	1749	11.9	6032	41.1	5969	40.7	915	6.2	8033	49.2	6795	41.6	250	1.5	417	2.6	820	5.0
DEKALB	463	4.6	736	7.3	7267	71.8	1654	16.3	4667	49.6	176	1.9	1203	12.8	1630	17.3	1729	18.4
ELMORE	4249	53.8	1175	14.9	2202	27.9	271	3.4	7524	61.5	1837	16.0	254	2.2	355	3.1	1513	13.2
ESCAMBIA	804	10.3	1544	19.8	5034	64.4	429	5.5	7134	69.2	1420	13.8	419	4.1	285	2.8	1047	10.2
ETOWAH	2263	9.8	3973	17.3	14801	64.3	1980	8.6	14239	53.6	2795	10.5	3113	11.7	2506	9.4	3919	14.7
FAYETTE	607	12.6	916	19.1	2923	60.8	358	7.5	3366	59.3	343	6.0	942	16.6	124	2.2	898	15.8
FRANKLIN	699	9.2	1390	18.3	5043	66.5	454	6.0	3886	44.4	319	3.6	2838	32.5	200	2.3	1500	17.2
GENEVA	815	11.8	948	13.7	4798	69.3	366	5.3	6566	81.5	493	6.1	230	2.9	92	1.1	672	8.3
GREENE	512	19.4	561	21.3	1289	48.9	275	10.4	1395	34.2	2188	53.6	103	2.5	142	3.5	252	6.2
HALE	836	27.5	605	19.9	1361	44.7	241	7.9	2819	44.0	2996	46.7	133	2.1	102	1.6	363	5.7
HENRY	523	11.3	783	16.9	3039	65.5	297	6.4	3830	72.4	939	17.7	43	.8	56	1.1	423	8.0
HOUSTON	1233	10.9	1439	12.8	7785	69.1	812	7.2	11968	76.7	1888	12.1	181	1.2	309	2.0	1250	8.0
JACKSON	412	5.8	749	10.5	5646	79.5	298	4.2	6277	62.8	422	4.2	517	5.2	1012	10.1	1768	17.7
JEFFERSON	32485	29.0	31474	28.1	45586	40.7	2385	2.1	62295	42.2	49132	33.3	12200	8.3	9131	6.2	14775	10.0
LAMAR	415	8.8	774	16.5	3170	67.4	344	7.3	4589	69.6	211	3.2	962	14.6	80	1.2	752	11.4
LAUDERDALE	1349	12.1	2329	20.8	6902	61.8	595	5.3	9716	57.4	1300	7.7	2629	15.5	1152	6.8	2125	12.6
LAWRENCE	682	8.4	1667	20.6	5338	66.1	392	4.9	5070	55.7	759	8.3	566	6.2	355	3.9	2354	25.9
LEE	622	7.8	1026	12.9	5980	75.3	317	4.0	6138	54.4	2193	19.5	1233	10.9	497	4.4	1212	10.8
LIMESTONE	592	9.2	681	10.6	4851	75.7	280	4.4	5202	54.0	944	9.8	696	7.2	1073	11.1	1721	17.9
LOWNDES	625	38.9	299	18.6	546	34.0	138	8.6	1443	56.0	631	24.5	46	1.8	68	2.6	389	15.1
MACON	561	11.7	2761	57.5	1361	28.3	121	2.5	1594	23.3	2849	41.7	1901	27.8	98	1.4	386	5.7
MADISON	1116	5.3	1694	8.1	17691	84.2	498	2.4	12098	40.1	4492	14.9	3991	13.2	5691	18.8	3934	13.0
MARENGO	1291	16.6	3109	39.9	2784	35.7	614	7.9	4625	47.5	4154	42.7	195	2.0	196	2.0	563	5.8

DEMOC. SENATOR 1966   *   DEMOC. GOVERNOR 1966

COUNTY	CROMMELIN #	%	DIXON #	%	SPARKMAN #	%	STEWART #	%	WALLACE #	%	FLOWERS #	%	ELLIOTT #	%	GILCHRIST #	%	OTHER #	%
MARION	860	10.8	1410	17.8	5013	63.2	653	8.2*	6133	61.9	159	1.6	1997	20.2	234	2.4	1380	13.9
MARSHALL	1190	10.3	1433	12.4	8269	71.7	635	5.5*	7609	51.7	253	1.7	1135	7.7	2057	14.0	3657	24.9
MOBILE	7139	18.1	5140	13.0	25176	63.7	2075	5.2*	36633	54.4	13724	20.4	5901	8.8	3636	5.4	7452	11.1
MONROE	681	10.6	1071	16.7	4163	64.9	498	7.8*	4752	65.1	1808	24.8	119	1.6	158	2.2	464	6.4
MONTGOMERY	8160	28.2	7558	26.1	11640	40.2	1606	5.5*	20493	48.0	13208	31.0	1428	3.3	2292	5.4	5230	12.3
MORGAN	1065	8.6	1746	14.1	9245	74.5	352	2.8*	6902	42.1	690	4.2	882	5.4	2612	15.9	5293	32.3
PERRY	956	22.3	1004	23.4	1927	44.9	406	9.5*	2671	42.4	3063	48.7	115	1.8	128	2.0	317	5.0
PICKENS	451	8.6	1567	30.0	2712	52.0	489	9.4*	4037	63.6	1175	18.5	451	7.1	132	2.1	552	8.7
PIKE	1011	18.2	1703	30.7	2320	41.8	518	9.3*	5021	60.5	1908	23.0	215	2.6	161	1.9	990	11.9
RANDOLF	408	10.3	789	19.9	2487	62.8	278	7.0*	4699	65.7	626	8.8	430	6.0	253	3.5	1143	16.0
RUSSELL	717	10.1	938	13.2	5088	71.4	379	5.3*	5888	53.4	2751	25.0	250	2.3	101	.9	2033	18.4
SHELBY	1743	28.2	1058	17.1	3048	49.4	325	5.3*	5858	63.1	804	8.7	656	7.1	459	4.9	1511	16.3
ST. CLAIR	1275	19.6	1274	19.6	3670	56.4	283	4.4*	4974	63.6	536	6.9	949	12.1	300	3.8	1056	13.5
SUMTER	507	12.8	1228	30.9	1919	48.3	320	8.1*	2047	38.2	2703	50.5	138	2.6	100	1.9	368	6.9
TALLADEGA	2764	18.4	2359	15.7	8944	59.5	971	6.5*	9352	55.9	2802	16.7	1414	8.5	842	5.0	2320	13.9
TALLAPOOSA	1616	23.3	1284	18.5	3661	52.7	382	5.5*	6473	54.4	1171	9.8	400	3.4	414	3.5	3451	29.0
TUSCALOOSA	2898	16.3	2339	13.2	11595	65.2	947	5.3*	13348	53.7	4196	16.9	2685	10.8	2459	9.9	2175	8.7
WALKER	2631	16.4	3064	19.1	9451	59.0	874	5.5*	9450	54.3	965	5.5	4747	27.3	421	2.4	1816	10.4
WASHINGTON	809	14.3	1509	26.7	2967	52.5	369	6.5*	4359	69.8	1081	17.3	195	3.1	133	2.1	479	7.7
WILCOX	581	11.8	540	11.0	3250	66.0	554	11.2*	2554	42.4	2872	47.7	60	1.0	86	1.4	449	7.5
WINSTON	85	5.4	116	7.4	1288	82.5	72	4.6*	812	46.3	14	.8	661	37.7	59	3.4	206	11.8
TOTALS	114622		133139		378295		37889	*	480841		172386		71972		49502		114137	
% OF VOTE	17.3		20.1		57.0		5.7	*	54.1		19.4		8.1		5.6		12.8	

GEOGRAPHIC CLASS

	CROMMELIN #	%	DIXON #	%	SPARKMAN #	%	STEWART #	%	WALLACE #	%	FLOWERS #	%	ELLIOTT #	%	GILCHRIST #	%	OTHER #	%
LOWLANDS	16424	15.	17870	17.	66734	62.	6496	6.*	102521	65.	23344	15.	8500	5.	6033	4.	16894	11.
BLACK BELT	25394	18.	36535	26.	67557	49.	9683	7.*	100405	52.	63750	33.	6249	3.	5298	3.	17322	9.
PIEDMONT	64412	19.	67350	20.	185966	56.	15178	5.*	227262	51.	82450	19.	39922	9.	31493	7.	60170	14.
MOUNTAIN	8392	10.	11384	13.	58038	69.	6532	8.*	50653	52.	2842	3.	17301	18.	6678	7.	19751	20.

DEMOGRAPHIC CLASS

	CROMMELIN #	%	DIXON #	%	SPARKMAN #	%	STEWART #	%	WALLACE #	%	FLOWERS #	%	ELLIOTT #	%	GILCHRIST #	%	OTHER #	%
METRO	54061	22.	52178	22.	126489	52.	9491	4.*	159106	47.	87547	26.	29318	9.	25715	8.	37485	11.
TOWN	8084	11.	15901	21.	46964	62.	4971	7.*	56601	57.	16306	16.	6393	6.	5935	6.	13903	14.
RURAL	52477	15.	65060	19.	204842	59.	23427	7.*	265134	59.	68533	15.	36261	8.	17852	4.	62749	14.

COUNTY	ALLEN #	%	SELDEN #	%	SMITH #	%	FOLSOM #	%	OTHER #	%*	ALLEN #	%	SELDEN #	%
AUTAUGA	1944	42.8	1581	34.8	483	10.6	342	7.5	194	4.3*	1614	56.8	1229	43.2
BALDWIN	4920	56.7	2850	32.9	500	5.8	172	2.0	230	2.7*	2841	52.6	2564	47.4
BARBOUR	2937	50.5	1181	20.3	1158	19.9	445	7.7	94	1.6*	2000	58.5	1420	41.5
BIBB	1098	28.0	2315	59.1	289	7.4	152	3.9	62	1.6*	864	36.4	1511	63.6
BLOUNT	1747	56.0	876	28.1	110	3.5	278	8.9	107	3.4*	1158	59.8	778	40.2
BULLOCK	1374	47.7	681	23.6	333	11.6	416	14.4	77	2.7*	817	70.9	336	29.1
BUTLER	2527	56.0	1308	29.0	453	10.0	150	3.3	78	1.7*	1464	66.9	724	33.1
CALHOUN	6257	58.1	2569	23.9	1282	11.9	229	2.1	429	4.0*	3937	63.8	2234	36.2
CHAMBERS	1692	39.8	1874	44.1	437	10.3	187	4.4	64	1.5*	1098	52.1	1010	47.9
CHEROKEE	2266	62.0	630	17.2	81	2.2	216	5.9	460	12.6*	2638	67.3	1280	32.7
CHILTON	1314	30.9	2492	58.6	194	4.6	156	3.7	95	2.2*	1277	38.3	2058	61.7
CHOCTAW	1094	31.6	1820	52.5	237	6.8	255	7.4	60	1.7*	860	48.9	900	51.1
CLARKE	2194	36.4	2494	41.3	906	15.0	282	4.7	156	2.6*	921	31.8	1976	68.2
CLAY	1768	51.7	1220	35.7	59	1.7	295	8.6	75	2.2*	2377	60.3	1567	39.7
CLEBURNE	1473	61.1	649	26.9	40	1.7	186	7.7	61	2.5*	453	53.7	391	46.3
COFFEE	2738	42.9	2087	32.7	795	12.4	696	10.9	71	1.1*	1800	56.5	1384	43.5
COLBERT	2995	39.1	2534	33.1	1491	19.5	464	6.1	176	2.3*	2083	39.9	3141	60.1
CONECUH	1679	42.2	1408	35.4	407	10.2	307	7.7	177	4.4*	755	50.1	752	49.9
COOSA	1134	39.3	922	31.9	478	16.6	223	7.7	130	4.5*	740	65.3	393	34.7
COVINGTON	3662	42.8	3771	44.1	674	7.9	315	3.7	129	1.5*	2863	54.5	2391	45.5
CRENSHAW	1105	36.6	1545	51.2	237	7.9	99	3.3	31	1.0*	897	62.8	531	37.2
CULLMAN	1896	31.4	2160	35.7	477	7.9	1393	23.0	120	2.0*	2635	50.6	2576	49.4
DALE	2578	45.1	2370	41.4	438	7.7	260	4.5	74	1.3*	1336	37.3	2243	62.7
DALLAS	2574	33.6	3359	43.8	1176	15.3	458	6.0	102	1.3*	2279	47.9	2474	52.1
DEKALB	2612	45.0	1877	32.4	383	6.6	772	13.3	156	2.7*	1582	55.1	1290	44.9
ELMORE	3844	45.0	2503	29.3	727	8.5	473	5.5	993	11.6*	3187	64.1	1785	35.9
ESCAMBIA	3349	43.8	3189	41.7	398	5.2	495	6.5	216	2.8*	2148	44.1	2723	55.9
ETOWAH	11297	67.4	2581	15.4	1839	11.0	515	3.1	527	3.1*	11068	73.0	4085	27.0
FAYETTE	2204	40.6	2154	39.6	178	3.3	780	14.4	118	2.2*	1512	57.5	1118	42.5
FRANKLIN	2507	44.1	1880	33.0	626	11.0	536	9.4	141	2.5*	1990	53.3	1747	46.7
GENEVA	1589	30.5	1497	28.7	1893	36.3	184	3.5	47	.9*	1290	42.9	1716	57.1
GREENE	543	22.5	1313	54.3	291	12.0	193	8.0	77	3.2*	1026	51.7	959	48.3
HALE	889	21.9	2202	54.3	526	13.0	360	8.9	78	1.9*	1483	38.7	2351	61.3
HENRY	2053	45.5	1424	31.6	723	16.0	217	4.8	96	2.1*	1986	56.0	1559	44.0
HOUSTON	4890	57.9	2369	28.1	790	9.4	198	2.3	194	2.3*	2667	55.0	2186	45.0
JACKSON	2549	39.4	2349	36.3	409	6.3	1052	16.2	115	1.8*	2566	48.3	2745	51.7
JEFFERSON	32619	38.7	27657	32.8	18968	22.5	2870	3.4	2191	2.6*	32109	45.9	37770	54.1
LAMAR	1954	48.0	1622	39.9	82	2.0	309	7.6	100	2.5*	837	57.4	620	42.6
LAUDERDALE	3162	42.2	2529	33.7	1056	14.1	553	7.4	200	2.7*	2881	47.4	3193	52.6
LAWRENCE	1500	38.4	1438	36.8	409	10.5	424	10.9	133	3.4*	1832	57.2	1370	42.8
LEE	2983	44.2	2312	34.2	1010	15.0	324	4.8	125	1.9*	2233	53.7	1929	46.3
LIMESTONE	2552	44.7	2092	36.6	503	8.8	362	6.3	203	3.6*	2187	53.1	1930	46.9
LOWNDES	975	43.4	569	25.3	135	6.0	477	21.2	89	4.0*	525	62.7	312	37.3
MACON	851	20.4	450	10.8	2082	49.9	625	15.0	164	3.9*	1115	44.2	1407	55.8
MADISON	6397	32.0	6922	34.6	4791	23.9	982	4.9	925	4.6*	5653	47.9	6143	52.1
MARENGO	1108	17.5	3543	55.9	1333	21.0	233	3.7	118	1.9*	2482	49.6	2524	50.4

COUNTY	ALLEN #	%	SELDEN #	%	SMITH #	%	FOLSOM #	%	OTHER #	%*	ALLEN #	%	SELDEN #	%
MARION	1391	52.0	946	35.4	68	2.5	229	8.6	39	1.5*	1011	62.8	598	37.2
MARSHALL	3579	49.6	2306	31.9	421	5.8	723	10.0	192	2.7*	3639	56.8	2767	43.2
MOBILE	21777	49.0	13616	30.7	5156	11.6	1945	4.4	1918	4.3*	18070	45.4	21757	54.6
MONROE	2414	50.1	1490	30.9	702	14.6	124	2.6	86	1.8*	1034	43.0	1370	57.0
MONTGOMERY	8126	38.6	6222	29.5	4670	22.2	1047	5.0	1012	4.8*	9340	61.2	5921	38.8
MORGAN	4748	40.8	4839	41.5	816	7.0	887	7.6	361	3.1*	5894	52.9	5244	47.1
PERRY	1133	28.8	1772	45.1	401	10.2	564	14.3	62	1.6*	1423	40.9	2053	59.1
PICKENS	1096	26.8	2480	60.7	251	6.1	200	4.9	57	1.4*	950	36.3	1669	63.7
PIKE	1901	42.4	1500	33.5	791	17.7	191	4.3	96	2.1*	2184	57.0	1645	43.0
RANDOLF	2112	58.8	934	26.0	74	2.1	387	10.8	87	2.4*	810	54.5	675	45.5
RUSSELL	2327	41.3	2495	44.3	207	3.7	437	7.8	163	2.9*	1434	45.8	1698	54.2
SHELBY	1913	37.6	2668	52.5	166	3.3	207	4.1	128	2.5*	1560	37.7	2581	62.3
ST. CLAIR	2681	58.2	1199	26.0	337	7.3	240	5.2	151	3.3*	2287	62.8	1357	37.2
SUMTER	367	15.8	1597	68.7	141	6.1	162	7.0	59	2.5*	551	31.0	1229	69.0
TALLADEGA	3939	31.8	6049	48.8	1187	9.6	830	6.7	384	3.1*	2931	47.2	3278	52.8
TALLAPOOSA	2556	45.1	2263	39.9	323	5.7	376	6.6	148	2.6*	4716	59.9	3156	40.1
TUSCALOOSA	5324	27.9	10531	55.1	2212	11.6	623	3.3	418	2.2*	5167	33.4	10308	66.6
WALKER	6392	45.5	4277	30.4	1858	13.2	1236	8.8	294	2.1*	6486	60.1	4305	39.9
WASHINGTON	1892	36.9	2114	41.3	631	12.3	258	5.0	229	4.5*	1293	40.7	1886	59.3
WILCOX	937	28.1	1407	42.2	569	17.1	291	8.7	131	3.9*	1201	47.8	1314	52.2
WINSTON	485	43.6	410	36.8	60	5.4	137	12.3	21	1.9*	464	59.8	312	40.2
TOTALS	224483		190283		72928		32004		16294	*	196511		192448	
% OF VOTE	41.9		35.5		13.6		6.0		3.0	*	50.5		49.5	

GEOGRAPHIC CLASS

LOWLANDS	48500	47.	35408	34.	11512	11.	4622	4.	3139	3.*	35205	47.	39381	53.
BLACK BELT	41043	37.	42296	38.	17975	16.	7776	7.	3226	3.*	37444	51.	35822	49.
PIEDMONT	109516	41.	94918	36.	38948	15.	13034	5.	8284	3.*	99693	50.	98847	50.
MOUNTAIN	25424	46.	17711	32.	4493	8.	6572	12.	1645	3.*	24169	57.	18398	43.

DEMOGRAPHIC CLASS

METRO	85540	42.	67529	33.	37636	18.	7982	4.	6991	3.*	81407	49.	85984	51.
TOWN	23958	46.	18160	35.	5327	10.	2762	5.	1446	3.*	19092	53.	17029	47.
RURAL	114985	41.	104594	38.	29965	11.	21260	8.	7857	3.*	96012	52.	89435	48.

COUNTY	BREWER #	%	WALLACE #	%	WOODS #	%	CARTER #	%	OTHER #	%	* BREWER #	%	WALLACE #	%
AUTAUGA	2639	33.4	3452	43.6	1409	17.8	258	3.3	155	2.0*	3697	43.9	4725	56.1
BALDWIN	5572	31.9	9850	56.5	1429	8.2	303	1.7	295	1.7*	6396	33.8	12534	66.2
BARBOUR	3464	37.3	4979	53.6	508	5.5	72	.8	268	2.9*	4122	41.6	5789	58.4
BIBB	1690	31.0	2580	47.3	947	17.4	145	2.7	87	1.6*	1962	36.1	3476	63.9
BLOUNT	3672	44.1	3028	36.3	1384	16.6	123	1.5	126	1.5*	4492	49.6	4572	50.4
										*				
BULLOCK	2137	43.3	1663	33.7	971	19.7	64	1.3	97	2.0*	3351	62.0	2050	38.0
BUTLER	2338	31.0	3786	50.2	1029	13.7	363	4.8	19	.3*	2937	37.6	4874	62.4
CALHOUN	9583	35.9	10415	39.0	5691	21.3	825	3.1	181	.7*	13639	45.6	16261	54.4
CHAMBERS	4905	42.2	5828	50.2	651	5.6	74	.6	163	1.4*	5028	41.6	7045	58.4
CHEROKEE	2299	34.5	3463	52.0	806	12.1	46	.7	42	.6*	2383	37.5	3977	62.5
CHILTON	2910	35.6	3607	44.1	1378	16.9	247	3.0	34	.4*	3534	40.1	5273	59.9
CHOCTAW	2812	38.6	3820	52.5	498	6.8	103	1.4	46	.6*	3098	42.1	4256	57.9
CLARKE	3824	39.5	4844	50.1	734	7.6	120	1.2	152	1.6*	4124	41.3	5872	58.7
CLAY	1971	34.4	2277	39.7	1282	22.4	182	3.2	19	.3*	2581	43.6	3344	56.4
CLEBURNE	1927	37.3	2392	46.3	667	12.9	140	2.7	37	.7*	2103	40.5	3092	59.5
COFFEE	4264	38.3	5520	49.6	835	7.5	323	2.9	185	1.7*	4357	37.1	7381	62.9
COLBERT	6691	38.9	6226	36.2	3913	22.7	302	1.8	77	.4*	7889	46.5	9086	53.5
CONECUH	2212	38.2	2948	50.9	387	6.7	226	3.9	22	.4*	2290	38.8	3613	61.2
COOSA	1781	41.6	1511	35.3	855	20.0	110	2.6	23	.5*	2095	49.4	2145	50.6
COVINGTON	4421	31.6	7604	54.4	1278	9.1	636	4.6	31	.2*	4560	30.7	10314	69.3
CRENSHAW	1977	32.9	2991	49.8	775	12.9	250	4.2	18	.3*	2220	36.7	3828	63.3
CULLMAN	8022	43.4	5658	30.6	4468	24.2	217	1.2	116	.6*	9667	53.2	8495	46.8
DALE	3284	31.8	5683	55.0	990	9.6	205	2.0	176	1.7*	3641	33.8	7145	66.2
DALLAS	9262	54.5	5760	33.9	1733	10.2	179	1.1	60	.4*	10903	60.6	7090	39.4
DEKALB	5633	45.9	4689	38.2	1820	14.8	38	.3	83	.7*	6736	52.8	6022	47.2
										*				
ELMORE	4361	35.1	5705	45.9	1664	13.4	468	3.8	243	2.0*	5077	40.6	7435	59.4
ESCAMBIA	4371	37.0	6567	55.6	649	5.5	187	1.6	29	.2*	4306	36.4	7510	63.6
ETOWAH	9946	33.3	9511	31.8	9620	32.2	709	2.4	119	.4*	15088	48.4	16102	51.6
FAYETTE	2957	39.5	2745	36.7	1626	21.7	138	1.8	23	.3*	3474	46.4	4013	53.6
FRANKLIN	3794	37.7	3701	36.8	2392	23.8	127	1.3	54	.5*	4495	46.2	5235	53.8
										*				
GENEVA	2306	26.3	5637	64.4	552	6.3	218	2.5	45	.5*	2219	24.4	6889	75.6
GREENE	730	36.7	1018	51.2	198	9.9	36	1.8	8	.4*	2721	69.9	1172	30.1
HALE	2340	46.5	2023	40.2	402	8.0	171	3.4	96	1.9*	3453	58.6	2439	41.4
HENRY	1776	32.2	3234	58.6	405	7.3	88	1.6	19	.3*	1966	35.4	3585	64.6
HOUSTON	5079	28.2	11065	61.5	1468	8.2	311	1.7	77	.4*	5515	29.0	13480	71.0
										*				
JACKSON	3641	32.0	5976	52.4	1687	14.8	15	.1	76	.7*	4211	34.2	8084	65.8
JEFFERSON	90124	53.8	53995	32.3	20979	12.5	1197	.7	1081	.6*	115632	60.6	75098	39.4
LAMAR	1973	27.9	3832	54.1	1030	14.6	210	3.0	32	.5*	2051	29.6	4874	70.4
LAUDERDALE	7848	40.3	7594	39.0	3771	19.4	191	1.0	67	.3*	9429	46.4	10875	53.6
LAWRENCE	2946	30.7	4108	42.8	2394	25.0	100	1.0	42	.4*	3690	37.7	6089	62.3
										*				
LEE	7009	51.2	5587	40.8	901	6.6	80	.6	108	.8*	7513	52.2	6875	47.8
LIMESTONE	4264	37.0	5199	45.1	1967	17.1	57	.5	46	.4*	5007	42.5	6775	57.5
LOWNDES	1907	45.2	1115	26.4	938	22.2	101	2.4	155	3.7*	2966	69.4	1306	30.6
MACON	4448	63.3	1286	18.3	1191	17.0	49	.7	48	.7*	5769	79.0	1529	21.0
MADISON	19681	43.7	14796	32.8	9519	21.1	273	.6	815	1.8*	27587	56.3	21429	43.7
										*				
MARENGO	4930	49.3	4014	40.2	798	8.0	152	1.5	102	1.0*	5543	55.0	4539	45.0

COUNTY	BREWER #	%	WALLACE #	%	WOODS #	%	CARTER #	%	OTHER #	% *	BREWER #	%	WALLACE #	%
MARION	3212	29.9	4132	38.5	3146	29.3	203	1.9	45	.4	4202	40.3	6229	59.7
MARSHALL	6491	39.1	6157	37.1	3774	22.7	115	.7	61	.4*	8166	46.9	9250	53.1
MOBILE	28357	36.7	38156	49.4	8627	11.2	853	1.1	1293	1.7*	34020	40.9	49131	59.1
MONROE	3221	41.2	4006	51.2	387	4.9	167	2.1	45	.6*	3242	41.9	4499	58.1
MONTGOMERY	21406	47.9	15258	34.2	6442	14.4	893	2.0	675	1.5*	27996	57.0	21142	43.0
MORGAN	11716	52.4	7446	33.3	3045	13.6	83	.4	67	.3*	13601	55.9	10737	44.1
PERRY	3354	55.5	1927	31.9	526	8.7	171	2.8	60	1.0*	3929	62.3	2374	37.7
PICKENS	3145	44.2	3037	42.7	745	10.5	153	2.2	33	.5*	3370	45.5	4030	54.5
PIKE	3506	39.6	4042	45.6	990	11.2	190	2.1	130	1.5*	4138	44.1	5249	55.9
RANDOLF	2862	33.2	4902	56.8	681	7.9	138	1.6	45	.5*	2750	36.5	4785	63.5
RUSSELL	3980	39.9	5469	54.9	397	4.0	59	.6	59	.6*	4434	39.6	6760	60.4
SHELBY	4309	40.3	4152	38.9	1860	17.4	147	1.4	215	2.0*	5104	45.1	6211	54.9
ST. CLAIR	3289	35.5	3591	38.7	2120	22.9	234	2.5	34	.4*	4190	45.0	5131	55.0
SUMTER	3271	63.2	1555	30.0	300	5.8	41	.8	12	.2*	3715	66.6	1867	33.4
TALLADEGA	8295	41.5	7505	37.5	3649	18.2	444	2.2	112	.6*	9780	48.3	10488	51.7
TALLAPOOSA	4674	36.1	4692	36.2	3033	23.4	330	2.5	227	1.8*	5931	45.8	7029	54.2
TUSCALOOSA	13910	47.6	11010	37.6	3329	11.4	288	1.0	715	2.4*	15937	51.0	15324	49.0
WALKER	6949	32.2	9527	44.2	4793	22.2	219	1.0	73	.3*	8797	38.7	13960	61.3
WASHINGTON	2072	30.9	3760	56.1	723	10.8	134	2.0	14	.2*	2126	31.9	4537	68.1
WILCOX	3198	57.4	1916	34.4	295	5.3	124	2.2	43	.8*	3734	62.1	2277	37.9
WINSTON	1208	46.5	921	35.4	436	16.8	26	1.0	8	.3*	1272	50.8	1230	49.2
TOTALS	428146		416443		149887		15441		9763	*	525951		559832	
% OF VOTE	42.0		40.8		14.7		1.5		1.0	*	48.4		51.6	

GEOGRAPHIC CLASS

	BREWER #	%	WALLACE #	%	WOODS #	%	CARTER #	%	OTHER #	% *	BREWER #	%	WALLACE #	%
LOWLANDS	61703	34.	96833	53.	17326	10.	3420	2.	2163	1.*	69360	36.	122749	64.
BLACK BELT	89900	45.	81152	41.	21283	11.	3780	2.	2304	1.*	111498	52.	101037	48.
PIEDMONT	231622	44.	191206	37.	86572	17.	7112	1.	4612	1.*	290672	52.	268992	48.
MOUNTAIN	44921	38.	47252	40.	24706	21.	1129	1.	684	1.*	54421	45.	67054	55.

DEMOGRAPHIC CLASS

	BREWER #	%	WALLACE #	%	WOODS #	%	CARTER #	%	OTHER #	% *	BREWER #	%	WALLACE #	%
METRO	183424	47.	142726	36.	58516	15.	4213	1.	4698	1.*	236260	54.	198226	46.
TOWN	47468	42.	47749	42.	16105	14.	1648	1.	511	0.*	57521	47.	65203	53.
RURAL	197254	38.	225968	44.	75266	15.	9580	2.	4554	1.*	232170	44.	296403	56.

COUNTY	SPARKMAN #	%	ALLEN #	%	EDINGTON #	%	MIMS #	%	OTHER #	%*	CIVL SERV #	%	AGAINST #	%
AUTAUGA	2244	35.1	2453	38.4	182	2.8	976	15.3	535	8.4*	472	57.2	353	42.8
BALDWIN	4161	33.8	4936	40.1	680	5.5	2323	18.9	195	1.6*	1717	69.0	770	31.0
BARBOUR	4158	61.8	1762	26.2	247	3.7	402	6.0	156	2.3*	537	53.0	476	47.0
BIBB	2164	45.0	1938	40.3	51	1.1	577	12.0	82	1.7*	396	49.4	405	50.6
BLOUNT	2631	51.6	1302	25.5	55	1.1	876	17.2	235	4.6*	568	37.1	961	62.9
BULLOCK	1038	39.0	1024	38.4	89	3.4	316	11.9	197	7.4*	273	61.2	173	38.8
BUTLER	2247	35.5	2890	45.7	140	2.2	890	14.1	156	2.5*	547	49.4	560	50.6
CALHOUN	6627	49.9	4754	35.8	267	2.0	1211	9.1	431	3.2*	1960	69.9	843	30.1
CHAMBERS	4026	51.4	2564	32.7	149	1.9	851	10.9	247	3.2*	977	61.0	624	39.0
CHEROKEE	3149	64.0	1097	22.3	124	2.5	247	5.0	301	6.1*	362	65.2	193	34.8
CHILTON	2205	50.4	1338	30.6	55	1.3	684	15.6	95	2.2*	481	37.9	789	62.1
CHOCTAW	3322	55.3	1479	24.6	45	.7	1016	16.9	150	2.5*	374	66.2	191	33.8
CLARKE	3433	40.9	3328	39.7	242	2.9	1272	15.2	111	1.3*	657	58.9	458	41.1
CLAY	2063	49.2	1233	29.4	59	1.4	710	16.9	124	3.0*	462	52.0	427	48.0
CLEBURNE	2202	49.0	1580	35.2	70	1.6	464	10.3	174	3.9*	295	70.1	126	29.9
COFFEE	5471	57.7	2324	24.5	223	2.4	1280	13.5	190	2.0*	415	37.9	681	62.1
COLBERT	6020	54.8	2829	25.8	256	2.3	1371	12.5	510	4.6*	1106	67.2	539	32.8
CONECUH	2005	38.3	1722	32.9	111	2.1	1143	21.9	249	4.8*	331	56.2	258	43.8
COOSA	1911	46.3	1257	30.5	130	3.2	736	17.8	92	2.2*	294	51.1	281	48.9
COVINGTON	4229	36.7	4618	40.0	242	2.1	1936	16.8	508	4.4*	822	61.6	513	38.4
CRENSHAW	1393	40.6	1375	40.1	82	2.4	515	15.0	66	1.9*	387	43.8	496	56.2
CULLMAN	5994	67.3	1804	20.2	90	1.0	757	8.5	265	3.0*	938	44.3	1177	55.7
DALE	5482	55.5	2303	23.3	202	2.0	1655	16.8	237	2.4*	481	49.8	485	50.2
DALLAS	2678	40.0	2383	35.6	135	2.0	1288	19.2	210	3.1*	1182	79.7	301	20.3
DEKALB	4813	74.6	801	12.4	49	.8	508	7.9	285	4.4*	1009	61.8	624	38.2
ELMORE	3498	35.3	4278	43.2	292	2.9	1470	14.8	363	3.7*	745	44.5	928	55.5
ESCAMBIA	3716	39.1	2960	31.1	315	3.3	2382	25.1	132	1.4*	705	75.0	235	25.0
ETOWAH	13317	50.0	8263	31.0	1063	4.0	3009	11.3	1002	3.8*	5137	63.0	3018	37.0
FAYETTE	2727	48.8	1119	20.0	61	1.1	1410	25.2	268	4.8*	445	43.5	579	56.5
FRANKLIN	2809	51.2	1108	20.2	28	.5	1094	19.9	448	8.2*	567	49.3	582	50.7
GENEVA	3770	64.9	1405	24.2	117	2.0	328	5.7	185	3.2*	457	57.3	341	42.7
GREENE	1088	67.7	344	21.4	30	1.9	117	7.3	27	1.7*	350	75.1	116	24.9
HALE	1823	46.0	1584	40.0	98	2.5	393	9.9	65	1.6*	597	82.8	124	17.2
HENRY	2608	57.4	949	20.9	51	1.1	735	16.2	203	4.5*	357	58.4	254	41.6
HOUSTON	4966	49.5	2657	26.5	228	2.3	1821	18.2	355	3.5*	667	59.4	455	40.6
JACKSON	6658	78.7	1033	12.2	151	1.8	421	5.0	193	2.3*	661	56.1	518	43.9
JEFFERSON	45150	53.6	23702	28.2	3343	4.0	9780	11.6	2197	2.6*	19344	71.5	7724	28.5
LAMAR	3492	66.0	771	14.6	57	1.1	471	8.9	500	9.5*	407	51.0	391	49.0
LAUDERDALE	6525	56.8	2927	25.5	473	4.1	968	8.4	587	5.1*	981	77.1	291	22.9
LAWRENCE	4576	61.3	1861	24.9	48	.6	616	8.3	361	4.8*	441	47.7	483	52.3
LEE	4873	54.5	2250	25.2	503	5.6	922	10.3	386	4.3*	919	78.9	246	21.1
LIMESTONE	4256	54.9	2609	33.6	166	2.1	392	5.1	332	4.3*	555	61.8	343	38.2
LOWNDES	1590	55.6	763	26.7	115	4.0	327	11.4	67	2.3*	370	55.6	295	44.4
MACON	3367	63.5	1324	25.0	168	3.2	225	4.2	218	4.1*	695	79.2	183	20.8
MADISON	20588	62.2	7041	21.3	1049	3.2	1536	4.6	2906	8.8*	1225	72.9	455	27.1
MARENGO	4199	53.5	2098	26.7	211	2.7	1155	14.7	188	2.4*	767	76.5	235	23.5

COUNTY	SPARKMAN #	%	ALLEN #	%	EDINGTON #	%	MIMS #	%	OTHER #	%	*	CIVL SERV #	%	AGAINST #	%
								DEMOC. SENATOR 1972			* SPECL. REFERENDUM 1951				
MARION	1392	48.6	508	17.7	11	.4	134	4.7	821	28.6	*	540	39.1	842	60.9
MARSHALL	3558	53.2	1737	26.0	189	2.8	914	13.7	288	4.3	*	1001	55.7	797	44.3
MOBILE	15252	29.8	21023	41.0	4104	8.0	9613	18.8	1241	2.4	*	5551	77.6	1606	22.4
MONROE	2648	41.7	1299	20.5	226	3.6	2121	33.4	53	.8	*	544	77.2	161	22.8
MONTGOMERY	11789	45.3	8226	31.6	1407	5.4	3608	13.9	971	3.7	*	4260	67.1	2093	32.9
											*				
MORGAN	8949	59.8	3933	26.3	259	1.7	1355	9.1	472	3.2	*	1470	46.9	1666	53.1
PERRY	2949	63.3	1102	23.6	78	1.7	446	9.6	85	1.8	*	479	81.2	111	18.8
PICKENS	2490	50.2	1399	28.2	59	1.2	738	14.9	273	5.5	*	364	43.5	472	56.5
PIKE	2772	44.1	2231	35.5	239	3.8	856	13.6	188	3.0	*	568	57.4	422	42.6
RANDOLF	2217	52.6	1218	28.9	121	2.9	375	8.9	284	6.7	*	295	35.9	526	64.1
											*				
RUSSELL	3601	51.9	1912	27.6	168	2.4	1014	14.6	245	3.5	*	1261	94.2	77	5.8
SHELBY	2052	45.6	1653	36.8	81	1.8	603	13.4	108	2.4	*	880	73.6	316	26.4
ST. CLAIR	2469	49.5	1625	32.6	212	4.3	557	11.2	120	2.4	*	566	62.1	345	37.9
SUMTER	2536	77.2	392	11.9	44	1.3	260	7.9	55	1.7	*	478	77.3	140	22.7
TALLADEGA	6702	51.7	3298	25.4	747	5.8	1905	14.7	312	2.4	*	1377	69.0	618	31.0
											*				
TALLAPOOSA	3907	44.2	2796	31.6	226	2.6	1545	17.5	373	4.2	*	928	55.9	732	44.1
TUSCALOOSA	12122	49.1	6643	26.9	1117	4.5	3777	15.3	1015	4.1	*	1858	63.0	1091	37.0
WALKER	7739	53.3	4133	28.5	139	1.0	2192	15.1	310	2.1	*	1155	43.4	1506	56.6
WASHINGTON	2456	38.6	2519	39.6	109	1.7	1160	18.2	122	1.9	*	392	68.1	184	31.9
WILCOX	2125	59.4	709	19.8	58	1.6	636	17.8	48	1.3	*	451	65.8	234	34.2
											*				
WINSTON	851	72.9	194	16.6	9	.8	76	6.5	38	3.3	*	377	46.1	440	53.9
											*				
TOTALS	331838		194690		22145		87461		24206		*	78230		44879	
% OF VOTE	50.3		29.5		3.4		13.2		3.7		*	63.5		36.5	
											*				
GEOGRAPHIC CLASS											*				
											*				
LOWLANDS	50896	39.	46120	36.	6302	5.	23013	18.	3231	2.	*	11594	67.	5766	33.
BLACK BELT	66710	49.	41373	30.	4143	3.	19934	15.	4450	3.	*	15914	67.	7687	33.
PIEDMONT	174638	53.	93480	28.	10855	3.	37295	11.	13341	4.	*	43544	65.	23786	35.
MOUNTAIN	39594	61.	13717	21.	845	1.	7219	11.	3184	5.	*	7178	48.	7640	52.
											*				
DEMOGRAPHIC CLASS											*				
											*				
METRO	118211	48.	74898	30.	12083	5.	31323	13.	9339	4.	*	37375	70.	15987	30.
TOWN	33346	53.	18566	29.	1530	2.	7657	12.	2300	4.	*	7521	67.	3633	33.
RURAL	180278	51.	101226	29.	8532	2.	48481	14.	12570	4.	*	33334	57.	25259	43.

		SPECL. REFERENDUM 1951*		SPECL. REFERENDUM 1956			
COUNTY	VOTER QUAL	AGAINST	FOR		AGAINST	
	# %	# %*	# %	# -%

COUNTY	#	%	#	%*	#	%	#	-%
AUTAUGA	323	42.6	435	57.4*	1033	79.2	271	20.8
BALDWIN	1628	64.6	893	35.4*	2418	67.1	1186	32.9
BARBOUR	400	41.3	568	58.7*	1354	77.2	400	22.8
BIBB	294	39.3	455	60.7*	1655	80.9	392	19.1
BLOUNT	424	28.6	1057	71.4*	638	28.9	1573	71.1
BULLOCK	306	61.9	188	38.1*	608	89.7	70	10.3
BUTLER	523	49.0	545	51.0*	1785	85.1	313	14.9
CALHOUN	1237	47.4	1370	52.6*	2264	42.9	3009	57.1
CHAMBERS	860	55.3	694	44.7*	1638	72.3	626	27.7
CHEROKEE	293	58.3	210	41.7*	503	47.4	558	52.6
CHILTON	367	29.0	897	71.0*	1141	61.0	731	39.0
CHOCTAW	455	73.2	167	26.8*	618	66.4	313	33.6
CLARKE	814	63.6	465	36.4*	2019	89.4	240	10.6
CLAY	438	57.5	324	42.5*	753	56.4	583	43.6
CLEBURNE	311	72.0	121	28.0*	379	46.9	429	53.1
COFFEE	313	30.9	700	69.1*	1642	76.4	508	23.6
COLBERT	678	44.0	862	56.0*	961	36.5	1672	63.5
CONECUH	329	55.2	267	44.8*	1427	90.3	153	9.7
COOSA	206	38.7	326	61.3*	717	62.9	423	37.1
COVINGTON	685	51.9	635	48.1*	2753	77.3	809	22.7
CRENSHAW	230	30.1	535	69.9*	1324	79.8	335	20.2
CULLMAN	680	33.3	1365	66.7*	1173	43.6	1518	56.4
DALE	597	57.5	442	42.5*	1661	83.3	334	16.7
DALLAS	1018	68.0	479	32.0*	3492	96.1	140	3.9
DEKALB	685	44.4	858	55.6*	1018	38.0	1660	62.0
ELMORE	611	38.9	958	61.1*	1470	53.2	1292	46.8
ESCAMBIA	464	62.4	280	37.6*	1398	69.0	627	31.0
ETOWAH	3672	47.8	4004	52.2*	3486	41.6	4899	58.4
FAYETTE	304	31.1	674	68.9*	634	35.8	1135	64.2
FRANKLIN	479	42.4	651	57.6*	474	28.8	1173	71.2
GENEVA	611	58.7	430	41.3*	1217	76.1	383	23.9
GREENE	331	72.1	128	27.9*	702	89.1	86	10.9
HALE	604	80.7	144	19.3*	1201	93.3	86	6.7
HENRY	425	62.5	255	37.5*	1205	85.6	203	14.4
HOUSTON	824	65.7	430	34.3*	3178	87.9	436	12.1
JACKSON	539	48.7	567	51.3*	784	47.8	856	52.2
JEFFERSON	11542	44.5	14412	55.5*	26154	60.0	17472	40.0
LAMAR	450	54.2	381	45.8*	614	44.9	753	55.1
LAUDERDALE	579	45.7	687	54.3*	805	29.9	1891	70.1
LAWRENCE	425	47.3	474	52.7*	500	40.9	723	59.1
LEE	640	56.7	488	43.3*	1496	72.7	563	27.3
LIMESTONE	342	41.2	489	58.8*	756	48.9	790	51.1
LOWNDES	326	50.7	317	49.3*	771	86.7	118	13.3
MACON	673	62.1	411	37.9*	773	56.1	604	43.9
MADISON	911	55.3	736	44.7*	2074	57.9	1505	42.1
MARENGO	807	75.2	266	24.8*	1936	95.0	101	5.0

COUNTY	VOTER QUAL #	%	AGAINST #	%*	FOR #	%	AGAINST #	%
MARION	395	30.4	904	69.6*	556	25.8	1598	74.2
MARSHALL	855	49.9	858	50.1*	1139	44.4	1426	55.6
MOBILE	5404	70.4	2269	29.6*	7139	56.1	5580	43.9
MONROE	594	77.9	169	22.1*	1346	87.1	200	12.9
MONTGOMERY	2804	45.8	3318	54.2*	6775	69.8	2927	30.2
MORGAN	1196	40.3	1774	59.7*	1387	35.0	2577	65.0
PERRY	381	66.6	191	33.4*	1414	92.4	117	7.6
PICKENS	531	55.8	421	44.2*	1699	89.0	209	11.0
PIKE	429	45.8	507	54.2*	2054	88.4	270	11.6
RANDOLF	214	26.9	582	73.1*	802	51.7	749	48.3
RUSSELL	1220	93.0	92	7.0*	801	58.1	577	41.9
SHELBY	570	59.6	386	40.4*	1677	62.7	997	37.3
ST. CLAIR	432	48.3	463	51.7*	1341	67.3	652	32.7
SUMTER	411	67.3	200	32.7*	922	75.6	297	24.4
TALLADEGA	969	52.7	869	47.3*	2785	67.3	1354	32.7
TALLAPOOSA	656	43.5	851	56.5*	1804	68.9	814	31.1
TUSCALOOSA	1291	45.3	1561	54.7*	3726	57.2	2788	42.8
WALKER	869	34.1	1676	65.9*	2013	41.7	2817	58.3
WASHINGTON	595	76.4	184	23.6*	1027	69.7	446	30.3
WILCOX	621	82.4	133	17.6*	1295	96.0	54	4.0
WINSTON	267	33.1	540	66.9*	282	29.5	675	70.5
TOTALS	60357		59988	*	128586		81066	
% OF VOTE	50.2		49.8	*	61.3		38.7	

GEOGRAPHIC CLASS

LOWLANDS	11351	63.	6798	37.*	23757	69.	10644	31.
BLACK BELT	14325	60.	9666	40.*	35230	82.	7749	18.
PIEDMONT	29195	46.	34838	54.*	61019	56.	48819	44.
MOUNTAIN	5486	39.	8686	61.*	8580	38.	13854	62.

DEMOGRAPHIC CLASS

METRO	25624	49.	26300	51.*	49354	58.	35171	42.
TOWN	6074	56.	4832	44.*	11927	58.	8630	42.
RURAL	28659	50.	28856	50.*	67305	64.	37265	36.

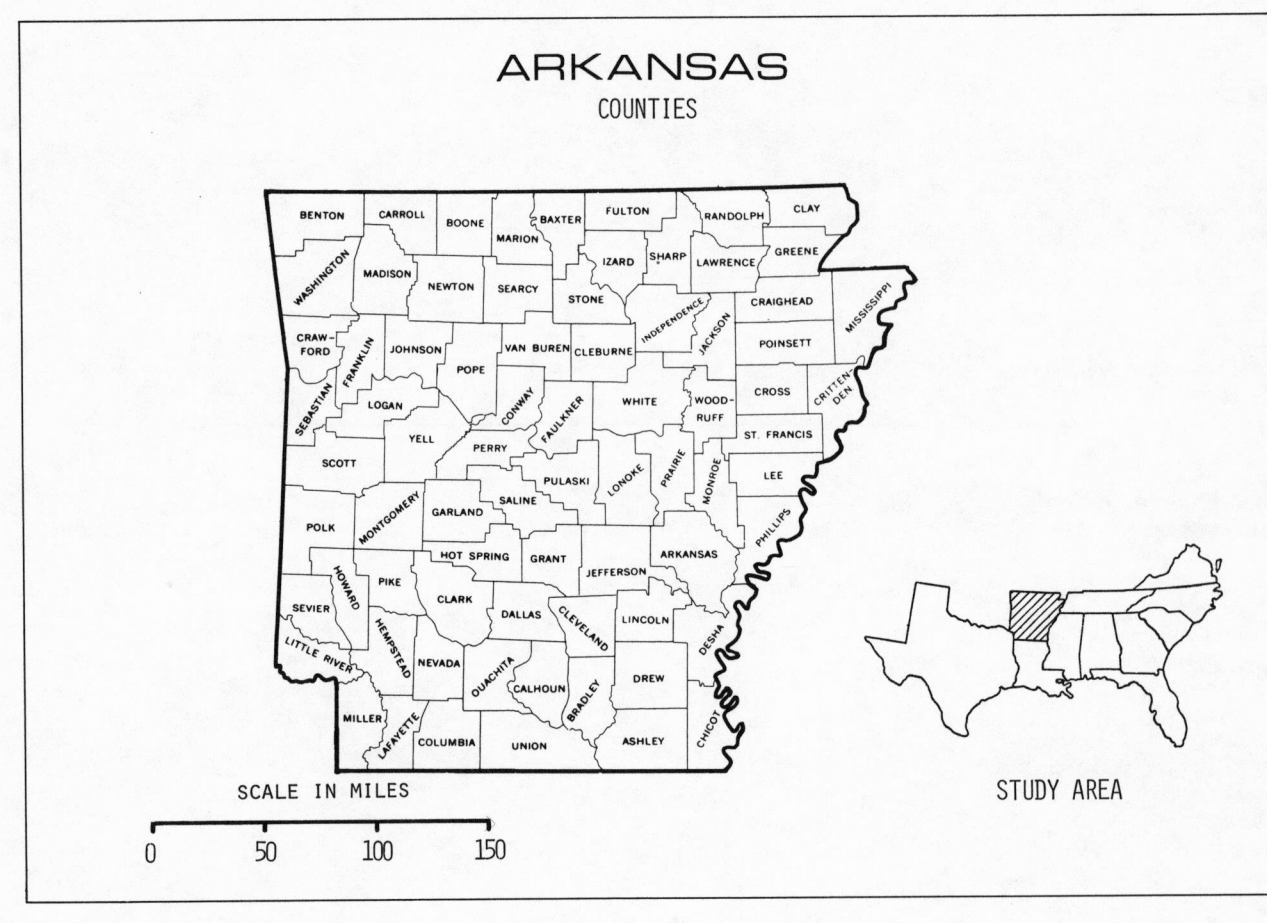

ARKANSAS
COUNTIES

BENTON | CARROLL | BOONE | BAXTER | FULTON | RANDOLPH | CLAY

MARION | IZARD | SHARP | LAWRENCE | GREENE

WASHINGTON | MADISON | NEWTON | SEARCY | STONE

CRAW-FORD | FRANKLIN | JOHNSON | VAN BUREN | CLEBURNE | INDEPENDENCE | JACKSON | CRAIGHEAD | POINSETT | MISSISSIPPI

SEBASTIAN | LOGAN | POPE | CONWAY | WHITE | WOOD-RUFF | CROSS | CRITTEN-DEN

SCOTT | YELL | PERRY | FAULKNER | PULASKI | LONOKE | PRAIRIE | MONROE | ST. FRANCIS | LEE

POLK | MONTGOMERY | GARLAND | SALINE | GRANT | LONOKE | PHILLIPS

PIKE | HOT SPRING | CLARK | DALLAS | CLEVELAND | JEFFERSON | ARKANSAS

SEVIER | HOWARD | HEMPSTEAD | NEVADA | OUACHITA | CALHOUN | BRADLEY | DREW | LINCOLN | DESHA

LITTLE RIVER | MILLER | LAFAYETTE | COLUMBIA | UNION | ASHLEY | CHICOT

SCALE IN MILES

0   50   100   150

STUDY AREA

ARKANSAS

The Arkansas Constitution required payment of
a noncumulative, $1-per-year poll tax until
the provision was eliminated for federal
elections by the Twenty-Fourth Amendment to
the United States Constitution, which became
effective in January, 1964. The provision was
eliminated for state elections by an amendment
to the Arkansas Constitution ratified later
in 1964. Haphazard registration procedures
and legislation relating to membership in the
Democratic party gave wide discretion to local
election officials and, prior to the mid-
1960s, frequently resulted in the disfranchisement of black voters and some re-
portedly questionable county election returns.

Black voter registration wavered between
60,000 and 70,000 during the 1950s, and
reached an estimated 72,600 in 1960, which was
38 percent of the black voting-age population
and 12.4 percent of the total voter registration. As in other southern states, voter
registration by both blacks and whites increased substantially during the 1960s. By
1970 the approximately 153,000 registered
blacks represented 17.4 percent of all
registered voters in the state.

The following data on presidential
elections in Arkansas are suggestive of
general trends in turnout and partisanship.
Turnout is expressed both in total votes cast
in the state and in the percentage of citizens
of voting age who cast ballots.

There are 22 Arkansas elections in this
section, 17 of them Democratic gubernatorial
primaries and 5 of them Democratic senatorial
primaries.

Gubernatorial Primaries

1. July 25, 1950: Sidney S. McMath 209,559
   (64.0%), Ben T. Laney 112,651 (34.4%),
   other 2 candidates 5,349 (1.6%). Total
   vote was 327,559; turnout of voting-age
   citizens was 29.5%.
2. July 29, 1952: Boyd Tackett 63,827
   (19.4%), Jack Holt 45,233 (13.7%), Ike
   Murry 27,937 (8.5%), Francis Cherry
   91,195 (27.7%), Sidney S. McMath 100,858
   (30.7%). Total vote was 329,050; turnout
   was 30.0%.
3. August 12, 1952: Francis Cherry 237,453
   (63.1%), Sidney S. McMath 139,044 (36.9%).
   Total vote was 376,497; turnout was 34.3%.
4. July 27, 1954: Francis Cherry 154,879
   (47.7%), Gus McMillan 18,857 (5.8%), Guy
   Jones 41,249 (12.7%), Orval E. Faubus
   109,614 (33.8%). Total vote was 324,599;
   turnout was 30.0%.
5. August 10, 1954: Francis Cherry 184,509
   (49.1%), Orval E. Faubus 191,328 (50.9%).
   Total vote was 375,837; turnout was 34.7%.
6. July 31, 1956 : Orval E. Faubus 180,760
   (58.1%), James D. Johnson 83,856 (26.9%),
   Jim Snoddy 43,630 (14.0%), other 2 candidates 2,981 (0.9%). Total vote was
   311,227; turnout was 29.1%.
7. July 29, 1958: Orval E. Faubus 264,346
   (68.8%), Chris Finkbeiner 60,373 (15.7%),
   Lee Ward 59,385 (15.5%). Total vote was
   384,104; turnout was 36.4%.
8. July 26, 1960: Orval E. Faubus 238,997
   (58.8%), Bruce Bennett 58,400 (14.4%),
   H. E. Williams 33,374 (8.2%), Joe Hardin
   66,499 (16.4%), one other candidate 9,547
   (2.2%). Total vote was 406,817; turnout
   was 39.0%.
9. July 31, 1962: Orval E. Faubus 208,996

(51.6%), Dale Alford 82,815 (20.4%), Sidney S. McMath 83,473 (20.6%), other 3 candidates 29,828 (7.4%). Total vote was 405,112; turnout was 37.9%.

10. July 28, 1964: Orval E. Faubus 239,890 (65.7%), Joe Hubbard 39,199 (10.7%), Ervin O. Dorsey 69,638 (19.1%), R. D. Burrow 16,310 (4.5%). Total vote was 365,037; turnout was 33.4%.

11. July 26, 1966: James D. Johnson 105,607 (25.1%), Frank Holt 92,711 (22.1%), Brooks Hays 64,814 (15.4%), Dale Alford 53,531 (12.7%), Sam Boyce 49,744 (11.9%), Raymond Rebsamen 35,608 (8.5%), one other candidate 18,051 (4.3%). Total vote was 420,066; turnout was 37.5%.

12. August 9, 1966: James D. Johnson 210,543 (51.9%), Frank Holt 195,442 (48.1%). Total vote was 405,985; turnout was 36.3%.

13. July 30, 1968: Frank Whitbeck 61,758 (14.9%), Bruce Bennett 65,095 (15.7%), Marion Crank 106,092 (25.6%), Ted Boswell 85,629 (20.6%), Mrs. James D. Johnson 86,038 (20.7%), Clyde E. Byrd 10,265 (2.5%). Total vote was 414,877; turnout was 36.3%.

14. August 13, 1968: Marion Crank 215,087 (63.3%), Mrs. James D. Johnson 124,880 (36.7%). Total vote was 339,967; turnout was 35.0%.

15. August 25, 1970: Robert C. Compton 19,336 (4.5%), Joseph Purcell 81,566 (18.9%), Hayes C. McClerkin 45,011 (10.5%), Bill Wells 32,543 (7.6%), Orval E. Faubus 156,578 (36.4%), Dale Bumpers 86,168 (20.0%), other 2 candidates 9,443 (2.2%). Total vote was 430,645; turnout was 36.8%.

16. September 8, 1970: Orval E. Faubus 182,008 (41.3%), Dale Bumpers 258,848 (58.7%). Total vote was 440,856; turnout was 37.7%.

17. May 30, 1972: Dale Bumpers 330,088 (66.7%), Byrum Hurst 81,239 (16.4%), Mack Harbour 55,172 (11.1%), George W. Davis 22,284 (4.5%), Les Gibbs 6,068 (1.2%). Total vote was 494,851; turnout was 38.1%.

Senatorial Primaries

1. July 27, 1954: John L. McClellan 164,905 (50.6%), Sidney S. McMath 127,941 (39.2%), other 2 candidates 33,168 (10.2%). Total vote was 326,014.

* (July 31, 1956: J. William Fulbright unopposed.)

* (July 26, 1960: John L. McClellan unopposed.)

2. July 31, 1962: J. William Fulbright 253,751 (66.1%), Winston G. Chandler 129,987 (33.9%). Total vote was 383,738.

* (July 26, 1966: John L. McClellan 310,526 (77.2%), Foster Johnson 91,746 (22.8%). Total vote was 402,272.)

3. July 30, 1968: J. William Fulbright 220,684 (52.9%), Bobby K. Hayes 52,906 (12.7%), Foster Johnson 11,395 (2.7%), James D. Johnson 132,038 (31.7%). Total vote was 417,023.

4. May 30, 1972: John L. McClellan 220,588 (44.7%), Foster Johnson 6,358 (1.3%), Ted Boswell 62,496 (12.7%), David H. Pryor 204,058 (41.3%). Total vote was 493,500.

5. June 13, 1972: John L. McClellan 242,983 (52.0%), David H. Pryor 224,262 (48.0%). Total vote was 467,245.

RETURNS FROM PRESIDENTIAL ELECTIONS

Year	Turnout		Partisan Vote
1948	242,475	(21.9%) [+]	Democrat 61.7%, Republican 21.0%, Dixiecrat 16.5%
1952	404,800	(36.9%)	Democrat 55.9%, Republican 43.8%
1956	406,572	(38.0%)	Democrat 52.5%, Republican 45.8%
1960	428,509	(41.1%)	Democrat 50.2%, Republican 43.1%, States' Rights 6.7%
1964	560,426	(51.2%)	Democrat 56.1%, Republican 43.4%
1968	619,969	(54.2%)	American Independent 38.9%, Republican 30.8%, Democrat 30.4%
1972	651,320	(50.2%)	Republican 68.9%, Democrat 30.7%

*Totals do not necessarily equal 100%, since minor party percentages are excluded.

[+]Percentage of citizens of voting age who voted is calculated on the basis of a straight-line interpolation of citizen population between census years.

COUNTY	MCMATH #	%	LANEY #	%	OTHER #	%*	TACKETT #	%	HOLT #	%	MURRY #	%	CHERRY #	%	MCMATH #	%
ARKANSAS	2272	57.4	1632	41.2	55	1.4*	497	12.3	599	14.8	1064	26.3	1069	26.4	814	20.1
ASHLEY	2451	52.7	2048	44.1	149	3.2*	453	13.3	579	17.0	660	19.3	839	24.6	881	25.8
BAXTER	1319	63.4	695	33.4	65	3.1*	377	16.7	618	27.5	138	6.1	167	7.4	951	42.2
BENTON	3064	65.2	1615	34.3	23	.5*	826	15.9	560	10.8	318	6.1	1951	37.5	1550	29.8
BOONE	2146	61.0	1332	37.9	38	1.1*	314	7.2	2365	54.5	186	4.3	395	9.1	1083	24.9
BRADLEY	1582	49.4	1473	46.0	148	4.6*	905	25.8	549	15.6	913	26.0	370	10.5	771	22.0
CALHOUN	1228	55.9	703	32.0	267	12.1*	1110	37.1	252	8.4	771	25.8	79	2.6	778	26.0
CARROLL	2147	73.6	726	24.9	46	1.6*	379	15.5	357	14.6	251	10.3	77	3.2	1380	56.5
CHICOT	1887	66.5	912	32.2	37	1.3*	196	8.4	237	10.2	457	19.7	299	12.9	1136	48.9
CLARK	3668	76.2	1032	21.5	111	2.3*	1548	33.0	785	16.7	427	9.1	824	17.6	1107	23.6
CLAY	2366	71.7	888	26.9	44	1.3*	322	9.1	560	15.8	114	3.2	1612	45.5	934	26.4
CLEBURNE	1724	61.8	980	35.1	87	3.1*	478	19.8	1152	47.8	75	3.1	212	8.8	492	20.4
CLEVELAND	1036	42.9	1091	45.2	286	11.9*	168	9.8	416	24.3	571	33.3	110	6.4	448	26.2
COLUMBIA	3333	72.3	1203	26.1	72	1.6*	1105	24.8	278	6.2	286	6.4	668	15.0	2117	47.5
CONWAY	3136	68.9	1397	30.7	19	.4*	919	18.2	846	16.7	119	2.4	440	8.7	2734	54.1
CRAIGHEAD	4481	65.1	2335	33.9	63	.9*	300	3.1	175	1.8	99	1.0	6636	69.0	2409	25.0
CRAWFORD	2272	69.1	979	29.8	37	1.1*	1677	39.7	292	6.9	112	2.6	1214	28.7	933	22.1
CRITTENDEN	622	20.9	2349	79.0	2	.1*	50	1.6	116	3.8	314	10.2	2160	70.2	438	14.2
CROSS	2386	58.6	1664	40.9	21	.5*	184	5.6	129	3.9	240	7.2	934	28.2	1828	55.1
DALLAS	1614	56.2	1073	37.4	185	6.4*	160	5.5	83	2.9	1822	62.6	69	2.4	775	26.6
DESHA	2197	64.2	1208	35.3	17	.5*	609	14.5	379	9.0	527	12.5	703	16.7	1994	47.3
DREW	2050	63.4	1082	33.5	99	3.1*	343	11.6	341	11.5	556	18.8	588	19.9	1134	38.3
FAULKNER	3943	64.4	2124	34.7	52	.8*	609	9.8	2014	32.6	397	6.4	1473	23.8	1692	27.4
FRANKLIN	2065	66.0	998	31.9	68	2.2*	773	23.6	624	19.1	146	4.5	610	18.6	1118	34.2
FULTON	1162	81.3	259	18.1	9	.6*	212	15.0	540	38.3	18	1.3	75	5.3	564	40.0
GARLAND	5443	55.1	4327	43.8	104	1.1*	2395	26.0	984	10.7	321	3.5	2815	30.6	2685	29.2
GRANT	1091	41.8	1423	54.5	98	3.8*	736	27.4	570	21.3	432	16.1	389	14.5	555	20.7
GREENE	3467	60.9	2150	37.7	79	1.4*	302	5.7	353	6.7	73	1.4	3060	57.7	1519	28.6
HEMSTEAD	3786	76.8	1098	22.3	47	1.0*	1921	38.8	619	12.5	165	3.3	1012	20.4	1239	25.0
HOTSPRING	2777	57.5	1827	37.8	228	4.7*	1232	23.7	590	11.3	794	15.2	1468	28.2	1124	21.6
HOWARD	2101	80.3	472	18.0	43	1.6*	2224	73.3	56	1.8	40	1.3	112	3.7	601	19.8
INDEPENDCE	3630	65.7	1841	33.3	58	1.0*	823	19.8	844	20.3	94	2.3	822	19.8	1578	37.9
IZARD	1948	79.6	480	19.6	20	.8*	631	20.5	854	27.8	41	1.3	236	7.7	1315	42.7
JACKSON	3518	69.4	1513	29.9	37	.7*	605	11.3	1029	19.2	258	4.8	1248	23.3	2220	41.4
JEFFERSON	7276	65.9	3603	32.6	161	1.5*	908	8.6	647	6.1	1200	11.4	4076	38.6	3723	35.3
JOHNSON	2493	69.3	1055	29.3	50	1.4*	608	16.4	1277	34.3	228	6.1	366	9.8	1239	33.3
LAFAYETTE	1594	62.6	897	35.2	55	2.2*	955	42.9	156	7.0	58	2.6	226	10.1	832	37.4
LAWRENCE	2336	61.2	1446	37.9	32	.8*	1045	24.3	748	17.4	232	5.4	1081	25.2	1189	27.7
LEE	611	30.4	1372	68.2	30	1.5*	64	3.1	99	4.8	447	21.7	613	29.7	838	40.7
LINCOLN	1250	52.2	1128	47.1	15	.6*	152	7.6	231	11.6	260	13.0	418	20.9	938	46.9
LITTLERIVR	1196	52.5	1044	45.8	37	1.6*	1765	71.5	90	3.6	44	1.8	126	5.1	442	17.9
LOGAN	3028	80.3	687	18.2	55	1.5*	1073	30.3	388	11.0	186	5.3	516	14.6	1375	38.9
LONOKE	3133	64.0	1702	34.8	62	1.3*	403	9.4	778	18.2	272	6.4	1324	31.0	1499	35.1
MADISON	2392	95.6	109	4.4	2	.1*	72	3.6	87	4.4	9	.5	20	1.0	1806	90.6
MARION	1062	56.9	763	40.9	41	2.2*	289	13.4	873	40.6	68	3.2	72	3.4	847	39.4
MILLER	3874	63.6	2153	35.3	66	1.1*	3309	52.1	644	10.1	139	2.2	733	11.5	1525	24.0

COUNTY	MCMATH #	%	LANEY #	%	OTHER #	%*	TACKETT #	%	HOLT #	%	MURRY #	%	CHERRY #	%	MCMATH #	%
MISSISSIP	6386	68.1	2928	31.2	57	.6*	629	6.7	779	8.3	1237	13.1	3382	35.9	3386	36.0
MONROE	1406	54.9	1146	44.7	11	.4	263	12.2	288	13.3	285	13.2	610	28.2	716	33.1
MONTGOMERY	1059	62.3	618	36.3	24	1.4*	1196	65.3	48	2.6	7	.4	104	5.7	476	26.0
NEVADA	2259	72.0	806	25.7	72	2.3*	852	27.1	318	10.1	110	3.5	869	27.7	992	31.6
NEWTON	1218	93.9	65	5.0	14	1.1*	83	7.1	222	19.1	12	1.0	17	1.5	831	71.3
QUACHITA	3757	58.1	2562	39.6	148	2.3*	1105	18.4	568	9.5	1318	21.9	1114	18.5	1905	31.7
PERRY	1042	59.1	691	39.2	30	1.7*	347	27.1	305	23.8	65	5.1	219	17.1	346	27.0
PHILLIPS	3204	71.1	1298	28.8	3	.1*	115	2.8	141	3.5	1303	31.9	1599	39.1	928	22.7
PIKE	1615	78.4	380	18.5	64	3.1*	1563	76.6	33	1.6	5	.2	68	3.3	372	18.2
POINSETT	2826	57.2	2085	42.2	32	.6*	316	6.0	248	4.7	128	2.4	2633	50.2	1919	36.6
POLK	1719	52.5	1440	43.9	118	3.6*	1966	64.3	182	6.0	151	4.9	294	9.6	464	15.2
POPE	3858	69.4	1631	29.3	74	1.3*	688	14.0	1138	23.1	238	4.8	1329	27.0	1528	31.1
PRAIRIE	1075	41.1	1516	57.9	27	1.0*	860	40.6	365	17.2	142	6.7	433	20.5	316	14.9
PULASKI	21974	65.1	11517	34.1	281	.8*	2667	7.7	4872	14.1	3629	10.5	14358	41.7	8944	25.9
RANDOLPH	2429	68.9	1029	29.2	68	1.9*	365	10.9	513	15.4	53	1.6	1177	35.3	1231	36.9
STFRANCIS	1610	43.9	2023	55.2	32	.9*	152	4.0	189	5.0	406	10.6	1755	46.0	1312	34.4
SALINE	3402	62.5	1776	32.6	267	4.9*	1117	20.5	1290	23.6	382	7.0	1152	21.1	1519	27.8
SCOTT	1808	71.5	672	26.6	48	1.9*	1139	47.7	48	2.0	48	2.0	113	4.7	1039	43.5
SEARCY	525	47.7	557	50.6	19	1.7*	89	8.7	576	56.5	67	6.6	35	3.4	252	24.7
SEBASTIAN	5546	63.4	3091	35.3	108	1.2*	4516	38.8	488	4.2	474	4.1	4237	36.4	1926	16.5
SEVIER	1558	58.5	1046	39.3	60	2.3*	1531	70.9	89	4.1	31	1.4	151	7.0	356	16.5
SHARP	1548	66.5	749	32.2	32	1.4*	549	26.3	245	11.8	27	1.3	238	11.4	1025	49.2
STONE	1334	81.0	302	18.3	11	.7*	218	18.0	201	16.6	45	3.7	222	18.3	525	43.4
UNION	5557	63.1	3102	35.2	145	1.6*	1871	17.3	1315	12.2	874	8.1	4810	44.6	1923	17.8
VANBUREN	1719	66.0	830	31.9	54	2.1*	207	10.8	838	43.6	65	3.4	171	8.9	642	33.4
WASHINGTON	4923	71.2	1918	27.7	75	1.1*	687	9.5	1223	16.9	361	5.0	3638	50.2	1337	18.5
WHITE	5057	70.7	2002	28.0	91	1.3*	961	14.8	1112	17.2	262	4.0	1242	19.2	2906	44.8
WOODRUFF	1856	63.5	1031	35.3	36	1.2*	276	12.2	251	11.1	148	6.6	548	24.3	1034	45.8
YELL	3132	76.2	952	23.2	28	.7*	1473	35.9	585	14.2	122	3.0	370	9.0	1558	37.9
TOTALS	209559		112651		5349	*	63827		45233		27937		91195		100858	
% OF VOTE	64.0		34.4		1.6	*	19.4		13.7		8.5		27.7		30.7	

ARKANSAS/33

```
              DEMOC.  GOVERNOR   1950      *                    DEMOC.  GOVERNOR   1952
                                           *
                                           *
COUNTY       MCMATH      LANEY      OTHER   *   TACKETT     HOLT      MURRY     CHERRY      MCMATH
              #     %     #     %    #    % *    #     %    #     %    #    %    #     %     #     %
-----------------------------------------------------------------------------------------------------------------
GEOGRAPHIC CLASS                            *
                                            *
LOWLANDS    103389 64.  55927 35.  2758 2. *  28639 19.  17033 11.  15200 10.  46279 31.  41233 28.
BLACK BELT   17851 55.  14437 44.   423 1. *   3900  9.   2817  7.   7227 17.  13076 31.  14664 35.
MOUNTAIN     88319 67.  42287 32.  2168 2. *  31288 23.  25383 18.   5510  4.  31840 23.  44961 32.
                                            *
                                            *
DEMOGRAPHIC CLASS                           *
                                            *
METRO        31394 65.  16761 34.   455 1. *  10492 20.   6004 11.   4242  8.  19328 37.  12395 24.
TOWN         35953 65.  19125 34.   642 1. *   6790 12.   5123  9.   4092  7.  25357 45.  15463 27.
RURAL       142212 64.  76765 34.  4252 2. *  46545 21.  34106 16.  19603  9.  46510 21.  73000 33.
```

ARKANSAS

```
          DEMOC.  RUNOFF    1952*         DEMOC.  GOVERNOR   1954
                                *
COUNTY      CHERRY     MCMATH   *  CHERRY      MCMILLAN    JONES      FAUBUS
             #     %    #     % *   #     %     #    %     #     %     #     %
------------------------------------------------------------------------------------
ARKANSAS    3791 74.3  1309 25.7*  2837 67.9   207  5.0   457 10.9   675 16.2
ASHLEY      3310 68.3  1534 31.7*  1926 53.6   372 10.4   560 15.6   735 20.5
BAXTER      1392 56.2  1085 43.8*   755 39.0   127  6.6   146  7.5   906 46.8
BENTON      4823 65.2  2578 34.8*  1769 28.0   166  2.6   307  4.9  4081 64.5
BOONE       3282 71.2  1330 28.8*  1043 34.1    80  2.6   365 11.9  1573 51.4
                                *
BRADLEY     2778 71.8  1090 28.2*  1874 53.0   365 13.1   463 13.1   835 23.6
CALHOUN     1312 58.8   919 41.2*   767 30.5   324 12.9   480 19.1   941 37.5
CARROLL     1114 37.6  1848 62.4*   423 20.9    31  1.5    67  3.3  1499 74.2
CHICOT      1693 52.6  1525 47.4*  1908 64.0   182  6.1   380 12.7   511 17.1
CLARK       3360 64.1  1885 35.9*  2803 53.7   364  7.0   666 12.7  1391 26.6
                                *
CLAY        3107 72.0  1211 28.0*  1465 44.8   175  5.4   509 15.6  1121 34.3
CLEBURNE    1783 72.7   670 27.3*   847 43.1   149  7.6   520 26.5   447 22.8
CLEVELAND   1563 68.3   724 31.7*   819 38.4   316 14.8   373 17.5   626 29.3
COLUMBIA    2247 45.3  2714 54.7*  1706 42.6   225  5.6   583 14.6  1492 37.2
CONWAY      2298 44.6  2851 55.4*  1521 41.1    83  2.2   741 20.0  1356 36.6
                                *
CRAIGHEAD   7284 72.1  2822 27.9*  4005 51.2   519  6.6   945 12.1  2354 30.1
CRAWFORD    3290 67.1  1612 32.9*   730 25.0    91  3.1   193  6.6  1909 65.3
CRITTENDEN  3491 84.9   623 15.1*  2393 83.8    93  3.3    87  3.0   281  9.8
CROSS       2031 47.7  2223 52.3*  1306 44.2   127  4.3   195  6.6  1330 45.0
DALLAS      1947 62.3  1179 37.7*  1319 41.5   368 11.6   344 10.8  1145 36.1
                                *
DESHA       2035 50.1  2030 49.9*  1819 63.1    79  2.7   311 10.8   674 23.4
DREW        2099 59.9  1406 40.1*  1191 46.0   252  9.7   341 13.2   804 31.1
FAULKNER    4492 69.8  1946 30.2*  1670 27.9    63  1.1  4003 66.9   245  4.1
FRANKLIN    2007 59.4  1371 40.6*   498 14.9   131  3.9   121  3.6  2598 77.6
```

	DEMOC. RUNOFF 1952*				DEMOC. GOVERNOR 1954							
COUNTY	CHERRY		MCMATH		CHERRY		MCMILLAN		JONES		FAUBUS	
	#	%	#	%*	#	%	#	%	#	%	#	%
FULTON	982	52.3	896	47.7*	543	37.2	95	6.5	183	12.5	640	43.8
GARLAND	7490	61.9	4616	38.1*	7035	60.6	624	5.4	1263	10.9	2696	23.2
GRANT	2204	74.4	758	25.6*	757	27.4	1472	53.3	174	6.3	361	13.1
GREENE	4050	66.3	2054	33.7*	1945	41.1	174	3.7	95	2.0	2521	53.2
HEMSTEAD	3539	63.8	2005	36.2*	2291	47.4	226	4.7	396	8.2	1916	39.7
HOTSPRING	4110	71.4	1650	28.6*	2855	45.8	455	7.3	908	14.6	2017	32.3
HOWARD	1972	61.4	1241	38.6*	1132	37.5	350	11.6	297	9.8	1237	41.0
INDEPENDCE	3380	64.6	1852	35.4*	1854	49.4	191	5.1	557	14.8	1152	30.7
IZARD	1719	50.0	1720	50.0*	345	25.7	82	6.1	279	20.8	637	47.4
JACKSON	3122	53.0	2769	47.0*	1784	51.4	219	6.3	623	18.0	843	24.3
JEFFERSON	7338	58.9	5111	41.1*	6409	56.4	759	6.7	1142	10.1	3047	26.8
JOHNSON	2218	56.8	1688	43.2*	738	24.6	102	3.4	226	7.5	1933	64.5
LAFAYETTE	1243	52.4	1127	47.6*	1281	49.7	269	10.4	305	11.8	723	28.0
LAWRENCE	3117	65.7	1626	34.3*	1323	38.5	205	6.0	345	10.0	1566	45.5
LEE	1597	57.1	1199	42.9*	1834	68.2	191	7.1	197	7.3	467	17.4
LINCOLN	1358	54.6	1131	45.4*	857	45.2	100	5.3	301	15.9	640	33.7
LITTLERIVR	1855	67.7	886	32.3*	790	37.5	188	8.9	244	11.6	885	42.0
LOGAN	2510	53.0	2225	47.0*	1301	35.2	194	5.3	355	9.6	1845	49.9
LONOKE	3226	61.0	2063	39.0*	2171	44.6	182	3.7	646	13.3	1865	38.3
MADISON	216	8.9	2211	91.1*	25	1.2	4	.2	27	1.2	2104	97.4
MARION	1251	54.9	1029	45.1*	351	20.9	150	8.9	307	18.3	870	51.8
MILLER	4390	63.1	2565	36.9*	3415	47.4	540	7.5	777	10.8	2466	34.3
MISSISSIP	5282	55.8	4184	44.2*	3466	53.0	243	3.7	314	4.8	2514	38.5
MONROE	1698	59.8	1141	40.2*	1717	61.1	183	6.5	285	10.1	624	22.2
MONTGOMERY	1066	57.7	781	42.3*	431	25.2	122	7.1	287	16.8	872	50.9
NEVADA	2008	57.8	1465	42.2*	1052	38.9	153	5.7	219	8.1	1280	47.3
NEWTON	296	23.4	969	76.6*	74	7.2	15	1.5	26	2.5	918	88.9
QUACHITA	4597	60.6	2987	39.4*	3910	50.0	775	9.9	868	11.1	2269	29.0
PERRY	1169	72.0	454	28.0*	426	32.1	51	3.8	598	45.0	253	19.1
PHILLIPS	3084	57.5	2284	42.5*	2859	70.3	157	3.9	414	10.2	637	15.7
PIKE	1196	54.6	995	45.4*	334	18.3	183	10.0	279	15.3	1033	56.5
POINSETT	4081	63.5	2341	36.5*	3358	60.8	428	7.7	808	14.6	931	16.9
POLK	2392	74.6	815	25.4*	1030	28.6	250	6.9	387	10.7	1938	53.8
POPE	3377	63.1	1975	36.9*	2282	40.3	175	3.1	714	12.6	2494	44.0
PRAIRIE	2490	82.5	527	17.5*	1555	65.4	200	8.4	232	9.8	389	16.4
PULASKI	26764	68.9	12053	31.1*	25155	66.4	731	1.9	4152	11.0	7545	20.1
RANDOLPH	2352	62.4	1415	37.6*	1299	32.6	216	5.4	344	8.6	2122	53.3
STFRANCIS	3087	62.0	1889	38.0*	2212	59.3	197	5.3	184	4.9	1136	30.5
SALINE	3853	64.1	2157	35.9*	3102	47.7	450	6.9	1567	24.1	1378	21.2
SCOTT	1135	46.5	1306	53.5*	307	19.2	89	5.6	323	20.2	881	55.1
SEARCY	779	65.2	415	34.8*	239	35.3	13	1.9	38	5.6	387	57.2
SEBASTIAN	9086	72.4	3460	27.6*	3766	42.5	344	3.9	1113	12.6	3639	41.1
SEVIER	1884	70.8	778	29.2*	918	44.3	194	9.4	283	13.6	679	32.7
SHARP	1170	50.5	1145	49.5*	651	41.3	112	7.1	284	18.0	531	33.7
STONE	1053	55.1	859	44.9*	374	25.2	107	7.2	665	44.9	336	22.7
UNION	8274	75.6	2671	24.4*	5893	54.0	742	6.8	1462	13.4	2825	25.9

```
                DEMOC.  RUNOFF    1952*        DEMOC.  GOVERNOR   1954
                                       *
      COUNTY    CHERRY      MCMATH    * CHERRY      MCMILLAN    JONES       FAUBUS
                #     %     #     %*    #     %     #     %     #     %     #     %
      ------------------------------------------------------------------------------------------------------
      VANBUREN  1632 63.4   944 36.6*   597 26.5    60  2.7   977 43.3   621 27.5
      WASHINGTON 6059 73.1  2235 26.9*  2621 35.9  127  1.7   188  2.6  4363 59.8
      WHITE     4291 58.7  3015 41.3*  2630 39.1   527  7.8   684 10.2  2884 42.9
      WOODRUFF  1587 53.9  1359 46.1*  1674 54.8   217  7.1   322 10.5   841 27.5
      YELL      2295 60.2  1518 39.8*  2517 57.0   135  3.1   428  9.7  1334 30.2
                                       *
      ------------------------------------------------------------------------------------------------------
                                       *
      TOTALS    237453     139044    * 154879      18857      41249      109614
      % OF VOTE  63.1        36.9    *   47.7        5.8       12.7        33.8
                                       *
                                       *
      GEOGRAPHIC CLASS                 *
                                       *
      LOWLANDS  109573 66.  57569 34.*  79736 54.  10169  7.  17466 12.  41205 28.
      BLACK BELT 30158 59.  20598 41.*  26282 60.   2795  6.   4272 10.  10726 24.
      MOUNTAIN   97722 62.  60877 38.*  48861 37.   5893  4.  19511 15.  57683 44.
                                       *
                                       *
      DEMOGRAPHIC CLASS                *
                                       *
      METRO      40240 69.  18078 31.*  32336 60.   1615  3.   6042 11.  13650 25.
      TOWN       41727 66.  21639 34.*  29429 53.   3014  5.   5314 10.  17799 32.
      RURAL     155486 61.  99327 39.*  93114 43.  14228  7.  29893 14.  78165 36.
```

ARKANSAS

```
                DEMOC.  RUNOFF    1954*        DEMOC.  GOVERNOR   1956
                                       *
      COUNTY    CHERRY      FAUBUS    * FAUBUS      JOHNSON     SNODDY      OTHER
                #     %     #     %*    #     %     #     %     #     %     #     %
      ------------------------------------------------------------------------------------------------------
      ARKANSAS  3332 70.4  1402 29.6*  1534 40.0  1401 36.5   865 22.6    34  .9
      ASHLEY    2060 49.9  2071 50.1*  2011 38.1  2939 55.7   289  5.5    39  .7
      BAXTER     891 36.2  1572 63.8*  1729 71.2   217  8.9   448 18.5    34 1.4
      BENTON    2189 29.6  5196 70.4*  2589 83.5   121  3.9   366 11.8    25  .8
      BOONE     1535 38.2  2483 61.8*  1716 73.8   101  4.3   488 21.0    20  .9
                                       *
      BRADLEY   2051 57.5  1516 42.5*  1444 37.5  1953 50.8   418 10.9    33  .9
      CALHOUN   1022 38.8  1612 61.2*   997 44.3  1091 48.4   139  6.2    26 1.2
      CARROLL    568 18.1  2569 81.9*  1651 93.3    32  1.8    84  4.7     2  .1
      CHICOT    2354 63.5  1354 36.5*  1465 52.1  1096 39.0   206  7.3    46 1.6
      CLARK     2776 49.4  2841 50.6*  2718 60.1  1240 27.4   507 11.2    57 1.3
                                       *
      CLAY      1951 46.6  2239 53.4*  1036 66.5   250 16.0   263 16.9     9  .6
      CLEBURNE  1209 46.9  1369 53.1*  1019 65.2   224 14.3   303 19.4    16 1.0
      CLEVELAND 1141 44.5  1425 55.5*   832 37.5  1254 56.6   124  5.6     6  .3
      COLUMBIA  2342 44.4  2933 55.6*  2157 55.1  1520 38.8   214  5.5    25  .6
      CONWAY    1820 40.5  2675 59.5*  3021 83.0   348  9.6   248  6.8    22  .6
```

```
              DEMOC.  RUNOFF    1954*         DEMOC.  GOVERNOR   1956
                                   *
COUNTY       CHERRY       FAUBUS       FAUBUS      JOHNSON      SNODDY       OTHER
              #     %      #     %*     #     %     #     %      #     %      #     %
----------------------------------*-----------------------------------------------------------------
CRAIGHEAD   4913  51.1   4708  48.9*  3945  53.7  1898  25.9  1461  19.9     36   .5
CRAWFORD    1027  24.8   3122  75.2*  1173  28.9   174   4.3  2700  66.6      8   .2
CRITTENDEN  3288  74.8   1108  25.2*  2093  65.7   994  31.2    95   3.0      4   .1
CROSS       1398  41.5   1968  58.5*  1515  67.7   354  15.8   363  16.2      5   .2
DALLAS      1615  45.1   1963  54.9*  1520  50.7  1209  40.3   237   7.9     33  1.1
                                   *
DESHA       2418  57.5   1785  42.5*  1923  55.1  1303  37.4   253   7.3      8   .2
DREW        1691  46.8   1920  53.2*  1408  45.0  1437  45.9   264   8.4     19   .6
FAULKNER    2775  45.1   3383  54.9*  3825  55.1  2214  31.9   740  10.7    160  2.3
FRANKLIN     605  16.5   3070  83.5*  2297  65.4   202   5.8   993  28.3     20   .6
FULTON       817  41.4   1156  58.6*  1049  66.6   205  13.0   300  19.1     20  1.3
                                   *
GARLAND     7874  62.5   4732  37.5*  4605  67.3  1220  17.8   869  12.7    152  2.2
GRANT       1279  42.3   1744  57.7*  1273  45.5  1227  43.9   258   9.2     40  1.4
GREENE      2517  45.5   3012  54.5*  2976  53.6  1873  33.8   636  11.5     64  1.2
HEMSTEAD    2756  54.9   2261  45.1*  2954  64.1  1177  25.7   417   9.1     37   .8
HOTSPRING   3311  49.4   3398  50.6*  2453  53.3  1531  33.3   554  12.0     62  1.3
                                   *
HOWARD      1477  43.4   1928  56.6*  1228  68.1   385  21.3   175   9.7     16   .9
INDEPENDCE  2391  47.9   2601  52.1*  2645  65.6   671  16.6   673  16.7     45  1.1
IZARD        549  27.2   1468  72.8*  1640  77.1   295  13.9   169   7.9     24  1.1
JACKSON     2404  46.3   2786  53.7*  2850  62.2   810  17.7   828  18.1     92  2.0
JEFFERSON   7189  57.0   5415  43.0*  5033  46.7  4688  43.5   981   9.1     86   .8
                                   *
JOHNSON     1037  26.6   2856  73.4*  1949  61.3   147   4.6  1072  33.7     10   .3
LAFAYETTE   1396  50.5   1367  49.5*   828  50.4   719  43.8    80   4.9     16  1.0
LAWRENCE    1462  36.9   2499  63.1*  2217  59.3  1132  30.3   355   9.5     36  1.0
LEE         1503  70.4    631  29.6*   867  53.1   652  39.9   108   6.6      6   .4
LINCOLN     1317  47.9   1435  52.1*  1110  56.5   714  36.3   131   6.7     11   .6
                                   *
LITTLERIVR  1425  49.5   1451  50.5*  1272  51.2  1043  42.0   118   4.7     53  2.1
LOGAN       1733  38.1   2814  61.9*  2779  65.7   490  12.2   726  18.1     26   .6
LONOKE      2566  46.2   2988  53.8*  2383  47.4  1897  37.7   723  14.4     23   .5
MADISON       47   1.6   2888  98.4*  1787  96.1     9   .5    62   3.3      1   .1
MARION       669  29.0   1634  71.0*  1363  66.7   270  13.2   384  18.8     27  1.3
                                   *
MILLER      3472  48.2   3726  51.8*  3355  45.3  3246  43.9   691   9.3    110  1.5
MISSISSIP   3723  45.0   4548  55.0*  6026  70.7  1943  22.8   514   6.0     46   .5
MONROE      1779  66.1    914  33.9*  1123  47.3  1015  42.7   220   9.3     18   .8
MONTGOMERY   525  27.6   1376  72.4*  1449  68.7   396  18.8   239  11.3     25  1.2
NEVADA      1551  46.2   1803  53.8*  1626  61.0   785  29.5   233   8.7     21   .8
                                   *
NEWTON       147  12.1   1065  87.9*   857  97.8     9  1.0     9  1.0      1   .1
QUACHITA    4319  49.9   4339  50.1*  3905  52.2  2823  37.7   703   9.4     53   .7
PERRY        540  38.1    876  61.9*   966  68.4   315  22.3   125   8.9      6   .4
PHILLIPS    3810  69.8   1651  30.2*  2696  66.4  1286  31.7    77   1.9      4   .1
PIKE         618  26.4   1720  73.6*   897  68.9   289  22.2    99   7.6     16  1.2
                                   *
POINSETT    3649  58.8   2559  41.2*  4277  67.3  1645  25.9   384   6.0     49   .8
POLK        1193  32.8   2440  67.2*  2226  68.0   979  29.9    21   .6     47  1.4
POPE        2565  43.8   3294  56.2*  2426  65.8   458  12.4   793  21.5      8   .2
PRAIRIE     2159  74.2    749  25.8*  1226  58.3   685  32.6   174   8.3     19   .9
PULASKI    27087  67.9  12820  32.1* 18841  55.1  8488  24.8  6417  18.8    426  1.2
                                   *
RANDOLPH    1382  31.8   2970  68.2*  2046  75.2   383  14.1   277  10.2     16   .6
```

COUNTY	DEMOC. RUNOFF 1954*				DEMOC. GOVERNOR 1956									
	CHERRY		FAUBUS		FAUBUS		JOHNSON		SNODDY		OTHER			
	#	%	#	%*	#	%	#	%	#	%	#	%		
STFRANCIS	2691	59.0	1872	41.0*	2108	41.8	2249	44.6	649	12.9	34	.7		
SALINE	3506	50.3	3470	49.7*	3972	58.8	1619	24.0	1108	16.4	60	.9		
SCOTT	553	24.1	1745	75.9*	1441	66.8	159	7.4	533	24.7	25	1.2		
SEARCY	303	30.3	698	69.7*	504	70.8	40	5.6	166	23.3	2	.3		
SEBASTIAN	5467	46.8	6205	53.2*	4476	46.8	819	8.6	4190	43.8	88	.9		
SEVIER	1176	47.1	1319	52.9*	871	62.2	412	29.4	104	7.4	13	.9		
SHARP	1014	45.3	1223	54.7*	843	65.3	265	20.5	176	13.6	6	.5		
STONE	734	36.0	1303	64.0*	724	65.3	288	26.0	87	7.8	10	.9		
UNION	7250	61.3	4577	38.7*	4635	41.5	5305	47.5	1076	9.6	161	1.4		
VANBUREN	721	26.8	1968	73.2*	2117	82.5	284	11.1	147	5.7	19	.7		
WASHINGTON	2976	35.9	5320	64.1*	5922	77.2	344	4.5	1310	17.1	91	1.2		
WHITE	3295	44.5	4108	55.5*	4371	65.6	1393	20.9	865	13.0	32	.5		
WOODRUFF	1693	52.0	1563	48.0*	1144	56.6	655	32.4	193	9.5	29	1.4		
YELL	1921	52.2	1759	47.8*	2811	75.2	552	14.8	363	9.7	12	.3		
TOTALS	184509		191328	*	180760		83856		43630		2981			
% OF VOTE	49.1		50.9	*	58.1		26.9		14.0		1.0			

GEOGRAPHIC CLASS

	CHERRY		FAUBUS		FAUBUS		JOHNSON		SNODDY		OTHER			
LOWLANDS	92330	55.	75392	45.*	77736	53.	48489	33.	18013	12.	1501	1.		
BLACK BELT	31053	60.	21058	40.*	21910	52.	16580	39.	3230	8.	295	1.		
MOUNTAIN	61126	39.	94878	61.*	81114	66.	18787	15.	22387	18.	1185	1.		

DEMOGRAPHIC CLASS

	CHERRY		FAUBUS		FAUBUS		JOHNSON		SNODDY		OTHER			
METRO	36026	61.	22751	39.*	26672	52.	12553	25.	11298	22.	624	1.		
TOWN	33925	54.	29300	46.*	30166	58.	15398	29.	6211	12.	572	1.		
RURAL	114558	45.	139277	55.*	123922	60.	55905	27.	26121	13.	1785	1.		

ARKANSAS

COUNTY	DEMOC. GOVERNOR 1958						DEMOC. GOVERNOR 1960							
	FAUBUS		FINKBEINR		WARD		FAUBUS		BENNETT		WILLIAMS		HARDIN	
	#	%	#	%	#	%*	#	%	#	%	#	%	#	%
ARKANSAS	3369	64.2	1205	23.0	672	12.8*	3154	61.5	774	15.1	265	5.2	933	18.2
ASHLEY	3648	77.3	680	14.4	392	8.3*	3698	62.9	934	15.9	345	5.9	900	15.3
BAXTER	1329	54.6	517	21.3	586	24.1*	1159	40.9	498	17.6	660	23.3	517	18.2
BENTON	4262	63.9	845	12.7	1560	23.4*	3758	59.3	1029	16.2	681	10.7	871	13.7
BOONE	2538	66.1	778	20.3	525	13.7*	1959	45.8	571	13.4	1245	29.1	498	11.7
BRADLEY	3124	73.4	648	15.2	484	11.4*	2925	69.1	548	12.9	305	7.2	458	10.8

	DEMOC. GOVERNOR 1958					DEMOC. GOVERNOR 1960					
COUNTY	FAUBUS		FINKBEINR		WARD		FAUBUS		BENNETT		WILLIAMS		HARDIN
	#	%	#	%	#	%*	#	%	#	%	#	%	#	%

COUNTY	FAUBUS #	%	FINKBEINR #	%	WARD #	%*	FAUBUS #	%	BENNETT #	%	WILLIAMS #	%	HARDIN #	%
CALHOUN	1691	68.8	503	20.5	264	10.7*	1700	64.5	593	22.5	199	7.5	145	5.5
CARROLL	1609	69.1	233	10.0	486	20.9*	1823	58.3	421	13.5	624	20.0	257	8.2
CHICOT	2471	67.3	738	20.1	463	12.6*	2323	52.9	716	16.3	294	6.7	1056	24.1
CLARK	3806	68.0	781	14.0	1008	18.0*	3266	64.7	536	10.6	114	2.3	1135	22.5
CLAY	2097	64.4	256	7.9	904	27.8*	2016	50.9	388	9.8	1094	27.6	461	11.6
CLEBURNE	1556	73.0	302	14.2	274	12.9*	1753	64.1	423	15.5	277	10.1	281	10.3
CLEVELAND	1898	82.3	204	8.8	205	8.9*	2073	79.2	313	12.0	101	3.9	131	5.0
COLUMBIA	4463	82.7	391	7.2	540	10.0*	2952	68.5	706	16.4	339	7.9	315	7.3
CONWAY	3897	78.1	558	11.2	537	10.8*	3602	76.3	397	8.4	351	7.4	372	7.9
CRAIGHEAD	5785	68.9	1126	13.4	1488	17.7*	4976	58.8	1360	16.1	714	8.4	1407	16.6
CRAWFORD	2565	58.9	1136	26.1	657	15.1*	2706	55.1	1388	28.3	242	4.9	576	11.7
CRITTENDEN	4185	94.4	77	1.7	171	3.9*	2521	72.7	526	15.2	167	4.8	256	7.4
CROSS	2917	91.8	118	3.7	144	4.5*	3274	80.8	203	5.0	141	3.5	433	10.7
DALLAS	2721	75.9	254	7.1	611	17.0*	2314	66.6	377	10.8	256	7.4	528	15.2
DESHA	2808	71.1	582	14.7	557	14.1*	2811	65.6	269	6.3	192	4.5	1012	23.6
DREW	2756	70.4	590	15.1	570	14.6*	2560	63.7	464	11.6	166	4.1	826	20.6
FAULKNER	5376	69.4	1140	14.7	1225	15.8*	5387	63.8	956	11.3	545	6.5	1557	18.4
FRANKLIN	2544	72.4	530	15.1	441	12.5*	1917	65.9	373	12.8	135	4.6	483	16.6
FULTON	1241	68.8	199	11.0	365	20.2*	1439	62.9	489	21.4	230	10.0	131	5.7
GARLAND	7052	57.6	2650	21.6	2550	20.8*	6919	55.6	2156	17.3	1091	8.8	2286	18.4
GRANT	2455	83.0	247	8.3	257	8.7*	2419	78.1	341	11.0	149	4.8	190	6.1
GREENE	2570	49.7	505	9.8	2096	40.5*	2572	43.4	791	13.3	1323	22.3	1240	20.9
HEMSTEAD	3829	72.3	715	13.5	749	14.2*	3461	62.9	925	16.8	278	5.1	835	15.2
HOTSPRING	4734	70.5	860	12.8	1122	16.7*	4023	65.6	810	13.2	374	6.1	922	15.0
HOWARD	2191	77.6	337	11.9	294	10.4*	2327	67.6	483	14.0	113	3.3	520	15.1
INDEPENDCE	3847	69.0	1009	18.1	719	12.9*	3427	60.2	697	12.2	973	17.1	598	10.5
IZARD	1777	81.7	161	7.4	236	10.9*	1398	67.2	348	16.7	248	11.9	86	4.1
JACKSON	3774	71.8	905	17.2	577	11.0*	3761	63.9	692	11.8	594	10.1	835	14.2
JEFFERSON	7645	56.3	2466	18.1	3476	25.6*	7512	52.1	1430	9.9	886	6.1	4595	31.9
JOHNSON	2321	70.4	586	17.8	389	11.8*	2597	67.9	659	17.2	184	4.8	383	10.0
LAFAYETTE	2213	77.3	339	11.8	310	10.8*	1704	64.7	447	17.0	216	8.2	265	10.1
LAWRENCE	2937	74.5	300	7.6	705	17.9*	2997	62.9	420	8.8	1201	25.2	144	3.0
LEE	2014	71.3	310	11.0	500	17.7*	1620	64.8	305	12.2	166	6.6	410	16.4
LINCOLN	1928	63.5	496	16.3	612	20.2*	1644	55.6	141	4.8	52	1.8	1119	37.9
LITTLERIVR	2264	79.0	419	14.6	182	6.4*	2076	68.1	596	19.6	148	4.9	228	7.5
LOGAN	3260	69.3	956	20.3	487	10.4*	2714	59.2	849	18.5	280	6.1	743	16.2
LONOKE	4381	79.3	571	10.3	573	10.4*	4594	73.0	548	8.7	356	5.7	799	12.7
MADISON	1921	94.8	27	1.3	78	3.8*	1797	91.5	73	3.7	28	1.4	66	3.4
MARION	1135	60.5	360	19.2	381	20.3*	1052	48.1	499	22.8	395	18.1	241	11.0
MILLER	5840	77.5	1194	15.8	500	6.6*	4911	64.9	1408	18.6	316	4.2	928	12.3
MISSISSIP	7314	89.0	432	5.3	470	5.7*	6558	68.5	1519	15.9	703	7.3	789	8.2
MONROE	2717	85.6	128	4.0	330	10.4*	2247	75.7	210	7.1	179	6.0	333	11.2
MONTGOMERY	1490	71.6	271	13.0	320	15.4*	1266	63.4	362	18.1	191	9.6	179	9.0
NEVADA	2199	73.1	374	12.4	437	14.5*	2284	65.9	505	14.6	184	5.3	495	14.3
NEWTON	1297	95.4	35	2.6	28	2.1*	1160	94.6	33	2.7	24	2.0	9	.7
QUACHITA	5302	63.9	1510	18.2	1479	17.8*	4467	51.3	1746	20.1	1460	16.8	1033	11.9

COUNTY	DEMOC. GOVERNOR 1958						*	DEMOC. GOVERNOR 1960							

COUNTY	FAUBUS		FINKBEINR		WARD		*	FAUBUS		BENNETT		WILLIAMS		HARDIN	
	#	%	#	%	#	%	*	#	%	#	%	#	%	#	%
PERRY	1095	80.0	152	11.1	122	8.9	*	1275	65.8	277	14.3	279	14.4	108	5.6
PHILLIPS	4206	78.2	830	15.4	340	6.3	*	2770	64.8	451	10.5	182	4.3	874	20.4
PIKE	2129	79.5	298	11.1	251	9.4	*	1751	68.4	459	17.9	112	4.4	237	9.3
POINSETT	5521	92.2	228	3.8	242	4.0	*	4682	72.4	913	14.1	419	6.5	454	7.0
POLK	2494	65.1	868	22.7	470	12.3	*	1939	51.9	955	25.6	463	12.4	376	10.1
							*								
POPE	4033	69.7	1054	18.2	700	12.1	*	3386	63.6	752	14.1	582	10.9	603	11.3
PRAIRIE	2472	87.2	220	7.8	144	5.1	*	2227	72.4	430	14.0	126	4.1	292	9.5
PULASKI	28903	57.0	11134	21.9	10690	21.1	*	28307	53.7	4280	8.1	3331	6.3	16832	31.9
RANDOLPH	2289	64.2	363	10.2	913	25.6	*	1910	53.7	478	13.4	772	21.7	397	11.2
STFRANCIS	3904	78.4	438	8.8	640	12.8	*	2665	67.4	418	10.6	301	7.6	570	14.4
							*								
SALINE	5071	68.0	1566	21.0	824	11.0	*	4015	63.1	848	13.3	443	7.0	1060	16.7
SCOTT	1424	61.6	487	21.1	401	17.3	*	1351	51.0	804	30.4	293	11.1	200	7.6
SEARCY	466	67.0	97	13.9	133	19.1	*	670	66.5	196	19.4	69	6.8	73	7.2
SEBASTIAN	6201	45.0	4563	33.1	3013	21.9	*	5800	47.2	2712	22.1	847	6.9	2922	23.8
SEVIER	1886	77.6	314	12.9	229	9.4	*	1840	67.6	391	14.4	110	4.0	379	13.9
							*								
SHARP	1407	73.8	164	8.6	335	17.6	*	1754	72.5	338	14.0	235	9.7	91	3.8
STONE	1010	70.9	242	17.0	173	12.1	*	1399	61.7	522	23.0	199	8.8	147	6.5
UNION	8788	74.6	1594	13.5	1403	11.9	*	4814	39.6	5825	47.9	662	5.4	866	7.1
VANBUREN	2201	78.3	275	9.8	335	11.9	*	1939	72.8	377	14.1	182	6.8	167	6.3
WASHINGTON	3964	63.0	919	14.6	1413	22.4	*	3168	47.1	770	11.4	656	9.7	2138	31.8
							*								
WHITE	5429	70.4	1346	17.4	940	12.2	*	4860	62.7	1118	14.4	698	9.0	1081	13.9
WOODRUFF	2039	78.4	181	7.0	380	14.6	*	1963	66.5	257	8.7	157	5.3	573	19.4
YELL	2351	74.8	486	15.5	308	9.8	*	2939	69.4	584	13.8	462	10.9	249	5.9

							*								
TOTALS	264346		60373		59385		*	238997		58400		33374		66499	
% OF VOTE		68.8		15.7		15.5	*		60.2		14.7		8.4		16.7

GEOGRAPHIC CLASS

							*								
LOWLANDS	125310	71.	27300	15.	25115	14.	*	113329	61.	27843	15.	12012	6.	33080	18.
BLACK BELT	38851	72.	6839	13.	8390	16.	*	32094	61.	5547	11.	3048	6.	11591	22.
MOUNTAIN	100185	66.	26234	17.	25880	17.	*	93574	59.	25010	16.	18314	12.	21828	14.

DEMOGRAPHIC CLASS

							*								
METRO	40944	57.	16891	23.	14203	20.	*	39018	54.	8400	12.	4494	6.	20682	28.
TOWN	40548	67.	9187	15.	10800	18.	*	33947	53.	13060	20.	4712	7.	12081	19.
RURAL	182854	73.	34295	14.	34382	14.	*	166032	64.	36940	14.	24168	9.	33736	13.

	DEMOC. GOVERNOR 1962				DEMOC. GOVERNOR 1964				
COUNTY	FAUBUS	ALFORD	MCMATH	OTHER	FAUBUS	HUBBARD	DORSEY	BURROW
	# %	# %	# %	# %	# %	# %	# %	# %
ARKANSAS	2744 49.4	1237 22.3	871 15.7	707 12.7*	2651 66.3	433 10.8	850 21.2	66 1.6
ASHLEY	3060 50.6	1070 17.7	1390 23.0	528 8.7*	3834 72.9	342 6.5	885 16.8	201 3.8
BAXTER	1423 38.3	473 12.7	1529 41.2	287 7.7*	1879 56.0	492 14.7	855 25.5	128 3.8
BENTON	3471 51.7	1545 23.0	1083 16.1	619 9.2*	3183 68.8	517 11.2	778 16.8	151 3.3
BOONE	2085 39.7	920 17.5	1777 33.8	470 8.9*	2279 52.3	651 15.0	1338 30.7	86 2.0
BRADLEY	2097 52.3	1017 25.3	687 17.1	212 5.3*	2519 66.7	299 7.9	889 23.5	72 1.9
CALHOUN	1533 56.8	584 21.6	490 18.1	93 3.4*	1832 71.5	209 8.2	474 18.5	48 1.9
CARROLL	1715 57.6	356 12.0	802 26.9	106 3.6*	2189 75.5	278 9.6	380 13.1	51 1.8
CHICOT	2157 49.7	863 19.9	955 22.0	364 8.4*	2916 72.9	429 10.7	559 14.0	96 2.4
CLARK	2549 46.4	973 17.7	1525 27.7	449 8.2*	2813 59.3	612 12.9	1232 26.0	89 1.9
CLAY	2069 48.8	977 23.0	1075 25.3	122 2.9*	2277 53.0	1075 25.0	326 7.6	615 14.3
CLEBURNE	1508 53.5	587 20.8	424 15.0	301 10.7*	1880 69.1	199 7.3	596 21.9	45 1.7
CLEVELAND	1669 67.7	494 20.0	252 10.2	50 2.0*	1933 80.1	129 5.3	314 13.0	36 1.5
COLUMBIA	2891 50.8	1164 20.5	1366 24.0	269 4.7*	3609 72.4	552 11.1	750 15.1	72 1.4
CONWAY	3214 59.3	1054 19.4	906 16.7	247 4.6*	2771 85.4	201 6.2	252 7.8	20 .6
CRAIGHEAD	4430 45.4	2662 27.3	1818 18.6	852 8.7*	4833 57.5	570 6.8	1184 14.1	1811 21.6
CRAWFORD	2340 46.6	1452 28.9	951 18.9	282 5.6*	3116 65.4	508 10.7	1054 22.1	90 1.9
CRITTENDEN	3056 83.6	204 5.6	312 8.5	82 2.2*	4576 92.8	167 3.4	134 2.7	53 1.1
CROSS	2378 70.9	546 16.3	330 9.8	100 3.0*	3127 81.2	149 3.9	516 13.4	57 1.5
DALLAS	1671 51.5	746 23.0	642 19.8	188 5.8*	2106 67.1	339 10.8	618 19.7	76 2.4
DESHA	2213 58.1	619 16.2	762 20.0	216 5.7*	3463 68.4	639 12.6	860 17.0	100 2.0
DREW	1700 51.4	802 24.2	559 16.9	249 7.5*	2047 69.8	265 9.0	580 19.8	41 1.4
FAULKNER	4419 53.1	1774 21.3	1515 18.2	612 7.4*	6174 68.7	857 9.5	1809 20.1	144 1.6
FRANKLIN	2640 62.2	835 19.7	509 12.0	263 6.2*	2511 71.0	367 10.4	492 13.9	168 4.7
FULTON	1533 62.4	255 10.4	565 23.0	102 4.2*	2041 74.4	226 8.2	269 9.8	208 7.6
GARLAND	6227 51.5	2330 19.3	2691 22.2	855 7.1*	6381 63.8	1105 11.0	2192 21.9	325 3.2
GRANT	1851 62.2	581 19.5	378 12.7	165 5.5*	1843 55.6	89 2.7	1354 40.8	31 .9
GREENE	2526 42.4	1172 19.7	1959 32.9	299 5.0*	3617 57.7	722 11.5	688 11.0	1241 19.8
HEMSTEAD	2791 52.2	1248 23.4	964 18.0	340 6.4*	3790 73.1	443 8.5	824 15.9	127 2.4
HOTSPRING	2955 47.3	1647 26.4	1156 18.5	486 7.8*	3426 53.7	336 5.3	2498 39.1	125 2.0
HOWARD	1751 51.1	1073 31.3	450 13.1	151 4.4*	2671 75.0	300 8.4	466 13.1	126 3.5
INDEPENDCE	3118 55.4	991 17.6	1144 20.3	372 6.6*	3495 62.8	607 10.9	1158 20.8	308 5.5
IZARD	1751 62.6	416 14.9	530 18.9	101 3.6*	1708 71.4	200 8.4	359 15.0	124 5.2
JACKSON	3094 53.0	1094 18.7	1356 23.2	298 5.1*	3598 60.8	869 14.7	785 13.3	670 11.3
JEFFERSON	5655 42.3	2434 18.2	3676 27.5	1618 12.1*	6259 56.9	1643 14.9	2777 25.2	327 3.0
JOHNSON	2072 55.8	729 19.6	672 18.1	242 6.5*	2849 68.1	664 15.9	612 14.6	59 1.4
LAFAYETTE	1735 58.3	400 13.4	656 22.0	186 6.2*	2335 79.5	178 6.1	376 12.8	48 1.6
LAWRENCE	2814 56.5	942 18.9	1089 21.9	138 2.8*	2604 47.9	145 2.7	239 4.4	2447 45.0
LEE	1212 57.4	154 7.3	327 15.5	420 19.9*	1717 73.7	224 9.6	317 13.6	71 3.0
LINCOLN	1574 50.7	681 22.0	686 22.1	161 5.2*	2230 67.4	188 5.7	846 25.6	45 1.4
LITTLERIVR	2064 66.7	484 15.6	390 12.6	157 5.1*	1702 78.5	152 7.0	250 11.5	63 2.9
LOGAN	2439 53.6	884 19.4	921 20.2	309 6.8*	3043 66.5	637 13.9	744 16.3	151 3.3
LONOKE	3289 56.0	1415 24.1	827 14.1	345 5.9*	3339 72.8	272 5.9	917 20.0	57 1.2
MADISON	2771 96.6	25 .9	62 2.2	12 .4*	2457 98.6	8 .3	26 1.0	2 .1
MARION	1202 51.9	323 13.9	635 27.4	158 6.8*	1401 56.0	236 9.4	749 30.0	114 4.6
MILLER	4327 56.6	1864 24.4	1090 14.3	361 4.7*	5484 76.2	470 6.5	989 13.7	254 3.5

COUNTY	FAUBUS #	FAUBUS %	ALFORD #	ALFORD %	MCMATH #	MCMATH %	OTHER #	OTHER %	FAUBUS #	FAUBUS %	HUBBARD #	HUBBARD %	DORSEY #	DORSEY %	BURROW #	BURROW %
MISSISSIP	7568	75.8	1010	10.1	1265	12.7	139	1.4*	5112	87.8	220	3.8	270	4.6	222	3.8
MONROE	1845	66.2	419	15.0	400	14.4	121	4.3*	2171	78.0	143	5.1	391	14.0	80	2.9
MONTGOMERY	1138	48.7	492	21.1	525	22.5	180	7.7*	1214	54.5	284	12.7	361	16.2	369	16.6
NEVADA	1882	53.7	684	19.5	685	19.6	252	7.2*	2076	68.6	406	13.4	451	14.9	94	3.1
NEWTON	1044	82.8	51	4.0	156	12.4	10	.8*	939	95.5	27	2.7	17	1.7	0	.0
								*								
QUACHITA	3371	37.7	2454	27.4	2651	29.7	464	5.2*	5108	59.2	1359	15.7	1940	22.5	226	2.6
PERRY	1191	54.2	535	24.4	333	15.2	138	6.3*	1285	70.9	152	8.4	354	19.5	21	1.2
PHILLIPS	2807	61.6	605	13.3	1021	22.4	125	2.7*	3741	73.6	773	15.2	470	9.3	97	1.9
PIKE	1348	47.1	1052	36.7	348	12.2	116	4.1*	1739	63.9	316	11.6	617	22.7	49	1.8
POINSETT	3688	68.7	850	15.8	593	11.0	239	4.5*	4312	80.4	308	5.7	407	7.6	337	6.3
								*								
POLK	1534	42.4	1001	27.7	641	17.7	443	12.2*	2212	59.3	334	8.9	1054	28.2	133	3.6
POPE	2681	45.2	1615	27.2	1111	18.7	523	8.8*	3465	58.2	1717	28.8	710	11.9	63	1.1
PRAIRIE	1761	62.5	633	22.5	230	8.2	193	6.9*	2293	78.2	115	3.9	449	15.3	74	2.5
PULASKI	18841	38.7	9933	20.4	14232	29.2	5686	11.7*	20606	53.6	5797	15.1	11283	29.4	737	1.9
RANDOLPH	1597	42.6	893	23.8	1146	30.6	110	2.9*	1591	44.4	619	17.3	338	9.4	1037	28.9
								*								
STFRANCIS	2783	60.9	774	16.9	799	17.5	216	4.7*	4507	79.9	492	8.7	542	9.6	103	1.8
SALINE	3419	43.7	2262	28.9	1333	17.0	814	10.4*	3317	53.8	385	6.2	2392	38.8	72	1.2
SCOTT	1047	50.4	517	24.9	389	18.7	124	6.0*	1115	61.2	222	12.2	442	24.2	44	2.4
SEARCY	523	68.0	109	14.2	103	13.4	34	4.4*	464	77.9	66	11.1	65	10.9	1	.2
SEBASTIAN	5461	42.7	3440	26.9	2523	19.7	1379	10.8*	5594	60.3	1142	12.3	2411	26.0	130	1.4
								*								
SEVIER	1757	59.2	567	19.1	398	13.4	248	8.4*	2361	78.0	271	9.0	363	12.0	30	1.0
SHARP	1704	62.7	430	15.8	502	18.5	82	3.0*	1191	69.4	78	4.5	148	8.6	298	17.4
STONE	1348	57.1	482	20.4	411	17.4	120	5.1*	1576	63.4	267	10.7	575	23.1	68	2.7
UNION	5710	45.8	3845	30.8	1664	13.3	1249	10.0*	7680	68.9	1269	11.4	2026	18.2	174	1.6
VANBUREN	2031	67.3	429	14.2	379	12.6	180	6.0*	1868	73.7	244	9.6	393	15.5	29	1.1
								*								
WASHINGTON	4273	54.1	966	12.2	1994	25.3	662	8.4*	4153	64.4	925	14.3	1150	17.8	222	3.4
WHITE	4571	54.6	1498	17.9	1707	20.4	600	7.2*	6131	65.9	692	7.4	2244	24.1	242	2.6
WOODRUFF	1998	63.3	344	10.9	628	19.9	186	5.9*	1893	71.2	299	11.2	363	13.7	103	3.9
YELL	2292	58.4	829	21.1	552	14.1	251	6.4*	1668	75.1	284	12.8	252	11.4	16	.7
								*								
TOTALS	208996		82815		83473		29828	*	239890		39199		69638		16310	
% OF VOTE		51.6		20.4		20.6		7.4 *		65.7		10.7		19.1		4.5

```
                 DEMOC.  GOVERNOR   1962            *          DEMOC.  GOVERNOR    1964

 COUNTY      FAUBUS        ALFORD        MCMATH        OTHER   *   FAUBUS        HUBBARD       DORSEY        BURROW
             #      %      #      %      #      %      #     %*   #      %      #      %      #      %      #      %
 ----------------------------------------------------------------*------------------------------------------------------
 GEOGRAPHIC CLASS                                               *
                                                               *
 LOWLANDS    100875 49.   43877 22.   42719 21.   16598  8.*  115133 65.   18738 11.   37103 21.    6348  4.
 BLACK BELT   23051 60.    5809 15.    7188 19.    2265  6.*   31655 76.    3871  9.    5476 13.     872  2.
 MOUNTAIN     85070 52.   33129 20.   33566 21.   10965  7.*   93102 64.   16590 11.   27059 19.    9090  6.
                                                               *
 DEMOGRAPHIC CLASS                                             *
                                                               *
 METRO        28629 41.   15237 22.   17845 26.    7426 11.*   31684 58.    7409 13.   14683 27.    1121  2.
 TOWN         36020 52.   14110 20.   14063 20.    5739  8.*   37334 66.    6161 11.   10158 18.    3177  6.
 RURAL       144347 54.   53468 20.   51565 19.   16663  6.*  170872 67.   25629 10.   44797 18.   12012  5.
```

ARKANSAS

```
                 DEMOC.  GOVERNOR    1966                     *  DEMOC.  RUNOFF     1966
                                                             *
 COUNTY      JOHNSON       HOLT          HAYS          ALFORD        BOYCE         REBSAMEN     JOHNSON       HOLT
             #      %      #      %      #      %      #     %    #      %      #     %*   #      %      #      %
 -----------------------------------------------------------------------------------*--------------------------------------------
 ARKANSAS    1190 24.6   1482 30.6    543 11.2    600 12.4    466  9.6    563 11.6*  2611 52.1   2397 47.9
 ASHLEY      3871 63.2    876 14.3    760 12.4    238  3.9    166  2.7    211  3.4*  4386 69.1   1963 30.9
 BAXTER       642 28.2    775 34.1    393 17.3    108  4.7    274 12.0     82  3.6*   873 43.0   1155 57.0
 BENTON       514 14.5   1161 32.7    989 27.8    323  9.1    379 10.7    186  5.2*  1318 41.5   1858 58.5
 BOONE        879 17.7   2562 51.6    512 10.3    283  5.7    560 11.3    165  3.3*  1724 42.3   2352 57.7

 BRADLEY     2045 52.3    611 15.6    484 12.4    404 10.3    168  4.3    201  5.1*  2481 64.5   1367 35.5
 CALHOUN     1184 49.2    205  8.5    310 12.9    459 19.1    156  6.5     94  3.9*  1308 63.4    754 36.6
 CARROLL      524 25.5    849 41.3    394 19.2     72  3.5    126  6.1     92  4.5*   888 46.1   1039 53.9
 CHICOT      1869 38.5    936 19.3   1028 21.2    497 10.2    171  3.5    354  7.3*  2197 46.1   2565 53.9
 CLARK       1174 20.4   1154 20.1   1238 21.5    967 16.8    737 12.8    482  8.4*  2825 46.0   3312 54.0

 CLAY         983 21.1   1082 23.3    922 19.8   1181 25.4    316  6.8    167  3.6*  2504 54.9   2057 45.1
 CLEBURNE     703 19.6    932 25.9    360 10.0    717 19.9    696 19.4    186  5.2*  2047 55.4   1648 44.6
 CLEVELAND   1221 48.4    403 16.0    326 12.9    276 10.9    193  7.6    106  4.2*  1593 70.4    669 29.6
 COLUMBIA    1400 33.4    938 22.4    756 18.1    523 12.5    227  5.4    343  8.2*  2466 53.5   2144 46.5
 CONWAY       258  6.7    358  9.3   2705 70.2    166  4.3    265  6.9    100  2.6*   856 20.6   3304 79.4

 CRAIGHEAD   2351 21.3   2818 25.5   1811 16.4   1880 17.0   1287 11.7    883  8.0*  5133 57.1   3864 42.9
 CRAWFORD    1968 40.5    842 17.3    850 17.5    514 10.6    310  6.4    373  7.7*  2405 58.2   1725 41.8
 CRITTENDEN   724 19.0   1972 51.7    417 10.9    233  6.1    184  4.8    288  7.5*  1780 39.8   2688 60.2
 CROSS       1615 37.6   1456 33.9    529 12.3    252  5.9    270  6.3    170  4.0*  2629 56.4   2034 43.6
 DALLAS      1252 42.7    438 14.9    467 15.9    359 12.2    206  7.0    209  7.1*  1674 59.4   1145 40.6
                                                                               *
 DESHA       1121 26.4   1049 24.7   1060 25.0    388  9.1    329  7.8    298  7.0*  2067 44.2   2610 55.8
 DREW        1825 43.9    610 14.7    709 17.0    502 12.1    201  4.8    314  7.5*  2395 60.1   1590 39.9
 FAULKNER    4025 46.0   1282 14.7   1009 11.5    896 10.2   1135 13.0    403  4.6*  6034 65.1   3228 34.9
 FRANKLIN    1439 35.7    885 22.0    610 15.1    457 11.3    438 10.9    202  5.0*  2663 58.7   1875 41.3
```

COUNTY	JOHNSON #	%	HOLT #	%	HAYS #	%	ALFORD #	%	BOYCE #	%	REBSAMEN #	%	JOHNSON #	%	HOLT #	%
FULTON	673	32.4	814	39.2	261	12.6	144	6.9	124	6.0	63	3.0*	905	57.2	677	42.8
GARLAND	1585	12.0	2279	17.3	1546	11.7	3181	24.1	1547	11.7	3059	23.2*	6509	46.7	7442	53.3
GRANT	625	28.0	452	20.3	205	9.2	434	19.5	291	13.0	224	10.0*	1553	61.7	963	38.3
GREENE	1273	19.5	1310	20.0	803	12.3	2028	31.0	892	13.6	235	3.6*	3857	60.8	2487	39.2
HEMSTEAD	1982	39.9	974	19.6	789	15.9	619	12.5	243	4.9	364	7.3*	3128	57.0	2361	43.0
HOTSPRING	1823	30.3	871	14.5	739	12.3	1183	19.7	915	15.2	489	8.1*	3761	63.5	2165	36.5
HOWARD	1746	43.7	604	15.1	401	10.0	674	16.9	348	8.7	225	5.6*	1748	63.1	1024	36.9
INDEPENDCE	724	13.1	1280	23.2	512	9.3	1068	19.4	1631	29.6	304	5.5*	3325	53.8	2857	46.2
IZARD	536	19.6	708	25.9	275	10.0	628	22.9	547	20.0	44	1.6*	1240	59.0	863	41.0
JACKSON	765	12.0	310	4.9	438	6.9	216	3.4	4519	71.1	109	1.7*	3577	60.0	2381	40.0
JEFFERSON	4432	27.6	3006	18.7	1831	11.4	2588	16.1	2122	13.2	2088	13.0*	9431	51.5	8874	48.5
JOHNSON	773	21.5	878	24.4	627	17.4	562	15.6	588	16.3	169	4.7*	1589	49.0	1654	51.0
LAFAYETTE	1040	43.2	343	14.3	470	19.5	210	8.7	194	8.1	149	6.2*	1204	58.2	864	41.8
LAWRENCE	989	24.3	1388	34.1	514	12.6	337	8.3	698	17.1	146	3.6*	2240	52.6	2017	47.4
LEE	1351	36.8	869	23.7	682	18.6	298	8.1	196	5.3	274	7.5*	1636	56.0	1288	44.0
LINCOLN	1121	34.5	1090	33.5	397	12.2	395	12.2	150	4.6	98	3.0*	1666	52.3	1518	47.7
LITTLERIVR	459	35.7	407	31.6	178	13.8	105	8.2	62	4.8	75	5.8*	743	46.3	861	53.7
LOGAN	942	22.0	1186	27.7	801	18.7	404	9.4	450	10.5	497	11.6*	1942	48.4	2072	51.6
LONOKE	1538	29.7	1065	20.6	475	9.2	818	15.8	804	15.5	479	9.2*	3237	61.1	2057	38.9
MADISON	96	6.8	1113	78.4	99	7.0	60	4.2	37	2.6	14	1.0*	237	14.1	1444	85.9
MARION	531	25.8	869	42.1	230	11.2	148	7.2	241	11.7	43	2.1*	1090	51.2	1038	48.8
MILLER	2217	29.7	1618	21.7	1378	18.4	1065	14.3	551	7.4	640	8.6*	4369	56.9	3304	43.1
MISSISSIP	926	17.2	2285	42.6	831	15.5	564	10.5	256	4.8	508	9.5*	3238	43.0	4299	57.0
MONROE	1314	33.3	1021	25.9	611	15.5	366	9.3	457	11.6	172	4.4*	2159	53.9	1849	46.1
MONTGOMERY	359	18.1	420	21.1	240	12.1	501	25.2	339	17.1	128	6.4*	1351	60.1	896	39.9
NEVADA	1586	41.9	705	18.6	530	14.0	461	12.2	299	7.9	207	5.5*	1836	57.6	1350	42.4
NEWTON	71	8.4	692	81.5	35	4.1	29	3.4	16	1.9	6	.7*	169	14.3	1012	85.7
QUACHITA	3473	35.6	1697	17.4	1850	19.0	1186	12.2	774	7.9	771	7.9*	5009	52.3	4573	47.7
PERRY	324	17.4	609	32.6	317	17.0	308	16.5	245	13.1	63	3.4*	867	50.7	844	49.3
PHILLIPS	2030	35.5	927	16.2	1892	33.0	410	7.2	130	2.3	337	5.9*	3199	47.7	3506	52.3
PIKE	390	24.7	304	19.2	93	5.9	564	35.7	146	9.2	84	5.3*	1145	66.3	582	33.7
POINSETT	1759	26.2	2006	29.9	791	11.8	768	11.4	1066	15.9	320	4.8*	3205	60.6	2085	39.4
POLK	859	28.5	715	23.7	618	20.5	341	11.3	268	8.9	210	7.0*	1290	54.7	1067	45.3
POPE	814	13.3	1294	21.2	1605	26.3	1109	18.2	876	14.4	401	6.6*	3071	56.1	2402	43.9
PRAIRIE	486	19.4	885	35.3	282	11.3	367	14.7	261	10.4	224	8.9*	1209	47.9	1315	52.1
PULASKI	7559	13.5	13261	23.7	10818	19.3	8324	14.9	7347	13.1	8612	15.4*	23141	40.3	34325	59.7
RANDOLPH	1057	30.0	916	26.0	550	15.6	261	7.4	588	16.7	152	4.3*	2174	57.2	1628	42.8
STFRANCIS	2780	46.8	988	16.6	1011	17.0	392	6.6	375	6.3	390	6.6*	3910	61.0	2501	39.0
SALINE	1839	22.1	1432	17.2	797	9.6	1544	18.5	1985	23.8	735	8.8*	5501	61.2	3489	38.8
SCOTT	1055	37.3	571	20.2	565	20.0	282	10.0	209	7.4	147	5.2*	1804	63.9	1020	36.1
SEARCY	145	17.6	494	60.1	59	7.2	50	6.1	63	7.7	11	1.3*	373	36.5	649	63.5
SEBASTIAN	3569	29.3	1768	14.5	2226	18.3	1067	8.8	728	6.0	2808	23.1*	7213	54.0	6149	46.0
SEVIER	515	28.4	537	29.6	318	17.5	126	7.0	176	9.7	140	7.7*	841	45.8	994	54.2
SHARP	495	29.7	581	34.9	136	8.2	158	9.5	211	12.7	83	5.0*	1329	72.5	503	27.5
STONE	307	12.8	615	25.6	190	7.9	416	17.3	822	34.2	55	2.3*	1472	64.4	814	35.6
UNION	5903	45.7	2049	15.9	1768	13.7	1373	10.6	539	4.2	1287	10.0*	7753	61.6	4843	38.4

DEMOC. GOVERNOR 1966   * DEMOC. RUNOFF 1966

COUNTY	JOHNSON #	%	HOLT #	%	HAYS #	%	ALFORD #	%	BOYCE #	%	REBSAMEN #	%*	JOHNSON #	%	HOLT #	%
VANBUREN	461	16.9	932	34.3	261	9.6	538	19.8	441	16.2	87	3.2*	1227	51.9	1137	48.1
WASHINGTON	1278	18.0	2146	30.2	1754	24.7	345	4.9	998	14.1	582	8.2*	2499	34.8	4678	65.2
WHITE	1279	15.0	2314	27.1	762	8.9	1359	15.9	2299	26.9	540	6.3*	4743	53.4	4140	46.6
WOODRUFF	601	21.6	497	17.9	399	14.4	311	11.2	802	28.9	169	6.1*	1695	53.3	1484	46.7
YELL	375	11.5	940	28.7	672	20.5	551	16.8	618	18.9	119	3.6*	1276	42.1	1754	57.9
												*				
TOTALS	105607		92711		64814		53531		49744		35608	*	210543		195442	
% OF VOTE	26.3		23.1		16.1		13.3		12.4		8.9	*	51.9		48.1	

GEOGRAPHIC CLASS

	JOHNSON #	%	HOLT #	%	HAYS #	%	ALFORD #	%	BOYCE #	%	REBSAMEN #	%*	JOHNSON #	%	HOLT #	%
LOWLANDS	51238	28.	40279	22.	29257	16.	24384	13.	22322	12.	18041	10.*	96175	52.	88994	48.
BLACK BELT	19635	33.	13136	22.	10265	17.	6447	11.	5316	9.	4826	8.*	32618	51.	30892	49.
MOUNTAIN	34734	22.	39296	25.	25292	16.	22700	14.	22106	14.	12741	8.*	81750	52.	75556	48.

DEMOGRAPHIC CLASS

	JOHNSON #	%	HOLT #	%	HAYS #	%	ALFORD #	%	BOYCE #	%	REBSAMEN #	%*	JOHNSON #	%	HOLT #	%
METRO	13345	18.	16647	22.	14422	19.	10456	14.	8626	11.	12060	16.*	34723	44.	43778	56.
TOWN	16475	25.	14583	22.	9541	15.	9931	15.	6749	10.	8407	13.*	34563	50.	34000	50.
RURAL	75787	29.	61481	24.	40851	16.	33144	13.	34369	13.	15141	6.*	141257	55.	117664	45.

ARKANSAS

DEMOC. GOVERNOR 1968   * DEMOC. RUNOFF 1968

COUNTY	WHITBECK #	%	BENNETT #	%	CRANK #	%	BOSWELL #	%	JOHNSON #	%	BYRD #	%*	CRANK #	%	JOHNSON #	%
ARKANSAS	691	13.5	766	15.0	1306	25.5	795	15.5	1437	28.1	125	2.4*	2508	58.5	1777	41.5
ASHLEY	396	7.5	717	13.6	772	14.7	981	18.7	2155	41.0	233	4.4*	1851	41.5	2605	58.5
BAXTER	357	17.1	313	15.0	386	18.5	461	22.0	424	20.3	150	7.2*	954	67.7	455	32.3
BENTON	691	14.8	1454	31.1	878	18.8	918	19.6	618	13.2	122	2.6*	2580	76.8	780	23.2
BOONE	1015	20.6	719	14.6	884	18.0	559	11.4	1633	33.2	112	2.3*	1555	55.3	1258	44.7
BRADLEY	580	13.7	617	14.6	459	10.8	889	21.0	1611	38.1	75	1.8*	1793	48.9	1874	51.1
CALHOUN	202	9.3	796	36.6	286	13.1	268	12.3	567	26.0	58	2.7*	897	56.1	701	43.9
CARROLL	459	18.6	413	16.7	576	23.3	237	9.6	719	29.1	70	2.8*	1119	66.2	571	33.8
CHICOT	266	11.3	436	18.5	583	24.7	349	14.8	644	27.3	81	3.4*	1222	58.2	876	41.8
CLARK	988	16.4	889	14.8	1375	22.8	1535	25.5	1088	18.1	146	2.4*	2849	66.4	1443	33.6
CLAY	881	18.2	1229	25.4	1142	23.6	555	11.5	835	17.3	194	4.0*	2844	62.8	1683	37.2
CLEBURNE	575	15.4	619	16.6	1230	33.0	557	14.9	596	16.0	155	4.2*	2361	71.3	950	28.7
CLEVELAND	184	9.7	368	19.4	421	22.2	238	12.6	653	34.4	32	1.7*	1092	57.0	824	43.0
COLUMBIA	1145	20.0	1211	21.2	1390	24.3	693	12.1	1160	20.3	122	2.1*	2275	62.3	1377	37.7
CONWAY	344	8.0	276	6.4	2786	65.0	484	11.3	317	7.4	80	1.9*	3318	88.3	441	11.7

DEMOC. GOVERNOR 1968   * DEMOC. RUNOFF 1968

COUNTY	WHITBECK #	WHITBECK %	BENNETT #	BENNETT %	CRANK #	CRANK %	BOSWELL #	BOSWELL %	JOHNSON #	JOHNSON %	BYRD #	BYRD %*	CRANK #	CRANK %	JOHNSON #	JOHNSON %
CRAIGHEAD	3045	27.5	1489	13.5	2231	20.2	1975	17.9	2114	19.1	204	1.8*	5055	59.7	3409	40.3
CRAWFORD	354	10.4	572	16.8	922	27.1	580	17.0	912	26.8	66	1.9*	1739	59.5	1185	40.5
CRITTENDEN	801	17.4	661	14.4	1801	39.2	517	11.3	724	15.8	88	1.9*	2693	75.0	900	25.0
CROSS	636	17.4	234	6.4	1089	29.8	701	19.2	947	25.9	51	1.4*	1843	59.9	1236	40.1
DALLAS	525	17.5	565	18.9	485	16.2	415	13.9	907	30.3	96	3.2*	1249	50.7	1214	49.3
DESHA	406	11.6	417	11.9	1064	30.5	696	19.9	847	24.3	61	1.7*	2054	64.5	1131	35.5
DREW	608	14.9	554	13.5	1071	26.2	615	15.0	1127	27.5	116	2.8*	2009	61.2	1273	38.8
FAULKNER	778	8.2	895	9.4	2949	30.9	2110	22.1	2525	26.5	280	2.9*	5250	61.4	3302	38.6
FRANKLIN	494	10.8	1071	23.3	1258	27.4	523	11.4	1118	24.4	125	2.7*	2529	62.1	1543	37.9
FULTON	368	15.0	687	28.0	596	24.3	306	12.5	429	17.5	66	2.7*	875	73.7	312	26.3
GARLAND	1608	11.8	3137	23.0	4095	30.0	2514	18.4	2039	14.9	246	1.8*	7458	73.5	2688	26.5
GRANT	318	8.2	698	17.9	1233	31.6	696	17.9	851	21.8	102	2.6*	1937	64.3	1074	35.7
GREENE	1111	16.9	1105	16.8	2054	31.3	1102	16.8	1053	16.0	139	2.1*	4046	64.6	2217	35.4
HEMSTEAD	825	18.1	478	10.5	1597	35.0	468	10.2	1111	24.3	88	1.9*	2137	62.4	1289	37.6
HOTSPRING	792	12.9	878	14.3	1146	18.7	1600	26.1	1556	25.4	156	2.5*	3011	57.2	2252	42.8
HOWARD	562	14.9	450	11.9	1420	37.7	458	12.1	769	20.4	111	2.9*	2452	63.0	1439	37.0
INDEPENDCE	898	16.0	612	10.9	2075	37.0	1152	20.6	744	13.3	124	2.2*	3314	75.6	1071	24.4
IZARD	515	16.5	876	28.1	550	17.7	508	16.3	573	18.4	93	3.0*	1124	61.7	698	38.3
JACKSON	973	16.4	742	12.5	1055	17.8	1198	20.2	1807	30.4	167	2.8*	2520	52.0	2325	48.0
JEFFERSON	2635	16.5	2880	18.0	1710	10.7	4576	28.6	3901	24.4	315	2.0*	7182	54.0	6125	46.0
JOHNSON	302	9.3	484	15.0	1325	41.0	498	15.4	557	17.2	69	2.1*	2137	72.9	794	27.1
LAFAYETTE	400	14.2	334	11.8	1148	40.7	204	7.2	665	23.5	73	2.6*	1014	53.3	887	46.7
LAWRENCE	850	15.7	821	15.2	1754	32.4	875	16.2	994	18.4	114	2.1*	2433	61.9	1499	38.1
LEE	421	14.3	302	10.3	1029	35.0	275	9.4	851	28.9	63	2.1*	1256	57.6	926	42.4
LINCOLN	298	9.9	600	19.9	774	25.6	404	13.4	895	29.7	47	1.6*	1931	65.9	998	34.1
LITTLERIVR	96	4.3	91	4.1	1813	81.8	70	3.2	129	5.8	17	.8*	2001	87.2	293	12.8
LOGAN	575	12.3	767	16.4	1623	34.8	635	13.6	835	17.9	232	5.0*	2339	67.5	1126	32.5
LONOKE	833	13.2	1078	17.0	1430	22.6	1116	17.6	1680	26.5	195	3.1*	3375	61.1	2153	38.9
MADISON	63	3.4	728	39.6	829	45.1	60	3.3	147	8.0	13	.7*	1791	92.8	138	7.2
MARION	383	17.8	354	16.5	503	23.4	261	12.1	582	27.1	68	3.2*	753	58.9	525	41.1
MILLER	552	8.2	778	11.5	3409	50.5	770	11.4	1087	16.1	157	2.3*	3188	68.8	1449	31.2
MISSISSIP	3260	30.4	1099	10.2	3909	36.5	896	8.4	1417	13.2	141	1.3*	5530	69.4	2435	30.6
MONROE	455	13.3	495	14.5	463	13.6	627	18.4	1329	38.9	47	1.4*	1637	51.5	1542	48.5
MONTGOMERY	402	17.1	467	19.9	609	25.9	306	13.0	461	19.6	102	4.3*	997	65.1	534	34.9
NEVADA	301	9.1	364	10.9	1142	34.3	438	13.2	965	29.0	115	3.5*	1344	55.8	1065	44.2
NEWTON	53	6.0	117	13.2	605	68.3	17	1.9	85	9.6	9	1.0*	889	92.1	76	7.9
QUACHITA	1335	14.0	1684	17.7	2122	22.3	2074	21.8	2077	21.9	212	2.2*	5165	59.7	3488	40.3
PERRY	221	10.7	285	13.8	787	38.0	343	16.6	367	17.7	68	3.3*	1070	68.4	495	31.6
PHILLIPS	1246	19.8	540	8.6	1597	25.4	1242	19.8	1608	25.6	55	.9*	3326	63.8	1885	36.2
PIKE	396	13.6	270	9.3	1196	41.0	353	12.1	624	21.4	79	2.7*	1815	65.3	963	34.7
POINSETT	2014	31.0	875	13.5	1687	26.0	532	8.2	1263	19.5	118	1.8*	2865	63.7	1632	36.3
POLK	493	12.2	745	18.4	1468	36.4	451	11.2	797	19.7	84	2.1*	2406	64.0	1351	36.0
POPE	1704	28.3	753	12.5	1400	23.3	1157	19.2	871	14.5	127	2.1*	3260	68.5	1499	31.5
PRAIRIE	405	13.8	486	16.6	886	30.2	354	12.1	714	24.3	88	3.0*	1641	66.7	821	33.3
PULASKI	6995	14.1	5169	10.5	8529	17.2	19256	38.9	7991	16.2	1506	3.0*	25816	63.3	14969	36.7
RANDOLPH	638	18.7	607	17.8	327	9.6	1093	32.0	636	18.6	112	3.3*	1656	61.5	1035	38.5

DEMOC. GOVERNOR 1968   * DEMOC. RUNOFF   1968

COUNTY	WHITBECK #	%	BENNETT #	%	CRANK #	%	BOSWELL #	%	JOHNSON #	%	BYRD #	%*	CRANK #	%	JOHNSON #	%
STFRANCIS	1082	16.8	808	12.5	1394	21.6	591	9.2	2441	37.8	140	2.2*	2832	52.1	2604	47.9
SALINE	598	6.3	951	10.1	965	10.2	5076	53.7	1681	17.8	182	1.9*	4864	53.5	4222	46.5
SCOTT	221	11.1	256	12.8	802	40.1	221	11.1	446	22.3	52	2.6*	1181	69.0	531	31.0
SEARCY	56	9.7	98	16.9	259	44.7	90	15.5	70	12.1	7	1.2*	566	85.2	98	14.8
SEBASTIAN.	2165	14.8	1772	12.1	4131	28.3	3190	21.9	3077	21.1	255	1.7*	8195	61.6	5110	38.4
SEVIER	227	7.9	241	8.4	1732	60.6	278	9.7	354	12.4	28	1.0*	1548	75.8	493	24.2
SHARP	134	7.4	211	11.6	1003	55.1	164	9.0	275	15.1	33	1.8*	1324	75.4	431	24.6
STONE	356	13.1	605	22.3	804	29.6	290	10.7	563	20.7	99	3.6*	1096	70.6	457	29.4
UNION	1160	9.9	5573	47.6	626	5.4	1850	15.8	2231	19.1	257	2.2*	4887	52.2	4476	47.8
VANBUREN	395	14.7	457	17.0	790	29.5	443	16.5	506	18.9	90	3.4*	1510	72.8	564	27.2
WASHINGTON	1449	14.7	2045	20.7	1461	14.8	3476	35.2	1263	12.8	193	2.0*	6883	73.2	2516	26.8
WHITE	1365	16.8	928	11.4	2099	25.9	2112	26.0	1422	17.5	188	2.3*	4792	66.4	2429	33.6
WOODRUFF	368	11.0	440	13.2	828	24.8	629	18.9	883	26.5	188	5.6*	1625	60.3	1068	39.7
YELL	465	10.2	593	12.9	1959	42.8	683	14.9	688	15.0	193	4.2*	2454	70.9	1005	29.1
TOTALS	61758		65095		106092		85629		86038		10265	*	215087		124880	
% OF VOTE	14.9		15.7		25.6		20.6		20.7		2.5	*	63.3		36.7	

GEOGRAPHIC CLASS

	WHITBECK #	%	BENNETT #	%	CRANK #	%	BOSWELL #	%	JOHNSON #	%	BYRD #	%*	CRANK #	%	JOHNSON #	%
LOWLANDS	29123	16.	28325	15.	44136	24.	40744	22.	38861	21.	4620	2.*	91589	61.	58172	39.
BLACK BELT	8903	15.	8478	15.	12876	22.	10525	18.	15695	27.	1254	2.*	28021	58.	20156	42.
MOUNTAIN	23732	14.	28292	17.	49080	29.	34360	20.	31482	18.	4391	3.*	95477	67.	46552	33.

DEMOGRAPHIC CLASS

	WHITBECK #	%	BENNETT #	%	CRANK #	%	BOSWELL #	%	JOHNSON #	%	BYRD #	%*	CRANK #	%	JOHNSON #	%
METRO	9712	14.	7719	11.	16069	23.	23216	33.	12155	17.	1918	3.*	37199	63.	21528	37.
TOWN	13157	18.	16223	22.	14032	19.	15287	21.	12965	18.	1356	2.*	36995	63.	21649	37.
RURAL	38889	14.	41153	15.	75991	28.	47126	17.	60918	22.	6991	3.*	140893	63.	81703	37.

ARKANSAS

DEMOC. GOVERNOR 1970   * DEMOC. RUNOFF   1970

COUNTY	COMPTON #	%	PURCELL #	%	MCCLERKIN #	%	WELLS #	%	FAUBUS #	%	BUMPERS #	%*	FAUBUS #	%	BUMPERS #	%
ARKANSAS	92	1.8	779	15.3	579	11.3	312	6.1	2540	49.8	801	15.7*	2836	50.7	2758	49.3
ASHLEY	313	5.0	1580	25.2	421	6.7	1198	19.1	2176	34.7	583	9.3*	2586	42.2	3545	57.8
BAXTER	19	.7	748	28.8	188	7.2	197	7.6	1001	38.5	448	17.2*	936	34.8	1757	65.2
BENTON	91	1.5	741	12.3	388	6.4	137	2.3	2214	36.7	2462	40.8*	2432	34.2	4673	65.8
BOONE	44	1.0	926	21.7	285	6.7	285	6.7	2050	48.1	676	15.8*	2162	47.4	2397	52.6
BRADLEY	47	1.2	1094	28.3	73	1.9	1893	48.9	578	14.9	186	4.8*	1750	49.2	1809	50.8

COUNTY	COMPTON #	COMPTON %	PURCELL #	PURCELL %	MCCLERKIN #	MCCLERKIN %	WELLS #	WELLS %	FAUBUS #	FAUBUS %	BUMPERS #	BUMPERS %	FAUBUS #	FAUBUS %	BUMPERS #	BUMPERS %
CALHOUN	371	17.1	476	21.9	125	5.8	290	13.4	705	32.5	205	9.4*	1133	49.7	1148	50.3
CARROLL	14	.8	310	16.9	133	7.2	150	8.2	1025	55.8	204	11.1*	1077	52.5	976	47.5
CHICOT	154	3.8	840	21.0	705	17.6	339	8.5	1422	35.5	544	13.6*	1390	45.1	1694	54.9
CLARK	125	2.3	1741	31.6	637	11.6	425	7.7	1640	29.7	945	17.1*	2123	35.8	3815	64.2
CLAY	25	.6	951	21.6	306	7.0	556	12.6	1864	42.4	696	15.8*	1975	38.7	3129	61.3
CLEBURNE	71	1.8	783	19.6	433	10.9	452	11.3	1631	40.9	620	15.5*	2132	49.5	2175	50.5
CLEVELAND	69	2.9	636	26.9	85	3.6	408	17.3	1037	43.9	126	5.3*	1513	66.8	753	33.2
COLUMBIA	909	14.7	1309	21.2	1068	17.3	386	6.3	1954	31.7	545	8.8*	2205	34.0	4288	66.0
CONWAY	43	1.0	317	7.1	147	3.3	170	3.8	3455	77.9	304	6.9*	3960	79.5	1020	20.5
CRAIGHEAD	80	.8	1966	19.3	1137	11.2	571	5.6	3428	33.7	2999	29.5*	3678	31.8	7888	68.2
CRAWFORD	174	2.8	662	10.5	527	8.3	326	5.2	2132	33.7	2505	39.6*	2022	32.3	4232	67.7
CRITTENDEN	62	1.0	728	12.1	850	14.1	246	4.1	2896	48.0	1248	20.7*	2061	45.2	2496	54.8
CROSS	34	.8	898	21.7	297	7.2	386	9.3	2104	50.8	419	10.1*	1834	51.7	1715	48.3
DALLAS	86	2.8	1182	38.4	184	6.0	230	7.5	1096	35.6	302	9.8*	1421	49.8	1431	50.2
DESHA	85	2.5	814	24.0	466	13.7	190	5.6	1348	39.8	487	14.4*	1741	49.1	1803	50.9
DREW	51	1.4	946	26.5	615	17.2	419	11.7	1044	29.3	493	13.8*	1608	45.2	1949	54.8
FAULKNER	161	1.7	1271	13.3	702	7.3	1076	11.2	3875	40.5	2480	25.9*	4585	44.6	5694	55.4
FRANKLIN	32	.7	147	3.0	102	2.1	151	3.1	1445	29.9	2951	61.1*	1604	32.7	3304	67.3
FULTON	24	.9	379	14.9	108	4.2	637	25.0	1129	44.4	266	10.5*	1255	60.4	823	39.6
GARLAND	674	5.4	1837	14.7	2357	18.9	713	5.7	5349	42.8	1558	12.5*	6148	47.1	6902	52.9
GRANT	66	1.9	921	27.1	233	6.8	306	9.0	1485	43.6	392	11.5*	1864	55.3	1509	44.7
GREENE	68	.9	1283	17.4	411	5.6	772	10.5	2147	29.2	2674	36.4*	2156	29.0	5291	71.0
HEMSTEAD	192	3.4	1678	29.5	1105	19.4	242	4.3	1973	34.7	497	8.7*	2154	35.6	3898	64.4
HOTSPRING	126	1.8	2720	39.7	503	7.3	515	7.5	2234	32.6	750	11.0*	2933	43.2	3854	56.8
HOWARD	50	1.3	885	23.2	943	24.8	260	6.8	1381	36.3	288	7.6*	1499	39.0	2345	61.0
INDEPENDCE	81	1.2	1415	21.0	289	4.3	808	12.0	2808	41.7	1333	19.8*	3189	44.7	3950	55.3
IZARD	37	1.2	558	17.5	141	4.4	523	16.4	1319	41.5	604	19.0*	1503	48.1	1620	51.9
JACKSON	65	1.1	643	11.2	359	6.2	638	11.1	2486	43.2	1559	27.1*	2745	45.3	3312	54.7
JEFFERSON	610	4.0	3625	23.9	1155	7.6	931	6.1	6702	44.3	2118	14.0*	8104	50.1	8077	49.9
JOHNSON	74	1.4	823	15.1	360	6.6	422	7.8	2182	40.1	1577	29.0*	2520	45.2	3059	54.8
LAFAYETTE	98	4.0	769	31.6	456	18.7	98	4.0	934	38.4	79	3.2*	1147	54.6	952	45.4
LAWRENCE	59	1.1	371	7.1	544	10.5	697	13.4	1999	38.5	1523	29.3*	1836	35.5	3333	64.5
LEE	19	.8	429	17.8	123	5.1	134	5.6	1405	58.3	299	12.4*	1313	61.7	816	38.3
LINCOLN	53	2.1	426	16.7	94	3.7	305	12.0	1444	56.7	225	8.8*	1807	68.5	832	31.5
LITTLERIVR	67	3.1	263	12.1	723	33.3	115	5.3	890	41.0	112	5.2*	967	53.2	852	46.8
LOGAN	93	1.9	338	7.1	156	3.3	228	4.8	1426	29.8	2542	53.1*	1537	30.3	3542	69.7
LONOKE	113	2.3	743	15.1	404	8.2	493	10.0	2529	51.3	652	13.2*	3508	53.3	3079	46.7
MADISON	6	.3	76	3.9	32	1.7	73	3.8	1629	84.5	111	5.8*	1906	86.1	307	13.9
MARION	36	1.5	404	17.3	199	8.5	302	12.9	943	40.3	454	19.4*	1013	37.4	1695	62.6
MILLER	205	2.6	567	7.1	4508	56.4	230	2.9	2317	29.0	168	2.1*	3276	46.4	3791	53.6
MISSISSIP	182	1.8	1411	14.2	1631	16.4	306	3.1	3940	39.7	2449	24.7*	4479	37.1	7584	62.9
MONROE	70	2.8	316	12.8	123	5.0	174	7.0	1505	60.7	290	11.7*	1820	66.1	933	33.9
MONTGOMERY	61	2.8	455	20.5	314	14.2	297	13.4	838	37.8	251	11.3*	1018	43.0	1348	57.0
NEVADA	400	10.5	1831	48.0	190	5.0	111	2.9	1126	29.5	157	4.1*	1454	40.5	2137	59.5
NEWTON	2	.2	152	16.4	27	2.9	36	3.9	680	73.4	29	3.1*	990	81.1	231	18.9
QUACHITA	1025	11.7	2013	23.0	1014	11.6	596	6.8	2822	32.2	1290	14.7*	3502	38.2	5655	61.8

COUNTY	COMPTON #	%	PURCELL #	%	MCCLERKIN #	%	WELLS #	%	FAUBUS #	%	BUMPERS #	%*	FAUBUS #	%	BUMPERS #	%
PERRY	95	4.7	363	17.8	274	13.5	227	11.1	767	37.7	310	15.2*	851	43.2	1119	56.8
PHILLIPS	92	1.8	2090	40.3	191	3.7	176	3.4	2037	39.3	602	11.6*	2244	45.7	2666	54.3
PIKE	75	3.0	595	23.6	434	17.2	230	9.1	854	33.8	335	13.3*	972	38.4	1556	61.6
POINSETT	56	.9	631	10.3	949	15.5	338	5.5	2901	47.3	1261	20.6*	2848	44.9	3496	55.1
POLK	132	3.9	612	18.2	500	14.9	444	13.2	1129	33.5	550	16.3*	1187	36.3	2085	63.7
POPE	162	2.1	1110	14.1	493	6.3	701	8.9	2545	32.4	2851	36.3*	2830	34.2	5433	65.8
PRAIRIE	60	2.3	304	11.5	179	6.8	317	12.0	1496	56.7	284	10.8*	1688	60.9	1085	39.1
PULASKI	1188	2.6	9186	20.3	6458	14.3	2460	5.4	14929	33.0	11058	24.4*	18344	35.4	33419	64.6
RANDOLPH	74	1.8	495	11.8	513	12.2	817	19.5	1115	26.6	1177	28.1*	1069	29.1	2609	70.9
STFRANCIS	133	2.2	907	14.9	287	4.7	300	4.9	3695	60.9	745	12.3*	3242	58.7	2282	41.3
SALINE	161	1.6	5622	55.4	594	5.9	557	5.5	2374	23.4	844	8.3*	3884	39.0	6064	61.0
SCOTT	139	6.3	333	15.2	133	6.1	248	11.3	607	27.7	733	33.4*	744	29.2	1808	70.8
SEARCY	6	.8	111	14.1	41	5.2	91	11.5	463	58.6	78	9.9*	629	65.0	339	35.0
SEBASTIAN	614	4.3	954	6.6	1332	9.2	422	2.9	3059	21.2	8020	55.7*	3157	18.5	13880	81.5
SEVIER	60	2.1	958	33.9	487	17.2	142	5.0	1010	35.7	172	6.1*	939	35.9	1677	64.1
SHARP	14	.7	327	15.3	82	3.8	364	17.0	1028	48.1	322	15.1*	1461	59.2	1006	40.8
STONE	37	1.3	880	30.5	251	8.7	306	10.6	1193	41.4	216	7.5*	1460	46.7	1669	53.3
UNION	7325	60.1	1269	10.4	434	3.6	780	6.4	1957	16.1	426	3.5*	3795	33.2	7627	66.8
VANBUREN	52	1.8	606	21.3	181	6.4	404	14.2	1226	43.2	372	13.1*	1554	49.1	1612	50.9
WASHINGTON	264	2.3	1645	14.3	1105	9.6	339	3.0	3303	28.8	4824	42.0*	3246	26.0	9244	74.0
WHITE	201	2.0	2417	23.7	798	7.8	705	6.9	4270	41.8	1826	17.9*	4822	44.8	5946	55.2
WOODRUFF	83	3.0	518	18.7	198	7.2	231	8.3	1292	46.7	447	16.1*	1006	41.9	1395	58.1
YELL	605	16.4	457	12.4	142	3.9	189	5.1	1046	28.4	1239	33.7*	1629	38.0	2655	62.0
TOTALS	19336		81566		45011		32543		156578		86168	*	182008		258848	
% OF VOTE	4.6		19.4		10.7		7.7		37.2		20.5	*	41.3		58.7	

GEOGRAPHIC CLASS

	COMPTON	%	PURCELL	%	MCCLERKIN	%	WELLS	%	FAUBUS	%	BUMPERS	%*	FAUBUS	%	BUMPERS	%
LOWLANDS	13271	7.	37448	21.	25157	14.	14137	8.	62682	35.	28817	16.*	77261	40.	114988	60.
BLACK BELT	1545	3.	12644	23.	4832	9.	3354	6.	25776	46.	7386	13.*	27296	52.	25377	48.
MOUNTAIN	4520	2.	31474	17.	15022	8.	15052	8.	68120	37.	49965	27.*	77451	40.	118483	60.

DEMOGRAPHIC CLASS

	COMPTON	%	PURCELL	%	MCCLERKIN	%	WELLS	%	FAUBUS	%	BUMPERS	%*	FAUBUS	%	BUMPERS	%
METRO	2007	3.	10707	16.	12298	18.	3112	5.	20305	30.	19246	28.*	24777	33.	51090	67.
TOWN	9135	13.	11753	16.	7819	11.	3640	5.	24679	35.	14374	20.*	29450	38.	47322	62.
RURAL	8194	3.	59106	21.	24894	9.	25791	9.	111594	40.	52548	19.*	127781	44.	160436	56.

ARKANSAS/49

DEMOC. SENATOR   1954   * DEMOC. SENATOR   1962

COUNTY	MCCLELLAN #	%	MCMATH #	%	OTHER #	% *	FULBRIGHT #	%	CHANDLER #	%
ARKANSAS	2514	60.0	1174	28.0	499	11.9*	3471	66.0	1788	34.0
ASHLEY	1823	50.1	1269	34.9	549	15.1*	4073	69.7	1770	30.3
BAXTER	922	48.7	807	42.6	166	8.8*	2463	71.6	977	28.4
BENTON	3798	60.5	2086	33.2	396	6.3*	4250	66.7	2120	33.3
BOONE	1667	54.4	1052	34.3	345	11.3*	3607	71.4	1443	28.6
BRADLEY	1758	48.9	1305	36.3	532	14.8*	2241	58.4	1597	41.6
CALHOUN	914	36.1	1341	53.0	276	10.9*	1592	62.7	946	37.3
CARROLL	878	43.7	1055	52.5	77	3.8*	1539	55.1	1254	44.9
CHICOT	1566	52.2	1174	39.1	260	8.7*	2695	69.4	1187	30.6
CLARK	2506	47.9	2150	41.1	579	11.1*	3637	68.2	1695	31.8
CLAY	1483	45.1	1417	43.1	386	11.7*	2789	72.8	1043	27.2
CLEBURNE	1282	64.9	478	24.2	214	10.8*	1902	69.5	833	30.5
CLEVELAND	1246	57.4	708	32.6	215	9.9*	1495	63.7	853	36.3
COLUMBIA	1763	43.7	2007	49.8	263	6.5*	3089	55.3	2497	44.7
CONWAY	1501	40.4	1986	53.5	225	6.1*	3768	72.3	1443	27.7
CRAIGHEAD	3960	48.6	3109	38.1	1087	13.3*	5909	62.5	3551	37.5
CRAWFORD	1505	51.3	1266	43.2	160	5.5*	2829	59.3	1944	40.7
CRITTENDEN	2316	81.0	411	14.4	134	4.7*	3030	83.9	580	16.1
CROSS	1739	58.6	951	32.0	280	9.4*	2671	82.6	564	17.4
DALLAS	1453	45.5	1370	42.9	368	11.5*	1839	59.3	1262	40.7
DESHA	1500	51.8	1132	39.1	266	9.2*	2531	71.4	1016	28.6
DREW	1376	52.3	936	35.6	318	12.1*	1854	60.3	1223	39.7
FAULKNER	3129	52.2	2223	37.1	643	10.7*	5421	67.6	2596	32.4
FRANKLIN	1414	42.3	1658	49.6	270	8.1*	2486	60.3	1637	39.7
FULTON	652	44.0	722	48.8	107	7.2*	1553	72.7	584	27.3
GARLAND	5980	51.5	4795	41.3	833	7.2*	7706	65.9	3986	34.1
GRANT	1060	38.2	1349	48.6	365	13.2*	1633	56.3	1269	43.7
GREENE	1990	42.3	2168	46.0	550	11.7*	3830	66.8	1900	33.2
HEMSTEAD	2458	51.1	1877	39.0	475	9.9*	3253	63.8	1842	36.2
HOTSPRING	2319	37.0	2819	45.0	1127	18.0*	3353	55.7	2670	44.3
HOWARD	1412	46.2	1327	43.5	314	10.3*	1919	58.4	1365	41.6
INDEPENDCE	1660	44.5	1728	46.3	343	9.2*	3677	67.0	1808	33.0
IZARD	414	30.8	823	61.2	108	8.0*	1795	71.4	719	28.6
JACKSON	1455	41.7	1587	45.5	444	12.7*	3806	70.6	1586	29.4
JEFFERSON	5451	47.5	4933	43.0	1091	9.5*	8414	66.7	4202	33.3
JOHNSON	1187	39.5	1579	52.5	239	8.0*	2143	59.9	1434	40.1
LAFAYETTE	1260	48.5	1182	45.5	158	6.1*	1549	57.3	1155	42.7
LAWRENCE	1626	47.2	1381	40.1	441	12.8*	3037	63.6	1739	36.4
LEE	1199	43.7	745	27.1	801	29.2*	1601	78.4	440	21.6
LINCOLN	963	50.4	741	38.8	205	10.7*	2027	71.0	827	29.0
LITTLERIVR	1369	65.2	516	24.6	215	10.2*	1832	66.1	938	33.9
LOGAN	1577	42.7	1808	49.0	308	8.3*	2880	65.9	1489	34.1
LONOKE	2474	50.7	1957	40.1	452	9.3*	3442	61.6	2147	38.4
MADISON	422	20.7	1577	77.3	40	2.0*	1791	73.6	643	26.4
MARION	840	46.4	784	43.3	188	10.4*	1632	74.8	550	25.2
MILLER	3864	52.8	2908	39.8	543	7.4*	4088	56.8	3103	43.2

COUNTY	DEMOC. SENATOR 1954						* DEMOC. SENATOR 1962			
	MCCLELLAN		MCMATH		OTHER		FULBRIGHT		CHANDLER	
	#	%	#	%	#	%*	#	%	#	%
MISSISSIP	4978	75.3	1420	21.5	211	3.2*	7064	79.5	1819	20.5
MONROE	1548	54.8	924	32.7	351	12.4*	1613	63.4	933	36.6
MONTGOMERY	706	38.2	924	50.0	217	11.7*	1293	61.0	827	39.0
NEVADA	1170	43.2	1297	47.9	243	9.0*	2055	62.5	1232	37.5
NEWTON	102	9.8	910	87.8	24	2.3*	988	88.0	135	12.0
QUACHITA	3628	45.5	3692	46.3	650	8.2*	5535	66.8	2745	33.2
PERRY	699	52.9	451	34.1	172	13.0*	1276	61.8	789	38.2
PHILLIPS	2065	50.1	1220	29.6	837	20.3*	3736	84.5	687	15.5
PIKE	816	40.0	1000	49.0	226	11.1*	1586	58.3	1133	41.7
POINSETT	3296	60.0	1805	32.9	390	7.1*	4055	78.0	1143	22.0
POLK	2080	57.8	1009	28.1	508	14.1*	1891	55.5	1518	44.5
POPE	2203	39.0	2553	45.2	893	15.8*	3669	64.0	2066	36.0
PRAIRIE	1463	64.3	523	23.0	288	12.7*	1942	72.6	732	27.4
PULASKI	20026	53.0	13601	36.0	4147	11.0*	30245	66.1	15539	33.9
RANDOLPH	1793	45.1	1757	44.2	423	10.6*	2336	65.0	1259	35.0
STFRANCIS	2089	56.0	1056	28.3	583	15.6*	2912	73.5	1050	26.5
SALINE	2388	36.7	3109	47.8	1003	15.4*	4617	60.4	3021	39.6
SCOTT	746	47.9	658	42.2	155	9.9*	1220	62.8	722	37.2
SEARCY	377	54.9	260	37.8	50	7.3*	596	82.3	128	17.7
SEBASTIAN	5463	61.0	2999	33.5	496	5.5*	7483	59.2	5159	40.8
SEVIER	1278	61.9	590	28.6	197	9.5*	1989	69.5	871	30.5
SHARP	726	47.5	719	47.0	84	5.5*	1732	70.1	739	29.9
STONE	579	39.5	767	52.3	121	8.2*	1338	68.0	631	32.0
UNION	6091	55.0	4038	36.5	942	8.5*	7559	62.8	4477	37.2
VANBUREN	1207	53.2	818	36.1	244	10.8*	1296	45.8	1535	54.2
WASHINGTON	4493	61.6	2263	31.0	534	7.3*	5497	71.0	2247	29.0
WHITE	3228	50.9	2552	40.2	563	8.9*	5461	67.2	2660	32.8
WOODRUFF	1406	45.9	1294	42.3	360	11.8*	1994	69.3	883	30.7
YELL	2616	59.8	1361	31.1	401	9.2*	2631	70.7	1092	29.3
TOTALS	164905		127941		33168	*	253751		129987	
% OF VOTE	50.6		39.2		10.2	*	66.1		33.9	

COUNTY	MCCLELLAN #	%	MCMATH #	%	OTHER #	%	FULBRIGHT #	%	CHANDLER #	%
DEMOC. SENATOR 1954							**DEMOC. SENATOR 1962**			
GEOGRAPHIC CLASS										
LOWLANDS	77940	52.	56256	38.	15601	10.	113802	65.	59962	35.
BLACK BELT	22816	51.	16182	36.	5414	12.	33941	70.	14222	30.
MOUNTAIN	64149	49.	55503	42.	12153	9.	106008	66.	55803	34.
DEMOGRAPHIC CLASS										
METRO	29353	54.	19508	36.	5186	10.	41816	64.	23801	36.
TOWN	30953	55.	20558	37.	4698	8.	42149	68.	20282	32.
RURAL	104599	48.	87875	41.	23284	11.	169786	66.	85904	34.

ARKANSAS

COUNTY	HAYES #	%	FULBRIGHT #	%	JOHNSON #	%	J.JOHNSON #	-%	MCCLELLAN #	%	JOHNSON #	%	BOSWELL #	%	PRYOR #	%
	DEMOC. SENATOR 1968								**DEMOC. SENATOR 1972**							
ARKANSAS	538	10.3	2821	53.9	77	1.5	1801	34.4	2693	59.5	26	.6	521	11.5	1287	28.4
ASHLEY	303	5.7	2228	42.1	109	2.1	2646	50.1	2116	33.1	170	2.7	357	5.6	3756	58.7
BAXTER	393	19.3	1121	55.0	64	3.1	459	22.5	1830	47.3	45	1.2	772	19.9	1226	31.7
BENTON	664	13.6	2860	58.8	191	3.9	1152	23.7	2292	49.9	31	.7	531	11.6	1735	37.8
BOONE	779	15.5	2311	46.1	124	2.5	1803	35.9	1285	41.7	79	2.6	315	10.2	1401	45.5
BRADLEY	431	10.0	1954	45.2	90	2.1	1852	42.8	1544	40.9	75	2.0	221	5.9	1937	51.3
CALHOUN	245	11.5	982	45.9	54	2.5	858	40.1	611	25.3	21	.9	165	6.8	1617	67.0
CARROLL	571	21.8	1105	42.2	43	1.6	900	34.4	798	51.1	31	2.0	187	12.0	546	35.0
CHICOT	137	5.8	1283	54.7	58	2.5	868	37.0	1583	48.2	59	1.8	148	4.5	1495	45.5
CLARK	984	16.0	3264	53.0	193	3.1	1716	27.9	2329	35.4	33	.5	614	9.3	3599	54.7
CLAY	717	14.3	2847	56.6	91	1.8	1374	27.3	2013	47.8	99	2.4	463	11.0	1634	38.8
CLEBURNE	712	18.9	2115	56.0	110	2.9	837	22.2	2055	50.7	44	1.1	493	12.2	1464	36.1
CLEVELAND	210	11.0	805	42.3	35	1.8	851	44.8	1088	51.7	9	.4	123	5.8	884	42.0
COLUMBIA	550	9.6	2909	50.8	127	2.2	2141	37.4	2651	46.4	69	1.2	207	3.6	2792	48.8
CONWAY	338	7.9	3424	79.8	60	1.4	467	10.9	1585	33.7	22	.5	405	8.6	2690	57.2
CRAIGHEAD	1336	11.9	5999	53.4	326	2.9	3583	31.9	6966	50.3	202	1.5	1565	11.3	5110	36.9
CRAWFORD	592	17.4	1196	35.2	101	3.0	1513	44.5	2565	41.3	115	1.9	1020	16.4	2504	40.4
CRITTENDEN	353	7.8	2792	61.5	130	2.9	1265	27.9	4644	59.6	225	2.9	1144	14.7	1778	22.8
CROSS	240	6.6	1974	54.6	44	1.2	1356	37.5	2918	58.4	82	1.6	477	9.6	1516	30.4
DALLAS	397	13.1	1374	45.2	96	3.2	1170	38.5	1363	35.1	37	1.0	313	8.1	2171	55.9
DESHA	287	8.1	2004	56.9	95	2.7	1136	32.3	1918	42.4	77	1.7	447	9.9	2085	46.1
DREW	395	9.5	2126	50.9	85	2.0	1569	37.6	1696	42.1	60	1.5	271	6.7	2002	49.7
FAULKNER	1310	13.6	4847	50.3	247	2.6	3225	33.5	4219	44.0	43	.4	1625	16.9	3710	38.7
FRANKLIN	814	17.2	1874	39.7	355	7.5	1677	35.5	2501	45.6	101	1.8	941	17.1	1944	35.4

	DEMOC. SENATOR 1968			*	DEMOC. SENATOR 1972			
COUNTY	HAYES	FULBRIGHT	JOHNSON	J.JOHNSON	MCCLELLAN	JOHNSON	BOSWELL	PRYOR
	# %	# %	# %	# %*	# %	# %	# %	# %
FULTON	825 31.1	1096 41.3	71 2.7	659 24.9*	1468 61.0	51 2.1	218 9.1	668 27.8
GARLAND	1963 14.3	7421 54.0	426 3.1	3933 28.6*	6633 38.8	158 .9	2119 12.4	8181 47.9
GRANT	667 17.2	1658 42.8	140 3.6	1407 36.3*	1478 44.2	17 .5	233 7.0	1613 48.3
GREENE	856 12.7	3612 53.5	231 3.4	2057 30.4*	3832 48.9	222 2.8	1068 13.6	2709 34.6
HEMSTEAD	447 9.6	2373 51.2	86 1.9	1733 37.4*	3320 51.3	89 1.4	387 6.0	2680 41.4
HOTSPRING	960 15.6	2588 42.1	222 3.6	2375 38.6*	2467 27.8	40 .4	685 7.7	5697 64.1
HOWARD	416 10.9	1874 49.2	93 2.4	1428 37.5*	1859 47.3	62 1.6	263 6.7	1748 44.5
INDEPENDCE	948 16.7	3661 64.4	93 1.6	985 17.3*	3103 48.1	44 .7	835 13.0	2465 38.2
IZARD	1494 45.8	1203 36.8	49 1.5	519 15.9*	1728 48.8	72 2.0	621 17.5	1120 31.6
JACKSON	766 12.8	2828 47.3	121 2.0	2263 37.9*	3841 53.7	61 .9	722 10.1	2530 35.4
JEFFERSON	1438 9.2	8399 53.5	438 2.8	5422 34.5*	7802 39.4	258 1.3	2649 13.4	9109 46.0
JOHNSON	729 22.2	1506 45.8	80 2.4	973 29.6*	2651 41.8	90 1.4	1152 18.2	2449 38.6
LAFAYETTE	304 10.6	1246 43.3	84 2.9	1241 43.2*	1067 46.7	29 1.3	73 3.2	1117 48.9
LAWRENCE	676 12.3	2895 52.8	103 1.9	1809 33.0*	2585 45.5	110 1.9	894 15.7	2098 36.9
LEE	252 8.5	1466 49.2	61 2.0	1203 40.3*	1851 61.3	67 2.2	272 9.0	828 27.4
LINCOLN	313 10.4	1495 49.6	114 3.8	1094 36.3*	1792 48.7	47 1.3	256 7.0	1588 43.1
LITTLERIVR	243 11.3	1168 54.5	76 3.5	658 30.7*	2138 56.6	70 1.9	238 6.3	1333 35.3
LOGAN	934 19.6	2231 46.8	175 3.7	1427 29.9*	2629 47.4	96 1.7	996 18.0	1820 32.8
LONOKE	868 13.5	3302 51.5	166 2.6	2074 32.4*	3670 51.3	80 1.1	746 10.4	2655 37.1
MADISON	413 22.5	1051 57.3	22 1.2	347 18.9*	1752 56.4	69 2.2	318 10.2	967 31.1
MARION	384 17.0	1089 48.1	71 3.1	719 31.8*	1315 45.6	94 3.3	467 16.2	1010 35.0
MILLER	684 10.0	3154 46.3	191 2.8	2778 40.8*	4509 48.4	144 1.5	520 5.6	4141 44.5
MISSISSIP	702 6.7	6744 64.7	199 1.9	2786 26.7*	7429 59.6	222 1.8	1756 14.1	3049 24.5
MONROE	376 11.0	1379 40.4	79 2.3	1581 46.3*	2282 53.2	69 1.6	550 12.8	1385 32.3
MONTGOMERY	489 20.7	1075 45.4	79 3.3	723 30.6*	863 37.8	43 1.9	325 14.2	1052 46.1
NEVADA	328 9.7	1664 49.4	48 1.4	1328 39.4*	1488 39.8	62 1.7	346 9.3	1844 49.3
NEWTON	173 20.2	484 56.5	22 2.6	178 20.8*	419 44.9	12 1.3	120 12.9	382 40.9
QUACHITA	922 9.6	5272 54.7	302 3.1	3150 32.7*	2418 23.5	68 .7	383 3.7	7428 72.1
PERRY	362 17.3	1075 51.3	73 3.5	585 27.9*	829 40.6	35 1.7	349 17.1	830 40.6
PHILLIPS	294 4.6	4008 63.0	40 .6	2020 31.8*	3129 57.1	34 .6	313 5.7	2003 36.6
PIKE	678 23.1	1279 43.6	68 2.3	908 31.0*	1670 47.6	46 1.3	299 8.5	1491 42.5
POINSETT	554 8.6	3614 55.9	135 2.1	2158 33.4*	4329 57.4	124 1.6	766 10.1	2328 30.8
POLK	736 17.4	1886 44.6	165 3.9	1446 34.2*	1702 44.6	79 2.1	595 15.6	1437 37.7
POPE	1250 20.9	3028 50.7	151 2.5	1549 25.9*	4102 45.6	87 1.0	1398 15.5	3417 37.9
PRAIRIE	341 11.6	1633 55.4	71 2.4	900 30.6*	1557 61.8	22 .9	249 9.9	690 27.4
PULASKI	4146 8.5	31031 64.0	1270 2.6	12057 24.9*	25835 40.3	664 1.0	12175 19.0	25509 39.7
RANDOLPH	554 16.1	1795 52.3	142 4.1	941 27.4*	1569 38.5	89 2.2	696 17.1	1723 42.3
STFRANCIS	421 6.5	2748 42.4	148 2.3	3163 48.8*	2668 49.1	104 1.9	703 12.9	1955 36.0
SALINE	1466 15.5	4499 47.6	482 5.1	3001 31.8*	2818 25.6	59 .5	2528 23.0	5596 50.9
SCOTT	413 20.4	794 39.3	65 3.2	748 37.0*	1395 35.8	83 2.1	906 23.2	1515 38.9
SEARCY	88 15.4	345 60.5	9 1.6	128 22.5*	418 55.5	19 2.5	105 13.9	211 28.0
SEBASTIAN	2036 13.7	6544 44.1	607 4.1	5644 38.1*	11047 50.1	162 .7	2561 11.6	8296 37.6
SEVIER	282 9.8	1586 55.1	85 3.0	927 32.2*	2074 59.0	61 1.7	280 8.0	1102 31.3
SHARP	255 13.9	1134 61.7	46 2.5	402 21.9*	1024 52.1	26 1.3	222 11.3	694 35.3
STONE	697 25.4	1357 49.4	50 1.8	645 23.5*	848 55.5	19 1.2	216 14.1	444 29.1
UNION	1158 9.9	5907 50.5	250 2.1	4391 37.5*	4623 36.1	132 1.0	904 7.1	7143 55.8

```
                 DEMOC.  SENATOR   1968           *        DEMOC.  SENATOR    1972
                                                  *
COUNTY      HAYES        FULBRIGHT    JOHNSON      J.JOHNSON   MCCLELLAN    JOHNSON      BOSWELL      PRYOR
            #     %      #      %     #     %      #     %*    #      %     #     %      #     %      #     %
--------------------------------------------------------------*------------------------------------------------------------------
VANBUREN    711  26.5   1235  46.1    92   3.4    643  24.0*  1288  44.3    47   1.6    452  15.5   1123  38.6
WASHINGTON  1137 11.1   6455  63.1   193   1.9   2443  23.9*  4861  38.1   125   1.0   2203  17.3   5570  43.7
WHITE       1359 16.7   4376  53.9   289   3.6   2102  25.9*  4407  49.3    47    .5   1036  11.6   3452  38.6
WOODRUFF    353  11.4   1541  49.8    75   2.4   1126  36.4*  1931  56.4    44   1.3    208   6.1   1240  36.2
YELL        749  16.3   2665  58.0   142   3.1   1042  22.7*  2812  52.1    49    .9    795  14.7   1740  32.2
                                                              *
-----------------------------------------------------------------*--------------------------------------------------------------------
                                                              *
TOTALS      52906       220684       11395       132038   * 220588        6358        62496        204058
% OF VOTE   12.7         52.9         2.7          31.7   *   44.7         1.3         12.7          41.3
                                                              *
                                                              *
GEOGRAPHIC CLASS                                              *
                                                              *
LOWLANDS    18716 10.   101458 55.   4595   2.    60786 33.*  97647 44.    2665   1.   25174 11.    95990 43.
BLACK BELT  4925   9.   29735  52.   1418   2.    21289 37.*  32030 48.    1050   2.    7076 11.    26754 40.
MOUNTAIN    29265 17.   89491  51.   5382   3.    49963 29.*  90911 44.    2643   1.   30246 15.    81314 40.
                                                              *
DEMOGRAPHIC CLASS                                             *
                                                              *
METRO       6866  10.   40729  58.   2068   3.    20479 29.*  41391 43.     970   1.   15256 16.    37946 40.
TOWN        7734  11.   40925  56.   1832   3.    22558 31.*  38314 43.    1097   1.   11196 13.    38162 43.
RURAL       38306 14.   139030 51.   7495   3.    89001 33.*  140883 46.   4291   1.   36044 12.    127950 41.
```

                                          ARKANSAS

```
                 DEMOC.  GOVERNOR   1972              * DEMOC.  RUNOFF    1972
                                                      *
COUNTY      BUMPERS      HURST        HARBOUR      DAVIS        GIBBS       MCCLELLAN    PRYOR
            #     %      #      %     #     %      #     %      #     %*    #     %      #     %
------------------------------------------------------------------------*------------------------------------------------------------------
ARKANSAS    3017 66.7    885  19.6   450   9.9     95   2.1     78   1.7*  3998  71.0   1630  29.0
ASHLEY      4831 75.6    827  12.9   438   6.9    147   2.3    148   2.3*  2650  44.0   3372  56.0
BAXTER      2962 76.2    481  12.4   293   7.5    111   2.9     40   1.0*  1127  42.9   1498  57.1
BENTON      3413 75.6    736  16.3   158   3.5    177   3.9     31    .7*  3261  59.5   2216  40.5
BOONE       2169 70.7    601  19.6   209   6.8     61   2.0     30   1.0*  1728  53.3   1512  46.7
                                                                *
BRADLEY     3073 79.5    340   8.8   308   8.0    105   2.7     40   1.0*  1693  46.3   1965  53.7
CALHOUN     1690 70.7    360  15.1   195   8.2    115   4.8     32   1.3*   707  29.9   1655  70.1
CARROLL     1066 68.0    371  23.7    65   4.1     44   2.8     21   1.3*  1170  58.4    834  41.6
CHICOT      2231 68.1    807  24.6   129   3.9     76   2.3     33   1.0*  1962  54.9   1611  45.1
CLARK       4431 67.7   1320  20.2   525   8.0    221   3.4     52    .8*  2566  40.5   3770  59.5
                                                                *
CLAY        2709 63.0    620  14.4   781  18.2    154   3.6     38    .9*  1677  52.3   1528  47.7
CLEBURNE    2649 65.6    602  14.9   560  13.9    178   4.4     51   1.3*  2644  57.6   1950  42.4
CLEVELAND   1354 65.0    313  15.0   325  15.6     56   2.7     35   1.7*  1462  58.0   1059  42.0
COLUMBIA    4295 76.0    632  11.2   359   6.4    308   5.5     56   1.0*  3703  58.5   2626  41.5
CONWAY      1941 41.4   2359  50.3   266   5.7     90   1.9     32    .7*  1185  25.8   3404  74.2
```

COUNTY	BUMPERS #	%	HURST #	%	HARBOUR #	%	DAVIS #	%	GIBBS #	%*	MCCLELLAN #	%	PRYOR #	%
CRAIGHEAD	9710	71.0	1346	9.8	2189	16.0	304	2.2	119	.9*	7333	57.8	5364	42.2
CRAWFORD	4499	71.7	1114	17.7	311	5.0	228	3.6	127	2.0*	3450	50.0	3444	50.0
CRITTENDEN	6633	80.3	890	10.8	433	5.2	109	1.3	198	2.4*	4761	57.2	3557	42.8
CROSS	3441	68.2	512	10.2	1021	20.2	0	.0	69	1.4*	2337	59.4	1600	40.6
DALLAS	2350	61.3	709	18.5	599	15.6	129	3.4	44	1.1*	1475	38.8	2330	61.2
DESHA	3371	75.1	648	14.4	321	7.2	89	2.0	57	1.3*	2516	50.2	2492	49.8
DREW	2997	75.3	531	13.3	308	7.7	101	2.5	43	1.1*	2208	48.5	2344	51.5
FAULKNER	6715	69.8	1556	16.2	910	9.5	251	2.6	188	2.0*	5180	53.4	4525	46.6
FRANKLIN	3807	69.3	1075	19.6	328	6.0	210	3.8	70	1.3*	2626	50.3	2595	49.7
FULTON	1072	42.3	101	4.0	1316	51.9	36	1.4	10	.4*	970	63.6	556	36.4
GARLAND	7509	43.9	8667	50.7	657	3.8	204	1.2	63	.4*	8191	50.6	7996	49.4
GRANT	2249	67.3	521	15.6	464	13.9	73	2.2	35	1.0*	1773	51.0	1701	49.0
GREENE	4314	53.8	519	6.5	2955	36.8	175	2.2	56	.7*	4247	56.7	3247	43.3
HEMSTEAD	4570	70.1	877	13.5	311	4.8	634	9.7	124	1.9*	3599	59.2	2476	40.8
HOTSPRING	5583	63.4	1925	21.9	901	10.2	297	3.4	96	1.1*	2592	34.0	5037	66.0
HOWARD	2224	56.2	316	8.0	123	3.1	1263	31.9	30	.8*	2215	55.6	1769	44.4
INDEPENDCE	4162	64.5	445	6.9	1713	26.5	108	1.7	28	.4*	3151	53.3	2763	46.7
IZARD	2195	61.5	305	8.5	902	25.3	82	2.3	88	2.5*	1429	52.2	1311	47.8
JACKSON	4683	65.9	1206	17.0	946	13.3	228	3.2	47	.7*	3845	60.1	2554	39.9
JEFFERSON	12679	64.2	3170	16.1	3161	16.0	341	1.7	399	2.0*	8907	44.3	11218	55.7
JOHNSON	4344	67.1	1400	21.6	317	4.9	191	3.0	220	3.4*	2099	49.5	2143	50.5
LAFAYETTE	1566	69.9	229	10.2	147	6.6	279	12.5	18	.8*	1404	50.7	1364	49.3
LAWRENCE	3611	63.4	830	14.6	976	17.1	234	4.1	48	.8*	2280	56.2	1776	43.8
LEE	460	15.2	473	15.6	2019	66.6	71	2.3	9	.3*	1707	75.1	567	24.9
LINCOLN	2451	66.9	725	19.8	346	9.4	77	2.1	67	1.8*	1731	57.6	1272	42.4
LITTLERIVR	1837	47.6	288	7.5	96	2.5	1601	41.5	34	.9*	1964	53.6	1697	46.4
LOGAN	3699	67.9	1016	18.7	402	7.4	279	5.1	48	.9*	2370	56.7	1810	43.3
LONOKE	4807	67.4	1220	17.1	770	10.8	176	2.5	155	2.2*	3894	59.8	2613	40.2
MADISON	1719	55.7	982	31.8	198	6.4	158	5.1	28	.9*	1200	64.1	671	35.9
MARION	2002	67.5	603	20.3	181	6.1	137	4.6	44	1.5*	729	43.3	956	56.7
MILLER	5963	63.7	1590	17.0	492	5.3	1187	12.7	136	1.5*	3612	56.7	2759	43.3
MISSISSIP	9435	74.2	985	7.8	1896	14.9	316	2.5	76	.6*	6316	65.7	3299	34.3
MONROE	2310	53.8	728	16.9	1070	24.9	126	2.9	63	1.5*	2730	64.0	1536	36.0
MONTGOMERY	1399	60.9	656	28.6	149	6.5	81	3.5	12	.5*	756	43.4	984	56.6
NEVADA	2618	69.9	578	15.4	263	7.0	238	6.4	46	1.2*	1640	52.8	1468	47.2
NEWTON	700	74.9	179	19.2	24	2.6	25	2.7	6	.6*	309	36.3	542	63.7
QUACHITA	7429	74.1	1680	16.8	510	5.1	288	2.9	115	1.1*	2651	26.3	7444	73.7
PERRY	1185	58.7	441	21.8	227	11.2	97	4.8	70	3.5*	871	48.6	922	51.4
PHILLIPS	3712	68.2	934	17.2	619	11.4	116	2.1	62	1.1*	3792	64.1	2125	35.9
PIKE	1958	55.7	964	27.4	165	4.7	385	11.0	41	1.2*	1795	51.9	1664	48.1
POINSETT	5547	72.8	1126	14.8	637	8.4	238	3.1	71	.9*	4854	64.2	2704	35.8
POLK	2199	56.9	516	13.3	217	5.6	898	23.2	38	1.0*	1197	46.5	1376	53.5
POPE	6406	70.6	1547	17.1	701	7.7	314	3.5	104	1.1*	4391	51.2	4192	48.8
PRAIRIE	1536	60.7	651	25.7	286	11.3	34	1.3	24	.9*	1884	74.3	651	25.7
PULASKI	46292	70.9	8521	13.1	7963	12.2	1774	2.7	715	1.1*	33570	49.6	34110	50.4
RANDOLPH	2650	64.8	715	17.5	501	12.3	166	4.1	55	1.3*	1295	44.9	1591	55.1

	DEMOC. GOVERNOR 1972									* DEMOC. RUNOFF 1972			

COUNTY	BUMPERS #	%	HURST #	%	HARBOUR #	%	DAVIS #	%	GIBBS #	%*	MCCLELLAN #	%	PRYOR #	%
STFRANCIS	3046	55.2	978	17.7	1286	23.3	120	2.2	93	1.7*	2799	58.4	1996	41.6
SALINE	6520	59.3	2000	18.2	2082	18.9	241	2.2	145	1.3*	3890	33.9	7585	66.1
SCOTT	2237	57.1	1014	25.9	288	7.4	314	8.0	65	1.7*	1252	36.9	2140	63.1
SEARCY	597	78.0	72	9.4	74	9.7	15	2.0	7	.9*	456	59.5	311	40.5
SEBASTIAN	17554	79.7	2999	13.6	799	3.6	512	2.3	170	.8*	11089	60.6	7217	39.4
										*				
SEVIER	638	17.9	137	3.8	52	1.5	2726	76.4	14	.4*	1566	63.7	894	36.3
SHARP	1132	58.3	257	13.2	449	23.1	66	3.4	39	2.0*	1842	68.1	864	31.9
STONE	1013	64.9	224	14.3	203	13.0	102	6.5	19	1.2*	987	66.4	499	33.6
UNION	9653	76.3	1803	14.3	640	5.1	370	2.9	185	1.5*	5879	46.3	6816	53.7
VANBUREN	2001	69.0	459	15.8	263	9.1	114	3.9	63	2.2*	1330	54.4	1113	45.6
										*				
WASHINGTON	9404	73.5	1711	13.4	969	7.6	545	4.3	158	1.2*	6682	49.7	6764	50.3
WHITE	5820	68.5	1082	12.7	1236	14.5	266	3.1	91	1.1*	5564	60.2	3682	39.8
WOODRUFF	2189	65.2	543	16.2	429	12.8	152	4.5	45	1.3*	1758	64.4	970	35.6
YELL	3855	71.8	696	13.0	300	5.6	455	8.5	61	1.1*	2510	60.1	1666	39.9

	BUMPERS #	%	HURST #	%	HARBOUR #	%	DAVIS #	%	GIBBS #	%*	MCCLELLAN #	%	PRYOR #	%
TOTALS	330088		81239		55172		22284		6068	*	242983		224262	
% OF VOTE	66.7		16.4		11.1		4.5		1.2	*	52.0		48.0	

GEOGRAPHIC CLASS

	BUMPERS #	%	HURST #	%	HARBOUR #	%	DAVIS #	%	GIBBS #	%*	MCCLELLAN #	%	PRYOR #	%
LOWLANDS	153903	69.	30490	14.	22468	10.	12895	6.	2575	1.*	110511	52.	103377	48.
BLACK BELT	42998	64.	10834	16.	10559	16.	1685	3.	1088	2.*	35542	53.	31038	47.
MOUNTAIN	133187	65.	39915	19.	22145	11.	7704	4.	2405	1.*	96930	52.	89847	48.

DEMOGRAPHIC CLASS

	BUMPERS #	%	HURST #	%	HARBOUR #	%	DAVIS #	%	GIBBS #	%*	MCCLELLAN #	%	PRYOR #	%
METRO	69809	72.	13110	14.	9254	10.	3473	4.	1021	1.*	48271	52.	44086	48.
TOWN	58390	66.	17682	20.	9512	11.	2080	2.	1000	1.*	43308	51.	41457	49.
RURAL	201889	65.	50447	16.	36406	12.	16731	5.	4047	1.*	151404	52.	138719	48.

FLORIDA
COUNTIES

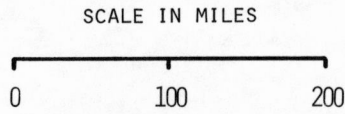

STUDY AREA

SCALE IN MILES

0   100   200

FLORIDA

Florida had no disfranchisement provisions, although the residency requirement of one year in the state and six months in the county was probably significant in such a rapidly growing state. Black registrants numbered approximately 120,000 in 1952, 180,000 in 1960, and 300,000 in 1970. White voter registration increased at such a rapid rate, however, that blacks remained about 10 percent of the total number of registered voters throughout the period.

The table below summarizes presidential voting in Florida. Turnout figures include both the total number of ballots cast and the estimated percentage of citizens of voting age who voted.

The following pages include 13 Democratic gubernatorial primaries. The 1954 contest was a special primary to fill the unexpired term of Dan McCarty, who died in 1953. Florida approved a constitutional amendment shifting gubernatorial elections away from presidential election years, and consequently the election of 1964 was for a two-year term. The constitution of 1968 provided for the reestablishment of a lieutenant governor's office and required that a governor and lieutenant governor be listed on the ballot as a ticket. Additionally, this section contains 7 Democratic senatorial primaries, 3 Republican primaries, the 1972 Democratic presidential primary, and the vote on 3 proposed constitutional amendments, for a total of 27 elections.

Gubernatorial Primaries

1. May 6, 1952: Alto Adams 126,426 (17.1%), Dan McCarty 361,367 (48.9%), Brailey Odham 232,574 (31.5%), other 2 candidates 18,079 (2.4%). Total vote was 738,446; turnout of voting-age citizens was 36.0%.
2. May 27, 1952: Dan McCarty 384,200 (53.3%), Brailey Odham 336,636 (46.7%). Total vote was 720,836; turnout was 35.2%.
3. May 4, 1954: LeRoy L. Collins 222,791 (33.4%), Charley E. Johns 255,784 (38.4%), Brailey Odham 187,782 (28.2%). Total vote was 666,357; turnout was 28.9%.
4. May 25, 1954: LeRoy L. Collins 380,323 (54.8%), Charley E. Johns 314,198 (45.2%). Total vote was 694,521; turnout was 30.1%.
5. May 8, 1956: C. Farris Bryant 110,469 (13.1%), LeRoy L. Collins 434,272 (51.7%), Sumter Lowry 179,019 (21.3%), other 3 candidates 116,321 (13.8%). Total vote was 840,081; turnout was 32.7%.
6. May 3, 1960: C. Farris Bryant 193,507 (20.7%), Haydon Burns 166,352 (17.8%), Doyle E. Carlton, Jr., 186,228 (19.9%), John McCarty 144,750 (15.4%), other 6 candidates 246,230 (26.3%). Total vote was 937,067; turnout was 30.3%.
7. May 24, 1960: C. Farris Bryant 512,757 (55.2%), Doyle E. Carlton, Jr., 416,052 (44.8%). Total vote was 928,809; turnout was 30.1%.
8. May 5, 1964: Haydon Burns 312,453 (27.5%), Fred O. Dickinson 184,865 (16.2%), Robert King High 207,280 (18.2%), Scott Kelly 205,078 (18.1%), other 2 candidates 226,163 (19.9%). Total vote was 1,135,839; turnout was 31.6%.
9. May 26, 1964: Haydon Burns 648,093 (58.2%), Robert King High 465,547 (41.8%).

Total vote was 1,113,640; turnout was 31.0%.

10. May 3, 1966: Haydon Burns 372,451 (35.3%), Robert King High 338,281 (32.1%), Scott Kelly 331,580 (31.5%), Sam Foor 11,343 (1.1%). Total vote was 1,053,655; turnout was 27.4%.

11. May 24, 1966: Haydon Burns 509,270 (46.1%), Robert King High 596,471 (53.9%). Total vote was 1,105,741; turnout was 28.7%.

12. September 8, 1970: Reubin Askew-Tom Adams 206,333 (27.2%), Earl Faircloth-George Tapper 227,413 (30.0%), Chuck Hall-Pat Thomas 139,384 (18.4%), John E. Mathews-Elton Gissendanner 186,053 (24.5%). Total vote was 759,183; turnout was 17.4%.

13. September 29, 1970: Reubin Askew-Tom Adams 447,025 (57.7%), Earl Faircloth-George Tapper 328,038 (42.3%). Total vote was 775,063; turnout was 17.8%.

Senatorial Primaries

1. May 5, 1950: Claude Pepper 319,754 (45.2%), George A. Smathers 387,215 (54.8%). Total vote was 706,969.

* (May 6, 1952: Spessard L. Holland won 84.2% against 1 opponent. Total vote was 576,526.)

* (May 8, 1956: George A. Smathers won 87.5% against 1 opponent. Total vote was 702,188.)

2. September 9, 1958: Spessard L. Holland 408,084 (55.9%), Claude Pepper 321,377 (44.1%). Total vote was 729,461.

* (May 8, 1962: George A. Smathers won 84.2% against 2 opponents. Total vote was 697,959.)

3. May 5, 1964: Spessard L. Holland 676,014 (70.0%), Brailey Odham 289,454 (30.0%). Total vote was 965,468.

4. May 7, 1968: LeRoy Collins 426,096 (49.5%), Earl Faircloth 397,642 (46.2%), other 2 candidates 36,825 (4.3%). Total vote was 860,563.

5. May 28, 1968: LeRoy Collins 410,689 (50.2%), Earl Faircloth 407,696 (49.8%). Total vote was 818,385.

6. September 8, 1970: C. Farris Bryant 240,222 (32.9%), Lawton Chiles 188,300 (25.8%), Joel T. Daves III 33,939 (4.6%), Alcee Hastings 91,948 (12.6%), Fred Schultz 175,745 (24.1%). Total vote was 730,154.

7. September 29, 1970: C. Farris Bryant 247,211 (34.3%), Lawton Chiles 474,420 (65.7%). Total vote was 721,631.

Republican Primaries

1. Governor September 8, 1970: Jack M. Eckerd-Robert H. Elrod 137,731 (38.4%), Claude R. Kirk, Jr.-Ray C. Osborne 172,888 (48.2%), L. A. Bafalis-Tom Dougherty 48,378 (13.5%). Total vote was 358,997; turnout of voting-age citizens was 8.2%.

2. Governor September 29, 1970: Jack M. Eckerd-Robert H. Elrod 152,327 (43.2%), Claude R. Kirk, Jr.-Ray C. Osborne 199,94 (56.8%). Total vote was 352,270; turnout was 8.1%.

3. Senator September 8, 1970: George Balme 10,947 (3.1%), Harold Carswell 121,281 (34.4%), William C. Cramer 220,553 (62.5%). Total vote was 352,781.

<u>Democratic Presidential Primary</u>

March 14, 1972: George Wallace 526,651
(41.6%), Edmund S. Muskie 112,523
(8.9%), George McGovern 78,232 (6.2%),
John V. Lindsay 82,386 (6.5%), Henry M.
Jackson 170,156 (13.5%), Hubert H.
Humphrey 234,658 (18.6%), Shirley Chisholm
43,989 (3.5%), other 4 candidates 15,959
(1.3%). Total vote was 1,264,554.

<u>Special Elections</u>

1. November 3, 1970: Constitutional
   amendment extending suffrage to those 18
   years of age. For 501,764 (39.9%),
   Against 754,281 (60.1%). Total vote was
   1,256,045.
2. November 3, 1970: Constitutional
   amendment permitting the issuance of
   state bonds for anti-pollution programs.
   For 819,629 (71.2%), Against 331,250
   (28.8%). Total vote was 1,150,879.
3. November 8, 1971: Constitutional
   amendment authorizing a state income tax
   on corporations. For 841,433 (70.3%),
   Against 355,023 (29.7%). Total vote was
   1,196,456.

RETURNS FROM PRESIDENTIAL ELECTIONS

Year	Turnout		Partisan Vote*
1948	577,643	(34.6%)[+]	Democrat 48.8%, Republican 33.6%, Dixiecrat 15.5%
1952	989,337	(48.3%)	Republican 55.0%, Democrat 45.0%
1956	1,125,762	(43.8%)	Republican 57.2%, Democrat 42.7%
1960	1,544,176	(50.0%)	Republican 51.5%, Democrat 48.5%
1964	1,854,481	(51.6%)	Democrat 51.1%, Republican 48.9%
1968	2,187,805	(53.3%)	Republican 40.5%, Democrat 30.9%, American Independent 28.5%
1972	2,583,283	(52.0%)	Republican 71.9%, Democrat 27.8%

*Totals do not necessarily equal 100%, since minor party percentages are excluded.

[+]Percentage of citizens of voting age who voted is calculated on the basis of a straight-line interpolation of citizen population between census years.

```
                  DEMOC.  GOVERNOR   1952        * DEMOC.  RUNOFF    1952
                                                 *
  COUNTY     ADAMS        MCCARTY       ODHAM       OTHER       MCCARTY       ODHAM
             #     %      #      %      #     %      #    %*     #      %      #     %
-----------------------------------------------------------------------------*------------------------------------------------------------
ALACHUA     1985 16.9   6521 55.5   3114 26.5    123  1.0*   6888 55.8   5447 44.2
BAKER        856 36.4    979 41.7    453 19.3     62  2.6*   1275 59.2    877 40.8
BAY         2011 15.5   4998 38.6   5737 44.3    206  1.6*   5336 44.3   6697 55.7
BRADFORD     490 14.2   2098 60.7    812 23.5     54  1.6*   1729 54.9   1422 45.1
BREVARD     1198 16.7   3952 55.2   1905 26.6    102  1.4*   4320 63.5   2487 36.5
                                                            *
BROWARD     4213 17.9  14275 60.7   4774 20.3    267  1.1*  12409 63.0   7302 37.0
CALHOUN      848 27.6   1682 54.6    482 15.7     66  2.1*   1806 61.6   1124 38.4
CHALOTTE     453 23.7    990 51.8    441 23.1     27  1.4*   1187 64.3    658 35.7
CITRUS       443 15.4   1238 43.1   1121 39.0     70  2.4*   1517 53.4   1325 46.6
CLAY         502 11.3   2738 61.8   1123 25.3     71  1.6*   2301 60.0   1531 40.0
                                                            *
COLLIER      385 18.8   1308 63.9    310 15.2     43  2.1*   1183 61.9    727 38.1
COLUMBIA    1286 21.3   2805 46.5   1855 30.8     85  1.4*   3333 57.2   2489 42.8
DADE       20389 15.0  68921 50.9  42951 31.7   3274  2.4*  73041 53.5  63407 46.5
DESOTA       535 16.1   1537 46.3   1194 36.0     51  1.5*   1629 51.4   1538 48.6
DIXIE        653 34.8    816 43.5    315 16.8     91  4.9*    945 51.7    884 48.3
                                                            *
DUVAL       7552 10.5  34883 48.5  28103 39.1   1384  1.9*  39175 50.4  38497 49.6
ESCAMBIA    4620 15.1  16851 55.0   8368 27.3    820  2.7*  17176 57.0  12938 43.0
FLAGLER      157 15.1    730 70.1    132 12.7     22  2.1*    705 68.2    329 31.8
FRANKLIN     577 27.0   1127 52.6    291 13.6    146  6.8*   1314 62.5    790 37.5
GADSDEN      595 12.1   2744 55.7   1361 27.6    223  4.5*   2685 56.1   2103 43.9
                                                            *
GILCHRIST    367 28.1    617 47.3    302 23.2     18  1.4*    742 56.7    566 43.3
GLADES       312 37.6    316 38.1    171 20.6     30  3.6*    393 60.6    255 39.4
GULF         516 22.5   1137 49.5    611 26.6     32  1.4*   1156 54.1    980 45.9
HAMILTON     864 35.1   1075 43.7    378 15.4    142  5.8*   1223 53.8   1049 46.2
HARDEE       688 17.2   1336 33.4   1910 47.8     64  1.6*   1623 41.3   2308 58.7
                                                            *
HENDRY       458 21.9    898 43.0    701 33.6     32  1.5*    924 48.7    972 51.3
HERNANDO     145  5.2   1434 51.3   1140 40.8     76  2.7*   1459 57.1   1096 42.9
HIGHLANDS    627 11.6   2395 44.2   2278 42.1    117  2.2*   2519 50.1   2510 49.9
HILLSBORO   7143 13.1  19543 35.9  26688 49.0   1061  1.9*  23941 44.0  30437 56.0
HOLMES      2333 41.7   2267 40.5    919 16.4     79  1.4*   2920 52.3   2665 47.7
                                                            *
INDRIVER    1048 27.0   2366 60.9    435 11.2     37  1.0*   2594 68.7   1182 31.3
JACKSON     2011 21.2   5380 56.7   1856 19.6    241  2.5*   5169 52.2   4727 47.8
JEFFERSON    559 24.5   1276 56.0    190  8.3    252 11.1*   1493 70.6    621 29.4
LAFAYETTE    375 21.2   1004 56.8    265 15.0    123  7.0*    941 67.6    452 32.4
LAKE        1427 13.6   4902 46.7   3903 37.1    276  2.6*   4406 47.3   4900 52.7
                                                            *
LEE         2423 33.7   3337 46.4   1322 18.4    106  1.5*   2834 48.1   3059 51.9
LEON        3262 24.3   7519 56.0   2076 15.5    558  4.2*   8571 64.6   4692 35.4
LEVEY        956 26.2   1488 40.7   1091 29.9    117  3.2*   1678 49.3   1724 50.7
LIBERTY      403 27.9    581 40.2    236 16.3    224 15.5*    704 49.5    719 50.5
MADISON     1088 30.0   1797 49.5    381 10.5    362 10.0*   1931 62.4   1163 37.6
                                                            *
MANATEE     1094 10.8   4737 46.6   4179 41.1    152  1.5*   4274 49.3   4389 50.7
MARION      1559 14.1   5427 49.0   3904 35.3    180  1.6*   5283 53.3   4620 46.7
MARTIN       831 24.3   2213 64.8    330  9.7     42  1.2*   2194 73.5    790 26.5
MONROE      1837 26.2   3466 49.5   1583 22.6    116  1.7*   3096 65.0   1667 35.0
NASSAU       471 10.9   2208 51.1   1585 36.7     59  1.4*   2032 51.2   1935 48.8
                                                            *
OKLALOOSA   2582 29.7   5211 60.0    779  9.0    110  1.3*   5144 60.3   3386 39.7
```

COUNTY	ADAMS #	%	MCCARTY #	%	ODHAM #	%	OTHER #	% *	MCCARTY #	%	ODHAM #	%
OKEECHOBE	555	31.5	733	41.6	430	24.4	46	2.6*	884	54.6	734	45.4
ORANGE	4444	16.7	10517	39.6	10541	39.7	1078	4.1*	11508	43.5	14939	56.5
OSCEOLA	1130	24.4	1611	34.8	1173	25.4	709	15.3*	2144	51.0	2064	49.0
PALMBEACH	5695	20.5	16570	59.6	5339	19.2	210	.8*	16480	64.8	8936	35.2
PASCO	958	13.0	3124	42.3	3139	42.5	157	2.1*	2875	43.8	3684	56.2
PINELLAS	5140	16.2	14058	44.3	11365	35.8	1149	3.6*	15523	49.9	15571	50.1
POLK	3766	11.7	13090	40.5	15017	46.5	429	1.3*	14180	44.0	18058	56.0
PUTNAM	1136	20.8	2897	53.2	1303	23.9	113	2.1*	3005	58.5	2131	41.5
STJOHNS	1202	17.3	3517	50.6	2101	30.3	124	1.8*	3310	51.8	3078	48.2
STLUCIE	2330	32.3	4569	63.4	280	3.9	30	.4*	5360	76.0	1690	24.0
SANTAROSA	1615	23.2	4402	63.2	851	12.2	99	1.4*	4389	67.8	2086	32.2
SARASOTA	1192	16.6	3324	46.3	2535	35.3	121	1.7*	3600	52.1	3310	47.9
SEMINOLE	613	8.7	1930	27.2	4252	60.0	291	4.1*	2664	38.2	4310	61.8
SUMTER	499	13.1	1755	46.0	1484	38.9	79	2.1*	1511	48.5	1605	51.5
SUWANNEE	1255	23.9	2355	44.9	1192	22.7	443	8.4*	2921	59.6	1982	40.4
TAYLOR	1162	37.0	1343	42.8	537	17.1	98	3.1*	1504	49.2	1553	50.8
UNION	204	12.9	1079	68.4	272	17.2	22	1.4*	976	64.6	534	35.4
VOLUSIA	3374	15.0	13456	59.8	5104	22.7	554	2.5*	14992	62.1	9151	37.9
WAKULLA	602	30.1	862	43.1	160	8.0	376	18.8*	1243	63.7	707	36.3
WALTON	2768	44.8	2826	45.7	490	7.9	101	1.6*	3510	56.4	2714	43.6
WASHINGTN	1659	33.9	2226	45.5	954	19.5	57	1.2*	2423	50.6	2363	49.4
TOTALS	126426		361367		232574		18079	*	384200		336636	
% OF VOTE	17.1		48.9		31.5		2.4	*	53.3		46.7	

GEOGRAPHIC CLASS

								*				
LOWLANDS	47975	19.	130574	51.	72269	28.	6304	2.*	139604	54.	116639	46.
BLACK BELT	3418	24.	7208	51.	2481	18.	1009	7.*	7725	60.	5191	40.
SOUTH FLA	75033	16.	223585	48.	157824	34.	10766	2.*	236871	52.	214806	48.

DEMOGRAPHIC CLASS

								*				
METRO	59196	15.	195618	49.	138129	34.	9243	2.*	209253	52.	192027	48.
TOWN	22180	18.	60280	50.	36768	30.	2243	2.*	64857	55.	53771	45.
RURAL	45050	21.	105469	49.	57677	27.	6593	3.*	110090	55.	90838	45.

```
         DEMOC.  GOVERNOR   1954    *  DEMOC.  RUNOFF    1954
                                     *
COUNTY     COLLINS      JOHNS      ODHAM        COLLINS      JOHNS
           #     %      #     %     #     %*    #     %      #     %
------------------------------------------------*---------------------------------------------------------
ALACHUA    3546 33.3   4893 45.9   2214 20.8*   5414 48.3   5805 51.7
BAKER       288 13.6   1581 74.4    256 12.0*    430 20.7   1648 79.3
BAY   ,    2538 21.8   5282 45.4   3818 32.8*   5488 46.9   6214 53.1
BRADFORD    131  3.6   3366 91.3    191  5.2*    278  7.2   3562 92.8
BREVARD    2750 37.4   3019 41.0   1587 21.6*   3416 49.4   3497 50.6
                                     *
BROWARD    9544 40.6   8381 35.6   5610 23.8*  14432 60.4   9465 39.6
CALHOUN     297 10.9   1991 73.4    425 15.7*    720 24.1   2266 75.9
CHALOTTE    785 41.1    594 31.1    530 27.8*   1017 58.9    711 41.1
CITRUS      684 27.3   1235 49.2    589 23.5*   1074 45.0   1314 55.0
CLAY        752 20.3   2276 61.5    672 18.2*   1214 34.1   2341 65.9
                                     *
COLLIER     967 36.1   1191 44.5    519 19.4*   1370 50.7   1331 49.3
COLUMBIA    977 18.0   3433 63.2   1022 18.8*   1667 32.6   3451 67.4
DADE      54661 42.4  31023 24.0  43345 33.6*101709 69.5  44564 30.5
DESOTA      750 32.5    932 40.3    628 27.2*   1335 56.3   1035 43.7
DIXIE       385 24.6    933 59.7    244 15.6*    572 36.7    987 63.3
                                     *
DUVAL     16803 25.5  26990 40.9  22218 33.7*  30276 46.5  34805 53.5
ESCAMBIA   5687 25.3  10849 48.2   5950 26.5*  11023 44.9  13515 55.1
FLAGLER     320 28.5    576 51.3    227 20.2*    447 43.6    578 56.4
FRANKLIN    549 27.6   1158 58.2    283 14.2*    699 36.8   1198 63.2
GADSDEN    1516 37.1   1894 46.3    681 16.6*   1894 47.6   2083 52.4
                                     *
GILCHRIST   186 16.9    773 70.3    141 12.8*    265 25.9    757 74.1
GLADES      250 36.0    331 47.7    113 16.3*    309 43.6    400 56.4
GULF        606 25.6   1087 45.9    673 28.4*   1098 43.1   1452 56.9
HAMILTON    605 27.4   1229 55.6    376 17.0*    832 36.7   1435 63.3
HARDEE      861 27.1   1084 34.1   1233 38.8*   1902 56.9   1439 43.1
                                     *
HENDRY      773 39.4    671 34.2    518 26.4*   1048 60.3    690 39.7
HERNANDO    401 16.9   1325 55.9    645 27.2*    944 38.9   1482 61.1
HIGHLANDS  2062 48.7    977 23.1   1193 28.2*   3167 68.5   1459 31.5
HILLSBORO 15678 32.0  16787 34.3  16480 33.7*  32158 60.8  20767 39.2
HOLMES      495 10.9   3058 67.4    985 21.7*   1180 24.7   3604 75.3
                                     *
INDRIVER   1520 46.8   1314 40.5    413 12.7*   1757 50.6   1713 49.4
JACKSON    1333 16.5   4863 60.2   1878 23.3*   2674 30.0   6225 70.0
JEFFERSON   833 41.2    730 36.1    461 22.8*   1140 56.0    896 44.0
LAFAYETTE   436 29.2    816 54.7    241 16.1*    579 40.3    859 59.7
LAKE       2634 29.0   4300 47.4   2147 23.6*   4081 45.1   4974 54.9
                                     *
LEE        2804 41.4   1799 26.6   2164 32.0*   4429 62.7   2630 37.3
LEON       7168 50.2   5370 37.6   1750 12.2*   8360 57.9   6069 42.1
LEVEY       524 16.5   1876 59.0    781 24.6*   1084 35.1   2002 64.9
LIBERTY     158 10.6   1008 67.5    328 22.0*    428 28.0   1101 72.0
MADISON     808 25.2   1929 60.2    466 14.5*   1215 37.3   2042 62.7
                                     *
MANATEE    4198 45.2   2749 29.6   2334 25.1*   5937 64.1   3325 35.9
MARION     3662 36.5   4160 41.5   2199 21.9*   4973 49.1   5162 50.9
MARTIN     1103 37.0   1113 37.3    765 25.7*   1586 55.0   1300 45.0
MONROE     2020 29.2   2572 37.1   2337 33.7*   2529 45.9   2978 54.1
NASSAU      943 21.2   2381 53.5   1129 25.4*   1412 36.9   2411 63.1
                                     *
OKLALOOSA  1451 21.3   3507 51.5   1849 27.2*   2775 37.6   4598 62.4
```

FLORIDA/65

```
              DEMOC.  GOVERNOR   1954   * DEMOC.  RUNOFF     1954
                                        *
   COUNTY     COLLINS      JOHNS        ODHAM     * COLLINS      JOHNS
              #      %     #      %     #      %* #      %     #      %
   -----------------------------------------------*------------------------------------------------------------------
   OKEECHOBE    509 31.4    764 47.1    348 21.5*    718 47.0    810 53.0
   ORANGE      6134 26.8  10267 44.9   6482 28.3* 10807 46.9  12236 53.1
   OSCEOLA     1483 36.4   1719 42.2    869 21.3*  1817 49.3   1866 50.7
   PALMBEACH   9561 37.8   8481 33.5   7282 28.8* 14314 56.7  10937 43.3
   PASCO       2006 34.3   1783 30.5   2051 35.1*  3494 60.6   2269 39.4
                                        *
   PINELLAS   10917 40.9   8574 32.1   7224 27.0* 19642 63.8  11154 36.2
   POLK        9946 39.2   6443 25.4   8998 35.4* 17281 65.0   9307 35.0
   PUTNAM      1720 28.9   2900 48.7   1340 22.5*  2861 44.8   3524 55.2
   STJOHNS     1826 28.2   3106 48.0   1545 23.9*  3135 47.8   3423 52.2
   STLUCIE     2846 49.1   2298 39.6    656 11.3*  3336 56.2   2605 43.8
                                        *
   SANTAROSA   1060 18.4   3567 62.1   1120 19.5*  2075 35.4   3782 64.6
   SARASOTA    2077 41.2   1389 27.6   1574 31.2*  3713 65.5   1955 34.5
   SEMINOLE     889 13.9   2179 34.1   3322 52.0*  2881 51.1   2757 48.9
   SUMTER       763 23.0   1827 55.1    724 21.8*  1273 37.6   2110 62.4
   SUWANNEE     935 20.4   2466 53.7   1189 25.9*  1694 38.4   2721 61.6
                                        *
   TAYLOR       744 25.6   1523 52.4    638 22.0*  1281 42.8   1710 57.2
   UNION         66  4.2   1447 91.7     65  4.1*    83  5.8   1338 94.2
   VOLUSIA     9703 41.5   8800 37.7   4853 20.8* 13414 56.7  10238 43.3
   WAKULLA      372 20.1   1242 67.2    233 12.6*   612 33.9   1191 66.1
   WALTON      1063 17.6   3164 52.4   1816 30.1*  2296 39.3   3544 60.7
                                        *
   WASHINGTN    729 18.2   2439 60.8    845 21.1*  1259 32.8   2581 67.2
   -----------------------------------------------*------------------------------------------------------------------
                                        *
   TOTALS    222791      255784      187782      * 380323     314198
   % OF VOTE    33.4        38.4        28.2      *   54.8       45.2
                                        *
                                        *
   GEOGRAPHIC CLASS                     *
                                        *
   LOWLANDS   57750 25.  114081 50.   58265 25.*  98352 42.  134424 58.
   BLACK BELT  4012 33.    6113 50.    2097 17.*   5390 44.    6856 56.
   SOUTH FLA 161029 38.  135590 32.  127420 30.* 276581 62.  172918 38.
                                        *
                                        *
   DEMOGRAPHIC CLASS                    *
                                        *
   METRO     128985 35.  121352 33.  114591 31.* 234361 60.  157443 40.
   TOWN       42648 39.   38846 35.   28364 26.*  63964 57.   47801 43.
   RURAL      51158 27.   95586 50.   44827 23.*  81998 43.  108954 57.
```

	DEMOC. GOVERNOR 1956								*		DEMOC. GOVERNOR 1960									
COUNTY	BRYANT #	%	COLLINS #	%	LOWRY #	%	OTHER #	%*		BRYANT #	%	BURNS #	%	CARLTON #	%	MCCARTY #	%	OTHER #	%
ALACHUA	3359	25.7	5272	40.3	2504	19.1	1955	14.9*		4735	30.0	2268	14.4	2032	12.9	2941	18.6	3824	24.2
BAKER	494	17.6	435	15.5	1173	41.7	708	25.2*		533	18.9	1073	38.0	304	10.8	274	9.7	642	22.7
BAY	2066	13.8	5166	34.6	3632	24.3	4061	27.2*		2188	14.9	661	4.5	2085	14.2	1324	9.0	8471	57.5
BRADFORD	1179	27.8	794	18.7	1452	34.3	814	19.2*		1419	33.9	1044	25.0	394	9.4	604	14.4	719	17.2
BREVARD	1591	18.9	5034	59.7	1269	15.1	536	6.4*		2891	19.5	2278	15.4	2608	17.6	4319	29.2	2708	18.3
BROWARD	1731	5.7	23858	78.0	2994	9.8	2017	6.6*		4016	9.9	2028	5.0	6254	15.4	7082	17.5	21154	52.2
CALHOUN	95	2.8	334	10.0	461	13.8	2448	73.3*		714	21.5	561	16.9	319	9.6	349	10.5	1380	41.5
CHALOTTE	220	9.0	1366	56.2	540	22.2	305	12.5*		597	18.0	878	26.4	870	26.2	506	15.2	473	14.2
CITRUS	353	10.9	1295	40.0	895	27.6	698	21.5*		1289	36.0	625	17.5	313	8.8	823	23.0	527	14.7
CLAY	853	17.3	1546	31.3	1546	31.3	993	20.1*		994	21.5	1729	37.5	594	12.9	496	10.7	803	17.4
COLLIER	293	8.3	1981	56.2	875	24.8	377	10.7*		900	27.7	325	10.0	1035	31.8	429	13.2	564	17.3
COLUMBIA	1504	22.1	1769	26.0	2413	35.5	1115	16.4*		2068	29.5	2074	29.6	755	10.8	696	9.9	1422	20.3
DADE	7916	5.1	112858	72.1	18696	11.9	17007	10.9*		18530	12.1	21234	13.8	38941	25.4	35823	23.3	38890	25.3
DESOTA	380	12.8	1039	34.9	1289	43.3	269	9.0*		710	20.3	273	7.8	1720	49.3	480	13.8	306	8.8
DIXIE	174	9.4	335	18.2	974	52.8	361	19.6*		713	33.2	245	11.4	368	17.2	368	17.2	451	21.0
DUVAL	16996	20.4	31761	38.1	16391	19.6	18269	21.9*		16227	17.0	42786	44.8	14265	14.9	6059	6.3	16185	16.9
ESCAMBIA	6702	19.1	16785	47.7	8117	23.1	3571	10.2*		11725	28.1	5104	12.2	6267	15.0	4282	10.2	14409	34.5
FLAGLER	274	21.3	346	26.9	500	38.9	167	13.0*		260	18.3	569	40.0	220	15.5	211	14.8	162	11.4
FRANKLIN	169	6.7	832	32.9	1002	39.6	526	20.8*		590	21.2	488	17.5	317	11.4	401	14.4	992	35.6
GADSDEN	777	18.1	1171	27.3	920	21.4	1425	33.2*		1461	34.1	272	6.3	563	13.1	721	16.8	1273	29.7
GILCHRIST	198	15.3	169	13.1	662	51.3	262	20.3*		524	35.8	191	13.1	143	9.8	290	19.8	315	21.5
GLADES	66	7.2	408	44.6	383	41.9	58	6.3*		145	15.9	41	4.5	324	35.6	265	29.1	136	14.9
GULF	173	5.5	880	28.2	1177	37.7	893	28.6*		559	16.3	193	5.6	660	19.3	357	10.4	1654	48.3
HAMILTON	544	20.7	438	16.6	1170	44.5	479	18.2*		749	29.1	551	21.4	333	12.9	288	11.2	656	25.5
HARDEE	460	11.2	1442	35.1	1629	39.6	582	14.2*		404	9.5	252	5.9	3161	74.2	233	5.5	209	4.9
HENDRY	176	6.1	1306	45.6	1239	43.3	143	5.0*		693	25.9	235	8.8	764	28.6	419	15.7	565	21.1
HERNANDO	199	6.2	810	25.2	915	28.5	1287	40.1*		1300	39.5	499	15.2	492	14.9	386	11.7	615	18.7
HIGHLANDS	463	8.9	3008	57.9	1287	24.8	433	8.3*		1315	19.9	623	9.4	2843	42.9	901	13.6	941	14.2
HILLSBORO	5425	8.8	35615	57.5	14426	23.3	6509	10.5*		16653	21.8	16177	21.2	24526	32.1	8521	11.2	10469	13.7
HOLMES	389	7.1	700	12.9	2924	53.7	1431	26.3*		119	2.2	88	1.7	248	4.7	90	1.7	4759	89.7
INDRIVER	481	11.3	2305	54.0	463	10.8	1022	23.9*		1043	20.3	563	11.0	1147	22.4	1921	37.5	453	8.8
JACKSON	681	6.6	2470	23.8	3347	32.3	3877	37.4*		1943	19.3	1482	14.7	1582	15.7	1094	10.9	3969	39.4
JEFFERSON	328	13.3	578	23.5	1031	41.9	523	21.3*		428	20.1	137	6.4	161	7.6	550	25.9	851	40.0
LAFAYETTE	217	12.8	194	11.5	935	55.3	345	20.4*		469	30.4	339	22.0	105	6.8	298	19.3	331	21.5
LAKE	3329	25.3	5288	40.2	3007	22.9	1516	11.5*		5205	42.0	1314	10.6	1563	12.6	1812	14.6	2508	20.2
LEE	2241	21.8	5384	52.3	1824	17.7	845	8.2*		1914	18.5	1969	19.0	1869	18.0	1381	13.3	3230	31.2
LEON	1451	9.7	8863	59.1	992	6.6	3692	24.6*		4110	22.9	806	4.5	4416	24.6	2092	11.7	6523	36.3
LEVEY	585	15.7	627	16.9	1702	45.8	806	21.7*		1671	48.7	391	11.4	288	8.4	583	17.0	500	14.6
LIBERTY	83	5.8	129	9.0	770	53.8	450	31.4*		448	27.7	142	8.8	168	10.4	251	15.5	607	37.6
MADISON	1175	28.1	771	18.5	1789	42.8	441	10.6*		1448	36.4	398	10.0	347	8.7	365	9.2	1424	35.8
MANATEE	1726	14.2	6965	57.2	2407	19.8	1072	8.8*		5259	35.8	2688	18.3	3738	25.4	1153	7.8	1853	12.6
MARION	6349	52.6	3216	26.7	1419	11.8	1075	8.9*		7678	62.3	884	7.2	1315	10.7	771	6.3	1671	13.6
MARTIN	212	5.1	2904	69.7	767	18.4	281	6.7*		644	13.3	1257	25.9	761	15.7	1373	28.3	819	16.9
MONROE	462	7.0	4371	66.3	782	11.9	976	14.8*		1907	22.5	1886	22.2	2181	25.7	1264	14.9	1239	14.6
NASSAU	1357	26.5	1556	30.4	1167	22.8	1039	20.3*		1377	28.3	1756	36.1	503	10.3	435	8.9	799	16.4
OKLALOOSA	977	9.7	3101	30.7	4261	42.2	1755	17.4*		1992	19.6	1896	18.6	1291	12.7	1445	14.2	3556	34.9

COUNTY	BRYANT #	%	COLLINS #	%	LOWRY #	%	OTHER #	%	BRYANT #	%	BURNS #	%	CARLTON #	%	MCCARTY #	%	OTHER #	%
OKEECHOBE	67	3.7	686	37.9	721	39.8	338	18.7	445	21.6	181	8.8	442	21.5	662	32.2	327	15.9
ORANGE	6311	20.1	17740	56.6	5302	16.9	1974	6.3	11738	30.9	3968	10.4	7473	19.7	7734	20.4	7076	18.6
OSCEOLA	845	18.6	2084	45.9	1256	27.7	354	7.8	1453	30.2	583	12.1	719	14.9	1303	27.1	757	15.7
PALMBEACH	2347	8.1	18590	63.8	6084	20.9	2115	7.3	2664	6.9	1831	4.8	3992	10.4	4449	11.6	25507	66.4
PASCO	495	7.3	2905	42.7	2484	36.5	921	13.5	2366	29.4	1463	18.2	1583	19.7	1410	17.6	1212	15.1
PINELLAS	4027	11.6	23710	68.3	3649	10.5	3340	9.6	10382	23.2	8599	19.2	9416	21.0	5554	12.4	10856	24.2
POLK	4153	12.0	16752	48.3	10676	30.8	3070	8.9	9124	22.6	5257	13.0	12571	31.2	7027	17.4	6353	15.8
PUTNAM	1622	21.7	2056	27.5	2367	31.7	1418	19.0	2188	29.4	2165	29.1	634	8.5	1248	16.7	1216	16.3
STJOHNS	1742	19.2	3990	44.0	2520	27.8	811	8.9	1442	17.6	3631	44.2	1507	18.4	696	8.5	932	11.4
STLUCIE	653	8.5	4669	60.5	1241	16.1	1153	14.9	894	10.0	504	5.7	1094	12.3	5772	64.8	643	7.2
SANTAROSA	757	9.7	2133	27.5	3483	44.8	1396	18.0	2014	25.0	1087	13.5	1240	15.4	954	11.8	2756	34.2
SARASOTA	601	9.1	4512	68.4	817	12.4	671	10.2	1442	19.1	1799	23.8	2443	32.3	962	12.7	914	12.1
SEMINOLE	1773	24.1	3598	48.9	1462	19.9	524	7.1	2547	29.2	1213	13.9	1774	20.3	1839	21.1	1354	15.5
SUMTER	856	21.4	796	19.9	1782	44.6	565	14.1	1984	53.3	461	12.4	437	11.7	437	11.7	403	10.8
SUWANNEE	1074	20.6	784	15.0	2844	54.5	520	10.0	1563	30.4	948	18.4	529	10.3	602	11.7	1505	29.2
TAYLOR	387	10.0	876	22.5	1946	50.1	676	17.4	1119	26.3	735	17.2	300	7.0	463	10.9	1644	38.6
UNION	237	13.4	91	5.2	468	26.5	967	54.8	486	29.8	417	25.6	183	11.2	298	18.3	245	15.0
VOLUSIA	4532	15.7	17542	60.7	4292	14.9	2514	8.7	5399	17.8	6934	22.9	3469	11.5	5606	18.5	8850	29.2
WAKULLA	216	9.5	486	21.4	686	30.2	885	38.9	316	15.3	276	13.4	274	13.3	181	8.8	1020	49.3
WALTON	458	7.3	1663	26.4	2732	43.4	1435	22.8	1075	16.0	692	10.3	542	8.1	684	10.2	3714	55.4
WASHINGTN	443	9.0	1134	23.0	2089	42.4	1260	25.6	309	7.4	335	8.0	453	10.8	143	3.4	2939	70.3
TOTALS	110469		434272		179019		116321		193507		166352		186228		144750		246230	
% OF VOTE	13.1		51.7		21.3		13.8		20.7		17.8		19.9		15.4		26.3	

GEOGRAPHIC CLASS

	BRYANT #	%	COLLINS #	%	LOWRY #	%	OTHER #	%	BRYANT #	%	BURNS #	%	CARLTON #	%	MCCARTY #	%	OTHER #	%
LOWLANDS	53261	18.	100493	34.	78656	27.	59981	21.	73568	23.	77056	24.	44301	14.	30980	10.	90115	29.
BLACK BELT	2890	20.	3366	23.	5293	37.	2926	20.	4231	30.	1399	10.	1728	12.	2189	16.	4340	31.
SOUTH FLA	54318	10.	330413	62.	95070	18.	53414	10.	115708	19.	87897	14.	140199	23.	111581	18.	151775	25.

DEMOGRAPHIC CLASS

	BRYANT #	%	COLLINS #	%	LOWRY #	%	OTHER #	%	BRYANT #	%	BURNS #	%	CARLTON #	%	MCCARTY #	%	OTHER #	%
METRO	51455	11.	280917	61.	75659	16.	54802	12.	91935	17.	101727	19.	111134	21.	79504	15.	144546	27.
TOWN	19518	14.	72531	53.	26760	19.	18937	14.	31713	21.	22084	14.	32160	21.	28369	18.	40047	26.
RURAL	39496	16.	80824	34.	76600	32.	42582	18.	69859	28.	42541	17.	42934	17.	36877	15.	61637	24.

COUNTY	BRYANT #	%	CARLTON #	%*	BURNS #	%	DICKINSON #	%	HIGH #	%	KELLY #	%	OTHER #	%
							DEMOC. GOVERNOR 1964							
ALACHUA	9891	64.9	5352	35.1*	4650	27.0	2471	14.3	2489	14.4	2782	16.1	4859	28.2
BAKER	1358	75.1	451	24.9*	1499	49.5	229	7.6	50	1.7	593	19.6	659	21.7
BAY	10611	72.6	4001	27.4*	4708	26.0	3174	17.6	1596	8.8	5552	30.7	3048	16.9
BRADFORD	3402	79.8	863	20.2*	2225	47.6	759	16.2	304	6.5	821	17.6	562	12.0
BREVARD	7407	55.0	6060	45.0*	6079	29.2	4039	19.4	2822	13.6	2937	14.1	4941	23.7
BROWARD	15450	35.3	28360	64.7*	14792	26.7	15636	28.2	13529	24.4	4745	8.6	6787	12.2
CALHOUN	2440	83.1	496	16.9*	1041	32.2	578	17.9	112	3.5	1211	37.4	294	9.1
CHALOTTE	1450	45.3	1751	54.7*	1239	25.2	892	18.1	603	12.3	1017	20.7	1165	23.7
CITRUS	2254	73.6	808	26.4*	1163	26.4	701	15.9	316	7.2	1083	24.6	1145	26.0
CLAY	3008	72.0	1167	28.0*	3530	56.1	685	10.9	280	4.4	767	12.2	1034	16.4
COLLIER	1542	51.6	1447	48.4*	879	21.6	1103	27.1	467	11.5	782	19.2	839	20.6
COLUMBIA	4725	74.2	1646	25.8*	3068	37.6	1281	15.7	922	11.3	2004	24.5	890	10.9
DADE	59045	34.5	112191	65.5*	42444	22.7	25267	13.5	80112	42.9	10679	5.7	28388	15.2
DESOTA	1468	44.0	1866	56.0*	682	19.4	189	5.4	453	12.9	1614	46.0	569	16.2
DIXIE	1647	81.1	383	18.9*	736	30.6	578	24.0	110	4.6	757	31.5	225	9.4
DUVAL	58957	66.3	29901	33.7*	64481	53.5	6575	5.5	17419	14.4	9460	7.8	22651	18.8
ESCAMBIA	28385	69.7	12333	30.3*	11718	25.5	7414	16.1	5303	11.5	15173	33.0	6392	13.9
FLAGLER	726	61.8	448	38.2*	721	43.6	152	9.2	139	8.4	192	11.6	451	27.3
FRANKLIN	1983	77.0	591	23.0*	838	26.7	816	26.0	425	13.6	794	25.3	263	8.4
GADSDEN	3383	83.6	663	16.4*	919	15.0	636	10.4	907	14.8	2911	47.5	760	12.4
GILCHRIST	1099	85.6	185	14.4*	386	24.6	457	29.2	33	2.1	461	29.4	229	14.6
GLADES	389	48.3	416	51.7*	155	13.3	317	27.2	134	11.5	390	33.4	170	14.6
GULF	2786	76.9	838	23.1*	955	22.9	697	16.7	438	10.5	1815	43.6	257	6.2
HAMILTON	1766	78.7	478	21.3*	909	30.7	692	23.4	467	15.8	586	19.8	309	10.4
HARDEE	944	23.6	3058	76.4*	755	15.6	192	4.0	238	4.9	2879	59.3	791	16.3
HENDRY	1634	61.6	1018	38.4*	477	16.0	757	25.4	466	15.6	896	30.1	384	12.9
HERNANDO	2037	69.1	912	30.9*	1052	26.3	564	14.1	349	8.7	1183	29.6	845	21.2
HIGHLANDS	2603	41.8	3631	58.2*	580	8.4	461	6.7	859	12.5	3888	56.5	1098	15.9
HILLSBORO	37633	49.0	39109	51.0*	24559	27.9	13060	14.8	13344	15.2	15127	17.2	21891	24.9
HOLMES	4163	90.8	422	9.2*	844	15.6	1326	24.4	83	1.5	2259	41.6	914	16.8
INDRIVER	2392	53.1	2109	46.9*	1814	26.4	1954	28.4	727	10.6	1003	14.6	1382	20.1
JACKSON	8140	74.4	2802	25.6*	2403	22.8	1779	16.9	1345	12.8	4228	40.2	773	7.3
JEFFERSON	1600	80.9	378	19.1*	692	26.1	506	19.1	279	10.5	542	20.4	634	23.9
LAFAYETTE	1443	91.4	135	8.6*	484	30.5	381	24.0	11	.7	558	35.2	151	9.5
LAKE	8832	73.3	3210	26.7*	2747	21.1	2234	17.2	1020	7.8	3653	28.1	3347	25.7
LEE	5746	54.1	4874	45.9*	3059	23.4	3457	26.4	1293	9.9	2246	17.2	3016	23.1
LEON	10466	58.4	7464	41.6*	3562	17.4	3199	15.7	2893	14.2	4298	21.1	6461	31.7
LEVEY	2753	82.7	574	17.3*	1170	28.5	725	17.7	299	7.3	1164	28.4	743	18.1
LIBERTY	1284	80.1	318	19.9*	369	21.1	412	23.6	18	1.0	808	46.3	139	8.0
MADISON	3006	82.4	641	17.6*	1011	21.7	891	19.2	646	13.9	1579	33.9	524	11.3
MANATEE	8145	55.3	6587	44.7*	2472	15.3	2131	13.2	2783	17.2	5173	32.0	3619	22.4
MARION	9296	74.8	3137	25.2*	4024	26.4	1628	10.7	3328	21.9	3670	24.1	2581	16.9
MARTIN	2167	54.3	1826	45.7*	1481	25.4	1872	32.1	1101	18.9	904	15.5	474	8.1
MONROE	3563	41.6	4999	58.4*	4488	38.2	1780	15.2	2918	24.9	1507	12.8	1041	8.9
NASSAU	3531	72.4	1349	27.6*	3206	54.3	643	10.9	606	10.3	918	15.6	527	8.9
OKLALOOSA	8117	75.4	2643	24.6*	5657	34.7	3633	22.3	622	3.8	4562	28.0	1815	11.1

```
              DEMOC.  RUNOFF    1960*              DEMOC.  GOVERNOR    1964
                                     *
  COUNTY      BRYANT       CARLTON      BURNS         DICKINSON   HIGH        KELLY        OTHER
              #     %      #     %*     #     %       #     %     #     %     #     %      #     %
------------------------------------*-----------------------------------------------------------------------------
OKEECHOBE    1194 58.9    833 41.1*    464 17.7     670 25.5    175  6.7    1029 39.2     288 11.0
ORANGE      20024 59.1  13834 40.9*  10300 23.6    7970 18.2   6044 13.8    7086 16.2   12292 28.1
OSCEOLA      2982 64.8   1623 35.2*   1350 22.8     959 16.2    407  6.9    1687 28.5    1513 25.6
PALMBEACH   20368 56.6  15619 43.4*   6890 14.9   26402 57.0   7904 17.1    2544  5.5    2610  5.6
PASCO        4685 62.0   2874 38.0*   2097 19.4    1136 10.5   1005  9.3    3248 30.0    3331 30.8
                                *
PINELLAS    21815 48.5  23131 51.5*  13527 23.2    6487 11.1   8405 14.4    6706 11.5   23220 39.8
POLK        22367 54.3  18847 45.7*   6229 12.2    4047  7.9   5695 11.2   27739 54.4    7326 14.4
PUTNAM       5271 76.5   1622 23.5*   3969 47.9    1177 14.2    690  8.3     998 12.0    1449 17.5
STJOHNS      5269 68.4   2430 31.6*   4757 53.4     662  7.4   1378 15.5     714  8.0    1390 15.6
STLUCIE      3803 49.2   3932 50.8*   2636 27.4    2297 23.9   1874 19.5    1051 10.9    1762 18.3
                                *
SANTAROSA    6396 75.4   2089 24.6*   2673 28.1    2108 22.1    242  2.5    2921 30.7    1584 16.6
SARASOTA     3369 45.2   4087 54.8*   2135 20.2    1027  9.7   1706 16.1    2313 21.8    3406 32.2
SEMINOLE     5273 64.7   2880 35.3*   2691 23.9    1667 14.8   1356 12.1    2312 20.6    3219 28.6
SUMTER       2785 80.0    697 20.0*   1347 33.7     501 12.5    326  8.1    1303 32.6     524 13.1
SUWANNEE     3878 83.3    778 16.7*   1603 28.8    1382 24.8    536  9.6    1253 22.5     798 14.3
                                *
TAYLOR       3712 90.2    402  9.8*    892 18.1    1585 32.1    457  9.3    1173 23.8     830 16.8
UNION        1268 86.7    194 13.3*   1036 56.2     236 12.8     46  2.5     346 18.8     181  9.8
VOLUSIA     14088 51.5  13241 48.5*   7540 20.9    3073  8.5   3380  9.3    2861  7.9   19303 53.4
WAKULLA      1598 75.7    512 24.3*    536 22.8     417 17.7    296 12.6     861 36.6     240 10.2
WALTON       4725 75.9   1501 24.1*   1860 28.3    1197 18.2    470  7.2    2515 38.3     530  8.1
                                *
WASHINGTN    3220 75.7   1035 24.3*   1198 24.2     942 19.0    230  4.6    2247 45.4     330  6.7
------------------------------------*-----------------------------------------------------------------------------
                                *
TOTALS     512757       416052     * 312453      184865      207280      205078       226163
% OF VOTE      55.2         44.8   *     27.5        16.2        18.2        18.1         19.9
                                *
GEOGRAPHIC CLASS                *
                                *
LOWLANDS   215548 71.   88062 29.* 140799 38.   49298 13.   43170 12.   77875 21.   63250 17.
BLACK BELT  10144 80.    2576 20.*   3686 21.    3042 17.    2433 14.    6008 34.    2397 14.
SOUTH FLA  287065 47.  325414 53.* 167968 23.  132525 18.  161677 22.  121195 16.  160516 22.
                                *
DEMOGRAPHIC CLASS               *
                                *
METRO      261677 49.  274478 51.* 188711 29.  108811 17.  152060 24.   71520 11.  124231 19.
TOWN        83904 56.   66797 44.*  39007 21.   24525 13.   23844 13.   50349 27.   50222 27.
RURAL      167176 69.   74777 31.*  84735 28.   51529 17.   31376 10.   83209 28.   51710 17.
```

SOUTHERN ELECTIONS/70

COUNTY	BURNS #	%	HIGH #	%*	BURNS #	%	HIGH #	%	KELLY #	%	FOOR #	%
ALACHUA	9762	58.5	6918	41.5*	4061	23.5	6909	40.0	6148	35.6	134	.8
BAKER	2664	86.4	418	13.6*	1086	37.2	317	10.9	1486	50.9	28	1.0
BAY	14368	81.0	3374	19.0*	5654	37.2	3386	22.3	6092	40.0	81	.5
BRADFORD	3471	79.1	918	20.9*	1459	35.5	765	18.6	1843	44.9	40	1.0
BREVARD	11600	61.1	7400	38.9*	7898	39.7	5840	29.3	6007	30.2	158	.8
BROWARD	27120	44.8	33467	55.2*	21355	35.7	25293	42.3	12485	20.9	664	1.1
CALHOUN	2562	89.3	308	10.7*	1039	37.0	283	10.1	1472	52.4	15	.5
CHALOTTE	2526	53.3	2211	46.7*	1685	36.4	1417	30.6	1492	32.2	33	.7
CITRUS	2844	72.8	1060	27.2*	1776	38.4	859	18.6	1927	41.7	64	1.4
CLAY	4650	80.5	1127	19.5*	2550	47.0	762	14.0	2055	37.9	62	1.1
COLLIER	2252	62.6	1348	37.4*	1808	46.6	693	17.9	1346	34.7	31	.8
COLUMBIA	5593	76.5	1722	23.5*	2391	39.1	981	16.1	2615	42.8	121	2.0
DADE	62812	29.0	153994	71.0*	61889	32.3	99056	51.7	27300	14.2	3341	1.7
DESOTA	2333	76.0	737	24.0*	1474	37.7	651	16.6	1753	44.8	35	.9
DIXIE	1540	84.8	276	15.2*	771	35.1	200	9.1	1200	54.6	25	1.1
DUVAL	80480	70.3	34071	29.7*	50351	44.3	30962	27.3	31452	27.7	848	.7
ESCAMBIA	34492	77.2	10172	22.8*	15011	36.5	7781	18.9	18118	44.0	257	.6
FLAGLER	1107	72.5	420	27.5*	593	37.8	397	25.3	570	36.3	10	.6
FRANKLIN	2150	75.0	716	25.0*	862	33.2	758	29.2	957	36.9	18	.7
GADSDEN	4608	78.8	1237	21.2*	2505	35.3	2078	29.3	2453	34.6	51	.7
GILCHRIST	1120	92.0	97	8.0*	503	35.9	145	10.3	741	52.9	12	.9
GLADES	814	73.4	295	26.6*	344	37.6	106	11.6	439	48.0	26	2.8
GULF	3284	80.9	777	19.1*	1360	40.2	396	11.7	1613	47.7	16	.5
HAMILTON	1698	74.6	578	25.4*	657	29.7	403	18.2	1119	50.7	30	1.4
HARDEE	3816	82.2	828	17.8*	766	25.4	330	10.9	1895	62.7	30	1.0
HENDRY	1788	69.9	771	30.1*	1021	40.5	393	15.6	1077	42.7	31	1.2
HERNANDO	2484	72.2	957	27.8*	1257	38.3	612	18.7	1368	41.7	42	1.3
HIGHLANDS	3351	63.4	1936	36.6*	1247	19.8	1282	20.4	3728	59.3	32	.5
HILLSBORO	53400	62.7	31739	37.3*	20972	26.0	26537	32.9	32429	40.2	808	1.0
HOLMES	4908	93.3	350	6.7*	1939	42.6	344	7.6	2254	49.5	13	.3
INDRIVER	3609	61.2	2289	38.8*	2037	38.2	1630	30.5	1605	30.1	66	1.2
JACKSON	7892	78.7	2141	21.3*	3387	38.2	1340	15.1	3934	44.4	194	2.2
JEFFERSON	1974	75.9	628	24.1*	1260	50.8	455	18.3	721	29.0	46	1.9
LAFAYETTE	1300	96.9	41	3.1*	585	41.8	59	4.2	735	52.5	22	1.6
LAKE	8918	78.3	2468	21.7*	5352	46.7	1925	16.8	4075	35.6	101	.9
LEE	8336	65.4	4414	34.6*	5681	48.5	2449	20.9	3486	29.7	106	.9
LEON	12532	64.5	6885	35.5*	8351	38.9	5608	26.1	7173	33.4	315	1.5
LEVEY	3028	78.2	846	21.8*	1188	41.1	437	15.1	1216	42.1	47	1.6
LIBERTY	1404	92.7	111	7.3*	636	39.8	230	14.4	721	45.2	9	.6
MADISON	3160	77.3	926	22.7*	1268	31.1	779	19.1	1998	49.0	31	.8
MANATEE	8281	60.0	5515	40.0*	3311	24.6	4312	32.0	5739	42.7	93	.7
MARION	9474	65.8	4920	34.2*	4932	37.8	2986	22.9	5022	38.5	104	.8
MARTIN	2514	50.9	2426	49.1*	2140	40.8	1291	24.6	1738	33.1	79	1.5
MONROE	5840	50.8	5662	49.2*	3804	50.3	2198	29.1	1365	18.1	189	2.5
NASSAU	4573	78.8	1231	21.2*	2265	49.1	828	17.9	1460	31.6	60	1.3
OKLALOOSA	12181	86.4	1916	13.6*	6382	51.7	1421	11.5	4472	36.2	72	.6

```
                  DEMOC.  RUNOFF    1964*            DEMOC.  GOVERNOR   1966
                                         *
        COUNTY   BURNS         HIGH       *  BURNS         HIGH         KELLY         FOOR
                 #      %      #     %*   *  #      %      #      %     #      %      #      %
        ------------------------------------------------------------------------------------------------
        OKEECHOBE  1919 77.6    554 22.4*    872 38.5    322 14.2   1027 45.4    42  1.9
        ORANGE    26718 65.5  14100 34.5*  18127 47.2   7536 19.6  12148 31.7   566  1.5
        OSCEOLA    3809 76.9   1144 23.1*   2551 53.9    715 15.1   1380 29.1    90  1.9
        PALMBEACH 23902 52.5  21633 47.5*  16910 40.5  13972 33.4  10522 25.2   386   .9
        PASCO      6433 64.2   3592 35.8*   2578 26.7   2769 28.7   4147 43.0   150  1.6
                                         *
        PINELLAS  24195 43.4  31546 56.6*  14320 25.5  27165 48.3  14492 25.8   280   .5
        POLK      31824 71.6  12614 28.4*   7504 18.8   7499 18.8  24599 61.6   303   .8
        PUTNAM     5818 78.4   1607 21.6*   3462 44.5   1813 23.3   2433 31.3    77  1.0
        STJOHNS    6551 75.8   2096 24.2*   4445 58.6   1619 21.4   1451 19.1    64   .8
        STLUCIE    4853 53.2   4271 46.8*   3178 31.1   3551 34.7   3403 33.3    90   .9
                                         *
        SANTAROSA  8031 88.3   1069 11.7*   2990 34.8    922 10.7   4624 53.8    55   .6
        SARASOTA   4551 50.4   4483 49.6*   2491 22.2   3394 30.2   5286 47.1    62   .6
        SEMINOLE   6753 68.9   3042 31.1*   3956 45.6   1433 16.5   3167 36.5   124  1.4
        SUMTER     2935 80.1    727 19.9*   1914 53.4    543 15.2   1081 30.2    46  1.3
        SUWANNEE   4299 82.2    930 17.8*   1944 38.9    640 12.8   2362 47.2    53  1.1
                                         *
        TAYLOR     3666 80.3    898 19.7*   1712 39.7    590 13.7   1994 46.2    21   .5
        UNION      1340 93.3     96  6.7*    642 43.6    141  9.6    679 46.2     9   .6
        VOLUSIA   18763 53.3  16452 46.7*   9646 27.9  14078 40.7  10640 30.7   242   .7
        WAKULLA    1742 77.4    508 22.6*    787 37.3    445 21.1    848 40.2    31  1.5
        WALTON     5392 86.2    862 13.8*   2169 40.2    649 12.0   2544 47.1    39   .7
                                         *
        WASHINGTN  3986 85.4    682 14.6*   1390 35.9    601 15.5   1859 48.0    23   .6
        ------------------------------------------------------------------------------------------------
                                         *
        TOTALS   648093       465547    *  372451       338281       331580       11343
        % OF VOTE   58.2         41.8   *    35.3         32.1         31.5          1.1
                                         *
                                         *
        GEOGRAPHIC CLASS                 *
                                         *
        LOWLANDS 265360 75.   88503 25.* 136897 41.   74715 22.  122143 36.    2875  1.
        BLACK BELT 12254 77.   3664 23.*   6034 36.    3821 23.    6730 40.     184  1.
        SOUTH FLA 370479 50.  373380 50.* 229520 33.  259745 37.  202707 29.   8284  1.
                                         *
                                         *
        DEMOGRAPHIC CLASS                *
                                         *
        METRO    333119 50.  330722 50.* 218935 35.  238302 38.  158946 25.    7150  1.
        TOWN     110829 63.   65073 37.*  50370 30.   49072 29.   68192 40.    1522  1.
        RURAL    204145 75.   69752 25.* 103146 39.   50907 19.  104442 40.    2671  1.
```

SOUTHERN ELECTIONS/72

DEMOC. RUNOFF   1966*   DEMOC. GOVERNOR   1970

COUNTY	BURNS #	%	HIGH #	%*	ASKEW #	%	FAIRCLOTH #	%	HALL #	%	MATHEWS #	%
ALACHUA	6661	37.1	11271	62.9*	5093	38.3	3253	24.5	2108	15.9	2827	21.3
BAKER	2034	67.4	983	32.6*	335	15.4	683	31.3	314	14.4	850	39.0
BAY	8241	55.2	6675	44.8*	3525	28.8	6440	52.5	1064	8.7	1226	10.0
BRADFORD	2281	56.0	1791	44.0*	796	22.2	1364	38.1	607	17.0	812	22.7
BREVARD	10996	49.9	11043	50.1*	8072	41.0	5830	29.6	2746	14.0	3017	15.3
BROWARD	27635	40.7	40183	59.3*	8735	20.6	14546	34.3	11211	26.4	7953	18.7
CALHOUN	1932	69.9	832	30.1*	874	44.8	651	33.4	231	11.8	194	9.9
CHALOTTE	2078	46.0	2438	54.0*	666	21.9	1507	49.5	186	6.1	687	22.6
CITRUS	2396	52.0	2212	48.0*	741	21.9	1229	36.3	288	8.5	1128	33.3
CLAY	3377	60.8	2177	39.2*	1116	25.8	1451	33.6	415	9.6	1342	31.0
COLLIER	2396	61.9	1472	38.1*	462	12.1	1471	38.6	1085	28.4	796	20.9
COLUMBIA	3993	62.5	2399	37.5*	780	16.8	2231	48.0	642	13.8	995	21.4
DADE	70351	33.0	142680	67.0*	24598	17.1	34319	23.9	53487	37.3	31126	21.7
DESOTA	2058	53.8	1764	46.2*	456	23.8	791	41.4	170	8.9	495	25.9
DIXIE	1325	70.6	552	29.4*	462	25.3	929	51.0	262	14.4	170	9.3
DUVAL	68568	56.9	51971	43.1*	14015	20.9	17959	26.8	7510	11.2	27613	41.2
ESCAMBIA	26474	63.9	14968	36.1*	25797	71.4	6568	18.2	1113	3.1	2638	7.3
FLAGLER	796	53.3	698	46.7*	484	41.1	336	28.5	105	8.9	252	21.4
FRANKLIN	1227	50.3	1212	49.7*	575	29.8	771	40.0	395	20.5	187	9.7
GADSDEN	4014	56.3	3114	43.7*	1082	20.7	852	16.3	2654	50.8	635	12.2
GILCHRIST	820	64.7	447	35.3*	201	16.8	696	58.3	147	12.3	150	12.6
GLADES	471	63.4	272	36.6*	213	28.1	256	33.8	40	5.3	248	32.8
GULF	2242	65.5	1180	34.5*	1046	31.8	1735	52.7	321	9.7	191	5.8
HAMILTON	1077	56.4	831	43.6*	513	30.9	696	42.0	149	9.0	300	18.1
HARDEE	1479	47.8	1613	52.2*	776	34.4	731	32.4	150	6.6	601	26.6
HENDRY	1561	61.5	977	38.5*	398	23.7	735	43.7	193	11.5	356	21.2
HERNANDO	1742	54.9	1431	45.1*	833	32.6	879	34.4	195	7.6	647	25.3
HIGHLANDS	2358	38.6	3745	61.4*	1451	34.5	1058	25.2	629	15.0	1065	25.3
HILLSBORO	27845	34.0	54127	66.0*	8988	16.6	19067	35.1	5106	9.4	21144	38.9
HOLMES	3299	72.8	1235	27.2*	955	29.2	836	25.6	624	19.1	853	26.1
INDRIVER	2905	55.0	2375	45.0*	596	20.0	1234	41.3	319	10.7	837	28.0
JACKSON	5404	66.9	2674	33.1*	2412	40.4	1831	30.7	798	13.4	929	15.6
JEFFERSON	1658	67.1	813	32.9*	439	22.7	743	38.4	358	18.5	393	20.3
LAFAYETTE	879	76.1	276	23.9*	323	29.6	479	43.9	142	13.0	147	13.5
LAKE	7072	63.2	4126	36.8*	1653	28.4	2107	36.2	798	13.7	1259	21.6
LEE	8461	62.4	5104	37.6*	1556	16.4	4216	44.4	954	10.1	2760	29.1
LEON	11917	54.6	9895	45.4*	6575	41.1	3026	18.9	1943	12.2	4447	27.8
LEVEY	1761	62.4	1061	37.6*	338	15.5	964	44.2	564	25.9	314	14.4
LIBERTY	1175	70.3	496	29.7*	481	36.7	513	39.2	195	14.9	121	9.2
MADISON	2277	61.5	1428	38.5*	875	29.0	1230	40.7	318	10.5	599	19.8
MANATEE	4321	32.7	8884	67.3*	1757	17.6	4096	41.1	930	9.3	3195	32.0
MARION	7797	58.1	5613	41.9*	2226	27.5	2546	31.4	891	11.0	2441	30.1
MARTIN	2496	49.7	2526	50.3*	632	24.2	992	37.9	393	15.0	597	22.8
MONROE	4834	55.1	3934	44.9*	976	13.8	2629	37.2	2347	33.2	1109	15.7
NASSAU	3289	66.2	1681	33.8*	557	17.7	1204	38.3	276	8.8	1104	35.1
OKLALOOSA	9726	75.4	3167	24.6*	5142	49.5	2689	25.9	843	8.1	1704	16.4

FLORIDA/73

COUNTY	BURNS #	%	HIGH #	%*	ASKEW #	%	FAIRCLOTH #	%	HALL #	%	MATHEWS #	%
OKEECHOBE	1426	60.7	923	39.3*	270	18.2	650	43.7	152	10.2	414	27.9
ORANGE	24092	56.4	18616	43.6*	6843	25.7	8077	30.3	5432	20.4	6298	23.6
OSCEOLA	3037	67.0	1496	33.0*	562	22.0	942	36.9	537	21.0	515	20.1
PALMBEACH	19575	44.7	24176	55.3*	9813	31.9	10112	32.9	5657	18.4	5190	16.9
PASCO	3275	36.9	5598	63.1*	1883	24.9	2751	36.3	688	9.1	2253	29.7
PINELLAS	18095	29.6	43124	70.4*	10268	23.9	13296	30.9	5331	12.4	14092	32.8
POLK	15129	38.4	24294	61.6*	7471	27.6	8349	30.8	4039	14.9	7258	26.8
PUTNAM	4598	59.3	3161	40.7*	1419	28.8	1262	25.6	845	17.1	1409	28.6
STJOHNS	5133	68.0	2417	32.0*	806	17.9	1129	25.1	614	13.6	1956	43.4
STLUCIE	4047	43.3	5306	56.7*	1985	33.3	1983	33.3	721	12.1	1266	21.3
SANTAROSA	5735	65.2	3065	34.8*	4052	55.6	1825	25.0	524	7.2	887	12.2
SARASOTA	2559	23.5	8310	76.5*	1326	19.1	2360	34.0	804	11.6	2441	35.2
SEMINOLE	5351	55.2	4343	44.8*	2318	29.7	2178	27.9	1269	16.3	2043	26.2
SUMTER	2239	66.1	1147	33.9*	496	20.5	1045	43.3	333	13.8	541	22.4
SUWANNEE	3204	68.6	1464	31.4*	871	23.7	1241	33.8	740	20.2	817	22.3
TAYLOR	2692	65.4	1422	34.6*	969	28.9	1114	33.3	483	14.4	783	23.4
UNION	1015	73.2	371	26.8*	190	17.5	354	32.7	299	27.6	241	22.2
VOLUSIA	13052	36.6	22566	63.4*	10668	46.0	5140	22.2	3541	15.3	3833	16.5
WAKULLA	1487	64.1	834	35.9*	498	31.5	611	38.7	294	18.6	176	11.1
WALTON	3511	63.4	2029	36.6*	1815	39.0	1494	32.1	611	13.1	738	15.8
WASHINGTN	2319	61.3	1463	38.7*	1234	40.2	1131	36.9	254	8.3	448	14.6
TOTALS	509270		596471	*	206333		227413		139384		186053	
% OF VOTE	46.1		53.9	*	27.2		30.0		18.4		24.5	

GEOGRAPHIC CLASS

	BURNS #	%	HIGH #	%*	ASKEW #	%	FAIRCLOTH #	%	HALL #	%	MATHEWS #	%
LOWLANDS	204912	59.	139480	41.*	85962	36.	69316	29.	26174	11.	58962	25.
BLACK BELT	9497	60.	6458	40.*	3122	25.	3777	30.	3519	28.	2175	17.
SOUTH FLA	294861	40.	450533	60.*	117249	23.	154320	30.	109691	22.	124916	25.

DEMOGRAPHIC CLASS

	BURNS #	%	HIGH #	%*	ASKEW #	%	FAIRCLOTH #	%	HALL #	%	MATHEWS #	%
METRO	282635	42.	389845	58.*	109057	25.	123944	28.	94847	21.	116054	26.
TOWN	74901	43.	97355	57.*	39175	32.	37396	31.	17521	14.	27167	22.
RURAL	151734	58.	109271	42.*	58101	30.	66073	34.	27016	14.	42832	22.

```
                DEMOC.  RUNOFF    1970* DEMOC.  SENATOR    1950
                                       *
  COUNTY        ASKEW            FAIRCLOTH    PEPPER         SMATHERS
                 #      %          #    %*    #      %        #     %
--------------------------------------------*--------------------------------------------------------------------------
ALACHUA        9723  69.2       4334  30.8*  3991  32.8     8174  67.2
BAKER           810  44.0       1029  56.0*   902  45.9     1065  54.1
BAY            6512  45.6       7784  54.4*  5557  62.2     3379  37.8
BRADFORD       1554  47.7       1707  52.3*  1079  35.6     1951  64.4
BREVARD       12503  67.3       6087  32.7*  3360  42.1     4616  57.9
                                       *
BROWARD       19466  47.2      21734  52.8*  5343  28.3    13570  71.7
CALHOUN        1402  67.2        684  32.8*  1882  67.7      897  32.3
CHALOTTE       1620  52.4       1470  47.6*   719  40.3     1064  59.7
CITRUS         2033  54.9       1668  45.1*  1133  46.5     1303  53.5
CLAY           1928  51.6       1807  48.4*  1101  34.0     2141  66.0
                                       *
COLLIER        1229  44.7       1520  55.3*   423  29.4     1014  70.6
COLUMBIA       1897  39.4       2919  60.6*  1758  32.7     3624  67.3
DADE          71496  49.7      72467  50.3* 66803  50.3    65886  49.7
DESOTA          984  56.2        766  43.8*  1615  50.9     1560  49.1
DIXIE           654  33.8       1281  66.2*   809  52.9      721  47.1
                                       *
DUVAL         34837  48.3      37280  51.7* 32822  43.6    42412  56.4
ESCAMBIA      34293  86.8       5211  13.2* 16542  58.2    11878  41.8
FLAGLER         609  62.1        372  37.9*   226  25.9      646  74.1
FRANKLIN        930  50.4        914  49.6*   947  53.1      838  46.9
GADSDEN        2727  62.6       1631  37.4*  1085  29.8     2557  70.2
                                       *
GILCHRIST       365  31.0        813  69.0*   683  58.6      483  41.4
GLADES          347  61.0        222  39.0*   407  51.0      391  49.0
GULF           1425  42.8       1903  57.2*  1291  63.3      749  36.7
HAMILTON        470  47.0        529  53.0*   976  45.7     1161  54.3
HARDEE         1281  61.4        807  38.6*  1691  45.1     2057  54.9
                                       *
HENDRY          868  51.4        820  48.6*   737  37.5     1227  62.5
HERNANDO       1240  58.0        898  42.0*  1043  46.7     1192  53.3
HIGHLANDS      2385  63.3       1382  36.7*  2509  46.2     2922  53.8
HILLSBORO     36408  59.7      24566  40.3* 29111  53.1    25749  46.9
HOLMES         1849  57.4       1374  42.6*  2997  58.1     2160  41.9
                                       *
INDRIVER       1361  44.4       1704  55.6*  1086  33.4     2162  66.6
JACKSON        3755  67.0       1848  33.0*  3794  44.6     4720  55.4
JEFFERSON       816  49.0        850  51.0*   658  32.1     1390  67.9
LAFAYETTE       582  51.7        543  48.3*   800  55.9      630  44.1
LAKE           3281  54.9       2695  45.1*  2858  27.7     7464  72.3
                                       *
LEE            4853  55.8       3846  44.2*  2403  35.2     4427  64.8
LEON          12140  74.4       4179  25.6*  5534  51.5     5214  48.5
LEVEY           750  34.7       1412  65.3*  1362  44.8     1680  55.2
LIBERTY         752  54.0        641  46.0*   926  70.3      391  29.7
MADISON        1428  52.3       1301  47.7*  1030  32.9     2102  67.1
                                       *
MANATEE        4950  53.4       4327  46.6*  3474  37.3     5843  62.7
MARION         4682  55.3       3791  44.7*  4355  42.6     5867  57.4
MARTIN         1453  52.6       1310  47.4*  1101  38.0     1793  62.0
MONROE         3226  42.0       4455  58.0*  3676  63.2     2145  36.8
NASSAU         1027  41.1       1471  58.9*  1522  39.7     2314  60.3
                                       *
OKLALOOSA      8442  80.5       2044  19.5*  2646  45.7     3138  54.3
```

FLORIDA/75

```
              DEMOC.  RUNOFF    1970* DEMOC.  SENATOR    1950
                                   *
  COUNTY      ASKEW       FAIRCLOTH    PEPPER        SMATHERS
              #     %     #     %*    #     %       #     %
-----------------------------------------------------------------------------------------
OKEECHOBE     545  54.2    461  45.8*   691  46.7     788  53.3
ORANGE      14897  56.8  11314  43.2*  9996  32.2   21092  67.8
OSCEOLA      1212  53.1   1069  46.9*  1313  34.5    2490  65.5
PALMBEACH   19381  60.8  12488  39.2* 10397  37.7   17152  62.3
PASCO        4470  58.8   3134  41.2*  2480  41.2    3534  58.8
                                   *
PINELLAS    30306  65.2  16186  34.8* 16021  46.7   18302  53.3
POLK        17792  59.3  12203  40.7* 14377  45.3   17363  54.7
PUTNAM       2895  61.5   1811  38.5*  1881  35.0    3487  65.0
STJOHNS      1978  50.9   1911  49.1*  2032  32.1    4293  67.9
STLUCIE      3544  53.1   3132  46.9*  2261  36.4    3952  63.6
                                   *
SANTAROSA    6552  79.6   1675  20.4*  3170  53.2    2787  46.8
SARASOTA     4404  62.9   2600  37.1*  2112  32.6    4375  67.4
SEMINOLE     4513  61.8   2795  38.2*  3054  43.4    3987  56.6
SUMTER        898  46.5   1033  53.5*  1946  53.7    1681  46.3
SUWANNEE     1728  47.7   1891  52.3*  2046  45.0    2499  55.0
                                   *
TAYLOR       1698  51.3   1610  48.7*  1670  60.9    1072  39.1
UNION         407  57.1    306  42.9*   398  27.8    1032  72.2
VOLUSIA     16612  71.6   6595  28.4* 11407  45.7   13531  54.3
WAKULLA       742  53.6    643  46.4*   772  47.9     841  52.1
WALTON       3209  67.4   1555  32.6*  2556  49.8    2577  50.2
                                   *
WASHINGTN    1899  60.7   1230  39.3*  2407  58.4    1713  41.6
-----------------------------------------------------------------------------------------
                                   *
TOTALS     447025        328038    * 319754        387215
% OF VOTE     57.7          42.3    *   45.2          54.8
                                   *
                                   *
GEOGRAPHIC CLASS                   *
                                   *
LOWLANDS   152026  61.   97973  39.* 110458  47.   125373  53.
BLACK BELT   5788  56.    4533  44.*   4156  35.     7601  65.
SOUTH FLA  289211  56.  225532  44.* 205140  45.   254241  55.
                                   *
                                   *
DEMOGRAPHIC CLASS                  *
                                   *
METRO      261084  56.  201246  44.* 187035  46.   216041  54.
TOWN        78806  62.   49128  38.*  51318  45.    62560  55.
RURAL      107135  58.   77664  42.*  81401  43.   108614  57.
```

```
           DEMOC.  SENATOR   1958* DEMOC.  SENATOR   1964
                                *
 COUNTY     HOLLAND     PEPPER      HOLLAND     ODHAM
            #      %    #      %*   #      %    #      %
------------------------------------------------------------------------------------------------------
ALACHUA     6596 64.2   3683 35.8* 11138 70.3   4705 29.7
BAKER       1042 46.9   1178 53.1*  1833 80.3    450 19.7
BAY         5429 49.1   5632 50.9* 11819 79.6   3026 20.4
BRADFORD    1544 51.4   1457 48.6*  3236 76.2   1011 23.8
BREVARD     7346 68.2   3430 31.8* 13938 72.9   5184 27.1
                                *
BROWARD    17269 57.8  12611 42.2* 25268 64.2  14116 35.8
CALHOUN     1153 44.1   1463 55.9*  2461 84.6    447 15.4
CHALOTTE    1554 66.5    784 33.5*  2893 68.7   1316 31.3
CITRUS      1685 61.3   1065 38.7*  2673 76.5    821 23.5
CLAY        2548 60.4   1670 39.6*  3712 78.7   1006 21.3
                                *
COLLIER     1629 65.2    868 34.8*  2607 78.0    736 22.0
COLUMBIA    3478 63.3   2015 36.7*  5732 76.9   1726 23.1
DADE       59372 41.6  83516 58.4* 90655 57.7  66588 42.3
DESOTA      1560 59.7   1051 40.3*  2627 77.6    760 22.4
DIXIE        810 50.7    787 49.3*  1843 82.4    395 17.6
                                *
DUVAL      43644 57.0  32924 43.0* 76744 72.6  28987 27.4
ESCAMBIA   12981 51.7  12111 48.3* 27195 76.6   8324 23.4
FLAGLER      684 71.8    269 28.2*  1012 70.7    420 29.3
FRANKLIN    1162 53.3   1020 46.7*  2316 77.4    675 22.6
GADSDEN     2014 81.3    463 18.7*  4787 80.4   1170 19.6
                                *
GILCHRIST    482 47.5    533 52.5*  1179 82.1    257 17.9
GLADES       392 56.9    297 43.1*   842 77.3    247 22.7
GULF        1074 36.3   1885 63.7*  3214 80.1    800 19.9
HAMILTON     792 46.4    914 53.6*  1911 73.3    695 26.7
HARDEE      2284 63.3   1327 36.7*  3179 80.7    758 19.3
                                *
HENDRY      1296 58.8    908 41.2*  1825 76.0    577 24.0
HERNANDO    1669 59.9   1117 40.1*  2294 74.4    789 25.6
HIGHLANDS   3118 64.2   1740 35.8*  4423 73.5   1598 26.5
HILLSBORO  32187 51.5  30268 48.5* 58503 73.4  21201 26.6
HOLMES      2635 69.0   1184 31.0*  3942 82.9    813 17.1
                                *
INDRIVER    2452 70.7   1018 29.3*  4472 74.6   1519 25.4
JACKSON     5146 67.8   2447 32.2*  6310 79.1   1669 20.9
JEFFERSON   1399 68.0    658 32.0*  1859 81.1    434 18.9
LAFAYETTE    778 56.6    597 43.4*  1245 88.9    156 11.1
LAKE        7492 77.1   2230 22.9*  9094 80.6   2195 19.4
                                *
LEE         5721 67.2   2797 32.8*  8076 75.9   2561 24.1
LEON        5819 49.2   6001 50.8* 13669 72.8   5101 27.2
LEVEY       1373 62.6    821 37.4*  3077 80.4    752 19.6
LIBERTY      605 44.6    753 55.4*  1299 83.6    254 16.4
MADISON     2243 62.8   1326 37.2*  3267 77.8    933 22.2
                                *
MANATEE     6665 68.7   3032 31.3*  8900 70.5   3721 29.5
MARION      6523 62.0   4000 38.0*  9541 68.1   4478 31.9
MARTIN      2254 69.1   1006 30.9*  3229 72.8   1209 27.2
MONROE      3144 41.6   4420 58.4*  6728 74.2   2338 25.8
NASSAU      2679 60.6   1740 39.4*  3278 77.1    972 22.9
                                *
OKLALOOSA   4553 58.3   3252 41.7* 10223 82.4   2188 17.6
```

```
              DEMOC.  SENATOR   1958* DEMOC.  SENATOR    1964
                                   *
    COUNTY      HOLLAND      PEPPER      HOLLAND      ODHAM
                #    %      #     %*     #     %      #     %
-------------------------------------------------------------------------------------------------
OKEECHOBE    1094 66.6     549 33.4*  1744 82.3      375 17.7
ORANGE      20545 72.9    7654 27.1* 28790 75.6     9303 24.4
OSCEOLA      2284 65.4    1208 34.6*  3935 79.3     1026 20.7
PALMBEACH   16794 62.9    9917 37.1* 27089 70.5    11309 29.5
PASCO        4004 65.8    2085 34.2*  6223 70.2     2644 29.8

PINELLAS    18861 57.4   14010 42.6* 31470 57.8    22953 42.2
POLK        18716 63.5   10780 36.5* 32620 76.2    10194 23.8
PUTNAM       3747 66.9    1856 33.1*  4866 77.3     1431 22.7
STJOHNS      4535 69.9    1953 30.1*  5075 72.3     1943 27.7
STLUCIE      3755 67.6    1800 32.4*  6158 68.9     2780 31.1
                                   *
SANTAROSA    3171 55.4    2552 44.6*  6219 84.2     1166 15.8
SARASOTA     3070 68.1    1438 31.9*  6236 71.9     2435 28.1
SEMINOLE     4433 67.2    2164 32.8*  7324 71.1     2982 28.9
SUMTER       1874 52.1    1726 47.9*  2651 78.9      708 21.1
SUWANNEE     2348 66.2    1201 33.8*  4401 82.2      953 17.8
                                   *
TAYLOR       1661 44.6    2065 55.4*  3944 83.4      784 16.6
UNION         762 55.3     616 44.7*  1407 83.9      270 16.1
VOLUSIA     12231 55.0    9996 45.0* 16880 54.1    14313 45.9
WAKULLA      1087 57.9     790 42.1*  1632 81.1      381 18.9
WALTON       2920 64.3    1623 35.7*  4274 84.6      778 15.4
                                   *
WASHINGTN    1917 63.0    1126 37.0*  3008 82.3      648 17.7
-------------------------------------------------------------------------------------------------
                                   *
TOTALS     408084       321377     * 676014       289454
% OF VOTE    55.9         44.1     *   70.0          30.0
                                   *
                                   *
GEOGRAPHIC CLASS                   *
                                   *
LOWLANDS   134886 57.   101204 43.* 240844 76.     76966 24.
BLACK BELT   6840 65.     3658 35.*  12666 78.      3479 22.
SOUTH FLA  266358 55.   216515 45.* 422504 67.    209009 33.
                                   *
                                   *
DEMOGRAPHIC CLASS                  *
                                   *
METRO      221653 52.   203011 48.* 365714 67.    182781 33.
TOWN        64481 58.    46547 42.* 113324 70.     47453 30.
RURAL      121950 63.    71819 37.* 196976 77.     59220 23.
```

SOUTHERN ELECTIONS/78

COUNTY	DEMOC. SENATOR 1968							* DEMOC. RUNOFF 1968			
	COLLINS		FAIRCLOTH		OTHER			COLLINS		FAIRCLOTH	
	#	%	#	%	#	%*		#	%	#	%
ALACHUA	8185	51.9	6950	44.0	648	4.1*		7751	49.5	7899	50.5
BAKER	536	21.4	1901	75.8	72	2.9*		534	18.2	2394	81.8
BAY	3852	26.3	10007	68.4	772	5.3*		3153	24.9	9506	75.1
BRADFORD	1179	31.3	2389	63.4	198	5.3*		742	26.4	2067	73.6
BREVARD	9541	53.2	7216	40.3	1156	6.5*		8033	50.8	7774	49.2
						*					
BROWARD	20299	62.5	11128	34.2	1067	3.3*		24057	65.0	12942	35.0
CALHOUN	549	21.6	1864	73.3	129	5.1*		513	18.0	2339	82.0
CHALOTTE	2383	52.8	1992	44.1	141	3.1*		1900	54.9	1560	45.1
CITRUS	1649	38.8	2391	56.3	209	4.9*		1466	39.0	2295	61.0
CLAY	1653	33.8	2940	60.0	303	6.2*		1430	27.6	3742	72.4
						*					
COLLIER	2047	51.9	1698	43.1	197	5.0*		1531	49.9	1536	50.1
COLUMBIA	1682	24.7	4286	63.0	834	12.3*		1814	25.1	5401	74.9
DADE	94497	67.1	42221	29.8	4392	3.1*		109987	67.6	52728	32.4
DESOTA	1115	35.2	1949	61.6	101	3.2*		1190	36.9	2037	63.1
DIXIE	505	22.7	1591	71.6	127	5.7*		415	20.6	1599	79.4
						*					
DUVAL	27750	42.5	34478	52.8	3106	4.8*		24943	41.0	35896	59.0
ESCAMBIA	13333	31.0	28073	65.2	1625	3.8*		12275	30.2	28411	69.8
FLAGLER	531	34.9	888	58.4	101	6.6*		412	35.4	752	64.6
FRANKLIN	766	26.6	2000	69.4	117	4.1*		693	24.6	2119	75.4
GADSDEN	2598	38.3	3839	56.5	355	5.2*		2096	38.2	3397	61.8
						*					
GILCHRIST	221	14.4	1250	81.2	69	4.5*		137	11.1	1098	88.9
GLADES	340	32.8	652	62.8	46	4.4*		245	32.9	500	67.1
GULF	793	22.8	2541	73.1	144	4.1*		646	21.1	2410	78.9
HAMILTON	854	35.1	1457	59.9	123	5.1*		734	32.6	1516	67.4
HARDEE	1025	28.0	2467	67.3	172	4.7*		785	26.1	2222	73.9
						*					
HENDRY	875	39.2	1244	55.7	114	5.1*		648	34.7	1218	65.3
HERNANDO	1481	41.1	1977	54.9	145	4.0*		1338	43.8	1717	56.2
HIGHLANDS	2968	47.3	3094	49.3	214	3.4*		2148	47.6	2369	52.4
HILLSBORO	43842	57.2	30673	40.0	2123	2.8*		40989	59.8	27584	40.2
HOLMES	659	16.8	3060	78.0	203	5.2*		413	8.6	4362	91.4
						*					
INDRIVER	2643	55.3	1927	40.3	208	4.4*		1770	56.3	1373	43.7
JACKSON	2239	28.3	5189	65.6	484	6.1*		1661	22.9	5601	77.1
JEFFERSON	943	36.6	1442	55.9	195	7.6*		1006	38.4	1613	61.6
LAFAYETTE	275	18.9	1100	75.6	80	5.5*		177	11.7	1335	88.3
LAKE	3327	39.0	4623	54.2	587	6.9*		2059	34.2	3967	65.8
						*					
LEE	7181	50.7	6573	46.4	409	2.9*		6938	50.3	6842	49.7
LEON	10906	51.5	9274	43.8	1004	4.7*		10499	51.5	9876	48.5
LEVEY	602	18.3	2500	76.1	182	5.5*		573	19.7	2337	80.3
LIBERTY	316	20.1	1189	75.5	69	4.4*		266	17.6	1244	82.4
MADISON	1295	32.8	2224	56.4	425	10.8*		1101	31.4	2400	68.6
						*					
MANATEE	6102	52.3	5127	44.0	433	3.7*		5099	52.7	4580	47.3
MARION	5036	37.5	7454	55.6	922	6.9*		3529	35.4	6437	64.6
MARTIN	1935	49.8	1815	46.7	138	3.5*		1096	48.0	1186	52.0
MONROE	5100	54.5	3911	41.8	346	3.7*		5545	58.8	3892	41.2
NASSAU	1423	31.7	2812	62.7	247	5.5*		1349	25.5	3939	74.5
						*					
OKLALOOSA	3454	26.4	9114	69.7	501	3.8*		2055	20.0	8213	80.0

FLORIDA/79

	DEMOC. SENATOR 1968				* DEMOC. RUNOFF 1968	

```
                  DEMOC.  SENATOR    1968    * DEMOC.  RUNOFF     1968
                                             *
COUNTY       COLLINS      FAIRCLOTH    OTHER  *   COLLINS       FAIRCLOTH
              #     %      #     %      #    %*    #     %       #     %
-------------------------------------------------------------------------------------------
OKEECHOBE    603  28.8   1407 67.3     82   3.9*  391  27.6    1025 72.4
ORANGE     15801  51.1  12839 41.5   2271   7.3* 13455 49.2   13894 50.8
OSCEOLA     1933  41.8   2371 51.3    315   6.8*  1154 36.1    2044 63.9
PALMBEACH  14709  55.6  10649 40.3   1092   4.1* 12957 58.8    9068 41.2
PASCO       4169  46.2   4499 49.9    349   3.9*  4008 50.6    3907 49.4
                                             *
PINELLAS   27120  68.9  11524 29.3    733   1.9* 31290 73.5   11279 26.5
POLK       16308  46.8  16944 48.7   1567   4.5* 15530 46.9   17587 53.1
PUTNAM      2805  37.2   4326 57.4    412   5.5*  2396 33.7    4705 66.3
STJOHNS     2283  37.1   3591 58.3    286   4.6*  1482 30.3    3410 69.7
STLUCIE     3891  49.6   3679 46.9    277   3.5*  2150 47.0    2428 53.0
                                             *
SANTAROSA   1792  21.2   6284 74.5    362   4.3*  1672 19.0    7151 81.0
SARASOTA    4911  69.9   1943 27.7    169   2.4*  4593 72.5    1742 27.5
SEMINOLE    4185  44.0   4684 49.2    653   6.9*  2957 40.2    4402 59.8
SUMTER      1142  32.9   2175 62.6    159   4.6*   994 30.2    2302 69.8
SUWANNEE    1463  27.4   3475 65.1    398   7.5*   961 21.8    3457 78.2
                                             *
TAYLOR      1309  28.1   3107 66.6    247   5.3*   970 23.6    3136 76.4
UNION        330  24.6    942 70.1     71   5.3*   247 18.2    1107 81.8
VOLUSIA    17664  58.6  10913 36.2   1564   5.2* 13673 57.7   10028 42.3
WAKULLA      542  26.1   1435 69.0    103   5.0*   481 23.2    1596 76.8
WALTON      1335  24.7   3794 70.3    265   4.9*   810 17.5    3825 82.5
                                             *
WASHINGTN    816  22.6   2571 71.3    217   6.0*   777 18.7    3378 81.3
-------------------------------------------------------------------------------------------
                                             *
TOTALS    426096        397642      36825   * 410689        407696
% OF VOTE   49.5          46.2        4.3   *   50.2          49.8
                                             *
                                             *
GEOGRAPHIC CLASS                             *
                                             *
LOWLANDS   99120  35.  172375 60.   14298   5.*  85776 32.   180742 68.
BLACK BELT  6030  36.    9614 57.    1144   7.*   5182 35.     9426 65.
SOUTH FLA 320946  58.  215653 39.   21383   4.* 319731 60.   217528 40.
                                             *
                                             *
DEMOGRAPHIC CLASS                            *
                                             *
METRO     257851  57.  181585 40.   16409   4.* 269953 58.   191802 42.
TOWN       77998  50.   70194 45.    6756   4.*  69832 50.    69800 50.
RURAL      90247  36.  145863 58.   13660   5.*  70904 33.   146094 67.
```

COUNTY	DEMOC. SENATOR 1970										* DEMOC. RUNOFF 1970			
	BRYANT		CHILES		DAVES		HASTINGS		SCHULTZ		BRYANT		CHILES	
	#	%	#	%	#	%	#	%	#	%*	#	%	#	%
ALACHUA	2558	18.5	4318	31.3	838	6.1	2636	19.1	3445	25.0*	2483	17.9	11414	82.1
BAKER	694	36.5	365	19.2	72	3.8	142	7.5	628	33.0*	611	36.0	1088	64.0
BAY	4362	40.0	1335	12.2	437	4.0	880	8.1	3893	35.7*	4513	35.3	8262	64.7
BRADFORD	1304	36.7	880	24.8	131	3.7	323	9.1	916	25.8*	1274	37.4	2134	62.6
BREVARD	9306	48.0	3171	16.4	840	4.3	1717	8.9	4356	22.5*	7849	44.5	9777	55.5
BROWARD	16404	38.8	6589	15.6	1526	3.6	10144	24.0	7636	18.1*	15614	40.2	23266	59.8
CALHOUN	734	40.4	294	16.2	74	4.1	88	4.8	627	34.5*	696	36.8	1194	63.2
CHALOTTE	1199	40.0	1017	34.0	118	3.9	131	4.4	529	17.7*	875	31.6	1891	68.4
CITRUS	1204	35.6	1236	36.5	121	3.6	204	6.0	617	18.2*	1246	34.8	2333	65.2
CLAY	1486	36.4	603	14.8	115	2.8	432	10.6	1442	35.4*	1332	38.0	2175	62.0
COLLIER	1937	55.5	624	17.9	151	4.3	231	6.6	545	15.6*	1216	47.3	1357	52.7
COLUMBIA	1713	37.3	1351	29.4	130	2.8	351	7.6	1049	22.8*	1488	30.8	3344	69.2
DADE	38710	31.2	32842	26.4	4818	3.9	14918	12.0	32899	26.5*	38148	30.7	86301	69.3
DESOTA	569	29.9	720	37.8	75	3.9	266	14.0	273	14.3*	509	31.3	1118	68.7
DIXIE	929	51.2	397	21.9	43	2.4	111	6.1	333	18.4*	864	45.1	1051	54.9
DUVAL	17944	25.2	9248	13.0	1805	2.5	15236	21.4	26912	37.8*	29564	41.7	41356	58.3
ESCAMBIA	12897	38.8	7126	21.4	1323	4.0	2771	8.3	9161	27.5*	13235	36.3	23184	63.7
FLAGLER	393	34.2	155	13.5	37	3.2	131	11.4	434	37.7*	320	36.1	566	63.9
FRANKLIN	733	40.9	254	14.2	68	3.8	318	17.7	421	23.5*	678	42.3	923	57.7
GADSDEN	1578	30.6	1470	28.5	194	3.8	1262	24.5	645	12.5*	1609	36.6	2791	63.4
GILCHRIST	478	43.0	338	30.4	27	2.4	50	4.5	218	19.6*	467	38.9	732	61.1
GLADES	354	45.6	205	26.4	20	2.6	34	4.4	163	21.0*	228	39.2	354	60.8
GULF	1165	38.2	263	8.6	158	5.2	314	10.3	1153	37.8*	998	34.9	1862	65.1
HAMILTON	683	39.1	388	22.2	68	3.9	254	14.6	352	20.2*	367	36.1	650	63.9
HARDEE	647	29.2	965	43.5	135	6.1	158	7.1	312	14.1*	452	23.7	1455	76.3
HENDRY	612	37.7	491	30.3	88	5.4	200	12.3	231	14.2*	602	40.2	896	59.8
HERNANDO	880	34.3	1045	40.7	96	3.7	214	8.3	334	13.0*	652	32.3	1365	67.7
HIGHLANDS	1118	27.7	1788	44.3	160	4.0	312	7.7	657	16.3*	793	21.7	2856	78.3
HILLSBORO	12549	23.9	25696	48.9	1232	2.3	4917	9.4	8172	15.5*	14212	25.1	42457	74.9
HOLMES	1006	42.2	757	31.7	137	5.7	108	4.5	377	15.8*	910	34.2	1750	65.8
INDRIVER	1234	42.1	396	13.5	212	7.2	282	9.6	810	27.6*	1230	41.7	1717	58.3
JACKSON	2555	47.1	901	16.6	446	8.2	399	7.3	1129	20.8*	2159	42.5	2920	57.5
JEFFERSON	635	35.0	569	31.4	59	3.3	302	16.7	247	13.6*	473	32.4	986	67.6
LAFAYETTE	533	49.8	233	21.8	25	2.3	41	3.8	239	22.3*	437	39.7	665	60.3
LAKE	2820	47.7	1140	19.3	321	5.4	661	11.2	968	16.4*	3153	53.3	2766	46.7
LEE	3844	41.8	2288	24.9	403	4.4	939	10.2	1726	18.8*	3062	38.2	4950	61.8
LEON	5399	33.9	4810	30.2	767	4.8	2669	16.8	2264	14.2*	4514	28.8	11149	71.2
LEVEY	567	28.3	829	41.3	70	3.5	127	6.3	414	20.6*	506	25.0	1515	75.0
LIBERTY	417	35.0	193	16.2	47	3.9	87	7.3	449	37.6*	473	40.1	707	59.9
MADISON	1373	42.5	828	25.6	101	3.1	358	11.1	572	17.7*	953	34.3	1825	65.7
MANATEE	2947	29.3	3908	38.8	315	3.1	519	5.2	2386	23.7*	2469	28.7	6120	71.3
MARION	3349	39.8	2050	24.3	293	3.5	1075	12.8	1654	19.6*	3417	42.7	4576	57.3
MARTIN	1196	46.9	388	15.2	213	8.3	190	7.4	565	22.1*	1148	43.0	1519	57.0
MONROE	3134	48.2	1537	23.7	184	2.8	510	7.8	1133	17.4*	3244	47.6	3574	52.4
NASSAU	1397	45.8	421	13.8	113	3.7	314	10.3	807	26.4*	1067	44.4	1338	55.6
OKLALOOSA	3893	41.8	2720	29.2	342	3.7	424	4.6	1926	20.7*	3209	32.2	6764	67.8

COUNTY	BRYANT #	%	CHILES #	%	DAVES #	%	HASTINGS #	%	SCHULTZ #	%*	BRYANT #	%	CHILES #	%
OKEECHOBE	519	41.9	266	21.5	106	8.6	70	5.7	277	22.4*	288	31.7	621	68.3
ORANGE	11867	43.5	4755	17.4	1876	6.9	4226	15.5	4563	16.7*	13832	53.4	12091	46.6
OSCEOLA	1174	45.6	708	27.5	178	6.9	211	8.2	301	11.7*	1090	49.6	1107	50.4
PALMBEACH	6838	22.0	7046	22.7	6476	20.9	4010	12.9	6679	21.5*	8688	29.1	21167	70.9
PASCO	2342	32.4	2734	37.8	240	3.3	381	5.3	1540	21.3*	1895	26.3	5323	73.7
PINELLAS	15235	36.1	9175	21.7	1604	3.8	3791	9.0	12421	29.4*	13808	31.7	29743	68.3
POLK	3975	14.2	17916	63.8	937	3.3	2418	8.6	2830	10.1*	5551	18.7	24196	81.3
PUTNAM	1577	33.4	599	12.7	152	3.2	665	14.1	1726	36.6*	1762	39.9	2659	60.1
STJOHNS	1267	28.0	874	19.3	157	3.5	511	11.3	1712	37.9*	1204	32.1	2549	67.9
STLUCIE	1896	31.9	1828	30.2	336	5.5	1010	16.7	989	16.3*	1784	29.6	4237	70.4
SANTAROSA	2639	39.6	1733	26.0	217	3.3	284	4.3	1796	26.9*	2588	34.6	4884	65.4
SARASOTA	3007	44.6	1611	23.9	346	5.1	507	7.5	1269	18.8*	2582	39.9	3892	60.1
SEMINOLE	3132	39.6	1720	21.8	590	7.5	1243	15.7	1222	15.5*	3312	46.6	3800	53.4
SUMTER	1136	46.1	565	22.9	86	3.5	209	8.5	469	19.0*	769	43.1	1016	56.9
SUWANNEE	1173	33.7	934	26.9	139	4.0	182	5.2	1050	30.2*	930	25.9	2660	74.1
TAYLOR	1405	44.0	718	22.5	87	2.7	314	9.8	669	21.0*	1251	40.1	1867	59.9
UNION	425	38.0	346	31.0	28	2.5	66	5.9	252	22.6*	197	26.8	538	73.2
VOLUSIA	5484	24.9	3736	17.0	1067	4.8	3705	16.8	8033	36.5*	6942	32.6	14376	67.4
WAKULLA	605	45.8	361	27.3	70	5.3	96	7.3	190	14.4*	518	41.1	741	58.9
WALTON	1934	45.9	828	19.6	153	3.6	181	4.3	1121	26.6*	1836	43.6	2379	56.4
WASHINGTN	1153	42.1	705	25.7	146	5.3	118	4.3	617	22.5*	1065	40.2	1581	59.8

TOTALS	240222		188300		33939		91948		175745	*	247211		474420	
% OF VOTE	32.9		25.8		4.6		12.6		24.1	*	34.3		65.7	

GEOGRAPHIC CLASS

LOWLANDS	78684	34.	46939	20.	8647	4.	31444	13.	69024	29.*	86566	37.	150527	63.
BLACK BELT	4623	36.	3460	27.	442	3.	2210	17.	1979	16.*	3630	35.	6606	65.
SOUTH FLA	156915	33.	137901	29.	24850	5.	58294	12.	104742	22.*	157015	33.	317287	67.

DEMOGRAPHIC CLASS

METRO	132444	31.	102477	24.	20660	5.	60013	14.	108443	26.*	147101	34.	279565	66.
TOWN	33659	28.	39379	33.	5315	4.	15274	13.	25582	21.*	34675	29.	86050	71.
RURAL	74119	40.	46444	25.	7964	4.	16661	9.	41720	22.*	65435	38.	108805	62.

COUNTY	REPUB. GOVERNOR 1970						REPUB. SENATOR 1970					
	ECKERD		KIRK		BAFALIS		CARSWELL		CRAMER		BALMER	
	#	%	#	%	#	%*	#	%	#	%	#	%
ALACHUA	1291	47.8	1157	42.9	252	9.3*	1119	41.7	1478	55.1	86	3.2
BAKER	0	.0	5	99.9	0	.0*	3	60.0	2	40.0	0	.0
BAY	183	23.3	429	54.7	172	21.9*	433	56.1	324	42.0	15	1.9
BRADFORD	35	33.7	61	58.7	8	7.7*	66	62.3	33	31.1	7	6.6
BREVARD	6250	37.2	7871	46.8	2683	16.0*	7449	45.2	8670	52.6	368	2.2
BROWARD	23737	42.9	24377	44.0	7248	13.1*	17664	32.9	34409	64.0	1670	3.1
CALHOUN	12	30.0	24	60.0	4	10.0*	32	80.0	7	17.5	1	2.5
CHALOTTE	1805	52.1	1227	35.4	431	12.4*	1413	41.8	1810	53.5	161	4.8
CITRUS	464	37.2	661	53.0	122	9.8*	314	25.6	853	69.6	58	4.7
CLAY	281	36.0	438	56.2	61	7.8*	461	59.3	297	38.2	19	2.4
COLLIER	2022	58.2	1192	34.3	258	7.4*	1479	43.5	1750	51.4	174	5.1
COLUMBIA	94	27.0	233	67.0	21	6.0*	203	58.5	134	38.6	10	2.9
DADE	12438	37.3	14184	42.5	6715	20.1*	10176	31.7	20146	62.7	1828	5.7
DESOTA	36	37.5	51	53.1	9	9.4*	29	33.0	57	64.8	2	2.3
DIXIE	1	20.0	4	80.0	0	.0*	2	40.0	3	60.0	0	.0
DUVAL	2768	26.2	6757	64.1	1022	9.7*	5473	53.8	4455	43.8	249	2.4
ESCAMBIA	740	25.8	940	32.8	1186	41.4*	1286	44.6	1519	52.7	80	2.8
FLAGLER	13	19.4	48	71.6	6	9.0*	39	60.9	22	34.4	3	4.7
FRANKLIN	33	22.6	98	67.1	15	10.3*	116	82.3	24	17.0	1	.7
GADSDEN	27	16.5	114	69.5	23	14.0*	109	66.9	41	25.2	13	8.0
GILCHRIST	1	20.0	2	40.0	2	40.0*	2	40.0	3	60.0	0	.0
GLADES	0	.0	11	91.7	1	8.3*	2	16.7	10	83.3	0	.0
GULF	6	19.4	19	61.3	6	19.4*	16	55.2	9	31.0	4	13.8
HAMILTON	4	23.5	13	76.5	0	.0*	15	75.0	5	25.0	0	.0
HARDEE	24	30.8	46	59.0	8	10.3*	31	38.7	47	58.7	2	2.5
HENDRY	21	26.9	42	53.8	15	19.2*	39	54.2	30	41.7	3	4.2
HERNANDO	418	46.5	348	38.8	132	14.7*	287	33.0	545	62.7	37	4.3
HIGHLANDS	538	39.5	731	53.7	92	6.8*	358	27.8	899	69.8	31	2.4
HILLSBORO	5033	39.3	5303	41.4	2458	19.2*	2773	21.8	9646	76.0	273	2.2
HOLMES	7	29.2	10	41.7	7	29.2*	15	65.2	7	30.4	1	4.3
INDRIVER	899	36.8	1089	44.6	452	18.5*	1033	43.4	1262	53.0	86	3.6
JACKSON	46	24.5	121	64.4	21	11.2*	141	73.8	43	22.5	7	3.7
JEFFERSON	19	18.8	75	74.3	7	6.9*	66	66.0	29	29.0	5	5.0
LAFAYETTE	2	18.2	9	81.8	0	.0*	8	99.9	0	.0	0	.0
LAKE	570	11.9	3948	82.4	274	5.7*	2553	53.9	2101	44.3	86	1.8
LEE	2862	37.4	2731	35.7	2058	26.9*	4241	56.6	2964	39.6	288	3.8
LEON	882	23.0	2490	64.8	470	12.2*	2679	69.7	1119	29.1	48	1.2
LEVEY	29	20.9	105	75.5	5	3.6*	73	52.5	62	44.6	4	2.9
LIBERTY	3	13.0	18	78.3	2	8.7*	14	60.9	9	39.1	0	.0
MADISON	16	20.8	54	70.1	7	9.1*	55	72.4	18	23.7	3	3.9
MANATEE	3458	42.2	4057	49.5	684	8.3*	2442	30.2	5368	66.4	280	3.5
MARION	349	18.9	1272	68.9	224	12.1*	774	42.6	977	53.7	67	3.7
MARTIN	689	35.4	1113	57.1	147	7.5*	703	36.8	1133	59.4	73	3.8
MONROE	290	38.6	340	45.2	122	16.2*	275	37.9	421	58.1	29	4.0
NASSAU	29	19.6	116	78.4	3	2.0*	115	77.7	32	21.6	1	.7
OKLALOOSA	256	28.0	386	42.3	271	29.7*	473	52.6	382	42.4	45	5.0

FLORIDA/83

```
              REPUB.  GOVERNOR   1970      *        REPUB.  SENATOR   1970
                                            *
COUNTY       ECKERD        KIRK        BAFALIS      CARSWELL       CRAMER       BALMER
              #     %      #     %      #     %*     #     %      #     %      #     %
----------------------------------------------------------*--------------------------------------------------------------------
OKEECHOBE       43  29.7     85  58.6     17  11.7*    69  48.9     63  44.7      9   6.4
ORANGE        3111  13.1  19181  80.5   1537   6.5* 11494  48.9  11605  49.4    394   1.7
OSCEOLA        184  10.6   1493  85.8     64   3.7*   752  44.5    898  53.1     41   2.4
PALMBEACH     9972  35.6  13566  48.4   4507  16.1*  9864  36.2  16728  61.3    689   2.5
PASCO         2671  45.1   2596  43.8    659  11.1*  1503  26.0   4000  69.3    273   4.7

PINELLAS     35629  50.1  26641  37.5   8845  12.4* 13656  19.1  55964  78.1   2033   2.8
POLK          2904  37.7   4241  55.0    566   7.3*  2557  33.7   4784  63.1    242   3.2
PUTNAM         150  24.6    414  68.0     45   7.4*   343  58.8    215  36.9     25   4.3
STJOHNS        271  32.9    499  60.6     54   6.6*   431  52.6    360  43.9     29   3.5
STLUCIE        858  35.4   1285  53.1    279  11.5*  1011  42.4   1283  53.8     89   3.7
                                            *
SANTAROSA      123  27.2    189  41.7    141  31.1*   229  50.9    207  46.0     14   3.1
SARASOTA      8537  49.4   6758  39.1   1994  11.5*  4372  25.7  12186  71.7    449   2.6
SEMINOLE       772  13.6   4556  80.4    340   6.0*  2692  48.0   2781  49.6    138   2.5
SUMTER          39  25.3     99  64.3     16  10.4*    65  43.3     77  51.3      8   5.3
SUWANNEE        17  31.5     35  64.8      2   3.7*    32  58.2     17  30.9      6  10.9
                                            *
TAYLOR          15  15.0     80  80.0      5   5.0*    78  77.2     22  21.8      1   1.0
UNION            4  30.8      9  69.2      0    .0*     7  53.8      4  30.8      2  15.4
VOLUSIA       3718  31.2   6646  55.8   1545  13.0*  4927  43.3   6088  53.5    374   3.3
WAKULLA          4   9.5     36  85.7      2   4.8*    30  75.0      9  22.5      1   2.5
WALTON          16  13.2     63  52.1     42  34.7*    42  36.2     66  56.9      8   6.9
                                            *
WASHINGTN       12   9.8     96  78.7     14  11.5*    78  63.4     41  33.3      4   3.3
----------------------------------------------------------*--------------------------------------------------------------------
                                            *
TOTALS      137731       172888        48378        * 121281       220553        10947
% OF VOTE     38.4          48.2          13.5        *  34.4          62.5           3.1
                                            *
                                            *
GEOGRAPHIC CLASS                            *
                                            *
LOWLANDS      7673  28.   16163  58.    4063  15.*  14813  54.   11882  43.     738   3.
BLACK BELT      66  18.     267  72.      38  10.*    247  67.     103  28.      21   6.
SOUTH FLA   129992  39.  156458  47.   44277  13.* 106221  33.  208568  64.   10188   3.
                                            *
DEMOGRAPHIC CLASS                           *
                                            *
METRO        93428  39.  110949  47.   33518  14.*  72386  31.  154472  66.    7216   3.
TOWN         21525  39.   26077  47.    7458  14.*  21614  40.   30647  57.    1620   3.
RURAL        22778  34.   35862  54.    7402  11.*  27281  42.   35434  55.    2111   3.
```

SOUTHERN ELECTIONS/84

```
         REPUB.  RUNOFF    1970* SPECL.  REFERENDUM 1970
                                *
COUNTY      ECKERD       KIRK          POLLUTION     AGAINST
            #      %      #      %*     #      %      #      %
---------------------------------------*---------------------------------------------------------------
ALACHUA    1335  52.3   1216  47.7*  13702  79.5    3526  20.5
BAKER         2  18.2      9  81.8*    513  59.4     350  40.6
BAY         296  40.2    441  59.8*   5735  52.3    5221  47.7
BRADFORD     33  35.9     59  64.1*   1837  66.0     948  34.0
BREVARD    6926  43.3   9070  56.7*  33575  74.8   11333  25.2
                                *
BROWARD   23479  44.6  29115  55.4*  90723  77.8   25897  22.2
CALHOUN       7  21.9     25  78.1*    510  44.1     646  55.9
CHALOTTE   1872  55.7   1491  44.3*   4601  70.0    1970  30.0
CITRUS      524  41.9    726  58.1*   2577  63.7    1471  36.3
CLAY        267  33.3    534  66.7*   3228  60.5    2104  39.5
                                *
COLLIER    1858  59.0   1289  41.0*   5071  69.8    2199  30.2
COLUMBIA     80  25.8    230  74.2*   1873  56.9    1417  43.1
DADE      14818  48.3  15842  51.7*145669  77.0   43444  23.0
DESOTA       45  41.7     63  58.3*   1008  53.9     863  46.1
DIXIE         0   .0      2  99.9*    520  53.1     460  46.9
                                *
DUVAL      2735  26.8   7485  73.2*  50539  72.9   18769  27.1
ESCAMBIA   1537  57.3   1144  42.7*  18625  55.1   15167  44.9
FLAGLER      16  23.5     52  76.5*    516  67.5     249  32.5
FRANKLIN     29  27.6     76  72.4*    520  53.3     456  46.7
GADSDEN      22  18.0    100  82.0*   2746  63.1    1606  36.9
                                *
GILCHRIST     3  99.9      0   .0*    406  53.5     353  46.5
GLADES        2  15.4     11  84.6*    344  63.8     195  36.2
GULF          5  35.7      9  64.3*    901  49.4     922  50.6
HAMILTON      4  26.7     11  73.3*    581  53.4     506  46.6
HARDEE       29  30.2     67  69.8*    706  39.3    1090  60.7
                                *
HENDRY       34  44.7     42  55.3*    766  67.7     365  32.3
HERNANDO    424  50.5    415  49.5*   1784  65.3     946  34.7
HIGHLANDS   608  46.3    706  53.7*   3124  65.4    1653  34.6
HILLSBORO  5935  45.6   7083  54.4*  53955  66.6   27106  33.4
HOLMES        6  27.3     16  72.7*    729  41.6    1024  58.4
                                *
INDRIVER   1094  43.0   1453  57.0*   4696  75.4    1536  24.6
JACKSON      52  33.8    102  66.2*   1455  44.6    1807  55.4
JEFFERSON    17  20.0     68  80.0*    476  52.3     434  47.7
LAFAYETTE     3  23.1     10  76.9*    200  24.9     604  75.1
LAKE        533  11.1   4279  88.9*   8479  60.9    5445  39.1
                                *
LEE        3665  51.3   3486  48.7*  14339  68.1    6702  31.9
LEON        964  27.1   2588  72.9*  14024  72.1    5429  27.9
LEVEY        27  20.8    103  79.2*    881  53.9     752  46.1
LIBERTY       1   5.9     16  94.1*    292  53.2     257  46.8
MADISON      11  17.7     51  82.3*   1092  54.9     898  45.1
                                *
MANATEE    3839  44.9   4702  55.1*  12802  67.2    6260  32.8
MARION      388  21.2   1442  78.8*   5653  60.6    3672  39.4
MARTIN      682  36.5   1187  63.5*   4079  74.6    1386  25.4
MONROE      362  47.6    398  52.4*   4172  63.7    2376  36.3
NASSAU       26  19.0    111  81.0*   1567  59.5    1067  40.5
                                *
OKLALOOSA   370  49.1    384  50.9*   7081  67.1    3468  32.9
```

```
                  REPUB.  RUNOFF    1970* SPECL.  REFERENDUM 1970
                                       *
   COUNTY        ECKERD      KIRK     *    POLLUTION    AGAINST
                 #     %    #     %*    #       %    #      %
--------------------------------------*--------------------------------------------------------
OKEECHOBE       53  42.4   72  57.6*   691   62.7    411  37.3
ORANGE        3170  13.4 20547 86.6* 45545   74.8  15384  25.2
OSCEOLA        156   8.7  1627 91.3*  3325   66.9   1648  33.1
PALMBEACH    11308  41.8 15713 58.2* 50398   80.5  12209  19.5
PASCO         3041  48.5  3227 51.5*  8613   59.8   5791  40.2
                                       *
PINELLAS     41459  56.3 32164 43.7* 82241   72.9  30604  27.1
POLK          2925  38.6  4648 61.4* 22280   63.6  12726  36.4
PUTNAM         122  22.0   433 78.0*  3394   64.2   1893  35.8
STJOHNS        231  30.4   529 69.6*  3917   70.3   1653  29.7
STLUCIE        889  37.4  1490 62.6*  5663   70.1   2415  29.9
                                       *
SANTAROSA      238  57.1   179 42.9*  3139   53.0   2787  47.0
SARASOTA      9005  51.6  8451 48.4* 22332   72.9   8312  27.1
SEMINOLE       798  14.5  4710 85.5*  9655   70.6   4028  29.4
SUMTER          24  18.9   103 81.1*   850   53.5    739  46.5
SUWANNEE        18  28.6    45 71.4*  1257   48.6   1329  51.4
                                       *
TAYLOR          10   9.0   101 91.0*  1073   58.3    766  41.7
UNION            4  44.4     5 55.6*   456   60.4    299  39.6
VOLUSIA       3837  32.4  8018 67.6* 23958   68.1  11221  31.9
WAKULLA          5  12.5    35 87.5*   373   43.2    491  56.8
WALTON          40  36.7    69 63.3*  1130   45.2   1368  54.8
                                       *
WASHINGTN       29  29.9    68 70.1*   667   44.6    827  55.4
--------------------------------------*--------------------------------------------------------
                                       *
TOTALS      152327       199943       * 819629      331250
% OF VOTE     43.2          56.8      *   71.2        28.8
                                       *
                                       *
GEOGRAPHIC CLASS                       *
                                       *
LOWLANDS      8879  34.   17518 66.* 146713  65.   80081  35.
BLACK BELT      56  19.     241 81.*   5239  59.    3639  41.
SOUTH FLA   143392  44.  182184 56.* 667677  73.  247530  27.
                                       *
                                       *
DEMOGRAPHIC CLASS                      *
                                       *
METRO       104441  45.  129093 55.* 537695  74.  188580  26.
TOWN         23278  43.   30736 57.* 126205  69.   57928  31.
RURAL        24608  38.   40114 62.* 155729  65.   84742  35.
```

COUNTY	18YR VOTE #	%	AGAINST #	%*	FOR #	%	AGAINST #	-%
ALACHUA	10937	59.1	7560	40.9*	17328	87.1	2568	12.9
BAKER	442	42.5	597	57.5*	724	69.2	322	30.8
BAY	5319	42.3	7262	57.7*	5153	54.5	4303	45.5
BRADFORD	1531	49.7	1552	50.3*	1711	70.8	706	29.2
BREVARD	22169	45.9	26134	54.1*	26237	69.4	11554	30.6
BROWARD	54873	43.3	71770	56.7*	82531	69.4	36456	30.6
CALHOUN	65	33.2	131	66.8*	637	56.1	498	43.9
CHALOTTE	2690	37.6	4471	62.4*	5853	75.1	1942	24.9
CITRUS	1565	34.5	2976	65.5*	3207	69.8	1390	30.2
CLAY	2267	46.9	2567	53.1*	3131	65.0	1686	35.0
COLLIER	3037	38.7	4803	61.3*	4975	66.4	2523	33.6
COLUMBIA	1505	40.4	2219	59.6*	1994	58.0	1445	42.0
DADE	95863	46.4	110778	53.6*	157484	82.4	33726	17.6
DESOTA	702	34.5	1334	65.5*	1433	75.1	476	24.9
DIXIE	564	48.2	605	51.8*	711	80.1	177	19.9
DUVAL	36092	49.6	36700	50.4*	46010	60.1	30542	39.9
ESCAMBIA	9183	24.6	28095	75.4*	23227	63.3	13482	36.7
FLAGLER	450	50.5	441	49.5*	587	66.7	293	33.3
FRANKLIN	467	41.3	663	58.7*	719	63.6	411	36.4
GADSDEN	1967	39.3	3037	60.7*	2214	53.3	1940	46.7
GILCHRIST	296	34.2	570	65.8*	612	76.0	193	24.0
GLADES	204	33.1	412	66.9*	438	74.4	151	25.6
GULF	763	36.8	1308	63.2*	875	56.9	662	43.1
HAMILTON	565	46.4	653	53.6*	567	58.9	396	41.1
HARDEE	403	19.6	1656	80.4*	1387	70.0	594	30.0
HENDRY	440	33.1	889	66.9*	893	61.3	563	38.7
HERNANDO	1105	37.0	1881	63.0*	2761	74.2	962	25.8
HIGHLANDS	1547	30.6	3512	69.4*	4683	78.4	1294	21.6
HILLSBORO	28939	32.6	59821	67.4*	59982	80.0	14983	20.0
HOLMES	844	39.1	1312	60.9*	818	57.0	616	43.0
INDRIVER	2781	39.8	4199	60.2*	4620	65.1	2477	34.9
JACKSON	1071	29.0	2618	71.0*	1922	50.5	1885	49.5
JEFFERSON	317	29.1	771	70.9*	623	42.8	832	57.2
LAFAYETTE	278	30.5	634	69.5*	294	46.3	341	53.7
LAKE	3507	23.1	11687	76.9*	4392	37.8	7219	62.2
LEE	7879	33.9	15335	66.1*	14212	62.9	8399	37.1
LEON	9046	42.7	12134	57.3*	15870	63.0	9303	37.0
LEVEY	621	33.8	1217	66.2*	1374	74.0	484	26.0
LIBERTY	320	45.3	387	54.7*	321	59.6	218	40.4
MADISON	930	39.2	1440	60.8*	828	41.6	1163	58.4
MANATEE	6731	32.6	13929	67.4*	15406	77.5	4473	22.5
MARION	3506	33.0	7124	67.0*	6276	60.6	4078	39.4
MARTIN	2456	40.2	3648	59.8*	4198	63.9	2371	36.1
MONROE	3667	49.8	3701	50.2*	5629	73.6	2023	26.4
NASSAU	1408	43.8	1803	56.2*	1847	64.8	1002	35.2
OKLALOOSA	4244	36.4	7425	63.6*	5637	57.4	4183	42.6

```
              SPECL.  REFERENDUM 1970* SPECL.  REFERENDUM 1971
                                    *
COUNTY      18YR VOTE    AGAINST   *   FOR          AGAINST
              #     %     #     %*   #      %      #      %
---------------------------------*------------------------------------------------
OKEECHOBE    505  37.6    838  62.4*   971  71.7    383  28.3
ORANGE     19241  29.2  46701  70.8* 22930  46.2  26693  53.8
OSCEOLA     1327  24.4   4117  75.6*  2187  46.8   2488  53.2
PALMBEACH  29430  43.6  38086  56.4* 55260  69.9  23755  30.1
PASCO       5181  32.3  10835  67.7* 15322  77.9   4347  22.1
                                    *
PINELLAS   51893  42.2  71183  57.8*102853  78.9  27488  21.1
POLK       12291  31.3  26966  68.7* 23524  68.2  10987  31.8
PUTNAM      2798  46.3   3242  53.7*  3162  55.7   2511  44.3
STJOHNS     2518  40.3   3731  59.7*  2502  45.8   2964  54.2
STLUCIE     3389  37.8   5588  62.2*  5079  56.4   3922  43.6
                                    *
SANTAROSA   1840  28.2   4688  71.8*  3594  53.5   3121  46.5
SARASOTA   10256  31.9  21909  68.1* 22830  76.4   7046  23.6
SEMINOLE    4508  30.5  10274  69.5*  5664  50.2   5617  49.8
SUMTER       442  24.5   1363  75.5*  1290  60.4    847  39.6
SUWANNEE    1205  40.2   1789  59.8*  1469  59.8    988  40.2
                                    *
TAYLOR       818  36.4   1427  63.6*  1048  56.3    815  43.7
UNION        421  46.9    476  53.1*   531  73.6    190  26.4
VOLUSIA    16117  41.1  23140  58.9* 25703  70.2  10904  29.8
WAKULLA      268  27.7    701  72.3*   541  51.1    518  48.9
WALTON      1091  37.7   1804  62.3*  1744  57.2   1307  42.8
                                    *
WASHINGTN    669  28.7   1662  71.3*   898  52.1    827  47.9
---------------------------------*------------------------------------------------
                                    *
TOTALS    501764         754281   * 841433        355023
% OF VOTE   39.9           60.1   *   70.3          29.7
                                    *
                                    *
GEOGRAPHIC CLASS                    *
                                    *
LOWLANDS  102847  42.  144444  58.* 153267  62.   92639  38.
BLACK BELT  3983  39.    6313  61.*   4670  51.    4482  49.
SOUTH FLA 394934  40.  603524  60.* 683496  73.  257902  27.
                                    *
                                    *
DEMOGRAPHIC CLASS                   *
                                    *
METRO     325514  41.  463134  59.* 550277  73.  207125  27.
TOWN       78901  39.  123595  61.* 135328  69.   59455  31.
RURAL      97349  37.  167552  63.* 155828  64.   88443  36.
```

DEMOC. PRESIDENT 1972

COUNTY	WALLACE #	%	MUSKIE #	%	MCGOVERN #	%	LINDSAY #	%	JACKSON #	%	HUMPHREY #	%	CHISHOLM #	%*
ALACHUA	7326	31.5	1746	7.5	5386	23.1	1778	7.6	1848	7.9	3532	15.2	1676	7.2*
BAKER	1524	81.0	31	1.6	11	.6	40	2.1	125	6.6	120	6.4	30	1.6*
BAY	10959	66.2	846	5.1	201	1.2	422	2.5	2526	15.2	756	4.6	856	5.2*
BRADFORD	2295	65.6	142	4.1	65	1.9	128	3.7	312	8.9	460	13.1	99	2.8*
BREVARD	12402	36.1	1341	3.9	1088	3.2	1533	4.5	6545	19.1	10852	31.6	553	1.6*
														*
BROWARD	31847	34.3	12023	13.0	8359	9.0	7478	8.1	11984	12.9	19041	20.5	2080	2.2*
CALHOUN	1666	80.6	48	2.3	34	1.6	35	1.7	136	6.6	100	4.8	47	2.3*
CHALOTTE	1768	36.7	603	12.5	133	2.8	295	6.1	1038	21.5	921	19.1	64	1.3*
CITRUS	2569	54.5	394	8.4	121	2.6	181	3.8	632	13.4	729	15.5	86	1.8*
CLAY	3582	57.8	304	4.9	170	2.7	225	3.6	1075	17.4	731	11.8	108	1.7*
														*
COLLIER	2068	47.9	411	9.5	283	6.6	191	4.4	596	13.8	706	16.3	64	1.5*
COLUMBIA	4143	72.2	193	3.4	130	2.3	171	3.0	409	7.1	503	8.8	189	3.3*
DADE	68126	27.7	25386	10.3	29678	12.1	15629	6.4	33308	13.5	64450	26.2	9055	3.7*
DESOTA	1556	64.9	141	5.9	31	1.3	150	6.3	209	8.7	270	11.3	42	1.8*
DIXIE	1121	76.8	38	2.6	23	1.6	45	3.1	102	7.0	86	5.9	44	3.0*
														*
DUVAL	53862	47.0	5510	4.8	2544	2.2	8859	7.7	16669	14.5	21370	18.7	5758	5.0*
ESCAMBIA	24921	51.1	3130	6.4	1201	2.5	1297	2.7	9971	20.4	6172	12.6	2110	4.3*
FLAGLER	711	60.7	94	8.0	14	1.2	61	5.2	98	8.4	184	15.7	10	.9*
FRANKLIN	1153	67.2	64	3.7	32	1.9	31	1.8	186	10.8	124	7.2	127	7.4*
GADSDEN	3804	49.4	250	3.2	87	1.1	369	4.8	563	7.3	1030	13.4	1594	20.7*
														*
GILCHRIST	1023	79.2	45	3.5	34	2.6	19	1.5	104	8.0	57	4.4	10	.8*
GLADES	611	71.0	43	5.0	12	1.4	19	2.2	80	9.3	85	9.9	10	1.2*
GULF	1934	73.6	85	3.2	20	.8	25	1.0	306	11.6	160	6.1	99	3.8*
HAMILTON	1164	70.3	63	3.8	15	.9	46	2.8	123	7.4	196	11.8	49	3.0*
HARDEE	2102	70.6	113	3.8	37	1.2	92	3.1	285	9.6	300	10.1	48	1.6*
														*
HENDRY	1546	64.6	81	3.4	38	1.6	77	3.2	243	10.2	343	14.3	64	2.7*
HERNANDO	1938	51.2	293	7.7	101	2.7	201	5.3	543	14.3	630	16.6	79	2.1*
HIGHLANDS	3094	52.5	456	7.7	146	2.5	326	5.5	822	14.0	948	16.1	99	1.7*
HILLSBORO	35328	38.9	10216	11.2	3529	3.9	9813	10.8	15194	16.7	13721	15.1	3008	3.3*
HOLMES	2648	86.7	87	2.8	28	.9	24	.8	187	6.1	56	1.8	23	.8*
														*
INDRIVER	2937	49.6	622	10.5	275	4.6	268	4.5	551	9.3	1153	19.5	113	1.9*
JACKSON	6626	74.4	219	2.5	95	1.1	265	3.0	429	4.8	503	5.6	769	8.6*
JEFFERSON	1334	59.0	68	3.0	31	1.4	93	4.1	141	6.2	253	11.2	341	15.1*
LAFAYETTE	852	83.5	24	2.4	3	.3	12	1.2	76	7.5	47	4.6	6	.6*
LAKE	6633	61.2	506	4.7	279	2.6	422	3.9	1327	12.2	1479	13.6	201	1.9*
														*
LEE	8864	50.5	1366	7.8	561	3.2	843	4.8	3065	17.5	2581	14.7	268	1.5*
LEON	10907	43.2	1547	6.1	2938	11.6	1614	6.4	2769	11.0	2689	10.6	2798	11.1*
LEVEY	1874	69.7	144	5.4	45	1.7	88	3.3	229	8.5	259	9.6	48	1.8*
LIBERTY	918	81.6	34	3.0	11	1.0	16	1.4	63	5.6	48	4.3	35	3.1*
MADISON	2381	66.8	71	2.0	34	1.0	212	6.0	197	5.5	385	10.8	282	7.9*
														*
MANATEE	6602	45.8	1502	10.4	494	3.4	1200	8.3	1863	12.9	2436	16.9	327	2.3*
MARION	8696	61.7	793	5.6	326	2.3	819	5.8	1439	10.2	1575	11.2	455	3.2*
MARTIN	2428	50.6	531	11.1	239	5.0	195	4.1	470	9.8	758	15.8	182	3.8*
MONROE	4620	53.7	626	7.3	513	6.0	813	9.5	922	10.7	893	10.4	216	2.5*
NASSAU	2419	61.0	158	4.0	73	1.8	165	4.2	461	11.6	532	13.4	157	4.0*
														*
OKLALOOSA	8578	62.0	677	4.9	333	2.4	289	2.1	3066	22.2	696	5.0	193	1.4*

FLORIDA/89

DEMOC. PRESIDENT 1972

COUNTY	WALLACE #	%	MUSKIE #	%	MCGOVERN #	%	LINDSAY #	%	JACKSON #	%	HUMPHREY #	%	CHISHOLM #	%*
OKEECHOBE	1429	73.0	107	5.5	33	1.7	54	2.8	117	6.0	201	10.3	16	.8*
ORANGE	21770	45.6	3696	7.7	2269	4.8	2260	4.7	7382	15.5	9389	19.7	996	2.1*
OSCEOLA	2562	56.9	279	6.2	16	.4	175	3.9	661	14.7	760	16.9	51	1.1*
PALMBEACH	22484	38.6	8170	14.0	4606	7.9	3572	6.1	6560	11.3	10751	18.4	2154	3.7*
PASCO	6065	44.5	1769	13.0	451	3.3	759	5.6	1563	11.5	2869	21.1	144	1.1*
PINELLAS	23420	27.5	14220	16.7	6154	7.2	9655	11.3	9753	11.5	20115	23.6	1830	2.1*
POLK	25128	54.2	2772	6.0	981	2.1	3487	7.5	7301	15.7	5908	12.7	794	1.7*
PUTNAM	4467	61.1	303	4.1	188	2.6	287	3.9	870	11.9	966	13.2	230	3.1*
STJOHNS	3757	58.9	292	4.6	134	2.1	223	3.5	851	13.3	783	12.3	336	5.3*
STLUCIE	4595	54.4	863	10.2	314	3.7	542	6.4	715	8.5	1050	12.4	375	4.4*
SANTAROSA	5421	66.5	290	3.6	183	2.2	143	1.8	1576	19.3	418	5.1	121	1.5*
SARASOTA	4664	33.8	1914	13.9	850	6.2	1463	10.6	1693	12.3	2547	18.4	686	5.0*
SEMINOLE	5801	46.5	791	6.3	491	3.9	522	4.2	1994	16.0	2575	20.7	293	2.4*
SUMTER	2116	69.0	125	4.1	54	1.8	100	3.3	267	8.7	367	12.0	36	1.2*
SUWANNEE	2750	71.1	116	3.0	63	1.6	108	2.8	364	9.4	326	8.4	139	3.6*
TAYLOR	2344	74.4	106	3.4	41	1.3	67	2.1	223	7.1	251	8.0	118	3.7*
UNION	978	78.7	34	2.7	33	2.7	23	1.9	68	5.5	90	7.2	16	1.3*
VOLUSIA	13723	39.0	3372	9.6	1471	4.2	1895	5.4	3981	11.3	9854	28.0	917	2.6*
WAKULLA	1454	79.2	34	1.9	23	1.3	52	2.8	109	5.9	100	5.4	65	3.5*
WALTON	3549	74.7	129	2.7	46	1.0	53	1.1	568	12.0	288	6.1	116	2.4*
WASHINGTN	2714	80.8	76	2.3	30	.9	72	2.1	253	7.5	130	3.9	84	2.5*
TOTALS	526651		112523		78232		82386		170156		234658		43989	*
% OF VOTE	42.2		9.0		6.3		6.6		13.6		18.8		3.5	*

GEOGRAPHIC CLASS

	WALLACE #	%	MUSKIE #	%	MCGOVERN #	%	LINDSAY #	%	JACKSON #	%	HUMPHREY #	%	CHISHOLM #	%*
LOWLANDS	187172	54.	17339	5.	14458	4.	17456	5.	47468	14.	44112	13.	16872	5.*
BLACK BELT	9294	58.	495	3.	179	1.	739	5.	1104	7.	1949	12.	2276	14.*
SOUTH FLA	330185	37.	94689	11.	63595	7.	64191	7.	121584	14.	188597	21.	24841	3.*

DEMOGRAPHIC CLASS

	WALLACE #	%	MUSKIE #	%	MCGOVERN #	%	LINDSAY #	%	JACKSON #	%	HUMPHREY #	%	CHISHOLM #	%*
METRO	282610	36.	82375	10.	58343	7.	58575	7.	110897	14.	165056	21.	26997	3.*
TOWN	90786	47.	15052	8.	13215	7.	12857	7.	24820	13.	29810	15.	8586	4.*
RURAL	153255	57.	15096	6.	6674	2.	10954	4.	34439	13.	39792	15.	8406	3.*

GEORGIA

COUNTIES

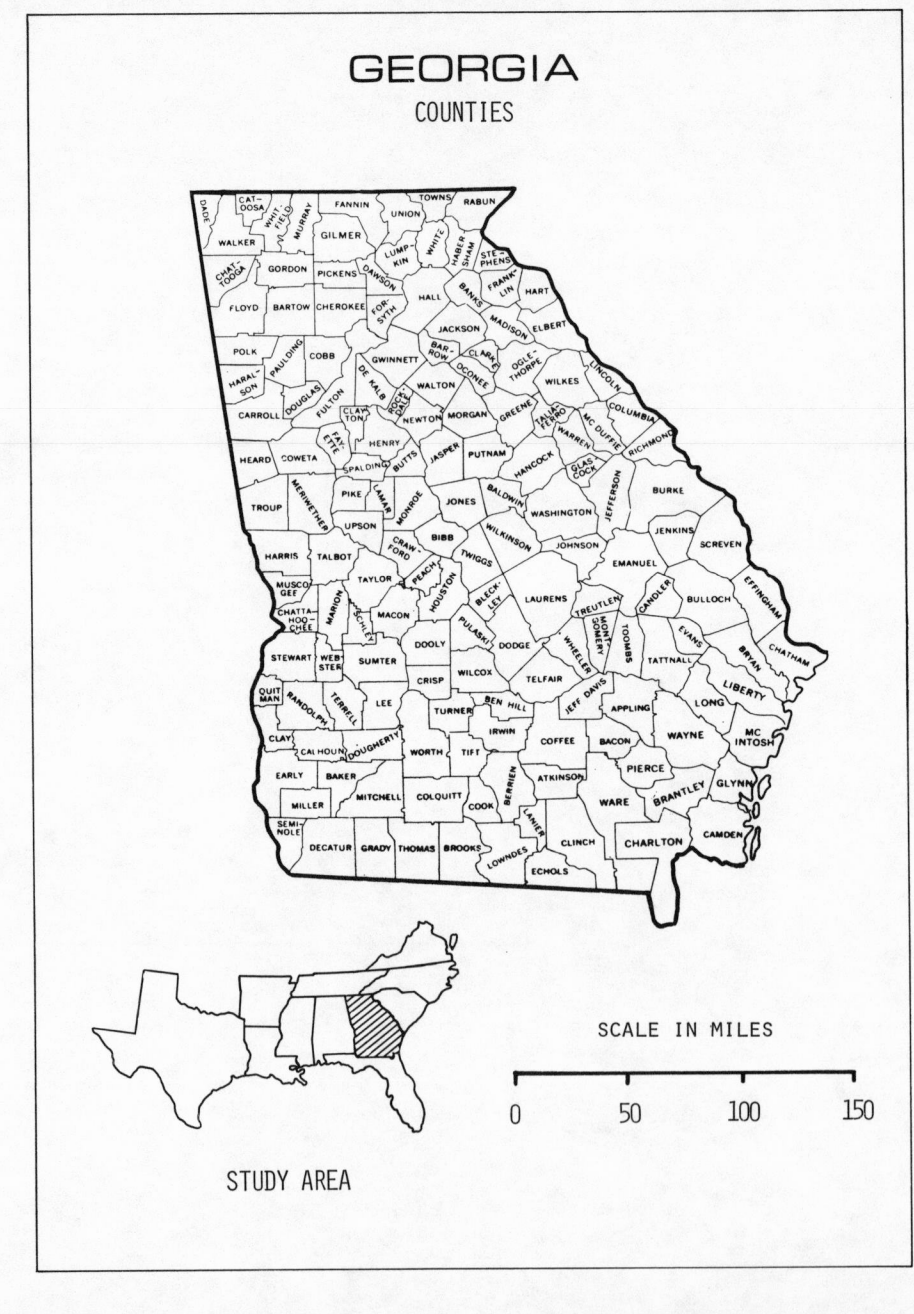

SCALE IN MILES

0   50   100   150

STUDY AREA

GEORGIA

County-unit votes rather than popular votes decided primary elections in Georgia prior to 1962. This system, which grossly discriminated against the metropolitan counties, assigned unit votes to each county and stipulated that the candidate in a primary election who carried a county won that county's unit votes. The 121 least populous counties cast 2 unit votes each, the 8 largest counties cast 6 each, and the 30 intermediate counties had 4 votes each. Thus the 121 predominantly rural counties, containing less than one-third of the people in 1960, cast a majority of the unit votes. Since black Georgians voted more freely in the cities than in the countryside, the county-unit system effectively limited the political influence of both urbanites and blacks. The Georgia Constitution also contained provisions for a literacy test, but this requirement was not widely enforced on the county level. Federal court decisions abrogated the county-unit system in 1962, and the literacy requirements fell victim to the Civil Rights Act of 1965.

Black voter registration in Georgia increased from approximately 140,000 in 1950 to an estimated 180,000 in 1960 and more than doubled to around 395,000 in 1970. In 1960 approximately 29 percent of potential black voters were registered, comprising 15 percent of all registered voters; in 1970 some 57 percent of voting-age blacks were on the registration lists, representing almost 20 percent of the total number of registered voters.

The following table summarizes presidential voting results in Georgia. Turnout figures are given both in total number of votes cast and in percentage of citizens of voting age casting ballots.

The pages below include 7 gubernatorial and 3 senatorial Democratic primaries and 2 constitutional amendment elections. In the gubernatorial primaries of 1950 and 1954, Herman E. Talmadge and Marvin Griffin received a majority of the county-unit ballots although winning only pluralities in the popular vote. There were two senatorial primaries on both August 8 and August 29, 1972. One was for the unexpired term of Richard B. Russell, who died in 1971, and the other was for a full six-year term, but the candidates were the same in each race. The first primary returns included here are for the unexpired term; the second primary returns are for the full term.

Gubernatorial Primaries

1. June 28, 1950: Herman E. Talmadge 287,637 (49.3%), Melvin E. Thompson 279,137 (47.9%), other 3 candidates 16,238 (2.8%). Total vote was 583,012; turnout of voting-age citizens was 26.8%.
2. September 8, 1954: Charlie Gowen 73,809 (11.4%), S. Marvin Griffin 234,681 (36.3%), Fred Hand 78,125 (12.1%), Tom Linder 87,240 (13.5%), Melvin E. Thompson 162,457 (25.1%), other 4 candidates 10,364 (1.6%). Total vote was 646,676; turnout was 28.5%.
* (September 10, 1958: S. Ernest Vandiver won 80.5% against 2 opponents. Total vote was 620,409; turnout was 26.2%.)
3. September 12, 1962: S. Marvin Griffin 332,746 (39.0%), Carl E. Sanders 494,978 (58.1%), other 3 candidates 24,774 (2.9%).

Total vote was 852,498; turnout was 34.6%.

4. September 14, 1966: Ellis Arnall 231,480 (29.4%), Garland T. Byrd 39,994 (5.1%), Jimmy Carter 164,562 (20.9%), James H. Gray 152,973 (19.4%), Lester G. Maddox 185,672 (23.5%), one other candidate 13,271 (1.7%). Total vote was 787,952; turnout was 30.6%.

5. September 28, 1966: Ellis Arnall 373,004 (45.7%), Lester G. Maddox 443,005 (54.3%). Total vote was 816,009; turnout was 31.7%.

6. September 9, 1970: Jimmy Carter 388,280 (48.6%), C. B. King 70,424 (8.8%), Carl E. Sanders 301,657 (37.8%), J. B. Stoner 17,663 (2.2%), other 5 candidates 20,475 (2.6%). Total vote was 798,499; turnout was 29.7%.

7. September 23, 1970: Jimmy Carter 506,462 (59.4%), Carl E. Sanders 345,906 (40.6%). Total vote was 852,368; turnout was 31.7%.

Senatorial Primaries

* (June 25, 1950: Walter F. George won 82.5% against 2 opponents. Total vote was 569,624.)

* (September 8, 1954: Richard B. Russell unopposed.)

* (September 12, 1956: Herman E. Talmadge won 80.3% against 1 opponent. Total vote was 620,479.)

* (September 14, 1960: Richard B. Russell unopposed.)

* (September 12, 1962: Herman E. Talmadge won 88.0% against 1 opponent. Total vote was 765,446.)

* (September 14, 1966: Richard B. Russell won 90.6% against 1 opponent. Total vote

was 658,131.)

1. September 11, 1968: Maynard H. Jackson, Jr., 207,171 (22.9%), Herman E. Talmadge 697,915 (77.1%). Total vote was 905,086.

2. August 8, 1972: David H. Gambrell 258,216 (34.3%), Sam Nunn 170,689 (22.7%) J. B. Stoner 38,261 (5.1%), S. Ernest Vandiver 151,908 (20.2%), Hosea Williams 45,613 (6.1%), other 10 candidates 87,520 (11.6%). Total vote was 752,207.

3. August 29, 1972: David H. Gambrell 283,414 (45.9%), Sam Nunn 334,670 (54.1%) Total vote was 618,084.

Special Elections

1. November 4, 1952: County-unit amendment making the county-unit system a constitutional requirement for the nomination of candidates. For 279,882 (47.5%), Against 309,170 (52.5%). Total vote was 589,052.

2. November 2, 1954: Private school amendment permitting the legislature to abolish the public schools and replace them with private schools in order to avoid desegregation. For 210,478 (53.7%) Against 181,157 (46.3%). Total vote was 391,635.

RETURNS FROM PRESIDENTIAL ELECTIONS

Year	Turnout		Partisan Vote*
1948	418,844	(20.0%)[+]	Democrat 60.8%, Dixiecrat 20.3%, Republican 18.3%
1952	655,785	(29.5%)	Democrat 69.7%, Republican 30.3%
1956	669,655	(28.9%)	Democrat 66.4%, Republican 33.3%
1960	733,349	(30.4%)	Democrat 62.5%, Republican 37.4%
1964	1,139,335	(45.2%)	Republican 54.1%, Democrat 45.9%
1968	1,250,266	(47.5%)	American Independent 42.8%, Republican 30.4%, Democrat 26.7%
1972	1,174,772	(38.5%)	Republican 75.0%, Democrat 24.6%

*Totals do not necessarily equal 100%, since minor party percentages are excluded.

[+]Percentage of citizens of voting age who voted is calculated on the basis of a straight-line interpolation of citizen population between census years.

COUNTY	DEMOC. GOVERNOR 1950 *						DEMOC. GOVERNOR 1954									
	TALMADGE		THOMPSON		OTHER		GOWEN		GRIFFIN		HAND		LINDER		THOMPSON	
	#	%	#	%	#	%	#	%	#	%	#	%	#	%	#	%
APPLING	1726	53.1	1500	46.1	27	.8*	130	3.7	960	27.5	62	1.8	1077	30.9	1257	36.1
ATKINSON	1026	48.8	1026	48.8	50	2.4*	41	2.1	621	31.1	33	1.7	558	28.0	743	37.2
BACON	1797	59.4	1189	39.3	37	1.2*	22	1.0	800	35.5	81	3.6	760	33.7	593	26.3
BAKER	541	54.3	412	41.3	44	4.4*	8	.7	606	53.6	133	11.8	136	12.0	247	21.9
BALDWIN	1871	54.4	1529	44.4	41	1.2*	327	7.9	1860	44.9	226	5.5	299	7.2	1429	34.5
BANKS	1030	62.3	607	36.7	17	1.0*	15	.8	891	44.8	28	1.4	487	24.5	569	28.6
BARROW	1592	51.4	1462	47.2	41	1.3*	156	5.7	1270	46.1	218	7.9	301	10.9	811	29.4
BARTON	2377	49.8	2330	48.8	64	1.3*	362	6.9	2155	40.9	522	9.9	826	15.7	1409	26.7
BEN HILL	1183	41.9	1479	52.4	160	5.7*	160	5.5	1107	38.2	221	7.6	413	14.2	999	34.4
BERRIEN	1175	45.1	1389	53.3	44	1.7*	23	1.0	759	32.1	117	4.9	564	23.8	902	38.1
BIBB	6219	38.4	9633	59.5	342	2.1*	3051	17.8	6765	39.4	571	3.3	859	5.0	5935	34.5
BLECKLEY	1369	64.8	717	33.9	27	1.3*	160	6.0	1342	50.6	36	1.4	597	22.5	517	19.5
BRANTLEY	733	57.0	534	41.6	18	1.4*	49	2.8	511	29.5	34	2.0	443	25.6	694	40.1
BROOKS	1338	44.2	1631	53.9	58	1.9*	96	3.1	1108	36.2	364	11.9	721	23.6	769	25.1
BRYAN	1094	61.7	665	37.5	13	.7*	48	3.2	678	44.9	16	1.1	73	4.8	696	46.1
BULLOCH	2841	54.9	2178	42.1	154	3.0*	346	7.0	2243	45.5	217	4.4	580	11.8	1545	31.3
BURKE	1023	58.5	699	39.9	28	1.6*	224	8.9	1214	48.2	110	4.4	210	8.3	759	30.2
BUTTS	1268	54.0	1023	43.6	57	2.4*	98	4.6	926	43.5	112	5.3	375	17.6	617	29.0
CALHOUN	746	60.1	449	36.2	47	3.8*	22	1.4	767	50.4	268	17.6	140	9.2	326	21.4
CAMDEN	950	60.4	586	37.3	36	2.3*	289	15.7	501	27.2	26	1.4	245	13.3	781	42.4
CHANDLER	984	57.7	664	38.9	57	3.3*	30	1.6	764	40.9	54	2.9	282	15.1	736	39.4
CARROLL	2571	49.9	2518	48.9	61	1.2*	446	7.7	2350	40.7	528	9.1	847	14.7	1606	27.8
CATOOSA	1291	58.8	853	38.9	51	2.3*	45	1.7	1256	48.8	68	2.6	257	10.0	948	36.8
CHARLTON	762	61.0	425	34.0	62	5.0*	57	4.5	474	37.4	44	3.5	504	39.7	190	15.0
CHATHAM	15652	62.1	8949	35.5	617	2.4*	4999	20.5	10469	42.9	1842	7.5	882	3.6	6214	25.5
CHATTAHOO	158	76.7	40	19.4	8	3.9*	10	5.3	137	72.1	2	1.1	21	11.1	20	10.5
CHATTOOGA	2572	49.8	2389	46.2	205	4.0*	287	6.0	1733	36.4	157	3.3	966	20.3	1619	34.0
CHEROKEE	1830	52.4	1537	44.0	123	3.5*	217	5.7	1744	46.1	324	8.6	642	17.0	854	22.6
CLARKE	2162	36.2	3237	54.2	569	9.5*	832	15.1	1172	21.3	1611	29.3	373	6.8	1511	27.5
CLAY	535	62.9	271	31.9	44	5.2*	19	2.5	355	47.0	67	8.9	58	7.7	256	33.9
CLAYTON	2152	56.0	1608	41.8	84	2.2*	516	11.2	2278	49.5	871	18.9	415	9.0	521	11.3
CLINCH	663	39.6	987	58.9	26	1.6*	17	1.3	144	10.6	58	4.3	374	27.6	760	56.2
COBB	4843	44.1	5936	54.0	207	1.9*	2153	14.9	6051	41.9	2957	20.5	1193	8.3	2075	14.4
COFFEE	2618	54.6	2074	43.2	105	2.2*	141	2.6	1527	28.3	117	2.2	1862	34.4	1758	32.5
COLQUITT	3030	54.8	2259	40.8	245	4.4*	172	2.9	2352	39.3	1203	20.1	1024	17.1	1227	20.5
COLUMBIA	877	75.5	269	23.1	16	1.4*	160	10.2	482	30.8	16	1.0	97	6.2	809	51.7
COOK	1101	49.9	1043	47.3	62	2.8*	64	2.6	763	31.5	147	6.1	452	18.7	995	41.1
COWETA	1733	37.4	2733	59.0	166	3.6*	765	14.0	1833	33.6	813	14.9	572	10.5	1465	26.9
CRAWFORD	724	64.5	390	34.8	8	.7*	16	1.3	754	63.4	25	2.1	129	10.8	266	22.4
CRISP	1537	48.1	1482	46.4	178	5.6*	323	8.8	1128	30.8	269	7.3	959	26.2	986	26.9
DADE	732	55.5	565	42.9	21	1.6*	4	.3	441	31.6	5	.4	480	34.4	467	33.4
DAWSON	855	57.8	604	40.9	19	1.3*	12	1.0	503	43.9	18	1.6	187	16.3	425	37.1
DECATUR	2192	54.3	1476	36.6	370	9.2*	35	.8	3321	76.6	354	8.2	356	8.2	270	6.2
DEKALB	8205	33.2	15714	63.6	782	3.2*	9650	28.4	8401	24.8	9703	28.6	2517	7.4	3653	10.8
DODGE	3307	64.4	1748	34.0	83	1.6*	240	4.3	2101	37.9	40	.7	944	17.0	2212	39.9
DOOLEY	1121	49.3	1091	47.9	64	2.8*	182	9.1	951	47.4	96	4.8	294	14.6	484	24.1

	DEMOC. GOVERNOR 1950			DEMOC. GOVERNOR 1954				
COUNTY	TALMADGE # %	THOMPSON # %	OTHER # %*	GOWEN # %	GRIFFIN # %	HAND # %	LINDER # %	THOMPSON # %
DOUGHERTY	2401 49.0	2378 48.5	123 2.5*	876 11.7	2805 37.6	1565 21.0	331 4.4	1888 25.3
DOUGLAS	1257 51.7	1138 46.8	35 1.4*	209 7.7	1382 50.6	275 10.1	201 7.4	665 24.3
EARLY	1290 54.7	998 42.3	72 3.1*	27 1.3	909 42.4	482 22.5	226 10.5	499 23.3
ECHOLS	528 75.1	168 23.9	7 1.0*	2 .3	124 17.8	5 .7	189 27.2	376 54.0
EFFINGHAM	1076 66.5	500 30.9	43 2.7*	53 3.1	754 43.7	40 2.3	307 17.8	570 33.1
ELBERT	2016 51.9	1754 45.1	117 3.0*	148 3.7	1729 43.6	284 7.2	686 17.3	1123 28.3
EMANUEL	2306 60.7	1323 34.8	173 4.6*	274 6.7	959 23.4	404 9.9	1205 29.4	1257 30.7
EVANS	1033 54.4	837 44.1	28 1.5*	110 5.3	1078 52.1	41 2.0	267 12.9	573 27.7
FANNIN	1169 63.9	615 33.6	46 2.5*	5 .4	188 15.3	53 4.3	92 7.5	894 72.6
FAYETTE	1112 59.9	724 39.0	20 1.1*	35 1.8	1098 57.3	56 2.9	68 3.6	658 34.4
FLOYD	7493 54.9	5509 40.3	658 4.8*	1571 14.7	4011 37.5	1073 10.0	1132 10.6	2900 27.1
FORSYTHE	1216 54.8	968 43.6	36 1.6*	39 1.8	913 41.0	47 2.1	596 26.8	630 28.3
FRANKLIN	1978 53.7	1644 44.6	64 1.7*	19 .5	1830 50.9	160 4.4	554 15.4	1034 28.7
FULTON	21318 32.6	42208 64.5	1959 3.0*	15746 21.4	19685 26.8	18546 25.2	4529 6.2	14963 20.4
GILMER	1240 55.1	1003 44.6	6 .3*	15 .7	683 29.7	33 1.4	137 6.0	1432 62.3
GLASCOCK	588 77.5	121 15.9	50 6.6*	12 1.4	570 65.9	8 .9	222 25.7	53 6.1
GLYNN	1710 30.2	3869 68.2	92 1.6*	4190 73.5	563 9.9	78 1.4	217 3.8	653 11.5
GORDON	1951 50.0	1844 47.3	106 2.7*	132 3.8	1718 49.6	109 3.1	377 10.9	1126 32.5
GRADY	1874 50.3	1639 44.0	216 5.8*	58 1.6	893 24.7	1379 38.1	697 19.2	594 16.4
GREENE	1300 49.1	1331 50.2	18 .7*	242 7.8	1279 41.1	208 6.7	222 7.1	1160 37.3
GWINNETT	3027 47.9	3168 50.1	125 2.0*	450 7.1	2599 41.0	469 7.4	1122 17.7	1701 26.8
HABERSHAM	1570 43.5	1920 53.2	117 3.2*	246 6.9	1511 42.2	208 5.8	657 18.4	957 26.7
HALL	3700 44.3	4435 53.2	208 2.5*	895 10.7	2516 30.0	538 6.4	2195 26.1	2250 26.8
HANCOCK	651 53.8	534 44.1	26 2.1*	142 10.5	647 48.0	55 4.1	177 13.1	328 24.3
HARALSON	1788 55.3	1354 41.9	93 2.9*	154 4.6	1284 38.7	249 7.5	917 27.6	713 21.5
HARRIS	955 47.7	1029 51.4	17 .8*	156 7.6	616 30.0	712 34.6	319 15.5	253 12.3
HART	2204 64.2	1161 33.8	69 2.0*	48 1.4	1890 54.9	442 12.8	576 16.7	488 14.2
HEARD	954 55.6	744 43.3	19 1.1*	28 2.0	569 40.4	77 5.5	264 18.8	469 33.3
HENRY	1973 58.3	1351 39.9	63 1.9*	331 8.9	1696 45.8	314 8.5	453 12.2	908 24.5
HOUSTON	1504 51.9	1366 47.1	30 1.0*	150 4.6	1548 47.2	260 7.9	285 8.7	1037 31.6
IRWIN	1414 51.8	1226 44.9	91 3.3*	39 1.3	1434 47.7	180 6.0	425 14.1	930 30.9
JACKSON	1945 46.0	2212 52.3	69 1.6*	199 4.6	1579 36.7	211 4.9	632 14.7	1682 39.1
JASPER	745 51.7	678 47.0	19 1.3*	84 5.3	816 51.9	127 8.1	56 3.6	489 31.1
JEFF DAVIS	949 63.0	504 33.4	54 3.6*	19 .7	430 16.0	46 1.7	1962 73.1	227 8.5
JEFFERSON	1536 68.5	654 29.2	51 2.3*	355 14.1	949 37.6	178 7.0	643 25.5	401 15.9
JENKINS	861 41.9	1146 55.7	49 2.4*	75 3.0	433 17.4	49 2.0	317 12.8	1612 64.8
JOHNSON	1304 66.7	583 29.8	67 3.4*	104 3.7	894 31.8	79 2.8	1328 47.2	409 14.5
JONES	984 53.6	747 40.7	105 5.7*	65 3.7	944 53.9	24 1.4	104 5.9	613 35.0
LAMAR	950 50.3	907 48.1	30 1.6*	177 7.3	1107 45.4	274 11.2	203 8.3	675 27.7
LANIER	378 30.2	844 67.5	29 2.3*	5 .5	112 11.2	25 2.5	233 23.4	621 62.3
LAURENS	3442 59.7	2097 36.4	222 3.9*	687 8.5	2068 25.5	182 2.2	3237 40.0	1924 23.8
LEE	526 80.4	119 18.2	9 1.4*	10 1.2	441 54.1	203 24.9	120 14.7	41 5.0
LIBERTY	771 38.5	1206 60.1	28 1.4*	192 8.9	550 25.6	26 1.2	136 6.3	1248 58.0
LINCOLN	907 68.2	345 26.0	77 5.8*	78 6.0	818 62.5	45 3.4	190 14.5	178 13.6
LONG	765 49.4	764 49.3	21 1.4*	22 1.7	214 16.3	6 .5	89 6.8	980 74.8
LOWNDES	1657 30.7	3668 67.9	77 1.4*	64 1.3	567 11.2	231 4.5	504 9.9	3713 73.1

COUNTY	TALMADGE #	%	THOMPSON #	%	OTHER #	%*	GOWEN #	%	GRIFFIN #	%	HAND #	%	LINDER #	%	THOMPSON #	%
LUMPKIN	1037	51.0	960	47.2	38	1.9*	66	3.2	677	32.3	52	2.5	546	26.1	752	35.9
MACON	1273	66.2	615	32.0	35	1.8*	153	6.4	1225	50.9	158	6.6	346	14.4	523	21.7
MADISON	1372	55.9	1035	42.2	48	2.0*	57	2.3	1115	45.4	112	4.6	399	16.2	775	31.5
MARION	508	63.9	276	34.7	11	1.4*	36	3.9	519	56.7	22	2.4	180	19.7	159	17.4
MCDUFFIE	1272	65.0	626	32.0	59	3.0*	257	12.8	1007	50.1	100	5.0	306	15.2	338	16.8
MCINTOSH	534	52.5	460	45.2	24	2.4*	297	21.2	367	26.2	26	1.9	145	10.4	564	40.3
MERIWETHR	1951	49.9	1915	49.0	41	1.0*	129	2.9	1642	37.1	1208	27.3	404	9.1	1041	23.5
MILLER	1101	63.2	586	33.7	54	3.1*	8	.4	850	46.7	100	5.5	760	41.8	101	5.6
MITCHELL	1799	57.4	1242	39.6	93	3.0*	42	1.0	242	5.6	3686	84.8	184	4.2	194	4.5
MONROE	1476	55.7	1093	41.2	81	3.1*	192	8.0	1121	46.9	186	7.8	216	9.0	674	28.2
MONTGOMRY	1349	74.3	436	24.0	31	1.7*	24	1.1	401	18.0	66	3.0	1211	54.4	526	23.6
MORGAN	1088	53.7	925	45.7	12	.6*	105	4.9	1061	50.0	210	9.9	418	19.7	329	15.5
MURRAY	992	57.7	709	41.2	18	1.0*	42	2.0	833	40.2	60	2.9	205	9.9	932	45.0
MUSCOGEE	4895	47.0	5221	50.1	295	2.8*	3530	29.9	5097	43.2	897	7.6	331	2.8	1946	16.5
NEWTON	1441	47.5	1534	50.5	60	2.0*	272	8.4	1528	47.3	431	13.3	331	10.2	669	20.7
OCONEE	934	59.4	601	38.2	38	2.4*	149	9.4	630	39.7	144	9.1	270	17.0	393	24.8
OGLETHRPE	1088	63.7	592	34.7	28	1.6*	31	1.8	985	56.0	142	8.1	224	12.7	377	21.4
PAULDING	1311	51.3	1204	47.1	43	1.7*	107	3.4	1654	53.1	94	3.0	271	8.7	989	31.7
PEACH	842	50.2	807	48.1	29	1.7*	188	8.9	1111	52.9	126	6.0	133	6.3	543	25.8
PICKENS	835	46.1	923	51.0	52	2.9*	48	2.4	972	49.4	59	3.0	153	7.8	736	37.4
PIERCE	1399	53.7	1179	45.2	29	1.1*	94	3.6	1098	42.6	123	4.8	448	17.4	814	31.6
PIKE	900	57.2	613	38.9	61	3.9*	69	4.6	710	47.6	154	10.3	256	17.1	304	20.4
POLK	2350	45.8	2542	49.5	244	4.8*	877	15.7	1688	30.1	879	15.7	796	14.2	1362	24.3
PULASKI	771	48.5	796	50.0	24	1.5*	57	2.9	842	43.3	25	1.3	221	11.4	798	41.1
PUTNAM	798	50.5	757	47.9	24	1.5*	74	4.4	825	49.0	228	13.5	71	4.2	487	28.9
QUITMAN	389	61.7	234	37.1	7	1.1*	12	2.0	126	20.8	101	16.6	310	51.1	58	9.6
RABUN	1029	55.7	767	41.5	53	2.9*	89	4.5	851	42.9	96	4.8	365	18.4	581	29.3
RANDOLPH	969	54.5	738	41.5	72	4.0*	93	4.1	930	41.3	306	13.6	469	20.8	456	20.2
RICHMOND	6483	54.7	4970	41.9	395	3.3*	5316	34.7	5385	35.2	724	4.7	745	4.9	3129	20.5
ROCKDALE	898	50.1	841	46.9	54	3.0*	167	8.2	919	44.9	180	8.8	264	12.9	519	25.3
SCHLEY	505	58.0	362	41.6	4	.5*	41	5.0	366	44.2	54	6.5	140	16.9	227	27.4
SCREVEN	1151	54.8	922	43.9	26	1.2*	57	2.7	929	44.5	36	1.7	183	8.8	883	42.3
SEMINOLE	1186	74.8	377	23.8	22	1.4*	19	1.0	852	46.1	138	7.5	531	28.7	308	16.7
SPALDING	2315	36.0	3765	58.5	359	5.6*	850	12.2	3599	51.8	802	11.5	514	7.4	1179	17.0
STEPHENS	1311	42.8	1601	52.3	152	5.0*	399	10.9	1420	38.6	321	8.7	672	18.3	862	23.5
STEWART	989	66.6	444	29.9	51	3.4*	75	4.5	1004	60.4	81	4.9	277	16.7	224	13.5
SUMTER	1772	50.1	1665	47.0	102	2.9*	157	3.9	1451	36.0	583	14.5	829	20.6	1013	25.1
TALBOT	650	58.3	456	40.9	9	.8*	40	4.2	492	51.7	68	7.2	84	8.8	267	28.1
TALIAFERO	358	32.8	727	66.6	7	.6*	28	2.5	421	37.5	53	4.7	105	9.3	516	45.9
TATTNALL	2167	52.8	1888	46.0	47	1.1*	41	.9	2054	43.6	44	.9	641	13.6	1926	40.9
TAYLOR	1138	56.6	847	42.2	24	1.2*	74	3.4	1107	50.8	68	3.1	355	16.3	574	26.4
TELFAIR	2898	90.5	278	8.7	26	.8*	46	1.3	2414	67.9	63	1.8	618	17.4	415	11.7
TERRELL	1277	64.5	618	31.2	84	4.2*	51	2.6	1180	59.8	210	10.6	204	10.3	328	16.6
THOMAS	2544	41.5	3434	56.0	153	2.5*	362	5.4	1151	17.2	1992	29.8	989	14.8	2195	32.8
TIFT	2041	48.8	1881	45.0	259	6.2*	301	6.5	2144	46.6	432	9.4	566	12.3	1162	25.2
TOOMBS	1802	59.5	1165	38.4	64	2.1*	73	1.9	941	25.0	273	7.3	1528	40.6	946	25.2

	DEMOC. GOVERNOR 1950					DEMOC. GOVERNOR 1954									
COUNTY	TALMADGE #	%	THOMPSON #	%	OTHER #	%*	GOWEN #	%	GRIFFIN #	%	HAND #	%	LINDER #	%	THOMPSON #	%
TOWNS	534	66.3	266	33.0	6	.7*	12	.9	744	58.1	35	2.7	124	9.7	366	28.6
TREUTLEN	1387	80.3	323	18.7	17	1.0*	48	2.7	90	5.1	49	2.8	1349	76.6	226	12.8
TROUP	2268	38.8	3384	57.9	193	3.3*	459	6.2	1778	24.1	3300	44.8	270	3.7	1562	21.2
TURNER	1375	59.0	825	35.4	131	5.6*	36	1.7	1124	52.3	139	6.5	525	24.4	327	15.2
TWIGGS	849	70.2	292	24.2	68	5.6*	45	2.9	871	56.4	27	1.7	373	24.2	227	14.7
UNION	1053	56.6	797	42.9	9	.5*	11	.6	668	38.6	34	2.0	407	23.5	611	35.3
UPSON	2086	42.5	2694	54.8	134	2.7*	392	7.9	1755	35.6	954	19.3	561	11.4	1273	25.8
WALKER	3146	60.5	1920	36.9	134	2.6*	168	3.3	2767	55.1	173	3.4	757	15.1	1154	23.0
WALTON	2064	54.7	1660	44.0	51	1.4*	178	4.7	2078	54.3	324	8.5	356	9.3	890	23.3
WARE	2338	44.2	2821	53.4	127	2.4*	378	6.4	2152	36.7	567	9.7	919	15.7	1851	31.5
WARREN	697	76.4	205	22.5	10	1.1*	94	9.2	471	45.9	149	14.5	260	25.3	53	5.2
WASHINGTON	1923	60.9	1141	36.1	93	2.9*	260	8.4	1122	36.2	191	6.2	844	27.2	685	22.1
WAYNE	1643	51.2	1538	47.9	31	1.0*	127	4.0	750	23.5	119	3.7	1047	32.9	1143	35.9
WEBSTER	480	75.2	141	22.1	17	2.7*	18	3.1	337	57.7	21	3.6	148	25.3	60	10.3
WHEELER	1055	65.5	518	32.2	38	2.4*	48	2.3	520	24.9	74	3.5	783	37.6	660	31.7
WHITE	1086	52.4	927	44.7	60	2.9*	30	1.2	790	32.8	182	7.6	723	30.0	684	28.4
WHITFIELD	2401	43.9	2870	52.5	199	3.6*	331	4.8	3096	45.3	486	7.1	576	8.4	2343	34.3
WILCOX	1601	57.3	1148	41.1	44	1.6*	59	2.3	875	34.7	68	2.7	754	29.9	767	30.4
WILKES	1089	54.1	846	42.0	79	3.9*	248	13.2	874	46.4	210	11.2	273	14.5	278	14.8
WILKINSON	1693	64.1	828	31.4	119	4.5*	58	2.8	1017	49.5	23	1.1	351	17.1	607	29.5
WORTH	1259	51.3	1133	46.1	64	2.6*	57	2.0	895	31.4	247	8.7	876	30.7	776	27.2
						*										
TOTALS	287637		279137		16238	*	73809		234681		78125		87240		162457	
% OF VOTE	49.3		47.9		2.8	*	11.6		36.9		12.3		13.7		25.5	

GEOGRAPHIC CLASS

						*										
LOWLANDS	86488	56.	64700	42.	3941	3.*	15028	9.	59999	35.	10532	6.	34014	20.	50324	30.
BLACK BELT	79853	53.	68036	45.	4165	3.*	19266	11.	68583	40.	18761	11.	20237	12.	42673	25.
PIEDMONT	85583	41.	116088	56.	6026	3.*	35162	15.	78814	34.	44530	19.	23226	10.	47762	21.
MOUNTAIN	35713	52.	30313	44.	2106	3.*	4353	6.	27285	40.	4302	6.	9763	14.	21698	32.

DEMOGRAPHIC CLASS

						*										
METRO	65173	41.	89073	56.	4513	3.*	43168	24.	58607	32.	33848	18.	10194	6.	37728	21.
TOWN	28442	43.	35163	53.	2396	4.*	11163	16.	23719	34.	11750	17.	5822	8.	17002	24.
RURAL	194022	54.	154901	43.	9329	3.*	19478	5.	152355	40.	32527	8.	71224	19.	107727	28.

COUNTY	GRIFFIN #	%	SANDERS #	%	OTHER #	%*	ARNALL #	%	BYRD #	%	CARTER #	%	GRAY #	%	MADDOX #	%
APPLING	1673	46.9	1791	50.2	102	2.9*	996	26.8	135	3.6	289	7.8	452	12.2	1839	49.6
ATKINSON	1189	55.5	903	42.2	49	2.3*	279	16.6	228	13.6	119	7.1	481	28.7	570	34.0
BACON	1393	52.3	1223	45.9	49	1.8*	304	14.1	64	3.0	151	7.0	330	15.3	1306	60.6
BAKER	938	83.8	175	15.6	6	.5*	300	24.4	20	1.6	44	3.6	751	61.2	113	9.2
BALDWIN	2435	47.7	2584	50.6	91	1.8*	1462	28.8	342	6.7	987	19.5	1172	23.1	1107	21.8
BANKS	973	45.6	1133	53.1	29	1.4*	259	15.4	92	5.5	268	15.9	330	19.6	734	43.6
BARROW	2073	45.6	2302	50.6	176	3.9*	534	13.8	138	3.6	1667	43.1	325	8.4	1201	31.1
BARTON	2687	46.0	3012	51.6	138	2.4*	1123	21.7	205	4.0	1779	34.4	676	13.1	1394	26.9
BEN HILL	1219	41.5	1647	56.1	70	2.4*	658	22.5	122	4.2	555	19.0	1142	39.1	445	15.2
BERRIEN	1716	53.7	1406	44.0	72	2.3*	375	14.6	113	4.4	225	8.8	1036	40.4	813	31.7
BIBB	12953	38.6	19882	59.2	763	2.3*	8376	33.1	2258	8.9	4835	19.1	5489	21.7	4385	17.3
BLECKLEY	1629	58.8	1094	39.5	47	1.7*	263	9.9	353	13.2	261	9.8	687	25.7	1106	41.4
BRANTLEY	1401	70.4	503	25.3	86	4.3*	340	19.2	83	4.7	73	4.1	118	6.7	1159	65.4
BROOKS	1469	53.9	1193	43.7	65	2.4*	579	19.6	116	3.9	273	9.2	1039	35.1	954	32.2
BRYAN	915	51.1	844	47.1	32	1.8*	401	27.0	166	11.2	117	7.9	222	14.9	581	39.1
BULLOCH	2600	41.5	3614	57.7	53	.8*	1714	27.0	491	7.7	957	15.1	742	11.7	2435	38.4
BURKE	1727	55.4	1360	43.6	31	1.0*	635	27.5	48	2.1	273	11.8	795	34.4	557	24.1
BUTTS	1221	46.0	1316	49.6	117	4.4*	478	24.8	72	3.7	410	21.3	342	17.7	627	32.5
CALHOUN	764	67.0	365	32.0	11	1.0*	217	15.6	30	2.2	161	11.6	951	68.5	29	2.1
CAMDEN	1198	47.8	1206	48.1	103	4.1*	881	36.9	109	4.6	170	7.1	331	13.8	899	37.6
CHANDLER	1053	50.6	996	47.9	30	1.4*	279	18.0	145	9.4	275	17.8	147	9.5	701	45.3
CARROLL	2366	31.5	4827	64.3	315	4.2*	1697	23.2	324	4.4	1683	23.0	1416	19.4	2187	29.9
CATOOSA	1906	51.5	1725	46.6	70	1.9*	1014	27.6	137	3.7	511	13.9	1156	31.5	851	23.2
CHARLTON	1030	60.7	639	37.7	28	1.6*	346	22.8	83	5.5	83	5.5	294	19.4	711	46.9
CHATHAM	11649	33.7	21179	61.3	1730	5.0*	14549	50.0	2716	9.3	3096	10.6	4256	14.6	4462	15.3
CHATTAHOO	232	75.3	68	22.1	8	2.6*	68	27.9	24	9.8	83	34.0	41	16.8	28	11.5
CHATTOOGA	1235	29.3	2894	68.7	83	2.0*	1096	31.2	140	4.0	628	17.9	564	16.0	1087	30.9
CHEROKEE	2911	47.8	2985	49.0	190	3.1*	974	23.4	161	3.9	1070	25.7	533	12.8	1421	34.2
CLARKE	1989	23.0	6442	74.4	227	2.6*	3264	34.7	205	2.2	3722	39.6	914	9.7	1303	13.8
CLAY	396	58.1	276	40.5	9	1.3*	200	30.9	27	4.2	79	12.2	300	46.3	42	6.5
CLAYTON	3778	39.0	5529	57.0	388	4.0*	2040	17.8	452	3.9	3156	27.5	1688	14.7	4124	36.0
CLINCH	1126	63.2	590	33.1	67	3.8*	214	15.8	83	6.1	95	7.0	280	20.6	685	50.5
COBB	7819	31.4	16107	64.8	941	3.8*	5063	22.6	666	3.0	8066	36.0	2463	11.0	6137	27.4
COFFEE	2542	45.0	2940	52.0	167	3.0*	1419	27.9	274	5.4	542	10.7	1709	33.6	1136	22.4
COLQUITT	4469	60.9	2724	37.1	140	1.9*	854	12.4	236	3.4	1552	22.6	2419	35.3	1801	26.2
COLUMBIA	1139	39.9	1662	58.2	55	1.9*	377	17.3	82	3.8	199	9.1	1220	55.9	306	14.0
COOK	1669	56.5	1210	41.0	75	2.5*	422	17.3	158	6.5	268	11.0	1142	46.7	455	18.6
COWETA	1783	32.1	3575	64.4	191	3.4*	3531	51.6	154	2.2	750	11.0	689	10.1	1723	25.2
CRAWFORD	640	50.0	614	48.0	25	2.0*	332	27.9	261	22.0	142	11.9	202	17.0	252	21.2
CRISP	2095	49.1	2028	47.5	145	3.4*	766	18.6	239	5.8	603	14.7	1397	34.0	1107	26.9
DADE	965	66.9	457	31.7	20	1.4*	326	30.2	48	4.4	220	20.4	230	21.3	257	23.8
DAWSON	662	49.0	638	47.3	50	3.7*	211	21.5	62	6.3	176	18.0	216	22.0	315	32.1
DECATUR	4906	87.9	630	11.3	46	.8*	986	20.9	29	.6	517	10.9	2868	60.7	323	6.8
DEKALB	13249	22.3	44536	74.8	1751	2.9*	16331	30.2	1914	3.5	18829	34.8	6180	11.4	10899	20.1
DODGE	3292	55.0	2611	43.6	86	1.4*	728	14.0	429	8.2	813	15.6	1649	31.7	1587	30.5
DOOLEY	1423	55.4	1068	41.6	77	3.0*	431	20.7	188	9.0	340	16.3	585	28.1	540	25.9

| | DEMOC. GOVERNOR 1962 | * | * | DEMOC. GOVERNOR 1966 | | | | |

COUNTY	GRIFFIN # %	SANDERS # %	OTHER # %*	ARNALL # %	BYRD # %	CARTER # %	GRAY # %	MADDOX # %
DOUGHERTY	5865 47.9	6174 50.4	205 1.7*	3203 21.6	147 1.0	939 6.3	10347 69.6	227 1.5
DOUGLAS	1959 47.3	2005 48.4	179 4.3*	712 15.2	116 2.5	1321 28.1	618 13.2	1931 41.1
EARLY	1755 76.7	498 21.8	34 1.5*	365 19.4	26 1.4	135 7.2	1134 60.4	217 11.6
ECHOLS	461 66.0	236 33.8	2 .3*	71 10.0	55 7.7	76 10.7	206 29.0	303 42.6
EFFINGHAM	1432 65.2	721 32.8	43 2.0*	389 18.6	360 17.2	228 10.9	337 16.1	782 37.3
ELBERT	1799 39.8	2520 55.8	199 4.4*	782 20.6	104 2.7	684 18.0	949 25.0	1282 33.7
EMANUEL	2319 44.6	2796 53.8	84 1.6*	1129 24.5	298 6.5	739 16.0	670 14.5	1780 38.6
EVANS	860 44.6	1038 53.8	30 1.6*	518 23.3	193 8.7	429 19.3	352 15.8	735 33.0
FANNIN	771 42.5	1036 57.0	9 .5*	762 54.8	26 1.9	136 9.8	334 24.0	133 9.6
FAYETTE	926 44.4	1067 51.2	93 4.5*	307 16.2	56 3.0	440 23.2	335 17.7	758 40.0
FLOYD	4359 31.7	8995 65.4	408 3.0*	2733 21.9	1134 9.1	4003 32.1	2032 16.3	2566 20.6
FORSYTHE	1572 47.6	1647 49.9	82 2.5*	492 20.5	136 5.7	596 24.8	272 11.3	904 37.7
FRANKLIN	1583 39.0	2377 58.6	95 2.3*	324 13.3	81 3.3	477 19.6	747 30.7	807 33.1
FULTON	27107 22.1	91773 74.7	3915 3.2*	46630 45.8	3295 3.2	23159 22.8	9188 9.0	19505 19.2
GILMER	893 36.0	1562 62.9	28 1.1*	457 28.0	16 1.0	166 10.2	594 36.4	399 24.4
GLASCOCK	773 71.0	157 14.4	159 14.6*	66 9.4	27 3.9	65 9.3	213 30.5	328 46.9
GLYNN	2648 36.5	4474 61.6	137 1.9*	3227 37.3	189 2.2	1414 16.4	1936 22.4	1874 21.7
GORDON	1852 43.0	2359 54.7	100 2.3*	867 25.8	89 2.6	1130 33.6	256 7.6	1020 30.3
GRADY	2034 54.1	1671 44.4	55 1.5*	663 17.4	177 4.6	666 17.5	1602 42.0	703 18.4
GREENE	951 31.2	2032 66.6	66 2.2*	753 34.1	67 3.0	599 27.2	303 13.7	483 21.9
GWINNETT	3992 41.4	4889 50.7	766 7.9*	1777 19.6	362 4.0	2553 28.1	1249 13.8	3138 34.6
HABERSHAM	1540 35.8	2675 62.1	92 2.1*	1212 25.1	143 3.0	1076 22.3	942 19.5	1455 30.1
HALL	4304 38.8	6574 59.2	219 2.0*	4181 37.0	376 3.3	3592 31.8	895 7.9	2266 20.0
HANCOCK	665 47.1	727 51.5	20 1.4*	1440 55.2	97 3.7	148 5.7	449 17.2	477 18.3
HARALSON	2112 51.1	1950 47.1	74 1.8*	544 20.6	140 5.3	541 20.5	313 11.8	1106 41.8
HARRIS	1240 47.9	1271 49.1	76 2.9*	504 25.7	170 8.7	478 24.4	304 15.5	505 25.8
HART	1789 52.4	1571 46.1	51 1.5*	753 20.1	121 3.2	446 11.9	1229 32.8	1193 31.9
HEARD	1221 54.6	963 43.1	52 2.3*	343 27.2	60 4.8	188 14.9	213 16.9	458 36.3
HENRY	1970 38.7	2986 58.6	140 2.7*	1226 24.0	201 3.9	1294 25.3	741 14.5	1650 32.3
HOUSTON	2798 40.1	3922 56.3	251 3.6*	1618 22.8	706 9.9	1910 26.9	1710 24.1	1153 16.2
IRWIN	1366 58.7	934 40.2	26 1.1*	380 16.8	228 10.1	263 11.6	958 42.3	438 19.3
JACKSON	1687 33.1	3306 64.8	111 2.2*	1164 24.8	180 3.8	1277 27.2	694 14.8	1377 29.3
JASPER	884 56.3	651 41.5	35 2.2*	368 24.4	76 5.0	331 21.9	179 11.9	554 36.7
JEFF DAVIS	1287 50.4	1198 46.9	70 2.7*	356 16.2	142 6.5	205 9.3	495 22.5	999 45.5
JEFFERSON	1835 55.7	1418 43.1	40 1.2*	1338 36.8	142 3.9	328 9.0	1116 30.7	712 19.6
JENKINS	1332 57.1	963 41.3	37 1.6*	346 22.9	64 4.2	328 21.7	265 17.5	510 33.7
JOHNSON	1431 62.1	839 36.4	34 1.5*	329 15.5	312 14.7	183 8.6	390 18.4	903 42.7
JONES	1362 58.7	902 38.9	55 2.4*	596 23.7	483 19.2	327 13.0	546 21.7	567 22.5
LAMAR	986 38.4	1514 59.0	65 2.5*	688 32.5	60 2.8	476 22.5	312 14.7	582 27.5
LANIER	878 55.2	681 42.8	31 1.9*	278 22.8	65 5.3	102 8.4	361 29.6	415 34.0
LAURINS	3934 47.2	4194 50.4	201 2.4*	1790 21.4	557 6.7	1205 14.4	2445 29.3	2360 28.2
LEE	718 77.5	191 20.6	18 1.9*	192 15.1	38 3.0	90 7.1	909 71.7	39 3.1
LIBERTY	1294 41.9	1758 57.0	33 1.1*	1793 52.8	277 8.1	302 8.9	299 8.8	728 21.4
LINCOLN	785 62.5	439 35.0	32 2.5*	356 22.4	61 3.8	151 9.5	440 27.6	584 36.7
LONG	1077 82.5	209 16.0	19 1.5*	1188 79.7	23 1.5	27 1.8	57 3.8	195 13.1
LOWNDES	2665 36.0	4523 61.1	215 2.9*	1942 30.4	227 3.6	1197 18.7	1706 26.7	1318 20.6

	DEMOC. GOVERNOR 1962					*	DEMOC. GOVERNOR 1966								

	DEMOC.	GOVERNOR	1962	*	DEMOC.	GOVERNOR	1966

COUNTY	GRIFFIN		SANDERS		OTHER		ARNALL		BYRD		CARTER		GRAY		MADDOX	
	#	%	#	%	#	%*	#	%	#	%	#	%	#	%	#	%
LUMPKIN	792	44.3 -	926	51.8	68	3.8*	360	21.1	62	3.6	655	38.5	208	12.2	418	24.5
MACON	1187	45.3	1374	52.4	59	2.3*	725	30.7	369	15.6	503	21.3	408	17.3	357	15.1
MADISON	1105	42.2	1434	54.7	82	3.1*	608	19.5	91	2.9	606	19.4	726	23.3	1091	34.9
MARION	501	56.6	366	41.4	18	2.0*	197	21.3	207	22.3	258	27.8	104	11.2	161	17.4
MCDUFFIE	1411	49.3	1398	48.8	55	1.9*	747	27.6	144	5.3	353	13.0	779	28.7	687	25.4
MCINTOSH	551	38.1	874	60.5	20	1.4*	921	53.5	100	5.8	126	7.3	172	10.0	402	23.4
MERIWETHR	1957	43.9	2387	53.6	112	2.5*	1472	32.0	330	7.2	721	15.7	946	20.6	1128	24.5
MILLER	1191	79.4	303	20.2	6	.4*	58	4.1	14	1.0	131	9.3	738	52.6	462	32.9
MITCHELL	3042	68.4	1349	30.3	56	1.3*	731	18.6	28	.7	362	9.2	2699	68.5	120	3.0
MONROE	1275	44.6	1515	53.0	68	2.4*	545	22.7	116	4.8	480	20.0	435	18.1	830	34.5
MONTGOMRY	788	46.0	892	52.1	33	1.9*	342	20.6	42	2.5	149	9.0	439	26.4	688	41.4
MORGAN	1150	47.9	1208	50.3	45	1.9*	286	13.0	68	3.1	1049	47.8	239	10.9	553	25.2
MURRAY	1161	47.3	1248	50.8	48	2.0*	597	37.8	117	7.4	371	23.5	119	7.5	374	23.7
MUSCOGEE	7297	34.0	13014	60.7	1138	5.3*	6011	31.5	1771	9.3	4939	25.9	3531	18.5	2815	14.8
NEWTON	1803	41.0	2420	55.0	179	4.1*	961	18.5	211	4.1	2107	40.5	449	8.6	1477	28.4
OCONEE	927	53.5	751	43.4	54	3.1*	328	15.9	73	3.5	636	30.9	374	18.2	648	31.5
OGLETHRPE	1001	59.9	637	38.1	34	2.0*	298	13.4	96	4.3	477	21.5	288	13.0	1061	47.8
PAULDING	2084	52.4	1793	45.1	98	2.5*	915	22.4	100	2.4	711	17.4	627	15.3	1732	42.4
PEACH	1091	43.8	1331	53.5	68	2.7*	1058	34.7	365	12.0	558	18.3	582	19.1	488	16.0
PICKENS	1161	53.7	943	43.6	60	2.8*	547	29.9	64	3.5	400	21.9	246	13.4	573	31.3
PIERCE	1518	55.6	1140	41.7	73	2.7*	655	21.3	168	5.5	208	6.8	112	3.6	1933	62.8
PIKE	833	46.5	898	50.1	61	3.4*	397	26.7	97	6.5	294	19.8	205	13.8	495	33.3
POLK	2320	36.3	3797	59.4	276	4.3*	1264	22.9	169	3.1	1736	31.4	746	13.5	1609	29.1
PULASKI	1655	70.9	648	27.8	32	1.4*	312	14.6	322	15.1	252	11.8	667	31.2	584	27.3
PUTNAM	1015	56.8	728	40.7	44	2.5*	403	22.2	56	3.1	555	30.5	311	17.1	493	27.1
QUITMAN	649	79.9	79	9.7	84	10.3*	251	41.6	23	3.8	191	31.7	112	18.6	26	4.3
RABUN	721	42.9	941	55.9	20	1.2*	493	28.1	28	1.6	316	18.0	569	32.4	350	19.9
RANDOLPH	1134	53.5	953	44.9	34	1.6*	648	28.8	122	5.4	232	10.3	1131	50.2	119	5.3
RICHMOND	6463	27.0	17003	71.0	467	2.0*	9602	46.1	703	3.4	3175	15.2	4515	21.7	2835	13.6
ROCKDALE	1158	39.6	1661	56.7	108	3.7*	690	25.9	107	4.0	697	26.2	338	12.7	832	31.2
SCHLEY	508	55.9	376	41.4	24	2.6*	163	25.1	85	13.1	141	21.7	108	16.6	153	23.5
SCREVEN	1323	49.2	1317	49.0	47	1.7*	776	32.7	119	5.0	491	20.7	298	12.5	692	29.1
SEMINOLE	1489	89.3	166	10.0	13	.8*	318	18.9	42	2.5	122	7.2	840	49.8	365	21.6
SPALDING	2103	28.6	4889	66.5	356	4.8*	1792	23.8	361	4.8	2642	35.1	821	10.9	1905	25.3
STEPHENS	1682	39.8	2463	58.4	76	1.8*	1052	34.4	173	5.7	490	16.0	589	19.3	751	24.6
STEWART	894	67.0	415	31.1	25	1.9*	197	20.1	66	6.7	306	31.2	279	28.5	132	13.5
SUMTER	2243	52.1	1906	44.3	153	3.6*	913	22.9	335	8.4	1346	33.7	748	18.7	652	16.3
TALBOT	558	48.0	586	50.4	19	1.6*	269	28.4	158	16.7	201	21.2	165	17.4	154	16.3
TALIAFERO	401	42.7	535	57.0	3	.3*	522	39.9	63	4.8	105	8.0	236	18.0	382	29.2
TATTNALL	2688	53.0	2319	45.7	62	1.2*	975	23.5	428	10.3	415	10.0	640	15.4	1686	40.7
TAYLOR	1275	57.8	828	37.5	103	4.7*	371	15.5	1427	59.6	146	6.1	192	8.0	259	10.8
TELFAIR	1799	48.9	1835	49.9	46	1.2*	994	24.5	287	7.1	467	11.5	961	23.6	1356	33.4
TERRELL	1499	65.7	730	32.0	52	2.3*	265	12.0	43	2.0	410	18.6	1298	58.9	187	8.5
THOMAS	2710	40.1	3849	56.9	207	3.1*	2062	37.6	113	2.1	973	17.8	1398	25.5	932	17.0
TIFT	2392	44.2	2886	53.3	133	2.5*	970	17.6	262	4.7	1369	24.8	1970	35.6	956	17.3
TOOMBS	1857	44.7	2207	53.1	94	2.3*	579	15.3	216	5.7	798	21.1	580	15.3	1610	42.6

COUNTY	DEMOC. GOVERNOR 1962					DEMOC. GOVERNOR 1966									
	GRIFFIN # %	SANDERS # %	OTHER # %*	ARNALL # %	BYRD # %	CARTER # %	GRAY # %	MADDOX # %
---	---	---	---	---	---	---	---	---
TOWNS	464 50.5	449 48.9	6 .7*	354 40.2	43 4.9	215 24.4	185 21.0	84 9.5
TREUTLEN	249 14.5	1449 84.6	14 .8*	104 6.5	20 1.3	179 11.3	966 60.8	321 20.2
TROUP	2661 29.7	6026 67.4	259 2.9*	1993 30.2	294 4.4	2106 31.9	812 12.3	1405 21.3
TURNER	1310 60.3	775 35.7	86 4.0*	223 11.0	104 5.1	284 14.1	1069 52.9	341 16.9
TWIGGS	884 60.8	532 36.6	38 2.6*	269 21.0	201 15.7	141 11.0	251 19.6	417 32.6
UNION	726 41.9	992 57.2	15 .9*	552 39.5	26 1.9	239 17.1	367 26.3	213 15.2
UPSON	2146 41.3	2945 56.6	109 2.1*	984 22.0	344 7.7	1054 23.6	1143 25.5	950 21.2
WALKER	2866 39.6	4246 58.7	126 1.7*	1537 25.4	201 3.3	1941 32.1	1206 19.9	1171 19.3
WALTON	2027 45.7	2143 48.3	266 6.0*	522 12.7	151 3.7	1482 36.1	311 7.6	1637 39.9
WARE	3162 39.0	4570 56.3	381 4.7*	2895 36.3	207 2.6	581 7.3	675 8.5	3611 45.3
WARREN	937 69.5	359 26.6	53 3.9*	543 32.1	77 4.5	144 8.5	439 25.9	490 28.9
WASHINGTON	1883 48.1	1960 50.0	74 1.9*	1013 27.7	203 5.5	558 15.3	979 26.8	906 24.8
WAYNE	1763 38.8	2622 57.7	163 3.6*	1128 20.7	224 4.1	651 11.9	897 16.4	2561 46.9
WEBSTER	396 78.6	98 19.4	10 2.0*	100 16.6	54 8.9	208 34.4	144 23.8	98 16.2
WHEELER	619 35.9	1082 62.8	23 1.3*	425 34.1	52 4.2	99 7.9	314 25.2	357 28.6
WHITE	1328 46.1	1476 51.3	75 2.6*	589 24.3	187 7.7	560 23.1	586 24.1	506 20.8
WHITFIELD	2494 32.4	4996 64.9	205 2.7*	2676 41.5	209 3.2	1854 28.7	528 8.2	1184 18.4
WILCOX	1530 60.7	938 37.2	54 2.1*	368 14.3	309 12.0	254 9.9	813 31.7	822 32.0
WILKES	1400 45.6	1582 51.6	86 2.8*	787 25.7	95 3.1	373 12.2	617 20.2	1188 38.8
WILKINSON	1852 69.3	755 28.2	67 2.5*	435 22.5	267 13.8	166 8.6	465 24.0	602 31.1
WORTH	2119 71.7	776 26.3	61 2.1*	499 13.6	60 1.6	271 7.4	2657 72.4	182 5.0
TOTALS	332746	494978	24774	231480	39994	164562	152973	185672
% OF VOTE	39.0	58.1	2.9	29.9	5.2	21.2	19.7	24.0
GEOGRAPHIC CLASS								
LOWLANDS	91901 47.	100113 51.	5542 3.*	49684 27.	12219 7.	25007 14.	43552 24.	53900 29.
BLACK BELT	104268 47.	113381 51.	5639 3.*	60791 29.	13571 7.	33951 16.	59919 29.	38349 19.
PIEDMONT	105674 30.	236117 67.	11696 3.*	102235 32.	11098 4.	87492 28.	37742 12.	77464 25.
MOUNTAIN	30903 40.	45367 58.	1897 2.*	18770 28.	3106 5.	18112 27.	11760 17.	15959 24.
DEMOGRAPHIC CLASS								
METRO	84583 27.	213561 69.	9969 3.*	98691 40.	11033 4.	54033 22.	39975 16.	42313 17.
TOWN	33982 33.	65477 64.	3563 3.*	32578 27.	6212 5.	33736 28.	18288 15.	28211 24.
RURAL	214181 49.	215940 49.	11242 3.*	100211 24.	22749 6.	76793 19.	94710 23.	115148 28.

```
        DEMOC. RUNOFF    1966*              DEMOC. GOVERNOR   1970
                                 *
COUNTY     ARNALL      MADDOX        CARTER       KING       SANDERS      STONER       OTHER
          #     %      #    %*      #     %      #     %     #      %     #     %     #     %
--------------------------------*-------------------------------------------------------------------------
APPLING   1078 32.1  2282 67.9*   1926 53.4    185  5.1   1135 31.5    115  3.2    244  6.8
ATKINSON   450 28.5  1129 71.5*    763 62.1     68  5.5    313 25.5     48  3.9     36  2.9
BACON      333 15.9  1760 84.1*    882 55.0     13   .8    630 39.3     34  2.1     46  2.9
BAKER      503 36.5   874 63.5*    476 40.0    385 32.4    211 17.7     93  7.8     24  2.0
BALDWIN   2060 43.6  2669 56.4*   2968 51.9    661 11.6   1942 34.0     80  1.4     64  1.1
                                 *
BANKS      349 21.3  1289 78.7*    941 56.5      2   .1    664 39.9     33  2.0     25  1.5
BARROW    1093 28.3  2771 71.7*   3010 66.8     94  2.1   1281 28.4     88  2.0     34   .8
BARTON    2010 38.7  3180 61.3*   3841 65.8    128  2.2   1748 29.9     66  1.1     57  1.0
BEN HILL   931 34.4  1779 65.6*   1765 62.1    348 12.2    637 22.4     54  1.9     39  1.4
BERRIEN    599 20.9  2264 79.1*   1304 61.9     53  2.5    616 29.2     91  4.3     44  2.1
                                 *
BIBB     13268 50.5 13025 49.5*   9689 43.1   2524 11.2   8490 37.8    797  3.5    978  4.4
BLECKLEY   441 18.0  2007 82.0*   1400 64.9     38  1.8    599 27.8     96  4.5     24  1.1
BRANTLEY   462 21.3  1705 78.7*    804 54.4     21  1.4    438 29.6     60  4.1    156 10.5
BROOKS     695 25.7  2014 74.3*   1495 57.8    288 11.1    594 23.0     92  3.6    116  4.5
BRYAN      547 34.0  1060 66.0*    807 61.3     53  4.0    350 26.6     58  4.4     49  3.7
                                 *
BULLOCH   2494 39.8  3775 60.2*   3497 54.6    328  5.1   2184 34.1     60   .9    333  5.2
BURKE     1269 41.7  1775 58.3*   1262 41.3    355 11.6   1186 38.8     56  1.8    200  6.5
BUTTS      833 36.5  1447 63.5*   1230 51.8    337 14.2    646 27.2    134  5.6     28  1.2
CALHOUN    334 28.8   824 71.2*    568 44.4    342 26.7    298 23.3     27  2.1     44  3.4
CAMDEN    1056 48.3  1130 51.7*   1176 38.5    349 11.4   1118 36.6    137  4.5    274  9.0
                                 *
CHANDLER   549 30.8  1235 69.2*    918 55.3    116  7.0    535 32.2     57  3.4     33  2.0
CARROLL   2950 36.8  5058 63.2*   4582 59.8    319  4.2   2419 31.6    234  3.1    104  1.4
CATOOSA    793 33.1  1601 66.9*   1393 45.2      3   .1   1535 49.8    107  3.5     42  1.4
CHARLTON   297 24.4   919 75.6*    785 48.9     49  3.1    501 31.2    148  9.2    122  7.6
CHATHAM  21390 61.4 13452 38.6*  12784 41.0   5124 16.4  10432 33.5    961  3.1   1856  6.0
                                 *
CHATTAHOO  124 41.2   177 58.8*    133 44.2     56 18.6    104 34.6      5  1.7      3  1.0
CHATTOOGA 1319 43.6  1706 56.4*   1389 42.1     32  1.0   1780 54.1     46  1.4     46  1.4
CHEROKEE  1368 31.6  2956 68.4*   2318 56.9     31   .8   1583 38.8     74  1.8     71  1.7
CLARKE    6113 63.0  3583 37.0*   4622 39.4   1550 13.2   5258 44.8    160  1.4    146  1.2
CLAY       283 43.1   374 56.9*    353 42.8    325 39.4    123 14.9      6   .7     18  2.2
                                 *
CLAYTON   3790 30.2  8776 69.8*   8700 62.3    190  1.4   4405 31.5    329  2.4    343  2.5
CLINCH     268 20.7  1027 79.3*    419 41.5     42  4.2    492 48.8     25  2.5     31  3.1
COBB     11094 43.0 14700 57.0*  13996 52.8    397  1.5  11129 41.9    411  1.5    597  2.3
COFFEE    1785 38.1  2895 61.9*   2972 58.1    246  4.8   1642 32.1    104  2.0    155  3.0
COLQUITT  1693 24.8  5129 75.2*   4485 70.1    485  7.6   1148 18.0    138  2.2    138  2.2
                                 *
COLUMBIA   741 30.5  1690 69.5*   1047 34.1    169  5.5   1790 58.3     34  1.1     31  1.0
COOK       635 26.6  1748 73.4*   1721 61.9    140  5.0    806 29.0     63  2.3     49  1.8
COWETA    3986 55.6  3186 44.4*   3667 57.4    291  4.6   2239 35.0    135  2.1     58   .9
CRAWFORD   499 39.4   769 60.6*    544 41.8    396 30.4    257 19.7     38  2.9     67  5.1
CRISP     1144 31.6  2478 68.4*   1983 60.8    386 11.8    613 18.8    154  4.7    124  3.8
                                 *
DADE       373 42.1   513 57.9*    470 46.7      1   .1    447 44.4     53  5.3     35  3.5
DAWSON     269 27.3   716 72.7*    552 61.3      3   .3    333 37.0      7   .8      6   .7
DECATUR   1492 32.4  3119 67.6*   2604 51.6    993 19.7   1122 22.2    154  3.1    174  3.4
DEKALB   33816 55.7 26873 44.3*  23494 42.1   2638  4.7  27621 49.5    825  1.5   1241  2.2
DODGE     1131 23.9  3605 76.1*   2863 65.8    276  6.3   1093 25.1     79  1.8     43  1.0
                                 *
DOOLEY     735 33.9  1434 66.1*    940 51.5    250 13.7    429 23.5     89  4.9    119  6.5
```

COUNTY	ARNALL #	%	MADDOX #	%*	CARTER #	%	KING #	%	SANDERS #	%	STONER #	%	OTHER #	%
DOUGHERTY	4526	39.6	6893	60.4*	6547	51.4	2321	18.2	3349	26.3	268	2.1	261	2.0
DOUGLAS	1361	26.6	3762	73.4*	3146	62.3	107	2.1	1540	30.5	116	2.3	138	2.7
EARLY	610	29.8	1436	70.2*	1304	51.6	388	15.3	756	29.9	43	1.7	38	1.5
ECHOLS	46	9.0	465	91.0*	362	63.2	4	.7	177	30.9	17	3.0	13	2.3
EFFINGHAM	623	26.6	1722	73.4*	1467	65.2	197	8.8	416	18.5	89	4.0	81	3.6
ELBERT	1278	35.5	2321	64.5*	2169	55.6	74	1.9	1516	38.8	99	2.5	45	1.2
EMANUEL	1487	33.8	2913	66.2*	3043	55.0	589	10.6	1683	30.4	83	1.5	133	2.4
EVANS	658	33.5	1306	66.5*	1088	62.5	40	2.3	522	30.0	46	2.6	45	2.6
FANNIN	980	72.3	376	27.7*	339	24.8	3	.2	995	72.7	6	.4	26	1.9
FAYETTE	543	26.7	1489	73.3*	1389	63.5	32	1.5	653	29.8	70	3.2	45	2.1
FLOYD	6219	46.3	7218	53.7*	7755	56.6	502	3.7	5038	36.7	162	1.2	256	1.9
FORSYTHE	691	26.3	1938	73.7*	1747	65.4	4	.1	854	32.0	28	1.0	39	1.5
FRANKLIN	750	27.0	2031	73.0*	1695	58.9	7	.2	1084	37.6	76	2.6	18	.6
FULTON	80278	65.0	43295	35.0*	32038	30.9	15928	15.4	52956	51.1	1367	1.3	1436	1.4
GILMER	543	36.7	938	63.3*	355	30.2	5	.4	773	65.7	15	1.3	28	2.4
GLASCOCK	56	8.0	647	92.0*	261	56.1	3	.6	185	39.8	6	1.3	10	2.2
GLYNN	4413	53.1	3893	46.9*	3034	39.6	157	2.1	3335	43.6	140	1.8	986	12.9
GORDON	1421	39.6	2169	60.4*	2109	57.7	16	.4	1441	39.5	34	.9	52	1.4
GRADY	1271	30.6	2882	69.4*	2390	60.3	389	9.8	928	23.4	94	2.4	161	4.1
GREENE	1415	52.0	1305	48.0*	759	34.6	119	5.4	1182	53.9	103	4.7	28	1.3
GWINNETT	3280	30.4	7518	69.6*	8702	66.1	109	.8	3939	29.9	221	1.7	196	1.5
HABERSHAM	1808	39.2	2809	60.8*	2294	55.2	14	.3	1721	41.4	47	1.1	77	1.9
HALL	6042	56.5	4651	43.5*	5976	51.1	115	1.0	5299	45.3	116	1.0	200	1.7
HANCOCK	1510	60.8	974	39.2*	981	27.2	1813	50.2	531	14.7	108	3.0	177	4.9
HARALSON	962	29.9	2260	70.1*	1957	56.3	28	.8	1391	40.0	74	2.1	28	.8
HARRIS	901	41.6	1264	58.4*	1503	56.9	303	11.5	761	28.8	41	1.6	32	1.2
HART	1108	35.4	2022	64.6*	1650	47.9	24	.7	1568	45.5	164	4.8	37	1.1
HEARD	476	33.7	938	66.3*	681	57.4	15	1.3	439	37.0	37	3.1	14	1.2
HENRY	2048	36.6	3542	63.4*	2715	55.2	191	3.9	1757	35.7	154	3.1	100	2.0
HOUSTON	3383	44.9	4157	55.1*	4436	51.4	959	11.1	2705	31.3	301	3.5	232	2.7
IRWIN	524	23.2	1730	76.8*	1113	71.9	115	7.4	250	16.1	39	2.5	32	2.1
JACKSON	1686	38.3	2719	61.7*	2852	54.8	78	1.5	2164	41.6	63	1.2	47	.9
JASPER	534	36.2	942	63.8*	701	51.1	128	9.3	474	34.5	46	3.4	23	1.7
JEFF DAVIS	459	23.0	1535	77.0*	1276	64.0	105	5.3	418	21.0	78	3.9	116	5.8
JEFFERSON	1696	43.8	2177	56.2*	1384	37.6	827	22.4	1223	33.2	74	2.0	176	4.8
JENKINS	635	33.3	1272	66.7*	1165	53.6	231	10.6	659	30.3	43	2.0	75	3.5
JOHNSON	456	21.2	1692	78.8*	1323	63.2	154	7.4	451	21.6	134	6.4	30	1.4
JONES	965	39.6	1472	60.4*	1186	56.3	105	5.0	717	34.0	68	3.2	31	1.5
LAMAR	941	38.8	1484	61.2*	1059	46.5	157	6.9	929	40.8	83	3.6	49	2.2
LANIER	298	27.7	777	72.3*	474	57.7	44	5.4	276	33.6	20	2.4	8	1.0
LAURINS	2979	32.6	6162	67.4*	5363	61.8	544	6.3	2296	26.4	406	4.7	76	.9
LEE	280	26.2	790	73.8*	509	47.7	200	18.7	268	25.1	52	4.9	39	3.7
LIBERTY	1918	64.2	1071	35.8*	1167	35.5	243	7.4	1646	50.1	65	2.0	166	5.1
LINCOLN	499	25.2	1480	74.8*	729	49.0	36	2.4	698	46.9	13	.9	12	.8
LONG	1472	86.8	223	13.2*	330	28.6	43	3.7	730	63.3	19	1.6	31	2.7
LOWNDES	2826	44.3	3559	55.7*	2542	47.3	358	6.7	2148	40.0	124	2.3	200	3.7

	DEMOC. RUNOFF 1966*						DEMOC. GOVERNOR 1970										
COUNTY	ARNALL		MADDOX		CARTER		KING		SANDERS		STONER		OTHER	
	#	%	#	%*	#	%	#	%	#	%	#	%	#	%
LUMPKIN	588	36.5	1023	63.5*	1131	60.7	5	.3	658	35.3	47	2.5	23	1.2
MACON	1167	44.1	1478	55.9*	976	52.8	432	23.4	343	18.5	50	2.7	49	2.6
MADISON	699	26.4	1952	73.6*	2160	67.8	42	1.3	833	26.2	98	3.1	52	1.6
MARION	321	35.1	594	64.9*	602	62.6	62	6.4	250	26.0	31	3.2	17	1.8
MCDUFFIE	927	35.6	1676	64.4*	1421	46.9	456	15.0	1081	35.6	54	1.8	21	.7
MCINTOSH	897	57.8	654	42.2*	730	39.0	145	7.7	828	44.2	47	2.5	123	6.6
MERIWETHR	1854	45.4	2234	54.6*	2486	55.6	209	4.7	1681	37.6	55	1.2	37	.8
MILLER	243	14.4	1449	85.6*	669	67.0	15	1.5	215	21.5	76	7.6	24	2.4
MITCHELL	1299	31.4	2836	68.6*	2193	50.5	861	19.8	943	21.7	201	4.6	146	3.4
MONROE	871	36.9	1491	63.1*	1354	47.5	326	11.4	1010	35.4	93	3.3	67	2.4
MONTGOMRY	554	26.8	1510	73.2*	809	54.6	52	3.5	548	37.0	39	2.6	33	2.2
MORGAN	871	37.7	1438	62.3*	1186	51.6	85	3.7	942	41.0	62	2.7	22	1.0
MURRAY	828	50.5	813	49.5*	1257	44.9	5	.2	1463	52.3	22	.8	52	1.9
MUSCOGEE	11272	57.2	8429	42.8*	11885	62.3	1339	7.0	5318	27.9	158	.8	392	2.1
NEWTON	2252	39.7	3419	60.3*	3188	57.7	310	5.6	1813	32.8	121	2.2	89	1.6
OCONEE	495	26.2	1391	73.8*	1353	68.2	42	2.1	530	26.7	34	1.7	25	1.3
OGLETHRPE	391	20.7	1501	79.3*	1330	66.4	103	5.1	434	21.7	80	4.0	57	2.8
PAULDING	1105	28.9	2713	71.1*	2105	62.3	51	1.5	1122	33.2	60	1.8	42	1.2
PEACH	1567	50.6	1527	49.4*	1188	40.5	826	28.2	698	23.8	77	2.6	145	4.9
PICKENS	699	39.8	1056	60.2*	684	47.4	4	.3	701	48.5	29	2.0	26	1.8
PIERCE	803	25.4	2364	74.6*	985	43.1	18	.8	880	38.5	68	3.0	335	14.7
PIKE	621	36.4	1086	63.6*	1135	52.6	410	19.0	451	20.9	132	6.1	30	1.4
POLK	2000	39.0	3127	61.0*	3963	62.4	208	3.3	1963	30.9	89	1.4	132	2.1
PULASKI	539	27.9	1393	72.1*	1212	65.2	54	2.9	531	28.6	42	2.3	19	1.0
PUTNAM	678	37.8	1115	62.2*	893	41.1	139	6.4	1040	47.8	60	2.8	42	1.9
QUITMAN	322	58.7	227	41.3*	307	45.0	152	22.3	183	26.8	25	3.7	15	2.2
RABUN	722	44.5	899	55.5*	1071	42.7	20	.8	1283	51.2	78	3.1	56	2.2
RANDOLPH	850	40.6	1244	59.4*	1267	45.0	701	24.9	581	20.7	212	7.5	52	1.8
RICHMOND	12255	54.4	10290	45.6*	6448	28.9	2744	12.3	12678	56.8	270	1.2	176	.8
ROCKDALE	1179	39.2	1831	60.8*	1422	52.4	131	4.8	1053	38.8	54	2.0	52	1.9
SCHLEY	269	38.9	422	61.1*	389	58.2	180	26.9	68	10.2	18	2.7	13	1.9
SCREVEN	1223	43.5	1587	56.5*	1395	59.8	262	11.2	588	25.2	29	1.2	57	2.4
SEMINOLE	358	22.9	1203	77.1*	888	50.9	238	13.6	549	31.5	39	2.2	30	1.7
SPALDING	3127	41.1	4474	58.9*	4258	57.0	586	7.8	2280	30.5	228	3.1	120	1.6
STEPHENS	1481	47.0	1668	53.0*	2333	55.3	35	.8	1654	39.2	78	1.8	122	2.9
STEWART	442	39.7	671	60.3*	809	57.7	325	23.2	181	12.9	54	3.9	33	2.4
SUMTER	2155	43.4	2807	56.6*	3210	63.2	649	12.8	837	16.5	166	3.3	221	4.3
TALBOT	496	46.4	573	53.6*	630	48.5	284	21.9	336	25.9	33	2.5	15	1.2
TALIAFERO	472	47.7	518	52.3*	459	29.7	333	21.5	714	46.2	18	1.2	22	1.4
TATTNALL	1238	32.0	2632	68.0*	1861	60.7	76	2.5	938	30.6	81	2.6	109	3.6
TAYLOR	677	33.4	1351	66.6*	1077	48.7	398	18.0	517	23.4	186	8.4	35	1.6
TELFAIR	1126	34.3	2156	65.7*	1334	47.7	390	14.0	800	28.6	155	5.5	116	4.2
TERRELL	468	23.9	1494	76.1*	1260	51.2	588	23.9	494	20.1	81	3.3	39	1.6
THOMAS	2822	47.9	3066	52.1*	3000	44.4	890	13.2	2685	39.8	76	1.1	100	1.5
TIFT	2000	36.3	3516	63.7*	2823	59.2	416	8.7	1281	26.9	88	1.8	157	3.3
TOOMBS	1032	25.6	2992	74.4*	1909	58.4	75	2.3	1042	31.9	117	3.6	125	3.8

```
            DEMOC.  RUNOFF     1966*                    DEMOC.  GOVERNOR   1970
                                   *
 COUNTY      ARNALL        MADDOX      CARTER       KING         SANDERS      STONER       OTHER
             #      %      #      %*   #      %     #      %     #      %     #      %     #      %
-----------------------------------*-----------------------------------------------------------------------------------
TOWNS         385  62.3     233  37.7*   389  31.6     4    .3     819  66.5     13   1.1      7    .6
TREUTLEN      194  11.3    1530  88.7*   533  36.3    11    .7     875  59.6     36   2.5     14   1.0
TROUP        3641  49.6    3706  50.4*  3951  52.3   257   3.4    3200  42.3     99   1.3     51    .7
TURNER        422  21.9    1504  78.1*  1115  57.6   178   9.2     566  29.2     49   2.5     28   1.4
TWIGGS        498  33.1    1006  66.9*   514  36.8   399  28.6     319  22.8    117   8.4     48   3.4

UNION         707  53.8     607  46.2*   944  51.8     4    .2     848  46.5      8    .4     18   1.0
UPSON        1792  38.1    2913  61.9*  3029  59.7   348   6.9    1470  29.0    162   3.2     64   1.3
WALKER       2282  41.6    3207  58.4*  2974  50.0    27    .5    2735  46.0    155   2.6     52    .9
WALTON       1179  27.4    3119  72.6*  2672  61.1   216   4.9    1342  30.7     75   1.7     71   1.6
WARE         3303  41.7    4613  58.3*  3655  52.4   446   6.4    2276  32.6    226   3.2    369   5.3
                                   *
WARREN        693  41.8     964  58.2*   468  47.4   147  14.9     342  34.7     18   1.8     12   1.2
WASHINGTON   1485  37.8    2441  62.2*  2780  42.4  2414  36.8    1176  17.9     68   1.0    116   1.8
WAYNE        1343  29.0    3289  71.0*  2147  48.6   130   2.9    1052  23.8     84   1.9   1007  22.8
WEBSTER       170  27.7     444  72.3*   381  64.4    80  13.5      88  14.9     31   5.2     12   2.0
WHEELER       555  34.0    1079  66.0*   468  46.1    65   6.4     431  42.4     40   3.9     12   1.2
                                   *
WHITE        1030  39.8    1558  60.2*  1264  55.5    22   1.0     948  41.7     21    .9     21    .9
WHITFIELD    3857  59.8    2588  40.2*  3277  46.0    50    .7    3600  50.5     39    .5    159   2.2
WILCOX        501  23.9    1597  76.1*  1219  69.7   103   5.9     338  19.3     75   4.3     13    .7
WILKES       1071  36.9    1828  63.1*  1268  48.7   266  10.2    1033  39.7     19    .7     19    .7
WILKINSON     602  26.9    1638  73.1*  1497  55.0   222   8.2     760  27.9    132   4.8    111   4.1
                                   *
WORTH         742  22.5    2554  77.5*  2087  59.9   459  13.2     664  19.1    178   5.1     96   2.8
-----------------------------------*-----------------------------------------------------------------------------------

TOTALS      373004        443005     * 388280       70424        301657       17663        20475
% OF VOTE    45.7          54.3      *  48.6          8.8          37.8         2.2          2.6
                                   *
GEOGRAPHIC CLASS                   *
                                   *
LOWLANDS     72077  38.  115894  62.*  92351  53.  14333   8.     55150  32.   5040   3.    7989   5.
BLACK BELT   91189  44.  117968  56.* 101616  48.  30827  14.     69450  33.   5767   3.    5716   3.
PIEDMONT    180905  51.  172806  49.* 156862  46.  24208   7.    146228  43.   5812   2.    5599   2.
MOUNTAIN     28833  44.   36337  56.*  37451  52.   1056   1.     30829  43.   1044   1.    1171   2.
                                   *
DEMOGRAPHIC CLASS                  *
                                   *
METRO       176805  59.  122257  41.* 102885  38.  32618  12.    120844  45.   4646   2.    6340   2.
TOWN         47909  45.   58679  55.*  56949  52.   5402   5.     41774  38.   2180   2.    3300   3.
RURAL       148290  36.  262069  64.* 228446  54.  32404   8.    139039  33.  10837   3.   10835   3.
```

```
              DEMOC.  RUNOFF    1970* DEMOC.  SENATOR    1968
                                    *
   COUNTY       CARTER       SANDERS       JACKSON       TALMADGE
               #      %      #      %*     #      %      #      %
----------------------------------------*----------------------------------------------------------

APPLING       2779  72.8   1038  27.2*    789  15.0   4455  85.0
ATKINSON       841  70.3    356  29.7*    393  16.0   2069  84.0
BACON         1279  70.6    533  29.4*    302   8.9   3100  91.1
BAKER          730  62.1    445  37.9*    502  29.1   1224  70.9
BALDWIN       3518  62.3   2133  37.7*   1644  25.1   4907  74.9
                                    *
BANKS         1321  64.2    738  35.8*    153   5.8   2499  94.2
BARROW        3328  74.0   1170  26.0*    485   9.7   4494  90.3
BARTON        3829  68.7   1746  31.3*    843  14.1   5135  85.9
BEN HILL      1875  73.2    685  26.8*    658  20.3   2580  79.7
BERRIEN       1846  75.3    604  24.7*    482  12.4   3400  87.6
                                    *
BIBB         13493  54.9  11068  45.1*   5809  23.7  18749  76.3
BLECKLEY      1690  75.0    563  25.0*    213   6.8   2922  93.2
BRANTLEY      1099  80.3    270  19.7*    225   8.2   2527  91.8
BROOKS        1819  72.8    678  27.2*    437  15.8   2326  84.2
BRYAN         1070  70.8    441  29.2*    431  17.6   2015  82.4
                                    *
BULLOCH       3584  59.8   2406  40.2*   1081  18.4   4788  81.6
BURKE         1829  49.8   1847  50.2*   1077  26.1   3042  73.9
BUTTS         1726  67.2    842  32.8*    599  17.6   2804  82.4
CALHOUN        822  64.3    457  35.7*    542  28.4   1368  71.6
CAMDEN        1617  62.1    986  37.9*    910  28.1   2333  71.9
                                    *
CHANDLER      1201  65.8    623  34.2*    291  12.7   1996  87.3
CARROLL       5721  68.8   2597  31.2*   1358  13.1   8973  86.9
CATOOSA       2121  64.3   1179  35.7*    538   7.8   6388  92.2
CHARLTON      1211  72.5    459  27.5*    517  22.9   1743  77.1
CHATHAM      18403  53.5  16020  46.5*  11593  38.7  18338  61.3
                                    *
CHATTAHOO      215  54.8    177  45.2*     44  16.6    221  83.4
CHATTOOGA     1842  56.4   1423  43.6*    687  12.2   4961  87.8
CHEROKEE      3149  65.2   1678  34.8*    555   9.1   5547  90.9
CLARKE        5678  50.8   5509  49.2*   2775  29.6   6596  70.4
CLAY           458  65.2    244  34.8*    295  32.1    623  67.9
                                    *
CLAYTON      10526  71.5   4196  28.5*   1769  12.6  12264  87.4
CLINCH         650  63.9    368  36.1*    259  12.8   1768  87.2
COBB         18035  62.7  10713  37.3*   4156  15.9  21951  84.1
COFFEE        3902  69.9   1684  30.1*   1175  17.9   5399  82.1
COLQUITT      5467  79.2   1434  20.8*    820  11.0   6602  89.0
                                    *
COLUMBIA      1493  38.5   2380  61.5*    517  14.8   2973  85.2
COOK          1781  74.9    596  25.1*    440  13.8   2751  86.2
COWETA        4490  68.1   2099  31.9*   1403  19.4   5816  80.6
CRAWFORD       862  58.5    612  41.5*    347  22.7   1181  77.3
CRISP         2623  77.4    766  22.6*    628  15.3   3481  84.7
                                    *
DADE           769  67.3    374  32.7*    185   8.7   1938  91.3
DAWSON         738  69.8    319  30.2*     83   4.1   1939  95.9
DECATUR       3338  63.2   1941  36.8*    804  24.5   2475  75.5
DEKALB       30032  51.4  28402  48.6*  17880  29.3  43103  70.7
DODGE         3350  78.9    896  21.1*    657  13.5   4221  86.5
                                    *
DOOLEY        1343  73.0    496  27.0*    389  16.7   1935  83.3
```

COUNTY	CARTER #	%	SANDERS #	%*	JACKSON #	%	TALMADGE #	%
DOUGHERTY	9469	69.6	4131	30.4*	2827	31.8	6075	68.2
DOUGLAS	3820	71.3	1538	28.7*	780	13.0	5204	87.0
EARLY	1777	69.8	769	30.2*	788	20.8	3006	79.2
ECHOLS	443	75.6	143	24.4*	51	6.8	698	93.2
EFFINGHAM	2183	80.7	521	19.3*	339	14.7	1967	85.3
ELBERT	3104	70.4	1307	29.6*	534	11.7	4014	88.3
EMANUEL	3423	69.1	1528	30.9*	1551	23.5	5063	76.5
EVANS	1250	72.9	464	27.1*	337	13.6	2148	86.4
FANNIN	428	33.9	836	66.1*	75	9.4	721	90.6
FAYETTE	1774	75.3	582	24.7*	243	8.8	2504	91.2
FLOYD	8621	64.7	4701	35.3*	2487	17.7	11529	82.3
FORSYTHE	2316	75.4	757	24.6*	230	5.5	3952	94.5
FRANKLIN	2139	67.0	1053	33.0*	343	6.4	4979	93.6
FULTON	43898	38.0	71666	62.0*	48972	46.4	56645	53.6
GILMER	673	45.4	808	54.6*	128	7.1	1678	92.9
GLASCOCK	421	68.1	197	31.9*	34	3.6	911	96.4
GLYNN	4903	63.4	2834	36.6*	2403	28.1	6151	71.9
GORDON	2784	66.7	1391	33.3*	648	9.8	5939	90.2
GRADY	2957	72.2	1137	27.8*	1146	21.2	4253	78.8
GREENE	1145	47.3	1278	52.7*	1563	39.8	2363	60.2
GWINNETT	10640	72.8	3966	27.2*	1509	10.3	13116	89.7
HABERSHAM	3139	66.3	1599	33.7*	506	9.0	5108	91.0
HALL	6806	56.4	5267	43.6*	1660	13.1	11030	86.9
HANCOCK	1406	65.6	738	34.4*	1796	56.0	1412	44.0
HARALSON	2560	67.3	1246	32.7*	609	10.6	5135	89.4
HARRIS	1766	65.4	933	34.6*	581	20.1	2303	79.9
HART	2054	67.4	995	32.6*	509	9.2	5046	90.8
HEARD	963	64.7	525	35.3*	227	10.2	1988	89.8
HENRY	3429	65.2	1827	34.8*	1353	19.8	5492	80.2
HOUSTON	6384	63.5	3675	36.5*	1553	18.4	6870	81.6
IRWIN	1482	86.9	223	13.1*	451	15.3	2499	84.7
JACKSON	3558	65.9	1840	34.1*	596	10.0	5344	90.0
JASPER	831	59.7	561	40.3*	475	23.2	1571	76.8
JEFF DAVIS	1971	74.6	670	25.4*	369	13.4	2386	86.6
JEFFERSON	2073	53.1	1829	46.9*	1211	28.1	3103	71.9
JENKINS	1442	63.5	828	36.5*	482	19.3	2012	80.7
JOHNSON	1741	77.7	501	22.3*	356	11.1	2848	88.9
JONES	1506	61.9	928	38.1*	819	24.1	2578	75.9
LAMAR	1474	62.1	901	37.9*	511	20.2	2024	79.8
LANIER	538	68.4	249	31.6*	352	19.9	1419	80.1
LAURINS	6346	70.2	2689	29.8*	2641	22.3	9225	77.7
LEE	805	68.7	366	31.3*	270	29.2	654	70.8
LIBERTY	1550	52.0	1432	48.0*	1589	43.7	2047	56.3
LINCOLN	998	56.4	773	43.6*	479	22.5	1651	77.5
LONG	1019	75.4	332	24.6*	383	22.8	1297	77.2
LOWNDES	3874	61.9	2388	38.1*	1505	26.8	4111	73.2

```
                DEMOC.  RUNOFF     1970* DEMOC.  SENATOR     1968
                                       *
        COUNTY      CARTER       SANDERS      JACKSON      TALMADGE
                   #      %      #       %*    #      %     #       %
        --------------------------------------*-----------------------------------------------------------------------------
        LUMPKIN     1375  72.3    526  27.7*    236   9.1   2363  90.9
        MACON       1388  64.5    765  35.5*    494  22.1   1743  77.9
        MADISON     2613  78.9    700  21.1*    282   7.6   3440  92.4
        MARION       739  75.0    246  25.0*    190  16.9    937  83.1
        MCDUFFIE    1973  57.3   1470  42.7*    819  21.6   2968  78.4
                                       *
        MCINTOSH    1109  61.6    691  38.4*    566  34.4   1080  65.6
        MERIWETHR   2714  63.1   1589  36.9*   1105  22.7   3773  77.3
        MILLER       994  87.2    146  12.8*    158   7.5   1937  92.5
        MITCHELL    2864  69.9   1233  30.1*    995  20.5   3852  79.5
        MONROE      1586  58.2   1140  41.8*    621  20.1   2472  79.9
                                       *
        MONTGOMRY   1013  60.5    661  39.5*    374  16.1   1942  83.9
        MORGAN      1520  62.5    913  37.5*    457  18.3   2042  81.7
        MURRAY      1477  60.9    947  39.1*    315  10.0   2831  90.0
        MUSCOGEE   17648  69.6   7723  30.4*   4747  25.7  13750  74.3
        NEWTON      3961  66.9   1961  33.1*   1212  20.3   4759  79.7
                                       *
        OCONEE      1548  78.6    421  21.4*    169   7.3   2149  92.7
        OGLETHRPE   1710  76.5    526  23.5*    255   9.6   2410  90.4
        PAULDING    2654  70.4   1114  29.6*    482   9.3   4691  90.7
        PEACH       1560  50.2   1549  49.8*    920  32.4   1918  67.6
        PICKENS      933  63.2    544  36.8*    108   6.5   1555  93.5
                                       *
        PIERCE      1314  66.4    664  33.6*    404  13.3   2631  86.7
        PIKE        1514  75.5    492  24.5*    471  20.2   1857  79.8
        POLK        4195  72.3   1609  27.7*   1067  14.7   6195  85.3
        PULASKI     1403  73.7    500  26.3*    222  10.6   1868  89.4
        PUTNAM      1088  51.6   1022  48.4*    938  28.9   2312  71.1
                                       *
        QUITMAN      461  71.4    185  28.6*    199  27.5    524  72.5
        RABUN       1514  63.1    887  36.9*    268   8.8   2780  91.2
        RANDOLPH    1497  66.3    762  33.7*    807  32.4   1682  67.6
        RICHMOND    8854  31.9  18890  68.1*   5798  36.8   9973  63.2
        ROCKDALE    1913  62.8   1132  37.2*    480  17.2   2306  82.8
                                       *
        SCHLEY       552  72.2    213  27.8*    238  27.5    627  72.5
        SCREVEN     1819  68.5    837  31.5*    669  20.3   2629  79.7
        SEMINOLE     998  74.7    338  25.3*    242  12.8   1655  87.2
        SPALDING    5579  70.0   2396  30.0*   1606  18.8   6957  81.2
        STEPHENS    3191  69.6   1394  30.4*    511  11.1   4113  88.9
                                       *
        STEWART      990  70.5    415  29.5*    338  20.4   1318  79.6
        SUMTER      3866  74.1   1350  25.9*   1147  21.3   4248  78.7
        TALBOT       826  58.7    580  41.3*    297  22.7   1013  77.3
        TALIAFERO    568  49.6    578  50.4*    393  38.5    627  61.5
        TATTNALL    2625  76.0    827  24.0*    824  13.6   5236  86.4
                                       *
        TAYLOR      1324  66.1    680  33.9*    609  20.5   2367  79.5
        TELFAIR     1842  58.3   1315  41.7*    969  21.7   3500  78.3
        TERRELL     1658  66.2    848  33.8*   1113  31.1   2462  68.9
        THOMAS      3998  57.5   2959  42.5*   1411  29.3   3398  70.7
        TIFT        3522  67.6   1687  32.4*    855  15.8   4557  84.2
                                       *
        TOOMBS      2644  73.5    951  26.5*    704  12.3   5013  87.7
```

SOUTHERN ELECTIONS/110

COUNTY	CARTER #	%	SANDERS #	%*	JACKSON #	%	TALMADGE #	%
TOWNS	393	52.6	354	47.4*	2	.2	924	99.8
TREUTLEN	896	49.5	913	50.5*	276	12.7	1895	87.3
TROUP	5574	66.0	2870	34.0*	1847	19.3	7710	80.7
TURNER	1480	68.9	667	31.1*	316	11.8	2369	88.2
TWIGGS	797	48.9	832	51.1*	724	30.6	1644	69.4
UNION	1028	63.0	604	37.0*	98	5.1	1830	94.9
UPSON	3576	70.9	1465	29.1*	904	16.6	4552	83.4
WALKER	3845	62.1	2342	37.9*	896	11.4	6939	88.6
WALTON	3380	72.5	1281	27.5*	1044	15.7	5593	84.3
WARE	4720	66.4	2393	33.6*	1673	19.7	6805	80.3
WARREN	717	58.0	519	42.0*	391	27.2	1044	72.8
WASHINGTON	3822	58.4	2720	41.6*	888	20.3	3479	79.7
WAYNE	3352	68.6	1534	31.4*	897	18.6	3916	81.4
WEBSTER	463	79.4	120	20.6*	123	16.9	606	83.1
WHEELER	803	59.6	544	40.4*	368	20.6	1419	79.4
WHITE	1518	63.2	884	36.8*	306	10.2	2694	89.8
WHITFIELD	4200	56.2	3271	43.8*	1259	16.1	6557	83.9
WILCOX	1527	80.1	380	19.9*	211	8.1	2384	91.9
WILKES	1537	54.1	1302	45.9*	538	18.1	2439	81.9
WILKINSON	1649	69.0	741	31.0*	880	25.7	2544	74.3
WORTH	2675	79.7	681	20.3*	434	17.0	2123	83.0

	CARTER #	%	SANDERS #	%*	JACKSON #	%	TALMADGE #	%
TOTALS	506462		345906	*	207171		697915	
% OF VOTE	59.4		40.6	*	22.9		77.1	

GEOGRAPHIC CLASS

	CARTER #	%	SANDERS #	%*	JACKSON #	%	TALMADGE #	%
LOWLANDS	122906	66.	63576	34.*	43899	20.	173938	80.
BLACK BELT	136759	60.	92507	40.*	56743	26.	165479	74.
PIEDMONT	201375	55.	163479	45.*	95794	26.	278494	74.
MOUNTAIN	45422	63.	26344	37.*	10735	12.	80004	88.

DEMOGRAPHIC CLASS

	CARTER #	%	SANDERS #	%*	JACKSON #	%	TALMADGE #	%
METRO	141797	47.	157900	53.*	97626	37.	166633	63.
TOWN	73894	64.	41675	36.*	21774	19.	90944	81.
RURAL	290771	67.	146331	33.*	87771	17.	440338	83.

COUNTY	GAMBRELL #	%	NUNN #	%	STONER #	%	VANDIVER #	%	WILLIAMS #	%	OTHER #	%*	GAMBRELL #	%	NUNN #	%
APPLING	1259	33.0	458	12.0	247	6.5	843	22.1	208	5.5	801	21.0*	1613	54.1	1367	45.9
ATKINSON	481	29.8	364	22.6	96	5.9	310	19.2	38	2.4	325	20.1*	171	31.6	370	68.4
BACON	870	38.9	166	7.4	62	2.8	280	12.5	8	.4	849	38.0*	1092	60.4	716	39.6
BAKER	366	23.2	328	20.8	129	8.2	248	15.7	270	17.1	236	15.0*	841	48.3	900	51.7
BALDWIN	1608	30.7	1372	26.2	255	4.9	728	13.9	585	11.2	685	13.1*	1598	39.7	2423	60.3
BANKS	799	33.3	293	12.2	97	4.0	894	37.2	5	.2	314	13.1*	934	39.5	1429	60.5
BARROW	1613	29.3	719	13.1	399	7.3	2228	40.5	87	1.6	455	8.3*	2147	42.0	2963	58.0
BARTON	2427	41.0	824	13.9	275	4.6	1220	20.6	108	1.8	1066	18.0*	1126	43.5	1465	56.5
BEN HILL	1032	29.3	1381	39.2	113	3.2	596	16.9	85	2.4	319	9.0*	1343	38.6	2139	61.4
BERRIEN	942	33.6	595	21.2	170	6.1	603	21.5	58	2.1	436	15.5*	1215	47.4	1346	52.6
BIBB	5512	31.4	6845	38.9	528	3.0	1768	10.1	770	4.4	2154	12.3*	6374	34.6	12027	65.4
BLECKLEY	756	26.6	1331	46.9	194	6.8	322	11.3	44	1.6	191	6.7*	811	28.3	2054	71.7
BRANTLEY	1018	42.4	276	11.5	111	4.6	464	19.3	18	.7	515	21.4*	1360	55.2	1106	44.8
BROOKS	568	35.1	432	26.7	104	6.4	225	13.9	38	2.3	251	15.5*	387	42.2	530	57.8
BRYAN	738	37.4	186	9.4	206	10.4	339	17.2	122	6.2	382	19.4*	610	53.0	540	47.0
BULLOCH	1423	31.3	1035	22.7	159	3.5	1071	23.5	126	2.8	738	16.2*	1897	42.9	2524	57.1
BURKE	982	29.3	901	26.8	137	4.1	390	11.6	467	13.9	480	14.3*	1350	42.0	1862	58.0
BUTTS	1239	41.6	460	15.4	263	8.8	586	19.7	237	8.0	194	6.5*	1546	55.5	1239	44.5
CALHOUN	391	31.9	296	24.2	18	1.5	212	17.3	169	13.8	138	11.3*	406	51.5	382	48.5
CAMDEN	1062	49.3	137	6.4	75	3.5	256	11.9	54	2.5	568	26.4*	312	42.0	431	58.0
CHANDLER	895	46.0	277	14.2	146	7.5	343	17.6	117	6.0	169	8.7*	1080	56.3	839	43.7
CARROLL	3249	35.8	1498	16.5	637	7.0	1774	19.6	137	1.5	1768	19.5*	4759	50.1	4732	49.9
CATOOSA	2960	44.8	705	10.7	786	11.9	1532	23.2	45	.7	577	8.7*	3399	50.7	3304	49.3
CHARLTON	669	45.4	93	6.3	62	4.2	217	14.7	68	4.6	366	24.8*	1072	71.9	418	28.1
CHATHAM	6882	31.5	3212	14.7	973	4.5	4740	21.7	1969	9.0	4052	18.6*	12370	60.5	8086	39.5
CHATTAHOO	178	32.4	166	30.2	22	4.0	91	16.5	42	7.6	51	9.3*	57	38.8	90	61.2
CHATTOOGA	2380	45.5	313	6.0	238	4.5	1687	32.2	94	1.8	520	9.9*	930	47.6	1024	52.4
CHEROKEE	1777	33.4	1049	19.7	465	8.7	1361	25.6	30	.6	640	12.0*	2215	44.0	2822	56.0
CLARKE	4163	37.2	1807	16.2	229	2.0	3117	27.9	942	8.4	925	8.3*	3682	50.5	3611	49.5
CLAY	285	28.6	193	19.4	30	3.0	188	18.8	153	15.4	147	14.8*	304	47.3	339	52.7
CLAYTON	5239	30.4	3732	21.6	1287	7.5	4895	28.4	174	1.0	1918	11.1*	5728	38.5	9165	61.5
CLINCH	707	41.2	148	8.6	52	3.0	387	22.6	71	4.1	350	20.4*	801	46.9	907	53.1
COBB	8149	36.0	5832	25.8	1085	4.8	5665	25.0	241	1.1	1644	7.3*	9519	44.3	11968	55.7
COFFEE	1677	38.6	897	20.6	193	4.4	664	15.3	100	2.3	815	18.8*	2269	47.5	2507	52.5
COLQUITT	2425	40.9	1532	25.8	277	4.7	703	11.8	98	1.7	899	15.1*	1686	43.6	2181	56.4
COLUMBIA	1213	29.4	1486	36.0	179	4.3	798	19.3	141	3.4	315	7.6*	979	30.3	2253	69.7
COOK	1030	33.2	758	24.4	167	5.4	626	20.2	80	2.6	440	14.2*	1329	45.0	1622	55.0
COWETA	1812	32.0	1421	25.1	448	7.9	1296	22.9	264	4.7	417	7.3*	1763	41.8	2453	58.2
CRAWFORD	402	25.7	541	34.6	84	5.4	170	10.9	173	11.1	192	12.3*	475	35.5	863	64.5
CRISP	829	23.8	1898	54.5	96	2.8	285	8.2	101	2.9	273	7.8*	1247	34.4	2375	65.6
DADE	890	43.4	124	6.1	361	17.6	392	19.1	6	.3	276	13.5*	1409	53.2	1239	46.8
DAWSON	578	35.7	320	19.8	120	7.4	471	29.1	3	.2	125	7.7*	724	41.0	1042	59.0
DECATUR	1870	35.3	1899	35.8	197	3.7	285	5.4	306	5.8	741	14.0*	1536	36.7	2817	63.3
DEKALB	9628	37.9	4654	18.3	762	3.0	5449	21.5	2151	8.5	2758	10.9*	10401	58.7	7328	41.3
DODGE	1697	33.1	2102	41.0	259	5.0	450	8.8	111	2.2	511	10.0*	1831	39.1	2857	60.9
DOOLEY	298	24.9	581	48.5	59	4.9	136	11.4	26	2.2	97	8.1*	349	31.0	777	69.0

COUNTY	GAMBRELL #	%	NUNN #	%	STONER #	%	VANDIVER #	%	WILLIAMS #	%	OTHER #	%*	GAMBRELL #	%	NUNN #	%
DOUGHERTY	2315	21.2	3973	36.4	174	1.6	1669	15.3	1230	11.3	1548	14.2*	4079	42.2	5595	57.8
DOUGLAS	1928	28.2	1218	17.8	728	10.7	1805	26.4	72	1.1	1080	15.8*	1952	38.6	3105	61.4
EARLY	931	37.9	597	24.3	109	4.4	372	15.1	135	5.5	314	12.8*	835	38.0	1360	62.0
ECHOLS	223	21.2	122	11.6	59	5.6	200	19.0	11	1.0	437	41.5*	58	30.1	135	69.9
EFFINGHAM	206	10.8	436	22.8	217	11.4	616	32.2	61	3.2	375	19.6*	1292	54.5	1078	45.5
ELBERT	1614	34.2	991	21.0	127	2.7	1611	34.2	92	2.0	279	5.9*	1930	43.0	2559	57.0
EMANUEL	3512	72.8	414	8.6	143	3.0	320	6.6	105	2.2	332	6.9*	3899	79.3	1019	20.7
EVANS	1032	47.0	288	13.1	159	7.2	358	16.3	69	3.1	290	13.2*	1283	63.6	734	36.4
FANNIN	313	50.8	53	8.6	21	3.4	115	18.7	3	.5	111	18.0*	188	59.3	129	40.7
FAYETTE	1080	36.0	560	18.6	264	8.8	806	26.8	12	.4	282	9.4*	892	41.6	1252	58.4
FLOYD	4684	33.9	2859	20.7	658	4.8	4104	29.7	146	1.1	1366	9.9*	4560	42.4	6193	57.6
FORSYTHE	1483	36.8	714	17.7	370	9.2	997	24.7	10	.2	461	11.4*	1491	43.4	1947	56.6
FRANKLIN	921	19.7	131	2.8	90	1.9	3283	70.2	14	.3	237	5.1*	580	33.1	1172	66.9
FULTON	26207	39.1	11231	16.8	2186	3.3	10510	15.7	12115	18.1	4739	7.1*	28904	61.7	17959	38.3
GILMER	509	39.2	196	15.1	33	2.5	439	33.8	10	.8	112	8.6*	485	47.8	529	52.2
GLASCOCK	253	29.0	255	29.2	97	11.1	161	18.5	12	1.4	94	10.8*	62	34.1	120	65.9
GLYNN	3145	47.5	998	15.1	104	1.6	1232	18.6	79	1.2	1070	16.1*	3018	52.0	2788	48.0
GORDON	2674	52.9	426	8.4	286	5.7	1103	21.8	33	.7	535	10.6*	3260	58.1	2355	41.9
GRADY	1536	35.3	1194	27.4	168	3.9	338	7.8	136	3.1	982	22.6*	682	41.0	980	59.0
GREENE	1458	50.3	253	8.7	142	4.9	709	24.5	163	5.6	173	6.0*	1392	53.5	1208	46.5
GWINNETT	5228	35.9	3078	21.2	832	5.7	4309	29.6	150	1.0	947	6.5*	5950	43.5	7737	56.5
HABERSHAM	2049	42.9	606	12.7	268	5.6	939	19.7	17	.4	897	18.8*	2598	49.7	2633	50.3
HALL	3627	32.0	4339	38.3	354	3.1	1577	13.9	191	1.7	1242	11.0*	3839	33.6	7595	66.4
HANCOCK	431	15.0	270	9.4	150	5.2	256	8.9	1601	55.8	161	5.6*	195	44.3	245	55.7
HARALSON	2088	41.7	652	13.0	529	10.6	1165	23.3	66	1.3	507	10.1*	1704	51.0	1638	49.0
HARRIS	740	31.4	784	33.3	87	3.7	434	18.4	142	6.0	170	7.2*	654	38.5	1045	61.5
HART	1592	32.1	450	9.1	142	2.9	2344	47.2	53	1.1	385	7.8*	2138	44.6	2655	55.4
HEARD	644	32.9	232	11.9	213	10.9	605	30.9	37	1.9	224	11.5*	1085	54.1	921	45.9
HENRY	2189	36.4	1011	16.8	479	8.0	1564	26.0	277	4.6	494	8.2*	2692	46.0	3164	54.0
HOUSTON	1473	12.2	8585	70.9	320	2.6	559	4.6	473	3.9	697	5.8*	1413	13.2	9313	86.8
IRWIN	698	29.4	905	38.2	135	5.7	345	14.6	88	3.7	200	8.4*	936	39.0	1461	61.0
JACKSON	1975	30.3	789	12.1	271	4.2	2643	40.5	123	1.9	726	11.1*	2643	40.6	3869	59.4
JASPER	525	34.9	273	18.2	101	6.7	223	14.8	191	12.7	190	12.6*	559	42.8	746	57.2
JEFF DAVIS	726	35.0	326	15.7	110	5.3	433	20.9	28	1.4	450	21.7*	663	47.6	729	52.4
JEFFERSON	959	32.4	658	22.2	148	5.0	390	13.2	441	14.9	364	12.3*	1039	44.0	1322	56.0
JENKINS	662	30.4	482	22.1	222	10.2	287	13.2	258	11.8	270	12.4*	1184	47.1	1328	52.9
JOHNSON	1059	36.6	793	27.4	250	8.6	447	15.4	171	5.9	174	6.0*	992	42.5	1340	57.5
JONES	827	23.2	1237	34.7	218	6.1	558	15.7	267	7.5	454	12.7*	420	24.8	1271	75.2
LAMAR	846	42.6	451	22.7	82	4.1	296	14.9	56	2.8	256	12.9*	869	46.6	997	53.4
LANIER	489	39.0	191	15.2	45	3.6	253	20.2	31	2.5	245	19.5*	674	50.1	671	49.9
LAURINS	2624	25.7	4856	47.6	626	6.1	902	8.8	499	4.9	701	6.9*	2974	30.3	6836	69.7
LEE	443	22.8	653	33.6	94	4.8	421	21.7	207	10.7	123	6.3*	328	34.0	637	66.0
LIBERTY	1402	48.4	379	13.1	74	2.6	506	17.5	233	8.0	303	10.5*	1245	55.4	1004	44.6
LINCOLN	605	31.4	311	16.1	75	3.9	468	24.3	305	15.8	162	8.4*	731	44.9	898	55.1
LONG	744	38.3	249	12.8	259	13.3	225	11.6	255	13.1	213	11.0*	991	44.8	1223	55.2
LOWNDES	2035	39.2	1217	23.4	150	2.9	796	15.3	92	1.8	902	17.4*	2476	42.3	3374	57.7

COUNTY	GAMBRELL #	%	NUNN #	%	STONER #	%	VANDIVER #	%	WILLIAMS #	%	OTHER #	%*	GAMBRELL #	%	NUNN #	%
LUMPKIN	1033	38.1	595	22.0	160	5.9	622	23.0	38	1.4	260	9.6*	1156	42.8	1545	57.2
MACON	595	26.7	894	40.2	42	1.9	263	11.8	171	7.7	261	11.7*	651	40.6	954	59.4
MADISON	1202	33.4	369	10.2	164	4.6	1420	39.4	33	.9	413	11.5*	1714	46.1	2008	53.9
MARION	250	24.7	310	30.7	51	5.0	214	21.2	49	4.8	137	13.6*	85	21.7	306	78.3
MCDUFFIE	1045	23.7	1022	23.2	229	5.2	949	21.5	847	19.2	314	7.1*	1573	45.4	1895	54.6
MCINTOSH	1256	51.0	236	9.6	158	6.4	384	15.6	215	8.7	216	8.8*	719	67.0	354	33.0
MERIWETHR	1357	32.8	802	19.4	253	6.1	1156	28.0	221	5.3	343	8.3*	2158	46.5	2479	53.5
MILLER	552	32.6	431	25.5	116	6.9	395	23.3	17	1.0	181	10.7*	510	38.1	828	61.9
MITCHELL	1323	31.3	1259	29.8	163	3.9	491	11.6	565	13.4	429	10.1*	1371	41.6	1925	58.4
MONROE	980	36.2	778	28.8	150	5.5	408	15.1	100	3.7	289	10.7*	731	40.1	1092	59.9
MONTGOMRY	729	33.8	382	17.7	135	6.3	451	20.9	141	6.5	319	14.8*	773	42.8	1032	57.2
MORGAN	1021	38.6	510	19.3	165	6.2	673	25.4	94	3.6	182	6.9*	920	46.0	1078	54.0
MURRAY	1475	43.0	422	12.3	175	5.1	909	26.5	14	.4	437	12.7*	1651	48.4	1761	51.6
MUSCOGEE	3171	24.3	5763	44.2	343	2.6	1922	14.7	1000	7.7	842	6.5*	3320	34.7	6237	65.3
NEWTON	1795	33.0	863	15.9	475	8.7	1374	25.3	238	4.4	696	12.8*	1305	41.3	1851	58.7
OCONEE	730	32.0	475	20.8	108	4.7	683	30.0	16	.7	267	11.7*	471	36.2	831	63.8
OGLETHRPE	675	36.1	206	11.0	96	5.1	576	30.8	82	4.4	233	12.5*	488	43.3	639	56.7
PAULDING	1718	31.2	779	14.1	668	12.1	1623	29.4	90	1.6	636	11.5*	2385	44.3	2993	55.7
PEACH	400	19.5	1236	60.3	53	2.6	133	6.5	49	2.4	180	8.8*	292	17.9	1340	82.1
PICKENS	162	35.4	70	15.3	40	8.7	111	24.2	8	1.7	67	14.6*	163	57.0	123	43.0
PIERCE	985	39.6	277	11.1	98	3.9	534	21.5	29	1.2	563	22.6*	239	38.3	385	61.7
PIKE	588	34.4	238	13.9	160	9.4	378	22.1	148	8.6	199	11.6*	347	44.6	465	55.4
POLK	2602	43.7	779	13.1	278	4.7	1359	22.8	125	2.1	813	13.7*	1941	50.0	1942	50.0
PULASKI	554	21.2	1513	58.0	80	3.1	227	8.7	123	4.7	111	4.3*	247	17.4	1173	82.6
PUTNAM	740	33.0	319	14.2	163	7.3	503	22.4	249	11.1	269	12.0*	1198	47.8	1310	52.2
QUITMAN	134	20.7	112	17.3	60	9.3	279	43.1	10	1.5	53	8.2*	69	26.3	193	73.7
RABUN	877	33.0	220	8.3	178	6.7	714	26.8	10	.4	661	24.8*	982	39.3	1517	60.7
RANDOLPH	806	34.2	590	25.0	98	4.2	449	19.0	224	9.5	192	8.1*	825	44.1	1046	55.9
RICHMOND	3006	25.6	3728	31.7	556	4.7	2372	20.2	1154	9.8	926	7.9*	3024	39.0	4733	61.0
ROCKDALE	1192	34.9	651	19.1	264	7.7	787	23.1	80	2.3	438	12.8*	656	44.1	832	55.9
SCHLEY	337	35.9	264	28.1	40	4.3	201	21.4	27	2.9	70	7.5*	115	34.7	216	65.3
SCREVEN	1096	43.4	269	10.7	154	6.1	546	21.6	106	4.2	352	14.0*	1562	61.4	982	38.6
SEMINOLE	875	44.3	315	16.0	115	5.8	347	17.6	44	2.2	278	14.1*	375	45.5	450	54.5
SPALDING	2807	38.6	1315	18.1	484	6.7	1546	21.3	258	3.6	857	11.8*	3173	49.7	3212	50.3
STEPHENS	2029	42.5	391	8.2	224	4.7	1181	24.7	38	.8	909	19.0*	2959	56.8	2247	43.2
STEWART	417	28.4	476	32.4	48	3.3	189	12.9	241	16.4	99	6.7*	196	33.1	396	66.9
SUMTER	1472	29.5	1879	37.7	199	4.0	825	16.5	168	3.4	442	8.9*	1406	36.7	2421	63.3
TALBOT	337	27.9	295	24.4	42	3.5	292	24.2	137	11.3	106	8.8*	223	37.1	378	62.9
TALIAFERO	219	23.6	215	23.2	14	1.5	185	20.0	200	21.6	94	10.1*	68	28.0	175	72.0
TATTNALL	1739	39.2	769	17.3	325	7.3	1112	25.1	57	1.3	436	9.8*	2060	56.1	1610	43.9
TAYLOR	455	20.3	825	36.9	73	3.3	290	13.0	380	17.0	215	9.6*	866	37.4	1447	62.6
TELFAIR	831	24.3	1217	35.6	206	6.0	535	15.6	127	3.7	505	14.8*	1115	34.2	2149	65.8
TERRELL	652	23.7	1055	38.4	67	2.4	369	13.4	373	13.6	232	8.4*	742	35.1	1374	64.9
THOMAS	2386	37.3	1362	21.3	241	3.8	846	13.2	473	7.4	1091	17.0*	2065	48.0	2236	52.0
TIFT	1877	39.7	1342	28.4	205	4.3	592	12.5	91	1.9	618	13.1*	2342	52.5	2116	47.5
TOOMBS	1818	37.8	839	17.4	421	8.7	876	18.2	160	3.3	700	14.5*	2385	50.0	2383	50.0

COUNTY	GAMBRELL #	%	NUNN #	%	STONER #	%	VANDIVER #	%	WILLIAMS #	%	OTHER #	%*	GAMBRELL #	%	NUNN #	%
TOWNS	311	33.9	102	11.1	51	5.6	369	40.2	5	.5	79	8.6*	397	53.3	348	46.7
TREUTLEN	861	39.3	404	18.4	157	7.2	566	25.8	37	1.7	165	7.5*	1168	46.7	1334	53.3
TROUP	2722	34.7	1816	23.2	367	4.7	1761	22.5	230	2.9	947	12.1*	3188	52.2	2922	47.8
TURNER	649	30.8	854	40.6	80	3.8	338	16.1	31	1.5	153	7.3*	845	36.2	1492	63.8
TWIGGS	434	21.3	770	37.7	159	7.8	200	9.8	331	16.2	147	7.2*	551	33.9	1075	66.1
												*				
UNION	898	42.8	170	8.1	208	9.9	617	29.4	9	.4	198	9.4*	1445	59.0	1005	41.0
UPSON	1527	25.0	503	8.2	255	4.2	635	10.4	355	5.8	2834	46.4*	2908	56.1	2277	43.9
WALKER	3270	45.6	455	6.3	703	9.8	2004	28.0	72	1.0	662	9.2*	1464	52.1	1344	47.9
WALTON	2041	39.6	654	12.7	427	8.3	1102	21.4	234	4.5	699	13.6*	2297	50.0	2301	50.0
WARE	2573	37.1	1448	20.9	234	3.4	961	13.9	191	2.8	1528	22.0*	3679	50.3	3633	49.7
												*				
WARREN	469	27.1	419	24.2	151	8.7	305	17.6	230	13.3	157	9.1*	611	39.0	957	61.0
WASHINGTON	1987	28.2	1456	20.7	393	5.6	676	9.6	1986	28.2	542	7.7*	2138	43.2	2816	56.8
WAYNE	1353	32.8	722	17.5	247	6.0	660	16.0	126	3.1	1013	24.6*	2006	45.1	2445	54.9
WEBSTER	251	36.5	245	35.6	19	2.8	68	9.9	43	6.3	62	9.0*	91	31.9	194	68.1
WHEELER	456	29.6	416	27.0	66	4.3	292	19.0	169	11.0	140	9.1*	604	49.5	616	50.5
												*				
WHITE	839	35.4	411	17.4	148	6.3	702	29.7	23	1.0	245	10.3*	662	42.5	896	57.5
WHITFIELD	2675	39.5	1114	16.5	273	4.0	1845	27.3	89	1.3	773	11.4*	2287	44.7	2830	55.3
WILCOX	597	23.7	1262	50.1	153	6.1	283	11.2	49	1.9	175	6.9*	651	27.3	1736	72.7
WILKES	746	31.7	561	23.8	86	3.7	648	27.5	143	6.1	170	7.2*	366	30.8	823	69.2
WILKINSON	757	33.9	573	25.6	180	8.1	221	9.9	218	9.8	286	12.8*	618	39.4	952	60.6
												*				
WORTH	828	26.9	1354	44.0	146	4.7	367	11.9	122	4.0	257	8.4*	817	32.3	1714	67.7
												*				
TOTALS	258216		170689		38261		151908		45613		87520	*	283414		334670	
% OF VOTE		34.3		22.7		5.1		20.2		6.1		11.6	*	45.9		54.1

GEOGRAPHIC CLASS

	GAMBRELL #	%	NUNN #	%	STONER #	%	VANDIVER #	%	WILLIAMS #	%	OTHER #	%*	GAMBRELL #	%	NUNN #	%
LOWLANDS	62421	34.	48960	27.	9208	5.	29251	16.	7327	4.	26826	15.*	74576	46.	89323	54.
BLACK BELT	58764	30.	57308	29.	8760	5.	30661	16.	18834	10.	20014	10.*	61830	41.	90772	59.
PIEDMONT	103425	35.	53657	18.	15033	5.	70742	24.	18594	6.	30900	11.*	116181	49.	121351	51.
MOUNTAIN	33606	41.	10764	13.	5260	6.	21254	26.	858	1.	9750	12.*	30827	48.	33224	52.

DEMOGRAPHIC CLASS

	GAMBRELL #	%	NUNN #	%	STONER #	%	VANDIVER #	%	WILLIAMS #	%	OTHER #	%*	GAMBRELL #	%	NUNN #	%
METRO	56721	34.	39406	24.	5522	3.	28430	17.	20389	12.	17019	10.*	68472	52.	61965	48.
TOWN	36990	33.	29609	27.	4918	4.	24636	22.	2826	3.	11854	11.*	40436	42.	56179	58.
RURAL	164505	35.	101674	21.	27821	6.	98842	21.	22398	5.	58647	12.*	174506	45.	216526	55.

COUNTY	SPECL. REFERENDUM 1952*				SPECL. REFERENDUM 1954			
	FOR		AGAINST		FOR		AGAINST	
	#	%	#	%*	#	%	#	%
APPLING	1432	59.1	989	40.9*	1105	70.5	462	29.5
ATKINSON	824	64.0	464	36.0*	600	60.5	391	39.5
BACON	1233	67.1	604	32.9*	666	68.7	304	31.3
BAKER	958	89.0	118	11.0*	662	94.4	39	5.6
BALDWIN	1846	54.2	1557	45.8*	1086	48.4	1160	51.6
BANKS	844	65.4	447	34.6*	478	59.7	323	40.3
BARROW	1542	56.0	1210	44.0*	1143	62.4	690	37.6
BARTON	2184	45.4	2624	54.6*	1550	52.0	1428	48.0
BEN HILL	1172	50.0	1173	50.0*	731	52.1	672	47.9
BERRIEN	1313	67.4	634	32.6*	1169	79.3	305	20.7
BIBB	8213	37.7	13581	62.3*	5633	48.0	6111	52.0
BLECKLEY	1401	80.8	333	19.2*	670	59.1	464	40.9
BRANTLEY	897	75.9	285	24.1*	584	61.6	364	38.4
BROOKS	1484	59.7	1000	40.3*	1132	69.2	504	30.8
BRYAN	1087	86.1	175	13.9*	530	80.4	129	19.6
BULLOCH	2258	53.0	1999	47.0*	1731	58.7	1217	41.3
BURKE	1278	71.3	514	28.7*	960	67.7	459	32.3
BUTTS	1384	66.3	704	33.7*	1029	74.6	351	25.4
CALHOUN	532	61.6	331	38.4*	468	76.3	145	23.7
CAMDEN	1148	80.8	273	19.2*	495	48.7	522	51.3
CHANDLER	1142	78.7	309	21.3*	576	67.8	273	32.2
CARROLL	2840	46.5	3265	53.5*	1801	53.9	1543	46.1
CATOOSA	1377	52.8	1230	47.2*	732	56.9	555	43.1
CHARLTON	959	90.7	98	9.3*	505	72.6	191	27.4
CHATHAM	13884	47.3	15446	52.7*	6714	47.1	7553	52.9
CHATTAHOO	113	66.5	57	33.5*	104	85.2	18	14.8
CHATTOOGA	1197	33.0	2426	67.0*	901	46.3	1047	53.7
CHEROKEE	2094	54.0	1785	46.0*	1048	51.4	990	48.6
CLARKE	1649	27.7	4310	72.3*	1269	29.9	2978	70.1
CLAY	438	69.9	189	30.1*	324	82.2	70	17.8
CLAYTON	2944	55.8	2334	44.2*	2365	66.5	1193	33.5
CLINCH	756	69.4	334	30.6*	307	54.5	256	45.5
COBB	5273	38.4	8467	61.6*	4668	41.8	6510	58.2
COFFEE	2520	63.0	1477	37.0*	1302	46.1	1522	53.9
COLQUITT	2348	46.8	2667	53.2*	2652	68.0	1250	32.0
COLUMBIA	847	68.0	398	32.0*	595	74.7	201	25.3
COOK	1640	66.5	826	33.5*	928	73.7	332	26.3
COWETA	1369	31.2	3014	68.8*	1515	49.6	1540	50.4
CRAWFORD	889	81.8	198	18.2*	487	73.1	179	26.9
CRISP	1564	50.1	1559	49.9*	844	52.7	757	47.3
DADE	539	49.9	542	50.1*	275	46.1	321	53.9
DAWSON	571	71.7	225	28.3*	525	52.3	478	47.7
DECATUR	2288	68.0	1076	32.0*	2345	86.8	358	13.2
DEKALB	8419	25.7	24383	74.3*	10573	39.3	16353	60.7
DODGE	2607	68.7	1187	31.3*	1941	70.9	798	29.1
DOOLEY	1289	65.8	671	34.2*	811	65.5	427	34.5

	SPECL. REFERENDUM 1952*				SPECL. REFERENDUM 1954			
COUNTY	FOR		AGAINST		FOR		AGAINST	
	#	%	#	%*	#	%	#	%
DOUGHERTY	1985	30.9	4436	69.1*	2821	50.9	2722	49.1
DOUGLAS	1417	52.8	1266	47.2*	1000	61.6	623	38.4
EARLY	1164	59.8	782	40.2*	633	58.3	453	41.7
ECHOLS	604	96.0	25	4.0*	252	71.6	100	28.4
EFFINGHAM	1157	79.0	307	21.0*	604	73.1	222	26.9
ELBERT	1731	51.5	1631	48.5*	1626	70.9	668	29.1
EMANUEL	2243	73.0	828	27.0*	1712	73.7	611	26.3
EVANS	1012	74.4	348	25.6*	497	60.8	321	39.2
FANNIN	1320	52.4	1197	47.6*	667	29.2	1615	70.8
FAYETTE	1032	68.3	478	31.7*	706	68.9	318	31.1
FLOYD	3730	31.6	8061	68.4*	2929	44.9	3594	55.1
FORSYTHE	1102	63.1	644	36.9*	425	49.2	438	50.8
FRANKLIN	1709	56.1	1335	43.9*	1264	65.2	676	34.8
FULTON	21459	29.4	51482	70.6*	23597	41.8	32883	58.2
GILMER	1335	60.3	879	39.7*	1140	57.1	857	42.9
GLASCOCK	514	89.7	59	10.3*	232	82.9	48	17.1
GLYNN	1463	33.0	2973	67.0*	704	17.7	3280	82.3
GORDON	954	30.8	2143	69.2*	701	43.4	913	56.6
GRADY	2003	64.1	1124	35.9*	1231	54.3	1034	45.7
GREENE	1285	48.6	1358	51.4*	937	56.2	731	43.8
GWINNETT	3356	48.3	3596	51.7*	2330	58.9	1624	41.1
HABERSHAM	1511	46.2	1761	53.8*	665	34.7	1249	65.3
HALL	3145	42.2	4314	57.8*	1743	38.9	2737	61.1
HANCOCK	716	57.9	520	42.1*	557	71.0	228	29.0
HARALSON	1930	61.1	1230	38.9*	1144	63.2	666	36.8
HARRIS	935	52.3	854	47.7*	994	50.2	987	49.8
HART	1957	63.3	1134	36.7*	1681	85.0	297	15.0
HEARD	720	57.5	533	42.5*	506	63.2	294	36.7
HENRY	1779	59.1	1230	40.9*	1328	63.1	776	36.9
HOUSTON	1796	56.2	1402	43.8*	1305	53.2	1147	46.8
IRWIN	1135	67.1	557	32.9*	748	56.5	576	43.5
JACKSON	1712	46.8	1945	53.2*	1368	55.7	1087	44.3
JASPER	682	52.8	610	47.2*	696	69.0	312	31.0
JEFF DAVIS	1215	74.4	418	25.6*	636	59.7	429	40.3
JEFFERSON	1346	66.7	673	33.3*	783	53.9	669	46.1
JENKINS	656	51.1	628	48.9*	415	53.3	364	46.7
JOHNSON	1622	80.6	390	19.4*	963	75.9	306	24.1
JONES	1145	71.9	448	28.1*	800	70.7	332	29.3
LAMAR	1146	58.1	825	41.9*	928	67.5	446	32.5
LANIER	463	47.1	520	52.9*	284	64.1	159	35.9
LAURINS	3693	63.9	2083	36.1*	2054	67.2	1001	32.8
LEE	465	80.0	116	20.0*	345	84.6	63	15.4
LIBERTY	1095	58.9	765	41.1*	508	37.2	856	62.8
LINCOLN	586	69.8	253	30.2*	427	69.9	184	30.1
LONG	1084	96.5	39	3.5*	492	80.5	119	19.5
LOWNDES	1862	38.4	2982	61.6*	1399	55.4	1127	44.6

	SPECL. REFERENDUM 1952*				SPECL. REFERENDUM 1954			
COUNTY	FOR		AGAINST		FOR		AGAINST	
	#	%	#	%*	#	%	#	%
LUMPKIN	704	55.7	560	44.3*	218	32.0	463	68.0
MACON	924	55.7	735	44.3*	736	62.9	434	37.1
MADISON	1051	53.0	931	47.0*	928	57.8	678	42.2
MARION	520	66.2	266	33.8*	462	81.8	103	18.2
MCDUFFIE	1074	57.2	803	42.8*	506	56.2	394	43.8
MCINTOSH	600	61.9	370	38.1*	463	55.4	372	44.6
MERIWETHR	1986	53.1	1751	46.9*	1877	72.3	720	27.7
MILLER	1174	84.0	223	16.0*	645	80.3	158	19.7
MITCHELL	2175	64.2	1215	35.8*	1032	55.9	813	44.1
MONROE	1268	62.7	753	37.3*	972	59.7	657	40.3
MONTGOMRY	1686	89.7	194	10.3*	891	83.5	176	16.5
MORGAN	1103	62.0	675	38.0*	937	71.7	370	28.3
MURRAY	910	46.0	1069	54.0*	525	49.3	539	50.7
MUSCOGEE	6139	35.8	11001	64.2*	6538	57.1	4914	42.9
NEWTON	1987	52.6	1791	47.4*	1356	60.3	894	39.7
OCONEE	916	60.9	587	39.1*	571	62.6	341	37.4
OGLETHRPE	1139	69.3	504	30.7*	779	72.4	297	27.6
PAULDING	1644	63.1	963	36.9*	1051	68.6	482	31.4
PEACH	1013	53.1	893	46.9*	922	64.8	500	35.2
PICKENS	918	52.9	818	47.1*	742	72.6	280	27.4
PIERCE	1507	70.7	625	29.3*	1407	79.0	374	21.0
PIKE	1207	67.9	570	32.1*	644	73.9	227	26.1
POLK	1892	34.1	3662	65.9*	1182	37.4	1980	62.6
PULASKI	1000	68.3	465	31.7*	711	68.0	335	32.0
PUTNAM	752	53.4	655	46.6*	561	58.1	405	41.9
QUITMAN	257	74.1	90	25.9*	172	80.0	43	20.0
RABUN	948	59.5	645	40.5*	337	37.4	563	62.6
RANDOLPH	984	55.6	786	44.4*	1027	76.2	321	23.8
RICHMOND	4109	27.3	10940	72.7*	2836	34.0	5495	66.0
ROCKDALE	1039	54.9	855	45.1*	801	60.7	519	39.3
SCHLEY	278	50.9	268	49.1*	251	68.6	115	31.4
SCREVEN	1207	65.8	626	34.2*	687	60.3	452	39.7
SEMINOLE	937	77.2	276	22.8*	1001	88.9	125	11.1
SPALDING	1952	32.8	3998	67.2*	2940	64.6	1611	35.4
STEPHENS	1298	43.6	1679	56.4*	1133	63.4	655	36.6
STEWART	851	74.2	296	25.8*	781	82.6	165	17.4
SUMTER	1444	42.5	1952	57.5*	1490	66.1	764	33.9
TALBOT	395	48.7	416	51.3*	457	69.8	198	30.2
TALIAFERO	411	43.6	531	56.4*	287	52.9	256	47.1
TATTNALL	2274	77.7	654	22.3*	1892	79.0	503	21.0
TAYLOR	1270	69.2	565	30.8*	778	64.9	420	35.1
TELFAIR	2692	92.3	226	7.7*	1909	89.0	236	11.0
TERRELL	1251	73.4	454	26.6*	977	85.0	173	15.0
THOMAS	2491	41.9	3455	58.1*	2060	49.5	2105	50.5
TIFT	2222	58.6	1573	41.4*	1735	70.2	736	29.8
TOOMBS	2348	72.8	879	27.2*	1661	77.5	483	22.5

```
              SPECL.   REFERENDUM 1952* SPECL.  REFERENDUM 1954
                                     *
  COUNTY     FOR         AGAINST       FOR         AGAINST
            #      %     #      %*     #      %    #      %
---------------------------------------------*-------------------------------------------------------
TOWNS        862  66.7   431  33.3*   311  25.3   919  74.7
TREUTLEN    1418  94.7    80   5.3*   926  92.6    74   7.4
TROUP       2686  33.6  5309  66.4*  2723  52.8  2439  47.2
TURNER      1096  68.9   495  31.1*   771  75.3   253  24.7
TWIGGS       933  81.4   213  18.6*   653  80.4   159  19.6
                                     *
UNION       1558  70.1   665  29.9*   287  36.4   502  63.6
UPSON       1779  43.2  2340  56.8*  1777  64.0   999  36.0
WALKER      2696  46.6  3087  53.4*  1154  38.0  1883  62.0
WALTON      2051  54.2  1735  45.8*  1741  72.0   677  28.0
WARE        3327  51.0  3192  49.0*  1975  59.6  1339  40.4
                                     *
WARREN       689  70.2   292  29.8*   526  78.7   142  21.3
WASHINGTON  1987  67.0   978  33.0*  1369  69.5   600  30.5
WAYNE       1952  78.5   535  21.5*  1261  72.1   487  27.9
WEBSTER      414  87.2    61  12.8*   309  89.3    37  10.7
WHEELER      917  73.8   325  26.2*   635  78.6   173  21.4
                                     *
WHITE        806  56.3   626  43.7*   285  34.8   534  65.2
WHITFIELD   2250  35.4  4114  64.6*  1231  42.5  1663  57.5
WILCOX      1221  66.8   608  33.2*   901  67.9   426  32.1
WILKES       937  52.3   856  47.7*   641  55.7   510  44.3
WILKINSON   1637  81.1   382  18.9*   844  78.0   238  22.0
                                     *
WORTH       1162  55.5   933  44.5*   984  71.9   384  28.1
---------------------------------------------*-------------------------------------------------------
                                     *
TOTALS    279882       309170    * 210478       181157
% OF VOTE   47.5         52.5    *   53.7         46.3
                                     *
                                     *
GEOGRAPHIC CLASS                     *
                                     *
LOWLANDS   85230  61.   54758  39.*  54328  62.   33709  38.
BLACK BELT 80597  51.   77831  49.*  61594  60.   41893  40.
PIEDMONT   85793  38.  139816  62.*  78199  48.   84172  52.
MOUNTAIN   28262  43.   36765  57.*  16357  43.   21383  57.
                                     *
DEMOGRAPHIC CLASS                    *
                                     *
METRO      64208  33.  131269  67.*  58712  44.   76031  56.
TOWN       26682  38.   43028  62.*  22277  47.   25218  53.
RURAL     188992  58.  134873  42.* 129489  62.   79908  38.
```

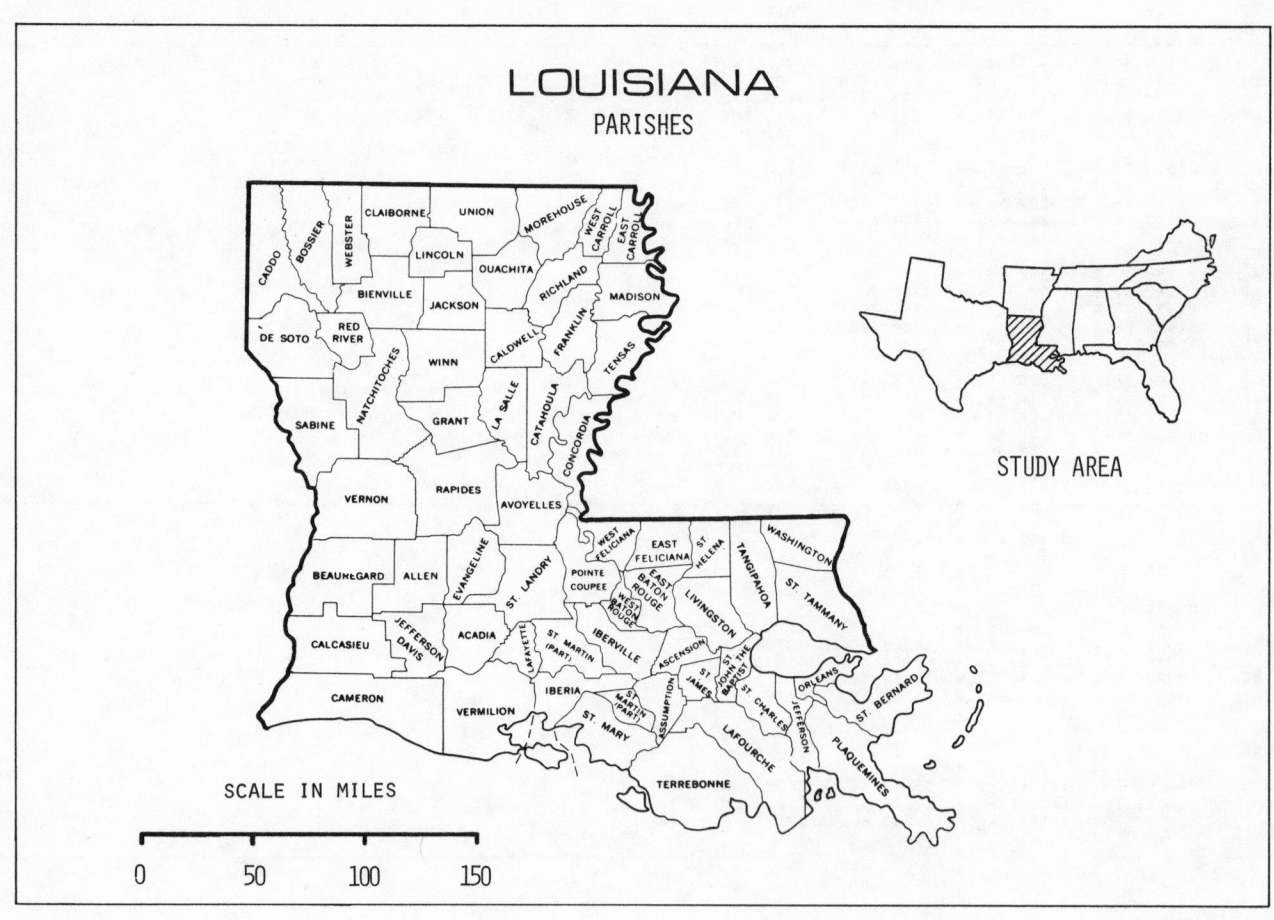

LOUISIANA
PARISHES

CADDO
BOSSIER
WEBSTER
CLAIBORNE
UNION
MOREHOUSE
WEST CARROLL
EAST CARROLL
LINCOLN
OUACHITA
RICHLAND
MADISON
BIENVILLE
JACKSON
DE SOTO
RED RIVER
WINN
CALDWELL
FRANKLIN
TENSAS
NATCHITOCHES
GRANT
LA SALLE
CATAHOULA
CONCORDIA
SABINE
VERNON
RAPIDES
AVOYELLES
BEAUREGARD
ALLEN
EVANGELINE
ST. LANDRY
WEST FELICIANA
EAST FELICIANA
ST. HELENA
TANGIPAHOA
WASHINGTON
ST. TAMMANY
POINTE COUPEE
EAST BATON ROUGE
WEST BATON ROUGE
LIVINGSTON
JEFFERSON DAVIS
ACADIA
LAFAYETTE
ST. MARTIN (PART)
IBERVILLE
ASCENSION
ST. JAMES
ST. JOHN THE BAPTIST
CALCASIEU
ST. CHARLES
ORLEANS
ST. BERNARD
CAMERON
VERMILION
IBERIA
ST. MARTIN (PART)
ASSUMPTION
ST. MARY
LAFOURCHE
JEFFERSON
PLAQUEMINES
TERREBONNE

SCALE IN MILES

0   50   100   150

STUDY AREA

LOUISIANA

Louisiana Democratic gubernatorial primaries consistently attracted almost half the citizens of voting age to the polls during the 1950s and more than half during the late 1960s and in 1971. As in other southern states, the number of registered voters increased substantially during this period. In 1950 there were some 818,000 registered voters, which was 51.9 percent of all citizens of voting age in the state; in 1960 registration was 1,152,151, or 63.9 percent of the citizenry; and in 1970 it was approximately 1,462,000 or 71.6 percent. The number of black registered voters grew from 7.5 percent of the total in 1950 to 13.8 percent in 1960 and to 21.8 percent in 1970. The Louisiana Constitution required that potential voters be able to read and understand any part of the constitutions of the United States and Louisiana or be able to interpret any section read to him, thus providing registrars with a device to limit black participation prior to the mid-1960s. In 1960, 31.1 percent of blacks of voting age were registered, compared to 57.4 percent in 1970. White registration remained relatively stable, with 76.9 percent of the voting-age population registered in 1960 and 77 percent in 1970.

The following table presents returns from recent presidential elections. Turnout figures include both total number of votes cast and the percentage of citizens of voting age who voted.

Included below are 9 Democratic gubernatorial primaries, 3 senatorial primaries, and the vote on a segregation amendment proposed during the conflict over school desegregation in New Orleans. Additionally, the 1956 primary for lieutenant governor is included as a demonstration of the relatively structured Democratic party factional competition that existed in Louisiana. Although listed separately on the ballot, candidates campaigned as part of a ticket or slate. In 1956 Earl K. Long and Lether E. Frazar headed the Long forces, and the major reform contenders were deLesseps S. Morrison-C. E. Barham, Frederick T. Preaus-A. Brown Moore, and James M. McLemore-J. Bentley Alexander. In 1960 the Long candidate failed to make the runoff, and the politics of economic class were displaced by the politics of race and religion.

Gubernatorial Primaries

1. January 15, 1952: Hale Boggs 142,542 (18.7%), William J. Dodd 90,925 (11.9%), Robert F. Kennon 163,434 (21.5%), Dudley J. LeBlanc 62,906 (8.3%), James M. McLemore 116,405 (15.3%), Carlos G. Spaht 173,987 (22.8%), other 3 candidates 11,535 (1.5%). Total vote was 761,734; turnout of voting-age citizens was 47.0%.
2. February 19, 1952: Robert F. Kennon 482,302 (61.4%), Carlos G. Spaht 302,653 (38.6%). Total vote was 784,955; turnout was 48.4%.
3. January 17, 1956: Francis C. Grevemberg 62,309 (7.6%), Earl K. Long 421,681 (51.4%), James M. McLemore 48,188 (5.9%), deLesseps S. Morrison 191,576 (23.4%), Frederick T. Preaus 95,955 (11.7%). Total vote was 819,709; turnout was 47.8%.
4. December 5, 1959: Jimmie H. Davis 213,551 (25.3%), William J. Dodd 85,436 (10.1%), deLesseps S. Morrison 278,956

(33.1%), James A. Noe 97,654 (11.6%), William M. Rainach 143,096 (17.0%), other 6 candidates received 23,917 (2.8%). Total vote was 842,610; turnout was 47.3%.

5. January 9, 1960: Jimmie H. Davis 487,681 (54.1%), deLesseps S. Morrison 414,110 (45.9%). Total vote was 901,791; turnout was 50.0%.

6. December 7, 1963: Shelby M. Jackson 103,949 (11.5%), Robert F. Kennon 127,870 (14.1%), Gillis W. Long 137,778 (15.2%), John J. McKeithen 157,304 (17.4%), deLesseps S. Morrison 299,702 (33.1%), other 5 candidates 79,872 (8.8%). Total vote was 906,475; turnout was 48.3%.

7. January 11, 1964: John J. McKeithen 492,905 (52.2%), deLesseps S. Morrison 451,161 (47.8%). Total vote was 944,066; turnout was 49.7%.

* (November 4, 1967: John J. McKeithen won 80.6% against 4 opponents. Total vote was 1,037,102; turnout was 52.7%.)

8. November 6, 1971: Jimmie H. Davis 138,756 (11.8%), Edwin W. Edwards 276,397 (23.6%), J. Bennett Johnston 208,830 (17.8%), Gillis W. Long 164,276 (14.0%), other 13 candidates 384,855 (32.8%). Total vote was 1,173,114; turnout was 51.1%.

9. December 18, 1971: Edwin W. Edwards 584,262 (50.2%), J. Bennett Johnston 579,774 (49.8%). Total vote was 1,164,036; turnout was 50.7%.

Primary for Lieutenant Governor

January 17, 1956: J. Bentley Alexander 53,593 (7.3%), C. E. Barham 195,616 (26.8%), Wesley H. Clanton 41,478 (5.7%),

Lether E. Frazar 327,679 (44.9%), A. Brown Moore 111,452 (15.3%). Total vote was 729,818.

Senatorial Primaries

1. July 25, 1950: Russell B. Long 359,330 (68.5%), Malcolm E. Lafargue 156,918 (29.9%), Newt V. Mills 8,611 (1.6%). Total vote was 524,859.

2. July 27, 1954: Allen J. Ellender 268,05 (59.1%), Frank B. Ellis 162,775 (35.9%), W. Gilbert Faulk 22,366 (4.9%). Total vote was 453,195.

* (July 31, 1956: Russell B. Long unopposed.)

* (July 23, 1960: Allen J. Ellender unopposed.)

* (July 28, 1962: Russell B. Long won 80. against 1 opponent. Total vote was 508,005.)

3. August 13, 1966: Allen J. Ellender 494,519 (74.2%), J. D. DeBlieux 94,154 (14.1%), Troyce E. Guice 78,137 (11.7%). Total vote was 666,810.

* (August 17, 1968: Russell B. Long won 87.0% against 1 opponent. Total vote wa 568,258.)

* (August 19, 1972: J. Bennett Johnston 79.4% against 1 opponent, with 73,088 votes going to Allen J. Ellender, deceased. Total vote was 784,362.)

Special Election

November 8, 1960: Segregation amendment providing for the recall of any official ordering the integration of any public

facility and "for abandonment of such
facility as a governmental function."
For 284,987 (65.3%), Against 151,685
(34.7%). Total vote was 436,672.

RETURNS FROM PRESIDENTIAL ELECTIONS

Year	Turnout		Partisan Vote*
1948	416,336	(27.1%)[+]	Dixiecrat 49.1%, Democrat 32.7%, Republican 17.5%
1952	651,952	(40.2%)	Democrat 52.9%, Republican 47.1%
1956	617,544	(36.0%)	Republican 53.3%, Democrat 39.5%, States' Rights 7.2%
1960	807,891	(44.8%)	Democrat 50.4%, Republican 28.6%, Independent 21.0%
1964	896,293	(47.2%)	Republican 56.8%, Democrat 43.2%
1968	1,097,450	(55.1%)	American Independent 48.3%, Democrat 28.2%, Republican 23.5%
1972	1,051,491	(45.4%)	Republican 65.3%, Democrat 28.4%, Other 6.3%

*Totals do not necessarily equal 100%, since minor party percentages are excluded.

[+]Percentage of citizens of voting age who voted is calculated on the basis of a straight-line interpolation of citizen population between census years.

	DEMOC. GOVERNOR 1952											* DEMOC. RUNOFF 1952			
COUNTY	BOGGS		DODD		KENNON		LEBLANC		MCLEMORE		SPAHT		KENNON		SPAHT	
	#	%	#	%	#	%	#	%	#	%	#	%*	#	%	#	%
ACADIA	1360	7.8	735	4.2	1241	7.1	7009	40.1	2112	12.1	5014	28.7*	9445	55.9	7465	44.1
ALLEN	328	4.1	4560	56.5	285	3.5	719	8.9	493	6.1	1685	20.9*	4118	54.0	3512	46.0
ASCENSN	2064	26.7	1292	16.7	1497	19.4	253	3.3	523	6.8	2102	27.2*	3561	47.1	3997	52.9
ASSUMPTN	705	14.8	367	7.7	1078	22.7	416	8.7	330	6.9	1859	39.1*	2550	53.5	2212	46.5
AVOYELLES	2359	19.9	790	6.7	1152	9.7	1464	12.3	2631	22.1	3483	29.3*	6496	52.4	5907	47.6
BEAUREGRD	802	12.3	1045	16.0	599	9.2	707	10.8	1100	16.9	2273	34.8*	3474	50.9	3350	49.1
BIENVILLE	623	12.6	420	8.5	1024	20.7	195	3.9	1113	22.5	1570	31.7*	2361	49.1	2443	50.9
BOSSIER	1108	15.0	487	6.6	2685	36.4	283	3.8	1799	24.4	1023	13.9*	4758	66.1	2439	33.9
CADDO	5424	18.2	1865	6.2	8419	28.2	475	1.6	10940	36.6	2757	9.2*	26988	75.0	9016	25.0
CALCASIEU	4499	16.3	4729	17.2	3428	12.4	4168	15.1	6877	25.0	3850	14.0*	20814	59.0	14468	41.0
CALDWELL	212	6.1	532	15.2	678	19.4	494	14.1	327	9.3	1257	35.9*	1873	51.4	1774	48.6
CAMERON	382	14.1	373	13.7	243	9.0	845	31.1	314	11.6	558	20.6*	1660	66.7	829	33.3
CATAHOULA	388	11.0	720	20.5	385	10.9	266	7.6	955	27.2	803	22.8*	1921	54.0	1634	46.0
CLAIBORNE	674	12.8	489	9.3	1649	31.4	97	1.8	1503	28.6	839	16.0*	3715	66.2	1893	33.8
CONCORDIA	366	11.9	357	11.6	679	22.1	354	11.5	598	19.4	723	23.5*	1906	58.3	1364	41.7
DESOTO	586	12.6	646	13.9	716	15.4	115	2.5	1600	34.4	984	21.2*	2875	60.2	1898	39.8
EBTNROUGE	6484	16.3	5057	12.7	15816	39.8	240	.6	4289	10.8	7892	19.8*	27996	64.0	15718	36.0
ECARROLL	387	16.5	136	5.8	280	12.0	183	7.8	797	34.0	558	23.8*	1593	62.3	963	37.7
EFELCIANA	158	6.7	174	7.3	1305	54.9	23	1.0	251	10.6	464	19.5*	1674	70.4	705	29.6
EVANGELIN	973	7.9	3230	26.3	1521	12.4	3046	24.8	858	7.0	2633	21.5*	6598	58.7	4646	41.3
FRANKLIN	931	13.2	853	12.1	1628	23.0	272	3.8	1475	20.9	1909	27.0*	4382	57.7	3206	42.3
GRANT	405	6.7	868	14.4	1491	24.8	355	5.9	750	12.5	2154	35.8*	3002	48.6	3173	51.4
IBERIA	1944	17.0	508	4.4	1846	16.1	3390	29.6	1974	17.2	1789	15.6*	8885	70.3	3750	29.7
IBERVILLE	1207	20.3	868	14.6	1467	24.7	114	1.9	388	6.5	1891	31.9*	3093	48.9	3230	51.1
JACKSON	952	16.5	633	10.9	1608	27.8	161	2.8	531	9.2	1899	32.8*	2485	41.0	3571	59.0
JEFFERSON	11511	31.9	4792	13.3	11133	30.8	1604	4.4	3387	9.4	3673	10.2*	27597	77.5	7996	22.5
JEFFDAVIS	795	8.7	1740	19.1	1720	18.8	2360	25.9	1282	14.0	1232	13.5*	6050	62.6	3607	37.4
LAFAYETTE	2574	14.5	630	3.6	1638	9.2	5929	33.4	3806	21.5	3152	17.8*	12452	67.4	6026	32.6
LAFOURCHE	1868	13.4	2818	20.3	5063	36.4	365	2.6	667	4.8	3119	22.4*	9601	64.5	5281	35.5
LASALLE	416	7.4	1248	22.3	972	17.4	251	4.5	1199	21.5	1503	26.9*	3093	54.0	2632	46.0
LINCOLN	1331	22.2	581	9.7	1247	20.8	113	1.9	1514	25.2	1217	20.3*	4069	63.0	2389	37.0
LIVINGSTN	895	11.6	1070	13.9	3423	44.5	267	3.5	196	2.5	1841	23.9*	4667	58.3	3335	41.7
MADISON	236	9.0	612	23.4	445	17.0	123	4.7	894	34.2	303	11.6*	1834	71.3	739	28.7
MOREHOUSE	915	14.1	903	13.9	1170	18.0	299	4.6	1930	29.7	1287	19.8*	4467	61.7	2771	38.3
NATCHTOCH	1140	11.0	2076	20.1	1098	10.6	681	6.6	2067	20.0	3285	31.7*	4970	47.5	5498	52.5
ORLEANS	54043	33.1	12082	7.4	33754	20.7	3067	1.9	17408	10.7	42723	26.2*	106070	63.8	60225	36.2
OUACHITE	2093	10.1	2733	13.2	6564	31.7	1354	6.5	3762	18.2	4185	20.2*	14511	64.8	7894	35.2
PLAQMINES	150	4.3	40	1.2	264	7.6	55	1.6	2893	83.2	75	2.2*	3388	96.4	125	3.6
PTCOUPEE	885	19.8	158	3.5	1497	33.4	60	1.3	463	10.3	1413	31.6*	2480	57.0	1869	43.0
RAPIDES	1900	7.1	4794	17.9	3216	12.0	1201	4.5	8492	31.7	7150	26.7*	16261	56.7	12419	43.3
REDRIVER	515	15.8	332	10.2	226	6.9	101	3.1	860	26.4	1222	37.5*	1230	35.8	2201	64.2
RICHLAND	905	16.0	423	7.5	1296	22.9	413	7.3	1154	20.4	1467	25.9*	3603	56.7	2751	43.3
SABINE	964	13.6	1821	25.7	881	12.4	429	6.0	907	12.8	2093	29.5*	2975	40.1	4440	59.9
STBERNARD	221	5.9	137	3.6	216	5.7	46	1.2	729	19.3	2419	64.2*	1203	30.0	2805	70.0
STCHARLES	1388	25.7	439	8.1	1080	20.0	166	3.1	509	9.4	1810	33.6*	2981	54.1	2528	45.9
STHELENA	202	8.5	572	24.0	958	40.1	62	2.6	117	4.9	477	20.0*	1483	58.9	1036	41.1

DEMOC. GOVERNOR 1952   * DEMOC. RUNOFF 1952

COUNTY	BOGGS #	%	DODD #	%	KENNON #	%	LEBLANC #	%	MCLEMORE #	%	SPAHT #	%*	KENNON #	%	SPAHT #	%
STJAMES	2176	51.6	483	11.4	427	10.1	78	1.8	83	2.0	973	23.1*	2145	50.1	2133	49.9
STJOHNBAP	1181	21.2	317	5.7	620	11.1	119	2.1	148	2.7	3190	57.2*	1737	36.3	3054	63.7
STLANDRY	2581	13.8	2552	13.7	1846	9.9	3748	20.1	3335	17.9	4614	24.7*	13162	66.7	6572	33.3
STMARTIN	1139	16.5	167	2.4	771	11.2	1600	23.2	671	9.7	2539	36.9*	3899	55.2	3169	44.8
STMARY	1428	17.0	2035	24.2	2444	29.1	830	9.9	908	10.8	751	8.9*	6334	72.6	2388	27.4
STTAMMANY	1487	15.9	666	7.1	3315	35.5	446	4.8	986	10.6	2425	26.0*	5873	62.2	3567	37.8
TANGPOHOA	3054	20.1	1800	11.8	5545	36.4	654	4.3	870	5.7	3301	21.7*	9833	62.1	5996	37.9
TENSAS	176	9.2	186	9.7	334	17.4	50	2.6	787	40.9	389	20.2*	1170	69.5	514	30.5
TERREBONN	1574	17.2	2347	25.7	3082	33.7	283	3.1	879	9.6	972	10.6*	7417	76.3	2301	23.7
UNION	967	14.9	779	12.0	1847	28.5	544	8.4	658	10.1	1690	26.1*	3462	52.8	3089	47.2
VERMILION	635	4.0	622	3.9	765	4.9	7907	50.2	1003	6.4	4820	30.6*	8394	55.6	6711	44.4
VERNON	844	10.5	2846	35.3	703	8.7	749	9.3	877	10.9	2052	25.4*	4327	51.0	4156	49.0
WASHNGTON	2027	15.9	2139	16.8	3036	23.8	465	3.6	2603	20.4	2489	19.5*	7011	55.6	5591	44.4
WEBSTER	1274	13.4	860	9.0	4607	48.4	169	1.8	933	9.8	1675	17.6*	6251	57.8	4562	42.2
WBTNROUGE	572	23.6	227	9.4	863	35.6	39	1.6	170	7.0	554	22.8*	1425	58.6	1007	41.4
WCARROLL	652	13.0	464	9.3	825	16.5	328	6.5	1480	29.5	1260	25.2*	3030	55.5	2430	44.5
WFELCIANA	61	5.6	157	14.3	332	30.3	4	.4	321	29.3	222	20.2*	698	71.2	282	28.8
WINN	446	7.2	543	8.8	1491	24.2	303	4.9	929	15.1	2456	39.8*	2926	46.2	3401	53.8
TOTALS	142542		90925		163434		62906		116405		173987	*	482302		302653	
% OF VOTE	19.0		12.1		21.8		8.4		15.5		23.2	*	61.4		38.6	

GEOGRAPHIC CLASS

	BOGGS		DODD		KENNON		LEBLANC		MCLEMORE		SPAHT	*	KENNON		SPAHT	
LOWLANDS	33122	13.	37530	15.	68391	27.	10860	4.	45076	18.	55863	22.*	160835	60.	107699	40.
BLACK BELT	18895	16.	14262	12.	22428	19.	8504	7.	22212	19.	31968	27.*	70282	58.	51559	42.
CATHOLC LA	90525	24.	39133	10.	72615	19.	43542	11.	49117	13.	86156	23.*	251185	64.	143395	36.

DEMOGRAPHIC CLASS

	BOGGS		DODD		KENNON		LEBLANC		MCLEMORE		SPAHT	*	KENNON		SPAHT	
METRO	84054	27.	31258	10.	79114	25.	10908	3.	46663	15.	65080	21.*	223976	66.	115317	34.
TOWN	11348	13.	11042	12.	15719	18.	11597	13.	20282	23.	18994	21.*	57987	62.	35331	38.
RURAL	47140	14.	48625	14.	68601	20.	40401	12.	49460	14.	89913	26.*	200339	57.	152005	43.

LOUISIANA

DEMOC. GOVERNOR 1956   DEMOC. LT-GOV. 1956

COUNTY	GREVMBERG #	%	LONG #	%	MCLEMORE #	%	MORRISON #	%	PREAUS #	%*	ALEXANDER #	%	BARHAM #	%	CLANTON #	%	FRAZAR #	%	MOORE #
ACADIA	1797	10.4	10118	58.8	393	2.3	4199	24.4	698	4.1*	1016	6.9	4180	28.5	1101	7.5	7588	51.8	760	5.
ALLEN	574	7.7	5025	67.7	254	3.4	1028	13.8	543	7.3*	353	5.4	1063	16.3	382	5.9	4168	64.0	547	8.

COUNTY	GREVMBERG #	%	LONG #	%	MCLEMORE #	%	MORRISON #	%	PREAUS #	%*	ALEXANDER #	%	BARHAM #	%	CLANTON #	%	FRAZAR #	%	MOORE #	%
ASCENSN	937	12.0	5183	66.2	294	3.8	1152	14.7	269	3.4*	508	7.7	1373	21.0	536	8.2	3735	57.1	385	5.9
ASSUMPTN	349	6.4	3481	64.1	173	3.2	1213	22.3	215	4.0*	192	4.8	1018	25.5	193	4.8	2314	58.0	271	6.8
AVOYELLES	1097	9.0	7392	60.5	427	3.5	2573	21.1	731	6.0*	572	5.1	2341	21.1	697	6.3	6526	58.8	971	8.7
BEAUREGRD	581	8.3	4734	67.6	400	5.7	543	7.7	750	10.7*	318	4.8	697	10.6	292	4.4	4672	71.0	601	9.1
BIENVILLE	128	2.5	3333	65.1	154	3.0	469	9.2	1037	20.2*	151	3.3	892	19.4	84	1.8	2560	55.6	914	19.9
BOSSIER	522	6.8	4170	54.4	280	3.7	660	8.6	2032	26.5*	328	4.5	1235	17.1	334	4.6	3417	47.4	1901	26.3
CADDO	2010	5.7	13624	38.8	1347	3.8	7292	20.8	10803	30.8*	1110	3.3	9267	27.8	1367	4.1	11247	33.7	10384	31.1
CALCASIEU	4695	15.7	16242	54.4	1495	5.0	4068	13.6	3381	11.3*	1437	5.3	3800	13.9	2898	10.6	16541	60.5	2662	9.7
CALDWELL	100	3.0	2208	66.8	138	4.2	335	10.1	522	15.8*	116	3.8	449	14.6	76	2.5	1946	63.1	497	16.1
CAMERON	196	8.4	1206	51.9	115	4.9	397	17.1	411	17.7*	124	6.5	379	19.8	93	4.9	980	51.1	341	17.8
CATAHOULA	174	5.2	2321	68.7	162	4.8	312	9.2	408	12.1*	153	4.8	579	18.1	84	2.6	1994	62.3	390	12.2
CLAIBORNE	290	5.7	2177	42.7	218	4.3	432	8.5	1986	38.9*	198	4.2	914	19.6	196	4.2	1597	34.2	1769	37.8
CONCORDIA	226	6.4	2135	60.9	160	4.6	371	10.6	612	17.5*	181	5.5	541	16.5	116	3.5	1853	56.4	592	18.0
DESOTO	192	3.5	3124	56.4	256	4.6	481	8.7	1487	26.8*	228	4.3	842	16.0	125	2.4	2655	50.6	1398	26.6
BTNROUGE	6296	13.1	18785	39.1	3851	8.0	9141	19.0	9930	20.7*	6195	13.7	10145	22.4	3973	8.8	14919	33.0	10036	22.2
ECARROLL	255	10.7	1432	60.2	117	4.9	285	12.0	288	12.1*	130	5.8	515	23.1	157	7.0	1131	50.7	296	13.3
EFELCIANA	212	5.9	2388	66.2	343	9.5	197	5.5	465	12.9*	296	10.0	461	15.5	106	3.6	1632	55.0	471	15.9
EVANGELIN	1171	9.6	8548	70.1	192	1.6	1963	16.1	337	2.8*	711	9.3	1677	21.9	734	9.6	4122	53.9	406	5.3
FRANKLIN	245	3.6	3868	57.6	318	4.7	618	9.2	1672	24.9*	320	5.1	941	15.1	151	2.4	3290	52.7	1539	24.7
GRANT	234	4.3	3562	65.1	122	2.2	859	15.7	698	12.7*	171	3.3	934	18.0	143	2.8	3220	62.1	714	13.8
IBERIA	1419	9.6	7849	53.2	561	3.8	4002	27.1	912	6.2*	737	5.8	3270	25.9	870	6.9	6290	49.8	1456	11.5
IBERVILLE	806	10.7	4859	64.8	350	4.7	1228	16.4	258	3.4*	721	10.9	1509	22.8	439	6.6	3643	55.0	314	4.7
JACKSON	163	3.0	3750	69.8	116	2.2	587	10.9	754	14.0*	175	3.4	712	14.0	110	2.2	3368	66.1	727	14.3
JEFFERSON	4207	9.2	19514	42.5	4774	10.4	14138	30.8	3328	7.2*	4041	12.8	13984	44.2	3235	10.2	4539	14.3	5868	18.5
JEFFDAVIS	907	10.0	4511	49.6	387	4.3	2613	28.7	683	7.5*	662	8.2	2620	32.6	540	6.7	3587	44.6	638	7.9
LAFAYETTE	1792	10.2	7704	43.8	527	3.0	6104	34.7	1446	8.2*	821	5.3	5029	32.2	1100	7.0	6669	42.7	1992	12.8
LAFOURCHE	1483	10.1	7361	50.1	644	4.4	4816	32.8	390	2.7*	772	5.9	4170	31.9	1021	7.8	6200	47.5	899	6.9
LASALLE	440	7.6	3730	64.7	162	2.8	613	10.6	817	14.2*	243	4.6	1080	20.4	261	4.9	2963	56.0	744	14.1
LINCOLN	144	2.2	2967	46.0	156	2.4	1350	20.9	1832	28.4*	138	2.2	2395	38.5	76	1.2	2485	39.9	1130	18.2
LIVINGSTN	774	8.9	5296	61.1	1314	15.2	347	4.0	941	10.9*	1124	16.2	822	11.8	514	7.4	3475	50.1	1008	14.5
MADISON	115	4.5	1411	55.8	96	3.8	337	13.3	569	22.5*	125	5.2	622	25.9	58	2.4	1110	46.2	487	20.3
MOREHOUSE	210	2.8	3563	48.1	535	7.2	624	8.4	2480	33.5*	358	5.3	942	14.0	177	2.6	2867	42.6	2390	35.5
NATCHTOCH	777	8.0	6082	62.9	377	3.9	1518	15.7	909	9.4*	466	5.1	1976	21.8	417	4.6	5210	57.4	1001	11.0
ORLEANS	8761	5.0	69419	39.8	14128	8.1	71436	40.9	10856	6.2*	12853	7.8	66566	40.2	6660	4.0	57656	34.8	22036	13.3
OUACHITE	1031	4.4	11343	48.7	769	3.3	3400	14.6	6747	29.0*	809	3.6	3443	15.5	642	2.9	10741	48.5	6534	29.5
PLAQMINES	202	5.2	741	18.9	120	3.1	460	11.7	2397	61.1*	77	2.1	397	10.8	148	4.0	391	10.7	2651	72.4
PTCOUPEE	305	6.1	3015	60.1	188	3.7	1314	26.2	197	3.9*	297	7.0	1354	32.1	169	4.0	2158	51.2	237	5.6
RAPIDES	2111	9.4	11651	51.7	909	4.0	4080	18.1	3789	16.8*	976	4.4	4572	20.8	1458	6.6	10964	50.0	3972	18.1
REDRIVER	143	3.3	3380	77.4	359	8.2	166	3.8	318	7.3*	313	8.9	422	12.0	85	2.4	2369	67.5	319	9.1
RICHLAND	327	5.1	3581	56.3	257	4.0	749	11.8	1444	22.7*	288	4.8	1020	16.9	211	3.5	3108	51.5	1404	23.3
SABINE	263	3.7	5384	75.1	183	2.6	618	8.6	718	10.0*	233	3.5	943	14.2	162	2.4	4593	69.2	711	10.7
STBERNARD	712	7.7	5328	57.3	885	9.5	1923	20.7	447	4.8*	696	8.3	1945	23.1	582	6.9	4490	53.3	717	8.5
STCHARLES	613	9.8	3723	59.5	342	5.5	1446	23.1	135	2.2*	417	8.5	1442	29.4	326	6.6	2458	50.1	266	5.4
STHELENA	135	3.9	2484	71.8	414	12.0	130	3.8	298	8.6*	343	13.0	380	14.4	74	2.8	1609	60.9	236	8.9
STJAMES	354	6.6	3865	72.0	150	2.8	927	17.3	69	1.3*	273	6.1	996	22.3	151	3.4	2920	65.3	132	3.0
STJOHNBAP	322	6.6	3329	68.7	212	4.4	900	18.6	82	1.7*	283	7.6	920	24.8	136	3.7	2252	60.7	119	3.2

DEMOC. GOVERNOR 1956 * DEMOC. LT-GOV. 1956

COUNTY	GREVMBERG #	%	LONG #	%	MCLEMORE #	%	MORRISON #	%	PREAUS #	%*	ALEXANDER #	%	BARHAM #	%	CLANTON #	%	FRAZAR #	%	MOORE #	%
STLANDRY	2964	11.8	16493	65.4	601	2.4	4351	17.3	805	3.2*	1565	8.8	3723	21.0	2608	14.7	9026	50.9	820	4.6
STMARTIN	464	6.1	4412	58.3	144	1.9	2264	29.9	288	3.8*	251	4.0	1743	27.5	283	4.5	3577	56.5	477	7.5
STMARY	716	7.6	4831	51.2	386	4.1	3085	32.7	416	4.4*	590	6.7	2776	31.6	451	5.1	4285	48.8	686	7.8
STTAMMANY	710	6.6	6565	60.6	1080	10.0	1888	17.4	585	5.4*	996	10.4	2011	21.1	501	5.3	5016	52.6	1013	10.6
TANGPOHOA	1418	8.6	9577	58.1	2360	14.3	1847	11.2	1269	7.7*	2148	15.0	2563	17.9	946	6.6	7132	49.9	1503	10.5
										*										
TENSAS	81	5.8	598	43.1	62	4.5	204	14.7	443	31.9*	73	5.4	348	25.8	49	3.6	514	38.1	365	27.1
TERREBONN	1035	9.1	5849	51.6	456	4.0	3442	30.4	544	4.8*	621	6.0	3064	29.6	769	7.4	4961	48.0	921	8.9
UNION	70	1.1	3419	51.6	112	1.7	405	6.1	2626	39.6*	169	2.8	701	11.6	41	.7	2790	46.1	2354	38.9
VERMILION	1081	7.1	8171	54.0	349	2.3	4922	32.5	606	4.0*	643	5.0	3889	30.2	635	4.9	6780	52.6	949	7.4
VERNON	431	5.6	5566	72.9	167	2.2	764	10.0	704	9.2*	337	4.8	1209	17.4	287	4.1	4420	63.6	699	10.1
										*										
WASHNGTON	1069	7.9	8767	64.7	1424	10.5	1373	10.1	924	6.8*	1376	12.2	2043	18.1	677	6.0	5771	51.2	1405	12.5
WEBSTER	439	4.2	6489	62.0	265	2.5	693	6.6	2572	24.6*	426	4.5	1267	13.3	251	2.6	5132	54.0	2432	25.6
WBTNROUGE	514	14.3	2123	59.2	202	5.6	455	12.7	290	8.1*	827	25.2	389	11.9	208	6.3	1597	48.7	257	7.8
WCARROLL	154	3.4	2835	62.3	201	4.4	547	12.0	814	17.9*	206	4.8	917	21.5	119	2.8	2256	52.8	776	18.
WFELCIANA	124	10.6	511	43.6	117	10.0	226	19.3	194	16.6*	98	9.6	330	32.4	68	6.7	326	32.0	198	19.4
										*										
WINN	242	3.8	4579	71.1	138	2.1	696	10.8	784	12.2*	218	3.7	869	14.9	125	2.1	3874	66.2	764	13.

										*										
TOTALS	62309		421681		48188		191576		95955	*	53593		195616		41478		327679		111452	
% OF VOTE		7.6		51.4		5.9		23.4		11.7		7.3		26.8		5.7		44.9		15.3

GEOGRAPHIC CLASS

										*										
LOWLANDS	19806	7.	143380	54.	15754	6.	38028	14.	49730	19.*	18180	7.	47521	19.	12745	5.	118078	48.	49712	20
BLACK BELT	9218	7.	80199	61.	5815	4.	18545	14.	17950	14.*	7864	7.	23450	21.	6054	5.	58226	52.	16659	15
CATHOLC LA	33285	8.	198102	47.	26619	6.	135003	32.	28275	7.*	27549	7.	124645	34.	22679	6.	151375	41.	45081	12

DEMOGRAPHIC CLASS

										*										
METRO	27000	8.	148927	42.	26364	7.	109475	31.	45045	13.*	26445	8.	107205	33.	18775	6.	115643	36.	57520	18
TOWN	8660	9.	51318	53.	5042	5.	21584	22.	10094	10.*	5555	6.	21158	24.	5790	7.	42562	49.	12364	14
RURAL	26649	7.	221436	60.	16782	5.	60517	17.	40816	11.*	21593	7.	67253	21.	16913	5.	169474	53.	41568	13

LOUISIANA

DEMOC. GOVERNOR 1959 * DEMOC. RUNOFF 1960

COUNTY	DAVIS #	%	DODD #	%	MORRISON #	%	NOE #	%	RAINACH #	%*	DAVIS #	%	MORRISON #	%
ACADIA	4606	28.3	2252	13.9	6260	38.5	1950	12.0	1186	7.3*	8106	42.7	10860	57.3
ALLEN	1333	18.2	2357	32.2	1926	26.3	1387	18.9	321	4.4*	4806	59.9	3224	40.1
ASCENSN	1623	19.0	1811	21.2	3497	40.9	1154	13.5	475	5.5*	3924	43.0	5212	57.0
ASSUMPTN	1351	26.6	342	6.7	2445	48.2	464	9.1	472	9.3*	2129	36.3	3738	63.7

COUNTY	DAVIS #	%	DODD #	%	MORRISON #	%	NOE #	%	RAINACH #	%*	DAVIS #	%	MORRISON #	%
AVOYELLES	2583	22.5	1098	9.6	3876	33.8	1548	13.5	2357	20.6*	6462	49.0	6726	51.0
BEAUREGRD	1892	26.9	730	10.4	1065	15.1	1840	26.1	1515	21.5*	4929	70.3	2079	29.7
BIENVILLE	985	22.3	193	4.4	190	4.3	512	11.6	2531	57.4*	3984	88.9	498	11.1
BOSSIER	2089	23.7	595	6.8	719	8.2	802	9.1	4597	52.2*	7144	81.2	1650	18.8
CADDO	11093	29.4	2214	5.9	6181	16.4	3104	8.2	15113	40.1*	29458	71.3	11883	28.7
CALCASIEU	10107	30.2	5702	17.0	10382	31.0	4232	12.6	3037	9.1*	20737	56.6	15893	43.4
CALDWELL	1153	37.2	331	10.7	274	8.8	738	23.8	607	19.6*	2810	85.7	468	14.3
CAMERON	968	37.7	369	14.4	668	26.0	397	15.5	163	6.4*	1376	54.2	1162	45.8
CATAHOULA	1098	31.8	237	6.9	194	5.6	1072	31.0	856	24.8*	3256	83.2	656	16.8
CLAIBORNE	665	14.2	83	1.8	99	2.1	152	3.2	3684	78.7*	4176	90.2	456	9.8
CONCORDIA	1322	30.0	290	6.6	366	8.3	822	18.7	1605	36.4*	3752	83.2	758	16.8
DESOTO	1282	24.2	276	5.2	398	7.5	969	18.3	2375	44.8*	4182	78.1	1174	21.9
EBTNROUGE	15586	29.8	8104	15.5	18383	35.2	3329	6.4	6873	13.1*	31946	54.6	26543	45.4
ECARROLL	587	26.1	69	3.1	202	9.0	227	10.1	1164	51.8*	2032	89.4	240	10.6
EFELCIANA	598	26.8	352	15.8	155	6.9	311	13.9	817	36.6*	1885	82.6	398	17.4
EVANGELIN	1322	11.5	3386	29.5	3839	33.4	1507	13.1	1433	12.5*	5554	40.6	8129	59.4
FRANKLIN	2221	34.1	499	7.7	389	6.0	1379	21.2	2022	31.1*	6357	87.4	920	12.6
GRANT	1480	29.5	340	6.8	532	10.6	1414	28.2	1248	24.9*	4420	78.2	1231	21.8
IBERIA	3105	20.9	1546	10.4	7065	47.7	1614	10.9	1496	10.1*	6215	37.4	10404	62.6
IBERVILLE	1200	15.8	1135	15.0	3229	42.5	1085	14.3	940	12.4*	3532	44.6	4393	55.4
JACKSON	2274	45.3	227	4.5	348	6.9	1430	28.5	737	14.7*	4450	83.2	900	16.8
JEFFERSON	12522	23.3	6804	12.6	23539	43.8	3419	6.4	7510	14.0*	28547	45.5	34183	54.5
JEFFDAVIS	2479	28.8	1179	13.7	3488	40.5	1009	11.7	464	5.4*	4188	44.7	5177	55.3
LAFAYETTE	4109	20.6	2621	13.1	10231	51.3	1536	7.7	1446	7.3*	7904	33.1	15965	66.9
LAFOURCHE	4121	25.7	1148	7.2	8334	52.0	1319	8.2	1097	6.8*	7830	40.7	11417	59.3
LASALLE	2165	42.1	326	6.3	321	6.2	1229	23.9	1102	21.4*	4884	87.1	723	12.9
LINCOLN	1494	27.1	258	4.7	818	14.8	722	13.1	2228	40.4*	4619	78.2	1291	21.8
LIVINGSTN	2490	26.8	2221	23.9	863	9.3	1568	16.9	2140	23.1*	8690	79.5	2246	20.5
MADISON	677	32.3	41	2.0	131	6.3	136	6.5	1110	53.0*	1915	87.4	275	12.6
MOREHOUSE	2019	35.4	467	8.2	723	12.7	718	12.6	1770	31.1*	5127	84.9	913	15.1
NATCHTOCH	1541	18.9	964	11.8	1404	17.2	1740	21.3	2522	30.9*	5372	63.6	3077	36.4
ORLEANS	40928	24.4	9440	5.6	86626	51.6	12604	7.5	18260	10.9*	71349	40.8	103554	59.2
OUACHITE	6406	33.5	1767	9.2	3389	17.7	3009	15.7	4561	23.8*	15278	74.8	5157	25.2
PLAQMINES	3822	67.3	152	2.7	1137	20.0	349	6.1	222	3.9*	4163	71.6	1652	28.4
PTCOUPEE	899	16.1	619	11.1	2338	41.9	946	17.0	772	13.9*	2574	40.7	3749	59.3
RAPIDES	7828	32.9	2004	8.4	6347	26.7	2926	12.3	4672	19.6*	17820	64.9	9643	35.1
REDRIVER	472	16.7	172	6.1	98	3.5	630	22.3	1453	51.4*	2753	89.5	322	10.5
RICHLAND	1590	31.9	346	6.9	510	10.2	820	16.4	1724	34.5*	4437	84.3	827	15.7
SABINE	1472	21.9	699	10.4	478	7.1	2173	32.4	1891	28.2*	5465	73.0	2019	27.0
STBERNARD	4204	37.8	927	8.3	2702	24.3	1997	17.9	1302	11.7*	7347	56.5	5662	43.5
STCHARLES	1472	21.1	641	9.2	3459	49.5	795	11.4	621	8.9*	2511	34.7	4733	65.3
STHELENA	537	19.3	285	10.2	418	15.0	777	27.9	770	27.6*	1828	62.3	1105	37.7
STJAMES	480	8.9	847	15.6	2999	55.4	823	15.2	268	4.9*	1515	25.4	4439	74.6
STJOHNBAP	758	16.3	331	7.1	2205	47.3	946	20.3	417	9.0*	1587	28.5	3986	71.5
STLANDRY	3206	14.7	3182	14.6	9251	42.4	1698	7.8	4473	20.5*	10770	40.4	15910	59.6
STMARTIN	964	13.5	610	8.6	3309	46.4	1403	19.7	842	11.8*	2964	33.2	5973	66.8

	DEMOC. GOVERNOR 1959										* DEMOC. RUNOFF 1960			
COUNTY	DAVIS		DODD		MORRISON		NOE		RAINACH		DAVIS		MORRISON	
	#	%	#	%	#	%	#	%	#	%*	#	%	#	%
STMARY	3554	31.0	1333	11.6	4913	42.9	723	6.3	926	8.1*	5915	45.0	7238	55.0
STTAMMANY	3994	33.2	1122	9.3	3797	31.5	1601	13.3	1522	12.6*	7690	58.0	5566	42.0
TANGPOHOA	3685	21.5	2207	12.9	4054	23.7	3335	19.5	3821	22.3*	11304	60.2	7479	39.8
TENSAS	760	45.2	26	1.5	115	6.8	109	6.5	670	39.9*	1516	90.4	161	9.6
TERREBONN	3193	25.3	826	6.5	6404	50.7	1164	9.2	1036	8.2*	6331	42.7	8480	57.3
										*				
UNION	1597	29.9	381	7.1	290	5.4	1282	24.0	1797	33.6*	4592	84.6	836	15.4
VERMILION	3073	21.5	1599	11.2	6218	43.4	2763	19.3	662	4.6*	5488	34.6	10392	65.4
VERNON	1593	21.1	1360	18.0	1087	14.4	1842	24.4	1673	22.1*	5781	71.7	2284	28.3
WASHNGTON	3943	33.0	1909	16.0	1726	14.4	2055	17.2	2312	19.4*	10361	77.2	3066	22.8
WEBSTER	2435	28.5	754	8.8	352	4.1	759	8.9	4237	49.6*	8118	90.4	865	9.6
										*				
WBTNROUGE	934	24.7	636	16.8	1569	41.5	354	9.4	290	7.7*	1798	45.8	2129	54.2
WCARROLL	1597	41.1	335	8.6	203	5.2	745	19.2	1001	25.8*	3766	89.4	448	10.6
WFELCIANA	337	31.8	82	7.7	152	14.3	74	7.0	416	39.2*	761	72.3	292	27.7
WINN	1678	28.8	277	4.8	276	4.7	2117	36.4	1472	25.3*	5201	80.2	1281	19.8
										*				
TOTALS	213551		85436		278956		97654		143096		* 487681		414110	
% OF VOTE	26.1		10.4		34.1		11.9		17.5		* 54.1		45.9	

GEOGRAPHIC CLASS

										*				
LOWLANDS	78881	30.	30497	11.	52805	20.	39757	15.	64068	24.*	202169	69.	90247	31.
BLACK BELT	25915	22.	11495	10.	30204	25.	16414	14.	34493	29.*	78601	61.	51051	39.
CATHOLC LA	108755	25.	43444	10.	195947	45.	41483	10.	44535	10.*	206911	43.	272812	57.

DEMOGRAPHIC CLASS

										*				
METRO	96642	27.	34031	9.	148500	41.	29697	8.	55354	15.*	197315	50.	197213	50.
TOWN	28471	28.	10428	10.	35194	34.	12094	12.	16861	16.*	63122	53.	54870	47.
RURAL	88438	25.	40977	12.	95262	27.	55863	16.	70881	20.*	227244	58.	162027	42.

LOUISIANA

	DEMOC. GOVERNOR 1963												* DEMOC. RUNOFF 1964			
COUNTY	JACKSON		KENNON		LONG		MCKEITHEN		MORRISON		OTHER		MCKEITHEN		MORRISON	
	#	%	#	%	#	%	#	%	#	%	#	%*	#	%	#	%
ACADIA	1303	6.9	1233	6.6	4256	22.6	3798	20.2	6316	33.6	1889	10.1*	10334	52.0	9528	48.0
ALLEN	805	10.3	673	8.6	1380	17.6	2320	29.7	2094	26.8	548	7.0*	4842	62.1	2957	37.9
ASCENSN	691	7.5	659	7.1	1850	20.0	1556	16.8	3902	42.2	587	6.3*	3900	40.6	5698	59.4
ASSUMPTN	174	3.0	546	9.5	1226	21.2	690	11.9	2263	39.2	876	15.2*	2139	35.8	3834	64.2
AVOYELLES	1656	13.0	799	6.3	2496	19.6	2324	18.3	3729	29.3	1702	13.4*	5822	47.6	6419	52.4
												*				
BEAUREGRD	1067	15.3	1187	17.0	1448	20.8	1646	23.6	1104	15.9	511	7.3*	4902	70.9	2015	29.1

COUNTY	JACKSON #	%	KENNON #	%	LONG #	%	MCKEITHEN #	%	MORRISON #	%	OTHER #	%*	MCKEITHEN #	%	MORRISON #	%
BIENVILLE	1573	31.8	1139	23.0	649	13.1	1023	20.6	354	7.1	216	4.4*	4099	81.7	917	18.3
BOSSIER	4131	42.0	2203	22.4	1109	11.3	1209	12.3	775	7.9	416	4.2*	7997	81.9	1764	18.1
CADDO.	8964	22.2	13212	32.7	4120	10.2	5132	12.7	6200	15.3	2821	7.0*	28330	69.3	12528	30.7
CALCASIEU	2370	5.9	4668	11.7	6527	16.4	6283	15.7	13239	33.2	6810	17.1*	20999	50.3	20718	49.7
CALDWELL	150	4.0	253	6.8	176	4.7	2695	72.3	357	9.6	97	2.6*	3432	91.5	320	8.5
CAMERON	250	8.4	363	12.2	797	26.7	444	14.9	677	22.7	452	15.2*	1458	52.3	1328	47.7
CATAHOULA	1239	34.4	379	10.5	316	8.8	1250	34.7	214	5.9	206	5.7*	3452	89.3	412	10.7
CLAIBORNE	1827	41.6	1107	25.2	415	9.4	470	10.7	127	2.9	449	10.2*	3754	87.5	538	12.5
CONCORDIA	2353	45.4	735	14.2	491	9.5	813	15.7	467	9.0	321	6.2*	4142	79.9	1042	20.1
DESOTO	1399	25.8	1699	31.4	999	18.4	568	10.5	487	9.0	263	4.9*	4120	77.2	1216	22.8
EBTNROUGE	7180	12.5	8495	14.7	6410	11.1	7812	13.6	21490	37.3	6259	10.9*	28920	45.5	34579	54.5
ECARROLL	337	19.2	698	39.7	110	6.3	318	18.1	206	11.7	88	5.0*	1294	77.5	375	22.5
EFELCIANA	839	33.2	602	23.8	388	15.3	344	13.6	225	8.9	130	5.1*	2046	81.6	460	18.4
EVANGELIN	1739	13.9	824	6.6	3914	31.4	2515	20.2	2245	18.0	1232	9.9*	7637	54.7	6327	45.3
FRANKLIN	1998	29.9	1489	22.3	471	7.0	1976	29.6	391	5.8	360	5.4*	6620	91.3	627	8.7
GRANT	745	13.3	964	17.2	853	15.2	1967	35.1	573	10.2	501	8.9*	4611	81.0	1084	19.0
IBERIA	898	5.1	1099	6.2	3199	18.0	2587	14.6	7087	39.9	2889	16.3*	7197	41.5	10163	58.5
IBERVILLE	436	4.9	844	9.6	2059	23.3	1316	14.9	3662	41.5	508	5.8*	3998	42.7	5363	57.3
JACKSON	1104	18.8	889	15.1	478	8.1	2340	39.8	757	12.9	313	5.3*	4925	77.0	1468	23.0
JEFFERSON	2972	4.8	8034	13.0	8552	13.9	9825	16.0	29484	47.9	2704	4.4*	27035	39.4	41631	60.6
JEFFDAVIS	554	6.0	584	6.3	1640	17.7	1135	12.2	2952	31.8	2425	26.1*	4719	49.7	4782	50.3
LAFAYETTE	1239	4.7	1459	5.5	3407	12.8	2903	10.9	7535	28.4	10029	37.7*	10360	37.8	17053	62.2
LAFOURCHE	613	3.0	1858	9.2	2578	12.8	3079	15.3	9621	47.7	2433	12.1*	7605	35.2	14001	64.8
LASALLE	1134	18.4	692	11.2	294	4.8	3340	54.2	433	7.0	271	4.4*	5876	89.8	665	10.2
LINCOLN	1593	22.5	1859	26.2	609	8.6	1013	14.3	1076	15.2	941	13.3*	5098	69.8	2207	30.2
LIVINGSTN	2102	18.2	1468	12.8	2949	25.5	2756	23.8	1397	12.1	891	7.7*	8731	76.3	2710	23.7
MADISON	707	28.5	567	22.8	247	10.0	362	14.6	309	12.4	290	11.7*	1956	77.1	581	22.9
MOREHOUSE	1228	18.3	2442	36.4	566	8.4	1379	20.6	533	7.9	559	8.3*	5718	84.9	1018	15.1
NATCHTOCH	2076	21.8	1278	13.4	2001	21.0	1559	16.3	1694	17.8	931	9.8*	6262	65.4	3316	34.6
ORLEANS	6167	3.8	19215	11.9	22991	14.2	20073	12.4	88812	54.9	4473	2.8*	53912	33.1	108915	66.9
OUACHITE	3557	15.1	6967	29.6	1667	7.1	6275	26.6	3133	13.3	1949	8.3*	18224	77.1	5411	22.9
PLAQMINES	73	1.3	4365	75.9	121	2.1	334	5.8	780	13.6	81	1.4*	4645	80.4	1132	19.6
PTCOUPEE	448	9.0	380	7.6	1089	21.9	695	14.0	2093	42.1	269	5.4*	1928	38.0	3151	62.0
RAPIDES	3504	12.6	3754	13.5	4220	15.2	6881	24.8	6027	21.7	3381	12.2*	18778	63.5	10775	36.5
REDRIVER	1261	41.5	444	14.6	644	21.2	504	16.6	76	2.5	113	3.7*	2878	91.1	280	8.9
RICHLAND	1298	24.2	1621	30.2	472	8.8	1263	23.6	385	7.2	321	6.0*	4678	85.5	792	14.5
SABINE	1586	22.4	1110	15.7	1969	27.8	1202	17.0	770	10.9	438	6.2*	5442	76.3	1694	23.7
STBERNARD	829	5.5	2126	14.2	2750	18.4	3197	21.4	5475	36.6	582	3.9*	8248	53.9	7057	46.1
STCHARLES	360	4.6	643	8.1	1331	16.8	1074	13.6	4174	52.8	327	4.1*	2620	29.5	6249	70.5
STHELENA	701	31.7	295	13.3	448	20.3	299	13.5	331	15.0	136	6.2*	1596	71.5	636	28.5
STJAMES	320	5.5	239	4.1	872	14.9	786	13.4	3418	58.3	224	3.8*	1589	26.0	4528	74.0
STJOHNBAP	275	4.9	369	6.6	897	16.1	856	15.4	2991	53.7	177	3.2*	1918	30.0	4466	70.0
STLANDRY	2033	8.4	1731	7.2	4554	18.9	4765	19.8	8332	34.6	2667	11.1*	12331	46.3	14282	53.7
STMARTIN	464	5.0	427	4.6	2494	26.8	703	7.5	3705	39.7	1529	16.4*	3938	38.6	6257	61.4
STMARY	413	3.1	886	6.6	1932	14.4	2698	20.2	5212	39.0	2238	16.7*	6308	42.6	8501	57.4
STTAMMANY	2039	13.4	2026	13.3	2242	14.7	3288	21.5	5016	32.9	654	4.3*	8838	55.1	7199	44.9

```
                    DEMOC.  GOVERNOR   1963                    * DEMOC.  RUNOFF    1964
                                                              *
COUNTY    JACKSON     KENNON      LONG       MCKEITHEN   MORRISON    OTHER      * MCKEITHEN    MORRISON
          #     %     #     %     #     %     #     %     #     %     #     %  *  #     %      #     %
----------------------------------------------------------------------------- *
TANGPOHOA 3828 20.4  2048 10.9  3764 20.1  3507 18.7  4784 25.5   807  4.3* 11889 60.8   7652 39.2
TENSAS     381 22.6   502 29.7   300 17.8   306 18.1    98  5.8   101  6.0*  1503 85.3    260 14.7
TERREBONN  854  5.4  1179  7.5  1732 11.0  2340 14.9  7835 49.8  1792 11.4*  6017 35.6  10880 64.4
UNION     1838 30.0  1486 24.3  1000 16.3   905 14.8   430  7.0   460  7.5*  5252 82.2   1134 17.8
VERMILION 1006  6.1  1040  6.3  3231 19.6  3703 22.4  5257 31.8  2271 13.8*  8923 51.2   8510 48.8
                                                                          *
VERNON    1124 13.2  1185 13.9  2428 28.5  2388 28.0   891 10.5   510  6.0*  6691 78.6   1825 21.4
WASHNGTON 4089 28.6  1119  7.8  2356 16.5  3119 21.8  2539 17.7  1089  7.6* 10734 71.9   4194 28.1
WEBSTER   2962 31.3  3121 32.9   910  9.6  1695 17.9   461  4.9   328  3.5*  8468 87.2   1245 12.8
WBTNROUGE  380  9.3   342  8.3   594 14.5   655 16.0  1779 43.4   352  8.6*  1732 42.4   2352 57.6
WCARROLL  1103 30.7   862 24.0   437 12.1   840 23.3   174  4.8   182  5.1*  3408 91.0    335  9.0
                                                                          *
WFELCIANA  309 24.8   204 16.3   102  8.2   349 28.0   164 13.1   120  9.6*   849 72.3    326 27.7
WINN      1301 19.8  1184 18.0  1251 19.1  1857 28.3   585  8.9   383  5.8*  5238 78.0   1479 22.0
----------------------------------------------------------------------------- *
                                                                          *
TOTALS   103949     127870     137778     157304     299702      79872  * 492905      451161
% OF VOTE   11.5       14.1       15.2       17.4       33.1        8.8  *   52.2        47.8
                                                                          *
                                                                          *
GEOGRAPHIC CLASS                                                          *
                                                                          *
LOWLANDS  55552 19.  55277 18.  41777 14.  64424 21.  60204 20.  23015  8.* 208980 67.  103445 33.
BLACK BELT 23946 18. 21132 16.  20203 16.  22309 17.  31461 24.  10412  8.*  83706 61.   53895 39.
CATHOLC LA 24451  5. 51461 11.  75798 16.  70571 15. 208037 44.  46445 10.* 200219 41.  293821 59.
                                                                          *
DEMOGRAPHIC CLASS                                                         *
                                                                          *
METRO     31210  8.  60591 16.  50267 13.  55400 14. 162358 42.  25016  7.* 177420 44.  223782 56.
TOWN      15544 12.  12939 10.  18773 15.  22236 18.  37273 29.  20178 16.*  69331 53.   61886 47.
RURAL     57195 14.  54340 14.  68738 17.  79668 20. 100071 25.  34678  9.* 246154 60.  165493 40.



                                         LOUISIANA


                    DEMOC.  GOVERNOR   1971                    * DEMOC.  RUNOFF    1971
                                                              *
COUNTY    DAVIS       EDWARDS     JOHNSTON    LONG       OTHER      * EDWARDS     JOHNSTON
          #     %     #     %     #     %     #     %     #     %  *  #     %      #     %
----------------------------------------------------------------------------- *
ACADIA    2399 10.6 14762 65.5   812  3.6  1419  6.3  3149 14.0* 18496 81.6   4169 18.4
ALLEN     2066 23.8  1327 15.3   759  8.8  1997 23.0  2517 29.0*  3699 43.0   4910 57.0
ASCENSN   2371 16.9  4248 30.3  2901 20.7  1145  8.2  3353 23.9*  6994 52.8   6244 47.2
ASSUMPTN   777 10.1  2403 31.3   571  7.4   769 10.0  3161 41.2*  5311 69.5   2333 30.5
AVOYELLES 1034  6.4  4272 26.3   996  6.1  2345 14.5  7573 46.7* 11061 68.2   5150 31.8
                                                                          *
BEAUREGRD 1914 20.3  1405 14.9   986 10.5   948 10.1  4164 44.2*  3386 36.3   5930 63.7
BIENVILLE 1147 17.3   530  8.0  1816 27.4   846 12.8  2291 34.6*  2606 42.8   3487 57.2
BOSSIER   1949 13.1  1979 13.3  6457 43.5  1358  9.1  3109 20.9*  5136 33.8  10056 66.2
```

SOUTHERN ELECTIONS/132

		DEMOC.	GOVERNOR	1971		* DEMOC.	RUNOFF	1971

COUNTY	DAVIS		EDWARDS		JOHNSTON		LONG		OTHER		EDWARDS		JOHNSTON	
	#	%	#	%	#	%	#	%	#	%*	#	%	#	%
CADDO	3919	7.6	3336	6.5	24112	47.0	6714	13.1	13260	25.8*	15991	29.3	38497	70.7
CALCASIEU	3723	7.8	19225	40.4	5482	11.5	2366	5.0	16769	35.3*	29734	61.9	18331	38.1
CALDWELL	899	20.6	366	8.4	398	9.1	459	10.5	2242	51.4*	1262	31.4	2753	68.6
CAMERON	714	20.3	1597	45.3	144	4.1	161	4.6	907	25.7*	2469	68.2	1149	31.8
CATAHOULA	984	19.6	505	10.1	597	11.9	621	12.4	2306	46.0*	2217	39.9	3341	60.1
CLAIBORNE	1127	17.0	278	4.2	2042	30.8	928	14.0	2253	34.0*	2071	32.9	4224	67.1
CONCORDIA	1860	22.9	1272	15.6	1443	17.7	963	11.8	2596	31.9*	3028	41.5	4271	58.5
DESOTO	915	11.4	580	7.2	2290	28.5	2533	31.5	1711	21.3*	3322	44.6	4122	55.4
EBTNROUGE	11374	14.3	15218	19.1	29601	37.2	9040	11.4	14374	18.1*	32618	39.3	50354	60.7
ECARROLL	807	20.4	409	10.3	425	10.7	753	19.0	1566	39.5*	1822	48.8	1910	51.2
EFELCIANA	1160	22.9	467	9.2	970	19.2	936	18.5	1523	30.1*	2168	44.1	2751	55.9
EVANGELIN	2553	16.0	5144	32.3	729	4.6	2890	18.1	4620	29.0*	10976	70.2	4669	29.8
FRANKLIN	2077	24.4	661	7.8	1313	15.4	939	11.0	3539	41.5*	2521	28.9	6212	71.1
GRANT	917	13.9	641	9.7	797	12.1	966	14.6	3284	49.7	2274	33.9	4435	66.1
IBERIA	2004	9.4	5165	24.1	2973	13.9	1525	7.1	9722	45.5*	15547	69.0	6971	31.0
IBERVILLE	1886	14.3	2717	20.7	2131	16.2	2327	17.7	4088	31.1*	8549	61.6	5332	38.4
JACKSON	1998	28.1	340	4.8	1179	16.6	1134	15.9	2462	34.6*	2637	37.8	4330	62.2
JEFFERSON	4114	4.6	27051	30.4	13701	15.4	11293	12.7	32883	36.9*	46099	49.7	46698	50.3
JEFFDAVIS	1134	10.2	5902	53.0	857	7.7	622	5.6	2613	23.5*	7710	71.9	3008	28.1
LAFAYETTE	2358	6.5	12088	33.2	4965	13.6	3064	8.4	13922	38.3*	25039	71.7	9879	28.3
LAFOURCHE	2078	7.7	9996	37.0	3227	11.9	2147	7.9	9585	35.5*	19895	70.9	8171	29.1
LASALLE	1010	13.9	239	3.3	615	8.5	508	7.0	4879	67.3*	1700	25.9	4857	74.1
LINCOLN	1153	13.2	953	10.9	3103	35.6	850	9.7	2663	30.5*	2452	28.9	6041	71.1
LIVINGSTN	5505	35.4	1989	12.8	3291	21.2	1766	11.4	2999	19.3*	6034	35.8	10821	64.2
MADISON	1097	19.3	168	3.0	502	8.8	450	7.9	3477	61.1*	1217	24.8	3682	75.2
MOREHOUSE	1860	19.3	1734	18.0	1821	18.9	1224	12.7	2997	31.1*	3436	38.9	5399	61.1
NATCHTOCH	1258	10.3	1435	11.7	1980	16.1	2756	22.5	4838	39.4*	5680	46.9	6422	53.1
ORLEANS	9537	5.7	39078	23.5	24515	14.8	41109	24.8	51762	31.2*	78057	49.8	78808	50.2
OUACHITE	5879	18.9	3893	12.5	7311	23.5	3159	10.2	10808	34.8*	10596	34.2	20362	65.8
PLAQMINES	198	2.3	1805	21.3	445	5.2	490	5.8	5545	65.4*	2295	30.2	5312	69.8
PTCOUPEE	1449	15.6	2019	21.7	1338	14.4	2065	22.2	2446	26.3*	5235	60.6	3399	39.4
RAPIDES	2888	8.4	4018	11.6	6267	18.1	6333	18.3	15065	43.6*	13648	39.6	20794	60.4
REDRIVER	772	17.0	272	6.0	949	21.0	1369	30.2	1166	25.8*	2299	52.2	2106	47.8
RICHLAND	1730	24.9	577	8.3	1201	17.3	726	10.4	2727	39.2*	2114	31.0	4708	69.0
SABINE	1023	12.2	629	7.5	1621	19.3	1724	20.5	3405	40.5*	2957	33.5	5883	66.5
STBERNARD	2985	13.2	6951	30.6	2539	11.2	2003	8.8	8212	36.2*	9458	50.4	9313	49.6
STCHARLES	787	6.9	3907	34.1	1328	11.6	2439	21.3	2988	26.1*	7191	61.2	4565	38.8
STHELENA	1258	27.9	707	15.7	590	13.1	834	18.5	1128	25.0*	2485	50.4	2444	49.6
STJAMES	511	6.4	2669	33.3	873	10.9	1250	15.6	2705	33.8*	5097	65.3	2706	34.7
STJOHNBAP	673	7.8	2520	29.1	833	9.6	1899	21.9	2745	31.7*	6323	65.7	3297	34.3
STLANDRY	3555	11.2	10298	32.5	2816	8.9	5806	18.3	9216	29.1*	21930	65.1	11780	34.9
STMARTIN	857	6.7	4500	35.1	724	5.6	1507	11.7	5245	40.9*	11635	81.5	2649	18.5
STMARY	1187	5.9	3460	17.2	2371	11.8	1489	7.4	11658	57.8*	11603	60.7	7516	39.3
STTAMMANY	3298	15.3	5738	26.7	4507	21.0	2102	9.8	5842	27.2*	8051	39.3	12419	60.7
TANGPOHOA	6597	26.3	5778	23.0	3856	15.4	3663	14.6	5185	20.7*	10374	44.4	12995	55.6
TENSAS	1036	25.9	169	4.2	538	13.5	273	6.8	1978	49.5*	1567	47.6	1726	52.4

```
                    DEMOC.  GOVERNOR   1971              *  DEMOC.  RUNOFF    1971
                                                         *
COUNTY      DAVIS        EDWARDS      JOHNSTON    LONG         OTHER      *  EDWARDS       JOHNSTON
            #      %     #      %     #      %    #      %     #      %*   #      %      #      %
--------------------------------------------------------------------------------------------------------
TERREBONN   1056   5.0  7731  36.3  3012  14.1  2002   9.4   7489  35.2*  14888  69.2   6625  30.8
UNION       1753  22.6  1029  13.3  1282  16.5   742   9.6   2955  38.1*   3034  38.3   4879  61.7
VERMILION   1982   9.8 10405  51.2   632   3.1  1726   8.5   5574  27.4*  15761  82.1   3437  17.9
VERNON      1866  17.4   855   8.0  1005   9.3  1769  16.5   5257  48.9*   3681  33.1   7442  66.9
WASHNGTON   4955  28.5  4211  24.2  3458  19.9  1533   8.8   3237  18.6*   6036  34.9  11276  65.1
                                                                         *
WEBSTER     2037  13.9   832   5.7  5410  36.8  2492  17.0   3930  26.7*   4281  31.8   9180  68.2
WBTNROUGE   1277  19.0   881  13.1  1546  23.1   427   6.4   2574  38.4*   3225  52.4   2931  47.6
WCARROLL    1769  33.6   424   8.0   548  10.4   651  12.4   1877  35.6*   1357  25.7   3914  74.3
WFELCIANA    526  16.9   333  10.7   548  17.6   440  14.1   1268  40.7*   1643  53.5   1430  46.5
WINN        1174  16.2   306   4.2   781  10.8  1492  20.6   3473  48.1*   2284  31.5   4969  68.5
                                                                         *
--------------------------------------------------------------------------------------------------------
                                                                         *
TOTALS    138756       276397       208830      164276      384855      *  584262        579774
% OF VOTE  11.8         23.6         17.8         14.0         32.8      *   50.2          49.8
                                                                         *
GEOGRAPHIC CLASS                                                         *
                                                                         *
LOWLANDS   65774  17.  55058  14. 104838  27.  51171  13. 116630  30.*  143253  36.  254397  64.
BLACK BELT 29911  16.  34052  18.  31639  17.  31363  16.  64656  34.*   96101  51.   92713  49.
CATHOLC LA 43071   7. 187287  32.  72353  12.  81742  14. 203569  35.*  344908  60.  232664  40.
                                                                         *
DEMOGRAPHIC CLASS                                                        *
                                                                         *
METRO      38546   8. 107801  23. 104722  23.  73681  16. 139856  30.*  213095  46.  253050  54.
TOWN       18195  11.  42143  25.  29671  18.  17818  11.  60756  36.*   89752  55.   74914  45.
RURAL      82015  15. 126453  23.  74437  14.  72777  13. 184243  34.*  281415  53.  251810  47.
```

LOUISIANA

```
                  DEMOC.  SENATOR    1950    *      DEMOC.  SENATOR    1954
                                             *
COUNTY      LONG         LAFARGE      MILLS   *   ELLENDER     ELLIS        FAULK
            #      %     #      %     #      %*   #      %     #      %     #      %
--------------------------------------------------------------------------------------------------------
ACADIA      8540  78.1  2299  21.0    97   .9*  5285  74.4  1630  23.0   186   2.6
ALLEN       3960  77.2  1132  22.1    39   .8*  2915  57.0  2071  40.5   125   2.4
ASCENSN     3877  78.4  1009  20.4    61  1.2*  2610  60.8  1554  36.2   129   3.0
ASSUMPTN    2876  86.0   443  13.2    25   .7*  1417  60.6   829  35.4    93   4.0
AVOYELLES   7934  79.8  1953  19.6    61   .6*  6400  69.9  2434  26.6   323   3.5
                                             *
BEAUREGRD   3569  75.9  1065  22.6    70  1.5*  3195  72.1  1054  23.8   182   4.1
BIENVILLE   3095  74.4   964  23.2   101  2.4*  2288  70.3   795  24.4   170   5.2
BOSSIER     3825  68.9  1549  27.9   174  3.1*  3230  70.2  1128  24.5   240   5.2
CADDO      14187  49.3 13690  47.5   920  3.2* 17758  63.1  8274  29.4  2121   7.5
CALCASIEU   9536  67.0  4453  31.3   250  1.8* 10248  51.8  8628  43.6   919   4.6
```

COUNTY	LONG #	%	LAFARGE #	%	MILLS #	%*	ELLENDER #	%	ELLIS #	%	FAULK #	%
CALDWELL	2221	82.1	425	15.7	59	2.2*	1397	60.0	657	28.2	275	11.8
CAMERON	1242	75.9	375	22.9	19	1.2*	944	81.0	176	15.1	46	3.9
CATAHOULA	2242	79.4	520	18.4	63	2.2*	1363	75.8	354	19.7	80	4.5
CLAIBORNE	1846	59.2	1196	38.3	78	2.5*	2534	73.5	709	20.6	204	5.9
CONCORDIA	1435	77.1	377	20.3	49	2.6*	1499	71.4	439	20.9	160	7.6
DESOTO	1818	60.2	1129	37.4	72	2.4*	1778	76.4	384	16.5	165	7.1
EBTNROUGE	19598	68.3	7999	27.9	1103	3.8*	17647	55.0	13202	41.1	1254	3.9
ECARROLL	1126	82.4	218	15.9	23	1.7*	1027	70.8	316	21.8	107	7.4
EFELCIANA	1128	69.5	440	27.1	55	3.4*	1537	63.2	805	33.1	90	3.7
EVANGELIN	5654	82.9	1136	16.7	32	.5*	4871	64.0	2531	33.2	214	2.8
FRANKLIN	3448	73.2	1092	23.2	169	3.6*	2978	67.4	1070	24.2	371	8.4
GRANT	3666	77.0	1040	21.9	53	1.1*	2603	69.0	978	25.9	191	5.1
IBERIA	4647	71.3	1782	27.3	92	1.4*	5165	64.5	2502	31.2	341	4.3
IBERVILLE	3707	82.2	762	16.9	41	.9*	2431	77.1	646	20.5	75	2.4
JACKSON	3151	78.7	785	19.6	66	1.6*	1798	61.6	928	31.8	191	6.5
JEFFERSON	13545	77.2	3850	21.9	151	.9*	9697	61.0	5827	36.7	370	2.3
JEFFDAVIS	4531	68.1	2036	30.6	85	1.3*	4075	66.4	1893	30.8	173	2.8
LAFAYETTE	5060	60.4	3128	37.4	184	2.2*	5217	56.8	3608	39.3	354	3.9
LAFOURCHE	7494	75.5	2314	23.3	119	1.2*	4188	61.4	2317	33.9	321	4.7
LASALLE	2940	72.3	1063	26.1	65	1.6*	2541	69.3	927	25.3	198	5.4
LINCOLN	2594	63.0	1441	35.0	83	2.0*	2393	60.0	1077	27.0	521	13.1
LIVINGSTN	4760	84.3	755	13.4	133	2.4*	3121	54.6	2386	41.7	213	3.7
MADISON	1020	65.0	497	31.7	53	3.4*	791	69.9	217	19.2	124	11.0
MOREHOUSE	2485	70.1	978	27.6	84	2.4*	1423	51.9	903	32.9	415	15.1
NATCHTOCH	5527	73.6	1848	24.6	134	1.8*	5105	74.6	1398	20.4	343	5.0
ORLEANS	73669	58.2	51776	40.9	1175	.9*	35299	46.1	39451	51.5	1810	2.4
OUACHITE	9290	65.9	4346	30.8	458	3.2*	4880	36.1	4519	33.4	4123	30.5
PLAQMINES	247	7.2	3176	92.6	7	.2*	1871	94.6	92	4.7	14	.7
PTCOUPEE	2229	74.5	726	24.3	38	1.3*	2238	75.5	648	21.9	79	2.7
RAPIDES	14323	68.1	6438	30.6	278	1.3*	9827	62.4	5200	33.0	716	4.5
REDRIVER	2080	83.5	359	14.4	51	2.0*	1851	78.6	421	17.9	84	3.6
RICHLAND	2919	75.0	871	22.4	100	2.6*	2612	64.3	1030	25.3	422	10.4
SABINE	4529	81.9	938	17.0	62	1.1*	2744	82.4	465	14.0	122	3.7
STBERNARD	2668	95.5	118	4.2	7	.3*	2751	84.0	510	15.6	14	.4
STCHARLES	2051	80.9	463	18.3	21	.8*	2276	57.8	1551	39.4	113	2.9
STHELENA	1496	79.4	336	17.8	52	2.8*	965	52.1	817	44.1	71	3.8
STJAMES	2742	86.9	401	12.7	13	.4*	1757	59.4	1140	38.5	63	2.1
STJOHNBAP	3127	87.6	413	11.6	30	.8*	1382	52.5	1178	44.8	70	2.7
STLANDRY	7803	73.8	2676	25.3	97	.9*	9665	62.4	5428	35.1	387	2.5
STMARTIN	3491	71.3	1346	27.5	56	1.1*	3315	66.7	1524	30.7	130	2.6
STMARY	3670	71.8	1390	27.2	49	1.0*	2535	52.8	1879	39.1	387	8.1
STTAMMANY	5491	78.4	1462	20.9	47	.7*	2234	43.6	2763	53.9	130	2.5
TANGPOHOA	9146	81.2	1912	17.0	202	1.8*	7420	54.6	5667	41.7	496	3.7
TENSAS	649	66.8	279	28.7	44	4.5*	833	73.4	222	19.6	80	7.0
TERREBONN	4589	75.9	1350	22.3	107	1.8*	4259	76.6	1115	20.1	184	3.3
UNION	3168	76.8	865	21.0	94	2.3*	1688	72.4	457	19.6	187	8.0

```
              DEMOC.  SENATOR    1950      *      DEMOC.  SENATOR    1954
   COUNTY     LONG          LAFARGE       MILLS      * ELLENDER      ELLIS         FAULK
              #      %      #      %      #      %*  #      %       #      %       #      %
-----------------------------------------------------*----------------------------------------------------------------
VERMILION    6908  67.7   3185  31.2    107   1.0*  5367  59.9   3350  37.4    236   2.6
VERNON       5408  83.9    965  15.0     69   1.1*  3784  76.7    946  19.2    201   4.1
WASHNGTON    7115  80.9   1534  17.4    145   1.6*  3759  50.3   3493  46.7    220   2.9
WEBSTER      4606  71.4   1656  25.7    192   3.0*  2954  60.1   1748  35.5    216   4.4
WBTNROUGE    1269  76.1    364  21.8     35   2.1*  1088  61.7    614  34.8     60   3.4
                                                   *
WCARROLL     2414  79.3    527  17.3    103   3.4*  1738  63.8    795  29.2    192   7.0
WFELCIANA     435  62.8    240  34.6     18   2.6*   644  74.1    196  22.6     29   3.3
WINN         3514  75.3   1063  22.8     91   1.9*  2849  71.2    909  22.7    246   6.1
-----------------------------------------------------*----------------------------------------------------------------
                                                   *
TOTALS     359330        156918        8611       * 268054       162775        22366
% OF VOTE    68.5          29.9          1.6       *  59.1         35.9          4.9
                                                   *
                                                   *
GEOGRAPHIC CLASS                                   *
                                                   *
LOWLANDS   133123  70.   51729  27.    4486   2.*  101445  59.   58921  34.    11919   7.
BLACK BELT  56854  74.   18050  24.    1445   2.*   50236  66.   21282  28.     4183   6.
CATHOLC LA 169353  65.   87139  34.    2680   1.*  116373  57.   82572  40.     6264   3.
                                                   *
                                                   *
DEMOGRAPHIC CLASS                                  *
                                                   *
METRO      139825  61.   86114  37.    4057   2.*   95529  51.   79901  43.    10597   6.
TOWN        42227  71.   15899  27.     987   2.*   34208  64.   17556  33.     2069   4.
RURAL      177278  75.   54905  23.    3567   2.*  138317  65.   65318  31.     9700   5.
```

LOUISIANA

```
              DEMOC.  SENATOR    1966      * SPECL.  REFERENDUM 1960
   COUNTY     ELLENDER      DEBLIEUX      GUICE      *  FOR           AGAINST
              #      %      #      %      #      %*  #      %       #      %
-------------------------------------------------------*----------------------------------------
ACADIA       9327  83.7   1213  10.9    610   5.5*  2717  64.2   1512  35.8
ALLEN        3654  80.1    509  11.2    396   8.7*  1654  54.8   1363  45.2
ASCENSN      4904  76.3   1097  17.1    424   6.6*  1354  41.9   1875  58.1
ASSUMPTN     3013  79.8    467  12.4    296   7.8*   509  43.0    675  57.0
AVOYELLES    9555  84.0    979   8.6    847   7.4*  2413  69.4   1063  30.6
                                                   *
BEAUREGRD    4009  77.6    512   9.9    643  12.5*  2091  59.4   1427  40.6
BIENVILLE    3318  76.6    416   9.6    599  13.8*  2056  85.2    356  14.8
BOSSIER      5727  81.2    368   5.2    958  13.6*  4810  83.0    983  17.0
CADDO       23883  71.2   5556  16.6   4098  12.2* 22119  77.2   6551  22.8
CALCASIEU   26220  69.7   5159  13.7   6214  16.5*  8726  43.4  11366  56.6
                                                   *
CALDWELL     1933  69.5    223   8.0    624  22.4*   815  78.3    226  21.7
CAMERON      2112  84.2    201   8.0    194   7.7*   443  56.6    340  43.4
```

COUNTY	ELLENDER #	ELLENDER %	DEBLIEUX #	DEBLIEUX %	GUICE #	GUICE %*	FOR #	FOR %	AGAINST #	AGAINST %
CATAHOULA	1885	68.3	75	2.7	801	29.0*	917	81.7	206	18.3
CLAIBORNE	2758	69.5	804	20.2	409	10.3*	2561	91.0	254	9.0
CONCORDIA	2952	57.9	226	4.4	1917	37.6*	1614	84.2	303	15.8
DESOTO	1958	62.0	886	28.0	316	10.0*	2698	87.5	386	12.5
EBTNROUGE	32203	60.3	16451	30.8	4738	8.9*	13191	36.3	23142	63.7
ECARROLL	1181	53.7	665	30.3	352	16.0*	950	90.8	96	9.2
EFELCIANA	2079	61.3	1006	29.7	307	9.1*	710	61.2	451	38.8
EVANGELIN	7137	85.5	638	7.6	568	6.8*	2506	78.6	683	21.4
FRANKLIN	2172	64.8	96	2.9	1083	32.3*	1617	81.5	366	18.5
GRANT	3404	81.5	186	4.5	588	14.1*	1511	74.7	511	25.3
IBERIA	7779	80.3	1041	10.7	868	9.0*	3039	68.8	1377	31.2
IBERVILLE	5378	77.6	1062	15.3	487	7.0*	1278	47.7	1404	52.3
JACKSON	3910	83.7	172	3.7	587	12.6*	1694	75.4	552	24.6
JEFFERSON	43029	82.6	4011	7.7	5071	9.7*	26594	68.5	12222	31.5
JEFFDAVIS	3993	79.7	523	10.4	497	9.9*	1808	51.0	1738	49.0
LAFAYETTE	13216	76.2	2246	12.9	1882	10.9*	4401	53.1	3893	46.9
LAFOURCHE	11875	85.6	1114	8.0	878	6.3*	3956	65.0	2128	35.0
LASALLE	4050	75.9	198	3.7	1091	20.4*	1543	73.4	559	26.6
LINCOLN	3212	72.6	574	13.0	636	14.4*	2527	75.6	814	24.4
LIVINGSTN	6758	80.3	816	9.7	843	10.0*	1792	47.9	1952	52.1
MADISON	1635	66.2	356	14.4	479	19.4*	1168	89.9	131	10.1
MOREHOUSE	2439	70.1	512	14.7	530	15.2*	3017	82.5	641	17.5
NATCHTOCH	6920	70.8	2169	22.2	681	7.0*	2848	74.9	954	25.1
ORLEANS	66056	72.3	17129	18.7	8191	9.0*	74673	67.1	36579	32.9
OUACHITE	13500	62.0	2718	12.5	5556	25.5*	9481	73.7	3380	26.3
PLAQMINES	5317	92.6	125	2.2	299	5.2*	3753	91.0	369	9.0
PTCOUPEE	3666	77.1	845	17.8	241	5.1*	778	65.3	414	34.7
RAPIDES	19645	76.3	3102	12.0	3008	11.7*	9590	68.0	4509	32.0
REDRIVER	2054	74.4	321	11.6	386	14.0*	1046	87.2	154	12.8
RICHLAND	1897	63.0	123	4.1	990	32.9*	1868	82.7	390	17.3
SABINE	3195	85.9	220	5.9	306	8.2*	2291	79.0	609	21.0
STBERNARD	4924	75.7	843	13.0	736	11.3*	5185	79.0	1377	21.0
STCHARLES	5187	80.9	667	10.4	560	8.7*	1734	50.6	1690	49.4
STHELENA	1645	76.2	316	14.6	199	9.2*	611	66.4	309	33.6
STJAMES	2875	78.7	588	16.1	189	5.2*	884	48.9	923	51.1
STJOHNBAP	2032	74.6	395	14.5	296	10.9*	1052	60.6	684	39.4
STLANDRY	12311	71.1	1659	9.6	3339	19.3*	3930	67.5	1891	32.5
STMARTIN	4342	84.1	456	8.8	366	7.1*	855	64.8	465	35.2
STMARY	6395	82.5	764	9.9	593	7.6*	2213	61.2	1403	38.8
STTAMMANY	8870	78.6	846	7.5	1563	13.9*	4104	67.9	1943	32.1
TANGPOHOA	11963	79.3	1627	10.8	1494	9.9*	4523	63.6	2594	36.4
TENSAS	1039	68.4	61	4.0	420	27.6*	826	89.0	102	11.0
TERREBONN	9001	84.4	966	9.1	698	6.5*	2901	49.4	2971	50.6
UNION	2560	75.9	132	3.9	679	20.1*	1673	75.3	550	24.7
VERMILION	8382	81.6	1257	12.2	634	6.2*	2400	68.2	1117	31.8
VERNON	5126	84.9	369	6.1	545	9.0*	2490	80.6	599	19.4

```
                DEMOC.  SENATOR    1966     * SPECL.  REFERENDUM 1960
                                            *
COUNTY        ELLENDER    DEBLIEUX    GUICE       FOR        AGAINST
              #      %     #      %    #      % *  #      %    #      %
-----------------------------------------------*-------------------------------------------------------
WASHNGTON    8650  66.7  1977  15.2  2346  18.1* 3873  68.3  1797  31.7
WEBSTER      6489  72.4  1318  14.7  1159  12.9* 4400  81.9   973  18.1
WBTNROUGE    2340  63.5  1146  31.1   197   5.3*  825  49.4   845  50.6
WCARROLL     1704  72.3    79   3.4   574  24.4* 1176  83.8   227  16.2
WFELCIANA     864  35.9  1359  56.4   185   7.7*  409  71.1   166  28.9
                                            *
WINN         2912  72.7   219   5.5   876  21.9* 1796  92.1   155   7.9
-----------------------------------------------*-------------------------------------------------------
                                            *
TOTALS      494519       94154       78137   * 284987       151685
% OF VOTE     74.2        14.1        11.7   *   65.3         34.7
                                            *
                                            *
GEOGRAPHIC CLASS                            *
                                            *
LOWLANDS    176030  71.  37673  15.  33473  14.* 97534  64.  54808  36.
BLACK BELT   69738  70.  16052  16.  14534  14.* 35782  74.  12709  26.
CATHOLC LA  248751  78.  40429  13.  30130   9.* 151671 64.  84168  36.
                                            *
                                            *
DEMOGRAPHIC CLASS                           *
                                            *
METRO       204891  71.  51024  18.  33868  12.* 154784 62.  93240  38.
TOWN         68942  77.  10543  12.  10496  12.* 33799  67.  16907  33.
RURAL       220686  77.  32587  11.  33773  12.* 96404  70.  41538  30.
```

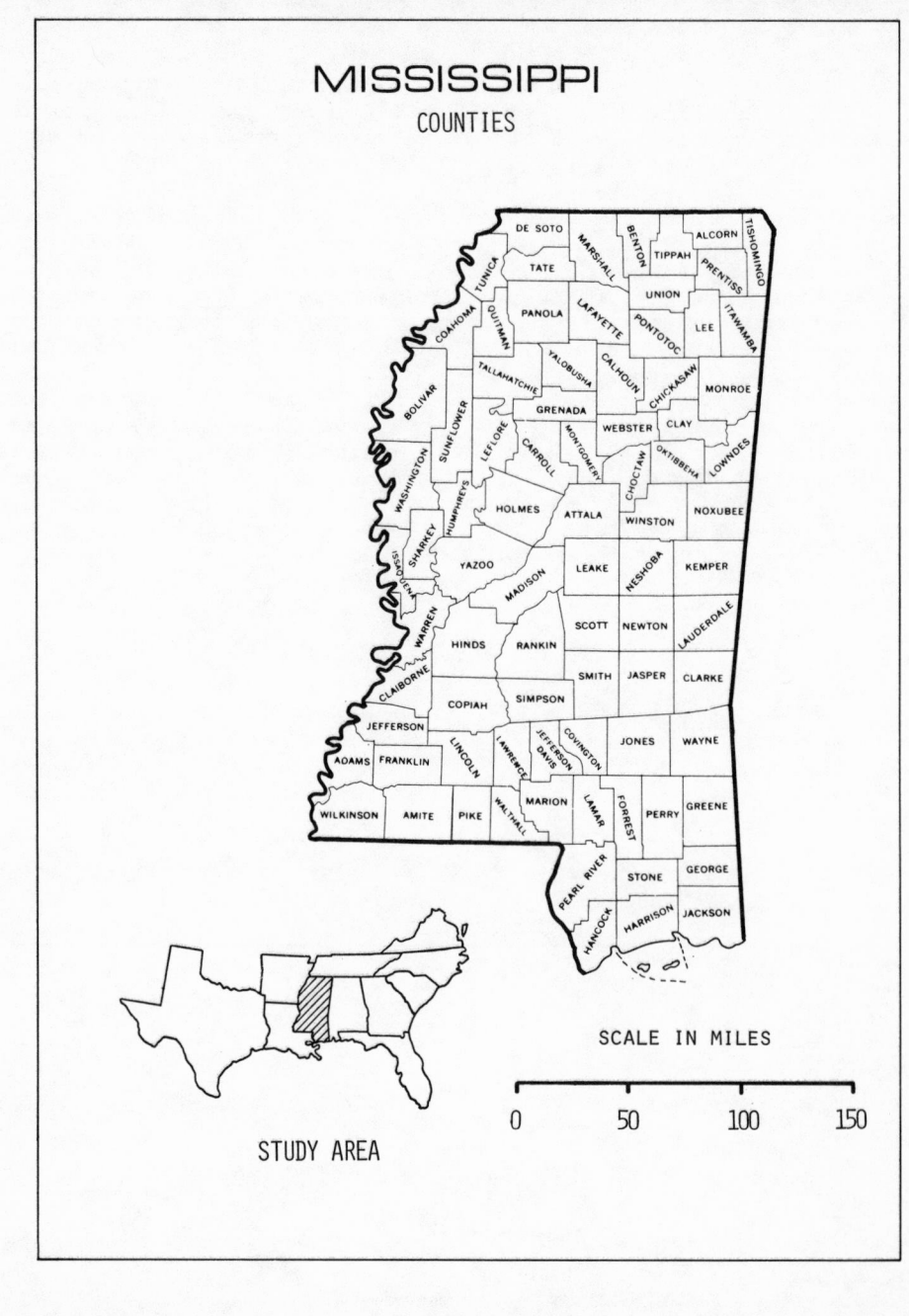

MISSISSIPPI
COUNTIES

SCALE IN MILES

0   50   100   150

STUDY AREA

MISSISSIPPI

No other state in the union erected such
stringent barriers to voting as did Mississippi. A potential voter had to pay the
poll tax of $2 or more (since counties could
add as much as $1 to the state tax) by
February 1 and at the same time show evi-
dence of having paid the tax for the two pre-
vious years. Residency requirements were two
years in the state and one year in the community. Prior to 1954 a registrant had to be
able to read a portion of the Mississippi
Constitution or interpret a section read to
him. In 1954 a constitutional amendment required a prospective voter to command the
ability to read, write, and demonstrate a
"reasonable interpretation" of a part of the
Mississippi Constitution to the satisfaction
of the registrar and further to show a
"reasonable understanding" of the obligations
and duties of citizenship. Additionally, the
potential voter had to complete unassisted a
written application for registration. As
Russell H. Barrett noted in 1960, Mississippi
was "the only southern state with a combi-
nation of 'understanding,' literacy, poll tax
and the two-year residence requirements."*
Later that same year, Mississippians ratified
a constitutional amendment (election results
reprinted below) requiring that a registrant

---

* Russell H. Barrett, "Suffrage and Elec-
tions," in Edward H. Hobbs (ed.), Yesterday's
Constitution Today: An Analysis of the
Mississippi Constitution of 1890 (University,
Miss.: Bureau of Public Administration,
1960), 98.

be of "good moral character." As an added
safeguard, the Mississippi legislature required that the names of all applicants for
registration be published locally.

Given all of this, it is not surprising
that few blacks voted in Mississippi prior
to the mid-1960s. During the 1950s there
were an estimated 20,000 black registrants.
In 1960 the figure was approximately 22,000,
slightly above 5 percent of the black voting-
age population. A dramatic increase in black
registration followed the 1965 Voting Rights
Act, so that in 1970 some 286,000 black
Mississippians, 71 percent of the black
voting-age population, were registered.
Consequently, less than 5 percent of Mississippi's registered voters were black during
the 1950s and hardly more than that in the
early 1960s; in 1970, however, almost 30
percent of the state's registrants were
blacks.

The following table sketching election
returns in recent presidential contests indi-
cates not only the surge in voter turnout but
also the massive shifts in partisan choice.
Turnout figures are given in both total
number of votes and, in parentheses, the
percentage of the voting-age citizens who
voted.

This section contains 12 Democratic
gubernatorial primaries, 1 senatorial primary,
and 5 referenda, for a total of 18 elections.

Gubernatorial Primaries

1. August 7, 1951: Ross R. Barnett 81,674
   (20.0%), Paul B. Johnson 86,117 (21.1%),
   Sam Lumpkin 83,951 (20.6%), Hugh White

95,321 (23.4%), other 4 candidates 60,632 (14.9%). Total vote was 407,695; turnout of voting-age citizens was 33.9%.

2. August 28, 1951: Paul B. Johnson 191,966 (48.8%), Hugh White 201,222 (51.2%). Total vote was 393,188; turnout was 32.7%.

3. August 2, 1955: Ross R. Barnett 92,785 (21.3%), J. P. Coleman 103,870 (23.8%), Paul B. Johnson 122,417 (28.1%), Fielding L. Wright 94,429 (21.7%), Mary D. Cain 22,469 (5.2%). Total vote was 435,970; turnout was 36.7%.

4. August 23, 1955: J. P. Coleman 233,240 (55.6%), Paul B. Johnson 186,024 (44.4%). Total vote was 419,264; turnout was 35.3%.

5. August 4, 1959: Ross R. Barnett 155,508 (35.5%), Carroll Gartin 151,043 (34.3%), Charles L. Sullivan 131,792 (29.9%), one other candidate 2,704 (0.6%). Total vote was 441,047; turnout was 37.6%.

6. August 25, 1959: Ross R. Barnett 230,557 (54.3%), Carroll Gartin 193,706 (45.7%). Total vote was 424,263; turnout was 36.1%.

7. August 6, 1963: James P. Coleman 156,299 (33.0%), Paul B. Johnson 182,540 (38.5%), Charles L. Sullivan 132,321 (27.9%), one other candidate 3,257 (0.7%). Total vote was 474,417; turnout was 39.8%.

8. August 27, 1963: J. P. Coleman 194,958 (42.7%), Paul B. Johnson 261,493 (57.3%). Total vote was 456,451; turnout was 38.3%.

9. August 8, 1967: Ross R. Barnett 76,053 (11.1%), James E. Swan 124,361 (18.2%), William L. Waller 60,090 (8.8%), John Bell Williams 197,778 (28.9%), William Winter 222,001 (32.5%), other 2 candidates 2,722 (0.5%). Total vote was 683,005; turnout was 56.0%.

10. August 29, 1967: John Bell Williams 371,817 (54.5%), William Winter 310,530 (45.5%). Total vote was 682,347; turnout was 55.9%.

11. August 3, 1971: Charles L. Sullivan 288,219 (37.8%), James E. Swan 128,946 (16.9%), William L. Waller 227,424 (29.8% Roy C. Adams 45,445 (6.0%), other 3 candidates 72,951 (9.6%). Total vote was 762,985; turnout was 55.0%.

12. August 24, 1971: Charles L. Sullivan 329,236 (45.8%), William L. Waller 389,952 (54.2%). Total vote was 719,188; turnout was 51.9%.

Senatorial Primaries

* (August 26, 1952: John C. Stennis won 89.4% against 1 opponent. Total vote was 214,182.)

1. August 24, 1954: James O. Eastland 137,836 (62.2%), Carroll Gartin 83,760 (37.8%). Total vote was 221,596.

* (August 26, 1958: John C. Stennis unopposed.)

* (June 7, 1960: James O. Eastland won 94.2% against 1 opponent. Total vote was 145,132.)

* (June 2, 1964: John C. Stennis won 97.4% against 1 opponent. Total vote was 178,467.)

* (June 7, 1966: James O. Eastland won 83.1% against 2 opponents. Total vote was 289,085.)

* (June 2, 1970: John C. Stennis unopposed

* (June 6, 1972: James O. Eastland won 203,847 (70.2%) against 2 opponents. Total vote was 290,256.)

Special Elections

1. August 26, 1952: Referendum to legalize
   the sale of alcoholic beverages. For
   80,822 (36.5%), Against 140,681 (63.5%).
   Total vote was 221,503.
2. June 7, 1960: Right-to-work amendment
   guaranteeing "that the right of persons
   to work shall not be denied or abridged
   on account of membership or nonmembership
   in a labor union." For 105,724 (69.0%),
   Against 47,459 (31.0%). Total vote was
   153,183.
3. November 8, 1960: Voter qualifications
   amendment requiring a person to be "of
   good moral character" to register. For
   161,352 (72.3%), Against 61,836 (27.7%).
   Total vote was 223,188.
4. June 3, 1968: Constitutional amendment
   lowering the residency requirement for
   voting from 2 years to 1 year. For
   136,846 (69.6%), Against 59,892 (30.4%).
   Total vote was 196,738.
5. June 3, 1968: Constitutional amendment
   providing for the Mississippi legislature
   to meet annually rather than biennially.
   For 98,842 (51.1%), Against 94,461
   (48.9%). Total vote was 193,303.

RETURNS FROM PRESIDENTIAL ELECTIONS

Year	Turnout		Partisan Vote*
1948	192,190	(16.0%)[+]	Dixiecrat 87.3%, Democrat 10.1%, Republican 2.6%
1952	285,532	(23.8%)	Democrat 60.4%, Republican 39.6%
1956	248,104	(21.0%)	Democrat 58.2%, Republican 24.5%, Independent 17.3%
1960	298,171	(25.5%)	Independent Democrat 39.0%, Democrat 36.3%, Republican 24.7%
1964	409,146	(34.1%)	Republican 87.1%, Democrat 12.9%
1968	654,509	(53.3%)	American Independent 63.5%, Democrat 23.0%, Republican 13.5%
1972	645,963	(46.4%)	Republican 78.2%, Democrat 19.6%

*Totals do not necessarily equal 100%, since minor party percentages are excluded.

[+]Percentage of citizens of voting age who voted is calculated on the basis of a straight-line interpolation of citizen population between census years.

COUNTY	BARNETT #	%	JOHNSON #	%	LUMPKIN #	%	WHITE #	%	OTHER #	%*	JOHNSON #	%	WHITE #	%
ADAMS	1016	22.9	630	14.2	693	15.6	1410	31.8	690	15.5*	1864	43.3	2445	56.7
ALCORN	1030	12.7	2549	31.4	2935	36.2	937	11.6	654	8.1*	5153	65.8	2675	34.2
AMITE	535	16.3	615	18.8	633	19.3	1085	33.1	407	12.4*	1325	41.9	1837	58.1
ATTALA	1412	26.6	994	18.7	768	14.4	1300	24.4	844	15.9*	2643	51.0	2543	49.0
BENTON	357	16.4	564	26.0	807	37.2	285	13.1	159	7.3*	1173	55.8	928	44.2
BOLIVAR	900	19.1	385	8.2	1312	27.8	1501	31.8	621	13.2*	1391	30.5	3170	69.5
CALHOUN	873	17.1	1821	35.6	1136	22.2	802	15.7	484	9.5*	2902	57.9	2108	42.1
CARROLL	684	22.2	1137	36.9	530	17.2	399	13.0	329	10.7*	1802	60.4	1183	39.6
CHICKASAW	695	17.4	828	20.8	1120	28.1	709	17.8	631	15.8*	1682	44.0	2137	56.0
CHOCTAW	595	19.2	733	23.6	591	19.1	913	29.4	269	8.7*	1241	40.8	1801	59.2
CLAIBORNE	229	15.7	164	11.2	349	23.9	366	25.0	355	24.3*	437	35.4	797	64.6
CLARKE	1092	23.8	1214	26.5	760	16.6	1183	25.8	338	7.4*	2379	55.5	1904	44.5
CLAY	168	5.0	453	13.5	913	27.2	1198	35.7	628	18.7*	1078	33.0	2184	67.0
COAHOMA	530	12.9	923	22.5	1292	31.5	856	20.9	500	12.2*	1454	36.4	2536	63.6
COPIAH	1243	24.8	858	17.1	620	12.4	1339	26.7	946	18.9*	2118	44.9	2599	55.1
COVINGTON	650	14.5	1236	27.6	469	10.5	1070	23.9	1047	23.4*	2108	47.3	2349	52.7
DESOTO	769	24.1	565	17.7	811	25.5	642	20.2	399	12.5*	1537	49.2	1584	50.8
FORREST	587	6.6	2971	33.6	645	7.3	2453	27.8	2180	24.7*	4931	56.8	3755	43.2
FRANKLIN	598	21.5	683	24.6	403	14.5	553	19.9	544	19.6*	1488	55.0	1215	45.0
GEORGE	838	27.4	772	25.2	511	16.7	498	16.3	440	14.4*	1513	55.2	1226	44.8
GREENE	194	6.4	341	11.3	265	8.8	530	17.6	1680	55.8*	1362	47.9	1480	52.1
GRENADA	500	16.1	819	26.5	355	11.5	902	29.1	520	16.8*	1601	51.2	1527	48.8
HANCOCK	581	12.3	1350	28.6	1367	28.9	726	15.4	700	14.8*	2960	61.7	1835	38.3
HARRISON	2290	15.3	4112	27.6	2436	16.3	3187	21.4	2899	19.4*	7716	53.3	6768	46.7
HINDS	7994	34.6	2144	9.3	4265	18.5	5689	24.6	3006	13.0*	7890	35.0	14631	65.0
HOLMES	670	18.4	476	13.1	757	20.8	1264	34.7	479	13.1*	1244	34.3	2385	65.7
HUMPHREYS	386	14.8	452	17.3	586	22.5	958	36.7	225	8.6*	1091	42.0	1504	58.0
ISSAQUENA	107	18.6	84	14.6	180	31.3	152	26.4	52	9.0*	291	51.4	275	48.6
ITAWAMBA	541	9.9	1488	27.4	2653	48.8	463	8.5	295	5.4*	3318	62.3	2010	37.7
JACKSON	2167	29.7	1089	14.9	965	13.2	1969	27.0	1100	15.1*	4277	59.4	2919	40.6
JASPER	1173	27.2	841	19.5	707	16.4	917	21.3	668	15.5*	2082	51.7	1942	48.3
JEFFERSON	104	7.4	108	7.7	241	17.2	224	16.0	724	51.7*	575	46.2	669	53.8
JEFFDAVIS	638	17.5	515	14.1	266	7.3	1917	52.5	312	8.6*	908	26.2	2564	73.8
JONES	1620	13.0	2249	18.0	1925	15.4	2277	18.3	4397	35.3*	7487	60.4	4917	39.6
KEMPER	594	16.4	1107	30.5	740	20.4	844	23.2	348	9.6*	1901	53.3	1668	46.7
LAFAYETTE	1223	27.0	1262	27.8	802	17.7	838	18.5	413	9.1*	2395	54.4	2010	45.6
LAMAR	526	11.7	830	18.5	464	10.3	1556	34.6	1121	24.9*	1717	42.8	2298	57.2
LAUDERDAL	2481	19.2	3031	23.4	2217	17.1	2668	20.6	2536	19.6*	6735	52.2	6156	47.8
LAWRENCE	900	25.2	1098	30.7	284	7.9	834	23.3	461	12.9*	2017	57.3	1503	42.7
LEAKE	4050	71.6	465	8.2	194	3.4	842	14.9	103	1.8*	3213	63.2	1874	36.8
LEE	492	5.2	1580	16.7	5885	62.2	1017	10.7	491	5.2*	4075	46.5	4693	53.5
LEFORE	833	16.3	740	14.5	1079	21.2	1636	32.1	813	15.9*	1775	36.1	3144	63.9
LINCOLN	1825	23.7	2052	26.7	849	11.0	1960	25.5	1001	13.0*	3442	47.4	3814	52.6
LOWNDES	544	10.4	453	8.6	1177	22.4	1427	27.2	1647	31.4*	1901	39.2	2951	60.8
MADISON	1157	33.9	264	7.7	682	20.0	951	27.9	356	10.4*	1017	31.1	2254	68.9
MARION	346	5.3	505	7.8	149	2.3	3430	52.8	2065	31.8*	1677	26.6	4621	73.4

COUNTY	BARNETT # %	JOHNSON # %	LUMPKIN # %	WHITE # %	OTHER # %*	JOHNSON # %	WHITE # %
MARSHALL	275 8.4	715 21.8	1317 40.2	673 20.5	297 9.1*	1343 41.8	1871 58.2
MONROE	627 8.7	1950 27.1	2313 32.2	1554 21.6	742 10.3*	3617 53.0	3203 47.0
MONTGMERY	744 22.2	813 24.3	340 10.1	973 29.0	481 14.4*	1779 47.9	1936 52.1
NESHOBA	2647 40.3	891 13.6	831 12.7	1706 26.0	490 7.5*	3068 47.4	3399 52.6
NEWTON	1408 29.8	1132 23.9	606 12.8	1109 23.4	476 10.1*	2306 50.8	2234 49.2
NOXUBEE	210 8.5	280 11.4	521 21.2	808 32.9	640 26.0*	718 30.6	1631 69.4
OKTIBBEHA	705 17.8	947 23.9	657 16.6	1029 25.9	629 15.9*	1564 40.3	2321 59.7
PANOLA	1501 32.7	691 15.0	1184 25.8	710 15.5	508 11.1*	2207 49.2	2280 50.8
PEARLRVER	1047 17.2	753 12.4	1678 27.5	1472 24.2	1144 18.8*	2492 41.8	3472 58.2
PERRY	308 11.1	668 24.1	251 9.0	702 25.3	848 30.5*	1599 57.2	1197 42.8
PIKE	829 12.2	870 12.8	1290 19.0	2259 33.3	1540 22.7*	2632 39.6	4019 60.4
PONTOTOC	1019 18.7	1095 20.1	2112 38.7	666 12.2	568 10.4*	2938 54.9	2413 45.1
PRENTISS	469 8.2	2307 40.2	1704 29.7	1001 17.4	259 4.5*	3787 68.4	1748 31.6
QUITMAN	328 10.7	1094 35.5	745 24.2	474 15.4	438 14.2*	1751 57.4	1299 42.6
RANKIN	2483 44.8	1053 19.0	707 12.8	802 14.5	500 9.0*	3062 54.8	2525 45.2
SCOTT	2078 41.3	1455 28.9	410 8.2	671 13.3	414 8.2*	2868 59.5	1949 40.5
SHARKEY	290 19.6	277 18.7	318 21.5	462 31.2	135 9.1*	621 42.9	827 57.1
SIMPSON	1888 32.5	1944 33.4	654 11.2	885 15.2	447 7.7*	3596 62.6	2147 37.4
SMITH	1743 31.6	1488 26.9	692 12.5	837 15.2	762 13.8*	3080 57.0	2327 43.0
STONE	274 12.7	234 10.9	314 14.6	1041 48.4	289 13.4*	715 35.2	1314 64.8
SUNFLOWER	490 10.3	950 20.0	1170 24.7	1446 30.5	686 14.5*	1738 39.8	2625 60.2
TALHATCHI	521 11.4	1503 32.9	1121 24.5	835 18.3	589 12.9*	2189 50.5	2147 49.5
TATE	827 28.1	443 15.1	700 23.8	547 18.6	426 14.5*	1184 40.1	1767 59.9
TIPPAH	857 16.5	1708 32.8	1252 24.1	1016 19.5	370 7.1*	3100 61.4	1948 38.6
TISHMINGO	449 9.0	1839 37.0	1713 34.5	593 11.9	375 7.5*	2817 56.9	2131 43.1
TUNICA	264 18.8	152 10.8	410 29.2	408 29.1	168 12.0*	487 40.6	712 59.4
UNION	755 12.0	1729 27.6	1947 31.0	1479 23.6	363 5.8*	3073 50.7	2987 49.3
WATHALL	511 14.7	773 22.3	435 12.6	1162 33.5	584 16.9*	1612 46.9	1823 53.1
WARREN	1567 23.3	830 12.3	1681 25.0	1885 28.0	759 11.3*	2369 41.0	3407 59.0
WASHINGTON	744 12.1	912 14.9	2164 35.3	1757 28.7	554 9.0*	1816 36.0	3231 64.0
WAYNE	520 12.3	1367 32.3	499 11.8	1126 26.6	714 16.9*	2062 51.4	1949 48.6
WEBSTER	810 22.0	1017 27.7	794 21.6	683 18.6	371 10.1*	1967 53.5	1709 46.5
WILKINSN	348 17.6	342 17.3	296 15.0	524 26.5	469 23.7*	711 41.0	1025 59.0
WINSTON	1618 32.0	916 18.1	788 15.6	1234 24.4	495 9.8*	2634 56.8	2003 43.2
YALOBUSHA	623 18.1	803 23.4	716 20.9	781 22.7	511 14.9*	1820 55.1	1483 44.9
YAZOO	1160 24.9	626 13.4	833 17.8	1334 28.6	714 15.3*	1758 38.8	2775 61.2
TOTALS	81674	86117	83951	95321	60632 *	191966	201222
% OF VOTE	20.0	21.1	20.6	23.4	14.9 *	48.8	51.2

```
                    DEMOC.  GOVERNOR   1951              * DEMOC.  RUNOFF    1951
                                                         *
COUNTY       BARNETT      JOHNSON      LUMPKIN      WHITE        OTHER      * JOHNSON      WHITE
             #      %     #      %     #      %     #      %     #      %  *  #      %     #      %
-------------------------------------------------------------------------*------------------------------------
GEOGRAPHIC CLASS                                                          *
                                                                         *
LOWLANDS    30493 21.   33835 23.   19948 14.   34692 24.   28049 19.*  75169 52.   68058 48.
BLACK BELT  40202 23.   29923 17.   35869 20.   46531 26.   24651 14.*  72831 43.   96640 57.
PIEDMONT    10979 13.   22359 27.   28134 34.   14098 17.    7932  9.*  43966 55.   36524 45.
                                                                         *
DEMOGRAPHIC CLASS                                                         *
                                                                         *
METRO        7994 35.    2144  9.    4265 18.    5689 25.    3006 13.*   7890 35.   14631 65.
TOWN        12212 15.   16851 21.   15309 19.   19556 24.   16975 21.*  38048 49.   39310 51.
RURAL       61468 20.   67122 22.   64377 21.   70076 23.   40651 13.* 146028 50.  147281 50.
```

```
                    DEMOC.  GOVERNOR   1955              * DEMOC.  RUNOFF    1955
                                                         *
COUNTY       BARNETT      COLEMAN      JOHNSON      WRIGHT       CAIN       * COLEMAN      JOHNSON
             #      %     #      %     #      %     #      %     #      %  *  #      %     #      %
-------------------------------------------------------------------------*------------------------------------
ADAMS         892 15.9    922 16.4   2015 35.9   1409 25.1    377  6.7*  2527 46.8   2872 53.2
ALCORN       1442 17.7   1863 22.9   3619 44.5   1026 12.6    177  2.2*  3543 44.9   4344 55.1
AMITE         471 13.8    625 18.3   1122 32.9    974 28.6    215  6.3*  1761 53.2   1550 46.8
ATTALA        776 14.2   2598 47.7   1153 21.2    740 13.6    179  3.3*  3475 65.1   1863 34.9
BENTON        675 28.7    730 31.0    442 18.8    442 18.8     64  2.7*  1239 57.6    912 42.4

BOLIVAR      1091 22.8    600 12.6    558 11.7   2290 47.9    238  5.0*  3189 66.6   1601 33.4
CALHOUN       926 17.4   2309 43.3   1302 24.4    407  7.6    388  7.3*  3419 65.0   1840 35.0
CARROLL       298 10.3   1252 43.4    844 29.2    400 13.9     93  3.2*  1622 57.2   1212 42.8
CHICKASAW     804 18.0   2470 55.3    583 13.1    429  9.6    177  4.0*  3340 75.8   1069 24.2
CHOCTAW       140  4.3   2589 80.3    302  9.4    140  4.3     53  1.6*  2623 84.6    478 15.4

CLAIBORNE     229 15.8     83  5.7    235 16.2    822 56.6     83  5.7*   851 59.9    570 40.1
CLARKE        687 15.5   1701 38.4   1363 30.8    401  9.1    278  6.3*  2050 50.7   1991 49.3
CLAY          272  7.7   1623 45.9    445 12.6   1003 28.4    190  5.4*  2526 76.7    766 23.3
COAHOMA       746 16.0    567 12.1    883 18.9   2215 47.4    263  5.6*  3004 62.6   1798 37.4
COPIAH       1147 23.9    803 16.7   1050 21.8   1564 32.5    245  5.1*  2531 56.7   1933 43.3
                                                                         *
COVINGTON    1256 27.5    615 13.5   2115 46.4    451  9.9    122  2.7*  1944 43.4   2538 56.6
DESOTO        789 24.5    822 25.5    531 16.5    874 27.1    207  6.4*  1831 58.0   1324 42.0
FORREST      1197 12.7    821  8.7   5371 56.9   1644 17.4    402  4.3*  3147 33.9   6126 66.1
FRANKLIN      702 24.2    594 20.5   1024 35.3    461 15.9    121  4.2*  1321 47.5   1459 52.5
GEORGE       1246 33.4    338  9.1   1613 43.3    417 11.2    114  3.1*  1558 44.8   1922 55.2
                                                                         *
GREENE       1156 36.9    280  8.9   1012 32.3    545 17.4    144  4.6*  1325 43.8   1698 56.2
GRENADA       543 15.1   1391 38.7    790 22.0    592 16.5    281  7.8*  2042 59.6   1383 40.4
HANCOCK       978 17.5    632 11.3   2490 44.6   1282 23.0    195  3.5*  2014 36.1   3558 63.9
HARRISON     2933 16.1    816  4.5   9174 50.2   3516 19.3   1825 10.0*  4671 25.5  13666 74.5
```

COUNTY	BARNETT #	%	COLEMAN #	%	JOHNSON #	%	WRIGHT #	%	CAIN #	%*	COLEMAN #	%	JOHNSON #	%
HINDS	8718	32.9	3138	11.8	3816	14.4	10042	37.9	803	3.0*	14304	56.6	10947	43.4
HOLMES	332	9.2	1326	36.6	524	14.5	1328	36.7	112	3.1*	2511	71.3	1011	28.7
HUMPHREYS	276	11.0	426	17.0	303	12.1	1335	53.3	164	6.5*	1462	61.7	907	38.3
ISSAQUENA	77	11.6	149	22.4	88	13.2	316	47.5	35	5.3*	368	59.6	249	40.4
ITAWAMBA	1584	26.6	1675	28.2	2165	36.4	283	4.8	240	4.0*	3139	54.6	2615	45.4
JACKSON	1751	19.3	1813	20.0	3942	43.5	1137	12.5	419	4.6*	3763	41.7	5255	58.3
JASPER	1016	25.6	694	17.5	1268	32.0	647	16.3	342	8.6*	2190	56.3	1701	43.7
JEFFERSON	258	15.4	343	20.5	347	20.7	615	36.7	112	6.7*	983	66.0	506	34.0
JEFFDAVIS	1250	30.6	768	18.8	1185	29.0	531	13.0	354	8.7*	2302	60.7	1489	39.3
JONES	2099	15.7	3190	23.8	5170	38.6	2245	16.8	673	5.0*	6572	50.6	6418	49.4
KEMPER	661	18.1	1356	37.2	881	24.2	440	12.1	310	8.5*	1961	57.5	1452	42.5
LAFAYETTE	971	21.1	1801	39.1	891	19.4	844	18.3	94	2.0*	2994	68.3	1389	31.7
LAMAR	1291	29.4	608	13.9	1682	38.4	643	14.7	161	3.7*	2243	53.3	1968	46.7
LAUDERDAL	2993	22.3	3747	28.0	3703	27.6	1896	14.2	1055	7.9*	6597	52.0	6098	48.0
LAWRENCE	1153	31.4	530	14.4	1468	39.9	408	11.1	118	3.2*	1593	44.5	1984	55.5
LEAKE	3524	67.9	454	8.8	775	14.9	315	6.1	119	2.3*	2543	50.7	2474	49.3
LEE	2738	25.9	3807	36.1	2759	26.1	1052	10.0	196	1.9*	6374	62.8	3768	37.2
LEFORE	558	10.4	1794	33.3	929	17.2	1855	34.4	252	4.7*	3947	73.6	1413	26.4
LINCOLN	1945	24.5	907	11.4	2986	37.6	1696	21.4	407	5.1*	3590	47.0	4050	53.0
LOWNDES	352	6.3	1890	33.8	866	15.5	2044	36.6	432	7.7*	4001	77.4	1165	22.6
MADISON	1091	29.7	342	9.3	791	21.5	1310	35.6	145	3.9*	1859	55.4	1494	44.6
MARION	1786	25.5	1627	23.2	2084	29.7	1292	18.4	228	3.2*	3821	59.0	2650	41.0
MARSHALL	538	15.7	685	20.0	748	21.9	1121	32.7	331	9.7*	1993	59.7	1344	40.3
MONROE	993	13.0	2939	38.4	2432	31.7	1030	13.4	269	3.5*	4436	60.8	2864	39.2
MONTGMERY	303	7.5	2124	52.3	748	18.4	697	17.2	188	4.6*	2846	70.9	1168	29.1
NESHOBA	1682	24.1	2109	30.2	2204	31.6	759	10.9	229	3.3*	3948	59.2	2717	40.8
NEWTON	1317	26.5	1481	29.8	1211	24.3	697	14.0	268	5.4*	2873	60.2	1903	39.8
NOXUBEE	339	14.0	933	38.5	264	10.9	635	26.2	255	10.5*	1562	73.1	575	26.9
OKTIBBEHA	581	12.8	1969	43.3	745	16.4	1039	22.9	210	4.6*	3403	76.0	1073	24.0
PANOLA	1397	28.5	579	11.8	835	17.1	1564	31.9	522	10.7*	3045	64.5	1675	35.5
PEARLRVER	1685	25.9	1162	17.8	1613	24.8	1863	28.6	188	2.9*	3295	55.5	2646	44.5
PERRY	567	19.1	167	5.6	1672	56.4	467	15.7	93	3.1*	998	34.3	1910	65.7
PIKE	889	13.0	1631	23.9	1460	21.4	2043	29.9	803	11.8*	3787	57.7	2780	42.3
PONTOTOC	2351	37.4	2014	32.1	1292	20.6	434	6.9	189	3.0*	4110	67.4	1987	32.6
PRENTISS	1849	29.0	1440	22.6	2615	41.0	367	5.7	114	1.8*	3150	49.8	3176	50.2
QUITMAN	391	12.8	384	12.6	833	27.2	1136	37.2	313	10.2*	1775	56.7	1356	43.3
RANKIN	2235	38.8	651	11.3	1460	25.4	1247	21.7	161	2.8*	2795	49.8	2815	50.2
SCOTT	1733	32.6	1063	20.0	1805	34.0	557	10.5	150	2.8*	2724	51.8	2536	48.2
SHARKEY	133	8.3	144	9.0	255	15.9	1017	63.4	54	3.4*	911	60.7	591	39.3
SIMPSON	2086	34.0	700	11.4	2309	37.6	833	13.6	216	3.5*	2619	43.2	3438	56.8
SMITH	2344	40.5	896	15.5	1869	32.3	461	8.0	214	3.7*	2442	44.9	2996	55.1
STONE	402	17.2	384	16.4	974	41.6	465	19.9	115	4.9*	1109	56.5	853	43.5
SUNFLOWER	530	11.7	565	12.5	792	17.5	2275	50.2	371	8.2*	2778	61.1	1770	38.9
TALHATCHI	998	21.8	773	16.9	954	20.9	1547	33.9	298	6.5*	2592	64.8	1406	35.2
TATE	538	16.7	994	30.8	482	14.9	1004	31.1	210	6.5*	2159	69.8	936	30.2
TIPPAH	785	14.3	2506	45.5	1758	31.9	346	6.3	109	2.0*	2904	57.7	2131	42.3

```
                    DEMOC.  GOVERNOR    1955              *  DEMOC.  RUNOFF      1955
                                                          *
COUNTY       BARNETT      COLEMAN     JOHNSON      WRIGHT      CAIN     *  COLEMAN     JOHNSON
             #     %      #     %     #     %      #     %     #    %*   #     %     #     %
-------------------------------------------------------------------------------------------------------
TISHMINGO    927 18.6   1334 26.7   2108 42.2    482  9.6    146  2.9*  2489 50.7   2423 49.3
TUNICA       286 18.6    186 12.1    110  7.1    849 55.2    108  7.0*   731 57.0    551 43.0
UNION        994 16.0   3134 50.5   1376 22.2    546  8.8    161  2.6*  4220 70.0   1807 30.0
WATHALL      968 25.2    907 23.6   1183 30.8    552 14.4    235  6.1*  1912 53.8   1642 46.2
WARREN      1191 16.0    499  6.7   1212 16.3   3707 49.8    842 11.3*  3953 59.7   2669 40.3

WASHINGTON   809 12.1   1195 17.9    578  8.7   3612 54.2    475  7.1*  4852 70.8   2005 29.2
WAYNE        598 13.2   1290 28.5   1683 37.2    564 12.5    395  8.7*  2298 53.1   2029 46.9
WEBSTER      363  8.2   3035 68.9    643 14.6    220  5.0    143  3.2*  3207 79.5    829 20.5
WILKINSN     337 16.8    119  5.9    519 25.9    735 36.7    292 14.6*   868 44.7   1074 55.3
WINSTON      473  9.4   2823 56.2   1254 25.0    323  6.4    151  3.0*  3263 67.0   1608 33.0
                                                                       *
YALOBUSHA    620 18.3   1051 31.0    866 25.5    631 18.6    225  6.6*  1967 61.6   1224 38.4
YAZOO        733 15.5    575 12.2    896 19.0   2286 48.5    224  4.8*  2556 55.6   2041 44.4
-------------------------------------------------------------------------------------------------------
                                                                       *
TOTALS      92785      103870      122417      94429       22469      * 233240      186024
% OF VOTE    21.3        23.8        28.1        21.7         5.2      *  55.6         44.4
                                                                       *
GEOGRAPHIC CLASS                                                       *
                                                                       *
LOWLANDS   37120 23.   27528 17.   60973 38.   25486 16.    8170  5.*  69989 46.   83765 54.
BLACK BELT 38446 21.   41536 22.   36733 20.   59293 32.   11411  6.* 109302 61.   70374 39.
PIEDMONT   17219 19.   34806 39.   24711 28.    9650 11.    2888  3.*  53949 63.   31885 37.
                                                                       *
DEMOGRAPHIC CLASS                                                      *
                                                                       *
METRO       8718 33.    3138 12.    3816 14.   10042 38.     803  3.*  14304 57.   10947 43.
TOWN       13770 15.   15441 17.   29901 33.   24143 27.    6596  7.*  43271 49.   44230 51.
RURAL      70297 22.   85291 27.   88700 28.   60244 19.   15070  5.* 175665 57.  130847 43.
```

MISSISSIPPI

```
              DEMOC.  GOVERNOR    1959    * DEMOC.  RUNOFF      1959
                                          *
COUNTY     BARNETT      GARTIN       SULLIVAN     BARNETT      GARTIN
           #     %      #     %      #     %*     #     %      #     %
------------------------------------------------------------------------------------------
ADAMS      2091 34.0   1976 32.1    2089 33.9*   3217 52.4    2927 47.6
ALCORN     2865 37.0   2797 36.1    2089 27.0*   4003 53.5    3474 46.5
AMITE      1720 52.4   1070 32.6     495 15.1*   1910 61.5    1195 38.5
ATTALA     2501 46.8   2031 38.0     807 15.1*   2757 55.4    2218 44.6
BENTON      674 32.7    852 41.3     536 26.0*   1000 55.1     814 44.9
                                          *
BOLIVAR    1473 28.3   1263 24.3    2464 47.4*   2878 56.7    2199 43.3
CALHOUN    2172 42.0   1858 35.9    1139 22.0*   2904 59.5    1979 40.5
CARROLL    1166 43.0    785 29.0     759 28.0*   1526 57.9    1109 42.1
```

COUNTY	BARNETT #	%	GARTIN #	%	SULLIVAN #	%*	BARNETT #	%	GARTIN #	%
	DEMOC. GOVERNOR 1959						* DEMOC. RUNOFF 1959			
CHICKASAW	1406	31.8	1964	44.4	1053	23.8*	2154	50.2	2140	49.8
CHOCTAW	1015	34.9	1464	50.3	429	14.8*	1309	46.3	1520	53.7
CLAIBORNE	546	38.2	425	29.7	459	32.1*	837	61.2	531	38.8
CLARKE	1730	38.3	1437	31.8	1351	29.9*	2564	59.1	1773	40.9
CLAY	671	19.9	1381	40.9	1326	39.3*	1586	47.7	1737	52.3
COAHOMA	360	7.8	791	17.1	3474	75.1*	2104	46.9	2381	53.1
COPIAH	2659	52.6	1380	27.3	1018	20.1*	2997	63.3	1740	36.7
COVINGTON	1781	41.5	1255	29.2	1258	29.3*	2629	62.0	1612	38.0
DESOTO	1260	35.8	1276	36.2	988	28.0*	1797	53.1	1586	46.9
FORREST	2053	19.8	3927	38.0	4366	42.2*	4091	42.0	5661	58.0
FRANKLIN	1467	54.8	782	29.2	427	16.0*	1708	67.5	822	32.5
GEORGE	1093	30.1	1058	29.1	1484	40.8*	2210	61.9	1358	38.1
GREENE	744	23.3	637	20.0	1806	56.7*	1859	58.3	1327	41.7
GRENADA	1184	32.5	1256	34.5	1198	32.9*	1858	51.3	1764	48.7
HANCOCK	1133	20.2	2002	35.8	2461	44.0*	2980	52.9	2653	47.1
HARRISON	4561	23.5	7316	37.6	7556	38.9*	9389	48.7	9883	51.3
HINDS	13339	46.6	8887	31.0	6400	22.4*	16707	59.4	11425	40.6
HOLMES	1437	40.8	1168	33.2	917	26.0*	2001	56.5	1538	43.5
HUMPHREYS	1051	42.7	495	20.1	914	37.2*	1547	66.2	789	33.8
ISSAQUENA	250	40.5	199	32.2	169	27.3*	381	62.6	228	37.4
ITAWAMBA	1785	29.3	2070	34.0	2232	36.7*	3080	50.6	3010	49.4
JACKSON	2995	26.6	5694	50.5	2583	22.9*	4617	42.4	6269	57.6
JASPER	1441	35.2	1586	38.8	1061	26.0*	2101	53.3	1843	46.7
JEFFERSON	649	39.6	556	33.9	433	26.4*	768	55.8	608	44.2
JEFFDAVIS	1299	41.5	719	23.0	1109	35.5*	1905	62.6	1138	37.4
JONES	2425	17.6	9061	65.9	2270	16.5*	3866	28.7	9621	71.3
KEMPER	1171	36.3	1255	38.9	801	24.8*	1751	56.9	1326	43.1
LAFAYETTE	1410	31.8	1986	44.9	1032	23.3*	1986	47.6	2185	52.4
LAMAR	1552	33.3	1192	25.6	1921	41.2*	2664	61.6	1659	38.4
LAUDERDAL	4019	30.4	5145	39.0	4038	30.6*	6623	49.9	6655	50.1
LAWRENCE	1922	55.0	816	23.3	757	21.7*	2334	69.2	1040	30.8
LEAKE	4128	82.1	598	11.9	302	6.0*	4139	83.8	799	16.2
LEE	2466	22.4	4770	43.4	3767	34.2*	4509	42.3	6147	57.7
LEFORE	1386	23.4	2141	36.2	2391	40.4*	2609	46.3	3022	53.7
LINCOLN	4074	50.4	1916	23.7	2090	25.9*	4771	64.6	2612	35.4
LOWNDES	831	14.3	2550	43.9	2431	41.8*	2331	40.8	3380	59.2
MADISON	1721	49.0	980	27.9	809	23.0*	2037	61.7	1263	38.3
MARION	3324	49.0	2111	31.1	1351	19.9*	3870	59.4	2647	40.6
MARSHALL	1174	33.7	1169	33.6	1136	32.7*	1776	54.6	1477	45.4
MONROE	1931	26.2	2783	37.7	2662	36.1*	3210	44.0	4083	56.0
MONTGMERY	1793	45.4	1183	29.9	977	24.7*	2228	58.5	1583	41.5
NESHOBA	2908	44.5	2196	33.6	1436	22.0*	3707	59.1	2562	40.9
NEWTON	2286	45.8	1193	23.9	1513	30.3*	3163	64.9	1710	35.1
NOXUBEE	617	27.8	754	34.0	847	38.2*	1246	56.1	977	43.9
OKTIBBEHA	1109	25.3	1814	41.3	1466	33.4*	2102	49.2	2170	50.8
PANOLA	1507	30.2	1381	27.7	2101	42.1*	2803	57.7	2058	42.3

```
              DEMOC.  GOVERNOR   1959     * DEMOC.  RUNOFF    1959
                                          *
 COUNTY      BARNETT      GARTIN       SULLIVAN    BARNETT       GARTIN
              #    %      #    %       #    %*     #    %        #    %
------------------------------------------------------------------------------------------
PEARLRVER    1749 28.4   2247 36.4   2169 35.2*   3323 54.6    2766 45.4
PERRY         833 27.1    969 31.6   1268 41.3*   1740 58.3    1246 41.7
PIKE         2797 41.8   2258 33.7   1643 24.5*   3739 57.4    2774 42.6
PONTOTOC     2212 35.6   1952 31.4   2046 32.9*   3676 59.6    2493 40.4
PRENTISS     1742 28.2   2160 34.9   2281 36.9*   3107 51.9    2884 48.1
                                          *
QUITMAN       666 22.5    650 22.0   1638 55.5*   1743 59.3    1196 40.7
RANKIN       4282 62.9   1342 19.7   1189 17.5*   4924 75.2    1624 24.8
SCOTT        3181 59.9   1129 21.3    998 18.8*   3684 70.1    1569 29.9
SHARKEY       500 32.9    441 29.0    578 38.1*    856 58.4     611 41.6
SIMPSON      3376 58.7   1247 21.7   1124 19.6*   4132 72.4    1578 27.6
                                          *
SMITH        2675 49.5   1174 21.7   1560 28.8*   3681 70.3    1555 29.7
STONE         523 22.4    820 35.1    990 42.4*   1071 49.1    1109 50.9
SUNFLOWER    1841 40.7   1108 24.5   1569 34.7*   2768 61.8    1709 38.2
TALHATCHI    1553 36.0    955 22.1   1804 41.8*   2498 63.1    1461 36.9
TATE          910 29.3   1170 37.6   1031 33.1*   1758 56.8    1335 43.2
                                          *
TIPPAH       2170 40.9   1866 35.2   1265 23.9*   2685 52.9    2389 47.1
TISHMINGO    1554 33.7   1877 40.7   1180 25.6*   2240 53.9    1918 46.1
TUNICA        130  9.3    459 32.8    812 58.0*    392 39.8     593 60.2
UNION        1438 23.9   2708 45.0   1875 31.1*   2356 40.7    3429 59.3
WATHALL      1887 48.9   1130 29.3    843 21.8*   2097 57.0    1584 43.0
                                          *
WARREN       2316 30.6   3449 45.6   1798 23.8*   2976 40.6    4352 59.4
WASHINGTON   1652 21.6   3223 42.1   2781 36.3*   2692 38.9    4231 61.1
WAYNE        1706 37.6   1476 32.6   1352 29.8*   2476 57.2    1852 42.8
WEBSTER      1687 41.8   1306 32.3   1046 25.9*   2278 60.1    1511 39.9
WILKINSN      671 38.6    516 29.7    553 31.8*   1066 62.4     643 37.6
                                          *
WINSTON      1976 41.2   1809 37.8   1006 21.0*   2824 58.5    2004 41.5
YALOBUSHA     992 32.2   1200 39.0    886 28.8*   1590 52.1    1459 47.9
YAZOO        2164 45.3   1051 22.0   1559 32.7*   3086 65.8    1604 34.2
-----------------------------------------*------------------------------------------------
                                          *
TOTALS     155508      151043       131792   * 230557        193706
% OF VOTE     35.5        34.5         30.1   *    54.3          45.7
```

```
              DEMOC.  GOVERNOR   1959    * DEMOC.  RUNOFF      1959
                                         *
COUNTY       BARNETT    GARTIN      SULLIVAN   BARNETT     GARTIN
              #    %     #    %      #    %*    #    %      #    %
-----------------------------------------*------------------------------------------------------------------
GEOGRAPHIC CLASS                         *

LOWLANDS     56925 35.  57360 35.  48891 30.* 86368 54.  72341 46.
BLACK BELT   71899 38.  59572 32.  56374 30.*102361 56.  78823 44.
PIEDMONT     26684 31.  34111 39.  26527 30.* 41828 50.  42542 50.


DEMOGRAPHIC CLASS                        *

METRO        13339 47.   8887 31.   6400 22.* 16707 59.  11425 41.
TOWN         21694 23.  39579 42.  33194 35.* 39898 43.  52113 57.
RURAL       120475 38. 102577 33.  92198 29.*173952 57. 130168 43.




                                              MISSISSIPPI


              DEMOC.  GOVERNOR   1963    * DEMOC.  RUNOFF      1963
                                         *
COUNTY       COLEMAN    JOHNSON     SULLIVAN   COLEMAN     JOHNSON
              #    %     #    %      #    %*    #    %      #    %
-----------------------------------------*------------------------------------------------------------------
ADAMS        1618 25.4  2011 31.6  2743 43.0* 2487 39.9  3747 60.1
ALCORN       2699 29.9  4036 44.7  2289 25.4* 2894 35.1  5341 64.9
AMITE         531 16.4  1973 61.1   726 22.5*  732 24.6  2244 75.4
ATTALA       2622 50.4  1883 36.2   698 13.4* 2802 55.2  2273 44.8
BENTON        454 23.0   995 50.5   522 26.5*  558 29.4  1339 70.6

BOLIVAR      1898 34.4  1413 25.6  2207 40.0* 2476 49.7  2509 50.3
CALHOUN      1529 28.8  2608 49.1  1177 22.1* 1863 37.9  3049 62.1
CARROLL      1038 39.9   991 38.1   573 22.0* 1180 46.7  1347 53.3
CHICKASAW    2141 45.1  1605 33.8  1003 21.1* 2283 50.6  2230 49.4
CHOCTAW      2388 75.8   609 19.3   154  4.9* 2374 77.0   711 23.0

CLAIBORNE     406 28.5   567 39.8   452 31.7*  519 37.3   873 62.7
CLARKE        895 20.6  2073 47.6  1383 31.8* 1099 26.1  3116 73.9
CLAY         1162 33.0  1520 43.2   839 23.8* 1435 42.5  1943 57.5
COAHOMA      1204 23.7   455  9.0  3419 67.3* 2671 59.8  1796 40.2
COPIAH       1518 29.0  2600 49.7  1116 21.3* 1846 36.3  3243 63.7

COVINGTON    1319 29.0  1875 41.3  1347 29.7* 1611 37.2  2718 62.8
DESOTO       1227 30.8  1395 35.0  1368 34.3* 1701 43.8  2187 56.3
FORREST      2449 22.5  5602 51.4  2838 26.1* 3489 32.4  7270 67.6
FRANKLIN      474 17.9  1631 61.6   544 20.5*  607 23.9  1934 76.1
GEORGE        707 18.7  1950 51.5  1126 29.8* 1031 27.5  2720 72.5

GREENE        577 16.2   963 27.0  2032 56.9* 1086 31.3  2387 68.7
GRENADA      1264 31.6  1573 39.3  1164 29.1* 1674 43.4  2180 56.6
HANCOCK      1542 27.9  2265 40.9  1725 31.2* 2176 39.5  3327 60.5
HARRISON     6914 30.8  7586 33.8  7943 35.4*10262 47.0 11574 53.0
```

COUNTY	DEMOC. GOVERNOR 1963						* DEMOC. RUNOFF 1963			
	COLEMAN		JOHNSON		SULLIVAN		COLEMAN		JOHNSON	
	#	%	#	%	#	%*	#	%	#	%
HINDS	13598	38.3	11976	33.8	9886	27.9*	17639	49.7	17838	50.3
HOLMES	1307	36.0	1378	38.0	945	26.0*	1463	43.7	1888	56.3
HUMPHREYS	704	31.2	910	40.3	643	28.5*	925	41.0	1331	59.0
ISSAQUENA	198	31.1	282	44.3	157	24.6*	227	38.3	366	61.7
ITAWAMBA	2587	39.5	2805	42.9	1154	17.6*	2876	45.3	3479	54.7
JACKSON	4819	35.8	5635	41.8	3015	22.4*	5846	45.3	7073	54.7
JASPER	1445	34.4	1615	38.4	1146	27.2*	1706	41.4	2415	58.6
JEFFERSON	375	25.1	597	40.0	522	34.9*	430	33.1	871	66.9
JEFFDAVIS	1082	33.3	1258	38.7	913	28.1*	1172	38.9	1838	61.1
JONES	7170	46.6	4635	30.1	3592	23.3*	7906	52.6	7136	47.4
KEMPER	883	30.7	1311	45.5	686	23.8*	1005	36.7	1730	63.3
LAFAYETTE	1845	39.9	1153	24.9	1628	35.2*	2459	55.3	1991	44.7
LAMAR	1092	22.2	2023	41.0	1814	36.8*	1603	33.8	3146	66.2
LAUDERDAL	4300	29.7	5846	40.4	4338	30.0*	5454	38.4	8760	61.6
LAWRENCE	728	19.2	2098	55.3	967	25.5*	952	27.4	2517	72.6
LEAKE	1191	24.3	2894	59.1	809	16.5*	1364	29.0	3344	71.0
LEE	5281	48.2	2823	25.8	2847	26.0*	6185	57.5	4579	42.5
LEFORE	2590	43.3	1255	21.0	2140	35.8*	3445	58.0	2492	42.0
LINCOLN	1727	22.2	3865	49.7	2184	28.1*	2386	30.2	5504	69.8
LOWNDES	2625	39.9	2225	33.8	1735	26.3*	3068	48.1	3317	51.9
MADISON	1592	40.1	1426	35.9	955	24.0*	1853	47.5	2051	52.5
MARION	1868	27.0	3055	44.1	2006	29.0*	2235	31.8	4790	68.2
MARSHALL	1130	31.6	1214	33.9	1236	34.5*	1471	42.1	2024	57.9
MONROE	2815	35.4	3363	42.3	1768	22.3*	3429	44.0	4368	56.0
MONTGMERY	1810	45.1	1319	32.9	880	22.0*	2001	52.1	1839	47.9
NESHOBA	2455	36.3	2910	43.0	1397	20.7*	2786	43.8	3569	56.2
NEWTON	1441	28.1	2177	42.4	1518	29.6*	1813	35.6	3286	64.4
NOXUBEE	609	26.0	1174	50.1	558	23.8*	719	32.6	1489	67.4
OKTIBBEHA	1995	42.9	1652	35.6	998	21.5*	2259	51.8	2106	48.2
PANOLA	1413	29.2	1512	31.2	1915	39.6*	2149	46.6	2461	53.4
PEARLRVER	1434	21.1	2982	44.0	2367	34.9*	2008	31.0	4467	69.0
PERRY	662	20.8	1328	41.7	1198	37.6*	833	27.5	2199	72.5
PIKE	1558	22.1	3534	50.2	1943	27.6*	2239	32.8	4596	67.2
PONTOTOC	2544	42.2	1838	30.5	1641	27.2*	2968	49.8	2987	50.2
PRENTISS	2279	35.2	2743	42.3	1460	22.5*	2521	40.0	3780	60.0
QUITMAN	882	27.6	1010	31.6	1308	40.9*	1355	42.8	1808	57.2
RANKIN	1961	22.8	4218	49.1	2413	28.1*	2697	31.8	5771	68.2
SCOTT	1539	27.2	2814	49.8	1299	23.0*	1836	33.6	3626	66.4
SHARKEY	416	28.0	617	41.6	451	30.4*	572	39.6	872	60.4
SIMPSON	1399	23.2	3477	57.7	1153	19.1*	1667	28.4	4206	71.6
SMITH	1338	24.5	2623	48.1	1491	27.3*	1619	30.7	3650	69.3
STONE	552	22.1	843	33.8	1100	44.1*	850	38.6	1351	61.4
SUNFLOWER	1439	32.6	1453	32.9	1524	34.5*	1812	44.2	2287	55.8
TALHATCHI	1309	31.4	1496	35.8	1369	32.8*	1685	40.0	2524	60.0
TATE	867	24.5	1482	41.8	1195	33.7*	1196	34.8	2242	65.2
TIPPAH	2177	37.1	2799	47.7	887	15.1*	2420	42.3	3300	57.7

DEMOC. GOVERNOR 1963 * DEMOC. RUNOFF 1963

COUNTY	COLEMAN #	%	JOHNSON #	%	SULLIVAN #	%*	COLEMAN #	%	JOHNSON #	%
TISHMINGO	1778	36.4	1767	36.2	1337	27.4*	1818	38.6	2895	61.4
TUNICA	535	41.1	167	12.8	600	46.1*	614	62.0	376	38.0
UNION	2798	42.0	2512	37.7	1346	20.2*	3098	47.9	3376	52.1
WATHALL	903	23.1	1907	48.9	1093	28.0*	1238	32.0	2629	68.0
WARREN	3337	39.8	2605	31.1	2432	29.0*	4080	50.0	4084	50.0
WASHINGTON	4985	54.7	1619	17.8	2514	27.6*	6060	67.6	2905	32.4
WAYNE	1231	24.4	2181	43.2	1637	32.4*	1463	31.0	3263	69.0
WEBSTER	1851	43.7	1647	38.9	733	17.3*	2036	49.4	2088	50.6
WILKINSN	328	18.0	668	36.6	827	45.4*	582	34.2	1119	65.8
WINSTON	2383	45.0	2154	40.7	753	14.2*	2717	52.0	2506	48.0
YALOBUSHA	890	26.7	1288	38.7	1151	34.6*	1175	37.3	1978	62.7
YAZOO	1673	32.0	2203	42.1	1359	26.0*	2117	41.8	2952	58.2
						*				
TOTALS	156299		182540		132321	*	194958		261493	
% OF VOTE	33.2		38.7		28.1	*	42.7		57.3	

GEOGRAPHIC CLASS

LOWLANDS	50119	28.	75024	42.	51883	29.*	64708	38.	107426	62.
BLACK BELT	68843	34.	72983	36.	59279	29.*	87958	45.	106576	55.
PIEDMONT	37337	40.	34533	37.	21159	23.*	42292	47.	47491	53.

DEMOGRAPHIC CLASS

METRO	13598	38.	11976	34.	9886	28.*	17639	50.	17838	50.
TOWN	37192	36.	33839	32.	33694	32.*	48922	48.	53081	52.
RURAL	105509	32.	136725	41.	88741	27.*	128397	40.	190574	60.

MISSISSIPPI

DEMOC. GOVERNOR 1967 * DEMOC. RUNOFF 1967

COUNTY	BARNETT #	%	SWAN #	%	WALLER #	%	WILLIAMS #	%	WINTER #	%*	WILLIAMS #	%	WINTER #	%
ADAMS	778	6.7	1391	12.0	2927	25.2	4889	42.1	1637	14.1*	6725	54.5	5624	45.5
ALCORN	2364	20.3	1267	10.9	806	6.9	3217	27.7	3971	34.2*	6436	58.0	4670	42.0
AMITE	560	12.4	326	7.2	183	4.1	2564	57.0	865	19.2*	3374	65.4	1786	34.6
ATTALA	1557	19.7	1526	19.3	317	4.0	2006	25.4	2497	31.6*	4044	53.7	3485	46.3
BENTON	449	15.5	350	12.1	96	3.3	1025	35.3	983	33.9*	1623	55.9	1282	44.1
BOLIVAR	857	8.8	619	6.4	964	9.9	3078	31.8	4174	43.1*	4577	46.7	5228	53.3
CALHOUN	813	12.4	1997	30.5	268	4.1	1875	28.6	1598	24.4*	4108	65.7	2143	34.3
CARROLL	569	15.3	950	25.5	95	2.5	1102	29.6	1011	27.1*	2234	57.7	1639	42.3

COUNTY	BARNETT #	BARNETT %	SWAN #	SWAN %	WALLER #	WALLER %	WILLIAMS #	WILLIAMS %	WINTER #	WINTER %*	WILLIAMS #	WILLIAMS %	WINTER #	WINTER %
CHICKASAW	716	11.1	1741	26.9	368	5.7	1754	27.1	1884	29.2*	3612	58.3	2586	41.7
CHOCTAW	399	10.2	1054	26.8	252	6.4	1043	26.6	1179	30.0*	2386	60.1	1583	39.9
CLAIBORNE	284	10.7	157	5.9	460	17.3	1075	40.4	685	25.7*	1599	42.1	2201	57.9
CLARKE	611	10.7	1610	28.3	186	3.3	1514	26.6	1777	31.2*	3143	56.4	2427	43.6
CLAY	667	10.8	1231	19.9	1113	18.0	1302	21.0	1881	30.4*	3027	48.5	3208	51.5
COAHOMA	575	5.7	256	2.5	2502	24.9	3272	32.5	3450	34.3*	4552	42.9	6061	57.1
COPIAH	1029	11.9	1245	14.4	1406	16.2	3046	35.1	1941	22.4*	4941	55.8	3915	44.2
COVINGTON	628	10.3	2395	39.4	343	5.6	1307	21.5	1405	23.1*	3743	64.5	2057	35.5
DESOTO	1254	16.0	214	2.7	602	7.7	2114	26.9	3662	46.7*	3893	48.0	4217	52.0
FORREST	779	4.8	5514	34.0	1131	7.0	3835	23.7	4943	30.5*	9635	58.8	6743	41.2
FRANKLIN	415	11.2	432	11.6	621	16.7	1742	46.8	511	13.7*	2259	64.0	1271	36.0
GEORGE	661	13.5	1426	29.1	175	3.6	1464	29.8	1181	24.1*	3169	66.3	1611	33.7
GREENE	383	9.1	1532	36.3	228	5.4	932	22.1	1148	27.2*	2321	58.3	1661	41.7
GRENADA	557	7.5	1322	17.8	291	3.9	1454	19.6	3783	51.1*	3003	39.8	4543	60.2
HANCOCK	653	9.2	1685	23.7	301	4.2	1456	20.5	3022	42.5*	3468	48.6	3668	51.4
HARRISON	2272	8.0	3639	12.8	1671	5.9	8720	30.6	12228	42.9*	14441	49.4	14781	50.6
HINDS	6178	11.5	4602	8.6	6347	11.9	17397	32.5	18981	35.5*	29331	52.9	26138	47.1
HOLMES	705	11.8	843	14.1	221	3.7	1730	29.0	2460	41.3*	3290	46.2	3835	53.8
HUMPHREYS	390	10.8	725	20.1	177	4.9	1060	29.4	1249	34.7*	1952	52.1	1798	47.9
ISSAQUENA	117	10.8	182	16.8	45	4.2	251	23.2	488	45.1*	494	46.0	581	54.0
ITAWAMBA	677	8.6	1979	25.3	562	7.2	1689	21.6	2928	37.4*	4059	51.6	3813	48.4
JACKSON	2753	14.0	3915	19.9	997	5.1	4178	21.2	7823	39.8*	10294	52.1	9470	47.9
JASPER	496	9.2	1679	31.1	196	3.6	1388	25.7	1636	30.3*	3106	58.7	2182	41.3
JEFFERSON	288	10.2	175	6.2	764	26.9	1093	38.6	515	18.2*	1537	43.2	2022	56.8
JEFFDAVIS	516	10.5	1353	27.4	256	5.2	1069	21.7	1738	35.2*	2531	52.1	2324	47.9
JONES	970	5.2	5734	30.9	1466	7.9	4673	25.2	5686	30.7*	10353	58.1	7457	41.9
KEMPER	452	12.5	779	21.6	99	2.7	1209	33.6	1064	29.5*	2113	61.2	1342	38.8
LAFAYETTE	385	5.7	336	5.0	2190	32.4	1400	20.7	2445	36.2*	3156	47.6	3481	52.4
LAMAR	272	4.3	3243	51.7	510	8.1	1366	21.8	878	14.0*	4320	71.7	1705	28.3
LAUDERDAL	1578	7.8	5495	27.0	1485	7.3	5742	28.3	6022	29.6*	11294	56.6	8671	43.4
LAWRENCE	708	15.1	1284	27.4	643	13.7	1205	25.7	851	18.1*	2841	62.9	1677	37.1
LEAKE	2954	40.2	990	13.5	849	11.5	1593	21.7	967	13.2*	3894	54.9	3196	45.1
LEE	952	5.9	2184	13.6	1177	7.3	4518	28.2	7202	44.9*	7781	49.0	8105	51.0
LEFORE	780	7.8	1573	15.7	862	8.6	3242	32.3	3569	35.6*	5554	53.7	4786	46.3
LINCOLN	1281	11.9	2468	23.0	771	7.2	3784	35.2	2441	22.7*	6820	64.8	3710	35.2
LOWNDES	902	8.1	1885	17.0	1293	11.6	3278	29.5	3748	33.7*	5684	50.5	5568	49.5
MADISON	1392	18.9	860	11.7	970	13.2	1870	25.4	2260	30.7*	4090	47.3	4564	52.7
MARION	731	7.7	3156	33.4	1204	12.7	2452	25.9	1916	20.3*	5807	64.0	3263	36.0
MARSHALL	941	13.7	369	5.4	279	4.1	1509	22.0	3759	54.8*	2835	38.6	4518	61.4
MONROE	1036	9.2	2870	25.5	577	5.1	2436	21.7	4318	38.4*	6017	53.6	5205	46.4
MONTGMERY	578	11.1	1122	21.5	204	3.9	1598	30.6	1714	32.9*	2902	54.8	2395	45.2
NESHOBA	1574	18.2	2327	26.9	317	3.7	2185	25.2	2252	26.0*	4626	57.0	3484	43.0
NEWTON	1124	15.4	2176	29.8	538	7.4	1853	25.4	1605	22.0*	4410	63.2	2567	36.8
NOXUBEE	326	9.0	496	13.7	136	3.8	1235	34.1	1427	39.4*	1868	55.7	1488	44.3
OKTIBBEHA	786	10.5	795	10.6	413	5.5	2179	29.0	3337	44.4*	3553	48.8	3727	51.2
PANOLA	686	8.2	494	5.9	919	11.0	2687	32.1	3585	42.8*	4470	51.2	4253	48.8

COUNTY	BARNETT		SWAN		WALLER		WILLIAMS		WINTER		WILLIAMS		WINTER	
	#	%	#	%	#	%	#	%	#	%*	#	%	#	%
PEARLRVER	911	9.3	2307	23.5	263	2.7	3020	30.7	3323	33.8*	5314	56.0	4172	44.0
PERRY	327	8.0	1819	44.5	328	8.0	741	18.1	869	21.3*	2390	61.0	1526	39.0
PIKE	854	8.3	1361	13.2	610	5.9	4161	40.2	3358	32.5*	6484	60.6	4210	39.4
PONTOTOC	1021	12.4	1214	14.8	757	9.2	2646	32.2	2581	31.4*	4739	57.7	3481	42.3
PRENTISS	1470	17.3	1620	19.1	351	4.1	2326	27.4	2712	32.0*	4730	56.4	3654	43.6
										*				
QUITMAN	551	11.2	244	5.0	849	17.3	1365	27.8	1903	38.7*	2645	49.3	2717	50.7
RANKIN	2212	17.2	3186	24.7	801	6.2	3172	24.6	3509	27.2*	7684	61.6	4785	38.4
SCOTT	1693	21.3	2227	28.0	467	5.9	1569	19.7	2007	25.2*	4834	62.0	2957	38.0
SHARKEY	241	10.2	449	18.9	443	18.7	552	23.3	685	28.9*	1088	46.8	1238	53.2
SIMPSON	1534	18.5	2297	27.7	951	11.5	1797	21.7	1704	20.6*	4774	59.2	3297	40.8
										*				
SMITH	1043	16.6	2254	35.8	381	6.1	1559	24.8	1060	16.8*	4038	65.9	2092	34.1
STONE	166	5.7	836	28.6	138	4.7	1061	36.3	725	24.8*	2127	70.3	900	29.7
SUNFLOWER	972	12.3	727	9.2	571	7.2	2554	32.4	3067	38.9*	3829	50.5	3747	49.5
TALHATCHI	785	12.4	691	10.9	364	5.7	1915	30.2	2592	40.8*	2684	47.3	2985	52.7
TATE	450	9.0	155	3.1	229	4.6	1601	32.1	2560	51.3*	2602	50.7	2527	49.3
										*				
TIPPAH	1127	15.4	1019	13.9	465	6.4	2274	31.1	2435	33.3*	4310	58.8	3014	41.2
TISHMINGO	917	13.0	1334	18.9	265	3.8	1973	28.0	2557	36.3*	3644	53.2	3204	46.8
TUNICA	224	11.7	49	2.6	145	7.5	853	44.4	650	33.8*	1275	53.8	1095	46.2
UNION	657	8.1	607	7.5	602	7.4	2375	29.4	3845	47.6*	3805	47.8	4162	52.2
WATHALL	425	7.8	998	18.4	276	5.1	2348	43.2	1389	25.6*	3394	63.2	1974	36.8
										*				
WARREN	771	6.0	872	6.8	2076	16.2	5923	46.2	3166	24.7*	7112	58.6	5030	41.4
WASHINGTON	1626	12.2	1461	11.0	1696	12.7	2946	22.1	5608	42.0*	5219	40.9	7550	59.1
WAYNE	640	9.6	2331	35.0	168	2.5	1336	20.1	2184	32.8*	3301	50.7	3212	49.3
WEBSTER	547	11.1	1630	33.0	221	4.5	1458	29.5	1080	21.9*	3199	66.8	1593	33.2
WILKINSN	227	6.2	119	3.3	1103	30.2	1635	44.7	574	15.7*	2057	51.6	1932	48.4
										*				
WINSTON	990	13.8	1052	14.7	923	12.9	2219	31.0	1977	27.6*	3767	55.1	3066	44.9
YALOBUSHA	508	10.8	418	8.9	435	9.3	1571	33.5	1758	37.5*	2582	57.6	1899	42.4
YAZOO	806	10.9	1116	15.1	439	6.0	3173	43.0	1843	25.0*	4895	63.6	2796	36.4
										*				
TOTALS	76053		124361		60090		197778		222001	*	371817		310530	
% OF VOTE	11.2		18.3		8.8		29.1		32.6	*	54.5		45.5	

	DEMOC. GOVERNOR 1967										*	DEMOC. RUNOFF 1967			
COUNTY	BARNETT #	%	SWAN #	%	WALLER #	%	WILLIAMS #	%	WINTER #	%*	WILLIAMS #	%	WINTER #	%
GEOGRAPHIC CLASS										*				
LOWLANDS	25504	11.	64856	27.	15463	7.	60921	26.	70559	30.*	135147	58.	97893	42.
BLACK BELT	36566	12.	36768	12.	34473	11.	102595	32.	106959	34.*	169004	52.	156375	48.
PIEDMONT	13983	11.	22737	18.	10154	8.	34262	27.	44483	35.*	67666	55.	56262	45.
DEMOGRAPHIC CLASS										*				
METRO	6178	12.	4602	9.	6347	12.	17397	33.	18981	35.*	29331	53.	26138	47.
TOWN	11031	7.	27820	18.	17109	11.	46520	30.	50057	33.*	80569	53.	72271	47.
RURAL	58844	12.	91939	19.	36634	8.	133861	28.	152963	32.*	261917	55.	212121	45.

MISSISSIPPI

	DEMOC. GOVERNOR 1971										*	DEMOC. RUNOFF 1971			
COUNTY	SULLIVAN #	%	SWAN #	%	WALLER #	%	ADAMS #	%	OTHER #	%*	SULLIVAN #	%	WALLER #	%
ADAMS	4264	35.4	2694	22.3	3850	31.9	270	2.2	976	8.1*	4197	40.9	6076	59.1
ALCORN	3143	27.3	1694	14.7	4299	37.3	1547	13.4	844	7.3*	4192	35.9	7483	64.1
AMITE	1596	33.3	860	18.0	1952	40.8	103	2.2	278	5.8*	2025	42.9	2699	57.1
ATTALA	2748	32.6	1554	18.4	2893	34.3	294	3.5	944	11.2*	3388	41.5	4773	58.5
BENTON	1165	36.7	528	16.6	927	29.2	398	12.5	157	4.9*	1527	46.4	1767	53.6
BOLIVAR	6437	60.1	1485	13.9	2209	20.6	186	1.7	400	3.7*	5803	62.9	3428	37.1
CALHOUN	2723	39.3	846	12.2	2020	29.2	504	7.3	828	12.0*	3130	48.1	3374	51.9
CARROLL	1079	28.4	856	22.6	723	19.1	195	5.1	942	24.8*	1454	42.0	2008	58.0
CHICKASAW	2676	37.8	1174	16.6	1609	22.7	856	12.1	760	10.7*	2913	42.6	3931	57.4
CHOCTAW	995	25.3	603	15.4	1055	26.9	243	6.2	1030	26.2*	1302	34.5	2472	65.5
CLAIBORNE	1416	47.2	656	21.9	618	20.6	127	4.2	183	6.1*	1130	55.9	891	44.1
CLARKE	2187	34.0	1151	17.9	2193	34.1	173	2.7	726	11.3*	2554	41.8	3555	58.2
CLAY	2519	38.1	1060	16.0	1818	27.5	671	10.2	541	8.2*	2996	47.8	3267	52.2
COAHOMA	8531	72.3	641	5.4	1263	10.7	409	3.5	953	8.1*	9262	81.1	2156	18.9
COPIAH	3215	32.7	2420	24.6	3130	31.9	383	3.9	674	6.9*	3731	42.2	5112	57.8
COVINGTON	1964	30.5	1744	27.1	1754	27.3	200	3.1	773	12.0*	2560	42.8	3422	57.2
DESOTO	4814	50.8	640	6.7	2604	27.5	947	10.0	479	5.1*	4975	54.5	4159	45.5
FORREST	6436	35.0	3311	18.0	4251	23.1	295	1.6	4085	22.2*	7646	45.9	9009	54.1
FRANKLIN	1233	31.0	1194	30.1	1122	28.2	90	2.3	333	8.4*	1476	43.4	1925	56.6
GEORGE	3047	50.8	1133	18.9	1109	18.5	104	1.7	601	10.0*	3060	54.4	2564	45.6
GREENE	2463	53.2	1035	22.3	700	15.1	76	1.6	357	7.7*	2682	63.9	1517	36.1
GRENADA	1878	24.9	1274	16.9	1065	14.1	219	2.9	3093	41.1*	3092	44.0	3936	56.0
HANCOCK	3922	47.5	1326	16.0	2078	25.1	123	1.5	816	9.9*	4503	54.8	3716	45.2
HARRISON	16637	49.2	4118	12.2	9681	28.7	489	1.4	2861	8.5*	17795	54.5	14874	45.5

MISSISSIPPI/157

```
                DEMOC.  GOVERNOR   1971              * DEMOC.  RUNOFF    1971
                                                     *
COUNTY      SULLIVAN    SWAN          WALLER      ADAMS        OTHER      * SULLIVAN      WALLER
            #      %     #      %      #      %    #      %     #      %*    #      %      #      %
--------------------------------------------------------------------------*-----------------------------------------
HINDS       21631 34.7  6432  10.3   27527 44.2  1840   3.0   4864   7.8* 25544 41.8    35568 58.2
HOLMES       2543 41.8  1100  18.1    1662 27.3   300   4.9    474   7.8*  2380 48.6     2519 51.4
HUMPHREYS    1607 39.0   835  20.3    1241 30.1   170   4.1    265   6.4*  2243 51.7     2094 48.3
ISSAQUENA     423 44.6   181  19.1     224 23.6    22   2.3     99  10.4*   589 54.1      500 45.9
ITAWAMBA     2635 31.2   719   8.5    1992 23.6  2473  29.2    638   7.5*  3577 42.4     4859 57.6
                                                             *
JACKSON     10341 44.1  3569  15.2    7071 30.1   413   1.8   2062   8.8* 10564 46.3    12275 53.7
JASPER       2217 35.4  1165  18.6    1881 30.1   196   3.1    797  12.7*  2456 42.4     3333 57.6
JEFFERSON     865 33.4   896  34.6     615 23.7    97   3.7    119   4.6*   789 42.2     1079 57.8
JEFFDAVIS    1799 32.0  1513  26.9    1530 27.2    94   1.7    680  12.1*  2140 39.4     3286 60.6
JONES        8048 34.4  4513  19.3    7419 31.8   490   2.1   2896  12.4*  8789 39.7    13359 60.3
                                                             *
KEMPER       1569 36.4   994  23.0    1134 26.3   234   5.4    384   8.9*  2185 53.6     1892 46.4
LAFAYETTE    2804 35.3   737   9.3    3676 46.3   335   4.2    387   4.9*  3293 47.3     3672 52.7
LAMAR        2108 29.7  2059  29.0    1851 26.0   123   1.7    966  13.6*  2617 39.5     4012 60.5
LAUDERDAL    7832 34.7  3954  17.5    7873 34.9   551   2.4   2356  10.4*  8509 40.4    12560 59.6
LAWRENCE     1263 23.9  1867  35.3    1737 32.8    95   1.8    327   6.2*  1657 34.5     3149 65.5

LEAKE        2337 30.4  1771  23.1    2531 33.0   504   6.6    536   7.0*  2890 38.2     4672 61.8
LEE          6182 37.1   893   5.4    3466 20.8  4762  28.6   1364   8.2*  7777 48.9     8131 51.1
LEFORE       5091 47.9  1791  16.8    2090 19.7   292   2.7   1372  12.9*  5953 59.3     4087 40.7
LINCOLN      3264 28.0  2656  22.8    4424 38.0   439   3.8    856   7.4*  3711 34.8     6947 65.2
LOWNDES      5408 43.7  2224  18.0    3111 25.2   435   3.5   1187   9.6*  5164 43.9     6598 56.1
                                                             *
MADISON      2159 25.4  1999  23.5    3122 36.7   332   3.9    894  10.5*  3285 44.5     4096 55.5
MARION       5001 46.7  2165  20.2    2187 20.4   159   1.5   1207  11.3*  5271 51.5     4965 48.5
MARSHALL     3726 47.0   856  10.8    1863 23.5   925  11.7    560   7.1*  4739 56.8     3603 43.2
MONROE       4384 37.7  1639  14.1    3412 29.4  1190  10.2    989   8.5*  4454 41.9     6164 58.1
MONTGMERY    1774 30.5   975  16.8    1312 22.6   636  10.9   1119  19.2*  2447 43.3     3205 56.7
                                                             *
NESHOBA      3063 31.2  2188  22.3    3492 35.6   426   4.3    638   6.5*  3469 37.1     5873 62.9
NEWTON       2366 29.0  1741  21.3    3061 37.5   301   3.7    701   8.6*  2762 36.8     4738 63.2
NOXUBEE      1297 37.2   503  14.4     932 26.7   284   8.1    474  13.6*  1661 47.8     1817 52.2
OKTIBBEHA    3169 39.5  1531  19.1    2042 25.4   575   7.2    712   8.9*  3240 48.9     3381 51.1
PANOLA       3160 35.5  1610  18.1    2814 31.6   821   9.2    496   5.6*  4223 46.3     4907 53.7
                                                             *
PEARLRVER    4441 41.9  2288  21.6    2670 25.2   157   1.5   1049   9.9*  5238 50.4     5161 49.6
PERRY        1786 38.1  1279  27.3     877 18.7   143   3.1    602  12.8*  2226 48.3     2386 51.7
PIKE         5583 49.5  1611  14.3    2862 25.4   193   1.7   1027   9.1*  4905 49.1     5092 50.9
PONTOTOC     3124 33.9   769   8.3    3738 40.5  1008  10.9    584   6.3*  3805 41.7     5318 58.3
PRENTISS     3418 34.6  1221  12.4    2561 26.0  2294  23.3    371   3.8*  4527 45.6     5410 54.4

QUITMAN      2411 47.3   835  16.4    1203 23.6   299   5.9    353   6.9*  2937 56.0     2310 44.0
RANKIN       5533 36.3  2769  18.2    5365 35.2   369   2.4   1196   7.9*  5519 38.3     8877 61.7
SCOTT        3178 33.8  2275  24.2    3101 33.0   281   3.0    562   6.0*  4070 46.4     4693 53.6
SHARKEY       854 35.3   529  21.9     762 31.5    99   4.1    173   7.2*  1133 46.9     1283 53.1
SIMPSON      2539 27.0  2244  23.9    3678 39.2   294   3.1    632   6.7*  3075 35.6     5570 64.4

SMITH        2045 30.3  1605  23.8    2179 32.3   205   3.0    712  10.6*  2421 39.8     3667 60.2
STONE        1289 35.7   559  15.5    1261 35.0    61   1.7    437  12.1*  1409 43.5     1833 56.5
SUNFLOWER    3855 43.4  1615  18.2    2610 29.4   325   3.7    470   5.3*  4071 52.7     3651 47.3
TALHATCHI    2563 39.0  1287  19.6    1742 26.5   310   4.7    671  10.2*  2808 47.3     3128 52.7
TATE         2294 38.6   406   6.8    1623 27.3  1300  21.9    313   5.3*  2906 48.9     3035 51.1
                                                             *
TIPPAH       2695 31.8  1101  13.0    2671 31.5  1497  17.7    502   5.9*  2977 37.2     5017 62.8
```

COUNTY	SULLIVAN # %	SWAN # %	WALLER # %	ADAMS # %	OTHER # %*	SULLIVAN # %	WALLER # %
TISHMINGO	1482 19.5	1311 17.2	840 11.0	3633 47.8	336 4.4*	2642 36.8	4530 63.2
TUNICA	1451 60.1	367 15.2	324 13.4	128 5.3	146 6.0*	1394 73.8	494 26.2
UNION	3647 37.5	484 5.0	3771 38.8	1427 14.7	396 4.1*	3653 40.4	5388 59.6
WATHALL	2124 36.8	1671 29.0	1289 22.3	139 2.4	548 9.5*	2405 45.4	2887 54.6
WARREN	6161 46.5	1081 8.2	4016 30.3	847 6.4	1152 8.7*	6130 47.4	6789 52.6
WASHINGTON	6304 43.6	1817 12.6	3612 25.0	373 2.6	2346 16.2*	6951 51.8	6473 48.2
WAYNE	1839 24.5	2069 27.6	2574 34.3	143 1.9	870 11.6*	3018 41.9	4190 58.1
WEBSTER	1461 26.7	948 17.3	1296 23.7	534 9.8	1232 22.5*	1792 33.8	3502 66.2
WILKINSN	1463 37.3	1172 29.9	1012 25.8	69 1.8	202 5.2*	1129 50.7	1099 49.3
WINSTON	2515 28.5	1986 22.5	3136 35.6	305 3.5	872 9.9*	3419 41.6	4806 58.4
YALOBUSHA	1865 34.9	1062 19.9	1471 27.6	325 6.1	615 11.5*	2299 46.0	2700 54.0
YAZOO	3145 30.2	3512 33.7	2965 28.4	271 2.6	529 5.1*	4606 46.9	5208 53.1

					*		
TOTALS	288219	128946	227424	45445	72951 *	329236	389952
% OF VOTE	37.8	16.9	29.8	6.0	9.6 *	45.8	54.2

GEOGRAPHIC CLASS

					*		
LOWLANDS	102592 38.	53618 20.	82586 30.	6110 2.	28288 10.*	115125 45.	142912 55.
BLACK BELT	138850 39.	58965 17.	105321 30.	16597 5.	33215 9.*	158913 48.	171191 52.
PIEDMONT	46777 34.	16363 12.	39517 29.	22738 17.	11448 8.*	55198 42.	75849 58.

DEMOGRAPHIC CLASS

					*		
METRO	21631 35.	6432 10.	27527 44.	1840 3.	4864 8.*	25544 42.	35568 58.
TOWN	74712 43.	26144 15.	47166 27.	4451 3.	20184 12.*	80396 50.	81981 50.
RURAL	191876 36.	96370 18.	152731 29.	39154 7.	47903 9.*	223296 45.	272403 55.

MISSISSIPPI

DEMOC. SENATOR 1954* SPECL. REFERENDUM 1952

COUNTY	EASTLAND # %	GARTIN # %*	FOR # %	AGAINST # %
ADAMS	1949 61.3	1229 38.7*	1920 73.1	706 26.9
ALCORN	1767 56.3	1370 43.7*	771 18.8	3338 81.2
AMITE	1140 69.6	498 30.4*	374 22.8	1266 77.2
ATTALA	1804 69.9	776 30.1*	987 31.6	2136 68.4
BENTON	546 64.9	295 35.1*	125 13.0	835 87.0
BOLIVAR	3113 91.0	308 9.0*	1178 53.2	1035 46.8
CALHOUN	1275 54.6	1062 45.4*	434 19.2	1829 80.8
CARROLL	916 81.1	214 18.9*	505 45.7	600 54.3

```
         DEMOC.  SENATOR   1954* SPECL.  REFERENDUM 1952
                                  *
COUNTY      EASTLAND     GARTIN       FOR          AGAINST
            #      %     #      %*    #       %    #       %
----------------------------------*--------------------------------------------------------------------
CHICKASAW   1150 54.7    951 45.3*    760 26.9    2064 73.1
CHOCTAW      971 64.3    538 35.7*    437 24.7    1331 75.3
CLAIBORNE    682 89.7     78 10.3*    466 51.8     433 48.2
CLARKE      1157 49.1   1200 50.9*    432 18.9    1856 81.1
CLAY         681 43.5    886 56.5*    686 31.9    1465 68.1
                                  *
COAHOMA     1812 71.9    707 28.1*   1347 61.7     835 38.3
COPIAH      2171 76.9    651 23.1*   1042 32.6    2153 67.4
COVINGTON   1585 62.6    946 37.4*    408 22.1    1438 77.9
DESOTO       993 72.0    386 28.0*    507 42.0     699 58.0
FORREST     3441 55.5   2758 44.5*   2396 40.9    3460 59.1
                                  *
FRANKLIN    1299 75.2    428 24.8*    315 22.2    1105 77.8
GEORGE       549 39.1    855 60.9*    411 28.0    1057 72.0
GREENE       549 42.9    731 57.1*    363 31.7     783 68.3
GRENADA     1139 65.7    594 34.3*    481 30.1    1115 69.9
HANCOCK     1535 66.0    789 34.0*   1118 62.2     680 37.8
                                  *
HARRISON    5992 57.7   4389 42.3*   5665 71.5    2254 28.5
HINDS      11785 64.3   6540 35.7*   8971 49.2    9279 50.8
HOLMES      1746 82.0    382 18.0*   1109 52.6    1000 47.4
HUMPHREYS   1322 90.1    146  9.9*    436 42.5     589 57.5
ISSAQUENA    192 86.1     31 13.9*     81 40.1     121 59.9
                                  *
ITAWAMBA     940 37.3   1582 62.7*    308 13.3    2004 86.7
JACKSON     1647 39.7   2499 60.3*   2112 53.0    1870 47.0
JASPER      1135 48.2   1218 51.8*    501 24.6    1538 75.4
JEFFERSON    841 86.4    132 13.6*    383 41.1     550 58.9
JEFFDAVIS    942 50.3    930 49.7*    263 16.9    1295 83.1
                                  *
JONES       3222 33.1   6508 66.9*   2899 39.5    4448 60.5
KEMPER      1002 58.6    708 41.4*    433 25.2    1287 74.8
LAFAYETTE   1179 59.8    793 40.2*    670 32.5    1394 67.5
LAMAR        896 63.5    515 36.5*    428 24.8    1301 75.2
LAUDERDAL   3039 40.4   4483 59.6*   3201 41.4    4533 58.6
                                  *
LAWRENCE    1027 68.2    478 31.8*    271 18.2    1214 81.8
LEAKE       2337 71.6    927 28.4*    661 23.2    2194 76.8
LEE         2230 47.5   2461 52.5*   1637 28.7    4064 71.3
LEFORE      2940 78.5    803 21.5*   1712 58.2    1228 41.8
LINCOLN     1876 61.1   1194 38.9*   1092 29.4    2621 70.6
                                  *
LOWNDES     1715 60.0   1143 40.0*   1474 41.0    2124 59.0
MADISON     1648 75.4    539 24.6*   1303 54.7    1079 45.3
MARION      1493 59.3   1026 40.7*    781 29.3    1884 70.7
MARSHALL    1230 71.2    498 28.8*    608 39.7     923 60.3
MONROE      1618 57.7   1184 42.3*   1261 27.7    3296 72.3
                                  *
MONTGMERY   1359 67.8    646 32.2*    630 36.4    1099 63.6
NESHOBA     2265 60.7   1466 39.3*    939 22.4    3256 77.6
NEWTON      1938 67.5    934 32.5*    697 23.5    2264 76.5
NOXUBEE      723 70.7    300 29.3*    422 34.4     805 65.6
OKTIBBEHA   1290 59.7    871 40.3*   1038 35.6    1878 64.4
                                  *
PANOLA      1400 72.3    537 27.7*    823 40.7    1200 59.3
```

```
           DEMOC.  SENATOR    1954* SPECL.  REFERENDUM 1952
                                *
  COUNTY      EASTLAND     GARTIN       FOR          AGAINST
               #     %      #      %*    #     %      #     -%
--------------------------------------------*--------------------------------------------------------------------
PEARLRVER    1236 46.2   1442 53.8*   611 20.9    2310 79.1
PERRY         686 53.2    603 46.8*   274 28.2     699 71.8
PIKE         2327 64.5   1280 35.5*  1544 35.9    2757 64.1
PONTOTOC     1413 69.3    627 30.7*   710 26.5    1972 73.5
PRENTISS     1149 57.9    837 42.1*   755 21.7    2729 78.3
                                *
QUITMAN      1030 88.6    132 11.4*   453 47.3     505 52.7
RANKIN       1975 71.2    798 28.8*   794 25.6    2302 74.4
SCOTT        2418 69.1   1083 30.9*   615 21.5    2250 78.5
SHARKEY       650 81.3    150 18.8*   308 45.2     374 54.8
SIMPSON      2280 63.4   1316 36.6*   771 26.7    2113 73.3
                                *
SMITH        2038 58.3   1456 41.7*   430 17.4    2047 82.6
STONE         816 65.0    439 35.0*   319 29.1     776 70.9
SUNFLOWER    3241 93.4    230  6.6*  1177 52.2    1079 47.8
TALHATCHI    1838 85.1    323 14.9*   693 36.5    1205 63.5
TATE         1271 77.8    363 22.2*   408 32.4     852 67.6
                                *
TIPPAH       1435 67.0    708 33.0*   239  8.4    2612 91.6
TISHMINGO     989 59.2    683 40.8*   447 17.1    2169 82.9
TUNICA        778 95.6     36  4.4*   361 67.6     173 32.4
UNION        1718 63.6    985 36.4*   320 10.7    2683 89.3
WATHALL       765 61.7    475 38.3*   233 14.8    1345 85.2
                                *
WARREN       2538 65.7   1324 34.3*  2612 62.6    1562 37.4
WASHINGTON   2281 70.3    964 29.7*  2446 68.7    1112 31.3
WAYNE        1158 59.9    776 40.1*   412 25.4    1207 74.6
WEBSTER      1101 66.6    552 33.4*   512 24.1    1610 75.9
WILKINSN      600 68.5    276 31.5*   444 43.1     585 56.9
                                *
WINSTON      1662 64.6    911 35.4*   541 19.0    2308 81.0
YALOBUSHA     908 65.5    479 34.5*   407 25.5    1187 74.5
YAZOO        2342 85.4    399 14.6*  1714 56.0    1347 44.0
--------------------------------*-----------------------------------------------------------------------
                                *
TOTALS     137836       83760     *  80822      140681
% OF VOTE    62.2         37.8    *   36.5         63.5
```

```
            DEMOC.  SENATOR    1954* SPECL.  REFERENDUM 1952
                                    *
     COUNTY      EASTLAND     GARTIN     FOR      AGAINST
                 #     %      #     %*   #     %   #      %
-----------------------------------*--------------------------------------------------------------------
GEOGRAPHIC CLASS                    *
                                    *
LOWLANDS       44818 54.     38684 46.*  27439 36.   48623 64.
BLACK BELT     72368 71.     29600 29.*  42648 43.   56839 57.
PIEDMONT       20650 57.     15476 43.*  10735 23.   35219 77.
                                    *
                                    *
DEMOGRAPHIC CLASS                   *
                                    *
METRO          11785 64.      6540 36.*   8971 49.    9279 51.
TOWN           28929 54.     24308 46.*  25672 54.   22262 46.
RURAL          97122 65.     52912 35.*  46179 30.  109140 70.
```

MISSISSIPPI

```
            SPECL.  REFERENDUM 1960* SPECL.  REFERENDUM 1960
                                    *
     COUNTY     RT TO WRK    AGAINST     VOTR QUAL   AGAINST
                #     %      #     %*    #     %     #     %
-----------------------------------*--------------------------------------------------------------------
ADAMS          1209 53.2    1065 46.8*  2145 81.6    483 18.4
ALCORN         1223 58.0     886 42.0*  1210 59.7    817 40.3
AMITE           714 69.5     313 30.5*  1266 74.7    428 25.3
ATTALA         1285 75.6     415 24.4*  1848 65.5    973 34.5
BENTON          273 87.8      38 12.2*   382 76.9    115 23.1
                                    *
BOLIVAR        2101 91.8     187  8.2*  2546 82.0    557 18.0
CALHOUN         922 88.0     126 12.0*  1332 90.2    145  9.8
CARROLL         601 81.8     134 18.2*  1138 93.0     85  7.0
CHICKASAW       985 75.4     322 24.6*  1497 87.6    211 12.4
CHOCTAW         567 67.8     269 32.2*   877 79.0    233 21.0
                                    *
CLAIBORNE       598 89.7      69 10.3*   808 89.7     93 10.3
CLARKE         1101 57.8     805 42.2*  1697 70.6    706 29.4
CLAY           1300 82.0     286 18.0*  1449 88.4    191 11.6
COAHOMA        1197 84.2     224 15.8*  2450 73.7    874 26.3
COPIAH         2151 83.5     426 16.5*  2546 84.3    474 15.7
                                    *
COVINGTON       590 59.7     399 40.3*  1071 70.6    447 29.4
DESOTO          650 88.1      88 11.9*  1386 84.3    258 15.7
FORREST        2234 66.2    1140 33.8*  4853 65.3   2575 34.7
FRANKLIN        404 40.4     596 59.6*  1084 85.3    187 14.7
GEORGE          444 60.3     292 39.7*   987 72.7    371 27.3
                                    *
GREENE          315 73.4     114 26.6*   629 69.2    280 30.8
GRENADA        1378 88.6     177 11.4*  1554 83.5    308 16.5
HANCOCK         513 70.0     220 30.0*  1334 58.9    929 41.1
HARRISON       4172 63.7    2380 36.3*  8876 73.5   3205 26.5
```

SPECL. REFERENDUM 1960* SPECL. REFERENDUM 1960

COUNTY	RT TO WRK #	%	AGAINST #	%*	VOTR QUAL #	%	AGAINST #	%
HINDS	11233	72.4	4283	27.6*	17970	70.1	7664	29.9
HOLMES	1322	91.0	131	9.0*	2125	90.6	220	9.4
HUMPHREYS	728	92.6	58	7.4*	1153	92.2	98	7.8
ISSAQUENA	126	90.0	14	10.0*	245	86.6	38	13.4
ITAWAMBA	784	62.3	474	37.7*	672	40.0	1010	60.0
JACKSON	957	21.6	3482	78.4*	2844	41.0	4090	59.0
JASPER	805	58.3	576	41.7*	1203	76.2	376	23.8
JEFFERSON	593	79.1	157	20.9*	832	86.9	125	13.1
JEFFDAVIS	689	81.8	153	18.2*	916	79.0	243	21.0
JONES	2202	37.5	3666	62.5*	3961	48.2	4256	51.8
KEMPER	618	57.3	460	42.7*	917	70.1	376	29.1
LAFAYETTE	1566	75.1	518	24.9*	1412	63.4	814	36.6
LAMAR	598	58.2	430	41.8*	1105	63.3	641	36.7
LAUDERDAL	2453	36.5	4261	63.5*	5842	64.9	3156	35.1
LAWRENCE	775	83.1	158	16.9*	862	83.0	176	17.0
LEAKE	1382	79.2	362	20.8*	2304	88.0	314	12.0
LEE	2125	67.8	1010	32.2*	2478	56.3	1926	43.7
LEFORE	1778	90.0	197	10.0*	3501	88.4	458	11.6
LINCOLN	2234	79.8	565	20.2*	2765	79.0	736	21.0
LOWNDES	1582	59.1	1097	40.9*	2595	83.1	529	16.9
MADISON	1872	87.9	258	12.1*	2017	81.8	448	18.2
MARION	1058	59.8	710	40.2*	1267	71.7	501	28.3
MARSHALL	632	94.3	38	5.7*	1346	92.1	115	7.9
MONROE	1639	66.9	811	33.1*	2160	70.0	925	30.0
MONTGMERY	973	81.4	223	18.6*	1433	89.7	165	10.3
NESHOBA	1971	70.0	845	30.0*	2368	74.5	812	25.5
NEWTON	1743	71.3	703	28.7*	2245	83.4	446	16.6
NOXUBEE	716	80.9	169	19.1*	1064	93.0	80	7.0
OKTIBBEHA	1166	78.4	321	21.6*	2237	86.5	349	13.5
PANOLA	1134	92.5	92	7.5*	2138	89.8	242	10.2
PEARLRVER	748	63.0	439	37.0*	1735	82.3	374	17.7
PERRY	434	62.5	260	37.5*	552	66.5	278	33.5
PIKE	1729	64.2	966	35.8*	2947	69.5	1296	30.5
PONTOTOC	847	82.3	182	17.7*	641	38.9	1005	61.1
PRENTISS	767	85.8	127	14.2*	680	48.2	730	51.8
QUITMAN	606	89.8	69	10.2*	931	83.1	189	16.9
RANKIN	1446	56.7	1106	43.3*	3296	80.2	816	19.8
SCOTT	1549	83.5	306	16.5*	2034	85.0	360	15.0
SHARKEY	403	91.4	38	8.6*	747	87.0	112	13.0
SIMPSON	1196	68.2	557	31.8*	1733	74.3	599	25.7
SMITH	1433	72.9	532	27.1*	1448	72.9	538	27.1
STONE	619	76.8	187	23.2*	718	74.8	242	25.2
SUNFLOWER	2177	95.1	111	4.9*	2693	90.1	297	9.9
TALHATCHI	1048	94.7	59	5.3*	1666	93.0	125	7.0
TATE	706	94.8	39	5.2*	1158	91.0	115	9.0
TIPPAH	1102	88.3	146	11.7*	919	69.3	408	30.7

SPECL. REFERENDUM 1960* SPECL. REFERENDUM 1960

COUNTY	RT TO WRK #	%	AGAINST #	%*	VOTR QUAL #	%	AGAINST #	%
TISHMINGO	927	60.8	598	39.2*	516	43.9	660	56.1
TUNICA	400	95.7	18	4.3*	699	88.0	95	12.0
UNION	914	79.1	241	20.9*	1074	55.2	872	44.8
WATHALL	495	69.4	218	30.6*	1257	84.9	223	15.1
WARREN	2484	66.9	1229	33.1*	3693	67.8	1751	32.2
WASHINGTON	2356	78.9	629	21.1*	3159	56.6	2419	43.4
WAYNE	858	65.0	461	35.0*	948	65.6	498	34.4
WEBSTER	961	77.8	275	22.2*	954	85.3	165	14.7
WILKINSN	441	82.9	91	17.1*	613	65.1	328	34.9
WINSTON	1568	63.2	914	36.8*	1902	83.0	390	17.0
YALOBUSHA	684	71.7	270	28.3*	1033	73.2	378	26.8
YAZOO	2445	92.5	198	7.5*	2664	89.9	299	10.1
TOTALS	105724		47459		161352		61836	
% OF VOTE	69.0		31.0		72.3		27.7	

GEOGRAPHIC CLASS

LOWLANDS	31643	57.	24018	43.*	55170	67.	27032	33.
BLACK BELT	57170	78.	16359	22.*	87165	78.	24354	22.
PIEDMONT	16911	70.	7082	30.*	19017	65.	10450	35.

DEMOGRAPHIC CLASS

METRO	11233	72.	4283	28.*	17970	70.	7664	30.
TOWN	21667	58.	15888	42.*	41075	68.	19706	32.
RURAL	72824	73.	27288	27.*	102307	75.	34466	25.

MISSISSIPPI

SPECL. REFERENDUM 1968* SPECL. REFERENDUM 1968

COUNTY	VOTR QUAL #	%	AGAINST #	%*	SESSIONS #	%	AGAINST #	%
ADAMS	1975	80.3	486	19.7*	587	25.1	1755	74.9
ALCORN	530	78.4	146	21.6*	437	65.2	233	34.8
AMITE	841	58.1	606	41.9*	533	37.9	875	62.1
ATTALA	1564	61.5	978	38.5*	791	31.8	1697	68.2
BENTON	346	83.0	71	17.0*	290	71.6	115	28.4
BOLIVAR	3331	74.2	1156	25.8*	1833	42.2	2507	57.8
CALHOUN	1625	65.1	870	34.9*	1563	66.8	778	33.2
CARROLL	848	51.0	814	49.0*	672	40.5	988	59.5

```
        SPECL.  REFERENDUM 1968*  SPECL.  REFERENDUM 1968
                                *
COUNTY     VOTR QUAL   AGAINST      SESSIONS   AGAINST
           #     %     #     %*     #     %    #     %
-----------------------------------------------------------------------------------------------------------
CHICKASAW  2149 80.5   521  19.5*  1740 67.6   835 32.4
CHOCTAW     526 37.7   868  62.3*   444 33.3   891 66.7
CLAIBORNE   889 74.0   312  26.0*   650 53.7   561 46.3
CLARKE     1550 79.2   407  20.8*  1367 68.8   620 31.2
CLAY       2314 76.6   706  23.4*  1397 46.2  1626 53.8
                                *
COAHOMA    1987 84.5   365  15.5*  1635 68.0   770 32.0
COPIAH     1885 66.6   947  33.4*  1062 37.4  1777 62.6
COVINGTON   686 54.2   580  45.8*   378 30.3   868 69.7
DESOTO      473 81.6   107  18.4*   363 62.6   217 37.4
FORREST    5042 69.5  2210  30.5*  3178 45.6  3785 54.4
                                *
FRANKLIN    837 65.3   445  34.7*   471 38.3   758 61.7
GEORGE      650 75.1   216  24.9*   533 63.2   311 36.8
GREENE      596 65.6   312  34.4*   369 42.3   503 57.7
GRENADA     700 81.6   158  18.4*   289 34.1   559 65.9
HANCOCK    1137 82.2   246  17.8*  1126 81.4   257 18.6
                                *
HARRISON   4862 74.0  1706  26.0*  4055 61.9  2499 38.1
HINDS     11716 65.6  6153  34.4*  6063 34.9 11290 65.1
HOLMES     2186 62.9  1289  37.1*  1621 50.6  1584 49.4
HUMPHREYS   836 49.6   851  50.4*   702 42.7   942 57.3
ISSAQUENA   257 57.2   192  42.8*   185 45.0   226 55.0
                                *
ITAWAMBA   1421 64.2   791  35.8*  1159 53.1  1022 46.9
JACKSON    4704 77.5  1366  22.5*  3972 67.8  1884 32.2
JASPER      777 57.2   581  42.8*   585 45.3   706 54.7
JEFFERSON   792 68.0   373  32.0*   505 47.9   549 52.1
JEFFDAVIS   864 65.5   456  34.5*   477 36.7   821 63.3
                                *
JONES      2658 62.5  1595  37.5*  1973 45.4  2371 54.6
KEMPER     1136 77.3   334  22.7*   836 58.9   583 41.1
LAFAYETTE   588 70.9   241  29.1*   559 68.3   259 31.7
LAMAR       998 59.9   667  40.1*   549 34.2  1054 65.8
LAUDERDAL  7302 81.1  1706  18.9*  6461 72.6  2439 27.4
                                *
LAWRENCE    746 69.7   325  30.3*   416 44.0   529 56.0
LEAKE      1152 49.3  1184  50.7*   475 20.6  1835 79.4
LEE        1139 80.5   276  19.5*   899 66.0   463 34.0
LEFORE     3765 75.6  1214  24.4*  3198 63.7  1822 36.3
LINCOLN    2018 70.7   835  29.3*  1140 41.6  1602 58.4
                                *
LOWNDES    3932 75.9  1251  24.1*  3600 69.5  1582 30.5
MADISON    1321 67.3   643  32.7*   687 37.4  1151 62.6
MARION      900 57.2   674  42.8*   485 32.8   993 67.2
MARSHALL   2554 71.2  1032  28.8*  2359 65.8  1228 34.2
MONROE     2620 73.4   948  26.6*  2399 67.6  1152 32.4
                                *
MONTGOMERY 1608 70.1   686  29.9*  1219 53.5  1061 46.5
NESHOBA    2057 63.6  1176  36.4*  1358 43.6  1754 56.4
NEWTON     2329 67.0  1149  33.0*  1562 45.7  1854 54.3
NOXUBEE    1243 70.0   533  30.0*  1129 62.1   688 37.9
OKTIBBEHA  2855 72.5  1083  27.5*  1862 47.6  2047 52.4
                                *
PANOLA      566 74.1   198  25.9*   506 66.9   250 33.1
```

COUNTY	VOTR QUAL #	%	AGAINST #	%*	SESSIONS #	%	AGAINST #	%
PEARLRVER	1395	68.8	633	31.2*	1063	53.5	925	46.5
PERRY	566	62.9	334	37.1*	299	34.2	576	65.8
PIKE	1921	73.6	689	26.4*	1281	50.0	1280	50.0
PONTOTOC	543	81.4	124	18.6*	490	73.0	181	27.0
PRENTISS	304	72.6	115	27.4*	261	62.1	159	37.9
QUITMAN	310	65.5	163	34.5*	138	30.2	319	69.8
RANKIN	1519	49.4	1556	50.6*	836	26.7	2290	73.3
SCOTT	1641	67.6	787	32.4*	1027	40.2	1526	59.8
SHARKEY	635	70.2	270	29.8*	591	66.7	295	33.3
SIMPSON	1147	60.6	745	39.4*	560	29.7	1323	70.3
SMITH	776	49.5	792	50.5*	395	25.3	1168	74.7
STONE	564	65.7	295	34.3*	387	47.1	435	52.9
SUNFLOWER	2560	67.1	1253	32.9*	2236	57.3	1665	42.7
TALHATCHI	652	77.0	195	23.0*	450	54.4	377	45.6
TATE	520	85.7	87	14.3*	389	64.2	217	35.8
TIPPAH	511	85.7	85	14.3*	501	77.6	145	22.4
TISHMINGO	484	80.1	120	19.9*	385	64.1	216	35.9
TUNICA	277	91.1	27	8.9*	172	57.0	130	43.0
UNION	718	77.4	210	22.6*	556	61.8	343	38.2
WATHALL	711	70.5	297	29.5*	415	42.5	561	57.5
WARREN	2650	76.5	816	23.5*	2217	63.5	1274	36.5
WASHINGTON	4291	77.3	1259	22.7*	3805	71.3	1530	28.7
WAYNE	973	63.1	570	36.9*	853	51.7	797	48.3
WEBSTER	1370	61.0	875	39.0*	784	36.4	1372	63.6
WILKINSN	359	39.3	555	60.7*	251	26.4	698	73.6
WINSTON	1502	67.4	726	32.6*	1054	48.5	1117	51.5
YALOBUSHA	1095	90.7	112	9.3*	991	82.7	208	17.3
YAZOO	2469	67.9	1167	32.1*	1751	49.2	1808	50.8
TOTALS	136846		59892	*	98842		94461	
% OF VOTE		69.6		30.4 *		51.1		48.9

```
        SPECL.  REFERENDUM 1968* SPECL.  REFERENDUM 1968
                              *
COUNTY    VOTR QUAL  AGAINST   *   SESSIONS   AGAINST
           #    %    #    %*   #     %     #     %
--------------------------------*----------------------------------------------
GEOGRAPHIC CLASS                *
                                *
LOWLANDS   46816 69.  20882 31.* 34342 51.  32363 49.
BLACK BELT 70729 70.  30963 30.* 48723 48.  52467 52.
PIEDMONT   19301 71.   8047 29.* 15777 62.   9631 38.
                                *
                                *
DEMOGRAPHIC CLASS               *
                                *
METRO      11716 66.   6153 34.*  6063 35.  11290 65.
TOWN       38464 75.  12608 25.* 30709 61.  19827 39.
RURAL      86666 68.  41131 32.* 62070 49.  63344 51.
```

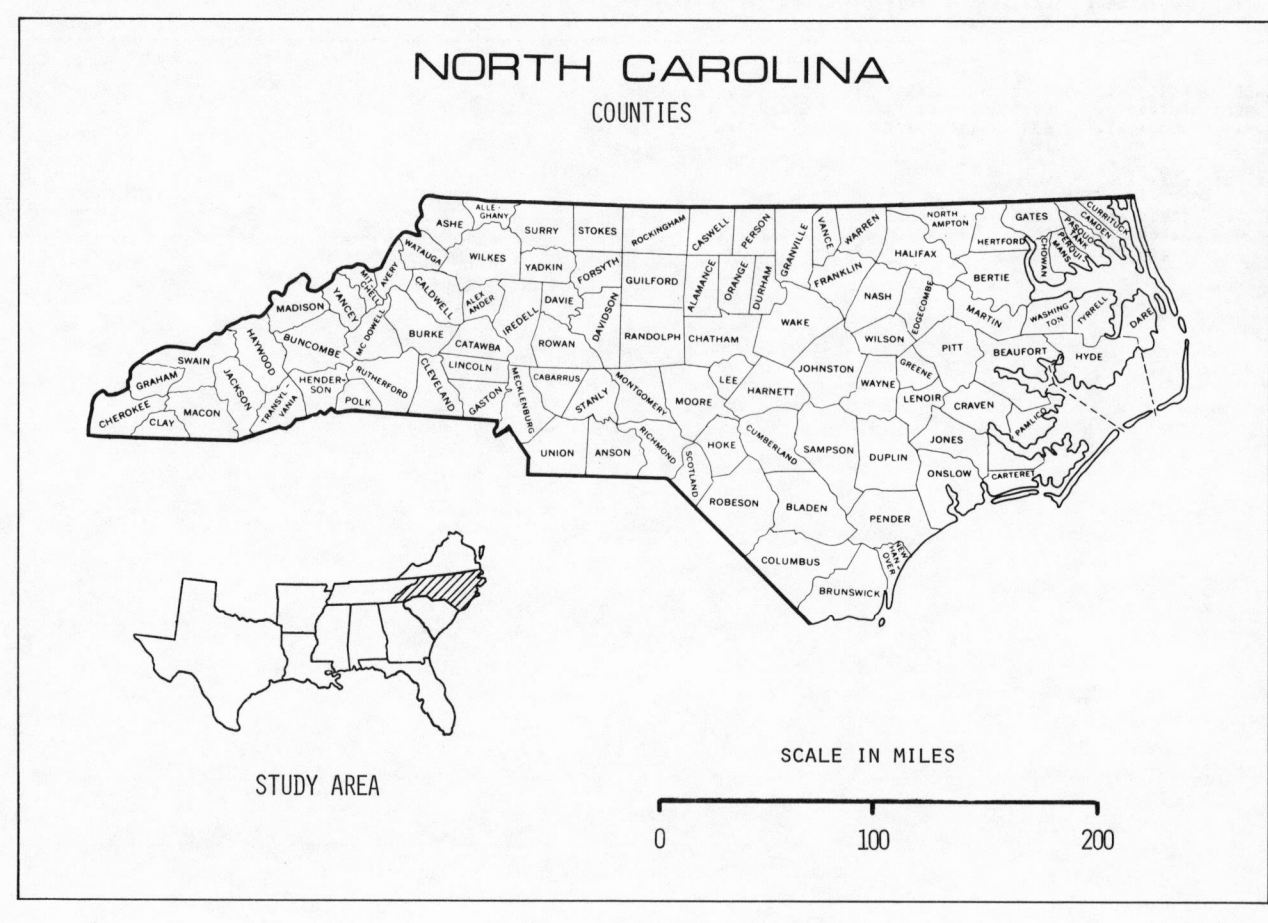

NORTH CAROLINA

COUNTIES

STUDY AREA

SCALE IN MILES

0   100   200

NORTH CAROLINA

The North Carolina Constitution required that every registrant "shall be able to read and write any section of the Constitution in the English language." This test was suspended in 40 of North Carolina's 100 counties as a result of the 1965 Voting Rights Act. The bulk of these counties were located in the heavily black eastern portion of the state. Black voter registration grew consistently during the 1950s. In 1947 there were some 75,000 black registrants; in 1958 there were almost 180,000, which was 30.9 percent of the black voting-age population; and in 1960, there were over 210,000, which was 31.2 percent of the potential. In both 1958 and 1960 black registrants were about 10 percent of all registered voters. Black registration continued to increase during the 1960s. In 1964 the 258,000 registered blacks were 11.7 percent of all registered voters in the state; in 1966 black registration had reached 281,000, or just over half of the voting-age black population; and in 1970 the approximately 305,000 registered blacks were 15.7 percent of North Carolina's registered voters. Despite this steady growth in black political participation, only 51.3 percent of voting-age blacks were registered in 1970, which was the lowest such figure of all southern states. Approximately 1,640,000 whites, or 68.1 percent of the white voting-age population, were registered in 1970.

The following table presents election returns in recent presidential elections. Turnout figures are expressed both in the number of ballots cast and the precentage of citizens of voting age who voted.

This section contains 8 Democratic guber-natorial primaries, 6 senatorial primaries, 3 Republican primaries, and the 1972 Democratic presidential primary. The 1954 senatorial primary included here is the contest for the regular senate term; W. Kerr Scott also won nomination for the unexpired term of the senate seat made vacant by the death of Willis Smith.

Gubernatorial Primaries

1. May 31, 1952: Hubert E. Olive 265,673 (47.1%), William B. Umstead 294,144 (52.1%), one other candidate 4,660 (0.8%). Total vote was 564,477; turnout of voting-age citizens was 24.0%.
* (May 26, 1956: Luther H. Hodges won 85.9% against 3 opponents. Total vote was 466,654; turnout was 19.0%.)
2. May 28, 1960: Terry Sanford 269,463 (41.3%), John D. Larkins, Jr., 100,757 (15.4%), Malcolm B. Seawell 101,148 (15.5%), I. Beverly Lake 181,692 (27.8%). Total vote was 653,060; turnout was 25.5%.
3. June 25, 1960: Terry Sanford 352,133 (56.1%), I. Beverly Lake 275,904 (43.9%). Total vote was 628,037; turnout was 24.6%.
4. May 30, 1964: I. Beverly Lake 217,172 (28.2%), L. Richardson Preyer 281,430 (36.6%), Dan K. Moore 257,872 (33.5%), other 3 candidates 12,616 (1.6%). Total vote was 769,090; turnout was 28.1%.
5. June 27, 1964: Dan K. Moore 480,431 (62.0%), L. Richardson Preyer 293,863 (38.0%). Total vote was 774,294; turnout was 28.3%.
6. May 4, 1968: Robert W. Scott 337,368 (48.1%), J. Melville Broughton, Jr., 233,924 (33.4%), Reginald A. Hawkins

169

129,808 (18.5%). Total vote was 701,100; turnout was 24.1%. (No runoff held; J. Melville Broughton, Jr., conceded.)
7. May 6, 1972: Hargrove Bowles 367,433 (45.5%), Reginald Hawkins 65,950 (8.2%), Wilbur Hobby 58,972 (7.3%), H. P. Taylor 304,910 (37.7%), other 2 candidates 10,822 (1.3%). Total vote was 808,087; turnout was 23.5%.
8. June 3, 1972: Hargrove Bowles 336,034 (54.3%), H. P. Taylor 282,345 (45.7%). Total vote was 618,379; turnout was 18.0%.

Senatorial Primaries

1. May 27, 1950: Willis Smith 250,222 (40.5%), Frank P. Graham 303,575 (49.1%), Robert R. Reynolds 58,752 (9.5%), one other candidate 5,900 (0.9%). Total vote was 618,449.
2. June 24, 1950: Frank P. Graham 261,843 (48.2%), Willis Smith 281,114 (51.8%). Total vote was 542,957.
3. May 29, 1954: W. Kerr Scott 312,053 (50.8%), Alton Lennon 286,730 (46.6%), other 5 candidates 15,875 (2.6%). Total vote was 614,658.
* (May 26, 1956: Sam J. Ervin, Jr., won 84.6% against 1 opponent. Total vote was 426,479.)
4. May 28, 1960: B. Everett Jordan 324,188 (54.3%), Addison Hewlett 217,899 (36.5%), Robert W. Gregory 31,463 (5.3%), Robert M. McIntosh 23,988 (4.0%). Total vote was 597,538.
* (May 26, 1962: Sam J. Ervin, Jr., unopposed.)
* (May 28, 1966: B. Everett Jordan won 79.3% against 1 opponent. Total vote was

562,002.
* (May 4, 1968: Sam J. Ervin, Jr., won 78.3% against 3 opponents. Total vote was 638,237.)
5. May 6, 1972: B. Everett Jordan 340,391 (44.3%), Nick Galifianakis 377,993 (49.2%), other 2 candidates 49,165 (6.4%). Total vote was 767,549.
6. June 3, 1972: Nick Galifianakis 333,458 (55.4%), B. Everett Jordan 267,997 (44.6%). Total vote was 601,455.

Republican Primaries

1. Governor May 6, 1972: James C. Gardner 84,896 (49.8%), James E. Holshouser 83,637 (49.0%), other 2 candidates 2,040 (1.2%). Total vote was 170,573; turnout of voting-age citizens was 5.0%.
2. Governor June 3, 1972: James C. Gardner 68,133 (49.4%), James E. Holshouser 69,916 (50.6%). Total vote was 138,049; turnout was 4.0%.
3. Senator May 6, 1972: James C. Johnson 45,303 (29.4%), William H. Booe 16,122 (10.5%), Jesse Helms 92,486 (60.1%). Total vote was 153,911.

Democratic Presidential Primary

May 6, 1972: George C. Wallace 413,518 (50.3%), Terry Sanford 306,014 (37.3%), Shirley Chisholm 61,723 (7.5%), other 2 candidates 40,155 (4.9%). Total vote was 821,410.

RETURNS FROM PRESIDENTIAL ELECTIONS

Year	Turnout		Partisan Vote*
1948	791,209	(35.5%)[+]	Democrat 58.0%, Republican 32.7%, Dixiecrat 8.8%
1952	1,210,910	(51.4%)	Democrat 53.9%, Republican 46.1%
1956	1,165,592	(47.5%)	Democrat 50.7%, Republican 49.3%
1960	1,368,556	(53.5%)	Democrat 52.1%, Republican 47.9%
1964	1,424,983	(52.1%)	Democrat 56.2%, Republican 43.8%
1968	1,587,493	(54.5%)	Republican 39.5%, American Independent 31.3%, Democrat 29.2%
1972	1,518,612	(44.2%)	Republican 69.5%, Democrat 28.9%

*Totals do not necessarily equal 100%, since minor party percentages are excluded.

[+]Percentage of citizens of voting age who voted is calculated on the basis of a straight-line interpolation of citizen population between census years.

COUNTY	OLIVE #	%	UMSTEAD #	%*	SANFORD #	%	LARKINS #	%	SEAWELL #	%	LAKE #	%
ALAMANCE	5948	58.4	4232	41.6*	4880	35.6	1656	12.1	1943	14.2	5210	38.1
ALEXANDER	914	41.2	1306	58.8*	873	55.3	349	22.1	84	5.3	272	17.2
ALLEGHANY	343	23.2	1133	76.8*	723	46.1	425	27.1	106	6.8	316	20.1
ANSON	1860	45.5	2230	54.5*	1058	39.3	159	5.9	504	18.7	974	36.1
ASHE	797	28.2	2033	71.8*	1340	63.9	534	25.5	74	3.5	148	7.1
AVERY	320	51.2	305	48.8*	666	81.2	50	6.1	60	7.3	44	5.4
BEAUFORT	1190	33.9	2318	66.1*	2148	35.1	810	13.2	284	4.6	2885	47.1
BERTIE	1754	60.2	1159	39.8*	1011	41.4	164	6.7	154	6.3	1115	45.6
BLADEN	2139	51.0	2058	49.0*	1886	36.1	473	9.0	544	10.4	2327	44.5
BRUNSWICK	1715	58.9	1199	41.1*	2419	52.1	315	6.8	307	6.6	1606	34.6
BUNCOMBE	9677	45.8	11467	54.2*	8083	40.0	7061	34.9	3010	14.9	2055	10.2
BURKE	3560	53.2	3133	46.8*	4084	67.0	417	6.8	966	15.9	624	10.2
CABARRUS	5573	54.1	4725	45.9*	4947	43.8	1101	9.8	2372	21.0	2872	25.4
CALDWELL	2946	51.7	2756	48.3*	3699	65.5	433	7.7	700	12.4	813	14.4
CAMDEN	420	35.5	762	64.5*	361	29.2	190	15.4	26	2.1	660	53.4
CARTERET	1621	39.2	2517	60.8*	1556	31.4	2618	52.8	228	4.6	561	11.3
CASWELL	1058	49.6	1073	50.4*	928	28.9	306	9.5	168	5.2	1809	56.3
CATAWBA	1852	29.4	4441	70.6*	2590	46.3	845	15.1	1273	22.8	881	15.8
CHATHAM	1637	42.8	2192	57.2*	1967	41.3	444	9.3	448	9.4	1908	40.0
CHEROKEE	616	27.5	1620	72.5*	1286	58.2	764	34.6	66	3.0	95	4.3
CHOWAN	377	38.6	599	61.4*	678	39.0	518	29.8	105	6.0	436	25.1
CLAY	182	25.2	539	74.8*	421	58.8	214	29.9	71	9.9	10	1.4
CLEVELAND	4014	44.3	5040	55.7*	4046	41.1	1292	13.1	2211	22.5	2285	23.2
COLUMBUS	3290	45.3	3979	54.7*	5035	39.1	1473	11.4	1308	10.1	5075	39.4
CRAVEN	2001	41.4	2831	58.6*	1611	19.4	5387	64.8	198	2.4	1112	13.4
CUMBERLAND	4257	49.8	4298	50.2*	9650	69.5	260	1.9	933	6.7	3032	21.9
CURRITUCK	392	27.4	1038	72.6*	677	37.4	309	17.1	76	4.2	747	41.3
DARE	539	38.1	875	61.9*	872	44.9	659	34.0	172	8.9	238	12.3
DAVIDSON	9031	91.8	807	8.2*	4658	45.9	687	6.8	2382	23.5	2418	23.8
DAVIE	768	56.8	583	43.2*	599	51.5	137	11.8	96	8.3	330	28.4
DUPLIN	3032	56.1	2375	43.9*	2537	37.6	1802	26.7	308	4.6	2104	31.2
DURHAM	8037	41.4	11378	58.6*	3148	15.9	1615	8.1	6888	34.7	8173	41.2
EDGECOMBE	4004	51.5	3769	48.5*	2263	39.3	623	10.8	478	8.3	2391	41.5
FORSYTH	10565	55.6	8422	44.4*	11172	42.5	4231	16.1	4902	18.6	5994	22.8
FRANKLIN	2331	55.5	1871	44.5*	1962	35.2	335	6.0	561	10.1	2723	48.8
GASTON	6985	51.4	6603	48.6*	5050	36.0	2258	16.1	3596	25.7	3109	22.2
GATES	397	35.8	712	64.2*	613	44.7	139	10.1	139	10.1	480	35.0
GRAHAM	481	44.7	594	55.3*	701	66.1	221	20.8	122	11.5	16	1.5
GRANVILLE	761	22.7	2597	77.3*	1647	32.1	725	14.1	630	12.3	2136	41.6
GREENE	1090	45.1	1326	54.9*	939	30.5	871	28.3	45	1.5	1227	39.8
GUILFORD	9546	44.5	11890	55.5*	11946	38.7	3515	11.4	8365	27.1	7064	22.9
HALIFAX	3897	45.0	4771	55.0*	2594	27.9	1175	12.6	1030	11.1	4506	48.4
HARNETT	3262	54.0	2777	46.0*	3142	38.7	345	4.3	594	7.3	4036	49.7
HAYWOOD	5037	73.1	1858	26.9*	4525	68.4	648	9.8	543	8.2	902	13.6
HENDERSON	985	36.5	1717	63.5*	1779	46.0	599	15.5	477	12.3	1011	26.2
HERTFORD	1229	58.4	876	41.6*	1379	57.5	225	9.4	234	9.8	561	23.4

COUNTY	DEMOC. GOVERNOR 1952*						DEMOC. GOVERNOR 1960						
	OLIVE		UMSTEAD		SANFORD		LARKINS		SEAWELL		LAKE		
	#	%	#	%*	#	%	#	%	#	%	#	%	
HOKE	565	40.2	839	59.8*	865	44.9	71	3.7	278	14.4	713	37.0
HYDE	507	47.3	564	52.7*	834	50.5	163	9.9	78	4.7	575	34.8
IREDELL	3717	37.5	6188	62.5*	3544	35.9	709	7.2	1201	12.2	4428	44.8
JACKSON	1298	41.7	1816	58.3*	2478	62.7	1004	25.4	234	5.9	239	6.0
JOHNSTON	4885	53.4	4256	46.6*	4718	43.5	1548	14.3	1293	11.9	3282	30.3
JONES	1023	57.1	768	42.9*	414	16.6	1841	73.7	30	1.2	213	8.5
LEE	1838	45.7	2186	54.3*	1324	25.9	121	2.4	2021	39.5	1653	32.3
LENOIR	2163	34.1	4187	65.9*	1045	12.7	5162	62.7	462	5.6	1570	19.1
LINCOLN	1815	40.8	2631	59.2*	2352	46.8	1269	25.3	743	14.8	658	13.1
MACON	821	42.3	1119	57.7*	1399	67.0	294	14.1	302	14.5	92	4.4
MADISON	835	42.8	1118	57.2*	1076	34.0	1982	62.7	62	2.0	43	1.4
MARTIN	1978	53.7	1704	46.3*	1661	35.8	793	17.1	229	4.9	1962	42.2
MCDOWELL	2464	54.8	2029	45.2*	2498	51.2	1505	30.9	319	6.5	554	11.4
MECKLENBRG	11950	40.8	17326	59.2*	12699	40.7	2528	8.1	10397	33.3	5581	17.9
MITCHELL	380	54.1	323	45.9*	551	78.0	39	5.5	72	10.2	44	6.2
MONTGOMERY	976	48.9	1018	51.1*	710	30.7	537	23.2	404	17.4	665	28.7
MOORE	1658	35.6	2997	64.4*	2561	52.4	211	4.3	1094	22.4	1020	20.9
NASH	4840	51.2	4618	48.8*	3755	41.2	583	6.4	670	7.4	4100	45.0
NEWHANOVER	4973	40.5	7317	59.5*	5177	33.1	2420	15.5	1903	12.2	6127	39.2
NORTHAMPTN	2086	48.9	2180	51.1*	2089	48.7	377	8.8	177	4.1	1647	38.4
ONSLOW	2177	56.4	1683	43.6*	1626	24.8	3712	56.6	278	4.2	944	14.4
ORANGE	1594	32.5	3314	67.5*	3054	38.4	710	8.9	1646	20.7	2552	32.1
PAMLICO	640	54.9	526	45.1*	637	35.9	780	44.0	28	1.6	329	18.5
PASQUOTANK	781	32.5	1620	67.5*	1681	39.6	904	21.3	255	6.0	1409	33.2
PENDER	1422	53.8	1219	46.2*	1136	37.0	601	19.6	151	4.9	1179	38.4
PERQUIMANS	1044	61.6	651	38.4*	704	40.8	362	21.0	60	3.5	600	34.8
PERSON	1711	41.9	2371	58.1*	1735	32.5	405	7.6	1193	22.4	2000	37.5
PITT	3336	45.7	3960	54.3*	4725	37.8	1891	15.1	555	4.4	5328	42.6
POLK	781	37.4	1310	62.6*	1175	56.9	286	13.8	182	8.8	423	20.5
RANDOLPH	2087	49.8	2102	50.2*	2248	34.1	960	14.6	1089	16.5	2289	34.8
RICHMOND	4046	60.0	2698	40.0*	4086	50.3	607	7.5	806	9.9	2619	32.3
ROBESON	4052	38.6	6451	61.4*	4900	45.9	300	2.8	3467	32.5	2008	18.8
ROCKINGHAM	3613	48.1	3893	51.9*	3663	37.9	1398	14.5	1250	12.9	3349	34.7
ROWAN	7187	58.2	5165	41.8*	6031	46.4	887	6.8	2769	21.3	3324	25.5
RUTHERFORD	2029	27.8	5258	72.2*	4373	49.5	1218	13.8	1492	16.9	1756	19.9
SAMPSON	2180	48.5	2313	51.5*	2542	49.4	1122	21.8	292	5.7	1193	23.2
SCOTLAND	1903	46.1	2228	53.9*	1867	67.4	131	4.7	347	12.5	427	15.4
STANLY	2109	47.0	2378	53.0*	2582	53.1	568	11.7	556	11.4	1157	23.8
STOKES	828	35.3	1520	64.7*	1606	41.0	839	21.4	107	2.7	1365	34.8
SURRY	4170	56.1	3266	43.9*	2671	46.8	1110	19.4	774	13.6	1154	20.2
SWAIN	977	55.5	784	44.5*	693	39.6	713	40.7	112	6.4	233	13.3
TRANSYLVNA	864	33.0	1755	67.0*	1594	51.4	246	7.9	407	13.1	853	27.5
TYRRELL	561	45.8	665	54.2*	866	78.0	110	9.9	25	2.3	109	9.8
UNION	2586	49.4	2650	50.6*	1989	38.4	266	5.1	1276	24.7	1644	31.8
VANCE	3478	62.4	2093	37.6*	2094	31.4	628	9.4	1809	27.2	2130	32.0
WAKE	12817	46.7	14654	53.3*	12046	42.4	2480	8.7	5951	21.0	7914	27.9

```
         DEMOC. GOVERNOR  1952*        DEMOC. GOVERNOR  1960
                           *
COUNTY    OLIVE      UMSTEAD    *  SANFORD     LARKINS     SEAWELL     LAKE
          #     %    #     %*      #     %    #     %    #     %    #     %
--------------------------------*------------------------------------------------------------------------
WARREN    1545 48.9  1615 51.1*   936 29.0   129  4.0   315  9.8  1845 57.2
WASHINGTON 1082 58.7  760 41.3*  1465 56.9   274 10.6   114  4.4   720 28.0
WATAUGA    253 15.8  1345 84.2*  1617 72.1   371 16.5   139  6.2   116  5.2
WAYNE     3634 48.1  3928 51.9*  3199 36.3  1986 22.5   632  7.2  3004 34.1
WILKES    1519 33.5  3011 66.5*  2766 64.0   637 14.7   479 11.1   441 10.2
                           *
WILSON    3429 47.9  3726 52.1*  2673 39.6  1074 15.9   656  9.7  2348 34.8
YADKIN    1204 60.5   787 39.5*  1153 55.3   399 19.1   112  5.4   422 20.2
YANCEY     832 63.6   477 36.4*  1431 85.4   119  7.1    74  4.4    51  3.0
--------------------------------*------------------------------------------------------------------------
                           *
TOTALS    265673     294144    * 269463     100757     101148     181692
% OF VOTE   47.5       52.5    *   41.3       15.4       15.5       27.8
                           *
                           *
GEOGRAPHIC CLASS           *
                           *
LOWLANDS  60147 47.  66765 53.* 67563 41.  28965 18.  18706 11.  49481 30.
BLACK BELT 57112 47. 63651 53.* 51029 37.  21297 16.  14296 10.  50228 37.
PIEDMONT 100895 49. 106952 51.* 94442 38.  26985 11.  56380 23.  67778 28.
MOUNTAIN  47519 46.  56776 54.* 56429 53.  23510 22.  11766 11.  14205 13.
                           *
                           *
DEMOGRAPHIC CLASS          *
                           *
METRO     62592 45.  75137 55.* 59094 38.  21430 14.  39513 25.  36781 23.
TOWN      51489 50.  51910 50.* 49640 40.  19318 16.  16299 13.  38315 31.
RURAL    151592 48. 167097 52.*160729 43.  60009 16.  45336 12. 106596 29.



                                          NORTH CAROLINA


         DEMOC.  RUNOFF    1960*     DEMOC. GOVERNOR  1964
                           *
COUNTY    SANFORD    LAKE      *  LAKE        PREYER      MOORE
          #     %    #     %*      #     %    #     %    #     %
--------------------------------*------------------------------------------------------------------------
ALAMANCE  5958 45.0  7282 55.0*  6127 40.5  5168 34.2  3825 25.3
ALEXANDER 1327 60.2   877 39.8*   226 10.3   611 28.0  1347 61.7
ALLEGHANY  803 50.0   804 50.0*   241 10.1   987 41.5  1148 48.3
ANSON     1528 44.5  1907 55.5*  1273 32.9  1372 35.5  1221 31.6
ASHE      1689 80.7   405 19.3*    95  2.1  1663 53.8  1331 43.1
                           *
AVERY      891 91.6    82  8.4*    23  2.1   503 45.7   574 52.2
BEAUFORT  2428 39.6  3702 60.4*  2742 43.6  1686 26.8  1868 29.7
BERTIE    1221 48.2  1312 51.8*  1288 47.3   927 34.1   507 18.6
BLADEN    2104 42.4  2863 57.6*  2668 49.5  1814 33.7   903 16.8
BRUNSWICK 2325 55.0  1899 45.0*  2333 45.7  1823 35.7   945 18.5
                           *
BUNCOMBE 12203 71.4  4888 28.6*  1212  4.6  6233 23.7 18850 71.7
```

SOUTHERN ELECTIONS/174

COUNTY	DEMOC. RUNOFF 1960*		DEMOC. GOVERNOR 1964			
	SANFORD	LAKE	LAKE	PREYER	MOORE	
	#	%	#	%*	#	%	#	%	#	%

COUNTY	SANFORD #	%	LAKE #	%*	LAKE #	%	PREYER #	%	MOORE #	%
BURKE	5564	81.0	1308	19.0*	524	5.6	4916	52.9	3856	41.5
CABARRUS	4980	57.7	3652	42.3*	1839	20.3	3162	34.9	4058	44.8
CALDWELL	3445	76.9	1034	23.1*	429	7.2	2676	45.0	2848	47.8
CAMDEN	418	40.4	616	59.6*	508	45.4	291	26.0	321	28.7
CARTERET	3297	59.7	2221	40.3*	1082	18.7	2516	43.5	2186	37.8
CASWELL	989	30.3	2279	69.7*	1366	43.4	794	25.2	991	31.5
CATAWBA	4270	71.7	1685	28.3*	957	11.5	2455	29.5	4916	59.0
CHATHAM	2251	46.6	2576	53.4*	2094	38.1	1844	33.6	1555	28.3
CHEROKEE	1625	75.7	523	24.3*	39	1.4	110	4.1	2544	94.5
CHOWAN	629	50.5	617	49.5*	798	48.0	644	38.7	221	13.3
CLAY	606	88.0	83	12.0*	15	2.2	101	14.6	574	83.2
CLEVELAND	5084	53.4	4444	46.6*	3948	27.8	4509	31.8	5741	40.4
COLUMBUS	5597	54.8	4618	45.2*	4958	43.0	3441	29.8	3138	27.2
CRAVEN	3603	44.3	4532	55.7*	2788	30.3	3412	37.0	3010	32.7
CUMBERLAND	10513	74.7	3564	25.3*	6312	41.4	6553	43.0	2385	15.6
CURRITUCK	773	49.4	791	50.6*	756	42.1	525	29.2	515	28.7
DARE	951	67.2	464	32.8*	472	24.7	636	33.3	804	42.1
DAVIDSON	4442	51.9	4114	48.1*	1878	17.3	4224	39.0	4735	43.7
DAVIE	917	58.7	644	41.3*	296	16.3	941	51.9	577	31.8
DUPLIN	3998	52.0	3687	48.0*	3569	45.2	2681	34.0	1643	20.8
DURHAM	10151	49.4	10406	50.6*	10940	42.5	10657	41.4	4171	16.2
EDGECOMBE	3077	52.4	2794	47.6*	2932	40.7	2403	33.4	1863	25.9
FORSYTH	14976	60.7	9709	39.3*	4235	15.4	14593	53.0	8704	31.6
FRANKLIN	2000	36.4	3493	63.6*	3865	59.8	1423	22.0	1177	18.2
GASTON	6874	59.6	4662	40.4*	3058	21.8	5284	37.7	5657	40.4
GATES	461	50.9	445	49.1*	505	36.2	341	24.4	550	39.4
GRAHAM	998	92.7	79	7.3*	9	.7	689	51.0	652	48.3
GRANVILLE	1985	37.0	3373	63.0*	3028	51.8	1561	26.7	1253	21.4
GREENE	1129	37.0	1924	63.0*	1766	53.1	690	20.8	868	26.1
GUILFORD	17284	59.2	11897	40.8*	5362	15.1	23418	66.0	6708	18.9
HALIFAX	3181	43.2	4187	56.8*	4947	39.6	3682	29.5	3852	30.9
HARNETT	4197	46.1	4908	53.9*	5664	60.3	2145	22.8	1583	16.9
HAYWOOD	4502	73.0	1663	27.0*	539	5.9	1802	19.8	6764	74.3
HENDERSON	2922	53.8	2510	46.2*	244	6.0	894	22.1	2903	71.8
HERTFORD	1442	66.6	722	33.4*	1527	35.9	1792	42.1	933	21.9
HOKE	1086	56.8	827	43.2*	847	33.3	1131	44.5	566	22.2
HYDE	726	58.7	511	41.3*	452	33.3	463	34.1	442	32.6
IREDELL	3779	45.4	4545	54.6*	1790	18.3	3591	36.6	4421	45.1
JACKSON	2331	71.2	945	28.8*	114	2.3	479	9.6	4391	88.1
JOHNSTON	5333	54.0	4552	46.0*	6450	49.0	3034	23.0	3682	28.0
JONES	1007	44.5	1257	55.5*	815	29.8	1025	37.5	894	32.7
LEE	2347	47.1	2638	52.9*	2051	39.0	1808	34.4	1394	26.5
LENOIR	3312	43.1	4373	56.9*	3496	37.5	2678	28.7	3156	33.8
LINCOLN	2623	61.5	1643	38.5*	611	10.7	2380	41.7	2720	47.6
MACON	1796	87.7	252	12.3*	59	1.7	689	20.1	2674	78.1
MADISON	3118	90.2	340	9.8*	65	1.2	2606	47.9	2765	50.9

```
              DEMOC.  RUNOFF    1960*       DEMOC.  GOVERNOR    1964
                                    *
 COUNTY        SANFORD     LAKE         LAKE        PREYER        MOORE
               #     %     #      %*    #     %     #      %     #      %
--------------------------------------------*------------------------------------------------------------------------
MARTIN        1882  46.0   2205  54.0*  2849  56.6  1213  24.1   969  19.3
MCDOWELL      2821  61.6   1755  38.4*   376   6.8  1429  26.0  3685  67.1
MECKLENBRG   19416  65.8  10098  34.2*  7688  19.3 18178  45.6 13987  35.1
MITCHELL       769  88.8     97  11.2*    29   2.8   300  29.2   697  67.9
MONTGOMERY    1154  40.6   1685  59.4*   575  19.2  1481  49.4   940  31.4

MOORE         3208  64.7   1754  35.3*  1639  28.6  2380  41.6  1706  29.8
NASH          4739  50.2   4704  49.8*  5676  53.1  2299  21.5  2710  25.4
NEWHANOVER    7985  49.9   8033  50.1*  6358  44.0  5399  37.3  2709  18.7
NORTHAMPTN    2123  52.6   1913  47.4*  2115  38.3  2331  42.2  1079  19.5
ONSLOW        3469  54.2   2929  45.8*  3109  38.1  2640  32.3  2412  29.6

ORANGE        4685  58.9   3267  41.1*  3127  31.8  4617  47.0  2079  21.2
PAMLICO        836  50.5    821  49.5*   466  22.5   680  32.8   925  44.7
PASQUOTANK    1805  50.4   1773  49.6*  2122  47.5  1851  41.4   496  11.1
PENDER        1556  50.2   1545  49.8*  1746  41.5  1628  38.7   837  19.9
PERQUIMANS     603  48.4    643  51.6*   813  47.8   559  32.9   329  19.3

PERSON        2407  43.4   3144  56.6*  2274  41.5  1621  29.6  1583  28.9
PITT          5158  49.0   5359  51.0*  4363  36.3  4099  34.1  3563  29.6
POLK          1165  56.0    917  44.0*   166  16.1   399  16.1  1912  77.2
RANDOLPH      3027  48.1   3260  51.9*  1568  26.0  2613  43.3  1852  30.7
RICHMOND      4354  56.1   3402  43.9*  2662  34.5  3387  43.9  1669  21.6

ROBESON       6615  61.5   4149  38.5*  3365  27.7  4750  39.1  4047  33.3
ROCKINGHAM    4130  43.6   5335  56.4*  2821  27.8  4182  41.3  3129  30.9
ROWAN         6057  52.6   5450  47.4*  2625  23.7  4291  38.7  4176  37.6
RUTHERFORD    4611  53.6   3988  46.4*  1169  13.0  2764  30.8  5041  56.2
SAMPSON       3334  62.0   2044  38.0*  2060  34.2  2476  41.1  1494  24.8

SCOTLAND      1913  70.5    801  29.5*  1434  33.8  1634  38.6  1169  27.6
STANLY        3279  63.5   1884  36.5*  1024  19.3  2433  45.9  1842  34.8
STOKES        1463  42.6   1971  57.4*   695  18.2  1426  37.3  1705  44.6
SURRY         3387  59.9   2267  40.1*   635   8.4  3305  43.9  3590  47.7
SWAIN         1148  62.4    691  37.6*    47   2.2   480  22.4  1612  75.4

TRANSYLVNA    1726  55.1   1406  44.9*   275   6.4  1044  24.4  2964  69.2
TYRRELL        760  84.4    141  15.6*   381  28.4   534  39.8   427  31.8
UNION         2434  44.7   3009  55.3*  1625  25.4  2290  35.8  2481  38.8
VANCE         2747  43.3   3594  56.7*  3768  45.6  2422  29.3  2065  25.0
WAKE         16692  58.3  11924  41.7* 15104  39.2 13378  34.8 10005  26.0

WARREN        1114  36.2   1962  63.8*  2716  54.0  1731  34.4   579  11.5
WASHINGTON    1563  59.5   1062  40.5*  1276  42.7  1239  41.5   472  15.8
WATAUGA       1766  87.4    255  12.6*    86   3.8  1020  45.4  1142  50.8
WAYNE         4172  47.5   4613  52.5*  4243  42.6  2865  28.8  2845  28.6
WILKES        4028  69.6   1761  30.4*   349   6.9  3271  64.3  1471  28.9

WILSON        3561  52.1   3271  47.9*  3280  36.6  2677  29.9  2995  33.5
YADKIN        1342  64.8    728  35.2*   223  10.9   757  37.0  1066  52.1
YANCEY        2063  92.6    166   7.4*    23    .9   881  36.1  1536  63.0
--------------------------------------------*------------------------------------------------------------------------
                                    *
TOTALS      352133        275904     * 217172      281430       257872
% OF VOTE      56.1          43.9     *   28.7        37.2         34.1


SOUTHERN ELECTIONS/176
```

```
        DEMOC.  RUNOFF    1960*      DEMOC.  GOVERNOR   1964
                                *
COUNTY     SANFORD      LAKE   *  LAKE         PREYER       MOORE
           #      %     #    %*   #      %     #      %     #     %
-------------------------------*--------------------------------------------------------
GEOGRAPHIC CLASS                *
                                *
LOWLANDS   89412  55.  73096 45.* 74818  40.  63465  34.  46918 25.
BLACK BELT 62434  48.  66622 52.* 67985  42.  51998  32.  41455 26.
PIEDMONT  126979  55. 104407 45.* 65767  24. 120920  44.  86685 32.
MOUNTAIN   73308  70.  31779 30.*  8602   6.  45047  33.  82814 61.
                                *
                                *
DEMOGRAPHIC CLASS               *
                                *
METRO      90722  61.  58922 39.* 44541  23.  86457  45.  62425 32.
TOWN       61647  54.  53053 46.* 44633  35.  44579  35.  37232 29.
RURAL     199764  55. 163929 45.*127998  29. 150394  34. 158215 36.
```

NORTH CAROLINA

```
        DEMOC.  RUNOFF    1964*      DEMOC.  GOVERNOR   1968
                                *
COUNTY     MOORE       PREYER  *  SCOTT        BROUGHTON    HAWKINS
           #      %     #    %*   #      %     #      %     #     %
-------------------------------*--------------------------------------------------------
ALAMANCE  10228 63.8  5792 36.2* 9606  66.1  3217  22.1  1703 11.7
ALEXANDER  1834 72.7   690 27.3* 1203  63.8   622  33.0    62  3.3
ALLEGHANY  1428 62.4   861 37.6* 2022  44.5  1394  30.7  1126 24.8
ANSON      2714 61.9  1674 38.1* 1073  70.1   439  28.7    18  1.2
ASHE       1624 50.8  1575 49.2* 1925  82.8   384  16.5    16   .7

AVERY       713 58.2   512 41.8*  531  80.6   118  17.9    10  1.5
BEAUFORT   4578 70.4  1929 29.6* 3049  48.8  2096  33.4  1132 18.0
BERTIE     1912 63.6  1096 36.4* 2440  45.9  1089  20.5  1784 33.6
BLADEN     3643 66.9  1806 33.1* 2369  36.0  2714  41.3  1492 22.7
BRUNSWICK  2626 54.2  2215 45.8* 1886  33.2  2326  40.9  1477 26.0

BUNCOMBE  21051 77.3  6197 22.7* 9567  52.5  6761  37.1  1911 10.5
BURKE      4868 48.8  5108 51.2* 5513  70.1  1609  20.5   741  9.4
CABARRUS   6013 65.6  3150 34.4* 6101  61.5  2664  26.9  1150 11.6
CALDWELL   3335 55.1  2720 44.9* 4304  65.6  1641  25.0   614  9.4
CAMDEN      735 69.1   328 30.9*  533  47.8   388  34.8   195 17.5

CARTERET   3257 55.3  2633 44.7* 3290  60.8  1630  30.1   488  9.0
CASWELL    2348 72.9   874 27.1* 1596  55.0   773  26.6   532 18.3
CATAWBA    6728 68.8  3054 31.2* 3641  55.6  2310  35.3   602  9.2
CHATHAM    3913 68.3  1816 31.7* 2349  50.9  1433  31.0   837 18.1
CHEROKEE   3141 94.3   190  5.7* 1233  75.0   391  23.8    19  1.2

CHOWAN      800 51.4   755 48.6* 1312  54.4   628  26.0   473 19.6
CLAY        880 87.4   127 12.6*  304  66.7   144  31.6     8  1.8
CLEVELAND  8416 62.2  5118 37.8* 5078  43.6  4883  42.0  1673 14.4
```

```
         DEMOC.  RUNOFF    1964*      DEMOC.  GOVERNOR   1968
                             *
 COUNTY      MOORE       PREYER      SCOTT       BROUGHTON    HAWKINS
             #     %     #     %*    #     %     #     %      #     %
---------------------------------------------------------------------------
COLUMBUS    6534 69.3   2891 30.7*  4497 46.8   3530 36.7   1582 16.5
CRAVEN      5459 62.0   3340 38.0*  3685 39.9   3552 38.4   2009 21.7
CUMBERLAND  9250 59.0   6418 41.0*  6181 42.9   5129 35.6   3106 21.5
CURRITUCK   1060 70.3    448 29.7*   793 47.9    720 43.5    142  8.6
DARE        1062 64.2    593 35.8*   841 50.7    759 45.8     59  3.6
                             *
DAVIDSON    7090 60.7   4583 39.3*  6192 65.1   2312 24.3   1001 10.5
DAVIE       1056 49.0   1100 51.0*  1098 55.4    480 24.2    405 20.4
DUPLIN      5255 63.7   2998 36.3*  3381 53.2   1788 28.1   1186 18.7
DURHAM     14101 56.5  10861 43.5*  7369 28.5   9484 36.7   9014 34.8
EDGECOMBE   4850 67.0   2392 33.0*  3303 38.1   2753 31.8   2606 30.1
                             *
FORSYTH    14620 48.3  15655 51.7* 10555 40.3   8402 32.1   7245 27.7
FRANKLIN    4896 77.7   1407 22.3*  3061 38.2   3284 40.9   1677 20.9
GASTON      9467 61.0   6054 39.0*  6591 50.0   5084 38.5   1515 11.5
GATES       1090 72.5    413 27.5*  1174 67.9    369 21.3    187 10.8
GRAHAM       720 53.0    638 47.0*   467 70.5    191 28.9      4   .6
                             *
GRANVILLE   4256 74.3   1469 25.7*  1831 35.1   2458 47.2    924 17.7
GREENE      2302 72.5    872 27.5*  1817 48.1   1069 28.3    892 23.6
GUILFORD   13608 36.0  24211 64.0* 14202 47.0   9194 30.4   6848 22.6
HALIFAX     7514 67.4   3641 32.6*  4004 43.0   3289 35.3   2013 21.6
HARNETT     7031 76.1   2206 23.9*  3576 47.8   3121 41.7    786 10.5
                             *
HAYWOOD     7977 80.6   1921 19.4*  3778 65.5   1853 32.1    135  2.3
HENDERSON   3747 78.6   1018 21.4*  1861 57.6   1295 40.1     77  2.4
HERTFORD    2041 56.8   1554 43.2*  1616 41.9   1118 29.0   1120 29.1
HOKE        1470 59.2   1013 40.8*  1457 38.9   1051 28.1   1238 33.0
HYDE         840 63.9    474 36.1*   850 60.4    308 21.9    250 17.8
                             *
IREDELL     6822 63.5   3918 36.5*  5203 57.6   2645 29.3   1192 13.2
JACKSON     4389 91.0    434  9.0*  1610 56.3   1206 42.2     44  1.5
JOHNSTON    8354 71.8   3284 28.2*  5041 51.8   3453 35.5   1234 12.7
JONES       1689 63.0    990 37.0*   972 42.9    531 23.4    762 33.6
LEE         3388 64.0   1906 36.0*  2559 54.1   1774 37.5    396  8.4
                             *
LENOIR      6558 70.4   2752 29.6*  4178 53.4   2020 25.8   1632 20.8
LINCOLN     3573 56.9   2704 43.1*  2556 55.7   1660 36.2    375  8.2
MACON       2923 81.5    664 18.5*  1260 80.1    294 18.7     19  1.2
MADISON     2367 85.5    401 14.5*  2030 76.5    593 22.3     32  1.2
MARTIN      3718 72.8   1392 27.2*  2812 50.8   1450 26.2   1278 23.1
                             *
MCDOWELL    3872 74.5   1326 25.5*  3012 69.4   1091 25.1    235  5.4
MECKLENBRG 23153 55.3  18712 44.7* 18131 48.4  11248 30.0   8053 21.5
MITCHELL     898 72.8    335 27.2*   585 86.9     81 12.0      7  1.0
MONTGOMERY  1671 47.7   1833 52.3*  2074 66.9    734 23.7    294  9.5
MOORE       3425 59.1   2369 40.9*  2959 48.5   1982 32.5   1164 19.1
                             *
NASH        7537 75.3   2468 24.7*  4188 38.5   3953 36.3   2748 25.2
NEWHANOVER  9597 63.0   5629 37.0*  5288 35.8   6452 43.6   3044 20.6
NORTHAMPTN  2973 56.0   2339 44.0*  2889 40.5   1951 27.4   2289 32.1
ONSLOW      4833 65.7   2520 34.3*  3608 51.8   2375 34.1    976 14.0
ORANGE      5283 53.8   4542 46.2*  4040 38.3   2761 26.2   3740 35.5
                             *
PAMLICO     1180 63.5    677 36.5*   909 50.0    486 26.7    423 23.3
```

SOUTHERN ELECTIONS/178

```
          DEMOC.  RUNOFF    1964*      DEMOC.  GOVERNOR   1968
                                  *
 COUNTY      MOORE        PREYER        SCOTT         BROUGHTON     HAWKINS
             #     %      #     %*      #     %        #     %       #    %
-------------------------------------------*--------------------------------------------
PASQUOTANK  2147 52.6   1934 47.4*    2032 42.4     1745 36.4     1019 21.2
PENDER      2564 59.6   1737 40.4*    1633 44.1     1341 36.2      728 19.7
PERQUIMANS   908 61.0    580 39.0*     931 46.3      645 32.1      435 21.6
PERSON      3733 69.5   1641 30.5*    2681 42.9     2045 32.7     1523 24.4
PITT        7596 62.9   4480 37.1*    6869 44.6     5176 33.6     3355 21.8
                                  *
POLK        1842 84.1    347 15.9*     896 56.5      593 37.4       98  6.2
RANDOLPH    3938 61.1   2504 38.9*    3500 63.7     1707 31.1      284  5.2
RICHMOND    4964 55.2   4026 44.8*    3607 50.4     1820 25.4     1726 24.1
ROBESON     8057 59.7   5438 40.3*    5977 43.2     4395 31.7     3475 25.1
ROCKINGHAM  6797 59.4   4654 40.6*    5835 47.8     4106 33.6     2263 18.5
                                  *
ROWAN       7746 61.9   4765 38.1*    6405 49.2     4256 32.7     2347 18.0
RUTHERFORD  6333 66.1   3253 33.9*    4225 62.1     2142 31.5      435  6.4
SAMPSON     3388 55.9   2673 44.1*    2647 51.7     1743 34.1      727 14.2
SCOTLAND    2452 62.6   1462 37.4*    1459 42.2     1289 37.3      707 20.5
STANLY      3201 54.3   2696 45.7*    3113 60.9     1554 30.4      442  8.7
                                  *
STOKES      2816 61.7   1745 38.3*    2053 56.5     1239 34.1      342  9.4
SURRY       4889 58.4   3483 41.6*    4056 55.1     2971 40.4      328  4.5
SWAIN       1704 76.8    516 23.2*     704 57.9      491 40.4       21  1.7
TRANSYLVNA  2966 73.7   1057 26.3*    1234 62.8      621 31.6      110  5.6
TYRRELL      648 51.3    615 48.7*     442 45.6      297 30.6      231 23.8
                                  *
UNION       4017 65.1   2150 34.9*    3504 54.9     2366 37.0      518  8.1
VANCE       5314 69.0   2385 31.0*    1842 20.9     4096 46.5     2869 32.6
WAKE       25127 63.5  14443 36.5*   12949 38.1    14949 44.0     6073 17.9
WARREN      3066 65.9   1589 34.1*    1153 26.2     1845 41.9     1409 32.0
WASHINGTON  1192 44.5   1484 55.5*    1371 42.7      987 30.7      856 26.6
                                  *
WATAUGA     1479 61.6    921 38.4*    1821 78.9      431 18.7       56  2.4
WAYNE       6738 67.1   3301 32.9*    3941 45.9     3157 36.8     1482 17.3
WILKES      2864 43.8   3680 56.2*    3166 77.2      787 19.2      148  3.6
WILSON      5904 65.5   3103 34.5*    4065 43.6     3602 38.6     1666 17.9
YADKIN      1612 62.9    950 37.1*    1172 71.3      375 22.8       96  5.8
                                  *
YANCEY      2145 76.3    666 23.7*    1076 85.4      166 13.2       18  1.4
-------------------------------------------*--------------------------------------------
                                  *
TOTALS    480431       293863      * 337368       233924       129808
% OF VOTE   62.0         38.0      *   48.1         33.4         18.5
```

```
          DEMOC.  RUNOFF      1964*     DEMOC.  GOVERNOR    1968
                                    *
COUNTY        MOORE       PREYER      SCOTT        BROUGHTON     HAWKINS
              #      %     #      %*    #      %     #      %     #      %
-------------------------------------*---------------------------------------------------------------
GEOGRAPHIC CLASS                     *
                                     *
LOWLANDS   117106 64.   66499 36.*  74687 45.   62842 38.   29212 18.
BLACK BELT 103734 66.   54516 34.*  71249 42.   57053 34.   40860 24.
PIEDMONT   160150 56.  127908 44.* 126754 49.   82237 32.   52077 20.
MOUNTAIN    99441 69.   44940 31.*  64678 62.   31792 31.    7659  7.
                                     *
DEMOGRAPHIC CLASS                    *
                                     *
METRO      111660 55.   90079 45.*  72773 42.   60038 35.   39144 23.
TOWN        83947 64.   47836 36.*  62528 48.   43510 34.   23606 18.
RURAL      284824 65.  155948 35.* 202067 51.  130376 33.   67058 17.



                                            NORTH CAROLINA


             DEMOC.  GOVERNOR    1972        * DEMOC.  RUNOFF      1972
                                            *
COUNTY      BOWLES       HAWKINS      HOBBY        TAYLOR      * BOWLES       TAYLOR
            #      %     #      %     #      %     #      %*    #      %     #      %
----------------------------------------------------------*------------------------------------------
ALAMANCE   6477 41.6    601  3.9   1564 10.0   6932 44.5*  5782 49.3   5956 50.7
ALEXANDER   988 47.7     22  1.1     71  3.4    989 47.8*   880 55.5    706 44.5
ALLEGHANY   928 50.3      7   .4     47  2.5    862 46.7*   628 43.7    809 56.3
ANSON       890 17.4    517 10.1     84  1.6   3618 70.8*   882 16.4   4493 83.6
ASHE       1246 44.0     12   .4     31  1.1   1541 54.5*  1116 47.7   1222 52.3
                                            *
AVERY       273 40.1      4   .6     14  2.1    389 57.2*   253 37.5    421 62.5
BEAUFORT   3085 49.8    442  7.1    300  4.8   2373 38.3*  2345 49.0   2437 51.0
BERTIE     1525 40.3    808 21.4     65  1.7   1382 36.6*  1325 38.7   2100 61.3
BLADEN     2635 49.4    592 11.1    221  4.1   1889 35.4*  2682 63.5   1542 36.5
BRUNSWICK  2568 48.3    784 14.7    428  8.0   1540 28.9*  2379 53.7   2053 46.3
                                            *
BUNCOMBE   9878 50.9    622  3.2   1344  6.9   7545 38.9*  9905 62.1   6037 37.9
BURKE      2617 39.5    275  4.2    592  8.9   3135 47.4*  2296 47.0   2586 53.0
CABARRUS   4149 41.3    414  4.1    435  4.3   5042 50.2*  3512 46.1   4107 53.9
CALDWELL   2435 48.4    234  4.7    227  4.5   2133 42.4*  2324 60.1   1543 39.9
CAMDEN      441 34.6    116  9.1     19  1.5    700 54.9*   246 35.2    453 64.8
                                            *
CARTERET   3263 55.3    233  3.9    286  4.8   2122 35.9*  2763 55.1   2250 44.9
CASWELL    1125 30.9    669 18.4    189  5.2   1662 45.6*  1567 45.7   1865 54.3
CATAWBA    4406 45.2    357  3.7    656  6.7   4322 44.4*  3879 51.4   3674 48.6
CHATHAM    2313 41.3    583 10.4    668 11.9   2036 36.4*  2169 48.3   2326 51.7
CHEROKEE   1257 60.7      8   .4     42  2.0    763 36.9*  1474 77.2    436 22.8
                                            *
CHOWAN      865 40.6    192  9.0     37  1.7   1036 48.6*   644 44.0    819 56.0
CLAY        326 46.5      5   .7     10  1.4    360 51.4*   251 62.3    152 37.7
CLEVELAND  5869 48.7    725  6.0    334  2.8   5119 42.5*  5275 49.3   5423 50.7
```

COUNTY	BOWLES #	%	HAWKINS #	%	HOBBY #	%	TAYLOR #	%*	BOWLES #	%	TAYLOR #	%
COLUMBUS	4549	46.0	381	3.9	592	6.0	4364	44.1*	4470	61.3	2819	38.7
CRAVEN	4596	52.6	700	8.0	622	7.1	2821	32.3*	3928	57.6	2894	42.4
CUMBERLAND	9569	42.6	2140	9.5	2082	9.3	8668	38.6*	9488	54.6	7894	45.4
CURRITUCK	688	38.8	71	4.0	41	2.3	972	54.9*	771	49.7	780	50.3
DARE	705	39.6	28	1.6	23	1.3	1025	57.6*	700	52.0	646	48.0
DAVIDSON	4667	43.2	525	4.9	706	6.5	4895	45.4*	4227	53.7	3646	46.3
DAVIE	797	39.5	100	5.0	95	4.7	1024	50.8*	691	45.9	813	54.1
DUPLIN	3451	47.9	702	9.7	327	4.5	2724	37.8*	2787	51.1	2669	48.9
DURHAM	9281	36.3	4337	17.0	4598	18.0	7369	28.8*	11963	60.2	7907	39.8
EDGECOMBE	5579	49.8	1041	9.3	292	2.6	4280	38.2*	4239	54.7	3516	45.3
FORSYTH	12789	43.4	3840	13.0	2107	7.1	10762	36.5*	11821	58.8	8274	41.2
FRANKLIN	3055	43.1	970	13.7	520	7.3	2536	35.8*	3164	57.8	2311	42.2
GASTON	8344	56.5	654	4.4	852	5.8	4924	33.3*	6758	59.3	4636	40.7
GATES	616	28.3	548	25.2	31	1.4	978	45.0*	369	37.4	617	62.6
GRAHAM	419	41.0	12	1.2	10	1.0	581	56.8*	537	66.1	275	33.9
GRANVILLE	3210	38.0	1340	15.9	845	10.0	3059	36.2*	3164	54.6	2630	45.4
GREENE	1727	61.8	174	6.2	89	3.2	805	28.8*	1148	57.4	853	42.6
GUILFORD	25009	56.6	3870	8.8	3590	8.1	11678	26.5*	22842	67.0	11245	33.0
HALIFAX	6421	57.4	1109	9.9	659	5.9	2994	26.8*	4498	59.1	3110	40.9
HARNETT	3702	48.7	408	5.4	1109	14.6	2380	31.3*	3321	58.7	2338	41.3
HAYWOOD	3712	54.7	46	.7	663	9.8	2366	34.9*	3574	60.9	2295	39.1
HENDERSON	1645	41.6	36	.9	177	4.5	2093	53.0*	1456	49.5	1488	50.5
HERTFORD	883	26.5	375	11.3	61	1.8	2011	60.4*	891	36.4	1557	63.6
HOKE	1568	53.4	104	3.5	98	3.3	1164	39.7*	1339	60.0	894	40.0
HYDE	673	50.0	146	10.8	50	3.7	477	35.4*	574	55.7	456	44.3
IREDELL	5374	50.0	522	4.9	607	5.6	4250	39.5*	4328	54.2	3664	45.8
JACKSON	1093	36.0	19	.6	126	4.2	1798	59.2*	1139	54.2	964	45.8
JOHNSTON	4856	49.0	478	4.8	733	7.4	3839	38.8*	4552	52.1	4178	47.9
JONES	1076	42.5	582	23.0	95	3.7	781	30.8*	859	45.7	1022	54.3
LEE	2955	53.1	256	4.6	390	7.0	1966	35.3*	2417	55.0	1974	45.0
LENOIR	5037	45.0	869	7.8	498	4.5	4777	42.7*	3942	52.3	3596	47.7
LINCOLN	2572	44.3	204	3.5	209	3.6	2821	48.6*	2139	47.5	2363	52.5
MACON	1247	53.9	25	1.1	50	2.2	993	42.9*	1215	64.9	656	35.1
MADISON	523	24.6	9	.4	42	2.0	1553	73.0*	580	37.4	969	62.6
MARTIN	2199	43.7	1038	20.6	214	4.3	1578	31.4*	2008	46.3	2327	53.7
MCDOWELL	2001	48.0	68	1.6	199	4.8	1902	45.6*	1575	47.1	1771	52.9
MECKLENBRG	23523	46.8	5935	11.8	3335	6.6	17428	34.7*	21002	53.4	18299	46.6
MITCHELL	282	40.2	6	.9	37	5.3	377	53.7*	296	50.4	291	49.6
MONTGOMERY	1186	32.2	479	13.0	160	4.4	1853	50.4*	1349	44.7	1672	55.3
MOORE	2845	43.9	533	8.2	483	7.4	2627	40.5*	3076	55.1	2506	44.9
NASH	7206	54.6	745	5.6	1084	8.2	4153	31.5*	6109	65.0	3287	35.0
NEWHANOVER	6654	48.7	973	7.1	1506	11.0	4541	33.2*	6288	52.2	5764	47.8
NORTHAMPTN	3743	57.5	477	7.3	268	4.1	2024	31.1*	2540	60.3	1674	39.7
ONSLOW	4190	46.8	465	5.2	426	4.8	3870	43.2*	3600	50.4	3549	49.6
ORANGE	4899	32.6	940	6.3	4611	30.7	4571	30.4*	5276	51.5	4964	48.5
PAMLICO	886	47.4	262	14.0	80	4.3	643	34.4*	730	52.9	650	47.1

COUNTY	BOWLES #	%	HAWKINS #	%	HOBBY #	%	TAYLOR #	%	BOWLES #	%	TAYLOR #	%
PASQUOTANK	1336	33.6	673	16.9	89	2.2	1882	47.3*	1232	36.8	2120	63.2
PENDER	1676	51.4	412	12.6	214	6.6	957	29.4*	1487	60.1	986	39.9
PERQUIMANS	535	36.3	274	18.6	27	1.8	636	43.2*	455	44.0	578	56.0
PERSON	2656	42.1	941	14.9	363	5.7	2356	37.3*	2823	58.1	2034	41.9
PITT	6106	46.2	1566	11.8	602	4.6	4942	37.4*	4356	41.9	6045	58.1
POLK	802	42.8	31	1.7	60	3.2	980	52.3*	775	47.7	850	52.3
RANDOLPH	4639	57.3	129	1.6	443	5.5	2880	35.6*	3820	61.5	2396	38.5
RICHMOND	2335	31.9	489	6.7	416	5.7	4077	55.7*	1777	33.3	3558	66.7
ROBESON	7465	43.5	1176	6.8	632	3.7	7896	46.0*	7381	55.3	5956	44.7
ROCKINGHAM	5878	50.3	630	5.4	1131	9.7	4047	34.6*	5069	59.4	3469	40.6
ROWAN	5052	45.6	725	6.5	580	5.2	4729	42.7*	4110	54.8	3396	45.2
RUTHERFORD	3373	48.9	137	2.0	146	2.1	3243	47.0*	2884	49.2	2976	50.8
SAMPSON	2607	46.7	338	6.1	255	4.6	2385	42.7*	2520	55.8	1998	44.2
SCOTLAND	1649	39.5	674	16.2	99	2.4	1749	41.9*	1559	44.5	1946	55.5
STANLY	2079	29.8	242	3.5	272	3.9	4389	62.9*	1726	30.0	4028	70.0
STOKES	1592	35.1	153	3.4	410	9.0	2383	52.5*	1341	48.4	1427	51.6
SURRY	3202	47.8	94	1.4	234	3.5	3168	47.3*	2683	52.2	2452	47.8
SWAIN	769	51.3	13	.9	31	2.1	687	45.8*	655	50.7	638	49.3
TRANSYLVNA	1487	50.2	37	1.2	150	5.1	1287	43.5*	1513	69.1	676	30.9
TYRRELL	499	45.4	160	14.6	46	4.2	393	35.8*	485	51.1	464	48.9
UNION	4878	55.9	369	4.2	281	3.2	3202	36.7*	4248	57.0	3203	43.0
VANCE	2866	38.2	990	13.2	965	12.9	2675	35.7*	3090	51.7	2882	48.3
WAKE	21972	45.3	4269	8.8	5864	12.1	16380	33.8*	23306	57.6	17143	42.4
WARREN	1649	42.6	876	22.6	255	6.6	1089	28.1*	1594	53.6	1378	46.4
WASHINGTON	1218	39.7	682	22.2	494	16.1	675	22.0*	978	42.4	1329	57.6
WATAUGA	1302	48.4	38	1.4	82	3.0	1267	47.1*	1349	60.8	870	39.2
WAYNE	6377	51.0	1449	11.6	617	4.9	4054	32.4*	6191	56.9	4694	43.1
WILKES	1804	43.0	71	1.7	175	4.2	2148	51.2*	1837	46.8	2089	53.2
WILSON	6067	49.5	1497	12.2	850	6.9	3840	31.3*	4650	57.8	3396	42.2
YADKIN	1008	49.2	46	2.2	100	4.9	895	43.7*	812	56.3	630	43.7
YANCEY	994	53.3	5	.3	33	1.8	834	44.7*	1011	61.8	625	38.2
TOTALS	367433		65950		58972		304910	*	336034		282345	
% OF VOTE		46.1		8.3		7.4		38.2	*	54.3		45.7

```
          DEMOC.  GOVERNOR   1972        * DEMOC.  RUNOFF    1972
                                         *
COUNTY     BOWLES      HAWKINS      HOBBY       TAYLOR     * BOWLES       TAYLOR
           #     %     #     %      #     %      #     %*   #     %       #     %
-----------------------------------------------------------*--------------------------------------------------
GEOGRAPHIC CLASS                                          *
                                                         *
LOWLANDS   91853  47.  15401  8.   16580  8.   73371 37.*  87409 55.   72794 45.
BLACK BELT 81540  45.  21392 12.    9692  5.   68638 38.*  69457 51.   66202 49.
PIEDMONT  142435  46.  26598  9.   26783  9.  111705 36.*  130984 56.  103621 44.
MOUNTAIN   51605  46.   2559  2.    5917  5.   51196 46.*  48184 55.   39728 45.
                                                         *
                                                         *
DEMOGRAPHIC CLASS                                        *
                                                         *
METRO     102452  47.  22873 11.  20838 10.   71162 33.*  100839 59.  68905 41.
TOWN       69411  47.  11929  8.    9878  7.   56729 38.*  59316 53.   53000 47.
RURAL     195570  45.  31148  7.   28256  7.  177019 41.*  175879 52.  160440 48.
```

NORTH CAROLINA

```
          DEMOC.  SENATOR    1950    * DEMOC.  RUNOFF    1950
                                     *
COUNTY     SMITH       GRAHAM       REYNOLDS    * GRAHAM      SMITH
           #     %      #     %      #     %*     #     %      #     %
-----------------------------------------------*----------------------------------------------
ALAMANCE   3137 38.2   4484 54.5    601  7.3*   4200 54.6   3494 45.4
ALEXANDER   687 48.6    600 42.5    126  8.9*    975 52.1    897 47.9
ALLEGHANY   784 37.0   1034 48.8    299 14.1*    590 33.6   1166 66.4
ANSON      2235 45.1   2313 46.7    407  8.2*   2290 44.8   2818 55.2
ASHE        413 22.3   1350 72.8     91  4.9*   1699 69.0    765 31.0
                                     *
AVERY       162 28.5    356 62.7     50  8.8*    394 66.2    201 33.8
BEAUFORT   2454 52.5   2025 43.4    191  4.2*   1722 33.3   3452 66.7
BERTIE     1386 44.1   1610 51.2    150  4.8*   1242 46.1   1454 53.9
BLADEN     2853 47.4   2590 43.0    574  9.5*   1872 39.3   2892 60.7
BRUNSWICK  1014 30.0   1910 56.5    456 13.5*   1536 46.9   1738 53.1
                                     *
BUNCOMBE   4760 19.1  12719 51.0   7484 30.0*  10185 61.7   6311 38.3
BURKE      2258 32.2   4469 63.7    294  4.2*   4334 64.0   2434 36.0
CABARRUS   5575 49.0   4034 35.5   1767 15.5*   2852 33.5   5664 66.5
CALDWELL   2980 48.6   2613 42.6    534  8.7*   1964 44.8   2416 55.2
CAMDEN      869 63.0    400 29.0    111  8.0*    321 33.1    650 66.9
                                     *
CARTERET   2038 40.6   2571 51.2    415  8.3*   1976 54.8   1629 45.2
CASWELL    1193 43.5   1265 46.1    284 10.4*    981 38.5   1569 61.5
CATAWBA    3834 48.5   3303 41.7    776  9.8*   2700 37.5   4492 62.5
CHATHAM    1635 41.9   1741 44.6    529 13.5*   1354 37.9   2217 62.1
CHEROKEE    679 28.3   1430 59.6    290 12.1*   1625 68.1    760 31.9
                                     *
CHOWAN      779 49.5    764 48.5     31  2.0*    682 49.3    700 50.7
CLAY        386 41.9    431 46.8    104 11.3*    329 47.8    359 52.2
CLEVELAND  6208 53.9   4332 37.6    968  8.4*   4701 40.2   7004 59.8
```

```
              DEMOC.  SENATOR    1950    * DEMOC.  RUNOFF    1950
                                         *
   COUNTY      SMITH        GRAHAM        REYNOLDS  GRAHAM        SMITH
               #      %     #      %      #      %*  #      %     #      %
------------------------------------------------------------------------------
   COLUMBUS    4962  53.0   3576  38.2    833   8.9* 2770  31.6   6000  68.4
   CRAVEN      2270  35.7   3194  50.2    895  14.1* 2176  40.4   3205  59.6
   CUMBERLAND  5055  51.2   4067  41.2    747   7.6* 3747  36.2   6595  63.8
   CURRITUCK   1238  57.7    711  33.2    195   9.1*  682  36.0   1212  64.0
   DARE         420  22.3   1286  68.3    177   9.4*  691  69.9    298  30.1
                                         *
   DAVIDSON    2610  35.0   4353  58.4    492   6.6* 4243  58.7   2982  41.3
   DAVIE        312  19.9   1137  72.4    121   7.7* 1049  77.0    313  23.0
   DUPLIN      2769  37.3   4305  58.0    349   4.7* 3185  49.5   3251  50.5
   DURHAM      6397  31.8  12630  62.7   1112   5.5*10973  63.1   6404  36.9
   EDGECOMBE   2942  39.5   4082  54.8    423   5.7* 3497  51.7   3271  48.3
                                         *
   FORSYTH     5219  34.2   8894  58.3   1144   7.5* 8213  60.9   5276  39.1
   FRANKLIN    3367  55.7   1817  30.1    858  14.2* 1800  31.5   3918  68.5
   GASTON      6701  47.0   6072  42.6   1473  10.3* 5975  45.1   7279  54.9
   GATES        834  59.0    478  33.8    101   7.1*  437  34.1    845  65.9
   GRAHAM       376  53.3    259  36.7     70   9.9*  329  42.1    452  57.9
                                         *
   GRANVILLE   2457  51.9   1711  36.1    567  12.0* 1343  31.8   2878  68.2
   GREENE       695  28.8   1584  65.6    135   5.6* 1328  59.0    921  41.0
   GUILFORD    9900  38.8  13758  54.0   1829   7.2*12606  55.4  10147  44.6
   HALIFAX     4457  50.8   3584  40.8    738   8.4* 2206  37.6   3659  62.4
   HARNETT     2502  38.7   3529  54.6    434   6.7* 3387  48.0   3663  52.0
                                         *
   HAYWOOD     2241  26.5   5595  66.3    606   7.2* 3974  69.8   1719  30.2
   HENDERSON   2420  44.9   2012  37.3    955  17.7* 2070  34.9   3869  65.1
   HERTFORD     976  35.2   1565  56.5    230   8.3*  997  48.6   1056  51.4
   HOKE         941  55.4    642  37.8    115   6.8*  518  34.4    989  65.6
   HYDE         451  35.5    738  58.0     83   6.5*  553  48.0    600  52.0
                                         *
   IREDELL     5278  47.6   4712  42.5   1107  10.0* 4192  40.9   6062  59.1
   JACKSON     1549  37.5   2249  54.4    333   8.1* 1293  52.2   1186  47.8
   JOHNSTON    4420  39.6   5963  53.4    789   7.1* 5093  43.1   6736  56.9
   JONES        568  28.1   1142  56.5    311  15.4*  634  48.6    670  51.4
   LEE         1978  42.8   2286  49.4    361   7.8* 1513  41.0   2173  59.0
                                         *
   LENOIR      1791  28.8   3711  59.6    723  11.6* 3163  54.8   2606  45.2
   LINCOLN     2233  40.0   2887  51.7    462   8.3* 2179  50.3   2149  49.7
   MACON        929  29.9   1904  61.4    270   8.7* 1323  72.3    506  27.7
   MADISON     1009  47.4    905  42.5    216  10.1* 1907  90.0    213  10.0
   MARTIN      1267  27.1   3218  68.7    196   4.2* 2390  62.5   1436  37.5
                                         *
   MCDOWELL    2067  42.4   1906  39.1    900  18.5* 2555  51.3   2424  48.7
   MECKLENBRG 14963  56.3  10245  38.6   1364   5.1* 9701  39.2  15067  60.8
   MITCHELL     109  20.1    393  72.6     39   7.2*  459  77.1    136  22.9
   MONTGOMERY  1293  48.8    971  36.7    383  14.5* 1028  35.4   1872  64.6
   MOORE       2548  47.7   2281  42.7    514   9.6* 2033  40.5   2988  59.5
                                         *
   NASH        3934  44.3   4464  50.2    488   5.5* 3812  44.6   4737  55.4
   NEWHANOVER  5310  36.9   6740  46.8   2346  16.3* 4761  43.1   6284  56.9
   NORTHAMPTN  2220  50.5   1908  43.4    266   6.1* 1352  40.5   1985  59.5
   ONSLOW      1206  29.5   2221  54.3    660  16.1* 1763  52.6   1591  47.4
   ORANGE      1234  17.9   5212  75.7    443   6.4* 4269  74.5   1462  25.5
                                         *
   PAMLICO      773  44.0    823  46.9    159   9.1*  586  40.8    852  59.2
```

| COUNTY | DEMOC. SENATOR 1950 | | | | | | DEMOC. RUNOFF 1950 | | | |
| | SMITH | | GRAHAM | | REYNOLDS | | GRAHAM | | SMITH | |
	#	%	#	%	#	%	#	%	#	%
PASQUOTANK	1764	53.0	1418	42.6	149	4.5	1179	42.8	1574	57.2
PENDER	1059	42.1	1110	44.1	349	13.9	796	36.5	1383	63.5
PERQUIMANS	1179	62.6	657	34.9	46	2.4	394	27.9	1016	72.1
PERSON	2092	44.7	2087	44.6	500	10.7	2099	41.7	2933	58.3
PITT	4519	48.9	4319	46.8	397	4.3	3430	42.9	4571	57.1
POLK	1199	47.0	980	38.4	374	14.6	1172	44.7	1450	55.3
RANDOLPH	2193	44.6	2381	48.4	342	7.0	2133	45.0	2605	55.0
RICHMOND	3847	42.0	4163	45.5	1144	12.5	3616	56.1	2824	43.9
ROBESON	4512	37.4	6850	56.8	704	5.8	4281	48.8	4489	51.2
ROCKINGHAM	2652	29.7	4937	55.3	1339	15.0	2879	57.7	2110	42.3
ROWAN	3870	34.7	6041	54.2	1233	11.1	4620	57.7	3382	42.3
RUTHERFORD	4203	50.2	2517	30.1	1645	19.7	2860	36.1	5070	63.9
SAMPSON	842	21.7	2943	75.8	96	2.5	2880	66.6	1444	33.4
SCOTLAND	2541	65.7	1116	28.9	208	5.4	840	24.8	2547	75.2
STANLY	2229	44.3	2242	44.6	559	11.1	2334	43.0	3100	57.0
STOKES	394	16.1	1912	78.1	141	5.8	1792	77.0	535	23.0
SURRY	2480	35.4	4044	57.7	481	6.9	4081	62.6	2436	37.4
SWAIN	1063	59.2	511	28.5	222	12.4	461	33.2	926	66.8
TRANSYLVNA	733	22.9	2011	62.9	455	14.2	1524	70.2	647	29.8
TYRRELL	548	46.5	492	41.8	138	11.7	414	43.2	544	56.8
UNION	2847	46.3	2762	44.9	536	8.7	2933	43.8	3759	56.2
VANCE	2623	39.4	3118	46.9	910	13.7	2777	46.2	3240	53.8
WAKE	10346	46.8	10405	47.1	1362	6.2	10247	42.4	13930	57.6
WARREN	1825	53.6	1267	37.2	314	9.2	1018	34.0	1972	66.0
WASHINGTON	558	29.3	1241	65.2	105	5.5	1229	56.7	937	43.3
WATAUGA	514	29.4	1217	69.6	18	1.0	1434	74.6	487	25.4
WAYNE	4347	42.1	5406	52.3	584	5.6	4199	45.7	4998	54.3
WILKES	1557	28.2	3721	67.4	239	4.3	3547	69.5	1557	30.5
WILSON	3204	45.1	3465	48.7	439	6.2	2915	40.3	4320	59.7
YADKIN	499	26.9	1238	66.7	120	6.5	1307	71.8	513	28.2
YANCEY	473	32.1	940	63.9	59	4.0	1173	59.6	796	40.4
TOTALS	250222		303575		58752		261843		281114	
% OF VOTE		40.8		49.6		9.6		48.2		51.8

```
              DEMOC.  SENATOR    1950    *  DEMOC.  RUNOFF     1950
                                          *
COUNTY     SMITH        GRAHAM       REYNOLDS  * GRAHAM       SMITH
           #      %     #      %     #     %*  #      %       #      %
--------------------------------------------*------------------------------------------
GEOGRAPHIC CLASS                            *

LOWLANDS   60339  42.   70405  49.   12707  9.*  58563  44.   74863  56.
BLACK BELT 60547  45.   64639  48.   10550  8.*  50691  43.   66247  57.
PIEDMONT   90236  42.   104405 49.   19366  9.*  94165  49.   97889  51.
MOUNTAIN   39100  33.   64126  54.   16129  14.* 58424  58.   42115  42.
                                            *
                                            *
DEMOGRAPHIC CLASS                           *

METRO      51585  38.   68651  51.   14295  11.* 61925  52.   57135  48.
TOWN       46451  42.   52421  48.   10733  10.* 43359  45.   52464  55.
RURAL      152186 41.   182503 50.   33724  9.*  156559 48.   171515 52.
```

NORTH CAROLINA

```
              DEMOC.  SENATOR    1954    *                DEMOC.  SENATOR    1960
                                         *
COUNTY     SCOTT        LENNON       OTHER   *  JORDAN       HEWLETT      GREGORY      MCINTOSH
           #     %      #     %      #    %*    #     %      #    %       #    %       #    %
--------------------------------------------*---------------------------------------------------
ALAMANCE   7687  78.3   1918  19.5   208  2.1* 9622  73.0   2762  21.0   437  3.3     356  2.7
ALEXANDER  646   37.2   1072  61.8   18   1.0*  844  64.3   340   25.9   88   6.7     41   3.1
ALLEGHANY  621   39.3   926   58.5   35   2.2*  707  63.2   229   20.5   99   8.9     83   7.4
ANSON      2089  42.8   2704  55.4   89   1.8* 1370  54.6   844   33.6   133  5.3     162  6.5
ASHE       1481  48.8   1526  50.3   28    .9*  882  47.1   843   45.1   99   5.3     47   2.5

AVERY      283   43.4   365   56.0   4     .6*  476  66.9   153   21.5   47   6.6     35   4.9
BEAUFORT   2472  54.0   1992  43.5   113  2.5* 3003  55.5   2073  38.3   177  3.3     162  3.0
BERTIE     2424  74.7   770   23.7   49   1.5*  787  34.7   1363  60.0   69   3.0     51   2.2
BLADEN     2502  42.9   3208  55.0   119  2.0* 2098  42.5   2510  50.9   158  3.2     168  3.4
BRUNSWICK  1624  39.1   2461  59.3   64   1.5*  929  21.9   2985  70.4   200  4.7     126  3.0
                                         *
BUNCOMBE   8112  42.7   10277 54.1   605  3.2* 12666 70.4   4095  22.8   571  3.2     663  3.7
BURKE      4197  64.4   2256  34.6   62   1.0* 3400  58.3   1917  32.9   233  4.0     284  4.9
CABARRUS   3803  38.1   5951  59.7   220  2.2* 6669  62.9   2398  22.6   844  8.0     690  6.5
CALDWELL   2265  36.3   3805  61.0   171  2.7* 3567  71.7   723   14.5   357  7.2     325  6.5
CAMDEN     477   45.5   551   52.5   21   2.0*  480  47.3   396   39.0   91   9.0     48   4.7
                                         *
CARTERET   2859  56.5   2147  42.4   54   1.1* 3164  67.6   1266  27.0   129  2.8     122  2.6
CASWELL    2165  60.9   1255  35.3   137  3.9* 1721  60.0   719   25.1   268  9.4     158  5.5
CATAWBA    3568  40.9   4947  56.7   209  2.4* 3646  69.9   987   18.9   244  4.7     337  6.5
CHATHAM    2738  60.4   1716  37.9   79   1.7* 2731  62.0   1286  29.2   193  4.4     195  4.4
CHEROKEE   1609  50.5   1494  46.9   82   2.6* 1558  77.6   273   13.6   82   4.1     94   4.7

CHOWAN     825   47.7   872   50.4   32   1.9*  862  55.7   524   33.9   95   6.1     66   4.3
CLAY       354   38.1   556   59.9   18   1.9*  471  71.0   134   20.2   33   5.0     25   3.8
CLEVELAND  4239  44.2   5191  54.1   158  1.6* 6377  70.9   1509  16.8   645  7.2     460  5.1
```

COUNTY	SCOTT #	%	LENNON #	%	OTHER #	%*	JORDAN #	%	HEWLETT #	%	GREGORY #	%	MCINTOSH #	%
COLUMBUS	3539	35.3	6335	63.2	157	1.6*	3809	33.5	6397	56.3	530	4.7	625	5.5
CRAVEN	3413	50.9	3164	47.2	133	2.0*	3802	50.1	3077	40.5	378	5.0	333	4.4
CUMBERLAND	5823	48.9	5686	47.8	391	3.3*	5874	45.6	5677	44.0	762	5.9	582	4.5
CURRITUCK	586	33.5	1080	61.8	81	4.6*	815	54.2	391	26.0	211	14.0	87	5.8
DARE	538	40.3	776	58.1	21	1.6*	1178	70.7	246	14.8	162	9.7	81	4.9
DAVIDSON	5648	68.9	2347	28.6	205	2.5*	5886	60.5	3137	32.3	370	3.8	330	3.4
DAVIE	700	60.8	406	35.2	46	4.0*	687	64.0	297	27.7	42	3.9	48	4.5
DUPLIN	5020	61.7	3021	37.1	92	1.1*	1865	30.5	3874	63.3	229	3.7	148	2.4
DURHAM	7503	58.6	4622	36.1	683	5.3*	12696	69.8	4313	23.7	800	4.4	368	2.0
EDGECOMBE	3592	61.1	2169	36.9	118	2.0*	2524	46.0	2659	48.5	178	3.2	122	2.2
FORSYTH	8320	48.7	8020	46.9	756	4.4*	13453	60.4	7001	31.4	1059	4.8	751	3.4
FRANKLIN	3494	61.4	2081	36.6	113	2.0*	2403	47.2	2072	40.7	392	7.7	224	4.4
GASTON	6134	33.4	11817	64.3	416	2.3*	8946	67.9	2269	17.2	870	6.6	1097	8.3
GATES	546	45.3	644	53.5	14	1.2*	339	32.6	481	46.2	148	14.2	73	7.0
GRAHAM	663	48.6	670	49.1	31	2.3*	572	68.1	166	19.8	62	7.4	40	4.8
GRANVILLE	2779	50.5	2400	43.6	324	5.9*	2445	54.9	1465	32.9	361	8.1	185	4.2
GREENE	2208	66.4	1071	32.2	44	1.3*	1387	48.2	1291	44.9	130	4.5	69	2.4
GUILFORD	8837	47.6	9130	49.2	585	3.2*	17172	58.3	9558	32.7	1576	5.4	962	3.3
HALIFAX	5352	55.8	3818	39.8	427	4.4*	3492	38.6	3430	37.9	1918	21.2	215	2.4
HARNETT	6224	77.4	1730	21.5	90	1.1*	3052	41.6	3193	43.6	897	12.2	189	2.6
HAYWOOD	5312	66.7	2522	31.6	135	1.7*	4941	78.4	845	13.4	298	4.7	216	3.4
HENDERSON	1283	34.4	2352	63.1	95	2.5*	2176	61.8	846	24.0	249	7.1	251	7.1
HERTFORD	1997	70.0	819	28.7	35	1.2*	882	40.0	1118	50.7	125	5.7	82	3.7
HOKE	1180	60.0	752	38.2	35	1.8*	671	35.7	1107	58.9	32	1.7	69	3.7
HYDE	1023	73.8	349	25.2	15	1.1*	671	50.5	543	40.9	62	4.7	52	3.9
IREDELL	3922	39.3	5742	57.5	324	3.2*	5944	65.1	1778	19.5	912	10.0	493	5.4
JACKSON	2014	49.7	1966	48.5	75	1.8*	2229	63.1	874	24.8	222	6.3	206	5.8
JOHNSTON	8197	69.9	3245	27.7	287	2.4*	4796	51.6	3786	40.7	476	5.1	242	2.6
JONES	1596	68.9	677	29.2	42	1.8*	829	37.9	1141	52.2	125	5.7	91	4.2
LEE	2733	64.1	1415	33.2	116	2.7*	2267	52.4	1815	42.0	120	2.8	122	2.8
LENOIR	4458	56.5	3261	41.3	176	2.2*	3581	46.5	3636	47.3	296	3.8	180	2.3
LINCOLN	2205	41.2	3067	57.3	82	1.5*	2431	54.6	1362	30.6	298	6.7	362	8.1
MACON	1620	58.6	1099	39.7	46	1.7*	1352	72.1	274	14.6	188	10.0	61	3.3
MADISON	1069	43.4	1364	55.4	30	1.2*	2355	80.2	406	13.9	87	3.0	73	2.5
MARTIN	3768	74.1	1164	22.9	150	3.0*	2624	60.9	1480	34.3	121	2.8	85	2.0
MCDOWELL	3037	61.2	1820	36.7	102	2.1*	2906	67.2	793	18.3	228	5.3	398	9.2
MECKLENBRG	7871	30.6	16870	65.7	945	3.7*	16542	58.0	9001	31.5	917	3.2	2072	7.3
MITCHELL	311	47.8	332	51.1	7	1.1*	464	77.1	89	14.8	19	3.2	30	5.0
MONTGOMERY	1373	54.0	1133	44.5	38	1.5*	1325	60.8	735	33.7	57	2.6	64	2.9
MOORE	2978	53.3	2499	44.7	108	1.9*	1637	34.6	2918	61.7	85	1.8	91	1.9
NASH	5446	62.1	3193	36.4	128	1.5*	3932	45.6	4238	49.1	323	3.7	135	1.6
NEWHANOVER	2576	17.1	12155	80.8	317	2.1*	1010	6.6	13971	90.9	174	1.1	219	1.4
NORTHAMPTN	2508	61.5	1514	37.1	59	1.4*	1344	34.6	2010	51.7	399	10.3	134	3.4
ONSLOW	2985	54.0	2485	45.0	58	1.0*	1842	34.0	3031	56.0	309	5.7	231	4.3
ORANGE	4062	68.1	1575	26.4	330	5.5*	3996	54.0	2892	39.1	289	3.9	221	3.0
PAMLICO	989	57.0	692	39.9	53	3.1*	543	36.5	833	55.9	63	4.2	50	3.4

NORTH CAROLINA/187

	DEMOC. SENATOR 1954					*	DEMOC. SENATOR 1960						
COUNTY	SCOTT		LENNON		OTHER		JORDAN		HEWLETT		GREGORY		MCINTOSH	
	#	%	#	%	#	%*	#	%	#	%	#	%	#	%
PASQUOTANK	799	37.0	1329	61.5	32	1.5*	2082	53.4	1386	35.5	320	8.2	113	2.9
PENDER	999	31.0	2190	67.9	38	1.2*	270	9.4	2457	85.6	76	2.6	68	2.4
PERQUIMANS	494	34.9	912	64.4	11	.8*	688	45.3	706	46.5	86	5.7	39	2.6
PERSON	2880	53.2	2152	39.7	385	7.1*	2504	56.1	1404	31.5	358	8.0	198	4.4
PITT	7234	57.8	5040	40.3	245	2.0*	5813	50.6	4894	42.6	497	4.3	291	2.5
POLK	927	34.2	1689	62.2	98	3.6*	1209	67.0	331	18.3	142	7.9	123	6.8
RANDOLPH	4426	68.4	1923	29.7	121	1.9*	3984	64.1	1887	30.3	150	2.4	198	3.2
RICHMOND	5020	56.7	3597	40.6	233	2.6*	3063	41.2	3247	43.7	389	5.2	731	9.8
ROBESON	7258	51.9	6470	46.3	256	1.8*	4690	47.6	4346	44.1	420	4.3	398	4.0
ROCKINGHAM	5708	57.4	3903	39.3	325	3.3*	4775	54.8	3049	35.0	518	5.9	366	4.2
ROWAN	5756	47.4	6107	50.3	289	2.4*	6246	52.3	3791	31.7	1209	10.1	708	5.9
RUTHERFORD	2805	31.6	5876	66.3	188	2.1*	5688	67.1	1500	17.7	799	9.4	491	5.8
SAMPSON	2794	63.3	1532	34.7	89	2.0*	1665	36.2	2633	57.2	172	3.7	132	2.9
SCOTLAND	2051	48.9	2031	48.4	116	2.8*	1410	54.3	999	38.5	75	2.9	114	4.4
STANLY	2555	51.6	2313	46.8	79	1.6*	2996	66.9	1074	24.0	201	4.5	204	4.6
STOKES	1322	50.2	1246	47.4	63	2.4*	1859	58.5	931	29.3	262	8.2	127	4.0
SURRY	4662	55.0	3553	41.9	265	3.1*	3825	72.1	1096	20.7	239	4.5	145	2.7
SWAIN	1048	57.0	741	40.3	51	2.8*	1332	85.1	118	7.5	67	4.3	48	3.1
TRANSYLVNA	1246	44.7	1477	53.0	65	2.3*	2058	71.8	309	10.8	217	7.6	281	9.8
TYRRELL	1089	77.5	307	21.9	9	.6*	230	25.8	540	60.5	79	8.8	44	4.9
UNION	2827	48.3	2855	48.8	174	3.0*	2835	61.5	1157	25.1	318	6.9	299	6.5
VANCE	2869	47.1	2941	48.3	282	4.6*	2806	44.7	2898	46.2	353	5.6	214	3.4
WAKE	14806	58.9	9464	37.6	879	3.5*	11184	42.5	14396	54.7	344	1.3	373	1.4
WARREN	1585	48.5	1590	48.7	92	2.8*	1552	52.5	1045	35.3	254	8.6	106	3.6
WASHINGTON	1256	71.2	481	27.3	26	1.5*	1014	44.0	1028	44.6	148	6.4	114	4.9
WATAUGA	482	30.8	1072	68.6	9	.6*	1243	63.1	569	28.9	98	5.0	59	3.0
WAYNE	3929	48.6	4012	49.7	139	1.7*	4738	57.3	3152	38.1	231	2.8	145	1.8
WILKES	1381	36.9	2320	61.9	46	1.2*	2603	64.8	1116	27.8	187	4.7	111	2.8
WILSON	3698	51.7	3335	46.6	125	1.7*	3652	57.6	2265	35.7	264	4.2	160	2.5
YADKIN	1232	72.8	420	24.8	41	2.4*	1323	73.1	338	18.7	87	4.8	63	3.5
YANCEY	443	34.1	843	64.8	14	1.1*	1134	68.5	392	23.7	62	3.7	68	4.1
TOTALS	312053		286730		15875	*	324188		217899		31463		23988	
% OF VOTE		50.8		46.6		2.6*		54.3		36.5		5.3		4.0

	DEMOC. SENATOR 1954						DEMOC. SENATOR 1960							
COUNTY	SCOTT #	%	LENNON #	%	OTHER #	%*	JORDAN #	%	HEWLETT #	%	GREGORY #	%	MCINTOSH #	%
GEOGRAPHIC CLASS						*								
LOWLANDS	79105	52.	69488	46.	3475	2.*	60236	40.	78961	53.	6038	4.	4791	3.
BLACK BELT	79761	56.	59898	42.	3359	2.*	58649	46.	55591	44.	7996	6.	4030	3.
PIEDMONT	99094	48.	101161	49.	6508	3.*	140387	62.	62501	28.	12522	6.	10523	5.
MOUNTAIN	54093	48.	56183	50.	2533	2.*	64916	68.	20846	22.	4907	5.	4644	5.
DEMOGRAPHIC CLASS						*								
METRO	55449	47.	58383	49.	4453	4.*	83713	59.	48364	34.	5267	4.	5189	4.
TOWN	54690	46.	61451	52.	2644	2.*	58675	50.	47474	41.	5762	5.	4550	4.
RURAL	201914	53.	166896	44.	8778	2.*	181800	54.	122061	36.	20434	6.	14249	4.

NORTH CAROLINA

	DEMOC. SENATOR 1972						DEMOC. RUNOFF 1972			
COUNTY	JORDAN #	%	GALFANAKS #	%	OTHER #	%*	GALFANAKS #	%	JORDAN #	%
ALAMANCE	7253	48.3	7022	46.7	754	5.0*	6010	50.9	5798	49.1
ALEXANDER	1263	62.0	670	32.9	105	5.2*	760	49.4	780	50.6
ALLEGHANY	1211	65.3	514	27.7	129	7.0*	518	38.3	833	61.7
ANSON	2811	55.5	1804	35.6	449	8.9*	2180	43.2	2865	56.8
ASHE	1856	68.0	764	28.0	108	4.0*	966	42.7	1294	57.3
AVERY	441	64.9	192	28.2	47	6.9*	264	40.6	386	59.4
BEAUFORT	3183	48.9	2919	44.8	411	6.3*	2528	53.8	2171	46.2
BERTIE	1621	49.2	1466	44.5	207	6.3*	1488	48.2	1596	51.8
BLADEN	3360	62.2	1504	27.8	539	10.0*	1747	42.2	2390	57.8
BRUNSWICK	2252	46.4	2129	43.9	471	9.7*	2314	55.4	1863	44.6
BUNCOMBE	8493	46.7	9012	49.5	687	3.8*	9322	60.3	6148	39.7
BURKE	3274	48.7	3011	44.8	435	6.5*	2791	57.7	2042	42.3
CABARRUS	3994	39.0	5808	56.7	450	4.4*	4351	57.4	3223	42.6
CALDWELL	2729	54.0	1958	38.8	365	7.2*	1954	52.3	1782	47.7
CAMDEN	679	62.4	272	25.0	138	12.7*	259	38.1	420	61.9
CARTERET	2905	49.1	2876	48.6	136	2.3*	2358	47.3	2624	52.7
CASWELL	1461	40.2	1894	52.1	280	7.7*	1721	50.5	1687	49.5
CATAWBA	5116	52.1	4114	41.9	581	5.9*	3930	53.6	3396	46.4
CHATHAM	1638	29.4	3507	63.0	424	7.6*	2960	67.0	1459	33.0
CHEROKEE	1552	76.6	322	15.9	151	7.5*	721	40.3	1070	59.7
CHOWAN	1428	67.2	559	26.3	137	6.5*	575	40.2	854	59.8
CLAY	493	71.0	123	17.7	78	11.2*	191	49.2	197	50.8
CLEVELAND	6186	51.2	5322	44.1	564	4.7*	5484	52.4	4982	47.6

	DEMOC. SENATOR 1972					*	DEMOC. RUNOFF 1972			
COUNTY	JORDAN		GALFANAKS		OTHER		GALFANAKS		JORDAN	
	#	%	#	%	#	%*	#	%	#	%
COLUMBUS	4751	53.1	3275	36.6	918	10.3*	3561	50.7	3456	49.3
CRAVEN	3644	45.3	4000	49.8	396	4.9*	3467	52.4	3154	47.6
CUMBERLAND	8326	37.8	12382	56.2	1326	6.0*	10278	59.9	6877	40.1
CURRITUCK	1105	59.7	484	26.2	261	14.1*	633	44.4	794	55.6
DARE	1389	75.8	361	19.7	83	4.5*	437	33.1	882	66.9
DAVIDSON	4537	42.3	5652	52.7	544	5.1*	4627	59.2	3193	40.8
DAVIE	1076	52.8	825	40.5	135	6.6*	470	33.7	925	66.3
DUPLIN	3697	53.3	2792	40.3	442	6.4*	2526	47.5	2794	52.5
DURHAM	7181	28.0	16338	63.7	2132	8.3*	13405	67.0	6616	33.0
EDGECOMBE	4474	44.2	5077	50.2	566	5.6*	3620	48.4	3861	51.6
FORSYTH	8231	29.3	18162	64.7	1668	5.9*	12295	62.5	7392	37.5
FRANKLIN	2957	46.4	2979	46.7	437	6.9*	2624	49.7	2655	50.3
GASTON	7675	51.2	6175	41.2	1132	7.6*	5777	51.6	5411	48.4
GATES	1095	51.4	749	35.1	288	13.5*	475	50.0	475	50.0
GRAHAM	623	61.2	313	30.7	82	8.1*	371	48.0	402	52.0
GRANVILLE	3541	45.0	3372	42.8	957	12.2*	2471	43.7	3188	56.3
GREENE	1369	48.5	1324	46.9	128	4.5*	898	45.1	1091	54.9
GUILFORD	12027	29.0	26688	64.4	2751	6.6*	22526	68.0	10583	32.0
HALIFAX	4940	46.4	4580	43.0	1125	10.6*	3662	49.0	3811	51.0
HARNETT	3955	50.7	3233	41.4	620	7.9*	2467	44.0	3140	56.0
HAYWOOD	3535	51.0	3054	44.0	349	5.0*	3436	59.1	2377	40.9
HENDERSON	1872	47.4	1805	45.7	273	6.9*	1652	57.0	1247	43.0
HERTFORD	1392	49.4	1263	44.8	165	5.9*	1361	59.7	917	40.3
HOKE	1057	36.3	1695	58.2	160	5.5*	1270	57.7	931	42.3
HYDE	877	64.3	412	30.2	74	5.4*	395	39.6	602	60.4
IREDELL	5740	50.9	4114	36.5	1426	12.6*	3835	48.6	4061	51.4
JACKSON	1965	64.7	822	27.1	251	8.3*	1143	55.3	923	44.7
JOHNSTON	4588	49.1	4237	45.3	528	5.6*	3830	46.0	4501	54.0
JONES	1282	49.1	1069	41.0	259	9.9*	1030	55.3	832	44.7
LEE	2235	47.2	2254	47.6	243	5.1*	2005	49.1	2078	50.9
LENOIR	3550	33.3	6560	61.5	557	5.2*	4804	63.9	2711	36.1
LINCOLN	2949	50.8	2531	43.6	327	5.6*	2337	53.4	2037	46.6
MACON	1460	63.5	655	28.5	185	8.0*	905	50.3	895	49.7
MADISON	1486	78.7	344	18.2	57	3.0*	459	31.3	1009	68.7
MARTIN	2416	52.6	2012	43.8	162	3.5*	1798	43.7	2314	56.3
MCDOWELL	2581	62.3	1287	31.0	278	6.7*	1521	47.2	1702	52.8
MECKLENBRG	19894	45.5	21743	49.8	2067	4.7*	22135	61.2	14058	38.8
MITCHELL	442	62.4	215	30.4	51	7.2*	274	47.5	303	52.5
MONTGOMERY	1930	51.9	1572	42.3	214	5.8*	1480	49.2	1528	50.8
MOORE	3247	49.0	2927	44.2	454	6.8*	2862	52.5	2587	47.5
NASH	6064	47.6	6094	47.8	585	4.6*	4435	47.9	4826	52.1
NEWHANOVER	5396	41.3	7060	54.0	610	4.7*	6702	56.6	5141	43.4
NORTHAMPTN	2234	40.3	2894	52.2	421	7.6*	2293	56.3	1779	43.7
ONSLOW	3458	38.7	5036	56.4	435	4.9*	3925	55.9	3095	44.1
ORANGE	4604	30.6	9466	62.9	978	6.5*	6627	64.2	3698	35.8
PAMLICO	1005	53.0	752	39.7	138	7.3*	643	47.4	713	52.6

| COUNTY | DEMOC. SENATOR 1972 | | | | | | DEMOC. RUNOFF 1972 | | | |
| | JORDAN | | GALFANAKS | | OTHER | | GALFANAKS | | JORDAN | |
	#	%	#	%	#	%*	#	%	#	%
PASQUOTANK	1650	45.4	1776	48.8	211	5.8*	1932	60.5	1259	39.5
PENDER	1641	52.9	1159	37.4	300	9.7*	1220	50.6	1191	49.4
PERQUIMANS	717	47.3	718	47.4	81	5.3*	634	62.5	381	37.5
PERSON	2243	36.6	3492	57.0	389	6.4*	2506	53.2	2203	46.8
PITT	5967	44.6	6638	49.6	776	5.8*	5547	54.1	4701	45.9
POLK	901	59.0	526	34.4	101	6.6*	724	49.0	754	51.0
RANDOLPH	2257	28.2	5537	69.2	208	2.6*	4562	73.4	1657	26.6
RICHMOND	2854	52.6	2275	41.9	301	5.5*	2285	46.8	2593	53.2
ROBESON	8871	54.4	5372	32.9	2078	12.7*	6541	51.6	6129	48.4
ROCKINGHAM	4398	36.6	6999	58.3	605	5.0*	5176	61.9	3192	38.1
ROWAN	5612	49.8	5112	45.4	536	4.8*	4199	56.4	3250	43.6
RUTHERFORD	4036	58.5	2526	36.6	340	4.9*	2762	47.7	3023	52.3
SAMPSON	2890	53.3	2167	40.0	363	6.7*	2104	47.6	2312	52.4
SCOTLAND	2038	56.1	1328	36.6	265	7.3*	1551	47.0	1748	53.0
STANLY	3657	53.2	2610	38.0	601	8.8*	2782	49.7	2819	50.3
STOKES	1608	34.2	2879	61.2	216	4.6*	1637	60.7	1060	39.3
SURRY	3376	50.7	2985	44.8	304	4.6*	2318	45.9	2735	54.1
SWAIN	780	58.7	360	27.1	188	14.2*	765	60.5	500	39.5
TRANSYLVNA	1655	55.4	1100	36.8	235	7.9*	1246	58.1	898	41.9
TYRRELL	492	43.3	513	45.2	131	11.5*	416	52.0	384	48.0
UNION	4626	53.6	3469	40.2	536	6.2*	3966	55.1	3227	44.9
VANCE	3348	48.4	2772	40.0	803	11.6*	2539	43.9	3250	56.1
WAKE	16554	35.3	27799	59.3	2523	5.4*	24208	61.0	15508	39.0
WARREN	1640	46.9	1624	46.4	234	6.7*	1398	47.9	1518	52.1
WASHINGTON	1273	39.9	1773	55.6	143	4.5*	1405	61.9	863	38.1
WATAUGA	1449	53.8	1150	42.7	96	3.6*	1195	55.1	975	44.9
WAYNE	5524	46.3	5726	48.0	673	5.6*	5159	49.7	5212	50.3
WILKES	1948	45.4	2180	50.8	161	3.8*	2193	57.4	1626	42.6
WILSON	5259	46.2	5462	48.0	657	5.8*	3828	47.8	4184	52.2
YADKIN	1137	54.4	808	38.7	145	6.9*	661	47.0	744	53.0
YANCEY	939	52.7	762	42.8	81	4.5*	860	56.0	676	44.0
TOTALS	340391		377993		49165	*	333458		267997	
% OF VOTE	44.3		49.2		6.4	*	55.4		44.6	

```
            DEMOC.  SENATOR   1972    * DEMOC.  RUNOFF    1972
                                      *
   COUNTY   JORDAN      GALFANAKS   OTHER    *  GALFANAKS   JORDAN
            #      %    #      %    #      %* #      %    #      %
--------------------------------------------*---------------------------------------------------------------
GEOGRAPHIC CLASS                             *
                                             *
LOWLANDS    82958 44.   94684 50.  11332  6.* 84292 54.  71495 46.
BLACK BELT  81504 48.   76714 45.  13313  8.* 66117 50.  65413 50.
PIEDMONT   117719 40.  161314 54.  18319  6.*137465 60.  91373 40.
MOUNTAIN    58210 53.   45281 41.   6201  6.* 45584 53.  39716 47.
                                             *
                                             *
DEMOGRAPHIC CLASS                            *
                                             *
METRO       72380 35.  119742 59.  11828  6.*103891 63.  60305 37.
TOWN        63030 44.   73022 51.   8037  6.* 60275 54.  50369 46.
RURAL      204981 49.  185229 44.  29300  7.*169292 52. 157323 48.
```

                            NORTH CAROLINA

```
               DEMOC.  PRESIDENT  1972              *     REPUB.  GOVERNOR  1972
                                                    *
   COUNTY   WALLACE     SANFORD     CHISHOLM    OTHER    GARDNER     HOLSHOUSR   OTHER
            #      %    #      %    #      %    #      %* #      %    #      %    #      %
--------------------------------------------------------*-------------------------------------------------------
ALAMANCE    8808 55.1   5966 37.3   530  3.3   691  4.3* 1500 51.6   1385 47.7   21   .7
ALEXANDER   1180 55.2    830 38.8    26  1.2   101  4.7*  686 61.9    413 37.3    9   .8
ALLEGHANY   1155 58.5    688 34.8    11   .6   122  6.2*  235 39.0    361 59.9    7  1.2
ANSON       2791 53.8   1676 32.3   447  8.6   274  5.3*   84 67.7     39 31.5    1   .8
ASHE        1092 37.6   1591 54.7    10   .3   213  7.3*  392 22.1   1376 77.5    7   .4
                                                    *
AVERY        312 44.4    339 48.2     9  1.3    43  6.1*  983 40.3   1429 58.6   28  1.1
BEAUFORT    3992 59.6   1991 29.7   441  6.6   278  4.1*  311 60.9    182 35.6   18  3.5
BERTIE      2050 49.4    951 22.9  1014 24.4   136  3.3*   37 74.0      8 16.0    5 10.0
BLADEN      3393 61.0   1592 28.6   279  5.0   299  5.4*  139 77.7     33 18.4    7  3.9
BRUNSWICK   3436 61.0   1573 27.9   315  5.6   305  5.4*  450 56.0    337 42.0   16  2.0
                                                    *
BUNCOMBE    9306 47.0   7628 38.5  1290  6.5  1570  7.9* 1651 39.4   2494 59.6   41  1.0
BURKE       2944 42.9   3337 48.6   177  2.6   406  5.9* 1501 47.9   1610 51.4   21   .7
CABARRUS    5785 55.9   3666 35.4   401  3.9   493  4.8* 1417 51.2   1332 48.1   20   .7
CALDWELL    2485 48.0   2167 41.9   222  4.3   298  5.8*  755 31.4   1633 67.9   18   .7
CAMDEN       917 65.4    353 25.2    69  4.9    64  4.6*   14 70.0      5 25.0    1  5.0
                                                    *
CARTERET    2665 44.9   2684 45.2   199  3.4   384  6.5* 1544 84.5    267 14.6   17   .9
CASWELL     2061 53.0   1350 34.7   273  7.0   203  5.2*  100 66.2     44 29.1    7  4.6
CATAWBA     4716 47.4   4243 42.7   398  4.0   585  5.9* 1567 34.9   2885 64.3   36   .8
CHATHAM     2949 50.7   2285 39.3   313  5.4   267  4.6*  806 68.1    372 31.4    6   .5
CHEROKEE    1028 49.3    772 37.0    19   .9   267 12.8*  480 53.6    405 45.3   10  1.1
                                                    *
CHOWAN      1096 50.5    823 37.9    88  4.1   164  7.6*   62 66.7     28 30.1    3  3.2
CLAY         305 46.4    278 42.3     4   .6    70 10.7*  341 59.9    223 39.2    5   .9
CLEVELAND   7146 58.7   3844 31.6   643  5.3   543  4.5*  505 54.7    408 44.2   11  1.2
```

COUNTY	DEMOC. PRESIDENT 1972									*	REPUB. GOVERNOR 1972							
	WALLACE		SANFORD		CHISHOLM		OTHER				GARDNER		HOLSHOUSR		OTHER		
	#	%	#	%	#	%	#	%*			#	%	#	%	#	%
COLUMBUS	6974	66.2	2693	25.6	360	3.4	509	4.8*			362	73.4	108	21.9	23	4.7
CRAVEN	5304	59.2	2594	28.9	653	7.3	413	4.6*			621	78.1	159	20.0	15	1.9
CUMBERLAND	11258	48.7	9062	39.2	1966	8.5	809	3.5*			1565	59.3	1049	39.8	24	.9
CURRITUCK	1287	65.2	522	26.5	49	2.5	115	5.8*			22	91.7	1	4.2	1	4.2
DARE	931	50.7	780	42.5	39	2.1	85	4.6*			201	79.4	49	19.4	3	1.2
										*						
DAVIDSON	5986	54.4	3960	36.0	533	4.8	528	4.8*			2509	58.5	1757	41.0	22	.5
DAVIE	1122	53.1	795	37.6	98	4.6	97	4.6*			1055	51.4	983	47.9	15	.7
DUPLIN	4684	62.8	2184	29.3	366	4.9	223	3.0*			458	78.4	110	18.8	16	2.7
DURHAM	10637	40.6	10458	39.9	4104	15.7	1000	3.8*			1790	54.9	1391	42.6	87	2.7
EDGECOMBE	5397	46.2	4415	37.8	1260	10.8	621	5.3*			593	76.3	159	20.5	25	3.2
										*						
FORSYTH	14345	45.8	12110	38.6	3563	11.4	1334	4.3*			2802	37.5	4545	60.8	126	1.7
FRANKLIN	4240	58.3	2452	33.7	321	4.4	254	3.5*			231	73.1	74	23.4	11	3.5
GASTON	9002	59.5	4667	30.8	611	4.0	849	5.6*			1526	53.4	1311	45.9	21	.7
GATES	997	42.6	1039	44.4	120	5.1	184	7.9*			22	84.6	3	11.5	1	3.8
GRAHAM	398	39.9	491	49.2	4	.4	105	10.5*			507	52.8	450	46.8	4	.4
										*						
GRANVILLE	4583	52.0	2858	32.4	970	11.0	398	4.5*			143	60.3	89	37.6	5	2.1
GREENE	2033	70.2	720	24.9	77	2.7	67	2.3*			213	80.1	35	13.2	18	6.8
GUILFORD	21729	48.5	16041	35.8	5273	11.8	1802	4.0*			4948	48.5	5099	50.0	146	1.4
HALIFAX	5963	51.9	3244	28.2	1663	14.5	614	5.3*			193	73.4	62	23.6	8	3.0
HARNETT	5124	63.0	2427	29.9	272	3.3	305	3.8*			912	75.4	289	23.9	9	.7
										- *						
HAYWOOD	3401	49.1	2696	38.9	119	1.7	710	10.3*			499	48.3	528	51.1	7	.7
HENDERSON	2050	51.5	1511	38.0	121	3.0	296	7.4*			1424	47.0	1582	52.2	25	.8
HERTFORD	1579	44.0	1204	33.5	659	18.4	149	4.1*			76	71.0	25	23.4	6	5.6
HOKE	1339	44.5	1451	48.2	105	3.5	117	3.9*			59	62.8	33	35.1	2	2.1
HYDE	779	56.0	491	35.3	71	5.1	51	3.7*			79	80.6	17	17.3	2	2.0
										- *						
IREDELL	6957	64.5	2955	27.4	387	3.6	488	4.5*			1680	62.2	1007	37.3	14	.5
JACKSON	1179	38.4	1381	45.0	77	2.5	433	14.1*			336	44.6	414	55.0	3	.4
JOHNSTON	6239	61.3	3203	31.5	425	4.2	313	3.1*			1185	78.6	310	20.6	12	.8
JONES	1433	53.9	653	24.5	466	17.5	109	4.1*			57	75.0	13	17.1	6	7.9
LEE	3343	57.3	2148	36.8	174	3.0	169	2.9*			339	59.6	218	38.3	12	2.1
										- *						
LENOIR	6923	64.0	2510	23.2	1001	9.3	379	3.5*			988	80.9	190	15.6	43	3.5
LINCOLN	2738	46.1	2697	45.4	172	2.9	335	5.6*			609	38.7	961	61.1	3	.2
MACON	1088	45.8	1059	44.6	19	.8	207	8.7*			292	52.4	256	46.0	9	1.6
MADISON	1053	51.0	677	32.8	27	1.3	309	15.0*			319	54.5	260	44.4	6	1.0
MARTIN	2731	51.5	1964	37.0	447	8.4	163	3.1*			141	76.2	37	20.0	7	3.8
										- *						
MCDOWELL	2555	60.3	1242	29.3	96	2.3	344	8.1*			309	46.6	347	52.3	7	1.1
MECKLENBRG	21786	41.9	21360	41.1	6805	13.1	1984	3.8*			6220	37.0	10415	61.9	184	1.1
MITCHELL	329	45.2	326	44.8	6	.8	67	9.2*			1195	37.9	1906	60.4	55	1.7
MONTGOMERY	1805	47.8	1550	41.1	270	7.2	150	4.0*			667	71.4	265	28.4	2	.2
MOORE	3255	48.1	2921	43.2	280	4.1	311	4.6*			1706	65.4	884	33.9	19	.7
										- *						
NASH	7523	55.0	4526	33.1	873	6.4	751	5.5*			1408	77.4	376	20.7	36	2.0
NEWHANOVER	7809	56.6	4128	29.9	1050	7.6	820	5.9*			1613	51.6	1377	44.1	133	4.3
NORTHAMPTN	2614	38.9	3235	48.1	667	9.9	209	3.1*			21	72.4	6	20.7	2	6.9
ONSLOW	5649	61.7	2503	27.4	460	5.0	537	5.9*			850	84.8	121	12.1	31	3.1
ORANGE	3759	24.4	9517	61.9	1404	9.1	696	4.5*			803	45.0	957	53.6	24	1.3
										*						
PAMLICO	1030	53.0	619	31.9	182	9.4	111	5.7*			116	80.6	26	18.1	2	1.4

COUNTY	DEMOC. PRESIDENT 1972											REPUB. GOVERNOR 1972						
	WALLACE #	%	SANFORD #	%	CHISHOLM #	%	OTHER #	%*	GARDNER #	%	HOLSHOUSR #	%	OTHER #	%
PASQUOTANK	1884	44.8	1899	45.1	228	5.4	196	4.7*	102	59.3	64	37.2	6	3.5
PENDER	2146	63.1	965	28.4	134	3.9	156	4.6*	126	67.7	57	30.6	3	1.6
PERQUIMANS	789	51.1	619	40.1	62	4.0	73	4.7*	24	60.0	15	37.5	1	2.5
PERSON	3434	52.4	1978	30.2	895	13.7	247	3.8*	246	62.9	133	34.0	12	3.1
PITT	7538	55.1	4341	31.7	1277	9.3	522	3.8*	1107	69.7	460	28.9	22	1.4
POLK	1094	57.4	663	34.8	32	1.7	118	6.2*	298	48.5	306	49.8	11	1.8
RANDOLPH	4210	51.3	3234	39.4	198	2.4	565	6.9*	3351	61.1	2085	38.0	50	.9
RICHMOND	4064	53.4	2650	34.8	557	7.3	342	4.5*	134	66.0	68	33.5	1	.5
ROBESON	8061	45.1	7533	42.1	1244	7.0	1042	5.8*	204	49.0	201	48.3	11	2.6
ROCKINGHAM	7305	60.3	3537	29.2	595	4.9	675	5.6*	807	53.2	692	45.6	17	1.1
ROWAN	6053	53.1	4263	37.4	450	4.0	624	5.5*	2212	42.8	2918	56.4	41	.8
RUTHERFORD	3814	55.4	2554	37.1	173	2.5	340	4.9*	399	30.5	900	68.7	11	.8
SAMPSON	2709	46.9	2389	41.3	334	5.8	346	6.0*	1488	52.5	1332	47.0	12	.4
SCOTLAND	1721	40.9	1819	43.2	495	11.8	172	4.1*	93	49.5	91	48.4	4	2.1
STANLY	3503	48.9	2955	41.2	268	3.7	439	6.1*	985	36.7	1678	62.6	18	.7
STOKES	3027	62.0	1482	30.4	125	2.6	249	5.1*	974	45.2	1159	53.8	20	.9
SURRY	3143	46.3	3187	46.9	125	1.8	337	5.0*	645	40.4	942	58.9	11	.7
SWAIN	680	50.1	488	36.0	14	1.0	175	12.9*	313	80.5	72	18.5	4	1.0
TRANSYLVNA	1486	49.3	1110	36.8	66	2.2	355	11.8*	288	32.1	597	66.6	12	1.3
TYRRELL	575	47.7	495	41.1	52	4.3	83	6.9*	29	85.3	5	14.7	0	.0
UNION	5129	57.7	2810	31.6	507	5.7	441	5.0*	526	58.1	363	40.1	17	1.9
VANCE	4142	54.0	2413	31.5	641	8.4	473	6.2*	174	47.7	187	51.2	4	1.1
WAKE	20502	41.2	23633	47.5	3737	7.5	1929	3.9*	4602	53.0	4005	46.1	82	.9
WARREN	1853	47.0	1126	28.5	755	19.1	210	5.3*	100	60.6	53	32.1	12	7.3
WASHINGTON	1459	44.7	1587	48.6	114	3.5	105	3.2*	102	68.9	43	29.1	3	2.0
WATAUGA	836	30.6	1692	61.9	51	1.9	153	5.6*	232	12.5	1611	87.1	6	.3
WAYNE	7134	56.4	3641	28.8	1444	11.4	426	3.4*	972	61.6	585	37.0	22	1.4
WILKES	1767	40.6	2304	52.9	68	1.6	214	4.9*	2706	46.8	3041	52.6	29	.5
WILSON	7179	55.5	3927	30.4	1168	9.0	650	5.0*	1026	74.0	340	24.5	20	1.4
YADKIN	1143	52.9	908	42.0	44	2.0	65	3.0*	1181	40.3	1721	58.8	26	.9
YANCEY	586	30.9	1146	60.4	27	1.4	137	7.2*	226	36.4	390	62.8	5	.8
TOTALS	413518		306014		61723		40155	*	84896		83637		2040	
% OF VOTE	50.3		37.3		7.5		4.9	*	49.8		49.0		1.2	

COUNTY	DEMOC. PRESIDENT 1972								REPUB. GOVERNOR 1972					
	WALLACE #	%	SANFORD #	%	CHISHOLM #	%	OTHER #	%*	GARDNER #	%	HOLSHOUSR #	%	OTHER #	%
GEOGRAPHIC CLASS								*						
LOWLANDS	107389	53.	74345	36.	13303	7.	8730	4.*	19451	62.	11477	37.	468	1.
BLACK BELT	97789	52.	64231	34.	17040	9.	8888	5.*	7747	72.	2792	26.	282	3.
PIEDMONT	154142	49.	119710	38.	27923	9.	14156	4.*	35699	47.	39013	52.	850	1.
MOUNTAIN	54198	48.	47728	42.	3457	3.	8381	7.*	21999	42.	30355	57.	440	1.
DEMOGRAPHIC CLASS								*						
METRO	98305	44.	91230	41.	24772	11.	9619	4.*	22013	43.	27949	55.	666	1.
TOWN	82886	55.	50586	33.	11158	7.	6884	5.*	14519	56.	11106	43.	392	2.
RURAL	232327	52.	164198	37.	25793	6.	23652	5.*	48364	52.	44582	47.	982	1.

NORTH CAROLINA

COUNTY	REPUB. RUNOFF 1972*				REPUB. SENATOR 1972					
	GARDNER #	%	HOLSHOUSR #	%*	JOHNSON #	%	BOOE #	%	HELMS #	%
ALAMANCE	1155	51.5	1088	48.5*	371	14.0	183	6.9	2098	79.1
ALEXANDER	746	72.4	284	27.6*	532	52.6	100	9.9	379	37.5
ALLEGHANY	111	34.3	213	65.7*	217	44.7	70	14.4	199	40.9
ANSON	74	57.8	54	42.2*	39	35.1	18	16.2	54	48.6
ASHE	285	20.7	1090	79.3*	299	22.8	143	10.9	871	66.3
AVERY	537	27.1	1441	72.9*	911	51.4	287	16.2	573	32.4
BEAUFORT	250	64.8	136	35.2*	92	21.4	30	7.0	308	71.6
BERTIE	30	83.3	6	16.7*	6	15.4	2	5.1	31	79.5
BLADEN	160	88.4	21	11.6*	35	20.7	8	4.7	126	74.6
BRUNSWICK	533	72.3	204	27.7*	235	33.3	61	8.6	410	58.1
BUNCOMBE	1319	34.7	2481	65.3*	1391	39.2	382	10.8	1779	50.1
BURKE	1498	54.8	1236	45.2*	635	21.8	234	8.0	2046	70.2
CABARRUS	948	50.2	939	49.8*	2216	80.6	104	3.8	429	15.6
CALDWELL	698	33.3	1397	66.7*	800	37.9	281	13.3	1029	48.8
CAMDEN	23	79.3	6	20.7*	5	17.9	4	14.3	19	67.9
CARTERET	1527	87.7	215	12.3*	210	12.3	55	3.2	1448	84.5
CASWELL	70	71.4	28	28.6*	24	18.5	12	9.2	94	72.3
CATAWBA	1214	30.2	2811	69.8*	1309	31.6	478	11.5	2354	56.8
CHATHAM	883	78.1	248	21.9*	118	10.0	38	3.2	1023	86.8
CHEROKEE	312	39.6	475	60.4*	272	39.6	109	15.9	306	44.5
CHOWAN	39	79.6	10	20.4*	34	39.5	10	11.6	42	48.8
CLAY	113	38.3	182	61.7*	242	55.1	70	15.9	127	28.9
CLEVELAND	360	52.9	320	47.1*	210	24.6	115	13.5	527	61.9

```
            REPUB.  RUNOFF     1972*     REPUB.  SENATOR     1972
                                  *
COUNTY        GARDNER      HOLSHOUSR    JOHNSON      BOOE        HELMS
              #      %      #      %*    #      %    #      %    #      %
-------------------------------------------------*----------------------------------------------------------------
COLUMBUS      382  78.6   104  21.4*   110  25.0    41   9.3   289  65.7
CRAVEN        501  83.5    99  16.5*   123  19.4    39   6.1   473  74.5
CUMBERLAND   1118  57.2   837  42.8*   261   9.9    50   1.9  2315  88.2
CURRITUCK      16  99.9     0    .0*     5  21.7     3  13.0    15  65.2
DARE          184  83.3    37  16.7*    67  30.7    20   9.2   131  60.1
                                  *
DAVIDSON     1903  51.3  1807  48.7*  1213  30.1   324   8.0  2498  61.9
DAVIE         736  42.5   995  57.5*   477  26.1   173   9.5  1178  64.4
DUPLIN        447  87.8    62  12.2*    31   5.4    14   2.5   524  92.1
DURHAM       1249  51.2  1189  48.8*   469  15.3   181   5.9  2424  78.9
EDGECOMBE     579  85.0   102  15.0*    67   9.4    22   3.1   625  87.5
                                  *
FORSYTH      1977  35.3  3618  64.7*  1929  29.5  1250  19.1  3358  51.4
FRANKLIN      233  78.5    64  21.5*    17   5.4    10   3.2   287  91.4
GASTON       1123  51.4  1060  48.6*   754  28.8   530  20.3  1330  50.9
GATES          14  87.5     2  12.5*    16  64.0     0    .0     9  36.0
GRAHAM        375  45.4   451  54.6*   458  68.6    75  11.2   135  20.2
                                  *
GRANVILLE      94  64.4    52  35.6*    31  14.2     6   2.7   182  83.1
GREENE        162  86.2    26  13.8*    18   7.4    18   7.4   208  85.2
GUILFORD     3634  47.1  4086  52.9*  3066  35.4  1105  12.7  4499  51.9
HALIFAX       138  72.6    52  27.4*    40  15.2     6   2.3   218  82.6
HARNETT       934  80.5   226  19.5*    47   3.9    19   1.6  1133  94.5
                                  *
HAYWOOD       353  43.6   457  56.4*   631  65.4    55   5.7   279  28.9
HENDERSON    1370  49.0  1427  51.0*  1194  42.2   275   9.7  1362  48.1
HERTFORD       62  84.9    11  15.1*    19  22.6     6   7.1    59  70.2
HOKE           38  65.5    20  34.5*     9   9.9     0    .0    82  90.1
HYDE           72  92.3     6   7.7*    23  27.4     4   4.8    57  67.9
                                  *
IREDELL      1347  60.8   869  39.2*   814  30.9   152   5.8  1667  63.3
JACKSON       395  44.3   496  55.7*   409  61.9    62   9.4   190  28.7
JOHNSTON     1292  82.8   269  17.2*   145   9.8    15   1.0  1313  89.1
JONES          58  86.6     9  13.4*    10  13.9     6   8.3    56  77.8
LEE           212  54.8   175  45.2*    43   8.0    11   2.0   484  90.0
                                  *
LENOIR        919  88.9   115  11.1*   146  12.5    40   3.4   985  84.1
LINCOLN       600  39.7   911  60.3*   472  31.6   167  11.2   857  57.3
MACON         189  46.2   220  53.8*   186  38.0    67  13.7   237  48.4
MADISON       236  48.3   253  51.7*   357  71.4    31   6.2   112  22.4
MARTIN        123  82.6    26  17.4*    20  12.0     6   3.6   141  84.4
                                  *
MCDOWELL      235  47.6   259  52.4*   150  25.7    38   6.5   396  67.8
MECKLENBRG   4711  34.9  8786  65.1*  5977  38.7  3259  21.1  6215  40.2
MITCHELL      283  21.0  1064  79.0*   835  37.2   403  17.9  1008  44.9
MONTGOMERY    579  62.4   349  37.6*   167  19.3    51   5.9   646  74.8
MOORE        1474  66.4   746  33.6*   186   7.3    46   1.8  2333  91.0
                                  *
NASH         1298  80.7   310  19.3*   160   9.0    35   2.0  1583  89.0
NEWHANOVER   1536  66.1   787  33.9*   561  20.5   237   8.7  1936  70.8
NORTHAMPTN     23  76.7     7  23.3*     4  13.8     2   6.9    23  79.3
ONSLOW        657  87.7    92  12.3*   239  25.5   112  12.0   586  62.5
ORANGE        583  44.7   721  55.3*   582  33.9   136   7.9   997  58.1
                                  *
PAMLICO       164  86.8    25  13.2*    32  27.6     6   5.2    78  67.2
```

```
        REPUB.  RUNOFF    1972*        REPUB.  SENATOR    1972
                                 *
  COUNTY    GARDNER      HOLSHOUSR    JOHNSON      BODE        HELMS
            #      %     #      %*    #      %     #      %    #      %
-------------------------------------------------*------------------------------------------------------------
PASQUOTANK   92 71.3     37 28.7*    41 28.7     30 21.0      72 50.3
PENDER      107 73.3     39 26.7*    37 21.4     13  7.5     123 71.1
PERQUIMANS   12 54.5     10 45.5*    15 50.0      4 13.3      11 36.7
PERSON      142 48.1    153 51.9*    18  4.7     10  2.6     359 92.8
PITT        903 72.5    343 27.5*   307 21.2    105  7.3    1035 71.5
                                 *
POLK        264 54.0    225 46.0*   245 50.7     53 11.0     185 38.3
RANDOLPH   2838 67.7   1354 32.3*  1066 21.9    345  7.1    3457 71.0
RICHMOND     83 50.3     82 49.7*    32 22.1     11  7.6     102 70.3
ROBESON     170 48.6    180 51.4*    68 16.9     34  8.5     300 74.6
ROCKINGHAM  629 50.7    611 49.3*   458 34.8    236 17.9     622 47.3

ROWAN      1418 41.9   1967 58.1*  1917 40.2    541 11.3    2313 48.5
RUTHERFORD  234 17.9   1076 82.1*   259 21.3     90  7.4     867 71.3
SAMPSON    1672 63.4    965 36.6*   117  4.2     18   .6    2652 95.2
SCOTLAND     59 39.1     92 60.9*    42 23.9      7  4.0     127 72.2
STANLY      734 31.5   1595 68.5*   959 39.9    368 15.3    1075 44.8

STOKES      624 43.2    821 56.8*   547 32.0    323 18.9     842 49.2
SURRY       564 45.6    673 54.4*   715 49.3    175 12.1     559 38.6
SWAIN       220 83.3     44 16.7*   288 79.6     20  5.5      54 14.9
TRANSYLVNA  154 25.6    448 74.4*   372 46.0     64  7.9     372 46.0
TYRRELL      46 93.9      3  6.1*    12 41.4      1  3.4      16 55.2
                                 *
UNION       322 54.4    270 45.6*   183 21.1    162 18.7     522 60.2
VANCE       152 51.7    142 48.3*    21  5.9      6  1.7     330 92.4
WAKE       3693 53.7   3181 46.3*  1462 17.4    295  3.5    6627 79.0
WARREN       59 57.8     43 42.2*    54 35.5     11  7.2      87 57.2
WASHINGTON   75 72.1     29 27.9*    28 20.9     12  9.0      94 70.1
                                 *
WATAUGA     213  9.4   2048 90.6*   469 30.8    170 11.2     885 58.1
WAYNE       896 68.2    417 31.8*   129  8.6     43  2.9    1332 88.6
WILKES     2598 48.7   2736 51.3*  1911 38.0    694 13.8    2425 48.2
WILSON      788 77.6    228 22.4*   120  8.8     26  1.9    1212 89.2
YADKIN      660 30.0   1540 70.0*   475 18.7    251  9.9    1813 71.4
                                 *
YANCEY      219 35.4    400 64.6*   163 32.9    102 20.6     231 46.6
-------------------------------------------------*------------------------------------------------------------
                                 *
TOTALS     68133       69916       *  45303      16122       92486
% OF VOTE   49.4        50.6       *   29.4       10.5        60.1
```

	REPUB. RUNOFF 1972*			REPUB. SENATOR 1972						
COUNTY	GARDNER		HOLSHOUSR		JOHNSON		BOVE		HELMS	
	#	%	#	%*	#	%	#	%	#	%

GEOGRAPHIC CLASS

LOWLANDS	17571	67.	8659	33.*	4127	14.	1126	4.	24489	82.
BLACK BELT	6672	76.	2073	24.*	1468	14.	464	5.	8288	81.
PIEDMONT	26769	45.	32106	55.*	22746	33.	9180	13.	36926	54.
MOUNTAIN	17121	39.	27078	61.*	16962	38.	5352	12.	22783	51.

DEMOGRAPHIC CLASS

METRO	16583	42.	23341	58.*	14294	31.	6472	14.	24902	55.
TOWN	11383	59.	7883	41.*	6849	28.	1881	8.	15610	64.
RURAL	40167	51.	38692	49.*	24160	29.	7769	9.	51974	62.

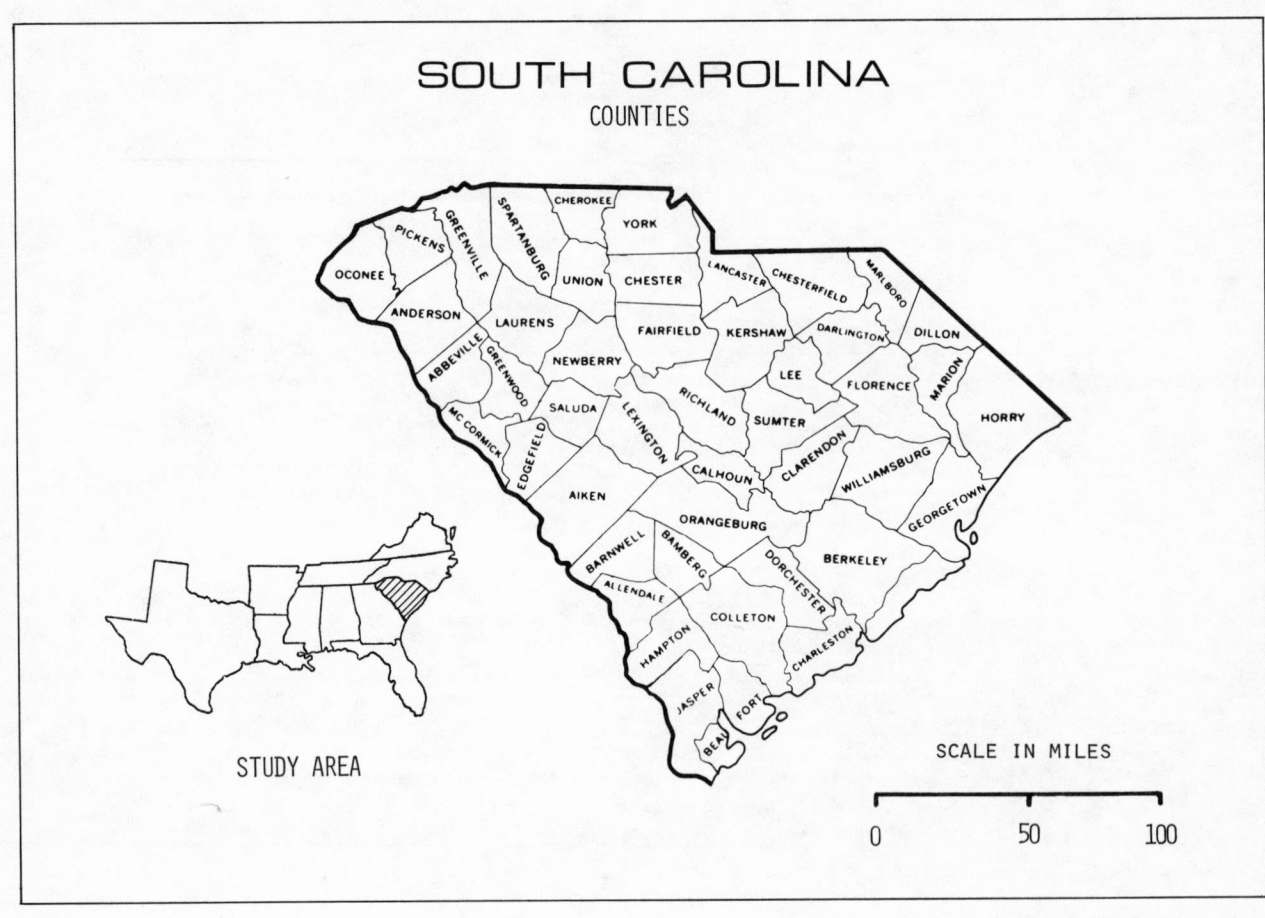

SOUTH CAROLINA
COUNTIES

OCONEE
PICKENS
GREENVILLE
SPARTANBURG
CHEROKEE
YORK
ANDERSON
UNION
CHESTER
LANCASTER
CHESTERFIELD
MARLBORO
ABBEVILLE
LAURENS
NEWBERRY
FAIRFIELD
KERSHAW
DARLINGTON
DILLON
GREENWOOD
MC CORMICK
SALUDA
LEXINGTON
RICHLAND
SUMTER
LEE
FLORENCE
MARION
HORRY
EDGEFIELD
AIKEN
CALHOUN
CLARENDON
WILLIAMSBURG
GEORGETOWN
ORANGEBURG
BERKELEY
BARNWELL
BAMBERG
DORCHESTER
ALLENDALE
COLLETON
HAMPTON
CHARLESTON
JASPER
BEAUFORT

STUDY AREA

SCALE IN MILES

0   50   100

SOUTH CAROLINA

When South Carolina required a general re-registration of voters in 1958, 536,205 people signed up. Of these, 57,978, or 10.8% of the total, were blacks. A decade later, in 1968, the state again cleansed the rolls. This time, 853,014 persons registered, of whom 200,778, which was 23.5 percent of the total, were blacks. In 1960, an estimated 57.1 percent of adult whites and 13.7 percent of adult blacks were registered; in 1970 the registered electorate included an estimated 62.3 percent of voting-age whites and 56.1 percent of voting-age blacks. Throughout the period, South Carolina had relatively lenient registration laws, although the state constitution did require that a registrant be able to read or write a section of the state constitution or to demonstrate payment of taxes on at least $300 worth of property in South Carolina.

The data in the table below summarize voting trends in recent presidential elections. Turnout figures are expressed both in the total number of ballots cast and the estimated percentage of citizens of voting age voting.

The following pages contain returns from 5 Democratic gubernatorial primaries, 6 senatorial primaries, and 3 referenda.

Gubernatorial Primaries

1. July 11, 1950: Lester L. Bates 63,143 (18.2%), James F. Byrnes 248,069 (71.6%), other 2 candidates 35,117 (10.1%). Total vote was 346,329; turnout of voting-age citizens was 30.2%.
2. June 8, 1954: Lester L. Bates 116,942 (38.7%), George Bell Timmerman, Jr., 185,541 (61.3%). Total vote was 302,483; turnout was 25.3%.
3. June 10, 1958: Ernest F. Hollings 158,159 (41.9%), William C. Johnston 86,983 (23.1%), Donald S. Russell 132,099 (35.0%). Total vote was 377,241; turnout was 30.3%.
4. June 24, 1958: Ernest F. Hollings 190,693 (56.8%), Donald S. Russell 145,162 (43.2%). Total vote was 335,855; turnout was 27.0%.
5. June 12, 1962: Donald S. Russell 199,619 (60.8%), Burnet R. Maybank, Jr., 103,015 (31.4%), other 3 candidates 25,661 (7.8%). Total vote was 328,295; turnout was 25.1%.
* (June 14, 1966: Robert E. McNair unopposed.)
* (June 9, 1970: John C. West unopposed.)

Senatorial Primaries

1. July 11, 1950: Olin D. Johnston 186,180 (54.0%), J. Strom Thurmond 158,904 (46.0%). Total vote was 345,084.
* (June 8, 1954: Burnet R. Maybank unopposed.)
* (June 12, 1956: Olin D. Johnston and J. Strom Thurmond both unopposed.)
* (June 14, 1960: J. Strom Thurmond won 89.5% against 1 opponent. Total vote was 305,931.)
2. June 12, 1962: Ernest F. Hollings 110,023 (34.3%), Olin D. Johnston 210,918 (65.7%). Total vote was 320,941.
3. June 14, 1966: John Bolt Culbertson 131,870 (44.1%), Bradley Morrah 167,401 (55.9%). Total vote was 299,271.
4. June 14, 1966: Ernest F. Hollings 196,405 (60.8%), Donald S. Russell 126,595 (39.2%).

Total vote was 323,000.
5. June 11, 1968: Ernest F. Hollings 308,016
   (78.4%), John Bolt Culbertson 84,913
   (21.6%). Total vote was 392,929.
6. August 29, 1972: Eugene N. Zeigler
   201,170 (58.7%), John Bolt Culbertson
   141,757 (41.3%). Total vote was 342,927.

Special Elections

1. November 4, 1952: Private school
   amendment relieving the state of the
   constitutional requirement to maintain
   a public school system and to permit the
   substitution of a system of private
   schools as a means to avoid desegregation.
   For 187,349 (67.1%), Against 91,823
   (32.9%). Total vote was 279,172.
2. November 8, 1966: Constitutional
   amendment "to permit women to serve on
   juries." For 175,790 (60.4%), Against
   115,178 (39.6%). Total vote was 290,968.
3. November 8, 1966: Constitutional
   amendment making possible "the con-
   sumption of alcoholic liquors and
   beverages on the premises where sold" on
   a local option basis. For 117,035
   (38.1%), Against 189,923 (61.9%). Total
   vote was 306,958.

RETURNS FROM PRESIDENTIAL ELECTIONS

Year	Turnout		Partisan Vote*
1948	142,571	(12.8%) [+]	Dixiecrat 72.1%, Democrat 24.1%, Republican 3.8%
1952	341,087	(29.1%)	Democrat 50.7%, Republican 49.3%
1956	300,583	(24.7%)	Democrat 45.4%, Republican 25.2%, Independent 29.4%
1960	386,688	(30.5%)	Democrat 51.2%, Republican 48.8%
1964	524,779	(39.0%)	Republican 58.9%, Democrat 41.1%
1968	666,978	(46.7%)	Republican 38.1%, American Independent 32.3%, Democrat 29.6%
1972	673,960	(40.0%)	Republican 70.8%, Democrat 27.7%

*Totals do not necessarily equal 100%, since minor party percentages are excluded.

[+]Percentage of citizens of voting age who voted is calculated on the basis of a straight-line interpolation of citizen population between census years.

	DEMOC. SENATOR 1950*				DEMOC. GOVERNOR 1950					
COUNTY	JOHNSTON		THURMOND		BATES		BYRNES		OTHER	
	#	%	#	%*	#	%	#	%	#	%
ABBEVILLE	3309	66.9	1640	33.1*	373	7.5	4112	83.0	470	9.5
AIKEN	3892	38.2	6300	61.8*	1994	19.6	7734	76.0	442	4.3
ALLENDALE	615	33.1	1241	66.9*	169	9.0	1561	83.6	138	7.4
ANDERSON	11694	75.9	3711	24.1*	1947	12.6	12637	81.7	891	5.8
BAMBERG	883	34.9	1645	65.1*	282	11.1	2178	85.4	91	3.6
BARNWELL	1851	61.6	1153	38.4*	466	15.4	2381	78.9	170	5.6
BEAUFORT	1605	53.9	1373	46.1*	766	26.8	1831	64.1	259	9.1
BERKELEY	1956	41.8	2719	58.2*	2073	45.0	2389	51.9	140	3.0
CALHOUN	800	56.5	617	43.5*	159	11.1	1206	84.5	62	4.3
CHARLESTON	11798	43.6	15238	56.4*	6610	24.5	17614	65.4	2715	10.1
CHEROKEE	5862	63.6	3350	36.4*	1761	19.0	6399	69.0	1120	12.1
CHESTER	4179	63.6	2387	36.4*	736	11.2	5165	78.4	688	10.4
CHSTRFILD	3937	53.9	3367	46.1*	1199	16.3	5519	74.9	647	8.8
CLARENDON	1535	37.4	2574	62.6*	717	17.4	3128	76.0	273	6.6
COLLETON	1395	34.0	2708	66.0*	914	22.2	2732	66.5	462	11.2
DARLINTON	6533	61.5	4097	38.5*	2325	22.0	7355	69.5	897	8.5
DILLON	2358	56.0	1853	44.0*	419	10.1	2739	66.2	982	23.7
DORCHSTR	1252	33.4	2492	66.6*	560	15.1	2975	80.2	174	4.7
EDGEFIELD	747	22.5	2580	77.5*	402	12.0	2689	80.5	251	7.5
FAIRFIELD	2164	65.1	1159	34.9*	800	23.8	2140	63.8	415	12.4
FLORENCE	5542	47.8	6058	52.2*	2096	18.1	8227	71.0	1264	10.9
GEORGTOWN	960	34.3	1837	65.7*	430	15.5	1833	65.9	518	18.6
GREENVILL	15099	52.5	13648	47.5*	3947	13.5	22920	78.1	2469	8.4
GREENWOOD	4014	52.5	3633	47.5*	729	9.5	6222	80.7	755	9.8
HAMPTON	1263	39.8	1910	60.2*	456	14.4	2496	78.9	213	6.7
HORRY	3531	43.8	4534	56.2*	964	11.8	6050	74.0	1159	14.2
JASPER	346	27.2	924	72.8*	294	23.5	823	65.8	133	10.6
KERSHAW	3030	58.9	2112	41.1*	1080	21.0	3713	72.3	341	6.6
LANCASTER	6659	69.0	2985	31.0*	1295	13.3	7146	73.6	1273	13.1
LAURENS	3360	48.4	3585	51.6*	465	6.7	5405	77.7	1084	15.6
LEE	1932	49.0	2008	51.0*	560	14.6	2954	77.0	324	8.4
LEXINGTON	5987	65.0	3226	35.0*	2040	22.1	6298	68.1	904	9.8
MARION	2090	60.1	1389	39.9*	615	17.7	2527	72.9	325	9.4
MARLBORO	2363	53.4	2063	46.6*	580	13.7	2861	67.5	797	18.8
MCCORMICK	270	29.1	657	70.9*	70	7.5	800	85.8	62	6.7
NEWBERRY	4142	53.2	3643	46.8*	756	9.0	3384	43.1	3719	47.3
OCONEE	2582	59.1	1790	40.9*	390	8.9	3570	81.2	439	10.0
ORANGBURG	3449	47.5	3810	52.5*	1322	18.1	5661	77.4	332	4.5
PICKENS	4181	57.4	3100	42.6*	594	8.1	6102	82.9	663	9.0
RICHLAND	15546	62.5	9309	37.5*	7424	29.6	15255	60.9	2363	9.4
SALNDA	1781	44.5	2223	55.5*	487	12.1	2940	73.0	603	15.0
SPARTNBRG	16407	65.8	8544	34.2*	7669	30.5	15998	63.6	1477	5.9
SUMTER	1923	35.6	3479	64.4*	1038	19.0	4133	75.8	285	5.2
UNION	3883	61.9	2390	38.1*	987	15.6	4146	65.7	1175	18.6
WMSBURG	1617	32.8	3314	67.2*	437	8.9	4058	82.2	441	8.9

COUNTY	DEMOC. SENATOR 1950* JOHNSTON #	%	THURMOND #	%*	DEMOC. GOVERNOR 1950 BATES #	%	BYRNES #	%	OTHER #	%
YORK	5858	56.4	4529	43.6*	1746	16.6	8063	76.6	712	6.8
				*						
TOTALS	186180		158904	*	63143		248069		35117	
% OF VOTE	54.0		46.0	*	18.2		71.6		10.1	
				*						
GEOGRAPHIC CLASS				*						
				*						
LOWLANDS	15015	49.	15433	51.*	5764	19.	21913	72.	2764	9.
BLACK BELT	78397	49.	81333	51.*	33034	21.	111593	70.	14856	9.
PIEDMONT	92768	60.	62138	40.*	24345	16.	114563	73.	17497	11.
				*						
DEMOGRAPHIC CLASS				*						
				*						
METRO	42443	53.	38195	47.*	17981	22.	55789	69.	7547	9.
TOWN	41424	61.	26321	39.*	14496	21.	49058	72.	4629	7.
RURAL	102313	52.	94388	48.*	30666	16.	143222	73.	22941	12.

SOUTH CAROLINA

COUNTY	DEMOC. GOVERNOR 1954* BATES #	%	TIMMERMN #	%*	DEMOC. GOVERNOR 1958 HOLLINGS #	%	JOHNSTON #	%	RUSSELL #	%
ABBEVILLE	1046	39.2	1623	60.8*	1499	33.5	2005	44.7	977	21.8
AIKEN	3006	31.3	6593	68.7*	5057	43.1	2649	22.6	4038	34.4
ALLENDALE	504	24.1	1588	75.9*	1090	51.2	299	14.1	738	34.7
ANDERSON	4366	43.6	5644	56.4*	4485	27.2	8476	51.5	3507	21.3
BAMBERG	939	36.1	1659	63.9*	1853	60.4	305	9.9	911	29.7
BARNWELL	357	12.9	2412	87.1*	2374	71.2	475	14.3	483	14.5
BEAUFORT	1263	48.9	1321	51.1*	1622	53.3	675	22.2	747	24.5
BERKELEY	2863	80.5	692	19.5*	2831	54.1	1706	32.6	696	13.3
CALHOUN	165	16.2	855	83.8*	512	40.3	111	8.7	647	50.9
CHARLESTON	9447	52.1	8693	47.9*	19511	68.4	4348	15.3	4649	16.3
CHEROKEE	4498	50.1	4478	49.9*	3210	36.1	2145	24.1	3541	39.8
CHESTER	1973	29.1	4811	70.9*	1617	29.7	1822	33.5	2001	36.8
CHSTRFILD	3194	33.8	6263	66.2*	2596	33.0	2967	37.7	2313	29.4
CLARENDON	1137	28.9	2802	71.1*	1576	50.3	497	15.9	1062	33.9
COLLETON	2574	54.8	2123	45.2*	3092	54.9	1027	18.2	1517	26.9
DARLINTON	4821	38.8	7599	61.2*	4874	49.0	1953	19.6	3114	31.3
DILLON	1387	32.2	2921	67.8*	2298	47.4	1045	21.5	1510	31.1
DORCHSTR	763	30.7	1725	69.3*	2642	59.5	742	16.7	1054	23.7

```
          DEMOC.  GOVERNOR  1954*        DEMOC.  GOVERNOR  1958
                                *
COUNTY    BATES          TIMMERMN      HOLLINGS    JOHNSTON    RUSSELL
          #       %      #       %*    #       %   #      %    #       %
---------------------------------*------------------------------------------------------
EDGEFIELD  494  19.5   2043  80.5*   1126  39.5    656  23.0  1068  37.5
FAIRFIELD  980  28.8   2425  71.2*   1483  37.3    893  22.4  1605  40.3
FLORENCE  4510  40.5   6639  59.5*   5951  46.0   2797  21.6  4195  32.4
GEORGTOWN 1333  49.8   1346  50.2*   1952  49.8    743  18.9  1227  31.3
                                *
GREENVILL 7080  36.6  12267  63.4*  11698  39.0   4522  15.1 13745  45.9
GREENWOOD 1917  35.9   3429  64.1*   2507  30.0   2526  30.2  3337  39.9
HAMPTON    917  31.1   2036  68.9*   1425  44.1    448  15.2  1072  36.4
HORRY     2814  32.8   5770  67.2*   4976  44.2   2495  22.2  3783  33.6
                                *
JASPER     752  38.7   1189  61.3*    722  38.8    359  19.3   779  41.9
KERSHAW   1712  26.6   4735  73.4*   4200  50.0   1443  17.2  2764  32.9
LANCASTER 2793  31.9   5960  68.1*   4505  41.4   2969  27.3  3406  31.3
LAURENS   2024  30.2   4682  69.8*   3203  39.6   2083  25.8  2793  34.6
                                *
LEE       1331  32.9   2718  67.1*   2230  53.3    770  18.4  1181  28.2
LEXINGTON 1407  17.2   6797  82.8*   4759  46.1   2488  24.1  3082  29.8
MARION    1354  34.7   2553  65.3*   1982  46.8   1000  23.6  1250  29.5
MARLBORO  1332  32.4   2774  67.6*   2110  38.8   1629  29.9  1701  31.3
                                *
MCCORMICK  267  21.5    972  78.5*    462  38.3    385  31.9   360  29.8
NEWBERRY  1675  24.9   5063  75.1*   2954  48.1   1537  25.0  1652  26.9
OCONEE    2041  48.1   2198  51.9*   1521  28.5   2010  37.6  1814  33.9
ORANGBURG 1884  36.3   3302  63.7*   3734  43.0   1203  13.9  3743  43.1
                                *
PICKENS   2158  38.5   3451  61.5*   2478  34.2   1509  20.8  3262  45.0
RICHLAND  8263  39.0  12923  61.0*   8065  30.2   5338  20.0 13323  49.9
SALNDA     789  25.3   2330  74.7*   1440  41.1    886  25.3  1179  33.6
SPARTNBRG 10308 54.2   8702  45.8*   7175  26.5   6486  23.9 13447  49.6
                                *
SUMTER    1729  35.9   3093  64.1*   3379  48.4    883  12.7  2716  38.9
UNION     3741  49.5   3817  50.5*   2458  28.7   2109  24.6  3989  46.6
WMSBURG   2127  40.3   3150  59.7*   3005  59.3    591  11.7  1469  29.0
YORK      4907  47.7   5375  52.3*   3920  33.9   2978  25.8  4652  40.3
                                *
---------------------------------*------------------------------------------------------
                                *
TOTALS   116942       185541     * 158159        86983       132099
% OF VOTE   38.7         61.3     *   41.9          23.1         35.0
```

```
          DEMOC.  GOVERNOR   1954*         DEMOC.  GOVERNOR  1958
                                     *
 COUNTY      BATES        TIMMERMN     HOLLINGS      JOHNSTON     RUSSELL
           #      %      #      %*    #       %     #       %    #       %
----------------------------------------*--------------------------------------------------------------
GEOGRAPHIC CLASS                        *
                                        *
LOWLANDS    8490 29.    20481 71.*   16414 45.    8307 23.    11650 32.
BLACK BELT 55915 38.    89778 62.*   86096 49.   33468 19.    56835 32.
PIEDMONT   52537 41.    75282 59.*   55649 34.   45208 27.    63614 39.
                                        *
                                        *
DEMOGRAPHIC CLASS                       *
                                        *
METRO      24790 42.    33883 58.*   39274 46.   14208 17.    31717 37.
TOWN       25820 47.    29453 53.*   24910 33.   21620 29.    28517 38.
RURAL      66332 35.   122205 65.*   93975 43.   51155 24.    71865 33.
```

SOUTH CAROLINA

```
          DEMOC.   RUNOFF     1958*       DEMOC.  GOVERNOR   1962
                                 *
 COUNTY     HOLLINGS     RUSSELL      RUSSELL      MAYBANK      OTHER
           #      %     #      %*    #      %     #      %     #      %
----------------------------------*------------------------------------------------------------------
ABBEVILLE   2766 68.5   1270 31.5*   1604 45.5   1729 49.1    191  5.4
AIKEN       6080 55.8   4820 44.2*   8350 66.4   3663 29.1    555  4.4
ALLENDALE   1238 57.6    913 42.4*   1302 60.2    723 33.4    137  6.3
ANDERSON    9716 66.6   4865 33.4*   8174 56.1   5677 38.9    726  5.0
                                 *
BAMBERG     2063 67.6    988 32.4*   1796 59.5   1065 35.3    158  5.2
BARNWELL    3590 87.7    504 12.3*   2218 54.8   1654 40.9    172  4.3
BEAUFORT    1723 70.4    726 29.6*   2330 68.2    884 25.9    201  5.9
BERKELEY    2622 74.1    917 25.9*   2778 61.2   1526 33.6    237  5.2
                                 *
CALHOUN      635 50.6    619 49.4*    655 68.0    219 22.7     89  9.2
CHARLESTON 21067 79.0   5585 21.0*  14016 59.7   7577 32.3   1880  8.0
CHEROKEE    3092 47.2   3454 52.8*   5153 54.1   3800 39.9    579  6.1
CHESTER     2664 54.0   2269 46.0*   4622 67.1   1965 28.5    297  4.3
                                 *
CHSTRFILD   4278 53.1   3774 46.9*   2914 46.8   3045 48.9    263  4.2
CLARENDON   1493 59.1   1033 40.9*   2029 63.9    887 27.9    261  8.2
COLLETON    2591 68.3   1201 31.7*   3097 60.9   1654 32.5    334  6.6
DARLINTON   4923 57.6   3624 42.4*   4056 58.2   2010 28.9    898 12.9
                                 *
DILLON      2518 62.1   1536 37.9*   1820 36.0    807 16.0   2430 48.1
DORCHSTR    2843 72.0   1106 28.0*   2571 59.3   1313 30.3    452 10.4
EDGEFIELD   1218 52.7   1093 47.3*   1490 74.9    435 21.9     65  3.3
FAIRFIELD   2041 52.8   1821 47.2*   1854 69.6    591 22.2    218  8.2
                                 *
FLORENCE    7309 59.1   5066 40.9*   7753 61.1   3825 30.1   1114  8.8
GEORGTOWN   2226 56.2   1732 43.8*   3527 65.0   1635 30.1    267  4.9
GREENVILL  13281 47.8  14515 52.2*  13156 62.3   6798 32.2   1180  5.6
```

```
                DEMOC.  RUNOFF    1958*      DEMOC.  GOVERNOR   1962
                                     *
COUNTY       HOLLINGS      RUSSELL       RUSSELL       MAYBANK       OTHER
               #     %      #     %*      #     %       #     %       #     %
-------------------------------------*-------------------------------------------------
GREENWOOD    3796  53.0   3366  47.0*   3985  64.4   1941  31.4    265   4.3
HAMPTON      1114  60.3    732  39.7*   1721  57.4   1115  37.2    163   5.4
HORRY        5710  58.4   4065  41.6*   5168  55.2   2609  27.9   1583  16.9
JASPER        819  59.3    561  40.7*    894  49.9    795  44.4    103   5.7
                                     *
KERSHAW      4689  61.4   2954  38.6*   3144  51.8   2236  36.8    688  11.3
LANCASTER    4292  55.2   3479  44.8*   5559  57.4   3533  36.5    592   6.1
LAURENS      4723  60.1   3137  39.9*   3441  54.2   2486  39.2    419   6.6
LEE          1580  49.8   1592  50.2*   2064  51.5   1236  30.9    706  17.6
                                     *
LEXINGTON    6003  63.4   3465  36.6*   4765  57.4   2623  31.6    907  10.9
MARION       1990  62.3   1204  37.7*   2042  62.2    837  25.5    406  12.4
MARLBORO     1541  51.3   1464  48.7*   2374  54.5   1444  33.2    535  12.3
MCCORMICK     505  55.9    398  44.1*    743  53.9    578  41.9     57   4.1
                                     *
NEWBERRY     3661  63.5   2101  36.5*   2979  50.7   2397  40.8    505   8.6
OCONEE       2205  54.5   1839  45.5*   2912  52.6   2385  43.1    236   4.3
ORANGBURG    4134  54.4   3472  45.6*   4359  67.2   1470  22.7    653  10.1
PICKENS      2444  45.4   2941  54.6*   3860  57.1   2541  37.6    363   5.4
                                     *
RICHLAND    11053  41.1  15826  58.9*  18286  73.2   4824  19.3   1856   7.4
SALNDA       1745  56.3   1354  43.7*   1992  56.6   1321  37.5    208   5.9
SPARTNBRG   11534  43.6  14903  56.4*  14868  68.5   5580  25.7   1242   5.7
SUMTER       3487  54.5   2906  45.5*   3518  71.2   1121  22.7    304   6.2
                                     *
UNION        4029  49.0   4201  51.0*   4382  64.2   2105  30.8    342   5.0
WMSBURG      2932  66.4   1482  33.6*   3067  60.7   1540  30.5    444   8.8
YORK         4730  52.4   4289  47.6*   6231  66.1   2816  29.9    380   4.0
-------------------------------------*-------------------------------------------------
                                     *
TOTALS     190693        145162     * 199619       103015        25661
% OF VOTE     56.8          43.2    *   60.8          31.4          7.8
                                     *
                                     *
GEOGRAPHIC CLASS                     *
                                     *
LOWLANDS    19516  60.   13076  40.*  20613  61.    9779  29.    3246  10.
BLACK BELT  94885  60.   62598  40.*  97796  62.   45082  29.   14924   9.
PIEDMONT    76292  52.   69488  48.*  81210  59.   48154  35.    7491   5.
                                     *
                                     *
DEMOGRAPHIC CLASS                    *
                                     *
METRO       45401  56.   35926  44.*  45458  65.   19199  28.    4916   7.
TOWN        36776  53.   32029  47.*  40544  64.   19019  30.    3766   6.
RURAL      108516  58.   77207  42.* 113617  58.   64797  33.   16979   9.
```

| | DEMOC. SENATOR 1962* | | | | DEMOC. SENATOR 1966 | | | |
| | HOLLINGS | | JOHNSTON | | CULBERTSN | | MORRAH | |
COUNTY	#	%	#	%*	#	%	#	%
ABBEVILLE	884	25.1	2641	74.9*	1188	32.0	2527	68.0
AIKEN	4459	36.1	7900	63.9*	3644	55.9	2873	44.1
ALLENDALE	957	45.8	1131	54.2*	899	40.7	1309	59.3
ANDERSON	3686	25.6	10690	74.4*	2987	32.7	6138	67.3
BAMBERG	1093	37.1	1856	62.9*	1028	35.5	1865	64.5
BARNWELL	1719	42.9	2288	57.1*	1373	34.3	2631	65.7
BEAUFORT	1045	30.3	2406	69.7*	1990	54.9	1638	45.1
BERKELEY	1174	25.7	3392	74.3*	2405	55.1	1962	44.9
CALHOUN	478	51.8	444	48.2*	796	50.7	773	49.3
CHARLESTON	9727	42.0	13458	58.0*	9132	48.7	9608	51.3
CHEROKEE	3199	32.9	6524	67.1*	3858	54.8	3183	45.2
CHESTER	1652	23.9	5255	76.1*	2903	56.8	2207	43.2
CHSTRFILD	1746	27.5	4598	72.5*	3050	48.4	3257	51.6
CLARENDON	1194	35.7	2151	64.3*	2925	52.8	2614	47.2
COLLETON	1607	32.7	3305	67.3*	2545	45.6	3031	54.4
DARLINTON	2706	39.9	4074	60.1*	2911	47.5	3214	52.5
DILLON	1586	31.2	3490	68.8*	2485	41.9	3448	58.1
DORCHSTR	1405	31.2	3097	68.8*	3608	54.9	2959	45.1
EDGEFIELD	739	37.8	1216	62.2*	948	46.6	1086	53.4
FAIRFIELD	674	26.7	1847	73.3*	1660	51.0	1595	49.0
FLORENCE	4541	35.8	8138	64.2*	5338	53.0	4737	47.0
GEORGTOWN	2172	39.5	3322	60.5*	2146	45.8	2540	54.2
GREENVILL	8529	44.0	10848	56.0*	2768	18.5	12184	81.5
GREENWOOD	2138	35.4	3894	64.6*	1943	28.6	4848	71.4
HAMPTON	1125	37.2	1901	62.8*	1424	49.8	1434	50.2
HORRY	3324	35.8	5971	64.2*	2752	43.6	3561	56.4
JASPER	563	30.4	1287	69.6*	1016	49.9	1020	50.1
KERSHAW	1986	34.9	3704	65.1*	2464	44.7	3046	55.3
LANCASTER	2663	28.1	6825	71.9*	5371	55.1	4380	44.9
LAURENS	1851	30.7	4175	69.3*	1413	23.9	4492	76.1
LEE	1541	37.9	2522	62.1*	1414	45.6	1685	54.4
LEXINGTON	2637	33.6	5210	66.4*	3311	37.3	5573	62.7
MARION	1143	34.8	2140	65.2*	2340	43.1	3092	56.9
MARLBORO	1310	29.7	3095	70.3*	1748	43.7	2254	56.3
MCCORMICK	340	26.0	969	74.0*	524	33.9	1021	66.1
NEWBERRY	1832	31.8	3927	68.2*	1885	40.8	2739	59.2
OCONEE	1197	22.1	4210	77.9*	1608	36.3	2819	63.7
ORANGBURG	2650	43.0	3507	57.0*	3720	51.2	3547	48.8
PICKENS	2232	34.9	4163	65.1*	953	20.9	3612	79.1
RICHLAND	7798	33.6	15413	66.4*	9868	42.7	13228	57.3
SALNDA	1001	28.8	2474	71.2*	1311	48.3	1404	51.7
SPARTNBRG	6669	31.1	14758	68.9*	6512	37.7	10757	62.3
SUMTER	1815	39.7	2756	60.3*	4675	53.3	4104	46.7
UNION	1995	28.8	4925	71.2*	3042	49.3	3130	50.7
WMSBURG	1815	36.3	3191	63.7*	4062	50.9	3916	49.1

```
            DEMOC.  SENATOR   1962* DEMOC.  SENATOR   1966
                                   *
   COUNTY     HOLLINGS    JOHNSTON *  CULBERTSN   MORRAH
              #      %    #      %*   #      %    #      %
---------------------------------------*---------------------------------------------------------------
   YORK       3426 37.0  5830 63.0*  5927 57.6  4360 42.4
---------------------------------------*---------------------------------------------------------------
                                   *
   TOTALS    110023     210918     * 131870     167401
   % OF VOTE   34.3        65.7    *   44.1        55.9
                                   *
                                   *
   GEOGRAPHIC CLASS                *
                                   *
   LOWLANDS   11465 35.  21487 65.* 11697 46.   13645 54.
   BLACK BELT 55510 36.  98949 64.* 76357 48.   83926 52.
   PIEDMONT   43048 32.  90482 68.* 43816 39.   69830 61.
                                   *
                                   *
   DEMOGRAPHIC CLASS               *
                                   *
   METRO      26054 40.  39719 60.* 21768 38.   35020 62.
   TOWN       20137 32.  42172 68.* 25439 46.   30096 54.
   RURAL      63832 33. 129027 67.* 84663 45.  102285 55.
```

SOUTH CAROLINA

```
            DEMOC.  SENATOR   1966* DEMOC.  SENATOR   1968
                                   *
   COUNTY     HOLLINGS    RUSSELL  *  HOLLINGS    CULBERTSON
              #      %    #      %*   #      %    #      %
-------------------------------------*-------------------------------------------------------------------
   ABBEVILLE  1671 43.9  2139 56.1*  3011 79.8   760 20.2
   AIKEN      3946 57.1  2964 42.9*  7782 83.4  1548 16.6
   ALLENDALE  1665 66.2   852 33.8*  1397 81.6   315 18.4
   ANDERSON   4172 44.7  5165 55.3*  9410 75.1  3115 24.9
                                   *
   BAMBERG    2005 63.1  1171 36.9*  2536 76.5   780 23.5
   BARNWELL   2847 67.4  1374 32.6*  3451 86.4   544 13.6
   BEAUFORT   2447 60.7  1581 39.3*  3971 69.5  1740 30.5
   BERKELEY   3524 76.7  1073 23.3*  6121 71.8  2410 28.2
                                   *
   CALHOUN    1284 79.2   338 20.8*   714 69.4   315 30.6
   CHARLESTON 15906 74.5 5458 25.5* 26609 77.0  7963 23.0
   CHEROKEE   4159 56.8  3157 43.2*  4349 72.7  1633 27.3
   CHESTER    2733 51.1  2615 48.9*  4570 82.8   951 17.2
                                   *
   CHSTRFILD  3627 53.6  3146 46.4*  6279 83.7  1220 16.3
   CLARENDON  4036 69.1  1803 30.9*  5005 68.3  2318 31.7
   COLLETON   3714 63.7  2118 36.3*  5977 76.5  1834 23.5
   DARLINTON  4202 64.7  2292 35.3*  6568 81.4  1499 18.6
                                   *
   DILLON     4153 66.4  2100 33.6*  5214 83.9   997 16.1
   DORCHSTR   4768 68.4  2200 31.6*  5907 66.8  2938 33.2
```

| | DEMOC. SENATOR 1966* | | | | DEMOC. SENATOR 1968 | | | |
| | HOLLINGS | | RUSSELL | | HOLLINGS | | CULBERTSON | |
COUNTY	#	%	#	%*	#	%	#	%
EDGEFIELD	1483	66.0	763	34.0*	2293	79.7	584	20.3
FAIRFIELD	1929	55.9	1520	44.1*	3608	70.6	1504	29.4
FLORENCE	5850	55.4	4709	44.6*	10958	87.6	1555	12.4
GEORGTOWN	2322	47.1	2608	52.9*	4725	67.1	2312	32.9
GREENVILL	10058	63.7	5739	36.3*	15536	81.6	3509	18.4
GREENWOOD	4576	65.0	2467	35.0*	5354	81.3	1231	18.7
HAMPTON	1738	59.2	1199	40.8*	4081	86.5	637	13.5
HORRY	4506	68.2	2102	31.8*	12076	85.8	1993	14.2
JASPER	1010	46.9	1145	53.1*	1666	67.2	813	32.8
KERSHAW	4069	68.6	1864	31.4*	4323	82.2	933	17.8
LANCASTER	6406	63.9	3616	36.1*	10330	85.6	1731	14.4
LAURENS	3914	64.2	2185	35.8*	5863	83.1	1190	16.9
LEE	2328	66.8	1155	33.2*	3453	71.3	1392	28.7
LEXINGTON	6462	68.9	2921	31.1*	8598	85.4	1467	14.6
MARION	3064	53.4	2675	46.6*	2752	71.7	1084	28.3
MARLBORO	2501	57.4	1859	42.6*	4437	83.1	901	16.9
MCCORMICK	752	46.9	850	53.1*	1851	83.4	368	16.6
NEWBERRY	3629	73.4	1312	26.6*	5762	79.0	1533	21.0
OCONEE	1972	43.7	2541	56.3*	5581	73.3	2029	26.7
ORANGBURG	5848	78.2	1627	21.8*	9703	70.3	4100	29.7
PICKENS	2739	57.6	2017	42.4*	5903	80.0	1472	20.0
RICHLAND	15062	55.2	12214	44.8*	15079	71.0	6173	29.0
SALNDA	1819	63.9	1027	36.1*	2835	74.5	971	25.5
SPARTNBRG	11791	54.5	9862	45.5*	20049	82.5	4240	17.5
SUMTER	6040	65.2	3226	34.8*	8811	72.6	3323	27.4
UNION	3437	54.6	2855	45.4*	7311	85.0	1291	15.0
WMSBURG	4060	47.3	4532	52.7*	7536	86.6	1165	13.4
YORK	6181	58.1	4459	41.9*	8671	77.4	2532	22.6
TOTALS	196405		126595	*	308016		84913	
% OF VOTE		60.8		39.2 *		78.4		21.6

```
             DEMOC.  SENATOR   1966* DEMOC.  SENATOR    1968
                                    *
  COUNTY     HOLLINGS    RUSSELL  *  HOLLINGS    CULBERTSON
             #      %    #     %* #      %    #       %
-------------------------------------*-------------------------------------------------
GEOGRAPHIC CLASS                    *
                                    *
LOWLANDS    17361 64.    9568 36.* 32427 83.    6748 17.
BLACK BELT 108893 62.   65340 38.* 159345 76.  49708 24.
PIEDMONT    70151 58.   51687 42.* 116244 80.  28457 20.
                                    *
                                    *
DEMOGRAPHIC CLASS                   *
                                    *
METRO       41026 64.   23411 36.* 57224 76.   17645 24.
TOWN        34034 55.   27421 45.* 57899 80.   14765 20.
RURAL      121345 62.   75763 38.* 192893 79.  52503 21.
```

SOUTH CAROLINA

```
             DEMOC.  SENATOR   1972* SPECL.  REFERENDUM 1952
                                    *
  COUNTY     CULBERTSN   ZEIGLER  *  FOR         AGAINST
             #      %    #     %* #      %    #       %
-------------------------------------*-------------------------------------------------
ABBEVILLE   1980 50.3   1960 49.7* 1002 40.4   1479 59.6
AIKEN       2935 37.6   4865 62.4* 5693 79.9   1435 20.1
ALLENDALE   1127 39.6   1719 60.4*  991 91.0     98  9.0
ANDERSON    7357 47.4   8176 52.6* 4067 32.9   8310 67.1
                                    *
BAMBERG     1132 33.8   2213 66.2* 1524 90.2    166  9.8
BARNWELL    1410 39.0   2202 61.0* 1023 75.3    335 24.7
BEAUFORT    1763 48.1   1900 51.9* 1549 71.0    632 29.0
BERKELEY    1130 35.1   2093 64.9* 2513 73.9    888 26.1
                                    *
CALHOUN      855 39.8   1291 60.2* 1287 95.6     59  4.4
CHARLESTON  5554 33.6  10967 66.4* 13549 67.4  6553 32.6
CHEROKEE    3999 52.6   3610 47.4* 1732 42.9   2301 57.1
CHESTER     2993 54.1   2535 45.9* 4180 80.6   1006 19.4
                                    *
CHSTRFILD   2055 32.6   4254 67.4* 3646 74.7   1238 25.3
CLARENDON   3111 54.3   2620 45.7* 2426 87.3    352 12.7
COLLETON    3616 45.7   4304 54.3* 3239 77.2    955 22.8
DARLINTON   4080 30.9   9111 69.1* 5576 67.3   2706 32.7
                                    *
DILLON      1127 27.0   3049 73.0* 2203 83.9    423 16.1
DORCHSTR    4063 47.2   4550 52.8* 2383 86.8    361 13.2
EDGEFIELD   1251 46.6   1435 53.4* 1920 92.9    146  7.1
FAIRFIELD   1986 53.6   1722 46.4* 2329 82.5    495 17.5
                                    *
FLORENCE    3208 23.5  10419 76.5* 7416 79.2   1949 20.8
GEORGTOWN   2770 32.7   5710 67.3* 2609 79.2    685 20.8
GREENVILL   4914 39.5   7517 60.5* 17124 51.8  15953 48.2
```

```
              DEMOC.  SENATOR    1972* SPECL.  REFERENDUM 1952
                                      *
 COUNTY        CULBERTSN   ZEIGLER   * FOR         AGAINST
               #      %    #      %  * #      %    #      %
-------------------------------------*-------------------------------------------------------
GREENWOOD      1022 33.1  2069 66.9* 3679 61.8  2277 38.2
HAMPTON        1810 48.7  1910 51.3* 2059 90.9   205  9.1
HORRY          5070 38.4  8146 61.6* 4602 77.9  1304 22.1
JASPER         1048 49.7  1060 50.3*  939 80.2   232 19.8
                                      *
KERSHAW        2295 45.7  2722 54.3* 3159 79.6   809 20.4
LANCASTER      5787 51.5  5454 48.5* 5113 80.4  1250 19.6
LAURENS        1730 35.1  3196 64.9* 4063 73.0  1503 27.0
LEE            1951 43.8  2507 56.2* 2056 86.6   317 13.4
                                      *
LEXINGTON      2409 39.6  3676 60.4* 5874 83.2  1187 16.8
MARION         1500 26.8  4087 73.2* 2821 82.3   606 17.7
MARLBORO       1853 34.6  3497 65.4* 1995 88.5   259 11.5
MCCORMICK      1352 53.9  1158 46.1*  800 75.4   261 24.6
                                      *
NEWBERRY       2716 45.2  3287 54.8* 4857 83.7   945 16.3
OCONEE         3271 50.8  3165 49.2* 2075 52.1  1910 47.9
ORANGBURG      4499 35.0  8362 65.0* 5506 84.3  1024 15.7
PICKENS        3729 40.1  5563 59.9* 2444 48.1  2636 51.9
                                      *
RICHLAND       9515 41.8 13246 58.2*13638 74.5  4677 25.5
SALNDA          751 40.6  1098 59.4* 2465 87.1   364 12.9
SPARTNBRG      9693 48.1 10458 51.9*13282 49.7 13463 50.3
SUMTER         3972 41.7  5542 58.3* 4984 81.1  1164 18.9
                                      *
UNION          3340 54.9  2749 45.1* 2866 56.7  2186 43.3
WMSBURG        3413 43.4  4458 56.6* 3213 89.6   374 10.4
YORK           4615 45.5  5538 54.5* 4878 52.9  4345 47.1
-------------------------------------*-------------------------------------------------------
                                      *
TOTALS       141757     201170       * 187349       91823
% OF VOTE      41.3        58.7       *  67.1        32.9
                                      *
                                      *
GEOGRAPHIC CLASS                      *
                                      *
LOWLANDS      12177 40.  18587 60.*  17718 80.   4558 20.
BLACK BELT    72621 39. 114489 61.*  96338 78.  27105 22.
PIEDMONT      56959 46.  68094 54.*  73293 55.  60160 45.
                                      *
                                      *
DEMOGRAPHIC CLASS                     *
                                      *
METRO         19983 39.  31730 61.*  44311 62.  27183 38.
TOWN          28845 42.  40133 58.*  34627 54.  29231 46.
RURAL         92929 42. 129307 58.* 108411 75.  35409 25.
```

SPECL. REFERENDUM 1966* SPECL. REFERENDUM 1966

COUNTY	WOMEN #	%	AGAINST #	%*	LIQUOR #	%	AGAINST #	%
ABBEVILLE	1472	53.9	1261	46.1*	615	22.5	2122	77.5
AIKEN	7549	68.9	3408	31.1*	5308	49.1	5508	50.9
ALLENDALE	782	51.7	731	48.3*	644	39.9	970	60.1
ANDERSON	6344	56.8	4834	43.2*	2790	24.1	8803	75.9
BAMBERG	1013	46.7	1156	53.3*	637	26.0	1812	74.0
BARNWELL	1222	49.0	1273	51.0*	724	25.4	2132	74.6
BEAUFORT	2458	68.2	1148	31.8*	2232	57.7	1639	42.3
BERKELEY	2601	62.6	1557	37.4*	1603	33.2	3223	66.8
CALHOUN	698	48.7	736	51.3*	423	28.0	1090	72.0
CHARLESTON	18937	65.9	9802	34.1*	17402	60.3	11467	39.7
CHEROKEE	2552	45.6	3046	54.4*	1163	20.2	4600	79.8
CHESTER	2242	64.0	1262	36.0*	1480	42.0	2043	58.0
CHSTRFILD	2046	50.5	2003	49.5*	1347	31.2	2971	68.8
CLARENDON	1377	40.7	2006	59.3*	975	26.6	2691	73.4
COLLETON	2055	47.7	2255	52.3*	1353	31.4	2962	68.6
DARLINTON	3869	65.3	2055	34.7*	2396	38.4	3847	61.6
DILLON	2344	63.9	1323	36.1*	2185	52.8	1951	47.2
DORCHSTR	1633	49.7	1654	50.3*	1117	29.7	2644	70.3
EDGEFIELD	197	18.4	875	81.6*	581	31.8	1245	68.2
FAIRFIELD	1323	56.3	1027	43.7*	1060	39.2	1646	60.8
FLORENCE	4877	57.2	3654	42.8*	1800	32.7	3710	67.3
GEORGTOWN	3618	64.8	1966	35.2*	3235	54.7	2678	45.3
GREENVILL	15481	63.8	8793	36.2*	9087	34.6	17199	65.4
GREENWOOD	3318	57.4	2459	42.6*	2117	27.7	5517	72.3
HAMPTON	250	47.7	274	52.3*	193	29.4	464	70.6
HORRY	3739	60.4	2448	39.6*	3512	48.8	3691	51.2
JASPER	767	58.1	554	41.9*	452	34.6	854	65.4
KERSHAW	3106	54.3	2616	45.7*	2210	37.1	3750	62.9
LANCASTER	3239	59.3	2219	40.7*	1339	20.6	5167	79.4
LAURENS	2371	56.4	1831	43.6*	1149	24.2	3593	75.8
LEE	776	49.1	806	50.9*	467	27.1	1257	72.9
LEXINGTON	6947	60.3	4583	39.7*	4421	38.1	7192	61.9
MARION	1832	62.8	1086	37.2*	1057	31.9	2252	68.1
MARLBORO	1798	64.7	979	35.3*	1061	42.8	1417	57.2
MCCORMICK	371	49.9	373	50.1*	227	22.4	787	77.6
NEWBERRY	3223	51.8	3004	48.2*	2085	32.1	4402	67.9
OCONEE	2231	54.8	1841	45.2*	1249	27.3	3332	72.7
ORANGBURG	3790	57.4	2809	42.6*	2885	38.2	4672	61.8
PICKENS	3662	57.2	2741	42.8*	1729	25.4	5078	74.6
RICHLAND	19287	72.6	7291	27.4*	15392	56.5	11873	43.5
SALNDA	1318	50.5	1291	49.5*	659	22.6	2261	77.4
SPARTNBRG	12774	63.3	7395	36.7*	6053	27.2	16201	72.8
SUMTER	4696	58.9	3279	41.1*	2741	32.1	5785	67.9
UNION	2074	50.9	2003	49.1*	905	20.1	3608	79.9
WMSBURG	2240	46.1	2623	53.9*	1761	34.0	3412	66.0

```
         SPECL.  REFERENDUM 1966* SPECL.  REFERENDUM 1966
                              *
COUNTY     WOMEN       AGAINST  * LIQUOR        AGAINST
           #     %     #     %* #      %     #     %
----------------------------------*----------------------------------------------------------------
YORK       5291 65.0   2848 35.0* 3214 42.2   4405 57.8
----------------------------------*----------------------------------------------------------------
                              *
TOTALS     175790      115178   * 117035      189923
% OF VOTE   60.4         39.6   *  38.1        61.9
                              *
                              *
GEOGRAPHIC CLASS              *
                              *
LOWLANDS   20693 64.   11587 36.* 15473 46.   18030 54.
BLACK BELT 87701 61.   56022 39.* 66061 44.   82634 56.
PIEDMONT   67396 59.   47569 41.* 35501 28.   89259 72.
                              *
                              *
DEMOGRAPHIC CLASS             *
                              *
METRO      53705 67.   25886 33.* 41881 51.   40539 49.
TOWN       33982 61.   22010 39.* 16598 30.   38904 70.
RURAL      88103 57.   67282 43.* 58556 35.  110480 65.
```

TENNESSEE

COUNTIES

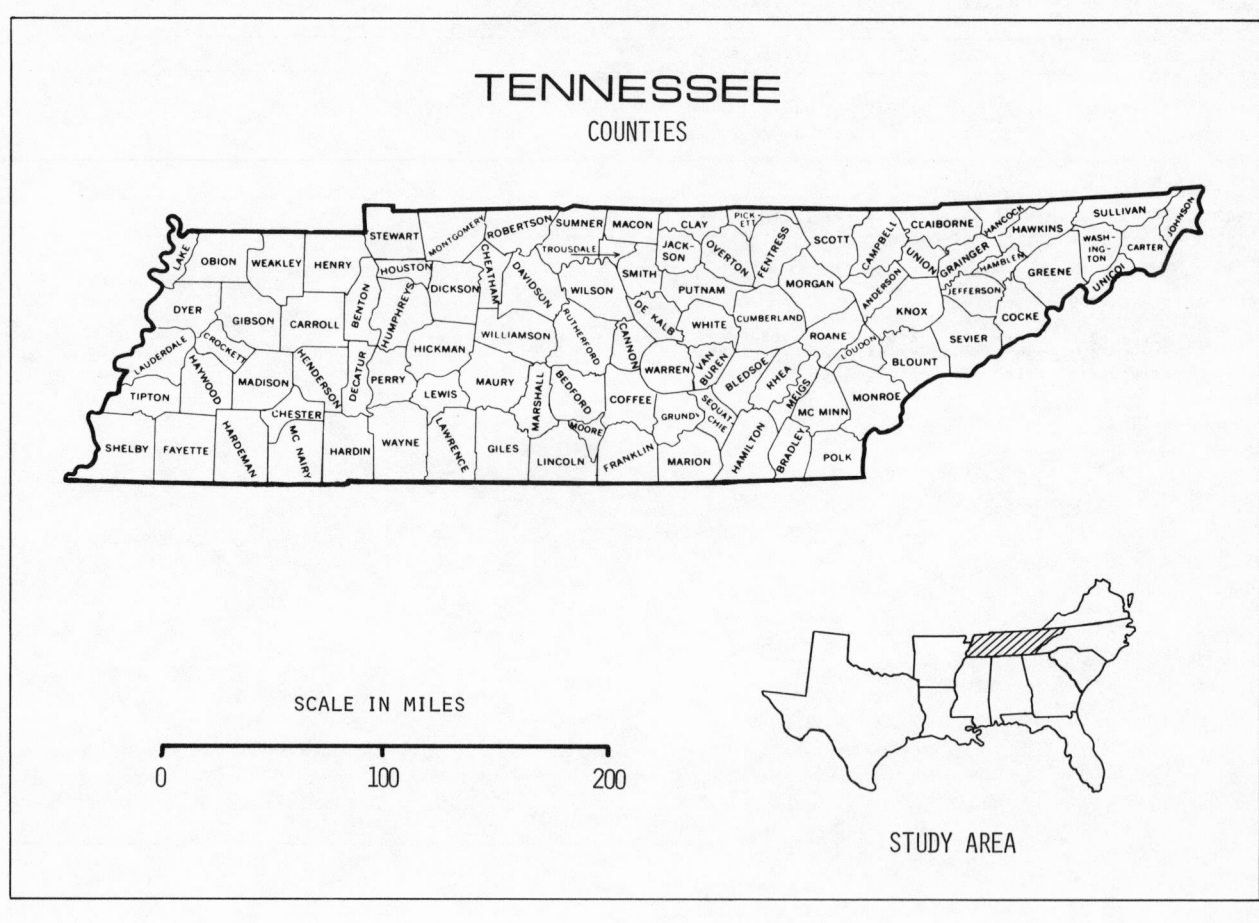

SCALE IN MILES

0   100   200

STUDY AREA

TENNESSEE

Tennessee had no requirements for registration beyond the customary residency, citizenship, and similar provisions. Tennessee had long required payment of a poll tax, but state laws in 1949 and 1951 drastically limited its effect, and the constitutional requirement for payment was eliminated altogether in 1953. Black voter registration grew rapidly during the 1950s and in 1960 reached 59.1 percent of the black voting-age population, which was the highest in the South. In 1970, the approximately 242,000 registered blacks were 71.6 percent of the black voting-age population. Since the number of white registrants also increased, the proportion of black names on the registration rolls changed little. In 1960 black registrants were 12.5 percent of all qualified voters; in 1970 they were 13.1 percent.

The response of Tennessee voters to recent presidential campaigns is suggested below. Turnout figures are expressed in both number of votes cast and in percentage of citizens of voting age who voted.

Included below are 14 primary elections. There are 7 Democratic gubernatorial primaries and 7 senatorial primaries. Tennessee was the only southern state where candidates were nominated by pluralities rather than having to obtain majorities in subsequent runoff elections. Prior to the 1954 elections, Tennessee voters approved a constitutional revision extending gubernatorial terms from two to four years.

Gubernatorial Primaries

1. August 3, 1950: Clifford R. Allen 208,634 (43.4%), Gordon Browning 267,855 (55.7%), Porter Freeman 1,907 (0.4%), John R. Neal 2,875 (0.6%). Total vote was 481,271; turnout of voting-age citizens was 24.4%.
2. August 7, 1952: Clifford R. Allen 75,269 (11.6%), Gordon Browning 245,156 (37.9%), Frank G. Clement 302,487 (46.7%), Clifford D. Pierce 24,184 (3.7%). Total vote was 647,096; turnout was 32.4%.
3. August 4, 1954: Gordon Browning 195,156 (27.6%), Frank G. Clement 481,808 (68.2%), Rawlston Schoolfield 29,866 (4.2%). Total vote was 706,830; turnout was 35.0%.
4. August 7, 1958: Clifford R. Allen 56,854 (8.3%), Buford Ellington 213,415 (31.1%), Edmund Orgill 204,382 (29.8%), Andrew T. Taylor 204,629 (29.9%), other 3 candidates received 6,011 (0.9%). Total vote was 685,291; turnout was 33.1%.
5. August 2, 1962: Frank G. Clement 309,333 (42.5%), William W. Farris 202,813 (27.9%), P. R. Olgiati 211,812 (29.1%), other 2 candidates received 3,240 (0.4%). Total vote was 727,198; turnout was 33.8%.
6. August 4, 1966: Buford Ellington 413,950 (53.5%), John J. Hooker 360,105 (46.5%). Total vote was 774,055; turnout was 34.2%.
7. August 6, 1970: John J. Hooker 261,580 (44.3%), Stanly Snodgrass 193,199 (32.7%), Robert L. Taylor 90,009 (15.3%), other 3 candidates 45,273 (7.7%). Total vote was 590,061; turnout was 24.8%.

Senatorial Primaries

1. August 7, 1952: Albert Gore 334,957

(56.5%), Kenneth D. McKellar 245,051
(41.4%), other 3 candidates 12,419 (2.1%).
Total vote was 592,427.

2. August 4, 1954: Estes Kefauver 440,497
(68.2%), Pat Sutton 186,363 (28.9%),
other 2 candidates 19,091 (3.0%). Total
vote was 645,951.

3. August 7, 1958: Prentice Cooper 253,091
(39.8%), Albert Gore 375,444 (59.0%), one
other candidate 7,711 (1.2%). Total vote
was 636,246.

4. August 4, 1960: Estes Kefauver 463,848
(64.6%), Andrew T. Taylor 249,336 (34.7%),
Jake Armstrong 4,867 (0.7%). Total vote
was 718,051.

* (August 6, 1964: Albert Gore won 84.7%
against 4 opponents. Total vote was
473,793.)

5. August 6, 1964: Ross Bass 330,213
(50.8%), M. M. Bullard 86,718 (13.3%),
Frank G. Clement 233,245 (35.9%). Total
vote was 650,176.

6. August 4, 1966: Ross Bass 366,079
(48.8%), Frank G. Clement 384,322 (51.2%).
Total vote was 750,401.

7. August 6, 1970: Hudley Crockett 238,767
(45.2%), Albert Gore 269,770 (51.0%),
Stanford Andress 9,871 (1.9%), Herman Frey
10,297 (1.9%). Total vote was 528,705.

* (August 3, 1972: Ray Blanton won 76.4%
against 4 opponents. Total vote was
382,508.)

RETURNS FROM PRESIDENTIAL ELECTIONS

Year	Turnout		Partisan Vote*
1948	550,283	(28.7%)[+]	Democrat 49.1%, Republican 36.9%, Dixiecrat 13.4%
1952	892,553	(44.7%)	Republican 50.0%, Democrat 49.7%
1956	939,404	(45.9%)	Republican 49.2%, Democrat 48.6%
1960	1,051,792	(50.3%)	Republican 52.9%, Democrat 45.8%
1964	1,143,946	(51.8%)	Democrat 55.5%, Republican 44.5%
1968	1,248,617	(53.8%)	Republican 37.8%, American Independent 34.0%, Democrat 28.1%
1972	1,201,182	(45.0%)	Republican 67.7%, Democrat 29.7%

*Totals do not necessarily equal 100%, since minor party percentages are excluded.

[+]Percentage of citizens of voting age who voted is calculated on the basis of a straight-line interpolation of citizen population between census years.

COUNTY	ALLEN #	%	BROWNING #	%	FREEMAN #	%	NEAL #	%*	ALLEN #	%	BROWNING #	%	CLEMENT #	%	PIERCE #	%
ANDERSON	2542	40.9	3550	57.1	29	.5	91	1.5*	482	5.5	3982	45.2	3264	37.1	1074	12.2
BEDFORD	1652	37.0	2797	62.6	7	.2	13	.3*	906	13.6	2306	34.6	3197	48.0	249	3.7
BENTON	2320	58.1	1648	41.3	9	.2	16	.4*	494	11.9	1427	34.5	2170	52.4	49	1.2
BLEDSOE	1298	63.1	751	36.5	3	.1	4	.2*	138	6.4	814	37.6	1198	55.4	13	.6
BLOUNT	1646	48.5	1662	49.0	58	1.7	28	.8*	816	15.9	2394	46.7	1774	34.6	144	2.8
BRADLEY	1863	56.0	1432	43.1	11	.3	19	.6*	1040	25.7	1554	38.4	1338	33.1	112	2.8
CAMPBELL	712	44.5	838	52.3	19	1.2	32	2.0*	294	9.8	1782	59.7	884	29.6	26	.9
CANNON	1423	44.4	1784	55.6	0	.0	0	.0*	346	9.2	1957	51.8	1447	38.3	26	.7
CARROLL	2335	37.4	3854	61.8	23	.4	24	.4*	333	5.3	3341	53.6	2493	40.0	65	1.0
CARTER	415	25.2	1226	74.4	0	.0	7	.4*	485	9.3	3121	59.7	1594	30.5	30	.6
CHEATHAM	1213	40.2	1778	58.9	7	.2	21	.7*	795	24.5	1165	35.9	1228	37.9	53	1.6
CHESTER	1699	52.1	1535	47.1	14	.4	12	.4*	380	11.0	1057	30.5	1975	57.0	52	1.5
CLAIBORNE	762	32.6	1536	65.8	15	.6	22	.9*	96	2.9	1965	60.4	1172	36.0	23	.7
CLAY	1626	67.4	776	32.2	6	.2	5	.2*	346	14.5	756	31.7	1275	53.4	10	.4
COCKE	702	24.0	2215	75.8	2	.1	3	.1*	105	3.1	2345	68.2	934	27.2	53	1.5
COFFEE	1858	45.9	2169	53.6	10	.2	11	.3*	905	14.8	2346	38.3	2641	43.1	238	3.9
CROCKETT	1447	41.7	1982	57.2	21	.6	18	.5*	234	5.7	1364	33.1	2448	59.3	79	1.9
CUMBERLND	2345	62.2	1408	37.3	7	.2	11	.3*	1060	23.5	1468	32.6	1929	42.8	52	1.2
DAVIDSON	11044	36.6	18843	62.4	240	.8	88	.3*	13007	22.8	17941	31.5	22922	40.2	3100	5.4
DECATUR	1169	46.7	1330	53.1	5	.2	1	.0*	109	4.0	1035	37.7	1583	57.7	15	.5
DEKALB	1329	33.9	2587	65.9	4	.1	5	.1*	403	10.6	1993	52.5	1365	36.0	35	.9
DICKSON	2451	49.0	2506	50.2	25	.5	15	.3*	578	9.0	954	14.8	4875	75.5	47	.7
DYER	3793	50.7	3660	48.9	11	.1	23	.3*	726	8.3	2663	30.6	5031	57.8	290	3.3
FAYETTE	522	40.2	763	58.8	1	.1	12	.9*	80	3.9	724	34.9	1022	49.2	251	12.1
FENTRESS	964	57.1	695	41.2	13	.8	16	.9*	312	15.4	613	30.3	1083	53.5	15	.7
FRANKLIN	3251	45.8	3747	52.8	40	.6	58	.8*	882	11.4	2806	36.4	3863	50.1	155	2.0
GIBSON	2606	29.2	6257	70.2	19	.2	29	.3*	379	3.3	5467	47.9	5267	46.2	291	2.6
GILES	2548	40.7	3671	58.6	25	.4	16	.3*	886	12.3	3001	41.6	2966	41.1	362	5.0
GRAINGER	610	54.7	497	44.6	4	.4	4	.4*	79	6.0	660	49.8	575	43.4	11	.8
GREENE	1480	35.9	2605	63.2	19	.5	17	.4*	332	6.8	2676	54.7	1849	37.8	37	.8
GRUNDY	2003	62.4	1190	37.1	4	.1	12	.4*	605	17.7	1034	30.2	1762	51.5	21	.6
HAMBLEN	1023	41.9	1412	57.8	1	.0	5	.2*	261	5.4	1462	30.5	3000	62.5	76	1.6
HAMILTON	12047	42.6	15640	55.3	189	.7	406	1.4*	3179	9.4	13841	40.9	15442	45.7	1358	4.0
HANCOCK	170	20.0	677	79.6	1	.1	2	.2*	33	3.1	574	56.8	397	39.3	7	.7
HARDEMAN	1144	27.6	2976	71.8	7	.2	15	.4*	376	8.3	2151	47.7	1823	40.4	157	3.5
HARDIN	716	35.3	1301	64.2	6	.3	5	.2*	216	9.7	1068	48.0	916	41.2	23	1.0
HAWKINS	1116	54.3	914	44.4	13	.6	14	.7*	287	8.8	1659	50.8	1254	38.4	67	2.1
HAYWOOD	495	20.8	1864	78.4	6	.3	12	.5*	151	4.0	1481	39.6	1933	51.7	177	4.7
HENDERSON	1271	44.3	1583	55.2	9	.3	4	.1*	151	6.2	1166	48.1	1076	44.4	29	1.2
HENRY	2884	43.1	3770	56.4	13	.2	23	.3*	794	10.5	2417	32.1	4182	55.5	146	1.9
HICKMAN	2331	48.0	2482	51.1	19	.4	22	.5*	1036	20.7	1578	31.5	2253	45.0	139	2.8
HOUSTON	951	44.0	1197	55.4	7	.3	7	.3*	245	10.0	931	37.8	1269	51.6	16	.7
HUMPHREYS	1790	49.9	1772	49.4	9	.3	13	.4*	833	18.2	1387	30.3	2298	50.1	65	1.4
JACKSON	2163	46.3	2485	53.2	6	.1	14	.3*	739	15.9	1998	43.1	1875	40.4	27	.6
JEFFERSON	373	41.9	510	57.2	2	.2	6	.7*	103	6.3	592	36.5	918	56.6	10	.6
JOHNSON	98	14.8	562	84.9	1	.2	1	.2*	23	2.6	600	68.0	255	28.9	4	.5

COUNTY	ALLEN #	%	BROWNING #	%	FREEMAN #	%	NEAL #	%*	ALLEN #	%	BROWNING #	%	CLEMENT #	%	PIERCE #	%
KNOX	6318	35.4	11077	62.1	99	.6	355	2.0*	2823	9.3	13644	45.1	13282	43.9	492	1.6
LAKE	1090	42.9	1421	55.9	17	.7	14	.6*	156	5.0	1126	35.9	1796	57.3	55	1.8
LAUDERDLE	2317	43.7	2977	56.1	7	.1	3	.1*	229	4.0	2432	42.6	2990	52.4	54	.9
LAWRENCE	4099	57.7	2971	41.9	16	.2	13	.2*	1111	14.4	2091	27.1	4381	56.8	124	1.6
LEWIS	1560	63.9	880	36.0	0	.0	3	.1*	125	5.3	615	26.1	1615	68.4	5	.2
LINCOLN	2720	40.7	3908	58.5	24	.4	25	.4*	859	10.7	3316	41.4	3676	45.9	165	2.1
LOUDON	796	35.9	1390	62.6	19	.9	14	.6*	366	11.0	1252	37.7	1656	49.9	44	1.3
MCMINN	2092	56.3	1589	42.8	13	.3	21	.6*	501	13.6	1547	41.8	1571	42.5	78	2.1
MCNAIRY	1963	42.6	2594	56.3	26	.6	28	.6*	505	9.8	1918	37.2	2647	51.4	79	1.5
MACON	863	40.9	1236	58.5	7	.3	6	.3*	534	20.2	788	29.9	1301	49.3	16	.6
MADISON	3351	33.8	6483	65.5	20	.2	50	.5*	802	6.0	4989	37.1	6847	50.9	822	6.1
MARION	2474	64.4	1329	34.6	10	.3	27	.7*	673	14.7	1254	27.4	2561	56.1	81	1.8
MARSHALL	2856	50.7	2754	48.9	9	.2	14	.2*	411	6.8	2242	37.0	2912	48.0	502	8.3
MAURY	2981	41.4	4188	58.1	22	.3	16	.2*	3067	28.0	2921	26.6	4265	38.9	710	6.5
MEIGS	365	39.0	559	59.7	8	.9	4	.4*	88	8.5	270	26.1	665	64.3	11	1.1
MONROE	1152	31.7	2452	67.5	13	.4	16	.4*	794	20.0	1938	48.8	1187	29.9	50	1.3
MONTGOMRY	1947	28.8	4756	70.2	35	.5	33	.5*	1017	11.8	3237	37.4	4271	49.4	123	1.4
MOORE	769	53.0	676	46.6	1	.1	5	.3*	242	15.3	560	35.4	753	47.6	27	1.7
MORGAN	467	27.4	1210	71.1	9	.5	16	.9*	249	6.8	1823	49.6	1569	42.7	32	.9
OBION	4911	54.4	4054	44.9	25	.3	40	.4*	754	10.1	2490	33.3	4092	54.7	151	2.0
OVERTON	2998	68.6	1357	31.0	8	.2	8	.2*	747	18.3	1103	27.1	2168	53.2	55	1.4
PERRY	1268	51.0	1186	47.7	18	.7	12	.5*	220	8.6	1002	39.1	1325	51.8	13	.5
PICKETT	493	61.9	300	37.7	2	.3	1	.1*	81	9.3	337	38.8	447	51.4	4	.5
POLK	1376	55.4	1095	44.1	3	.1	8	.3*	206	7.2	1497	52.0	1164	40.4	14	.5
PUTNAM	3298	52.2	2979	47.2	12	.2	23	.4*	785	11.4	1911	27.8	4085	59.4	97	1.4
RHEA	968	47.0	1044	50.7	9	.4	38	1.8*	274	11.9	818	35.5	1183	51.4	27	1.2
ROANE	2051	63.0	1157	35.6	14	.4	31	1.0*	585	10.8	1844	34.2	2751	51.0	218	4.0
ROBERTSON	2830	41.0	3973	57.5	41	.6	60	.9*	1144	16.9	3141	46.5	2352	34.8	118	1.7
RUTHERFRD	3369	41.9	4615	57.4	24	.3	39	.5*	1577	14.9	3947	37.3	4599	43.5	450	4.3
SCOTT	679	56.8	499	41.7	11	.9	7	.6*	112	3.4	1584	47.7	1610	48.5	17	.5
SEQUATCH	1419	75.5	446	23.7	6	.3	8	.4*	104	5.3	335	17.2	1494	76.8	12	.6
SEVIER	518	32.5	1071	67.2	2	.1	3	.2*	138	4.7	2083	71.7	643	22.1	43	1.5
SHELBY	20570	39.3	31189	59.6	174	.3	437	.8*	4285	4.5	31168	32.6	51479	53.9	8638	9.0
SMITH	1230	34.0	2369	65.5	8	.2	11	.3*	678	13.9	1829	37.5	2301	47.2	70	1.4
STEWART	1425	37.8	2323	61.6	12	.3	10	.3*	439	12.4	1753	49.6	1318	37.3	23	.7
SULLIVAN	2883	35.8	5027	62.4	66	.8	82	1.0*	1390	10.5	5750	43.6	5855	44.4	194	1.5
SUMNER	4604	58.1	3285	41.5	17	.2	16	.2*	2037	26.8	2505	33.0	2918	38.5	129	1.7
TIPTON	2000	35.3	3600	63.6	24	.4	40	.7*	427	6.2	2644	38.4	3583	52.0	230	3.3
TROUSDALE	1270	54.2	1044	44.5	9	.4	21	.9*	386	20.9	676	36.5	758	41.0	31	1.7
UNICOI	294	29.5	700	70.3	2	.2	0	.0*	111	6.4	782	45.3	830	48.0	5	.3
UNION	368	48.1	388	50.7	6	.8	3	.4*	89	7.1	504	40.3	640	51.1	19	1.5
VN BUREN	1102	77.6	313	22.0	1	.1	4	.3*	217	15.1	370	25.7	830	57.8	20	1.4
WARREN	3254	63.3	1859	36.2	16	.3	13	.3*	2009	30.8	1798	27.6	2605	40.0	104	1.6
WASHINGTN	1486	37.6	2442	61.8	7	.2	17	.4*	698	8.3	4302	51.4	3298	39.4	72	.9
WAYNE	682	35.1	1254	64.6	4	.2	2	.1*	358	17.6	743	36.6	912	44.9	18	.9
WEAKLEY	2641	37.1	4422	62.2	28	.4	21	.3*	438	5.8	3470	46.1	3521	46.8	90	1.2

```
              DEMOC.  GOVERNOR   1950          *           DEMOC.  GOVERNOR   1952
                                               *
   COUNTY     ALLEN        BROWNING    FREEMAN    NEAL     *  ALLEN        BROWNING    CLEMENT      PIERCE
              #     %      #     %     #    %     #    %*     #     %      #     %     #     %      #    %
   -------------------------------------------------------*-----------------------------------------------------------
   WHITE      2132 59.2   1450 40.2    9   .2    12  .3*    1235 25.9   1450 30.4   2003 42.0     79  1.7
   WILLIAMSN  3267 47.4   3569 51.8   18   .3    33  .5*    1510 21.4   2904 41.1   2439 34.5    218  3.1
   WILSON     2868 41.6   3958 57.4   36   .5    30  .4*    1623 20.1   2837 35.2   3324 41.2    276  3.4
   -------------------------------------------------------*-----------------------------------------------------------
                                               *
   TOTALS     208634      267855      1907      2875   *   75269       245156      302487       24184
   % OF VOTE  43.4         55.7        .4        .6    *   11.6         37.9        46.7         3.7
                                               *
                                               *
   GEOGRAPHIC CLASS                            *
                                               *
   LOWLANDS   52773 41.   75974 58.   389  0.   741  1.*   10474  6.   64865 35.   97204 53.    11104  6.
   BLACK BELT  1017 28.    2627 71.     7  0.    24  1.*     231  4.    2205 38.    2955 51.      428  7.
   PIEDMONT   82081 45.   99734 54.   739  0.   682  0.*   42294 18.   79967 34.  103680 44.     7718  3.
   MOUNTAIN   72763 44.   89520 54.   772  0.  1428  1.*   22270 10.   98119 44.   98648 44.     4934  2.
                                               *
   DEMOGRAPHIC CLASS                           *
                                               *
   METRO      49979 39.   76749 60.   702  1.  1286  1.*   23294 11.   76594 35.  103125 48.    13588  6.
   TOWN       13232 35.   23670 63.   158  0.   278  1.*    4168  9.   19740 41.   23271 48.     1287  3.
   RURAL     145423 46.  167436 53.  1047  0.  1311  0.*   47807 13.  148822 39.  176091 46.     9309  2.


                                          TENNESSEE


              DEMOC.  GOVERNOR   1954       *          DEMOC.  GOVERNOR   1958
                                           *
   COUNTY     BROWNING    CLEMENT    SCHOOLFLD   ALLEN      *  ELLINGTON   ORGILL      TAYLOR
              #     %     #     %    #    %*     #     %       #     %     #     %     #     %
   -------------------------------------------*------------------------------------------------------------
   ANDERSON   3401 32.2  6765 64.1  391  3.7*   925  9.1    1817 17.9   6085 60.0   1316 13.0
   BEDFORD    2178 29.7  4463 60.7  689  9.4*   435  7.4    2620 44.5   1653 28.1   1181 20.1
   BENTON     1802 41.0  2393 54.5  195  4.4*   362  8.6    1184 28.1   1217 28.9   1455 34.5
   BLEDSOE     551 21.6  1835 72.1  160  6.3*    81  4.3     910 47.9    627 33.0    280 14.8
   BLOUNT     1473 24.7  4386 73.7   96  1.6*   513  8.7    2112 35.8   1968 33.4   1300 22.1
                                           *
   BRADLEY     856 12.7  5722 84.6  184  2.7*   322  5.9    2031 37.0    914 16.7   2216 40.4
   CAMPBELL   1308 34.6  2280 60.3  190  5.0*   162  4.9    1013 30.7   1563 47.3    566 17.1
   CANNON     1598 39.9  2295 57.3  109  2.7*   473 13.0    1558 42.7   1004 27.5    611 16.8
   CARROLL    4084 53.4  3472 45.4   97  1.3*   236  3.7    1706 27.0    731 11.6   3645 57.7
   CARTER     1933 25.5  5556 73.2  105  1.4*   568  9.7    1373 23.5   1413 24.2   2496 42.7
                                           *
   CHEATHAM   1534 40.7  1980 52.5  257  6.8*  1197 35.3    1173 34.6    831 24.5    189  5.6
   CHESTER    1019 24.9  3015 73.7   58  1.4*    73  1.9     896 23.6    500 13.2   2332 61.4
   CLAIBORNE  1157 35.2  2049 62.4   78  2.4*   104  3.8    1310 47.4    823 29.8    527 19.1
   CLAY        609 22.6  2019 75.1   61  2.3*   127  6.2     779 38.0    990 48.3    154  7.5
   COCKE      1368 29.9  3189 69.6   23   .5*    80  2.0    2251 55.1   1239 30.3    518 12.7
                                           *
   COFFEE     2455 34.4  4120 57.7  560  7.8*  1559 19.9    2011 25.6   2718 34.7   1554 19.8
```

SOUTHERN ELECTIONS/222

COUNTY	BROWNING #	%	CLEMENT #	%	SCHOOLFLD #	%*	ALLEN #	%	ELLINGTON #	%	ORGILL #	%	TAYLOR #	%
CROCKETT	1340	32.7	2649	64.7	105	2.6*	31	1.0	1104	34.6	170	5.3	1887	59.1
CUMBERLND	1308	27.2	3289	68.4	211	4.4*	252	6.7	1255	33.3	1239	32.9	1022	27.1
DAVIDSON	21473	32.6	40689	61.8	3674	5.6*	19279	28.8	19616	29.3	19815	29.6	8173	12.2
DECATUR	1144	35.3	2007	61.9	92	2.8*	64	2.3	617	22.2	544	19.6	1553	55.9
DEKALB	1678	37.0	2741	60.5	113	2.5*	599	16.9	1516	42.7	1129	31.8	305	8.6
DICKSON	1069	17.1	5067	80.9	130	2.1*	800	15.0	2442	45.7	1399	26.2	699	13.1
DYER	2162	23.6	6720	73.3	286	3.1*	84	1.0	3665	45.3	1326	16.4	3024	37.3
FAYETTE	684	32.6	1344	64.0	71	3.4*	17	.8	356	15.8	119	5.3	1762	78.2
FENTRESS	406	15.7	2155	83.2	29	1.1*	160	7.2	1020	46.1	716	32.3	318	14.4
FRANKLIN	3133	38.6	4544	55.9	446	5.5*	786	11.6	1931	28.4	2828	41.6	1260	18.5
GIBSON	5718	42.0	7754	56.9	155	1.1*	143	1.3	2949	27.7	1298	12.2	6264	58.8
GILES	3064	40.3	4257	56.0	284	3.7*	392	6.1	1768	27.7	3681	57.7	543	8.5
GRAINGER	502	30.4	1129	68.4	20	1.2*	92	6.1	742	49.4	337	22.4	332	22.1
GREENE	1077	20.3	4189	78.8	47	.9*	128	2.6	2300	45.9	498	9.9	2086	41.6
GRUNDY	541	13.5	3291	82.1	175	4.4*	303	9.5	1341	41.9	675	21.1	884	27.6
HAMBLEN	1064	22.3	3628	76.2	70	1.5*	115	2.5	2187	46.9	1859	39.8	504	10.8
HAMILTON	5209	14.8	25411	72.0	4674	13.2*	1179	3.1	9368	24.9	11289	30.0	15831	42.0
HANCOCK	451	35.4	821	64.5	1	.1*	24	2.4	530	52.4	283	28.0	175	17.3
HARDEMAN	1917	39.2	2832	57.9	141	2.9*	111	2.4	919	19.8	282	6.1	3332	71.7
HARDIN	1064	26.9	2814	71.3	71	1.8*	110	2.5	1698	38.5	480	10.9	2118	48.1
HAWKINS	1045	27.0	2782	71.9	43	1.1*	125	4.2	1264	42.0	702	23.3	916	30.5
HAYWOOD	1208	32.2	2495	66.6	44	1.2*	32	.9	787	21.7	129	3.6	2682	73.9
HENDERSON	1297	30.6	2896	68.3	48	1.1*	104	2.7	1410	36.1	148	3.8	2243	57.4
HENRY	2918	37.0	4633	58.8	325	4.1*	291	4.3	1896	27.8	1538	22.6	3089	45.3
HICKMAN	1764	36.6	2848	59.1	211	4.4*	667	15.8	1448	34.4	1167	27.7	932	22.1
HOUSTON	1076	42.7	1386	55.0	58	2.3*	135	6.2	797	36.6	868	39.9	378	17.4
HUMPHREYS	1341	30.6	2826	64.6	209	4.8*	561	14.1	1437	36.2	1091	27.5	882	22.2
JACKSON	1285	25.2	3729	73.2	78	1.5*	233	5.3	2085	47.7	1267	29.0	783	17.9
JEFFERSON	634	22.6	2115	75.5	54	1.9*	50	3.0	796	47.6	385	23.0	440	26.3
JOHNSON	328	25.5	954	74.2	4	.3*	26	3.0	494	56.8	32	3.7	318	36.6
KNOX	7498	25.1	21480	72.0	865	2.9*	2665	8.9	9499	31.7	12795	42.7	5013	16.7
LAKE	1087	31.7	2342	68.3	0	.0*	68	2.3	928	30.8	365	12.1	1650	54.8
LAUDERDLE	1965	24.9	5830	73.9	89	1.1*	141	2.0	2461	34.7	642	9.0	3852	54.3
LAWRENCE	1857	23.3	5714	71.7	401	5.0*	364	4.8	3816	50.7	2467	32.8	883	11.7
LEWIS	503	20.2	1942	78.1	42	1.7*	35	1.4	1938	75.6	465	18.1	125	4.9
LINCOLN	2992	39.1	4361	57.1	291	3.8*	410	5.6	2620	35.5	2963	40.2	1379	18.7
LOUDON	1143	27.3	2778	66.4	263	6.3*	282	8.9	1197	37.6	1158	36.4	543	17.1
MCMINN	1141	25.3	3228	71.7	134	3.0*	94	2.7	1786	50.9	1092	31.1	534	15.2
MCNAIRY	1963	30.6	4341	67.7	108	1.7*	123	1.9	1828	28.0	658	10.1	3930	60.1
MACON	742	23.2	2332	72.9	124	3.9*	272	13.0	768	36.8	821	39.3	227	10.9
MADISON	5647	32.7	11065	64.0	574	3.3*	215	1.2	1832	10.6	1271	7.4	13963	80.8
MARION	871	16.4	4011	75.5	431	8.1*	207	4.1	2018	40.1	1601	31.8	1210	24.0
MARSHALL	1889	30.7	4073	66.3	184	3.0*	275	4.1	4658	69.7	1547	23.1	205	3.1
MAURY	3003	27.3	5992	54.4	2021	18.3*	1044	9.3	3931	35.2	3014	27.0	3188	28.5
MEIGS	203	14.4	1124	80.0	78	5.6*	50	4.7	399	37.5	329	30.9	287	26.9
MONROE	1256	27.7	3183	70.1	103	2.3*	393	8.1	1848	37.9	2099	43.1	533	10.9

COUNTY	DEMOC. GOVERNOR 1954						DEMOC. GOVERNOR 1958							
	BROWNING #	%	CLEMENT #	%	SCHOOLFLD #	%	ALLEN #	%	ELLINGTON #	%	ORGILL #	%	TAYLOR #	%
MONTGOMRY	3252	31.7	6701	65.3	312	3.0*	736	7.5	3265	33.3	4933	50.4	858	8.8
MOORE	486	32.2	917	60.8	104	6.9*	162	11.2	526	36.2	373	25.7	391	26.9
MORGAN	1065	26.2	2884	70.8	123	3.0*	157	5.0	1038	33.3	1542	49.5	378	12.1
OBION	1876	23.0	6059	74.4	214	2.6*	133	1.9	2141	30.9	1536	22.2	3112	45.0
OVERTON	1013	20.2	3886	77.4	119	2.4*	326	7.7	1913	45.1	1580	37.2	426	10.0
PERRY	1100	41.3	1465	55.0	100	3.8*	197	7.9	924	36.9	728	29.1	654	26.1
PICKETT	246	27.3	645	71.5	11	1.2*	20	2.9	380	56.0	164	24.2	114	16.8
POLK	943	31.9	1973	66.8	39	1.3*	61	3.1	1038	52.3	319	16.1	566	28.5
PUTNAM	1840	19.7	7194	77.2	283	3.0*	627	7.2	3388	39.0	3604	41.4	1078	12.4
RHEA	496	15.2	2445	74.9	325	10.0*	116	4.4	777	29.2	777	29.2	988	37.2
ROANE	1585	19.4	5771	70.7	808	9.9*	523	6.6	2308	29.3	3385	43.0	1655	21.0
ROBERTSON	2707	34.4	4788	60.8	380	4.8*	997	16.5	2264	37.4	1776	29.4	1014	16.8
RUTHERFRD	3327	31.5	6631	62.7	614	5.8*	587	6.6	3229	36.5	3412	38.6	1610	18.2
SCOTT	526	13.7	3263	85.2	40	1.0*	146	8.4	764	44.2	364	21.1	454	26.3
SEQUATCH	258	13.0	1636	82.2	97	4.9*	80	4.8	684	40.8	275	16.4	637	38.0
SEVIER	1048	34.8	1928	64.0	35	1.2*	68	3.4	797	39.8	478	23.9	657	32.8
SHELBY	16198	20.3	62044	77.7	1582	2.0*	3216	3.0	18631	17.4	40951	38.3	44190	41.3
SMITH	2065	34.9	3611	61.0	248	4.2*	399	8.0	1639	32.8	1759	35.2	1202	24.0
STEWART	1607	46.1	1763	50.6	115	3.3*	312	9.5	969	29.6	1459	44.5	537	16.4
SULLIVAN	3434	21.4	12444	77.5	176	1.1*	743	5.6	6090	45.8	2779	20.9	3676	27.7
SUMNER	2486	25.1	6572	66.3	857	8.6*	1649	17.7	2687	28.8	3158	33.9	1821	19.5
TIPTON	1647	21.5	5954	77.6	67	.9*	85	1.1	3688	47.9	816	10.6	3112	40.4
TROUSDALE	562	24.4	1547	67.2	194	8.4*	319	17.0	556	29.7	674	36.0	322	17.2
UNICOI	403	20.8	1517	78.3	18	.9*	152	9.2	459	27.9	305	18.5	730	44.3
UNION	336	25.1	982	73.3	21	1.6*	44	3.4	872	67.4	278	21.5	100	7.7
VN BUREN	312	19.7	1199	75.9	69	4.4*	102	7.9	642	49.9	350	27.2	192	14.9
WARREN	1829	27.0	4615	68.2	322	4.8*	651	10.0	1983	30.5	2218	34.1	1645	25.3
WASHINGTN	2334	22.6	7873	76.3	112	1.1*	428	4.9	3169	36.3	1602	18.4	3528	40.4
WAYNE	686	25.6	1820	67.9	176	6.4*	202	7.8	1285	49.5	425	16.4	684	26.3
WEAKLEY	3658	43.5	4684	55.7	64	.8*	100	1.7	2485	41.1	574	9.5	2884	47.7
WHITE	1415	30.1	3117	66.3	172	3.7*	437	10.7	1410	34.5	1613	39.4	629	15.4
WILLIAMSN	2740	32.4	5157	61.1	549	6.5*	978	13.9	2429	34.6	3109	44.3	506	7.2
WILSON	2690	30.7	5393	61.5	690	7.9*	1353	16.5	2976	36.2	2209	26.9	1682	20.5
TOTALS	195156		481808		29866	*	56854		213415		204382		204629	
% OF VOTE	27.6		68.2		4.2	*	8.4		31.4		30.1		30.1	

```
        DEMOC. GOVERNOR  1954    *        DEMOC. GOVERNOR  1958
                                 *
COUNTY    BROWNING    CLEMENT   SCHOOLFLD   ALLEN      ELLINGTON   ORGILL      TAYLOR
          #     %     #     %   #     %*   #     %    #     %     #     %     #     %
----------------------------------------*-----------------------------------------------------------------------------------
GEOGRAPHIC CLASS                         *

LOWLANDS   48954 27.  127974 71.  3855  2.*  5053  3.  44779 23.  52486 27.  94146 48.
BLACK BELT  1892 32.    3839 66.   115  2.*    49  1.   1143 19.    248  4.   4444 76.
PIEDMONT   81110 31.  163850 63. 14569  6.* 38586 16.  84095 35.  81181 34.  36819 15.
MOUNTAIN   63200 24.  186145 71. 11327  4.* 13166  6.  83398 35.  70467 30.  69220 29.
                                         *
DEMOGRAPHIC CLASS                        *

METRO      50378 24.  149624 71. 10795  5.* 26339 11.  57114 24.  84850 35.  73207 30.
TOWN       12297 29.   29267 69.  1068  3.*  2237  4.  16543 31.  12444 23.  22529 42.
RURAL     132481 29.  302917 67. 18003  4.* 28278  7. 139758 36. 107088 28. 108893 28.



                              TENNESSEE


         DEMOC. GOVERNOR  1962    * DEMOC. GOVERNOR  1966
                                  *
COUNTY     CLEMENT     FARRIS     OLGIATI   ELLINGTON   HOOKER
           #     %     #     %    #     %*   #     %    #     %
-----------------------------------------*--------------------------------------------------------------------------------
ANDERSON   2881 23.2   716  5.8  8834 71.1* 5157 50.3  5095 49.7
BEDFORD    2427 40.0  2562 42.2  1077 17.8* 3596 51.4  3401 48.6
BENTON     1882 44.1   694 16.3  1693 39.7* 1927 43.2  2538 56.8
BLEDSOE    1301 57.7   496 22.0   456 20.2* 1193 57.2   893 42.8
BLOUNT     2679 41.8   338  5.3  3391 52.9* 3942 58.8  2764 41.2
                                  *
BRADLEY    2896 48.6  1728 29.0  1337 22.4* 2712 49.4  2778 50.6
CAMPBELL   1788 40.5    80  1.8  2551 57.7* 1877 47.6  2065 52.4
CANNON     1961 51.9  1194 31.6   620 16.4* 1928 45.1  2349 54.9
CARROLL    3034 44.5  2153 31.6  1626 23.9* 3104 49.0  3231 51.0
CARTER     1393 43.6   113  3.5  1690 52.9* 3112 51.8  2891 48.2
                                  *
CHEATHAM   1516 43.8  1005 29.0   939 27.1* 1926 50.9  1856 49.1
CHESTER    1951 51.6   698 18.5  1133 30.0* 1739 47.8  1898 52.2
CLAIBORNE  1634 60.6   137  5.1   924 34.3* 1633 52.0  1508 48.0
CLAY       1376 61.2   483 21.5   388 17.3* 1233 50.6  1205 49.4
COCKE      2808 60.2   147  3.2  1709 36.6* 1900 44.6  2358 55.4
                                  *
COFFEE     2847 32.7  2972 34.1  2890 33.2* 4301 51.0  4130 49.0
CROCKETT   1586 51.3  1090 35.3   416 13.5* 1937 62.0  1186 38.0
CUMBERLND  1729 39.1   970 21.9  1725 39.0* 1687 49.4  1729 50.6
DAVIDSON  34831 44.7 26721 34.3 16418 21.1*61208 61.0 39078 39.0
DECATUR    1190 42.5   575 20.5  1036 37.0* 1454 47.4  1614 52.6
                                  *
DEKALB     1871 49.2   998 26.3   932 24.5* 1796 42.4  2440 57.6
DICKSON    3591 61.5  1354 23.2   895 15.3* 3857 57.9  2810 42.1
DYER       4213 41.9  5032 50.1   799  8.0* 5135 57.0  3881 43.0
```

	DEMOC. GOVERNOR 1962						* DEMOC. GOVERNOR 1966			
COUNTY	CLEMENT		FARRIS		OLGIATI		ELLINGTON		HOOKER	
	#	%	#	%	#	%*	#	%	#	%
FAYETTE	1888	59.3	986	31.0	309	9.7*	2368	51.7	2211	48.3
FENTRESS	1298	47.5	370	13.5	1067	39.0*	1052	52.1	966	47.9
FRANKLIN	2900	36.5	1660	20.9	3380	42.6*	4468	49.5	4550	50.5
GIBSON	4870	43.0	4569	40.3	1893	16.7*	6169	54.5	5151	45.5
GILES	2822	43.2	2709	41.5	1002	15.3*	3658	50.5	3583	49.5
GRAINGER	612	46.2	251	18.9	463	34.9*	807	51.4	762	48.6
GREENE	2867	57.6	127	2.5	1987	39.9*	3977	64.6	2181	35.4
GRUNDY	1311	44.3	209	7.1	1442	48.7*	1618	48.6	1712	51.4
HAMBLEN	2188	48.9	431	9.6	1855	41.5*	2823	60.6	1838	39.4
HAMILTON	15997	34.0	10053	21.4	21010	44.6*	21012	52.4	19114	47.6
HANCOCK	489	60.5	23	2.8	296	36.6*	635	54.3	535	45.7
HARDEMAN	1956	45.7	1844	43.1	480	11.2*	2599	60.8	1676	39.2
HARDIN	2562	53.0	1316	27.2	959	19.8*	2391	52.9	2125	47.1
HAWKINS	1183	40.4	64	2.2	1681	57.4*	2291	60.0	1529	40.0
HAYWOOD	2046	57.3	1286	36.0	239	6.7*	1976	54.5	1653	45.5
HENDERSON	2105	47.7	956	21.7	1354	30.7*	1892	48.7	1992	51.3
HENRY	2491	38.2	3098	47.5	934	14.3*	3106	44.6	3851	55.4
HICKMAN	2075	46.3	1932	43.1	472	10.5*	2048	43.4	2672	56.6
HOUSTON	1133	53.9	714	34.0	255	12.1*	919	38.2	1485	61.8
HUMPHREYS	2187	49.9	1334	30.4	863	19.7*	1883	41.1	2700	58.9
JACKSON	2681	63.3	270	6.4	1285	30.3*	2531	61.4	1588	38.6
JEFFERSON	987	47.1	145	6.9	963	46.0*	1828	61.9	1123	38.1
JOHNSON	473	74.0	36	5.6	130	20.3*	511	58.6	361	41.4
KNOX	12743	35.9	3348	9.4	19377	54.6*	18808	56.1	14720	43.9
LAKE	1601	52.5	1058	34.7	391	12.8*	1592	73.5	574	26.5
LAUDERDLE	3414	48.3	2985	42.2	669	9.5*	3660	50.0	3658	50.0
LAWRENCE	3438	45.5	2106	27.9	2017	26.7*	4654	48.7	4893	51.3
LEWIS	1984	76.3	478	18.4	138	5.3*	1728	55.6	1382	44.4
LINCOLN	2705	38.0	1805	25.3	2613	36.7*	3437	49.3	3533	50.7
LOUDON	1634	39.3	160	3.8	2369	56.9*	1674	52.9	1488	47.1
MCMINN	2077	40.6	498	9.7	2538	49.6*	2969	63.2	1731	36.8
MCNAIRY	2584	44.3	1658	28.4	1596	27.3*	2314	49.3	2377	50.7
MACON	1008	46.7	640	29.7	510	23.6*	1360	54.9	1119	45.1
MADISON	7934	49.8	5430	34.1	2558	16.1*	8329	52.6	7516	47.4
MARION	3116	59.7	708	13.6	1393	26.7*	2391	51.6	2246	48.4
MARSHALL	2599	50.0	1436	27.6	1159	22.3*	4699	70.7	1950	29.3
MAURY	4063	38.7	2449	23.3	3995	38.0*	6127	54.4	5146	45.6
MEIGS	518	40.4	374	29.2	390	30.4*	489	48.4	521	51.6
MONROE	2168	44.4	377	7.7	2336	47.9*	2539	54.3	2139	45.7
MONTGOMRY	4559	45.2	3468	34.4	2060	20.4*	5295	46.6	6057	53.4
MOORE	484	35.9	464	34.4	402	29.8*	792	48.6	836	51.4
MORGAN	1234	34.6	161	4.5	2172	60.9*	1311	58.0	950	42.0
OBION	2412	34.1	3272	46.2	1397	19.7*	4425	58.1	3193	41.9
OVERTON	2053	51.7	297	7.5	1622	40.8*	2628	50.7	2558	49.3
PERRY	910	42.5	984	45.9	248	11.6*	1017	42.7	1362	57.3
PICKETT	422	52.2	111	13.7	275	34.0*	380	49.5	387	50.5

		DEMOC.	GOVERNOR	1962	*	DEMOC.	GOVERNOR	1966	
COUNTY	CLEMENT		FARRIS		OLGIATI		ELLINGTON		HOOKER	
	#	%	#	%	#	%*	#	%	#	%
POLK	1430	62.6	219	9.6	636	27.8*	1139	66.5	574	33.5
PUTNAM	3681	44.0	1284	15.4	3393	40.6*	4524	47.4	5016	52.6
RHEA	1473	45.9	847	26.4	889	27.7*	1699	56.5	1306	43.5
ROANE	3112	36.6	547	6.4	4848	57.0*	3083	48.5	3277	51.5
ROBERTSON	2146	41.9	1918	37.4	1063	20.7*	3547	53.0	3146	47.0
RUTHERFRD	4556	40.1	4564	40.2	2242	19.7*	7652	55.8	6053	44.2
SCOTT	1442	44.4	140	4.3	1664	51.3*	666	42.9	886	57.1
SEQUATCH	929	58.1	315	19.7	356	22.2*	947	54.6	788	45.4
SEVIER	825	41.8	116	5.9	1034	52.4*	1600	59.4	1092	40.6
SHELBY	39782	35.2	51219	45.3	22005	19.5*	61057	49.5	62350	50.5
SMITH	2264	46.8	1485	30.7	1090	22.5*	2497	50.1	2483	49.9
STEWART	1345	41.9	1539	47.9	329	10.2*	1047	34.1	2027	65.9
SULLIVAN	6730	54.4	487	3.9	5145	41.6*	8905	55.4	7161	44.6
SUMNER	5207	46.9	2106	19.0	3787	34.1*	7656	53.5	6642	46.5
TIPTON	4330	55.4	2767	35.4	714	9.1*	4413	58.2	3165	41.8
TROUSDALE	761	53.7	387	27.3	268	18.9*	1016	52.2	930	47.8
UNICOI	565	49.3	59	5.1	523	45.6*	889	54.8	734	45.2
UNION	984	64.9	29	1.9	504	33.2*	881	59.3	605	40.7
VN BUREN	928	61.1	275	18.1	315	20.8*	899	54.6	747	45.4
WARREN	2745	40.3	2632	38.6	1434	21.1*	3140	45.3	3790	54.7
WASHINGTN	3563	57.1	426	6.8	2251	36.1*	5804	63.9	3278	36.1
WAYNE	1347	50.6	875	32.9	440	16.5*	1243	44.0	1585	56.0
WEAKLEY	2822	45.5	2630	42.4	747	12.1*	3446	55.7	2738	44.3
WHITE	1348	38.6	844	24.2	1300	37.2*	2251	54.1	1913	45.9
WILLIAMSN	3256	43.9	1665	22.4	2500	33.7*	4984	56.7	3813	43.3
WILSON	3596	42.6	2532	30.0	2312	27.4*	5431	54.1	4614	45.9

| TOTALS | 309333 | | 202813 | | 211812 | * | 413950 | | 360105 | |
| % OF VOTE | 42.7 | | 28.0 | | 29.3 | * | 53.5 | | 46.5 | |

GEOGRAPHIC CLASS

LOWLANDS	81244	40.	86386	42.	35829	18.*	109534	51.	103375	49.
BLACK BELT	3934	58.	2272	34.	548	8.*	4344	53.	3864	47.
PIEDMONT	114045	45.	78065	31.	63651	25.*	164741	55.	136389	45.
MOUNTAIN	110110	43.	36090	14.	111784	43.*	135331	54.	116477	46.

DEMOGRAPHIC CLASS

METRO	103353	38.	91341	33.	78810	29.*	162085	55.	135262	45.
TOWN	24974	51.	10242	21.	13869	28.*	31156	55.	25850	45.
RURAL	181006	45.	101230	25.	119133	30.*	220709	53.	198993	47.

	DEMOC. GOVERNOR 1970							*	DEMOC. SENATOR 1952					
COUNTY	HOOKER		SNODGRASS		TAYLOR		OTHER		GORE		MCKELLAR		OTHER	
	#	%	#	%	#	%	#	%*	#	%	#	%	#	%
ANDERSON	3480	40.4	2884	33.5	1086	12.6	1159	13.5*	4600	55.1	3656	43.8	88	1.1
BEDFORD	2686	43.9	1984	32.5	804	13.2	640	10.5*	4343	67.6	1983	30.9	100	1.6
BENTON	1970	47.7	1353	32.8	406	9.8	401	9.7*	2157	57.4	1516	40.3	88	2.3
BLEDSOE	508	29.9	1111	65.4	62	3.6	19	1.1*	987	55.3	720	40.3	78	4.4
BLOUNT	3143	57.2	1491	27.1	569	10.4	293	5.3*	2608	53.7	2137	44.0	112	2.3
BRADLEY	2326	59.6	1104	28.3	299	7.7	172	4.4*	1894	56.1	1366	40.5	117	3.5
CAMPBELL	1626	57.6	972	34.5	95	3.4	128	4.5*	1089	39.4	1567	56.7	106	3.8
CANNON	1204	42.2	921	32.3	477	16.7	251	8.8*	2613	77.9	710	21.2	31	.9
CARROLL	2138	42.0	2095	41.2	406	7.8	449	8.8*	3242	62.1	1856	35.5	123	2.4
CARTER	1432	58.6	568	23.3	309	12.6	134	5.5*	1948	40.5	2730	56.8	130	2.7
CHEATHAM	1062	33.4	983	30.9	327	10.3	805	25.3*	1959	66.0	960	32.4	47	1.6
CHESTER	1313	51.2	859	33.5	348	13.6	45	1.8*	1841	63.0	1000	34.2	80	2.7
CLAIBORNE	1109	58.6	532	28.1	141	7.5	110	5.8*	997	37.9	1517	57.6	120	4.6
CLAY	923	48.1	513	26.7	364	19.0	120	6.3*	1424	66.4	688	32.1	31	1.4
COCKE	1337	78.2	157	9.2	110	6.4	105	6.1*	1200	45.0	1405	52.7	60	2.3
COFFEE	2084	36.7	2399	42.3	438	7.7	753	13.3*	4002	68.0	1830	31.1	57	1.0
CROCKETT	634	28.0	795	35.1	790	34.8	48	2.1*	2279	60.8	1417	37.8	55	1.5
CUMBERLND	1468	51.9	1017	36.0	219	7.7	124	4.4*	2388	58.7	1574	38.7	103	2.5
DAVIDSON	32453	37.5	38522	44.6	6341	7.3	9114	10.5*	27044	60.4	17353	38.7	408	.9
DECATUR	1428	58.4	589	24.1	341	13.9	88	3.6*	1638	68.2	731	30.4	34	1.4
DEKALB	1506	50.3	1213	40.5	128	4.3	146	4.9*	1927	56.9	1440	42.5	20	.6
DICKSON	1975	32.5	2210	36.4	460	7.6	1426	23.5*	4542	76.1	1345	22.5	80	1.3
DYER	2283	42.2	992	18.4	1725	31.9	405	7.5*	5603	70.5	2178	27.4	165	2.1
FAYETTE	1601	47.5	559	16.6	1086	32.2	126	3.7*	1032	51.4	964	48.0	12	.6
FENTRESS	745	54.3	472	34.4	107	7.8	48	3.5*	1178	64.9	597	32.9	39	2.1
FRANKLIN	1959	30.3	3452	53.4	554	8.6	497	7.7*	4142	56.0	3020	40.9	228	3.1
GIBSON	3454	37.7	2671	29.2	2556	27.9	478	5.2*	6588	60.8	4047	37.3	206	1.9
GILES	1470	49.6	804	27.1	436	14.7	256	8.6*	4221	66.3	1910	30.0	237	3.7
GRAINGER	845	70.4	179	14.9	161	13.4	16	1.3*	182	15.5	952	81.2	38	3.2
GREENE	1559	39.6	772	19.6	971	24.7	637	16.2*	1762	38.3	2729	59.3	114	2.5
GRUNDY	1275	46.4	1187	43.2	129	4.7	155	5.6*	1536	50.6	1416	46.7	83	2.7
HAMBLEN	1770	51.2	724	20.9	847	24.5	116	3.4*	1879	42.5	2455	55.5	86	1.9
HAMILTON	15445	51.9	10864	36.5	1993	6.7	1430	4.8*	16160	50.7	14596	45.8	1101	3.5
HANCOCK	239	44.4	207	38.5	43	8.0	49	9.1*	401	49.4	382	47.0	29	3.6
HARDEMAN	1078	29.0	963	25.9	1292	34.8	378	10.2*	2364	59.0	1507	37.6	139	3.5
HARDIN	1929	55.4	777	22.3	604	17.3	174	5.0*	884	45.5	1015	52.2	45	2.3
HAWKINS	1109	45.0	1002	40.6	211	8.6	145	5.9*	970	32.3	1922	64.0	112	3.7
HAYWOOD	888	32.3	410	14.9	1393	50.6	60	2.2*	2092	59.6	1367	38.9	54	1.5
HENDERSON	780	49.4	626	39.6	139	8.8	35	2.2*	1359	61.9	801	36.5	34	1.5
HENRY	2585	47.6	2226	41.0	327	6.0	290	5.3*	4406	63.0	2408	34.4	184	2.6
HICKMAN	1499	49.6	736	24.4	295	9.8	491	16.3*	2847	65.0	1440	32.9	90	2.1
HOUSTON	908	52.9	429	25.0	165	9.6	214	12.5*	1388	65.1	655	30.7	89	4.2
HUMPHREYS	1799	46.8	1134	29.5	390	10.1	522	13.6*	2490	60.2	1460	35.3	189	4.6
JACKSON	1639	66.0	498	20.1	204	8.2	142	5.7*	2879	65.8	1469	33.6	30	.7
JEFFERSON	719	41.9	196	11.4	739	43.1	62	3.6*	423	30.1	941	67.1	39	2.8
JOHNSON	450	61.4	197	26.9	44	6.0	42	5.7*	263	33.5	512	65.2	10	1.3

	DEMOC. GOVERNOR 1970							*	DEMOC. SENATOR 1952					
COUNTY	HOOKER #	%	SNODGRASS #	%	TAYLOR #	%	OTHER #	%*	GORE #	%	MCKELLAR #	%	OTHER #	%
KNOX	10864	46.2	6177	26.3	4844	20.6	1615	6.9*	15374	54.0	11935	41.9	1178	4.1
LAKE	894	43.8	681	33.4	345	16.9	119	5.8*	1276	49.5	1213	47.0	90	3.5
LAUDERDLE	2472	43.9	624	11.1	2412	42.8	126	2.2*	3244	65.6	1617	32.7	83	1.7
LAWRENCE	3637	63.1	1375	23.9	366	6.4	382	6.6*	3721	55.8	2818	42.2	134	2.0
LEWIS	924	39.2	1264	53.6	78	3.3	94	4.0*	677	30.6	1520	68.6	18	.8
LINCOLN	2566	44.0	2150	36.9	582	10.0	536	9.2*	5072	67.2	2323	30.8	148	2.0
LOUDON	1224	51.6	780	32.9	284	12.0	86	3.6*	1013	33.2	1932	63.3	108	3.5
MCMINN	2185	63.2	1018	29.4	127	3.7	127	3.7*	1378	41.9	1763	53.6	148	4.5
MCNAIRY	1686	42.8	1353	34.3	732	18.6	171	4.3*	2765	63.0	1467	33.4	160	3.6
MACON	933	55.3	481	28.5	166	9.8	108	6.4*	1578	67.2	755	32.2	15	.6
MADISON	4421	35.7	4714	38.0	2550	20.6	716	5.8*	8578	65.2	4405	33.5	174	1.3
MARION	1893	67.2	496	17.6	131	4.6	298	10.6*	1877	47.6	1854	47.0	211	5.4
MARSHALL	1982	40.5	1833	37.5	829	16.9	249	5.1*	3604	62.7	2092	36.4	50	.9
MAURY	4523	47.2	3149	32.9	1037	10.8	868	9.1*	6328	62.5	3495	34.5	301	3.0
MEIGS	357	50.8	276	39.3	27	3.8	43	6.1*	388	45.4	435	50.9	32	3.7
MONROE	1894	48.7	1502	38.6	268	6.9	223	5.7*	1470	39.6	2111	56.9	132	3.6
MONTGOMRY	4630	55.0	2264	26.9	763	9.1	768	9.1*	5373	65.3	2757	33.5	104	1.3
MOORE	597	40.6	498	33.9	186	12.6	190	12.9*	1055	69.6	452	29.8	8	.5
MORGAN	902	43.9	920	44.7	139	6.8	95	4.6*	1514	50.0	1333	44.1	179	5.9
OBION	2167	44.8	2083	43.0	332	6.9	258	5.3*	5129	74.7	1621	23.6	114	1.7
OVERTON	1440	57.7	654	26.2	307	12.3	95	3.8*	2002	48.1	2127	51.1	31	.7
PERRY	1006	60.5	395	23.8	115	6.9	147	8.8*	1357	60.2	758	33.6	140	6.2
PICKETT	377	62.3	150	24.8	48	7.9	30	5.0*	504	65.8	256	33.4	6	.8
POLK	1165	67.8	357	20.8	124	7.2	73	4.2*	1370	63.4	747	34.6	45	2.1
PUTNAM	3100	47.3	2416	36.9	568	8.7	470	7.2*	2490	37.3	4154	62.2	37	.6
RHEA	851	33.7	1467	58.1	156	6.2	51	2.0*	1047	50.8	907	44.0	107	5.2
ROANE	2778	46.6	2303	38.7	494	8.3	382	6.4*	2544	49.4	2458	47.7	151	2.9
ROBERTSON	3029	44.6	2354	34.7	388	5.7	1019	15.0*	4789	74.2	1569	24.3	99	1.5
RUTHERFRD	4095	35.1	4355	37.3	1584	13.6	1646	14.1*	7001	71.6	2651	27.1	132	1.3
SCOTT	663	68.6	176	18.2	88	9.1	39	4.0*	948	39.9	1295	54.5	133	5.6
SEQUATCH	708	62.2	321	28.2	57	5.0	53	4.7*	831	57.7	513	35.6	95	6.6
SEVIER	917	50.4	364	20.0	456	25.1	83	4.6*	1026	40.4	1452	57.2	59	2.3
SHELBY	41508	42.4	21351	21.8	29829	30.5	5246	5.4*	44798	47.9	47859	51.1	939	1.0
SMITH	1994	47.0	1318	31.1	455	10.7	472	11.1*	3398	71.0	1367	28.6	22	.5
STEWART	1297	55.5	712	30.4	122	5.2	208	8.9*	2087	69.8	842	28.2	62	2.1
SULLIVAN	5332	56.7	2969	31.6	578	6.2	517	5.5*	7351	59.0	4738	38.0	372	3.0
SUMNER	3965	36.3	4827	44.2	979	9.0	1146	10.5*	4972	66.3	2469	32.9	58	.8
TIPTON	3556	58.3	1112	18.2	1275	20.9	157	2.6*	3532	56.1	2611	41.5	150	2.4
TROUSDALE	670	48.9	372	27.2	205	15.0	123	9.0*	1409	79.4	351	19.8	15	.8
UNICOI	487	48.5	327	32.6	136	13.5	54	5.4*	674	42.6	872	55.1	37	2.3
UNION	493	48.7	399	39.4	81	8.0	39	3.9*	457	40.4	570	50.4	103	9.1
VN BUREN	621	44.9	663	47.9	37	2.7	63	4.6*	895	71.8	313	25.1	38	3.0
WARREN	2127	43.0	1935	39.1	387	7.8	500	10.1*	3195	53.6	2598	43.6	166	2.8
WASHINGTN	2091	40.2	1776	34.1	1082	20.8	257	4.9*	3643	46.3	3988	50.7	234	3.0
WAYNE	1147	61.6	441	23.7	143	7.7	132	7.1*	993	63.2	546	34.7	33	2.1
WEAKLEY	2575	42.0	2605	42.5	769	12.5	186	3.0*	4383	62.4	2542	36.2	94	1.3

```
                     DEMOC. GOVERNOR  1970          *       DEMOC. SENATOR  1952
                                                    *
COUNTY       HOOKER      SNODGRASS    TAYLOR     OTHER       GORE       MCKELLAR      OTHER
             #     %     #     %      #     %    #     %*    #     %    #     %       #     %
-------------------------------------------------------*------------------------------------------------------
WHITE        1666 50.3   1237 37.4    229  6.9   178  5.4*   2506 58.1  1721 39.9     87  2.0
WILLIAMSN    2270 31.5   2867 39.8    1326 18.4  741 10.3*   3843 58.6  2620 39.9     97  1.5
WILSON       3068 39.8   2989 38.7    862 11.2   796 10.3*   5727 73.3  2015 25.8     69   .9
-------------------------------------------------------*------------------------------------------------------
                                                    *
TOTALS       261580      193199       90009      45273   *   334957     245051       12419
% OF VOTE    44.3        32.7         15.3       7.7     *   56.5       41.4         2.1
                                                    *
                                                    *
GEOGRAPHIC CLASS                                    *
                                                    *
LOWLANDS     70910 42.   43029 26.    44956 27.   8853  5.*   96178 55.  75941 43.    2561  1.
BLACK BELT   2489 41.    969 16.      2479 40.    186   3.*   3124 57.   2331 42.     66   1.
PIEDMONT     98202 41.   93223 39.    22101  9.   25523 11.*  134284 63. 74899 35.    3296  2.
MOUNTAIN     89979 51.   55978 32.    20473 12.   10711  6.*  101371 51. 91880 46.    6496  3.
                                                    *
                                                    *
DEMOGRAPHIC CLASS                                   *
                                                    *
METRO        100270 42.  76914 32.    43007 18.   17405  7.*  103376 52. 91743 46.    3626  2.
TOWN         18244 47.   12447 32.    5820 15.    2374   6.*  31424 58.  21999 40.    1058  2.
RURAL        143066 46.  103838 33.   41182 13.   25494  8.*  200157 59. 131309 39.   7735  2.
```

TENNESSEE

```
                   DEMOC. SENATOR  1954    * DEMOC. SENATOR    1958
                                           *
COUNTY        KEFAUVER     SUTTON      OTHER     * COOPER       GORE
              #     %      #     %     #     %*  #     %      #     %
-------------------------------------------------*------------------------------------------------------
ANDERSON      7967 80.8    1613 16.4   283  2.9* 1765 19.2    7432 80.8
BEDFORD       3736 53.6    3134 45.0   98   1.4* 1956 33.8    3829 66.2
BENTON        3197 80.8    676 17.1    91   2.3* 1421 35.3    2601 64.7
BLEDSOE       1649 77.8    394 18.6    77   3.6* 811 45.3     978 54.7
BLOUNT        4702 82.2    902 15.8    115  2.0* 2027 35.1    3740 64.9
                                           *
BRADLEY       4405 73.1    1439 23.9   183  3.0* 3336 65.2    1781 34.8
CAMPBELL      2739 77.5    678 19.2    115  3.3* 1147 36.4    2006 63.6
CANNON        2418 69.6    990 28.5    68   2.0* 1192 33.6    2354 66.4
CARROLL       4343 67.0    1968 30.4   169  2.6* 2360 41.2    3363 58.8
CARTER        4718 68.8    1859 27.1   285  4.2* 2307 44.1    2927 55.9
                                           *
CHEATHAM      2435 66.6    1139 31.1   84   2.3* 880 27.5     2323 72.5
CHESTER       2002 54.8    1562 42.8   89   2.4* 2057 60.6    1337 39.4
CLAIBORNE     2263 80.6    427 15.2    116  4.1* 1121 46.3    1301 53.7
CLAY          1434 72.7    463 23.5    75   3.8* 698 35.8     1250 64.2
COCKE         2279 59.8    1376 36.1   159  4.2* 1412 49.6    1436 50.4
                                           *
COFFEE        4657 67.5    2103 30.5   140  2.0* 2436 31.9    5206 68.1
```

	DEMOC. SENATOR	1954	* DEMOC. SENATOR	1958	

COUNTY	KEFAUVER #	KEFAUVER %	SUTTON #	SUTTON %	OTHER #	OTHER %*	COOPER #	COOPER %	GORE #	GORE %
CROCKETT	1857	48.7	1923	50.4	36	.9*	1945	63.8	1103	36.2
CUMBERLND	2774	66.4	1144	27.4	258	6.2*	1241	34.7	2336	65.3
DAVIDSON	43444	72.1	14788	24.6	1991	3.3*	16454	27.7	42876	72.3
DECATUR	1685	57.7	1194	40.9	40	1.4*	1077	42.7	1445	57.3
DEKALB	2379	61.0	1497	38.3	29	.7*	1506	45.7	1788	54.3
DICKSON	3724	62.9	2116	35.8	78	1.3*	1074	21.1	4022	78.9
DYER	4926	56.2	3754	42.9	78	.9*	4439	58.3	3172	41.7
FAYETTE	850	41.8	1148	56.5	35	1.7*	1718	79.0	458	21.0
FENTRESS	1384	66.4	596	28.6	104	5.0*	946	45.5	1135	54.5
FRANKLIN	5243	66.0	2538	32.0	157	2.0*	1848	28.3	4690	71.7
GIBSON	8185	65.5	4176	33.4	144	1.2*	5293	52.1	4864	47.9
GILES	5257	73.0	1811	25.2	131	1.8*	1423	24.2	4465	75.8
GRAINGER	1054	75.0	302	21.5	49	3.5*	893	68.0	421	32.0
GREENE	3935	84.2	649	13.9	89	1.9*	2656	61.0	1695	39.0
GRUNDY	3032	81.2	622	16.7	78	2.1*	1642	54.2	1389	45.8
HAMBLEN	2503	65.1	1202	31.2	142	3.7*	2093	50.2	2079	49.8
HAMILTON	23766	72.7	8261	25.3	653	2.0*	21327	60.6	13875	39.4
HANCOCK	640	64.5	328	33.1	24	2.4*	693	78.9	185	21.1
HARDEMAN	2315	53.6	1855	43.0	146	3.4*	2765	66.2	1410	33.8
HARDIN	2196	67.8	968	29.9	75	2.3*	1482	38.3	2392	61.7
HAWKINS	2612	76.1	710	20.7	109	3.2*	1156	41.1	1658	58.9
HAYWOOD	1629	44.9	1972	54.3	31	.9*	2411	70.1	1030	29.9
HENDERSON	1974	55.1	1538	42.9	69	1.9*	1671	47.9	1816	52.1
HENRY	5287	73.1	1814	25.1	135	1.9*	2055	31.9	4396	68.1
HICKMAN	2814	61.3	1681	36.6	92	2.0*	1397	35.3	2558	64.7
HOUSTON	1438	59.5	925	38.3	54	2.2*	520	25.9	1489	74.1
HUMPHREYS	2233	53.3	1911	45.6	43	1.0*	1105	29.3	2672	70.7
JACKSON	2952	67.7	1281	29.4	130	3.0*	1658	39.4	2549	60.6
JEFFERSON	1474	60.6	905	37.2	52	2.1*	862	55.9	679	44.1
JOHNSON	793	74.7	234	22.0	35	3.3*	385	49.5	393	50.5
KNOX	20856	75.3	6104	22.1	721	2.6*	8971	33.8	17605	66.2
LAKE	1628	55.2	1215	41.2	107	3.6*	1404	52.7	1259	47.3
LAUDERDLE	4511	62.9	2476	34.5	180	2.5*	3616	56.8	2752	43.2
LAWRENCE	3267	42.7	4247	55.6	131	1.7*	2587	38.6	4108	61.4
LEWIS	1742	74.7	554	23.8	35	1.5*	746	33.0	1517	67.0
LINCOLN	5307	72.0	1870	25.4	190	2.6*	2266	31.9	4838	68.1
LOUDON	2704	67.8	1195	30.0	89	2.2*	1023	34.2	1970	65.8
MCMINN	3860	88.2	461	10.5	55	1.3*	1498	44.4	1875	55.6
MCNAIRY	3163	56.8	2234	40.1	174	3.1*	2965	51.8	2764	48.2
MACON	1447	58.2	1003	40.3	36	1.4*	656	31.2	1449	68.8
MADISON	9762	61.0	5944	37.2	289	1.8*	7953	47.3	8869	52.7
MARION	3397	67.3	1311	26.0	338	6.7*	2851	60.7	1846	39.3
MARSHALL	4320	73.5	1500	25.5	57	1.0*	1853	29.1	4519	70.9
MAURY	6927	65.7	3333	31.6	284	2.7*	5098	48.2	5470	51.8
MEIGS	1081	85.0	155	12.2	36	2.8*	404	44.2	511	55.8
MONROE	4059	92.7	255	5.8	63	1.4*	1910	44.4	2394	55.6

| COUNTY | DEMOC. SENATOR 1954 | | | | | | DEMOC. SENATOR 1958 | | | | |
| | KEFAUVER | | SUTTON | | OTHER | | COOPER | | GORE | |
	#	%	#	%	#	%*	#	%	#	%
MONTGOMRY	5958	62.6	3333	35.0	234	2.5*	2159	23.3	7106	76.7
MOORE	871	64.0	471	34.6	18	1.3*	376	27.0	1019	73.0
MORGAN	2282	63.5	1182	32.9	132	3.7*	1302	47.3	1451	52.7
OBION	5119	70.4	1967	27.1	185	2.5*	3154	49.2	3257	50.8
OVERTON	3327	77.8	810	18.9	142	3.3*	1532	39.2	2375	60.8
PERRY	1322	52.2	1165	46.0	44	1.7*	920	40.4	1357	59.6
PICKETT	660	86.6	84	11.0	18	2.4*	99	15.4	542	84.6
POLK	1595	71.4	537	24.0	101	4.5*	972	53.0	862	47.0
PUTNAM	5354	62.8	3063	35.9	115	1.3*	3519	41.0	5063	59.0
RHEA	2387	77.8	547	17.8	133	4.3*	1320	52.7	1186	47.3
ROANE	5246	67.6	2348	30.2	172	2.2*	2752	36.6	4772	63.4
ROBERTSON	5185	70.0	1986	26.8	234	3.2*	1324	22.4	4598	77.6
RUTHERFRD	7066	71.7	2566	26.0	225	2.3*	2347	27.4	6220	72.6
SCOTT	1909	68.6	729	26.2	146	5.2*	821	54.4	688	45.6
SEQUATCH	1318	72.8	436	24.1	56	3.1*	907	59.6	614	40.4
SEVIER	1594	61.7	40	1.5	949	36.7*	1008	55.5	809	44.5
SHELBY	47246	66.0	20367	28.4	3981	5.6*	40144	40.7	58548	59.3
SMITH	3353	64.7	1702	32.8	131	2.5*	1251	24.9	3772	75.1
STEWART	1991	57.9	1382	40.2	68	2.0*	755	25.6	2192	74.4
SULLIVAN	13279	85.1	2038	13.1	293	1.9*	4199	36.7	7256	63.3
SUMNER	7139	74.4	2132	22.2	330	3.4*	1812	20.1	7212	79.9
TIPTON	4013	58.3	2742	39.8	133	1.9*	4941	70.1	2108	29.9
TROUSDALE	1367	67.6	613	30.3	43	2.1*	474	25.8	1362	74.2
UNICOI	1586	89.6	151	8.5	33	1.9*	491	32.0	1044	68.0
UNION	777	72.2	239	22.2	60	5.6*	527	43.0	700	57.0
VN BUREN	926	63.5	474	32.5	59	4.0*	593	49.4	607	50.6
WARREN	4132	63.0	2313	35.3	110	1.7*	2738	44.2	3455	55.8
WASHINGTN	6857	72.1	2315	24.4	334	3.5*	2816	34.7	5299	65.3
WAYNE	1257	56.5	957	43.0	11	.5*	940	43.8	1208	56.2
WEAKLEY	4706	64.7	2454	33.7	118	1.6*	2289	39.4	3516	60.6
WHITE	2983	66.4	1324	29.5	185	4.1*	1506	37.6	2494	62.3
WILLIAMSN	4640	58.0	3205	40.1	149	1.9*	2324	34.4	4423	65.6
WILSON	5722	70.5	2268	27.9	130	1.6*	2317	29.0	5679	71.0
TOTALS	440497		186363		19091	*	253091		375444	
% OF VOTE		68.2		28.9		3.0*		40.3		59.7

```
            DEMOC.  SENATOR   1954     * DEMOC.  SENATOR    1958
                                       *
COUNTY      KEFAUVER      SUTTON        OTHER     * COOPER        GORE
            #      %      #      %      #      %* #      %      #      %
----------------------------------------------------*-------------------------------------------------
GEOGRAPHIC CLASS                                 *

LOWLANDS    104754 64.    52925 32.     5712  3.* 83476 46.     99192 54.
BLACK BELT    2479 44.     3120 55.       66  1.*  4129 74.      1488 26.
PIEDMONT    161899 68.    71980 30.     5862  2.* 68928 31.    155837 69.
MOUNTAIN    171365 72.    58338 25.     7451  3.* 96558 45.    118927 55.
                                                 *
                                                 *
DEMOGRAPHIC CLASS                                *
                                                 *
METRO       135312 70.    49520 26.     7346  4.* 86896 40.    132904 60.
TOWN         46326 72.    16445 26.     1575  2.* 20985 36.     38041 64.
RURAL       258859 66.   120398 31.    10170  3.*145210 42.    204499 58.
```


TENNESSEE


```
            DEMOC.  SENATOR   1960     *         DEMOC.  SENATOR    1964
                                       *
COUNTY      ARMSTRONG   KEFAUVER    TAYLOR      *  BASS        BULLARD     CLEMENT
            #     %     #      %    #      %*   #      %    #      %    #      %
----------------------------------------------*----------------------------------------------------
ANDERSON     75  .7   9982 89.2  1139 10.2*  5442 62.6   998 11.5   2256 25.9
BEDFORD      53  .7   5195 69.2  2259 30.1*  3985 51.1   447  5.7   3365 43.2
BENTON       21  .6   2611 69.3  1135 30.1*  2146 54.3   309  7.8   1494 37.8
BLEDSOE       9  .5    820 49.5   826 49.9*   435 24.3   120  6.7   1233 69.0
BLOUNT       27  .4   5250 86.1   821 13.5*  1849 44.5   466 11.2   1840 44.3
                                       *
BRADLEY      32  .6   3661 66.9  1776 32.5*  2169 44.1   869 17.7   1876 38.2
CAMPBELL     21  .5   3352 82.6   687 16.9*  1019 34.7   223  7.6   1693 57.7
CANNON       17  .5   2421 71.3   957 28.2*  1337 35.1  1468 38.5   1007 26.4
CARROLL      32  .5   3193 54.5  2636 45.0*  2731 48.7   518  9.2   2363 42.1
CARTER       20  .3   6092 79.5  1551 20.2*  1506 35.8   295  7.0   2400 57.1
                                       *
CHEATHAM     25  .8   2285 75.0   735 24.1*  2452 69.1   205  5.8    889 25.1
CHESTER      21  .6   1200 33.9  2324 65.6*  1423 45.4   291  9.3   1421 45.3
CLAIBORNE    33 1.3   2372 90.3   222  8.5*   944 34.9   259  9.6   1500 55.5
CLAY         17 1.0   1338 76.2   402 22.9*  1053 50.2    60  2.9    983 46.9
COCKE        18  .5   2582 71.5  1009 28.0*   178  4.0  2799 62.4   1510 33.7
                                       *
COFFEE       34  .4   5969 75.2  1933 24.4*  5455 64.4   744  8.8   2267 26.8
CROCKETT     12  .3   1030 26.3  2871 73.4*   682 27.3   672 26.9   1141 45.7
CUMBERLND    31  .8   2777 72.0  1048 27.2*  2008 59.1   122  3.6   1266 37.3
DAVIDSON    276  .4  55805 71.4 22068 28.2* 50230 63.1  6382  8.0  23044 28.9
DECATUR      17  .6   1411 46.9  1579 52.5*  1374 54.2   232  9.2    929 36.6
                                       *
DEKALB        9  .3   1889 72.0   727 27.7*  1882 51.1   410 11.1   1388 37.7
DICKSON      32  .6   4279 79.0  1105 20.4*  2605 48.6   185  3.4   2573 48.0
DYER         41  .5   3107 38.4  4951 61.1*  2668 31.3  1518 17.8   4333 50.9
```

COUNTY	ARMSTRONG #	%	KEFAUVER #	%	TAYLOR #	%*	BASS #	%	BULLARD #	%	CLEMENT #	%
FAYETTE	14	.4	368	11.5	2805	88.0*	1931	38.3	1332	26.4	1773	35.2
FENTRESS	8	.5	1396	83.2	274	16.3*	1246	61.8	64	3.2	706	35.0
FRANKLIN	26	.3	5418	71.3	2154	28.3*	4779	57.5	607	7.3	2925	35.2
GIBSON	35	.3	5023	47.2	5586	52.5*	3382	44.7	1274	16.8	2907	38.4
GILES	36	.6	5247	80.4	1246	19.1*	4231	68.4	476	7.7	1481	23.9
GRAINGER	11	.8	1126	86.5	164	12.6*	461	38.7	263	22.1	466	39.2
GREENE	32	.6	3882	78.1	1055	21.2*	1166	25.8	1140	25.2	2222	49.1
GRUNDY	18	.7	1785	67.8	829	31.5*	1567	48.4	302	9.3	1367	42.2
HAMBLEN	45	1.0	3329	75.2	1053	23.8*	2428	53.4	666	14.6	1457	32.0
HAMILTON	465	1.0	25174	56.0	19284	42.9*	15779	46.3	8286	24.3	10026	29.4
HANCOCK	4	.6	594	86.6	88	12.8*	219	28.6	64	8.3	484	63.1
HARDEMAN	21	.5	910	23.3	2980	76.2*	765	20.4	1091	29.1	1887	50.4
HARDIN	26	.6	2375	51.3	2233	48.2*	1413	36.6	432	11.2	2016	52.2
HAWKINS	31	1.0	2692	87.8	342	11.2*	1342	41.6	298	9.2	1585	49.1
HAYWOOD	12	.3	721	19.4	2991	80.3*	591	23.1	749	29.3	1218	47.6
HENDERSON	9	.3	1054	33.7	2064	66.0*	1665	46.2	564	15.6	1377	38.2
HENRY	31	.5	3673	55.1	2960	44.4*	2748	51.4	766	14.3	1833	34.3
HICKMAN	28	.6	3147	71.3	1241	28.1*	2639	59.2	391	8.8	1429	32.0
HOUSTON	24	1.2	1664	83.5	306	15.3*	1675	70.1	70	2.9	644	27.0
HUMPHREYS	27	.6	3196	76.1	975	23.2*	2774	67.0	251	6.1	1114	26.9
JACKSON	31	.9	2389	69.3	1027	29.8*	1911	50.5	71	1.9	1801	47.6
JEFFERSON	12	.6	1386	66.4	690	33.0*	653	30.9	535	25.3	927	43.8
JOHNSON	4	.5	633	75.1	206	24.4*	223	32.6	48	7.0	414	60.4
KNOX	419	1.3	25771	79.5	6242	19.2*	12975	52.3	4524	18.2	7314	29.5
LAKE	56	2.0	1370	49.7	1332	48.3*	494	20.1	166	6.8	1796	73.1
LAUDERDLE	88	1.4	2533	39.2	3840	59.4*	1377	26.3	1098	21.0	2756	52.7
LAWRENCE	28	.4	5301	68.6	2404	31.1*	5190	66.0	507	6.5	2162	27.5
LEWIS	6	.3	848	41.6	1183	58.1*	550	23.1	35	1.5	1794	75.4
LINCOLN	35	.5	6109	81.3	1371	18.2*	4351	62.8	500	7.2	2072	29.9
LOUDON	21	.6	3287	87.0	471	12.5*	938	41.0	375	16.4	975	42.6
MCMINN	141	2.8	4386	86.7	534	10.6*	1769	38.9	359	7.9	2423	53.2
MCNAIRY	27	.5	2327	41.8	3208	57.7*	1736	37.8	562	12.2	2291	49.9
MACON	10	.5	1493	72.8	547	26.7*	1254	55.6	137	6.1	865	38.3
MADISON	162	.8	5850	28.8	14288	70.4*	6392	44.4	3079	21.4	4925	34.2
MARION	71	1.3	2887	53.9	2403	44.8*	1290	30.0	558	13.0	2445	57.0
MARSHALL	25	.5	4131	75.1	1347	24.5*	3116	60.7	342	6.7	1674	32.6
MAURY	80	.8	6387	63.4	3606	35.8*	5888	52.0	1613	14.2	3826	33.8
MEIGS	8	.8	782	75.7	243	23.5*	306	31.8	138	14.3	518	53.8
MONROE	42	.9	4443	92.6	314	6.5*	1033	25.9	651	16.3	2299	57.7
MONTGOMRY	83	.8	8817	81.8	1883	17.5*	7553	68.7	575	5.2	2870	26.1
MOORE	12	.9	994	73.0	355	26.1*	886	61.7	86	6.0	464	32.3
MORGAN	17	.6	1905	69.6	816	29.8*	667	37.3	73	4.1	1046	58.6
OBION	42	.6	4059	53.3	3513	46.1*	2333	41.8	743	13.3	2502	44.9
OVERTON	20	.5	2911	78.5	775	20.9*	2420	60.5	121	3.0	1460	36.5
PERRY	9	.4	1583	70.1	667	29.5*	1323	58.4	159	7.0	784	34.6
PICKETT	0	.0	538	81.9	119	18.1*	420	55.9	9	1.2	323	43.0

	DEMOC. SENATOR 1960					*	DEMOC. SENATOR 1964				
COUNTY	ARMSTRONG		KEFAUVER		TAYLOR		BASS		BULLARD		CLEMENT	
	#	%	#	%	#	%*	#	%	#	%	#	%
POLK	9	.5	1412	75.8	441	23.7*	392	31.5	116	9.3	736	59.2
PUTNAM	30	.4	5933	72.9	2180	26.8*	4565	59.7	335	4.4	2751	36.0
RHEA	20	.8	1527	62.8	883	36.3*	1191	42.5	484	17.3	1130	40.3
ROANE	58	.8	5923	82.6	1188	16.6*	2762	53.1	488	9.4	1948	37.5
ROBERTSON	34	.6	4299	74.2	1459	25.2*	4838	69.6	478	6.9	1636	23.5
RUTHERFRD	75	.7	7783	73.4	2748	25.9*	6875	59.9	1037	9.0	3564	31.1
SCOTT	26	1.7	1294	83.5	229	14.8*	593	42.9	41	3.0	749	54.2
SEQUATCH	19	1.3	813	53.6	684	45.1*	794	43.2	309	16.8	736	40.0
SEVIER	9	.5	1523	84.8	265	14.7*	456	21.1	664	30.7	1041	48.2
SHELBY	808	.7	64349	54.3	53424	45.1*	47596	47.4	18607	18.5	34127	34.0
SMITH	13	.3	3472	77.2	1013	22.5*	2383	54.5	242	5.5	1746	39.9
STEWART	20	.6	2748	85.4	448	13.9*	2505	80.3	110	3.5	504	16.2
SULLIVAN	109	.6	13575	79.8	3328	19.6*	6953	50.7	1994	14.5	4765	34.8
SUMNER	54	.6	7233	80.0	1749	19.4*	6769	66.0	623	6.1	2868	28.0
TIPTON	58	.8	2544	36.1	4443	63.1*	1462	21.2	1226	17.8	4210	61.0
TROUSDALE	35	1.9	1450	78.9	352	19.2*	899	54.8	92	5.6	650	39.6
UNICOI	5	.3	1584	90.7	157	9.0*	875	54.5	127	7.9	604	37.6
UNION	12	1.0	724	59.9	473	39.1*	299	31.5	72	7.6	579	60.9
VN BUREN	10	.7	1024	69.8	434	29.6*	717	48.1	43	2.9	730	49.0
WARREN	38	.6	4687	73.9	1615	25.5*	4372	64.1	470	6.9	1974	29.0
WASHINGTN	59	.5	7627	71.0	3062	28.5*	3223	44.5	940	13.0	3084	42.6
WAYNE	20	.8	1262	53.6	1072	45.5*	867	49.9	93	5.4	778	44.8
WEAKLEY	19	.3	2607	47.5	2865	52.2*	2238	43.3	503	9.7	2424	46.9
WHITE	30	.7	2901	70.6	1177	28.7*	2215	65.1	151	4.4	1038	30.5
WILLIAMSN	35	.4	5250	67.1	2540	32.5*	4908	64.1	630	8.2	2120	27.7
WILSON	37	.5	5789	71.0	2332	28.6*	4044	54.0	1101	14.7	2339	31.3
TOTALS	4867		463848		249336	*	330213		86718		233245	
% OF VOTE	.7		64.6		34.7	*	50.8		13.3		35.9	
GEOGRAPHIC CLASS						*						
LOWLANDS	1415	1.	100866	48.	106512	51.*	75706	43.	31343	18.	67756	39.
BLACK BELT	26	0.	1089	16.	5796	84.*	2522	33.	2081	27.	2991	39.
PIEDMONT	1299	1.	182639	73.	65525	26.*	157691	61.	19274	7.	81420	32.
MOUNTAIN	2127	1.	179254	71.	71503	28.*	94294	45.	34020	16.	81078	39.
DEMOGRAPHIC CLASS						*						
METRO	1968	1.	171099	62.	101018	37.*	126580	53.	37799	16.	74511	31.
TOWN	533	1.	49180	66.	24753	33.*	22610	55.	5592	14.	13135	32.
RURAL	2366	1.	243569	66.	123565	33.*	181023	49.	43327	12.	145599	39.

COUNTY	BASS #	%	CLEMENT #	%*	ANDRESS #	%	CROCKETT #	%	FREY #	%	GORE #	%
ANDERSON	5313	55.5	4266	44.5*	224	2.9	2112	27.3	210	2.7	5187	67.1
BEDFORD	3356	49.3	3450	50.7*	56	1.0	2856	49.0	108	1.9	2803	48.1
BENTON	2565	57.1	1926	42.9*	31	.8	2120	53.0	42	1.0	1810	45.2
BLEDSOE	816	40.1	1221	59.9*	22	1.5	429	29.3	27	1.8	986	67.3
BLOUNT	3405	51.8	3164	48.2*	104	2.1	1292	26.6	137	2.8	3323	68.4
BRADLEY	2629	48.4	2806	51.6*	74	2.1	1218	34.3	76	2.1	2182	61.5
CAMPBELL	2056	53.7	1773	46.3*	70	3.3	361	16.8	112	5.2	1600	74.7
CANNON	2149	50.6	2094	49.4*	59	2.4	974	39.3	91	3.7	1356	54.7
CARROLL	3195	51.5	3009	48.5*	95	2.1	2486	54.2	86	1.9	1918	41.8
CARTER	2779	47.3	3095	52.7*	67	3.0	635	28.7	52	2.4	1455	65.9
CHEATHAM	2110	56.0	1661	44.0*	45	1.6	1317	46.0	49	1.7	1451	50.7
CHESTER	1719	48.3	1840	51.7*	38	1.7	1245	54.7	46	2.0	946	41.6
CLAIBORNE	1628	54.0	1389	46.0*	65	4.9	235	17.6	36	2.7	997	74.8
CLAY	1066	43.9	1360	56.1*	45	3.0	525	35.2	33	2.2	890	59.6
COCKE	1827	46.3	2119	53.7*	53	4.9	271	24.9	65	6.0	701	64.3
COFFEE	3773	45.6	4507	54.4*	73	1.3	2928	53.2	43	.8	2457	44.7
CROCKETT	1160	38.4	1859	61.6*	18	.8	1752	81.4	21	1.0	361	16.8
CUMBERLND	1811	54.7	1499	45.3*	68	2.7	830	33.0	70	2.8	1544	61.5
DAVIDSON	45665	47.0	51511	53.0*	413	.5	39686	49.1	688	.9	40010	49.5
DECATUR	1673	55.4	1348	44.6*	38	1.6	891	38.6	37	1.6	1344	58.2
DEKALB	2227	55.2	1806	44.8*	49	1.8	1376	50.8	32	1.2	1251	46.2
DICKSON	2472	37.2	4169	62.8*	101	1.8	2701	47.9	190	3.4	2652	47.0
DYER	3288	38.2	5322	61.8*	183	4.2	2642	60.4	167	3.8	1379	31.5
FAYETTE	2047	45.7	2430	54.3*	84	2.8	1450	48.6	103	3.5	1347	45.1
FENTRESS	940	46.9	1066	53.1*	20	1.8	282	25.8	30	2.7	763	69.7
FRANKLIN	4741	53.2	4166	46.8*	90	1.5	2906	48.2	92	1.5	2940	48.8
GIBSON	5173	46.8	5875	53.2*	208	2.4	5874	69.0	215	2.5	2214	26.0
GILES	3867	54.8	3185	45.2*	42	1.4	1372	45.9	58	1.9	1519	50.8
GRAINGER	937	61.6	584	38.4*	29	2.5	156	13.7	25	2.2	930	81.6
GREENE	2413	40.6	3531	59.4*	114	3.4	969	29.2	84	2.5	2155	64.9
GRUNDY	1882	56.7	1435	43.3*	56	2.4	772	32.7	47	2.0	1489	63.0
HAMBLEN	2279	50.8	2203	49.2*	70	2.6	773	28.9	82	3.1	1753	65.5
HAMILTON	17917	46.2	20863	53.8*	414	1.6	10752	40.5	750	2.8	14621	55.1
HANCOCK	452	40.1	675	59.9*	14	4.3	49	15.2	12	3.7	248	76.8
HARDEMAN	1553	38.4	2491	61.6*	265	8.3	1835	57.6	200	6.3	887	27.8
HARDIN	1963	44.7	2427	55.3*	77	2.5	1561	51.4	79	2.6	1321	43.5
HAWKINS	1826	48.2	1964	51.8*	96	4.4	486	22.2	63	2.9	1543	70.5
HAYWOOD	1544	43.7	1991	56.3*	47	1.8	1659	63.6	30	1.1	873	33.5
HENDERSON	1930	50.8	1866	49.2*	17	1.0	896	55.0	19	1.2	698	42.8
HENRY	3811	55.6	3043	44.4*	52	1.0	2870	55.7	49	1.0	2183	42.4
HICKMAN	2963	63.4	1711	36.6*	48	1.8	1028	37.9	49	1.8	1584	58.5
HOUSTON	1527	63.6	875	36.4*	38	2.5	392	25.4	26	1.7	1087	70.4
HUMPHREYS	2807	61.6	1750	38.4*	45	1.3	1337	37.4	46	1.3	2151	60.1
JACKSON	1635	40.0	2457	60.0*	26	1.1	590	25.0	34	1.4	1706	72.4
JEFFERSON	1239	43.1	1635	56.9*	45	3.0	424	28.2	51	3.4	986	65.5
JOHNSON	356	41.8	495	58.2*	33	5.9	133	23.8	26	4.7	367	65.7

COUNTY	BASS #	%	CLEMENT #	%*	ANDRESS #	%	CROCKETT #	%	FREY #	%	GORE #	%
KNOX	16114	51.8	14966	48.2*	587	2.9	5442	26.6	633	3.1	13802	67.4
LAKE	705	30.7	1591	69.3*	104	6.0	763	44.1	69	4.0	795	46.2
LAUDERDLE	3333	47.9	3623	52.1*	129	2.6	3081	61.0	92	1.8	1751	34.7
LAWRENCE	4911	52.2	4499	47.8*	83	1.5	2456	45.8	67	1.2	2757	51.4
LEWIS	1467	47.9	1595	52.1*	32	1.4	777	34.4	33	1.5	1414	62.7
LINCOLN	3603	52.9	3214	47.1*	54	1.0	2676	49.1	68	1.2	2651	48.7
LOUDON	1414	48.6	1494	51.4*	49	2.4	461	22.8	43	2.1	1466	72.6
MCMINN	1986	43.0	2633	57.0*	49	1.7	630	21.6	80	2.7	2164	74.0
MCNAIRY	2295	50.6	2240	49.4*	186	5.4	1378	40.1	124	3.6	1734	50.7
MACON	1244	50.9	1200	49.1*	19	1.1	487	29.1	17	1.0	1153	68.8
MADISON	7195	46.9	8149	53.1*	213	1.8	7845	66.2	300	2.5	3490	29.5
MARION	2184	47.7	2398	52.3*	83	3.4	740	30.5	101	4.2	1505	62.0
MARSHALL	2997	47.6	3300	52.4*	30	.7	2178	49.9	18	.4	2135	49.0
MAURY	4962	46.3	5757	53.7*	53	.7	5002	64.9	72	.9	2580	33.5
MEIGS	493	50.7	480	49.3*	19	3.1	154	25.1	24	3.9	416	67.9
MONROE	2717	60.9	1744	39.1*	95	2.8	609	17.8	138	4.0	2583	75.4
MONTGOMRY	6216	57.2	4648	42.8*	339	4.5	3077	41.2	266	3.6	3793	50.7
MOORE	850	54.6	706	45.4*	26	1.9	539	40.2	19	1.4	756	56.4
MORGAN	1116	50.4	1098	49.6*	60	3.5	694	40.0	55	3.2	925	53.3
OBION	3910	52.8	3490	47.2*	110	2.6	2426	58.4	69	1.7	1546	37.2
OVERTON	2690	52.2	2461	47.8*	21	.9	1010	42.3	25	1.0	1332	55.8
PERRY	1424	60.9	914	39.1*	21	1.4	396	26.5	27	1.8	1052	70.3
PICKETT	408	54.7	338	45.3*	5	.9	116	20.2	5	.9	449	78.1
POLK	879	53.0	778	47.0*	34	2.3	235	16.1	21	1.4	1171	80.2
PUTNAM	5037	53.3	4408	46.7*	56	.9	2926	46.8	60	1.0	3207	51.3
RHEA	1380	46.7	1573	53.3*	52	2.4	662	30.0	38	1.7	1454	65.9
ROANE	2928	49.9	2935	50.1*	94	2.0	1630	34.3	91	1.9	2931	61.8
ROBERTSON	3416	53.1	3020	46.9*	171	2.9	2334	39.8	176	3.0	3179	54.2
RUTHERFRD	6269	46.4	7247	53.6*	144	1.4	5609	52.7	380	3.6	4520	42.4
SCOTT	860	57.0	650	43.0*	26	3.3	100	12.7	23	2.9	638	81.1
SEQUATCH	840	49.4	862	50.6*	19	1.9	386	39.1	33	3.3	550	55.7
SEVIER	1251	47.7	1371	52.3*	56	4.0	368	26.1	66	4.7	921	65.3
SHELBY	56797	47.7	62366	52.3*	1729	2.0	41240	48.9	1194	1.4	40206	47.7
SMITH	2304	46.8	2622	53.2*	58	1.4	1280	30.5	79	1.9	2780	66.2
STEWART	2278	75.1	757	24.9*	47	2.2	481	22.6	62	2.9	1539	72.3
SULLIVAN	7493	49.0	7795	51.0*	194	2.5	2521	32.5	242	3.1	4809	61.9
SUMNER	6888	48.8	7219	51.2*	106	1.0	4967	46.7	166	1.6	5401	50.8
TIPTON	2721	37.2	4585	62.8*	135	2.4	3495	61.4	126	2.2	1940	34.1
TROUSDALE	813	42.6	1095	57.4*	26	2.1	439	34.7	31	2.5	768	60.8
UNICOI	844	53.0	748	47.0*	24	2.6	183	19.8	49	5.3	666	72.2
UNION	678	48.1	733	51.9*	33	4.5	192	26.1	17	2.3	495	67.2
VN BUREN	758	46.3	878	53.7*	34	3.1	444	40.5	21	1.9	598	54.5
WARREN	3849	56.4	2970	43.6*	72	1.6	2213	49.7	79	1.8	2091	46.9
WASHINGTN	3571	40.1	5339	59.9*	142	3.0	1667	35.7	74	1.6	2786	59.7
WAYNE	1463	53.4	1279	46.6*	34	2.1	795	49.8	21	1.3	745	46.7
WEAKLEY	2836	47.3	3159	52.7*	120	2.1	3261	56.4	126	2.2	2278	39.4

	DEMOC.	SENATOR	1966*		DEMOC.	SENATOR	1970			
COUNTY	BASS		CLEMENT	ANDRESS		CROCKETT		FREY		GORE	
	#	%	#	%*	#	%	#	%	#	%	#	%
WHITE	2226	54.0	1896	46.0*	31	1.0	1480	46.0	19	.6	1684	52.4
WILLIAMSN	4434	51.2	4226	48.8*	68	1.0	4007	60.4	72	1.1	2490	37.5
WILSON	4548	45.9	5361	54.1*	78	1.1	3467	47.2	98	1.3	3706	50.4
TOTALS	366079		384322	*	9871		238767		10297		269770	
% OF VOTE	48.8		51.2	*	1.9		45.2		1.9		51.0	
				*							
GEOGRAPHIC CLASS				*							
				*							
LOWLANDS	96766	47.	109319	53.*	3335	2.	80449	54.	2716	2.	61786	42.
BLACK BELT	3591	45.	4421	55.*	131	2.	3109	56.	133	2.	2220	40.
PIEDMONT	146217	50.	147704	50.*	2542	1.	104513	47.	3239	1.	111148	50.
MOUNTAIN	119505	49.	122878	51.*	3863	3.	50696	33.	4209	3.	94616	62.
				*							
DEMOGRAPHIC CLASS				*							
				*							
METRO	136493	48.	149706	52.*	3143	1.	97120	46.	3265	2.	108639	51.
TOWN	32067	50.	32400	50.*	816	3.	14216	48.	890	3.	13845	47.
RURAL	197519	49.	202216	51.*	5912	2.	127431	44.	6142	2.	147286	51.

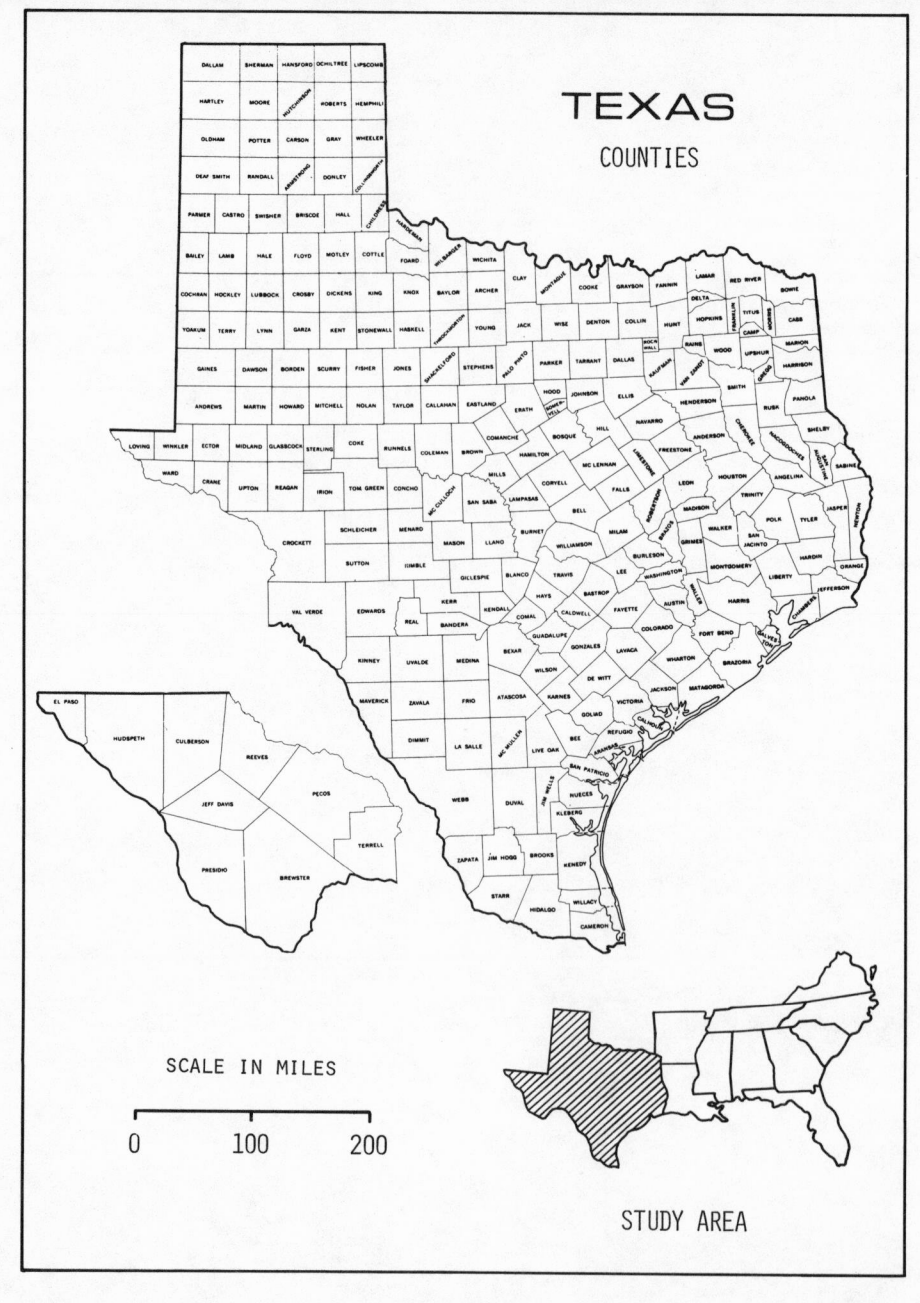

TEXAS
COUNTIES

SCALE IN MILES

0   100   200

STUDY AREA

TEXAS

The principal disfranchisement measure in Texas was the $1.50 poll tax (or $1.75 if county officials chose to add an optional 25¢ local assessment), payable no later than January 31 by those citizens 21 to 59 years of age who wished to cast ballots later in the year. In 1963 Texas voters defeated a state constitutional amendment repealing the poll tax (results reprinted below). When the Twenty-Fourth Amendment to the United States Constitution abolished the poll tax for voting in contests for national office, Texas continued to require a payment receipt for voting in state and local elections until the tax was eliminated entirely by a federal court decision in 1966.

The number of people paying the poll tax was considerably higher in presidential election years than at other times. In 1952 the almost 2.5 million estimated qualified voters (those who had paid the poll tax or who were 60 years of age or older) included an estimated 182,000 black citizens. By 1968 registration exceeded four million, more than half a million of whom were blacks. In 1952 eligible black voters were 7.4 percent of the state electorate; in 1970 they made up 13.3 percent. The 550,000 black registrants in 1970 were 72.6 percent of the black voting-age population, while the almost 3.6 million registered whites were 62 percent of white adults.

The Texas vote in presidential elections from 1948 to 1972 is outlined in the following table. Turnout is expressed both in number of votes cast and in percentage of voting-age citizens voting.

Reprinted below are 15 Democratic guber-natorial primaries, 7 senatorial primaries, 3 special senatorial elections, and 1 referendum, making a total of 26 elections. The 1951 special senatorial election was to fill the seat vacated by the resignation of Price Daniel; there was no runoff election. The 1961 special senatorial election and runoff were to fill the seat formerly held by Lyndon B. Johnson.

Gubernatorial Primaries

* (July 22, 1950: Allan Shivers won 76.4% against 6 opponents. Total vote was 1,086,564; turnout of voting-age citizens was 23.7%.)

1. July 26, 1952: Allan Shivers 833,859 (61.5%), Ralph W. Yarborough 488,343 (36.0%), Allene M. Trayler 34,186 (2.5%). Total vote was 1,356,388; turnout was 28.4%.

2. July 24, 1954: Allan Shivers 668,913 (49.5%), Ralph W. Yarborough 645,994 (47.8%), other 2 candidates 35,845 (2.7%). Total vote was 1,350,752; turnout was 27.2%.

3. August 28, 1954: Allan Shivers 775,079 (53.2%), Ralph W. Yarborough 683,132 (46.8%). Total vote was 1,458,211; turnout was 29.4%.

4. July 28, 1956: Price Daniel 628,817 (39.9%), J. Evetts Haley 88,777 (5.6%), J. J. Holmes 10,165 (0.6%), W. Lee O'Daniel 347,755 (22.1%), Reuben Senterfitt 37,783 (2.4%), Ralph W. Yarborough 463,396 (29.4%). Total vote was 1,576,693; turnout was 30.6%.

5. August 25, 1956: Price Daniel 698,001 (50.1%), Ralph W. Yarborough 694,830

(49.9%). Total vote was 1,392,831; turnout was 27.0%.

6. July 26, 1958: Price Daniel 799,107 (60.7%), Henry B. Gonzalez 245,969 (18.7%), Joe A. Irwin 33,643 (2.6%), W. Lee O'Daniel 238,797 (18.1%). Total vote was 1,317,516; turnout was 24.7%.

7. May 7, 1960: Jack Cox 619,834 (40.5%), Price Daniel 908,992 (59.5%). Total vote was 1,528,826; turnout was 27.6%.

8. May 5, 1962: John Connally 431,498 (29.8%), Price Daniel 248,524 (17.2%), Marshall Formby 139,094 (9.6%), Edwin A. Walker 138,387 (9.6%), Will Wilson 171,617 (11.9%), Don Yarborough 317,986 (22.0%). Total vote was 1,447,106; turnout was 25.2%.

9. June 2, 1962: John Connally 565,169 (51.2%), Don Yarborough 538,924 (48.8%). Total vote was 1,104,093; turnout was 19.2%.

10. May 2, 1964: John Connally 1,125,884 (69.1%), Don Yarborough 471,411 (28.9%), other 2 candidates 33,002 (2.0%). Total vote was 1,630,297; turnout was 27.4%.

11. May 7, 1966: John Connally 932,641 (74.3%), Stanley C. Woods 291,651 (23.2%), Johnnie Mae Hackworthe 31,105 (2.5%). Total vote was 1,255,397; turnout was 20.4%.

12. May 4, 1968: Preston Smith 386,875 (22.1%), John Hill 154,908 (8.8%), Waggoner Carr 257,543 (14.7%), Eugene Locke 218,118 (12.5%), Dolph Briscoe 225,686 (12.9%), Don Yarborough 421,617 (24.1%), other 4 candidates 85,914 (4.9%). Total vote was 1,750,661; turnout was 27.5%.

13. June 1, 1968: Preston Smith 767,490 (55.3%), Don Yarborough 621,226 (44.7%).

Total vote was 1,388,716; turnout was 21.8%.

* (May 2, 1970: Preston Smith was unopposed.)

14. May 6, 1972: Ben Barnes 392,358 (17.9%), Dolph Briscoe 963,417 (43.9%), Frances Farenthold 612,051 (27.9%), other 4 candidates 225,099 (10.3%). Total vote was 2,192,925; turnout was 29.4%.

15. June 3, 1972: Dolph Briscoe 1,100,599 (55.3%), Francis Farenthold 889,544 (44.7%). Total vote was 1,990,143; turnout was 26.7%.

Senatorial Primaries

1. July 26, 1952: Price Daniel 940,770 (72.5%), Lindley Beckworth 285,843 (22.0%), E. W. Napier 70,232 (5.4%). Total vote was 1,296,845.

2. July 24, 1954: Lyndon B. Johnson 882,455 (71.4%), Dudley T. Doughtery 354,188 (28.6%). Total vote was 1,236,643.

3. April 2, 1957: Martin Dies 290,869 (30.7%), Thad Hutcheson 219,591 (22.9%), Ralph W. Yarborough 364,881 (38.1%), other 20 candidates 82,242 (8.6%). Total vote was 957,583.

4. July 26, 1958: Ralph W. Yarborough 760,511 (59.1%), William T. Blakley 525,418 (40.9%). Total vote was 1,285,929.

* (May 7, 1960: Lyndon B. Johnson unopposed.)

5. April 4, 1961: William A. Blakley 190,81 (18.8%), Henry B. Gonzalez 97,659 (9.6%), Maury Maverick, Jr., 104,992 (10.4%), John G. Tower 327,308 (32.3%), Will Wils 121,961 (12.0%), James C. Wright 171,328

(16.9%). There were 65 other candidates.
6. May 23, 1961: William A. Blakley 437,874
   (49.4%), John G. Tower 448,217 (50.6%).
   Total vote was 886,091.
7. May 2, 1964: Ralph W. Yarborough 905,041
   (57.4%), Gordon McLendon 672,573 (42.6%).
   Total vote was 1,577,614.
* (May 7, 1966: Waggoner Carr won 79.9%
   against 1 opponent. Total vote was
   1,126,121.)
8. May 2, 1970: Lloyd Bentsen 814,226
   (52.8%), Ralph W. Yarborough 726,447
   (47.2%). Total vote was 1,540,673.
9. May 6, 1972: Ralph W. Yarborough
   1,032,606 (50.0%), Barefoot Sanders
   787,504 (38.1%), Hugh Wilson 125,468
   (6.1%), Thomas M. Cartlidge 66,240 (3.2%),
   Alfonso Veloz 53,943 (2.6%). Total vote
   was 2,065,761.
10. June 3, 1972: Barefoot Sanders 1,008,499
    (52.1%), Ralph W. Yarborough 928,087
    (47.9%). Total vote was 1,936,586.

Special Election

   November 9, 1963: Poll tax repeal
   amendment. For repeal 543,120 (43.4%),
   Against repeal 316,775 (56.6%). Total
   vote was 559,895.

RETURNS FROM PRESIDENTIAL ELECTIONS

Year	Turnout		Partisan Vote*
1948	1,249,577	(28.3%)[+]	Democrat 66.0%, Republican 24.3%, Dixiecrat 9.7%
1952	2,075,946	(43.5%)	Republican 53.1%, Democrat 46.7%
1956	1,955,168	(37.9%)	Republican 55.3%, Democrat 44.0%
1960	2,311,084	(41.8%)	Democrat 50.5%, Republican 48.5%
1964	2,626,811	(44.2%)	Democrat 63.3%, Republican 36.5%
1968	3,079,216	(48.4%)	Democrat 41.1%, Republican 39.9%, American Independent 19.0%
1972	3,471,281	(46.6%)	Republican 66.2%, Democrat 33.3%

*Totals do not necessarily equal 100%, since minor party percentages are excluded.

[+]Percentage of citizens of voting age who voted is calculated on the basis of a straight-line interpolation of citizen population between census years.

	DEMOC. GOVERNOR 1952			* DEMOC. GOVERNOR 1954	
COUNTY	SHIVERS # %	R. YARBRO # %	TRAYLOR # %*	SHIVERS # %	R. YARBRO # %
ANDERSON	3951 62.1	2298 36.1	109 1.7*	3634 50.4	3581 49.6
ANDREWS	1030 65.1	519 32.8	32 2.0*	706 43.6	914 56.4
ANGELINA	5516 49.5	5300 47.5	335 3.0*	4124 41.7	5767 58.3
ARANSAS	645 62.5	351 34.0	36 3.5*	598 63.8	340 36.2
ARCHER	1307 59.6	840 38.3	45 2.1*	698 39.7	1061 60.3
ARMSTRONG	696 72.9	241 25.2	18 1.9*	403 53.0	357 47.0
ATASCOSA	2451 48.4	1120 22.1	1495 29.5*	1868 50.1	1863 49.9
AUSTIN	2896 78.2	738 19.9	68 1.8*	2186 69.2	973 30.8
BAILEY	1324 68.7	537 27.9	65 3.4*	881 48.4	940 51.6
BANDERA	1181 74.2	360 22.6	50 3.1*	943 76.4	292 23.6
BASTROP	2259 54.8	1748 42.4	112 2.7*	1550 40.8	2247 59.2
BAYLOR	1411 65.7	695 32.3	43 2.0*	827 46.4	957 53.6
BEE	2772 72.0	1001 26.0	77 2.0*	2492 59.9	1670 40.1
BELL	6577 51.2	5985 46.6	275 2.1*	3348 30.8	7514 69.2
BEXAR	24753 63.1	12538 32.0	1908 4.9*	31196 54.6	25900 45.4
BLANCO	250 55.6	195 43.3	5 1.1*	442 56.7	338 43.3
BORDEN	228 62.1	123 33.5	16 4.4*	198 55.5	159 44.5
BOSQUE	1791 50.3	1659 46.6	110 3.1*	1629 45.7	1934 54.3
BOWIE	8409 69.5	3329 27.5	366 3.0*	5235 43.0	6929 57.0
BRAZORIA	8350 66.7	3925 31.3	248 2.0*	5320 52.6	4787 47.4
BRAZOS	4658 73.4	1593 25.1	91 1.4*	3335 49.5	3398 50.5
BREWSTER	882 72.1	319 26.1	23 1.9*	757 65.0	408 35.0
BRISCOE	768 75.5	233 22.9	16 1.6*	604 52.8	540 47.2
BROOKS	966 63.6	503 33.1	51 3.4*	737 41.3	1048 58.7
BROWN	4045 57.8	2831 40.4	127 1.8*	2959 49.7	2991 50.3
BURLESON	2390 66.2	1071 29.7	150 4.2*	1583 43.4	2064 56.6
BURNET	1507 59.4	988 38.9	44 1.7*	1164 45.8	1376 54.2
CALDWELL	2215 53.6	1853 44.8	67 1.6*	1696 45.4	2040 54.6
CALHOUN	1646 81.5	335 16.6	39 1.9*	1385 65.5	730 34.5
CALLAHAN	891 32.9	1758 65.0	57 2.1*	1080 43.0	1434 57.0
CAMERON	7113 71.3	2513 25.2	357 3.6*	7790 61.6	4861 38.4
CAMP	1661 68.2	671 27.5	104 4.3*	1020 47.6	1122 52.4
CARSON	1074 61.6	636 36.5	34 1.9*	802 47.5	885 52.5
CASS	3978 80.1	915 18.4	72 1.5*	2595 52.9	2307 47.1
CASTRO	1198 68.9	515 29.6	25 1.4*	877 51.6	821 48.4
CHAMBERS	1563 76.1	453 22.1	38 1.9*	1155 64.9	625 35.1
CHEROKEE	3992 52.9	3287 43.6	268 3.6*	2561 40.8	3711 59.2
CHILDRESS	2195 63.7	1173 34.0	80 2.3*	1418 50.0	1419 50.0
CLAY	1692 55.9	1259 41.6	74 2.4*	1003 34.9	1874 65.1
COCHRAN	1295 72.7	427 24.0	59 3.3*	682 46.9	771 53.1
COKE	909 58.3	589 37.8	61 3.9*	509 48.4	542 51.6
COLEMAN	2333 55.7	1796 42.9	56 1.3*	1969 54.1	1672 45.9
COLLIN	3415 48.3	3496 49.4	163 2.3*	3036 41.6	4256 58.4
CLNGSWORTH	1788 68.8	746 28.7	64 2.5*	992 45.7	1180 54.3
COLORADO	3734 79.3	846 18.0	127 2.7*	2804 66.3	1425 33.7
COMAL	2896 75.1	876 22.7	83 2.2*	2724 74.0	958 26.0

COUNTY	SHIVERS #	%	R. YARBRO #	%	TRAYLOR #	%*	SHIVERS #	%	R. YARBRO #	%
COMANCHEE	2115	46.5	2287	50.3	149	3.3*	1694	41.6	2377	58.4
CONCHO	840	58.7	564	39.4	28	2.0*	527	51.2	503	48.8
COOKE	3845	66.1	1875	32.2	94	1.6*	3145	64.8	1712	35.2
CORYELL	1674	44.9	1940	52.0	115	3.1*	1446	39.2	2241	60.8
COTTLE	972	58.6	648	39.1	39	2.4*	459	28.5	1149	71.5
CRANE	789	55.5	603	42.4	29	2.0*	481	35.4	877	64.6
CROCKETT	705	76.1	197	21.3	24	2.6*	768	67.8	364	32.2
CROSBY	1346	59.2	859	37.8	70	3.1*	800	35.7	1440	64.3
CULBERSON	411	78.9	99	19.0	11	2.1*	348	67.3	169	32.7
DALLAM	1812	76.6	483	20.4	70	3.0*	846	47.9	921	52.1
DALLAS	41582	61.9	24009	35.7	1609	2.4*	38454	56.3	29872	43.7
DAWSON	2881	68.6	1232	29.3	87	2.1*	1706	55.3	1377	44.7
DEAFSMITH	2113	73.3	711	24.7	59	2.0*	1506	69.2	670	30.8
DELTA	1243	53.8	1012	43.8	57	2.5*	801	35.8	1437	64.2
DENTON	4367	50.9	4064	47.4	146	1.7*	3686	45.2	4473	54.8
DEWITT	3177	81.0	667	17.0	79	2.0*	3516	72.2	1356	27.8
DICKENS	1199	55.5	893	41.3	70	3.2*	627	36.1	1109	63.9
DIMMIT	1029	70.0	394	26.8	46	3.1*	878	66.5	443	33.5
DONLEY	1228	61.0	696	34.6	88	4.4*	929	53.6	804	46.4
DUVAL	883	29.7	2061	69.3	29	1.0*	1378	31.4	3016	68.6
EASTLAND	3617	49.9	3394	46.8	235	3.2*	2941	49.6	2991	50.4
ECTOR	5842	68.1	2522	29.4	218	2.5*	4288	55.0	3505	45.0
EDWARDS	620	76.4	159	19.6	33	4.1*	584	73.6	210	26.4
ELLIS	4231	54.2	3474	44.5	98	1.3*	2937	44.0	3740	56.0
ELPASO	14376	74.7	4521	23.5	359	1.9*	8962	58.8	6267	41.2
ERATH	2740	49.7	2689	48.7	89	1.6*	2283	48.3	2443	51.7
FALLS	1393	49.9	1335	47.8	63	2.3*	1725	40.4	2540	59.6
FANNIN	3632	46.5	3840	49.2	335	4.3*	2355	34.4	4489	65.6
FAYETTE	3608	72.4	1261	25.3	116	2.3*	3695	63.6	2116	36.4
FISHER	1189	41.2	1602	55.5	96	3.3*	941	39.3	1452	60.7
FLOYD	2405	73.5	810	24.7	58	1.8*	1431	50.6	1395	49.4
FOARD	860	69.7	335	27.2	38	3.1*	484	40.0	725	60.0
FORTBEND	3119	72.9	1083	25.3	77	1.8*	2490	62.3	1508	37.7
FRANKLIN	971	46.8	1045	50.3	61	2.9*	745	35.7	1343	64.3
FREESTONE	2622	61.9	1503	35.5	112	2.6*	2043	45.5	2446	54.5
FRIO	1192	66.4	506	28.2	96	5.4*	867	51.5	817	48.5
GAINES	1902	67.3	804	28.4	121	4.3*	1357	52.6	1221	47.4
GALVESTON	12298	67.2	5306	29.0	694	3.8*	10990	54.4	9218	45.6
GARZA	1106	70.2	406	25.8	64	4.1*	737	49.4	754	50.6
GILLESPIE	1453	89.2	159	9.8	17	1.0*	860	83.7	167	16.3
GLASCOCK	298	67.1	135	30.4	11	2.5*	267	64.0	150	36.0
GOLIAD	437	73.8	143	24.2	12	2.0*	1037	69.3	460	30.7
GONZALES	2083	71.3	769	26.3	71	2.4*	1446	52.9	1289	47.1
GRAY	3222	75.0	973	22.6	103	2.4*	2751	57.8	2011	42.2
GRAYSON	6471	49.9	6136	47.3	367	2.8*	4391	39.1	6827	60.9
GREGG	6990	60.6	4181	36.3	358	3.1*	5500	49.1	5705	50.9

COUNTY	SHIVERS #	%	R. YARBRO #	%	TRAYLOR #	%*	SHIVERS #	%	R. YARBRO #	%
GRIMES	1129	75.2	348	23.2	24	1.6*	1151	56.0	905	44.0
GUADALUPE	1033	73.8	343	24.5	24	1.7*	1518	66.9	751	33.1
HALE	2939	71.3	1116	27.1	68	1.6*	2418	61.3	1525	38.7
HALL	1579	60.4	978	37.4	59	2.3*	1035	44.0	1316	56.0
HAMILTON	1643	50.9	1473	45.6	112	3.5*	1718	53.6	1487	46.4
HANSFORD	744	77.5	192	20.0	24	2.5*	927	71.4	371	28.6
HARDEMAN	1757	66.1	849	31.9	54	2.0*	1187	52.2	1089	47.8
HARDIN	1758	34.3	3252	63.4	122	2.4*	1514	30.8	3396	69.2
HARRIS	75524	62.8	42087	35.0	2628	2.2*	51888	53.1	45915	46.9
HARRISON	4985	70.6	1935	27.4	141	2.0*	3725	53.1	3290	46.9
HARTLEY	624	81.7	122	16.0	18	2.4*	320	50.0	320	50.0
HASKELL	1443	40.8	2002	56.6	89	2.5*	1260	33.2	2536	66.8
HAYS	1266	58.3	888	40.9	17	.8*	1768	53.8	1518	46.2
HEMPHILL	1010	84.2	154	12.8	35	2.9*	757	61.9	465	38.1
HENDERSON	1763	26.0	4846	71.5	170	2.5*	1760	25.6	5127	74.4
HIDALGO	12879	80.6	2747	17.2	358	2.2*	11640	65.8	6054	34.2
HILL	3833	51.2	3425	45.7	229	3.1*	2768	39.0	4337	61.0
HOCKLEY	3126	65.6	1493	31.3	147	3.1*	1992	50.7	1937	49.3
HOOD	1026	49.9	991	48.2	40	1.9*	866	40.0	1301	60.0
HOPKINS	3518	59.3	2253	38.0	161	2.7*	2139	40.5	3143	59.5
HOUSTON	3009	64.4	1486	31.8	178	3.8*	2254	51.7	2103	48.3
HOWARD	3040	47.1	3303	51.2	109	1.7*	2538	44.0	3225	56.0
HUDSPETH	487	79.2	113	18.4	15	2.4*	463	70.9	190	29.1
HUNT	5280	67.3	2451	31.2	116	1.5*	4496	54.4	3773	45.6
HUTCHISON	3769	60.2	2330	37.2	161	2.6*	1963	37.6	3264	62.4
IRION	344	56.8	240	39.6	22	3.6*	250	49.6	254	50.4
JACK	1470	60.5	904	37.2	54	2.2*	1072	53.3	940	46.7
JACKSON	2574	75.5	713	20.9	121	3.6*	2203	65.7	1149	34.3
JASPER	1892	44.2	2319	54.1	72	1.7*	1944	39.2	3016	60.8
JEFFDAVIS	372	77.3	94	19.5	15	3.1*	232	62.9	137	37.1
JEFFERSON	16594	52.1	14937	46.9	309	1.0*	15677	48.7	16543	51.3
JIMHOGG	547	75.2	160	22.0	20	2.8*	513	48.7	541	51.3
JIMWELLS	4449	70.5	1724	27.3	136	2.2*	4061	55.3	3280	44.7
JOHNSON	2744	51.6	2471	46.5	98	1.9*	2914	44.3	3653	55.6
JONES	2735	54.2	2197	43.6	110	2.2*	2008	48.4	2141	51.6
KARNES	2908	75.0	885	22.8	84	2.2*	2140	53.6	1856	46.4
KAUFMAN	3750	60.7	2324	37.6	102	1.7*	2399	47.5	2656	52.5
KENDALL	311	78.9	82	20.8	1	.3*	449	76.2	140	23.8
KENEDY	77	89.5	3	3.5	6	7.0*	129	97.7	3	2.3
KENT	409	49.0	401	48.0	25	3.0*	308	38.4	494	61.6
KERR	2891	71.6	1086	26.9	63	1.6*	2703	74.1	946	25.9
KIMBLE	837	61.1	494	36.1	38	2.8*	958	63.0	563	37.0
KING	81	52.9	71	46.4	1	.7*	89	36.0	158	64.0
KINNEY	139	74.7	42	22.6	5	2.7*	294	58.4	209	41.6
KLEBERG	2143	54.2	1652	41.8	160	4.0*	1346	43.2	1770	56.8
KNOX	1495	60.5	942	38.1	36	1.5*	1006	44.6	1250	55.4

	DEMOC. GOVERNOR 1952						* DEMOC. GOVERNOR 1954				

COUNTY	SHIVERS		R. YARBRO		TRAYLOR		SHIVERS		R. YARBRO	
	#	%	#	%	#	%*	#	%	#	%
LAMAR	6377	68.9	2637	28.5	247	2.7*	4459	49.5	4557	50.5
LAMB	2771	62.3	1572	35.3	108	2.4*	2144	51.6	2008	48.4
LAMPASAS	1513	65.7	748	32.5	42	1.8*	1180	52.3	1076	47.7
LASALLE	806	71.1	302	26.7	25	2.2*	535	61.7	332	38.3
LABACA	3092	75.0	948	23.0	83	2.0*	2723	60.8	1755	39.2
LEE	1601	63.8	855	34.1	54	2.2*	1173	49.3	1208	50.7
LEON	1825	62.2	1061	36.1	49	1.7*	1416	44.4	1774	55.6
LIBERTY	4806	71.5	1741	25.9	174	2.6*	3040	54.3	2557	45.7
LIMESTONE	3560	57.3	2542	40.9	116	1.9*	2368	40.1	3544	59.9
LIPSCOMB	638	86.6	86	11.7	13	1.8*	478	72.9	178	27.1
LIVEOAK	1636	75.5	483	22.3	47	2.2*	1339	65.8	697	34.2
LLANO	1052	54.8	807	42.0	62	3.2*	536	42.9	712	57.1
LOVING	57	80.3	12	16.9	2	2.8*	68	86.1	11	13.9
LUBBOCK	11126	69.0	4687	29.1	309	1.9*	7302	53.5	6348	46.5
LYNN	1870	68.0	799	29.1	80	2.9*	1091	49.1	1130	50.9
MADISON	1159	59.3	765	39.2	29	1.5*	881	44.3	1106	55.7
MARION	1544	76.1	403	19.9	81	4.0*	960	56.4	743	43.6
MARTIN	927	59.0	602	38.3	42	2.7*	492	41.2	702	58.8
MASON	1039	61.2	630	37.1	30	1.8*	920	64.2	513	35.8
MATAGORDA	3723	76.8	952	19.6	175	3.6*	3592	71.0	1466	29.0
MAVERICK	939	75.8	241	19.5	58	4.7*	791	74.1	277	25.9
MCCULLOCH	1887	59.8	1206	38.2	60	1.9*	1927	57.1	1447	42.9
MCLENNAN	11985	54.0	9759	44.0	438	2.0*	8979	39.1	14010	60.9
MCMULLEN	324	79.8	62	15.3	20	4.9*	313	64.8	170	35.2
MEDINA	684	64.7	343	32.5	30	2.8*	948	57.9	690	42.1
MENARD	838	62.7	455	34.0	44	3.3*	688	62.1	420	37.9
MIDLAND	4513	73.5	1511	24.6	116	1.9*	4316	66.2	2203	33.8
MILAN	2687	55.3	2033	41.8	139	2.9*	2394	45.4	2884	54.6
MILLS	973	46.7	1062	50.9	50	2.4*	912	47.8	996	52.2
MITCHELL	1857	57.3	1298	40.1	85	2.6*	1214	42.4	1648	57.6
MONTAGE	2758	52.8	2350	45.0	117	2.2*	1782	42.6	2405	57.4
MONTGOMRY	4443	75.7	1227	20.9	197	3.4*	3325	52.0	3074	48.0
MOORE	2279	71.9	826	26.0	66	2.1*	1027	41.4	1453	58.6
MORRIS	903	73.4	290	23.6	38	3.1*	1218	40.7	1775	59.3
MOTLEY	1655	63.6	874	33.6	72	2.8*	628	58.4	447	41.6
NACDOCHES	4654	69.4	1857	27.7	191	2.8*	2677	44.3	3370	55.7
NAVARRO	3554	46.4	3935	51.4	165	2.2*	2520	37.7	4170	62.3
NEWTON	1049	40.5	1443	55.7	97	3.7*	893	36.1	1579	63.9
NOLAN	3262	58.3	2191	39.1	146	2.6*	1726	42.2	2368	57.8
NUECES	12860	50.9	11801	46.7	602	2.4*	11685	47.3	13002	52.7
OCHILTREE	1507	85.7	215	12.2	36	2.0*	968	74.3	335	25.7
OLDHAM	373	65.2	192	33.6	7	1.2*	303	51.3	288	48.7
ORANGE	4955	49.4	4816	48.0	268	2.7*	3467	36.9	5925	63.1
PALOPINTO	2802	59.5	1786	37.9	120	2.5*	2298	51.9	2128	48.1
PANOLA	3325	57.4	2365	40.8	104	1.8*	2896	47.0	3261	53.0
PARKER	3200	58.6	2121	38.9	138	2.5*	3029	50.0	3029	50.0

	DEMOC. GOVERNOR 1952						* DEMOC. GOVERNOR 1954				
COUNTY	SHIVERS		R. YARBRO		TRAYLOR		SHIVERS		R. YARBRO	
	#	%	#	%	#	%*	#	%	#	%
PARMER	990	77.7	255	20.0	29	2.3*	1097	69.8	474	30.2
PECOS	1699	67.7	716	28.5	95	3.8*	1403	54.0	1194	46.0
POLK	2348	60.7	1390	35.9	131	3.4*	1615	49.1	1675	50.9
POTTER	4695	70.6	1864	28.0	91	1.4*	5136	46.5	5913	53.5
PRESIDIO	791	72.8	244	22.4	52	4.8*	789	66.7	394	33.3
RAINES	743	57.2	514	39.5	43	3.3*	575	45.6	686	54.4
RANDALL	2868	75.1	891	23.3	62	1.6*	2100	55.9	1655	44.1
REAGAN	649	70.5	256	27.8	16	1.7*	623	54.9	511	45.1
REAL	541	68.8	213	27.1	32	4.1*	235	62.0	144	38.0
REDRIVER	3576	63.9	1804	32.2	214	3.8*	2209	40.2	3286	59.8
REEVES	1908	73.7	603	23.3	79	3.1*	1545	61.7	959	38.3
REFUGIO	1458	73.7	481	24.3	39	2.0*	1145	59.5	779	40.5
ROBERTS	192	83.8	31	13.5	6	2.6*	331	76.8	100	23.2
ROBERTSON	1848	58.1	1262	39.7	69	2.2*	1354	35.1	2507	64.9
ROCKWALL	1157	61.8	686	36.6	30	1.6*	575	45.5	689	54.5
RUNNELLS	1419	55.8	1087	42.8	36	1.4*	1879	62.4	1134	37.6
RUSK	6892	66.5	3069	29.6	408	3.9*	5154	50.6	5032	49.4
SABINE	1459	55.5	1068	40.6	103	3.9*	959	38.9	1505	61.1
SNAUGSTNE	1550	60.1	923	35.8	107	4.1*	935	37.6	1550	62.4
SNJACINTO	706	64.8	342	31.4	41	3.8*	546	42.9	726	57.1
SNPATRICIO	2777	59.1	1797	38.3	122	2.6*	2680	48.3	2869	51.7
SANSABA	728	37.4	1167	60.0	50	2.6*	832	34.5	1579	65.5
SCHLEICHER	792	68.6	341	29.5	21	1.8*	648	63.3	376	36.7
SCURRY	3069	63.4	1614	33.3	157	3.2*	1600	44.3	2014	55.7
SHACKELFRD	1000	51.9	860	44.6	68	3.5*	808	54.3	679	45.7
SHELBY	3962	56.3	2940	41.8	139	2.0*	2459	35.4	4486	64.6
SHERMAN	720	85.0	108	12.8	19	2.2*	647	71.3	260	28.7
SMITH	8236	52.4	7288	46.3	201	1.3*	7792	50.0	7777	50.0
SOMERVELL	561	57.0	394	40.0	29	2.9*	519	50.7	504	49.3
STARR	3378	89.8	165	4.4	219	5.8*	3188	78.8	859	21.2
STEPHENS	2036	57.8	1366	38.8	121	3.4*	1762	55.4	1416	44.6
STERLING	287	74.9	88	23.0	8	2.1*	244	66.7	122	33.3
STONEWALL	664	54.5	508	41.7	46	3.8*	465	37.1	787	62.9
SUTTON	417	82.4	77	15.2	12	2.4*	517	65.8	269	34.2
SWISHER	1559	62.6	893	35.9	38	1.5*	1025	51.6	963	48.4
TARRANT	36060	58.0	24942	40.1	1135	1.8*	29588	50.4	29104	49.6
TAYLOR	6557	49.2	6587	49.5	171	1.3*	4783	52.4	4347	47.6
TERRELL	234	75.5	74	23.9	2	.6*	341	58.8	239	41.2
TERRY	2760	75.1	827	22.5	90	2.4*	1376	51.7	1287	48.3
THRCKMORTN	638	43.9	781	53.8	34	2.3*	629	46.4	727	53.6
TITUS	3032	56.9	2136	40.1	162	3.0*	1788	40.1	2676	59.9
TOMGREEN	7028	63.1	3780	33.9	333	3.0*	5930	59.3	4067	40.7
TRAVIS	16576	55.1	13179	43.8	340	1.1*	15803	54.6	13136	45.4
TRINITY	1576	67.0	682	29.0	95	4.0*	1253	49.1	1301	50.9
TYLER	1560	54.4	1215	42.3	94	3.3*	2159	67.2	1054	32.8
UPSHUR	3028	51.6	2595	44.2	245	4.2*	2642	42.8	3528	57.2

	DEMOC. GOVERNOR 1952			* DEMOC. GOVERNOR 1954	
COUNTY	SHIVERS	R. YARBRO	TRAYLOR	SHIVERS	R. YARBRO
	# %	# %	# %*	# %	# %
UPTON	1053 68.2	463 30.0	29 1.9*	765 50.2	758 49.8
UVALDE	2155 71.0	784 25.8	96 3.2*	1952 66.3	992 33.7
VALVERDE	1645 73.7	490 22.0	96 4.3*	1489 55.0	1217 45.0
VANZANDT	2917 45.8	3326 52.2	130 2.0*	2104 35.2	3867 64.8
VICTORIA	3460 73.0	1209 25.5	71 1.5*	3839 58.7	2705 41.3
WALKER	2521 74.1	790 23.2	93 2.7*	1912 50.9	1841 49.1
WALLER	1886 77.2	502 20.5	56 2.3*	1108 58.0	802 42.0
WARD	1875 62.1	1060 35.1	84 2.8*	1641 51.2	1563 48.8
WASHINGTON	2645 84.3	455 14.5	38 1.2*	3252 72.8	1218 27.2
WEBB	6066 95.4	272 4.3	18 .3*	6800 91.5	630 8.5
WHARTON	5867 76.1	1554 20.2	289 3.7*	4370 61.9	2689 38.1
WHEELER	1737 73.1	591 24.9	49 2.1*	1021 41.5	1440 58.5
WICHITA	9986 62.1	5809 36.1	280 1.7*	5457 39.9	8223 60.1
WILBARGER	3148 65.1	1602 33.1	88 1.8*	2052 51.1	1962 48.9
WILLACY	2532 80.8	538 17.2	64 2.0*	2052 67.4	992 32.6
WILLIAMSON	3158 54.3	2556 43.9	102 1.8*	2929 45.0	3573 55.0
WILSON	2656 69.2	1034 26.9	150 3.9*	1839 47.2	2059 52.8
WINKLER	1456 62.5	777 33.4	95 4.1*	1087 46.3	1262 53.7
WISE	2441 47.8	2522 49.4	141 2.8*	1755 35.9	3139 64.1
WOOD	2481 52.6	2152 45.6	87 1.8*	2057 42.4	2794 57.6
YOAKUM	824 58.2	550 38.8	42 3.0*	761 46.7	869 53.3
YOUNG	2303 58.9	1508 38.5	102 2.6*	1385 45.9	1630 54.1
ZAPATA	398 91.9	29 6.7	6 1.4*	541 95.2	27 4.8
ZAVALA	1122 76.6	289 19.7	53 3.6*	1064 67.4	515 32.6
TOTALS	833859	488343	34186 *	668913	645994
% OF VOTE	61.5	36.0	2.5 *	50.9	49.1

GEOGRAPHIC CLASS

			*		
LOWLANDS	324062 60.	201546 37.	13144 2.*	243786 48.	266190 52.
BLACK BELT	10969 69.	4444 28.	388 2.*	7693 49.	8068 51.
WEST TEXAS	418427 61.	256169 37.	16398 2.*	345513 51.	326889 49.
MEX. TEXAS	80401 73.	26184 24.	4256 4.*	71921 62.	44847 38.

DEMOGRAPHIC CLASS

			*		
METRO	347134 61.	208057 37.	12750 2.*	293397 53.	264829 47.
TOWN	79809 62.	45295 35.	2950 2.*	61202 49.	63398 51.
RURAL	406916 62.	234991 36.	18486 3.*	314314 50.	317267 50.

	DEMOC. RUNOFF 1954*			DEMOC. GOVERNOR 1956					
COUNTY	SHIVERS	R. YARBRO	DANIEL	HALEY	HOLMES	ODANIEL	SENT	R. YARBRO	
	# %	# %*	# %	# %	# %	# %	# %	# %	
ANDERSON	4146 51.6	3888 48.4*	2121 28.3	364 4.8	51 .7	2238 29.8	334 4.4	2398 31.9	
ANDREWS	710 45.4	854 54.6*	718 29.7	216 8.9	11 .5	729 30.1	69 2.9	678 28.0	
ANGELINA	4937 45.4	5946 54.6*	3141 28.7	305 2.8	68 .6	2705 24.7	86 .8	4644 42.4	
ARANSAS	583 64.6	319 35.4*	483 44.4	14 1.3	13 1.2	241 22.2	16 1.5	321 29.5	
ARCHER	700 45.7	832 54.3*	626 31.5	105 5.3	22 1.1	498 25.0	114 5.7	625 31.4	
ARMSTRONG	360 61.5	225 38.5*	324 38.8	180 21.5	0 .0	166 19.9	3 .4	163 19.5	
ATASCOSA	1790 48.1	1935 51.9*	1680 42.9	61 1.6	16 .4	975 24.9	32 .8	1155 29.5	
AUSTIN	2203 72.9	820 27.1*	1622 41.1	94 2.4	77 1.9	1474 37.3	75 1.9	608 15.4	
BAILEY	1049 53.4	917 46.6*	730 37.9	221 11.5	7 .4	473 24.6	51 2.6	443 23.0	
BANDERA	904 82.8	188 17.2*	810 57.4	38 2.7	7 .5	367 26.0	17 1.2	171 12.1	
BASTROP	1858 44.7	2303 55.3*	1413 30.9	93 2.0	32 .7	1586 34.6	67 1.5	1389 30.3	
BAYLOR	947 53.5	822 46.5*	726 35.8	114 5.6	12 .6	701 34.6	45 2.2	428 21.1	
BEE	2596 63.3	1508 36.7*	1634 36.7	56 1.3	28 .6	1511 33.9	77 1.7	1145 25.7	
BELL	4135 38.2	6679 61.8*	3581 27.4	385 2.9	86 .7	4815 36.8	713 5.5	3499 26.8	
BEXAR	38099 55.0	31174 45.0*	41913 55.1	799 1.1	607 .8	8472 11.1	780 1.0	23465 30.9	
BLANCO	579 60.7	375 39.3*	282 43.1	3 .5	4 .6	181 27.6	13 2.0	172 26.3	
BORDEN	158 46.5	182 53.5*	140 32.6	67 15.6	1 .2	137 31.9	7 1.6	78 18.1	
BOSQUE	1868 48.8	1959 51.2*	1204 32.8	281 7.6	24 .7	1284 34.9	157 4.3	725 19.7	
BOWIE	5688 46.3	6591 53.7*	5062 34.6	514 3.5	72 .5	4803 32.9	137 .9	4032 27.6	
BRAZORIA	6012 51.2	5722 48.8*	4617 37.0	207 1.7	40 .3	2983 23.9	250 2.0	4393 35.2	
BRAZOS	3739 51.4	3542 48.6*	2718 40.5	160 2.4	32 .5	2022 30.1	200 3.0	1576 23.5	
BREWSTER	769 67.9	363 32.1*	651 56.6	114 9.9	5 .4	163 14.2	15 1.3	202 17.6	
BRISCOE	601 51.3	570 48.7*	295 26.1	270 23.9	5 .4	310 27.4	16 1.4	234 20.7	
BROOKS	755 38.3	1216 61.7*	551 29.2	34 1.8	21 1.1	488 25.9	26 1.4	765 40.6	
BROWN	3250 55.0	2664 45.0*	2393 34.0	593 8.4	35 .5	1871 26.6	557 7.9	1587 22.6	
BURLESON	1345 42.6	1814 57.4*	865 25.1	78 2.3	35 1.0	1548 44.9	60 1.7	859 24.9	
BURNET	1144 51.9	1060 48.1*	763 28.2	64 2.4	5 .2	882 32.6	304 11.3	684 25.3	
CALDWELL	2096 48.8	2200 51.2*	1499 37.0	44 1.1	28 .7	1158 28.6	127 3.1	1192 29.4	
CALHOUN	1108 64.9	598 35.1*	1112 39.1	44 1.5	8 .3	990 34.8	69 2.4	621 21.8	
CALLAHAN	1339 49.2	1383 50.8*	757 36.7	175 8.5	17 .8	569 27.6	82 4.0	465 22.5	
CAMERON	9099 65.8	4734 34.2*	7907 50.8	283 1.8	127 .8	1625 10.4	553 3.6	5073 32.6	
CAMP	910 42.9	1210 57.1*	691 28.0	98 4.0	5 .2	1105 44.8	10 .4	559 22.6	
CARSON	830 51.5	783 48.5*	493 33.4	151 10.2	2 .1	335 22.7	23 1.6	472 32.0	
CASS	3011 53.2	2644 46.8*	2002 35.1	260 4.6	13 .2	1794 31.5	34 .6	1599 28.0	
CASTRO	757 55.1	616 44.9*	579 36.2	175 10.9	2 .1	284 17.7	14 .9	547 34.2	
CHAMBERS	1274 62.5	764 37.5*	1266 47.0	47 1.7	10 .4	618 23.0	21 .8	729 27.1	
CHEROKEE	2876 42.6	3873 57.4*	1991 28.1	250 3.5	42 .6	2224 31.4	109 1.5	2459 34.8	
CHILDRESS	1390 48.6	1471 51.4*	1010 30.8	461 14.0	27 .8	909 27.7	67 2.0	810 24.7	
CLAY	1179 41.2	1681 58.8*	854 28.3	198 6.6	21 .7	872 28.9	67 2.2	1001 33.2	
COCHRAN	641 49.4	657 50.6*	527 32.1	141 8.6	7 .4	394 24.0	227 13.8	347 21.1	
COKE	582 58.0	421 42.0*	303 25.5	98 8.3	4 .3	495 41.7	89 7.5	197 16.6	
COLEMAN	2133 54.7	1770 45.3*	1368 34.5	346 8.7	20 .5	1300 32.8	266 6.7	665 16.8	
COLLIN	3380 43.4	4417 56.6*	2733 31.8	432 5.0	17 .2	2687 31.3	92 1.1	2634 30.6	
CLNGSWORTH	1082 48.1	1169 51.9*	658 29.8	247 11.2	7 .3	633 28.7	19 .9	645 29.2	
COLORADO	2662 66.1	1368 33.9*	1373 35.7	113 2.9	19 .5	1707 44.4	57 1.5	572 14.9	
COMAL	2751 74.7	930 25.3*	2187 60.1	43 1.2	8 .2	608 16.7	42 1.2	751 20.6	

DEMOC. RUNOFF   1954*   DEMOC. GOVERNOR   1956

COUNTY	SHIVERS #	%	R. YARBRO #	%*	DANIEL #	%	HALEY #	%	HOLMES #	%	ODANIEL #	%	SENT #	%	R. YARBRO #	%
COMANCHEE	1622	43.3	2127	56.7*	1060	25.6	431	10.4	8	.2	1538	37.1	130	3.1	977	23.6
CONCHO	572	52.4	519	47.6*	386	29.9	87	6.7	6	.5	492	38.1	61	4.7	259	20.1
COOKE	3366	64.9	1819	35.1*	2521	43.4	429	7.4	32	.6	1570	27.0	70	1.2	1193	20.5
CORYELL	1531	44.8	1889	55.2*	1182	27.8	137	3.2	13	.3	1830	43.0	263	6.2	826	19.4
COTTLE	470	32.4	982	67.6*	443	24.9	236	13.3	4	.2	443	24.9	17	1.0	637	35.8
CRANE	494	39.0	772	61.0*	428	28.2	179	11.8	9	.6	358	23.6	38	2.5	504	33.2
CROCKETT	624	61.1	398	38.9*	469	37.8	98	7.9	3	.2	316	25.5	34	2.7	320	25.8
CROSBY	840	35.6	1518	64.4*	738	26.7	159	5.8	19	.7	682	24.7	68	2.5	1096	39.7
CULBERSON	318	72.4	121	27.6*	316	49.2	46	7.2	1	.2	194	30.2	19	3.0	66	10.3
DALLAM	860	51.3	818	48.7*	687	47.2	115	7.9	5	.3	274	18.8	11	.8	364	25.0
DALLAS	57737	59.8	38782	40.2*	54473	47.7	8371	7.3	979	.9	16509	14.4	1066	.9	32866	28.8
DAWSON	1776	56.5	1369	43.5*	1528	40.2	239	6.3	10	.3	1240	32.6	69	1.8	719	18.9
DEAFSMITH	1513	69.4	666	30.6*	1265	51.3	335	13.6	6	.2	402	16.3	69	2.8	389	15.8
DELTA	947	38.9	1489	61.1*	538	24.0	74	3.3	7	.3	1003	44.7	24	1.1	599	26.7
DENTON	3611	48.8	3787	51.2*	3128	34.0	862	9.4	34	.4	2427	26.4	86	.9	2652	28.9
DEWITT	3620	73.8	1286	26.2*	2659	46.9	50	.9	33	.6	2060	36.4	74	1.3	790	13.9
DICKENS	720	39.1	1121	60.9*	535	26.1	142	6.9	12	.6	601	29.4	44	2.2	712	34.8
DIMMIT	1013	66.7	505	33.3*	429	39.2	5	.5	2	.2	381	34.9	30	2.7	246	22.5
DONLEY	838	56.1	657	43.9*	653	35.0	348	18.6	1	.1	576	30.8	16	.9	274	14.7
DUVAL	1220	26.9	3310	73.1*	3402	78.7	25	.6	12	.3	366	8.5	53	1.2	466	10.8
EASTLAND	3530	53.8	3032	46.2*	1890	32.0	480	8.1	32	.5	2172	36.8	196	3.3	1131	19.2
ECTOR	5523	61.6	3448	38.4*	5173	42.7	1274	10.5	160	1.3	2608	21.5	530	4.4	2376	19.6
EDWARDS	556	75.9	177	24.1*	404	49.4	77	9.4	2	.2	197	24.1	40	4.9	97	11.9
ELLIS	2980	43.1	3938	56.9*	2689	32.7	718	8.7	34	.4	2049	24.9	68	.8	2667	32.4
ELPASO	10304	58.4	7339	41.6*	10675	50.8	532	2.5	193	.9	2120	10.1	163	.8	7327	34.9
ERATH	2442	48.3	2619	51.7*	1864	35.1	359	6.8	17	.3	1655	31.2	161	3.0	1251	23.6
FALLS	1896	44.8	2332	55.2*	1213	31.9	110	2.9	11	.3	1326	34.9	71	1.9	1071	28.2
FANNIN	2091	31.9	4471	68.1*	1547	22.5	284	4.1	26	.4	2296	33.4	76	1.1	2643	38.5
FAYETTE	3753	72.4	1433	27.6*	2633	37.8	278	4.0	41	.6	3049	43.8	137	2.0	829	11.9
FISHER	1062	40.9	1537	59.1*	604	23.1	160	6.1	19	.7	870	33.3	79	3.0	884	33.8
FLOYD	1671	55.5	1341	44.5*	1480	47.0	366	11.6	17	.5	637	20.2	30	1.0	622	19.7
FOARD	374	41.6	526	58.4*	284	31.9	103	11.6	4	.4	204	22.9	25	2.8	271	30.4
FORTBEND	2931	58.7	2058	41.3*	1886	36.6	150	2.9	20	.4	1825	35.4	157	3.0	1118	21.7
FRANKLIN	870	38.1	1414	61.9*	444	21.7	90	4.4	11	.5	946	46.2	18	.9	540	26.4
FREESTONE	2082	43.7	2680	56.3*	1441	31.7	170	3.7	30	.7	1446	31.8	46	1.0	1419	31.2
FRIO	899	46.5	1033	53.5*	642	39.9	26	1.6	4	.2	313	19.5	9	.6	615	38.2
GAINES	1308	50.9	1260	49.1*	942	36.3	248	9.5	81	3.1	697	26.8	65	2.5	564	21.7
GALVESTON	14085	56.2	10974	43.8*	10157	37.7	677	2.5	208	.8	2764	10.2	646	2.4	12524	46.4
GARZA	619	47.5	685	52.5*	436	31.9	130	9.5	8	.6	475	34.8	29	2.1	287	21.0
GILLESPIE	1576	90.5	166	9.5*	629	65.7	4	.4	3	.3	205	21.4	52	5.4	65	6.8
GLASCOCK	253	71.5	101	28.5*	133	33.8	94	23.9	5	1.3	92	23.4	17	4.3	52	13.2
GOLIAD	778	74.0	274	26.0*	690	45.3	24	1.6	5	.3	636	41.8	4	.3	163	10.7
GONZALES	1947	55.9	1539	44.1*	1620	44.8	45	1.2	32	.9	1126	31.1	65	1.8	728	20.1
GRAY	3161	61.0	2024	39.0*	2022	37.5	641	11.9	34	.6	1599	29.7	59	1.1	1036	19.2
GRAYSON	4905	41.5	6912	58.5*	4634	32.8	570	4.0	64	.5	3070	21.8	182	1.3	5588	39.6
GREGG	7268	52.4	6597	47.6*	5264	37.9	609	4.4	103	.7	4342	31.3	183	1.3	3372	24.3

COUNTY	SHIVERS # %	R. YARBRO # %*	DANIEL # %	HALEY # %	HOLMES # %	ODANIEL # %	SENT # %	R. YARBRO # %
GRIMES	1321 59.8	887 40.2*	740 33.4	263 11.9	8 .4	773 34.9	20 .9	413 18.6
GUADALUPE	2498 69.9	1074 30.1*	1456 48.9	15 .5	13 .4	761 25.5	46 1.5	688 23.1
HALE	2920 64.8	1584 35.2*	2663 47.3	405 7.2	19 .3	1183 21.0	131 2.3	1228 21.8
HALL	966 43.2	1272 56.8*	484 25.3	385 20.1	6 .3	456 23.8	45 2.3	539 28.1
HAMILTON	1649 59.9	1103 40.1*	1074 32.3	188 5.7	12 .4	1419 42.7	206 6.2	427 12.8
HANSFORD	709 73.2	259 26.8*	490 53.9	133 14.6	3 .3	159 17.5	18 2.0	106 11.7
HARDEMAN	1249 57.6	919 42.4*	786 38.1	190 9.2	7 .3	648 31.4	26 1.3	404 19.6
HARDIN	1798 33.4	3582 66.6*	1869 32.2	113 1.9	13 .2	936 16.1	84 1.4	2787 48.0
HARRIS	75049 53.1	66187 46.9*	59344 45.2	4489 3.4	1122 .9	16384 12.5	3664 2.8	46149 35.2
HARRISON	4185 58.4	2981 41.6*	3026 41.3	591 8.1	16 .2	1339 18.3	69 .9	2286 31.2
HARTLEY	351 59.2	242 40.8*	391 52.1	94 12.5	2 .3	97 12.9	3 .4	163 21.7
HASKELL	1472 37.4	2467 62.6*	693 17.9	223 5.8	17 .4	1696 43.9	102 2.6	1130 29.3
HAYS	1744 55.8	1382 44.2*	1367 44.8	35 1.1	19 .6	637 20.9	71 2.3	919 30.2
HEMPHILL	523 61.9	322 38.1*	355 43.9	139 17.2	2 .2	145 17.9	11 1.4	156 19.3
HENDERSON	1969 25.9	5638 74.1*	1159 18.5	240 3.8	20 .3	1603 25.7	167 2.7	3060 49.0
HIDALGO	12801 64.9	6925 35.1*	10363 51.3	268 1.3	130 .6	2219 11.0	807 4.0	6395 31.7
HILL	2771 42.7	3724 57.3*	2431 33.1	588 8.0	19 .3	2112 28.8	135 1.8	2049 27.9
HOCKLEY	2097 52.4	1904 47.6*	1926 37.2	298 5.8	51 1.0	1292 25.3	127 2.5	1420 27.8
HOOD	1026 42.6	1381 57.4*	528 23.6	275 12.3	20 .9	736 32.9	31 1.4	645 28.9
HOPKINS	2362 43.2	3103 56.8*	1606 28.0	246 4.3	26 .5	2253 39.3	58 1.0	1545 26.9
HOUSTON	2146 48.3	2301 51.7*	1187 24.3	195 4.0	11 .2	1951 40.0	53 1.1	1478 30.3
HOWARD	2850 45.5	3418 54.5*	2308 36.2	544 8.5	33 .5	1292 20.3	133 2.1	2070 32.4
HUDSPETH	306 68.6	140 31.4*	412 55.9	59 8.0	8 1.1	137 18.6	13 1.8	108 14.7
HUNT	5390 57.9	3923 42.1*	3648 41.8	244 2.8	29 .3	2665 30.5	76 .9	2066 23.7
HUTCHISON	2629 45.7	3125 54.3*	1886 31.5	631 10.5	54 .9	1223 20.4	72 1.2	2120 35.4
IRION	228 60.8	147 39.2*	193 35.9	61 11.3	6 1.1	181 33.6	31 5.8	66 12.3
JACK	1050 57.6	773 42.4*	711 31.3	311 13.7	7 .3	777 34.3	40 1.8	422 18.6
JACKSON	1763 65.4	933 34.6*	1389 37.4	106 2.9	18 .5	1490 40.1	65 1.7	650 17.5
JASPER	2302 43.1	3045 56.9*	1974 36.7	240 4.5	31 .6	773 14.4	57 1.1	2304 42.8
JEFFDAVIS	255 56.8	194 43.2*	140 42.4	47 14.2	10 3.0	50 15.2	7 2.1	76 23.0
JEFFERSON	21205 50.1	21079 49.9*	20745 48.6	1112 2.6	262 .6	2131 5.0	561 1.3	17854 41.8
JIMHOGG	664 53.1	587 46.9*	374 31.2	19 1.6	7 .6	265 22.1	6 .5	529 44.1
JIMWELLS	3681 55.0	3010 45.0*	2827 41.2	95 1.4	32 .5	1872 27.3	192 2.8	1847 26.9
JOHNSON	3120 47.8	3401 52.2*	1548 26.9	1447 25.2	20 .3	1060 18.4	46 .8	1631 28.4
JONES	2084 50.4	2049 49.6*	1430 32.2	269 6.1	46 1.0	1314 29.6	159 3.6	1221 27.5
KARNES	2023 57.8	1474 42.2*	1786 49.1	71 2.0	16 .4	986 27.1	41 1.1	741 20.4
KAUFMAN	2678 48.7	2818 51.3*	1850 31.3	311 5.3	37 .6	1847 31.2	98 1.7	1768 29.9
KENDALL	835 83.7	163 16.3*	394 66.3	6 1.0	0 .0	102 17.2	7 1.2	85 14.3
KENEDY	148 94.9	8 5.1*	92 84.4	0 .0	2 1.8	11 10.1	3 2.8	1 .9
KENT	241 40.8	350 59.2*	181 20.6	177 20.2	5 .6	284 32.3	14 1.6	217 24.7
KERR	3027 78.1	850 21.9*	1674 60.6	47 1.7	14 .5	617 22.3	87 3.1	325 11.8
KIMBLE	900 63.5	518 36.5*	485 33.6	217 15.0	22 1.5	412 28.6	90 6.2	217 15.0
KING	91 36.8	156 63.2*	39 15.9	62 25.3	10 4.1	71 29.0	2 .8	61 24.9
KINNEY	301 56.2	235 43.8*	215 37.7	18 3.2	3 .5	73 12.8	9 1.6	252 44.2
KLEBERG	1334 41.3	1894 58.7*	1333 31.7	43 1.0	32 .8	582 13.9	81 1.9	2131 50.7
KNOX	1127 49.8	1134 50.2*	636 30.5	184 8.8	15 .7	684 32.8	34 1.6	530 25.4

COUNTY	SHIVERS #	%	R. YARBRO #	%*	DANIEL #	%	HALEY #	%	HOLMES #	%	ODANIEL #	%	SENT #	%	R. YARBRO #	%
LAMAR	4568	51.1	4380	48.9*	3285	34.2	403	4.2	65	.7	3853	40.1	223	2.3	1780	18.5
LAMB	2260	55.3	1830	44.7*	1608	35.6	467	10.3	14	.3	911	20.2	130	2.9	1388	30.7
LAMPASAS	1449	53.0	1283	47.0*	559	20.8	78	2.9	37	1.4	1031	38.4	639	23.8	343	12.8
LASALLE	541	51.5	510	48.5*	368	40.8	6	.7	2	.2	151	16.7	62	6.9	314	34.8
LABACA	3335	69.4	1469	30.6*	2402	43.9	108	2.0	32	.6	2042	37.4	90	1.6	792	14.5
LEE	1192	52.3	1089	47.7*	629	23.5	244	9.1	7	.3	1049	39.1	26	1.0	726	27.1
LEON	1671	45.1	2038	54.9*	729	23.4	138	4.4	12	.4	1304	41.8	106	3.4	830	26.6
LIBERTY	3127	56.4	2421	43.6*	3424	48.0	92	1.3	24	.3	2045	28.6	96	1.3	1459	20.4
LIMESTONE	2677	40.9	3872	59.1*	2038	35.5	160	2.8	55	1.0	1463	25.5	101	1.8	1918	33.4
LIPSCOMB	522	74.0	183	26.0*	471	48.8	68	7.0	1	.1	213	22.1	9	.9	203	21.0
LIVEOAK	1246	69.8	540	30.2*	579	40.0	30	2.1	7	.5	532	36.8	63	4.4	235	16.3
LLANO	809	55.3	654	44.7*	463	26.5	50	2.9	10	.6	610	34.9	156	8.9	459	26.3
LOVING	51	91.1	5	8.9*	25	26.9	38	40.9	0	.0	27	29.0	1	1.1	2	2.2
LUBBOCK	9133	57.4	6788	42.6*	9445	47.3	1131	5.7	98	.5	3309	16.6	600	3.0	5371	26.9
LYNN	1011	50.4	993	49.6*	1023	38.3	194	7.3	15	.6	727	27.2	31	1.2	679	25.4
MADISON	994	47.6	1096	52.4*	533	26.3	98	4.8	11	.5	893	44.1	38	1.9	454	22.4
MARION	829	55.8	657	44.2*	652	32.7	137	6.9	43	2.2	721	36.2	12	.6	428	21.5
MARTIN	396	41.4	561	58.6*	215	23.3	218	23.7	5	.5	293	31.8	23	2.5	167	18.1
MASON	828	67.5	399	32.5*	449	32.7	38	2.8	2	.1	482	35.1	76	5.5	326	23.7
MATAGORDA	3145	70.0	1347	30.0*	2767	47.9	100	1.7	27	.5	1784	30.9	120	2.1	983	17.0
MAVERICK	913	65.9	473	34.1*	1001	51.6	15	.8	4	.2	230	11.8	16	.8	675	34.8
MCCULLOCH	1998	57.7	1465	42.3*	665	22.5	160	5.4	15	.5	1396	47.2	370	12.5	353	11.9
MCLENNAN	11740	46.5	13531	53.5*	10518	40.5	767	3.0	114	.4	5399	20.8	638	2.5	8507	32.8
MCMULLEN	242	65.4	128	34.6*	277	52.3	7	1.3	4	.8	151	28.5	15	2.8	76	14.3
MEDINA	1544	65.7	806	34.3*	1320	55.2	23	1.0	33	1.4	552	23.1	33	1.4	430	18.0
MENARD	703	60.3	463	39.7*	333	28.2	113	9.6	16	1.4	485	41.0	66	5.6	169	14.3
MIDLAND	5005	71.3	2018	28.7*	3914	50.1	1425	18.2	52	.7	914	11.7	296	3.8	1209	15.5
MILAN	2423	46.0	2850	54.0*	1367	25.9	181	3.4	32	.6	2277	43.2	104	2.0	1315	24.9
MILLS	951	52.3	866	47.7*	426	19.3	115	5.2	7	.3	881	39.9	500	22.6	281	12.7
MITCHELL	1270	43.2	1668	56.8*	855	27.5	192	6.2	25	.8	1077	34.6	142	4.6	820	26.4
MONTAGE	1794	45.9	2115	54.1*	1545	30.7	482	9.6	10	.2	1692	33.6	66	1.3	1237	24.6
MONTGOMRY	3073	45.6	3664	54.4*	2001	28.8	190	2.7	27	.4	2745	39.6	112	1.6	1861	26.8
MOORE	858	44.6	1064	55.4*	890	28.9	323	10.5	17	.6	845	27.4	42	1.4	967	31.4
MORRIS	1434	43.2	1888	56.8*	864	24.0	290	8.1	9	.3	1302	36.2	23	.6	1110	30.9
MOTLEY	547	63.2	319	36.8*	310	26.8	298	25.8	8	.7	281	24.3	13	1.1	247	21.3
NACDOCHES	3165	46.1	3704	53.9*	2549	35.4	180	2.5	47	.7	1368	19.0	128	1.8	2926	40.7
NAVARRO	2884	40.5	4245	59.5*	2731	32.8	424	5.1	25	.3	1933	23.2	97	1.2	3121	37.5
NEWTON	794	33.7	1565	66.3*	884	31.6	76	2.7	27	1.0	497	17.8	42	1.5	1268	45.4
NOLAN	2044	47.1	2295	52.9*	1587	34.7	180	3.9	39	.9	1330	29.1	181	4.0	1252	27.4
NUECES	14352	49.9	14408	50.1*	12851	41.7	414	1.3	302	1.0	4816	15.6	592	1.9	11859	38.5
OCHILTREE	862	78.9	230	21.1*	881	52.4	123	7.3	6	.4	425	25.3	13	.8	234	13.9
OLDHAM	290	53.6	251	46.4*	281	44.0	72	11.3	3	.5	138	21.6	7	1.1	137	21.5
ORANGE	4114	40.3	6091	59.7*	4027	41.3	294	3.0	33	.3	953	9.8	151	1.5	4287	44.0
PALOPINTO	2542	55.9	2009	44.1*	1843	37.6	439	9.0	24	.5	1408	28.7	40	.8	1148	23.4
PANOLA	3102	49.2	3202	50.8*	1411	23.8	698	11.8	27	.5	2049	34.6	44	.7	1696	28.6
PARKER	3295	52.3	3002	47.7*	1785	28.8	729	11.8	17	.3	2117	34.2	127	2.1	1420	22.9

COUNTY	SHIVERS #	%	R. YARBRO #	%	DANIEL #	%	HALEY #	%	HOLMES #	%	ODANIEL #	%	SENT #	%	R. YARBRO #	%
PARMER	1040	72.4	397	27.6*	851	47.4	316	17.6	10	.6	341	19.0	29	1.6	247	13.8
PECOS	1368	51.6	1282	48.4*	953	38.2	290	11.6	14	.6	484	19.4	155	6.2	599	24.0
POLK	1969	53.1	1739	46.9*	1098	28.4	103	2.7	21	.5	1702	44.1	112	2.9	824	21.3
POTTER	7007	53.1	6178	46.9*	4750	41.2	1385	12.0	51	.4	1609	14.0	136	1.2	3595	31.2
PRESIDIO	479	65.0	258	35.0*	548	63.6	47	5.5	4	.5	58	6.7	24	2.8	181	21.0
RAINES	490	42.2	672	57.8*	552	43.5	14	1.1	4	.3	472	37.2	6	.5	221	17.4
RANDALL	2571	63.4	1487	36.6*	1881	39.4	1246	26.1	9	.2	507	10.6	87	1.8	1041	21.8
REAGAN	380	57.8	278	42.2*	350	28.5	213	17.3	7	.6	337	27.4	237	19.3	84	6.8
REAL	319	68.3	148	31.7*	276	42.6	19	2.9	3	.5	244	37.7	9	1.4	97	15.0
REDRIVER	2107	40.9	3041	59.1*	1581	29.6	215	4.0	25	.5	2311	43.3	44	.8	1164	21.8
REEVES	1766	64.7	965	35.3*	1053	35.0	561	18.6	29	1.0	657	21.8	174	5.8	535	17.8
REFUGIO	1164	62.1	710	37.9*	1117	43.4	43	1.7	12	.5	839	32.6	40	1.6	524	20.3
ROBERTS	295	80.8	70	19.2*	217	61.0	47	13.2	0	.0	61	17.1	2	.6	29	8.1
ROBERTSON	1488	37.4	2492	62.6*	866	26.7	88	2.7	20	.6	915	28.2	61	1.9	1292	39.9
ROCKWALL	745	47.1	837	52.9*	746	37.7	115	5.8	1	.1	660	33.3	27	1.4	432	21.8
RUNNELLS	1984	65.6	1040	34.4*	1201	32.5	259	7.0	34	.9	1291	34.9	346	9.4	569	15.4
RUSK	5973	52.0	5515	48.0*	3805	37.8	459	4.6	216	2.1	3035	30.2	150	1.5	2399	23.8
SABINE	1132	41.1	1625	58.9*	704	26.6	89	3.4	36	1.4	909	34.4	46	1.7	862	32.6
SNAUGSTNE	1304	46.3	1512	53.7*	655	26.3	86	3.4	18	.7	836	33.5	39	1.6	861	34.5
SNJACINTO	473	34.9	883	65.1*	307	20.2	15	1.0	16	1.1	754	49.6	40	2.6	389	25.6
SNPATRICIO	2649	52.3	2412	47.7*	2383	35.8	90	1.4	89	1.3	1615	24.3	115	1.7	2359	35.5
SANSABA	891	36.3	1565	63.7*	106	4.0	39	1.5	4	.2	697	26.3	1550	58.5	252	9.5
SCHLEICHER	686	66.0	353	34.0*	321	34.1	112	11.9	15	1.6	333	35.4	33	3.5	127	13.5
SCURRY	1675	51.6	1570	48.4*	1637	32.0	635	12.4	24	.5	1745	34.1	113	2.2	960	18.8
SHACKELFRD	801	56.3	622	43.7*	485	32.9	259	17.6	7	.5	407	27.6	54	3.7	261	17.7
SHELBY	2626	38.6	4182	61.4*	1672	25.3	188	2.8	57	.9	1440	21.8	94	1.4	3163	47.8
SHERMAN	627	73.5	226	26.5*	365	51.8	70	9.9	1	.1	174	24.7	7	1.0	88	12.5
SMITH	8348	52.3	7616	47.7*	7875	42.4	327	1.8	58	.3	4129	22.2	265	1.4	5904	31.8
SOMERVELL	459	52.6	413	47.4*	225	21.4	102	9.7	3	.3	531	50.5	10	1.0	181	17.2
STARR	1328	53.2	1168	46.8*	3428	82.8	9	.2	2	.0	131	3.2	10	.2	561	13.5
STEPHENS	1939	57.2	1451	42.8*	1047	33.0	229	7.2	37	1.2	1207	38.0	101	3.2	554	17.4
STERLING	214	69.9	92	30.1*	191	41.5	48	10.4	7	1.5	125	27.2	21	4.6	68	14.8
STONEWALL	540	39.5	828	60.5*	327	22.4	152	10.4	22	1.5	610	41.8	23	1.6	326	22.3
SUTTON	554	68.7	252	31.3*	265	46.2	41	7.2	3	.5	134	23.4	14	2.4	116	20.2
SWISHER	1029	55.7	818	44.3*	638	24.9	332	13.0	17	.7	391	15.3	152	5.9	1033	40.3
TARRANT	34653	54.2	29310	45.8*	27447	35.2	15167	19.5	307	.4	10444	13.4	1304	1.7	23255	29.8
TAYLOR	5833	55.4	4691	44.6*	6008	43.4	399	2.9	126	.9	2617	18.9	1002	7.2	3695	26.7
TERRELL	250	60.5	163	39.5*	277	41.7	38	5.7	4	.6	78	11.7	37	5.6	230	34.6
TERRY	1432	53.0	1272	47.0*	1373	37.8	253	7.0	37	1.0	879	24.2	103	2.8	989	27.2
THRCKMORTN	744	50.1	740	49.9*	297	20.3	148	10.1	9	.6	644	44.0	19	1.3	348	23.8
TITUS	1898	39.3	2936	60.7*	1171	22.2	450	8.5	17	.3	2258	42.9	41	.8	1327	25.2
TOMGREEN	6831	62.5	4097	37.5*	4641	37.3	713	5.7	111	.9	3981	32.0	838	6.7	2150	17.3
TRAVIS	18416	57.4	13693	42.6*	17267	44.6	404	1.0	354	.9	6116	15.8	1818	4.7	12733	32.9
TRINITY	1059	47.1	1191	52.9*	448	22.0	26	1.3	14	.7	930	45.6	34	1.7	589	28.9
TYLER	2367	67.9	1118	32.1*	1591	51.1	37	1.2	7	.2	696	22.4	65	2.1	716	23.0
UPSHUR	3068	45.4	3693	54.6*	1535	27.5	233	4.2	20	.4	2390	42.8	44	.8	1368	24.5

	DEMOC. RUNOFF 1954*					DEMOC. GOVERNOR 1956												
COUNTY	SHIVERS		R. YARBRO		DANIEL		HALEY		HOLMES		ODANIEL		SENT		R. YARBRO	
	#	%	#	%*	#	%	#	%	#	%	#	%	#	%	#	%
UPTON	628	47.5	693	52.5*	479	27.7	274	15.8	28	1.6	523	30.2	94	5.4	334	19.3
UVALDE	1731	70.6	721	29.4*	1747	48.8	83	2.3	14	.4	1142	31.9	50	1.4	544	15.2
VALVERDE	1343	55.1	1095	44.9*	909	55.1	40	2.4	14	.8	155	9.4	36	2.2	496	30.1
VANZANDT	1750	35.6	3161	64.4*	1427	25.1	240	4.2	22	.4	1941	34.1	71	1.2	1984	34.9
VICTORIA	3724	61.2	2360	38.8*	3145	38.8	132	1.6	54	.7	2643	32.6	150	1.9	1979	24.4
WALKER	2091	54.8	1727	45.2*	1222	32.6	107	2.9	7	.2	1185	31.6	86	2.3	1142	30.5
WALLER	1122	58.7	791	41.3*	894	33.4	153	5.7	13	.5	954	35.7	31	1.2	629	23.5
WARD	1541	54.0	1311	46.0*	889	28.0	722	22.7	32	1.0	849	26.7	85	2.7	603	19.0
WASHINGTON	3085	75.4	1005	24.6*	1934	43.0	122	2.7	10	.2	1778	39.5	47	1.0	606	13.5
WEBB	6215	87.9	854	12.1*	4858	63.0	60	.8	30	.4	577	7.5	89	1.2	2100	27.2
WHARTON	4352	63.7	2475	36.3*	3069	41.7	135	1.8	33	.4	2146	29.2	254	3.5	1723	23.4
WHEELER	1062	42.2	1457	57.8*	660	27.2	369	15.2	9	.4	704	29.0	24	1.0	664	27.3
WICHITA	7264	45.7	8627	54.3*	8162	40.9	506	2.5	115	.6	3104	15.5	353	1.8	7724	38.7
WILBARGER	2245	56.2	1748	43.8*	1637	42.6	213	5.5	12	.3	958	24.9	126	3.3	899	23.4
WILLACY	2150	68.1	1006	31.9*	1375	49.7	40	1.4	17	.6	715	25.8	157	5.7	464	16.8
WILLIAMSON	3343	50.8	3234	49.2*	2176	31.8	172	2.5	28	.4	2478	36.2	285	4.2	1710	25.0
WILSON	1578	47.5	1745	52.5*	1400	33.6	23	.6	17	.4	1092	26.2	28	.7	1611	38.6
WINKLER	977	50.6	955	49.4*	761	26.5	759	26.5	30	1.0	714	24.9	77	2.7	526	18.3
WISE	1631	39.9	2457	60.1*	1158	26.0	481	10.8	50	1.1	1374	30.9	84	1.9	1302	29.3
WOOD	2117	43.1	2798	56.9*	1553	32.8	179	3.8	12	.3	1505	31.8	48	1.0	1435	30.3
YOAKUM	844	47.7	924	52.3*	509	30.8	206	12.5	11	.7	454	27.4	77	4.7	397	24.0
YOUNG	1724	51.1	1649	48.9*	1338	34.3	282	7.2	13	.3	1183	30.3	80	2.0	1010	25.9
ZAPATA	414	91.8	37	8.2*	731	79.5	1	.1	5	.5	14	1.5	2	.2	167	18.2
ZAVALA	1035	63.2	603	36.8*	656	41.3	42	2.6	2	.1	533	33.5	21	1.3	336	21.1
TOTALS	775079		683132	*	628817		88777		10165		347755		37783		463396	
% OF VOTE	53.2		46.8	*	39.9		5.6		.6		22.1		2.4		29.4	

GEOGRAPHIC CLASS

LOWLANDS	291386	50.	296551	50.*	223009	38.	20966	4.	3644	1.	139469	24.	11224	2.	194204	33.
BLACK BELT	8097	51.	7804	49.*	5745	34.	984	6.	108	1.	4683	28.	213	1.	5024	30.
WEST TEXAS	402855	55.	331818	45.*	334130	40.	63892	8.	5517	1.	182532	22.	23352	3.	225925	27.
MEX. TEXAS	72741	61.	46959	39.*	65933	50.	2935	2.	896	1.	21071	16.	2994	2.	38243	29.

DEMOGRAPHIC CLASS

METRO	375700	55.	308210	45.*	337212	45.	41043	5.	5481	1.	105384	14.	16182	2.	244055	33.
TOWN	68046	52.	63366	48.*	54132	38.	7604	5.	803	1.	35738	25.	3334	2.	42493	29.
RURAL	331333	52.	311556	48.*	237473	35.	40130	6.	3881	1.	206633	30.	18267	3.	176848	26.

```
                 DEMOC.  RUNOFF    1956*              DEMOC.  GOVERNOR   1958
                                     *
    COUNTY      DANIEL        R. YARBRO    DANIEL        GONZALEZ     IRWIN        ODANIEL
                #     %       #     %*     #     %       #     %      #     %      #     %
--------------------------------------------------------------------------------------------------------
ANDERSON       2857  46.8    3250  53.2*   4043  60.9    745  11.2    174  2.6    1675  25.2
ANDREWS         892  44.6    1108  55.4*    689  28.5    157   6.5     62  2.6    1511  62.5
ANGELINA       3781  39.0    5912  61.0*   5879  58.4    963   9.6    282  2.8    2948  29.3
ARANSAS         513  54.4     430  45.6*    854  63.8    200  14.9     52  3.9     233  17.4
ARCHER          676  45.0     827  55.0*   1086  58.7    192  10.4     96  5.2     477  25.8

ARMSTRONG       253  49.2     261  50.8*    485  76.5     37   5.8     13  2.1      99  15.6
ATASCOSA       2063  51.6    1935  48.4*   2124  56.7   1102  29.4     42  1.1     475  12.7
AUSTIN         2460  62.9    1453  37.1*   1651  66.5    124   5.0     32  1.3     674  27.2
BAILEY          506  40.3     749  59.7*   1022  65.6    103   6.6     62  4.0     370  23.8
BANDERA         617  77.8     176  22.2*   1070  75.9    105   7.4     23  1.6     212  15.0

BASTROP        1598  42.6    2153  57.4*   2294  58.5    471  12.0     59  1.5    1096  28.0
BAYLOR          584  50.0     583  50.0*   1105  72.4     68   4.5     27  1.8     327  21.4
BEE            1435  50.9    1384  49.1*   1646  47.7   1279  37.0     50  1.4     478  13.8
BELL           4077  36.4    7126  63.6*   6293  61.0    906   8.8    283  2.7    2839  27.5
BEXAR         38985  58.3   27870  41.7*  33939  50.1  26029  38.4   1263  1.9    6495   9.6

BLANCO          319  52.3     291  47.7*    332  63.8     37   7.1     13  2.5     138  26.5
BORDEN          146  45.1     178  54.9*    240  59.7     18   4.5     29  7.2     115  28.6
BOSQUE         1497  46.7    1709  53.3*   2021  65.2    235   7.6     75  2.4     768  24.8
BOWIE          5676  49.5    5798  50.5*   7182  68.8   1128  10.8    145  1.4    1981  19.0
BRAZORIA       4915  42.8    6571  57.2*   8146  64.8   1829  14.5    349  2.8    2255  17.9

BRAZOS         2593  46.6    2976  53.4*   4616  62.5   1142  15.5    121  1.6    1508  20.4
BREWSTER        475  62.5     285  37.5*    779  60.2    339  26.2     36  2.8     140  10.8
BRISCOE         261  43.2     343  56.8*    655  63.0     92   8.8     31  3.0     262  25.2
BROOKS          568  44.5     707  55.5*    569  26.0   1411  64.5     18   .8     188   8.6
BROWN          2333  46.5    2681  53.5*   3963  60.2    502   7.6    222  3.4    1898  28.8

BURLESON       1695  45.2    2058  54.8*   1704  53.5    354  11.1     62  1.9    1067  33.5
BURNET          818  42.7    1097  57.3*   1405  59.9    136   5.8    101  4.3     702  29.9
CALDWELL       1953  46.1    2283  53.9*   2367  67.1    464  13.2     66  1.9     630  17.9
CALHOUN        1292  54.5    1078  45.5*   1623  57.2    570  20.1     71  2.5     574  20.2
CALLAHAN        710  44.3     892  55.7*   1293  62.9    138   6.7     72  3.5     554  26.9

CAMERON        7201  62.4    4333  37.6*   7665  53.1   5806  40.2    208  1.4     752   5.2
CAMP           1056  49.8    1065  50.2*   1371  59.1    226   9.7     61  2.6     661  28.5
CARSON          542  40.8     788  59.2*    860  63.8    191  14.2     28  2.1     269  20.0
CASS           1893  47.8    2069  52.2*   3472  69.1    373   7.4     79  1.6    1102  21.9
CASTRO          631  38.6    1002  61.4*    950  60.1    231  14.6     64  4.1     335  21.2

CHAMBERS       1289  58.6     909  41.4*   1421  66.9    219  10.3     45  2.1     438  20.6
CHEROKEE       2643  42.1    3640  57.9*   3097  56.3    558  10.1    111  2.0    1734  31.5
CHILDRESS      1392  45.8    1649  54.2*   1334  68.4    136   7.0     69  3.5     410  21.0
CLAY           1212  41.9    1678  58.1*   1712  65.6    270  10.3     80  3.1     549  21.0
COCHRAN         657  43.3     859  56.7*    864  59.7     67   4.6     65  4.5     451  31.2

COKE            349  42.1     479  57.9*    856  60.2     96   6.8     65  4.6     405  28.5
COLEMAN        1627  53.4    1422  46.6*   1998  65.1    170   5.5     59  1.9     842  27.4
COLLIN         3495  42.0    4831  58.0*   4493  65.4    453   6.6    174  2.5    1746  25.4
CLNGSWORTH      727  40.3    1076  59.7*   1267  69.4     90   4.9     48  2.6     420  23.0
COLORADO       1785  54.6    1486  45.4*   2618  61.7    500  11.8     55  1.3    1070  25.2

COMAL          2020  69.6     881  30.4*   1815  72.3    338  13.5     35  1.4     322  12.8
```

| | DEMOC. RUNOFF 1956* | | | | DEMOC. GOVERNOR 1958 | | | | | | | |
| COUNTY | DANIEL | | R. YARBRO | | DANIEL | | GONZALEZ | | IRWIN | | ODANIEL | |
	#	%	#	%*	#	%	#	%	#	%	#	%
COMANCHEE	1607	39.4	2476	60.6*	1643	56.9	224	7.8	118	4.1	902	31.2
CONCHO	355	38.8	560	61.2*	548	52.4	127	12.2	43	4.1	327	31.3
COOKE	2829	60.1	1881	39.9*	3383	68.6	436	8.8	98	2.0	1013	20.5
CORYELL	1363	40.7	1983	59.3*	2196	66.8	99	3.0	84	2.6	908	27.6
COTTLE	275	26.8	753	73.2*	784	57.9	119	8.8	71	5.2	379	28.0
CRANE	527	35.0	978	65.0*	615	60.4	96	9.4	47	4.6	261	25.6
CROCKETT	294	55.4	237	44.6*	397	62.5	80	12.6	15	2.4	143	22.5
CROSBY	521	23.1	1739	76.9*	1094	61.5	180	10.1	86	4.8	420	23.6
CULBERSON	242	68.8	110	31.3*	298	68.0	86	19.6	10	2.3	44	10.0
DALLAM	503	46.2	585	53.8*	942	66.8	143	10.1	39	2.8	286	20.3
DALLAS	68409	58.8	48017	41.2*	60995	65.5	18318	19.7	1947	2.1	11903	12.8
DAWSON	1317	47.0	1485	53.0*	1973	66.5	182	6.1	87	2.9	727	24.5
DEAFSMITH	1196	60.4	784	39.6*	1199	71.8	189	11.3	46	2.8	237	14.2
DELTA	946	43.7	1219	56.3*	1035	62.7	81	4.9	33	2.0	502	30.4
DENTON	3186	48.6	3368	51.4*	4382	63.4	922	13.3	140	2.0	1471	21.3
DEWITT	3158	69.5	1389	30.5*	2519	67.5	532	14.3	39	1.0	641	17.2
DICKENS	735	36.4	1283	63.6*	1051	65.2	93	5.8	58	3.6	411	25.5
DIMMIT	447	55.9	353	44.1*	752	55.2	430	31.5	12	.9	169	12.4
DONLEY	908	49.7	919	50.3*	936	74.5	71	5.7	22	1.8	227	18.1
DUVAL	3523	70.2	1494	29.8*	776	17.8	3327	76.5	45	1.0	202	4.6
EASTLAND	2060	45.5	2469	54.5*	3056	56.9	368	6.9	140	2.6	1804	33.6
ECTOR	5745	52.9	5120	47.1*	3833	61.2	974	15.6	200	3.2	1253	20.0
EDWARDS	444	77.6	128	22.4*	474	75.5	33	5.3	20	3.2	101	16.1
ELLIS	3090	45.9	3649	54.1*	3155	70.0	454	10.1	95	2.1	801	17.8
ELPASO	8473	54.6	7058	45.4*	10661	53.6	7648	38.4	561	2.8	1037	5.2
ERATH	2279	45.7	2713	54.3*	2483	60.7	356	8.7	132	3.2	1121	27.4
FALLS	1422	42.0	1966	58.0*	1976	58.5	412	12.2	112	3.3	877	26.0
FANNIN	1484	33.4	2955	66.6*	3318	63.2	411	7.8	112	2.1	1405	26.8
FAYETTE	2950	65.7	1538	34.3*	2696	60.0	479	10.7	52	1.2	1269	28.2
FISHER	461	26.4	1286	73.6*	1357	60.1	183	8.1	117	5.2	601	26.6
FLOYD	994	51.8	925	48.2*	1706	72.6	71	3.0	83	3.5	490	20.9
FOARD	275	40.1	411	59.9*	727	70.0	58	5.6	52	5.0	202	19.4
FORTBEND	2172	53.3	1900	46.7*	2712	61.9	657	15.0	55	1.3	956	21.8
FRANKLIN	636	39.7	968	60.3*	1140	59.0	124	6.4	48	2.5	619	32.1
FREESTONE	1438	49.8	1451	50.2*	2317	62.7	351	9.5	84	2.3	946	25.6
FRIO	562	43.6	727	56.4*	1094	54.9	627	31.5	31	1.6	240	12.0
GAINES	1012	42.4	1377	57.6*	1528	60.1	157	6.2	98	3.9	759	29.9
GALVESTON	12360	42.7	16580	57.3*	11557	57.3	5238	25.9	988	4.9	2402	11.9
GARZA	598	43.0	792	57.0*	746	61.2	56	4.6	43	3.5	373	30.6
GILLESPIE	854	87.4	123	12.6*	727	76.7	82	8.6	12	1.3	127	13.4
GLASCOCK	143	55.4	115	44.6*	221	59.4	21	5.6	13	3.5	117	31.5
GOLIAD	640	69.9	275	30.1*	749	60.9	265	21.5	15	1.2	201	16.3
GONZALES	1692	56.6	1299	43.4*	2481	74.1	264	7.9	61	1.8	541	16.2
GRAY	1958	48.2	2101	51.8*	2978	63.3	397	8.4	130	2.8	1201	25.5
GRAYSON	5047	41.3	7171	58.7*	5550	67.8	900	11.0	176	2.2	1556	19.0
GREGG	6097	57.7	4471	42.3*	6750	62.0	1209	11.1	539	5.0	2388	21.9

COUNTY	DANIEL #	%	R. YARBRO #	%*	DANIEL #	%	GONZALEZ #	%	IRWIN #	%	ODANIEL #	%
GRIMES	1065	43.9	1361	56.1*	1087	64.6	147	8.7	59	3.5	389	23.1
GUADALUPE	1890	64.6	1037	35.4*	1631	67.7	504	20.9	23	1.0	250	10.4
HALE	2325	49.6	2358	50.4*	3473	68.1	337	6.6	129	2.5	1160	22.7
HALL	609	33.6	1201	66.4*	1331	69.9	155	8.1	54	2.8	365	19.2
HAMILTON	1300	52.9	1156	47.1*	1282	60.9	92	4.4	46	2.2	686	32.6
HANSFORD	419	69.0	188	31.0*	634	72.2	67	7.6	29	3.3	148	16.9
HARDEMAN	761	53.4	665	46.6*	1391	73.2	102	5.4	62	3.3	345	18.2
HARDIN	1736	36.9	2968	63.1*	2817	56.0	783	15.6	115	2.3	1315	26.1
HARRIS	69564	49.4	71377	50.6*	78635	60.8	30917	23.9	3999	3.1	15743	12.2
HARRISON	4001	60.4	2623	39.6*	5320	72.4	800	10.9	200	2.7	1028	14.0
HARTLEY	272	54.5	227	45.5*	436	73.3	43	7.2	15	2.5	101	17.0
HASKELL	829	29.3	1997	70.7*	1844	58.9	239	7.6	118	3.8	931	29.7
HAYS	1374	50.4	1350	49.6*	1782	66.5	426	15.9	56	2.1	417	15.6
HEMPHILL	265	62.2	161	37.8*	705	75.9	48	5.2	8	.9	168	18.1
HENDERSON	1779	27.7	4648	72.3*	3003	54.2	743	13.4	159	2.9	1632	29.5
HIDALGO	9278	62.7	5514	37.3*	8261	45.5	8493	46.7	244	1.3	1174	6.5
HILL	2984	45.9	3515	54.1*	4218	61.7	369	5.4	128	1.9	2120	31.0
HOCKLEY	1837	39.2	2853	60.8*	2930	64.5	282	6.2	130	2.9	1199	26.4
HOOD	493	35.3	904	64.7*	1218	63.2	183	9.5	74	3.8	452	23.5
HOPKINS	2339	44.7	2890	55.3*	3006	58.5	350	6.8	158	3.1	1623	31.6
HOUSTON	1560	40.7	2272	59.3*	1951	50.4	391	10.1	86	2.2	1444	37.3
HOWARD	2572	38.8	4058	61.2*	2904	58.3	726	14.6	232	4.7	1117	22.4
HUDSPETH	296	69.2	132	30.8*	389	68.0	107	18.7	18	3.1	58	10.1
HUNT	3758	54.1	3184	45.9*	4536	70.8	460	7.2	104	1.6	1306	20.4
HUTCHISON	2163	40.0	3240	60.0*	3196	63.9	781	15.6	173	3.5	854	17.1
IRION	214	50.5	210	49.5*	306	56.8	48	8.9	13	2.4	172	31.9
JACK	904	51.0	869	49.0*	1349	61.3	155	7.0	90	4.1	606	27.5
JACKSON	1210	51.3	1149	48.7*	1913	59.6	500	15.6	53	1.7	744	23.2
JASPER	2191	46.6	2509	53.4*	3255	67.6	405	8.4	135	2.8	1017	21.1
JEFFDAVIS	108	61.0	69	39.0*	184	58.4	105	33.3	5	1.6	21	6.7
JEFFERSON	20834	50.5	20451	49.5*	19868	67.0	6578	22.2	1025	3.5	2162	7.3
JIMHOGG	293	48.6	310	51.4*	285	20.0	1109	77.8	6	.4	25	1.8
JIMWELLS	2932	48.3	3133	51.7*	2282	35.0	3418	52.4	98	1.5	729	11.2
JOHNSON	2141	42.7	2872	57.3*	2799	62.3	472	10.5	176	3.9	1044	23.2
JONES	1621	40.7	2363	59.3*	2307	69.1	171	5.1	115	3.4	744	22.3
KARNES	1587	58.3	1134	41.7*	2635	63.2	906	21.7	54	1.3	576	13.8
KAUFMAN	2880	49.7	2910	50.3*	3371	69.4	313	6.4	69	1.4	1104	22.7
KENDALL	514	79.6	132	20.4*	393	78.3	42	8.4	7	1.4	60	12.0
KENEDY	96	96.0	4	4.0*	73	79.3	10	10.9	1	1.1	8	8.7
KENT	243	32.4	508	67.6*	588	67.8	35	4.0	23	2.7	221	25.5
KERR	1923	76.1	604	23.9*	2333	70.2	289	8.7	62	1.9	638	19.2
KIMBLE	863	58.6	609	41.4*	311	32.3	580	60.2	13	1.3	60	6.2
KING	39	25.5	114	74.5*	139	65.3	12	5.6	7	3.3	55	25.8
KINNEY	302	50.5	296	49.5*	287	48.6	213	36.1	10	1.7	80	13.6
KLEBERG	1482	34.0	2877	66.0*	1555	46.6	1399	41.9	71	2.1	314	9.4
KNOX	709	45.2	859	54.8*	1199	72.0	77	4.6	42	2.5	347	20.8

```
          DEMOC.  RUNOFF    1956*          DEMOC.  GOVERNOR   1958
                                *
COUNTY      DANIEL      R. YARBRO     DANIEL       GONZALEZ      IRWIN       ODANIEL
            #    %       #    %*      #     %       #    %       #    %       #    %
---------------------------------------------------------------------------------------
LAMAR      4639 54.1   3941 45.9*   4545 61.4    600   8.1    147  2.0    2110 28.5
LAMB       1217 36.0   2159 64.0*   2427 64.5    287   7.6    101  2.7     947 25.2
LAMPASAS    930 48.4    991 51.6*   1423 67.2    115   5.4     49  2.3     532 25.1
LASALLE     333 43.8    428 56.2*    632 55.5    403  35.4     23  2.0      80  7.0
LABACA     2822 62.9   1661 37.1*   2529 65.9    447  11.6     49  1.3     814 21.2

LEE        1040 42.9   1386 57.1*   1219 52.3    274  11.7     37  1.6     803 34.4
LEON        753 40.6   1100 59.4*   1962 62.3    280   8.9     50  1.6     859 27.3
LIBERTY    3312 59.0   2304 41.0*   3552 67.9    520   9.9     83  1.6    1073 20.5
LIMESTONE  2146 44.2   2707 55.8*   2892 61.8    537  11.5    114  2.4    1137 24.3
LIPSCOMB    296 64.5    163 35.5*    670 73.0     46   5.0     11  1.2     191 20.8
                                *
LIVEOAK     670 61.4    421 38.6*   1112 62.2    306  17.1     38  2.1     333 18.6
LLANO       683 38.4   1095 61.6*    691 54.4    136  10.7     57  4.5     386 30.4
LOVING       23 57.5     17 42.5*     45 47.4      9   9.5      3  3.2      38 40.0
LUBBOCK    7918 48.0   8585 52.0*   9906 70.5   1259   9.0    400  2.8    2482 17.7
LYNN        864 40.9   1248 59.1*   1409 69.5     78   3.8     50  2.5     489 24.1
                                *
MADISON     591 45.1    719 54.9*   1145 61.4    134   7.2     42  2.3     543 29.1
MARION      708 58.0    512 42.0*   1218 71.2    109   6.4     31  1.8     353 20.6
MARTIN      196 28.8    484 71.2*    475 58.1     51   6.2     21  2.6     271 33.1
MASON       500 48.1    539 51.9*    664 55.7     93   7.8     33  2.8     403 33.8
MATAGORDA  2753 61.6   1715 38.4*   2225 63.5    577  16.5     47  1.3     657 18.7
                                *
MAVERICK    748 67.4    361 32.6*    602 35.4   1000  58.9     15   .9      82  4.8
MCCULLOCH  1089 44.7   1349 55.3*   1354 57.1    161   6.8     67  2.8     791 33.3
MCLENNAN  11551 47.3  12862 52.7*  14911 65.0   3096  13.5    556  2.4    4377 19.1
MCMULLEN    210 68.9     95 31.1*    325 62.3    107  20.5      6  1.1      84 16.1
MEDINA     1393 64.8    756 35.2*   1555 66.1    474  20.1     28  1.2     297 12.6
                                *
MENARD      588 51.0    564 49.0*    510 50.6    125  12.4     22  2.2     351 34.8
MIDLAND    5575 65.9   2882 34.1*   4028 60.3    806  13.7    129  2.2     934 15.8
MILAN      1620 38.8   2551 61.2*   2917 50.9    451   7.9    160  2.8    2207 38.5
MILLS       546 46.4    630 53.6*    972 59.6     77   4.7     47  2.9     536 32.8
MITCHELL   1016 32.2   2136 67.8*   1562 59.5    216   8.2     95  3.6     759 28.8
                                *
MONTAGE    1345 46.3   1563 53.7*   2285 63.5    255   7.1     80  2.2     976 27.1
MONTGOMRY  2379 42.9   3170 57.1*   3148 56.3    440   7.9    115  2.1    1891 33.8
MOORE      1123 40.6   1642 59.4*   1531 62.6    293  12.0     77  3.1     544 22.2
MORRIS     1475 43.6   1908 56.4*   1778 63.0    275   9.7     86  3.0     685 24.3
MOTLEY      448 50.9    433 49.1*    622 61.8     66   6.6     40  4.0     279 27.7
                                *
NACDOCHES  3247 44.3   4076 55.7*   3995 67.5    448   7.6    126  2.1    1347 22.8
NAVARRO    2915 44.5   3634 55.5*   3656 60.9    975  16.2    129  2.1    1244 20.7
NEWTON      901 39.9   1358 60.1*   1607 60.2    219   8.2     52  1.9     791 29.6
NOLAN      1381 40.7   2010 59.3*   2447 62.8    317   8.1    133  3.4     998 25.6
NUECES    15067 46.5  17344 53.5*  13058 53.1   8384  34.1    598  2.4    2552 10.4
                                *
OCHILTREE   434 70.0    186 30.0*   1048 71.3    117   8.0     20  1.4     284 19.3
OLDHAM      191 53.5    166 46.5*    375 68.3     68  12.4      7  1.3      99 18.0
ORANGE     3817 44.6   4732 55.4*   5973 68.5   1130  13.0    200  2.3    1411 16.2
PALOPINTO  1810 49.1   1876 50.9*   2482 61.0    397   9.8     94  2.3    1096 26.9
PANOLA     3046 52.2   2791 47.8*   3265 72.4    201   4.5    121  2.7     922 20.4

PARKER     2332 46.1   2730 53.9*   2579 59.2    292   6.7    123  2.8    1359 31.2
```

COUNTY	DANIEL #	%	R. YARBRO #	%*	DANIEL #	%	GONZALEZ #	%	IRWIN #	%	ODANIEL #	%
PARMER	1036	62.3	627	37.7*	1329	73.3	68	3.8	29	1.6	386	21.3
PECOS	695	50.5	680	49.5*	1385	57.2	514	21.2	92	3.8	430	17.8
POLK	1423	46.4	1644	53.6*	1944	56.2	267	7.7	72	2.1	1179	34.1
POTTER	5380	47.4	5959	52.6*	5781	68.6	1452	17.2	249	3.0	947	11.2
PRESIDIO	359	63.3	208	36.7*	424	45.2	464	49.4	9	1.0	42	4.5
RAINES	630	61.4	396	38.6*	585	62.6	30	3.2	20	2.1	300	32.1
RANDALL	2535	56.6	1943	43.4*	3093	74.5	491	11.8	112	2.7	458	11.0
REAGAN	467	47.3	521	52.7*	797	66.5	85	7.1	50	4.2	266	22.2
REAL	194	60.2	128	39.8*	425	62.0	56	8.2	26	3.8	179	26.1
REDRIVER	2159	49.5	2201	50.5*	2494	58.7	222	5.2	73	1.7	1463	34.4
REEVES	1669	54.1	1415	45.9*	1366	64.0	356	16.7	63	2.9	351	16.4
REFUGIO	1065	52.6	961	47.4*	1052	59.5	453	25.6	25	1.4	238	13.5
ROBERTS	184	70.5	77	29.5*	201	71.0	28	9.9	6	2.1	48	17.0
ROBERTSON	964	31.9	2057	68.1*	1860	56.3	503	15.2	80	2.4	858	26.0
ROCKWALL	623	52.6	561	47.4*	1116	67.8	98	6.0	31	1.9	402	24.4
RUNNELLS	1729	55.3	1396	44.7*	1791	62.5	177	6.2	126	4.4	773	27.0
RUSK	4501	52.1	4141	47.9*	5335	60.4	910	10.3	146	1.7	2442	27.6
SABINE	757	40.7	1102	59.3*	1440	65.6	110	5.0	61	2.8	583	26.6
SNAUGSTNE	766	39.8	1157	60.2*	1306	59.6	134	6.1	107	4.9	645	29.4
SNJACINTO	302	31.3	664	68.7*	375	47.2	124	15.6	14	1.8	282	35.5
SNPATRICIO	2103	42.3	2866	57.7*	3163	54.4	1677	28.9	144	2.5	825	14.2
SANSABA	406	23.3	1337	76.7*	1111	56.3	141	7.1	101	5.1	622	31.5
SCHLEICHER	511	53.7	440	46.3*	451	56.2	46	5.7	31	3.9	275	34.2
SCURRY	1985	42.1	2728	57.9*	2537	59.9	291	6.9	169	4.0	1237	29.2
SHACKELFRD	593	52.3	540	47.7*	834	61.4	78	5.7	24	1.8	422	31.1
SHELBY	2282	37.5	3806	62.5*	3655	60.7	442	7.3	211	3.5	1711	28.4
SHERMAN	262	63.7	149	36.3*	525	77.4	67	9.9	13	1.9	73	10.8
SMITH	10001	54.5	8338	45.5*	8286	63.0	1923	14.6	297	2.3	2643	20.1
SOMERVELL	478	43.4	623	56.6*	485	48.2	71	7.1	65	6.5	385	38.3
STARR	1250	73.4	453	26.6*	921	24.5	2796	74.4	5	.1	35	.9
STEPHENS	1045	47.1	1173	52.9*	1571	63.9	173	7.0	49	2.0	667	27.1
STERLING	136	57.9	99	42.1*	285	71.1	21	5.2	14	3.5	81	20.2
STONEWALL	530	37.0	901	63.0*	745	61.1	65	5.3	35	2.9	375	30.7
SUTTON	286	62.7	170	37.3*	351	60.4	155	26.7	9	1.5	66	11.4
SWISHER	811	36.9	1386	63.1*	1241	53.1	430	18.4	557	23.8	108	4.6
TARRANT	37527	52.3	34266	47.7*	36483	65.7	9896	17.8	1632	2.9	7540	13.6
TAYLOR	5475	48.8	5735	51.2*	6870	67.8	769	7.6	306	3.0	2191	21.6
TERRELL	142	52.6	128	47.4*	303	66.6	75	16.5	11	2.4	66	14.5
TERRY	1311	41.2	1871	58.8*	1804	63.1	230	8.1	119	4.2	704	24.6
THRCKMORTN	304	30.6	689	69.4*	588	57.5	85	8.3	47	4.6	303	29.6
TITUS	2032	46.9	2297	53.1*	2551	61.5	363	8.7	146	3.5	1089	26.2
TOMGREEN	4923	49.3	5070	50.7*	5358	56.3	1379	14.5	171	1.8	2612	27.4
TRAVIS	17628	52.1	16232	47.9*	17971	59.1	7428	24.4	717	2.4	4310	14.2
TRINITY	693	37.2	1170	62.8*	1164	48.6	235	9.8	42	1.8	952	39.8
TYLER	1645	65.4	872	34.6*	2073	68.9	164	5.5	42	1.4	730	24.3
UPSHUR	1806	48.8	1893	51.2*	3234	57.7	434	7.7	129	2.3	1806	32.2

```
       DEMOC.  RUNOFF   1956*           DEMOC.  GOVERNOR   1958
                                 *
COUNTY    DANIEL       R. YARBRO   DANIEL      GONZALEZ     IRWIN       ODANIEL
          #    %       #    %*     #    %      #    %       #    %      #    %
----------------------------------------*-------------------------------------------------------------------
UPTON       497 45.7    590 54.3*   766 57.1    121  9.0    61  4.5    394 29.4
UVALDE     2159 62.6   1291 37.4*  2099 63.7    546 16.6    76  2.3    576 17.5
VALVERDE    893 62.7    532 37.3*  1375 56.7    904 37.3    18   .7    129  5.3
VANZANDT   1910 37.3   3207 62.7*  2845 55.3    489  9.5   142  2.8   1667 32.4
VICTORIA   2993 51.8   2789 48.2*  3410 57.1   1323 22.1   114  1.9   1126 18.9
                                 *
WALKER     1803 50.0   1804 50.0*  2110 61.9    520 15.2    42  1.2    739 21.7
WALLER     1093 49.2   1129 50.8*  1102 61.7    231 12.9    21  1.2    433 24.2
WARD        734 39.9   1105 60.1*  1584 63.8    265 10.7    72  2.9    563 22.7
WASHINGTON 1741 69.6    761 30.4*  1960 67.1    185  6.3    29  1.0    749 25.6
WEBB       4063 63.5   2336 36.5*  2540 24.3   7670 73.3    34   .3    224  2.1
                                 *
WHARTON    2757 50.5   2704 49.5*  3911 60.0   1147 17.6   115  1.8   1346 20.6
WHEELER     671 37.7   1109 62.3*  1552 70.1    105  4.7    42  1.9    514 23.2
WICHITA    9003 45.4  10814 54.6*  8902 66.3   2356 17.6   355  2.6   1810 13.5
WILBARGER  1497 54.5   1252 45.5*  3076 73.9    226  5.4   112  2.7    751 18.0
WILLACY    1516 66.5    764 33.5*  1274 59.3    584 27.2    25  1.2    264 12.3
                                 *
WILLIAMSON 2491 43.1   3289 56.9*  3511 61.4    488  8.5   122  2.1   1598 27.9
WILSON     2091 45.3   2527 54.7*  2014 55.8    883 24.5    57  1.6    655 18.1
WINKLER    1076 47.0   1215 53.0*  1096 59.8    161  8.8    61  3.3    514 28.1
WISE       1177 36.3   2062 63.7*  2350 57.9    424 10.4   149  3.7   1139 28.0
WOOD       1778 46.4   2051 53.6*  3220 64.1    448  8.9   148  2.9   1211 24.1
                                 *
YOAKUM      418 37.2    707 62.8*  1135 61.4     92  5.0    63  3.4    560 30.3
YOUNG      1342 46.0   1575 54.0*  2493 71.2    270  7.7    91  2.6    646 18.5
ZAPATA      421 76.7    128 23.3*    72  8.0    826 91.6     0   .0      4   .4
ZAVALA      784 54.1    666 45.9*   935 54.8    566 33.2    25  1.5    181 10.6
----------------------------------------*-------------------------------------------------------------------
                                 *
TOTALS   698001       694830    * 799107     245969      33643      238797
% OF VOTE  50.1         49.9    *   60.7       18.7        2.6        18.1
                                 *
                                 *
GEOGRAPHIC CLASS                 *
                                 *
LOWLANDS  260068 48.  283643 52.* 315220 62.   77303 15.  13596 3.  102674 20.
BLACK BELT  7068 50.    6985 50.*   9875 66.    1767 12.    346 2.    2954 2).
WEST TEXAS 371676 51.  360481 49.* 415172 62.  111089 17.  17709 3.  123427 18.
MEX. TEXAS 59189 58.   43721 42.*  58840 47.   55810 44.   1992 2.    9742  8.
                                 *
                                 *
DEMOGRAPHIC CLASS                *
                                 *
METRO     377325 52.  343283 48.* 374402 61.  150184 24.  15980 3.   77761 13.
TOWN       58468 49.   60965 51.*  68791 59.   24482 21.   2909 2.   21117 18.
RURAL     262208 47.  290582 53.* 355914 61.   71303 12.  14754 3.  139919 24.
```

COUNTY	DEMOC. GOVERNOR 1960* COX #	%	DANIEL #	%*	DEMOC. GOVERNOR 1962 CONNALLY #	%	DANIEL #	%	FORMBY #	%	WALKER #	%	WILSON #	%	D. YARBRO #	%
ANDERSON	3089	38.4	4960	61.6*	1374	21.3	1571	24.4	400	6.2	892	13.8	890	13.8	1322	20.5
ANDREWS	1357	43.9	1736	56.1*	447	14.0	183	5.7	877	27.5	246	7.7	583	18.3	854	26.8
ANGELINA	5914	46.2	6892	53.8*	1843	16.7	2065	18.7	166	1.5	1069	9.7	2034	18.4	3873	35.0
ARANSAS	642	33.4	1279	66.6*	406	22.6	261	22.6	72	6.2	58	5.0	136	11.8	222	19.2
ARCHER	1120	57.9	815	42.1*	821	44.2	237	12.8	301	16.2	67	3.6	206	11.1	226	12.2
ARMSTRONG	286	37.0	487	63.0*	100	12.8	108	13.8	370	47.4	81	10.4	71	9.1	51	6.5
ATASCOSA	1789	42.1	2464	57.9*	2424	58.1	752	18.0	112	2.7	171	4.1	352	8.4	364	8.7
AUSTIN	1250	36.0	2222	64.0*	553	26.4	396	18.9	62	3.0	245	11.7	271	12.9	569	27.1
BAILEY	1045	49.9	1048	50.1*	157	9.2	161	9.4	757	44.2	199	11.6	184	10.7	256	14.9
BANDERA	449	32.1	948	67.9*	480	34.1	309	21.9	32	2.3	331	23.5	179	12.7	78	5.5
BASTROP	1749	42.8	2337	57.2*	1233	40.2	505	16.4	143	4.7	213	6.9	268	8.7	708	23.1
BAYLOR	786	56.5	605	43.5*	639	37.5	166	10.3	353	21.8	71	4.4	201	12.4	186	11.5
BEE	2232	49.8	2251	50.2*	1190	34.3	670	19.3	201	5.8	175	5.0	551	15.9	687	19.8
BELL	4312	36.4	7521	63.6*	4579	45.0	1579	15.5	661	6.5	512	5.0	829	8.1	2017	19.8
BEXAR	24104	32.3	50579	67.7*	41800	52.7	13602	17.1	1601	2.0	4347	5.5	6048	7.6	11955	15.1
BLANCO	252	46.1	295	53.9*	347	52.3	95	14.3	18	2.7	34	5.1	80	12.0	90	13.6
BORDEN	207	46.8	235	53.2*	104	15.5	50	7.5	54	8.0	72	10.7	33	4.9	358	53.4
BOSQUE	1321	43.0	1749	57.0*	1048	32.7	547	17.1	367	11.4	280	8.7	446	13.9	519	16.2
BOWIE	4055	36.2	7153	63.8*	2055	19.1	3260	30.3	352	3.3	923	8.6	2148	20.0	2009	18.7
BRAZORIA	6012	37.7	9920	62.3*	3127	21.1	2569	17.3	644	4.3	1569	10.6	1481	10.0	5458	36.8
BRAZOS	3435	38.7	5435	61.3*	2153	26.9	1626	20.3	484	6.1	384	4.8	1367	17.1	1977	24.7
BREWSTER	569	43.9	727	56.1*	265	20.2	282	21.5	206	15.7	110	8.4	310	23.7	136	10.4
BRISCOE	592	55.5	474	44.5*	106	10.8	91	9.3	523	53.3	41	4.2	90	9.2	130	13.3
BROOKS	1191	49.0	1238	51.0*	683	52.6	184	14.2	79	6.1	37	2.9	104	8.0	211	16.3
BROWN	4098	58.2	2946	41.8*	2156	34.3	735	11.7	581	9.3	1240	19.7	949	15.1	619	9.9
BURLESON	1572	43.0	2080	57.0*	920	28.5	543	16.8	72	2.2	199	6.2	544	16.8	952	29.5
BURNET	1129	47.0	1271	53.0*	922	44.5	262	12.6	151	7.3	123	5.9	175	8.4	439	21.2
CALDWELL	1497	45.8	1772	54.2*	1639	46.0	693	19.5	145	4.1	204	5.7	458	12.9	423	11.9
CALHOUN	1719	45.1	2095	54.9*	902	31.1	532	18.3	100	3.4	126	4.3	261	9.0	983	33.8
CALLAHAN	1495	56.1	1168	43.9*	567	22.1	340	13.3	449	17.5	466	18.2	589	23.0	153	6.0
CAMERON	7721	45.7	9191	54.3*	3894	32.6	1369	11.5	1381	11.6	931	7.8	871	7.3	3505	29.3
CAMP	733	31.4	1603	68.6*	449	22.3	370	18.4	153	7.6	179	8.9	234	11.6	625	31.1
CARSON	752	43.2	989	56.8*	288	17.7	208	12.8	313	19.3	123	7.6	199	12.2	494	30.4
CASS	1772	32.9	3607	67.1*	986	18.2	1166	21.5	580	10.7	795	14.6	712	13.1	1191	21.9
CASTRO	741	45.3	894	54.7*	134	8.6	120	7.7	789	50.7	57	3.7	176	11.3	281	18.0
CHAMBERS	1184	41.4	1675	58.6*	659	23.8	595	21.5	105	3.8	212	7.7	423	15.3	770	27.9
CHEROKEE	3205	40.4	4724	59.6*	1525	25.9	1009	17.1	378	6.4	395	6.7	1039	17.6	1544	26.2
CHILDRESS	832	34.9	1551	65.1*	540	25.4	321	15.1	655	30.8	131	6.2	210	9.9	271	12.7
CLAY	812	44.1	1031	55.9*	1016	39.8	302	11.8	232	9.1	103	4.0	422	16.5	478	18.7
COCHRAN	749	44.3	943	55.7*	176	14.0	149	11.8	564	44.8	75	6.0	148	11.8	147	11.7
COKE	629	43.2	827	56.8*	308	23.3	141	10.7	237	18.0	207	15.7	289	21.9	138	10.5
COLEMAN	1843	48.2	1984	51.8*	609	22.0	489	17.7	206	7.4	705	25.5	598	21.6	161	5.8
COLLIN	2993	39.5	4578	60.5*	1907	32.3	1000	16.9	662	11.2	402	6.8	790	13.4	1151	19.5
CLNGSWORTH	761	38.5	1218	61.5*	203	12.1	193	11.5	845	50.5	120	7.2	198	11.8	115	6.9
COLORADO	1637	38.6	2602	61.4*	880	24.9	594	16.8	120	3.4	434	12.3	577	16.3	931	26.3
COMAL	1425	44.2	1797	55.8*	2062	52.8	657	16.8	151	3.9	245	6.3	481	12.3	312	8.0

```
            DEMOC. GOVERNOR   1960*                    DEMOC. GOVERNOR   1962
                                  *
   COUNTY     COX          DANIEL        CONNALLY      DANIEL      FORMBY       WALKER       WILSON      D. YARBRO
              #     %       #     %*      #     %       #    %      #    %       #    %       #    %      #    %
--------------------------------------------------------------------------------------------------------------------
COMANCHEE    2257 55.3    1822 44.7*    1033 37.9     221  8.1    303 11.1     420 15.4     328 12.0    424 15.5
CONCHO        548 46.8     622 53.2*     211 25.1      80  9.5     88 10.5     136 16.2     201 24.0    123 14.7
COOKE        2034 35.1    3757 64.9*    1303 26.6     821 16.8    589 12.0     689 14.1     719 14.7    777 15.9
CORYELL      1528 38.9    2401 61.1*    1242 38.0     576 17.6    199  6.1     214  6.5     416 12.7    621 19.0
COTTLE        422 50.6     412 49.4*     508 42.1      91  7.5    408 33.8      63  5.2      73  6.0     65  5.4

CRANE         756 44.3     949 55.7*     271 19.3      85  6.1    219 15.6     251 17.9     239 17.0    337 24.0
CROCKETT      437 41.9     605 58.1*     243 22.4     138 12.7     71  6.6     121 11.2     359 33.1    151 13.9
CROSBY        937 34.4    1790 65.6*     213  9.5     194  8.6   1395 62.1      61  2.7     134  6.0    248 11.0
CULBERSON     151 39.1     235 60.9*     145 24.1      91 15.1     86 14.3      67 11.1     142 23.6     70 11.6
DALLAM        341 27.6     893 72.4*     213 16.3     190 14.5    351 26.9     110  8.4     181 13.8    262 20.0

DALLAS      29920 40.0   44937 60.0*   37781 36.0   16758 16.0   6303  6.0   13582 12.9   14041 13.4  16463 15.7
DAWSON       2032 52.3    1853 47.7*     540 21.0     273 10.6    945 36.8     130  5.1     274 10.7    408 15.9
DEAFSMITH    1453 52.3    1323 47.7*     142  5.7      74  3.0   1851 74.7      75  3.0     187  7.5    150  6.1
DELTA         698 36.8    1201 63.2*     596 34.6     299 17.4     98  5.7      92  5.3     389 22.6    247 14.4
DENTON       2944 40.7    4287 59.3*    1650 26.6    1104 17.8    672 10.8     427  6.9     751 12.1   1602 25.8

DEWITT       1543 43.7    1987 56.3*    1225 31.6     737 19.0    644 16.6     312  8.1     571 14.8    382  9.9
DICKENS       818 45.9     966 54.1*      89  5.2      84  4.9   1396 80.9      35  2.0      40  2.3     82  4.8
DIMMIT        360 27.9     929 72.1*     670 36.3     579 31.4    145  7.9     129  7.0     191 10.3    132  7.2
DONLEY        741 42.0    1025 58.0*     261 19.8     126  9.5    419 31.7     144 10.9     279 21.1     91  6.9
DUVAL        1487 38.9    2338 61.1*    2641 80.0     217  6.6     33  1.0      48  1.5     179  5.4    184  5.6

EASTLAND     4123 67.4    1995 32.6*    1522 27.4     681 12.3    837 15.1     944 17.0    1001 18.0    562 10.1
ECTOR        7081 56.3    5502 43.7*    1984 18.0     951  8.6   1142 10.4    2590 23.6    2220 20.2   2110 19.2
EDWARDS       209 32.3     439 67.7*     272 38.4      89 12.6     56  7.9     139 19.6     132 18.6     20  2.8
ELLIS        2969 36.1    5247 63.9*    1755 30.8     997 17.5    466  8.2     574 10.1     871 15.3   1039 18.2
ELPASO       4140 33.6    8164 66.4*    4090 22.4    4038 22.2    875  4.8     711  3.9    3554 19.5   4957 27.2

ERATH        1691 45.2    2048 54.8*    1432 32.7     778 17.8    551 12.6     487 11.1     484 11.0    649 14.8
FALLS        1957 42.9    2610 57.1*    1300 40.2     558 17.3    180  5.6     158  4.9     364 11.3    670 20.7
FANNIN       1809 33.5    3588 66.5*    2374 45.4     877 16.8    200  3.8     245  4.7     755 14.4    780 14.9
FAYETTE      1820 37.9    2980 62.1*    1540 31.7     880 18.1    168  3.5     338  7.0     849 17.5   1078 22.2
FISHER       1112 42.8    1488 57.2*     493 21.1     233 10.0    420 18.0     113  4.8     437 18.7    636 27.3

FLOYD         614 36.4    1074 63.6*     128  5.9     147  6.8   1523 70.0     119  5.5     144  6.6    114  5.2
FOARD         438 44.3     550 55.7*     316 48.3      81 12.4     96 14.7      44  6.7      66 10.1     51  7.8
FORTBEND     2801 38.6    4462 61.4*    1376 20.8    1557 23.5    231  3.5     904 13.7     695 10.5   1850 28.0
FRANKLIN      611 32.8    1251 67.2*     487 27.8     286 16.3    157  9.0      91  5.2     373 21.3    357 20.4
FREESTONE    1404 38.9    2208 61.1*     635 18.9     430 12.8    500 14.9     307  9.1     586 17.5    899 26.8

FRIO          680 37.1    1151 62.9*     969 48.6     441 22.1     80  4.0     139  7.0     194  9.7    171  8.6
GAINES       1299 43.8    1669 56.2*     265 14.1     186  9.9    687 36.4     134  7.1     316 16.8    298 15.8
GALVESTON    9884 38.5   15757 61.5*    4170 17.1    5160 21.2    905  3.7    1510  6.2    2129  8.7   10478 43.0
GARZA         777 44.1     984 55.9*     184 13.1     154 11.0    567 40.4     107  7.6      95  6.8    296 21.1
GILLESPIE     140 26.5     389 73.5*     424 49.4     113 13.2     24  2.8     128 14.9     138 16.1     32  3.7

GLASCOCK      225 52.4     204 47.6*      80 23.3      26  7.6     57 16.6      60 17.5      89 25.9     31  9.0
GOLIAD        514 38.2     832 61.8*     280 27.5     329 32.3     54  5.3     134 13.2     114 11.2    107 10.5
GONZALES      903 36.8    1552 63.2*    1867 52.7     724 20.5     99  2.8     214  6.0     439 12.4    197  5.6
GRAY         2997 49.8    3016 50.2*     776 20.0     499 12.9    875 22.6     449 11.6     693 17.9    583 15.0
GRAYSON      3932 34.0    7616 66.0*    3569 29.7    2133 17.7    755  6.3     684  5.7    1730 14.4   3156 26.2

GREGG        4806 45.5    5759 54.5*    2762 27.8    1214 12.2   1209 12.2    1916 19.3    1460 14.7   1381 13.9
```

COUNTY	COX #	%	DANIEL #	%*	CONNALLY #	%	DANIEL #	%	FORMBY #	%	WALKER #	%	WILSON #	%	D. YARBRO #	%
GRIMES	784	36.5	1363	63.5*	576	19.4	450	15.2	75	2.5	280	9.4	325	11.0	1262	42.5
GUADALUPE	1275	44.1	1618	55.9*	1903	49.4	547	14.2	87	2.3	175	4.5	910	23.6	233	6.0
HALE	2369	45.2	2875	54.8*	399	5.8	322	4.7	4955	72.6	302	4.4	444	6.5	404	5.9
HALL	862	49.2	890	50.8*	334	17.1	193	9.9	889	45.6	143	7.3	216	11.1	176	9.0
HAMILTON	1561	54.2	1317	45.8*	640	27.2	321	13.7	297	12.6	320	13.6	414	17.6	357	15.2
HANSFORD	441	35.6	797	64.4*	164	12.9	243	19.1	354	27.8	208	16.3	242	19.0	64	5.0
HARDEMAN	1036	41.6	1454	58.4*	478	29.0	296	18.0	398	24.1	117	7.1	211	12.8	149	9.0
HARDIN	2393	37.1	4051	62.9*	831	15.8	785	15.0	94	1.8	402	7.7	649	12.4	2486	47.4
HARRIS	52508	34.8	98329	65.2*	31985	20.6	33483	21.6	3138	2.0	19315	12.5	10862	7.0	56154	36.2
HARRISON	2857	30.2	6616	69.8*	1678	18.7	1600	17.8	406	4.5	2227	24.8	1866	20.7	1218	13.5
HARTLEY	249	31.8	534	68.2*	140	19.3	83	11.4	280	38.5	39	5.4	104	14.3	81	11.1
HASKELL	1725	48.0	1866	52.0*	715	24.6	385	13.3	573	19.8	188	6.5	619	21.3	421	14.5
HAYS	1669	41.6	2346	58.4*	1475	38.2	1032	26.7	256	6.6	182	4.7	425	11.0	490	12.7
HEMPHILL	358	35.0	666	65.0*	72	10.4	90	13.0	346	50.0	60	8.7	69	10.0	55	7.9
HENDERSON	2164	34.5	4103	65.5*	1589	27.8	1005	17.6	569	9.9	342	6.0	574	10.0	1640	28.7
HIDALGO	9410	41.2	13417	58.8*	5900	33.3	2406	13.6	1816	10.2	2083	11.7	921	5.2	4606	26.0
HILL	2292	35.7	4128	64.3*	1972	34.8	1531	27.0	452	8.0	359	6.3	624	11.0	728	12.8
HOCKLEY	1974	40.0	2962	60.0*	564	16.1	463	13.2	1568	44.6	152	4.3	270	7.7	496	14.1
HOOD	914	44.9	1123	55.1*	348	28.4	158	12.9	110	9.0	178	14.5	177	14.4	254	20.7
HOPKINS	1774	40.6	2595	59.4*	547	11.9	562	12.3	1885	41.1	178	3.9	981	21.4	428	9.3
HOUSTON	2262	45.7	2691	54.3*	976	20.7	669	14.2	195	4.1	349	7.4	830	17.6	1687	35.8
HOWARD	2241	32.9	4565	67.1*	1010	16.0	767	12.2	887	14.1	384	6.1	922	14.6	2330	37.0
HUDSPETH	218	29.9	511	70.1*	222	36.5	101	16.6	66	10.8	79	13.0	77	12.6	64	10.5
HUNT	2883	36.3	5061	63.7*	1749	28.2	1347	21.7	554	8.9	613	9.9	905	14.6	1030	16.6
HUTCHISON	3038	41.2	4336	58.8*	1068	19.0	697	12.4	1034	18.4	746	13.2	638	11.3	1450	25.7
IRION	231	49.3	238	50.7*	102	23.1	66	14.9	57	12.9	5	1.1	99	22.4	113	25.6
JACK	1419	58.0	1026	42.0*	606	28.8	188	8.9	547	26.0	195	9.3	284	13.5	287	13.6
JACKSON	1501	38.9	2356	61.1*	921	29.7	550	17.7	128	4.1	262	8.4	459	14.8	783	25.2
JASPER	1893	39.6	2884	60.4*	969	21.5	800	17.8	245	5.4	259	5.7	587	13.0	1646	36.5
JEFFDAVIS	103	49.5	105	50.5*	42	11.4	42	11.4	61	16.6	37	10.1	52	14.1	134	36.4
JEFFERSON	10710	35.4	19511	64.6*	11313	26.5	6058	14.2	2353	5.5	4009	9.4	3644	8.5	15360	35.9
JIMHOGG	503	37.6	833	62.4*	911	59.1	343	22.3	41	2.7	32	2.1	80	5.2	134	8.7
JIMWELLS	3457	50.8	3349	49.2*	2843	39.9	1738	24.4	384	5.4	333	4.7	811	11.4	1022	14.3
JOHNSON	2902	40.6	4238	59.4*	1647	32.3	670	13.1	475	9.3	945	18.5	532	10.4	833	16.3
JONES	2481	52.1	2284	47.9*	676	20.2	413	12.4	835	25.0	239	7.2	809	24.2	368	11.0
KARNES	1534	42.7	2057	57.3*	2702	60.7	885	19.9	86	1.9	155	3.5	433	9.7	192	4.3
KAUFMAN	2226	38.0	3629	62.0*	1389	30.8	999	22.1	417	9.2	567	12.6	534	11.8	608	13.5
KENDALL	103	36.3	181	63.7*	215	44.5	78	16.1	15	3.1	94	19.5	52	10.8	29	6.0
KENEDY	30	21.6	109	78.4*	51	46.4	36	32.7	2	1.8	0	.0	11	10.0	10	9.1
KENT	355	47.9	386	52.1*	70	9.4	82	11.0	390	52.3	20	2.7	90	12.1	93	12.5
KERR	1498	40.6	2191	59.4*	798	25.3	507	16.0	102	3.2	1292	40.9	309	9.8	151	4.8
KIMBLE	379	54.1	322	45.9*	390	32.6	167	14.0	93	7.8	269	22.5	189	15.8	87	7.3
KING	104	54.5	87	45.5*	41	18.6	24	10.9	113	51.1	13	5.9	12	5.4	18	8.1
KINNEY	80	27.9	207	72.1*	101	49.5	49	24.0	8	3.9	10	4.9	25	12.3	11	5.4
KLEBERG	1853	36.1	3287	63.9*	980	24.9	1167	29.6	246	6.2	241	6.1	364	9.2	941	23.9
KNOX	784	44.5	977	55.5*	651	33.1	308	15.7	524	26.6	73	3.7	230	11.7	182	9.2

DEMOC. GOVERNOR 1960*   DEMOC. GOVERNOR 1962

COUNTY	COX #	%	DANIEL #	%*	CONNALLY #	%	DANIEL #	%	FORMBY #	%	WALKER #	%	WILSON #	%	D. YARBRO #	%
LAMAR	3327	34.5	6307	65.5*	1459	24.1	1323	21.8	588	9.7	390	6.4	1392	23.0	911	15.0
LAMB	2031	43.8	2604	56.2*	414	11.8	275	7.8	1839	52.2	157	4.5	309	8.8	527	15.0
LAMPASAS	1099	49.2	1136	50.8*	1080	43.4	272	10.9	183	7.4	249	10.0	299	12.0	406	16.3
LASALLE	278	44.3	349	55.7*	639	76.7	97	11.6	8	1.0	17	2.0	47	5.6	25	3.0
LABACA	1788	39.3	2758	60.7*	1114	32.2	369	10.7	110	3.2	213	6.2	1050	30.3	606	17.5
LEE	1020	46.5	1173	53.5*	763	31.9	362	15.1	59	2.5	176	7.4	363	15.2	667	27.9
LEON	1137	37.4	1903	62.6*	707	23.0	668	21.7	170	5.5	215	7.0	328	10.7	987	32.1
LIBERTY	2969	42.5	4015	57.5*	1095	17.8	2067	33.6	119	1.9	421	6.8	817	13.3	1639	26.6
LIMESTONE	2034	39.2	3152	60.8*	1149	25.2	855	18.7	288	6.3	362	7.9	525	11.5	1384	30.3
LIPSCOMB	273	27.1	733	72.9*	147	14.3	251	24.5	244	23.8	118	11.5	162	15.8	104	10.1
LIVEOAK	874	49.6	888	50.4*	605	29.1	390	18.8	426	20.5	198	9.5	238	11.5	219	10.5
LLANO	918	52.7	825	47.3*	451	35.1	148	11.5	67	5.2	84	6.5	154	12.0	380	29.6
LOVING	48	55.2	39	44.8*	7	9.7	10	13.9	27	37.5	12	16.7	8	11.1	8	11.1
LUBBOCK	7297	36.9	12502	63.1*	2771	14.8	2015	10.8	7925	42.3	1968	10.5	1192	6.4	2848	15.2
LYNN	1248	42.5	1686	57.5*	314	16.9	239	12.9	838	45.1	132	7.1	135	7.3	200	10.8
MADISON	721	36.4	1258	63.6*	485	37.1	354	27.1	47	3.6	183	14.0	183	14.0	56	4.3
MARION	379	31.3	831	68.7*	272	19.3	369	26.2	63	4.5	288	20.5	222	15.8	192	13.7
MARTIN	453	47.7	496	52.3*	190	23.7	78	9.7	185	23.1	87	10.9	152	19.0	108	13.5
MASON	818	58.2	587	41.8*	325	24.7	144	10.9	79	6.0	195	14.8	376	28.5	198	15.0
MATAGORDA	2048	43.2	2695	56.8*	792	17.9	1204	27.2	202	4.6	647	14.6	617	14.0	958	21.7
MAVERICK	301	18.0	1368	82.0*	701	39.2	594	33.2	39	2.2	123	6.9	127	7.1	205	11.5
MCCULLOCH	1150	46.7	1310	53.3*	927	38.3	269	11.1	189	7.8	278	11.5	544	22.5	215	8.9
MCLENNAN	9316	32.5	19327	67.5*	8640	33.3	5642	21.7	1748	6.7	1350	5.2	2465	9.5	6128	23.6
MCMULLEN	151	42.3	206	57.7*	153	45.1	59	17.4	39	11.5	43	12.7	26	7.7	19	5.6
MEDINA	668	37.3	1122	62.7*	1703	57.0	577	19.3	41	1.4	185	6.2	291	9.7	190	6.4
MENARD	588	49.9	591	50.1*	161	25.2	66	10.3	46	7.2	155	24.2	154	24.1	58	9.1
MIDLAND	5680	50.9	5479	49.1*	2173	29.3	675	9.1	781	10.5	1529	20.7	1456	19.7	790	10.7
MILAN	2295	45.6	2737	54.4*	1284	29.0	674	15.2	210	4.7	255	5.8	437	9.9	1564	35.4
MILLS	1181	55.6	942	44.4*	436	29.2	170	11.4	184	12.3	302	20.2	222	14.9	180	12.0
MITCHELL	1275	39.2	1978	60.8*	377	16.4	235	10.2	702	30.6	151	6.6	281	12.2	550	24.0
MONTAGE	2025	42.7	2713	57.3*	1607	37.2	531	12.3	571	13.2	501	11.6	566	13.1	545	12.6
MONTGOMRY	3361	45.5	4027	54.5*	1321	21.8	1360	22.4	121	2.0	755	12.4	684	11.3	1828	30.1
MOORE	1085	41.3	1541	58.7*	270	13.8	238	12.2	686	35.1	159	8.1	257	13.2	342	17.5
MORRIS	1013	25.6	2938	74.4*	656	16.6	676	17.1	396	10.0	519	13.2	397	10.1	1302	33.0
MOTLEY	353	41.6	496	58.4*	51	7.2	43	6.1	498	70.7	42	6.0	23	3.3	47	6.7
NACDOCHES	3642	45.2	4412	54.8*	1605	24.3	1167	17.7	569	8.6	460	7.0	1069	16.2	1739	26.3
NAVARRO	3078	38.8	4858	61.2*	1765	29.2	1200	19.9	628	10.4	460	7.6	778	12.9	1204	20.0
NEWTON	1064	36.9	1819	63.1*	451	17.5	641	24.9	61	2.4	223	8.7	393	15.3	805	31.3
NOLAN	2262	46.4	2608	53.6*	994	21.8	531	11.7	803	17.6	490	10.8	720	15.8	1018	22.3
NUECES	12454	37.7	20574	62.3*	10699	34.0	7721	24.6	2010	6.4	1615	5.1	3290	10.5	6110	19.4
OCHILTREE	664	43.1	875	56.9*	214	12.0	245	13.7	722	40.4	274	15.3	225	12.6	107	6.0
OLDHAM	261	41.3	371	58.7*	150	20.9	98	13.6	238	33.1	54	7.5	103	14.3	75	10.4
ORANGE	4129	39.5	6319	60.5*	1991	18.5	1920	17.8	305	2.8	804	7.5	950	8.8	4819	44.7
PALOPINTO	2502	51.3	2378	48.7*	1072	31.8	542	16.1	458	13.6	380	11.3	460	13.6	464	13.7
PANOLA	3343	57.0	2518	43.0*	708	15.5	767	16.8	278	6.1	1600	35.1	508	11.1	698	15.3
PARKER	3227	46.1	3769	53.9*	1793	33.0	836	15.4	464	8.5	760	14.0	846	15.6	737	13.6

COUNTY	COX #	%	DANIEL #	%*	CONNALLY #	%	DANIEL #	%	FORMBY #	%	WALKER #	%	WILSON #	%	D. YARBRO #	%
PARMER	906	48.9	948	51.1*	102	6.3	117	7.2	892	55.1	119	7.4	114	7.0	274	16.9
PECOS	1329	43.4	1735	56.6*	680	25.9	545	20.7	350	13.3	223	8.5	483	18.4	349	13.3
POLK	1544	41.2	2204	58.8*	624	17.8	800	22.9	113	3.2	403	11.5	491	14.0	1070	30.6
POTTER	6844	41.6	9605	58.4*	2928	27.7	1425	13.5	2401	22.7	828	7.8	1023	9.7	1958	18.5
PRESIDIO	486	39.4	747	60.6*	270	23.4	244	21.1	136	11.8	113	9.8	235	20.3	157	13.6
RAINES	357	35.9	638	64.1*	189	22.3	249	29.4	74	8.7	58	6.9	161	19.0	115	13.6
RANDALL	3291	44.0	4182	56.0*	1113	21.3	571	10.9	1737	33.2	530	10.1	535	10.2	746	14.3
REAGAN	571	48.9	596	51.1*	293	28.3	90	8.7	168	16.2	107	10.3	210	20.3	166	16.1
REAL	259	39.8	392	60.2*	132	34.4	65	16.9	19	4.9	82	21.4	67	17.4	19	4.9
REDRIVER	2005	47.8	2191	52.2*	1146	27.1	1102	26.0	451	10.6	195	4.6	720	17.0	621	14.7
REEVES	1773	54.6	1472	45.4*	975	32.7	535	18.0	202	6.8	192	6.4	560	18.8	515	17.3
REFUGIO	1094	40.9	1583	59.1*	676	40.7	412	24.8	78	4.7	81	4.9	179	10.8	236	14.2
ROBERTS	141	39.4	217	60.6*	52	12.9	54	13.4	169	41.8	45	11.1	61	15.1	23	5.7
ROBERTSON	1290	35.4	2351	64.6*	893	25.2	525	14.8	156	4.4	192	5.4	282	8.0	1490	42.1
ROCKWALL	678	39.1	1054	60.9*	442	26.7	262	15.8	445	26.9	104	6.3	182	11.0	220	13.3
RUNNELLS	1711	60.1	1135	39.9*	480	20.1	271	11.3	368	15.4	373	15.6	740	30.9	159	6.6
RUSK	3774	41.7	5266	58.3*	1967	23.8	1329	16.1	905	10.9	846	10.2	1134	13.7	2096	25.3
SABINE	956	36.5	1665	63.5*	344	18.0	396	20.7	76	4.0	154	8.0	353	18.4	593	30.9
SNAUGSTNE	1197	44.0	1525	56.0*	389	17.5	447	20.2	65	2.9	250	11.3	373	16.8	694	31.3
SNJACINTO	633	43.0	838	57.0*	282	18.8	299	19.9	23	1.5	157	10.4	158	10.5	585	38.9
SNPATRICIO	3827	52.9	3414	47.1*	2281	33.5	1413	20.7	648	9.5	261	3.8	833	12.2	1382	20.3
SANSABA	645	48.2	693	51.8*	735	34.7	248	11.7	147	6.9	257	12.1	315	14.9	419	19.8
SCHLEICHER	263	41.2	375	58.8*	156	24.2	91	14.1	63	9.8	109	16.9	112	17.4	114	17.7
SCURRY	2249	42.4	3061	57.6*	616	13.9	439	9.9	1333	30.1	288	6.5	583	13.2	1173	26.5
SHACKELFRD	1114	73.0	413	27.0*	146	16.6	73	8.3	254	28.8	135	15.3	211	23.9	63	7.1
SHELBY	2236	31.7	4808	68.3*	1388	26.1	837	15.7	434	8.2	873	16.4	718	13.5	1065	20.0
SHERMAN	347	38.8	547	61.2*	106	14.3	141	19.0	201	27.1	156	21.0	101	13.6	37	5.0
SMITH	7038	41.7	9853	58.3*	3327	28.8	1947	16.9	1720	14.9	758	6.6	1582	13.7	2204	19.1
SOMERVELL	450	46.5	518	53.5*	219	26.7	157	19.2	76	9.3	107	13.1	116	14.2	144	17.6
STARR	219	6.0	3419	94.0*	3181	88.3	58	1.6	18	.5	43	1.2	161	4.5	143	4.0
STEPHENS	2658	81.3	613	18.7*	811	33.8	251	10.4	290	12.1	244	10.2	514	21.4	292	12.2
STERLING	232	54.7	192	45.3*	65	27.9	21	9.0	67	28.8	25	10.7	29	12.4	26	11.2
STONEWALL	672	48.3	720	51.7*	130	11.3	117	10.2	431	37.5	53	4.6	158	13.8	259	22.6
SUTTON	422	44.7	522	55.3*	175	22.5	229	29.5	82	10.6	126	16.2	106	13.6	59	7.6
SWISHER	841	36.6	1454	63.4*	157	7.5	287	13.7	826	39.4	56	2.7	191	9.1	579	27.6
TARRANT	36189	47.6	39814	52.4*	28957	41.0	9239	13.1	5985	8.5	8542	12.1	6050	8.6	11910	16.8
TAYLOR	8186	53.8	7039	46.2*	3045	22.9	1789	13.4	3100	23.3	1486	11.2	2588	19.5	1295	9.7
TERRELL	228	40.4	337	59.6*	86	12.9	73	10.9	39	5.8	105	15.7	185	27.7	180	26.9
TERRY	1851	56.2	1444	43.8*	469	20.9	218	9.7	746	33.3	125	5.6	211	9.4	472	21.1
THRCKMORTN	933	68.1	438	31.9*	413	44.5	75	8.1	126	13.6	53	5.7	129	13.9	133	14.3
TITUS	1862	34.0	3614	66.0*	790	16.1	910	18.6	521	10.6	412	8.4	656	13.4	1609	32.9
TOMGREEN	3992	46.5	4587	53.5*	2359	22.8	1191	11.5	1061	10.3	1398	13.5	2108	20.4	2229	21.5
TRAVIS	14881	36.4	25971	63.6*	13027	32.3	8615	21.4	2378	5.9	1747	4.3	4778	11.9	9742	24.2
TRINITY	1365	53.8	1171	46.2*	405	16.9	427	17.8	54	2.2	172	7.2	463	19.3	880	36.7
TYLER	1209	43.2	1588	56.8*	534	19.6	494	18.1	95	3.5	245	9.0	509	18.7	852	31.2
UPSHUR	2140	34.4	4078	65.6*	1233	23.3	796	15.0	473	8.9	617	11.6	660	12.5	1522	28.7

	DEMOC. GOVERNOR 1960*				DEMOC. GOVERNOR 1962									
COUNTY	COX		DANIEL		CONNALLY		DANIEL		FORMBY		WALKER		WILSON		D. YARBRO
	#	%	#	%*	#	%	#	%	#	%	#	%	#	%	#	%
UPTON	670	43.4	874	56.6*	342	22.8	155	10.3	212	14.1	210	14.0	340	22.7	241	16.1
UVALDE	1063	39.6	1624	60.4*	1169	38.4	646	21.2	154	5.1	333	10.9	519	17.0	226	7.4
VALVERDE	870	29.0	2131	71.0*	1178	49.7	563	23.7	74	3.1	131	5.5	186	7.8	239	10.1
VANZANDT	1159	36.5	2013	63.5*	1476	29.1	986	19.4	400	7.9	378	7.4	738	14.5	1100	21.7
VICTORIA	3777	38.7	5992	61.3*	1979	33.0	1677	28.0	170	2.8	438	7.3	624	10.4	1108	18.5
WALKER	1577	42.3	2150	57.7*	661	22.3	680	22.9	69	2.3	406	13.7	336	11.3	818	27.5
WALLER	883	31.3	1935	68.7*	421	16.8	643	25.6	102	4.1	347	13.8	259	10.3	735	29.3
WARD	2010	54.3	1689	45.7*	847	27.9	345	11.3	240	7.9	471	15.5	542	17.8	596	19.6
WASHINGTON	1730	37.4	2899	62.6*	804	30.3	554	20.9	60	2.3	215	8.1	333	12.5	688	25.9
WEBB	3612	37.6	5983	62.4*	4623	73.8	816	13.0	35	.6	45	.7	247	3.9	496	7.9
WHARTON	2077	34.3	3976	65.7*	1447	26.7	929	17.1	153	2.8	395	7.3	691	12.7	1813	33.4
WHEELER	589	31.9	1258	68.1*	197	11.4	253	14.6	708	40.8	183	10.5	217	12.5	177	10.2
WICHITA	9898	47.0	11151	53.0*	5883	39.2	2347	15.6	1267	8.4	532	3.5	2118	14.1	2873	19.1
WILBARGER	1173	43.0	1553	57.0*	733	22.7	542	16.8	879	27.2	430	13.3	390	12.1	252	7.8
WILLACY	1239	39.6	1891	60.4*	998	35.2	528	18.6	302	10.6	344	12.1	208	7.3	458	16.1
WILLIAMSON	2463	44.1	3122	55.9*	2584	40.4	1231	19.3	233	3.6	326	5.1	681	10.7	1334	20.9
WILSON	1346	36.2	2376	63.8*	3631	82.0	350	7.9	31	.7	103	2.3	169	3.8	144	3.3
WINKLER	1479	51.5	1395	48.5*	458	18.0	180	7.1	631	24.9	408	16.1	345	13.6	516	20.3
WISE	1928	45.5	2314	54.5*	1289	34.5	514	13.7	467	12.5	447	11.9	491	13.1	533	14.2
WOOD	1548	35.3	2834	64.7*	964	23.7	720	17.7	569	14.0	231	5.7	646	15.9	936	23.0
YOAKUM	1059	43.8	1359	56.2*	330	15.9	208	10.0	618	29.8	185	8.9	247	11.9	487	23.5
YOUNG	1492	44.6	1852	55.4*	1073	37.6	305	10.7	356	12.5	290	10.2	345	12.1	488	17.1
ZAPATA	177	33.8	346	66.2*	762	78.9	142	14.7	5	.5	22	2.3	8	.8	27	2.8
ZAVALA	496	38.8	781	61.2*	724	45.7	306	19.3	70	4.4	78	4.9	260	16.4	145	9.2
TOTALS	619834		908992	*	431498		248524		139094		138387		171617		317986	
% OF VOTE		40.5		59.5	*	29.8		17.2		9.6		9.6		11.9		22.0

GEOGRAPHIC CLASS

				*												
LOWLANDS	223384	38.	368623	62.*	130109	23.	110081	20.	30048	5.	55511	10.	62777	11.	168244	30.
BLACK BELT	6042	32.	12571	68.*	3546	20.	3436	19.	750	4.	3211	18.	2787	16.	4220	24.
WEST TEXAS	337901	43.	450309	57.*	249652	33.	113204	15.	100472	13.	71898	10.	93019	12.	123590	16.
MEX. TEXAS	52507	40.	77489	60.*	48191	40.	21803	18.	7824	6.	7767	6.	13034	11.	21932	18.

DEMOGRAPHIC CLASS

				*												
METRO	279639	39.	437327	61.*	229495	31.	130021	18.	48766	7.	70520	10.	75364	1.	176393	24.
TOWN	58755	39.	90543	61.*	35284	29.	21301	17.	12552	10.	12204	10.	15681	13.	26252	21.
RURAL	281440	42.	381122	58.*	166719	28.	97202	16.	77776	13.	55663	9.	80572	14.	115341	19.

```
          DEMOC.  RUNOFF    1962*        DEMOC.  GOVERNOR    1964

  COUNTY      CONNALLY     D. YARBRO     CONNALLY     D. YARBRO     OTHER
             #       %     #       %*    #       %     #       %     #       %
-----------------------------------------------------------------------------------------------------------

ANDERSON    2063  44.1   2611  55.9*   6544  75.5   1933  22.3     188   2.2
ANDREWS     1048  38.6   1667  61.4*   2226  64.6   1101  31.9     120   3.5
ANGELINA    3463  36.1   6142  63.9*   7301  50.5   7049  48.7     117    .8
ARANSAS      391  44.9    479  55.1*   1248  57.8    890  41.2      20    .9
ARCHER       649  56.2    505  43.8*   1343  69.7    552  28.6      33   1.7

ARMSTRONG    234  58.9    163  41.1*    638  79.3    143  17.8      24   3.0
ATASCOSA    2815  72.2   1085  27.8*   2447  78.5    620  19.9      52   1.7
AUSTIN       917  48.2    985  51.8*   1710  70.0    678  27.7      56   2.3
BAILEY       321  37.4    537  62.6*    885  65.3    419  30.9      52   3.8
BANDERA      508  59.1    352  40.9*   1157  73.4    359  22.8      61   3.9

BASTROP     1264  48.8   1326  51.2*   2504  63.0   1423  35.8      47   1.2
BAYLOR       778  60.9    500  39.1*    961  77.4    263  21.2      17   1.4
BEE         1129  45.8   1336  54.2*   2510  65.2   1275  33.1      67   1.7
BELL        4337  53.4   3779  46.6*   9402  69.6   4000  29.6     104    .8
BEXAR      41915  64.3  23296  35.7*  49793  60.0  31056  37.4    2208   2.7

BLANCO       263  54.0    224  46.0*    445  74.0    149  24.8       7   1.2
BORDEN        62  26.6    171  73.4*    260  67.0    115  29.6      13   3.4
BOSQUE      1153  54.8    951  45.2*   2279  78.5    554  19.1      69   2.4
BOWIE       3197  47.0   3598  53.0*   9146  69.7   3529  26.9     447   3.4
BRAZORIA    4559  41.0   6574  59.0*  11027  65.5   5606  33.3     202   1.2

BRAZOS      2891  46.5   3323  53.5*   6400  72.1   2365  26.6     114   1.3
BREWSTER     527  47.1    592  52.9*   1338  74.8    420  23.5      31   1.7
BRISCOE      283  49.8    285  50.2*    918  75.2    283  23.2      19   1.6
BROOKS       424  46.2    493  53.8*   1687  71.1    642  27.0      45   1.9
BROWN       2816  54.7   2333  45.3*   4017  75.6   1201  22.6      95   1.8

BURLESON    1179  41.2   1680  58.8*   1918  64.7    984  33.2      62   2.1
BURNET      1024  54.2    864  45.8*   1921  67.5    902  31.7      21    .7
CALDWELL    1456  61.9    897  38.1*   2565  75.9    772  22.9      41   1.2
CALHOUN     1182  47.2   1323  52.8*   2194  62.5   1286  36.6      33    .9
CALLAHAN    1339  57.3    996  42.7*   1711  69.4    712  28.9      42   1.7

CAMERON     4156  50.2   4116  49.8*   8881  57.1   6090  39.1     586   3.8
CAMP         623  45.2    754  54.8*   1443  67.9    619  29.1      63   3.0
CARSON       409  37.9    669  62.1*   1202  69.5    490  28.3      38   2.2
CASS        1978  50.3   1957  49.7*   3228  73.6   1052  24.0     107   2.4
CASTRO       501  37.6    830  62.4*    897  64.1    482  34.4      21   1.5

CHAMBERS     880  47.2    984  52.8*   1863  59.0   1231  39.0      62   2.0
CHEROKEE    1977  43.7   2542  56.3*   5532  65.5   2777  32.9     134   1.6
CHILDRESS    599  53.0    532  47.0*   1622  61.6    976  37.1      34   1.3
CLAY         659  54.6    548  45.4*   1864  70.9    722  27.5      44   1.7
COCHRAN      558  47.8    610  52.2*   1089  71.9    378  25.0      47   3.1

COKE         305  49.6    310  50.4*    551  77.9    132  18.7      24   3.4
COLEMAN     1105  52.8    986  47.2*   2383  68.8    995  28.7      86   2.5
COLLIN      2232  54.1   1891  45.9*   6645  82.5   1311  16.3      98   1.2
CLNGSWORTH   286  46.6    328  53.4*   1291  76.2    373  22.0      31   1.8
COLORADO    1467  45.7   1746  54.3*   3480  71.4   1322  27.1      74   1.5

COMAL       2181  65.1   1168  34.9*   2475  74.2    841  25.2      21    .6
```

```
            DEMOC.  RUNOFF    1962*        DEMOC.  GOVERNOR   1964
                                  *
 COUNTY    CONNALLY    D. YARBRO    CONNALLY    D. YARBRO   OTHER
            #     %     #     %*     #     %     #     %     #     %
-------------------------------------------------------------------------------------------------------------------------------------------
```

COUNTY	CONNALLY #	%	D. YARBRO #	%*	CONNALLY #	%	D. YARBRO #	%	OTHER #	%
COMANCHEE	911	53.0	807	47.0*	2494	77.2	679	21.0	57	1.8
CONCHO	255	46.9	289	53.1*	951	81.3	193	16.5	26	2.2
COOKE	1681	57.2	1257	42.8*	4980	82.0	997	16.4	95	1.6
CORYELL	1274	54.8	1049	45.2*	2151	73.8	733	25.2	30	1.0
COTTLE	405	66.2	207	33.8*	1071	79.8	251	18.7	20	1.5
CRANE	489	39.7	744	60.3*	937	68.5	390	28.5	40	2.9
CROCKETT	504	51.2	481	48.8*	831	80.1	178	17.1	29	2.8
CROSBY	562	38.1	914	61.9*	1693	72.0	631	26.8	28	1.2
CULBERSON	183	58.7	129	41.3*	539	71.8	193	25.7	19	2.5
DALLAM	423	47.2	473	52.8*	811	71.3	298	26.2	29	2.5
DALLAS	45633	62.5	27335	37.5*	99086	80.2	21551	17.4	2908	2.4
DAWSON	1121	52.5	1015	47.5*	2929	75.2	897	23.0	70	1.8
DEAFSMITH	660	57.6	486	42.4*	1909	73.0	557	21.3	150	5.7
DELTA	934	58.6	660	41.4*	1373	81.4	277	16.4	37	2.2
DENTON	2439	51.4	2307	48.6*	6534	76.8	1912	22.5	60	.7
DEWITT	1854	57.5	1369	42.5*	3857	80.0	901	18.7	65	1.3
DICKENS	399	43.5	518	56.5*	1057	67.6	474	30.3	32	2.0
DIMMIT	907	63.5	521	36.5*	1268	82.4	255	16.6	16	1.0
DONLEY	511	52.8	456	47.2*	1319	71.5	483	26.2	43	2.3
DUVAL	3081	93.3	223	6.7*	3985	94.2	232	5.5	12	.3
EASTLAND	2721	52.7	2443	47.3*	3935	68.4	1686	29.3	128	2.2
ECTOR	2821	44.2	3555	55.8*	6517	68.5	2784	29.3	208	2.2
EDWARDS	483	72.9	180	27.1*	626	88.2	69	9.7	15	2.1
ELLIS	2726	56.4	2110	43.6*	4986	81.2	1109	18.1	49	.8
ELPASO	7713	45.0	9435	55.0*	18584	67.9	7872	28.7	928	3.4
ERATH	1600	52.3	1460	47.7*	3546	81.0	740	16.9	94	2.1
FALLS	1228	50.3	1215	49.7*	3111	73.5	1060	25.1	59	1.4
FANNIN	2962	63.1	1734	36.9*	5162	78.3	1352	20.5	80	1.2
FAYETTE	2323	50.8	2248	49.2*	2878	68.5	1234	29.4	88	2.1
FISHER	533	37.4	894	62.6*	1714	70.9	683	28.3	20	.8
FLOYD	866	54.3	728	45.7*	1812	74.4	574	23.6	49	2.0
FOARD	237	63.7	135	36.3*	379	74.6	120	23.6	9	1.8
FORTBEND	2047	46.3	2375	53.7*	5670	69.8	2322	28.6	128	1.6
FRANKLIN	579	49.9	582	50.1*	1411	76.7	384	20.9	45	2.4
FREESTONE	1109	44.7	1373	55.3*	2807	74.4	890	23.6	78	2.1
FRIO	642	70.9	264	29.1*	1677	77.4	455	21.0	34	1.6
GAINES	538	44.5	670	55.5*	1750	70.3	648	26.0	91	3.7
GALVESTON	8758	41.8	12202	58.2*	13872	57.4	9422	39.0	892	3.7
GARZA	514	37.2	869	62.8*	1163	66.2	547	31.2	46	2.6
GILLESPIE	572	80.7	137	19.3*	671	87.3	96	12.5	2	.3
GLASCOCK	105	54.7	87	45.3*	179	77.5	40	17.3	12	5.2
GOLIAD	500	57.0	377	43.0*	673	64.3	356	34.0	17	1.6
GONZALES	1810	71.7	715	28.3*	2543	83.2	469	15.4	43	1.4
GRAY	1454	48.2	1561	51.8*	2151	67.1	992	30.9	64	2.0
GRAYSON	3639	46.6	4175	53.4*	8603	75.5	2644	23.2	150	1.3
GREGG	3483	55.7	2775	44.3*,	8630	69.2	3167	25.4	667	5.4

```
              DEMOC.  RUNOFF    1962*        DEMOC.  GOVERNOR   1964
                                    *
  COUNTY      CONNALLY    D. YARBRO     CONNALLY     D. YARBRO     OTHER
               #    %     #     %*     #     %     #     %      #     %
--------------------------------------------------------------------------------

GRIMES         749 36.7  1294 63.3*  2236 67.9  1021 31.0     38  1.2
GUADALUPE     2434 69.7  1060 30.3*  2142 73.6   737 25.3     30  1.0
HALE          2152 47.1  2421 52.9*  4360 70.3  1644 26.5    198  3.2
HALL           587 54.3   494 45.7*  1659 74.7   524 23.6     39  1.8
HAMILTON       325 29.1   791 70.9*  2355 79.0   574 19.3     51  1.7
                                *
HANSFORD       244 61.6   152 38.4*   384 79.0    94 19.3      9  1.8
HARDEMAN       534 63.6   305 36.4*  1948 78.0   503 20.1     46  1.8
HARDIN         827 26.8  2264 73.2*  3079 42.0  4132 56.4    114  1.6
HARRIS       54252 45.0 66218 55.0*104101 62.1 61698 36.8   1924  1.1
HARRISON      2862 51.8  2661 48.2*  5791 78.4  1321 17.9    275  3.7

HARTLEY        288 62.6   172 37.4*   413 80.2    96 18.6      6  1.2
HASKELL       1148 49.7  1161 50.3*  2270 66.4  1115 32.6     35  1.0
HAYS          1734 56.8  1317 43.2*  3210 71.1  1264 28.0     43  1.0
HEMPHILL       103 50.5   101 49.5*   845 77.5   228 20.9     17  1.6
HENDERSON     1575 42.1  2164 57.9*  4742 70.4  1876 27.9    118  1.8
                                *
HIDALGO       7245 49.6  7375 50.4* 12564 56.7  8588 38.8   1009  4.6
HILL          2296 53.4  2004 46.6*  5057 81.4  1099 17.7     54   .9
HOCKLEY       1384 50.3  1367 49.7*  3190 74.8  1005 23.6     68  1.6
HOOD           402 46.4   464 53.6*  1252 78.6   314 19.7     27  1.7
HOPKINS       1544 50.7  1501 49.3*  4096 78.3  1037 19.8     96  1.8

HOUSTON       1601 36.3  2809 63.7*  2783 52.6  2443 46.2     64  1.2
HOWARD        1433 33.1  2894 66.9*  4665 62.8  2600 35.0    166  2.2
HUDSPETH       250 55.7   199 44.3*   446 64.9   214 31.1     27  3.9
HUNT          2379 57.0  1798 43.0*  7257 82.3  1392 15.8    165  1.9
HUTCHISON     1723 43.0  2283 57.0*  3403 59.3  2216 38.6    122  2.1
                                *
IRION          135 43.8   173 56.2*   412 82.9    63 12.7     22  4.4
JACK           678 53.8   582 46.2*  1526 72.4   538 25.5     44  2.1
JACKSON        642 42.5   870 57.5*  2498 72.5   880 25.5     67  1.9
JASPER        1071 31.3  2348 68.7*  2911 52.1  2599 46.5     81  1.4
JEFFDAVIS      123 28.0   316 72.0*   149 64.5    79 34.2      3  1.3
                                *
JEFFERSON    14472 40.4 21328 59.6* 29232 51.3 24381 42.8   3360  5.9
JIMHOGG       1275 71.4   510 28.6*  1037 63.0   591 35.9     17  1.0
JIMWELLS      3404 47.4  3778 52.6*  5853 68.2  2606 30.4    119  1.4
JOHNSON       1831 51.9  1697 48.1*  6275 80.4  1402 18.0    125  1.6
JONES         1326 48.0  1438 52.0*  3306 75.5  1026 23.4     47  1.1

KARNES        2028 77.5   589 22.5*  2944 80.2   670 18.3     56  1.5
KAUFMAN       1449 58.9  1010 41.1*  5074 83.3   948 15.6     67  1.1
KENDALL        256 69.8   111 30.2*   317 86.6    45 12.3      4  1.1
KENEDY          67 77.0    20 23.0*   100 92.6     8  7.4      0   .0
KENT           249 32.8   509 67.2*   480 65.3   242 32.9     13  1.8

KERR           942 59.6   639 40.4*  1895 79.9   415 17.5     62  2.6
KIMBLE         317 63.0   186 37.0*  1009 84.2   170 14.2     20  1.7
KING            77 65.3    41 34.7*   183 80.3    41 18.0      4  1.8
KINNEY          80 72.7    30 27.3*   369 76.4   100 20.7     14  2.9
KLEBERG       1666 48.7  1753 51.3*  3258 62.6  1896 36.4     53  1.0

KNOX          1034 59.8   696 40.2*  1141 78.1   300 20.5     20  1.4
```

```
              DEMOC.  RUNOFF     1962*        DEMOC.  GOVERNOR    1964
                                    *
COUNTY        CONNALLY      D. YARBRO    CONNALLY      D. YARBRO    OTHER
                #     %       #     %*     #      %      #     %      #    %
----------------------------------------*---------------------------------------------------------
LAMAR         3127  55.1   2544  44.9*   6247  77.6   1564  19.4    241   3.0
LAMB          1330  49.3   1370  50.7*   2709  70.7   1056  27.6     64   1.7
LAMPASAS       745  61.1    475  38.9*   1495  69.7    608  28.3     43   2.0
LASALLE        364  81.8     81  18.2*    896  84.1    158  14.8     11   1.0
LABACA        1651  63.2    963  36.8*   3949  82.5    773  16.2     62   1.3

LEE            851  40.9   1231  59.1*   1192  57.5    857  41.4     23   1.1
LEON          1353  42.1   1859  57.9*   1851  66.0    916  32.7     37   1.3
LIBERTY       1367  32.6   2823  67.4*   4174  61.7   2467  36.5    121   1.8
LIMESTONE     1540  41.6   2162  58.4*   3311  69.7   1377  29.0     65   1.4
LIPSCOMB       437  60.0    291  40.0*    737  77.2    189  19.8     29   3.0
                                    *
LIVEOAK       1107  51.3   1052  48.7*   1662  74.4    542  24.3     29   1.3
LLANO          484  46.4    560  53.6*   1204  63.2    662  34.8     39   2.0
LOVING           9  37.5     15  62.5*     39  53.4     28  38.4      6   8.2
LUBBOCK       6831  49.6   6944  50.4*  15447  74.4   5031  24.2    287   1.4
LYNN          1061  65.8    551  34.2*   2021  80.8    433  17.3     48   1.9

MADISON        807  43.2   1059  56.8*   1370  71.5    487  25.4     58   3.0
MARION         402  63.7    229  36.3*   1223  76.8    284  17.8     86   5.4
MARTIN         253  53.6    219  46.4*    619  78.4    158  20.1     11   1.4
MASON          305  48.6    322  51.4*    813  70.8    310  27.0     26   2.3
MATAGORDA     1236  53.1   1092  46.9*   3559  70.4   1429  28.3     69   1.4
                                    *
MAVERICK       669  67.6    321  32.4*   1958  78.4    506  20.2     35   1.4
MCCULLOCH      771  55.9    609  44.1*   1657  72.6    579  25.4     45   2.0
MCLENNAN     10236  49.0  10653  51.0*  19501  69.7   8219  29.4    241    .9
MCMULLEN       124  60.8     80  39.2*    223  71.9     79  25.5      8   2.6
MEDINA        1626  70.1    694  29.9*   1853  79.3    462  19.8     22    .9
                                    *
MENARD         230  53.7    198  46.3*    320  75.8     91  21.6     11   2.6
MIDLAND       3598  63.8   2043  36.2*   6562  74.0   2170  24.5    137   1.5
MILAN         1395  40.5   2046  59.5*   2870  60.2   1861  39.0     40    .8
MILLS          399  52.6    360  47.4*   1368  71.7    499  26.2     41   2.1
MITCHELL       889  46.1   1039  53.9*   1475  74.6    483  24.4     18    .9
                                    *
MONTAGE       1035  54.3    872  45.7*   2919  69.7   1143  27.3    127   3.0
MONTGOMRY     1690  40.8   2451  59.2*   5122  67.1   2278  29.9    231   3.0
MOORE          624  46.5    717  53.5*   2042  64.3   1059  33.3     76   2.4
MORRIS        1788  48.0   1935  52.0*   2547  73.9    771  22.4    129   3.7
MOTLEY         239  54.7    198  45.3*    735  74.6    232  23.6     18   1.8

NACDOCHES     1971  43.5   2563  56.5*   5300  63.2   2977  35.5    110   1.3
NAVARRO       2493  52.4   2265  47.6*   4620  75.5   1443  23.6     60   1.0
NEWTON         723  33.1   1459  66.9*   1403  50.1   1346  48.0     54   1.9
NOLAN         1607  41.7   2246  58.3*   3705  77.1   1049  21.8     52   1.1
NUECES       13702  49.9  13768  50.1*  21894  61.7  13329  37.5    278    .8
                                    *
OCHILTREE      942  64.7    513  35.3*    725  77.6    181  19.4     28   3.0
OLDHAM         170  55.0    139  45.0*    352  74.9    107  22.8     11   2.3
ORANGE        2802  31.2   6189  68.8*   6405  53.8   5245  44.0    264   2.2
PALOPINTO     1341  57.9    976  42.1*   3670  80.8    790  17.4     83   1.8
PANOLA        1661  53.4   1452  46.6*   3153  72.9    903  20.9    268   6.2
                                    *
PARKER        2584  57.1   1942  42.9*   4654  78.1   1201  20.2    105   1.8
```

```
               DEMOC.  RUNOFF      1962*        DEMOC.  GOVERNOR    1964
                                        *
   COUNTY     CONNALLY      D. YARBRO     CONNALLY      D. YARBRO     OTHER
               #      %     #      %*     #      %      #      %      #      %
--------------------------------------------*----------------------------------------------------------------
PARMER         450  45.7   535  54.3*   1001  66.8    451  30.1     47  3.1
PECOS          662  55.8   524  44.2*   1725  72.8    564  23.8     81  3.4
POLK           695  36.9  1189  63.1*   2472  59.3   1605  38.5     92  2.2
POTTER        4837  56.4  3737  43.6*   8145  66.1   3998  32.4    186  1.5
PRESIDIO       212  55.6   169  44.4*   1017  71.6    368  25.9     35  2.5
                                        *
RAINES         450  53.5   391  46.5*    870  80.8    184  17.1     23  2.1
RANDALL       2531  62.1  1546  37.9*   4069  74.9   1281  23.6     81  1.5
REAGAN         419  53.5   364  46.5*    766  73.6    242  23.2     33  3.2
REAL           130  71.8    51  28.2*    391  87.3     50  11.2      7  1.6
REDRIVER      1823  51.4  1722  48.6*   3537  77.1    937  20.4    112  2.4
                                        *
REEVES        1041  64.6   571  35.4*   2218  76.5    600  20.7     81  2.8
REFUGIO        584  52.7   525  47.3*   1450  72.6    520  26.0     28  1.4
ROBERTS         93  57.8    68  42.2*    161  78.5     39  19.0      5  2.4
ROBERTSON      887  32.3  1858  67.7*   1746  58.4   1215  40.6     29  1.0
ROCKWALL       397  58.7   279  41.3*   1359  85.4    212  13.3     20  1.3
                                        *
RUNNELLS       937  52.8   837  47.2*   2439  75.2    712  21.9     93  2.9
RUSK          3270  43.6  4232  56.4*   6203  70.3   2052  23.3    566  6.4
SABINE         400  26.6  1101  73.4*   1207  49.3   1153  47.1     89  3.6
SNAUGSTNE      768  33.9  1496  66.1*   1188  51.9   1038  45.3     65  2.8
SNJACINTO      581  33.3  1164  66.7*   1134  52.0    975  44.7     70  3.2
                                        *
SNPATRICIO    2686  44.3  3384  55.7*   4725  60.8   2951  38.0     96  1.2
SANSABA        901  47.1  1012  52.9*   1531  67.3    718  31.5     27  1.2
SCHLEICHER     188  44.9   231  55.1*    509  78.9    124  19.2     12  1.9
SCURRY        1305  34.3  2498  65.7*   3250  67.8   1440  30.0    107  2.2
SHACKELFRD     317  55.4   255  44.6*   1031  69.2    432  29.0     26  1.7
                                        *
SHELBY        2231  46.5  2563  53.5*   4440  65.9   1959  29.1    341  5.1
SHERMAN        190  62.1   116  37.9*    447  70.1    163  25.5     28  4.4
SMITH         4866  51.8  4526  48.2*  11153  70.8   4201  26.7    395  2.5
SOMERVELL      179  47.5   198  52.5*    769  78.1    197  20.0     19  1.9
STARR         1716  92.0   149   8.0*   3581  85.9    537  12.9     49  1.2
                                        *
STEPHENS      1055  52.6   952  47.4*   2187  76.7    617  21.6     47  1.6
STERLING        77  56.2    60  43.8*    140  80.5     34  19.5      0   .0
STONEWALL      149  25.9   426  74.1*    847  62.0    499  36.5     21  1.5
SUTTON         464  69.2   207  30.8*    454  87.3     54  10.4     12  2.3
SWISHER        349  28.7   868  71.3*   1553  63.4    863  35.2     33  1.3
                                        *
TARRANT      31296  60.7 20221  39.3*  62265  80.1  14697  18.9    769  1.0
TAYLOR        4943  57.6  3640  42.4*  12086  78.5   3151  20.5    159  1.0
TERRELL         83  32.0   176  68.0*    269  70.6    104  27.3      8  2.1
TERRY          989  53.4   862  46.6*   3031  77.6    827  21.2     50  1.3
THRCKMORTN     389  58.8   273  41.2*    911  71.2    353  27.6     16  1.2
                                        *
TITUS         1330  42.6  1795  57.4*   2731  75.9    787  21.9     82  2.3
TOMGREEN      3234  45.4  3896  54.6*   8905  82.7   1712  15.9    156  1.4
TRAVIS       17406  49.5 17729  50.5*  29899  66.7  14633  32.6    296   .7
TRINITY        487  27.0  1316  73.0*   1278  48.3   1311  49.6     56  2.1
TYLER          977  40.3  1447  59.7*   1589  55.4   1203  41.9     78  2.7
                                        *
UPSHUR        2299  44.2  2901  55.8*   3836  65.3   1766  30.1    271  4.6
```

```
          DEMOC.  RUNOFF     1962*       DEMOC.  GOVERNOR    1964
                                *
COUNTY      CONNALLY      D. YARBRO    CONNALLY      D. YARBRO    OTHER
            #     %       #     %*     #     %       #     %      #     %
---------------------------------------*----------------------------------------------------------------
UPTON        690  45.6    822  54.4*    793  68.0    334  28.6     39  3.3
UVALDE      1462  64.9    791  35.1*   3019  81.4    600  16.2     89  2.4
VALVERDE    1458  63.4    842  36.6*   2616  74.2    877  24.9     34  1.0
VANZANDT    1656  46.1   1940  53.9*   3861  77.9    994  20.1     99  2.0
VICTORIA    1716  50.0   1714  50.0*   5454  71.8   2043  26.9     97  1.3
                                *
WALKER       977  41.9   1353  58.1*   2698  69.9   1095  28.4     67  1.7
WALLER       974  40.9   1408  59.1*   1448  66.9    642  29.7     73  3.4
WARD        1164  49.5   1187  50.5*   1884  68.9    786  28.7     66  2.4
WASHINGTON   957  45.0   1169  55.0*   1288  76.0    382  22.5     25  1.5
WEBB        4624  70.2   1966  29.8*   5813  77.1   1646  21.8     78  1.0
                                *
WHARTON     2079  46.8   2365  53.2*   5263  71.5   2006  27.2     94  1.3
WHEELER      467  50.8    452  49.2*   1093  73.9    339  22.9     47  3.2
WICHITA     6442  55.0   5277  45.0*  12007  67.2   5693  31.8    175  1.0
WILBARGER   1114  62.6    665  37.4*   3047  72.2   1099  26.0     75  1.8
WILLACY     1203  57.7    881  42.3*   2110  73.2    723  25.1     48  1.7
                                *
WILLIAMSON  2516  50.0   2512  50.0*   4786  69.3   2041  29.6     79  1.1
WILSON      3237  83.8    627  16.2*   3029  75.8    938  23.5     27   .7
WINKLER      833  41.0   1200  59.0*   2093  63.4   1091  33.1    116  3.5
WISE        1895  53.9   1621  46.1*   3057  79.7    701  18.3     77  2.0
WOOD        1662  46.4   1923  53.6*   3430  74.5   1066  23.1    110  2.4
                                *
YOAKUM       664  41.1    953  58.9*   1464  68.7    614  28.8     52  2.4
YOUNG        892  57.5    660  42.5*   2710  73.0    929  25.0     73  2.0
ZAPATA       488  88.7     62  11.3*   1103  90.3    108   8.8     11   .9
ZAVALA       672  60.8    434  39.2*   1769  59.0   1199  40.0     29  1.0
---------------------------------------*----------------------------------------------------------------
                                *
TOTALS    565169       538924      *1125884       471411       33002
% OF VOTE    51.2         48.8     *   69.1         28.9          2.0
                                *
                                *
GEOGRAPHIC CLASS                *
                                *
LOWLANDS  194863  45.  241477  55.* 410714  65.  211268  33.   14385  2.
BLACK BELT  5706  44.    7320  56.*  11342  70.    4437  27.     533  3.
WEST TEXAS 309038  56.  246587  44.* 602213  73.  212173  26.   14374  2.
MEX. TEXAS  55562  56.   43540  44.* 101615  68.   43533  29.    3710  3.
                                *
                                *
DEMOGRAPHIC CLASS               *
                                *
METRO     298222  52.  271734  48.* 559294  68.  252108  30.   16882  2.
TOWN       46443  50.   46733  50.*  97644  69.   40638  29.    3382  2.
RURAL     220504  50.  220457  50.* 468946  71.  178665  27.   12738  2.
```

COUNTY	CONNALLY #	%	WOODS #	%	HACKWORTHE #	%*	SMITH #	%	HILL #	%	CARR #	%	LOCKE #	%	BRISCOE #	%	D. YARBRO #	%
ANDERSON	3663	75.6	1073	22.1	112	2.3*	1541	23.7	766	11.8	1187	18.2	835	12.8	775	11.9	1403	21.6
ANDREWS	2007	65.1	997	32.4	77	2.5*	911	36.4	165	6.6	400	16.0	171	6.8	238	9.5	619	24.7
ANGELINA	7710	67.5	3453	30.2	256	2.2*	2325	21.2	1254	11.4	1288	11.7	764	7.0	1247	11.4	4085	37.3
ARANSAS	715	71.1	256	25.4	35	3.5*	419	17.2	232	9.5	248	10.2	406	16.6	412	16.9	726	29.7
ARCHER	1507	76.9	403	20.6	49	2.5*	454	26.3	385	22.3	133	7.7	161	9.3	400	23.2	194	11.2
ARMSTRONG	570	81.5	113	16.2	16	2.3*	95	14.4	47	7.1	144	21.8	118	17.9	171	25.9	86	13.0
ATASCOSA	2236	76.9	614	21.1	59	2.0*	437	10.6	106	2.6	253	6.1	291	7.0	2235	54.1	806	19.5
AUSTIN	2461	84.3	343	11.8	115	3.9*	994	37.6	151	5.7	332	12.6	196	7.4	459	17.4	511	19.3
BAILEY	1066	80.2	232	17.5	31	2.3*	566	37.0	79	5.2	451	29.5	117	7.6	119	7.8	198	12.9
BANDERA	1269	77.8	327	20.0	36	2.2*	193	14.4	43	3.2	92	6.9	180	13.4	770	57.4	64	4.8
BASTROP	2566	74.8	779	22.7	86	2.5*	611	17.9	297	8.7	652	19.1	360	10.6	828	24.3	659	19.3
BAYLOR	1543	82.9	284	15.3	34	1.8*	753	41.6	139	7.7	248	13.7	187	10.3	305	16.9	176	9.7
BEE	2958	78.2	739	19.5	84	2.2*	472	13.2	190	5.3	264	7.4	277	7.8	1225	34.3	1141	32.0
BELL	6205	77.5	1661	20.8	138	1.7*	2741	23.4	1901	16.2	2326	19.8	1261	10.7	1325	11.3	2179	18.6
BEXAR	62603	71.2	22300	25.4	3019	3.4*	16103	19.4	3362	4.0	6525	7.8	11948	14.4	18643	22.4	26604	32.0
BLANCO	605	78.6	156	20.3	9	1.2*	134	19.7	33	4.9	72	10.6	69	10.2	326	48.0	45	6.6
BORDEN	313	71.1	118	26.8	9	2.0*	134	34.1	11	2.8	51	13.0	27	6.9	115	29.3	55	14.0
BOSQUE	2081	78.1	496	18.6	87	3.3*	1009	36.5	155	5.6	576	20.8	215	7.8	451	16.3	359	13.0
BOWIE	3848	70.1	1500	27.3	144	2.6*	3963	38.1	1022	9.8	1374	13.2	566	5.4	752	7.2	2715	26.1
BRAZORIA	6770	68.1	3023	30.4	141	1.4*	2878	19.4	2096	14.1	2133	14.4	1437	9.7	1660	11.2	4629	31.2
BRAZOS	6919	80.3	1537	17.8	163	1.9*	1392	12.6	1176	10.6	2223	20.1	1952	17.6	1486	13.4	2848	25.7
BREWSTER	950	71.6	361	27.2	16	1.2*	263	17.8	63	4.3	152	10.3	184	12.4	501	33.9	315	21.3
BRISCOE	428	82.8	73	14.1	16	3.1*	194	19.9	55	5.6	194	19.9	79	8.1	265	27.1	190	19.4
BROOKS	1531	82.7	252	13.6	68	3.7*	98	7.9	57	4.6	99	8.0	193	15.6	316	25.5	474	38.3
BROWN	3094	81.2	655	17.2	61	1.6*	1727	24.7	915	13.1	1017	14.5	604	8.6	1469	21.0	1268	18.1
BURLESON	2306	79.1	480	16.5	130	4.5*	536	27.2	133	6.8	390	19.8	138	7.0	236	12.0	536	27.2
BURNET	1293	74.8	398	23.0	38	2.2*	507	15.8	349	10.9	605	18.9	355	11.1	1135	35.4	258	8.0
CALDWELL	2323	80.1	546	18.8	31	1.1*	695	17.9	228	5.9	539	13.9	352	9.1	1499	38.7	563	14.5
CALHOUN	2656	76.0	733	21.0	104	3.0*	877	19.2	475	10.4	410	9.0	599	13.1	455	10.0	1753	38.4
CALLAHAN	1820	74.5	551	22.5	73	3.0*	664	28.8	225	9.8	220	9.6	282	12.3	561	24.4	350	15.2
CAMERON	7406	66.9	2820	25.5	852	7.7*	2099	15.7	684	5.1	1115	8.3	3565	26.6	1560	11.7	4366	32.6
CAMP	1456	73.1	483	24.2	53	2.7*	627	31.7	112	5.7	246	12.4	130	6.6	124	6.3	739	37.4
CARSON	1029	75.1	322	23.5	19	1.4*	158	12.6	147	11.7	256	20.3	214	17.0	176	14.0	307	24.4
CASS	3273	75.7	907	21.0	142	3.3*	1139	42.4	177	6.6	314	11.7	214	8.0	142	5.3	699	26.0
CASTRO	946	69.9	363	26.8	44	3.3*	476	22.4	123	5.8	443	20.8	168	7.9	392	18.4	524	24.6
CHAMBERS	1204	70.3	450	26.3	59	3.4*	658	28.1	424	18.1	347	14.8	150	6.4	269	11.5	496	21.2
CHEROKEE	2683	66.1	1205	29.7	173	4.3*	1826	27.9	1104	16.9	785	12.0	585	8.9	1002	15.3	1247	19.0
CHILDRESS	1360	71.6	483	25.4	57	3.0*	814	47.7	117	6.9	191	11.2	144	8.4	217	12.7	224	13.1
CLAY	1793	73.3	607	24.8	47	1.9*	526	27.1	320	16.5	244	12.6	201	10.3	341	17.5	312	16.0
COCHRAN	1053	79.8	227	17.2	40	3.0*	664	48.3	47	3.4	352	25.6	69	5.0	138	10.0	104	7.6
COKE	934	81.5	191	16.7	21	1.8*	288	29.1	70	7.1	141	14.3	86	8.7	307	31.0	97	9.8
COLEMAN	2310	74.2	721	23.2	81	2.6*	699	29.8	248	10.6	354	15.1	370	15.8	244	10.4	428	18.3
COLLIN	5475	82.4	967	14.6	200	3.0*	2824	25.3	756	6.8	2992	26.8	2040	18.2	725	6.5	1844	16.5
CLNGSWORTH	1257	85.7	185	12.6	25	1.7*	470	32.9	127	8.9	312	21.8	117	8.2	253	17.7	149	10.4
COLORADO	2621	81.2	506	15.7	102	3.2*	899	21.3	767	18.2	420	10.0	453	10.7	916	21.7	763	18.1
COMAL	2273	79.8	534	18.7	42	1.5*	894	35.7	70	2.8	279	11.1	253	10.1	599	23.9	410	16.4

COUNTY	CONNALLY #	%	WOODS #	%	HACKWORTHE #	%*	SMITH #	%	HILL #	%	CARR #	%	LOCKE #	%	BRISCOE #	%	D. YARBRO #	%
COMANCHEE	1795	76.6	485	20.7	63	2.7*	964	29.6	220	6.8	732	22.5	540	16.6	473	14.5	325	10.0
CONCHO	577	79.4	126	17.3	24	3.3*	173	19.4	63	7.1	95	10.7	63	7.1	427	48.0	69	7.8
COOKE	4513	82.6	874	16.0	76	1.4*	1125	25.9	651	15.0	842	19.3	565	13.0	370	8.5	799	18.4
CORYELL	2924	78.8	720	19.4	66	1.8*	1178	28.1	335	8.0	754	18.0	240	5.7	1201	28.6	488	11.6
COTTLE	935	84.9	157	14.3	9	.8*	431	41.0	49	4.7	149	14.2	87	8.3	166	15.8	170	16.2
CRANE	665	71.0	249	26.6	23	2.5*	292	26.9	67	6.2	162	14.9	129	11.9	208	19.1	229	21.1
CROCKETT	1000	83.6	163	13.6	33	2.8*	91	8.2	47	4.2	110	9.9	55	4.9	633	56.8	179	16.1
CROSBY	1689	82.7	322	15.8	31	1.5*	1209	50.4	40	1.7	539	22.5	119	5.0	207	8.6	283	11.8
CULBERSON	540	78.8	134	19.6	11	1.6*	214	29.6	99	13.7	80	11.0	38	5.2	195	26.9	98	13.5
DALLAM	999	77.3	260	20.1	33	2.6*	142	12.8	264	23.8	282	25.4	145	13.1	128	11.5	148	13.3
DALLAS	61751	81.5	12877	17.0	1123	1.5*	24894	16.9	7850	5.3	33853	23.0	42679	29.0	6250	4.2	31539	21.4
DAWSON	1851	78.2	459	19.4	56	2.4*	1666	56.8	72	2.5	643	21.9	106	3.6	205	7.0	241	8.2
DEAFSMITH	1961	82.2	374	15.7	50	2.1*	841	27.6	244	8.0	451	14.8	536	17.6	586	19.2	389	12.8
DELTA	1246	83.3	221	14.8	29	1.9*	477	27.3	253	14.5	434	24.8	131	7.5	243	13.9	209	12.0
DENTON	2459	77.4	621	19.6	96	3.0*	2187	20.1	953	8.8	2001	18.4	2313	21.3	1037	9.6	2364	21.8
DEWITT	2330	80.3	526	18.1	47	1.6*	787	27.2	206	7.1	581	20.1	196	6.8	816	28.2	303	10.5
DICKENS	585	75.0	181	23.2	14	1.8*	606	42.2	29	2.0	343	23.9	107	7.5	122	8.5	229	15.9
DIMMIT	1481	78.3	367	19.4	44	2.3*	34	3.2	14	1.3	5	.5	51	4.8	614	58.0	340	32.1
DONLEY	1056	80.2	228	17.3	33	2.5*	346	26.0	119	8.9	289	21.7	184	13.8	258	19.4	137	10.3
DUVAL	3789	98.1	38	1.0	36	.9*	818	21.1	19	.5	41	1.1	2609	67.3	226	5.8	165	4.3
EASTLAND	3347	75.9	949	21.5	114	2.6*	1572	35.5	538	12.2	641	14.5	379	8.6	551	12.4	746	16.9
ECTOR	5222	69.2	1966	26.0	360	4.8*	2893	27.4	885	8.4	2156	20.4	1324	12.5	858	8.1	2441	23.1
EDWARDS	559	82.9	95	14.1	20	3.0*	71	12.9	7	1.3	38	6.9	10	1.8	416	75.6	8	1.5
ELLIS	4210	82.1	793	15.5	123	2.4*	1895	29.8	280	4.4	1730	27.2	714	11.2	680	10.7	1057	16.6
ELPASO	15025	63.2	6830	28.7	1936	8.1*	7152	24.4	3196	10.9	3391	11.6	3060	10.5	2104	7.2	10369	35.4
ERATH	3101	81.5	624	16.4	81	2.1*	1464	34.9	507	12.1	933	22.2	333	7.9	522	12.4	439	10.5
FALLS	2270	80.2	497	17.5	65	2.3*	1022	21.1	260	5.4	834	17.2	779	16.1	996	20.5	958	19.8
FANNIN	3021	79.7	681	18.0	88	2.3*	1202	21.7	307	5.5	1855	33.5	512	9.2	343	6.2	1319	23.8
FAYETTE	2460	76.5	550	17.1	205	6.4*	1105	27.5	496	12.3	716	17.8	474	11.8	780	19.4	453	11.3
FISHER	1611	79.4	373	18.4	46	2.3*	713	34.0	116	5.5	168	8.0	220	10.5	406	19.3	476	22.7
FLOYD	585	79.8	136	18.6	12	1.6*	861	41.0	51	2.4	608	28.9	131	6.2	235	11.2	216	10.3
FOARD	539	82.2	103	15.7	14	2.1*	381	41.9	43	4.7	107	11.8	96	10.5	180	19.8	103	11.3
FORTBEND	5426	77.3	1378	19.6	211	3.0*	1993	27.4	459	6.3	697	9.6	552	7.6	1790	24.6	1783	24.5
FRANKLIN	1336	79.9	293	17.5	43	2.6*	578	33.0	157	9.0	350	20.0	163	9.3	190	10.8	315	18.0
FREESTONE	2750	81.2	556	16.4	79	2.3*	791	23.9	431	13.0	749	22.6	282	8.5	387	11.7	669	20.2
FRIO	1509	83.6	268	14.9	27	1.5*	85	3.4	33	1.3	97	3.8	63	2.5	1585	62.6	669	26.4
GAINES	1000	73.7	317	23.4	39	2.9*	1535	55.6	76	2.8	563	20.4	133	4.8	198	7.2	258	9.3
GALVESTON	15284	68.5	6489	29.1	524	2.4*	5005	18.6	2449	9.1	3344	12.4	3264	12.1	1208	4.5	11672	43.3
GARZA	1078	75.7	310	21.8	36	2.5*	682	44.3	25	1.6	331	21.5	114	7.4	177	11.5	211	13.7
GILLESPIE	772	84.5	125	13.7	17	1.9*	276	35.5	26	3.3	87	11.2	65	8.4	275	35.4	48	6.2
GLASCOCK	118	75.2	35	22.3	4	2.5*	76	22.8	7	2.1	63	18.9	57	17.1	98	29.4	32	9.6
GOLIAD	535	75.7	161	22.8	11	1.6*	188	16.2	56	4.8	191	16.5	153	13.2	247	21.3	326	28.1
GONZALES	1490	83.7	278	15.6	12	.7*	835	21.8	223	5.8	254	6.6	182	4.7	2079	54.2	263	6.9
GRAY	2995	69.8	1157	27.0	139	3.2*	634	14.5	630	14.4	1043	23.9	678	15.5	575	13.2	803	18.4
GRAYSON	6852	74.1	2159	23.4	235	2.5*	3019	25.4	824	6.9	2807	23.6	1780	15.0	617	5.2	2857	24.0
GREGG	8530	76.6	2236	20.1	364	3.3*	3049	32.5	2739	29.2	695	7.4	1083	11.5	563	6.0	1265	13.5

COUNTY	CONNALLY #	%	WOODS #	%	HACKWORTHE #	%*	SMITH #	%	HILL #	%	CARR #	%	LOCKE #	%	BRISCOE #	%	D. YARBRO #	%
GRIMES	2474	80.1	527	17.1	86	2.8*	650	24.6	177	6.7	400	15.2	239	9.1	596	22.6	575	21.8
GUADALUPE	2597	79.4	594	18.2	79	2.4*	866	21.8	223	5.6	512	12.9	507	12.8	1352	34.1	505	12.7
HALE	2682	78.8	661	19.4	61	1.8*	2193	36.5	408	6.8	1761	29.3	469	7.8	549	9.1	636	10.6
HALL	956	83.9	165	14.5	19	1.7*	454	27.2	105	6.3	375	22.5	216	12.9	248	14.9	271	16.2
HAMILTON	1816	77.0	440	18.7	103	4.4*	718	30.1	180	7.5	574	24.1	191	8.0	493	20.7	230	9.6
HANSFORD	798	85.3	120	12.8	17	1.8*	183	20.7	142	16.0	257	29.0	97	10.9	139	15.7	68	7.7
HARDEMAN	1336	82.4	260	16.0	25	1.5*	1011	50.8	94	4.7	197	9.9	188	9.5	218	11.0	281	14.1
HARDIN	3944	58.8	2588	38.6	177	2.6*	1312	18.0	586	8.0	1387	19.0	507	6.9	581	8.0	2923	40.1
HARRIS	96663	67.3	44788	31.2	2263	1.6*	52220	26.2	20958	10.5	19736	9.9	22181	11.1	8804	4.4	75780	38.0
HARRISON	6342	81.7	1292	16.6	131	1.7*	3013	37.2	668	8.2	1107	13.7	1372	16.9	452	5.6	1491	18.4
HARTLEY	655	83.5	117	14.9	12	1.5*	99	14.1	120	17.1	164	23.4	120	17.1	120	17.1	77	11.0
HASKELL	2053	73.6	648	23.2	87	3.1*	1057	34.5	209	6.8	381	12.4	358	11.7	445	14.5	616	20.1
HAYS	3061	81.1	657	17.4	58	1.5*	863	22.8	382	10.1	371	9.8	390	10.3	1068	28.2	716	18.9
HEMPHILL	679	83.4	108	13.3	27	3.3*	122	16.3	115	15.3	182	24.3	94	12.5	151	20.1	86	11.5
HENDERSON	4389	67.9	1903	29.4	171	2.6*	973	19.0	317	6.2	1272	24.8	426	8.3	653	12.7	1489	29.0
HIDALGO	14761	75.2	4656	23.7	224	1.1*	6218	23.5	624	2.4	1500	5.7	4184	15.8	4368	16.5	9569	36.2
HILL	3048	88.6	362	10.5	32	.9*	1447	35.2	312	7.6	885	21.5	425	10.3	519	12.6	519	12.6
HOCKLEY	2450	76.9	621	19.5	114	3.6*	1679	42.9	142	3.6	1066	27.2	247	6.3	340	8.7	438	11.2
HOOD	1342	76.9	368	21.1	36	2.1*	369	26.3	145	10.3	323	23.0	115	8.2	229	16.3	222	15.8
HOPKINS	3475	80.8	740	17.2	84	2.0*	1415	27.3	686	13.2	1294	25.0	597	11.5	306	5.9	886	17.1
HOUSTON	3200	75.7	950	22.5	80	1.9*	924	18.5	1104	22.1	668	13.4	336	6.7	540	10.8	1416	28.4
HOWARD	3638	67.4	1658	30.7	100	1.9*	1134	18.3	203	3.3	1635	26.3	663	10.7	656	10.6	1915	30.9
HUDSPETH	455	80.0	95	16.7	19	3.3*	156	24.1	135	20.8	70	10.8	69	10.6	113	17.4	105	16.2
HUNT	4252	75.6	1190	21.2	180	3.2*	2039	22.0	1169	12.6	3030	32.6	959	10.3	646	7.0	1446	15.6
HUTCHISON	2624	58.8	1763	39.5	72	1.6*	730	19.2	357	9.4	668	17.5	502	13.2	327	8.6	1226	32.2
IRION	391	73.9	126	23.8	12	2.3*	43	10.3	37	8.9	55	13.2	18	4.3	222	53.4	41	9.9
JACK	1571	80.7	336	17.3	40	2.1*	611	31.3	218	11.2	264	13.5	163	8.4	437	22.4	259	13.3
JACKSON	2890	78.9	647	17.7	124	3.4*	666	18.0	424	11.5	519	14.0	303	8.2	1033	27.9	758	20.5
JASPER	3265	64.6	1680	33.2	108	2.1*	1106	26.7	321	7.7	907	21.9	251	6.1	536	12.9	1026	24.7
JEFFDAVIS	356	79.3	83	18.5	10	2.2*	67	22.3	34	11.3	16	5.3	32	10.6	90	29.9	62	20.6
JEFFERSON	17469	61.8	10319	36.5	483	1.7*	6894	22.7	2729	9.0	4504	14.8	2674	8.8	2751	9.1	10783	35.5
JIMHOGG	829	85.2	125	12.8	19	2.0*	215	16.1	48	3.6	62	4.6	131	9.8	382	28.6	500	37.4
JIMWELLS	5809	80.2	1269	17.5	163	2.3*	889	10.9	354	4.3	686	8.4	720	8.8	1874	23.0	3638	44.6
JOHNSON	2698	75.8	798	22.4	65	1.8*	2044	24.1	585	6.9	2284	26.9	1023	12.1	713	8.4	1833	21.6
JONES	2375	82.8	439	15.3	53	1.8*	1377	34.7	327	8.2	358	9.0	451	11.4	885	22.3	571	14.4
KARNES	2095	75.1	641	23.0	55	2.0*	633	18.3	134	3.9	388	11.2	353	10.2	1515	43.9	430	12.5
KAUFMAN	5014	82.6	910	15.0	145	2.4*	1642	26.2	596	9.5	1553	24.8	801	12.8	492	7.8	1185	18.9
KENDALL	251	87.5	35	12.2	1	.3*	78	16.0	7	1.4	47	9.6	65	13.3	253	51.8	38	7.8
KENEDY	98	86.7	8	7.1	7	6.2*	17	11.4	3	2.0	5	3.4	40	26.8	65	43.6	19	12.8
KENT	581	75.2	167	21.6	25	3.2*	259	36.5	19	2.7	98	13.8	58	8.2	154	21.7	121	17.1
KERR	1826	81.4	362	16.1	56	2.5*	714	21.5	234	7.1	446	13.4	391	11.8	1234	37.2	299	9.0
KIMBLE	811	80.8	166	16.5	27	2.7*	335	28.8	31	2.7	66	5.7	48	4.1	637	54.8	46	4.0
KING	173	82.4	34	16.2	3	1.4*	109	51.4	2	.9	26	12.3	26	12.3	41	19.3	8	3.8
KINNEY	438	79.1	96	17.3	20	3.6*	32	5.2	9	1.5	27	4.4	60	9.8	388	63.4	96	15.7
KLEBERG	3739	75.9	1047	21.3	137	2.8*	800	15.3	396	7.6	374	7.1	389	7.4	1013	19.3	2273	43.3
KNOX	1192	80.9	253	17.2	28	1.9*	774	48.4	105	6.6	207	12.9	95	5.9	272	17.0	146	9.1

COUNTY	CONNALLY #	%	WOODS #	%	HACKWORTHE #	%*	SMITH #	%	HILL #	%	CARR #	%	LOCKE #	%	BRISCOE #	%	D. YARBRO #	%
LAMAR	4960	78.3	1182	18.7	189	3.0*	1726	22.4	374	4.9	2854	37.0	472	6.1	329	4.3	1955	25.4
LAMB	2314	77.2	587	19.6	96	3.2*	1866	38.6	76	1.6	1326	27.4	341	7.1	569	11.8	654	13.5
LAMPASAS	1136	77.3	299	20.4	34	2.3*	567	23.0	172	7.0	500	20.3	187	7.6	766	31.1	273	11.1
LASALLE	760	78.4	183	18.9	27	2.8*	56	6.9	32	3.9	40	4.9	30	3.7	499	61.3	157	19.3
LABACA	2639	77.7	655	19.3	102	3.0*	1285	36.1	268	7.5	501	14.1	266	7.5	799	22.5	436	12.3
LEE	1358	70.1	497	25.7	81	4.2*	333	26.0	109	8.5	214	16.7	74	5.8	337	26.3	214	16.7
LEON	949	70.1	198	14.6	207	15.3*	517	22.7	162	7.1	410	18.0	202	8.9	590	25.9	401	17.6
LIBERTY	3164	67.9	1395	29.9	99	2.1*	2173	31.7	755	11.0	825	12.0	413	6.0	644	9.4	2041	29.8
LIMESTONE	2733	78.6	652	18.7	93	2.7*	841	20.9	176	4.4	884	21.9	264	6.5	870	21.6	998	24.7
LIPSCOMB	707	84.8	118	14.1	9	1.1*	99	17.3	49	8.6	207	36.2	51	8.9	95	16.6	71	12.4
LIVEOAK	1405	74.4	424	22.5	59	3.1*	337	14.2	83	3.5	231	9.7	181	7.6	1161	48.8	388	16.3
LLANO	961	71.8	355	26.5	22	1.6*	410	19.6	189	9.0	357	17.1	196	9.4	763	36.5	178	8.5
LOVING	46	73.0	15	23.8	2	3.2*	18	24.3	3	4.1	9	12.2	5	6.8	29	39.2	10	13.5
LUBBOCK	9129	76.8	2581	21.7	172	1.4*	14935	47.4	868	2.8	7055	22.4	2116	6.7	1357	4.3	5145	16.3
LYNN	1680	81.8	294	14.3	81	3.9*	1501	57.2	52	2.0	574	21.9	136	5.2	182	6.9	181	6.9
MADISON	1326	78.7	321	19.1	38	2.3*	363	18.1	194	9.7	360	17.9	134	6.7	533	26.6	423	21.1
MARION	1388	80.3	304	17.6	36	2.1*	529	42.0	85	6.7	164	13.0	145	11.5	52	4.1	285	22.6
MARTIN	409	75.9	109	20.2	21	3.9*	229	39.7	14	2.4	121	21.0	45	7.8	126	21.8	42	7.3
MASON	668	79.0	165	19.5	13	1.5*	222	14.6	57	3.8	149	9.8	73	4.8	919	60.5	98	6.5
MATAGORDA	3371	80.8	716	17.2	84	2.0*	1408	24.7	867	15.2	898	15.8	390	6.8	817	14.3	1315	23.1
MAVERICK	2154	84.5	334	13.1	60	2.4*	143	6.0	28	1.2	106	4.5	635	26.7	931	39.2	533	22.4
MCCULLOCH	1477	79.5	346	18.6	34	1.8*	635	27.1	87	3.7	257	11.0	162	6.9	1017	43.4	185	7.9
MCLENNAN	9919	71.5	3733	26.9	213	1.5*	5659	19.5	2277	7.8	5924	20.4	3681	12.7	3196	11.0	8300	28.6
MCMULLEN	243	67.7	101	28.1	15	4.2*	46	10.0	14	3.0	57	12.4	25	5.4	259	56.3	59	12.8
MEDINA	1821	83.6	314	14.4	44	2.0*	320	11.6	28	1.0	114	4.1	154	5.6	1722	62.4	423	15.3
MENARD	601	79.6	130	17.2	24	3.2*	119	20.8	35	6.1	73	12.7	26	4.5	244	42.6	76	13.3
MIDLAND	4562	77.6	1231	20.9	87	1.5*	1856	19.7	604	6.4	2205	23.4	1694	17.9	1497	15.9	1582	16.8
MILAN	2678	72.6	907	24.6	106	2.9*	1030	21.2	397	8.2	914	18.8	309	6.4	953	19.6	1257	25.9
MILLS	744	74.6	213	21.4	40	4.0*	311	19.2	80	5.0	326	20.2	112	6.9	647	40.0	140	8.7
MITCHELL	1779	77.7	480	21.0	32	1.4*	711	30.7	51	2.2	333	14.4	339	14.6	495	21.4	385	16.6
MONTAGE	2461	78.3	557	17.7	125	4.0*	1307	32.0	311	7.6	665	16.3	460	11.3	691	16.9	651	15.9
MONTGOMRY	6050	74.0	1808	22.1	316	3.9*	2468	28.9	1520	17.8	1048	12.3	745	8.7	784	9.2	1978	23.2
MOORE	2100	72.4	711	24.5	88	3.0*	559	16.2	517	15.0	821	23.8	410	11.9	357	10.4	783	22.7
MORRIS	2272	79.2	534	18.6	61	2.1*	1037	33.8	226	7.4	367	11.9	319	10.4	195	6.3	928	30.2
MOTLEY	718	79.5	168	18.6	17	1.9*	432	45.4	38	4.0	229	24.1	59	6.2	94	9.9	99	10.4
NACDOCHES	5122	77.2	1288	19.4	222	3.3*	1375	18.9	1182	16.2	691	9.5	397	5.5	1778	24.4	1855	25.5
NAVARRO	4595	78.7	1114	19.1	132	2.3*	1281	16.5	642	8.3	2128	27.4	1035	13.3	805	10.4	1879	24.2
NEWTON	2103	69.9	808	26.9	96	3.2*	709	26.2	181	6.7	565	20.9	159	5.9	344	12.7	745	27.6
NOLAN	2780	72.8	981	25.7	60	1.6*	1009	25.1	478	11.9	438	10.9	575	14.3	849	21.1	676	16.8
NUECES	20715	73.9	5431	19.4	1876	6.7*	5007	12.1	5118	12.3	2252	5.4	5002	12.1	7546	18.2	16566	39.9
OCHILTREE	706	81.9	138	16.0	18	2.1*	367	36.6	103	10.3	218	21.8	121	12.1	122	12.2	71	7.1
OLDHAM	441	86.0	69	13.5	3	.6*	67	11.4	54	9.2	107	18.2	112	19.1	166	28.3	81	13.8
ORANGE	5297	59.6	3391	38.1	206	2.3*	3515	24.1	652	4.5	3279	22.5	1065	7.3	714	4.9	5377	36.8
PALOPINTO	2921	80.5	640	17.6	66	1.8*	1407	24.7	934	16.4	1264	22.2	549	9.6	607	10.7	934	16.4
PANOLA	2395	73.9	728	22.5	117	3.6*	1249	29.7	238	5.7	525	12.5	186	4.4	1227	29.2	776	18.5
PARKER	3197	75.9	920	21.8	96	2.3*	1383	22.0	1352	21.5	1228	19.5	470	7.5	493	7.8	1359	21.6

COUNTY	CONNALLY #	%	WOODS #	%	HACKWORTHE #	%*	SMITH #	%	HILL #	%	CARR #	%	LOCKE #	%	BRISCOE #	%	D. YARBRO #	%
PARMER	1059	80.3	229	17.4	31	2.4*	701	45.3	89	5.7	389	25.1	102	6.6	129	8.3	138	8.9
PECOS	994	77.0	275	21.3	22	1.7*	505	19.9	113	4.4	320	12.6	216	8.5	885	34.8	504	19.8
POLK	2538	73.8	769	22.4	130	3.8*	1169	29.2	522	13.0	648	16.2	258	6.4	309	7.7	1102	27.5
POTTER	4004	76.4	1177	22.5	60	1.1*	1097	9.4	1335	11.4	2332	20.0	2584	22.1	1093	9.4	3228	27.7
PRESIDIO	995	82.6	176	14.6	34	2.8*	254	20.3	57	4.6	134	10.7	167	13.4	274	21.9	364	29.1
RAINES	718	71.2	257	25.5	33	3.3*	147	20.6	155	21.7	179	25.1	69	9.7	38	5.3	126	17.6
RANDALL	2093	79.2	526	19.9	25	.9*	1065	13.5	960	12.2	1616	20.5	1778	22.5	1013	12.8	1457	18.5
REAGAN	536	75.9	154	21.8	16	2.3*	195	19.6	116	11.6	228	22.9	81	8.1	286	28.7	90	9.0
REAL	167	84.3	28	14.1	3	1.5*	56	9.7	9	1.6	23	4.0	27	4.7	448	77.9	12	2.1
REDRIVER	2605	81.4	519	16.2	75	2.3*	1346	38.0	309	8.7	1045	29.5	224	6.3	303	8.5	319	9.0
REEVES	1948	83.2	355	15.2	37	1.6*	730	26.5	115	4.2	398	14.4	242	8.8	828	30.0	446	16.2
REFUGIO	1207	76.3	338	21.4	36	2.3*	481	16.2	270	9.1	310	10.5	303	10.2	819	27.6	780	26.3
ROBERTS	347	86.3	48	11.9	7	1.7*	53	15.5	32	9.4	116	34.0	61	17.9	44	12.9	35	10.3
ROBERTSON	2069	74.7	624	22.5	75	2.7*	720	18.8	261	6.8	565	14.7	338	8.8	600	15.6	1352	35.2
ROCKWALL	1139	85.4	170	12.8	24	1.8*	379	21.4	754	42.5	311	17.5	101	5.7	66	3.7	164	9.2
RUNNELLS	1270	81.5	247	15.8	42	2.7*	1121	37.6	160	5.4	279	9.4	240	8.1	921	30.9	257	8.6
RUSK	5155	69.6	2011	27.1	242	3.3*	1337	18.0	2338	31.5	680	9.2	453	6.1	1382	18.6	1240	16.7
SABINE	1426	72.7	448	22.8	88	4.5*	987	40.2	102	4.2	433	17.6	89	3.6	309	12.6	536	21.8
SNAUGSTNE	1670	73.9	492	21.8	99	4.4*	726	34.5	191	9.1	235	11.2	97	4.6	383	18.2	473	22.5
SNJACINTO	893	62.8	459	32.3	71	5.0*	386	22.0	236	13.4	246	14.0	127	7.2	102	5.8	659	37.5
SNPATRICIO	3981	74.6	1236	23.2	120	2.2*	850	10.6	894	11.1	662	8.2	491	6.1	2256	28.0	2893	36.0
SANSABA	1071	78.8	255	18.8	33	2.4*	381	19.0	89	4.4	401	20.0	163	8.1	780	38.9	189	9.4
SCHLEICHER	683	76.2	179	20.0	34	3.8*	83	10.0	49	5.9	157	19.0	39	4.7	419	50.7	80	9.7
SCURRY	2974	73.7	943	23.4	117	2.9*	1325	35.4	91	2.4	526	14.1	651	17.4	617	16.5	530	14.2
SHACKELFRD	1164	80.4	248	17.1	35	2.4*	332	23.8	525	37.7	86	6.2	92	6.6	175	12.6	183	13.1
SHELBY	4105	74.8	1177	21.4	209	3.8*	1925	32.4	963	16.2	655	11.0	285	4.8	625	10.5	1491	25.1
SHERMAN	598	85.2	88	12.5	16	2.3*	102	14.0	92	12.6	223	30.6	82	11.3	121	16.6	108	14.8
SMITH	8539	72.0	3063	25.8	264	2.2*	2217	15.3	2249	15.5	3171	21.8	1570	10.8	1859	12.8	3453	23.8
SOMERVELL	541	79.4	120	17.6	20	2.9*	136	17.8	28	3.7	219	28.7	100	13.1	130	17.1	149	19.6
STARR	2985	94.6	130	4.1	42	1.3*	261	7.0	24	.6	66	1.8	1105	29.7	654	17.6	1607	43.2
STEPHENS	1803	82.6	347	15.9	34	1.6*	833	28.5	430	14.7	394	13.5	294	10.0	506	17.3	470	16.1
STERLING	106	82.2	20	15.5	3	2.3*	49	14.1	5	1.4	41	11.8	30	8.6	180	51.7	43	12.4
STONEWALL	897	78.7	217	19.0	26	2.3*	449	41.4	28	2.6	88	8.1	88	8.1	234	21.6	197	18.2
SUTTON	310	84.5	54	14.7	3	.8*	159	26.0	31	5.1	76	12.4	45	7.4	235	38.5	65	10.6
SWISHER	915	77.8	229	19.5	32	2.7*	813	28.6	162	5.7	466	16.4	214	7.5	293	10.3	895	31.5
TARRANT	36924	73.2	12814	25.4	678	1.3*	15776	19.4	11780	14.5	15995	19.6	13545	16.6	6910	8.5	17468	21.4
TAYLOR	8827	83.0	1707	16.1	101	.9*	5713	34.0	1365	8.1	2273	13.5	2929	17.4	2104	12.5	2424	14.4
TERRELL	271	77.4	76	21.7	3	.9*	46	11.1	12	2.9	41	9.9	21	5.0	233	56.0	63	15.1
TERRY	2207	78.7	523	18.7	74	2.6*	1561	40.0	104	2.7	1019	26.1	422	10.8	289	7.4	510	13.1
THRCKMORTN	869	79.4	199	18.2	26	2.4*	298	26.7	154	13.8	113	10.1	108	9.7	291	26.1	153	13.7
TITUS	1814	80.6	388	17.2	50	2.2*	1422	29.9	248	5.2	675	14.2	412	8.7	351	7.4	1640	34.5
TOMGREEN	7196	78.7	1705	18.7	237	2.6*	2163	17.3	1154	9.2	2293	18.3	1384	11.1	3895	31.2	1611	12.9
TRAVIS	23794	74.3	7885	24.6	362	1.1*	9816	19.3	7939	15.6	6502	12.8	7055	13.9	8379	16.5	11217	22.0
TRINITY	2014	75.1	587	21.9	82	3.1*	647	30.0	285	12.3	264	12.3	154	7.1	173	8.0	632	29.3
TYLER	1433	60.7	867	36.8	59	2.5*	737	23.6	272	8.7	687	22.0	213	6.8	411	13.2	801	25.7
UPSHUR	2565	67.1	1155	30.2	104	2.7*	876	22.4	658	16.8	322	8.2	279	7.1	539	13.8	1240	31.7

COUNTY	CONNALLY #	%	WOODS #	%	HACKWORTHE #	%*	SMITH #	%	HILL #	%	CARR #	%	LOCKE #	%	BRISCOE #	%	D. YARBRO #	%
UPTON	726	70.4	265	25.7	40	3.9*	310	22.9	87	6.4	194	14.3	187	13.8	404	29.9	170	12.6
UVALDE	1802	71.9	639	25.5	67	2.7*	97	2.0	18	.4	50	1.0	89	1.8	4106	83.6	549	11.2
VALVERDE	2699	79.7	622	18.4	66	1.9*	342	7.9	92	2.1	277	6.4	422	9.8	1655	38.3	1537	35.5
VANZANDT	2987	65.2	1508	32.9	87	1.9*	842	18.5	349	7.7	1583	34.8	429	9.4	458	10.1	885	19.5
VICTORIA	5655	77.8	1471	20.2	147	2.0*	1702	19.4	1367	15.5	1255	14.3	1095	12.5	1526	17.4	1847	21.0
WALKER	2274	79.3	535	18.7	59	2.1*	1474	33.4	709	16.1	450	10.2	308	7.0	277	6.3	1196	27.1
WALLER	2315	85.1	353	13.0	52	1.9*	556	25.5	183	8.4	258	11.8	138	6.3	314	14.4	729	33.5
WARD	1777	69.0	743	28.8	57	2.2*	1143	36.3	152	4.8	611	19.4	264	8.4	435	13.8	541	17.2
WASHINGTON	2007	85.7	282	12.0	54	2.3*	867	40.1	356	16.5	188	8.7	124	5.7	346	16.0	282	13.0
WEBB	8082	94.2	446	5.2	55	.6*	277	3.7	92	1.2	120	1.6	416	5.6	4488	60.2	2057	27.6
WHARTON	4738	80.9	896	15.3	225	3.8*	1239	24.6	932	18.5	615	12.2	467	9.3	855	17.0	925	18.4
WHEELER	1571	82.3	300	15.7	37	1.9*	324	18.3	175	9.9	552	31.2	209	11.8	271	15.3	241	13.6
WICHITA	7325	73.9	2418	24.4	175	1.8*	4365	27.7	2550	16.2	1633	10.3	1994	12.6	1578	10.0	3662	23.2
WILBARGER	2561	85.4	398	13.3	39	1.3*	1403	40.5	185	5.3	510	14.7	532	15.3	481	13.9	355	10.2
WILLACY	2531	81.3	520	16.7	61	2.0*	493	16.2	66	2.2	253	8.3	530	17.4	967	31.8	732	24.1
WILLIAMSON	4646	77.0	1224	20.3	165	2.7*	2320	33.6	477	6.9	1023	14.8	440	6.4	1865	27.0	776	11.2
WILSON	3025	73.5	969	23.6	120	2.9*	417	9.9	290	6.9	213	5.0	919	21.8	1590	37.6	796	18.8
WINKLER	1320	70.4	505	26.9	50	2.7*	918	34.1	416	15.5	393	14.6	265	9.9	267	9.9	430	16.0
WISE	978	73.1	323	24.1	37	2.8*	1085	27.4	605	15.3	790	19.9	334	8.4	562	14.2	584	14.7
WOOD	2467	73.2	843	25.0	62	1.8*	925	20.2	864	18.8	1022	22.3	579	12.6	396	8.6	799	17.4
YOAKUM	1488	69.8	597	28.0	46	2.2*	1041	50.3	60	2.9	534	25.8	86	4.2	100	4.8	249	12.0
YOUNG	2402	83.8	416	14.5	47	1.6*	763	22.0	1371	39.6	316	9.1	256	7.4	307	8.9	449	13.0
ZAPATA	957	96.2	37	3.7	1	.1*	597	81.4	4	.5	9	1.2	16	2.2	52	7.1	55	7.5
ZAVALA	1514	65.0	725	31.1	89	3.8*	84	3.7	29	1.3	49	2.2	48	2.1	1216	54.2	818	36.5
TOTALS	932641		291651		31105	*	386875		154908		257543		218118		225686		421617	
% OF VOTE	74.3		23.2		2.5	*	23.2		9.3		15.5		13.1		13.6		25.3	

GEOGRAPHIC CLASS

LOWLANDS	347232	71.	130079	27.	11217	2.*	149800	25.	67455	11.	92416	15.	60354	10.	55607	9.	185249	30.
BLACK BELT	13007	79.	3032	18.	365	2.*	5204	30.	1433	8.	2340	14.	2120	12.	1520	9.	4516	26.
WEST TEXAS	474345	76.	132534	21.	15036	2.*	205311	23.	77755	9.	150895	17.	134719	15.	127711	15.	182913	21.
MEX. TEXAS	98057	76.	26006	20.	4487	3.*	26560	17.	8265	5.	11892	8.	20925	13.	40848	26.	48939	31.

DEMOGRAPHIC CLASS

METRO	439584	72.	157471	26.	15190	2.*	193619	22.	81118	9.	131032	15.	136296	15.	87546	10.	258359	29.
TOWN	88176	76.	25349	22.	2455	2.*	31580	21.	14168	9.	24918	17.	21277	14.	17966	12.	39566	26.
RURAL	404881	77.	108831	21.	13460	3.*	161676	26.	59622	10.	101593	16.	60545	10.	120174	19.	123692	20.

```
        DEMOC.  RUNOFF     1968*        DEMOC.  GOVERNOR   1972
                             *
 COUNTY     SMITH         D. YARBRO     BARNES        BRISCOE      FARENTHOLD
            #      %       #      %*    #      %      #      %      #      %
---------------------------------------------------------------------------------------------------------
ANDERSON   2777 51.5    2620 48.5*   1550 21.9    4628 65.4     900 12.7
ANDREWS    1002 68.6     459 31.4*    373 16.9    1305 59.0     534 24.1
ANGELINA   3209 46.6    3682 53.4*   2329 17.0    5773 42.1    5606 40.9
ARANSAS     862 50.6     840 49.4*    301 12.7    1235 52.0     838 35.3
ARCHER      965 63.9     546 36.1*    239 13.7    1237 70.8     272 15.6
                             *
ARMSTRONG   254 62.4     153 37.6*    153 19.4     539 68.3      97 12.3
ATASCOSA   1732 67.1     848 32.9*    712 16.0    3067 68.8     678 15.2
AUSTIN     1144 69.9     493 30.1*    565 17.3    2051 62.9     645 19.8
BAILEY     1048 76.2     327 23.8*    357 28.5     780 62.2     117  9.3
BANDERA     676 82.7     141 17.3*    154  8.2    1447 77.1     275 14.7

BASTROP    1185 57.2     887 42.8*    578 15.7    2448 66.5     656 17.8
BAYLOR     1007 76.6     308 23.4*    206 12.0    1227 71.3     289 16.8
BEE        1589 46.4    1835 53.6*    550 12.1    2394 52.7    1597 35.2
BELL       5575 54.4    4666 45.6*   2765 17.4    9305 58.4    3854 24.2
BEXAR     39292 52.0   36288 48.0*  23962 22.0   53599 49.1   31501 28.9

BLANCO      373 77.4     109 22.6*     68  9.1     573 76.8     105 14.1
BORDEN      260 78.1      73 21.9*     49 13.8     256 72.1      50 14.1
BOSQUE     1339 65.6     703 34.4*    653 18.6    2409 68.6     449 12.8
BOWIE      5450 63.6    3119 36.4*   2836 26.4    5686 52.9    2217 20.6
BRAZORIA   5376 45.1    6547 54.9*   2960 13.9    8408 39.6    9873 46.5
                             *
BRAZOS     4331 49.7    4378 50.3*   1684 13.6    6486 52.4    4209 34.0
BREWSTER    567 67.2     277 32.8*    203 15.8     822 63.9     262 20.4
BRISCOE     459 61.4     288 38.6*    204 25.2     534 65.9      72  8.9
BROOKS      422 30.5     960 69.5*    661 23.6     781 27.8    1363 48.6
BROWN      3973 68.0    1866 32.0*   3502 47.0    3350 44.9     601  8.1
                             *
BURLESON    745 49.9     747 50.1*    692 22.2    1571 50.4     853 27.4
BURNET     1504 67.9     711 32.1*    504 13.3    2620 69.3     659 17.4
CALDWELL   1798 64.6     985 35.4*    559 13.9    2748 68.1     726 18.0
CALHOUN    2190 46.4    2530 53.6*    690 13.3    2213 42.6    2291 44.1
CALLAHAN   1553 66.1     796 33.9*    424 17.7    1688 70.3     290 12.1
                             *
CAMERON    5957 52.0    5502 48.0*   5532 27.4    9937 49.3    4692 23.3
CAMP        991 50.7     964 49.3*    513 23.9    1237 57.6     398 18.5
CARSON      426 50.4     420 49.6*    375 26.2     813 56.7     245 17.1
CASS       1331 64.1     746 35.9*   1282 24.4    3119 59.4     853 16.2
CASTRO      572 49.2     591 50.8*    487 26.1    1177 63.0     203 10.9

CHAMBERS   1209 53.6    1045 46.4*    390 14.7    1391 52.6     864 32.7
CHEROKEE   2247 52.3    2051 47.7*   1095 16.2    4200 62.1    1472 21.8
CHILDRESS   958 75.8     306 24.2*    176 11.6    1190 78.3     154 10.1
CLAY        671 61.7     417 38.3*    276 12.2    1567 69.3     417 18.5
COCHRAN    1055 85.1     185 14.9*    356 25.9     824 59.8     197 14.3
                             *
COKE        452 81.1     105 18.9*    191 18.8     711 70.1     112 11.0
COLEMAN    1530 69.6     667 30.4*    755 26.1    1916 66.3     221  7.6
COLLIN     6740 64.1    3779 35.9*   3674 31.2    6199 52.6    1919 16.3
CLNGSWORTH  646 72.6     244 27.4*    226 16.4    1027 74.7     121  8.8
COLORADO   2055 61.1    1310 38.9*    666 15.0    2830 63.6     957 21.5
                             *
COMAL      1327 69.5     581 30.5*    775 16.9    2896 63.0     926 20.1
```

```
           DEMOC.  RUNOFF    1968*      DEMOC.  GOVERNOR   1972
                               *
  COUNTY      SMITH       D. YARBRO    BARNES      BRISCOE      FARENTHOLD
            #      %     #      %*    #      %    #      %     #       %
```

COUNTY	SMITH #	%	D. YARBRO #	%*	BARNES #	%	BRISCOE #	%	FARENTHOLD #	%
COMANCHEE	1679	70.5	704	29.5*	2031	46.8	2031	46.8	280	6.4
CONCHO	655	72.5	249	27.5*	132	13.4	772	78.2	83	8.4
COOKE	2184	71.7	863	28.3*	883	15.3	3559	61.7	1330	23.0
CORYELL	2291	67.5	1103	32.5*	741	15.2	3432	70.4	702	14.4
COTTLE	445	67.4	215	32.6*	232	28.8	474	58.9	99	12.3
CRANE	469	60.5	306	39.5*	209	13.7	1108	72.6	210	13.8
CROCKETT	719	65.0	387	35.0*	128	11.0	782	67.4	251	21.6
CROSBY	1456	74.4	501	25.6*	362	19.8	1148	62.9	316	17.3
CULBERSON	343	64.0	193	36.0*	145	22.4	435	67.1	68	10.5
DALLAM	402	64.2	224	35.8*	189	29.1	364	56.1	96	14.8
DALLAS	80141	62.8	47540	37.2*	41910	26.1	66069	41.2	52485	32.7
DAWSON	2109	86.5	328	13.5*	255	10.1	1855	73.3	419	16.6
DEAFSMITH	1180	68.4	544	31.6*	600	26.4	1489	65.5	186	8.2
DELTA	1097	64.2	612	35.8*	574	35.1	732	44.7	330	20.2
DENTON	5137	58.9	3583	41.1*	3285	20.5	6993	43.7	5714	35.7
DEWITT	1798	73.7	641	26.3*	711	17.3	2686	65.3	714	17.4
DICKENS	1016	73.4	368	26.6*	317	25.6	745	60.3	174	14.1
DIMMIT	562	62.3	340	37.7*	354	18.1	1386	70.7	221	11.3
DONLEY	445	63.0	261	37.0*	279	22.6	816	66.0	141	11.4
DUVAL	3265	89.1	400	10.9*	3739	86.0	322	7.4	286	6.6
EASTLAND	1808	64.0	1017	36.0*	1006	21.2	2984	63.0	745	15.7
ECTOR	4362	63.7	2482	36.3*	1504	15.8	6157	64.5	1879	19.7
EDWARDS	347	92.0	30	8.0*	27	4.7	530	91.7	21	3.6
ELLIS	3342	66.8	1663	33.2*	2270	25.4	5172	57.8	1509	16.9
ELPASO	12545	46.1	14667	53.9*	8928	23.2	11499	29.9	18010	46.9
ERATH	1937	68.3	899	31.7*	2031	35.6	3033	53.2	640	11.2
FALLS	2030	56.6	1554	43.4*	889	19.9	2852	64.0	718	16.1
FANNIN	2380	54.5	1983	45.5*	1542	24.8	3684	59.3	991	15.9
FAYETTE	1961	68.7	895	31.3*	735	15.6	2963	62.9	1012	21.5
FISHER	1070	58.5	759	41.5*	345	17.5	1359	68.7	273	13.8
FLOYD	1250	80.6	300	19.4*	701	29.3	1387	58.0	302	12.6
FOARD	299	73.8	106	26.2*	41	9.1	357	79.0	54	11.9
FORTBEND	4272	58.6	3018	41.4*	1124	13.8	4149	50.8	2888	35.4
FRANKLIN	1101	57.7	807	42.3*	341	23.2	919	62.4	213	14.5
FREESTONE	1490	54.5	1245	45.5*	938	30.3	1745	56.4	409	13.2
FRIO	1118	56.1	874	43.9*	171	6.5	2122	80.9	330	12.6
GAINES	1308	82.9	270	17.1*	342	18.4	1194	64.3	322	17.3
GALVESTON	8415	36.6	14577	63.4*	5022	15.8	8551	26.9	18203	57.3
GARZA	608	74.6	207	25.4*	175	14.8	721	61.2	283	24.0
GILLESPIE	634	88.4	83	11.6*	89	6.5	1134	83.3	138	10.1
GLASCOCK	104	77.6	30	22.4*	52	15.0	268	77.5	26	7.5
GOLIAD	405	57.9	294	42.1*	224	20.3	682	61.8	197	17.9
GONZALES	1559	78.1	438	21.9*	387	12.4	2370	75.9	364	11.7
GRAY	1357	59.2	936	40.8*	786	20.6	2501	65.6	526	13.8
GRAYSON	4908	52.1	4519	47.9*	3564	24.0	7688	51.7	3626	24.4
GREGG	5855	72.3	2247	27.7*	1978	14.2	10205	73.2	1761	12.6

```
              DEMOC.  RUNOFF      1968*      DEMOC.  GOVERNOR    1972
                                      *
    COUNTY      SMITH         D. YARBRO    BARNES        BRISCOE       FARENTHOLD
                #      %      #      %*    #      %      #      %      #      %
    --------------------------------------------------------------------------------------------------
    GRIMES      1304  56.4   1008  43.6*   789  25.2   1882  60.1    462  14.7
    GUADALUPE   1846  67.5    890  32.5*  1033  16.4   3945  62.7   1312  20.9
    HALE        3175  81.0    746  19.0*  1083  21.1   3199  62.4    843  16.4
    HALL         820  69.6    359  30.4*   327  23.0    971  68.2    125   8.8
    HAMILTON     971  75.6    314  24.4*   411  19.1   1538  71.5    201   9.3
                                      *
    HANSFORD     286  73.1    105  26.9*   300  26.2    728  63.6    117  10.2
    HARDEMAN     996  67.2    487  32.8*   171  15.3    771  69.0    176  15.7
    HARDIN      1765  37.5   2937  62.5*  1464  19.2   2910  38.2   3249  42.6
    HARRIS     81400  46.0  95616  54.0*  49378 18.5  92555  34.7  125066 46.8
    HARRISON    4370  63.1   2561  36.9*  2105  29.4   3895  54.5   1152  16.1
                                      *
    HARTLEY      319  72.5    121  27.5*   101  19.4    373  71.7     46   8.8
    HASKELL     1484  62.2    902  37.8*   538  19.8   1897  69.9    279  10.3
    HAYS        1756  56.8   1338  43.2*   746  11.7   3367  53.0   2237  35.2
    HEMPHILL     169  61.9    104  38.1*   170  22.8    455  60.9    122  16.3
    HENDERSON   1696  45.6   2020  54.4*  2262  27.5   4178  50.8   1789  21.7
                                      *
    HIDALGO    13619  46.4  15717  53.6*  6603  23.2  13297  46.7   8543  30.0
    HILL        2423  68.7   1103  31.3*  1022  17.9   4103  72.1    569  10.0
    HOCKLEY     2409  81.4    551  18.6*   671  17.6   2367  62.1    775  20.3
    HOOD         553  63.3    320  36.7*   732  29.2   1445  57.7    329  13.1
    HOPKINS     3065  64.4   1695  35.6*  1280  25.0   2969  58.0    871  17.0
                                      *
    HOUSTON     2217  46.3   2573  53.7*   708  14.0   2643  52.1   1721  33.9
    HOWARD      2311  45.6   2755  54.4*   734  14.9   2614  53.1   1576  32.0
    HUDSPETH     413  58.4    294  41.6*   129  25.9    295  59.1     75  15.0
    HUNT        3905  62.8   2312  37.2*  2385  25.4   3951  42.0   3063  32.6
    HUTCHISON   1240  48.2   1335  51.8*  1155  28.2   2286  55.8    659  16.1
                                      *
    IRION        272  70.5    114  29.5*    58  12.1    348  72.7     73  15.2
    JACK         765  69.9    330  30.1*   554  23.6   1314  56.0    478  20.4
    JACKSON     1826  60.0   1219  40.0*   453  12.5   2105  57.9   1079  29.7
    JASPER      1783  49.9   1788  50.1*  1230  20.2   2532  41.5   2337  38.3
    JEFFDAVIS    133  57.8     97  42.2*    41  10.8    271  71.1     69  18.1
                                      *
    JEFFERSON  11637  35.0  21629  65.0*  6715  15.2  18668  42.2  18881  42.7
    JIMHOGG      351  33.9    684  66.1*   518  30.0    383  22.2    826  47.8
    JIMWELLS    2888  32.2   6075  67.8*  2204  23.6   3079  33.0   4058  43.4
    JOHNSON     3172  58.9   2212  41.1*  2007  22.5   5075  57.0   1826  20.5
    JONES       2237  69.5    984  30.5*   511  15.0   2533  74.4    360  10.6
                                      *
    KARNES      2269  62.2   1379  37.8*   614  16.3   2512  66.7    639  17.0
    KAUFMAN     2357  69.2   1048  30.8*  1439  26.8   3064  57.0    873  16.2
    KENDALL      307  81.9     68  18.1*    75   9.4    608  76.4    113  14.2
    KENEDY        77  60.2     51  39.8*    28  16.3    105  61.0     39  22.7
    KENT         268  72.4    102  27.6*   134  21.8    418  68.1     62  10.1
                                      *
    KERR        1492  79.2    392  20.8*   433  10.2   3164  74.7    638  15.1
    KIMBLE       548  84.2    103  15.8*    57   4.7   1031  85.9    112   9.3
    KING          57  89.1      7  10.9*    41  24.4    112  66.7     15   8.9
    KINNEY       301  54.9    247  45.1*   116  23.5    348  70.4     30   6.1
    KLEBERG     1703  35.7   3061  64.3*   610   8.8   2916  42.0   3417  49.2
                                      *
    KNOX         721  78.3    200  21.7*   219  16.2    963  71.2    170  12.6
```

COUNTY	SMITH #	%	D. YARBRO #	%	BARNES #	%	BRISCOE #	%	FARENTHOLD #	%
LAMAR	3066	59.1	2124	40.9*	3042	34.7	4643	53.0	1080	12.3
LAMB	2723	80.8	646	19.2*	437	17.0	1856	72.4	271	10.6
LAMPASAS	1643	68.2	767	31.8*	298	11.0	2126	78.3	290	10.7
LASALLE	308	56.6	236	43.4*	167	13.4	966	77.7	110	8.8
LABACA	1685	72.2	648	27.8*	480	11.1	2580	59.6	1271	29.3
LEE	671	60.1	446	39.9*	427	17.1	1499	60.0	572	22.9
LEON	783	55.8	619	44.2*	395	16.7	1556	65.8	415	17.5
LIBERTY	3571	50.8	3464	49.2*	1325	17.4	3831	50.3	2457	32.3
LIMESTONE	1651	56.8	1257	43.2*	897	21.6	2755	66.4	499	12.0
LIPSCOMB	207	60.0	138	40.0*	226	35.8	348	55.1	58	9.2
LIVEOAK	1675	59.0	1164	41.0*	332	13.4	1692	68.4	448	18.1
LLANO	1091	71.6	433	28.4*	228	10.4	1632	74.8	322	14.8
LOVING	23	69.7	10	30.3*	18	25.0	45	62.5	9	12.5
LUBBOCK	20564	76.7	6238	23.3*	3556	15.5	11358	49.5	8036	35.0
LYNN	2122	86.0	345	14.0*	265	13.6	1325	67.9	360	18.5
MADISON	708	58.7	498	41.3*	654	27.8	1337	56.9	360	15.3
MARION	623	61.9	383	38.1*	436	24.5	1003	56.3	341	19.2
MARTIN	370	80.4	90	19.6*	142	17.8	534	66.9	122	15.3
MASON	1176	72.2	452	27.8*	135	10.8	972	78.1	138	11.1
MATAGORDA	3500	56.4	2702	43.6*	914	17.6	2719	52.4	1555	30.0
MAVERICK	620	49.7	627	50.3*	1360	45.1	1177	39.1	476	15.8
MCCULLOCH	999	75.2	330	24.8*	506	18.7	1985	73.5	209	7.7
MCLENNAN	13046	51.4	12313	48.6*	4726	13.7	20509	59.5	9240	26.8
MCMULLEN	169	72.5	64	27.5*	79	18.9	308	73.9	30	7.2
MEDINA	1184	63.8	671	36.2*	461	9.4	3782	76.8	681	13.8
MENARD	313	72.0	122	28.0*	114	12.1	708	75.2	119	12.6
MIDLAND	4564	67.7	2178	32.3*	1884	19.4	5741	59.2	2075	21.4
MILAN	1872	47.0	2109	53.0*	669	12.5	2905	54.5	1759	33.0
MILLS	480	75.8	153	24.2*	303	17.8	1222	71.8	177	10.4
MITCHELL	1004	62.1	613	37.9*	351	14.2	1761	71.2	362	14.6
MONTAGE	2363	64.6	1293	35.4*	656	18.9	2347	67.6	471	13.6
MONTGOMRY	3259	58.6	2306	41.4*	3023	23.2	5750	44.1	4266	32.7
MOORE	886	49.2	916	50.8*	605	29.0	1116	53.4	367	17.6
MORRIS	1042	59.9	698	40.1*	458	14.7	1904	61.3	746	24.0
MOTLEY	474	82.6	100	17.4*	182	24.3	472	62.9	96	12.8
NACDOCHES	3115	55.4	2509	44.6*	1156	12.5	4575	49.6	3500	37.9
NAVARRO	3850	52.4	3492	47.6*	2093	27.2	4356	56.6	1248	16.2
NEWTON	974	42.6	1312	57.4*	729	25.2	1060	36.6	1107	38.2
NOLAN	2394	63.9	1355	36.1*	639	16.3	2777	70.7	512	13.0
NUECES	16001	38.6	25459	61.4*	5918	11.9	19497	39.2	24292	48.9
OCHILTREE	491	77.9	139	22.1*	430	25.2	1088	63.7	191	11.2
OLDHAM	151	64.3	84	35.7*	110	22.7	320	66.0	55	11.3
ORANGE	5753	37.8	9468	62.2*	3132	18.2	6648	38.7	7395	43.1
PALOPINTO	2686	59.5	1832	40.5*	1507	27.0	3160	56.7	909	16.3
PANOLA	2853	65.1	1531	34.9*	804	17.0	3565	75.3	364	7.7
PARKER	3274	56.2	2548	43.8*	1586	20.2	4480	57.1	1783	22.7

```
        DEMOC.  RUNOFF   1968*      DEMOC.  GOVERNOR   1972
                           *
COUNTY    SMITH      D. YARBRO   BARNES      BRISCOE    FARENTHOLD
          #     %    #     %*    #     %     #     %     #     %
-------------------------------------------------------------------------------------------------

PARMER    854  77.6  246  22.4*   226  16.8   978  72.6   143  10.6
PECOS    1252  58.6  883  41.4*   363  14.7  1744  70.6   363  14.7
POLK     1912  51.3 1812  48.7*   938  21.7  2124  49.1  1261  29.2
POTTER   3580  40.4 5286  59.6*  3811  32.7  5544  47.6  2290  19.7
PRESIDIO  713  50.5  699  49.5*   223  22.1   686  68.0   100   9.9
                           *
RAINES    282  57.7  207  42.3*   394  29.6   759  57.1   176  13.2
RANDALL  2886  53.3 2527  46.7*  2166  26.3  4526  54.9  1557  18.9
REAGAN    292  79.6   75  20.4*   134  16.2   564  68.4   127  15.4
REAL      332  93.5   23   6.5*    46   7.2   575  90.3    16   2.5
REDRIVER 2594  68.4 1198  31.6*   882  20.2  3078  70.5   408   9.3
                           *
REEVES   1166  69.8  504  30.2*   491  17.0  1866  64.8   523  18.2
REFUGIO  1191  61.0  763  39.0*   390  14.0  1405  50.4   992  35.6
ROBERTS   111  66.1   57  33.9*    77  32.2   136  56.9    26  10.9
ROBERTSON 1513 40.8 2191  59.2*   584  14.9  2175  55.4  1167  29.7
ROCKWALL  698  75.8  223  24.2*   735  32.3  1199  52.6   345  15.1
                           *
RUNNELLS 1966  79.6  505  20.4*   428  15.2  2142  76.1   245   8.7
RUSK     3793  53.7 3268  46.3*  1732  21.9  5017  63.5  1151  14.6
SABINE    461  51.2  440  48.8*   512  25.3   969  47.9   542  26.8
SNAUGSTNE 548  57.3  408  42.7*   427  19.6  1241  56.8   515  23.6
SNJACINTO 526  42.6  710  57.4*   506  25.9   885  45.3   564  28.8
                           *
SNPATRICIO 3174 43.4 4145 56.6*  1412  13.0  4936  45.3  4554  41.8
SANSABA  1440  67.7  688  32.3*   310  15.9  1469  75.6   165   8.5
SCHLEICHER 498 71.6  198  28.4*   116  13.2   648  74.0   112  12.8
SCURRY   1647  62.2 1003  37.8*   520  12.8  3061  75.4   479  11.8
SHACKELFRD 926 64.1  519  35.9*   261  18.8   973  70.2   152  11.0
                           *
SHELBY   2781  49.7 2811  50.3*  1284  23.8  3163  58.7   940  17.4
SHERMAN   317  60.4  208  39.6*   160  29.0   329  59.7    62  11.3
SMITH    6760  52.9 6011  47.1*  2714  15.2 11378  63.9  3716  20.9
SOMERVELL 272  58.4  194  41.6*   226  22.0   684  66.5   118  11.5
STARR    1337  31.9 2854  68.1*  1176  35.5  1612  48.7   521  15.7
                           *
STEPHENS 1706  63.4  983  36.6*   689  21.9  2044  65.0   412  13.1
STERLING  159  78.7   43  21.3*    19   7.7   205  83.0    23   9.3
STONEWALL 463  60.8  299  39.2*   162  20.5   561  70.8    69   8.7
SUTTON    328  79.2   86  20.8*    61  10.5   461  79.3    59  10.2
SWISHER   970  50.2  962  49.8*   763  40.1   797  41.8   345  18.1
                           *
TARRANT 34552 58.0 25012 42.0* 25313  23.8 46375  43.5 34852  32.7
TAYLOR   8431  69.0 3791  31.0*  2661  16.4 10743  66.4  2775  17.2
TERRELL   185  64.5  102  35.5*    50  10.7   345  74.0    71  15.2
TERRY    1866  80.2  461  19.8*   499  19.9  1545  61.7   459  18.3
THRCKMORTN 676 64.8  368  35.2*   221  20.6   722  67.4   129  12.0
                           *
TITUS    2457  55.6 1961  44.4*   743  20.2  2291  62.2   651  17.7
TOMGREEN 5020  68.5 2310  31.5*  1665  13.2  7903  62.8  3026  24.0
TRAVIS  24841 57.2 18625 42.8*  8261  10.0 34234  41.6 39828  48.4
TRINITY   573  48.4  612  51.6*   406  16.8  1394  57.8   611  25.3
TYLER    1551  48.9 1624  51.1*   776  22.3  1679  48.2  1030  29.6
                           *
UPSHUR   1497  45.8 1770  54.2*  1063  19.4  3608  65.9   802  14.7
```

COUNTY	DEMOC. RUNOFF 1968*		DEMOC. GOVERNOR 1972						
	SMITH		D. YARBRO		BARNES		BRISCOE		FARENTHOLD	
	#	%	#	%*	#	%	#	%	#	%
UPTON	731	66.5	369	33.5*	216	21.0	662	64.2	153	14.8
UVALDE	2216	74.0	779	26.0*	207	4.2	4445	91.1	229	4.7
VALVERDE	1017	53.8	872	46.2*	1160	29.0	2264	56.6	577	14.4
VANZANDT	1534	53.2	1350	46.8*	1183	21.4	3580	64.8	760	13.8
VICTORIA	4346	56.4	3355	43.6*	2308	18.2	6843	54.0	3530	27.8
WALKER	1699	56.9	1288	43.1*	1032	18.2	2493	43.9	2152	37.9
WALLER	733	53.1	647	46.9*	920	27.3	1736	51.5	713	21.2
WARD	1707	58.2	1228	41.8*	421	19.6	1399	65.3	324	15.1
WASHINGTON	1263	77.2	373	22.8*	417	11.2	2794	74.8	526	14.1
WEBB	4124	51.8	3838	48.2*	5191	46.3	3588	32.0	2439	21.7
WHARTON	2573	64.4	1420	35.6*	1319	21.8	2680	44.3	2047	33.9
WHEELER	761	61.2	483	38.8*	248	20.7	836	69.9	112	9.4
WICHITA	7084	56.3	5509	43.7*	2709	14.2	10795	56.6	5567	29.2
WILBARGER	1764	80.1	438	19.9*	431	17.7	1706	69.9	304	12.5
WILLACY	1466	57.8	1072	42.2*	817	25.0	1916	58.7	533	16.3
WILLIAMSON	4155	72.3	1589	27.7*	691	8.8	5129	65.7	1990	25.5
WILSON	2659	56.8	2025	43.2*	885	19.4	2966	65.1	704	15.5
WINKLER	1954	64.9	1057	35.1*	641	23.6	1660	61.1	415	15.3
WISE	1661	67.2	809	32.8*	915	18.8	3212	66.0	740	15.2
WOOD	2370	51.7	2212	48.3*	891	21.5	2652	64.0	601	14.5
YOAKUM	1019	82.7	213	17.3*	296	16.0	1210	65.3	346	18.7
YOUNG	1915	69.9	826	30.1*	652	17.1	2520	66.0	647	16.9
ZAPATA	506	80.2	125	19.8*	401	32.2	514	41.3	329	26.4
ZAVALA	801	61.9	492	38.1*	62	4.5	1233	90.3	70	5.1
TOTALS	767490		621226	*	392358		963417		612051	
% OF VOTE	55.3		44.7	*	19.9		49.0		31.1	

GEOGRAPHIC CLASS

LOWLANDS	262157	49.	268051	51.*	141869	19.	347766	46.	269805	36.
BLACK BELT	6252	59.	4301	41.*	4551	25.	9694	53.	3937	22.
WEST TEXAS	431430	61.	279262	39.*	200612	20.	519950	52.	281827	28.
MEX. TEXAS	67651	49.	69612	51.*	44813	24.	84770	46.	56084	30.

DEMOGRAPHIC CLASS

METRO	405485	52.	367963	48.*	217841	20.	468271	42.	418863	38.
TOWN	67442	52.	63331	48.*	38114	21.	94126	52.	48662	27.
RURAL	294563	61.	189932	39.*	136403	20.	401020	59.	144526	21.

```
           DEMOC.  RUNOFF    1972*       DEMOC.  SENATOR    1952
                                  *
  COUNTY      BRISCOE      FARENTHOLD  DANIEL       BECKWORTH   NAPIER
             #      %      #      %*    #      %    #      %     #     %
-------------------------------------------------------------------------------------------------------
ANDERSON    5638 73.8    1997 26.2*  4220 67.3   1797 28.6    256  4.1
ANDREWS     1149 62.9     679 37.1*  1024 67.9    373 24.8    110  7.3
ANGELINA    7703 52.8    6897 47.2*  7132 67.4   3162 29.9    280  2.6
ARANSAS     1134 60.1     752 39.9*   744 76.3    188 19.3     43  4.4
ARCHER      1019 66.3     519 33.7*  1150 56.7    269 13.3    611 30.1
                                  *
ARMSTRONG    436 78.8     117 21.2*   737 82.6     82  9.2     73  8.2
ATASCOSA    3529 70.5    1474 29.5*  2653 82.1    431 13.3    147  4.5
AUSTIN      2066 63.1    1207 36.9*  3052 83.8    524 14.4     64  1.8
BAILEY       994 76.8     300 23.2*  1439 78.5    239 13.0    154  8.4
BANDERA     1586 74.1     553 25.9*  1284 84.6    187 12.3     47  3.1

BASTROP     2567 70.6    1070 29.4*  2894 74.2    859 22.0    146  3.7
BAYLOR      1185 68.3     549 31.7*  1393 69.6    195  9.7    413 20.6
BEE         2407 64.2    1345 35.8*  3008 83.0    467 12.9    148  4.1
BELL       10217 61.2    6468 38.8*  9420 75.2   2643 21.1    460  3.7
BEXAR      72207 55.8   57218 44.2* 25469 75.3   5245 15.5   3123  9.2

BLANCO       641 79.4     166 20.6*   347 78.2     87 19.6     10  2.3
BORDEN       267 74.2      93 25.8*   285 83.1     31  9.0     27  7.9
BOSQUE      2288 73.7     817 26.3*  2527 73.7    762 22.2    142  4.1
BOWIE       6891 57.5    5098 42.5*  8495 72.4   2776 23.7    465  4.0
BRAZORIA    9340 43.1   12336 56.9*  9330 75.4   2639 21.3    404  3.3

BRAZOS      6634 54.8    5471 45.2*  4746 74.8   1472 23.2    125  2.0
BREWSTER     729 66.5     368 33.5*  1031 84.9    167 13.8     16  1.3
BRISCOE      470 75.8     150 24.2*   862 87.1     63  6.4     65  6.6
BROOKS      1081 32.8    2213 67.2*  1034 75.7    221 16.2    111  8.1
BROWN       3972 77.8    1133 22.2*  5021 74.1   1537 22.7    214  3.2
                                  *
BURLESON    1992 53.5    1731 46.5*  2369 70.1    841 24.9    168  5.0
BURNET      2349 71.8     924 28.2*  2056 84.4    280 11.5     99  4.1
CALDWELL    2780 73.8     989 26.2*  3141 81.6    613 15.9     94  2.4
CALHOUN     2536 48.0    2751 52.0*  1728 90.4    142  7.4     41  2.1
CALLAHAN    1775 75.1     590 24.9*  1639 65.1    658 26.2    219  8.7
                                  *
CAMERON    11369 51.7   10617 48.3*  7590 79.6   1088 11.4    860  9.0
CAMP        1608 64.8     873 35.2*   996 39.0   1541 60.3     19   .7
CARSON       857 63.7     489 36.3*  1239 73.0    353 20.8    106  6.2
CASS        2681 64.4    1479 35.6*  3669 77.8    965 20.5     83  1.8
CASTRO      1104 71.5     439 28.5*  1346 80.6    252 15.1     72  4.3
                                  *
CHAMBERS    1605 54.9    1317 45.1*  1695 83.8    275 13.6     53  2.6
CHEROKEE    4237 62.0    2592 38.0*  4438 61.0   2597 35.7    246  3.4
CHILDRESS   1026 79.6     263 20.4*  2230 67.9    487 14.8    567 17.3
CLAY        1538 64.4     851 35.6*  1692 61.8    358 13.1    689 25.2
COCHRAN      984 69.9     423 30.1*  1353 79.8    200 11.8    142  8.4

COKE         691 77.9     196 22.1*  1010 74.3    286 21.0     64  4.7
COLEMAN     1830 78.8     492 21.2*  2961 73.5    817 20.3    253  6.3
COLLIN      6203 66.3    3147 33.7*  4870 72.2   1491 22.1    385  5.7
CLNGSWORTH  1170 79.5     301 20.5*  1976 80.5    208  8.5    271 11.0
COLORADO    3083 61.2    1958 38.8*  3845 86.3    481 10.8    128  2.9
                                  *
COMAL       2498 70.4    1050 29.6*  3258 87.5    381 10.2     84  2.3
```

```
         DEMOC.  RUNOFF     1972*       DEMOC.  SENATOR    1952
                               *
COUNTY       BRISCOE      FARENTHOLD    DANIEL        BECKWORTH     NAPIER
             #      %     #      %*     #      %      #      %      #      %
--------------------------------------------------------------------------------------------------
COMANCHEE   2864 72.9   1066 27.1*    2539 60.6    1293 30.9     355  8.5
CONCHO       771 77.1    229 22.9*    1048 77.1     257 18.9      55  4.0
COOKE       3616 70.7   1501 29.3*    4188 76.2     902 16.4     407  7.4
CORYELL     2869 74.2    999 25.8*    2515 73.5     798 23.3     110  3.2
COTTLE       531 73.0    196 27.0*    1066 70.9     198 13.2     239 15.9
                               *
CRANE        839 72.0    326 28.0*    1040 73.1     259 18.2     124  8.7
CROCKETT     761 69.3    337 30.7*     648 76.2     149 17.5      53  6.2
CROSBY      1206 73.5    434 26.5*    1570 73.0     359 16.7     223 10.4
CULBERSON    341 76.3    106 23.7*     362 74.9     100 20.7      21  4.3
DALLAM       373 62.9    220 37.1*    1806 80.6     264 11.8     171  7.6
                               *
DALLAS     90489 53.0  80153 47.0*   43430 67.7   18501 28.8    2260  3.5
DAWSON      1953 76.3    605 23.7*    3486 85.2     402  9.8     205  5.0
DEAFSMITH   1714 77.4    500 22.6*    2280 82.4     335 12.1     152  5.5
DELTA       1040 70.6    433 29.4*    1379 65.8     621 29.6      95  4.5
DENTON      9249 55.7   7360 44.3*    5528 67.8    2197 26.9     432  5.3
                               *
DEWITT      2375 70.5    996 29.5*    3517 92.0     251  6.6      55  1.4
DICKENS      584 66.3    297 33.7*    1413 72.5     272 14.0     263 13.5
DIMMIT      1226 64.1    686 35.9*    1076 82.4     178 13.6      52  4.0
DONLEY       764 70.3    323 29.7*    1433 79.7     204 11.3     161  9.0
DUVAL       3424 79.4    889 20.6*    2822 92.2     198  6.5      41  1.3
                               *
EASTLAND    3053 69.5   1340 30.5*    4672 65.8    1885 26.6     538  7.6
ECTOR       7450 68.8   3374 31.2*    6569 77.3    1441 16.9     492  5.8
EDWARDS      452 92.4     37  7.6*     677 89.7      50  6.6      28  3.7
ELLIS       4183 66.7   2086 33.3*    5201 70.1    1933 26.1     283  3.8
ELPASO     18099 38.8  28518 61.2*   14563 75.6    4114 21.4     582  3.0
                               *
ERATH       3885 71.7   1533 28.3*    2743 62.5    1415 32.3     228  5.2
FALLS       2423 64.0   1363 36.0*    1796 65.2     876 31.8      84  3.0
FANNIN      3477 69.1   1557 30.9*    5085 67.1    1806 23.8     684  9.0
FAYETTE     2723 60.8   1752 39.2*    3925 80.4     523 10.7     436  8.9
FISHER      1079 71.0    440 29.0*    1762 68.5     526 20.4     285 11.1
                               *
FLOYD       1730 75.3    567 24.7*    2500 82.2     330 10.9     211  6.9
FOARD        303 80.2     75 19.8*     837 71.9     135 11.6     192 16.5
FORTBEND    4220 52.0   3900 48.0*    3293 79.4     727 17.5     125  3.0
FRANKLIN     764 75.8    244 24.2*    1281 64.0     669 33.4      53  2.6
FREESTONE   2365 69.9   1019 30.1*    3081 78.9     671 17.2     155  4.0
                               *
FRIO        1763 77.5    512 22.5*    1367 84.4     160  9.9      93  5.7
GAINES      1484 64.8    805 35.2*    1933 72.2     461 17.2     282 10.5
GALVESTON  10848 33.0  22014 67.0*   13250 76.4    3099 17.9     989  5.7
GARZA        702 57.6    517 42.4*    1094 73.8     225 15.2     163 11.0
GILLESPIE   1119 79.2    294 20.8*    1525 94.7      69  4.3      16  1.0
                               *
GLASCOCK     199 81.9     44 18.1*     321 76.8      64 15.3      33  7.9
GOLIAD       645 65.0    347 35.0*     512 90.8      36  6.4      16  2.8
GONZALES    2168 78.4    598 21.6*    2322 86.8     284 10.6      68  2.5
GRAY        2185 68.9    988 31.1*    3285 81.0     455 11.2     316  7.8
GRAYSON     7701 64.0   4335 36.0*    8297 66.5    3369 27.0     816  6.5
                               *
GREGG       9702 78.9   2598 21.1*    4908 42.6    6456 56.0     157  1.4
```

```
           DEMOC.  RUNOFF    1972*      DEMOC.  SENATOR   1952
                               *
 COUNTY       BRISCOE      FARENTHOLD   DANIEL        BECKWORTH    NAPIER
            #      %      #      %*     #      %      #      %      #      %
--------------------------------------------------------------------------------------------------
GRIMES     2138  64.0   1205  36.0*  1250  84.6    197  13.3     30   2.0
GUADALUPE  3608  64.7   1970  35.3*  1212  87.4    116   8.4     59   4.3
HALE       3845  73.6   1378  26.4*  3403  83.9    466  11.5    185   4.6
HALL       1124  76.0    355  24.0*  1951  78.9    296  12.0    227   9.2
HAMILTON   1370  75.9    436  24.1*  2357  79.2    439  14.7    181   6.1
                               *
HANSFORD    824  76.9    247  23.1*   780  85.3     91  10.0     43   4.7
HARDEMAN    676  67.9    320  32.1*  1915  75.0    317  12.4    322  12.6
HARDIN     4454  50.6   4343  49.4*  3574  73.9   1138  23.5    127   2.6
HARRIS   111678  38.8 176244  61.2* 86211  73.1  28108  23.8   3537   3.0
HARRISON   4858  65.4   2566  34.6*  4078  59.0   2672  38.6    166   2.4
                               *
HARTLEY     396  69.6    173  30.4*   606  81.3     90  12.1     49   6.6
HASKELL    1518  77.8    432  22.2*  2015  59.5    796  23.5    576  17.0
HAYS       3292  59.9   2203  40.1*  1719  81.5    324  15.4     66   3.1
HEMPHILL    293  59.9    196  40.1*   835  79.2    123  11.7     96   9.1
HENDERSON  4953  62.7   2947  37.3*  3714  55.6   2464  36.9    507   7.6

HIDALGO   16907  53.0  15002  47.0* 12837  87.2   1135   7.7    755   5.1
HILL       4691  76.6   1436  23.4*  5690  79.3   1225  17.1    262   3.7
HOCKLEY    3076  68.9   1391  31.1*  3229  69.6    862  18.6    547  11.8
HOOD       1634  71.0    668  29.0*  1338  67.8    474  24.0    161   8.2
HOPKINS    3583  72.2   1378  27.8*  3833  67.1   1709  29.9    168   2.9
                               *
HOUSTON    2556  59.5   1740  40.5*  3115  70.9   1157  26.3    121   2.8
HOWARD     2865  60.5   1867  39.5*  4200  68.1   1664  27.0    305   4.9
HUDSPETH    300  66.4    152  33.6*   442  74.0    123  20.6     32   5.4
HUNT       4233  57.5   3128  42.5*  5663  74.5   1721  22.6    219   2.9
HUTCHISON  1944  60.1   1292  39.9*  4467  74.2   1136  18.9    416   6.9
                               *
IRION       309  72.2    119  27.8*   432  75.8    108  18.9     30   5.3
JACK       1773  69.5    777  30.5*  1425  64.2    367  17.1    358  16.7
JACKSON    2052  60.8   1321  39.2*  2493  79.7    524  16.7    112   3.6
JASPER     3665  50.4   3613  49.6*  3129  77.8    801  19.9     93   2.3
JEFFDAVIS   204  65.2    109  34.8*   335  76.8     78  17.9     23   5.3
                               *
JEFFERSON 20063  45.8  23758  54.2* 17877  63.2   9008  31.8   1398   4.9
JIMHOGG     542  32.2   1142  67.8*   556  87.6     66  10.4     13   2.0
JIMWELLS   3555  41.9   4931  58.1*  4777  83.2    762  13.3    202   3.5
JOHNSON    6082  68.3   2829  31.7*  3761  74.0   1110  21.8    214   4.2
JONES      2465  73.7    880  26.3*  3040  65.3   1134  24.4    483  10.4
                               *
KARNES     2544  68.8   1152  31.2*  3447  91.5    253   6.7     68   1.8
KAUFMAN    2808  68.6   1283  31.4*  3878  64.4   1964  32.6    179   3.0
KENDALL     660  76.2    206  23.8*   341  87.0     42  10.7      9   2.3
KENEDY      111  63.4     64  36.6*    66  78.6     17  20.2      1   1.2
KENT        538  78.7    146  21.3*   476  61.9    241  31.3     52   6.8
                               *
KERR       2518  75.5    817  24.5*  3337  85.4    463  11.9    106   2.7
KIMBLE     1015  84.3    189  15.7*  1024  79.8    181  14.1     79   6.2
KING         95  81.9     21  18.1*   108  74.0     20  13.9     16  11.1
KINNEY      335  69.1    150  30.9*   119  76.3     32  20.5      5   3.2
KLEBERG    3093  45.8   3658  54.2*  2671  72.6    858  23.3    152   4.1
                               *
KNOX       1080  74.5    370  25.5*  1465  65.0    485  21.5    304  13.5
```

	DEMOC. RUNOFF 1972*				DEMOC. SENATOR 1952				

COUNTY	BRISCOE		FARENTHOLD		DANIEL		BECKWORTH		NAPIER	
	#	%	#	%*	#	%	#	%	#	%
LAMAR	6647	69.5	2917	30.5*	6941	79.2	1396	15.9	427	4.9
LAMB	1913	74.6	652	25.4*	3341	79.9	459	11.0	380	9.1
LAMPASAS	1686	77.6	486	22.4*	1843	82.8	323	14.5	61	2.7
LASALLE	887	80.1	221	19.9*	897	85.4	112	10.7	41	3.9
LABACA	2272	65.4	1200	34.6*	3337	85.9	414	10.7	132	3.4
LEE	1414	65.2	755	34.8*	1981	82.5	341	14.2	79	3.3
LEON	1243	66.4	628	33.6*	2036	74.3	656	24.0	47	1.7
LIBERTY	4241	49.2	4374	50.8*	5593	83.2	915	13.6	213	3.2
LIMESTONE	3064	72.8	1145	27.2*	4701	78.7	1077	18.0	199	3.3
LIPSCOMB	259	62.9	153	37.1*	523	81.8	66	10.3	50	7.8
LIVEOAK	1651	76.7	502	23.3*	1841	88.5	168	8.1	72	3.5
LLANO	1488	73.0	549	27.0*	1470	82.4	251	14.1	63	3.5
LOVING	39	92.9	3	7.1*	53	82.8	7	10.9	4	6.3
LUBBOCK	16509	58.7	11623	41.3*	12042	75.9	2363	14.9	1457	9.2
LYNN	1484	75.3	488	24.7*	2069	77.1	383	14.3	232	8.6
MADISON	1195	65.9	617	34.1*	1502	80.7	255	13.7	105	5.6
MARION	1325	61.7	822	38.3*	1170	61.4	670	35.2	66	3.5
MARTIN	490	73.5	177	26.5*	1086	73.5	300	20.3	91	6.2
MASON	899	79.8	227	20.2*	1287	85.0	170	11.2	58	3.8
MATAGORDA	2565	54.4	2150	45.6*	4028	86.6	467	10.0	157	3.4
MAVERICK	1386	43.6	1790	56.4*	1046	89.2	95	8.1	32	2.7
MCCULLOCH	1973	81.8	440	18.2*	2497	82.5	375	12.4	154	5.1
MCLENNAN	21532	60.6	13996	39.4*	15716	72.2	5235	24.1	806	3.7
MCMULLEN	275	84.1	52	15.9*	327	85.6	46	12.0	9	2.4
MEDINA	2929	75.7	941	24.3*	879	86.3	120	11.8	20	2.0
MENARD	508	74.4	175	25.6*	954	75.2	243	19.2	71	5.6
MIDLAND	5739	64.4	3172	35.6*	4719	78.2	1031	17.1	283	4.7
MILAN	2991	57.2	2239	42.8*	3670	77.9	801	17.0	238	5.1
MILLS	995	80.7	238	19.3*	1392	69.9	510	25.6	88	4.4
MITCHELL	1104	70.4	464	29.6*	2130	67.9	824	26.3	181	5.8
MONTAGE	1906	72.6	721	27.4*	3465	70.7	638	13.0	795	16.2
MONTGOMRY	6430	53.1	5675	46.9*	4587	81.5	795	14.1	246	4.4
MOORE	1170	61.8	724	38.2*	2158	71.0	728	24.0	152	5.0
MORRIS	2454	62.0	1507	38.0*	1567	60.3	975	37.5	57	2.2
MOTLEY	439	75.4	143	24.6*	909	79.6	99	8.7	134	11.7
NACDOCHES	4949	57.5	3658	42.5*	4521	69.9	1607	24.9	337	5.2
NAVARRO	5377	67.6	2580	32.4*	5355	72.7	1724	23.4	289	3.9
NEWTON	1877	46.6	2155	53.4*	1860	79.2	396	16.9	93	4.0
NOLAN	2630	73.2	963	26.8*	3728	68.3	908	16.6	825	15.1
NUECES	24001	46.8	27321	53.2*	17391	75.0	4465	19.2	1342	5.8
OCHILTREE	924	82.1	202	17.9*	1404	86.0	138	8.5	90	5.5
OLDHAM	294	72.4	112	27.6*	424	77.2	94	17.1	31	5.6
ORANGE	7988	46.5	9195	53.5*	7694	79.9	1620	16.8	314	3.3
PALOPINTO	3343	69.0	1501	31.0*	2870	64.1	1302	29.1	306	6.8
PANOLA	3498	78.3	969	21.7*	2358	41.0	3314	57.6	79	1.4
PARKER	5642	69.4	2492	30.6*	3429	68.1	1174	23.3	432	8.6

COUNTY	DEMOC. RUNOFF 1972* BRISCOE # %	FARENTHOLD # %*	DEMOC. SENATOR 1952 DANIEL # %	BECKWORTH # %	NAPIER # %
PARMER	988 79.4	256 20.6*	1018 82.3	134 10.8	85 6.9
PECOS	1394 65.7	727 34.3*	1894 78.2	371 15.3	158 6.5
POLK	2566 55.8	2035 44.2*	2718 75.9	712 19.9	149 4.2
POTTER	5550 52.6	4995 47.4*	5148 79.4	1050 16.2	286 4.4
PRESIDIO	469 75.6	151 24.4*	806 79.2	161 15.8	51 5.0
RAINES	579 67.0	285 33.0*	1016 81.1	212 16.9	25 2.0
RANDALL	2798 37.1	4736 62.9*	3044 81.2	483 12.9	221 5.9
REAGAN	413 71.1	168 28.9*	693 78.1	147 16.6	47 5.3
REAL	506 92.8	39 7.2*	508 83.3	65 10.7	37 6.1
REDRIVER	2976 72.6	1125 27.4*	3630 70.8	1261 24.6	236 4.6
REEVES	1327 68.4	612 31.6*	1904 76.4	477 19.1	110 4.4
REFUGIO	1845 56.6	1414 43.4*	1528 84.7	220 12.2	57 3.2
ROBERTS	196 78.7	53 21.3*	193 86.2	17 7.6	14 6.3
ROBERTSON	1802 50.6	1757 49.4*	2237 73.0	739 24.1	89 2.9
ROCKWALL	1042 71.9	408 28.1*	1281 70.5	449 24.7	86 4.7
RUNNELLS	1918 80.9	452 19.1*	1938 79.0	413 16.8	103 4.2
RUSK	5740 73.8	2043 26.2*	4300 42.6	5330 52.8	470 4.7
SABINE	884 54.3	743 45.7*	1959 79.2	408 16.5	106 4.3
SNAUGSTNE	1400 58.9	975 41.1*	1711 70.4	522 21.5	199 8.2
SNJACINTO	746 49.8	753 50.2*	759 78.7	170 17.6	36 3.7
SNPATRICIO	5440 51.3	5158 48.7*	3458 77.9	877 19.7	106 2.4
SANSABA	1216 79.7	310 20.3*	1309 71.9	425 23.4	86 4.7
SCHLEICHER	647 80.0	162 20.0*	907 82.5	141 12.8	51 4.6
SCURRY	2864 74.6	977 25.4*	3419 73.0	912 19.5	355 7.6
SHACKELFRD	728 75.0	243 25.0*	1340 73.5	328 18.0	154 8.5
SHELBY	4118 63.8	2341 36.2*	4337 60.5	2657 37.0	178 2.5
SHERMAN	298 72.0	116 28.0*	634 80.3	102 12.9	54 6.8
SMITH	13157 67.9	6206 32.1*	7560 48.3	7966 50.9	130 .8
SOMERVELL	640 73.8	227 26.2*	716 78.7	149 16.4	45 4.9
STARR	3297 64.0	1852 36.0*	3451 92.6	256 6.9	21 .6
STEPHENS	2248 68.4	1039 31.6*	2627 76.1	629 18.2	194 5.6
STERLING	184 79.3	48 20.7*	300 80.0	55 14.7	20 5.3
STONEWALL	540 74.5	185 25.5*	769 67.2	202 17.7	173 15.1
SUTTON	398 77.4	116 22.6*	404 82.8	78 16.0	6 1.2
SWISHER	1128 60.5	737 39.5*	2029 87.2	199 8.6	99 4.3
TARRANT	57097 55.4	46027 44.6*	43983 71.7	13573 22.1	3808 6.2
TAYLOR	10292 70.0	4420 30.0*	8953 70.0	3013 23.6	822 6.4
TERRELL	286 77.5	83 22.5*	143 69.4	55 26.7	8 3.9
TERRY	1748 74.8	589 25.2*	2919 79.9	369 10.1	364 10.0
THRCKMORTN	460 71.5	183 28.5*	819 62.0	278 21.0	225 17.0
TITUS	2353 71.8	923 28.2*	3294 63.7	1717 33.2	158 3.1
TOMGREEN	7581 65.8	3940 34.2*	7887 73.6	2106 19.7	720 6.7
TRAVIS	44408 51.4	41915 48.6*	22923 77.5	5614 19.0	1023 3.5
TRINITY	1092 51.6	1026 48.4*	1538 71.5	452 21.0	160 7.4
TYLER	2116 55.3	1707 44.7*	2277 86.5	307 11.7	49 1.9
UPSHUR	3077 73.6	1101 26.4*	1516 25.0	4486 74.1	51 .8

```
DEMOC. RUNOFF    1972*   DEMOC. SENATOR   1952
                                 *
COUNTY    BRISCOE      FARENTHOLD  DANIEL       BECKWORTH    NAPIER
          #      %     #      %*   #      %     #      %     #      %
```

COUNTY	BRISCOE #	%	FARENTHOLD #	%*	DANIEL #	%	BECKWORTH #	%	NAPIER #	%
UPTON	596	66.3	303	33.7*	1154	77.8	251	16.9	78	5.3
UVALDE	4376	92.5	354	7.5*	2462	88.0	248	8.9	87	3.1
VALVERDE	2210	56.2	1723	43.8*	1677	83.1	281	13.9	61	3.0
VANZANDT	3324	70.5	1390	29.5*	2194	34.5	4044	63.6	116	1.8
VICTORIA	5964	57.4	4430	42.6*	3867	83.4	605	13.0	167	3.6
WALKER	2771	50.3	2733	49.7*	2679	83.8	416	13.0	102	3.2
WALLER	1645	58.1	1186	41.9*	1972	85.3	274	11.8	67	2.9
WARD	1153	71.6	457	28.4*	2086	71.7	622	21.4	202	6.9
WASHINGTON	3519	73.2	1287	26.8*	2552	85.5	374	12.5	59	2.0
WEBB	7208	61.5	4519	38.5*	6105	98.5	71	1.1	20	.3
WHARTON	3158	50.1	3145	49.9*	6086	84.1	851	11.8	298	4.1
WHEELER	787	75.1	261	24.9*	1624	74.6	330	15.2	224	10.3
WICHITA	8447	54.1	7153	45.9*	8117	52.0	2531	16.2	4976	31.8
WILBARGER	1945	78.2	541	21.8*	3188	68.5	673	14.5	794	17.1
WILLACY	2034	58.3	1455	41.7*	2462	82.9	310	10.4	199	6.7
WILLIAMSON	5355	70.5	2244	29.5*	4567	80.7	879	15.5	210	3.7
WILSON	3123	70.3	1318	29.7*	2900	83.0	475	13.6	119	3.4
WINKLER	1952	66.7	975	33.3*	1775	78.7	341	15.1	138	6.1
WISE	2849	75.9	905	24.1*	3641	71.6	914	18.0	533	10.5
WOOD	3065	73.6	1097	26.4*	2086	44.2	2575	54.5	63	1.3
YOAKUM	1336	71.7	528	28.3*	1048	77.8	161	12.0	138	10.2
YOUNG	2080	67.7	991	32.3*	2809	74.2	554	14.6	423	11.2
ZAPATA	366	47.0	412	53.0*	398	94.1	13	3.1	12	2.8
ZAVALA	1059	92.5	86	7.5*	1199	89.4	109	8.1	33	2.5

```
                      *
TOTALS    1100599     889544  * 940770      285843       70232
% OF VOTE    55.3       44.7  *   72.5         22.0          5.4
                      *
GEOGRAPHIC CLASS      *
                      *
LOWLANDS   394291 51. 385445 49.* 360933 69.  142592 27.   18024  3.
BLACK BELT  10376 59.   7084 41.*  10216 67.    4525 30.     424  3.
WEST TEXAS 591873 59. 405170 41.* 479317 74.  124234 19.   47263  7.
MEX. TEXAS 104059 53.  91845 47.*  86116 83.   13590 13.    4114  4.
                      *
DEMOGRAPHIC CLASS     *
                      *
METRO      578603 49. 591476 51.* 391692 72.  124018 23.   29693  5.
TOWN       102467 58.  73932 42.*  88421 72.   29027 24.    5406  4.
RURAL      419529 65. 224136 35.* 460657 73.  132798 21.   35133  6.
```

SOUTHERN ELECTIONS/292

	DEMOC. SENATOR 1954*					DEMOC. SENATOR 1957					
COUNTY	DOUGHERTY		JOHNSON		DIES		HUTCHESON		R. YARBRO		OTHER	
	#	%	#	%*	#	%	#	%	#	%	#	%
ANDERSON	2553	35.2	4696	64.8*	1394	43.0	338	10.4	1380	42.6	130	4.0
ANDREWS	352	22.7	1202	77.3*	197	21.1	170	18.2	497	53.3	69	7.4
ANGELINA	3022	32.0	6430	68.0*	2646	46.5	356	6.3	2556	44.9	130	2.3
ARANSAS	357	40.2	531	59.8*	111	19.6	173	30.5	242	42.7	41	7.2
ARCHER	440	25.3	1296	74.7*	159	18.2	116	13.3	465	53.3	133	15.2
ARMSTRONG	106	14.2	638	85.8*	102	29.2	38	10.9	181	51.9	28	8.0
ATASCOSA	1298	39.2	2011	60.8*	600	30.7	400	20.5	860	44.0	95	4.9
AUSTIN	1085	34.4	2070	65.6*	743	45.8	410	25.3	338	20.8	132	8.1
BAILEY	313	18.0	1423	82.0*	156	21.0	119	16.0	391	52.7	76	10.2
BANDERA	417	33.8	816	66.2*	232	35.4	282	43.1	109	16.6	32	4.9
BASTROP	854	22.3	2976	77.7*	360	16.2	258	11.6	1336	60.1	269	12.1
BAYLOR	411	23.2	1358	76.8*	203	25.2	95	11.8	401	49.8	107	13.3
BEE	2824	67.5	1361	32.5*	697	39.3	468	26.4	500	28.2	110	6.2
BELL	2804	25.7	8087	74.3*	1512	21.8	657	9.5	4082	59.0	670	9.7
BEXAR	18685	41.4	26412	58.6*	10521	20.0	19017	36.2	18161	34.6	4800	9.1
BLANCO	173	21.9	616	78.1*	109	16.1	223	32.8	277	40.8	70	10.3
BORDEN	87	24.5	268	75.5*	52	16.0	25	12.0	109	52.4	22	10.6
BOSQUE	1166	32.8	2387	67.2*	544	31.4	262	15.1	830	47.9	95	5.5
BOWIE	2975	25.5	8706	74.5*	2701	45.6	624	10.5	2408	40.7	187	3.2
BRAZORIA	2174	26.9	5914	73.1*	1983	21.0	2212	23.5	3864	41.0	1368	14.5
BRAZOS	1847	28.7	4593	71.3*	903	22.6	759	19.0	1379	34.5	960	24.0
BREWSTER	268	24.1	844	75.9*	237	37.4	160	25.3	208	32.9	28	4.4
BRISCOE	207	18.8	892	81.2*	119	27.9	47	11.0	237	55.5	24	5.6
BROOKS	580	38.8	914	61.2*	162	15.2	275	25.9	590	55.5	36	3.4
BROWN	1985	33.0	4038	67.0*	1217	31.9	743	19.4	1621	42.4	240	6.3
BURLESON	707	19.5	2916	80.5*	382	28.1	122	9.0	692	50.8	165	12.1
BURNET	474	18.9	2031	81.1*	196	13.7	302	21.1	748	52.3	185	12.9
CALDWELL	1048	27.4	2772	72.6*	439	21.8	300	14.9	1090	54.0	189	9.4
CALHOUN	468	23.8	1498	76.2*	286	22.6	303	24.0	443	35.0	232	18.4
CALLAHAN	570	23.7	1831	76.3*	387	33.7	168	14.6	549	47.7	46	4.0
CAMERON	3917	34.3	7515	65.7*	2467	29.9	2545	30.8	2880	34.8	372	4.5
CAMP	396	17.7	1844	82.3*	386	40.5	49	5.1	488	51.2	30	3.1
CARSON	281	17.5	1327	82.5*	270	22.4	232	19.3	552	45.9	40	3.3
CASS	929	20.0	3723	80.0*	1323	50.3	187	7.1	1025	39.0	96	3.6
CASTRO	241	14.9	1381	85.1*	198	22.4	107	12.1	521	58.9	59	6.7
CHAMBERS	431	25.9	1233	74.1*	662	47.3	218	15.6	361	25.8	160	11.4
CHEROKEE	1664	27.2	4446	72.8*	1673	43.9	331	8.7	1632	42.8	174	4.6
CHILDRESS	482	17.2	2318	82.8*	434	34.9	120	9.7	563	45.3	126	10.1
CLAY	516	20.6	1992	79.4*	195	15.8	164	13.2	704	56.9	175	14.1
COCHRAN	327	25.2	969	74.8*	143	26.2	68	12.5	228	41.8	106	19.4
COKE	223	22.3	776	77.7*	205	33.0	85	13.7	303	48.7	29	4.7
COLEMAN	962	26.4	2683	73.6*	701	39.4	237	13.3	727	40.9	113	6.4
COLLIN	1887	25.7	5443	74.3*	1513	31.2	712	14.7	2397	49.5	220	4.5
CLNGSWORTH	360	17.3	1726	82.7*	356	33.9	102	9.7	515	49.0	78	7.4
COLORADO	1494	35.7	2687	64.3*	657	29.5	733	32.9	616	27.6	223	10.0
COMAL	1157	31.3	2539	68.7*	580	29.9	895	46.1	405	20.9	61	3.1

```
          DEMOC.  SENATOR    1954*          DEMOC.  SENATOR    1957
                                *
  COUNTY     DOUGHERTY    JOHNSON     DIES          HUTCHESON   R. YARBRO   OTHER
             #      %      #      %*    #      %     #     %     #     %     #     %
-----------------------------------------------------------------------------------------------------------------
COMANCHEE   1328  33.1   2684  66.9*   612  30.0    250  12.3  1021  50.1   156   7.7
CONCHO       213  21.0    802  79.0*   132  22.6     68  11.6   354  60.6    30   5.1
COOKE       1663  36.8   2857  63.2*  1391  51.2    403  14.8   842  31.0    81   3.0
CORYELL      968  27.9   2507  72.1*   428  25.1    178  10.4   958  56.2   140   8.2
COTTLE       232  15.8   1239  84.2*   178  23.4     62   8.1   468  61.4    54   7.1
                                *
CRANE        360  26.9    980  73.1*   146  26.5     94  17.1   286  51.9    25   4.5
CROCKETT     300  28.6    748  71.4*   122  38.0     87  27.1    95  29.6    17   5.3
CROSBY       501  22.6   1716  77.4*   199  16.2     84   6.8   844  68.6   103   8.4
CULBERSON     90  18.0    410  82.0*   114  43.5     57  21.8    52  19.8    39  14.9
DALLAM       293  17.3   1404  82.7*   237  23.8    201  20.2   513  51.5    46   4.6
                                *
DALLAS     20323  33.2  40873  66.8* 32564  34.3  30709  32.3 25886  27.2  5836   6.1
DAWSON       818  26.1   2321  73.9*   412  30.8    197  14.7   550  41.2   177  13.2
DEAFSMITH    368  17.1   1779  82.9*   324  26.7    303  24.9   526  43.3    62   5.1
DELTA        481  22.7   1638  77.3*   351  40.8     43   5.0   424  49.2    43   5.0
DENTON      2485  31.9   5298  68.1*  1424  34.0    891  21.3  1679  40.1   195   4.7
                                *
DEWITT      1830  39.9   2756  60.1*   821  35.7    769  33.5   503  21.9   205   8.9
DICKENS      338  20.5   1307  79.5*   144  15.5    110  11.8   575  61.8   102  11.0
DIMMIT       383  31.1    848  68.9*   148  25.6    185  32.0   205  35.4    41   7.1
DONLEY       293  18.4   1303  81.6*   231  33.9    101  14.8   297  43.6    52   7.6
DUVAL       1445  33.1   2926  66.9*   764  29.9    462  18.1   974  38.1   357  14.0
                                *
EASTLAND    1976  32.8   4041  67.2*  1245  38.5    494  15.3  1339  41.4   158   4.9
ECTOR       1890  27.7   4936  72.3*  1429  36.1   1081  27.3  1174  29.7   271   6.9
EDWARDS      306  39.7    465  60.3*   100  32.4    133  43.0    59  19.1    17   5.5
ELLIS       2179  34.7   4105  65.3*  1725  37.4    471  10.2  2272  49.3   142   3.1
ELPASO      2058  13.8  12822  86.2*  3592  25.1   3398  23.7  6840  47.8   480   3.4
                                *
ERATH       1397  30.4   3191  69.6*   888  36.4    376  15.4   988  40.5   187   7.7
FALLS       1360  32.6   2810  67.4*   757  34.6    210   9.6  1002  45.8   219  10.0
FANNIN      1753  25.7   5074  74.3*   717  25.5    233   8.3  1741  62.0   116   4.1
FAYETTE     1785  30.8   4011  69.2*  1081  35.5    717  23.6   862  28.3   381  12.5
FISHER       370  17.2   1778  82.8*   237  21.9     89   8.2   694  64.3    60   5.6
                                *
FLOYD        616  23.0   2059  77.0*   471  34.5    158  11.6   635  46.5   101   7.4
FOARD        237  21.9    846  78.1*   115  25.5     35   7.8   245  54.3    56  12.4
FORTBEND    1118  31.8   2401  68.2*  1660  46.6    669  18.8   988  27.7   244   6.9
FRANKLIN     597  29.3   1441  70.7*   231  27.5     69   8.2   506  60.3    33   3.9
FREESTONE   1258  31.5   2734  68.5*   834  42.0    201  10.1   869  43.7    83   4.2
                                *
FRIO         622  39.6    947  60.4*   187  20.9    206  23.0   473  52.9    28   3.1
GAINES       571  23.0   1914  77.0*   422  33.8    130  10.4   584  46.8   111   8.9
GALVESTON   3074  17.1  14895  82.9*  3546  21.9   4232  26.1  7118  43.9  1314   8.1
GARZA        378  26.8   1033  73.2*   146  27.6     80  15.1   231  43.7    72  13.6
GILLESPIE    447  43.8    574  56.2*   229  19.3    822  69.3    92   7.8    43   3.6
                                *
GLASCOCK     128  29.2    310  70.8*    87  46.3     42  22.3    46  24.5    13   6.9
GOLIAD       697  51.6    654  48.4*   137  30.8    186  41.8    89  20.0    33   7.4
GONZALES     945  34.3   1807  65.7*   726  37.6    280  14.5   797  41.3   129   6.7
GRAY        1297  27.7   3388  72.3*  1088  32.9    799  24.2  1323  40.0    96   2.9
GRAYSON     2646  24.0   8385  76.0*  1799  27.1   1155  17.4  3464  52.2   213   3.2
                                *
GREGG       2686  27.8   6983  72.2*  3976  55.8    854  12.0  1959  27.5   334   4.7
```

SOUTHERN ELECTIONS/294

COUNTY	DOUGHERTY #	%	JOHNSON #	%*	DIES #	%	HUTCHESON #	%	R. YARBRO #	%	OTHER #	%
GRIMES	441	22.8	1491	77.2*	367	22.3	179	10.9	763	46.3	340	20.6
GUADALUPE	872	37.5	1452	62.5*	509	21.5	1063	44.8	670	28.3	129	5.4
HALE	923	24.0	2923	76.0*	918	31.6	571	19.6	1202	41.3	216	7.4
HALL	303	13.5	1936	86.5*	301	26.8	87	7.7	672	59.7	65	5.8
HAMILTON	1133	37.3	1907	62.7*	692	45.9	184	12.2	511	33.9	122	8.1
HANSFORD	220	18.3	979	81.7*	204	36.6	139	24.9	200	35.8	15	2.7
HARDEMAN	719	31.7	1550	68.3*	460	40.9	133	11.8	446	39.6	87	7.7
HARDIN	976	23.3	3207	76.7*	974	36.6	189	7.1	1392	52.3	106	4.0
HARRIS	26700	30.5	60922	69.5*	36482	23.6	46248	29.9	51054	33.0	21115	13.6
HARRISON	1341	19.0	5707	81.0*	1928	60.2	287	9.0	902	28.2	86	2.7
HARTLEY	85	13.8	530	86.2*	113	30.5	67	18.1	176	47.4	15	4.0
HASKELL	807	22.1	2843	77.9*	467	31.2	116	7.8	819	54.7	94	6.3
HAYS	723	22.1	2555	77.9*	412	22.1	335	18.0	855	45.8	263	14.1
HEMPHILL	162	14.4	963	85.6*	218	32.2	122	18.0	291	43.0	46	6.8
HENDERSON	1659	24.6	5095	75.4*	879	28.7	283	9.2	1830	59.6	76	2.5
HIDALGO	5573	35.6	10077	64.4*	3448	28.0	3516	28.5	4497	36.5	862	7.0
HILL	2037	30.1	4723	69.9*	1108	33.0	278	8.3	1694	50.4	279	8.3
HOCKLEY	979	24.8	2965	75.2*	588	23.5	359	14.4	1243	49.7	310	12.4
HOOD	548	28.9	1349	71.1*	215	24.7	119	13.6	477	54.7	61	7.0
HOPKINS	1506	28.5	3769	71.5*	989	38.1	219	8.4	1221	47.0	170	6.5
HOUSTON	1067	25.8	3075	74.2*	714	32.6	281	12.8	1021	46.6	174	7.9
HOWARD	1256	21.9	4479	78.1*	752	27.6	466	17.1	1406	51.6	100	3.7
HUDSPETH	75	12.5	527	87.5*	126	50.2	40	15.9	81	32.3	4	1.6
HUNT	2731	34.7	5136	65.3*	1840	46.9	550	14.0	1373	35.0	161	4.1
HUTCHISON	1407	27.8	3656	72.2*	893	26.5	782	23.2	1606	47.6	95	2.8
IRION	150	29.1	365	70.9*	74	33.2	52	23.3	77	34.5	20	9.0
JACK	592	31.9	1261	68.1*	367	35.6	179	17.4	416	40.3	69	6.7
JACKSON	944	28.4	2378	71.6*	507	36.6	272	19.6	457	33.0	149	10.8
JASPER	1023	22.7	3474	77.3*	1289	50.7	196	7.7	967	38.0	90	3.5
JEFFDAVIS	79	24.9	238	75.1*	48	31.8	34	22.5	47	31.1	22	14.6
JEFFERSON	7430	27.7	19435	72.3*	9892	35.7	4836	17.5	11039	39.9	1914	6.9
JIMHOGG	304	32.0	647	68.0*	156	44.8	53	15.2	131	37.6	8	2.3
JIMWELLS	3281	52.0	3029	48.0*	512	19.6	758	29.0	1185	45.4	157	6.0
JOHNSON	1996	32.3	4178	67.7*	1069	32.8	564	17.3	1499	46.0	125	3.8
JONES	896	22.3	3122	77.7*	749	32.1	287	12.3	1158	49.7	137	5.9
KARNES	1688	46.5	1943	53.5*	591	37.0	308	19.3	612	38.3	85	5.3
KAUFMAN	1545	31.9	3304	68.1*	1311	42.9	374	12.2	1263	41.4	106	3.5
KENDALL	230	39.9	346	60.1*	183	22.8	483	60.3	102	12.7	33	4.1
KENEDY	112	83.6	22	16.4*	23	21.1	76	69.7	6	5.5	4	3.7
KENT	149	20.2	590	79.8*	135	36.7	22	6.0	194	52.7	17	4.6
KERR	1134	33.0	2301	67.0*	622	28.3	1015	46.1	437	19.9	126	5.7
KIMBLE	674	43.9	862	56.1*	335	31.3	296	27.6	345	32.2	95	8.9
KING	40	17.8	185	82.2*	29	22.0	8	6.1	80	60.6	15	11.4
KINNEY	152	38.2	246	61.8*	69	29.0	43	18.1	85	35.7	41	17.2
KLEBERG	1064	35.9	1897	64.1*	402	19.4	535	25.9	931	45.0	200	9.7
KNOX	400	18.4	1777	81.6*	271	26.2	87	8.4	555	53.6	122	11.8

| COUNTY | DEMOC. SENATOR 1954* | | | | | | DEMOC. SENATOR 1957 | | | | | |
| | DOUGHERTY | | JOHNSON | | DIES | | HUTCHESON | | R. YARBRO | | OTHER | |
	#	%	#	%*	#	%	#	%	#	%	#	%
LAMAR	2547	28.9	6280	71.1*	1368	42.3	385	11.9	1205	37.2	278	8.6
LAMB	917	22.0	3246	78.0*	493	19.4	430	16.9	1407	55.5	207	8.2
LAMPASAS	707	30.9	1583	69.1*	342	30.9	173	15.6	469	42.4	122	11.0
LASALLE	182	22.0	644	78.0*	179	34.8	64	12.5	253	49.2	18	3.5
LABACA	1416	31.5	3084	68.5*	1059	44.6	441	18.6	637	26.8	240	10.1
LEE	604	24.7	1841	75.3*	238	18.8	215	16.9	614	48.4	202	15.9
LEON	585	20.5	2268	79.5*	520	42.0	81	6.5	525	42.4	113	9.1
LIBERTY	1437	28.3	3644	71.7*	1717	48.4	456	12.9	1027	29.0	346	9.8
LIMESTONE	1546	27.4	4089	72.6*	910	30.3	234	7.8	1682	55.9	181	6.0
LIPSCOMB	79	13.5	508	86.5*	98	23.0	132	31.0	150	35.2	46	10.8
LIVEOAK	1194	60.5	778	39.5*	221	28.1	274	34.9	242	30.8	49	6.2
LLANO	285	23.4	935	76.6*	131	14.7	152	17.1	518	58.2	89	10.0
LOVING	11	14.9	63	85.1*	18	33.3	12	22.2	23	42.6	1	1.9
LUBBOCK	3636	26.9	9874	73.1*	2804	29.5	2129	22.4	3811	40.1	762	8.0
LYNN	516	23.3	1698	76.7*	333	29.0	128	11.1	535	46.6	152	13.2
MADISON	432	23.1	1439	76.9*	289	34.2	97	11.5	345	40.8	114	13.5
MARION	225	14.2	1359	85.8*	432	61.8	81	11.6	141	20.2	45	6.4
MARTIN	251	21.1	937	78.9*	123	27.0	36	7.9	240	52.7	56	12.3
MASON	546	39.6	832	60.4*	107	15.8	260	38.5	247	36.5	62	9.2
MATAGORDA	1591	32.1	3372	67.9*	844	31.4	837	31.1	709	26.4	298	11.1
MAVERICK	163	16.8	809	83.2*	156	18.6	133	15.9	523	62.5	25	3.0
MCCULLOCH	691	20.5	2681	79.5*	472	34.4	246	17.9	539	39.3	115	8.4
MCLENNAN	6548	28.9	16092	71.1*	4151	26.5	2453	15.7	7686	49.1	1366	8.7
MCMULLEN	274	56.5	211	43.5*	90	43.3	52	25.0	55	26.4	11	5.3
MEDINA	513	32.3	1075	67.7*	597	30.9	626	32.4	605	31.3	105	5.4
MENARD	332	31.5	723	68.5*	103	24.6	129	30.9	142	34.0	44	10.5
MIDLAND	2074	34.1	4011	65.9*	1595	33.1	2123	44.0	752	15.6	350	7.3
MILAN	1650	34.9	3078	65.1*	785	29.6	305	11.5	1334	50.3	229	8.6
MILLS	646	33.7	1273	66.3*	248	33.8	111	16.1	317	43.2	57	7.8
MITCHELL	704	25.0	2114	75.0*	371	27.4	185	13.7	729	53.8	69	5.1
MONTAGE	1130	27.9	2920	72.1*	668	31.9	243	11.6	986	47.1	196	9.4
MONTGOMRY	1917	30.8	4314	69.2*	974	34.3	478	16.8	1120	39.5	266	9.4
MOORE	471	19.8	1912	80.2*	360	20.0	356	19.8	989	54.9	95	5.3
MORRIS	573	19.6	2356	80.4*	609	44.7	95	7.0	613	45.0	44	3.2
MOTLEY	208	20.7	795	79.3*	204	48.0	33	7.8	137	32.2	51	12.0
NACDOCHES	1521	25.1	4528	74.9*	1505	43.2	253	7.3	1545	44.3	182	5.2
NAVARRO	1866	27.1	5008	72.9*	1441	32.9	481	11.0	2248	51.4	206	4.7
NEWTON	514	24.8	1558	75.2*	601	48.4	77	6.2	529	42.6	34	2.7
NOLAN	846	20.7	3247	79.3*	520	26.1	346	17.4	1041	52.3	84	4.2
NUECES	8408	37.9	13797	62.1*	3784	22.1	4397	25.7	6924	40.5	1980	11.6
OCHILTREE	262	22.9	881	77.1*	333	48.8	160	23.4	161	23.6	29	4.2
OLDHAM	68	12.0	499	88.0*	69	20.0	73	21.2	189	54.8	14	4.1
ORANGE	2036	21.9	7245	78.1*	2478	42.9	682	11.8	2425	42.0	191	3.3
PALOPINTO	1261	34.3	2420	65.7*	844	33.9	414	16.6	1107	44.5	123	4.9
PANOLA	1114	18.7	4842	81.3*	1245	59.5	88	4.2	715	34.1	46	2.2
PARKER	1542	26.4	4306	73.6*	599	23.4	595	23.3	1222	47.8	142	5.6

COUNTY	DOUGHERTY #	%	JOHNSON #	%*	DIES #	%	HUTCHESON #	%	R. YARBRO #	%	OTHER #	%
PARMER	283	19.4	1173	80.6*	296	32.0	148	16.0	356	38.4	126	13.6
PECOS	607	23.8	1942	76.2*	356	34.3	248	23.9	365	35.1	70	6.7
POLK	700	25.8	2017	74.2*	747	43.5	140	8.2	697	40.6	132	7.7
POTTER	1904	17.7	8867	82.3*	2346	29.0	2011	24.9	3308	40.9	416	5.1
PRESIDIO	252	22.4	875	77.6*	157	39.3	90	22.6	107	26.8	45	11.3
RAINES	287	24.8	871	75.2*	175	40.3	59	13.6	180	41.5	20	4.6
RANDALL	673	17.9	3078	82.1*	781	27.4	816	28.6	961	33.7	291	10.2
REAGAN	277	23.3	910	76.7*	140	38.8	58	16.1	140	38.8	23	6.4
REAL	129	35.0	240	65.0*	71	22.8	129	41.5	96	30.9	15	4.8
REDRIVER	1265	25.1	3769	74.9*	917	40.1	163	7.1	1104	48.3	104	4.5
REEVES	441	18.4	1950	81.6*	415	42.9	173	17.9	307	31.7	72	7.4
REFUGIO	784	46.4	907	53.6*	368	34.6	270	25.4	349	32.8	77	7.2
ROBERTS	122	29.0	298	71.0*	96	39.5	74	30.5	61	25.1	12	4.9
ROBERTSON	972	26.2	2736	73.8*	489	22.9	185	8.7	1266	59.3	195	9.1
ROCKWALL	398	32.2	837	67.8*	349	42.7	78	9.5	355	43.4	36	4.4
RUNNELLS	823	27.3	2193	72.7*	1430	39.9	562	15.7	1308	36.5	285	7.9
RUSK	2047	24.6	6276	75.4*	2416	59.0	394	9.6	1097	26.8	187	4.6
SABINE	446	19.0	1899	81.0*	407	47.2	61	7.1	340	39.4	55	6.4
SNAUGSTNE	505	31.5	1096	68.5*	427	45.9	29	3.1	420	45.1	55	5.9
SNJACINTO	268	25.9	765	74.1*	140	21.4	52	8.0	392	59.9	70	10.7
SNPATRICIO	2143	42.4	2909	57.6*	847	25.4	720	21.6	1469	44.0	300	9.0
SANSABA	655	27.1	1764	72.9*	216	20.4	102	9.6	675	63.9	64	6.1
SCHLEICHER	255	25.2	755	74.8*	140	26.5	187	35.3	178	33.6	24	4.5
SCURRY	760	22.6	2609	77.4*	597	36.6	285	17.5	626	38.4	124	7.6
SHACKELFRD	399	30.3	916	69.7*	246	39.1	118	18.8	229	36.4	36	5.7
SHELBY	1890	27.2	5071	72.8*	1403	50.4	109	3.9	1178	42.3	95	3.4
SHERMAN	129	15.6	699	84.4*	119	33.0	54	15.0	172	47.6	16	4.4
SMITH	4387	28.7	10907	71.3*	3694	40.0	1880	20.4	3319	36.0	334	3.6
SOMERVELL	300	32.2	632	67.8*	101	29.0	62	17.8	163	46.8	22	6.3
STARR	328	8.0	3783	92.0*	53	3.6	80	5.4	1335	89.6	22	1.5
STEPHENS	1017	32.5	2115	67.5*	592	40.7	333	22.9	487	33.5	42	2.9
STERLING	80	22.7	273	77.3*	82	47.4	32	18.5	52	30.1	7	4.0
STONEWALL	254	20.8	966	79.2*	82	18.0	37	8.1	285	62.6	51	11.2
SUTTON	210	26.6	578	73.4*	126	33.3	156	41.3	81	21.4	15	4.0
SWISHER	281	14.5	1656	85.5*	170	13.5	166	13.2	847	67.3	75	6.0
TARRANT	18406	31.2	40528	68.8*	19486	37.7	11645	22.5	17940	34.7	2645	5.1
TAYLOR	1872	20.3	7368	79.7*	2700	35.4	1650	21.6	2835	37.1	450	5.9
TERRELL	168	31.3	368	68.7*	64	26.0	84	34.1	83	33.7	15	6.1
TERRY	594	23.3	1957	76.7*	283	23.7	157	13.2	619	51.9	133	11.2
THRCKMORTN	295	22.9	995	77.1*	114	20.2	53	9.4	350	62.2	46	8.2
TITUS	1258	29.2	3051	70.8*	734	38.4	161	8.4	939	49.2	76	4.0
TOMGREEN	2780	27.7	7272	72.3*	1879	33.5	1499	26.7	1823	32.5	404	7.2
TRAVIS	8057	27.8	20970	72.2*	3041	11.8	5665	22.0	10174	39.6	6828	26.6
TRINITY	653	28.8	1611	71.2*	333	30.4	95	8.7	590	53.8	79	7.2
TYLER	718	26.3	2010	73.7*	867	56.0	169	10.9	447	28.9	65	4.2
UPSHUR	802	13.2	5254	86.8*	930	44.2	171	8.1	922	43.8	83	3.9

```
         DEMOC.  SENATOR   1954*          DEMOC.  SENATOR    1957
                                *
COUNTY      DOUGHERTY    JOHNSON      DIES          HUTCHESON      R. YARBRO     OTHER
            #      %     #      %*    #      %      #      %       #      %      #      %
------------------------------------------------*-----------------------------------------------------------------------------
UPTON       427  27.7  1117  72.3*   365  36.5    194  19.4     380  38.0      60   6.0
UVALDE     1160  40.0  1738  60.0*   427  27.0    635  40.2     430  27.2      88   5.6
VALVERDE    520  19.8  2103  80.2*   377  35.3    335  31.3     312  29.2      45   4.2
VANZANDT   1334  22.8  4529  77.2*   815  31.7    273  10.6    1377  53.5     108   4.2
VICTORIA   2098  33.8  4100  66.2*   822  27.8    948  32.0     919  31.0     272   9.2
                                *
WALKER     1330  36.1  2353  63.9*   526  24.4    253  11.8     811  37.7     562  26.1
WALLER      512  29.6  1219  70.4*   451  34.1    228  17.2     419  31.7     224  16.9
WARD        900  29.1  2197  70.9*   555  36.9    337  22.4     570  37.9      42   2.8
WASHINGTON 1356  30.8  3049  69.2*   581  36.2    521  32.5     412  25.7      91   5.7
WEBB        516   6.7  7156  93.3*  4238  74.5    396   7.0     948  16.7     107   1.9
                                *
WHARTON    2143  31.1  4749  68.9*  1285  31.5    872  21.4    1545  37.9     379   9.3
WHEELER     497  21.0  1865  79.0*   281  27.0    163  15.6     542  52.0      56   5.4
WICHITA    3400  25.6  9870  74.4*  2306  20.8   2341  21.1    5273  47.5    1177  10.6
WILBARGER   890  22.8  3021  77.2*   937  49.9    337  17.9     534  28.4      71   3.8
WILLACY     801  27.7  2093  72.3*   679  46.0    319  21.6     359  24.3     119   8.1
                                *
WILLIAMSON 1533  23.6  4969  76.4*   875  23.6    493  13.3    1859  50.1     482  13.0
WILSON     1434  39.6  2191  60.4*   260  14.7    425  24.0    1008  56.8      81   4.6
WINKLER     576  24.4  1783  75.6*   437  36.9    191  16.1     521  44.0      35   3.0
WISE       1069  22.0  3784  78.0*   553  27.1    342  16.8    1033  50.7     110   5.4
WOOD       1311  28.2  3342  71.8*   998  39.2    269  10.6    1168  45.8     113   4.4
                                *
YOAKUM      391  24.2  1224  75.8*   290  32.4    131  14.6     420  46.9      54   6.0
YOUNG       836  28.7  2076  71.3*   565  27.7    334  16.4     969  47.5     172   8.4
ZAPATA       14   2.4   559  97.6*    93  13.4    220  31.7     377  54.3       4    .6
ZAVALA      481  33.9   938  66.1*   192  26.9    201  28.2     254  35.6      66   9.3
------------------------------------------------*-----------------------------------------------------------------------------
                                *
TOTALS    354188        882455    * 290869      219591         364881        82242
% OF VOTE    28.6          71.4    *   30.4        22.9           38.1          8.6
                                *
                                *
GEOGRAPHIC CLASS                *
                                *
LOWLANDS  131063  28.  342591  72.* 122805  31.   80255  21.   149890  38.   37768  10.
BLACK BELT  3318  22.   11786  78.*   3440  43.     833  10.     3120  39.     620   8.
WEST TEXAS186513  29.  451889  71.* 141945  29.  120689  25.   183680  38.   39863   8.
MEX. TEXAS 33294  30.   76189  70.*  22679  31.   17814  25.    28191  39.    3991   5.
                                *
                                *
DEMOGRAPHIC CLASS               *
                                *
METRO     151076  30.  360473  70.* 157696  28.  151561  27.   193778  35.   53299  10.
TOWN       34871  29.   84045  71.*  23049  32.   14089  20.    29746  41.    5015   7.
RURAL     168241  28.  437937  72.* 110124  33.   53941  16.   141357  43.   23928   7.
```

COUNTY	DEMOC. SENATOR 1958*				DEMOC. SENATOR 1961											
	BLAKLEY #	%	R. YARBRO #	%*	BLAKLEY #	%	GONZALEZ #	%	MAVERICK #	%	TOWER #	%	WILSON #	%	WRIGHT #	%
ANDERSON	2648	39.9	3985	60.1*	705	25.2	75	2.7	374	13.4	879	31.4	432	15.4	333	11.9
ANDREWS	995	41.0	1432	59.0*	406	29.3	21	1.5	103	7.4	389	28.1	217	15.7	250	18.0
ANGELINA	3488	34.5	6613	65.5*	843	17.4	35	.7	1178	24.3	1461	30.1	353	7.3	981	20.2
ARANSAS	462	34.3	883	65.7*	174	24.8	64	9.1	88	12.6	198	28.2	106	15.1	71	10.1
ARCHER	668	36.3	1174	63.7*	200	22.2	67	7.4	50	5.5	204	22.6	128	14.2	253	28.0
ARMSTRONG	191	30.4	437	69.6*	94	27.6	3	.9	6	1.8	131	38.4	27	7.9	80	23.5
ATASCOSA	1205	34.6	2281	65.4*	315	16.1	416	21.3	182	9.3	607	31.1	216	11.1	217	11.1
AUSTIN	1231	51.4	1164	48.6*	380	27.6	45	3.3	112	8.1	524	38.0	184	13.4	133	9.7
BAILEY	653	41.7	913	58.3*	188	17.9	15	1.4	65	6.2	435	41.5	213	20.3	133	12.7
BANDERA	774	56.0	609	44.0*	108	19.7	23	4.2	44	8.0	276	50.5	68	12.4	28	5.1
BASTROP	1178	30.3	2706	69.7*	547	24.9	114	5.2	391	17.8	384	17.4	350	15.9	415	18.9
BAYLOR	563	37.7	932	62.3*	163	24.2	21	3.1	37	5.5	153	22.7	103	15.3	197	29.2
BEE	1321	39.7	2008	60.3*	213	11.7	382	21.0	166	9.1	654	35.9	224	12.3	182	10.0
BELL	2851	27.7	7460	72.3*	1085	16.8	161	2.5	809	12.5	1000	15.5	876	13.6	2517	39.0
BEXAR	25698	42.0	35532	58.0*	5582	8.3	25991	38.4	9219	13.6	20018	29.6	4747	7.0	2094	3.1
BLANCO	212	40.7	309	59.3*	178	28.1	19	3.0	31	4.9	211	33.3	85	13.4	110	17.4
BORDEN	194	49.1	201	50.9*	54	24.0	7	3.1	11	4.9	47	20.9	26	11.6	80	35.6
BOSQUE	1128	36.8	1936	63.2*	498	27.4	20	1.1	100	5.5	382	21.0	206	11.3	614	33.7
BOWIE	3875	37.2	6555	62.8*	2081	38.4	85	1.6	409	7.5	1118	20.6	1032	19.0	695	12.8
BRAZORIA	5008	45.2	6083	54.8*	937	11.1	254	3.0	2018	23.9	3821	45.2	929	11.0	502	5.9
BRAZOS	2459	33.3	4928	66.7*	1374	31.4	266	6.1	385	8.8	1072	24.5	819	18.7	462	10.6
BREWSTER	468	38.3	754	61.7*	114	15.8	94	13.0	27	3.7	238	32.9	197	27.2	53	7.3
BRISCOE	348	33.6	687	66.4*	62	15.0	5	1.2	4	1.0	101	24.5	50	12.1	190	46.1
BROOKS	476	23.4	1556	76.6*	103	7.7	679	51.0	27	2.0	185	13.9	211	15.9	126	9.5
BROWN	2825	43.0	3743	57.0*	573	18.4	28	.9	235	7.6	820	26.4	303	9.7	1151	37.0
BURLESON	1012	31.8	2169	68.2*	415	32.9	65	5.2	203	16.1	114	9.0	330	26.2	134	10.6
BURNET	892	37.7	1473	62.3*	389	27.1	6	.4	121	8.4	299	20.8	177	12.3	444	30.9
CALDWELL	1262	36.5	2191	63.5*	499	29.2	115	6.7	111	6.5	393	23.0	315	18.4	276	16.1
CALHOUN	1042	37.8	1718	62.2*	248	12.1	372	18.1	162	7.9	463	22.6	520	25.3	288	14.0
CALLAHAN	896	43.6	1160	56.4*	310	23.8	11	.8	113	8.7	257	19.7	155	11.9	458	35.1
CAMERON	7247	51.4	6850	48.6*	1921	20.1	2155	22.5	288	3.0	3916	40.9	764	8.0	533	5.6
CAMP	1021	43.4	1330	56.6*	303	34.2	10	1.1	223	25.1	156	17.6	112	12.6	83	9.4
CARSON	484	35.6	876	64.4*	106	10.3	8	.8	63	6.1	295	28.7	85	8.3	472	45.9
CASS	2190	44.4	2740	55.6*	844	42.5	7	.4	355	17.9	386	19.4	249	12.5	145	7.3
CASTRO	476	30.2	1100	69.8*	125	14.2	16	1.8	32	3.6	195	22.1	151	17.1	363	41.2
CHAMBERS	955	46.4	1103	53.6*	204	23.6	31	3.6	100	11.5	283	32.7	151	17.4	97	11.2
CHEROKEE	2040	35.8	3663	64.2*	868	28.2	39	1.3	305	9.9	816	26.5	451	14.6	601	19.5
CHILDRESS	718	37.0	1221	63.0*	343	30.0	9	.8	105	9.2	271	23.7	154	13.5	262	22.9
CLAY	849	31.9	1814	68.1*	294	22.8	17	1.3	140	10.8	313	24.2	206	16.0	321	24.9
COCHRAN	571	39.2	885	60.8*	189	27.5	8	1.2	18	2.6	178	25.9	157	22.8	138	20.1
COKE	453	32.8	930	67.2*	182	31.0	6	1.0	29	4.9	138	23.5	86	14.7	146	24.9
COLEMAN	1445	46.7	1646	53.3*	632	32.1	10	.5	44	2.2	495	25.2	258	13.1	527	26.8
COLLIN	2346	34.0	4561	66.0*	1078	26.3	27	.7	229	5.6	756	18.5	428	10.5	1576	38.5
CLNGSWORTH	655	35.4	1196	64.6*	157	24.0	5	.8	16	2.4	192	29.4	125	19.1	159	24.3
COLORADO	1958	46.0	2294	54.0*	309	18.1	85	5.0	200	11.7	749	43.8	233	13.6	133	7.8
COMAL	1304	52.2	1193	47.8*	383	19.9	267	13.9	133	6.9	967	50.3	118	6.1	56	2.9

COUNTY	BLAKLEY #	%	R. YARBRO #	%*	BLAKLEY #	%	GONZALEZ #	%	MAVERICK #	%	TOWER #	%	WILSON #	%	WRIGHT #	%
COMANCHEE	967	32.8	1978	67.2*	388	22.4	7	.4	79	4.6	426	24.6	145	8.4	686	39.6
CONCHO	418	40.4	616	59.6*	158	28.6	20	3.6	15	2.7	126	22.8	89	16.1	145	26.2
COOKE	2298	46.9	2603	53.1*	1631	32.7	109	2.2	489	9.8	1319	26.5	758	15.2	679	13.6
CORYELL	1194	36.5	2076	63.5*	623	34.1	19	1.0	106	5.8	291	15.9	242	13.3	544	29.8
COTTLE	359	26.6	990	73.4*	164	28.3	10	1.7	24	4.1	78	13.5	69	11.9	234	40.4
CRANE	418	36.8	717	63.2*	150	24.7	13	2.1	86	14.2	215	35.4	74	12.2	69	11.4
CROCKETT	296	47.7	324	52.3*	134	38.7	22	6.4	7	2.0	108	31.2	43	12.4	32	9.2
CROSBY	476	26.3	1334	73.7*	97	10.4	20	2.1	72	7.7	222	23.8	176	18.8	347	37.2
CULBERSON	234	56.1	183	43.9*	61	21.7	15	5.3	3	1.1	116	41.3	61	21.7	25	8.9
DALLAM	591	41.9	819	58.1*	140	18.6	8	1.1	84	11.2	250	33.2	116	15.4	154	20.5
DALLAS	41203	48.7	43395	51.3*	36284	32.8	4138	3.7	7120	6.4	40296	36.4	11802	10.7	10955	9.9
DAWSON	1270	42.5	1716	57.5*	445	21.9	179	8.8	63	3.1	519	25.5	323	15.9	506	24.9
DEAFSMITH	761	44.9	934	55.1*	219	14.9	28	1.9	27	1.8	610	41.6	170	11.6	412	28.1
DELTA	586	35.2	1080	64.8*	250	38.2	1	.2	16	2.4	54	8.2	206	31.5	128	19.5
DENTON	2930	42.3	3997	57.7*	1103	22.6	177	3.6	328	6.7	1359	27.9	496	10.2	1413	29.0
DEWITT	1964	54.4	1647	45.6*	512	22.2	179	7.8	171	7.4	1015	44.0	173	7.5	256	11.1
DICKENS	499	30.9	1117	69.1*	103	16.6	14	2.3	31	5.0	122	19.7	124	20.0	225	36.3
DIMMIT	614	48.7	646	51.3*	76	10.8	268	38.1	43	6.1	220	31.3	66	9.4	31	4.4
DONLEY	481	39.9	724	60.1*	122	19.5	9	1.4	19	3.0	196	31.3	87	13.9	193	30.8
DUVAL	674	20.6	2594	79.4*	49	1.6	283	9.1	14	.4	177	5.7	2585	82.7	19	.6
EASTLAND	2300	43.0	3055	57.0*	718	23.2	31	1.0	127	4.1	725	23.4	191	6.2	1309	42.2
ECTOR	3371	55.4	2709	44.6*	1307	21.1	175	2.8	426	6.9	3109	50.3	445	7.2	721	11.7
EDWARDS	417	67.7	199	32.3*	52	21.1	0	.0	15	6.1	157	63.6	23	9.3	0	.0
ELLIS	1824	40.4	2693	59.6*	1189	29.2	67	1.6	542	13.3	725	17.8	543	13.3	1004	24.7
ELPASO	6014	36.5	10474	63.5*	2808	9.2	7312	24.0	1945	6.4	10920	35.9	5206	17.1	2220	7.3
ERATH	1483	36.2	2609	63.8*	582	22.2	27	1.0	88	3.4	646	24.7	146	5.6	1127	43.1
FALLS	1312	37.2	2217	62.8*	644	35.5	59	3.3	93	5.1	246	13.6	378	20.8	393	21.7
FANNIN	1358	25.7	3932	74.3*	552	21.4	21	.8	217	8.4	288	11.2	455	17.7	1043	40.5
FAYETTE	2094	46.8	2380	53.2*	595	25.7	189	8.2	275	11.9	616	26.6	363	15.7	274	11.9
FISHER	678	30.0	1580	70.0*	230	18.9	16	1.3	42	3.5	129	10.6	64	5.3	734	60.4
FLOYD	952	40.3	1409	59.7*	256	18.2	35	2.5	33	2.4	432	30.8	174	12.4	474	33.8
FOARD	331	31.4	724	68.6*	80	21.0	4	1.0	26	6.8	54	14.2	82	21.5	135	35.4
FORTBEND	2055	46.8	2333	53.2*	457	14.1	367	11.3	459	14.1	1292	39.7	494	15.2	183	5.6
FRANKLIN	713	37.9	1169	62.1*	149	22.3	9	1.3	56	8.4	94	14.1	274	41.1	85	12.7
FREESTONE	1538	41.2	2193	58.8*	620	39.5	31	2.0	257	16.4	291	18.5	221	14.1	151	9.6
FRIO	688	38.3	1109	61.7*	187	15.4	435	35.8	73	6.0	274	22.6	152	12.5	94	7.7
GAINES	901	36.1	1594	63.9*	250	24.2	10	1.0	53	5.1	304	29.5	175	17.0	240	23.3
GALVESTON	6522	33.4	13019	66.6*	1238	8.0	2313	15.0	2916	18.9	5663	36.8	1948	12.6	1330	8.6
GARZA	484	39.9	729	60.1*	108	16.7	39	6.0	45	7.0	183	28.3	109	16.9	162	25.1
GILLESPIE	653	69.7	284	30.3*	106	7.9	39	2.9	22	1.6	923	68.8	168	12.5	84	6.3
GLASCOCK	200	55.2	162	44.8*	69	34.2	3	1.5	5	2.5	55	27.2	40	19.8	30	14.9
GOLIAD	563	49.7	569	50.3*	74	14.1	60	11.4	35	6.7	265	50.4	46	8.7	46	8.7
GONZALES	1433	41.8	1999	58.2*	476	28.4	89	5.3	123	7.3	420	25.1	291	17.4	276	16.5
GRAY	2307	49.3	2369	50.7*	549	15.2	26	.7	160	4.4	2014	55.6	344	9.5	527	14.6
GRAYSON	2614	31.9	5581	68.1*	2079	27.8	89	1.2	1473	19.7	1523	20.3	696	9.3	1628	21.7
GREGG	6275	58.4	4472	41.6*	2567	39.4	159	2.4	371	5.7	1985	30.4	987	15.1	450	6.9

	DEMOC. SENATOR 1958*		DEMOC. SENATOR 1961					
COUNTY	BLAKLEY # %	R. YARBRO # %*	BLAKLEY # %	GONZALEZ # %	MAVERICK # %	TOWER # %	WILSON # %	WRIGHT # %
GRIMES	682 39.5	1044 60.5*	429 35.4	17 1.4	111 9.2	285 23.5	185 15.3	185 15.3
GUADALUPE	1026 43.1	1354 56.9*	345 11.9	363 12.5	283 9.7	1349 46.5	393 13.5	171 5.9
HALE	2151 42.3	2936 57.7*	465 16.0	50 1.7	106 3.7	1060 36.6	314 10.8	904 31.2
HALL	431 23.8	1377 76.2*	216 25.8	2 .2	18 2.1	136 16.2	91 10.9	375 44.7
HAMILTON	995 47.5	1100 52.5*	302 26.8	8 .7	55 4.9	393 34.9	83 7.4	284 25.2
HANSFORD	500 53.9	427 46.1*	118 18.0	2 .3	11 1.7	384 58.7	79 12.1	60 9.2
HARDEMAN	863 45.5	1033 54.5*	371 36.3	11 1.1	90 8.8	325 31.8	68 6.6	158 15.4
HARDIN	1210 25.2	3590 74.8*	256 11.4	95 4.2	739 32.9	326 14.5	372 16.6	457 20.4
HARRIS	54711 42.4	74211 57.6*	13458 10.2	10250 7.8	21421 16.2	60016 45.5	17519 13.3	9233 7.0
HARRISON	4612 61.9	2839 38.1*	2030 44.4	31 .7	344 7.5	619 13.5	1425 31.2	121 2.6
HARTLEY	297 49.0	309 51.0*	86 26.7	2 .6	12 3.7	111 34.5	50 15.5	61 18.9
HASKELL	950 30.4	2176 69.6*	303 21.4	12 .8	67 4.7	115 8.1	212 14.9	710 50.0
HAYS	1109 41.5	1562 58.5*	581 23.8	503 20.6	204 8.4	522 21.4	323 13.2	305 12.5
HEMPHILL	351 38.4	563 61.6*	93 16.6	4 .7	24 4.3	274 48.8	77 13.7	89 15.9
HENDERSON	1426 25.5	4168 74.5*	599 22.0	94 3.4	270 9.9	733 26.9	411 15.1	620 22.7
HIDALGO	7982 46.1	9319 53.9*	2451 17.5	3733 26.7	301 2.2	5422 38.8	1086 7.8	996 7.1
HILL	2373 35.1	4394 64.9*	1078 34.2	47 1.5	153 4.9	403 12.8	292 9.3	1180 37.4
HOCKLEY	1781 39.3	2752 60.7*	308 16.1	115 6.0	73 3.8	564 29.6	243 12.7	605 31.7
HOOD	551 29.7	1306 70.3*	41 4.6	1 .1	8 .9	114 12.8	25 2.8	702 78.8
HOPKINS	1957 38.2	3168 61.8*	345 15.9	19 .9	62 2.9	369 17.0	1047 48.3	325 15.0
HOUSTON	1364 35.6	2470 64.4*	501 28.8	25 1.4	342 19.6	378 21.7	185 10.6	310 17.8
HOWARD	1650 33.2	3313 66.8*	538 17.4	85 2.8	535 17.3	817 26.5	343 11.1	767 24.9
HUDSPETH	217 39.2	337 60.8*	46 15.3	13 4.3	12 4.0	72 23.9	44 14.6	114 37.9
HUNT	2774 43.7	3579 56.3*	855 29.7	56 1.9	341 11.9	691 24.0	327 11.4	605 21.0
HUTCHISON	1729 34.5	3279 65.5*	607 14.7	26 .6	748 18.2	1885 45.7	256 6.2	599 14.5
IRION	307 58.3	220 41.7*	114 40.6	10 3.6	14 5.0	83 29.5	16 5.7	44 15.7
JACK	920 42.8	1232 57.2*	241 18.3	19 1.4	32 2.4	437 33.2	77 5.9	510 38.8
JACKSON	1348 44.8	1664 55.2*	210 14.5	203 14.0	171 11.8	432 29.8	310 21.4	123 8.5
JASPER	1444 30.2	3340 69.8*	274 15.4	27 1.5	188 10.6	384 21.6	251 14.1	656 36.9
JEFFDAVIS	109 38.2	176 61.8*	46 27.5	7 4.2	11 6.6	61 36.5	20 12.0	22 13.2
JEFFERSON	11520 38.4	18474 61.6*	3237 11.6	1532 5.5	7468 26.8	7352 26.4	1721 6.2	6514 23.4
JIMHOGG	214 19.7	875 80.3*	17 5.3	168 52.5	3 .9	32 10.0	89 27.8	11 3.4
JIMWELLS	1666 28.9	4096 71.1*	199 5.6	1440 40.8	109 3.1	725 20.5	486 13.8	570 16.2
JOHNSON	1609 36.8	2768 63.2*	485 12.3	25 .6	279 7.1	1025 26.0	63 1.6	2063 52.4
JONES	1342 40.0	2014 60.0*	631 30.2	16 .8	61 2.9	415 19.9	167 8.0	799 38.2
KARNES	1516 39.2	2353 60.8*	219 13.4	383 23.5	87 5.3	477 29.3	293 18.0	170 10.4
KAUFMAN	2092 43.2	2751 56.8*	1060 40.3	31 1.2	132 5.0	482 18.3	370 14.1	553 21.0
KENDALL	321 64.3	178 35.7*	86 11.1	24 3.1	44 5.7	545 70.2	46 5.9	31 4.0
KENEDY	69 79.3	18 20.7*	20 14.6	7 5.1	0 .0	19 13.9	90 65.7	1 .7
KENT	285 33.4	569 66.6*	98 27.4	10 2.8	15 4.2	39 10.9	103 28.8	93 26.0
KERR	1972 57.4	1462 42.6*	442 18.9	99 4.2	110 4.7	1300 55.5	210 9.0	182 7.8
KIMBLE	563 58.3	403 41.7*	182 28.3	13 2.0	18 2.8	265 41.3	94 14.6	70 10.9
KING	67 32.5	139 67.5*	28 27.2	1 1.0	1 1.0	19 18.4	21 20.4	33 32.0
KINNEY	206 37.7	341 62.3*	28 14.8	31 16.4	5 2.6	69 36.5	38 20.1	18 9.5
KLEBERG	919 28.2	2339 71.8*	202 8.5	782 33.0	300 12.7	580 24.5	287 12.1	218 9.2
KNOX	607 36.5	1058 63.5*	248 26.5	14 1.5	31 3.3	169 18.0	111 11.8	364 38.8

COUNTY	BLAKLEY #	%	R. YARBRO #	%*	BLAKLEY #	%	GONZALEZ #	%	MAVERICK #	%	TOWER #	%	WILSON #	%	WRIGHT #	%
LAMAR	3079	41.2	4397	58.8*	1281	30.4	25	.6	199	4.7	744	17.6	1563	37.1	406	9.6
LAMB	1281	34.4	2438	65.6*	399	19.8	44	2.2	104	5.2	680	33.8	320	15.9	467	23.2
LAMPASAS	874	41.9	1210	58.1*	251	25.7	8	.8	50	5.1	259	26.5	107	11.0	301	30.8
LASALLE	365	35.2	671	64.8*	76	16.4	75	16.2	22	4.8	84	18.1	184	39.7	22	4.8
LABACA	1207	31.6	2612	68.4*	455	20.4	130	5.8	166	7.5	471	21.2	895	40.2	109	4.9
LEE	707	29.2	1716	70.8*	267	26.1	15	1.5	83	8.1	361	35.3	127	12.4	169	16.5
LEON	1150	37.9	1885	62.1*	394	43.4	21	2.3	115	12.7	111	12.2	163	18.0	104	11.5
LIBERTY	2243	44.3	2824	55.7*	647	23.2	63	2.3	544	19.5	969	34.8	302	10.8	259	9.3
LIMESTONE	1719	36.3	3011	63.7*	792	39.5	34	1.7	208	10.4	321	16.0	255	12.7	395	19.7
LIPSCOMB	342	38.4	549	61.6*	72	15.4	2	.4	28	6.0	273	58.5	60	12.8	32	6.9
LIVEOAK	824	49.0	859	51.0*	162	15.4	168	16.0	71	6.8	437	41.6	142	13.5	71	6.8
LLANO	443	34.2	852	65.8*	285	28.4	10	1.0	65	6.5	225	22.4	70	7.0	348	34.7
LOVING	48	51.1	46	48.9*	5	15.2	0	.0	0	.0	14	42.4	5	15.2	9	27.3
LUBBOCK	6588	46.2	7676	53.8*	1632	13.3	621	5.1	1171	9.6	5034	41.2	1308	10.7	2464	20.1
LYNN	788	38.8	1242	61.2*	313	28.4	32	2.9	23	2.1	198	18.0	273	24.8	263	23.9
MADISON	615	32.8	1261	67.2*	295	44.0	21	3.1	53	7.9	110	16.4	151	22.5	40	6.0
MARION	983	58.5	696	41.5*	353	58.3	14	2.3	36	5.9	119	19.6	75	12.4	9	1.5
MARTIN	319	39.4	491	60.6*	149	35.2	10	2.4	23	5.4	44	10.4	64	15.1	133	31.4
MASON	525	44.5	654	55.5*	119	16.8	10	1.4	22	3.1	309	43.6	48	6.8	201	28.3
MATAGORDA	1534	45.1	1870	54.9*	318	14.9	248	11.6	142	6.7	781	36.6	378	17.7	266	12.5
MAVERICK	540	37.0	920	63.0*	54	7.4	368	50.3	19	2.6	184	25.2	90	12.3	16	2.2
MCCULLOCH	1020	43.3	1335	56.7*	291	23.5	52	4.2	26	2.1	282	22.8	157	12.7	428	34.6
MCLENNAN	7851	33.9	15291	66.1*	4827	32.2	499	3.3	2522	16.8	2843	18.9	2238	14.9	2082	13.9
MCMULLEN	234	49.4	240	50.6*	46	22.0	29	13.9	9	4.3	65	31.1	19	9.1	41	19.6
MEDINA	896	39.3	1386	60.7*	448	14.7	428	14.0	563	18.4	1049	34.3	387	12.7	181	5.9
MENARD	482	48.9	503	51.1*	83	17.2	12	2.5	23	4.8	210	43.6	62	12.9	92	19.1
MIDLAND	3482	59.6	2357	40.4*	1098	14.3	230	3.0	214	2.8	4320	56.6	790	10.3	1003	13.1
MILAN	2094	36.7	3613	63.3*	622	29.5	56	2.7	233	11.0	372	17.6	381	18.0	447	21.2
MILLS	601	37.4	1006	62.6*	197	30.2	8	1.2	28	4.3	182	27.9	34	5.2	203	31.1
MITCHELL	887	34.6	1673	65.4*	337	23.8	11	.8	143	10.1	254	17.9	163	11.5	508	35.9
MONTAGE	1353	37.5	2252	62.5*	704	31.8	30	1.4	159	7.2	525	23.7	304	13.7	492	22.2
MONTGOMRY	1960	35.3	3593	64.7*	550	24.9	47	2.1	325	14.7	689	31.2	267	12.1	331	15.0
MOORE	869	35.7	1564	64.3*	264	16.2	14	.9	281	17.3	673	41.4	139	8.5	255	15.7
MORRIS	1341	46.9	1519	53.1*	870	47.5	13	.7	473	25.8	237	12.9	124	6.8	114	6.2
MOTLEY	433	44.0	552	56.0*	169	41.7	3	.7	18	4.4	76	18.8	39	9.6	100	24.7
NACDOCHES	2095	35.2	3865	64.8*	885	39.7	40	1.8	240	10.8	471	21.1	251	11.3	341	15.3
NAVARRO	2137	35.2	3938	64.8*	1452	32.4	56	1.3	880	19.7	798	17.8	673	15.0	618	13.8
NEWTON	678	25.5	1986	74.5*	112	15.5	30	4.2	92	12.7	93	12.9	202	28.0	193	26.7
NOLAN	1517	38.8	2394	61.2*	461	20.4	44	1.9	222	9.8	497	22.0	257	11.4	780	34.5
NUECES	7740	33.4	15417	66.6*	2885	11.3	7543	29.5	2644	10.3	6295	24.6	3591	14.0	2653	10.4
OCHILTREE	766	50.4	753	49.6*	126	11.2	9	.8	16	1.4	759	67.2	82	7.3	137	12.1
OLDHAM	226	40.7	329	59.3*	71	20.5	8	2.3	15	4.3	96	27.7	94	27.2	62	17.9
ORANGE	2766	31.9	5901	68.1*	637	14.6	78	1.8	1239	28.4	1035	23.7	388	8.9	992	22.7
PALOPINTO	1720	43.2	2258	56.8*	395	13.9	19	.7	142	5.0	658	23.2	87	3.1	1541	54.2
PANOLA	2774	59.6	1883	40.4*	1047	65.7	17	1.1	81	5.1	244	15.3	140	8.8	65	4.1
PARKER	1593	37.3	2679	62.7*	227	5.9	11	.3	71	1.8	716	18.6	69	1.8	2761	71.6

COUNTY	BLAKLEY #	%	R. YARBRO #	%*	BLAKLEY #	%	GONZALEZ #	%	MAVERICK #	%	TOWER #	%	WILSON #	%	WRIGHT #	%
PARMER	714	39.6	1090	60.4*	257	20.4	16	1.3	119	8.8	417	33.2	314	25.0	143	11.4
PECOS	1117	46.7	1275	53.3*	633	38.0	344	20.7	29	1.7	376	22.6	127	7.6	156	9.4
POLK	1383	41.0	1990	59.0*	269	27.0	28	2.8	147	14.8	202	20.3	168	16.9	181	18.2
POTTER	3962	46.7	4514	53.3*	1832	17.2	266	2.5	1429	13.4	4468	42.0	1221	11.5	1426	13.4
PRESIDIO	353	40.6	516	59.4*	116	20.0	185	31.9	16	2.8	142	24.5	90	15.5	31	5.3
RAINES	269	28.9	661	71.1*	77	21.4	4	1.1	51	14.2	60	16.7	29	8.1	139	38.6
RANDALL	2160	51.6	2028	48.4*	1045	21.2	88	1.8	405	8.2	2310	46.8	491	10.0	594	12.0
REAGAN	564	45.2	683	54.8*	299	55.4	23	4.3	11	2.0	85	15.7	52	9.6	70	13.0
REAL	298	47.2	334	52.8*	44	19.0	9	3.9	14	6.0	102	44.0	45	19.4	18	7.8
REDRIVER	1600	38.5	2560	61.5*	725	47.0	10	.6	34	2.2	187	12.1	300	19.5	285	18.5
REEVES	920	43.0	1219	57.0*	481	30.7	120	7.7	76	4.9	553	35.3	197	12.6	138	8.8
REFUGIO	557	33.8	1089	66.2*	228	18.3	255	20.4	72	5.8	312	25.0	234	18.8	146	11.7
ROBERTS	176	61.8	109	38.2*	56	26.2	0	.0	0	.0	115	53.7	21	9.8	22	10.3
ROBERTSON	1011	29.8	2385	70.2*	453	28.3	81	5.1	338	21.1	152	9.5	218	13.6	358	22.4
ROCKWALL	685	41.0	985	59.0*	326	42.2	3	.4	34	4.4	104	13.5	88	11.4	218	28.2
RUNNELLS	1549	52.2	1418	47.8*	618	31.4	49	2.5	30	1.5	523	26.6	277	14.1	469	23.9
RUSK	4229	49.8	4259	50.2*	1302	31.7	104	2.5	246	6.0	1721	41.9	488	11.9	242	5.9
SABINE	717	32.6	1481	67.4*	96	17.9	10	1.9	49	9.2	89	16.6	129	24.1	162	30.3
SNAUGSTNE	786	35.6	1421	64.4*	173	23.7	11	1.5	60	8.2	226	31.0	96	13.2	164	22.5
SNJACINTO	205	27.4	542	72.6*	175	23.2	15	2.0	89	11.8	122	16.2	199	26.4	153	20.3
SNPATRICIO	1861	33.1	3762	66.9*	331	8.7	1139	30.0	391	10.3	778	20.5	715	18.8	446	11.7
SANSABA	614	31.4	1339	68.6*	194	19.5	31	3.1	37	3.7	157	15.8	134	13.5	441	44.4
SCHLEICHER	385	47.7	422	52.3*	81	16.7	13	2.7	6	1.2	221	45.7	44	9.1	119	24.6
SCURRY	1827	43.5	2375	56.5*	300	16.0	22	1.2	88	4.7	505	26.9	182	9.7	783	41.6
SHACKELFRD	717	54.1	609	45.9*	217	36.2	6	1.0	32	5.3	131	21.9	48	8.0	165	27.5
SHELBY	2335	38.6	3720	61.4*	527	41.0	23	1.8	99	7.7	76	5.9	210	16.3	351	27.3
SHERMAN	325	47.6	358	52.4*	134	33.3	1	.2	9	2.2	203	50.4	24	6.0	32	7.9
SMITH	6057	45.6	7228	54.4*	1809	18.6	209	2.1	879	9.0	4379	45.0	1280	13.2	1175	12.1
SOMERVELL	389	39.3	601	60.7*	72	18.9	0	.0	14	3.7	85	22.3	18	4.7	192	50.4
STARR	265	7.9	3102	92.1*	34	1.9	417	23.0	6	.3	55	3.0	1291	71.2	9	.5
STEPHENS	1177	48.5	1252	51.5*	254	22.3	16	1.4	64	5.6	408	35.8	147	12.9	251	22.0
STERLING	224	57.3	167	42.7*	100	48.1	7	3.4	8	3.8	49	23.6	17	8.2	27	13.0
STONEWALL	383	31.4	835	68.6*	83	24.1	3	.9	21	6.1	40	11.6	72	20.9	125	36.3
SUTTON	322	55.0	263	45.0*	128	27.9	86	18.8	3	.7	164	35.8	29	6.3	48	10.5
SWISHER	605	25.5	1764	74.5*	174	14.4	9	.7	14	1.2	296	24.5	113	9.4	600	49.8
TARRANT	23808	42.7	31991	57.3*	4830	7.4	1278	2.0	3211	4.9	19714	30.1	1467	2.2	34901	53.4
TAYLOR	5425	53.7	4679	46.3*	2351	28.4	131	1.6	479	5.8	2423	29.2	663	8.0	2242	27.0
TERRELL	189	43.2	249	56.8*	54	26.5	23	11.3	19	9.3	80	39.2	22	10.8	6	2.9
TERRY	1032	36.5	1794	63.5*	328	20.3	63	3.9	57	3.5	583	36.0	185	11.4	403	24.9
THRCKMORTN	304	29.6	724	70.4*	132	29.3	5	1.1	26	5.8	91	20.2	49	10.9	147	32.7
TITUS	1617	37.4	2709	62.6*	757	38.9	15	.8	264	13.6	272	14.0	315	16.2	324	16.6
TOMGREEN	4409	46.2	5137	53.8*	1141	16.4	495	7.1	432	6.2	2643	38.0	713	10.3	1532	22.0
TRAVIS	12587	41.5	17759	58.5*	6478	21.3	2563	8.4	3559	11.7	7774	25.5	4299	14.1	5804	19.0
TRINITY	735	31.7	1582	68.3*	178	27.9	8	1.3	72	11.3	162	25.4	118	18.5	101	15.8
TYLER	1422	47.2	1591	52.8*	166	16.8	22	2.2	141	14.2	305	30.8	126	12.7	230	23.2
UPSHUR	2470	44.0	3139	56.0*	527	29.1	14	.8	303	16.8	310	17.1	352	19.5	302	16.7

```
         DEMOC.  SENATOR   1958*                        DEMOC.  SENATOR   1961
                              *
COUNTY     BLAKLEY     R. YARBRO  * BLAKLEY      GONZALEZ     MAVERICK     TOWER       WILSON       WRIGHT
           #     %     #     %*   #     %       #     %      #     %      #     %     #     %      #     %
------------------------------------*------------------------------------------------------------------------------
UPTON       560 41.6   787 58.4*   194 27.9    15   2.2     23   3.3    201 28.9     86 12.4     177 25.4
UVALDE     1526 47.5  1690 52.5*   191 12.2   151   9.7     90   5.8    842 53.9    214 13.7      73  4.7
VALVERDE   1026 43.0  1360 57.0*   196 14.3   414  30.2     86   6.3    478 34.9     64  4.7     133  9.7
VANZANDT   1631 32.1  3451 67.9*   515 25.1    17   .8     191   9.3    472 23.0    422 20.6     435 21.2
VICTORIA   2112 36.7  3638 63.3*   586 11.2   661  12.6    541  10.3   1706 32.5    872 16.6     878 16.7
                              *
WALKER     1283 37.7  2116 62.3*   344 24.6    31   2.2    158  11.3    413 29.5    275 19.6     180 12.8
WALLER      778 41.7  1088 58.3*   176 17.9    38   3.9     91   9.2    441 44.8    162 16.4      77  7.8
WARD       1112 45.2  1347 54.8*   401 27.1    45   3.0     63   4.3    548 37.1    171 11.6     250 16.9
WASHINGTON 1714 59.1  1185 40.9*   302 20.8    26   1.8     46   3.2    775 53.3    113  7.8     192 13.2
WEBB       2576 28.5  6468 71.5*   235  4.2  4573  81.2     91   1.6    389  6.9    295  5.2      48   .9
                              *
WHARTON    2639 41.1  3778 58.9*   560 14.0   621  15.5    496  12.4   1417 35.4    627 15.7     283  7.1
WHEELER     848 39.3  1311 60.7*   264 27.5     2   .2      21   2.2    348 36.3    124 12.9     200 20.9
WICHITA    5345 39.6  8164 60.4*  2857 21.1   476   3.5   1437  10.6   4964 36.6   1650 12.2    2182 16.1
WILBARGER  1940 46.6  2219 53.4*   546 33.2    26   1.6    107   6.5    416 25.3    303 18.4     249 15.1
WILLACY    1130 56.4   875 43.6*   716 39.6   206  11.4     46   2.5    521 28.8    224 12.4      93  5.1
                              *
WILLIAMSON 2241 39.1  3496 60.9*  1203 29.4   225   5.5    444  10.8    685 16.7    659 16.1     880 21.5
WILSON     1066 30.9  2385 69.1*   170 12.5   319  23.4     89   6.5    330 24.2    256 18.8     199 14.6
WINKLER     721 39.6  1099 60.4*   227 17.8    26   2.0     97   7.6    518 40.6    184 14.4     223 17.5
WISE       1339 31.9  2857 68.1*   287 14.4    14   .7      91   4.6    508 25.5     94  4.7     995 50.0
WOOD       1848 36.4  3226 63.6*   634 27.7    26   1.1    178   7.8    612 26.7    374 16.3     464 20.3
                              *
YOAKUM      615 32.6  1273 67.4*   107 12.1     8   .9      49   5.5    318 35.9    194 21.9     211 23.8
YOUNG      1367 38.8  2157 61.2*   405 21.5    10   .5      98   5.2    540 28.6    140  7.4     692 36.7
ZAPATA       73  9.9   668 90.1*     1   .2   367  90.6      7   1.7     23  5.7      7  1.7       0   .0
ZAVALA      664 43.2   873 56.8*    77 11.7   247  37.5     31   4.7    241 36.6     56  8.5       6   .9
------------------------------------*------------------------------------------------------------------------------
                              *
TOTALS    525418      760511    * 190818      97659       104992       327308      121961       171328
% OF VOTE    40.9        59.1   *    18.8        9.6         10.4         32.3         12.0         16.9
                              *
                              *
GEOGRAPHIC CLASS              *
                              *
LOWLANDS  200962 40.  305265 60.* 63851 19.   18776  6.    53284 16.   115781 34.   46924 14.    42369 12.
BLACK BELT  7589 50.    7550 50.*  3187 37.     179  2.      898 11.     1453 17.     2079 24.      718  8.
WEST TEXAS 272624 42. 376710 58.*111614 20.   51596  9.    45776  8.   179717 32.   57183 10.   121454 21.
MEX. TEXAS  44243 38.   70986 62.* 12166 13.   27108 28.     5034  5.    30357 31.   15775 16.     6787  7.
                              *
                              *
DEMOGRAPHIC CLASS             *
                              *
METRO     252757 42.  343801 58.*100528 16.   72913 12.    70519 11.   218689 35.   65087 10.    92799 15.
TOWN       47482 41.   67993 59.* 19148 23.    7805  9.     7888  9.    24559 29.    11700 14.    12764 15.
RURAL     225179 39.  348717 61.* 71142 23.   16941  5.    26585  9.    84060 27.    45174 15.    65765 21.
```

COUNTY	BLAKLEY #	%	TOWER #	%	R. YARBRO #	%	MCCLENDON #	%
ANDERSON	1563	54.9	1282	45.1*	3774	44.2	4769	55.8
ANDREWS	530	52.4	482	47.6*	1709	52.0	1578	48.0
ANGELINA	2545	57.6	1872	42.4*	7595	52.7	6826	47.3
ARANSAS	247	47.6	272	52.4*	1074	57.4	798	42.6
ARCHER	641	69.4	282	30.6*	1332	71.2	539	28.8
ARMSTRONG	187	57.2	140	42.8*	427	55.5	342	44.5
ATASCOSA	853	51.7	797	48.3*	1823	59.5	1240	40.5
AUSTIN	671	44.0	855	56.0*	1304	54.4	1093	45.6
BAILEY	435	44.4	545	55.6*	721	52.4	654	47.6
BANDERA	252	38.5	402	61.5*	737	48.1	794	51.9
BASTROP	1402	69.5	614	30.5*	2639	67.2	1288	32.8
BAYLOR	506	68.4	234	31.6*	832	68.6	380	31.4
BEE	732	44.0	930	56.0*	2159	58.5	1531	41.5
BELL	3801	69.9	1640	30.1*	8940	67.4	4327	32.6
BEXAR	22821	45.7	27161	54.3*	50264	65.8	26145	34.2
BLANCO	371	54.5	310	45.5*	357	58.9	249	41.1
BORDEN	121	63.0	71	37.0*	211	58.3	151	41.7
BOSQUE	984	62.2	597	37.8*	1601	54.1	1360	45.9
BOWIE	2622	56.6	2007	43.4*	6939	55.3	5615	44.7
BRAZORIA	3748	44.6	4650	55.4*	9265	58.9	6458	41.1
BRAZOS	2114	57.9	1540	42.1*	5447	62.3	3294	37.7
BREWSTER	301	46.5	346	53.5*	1029	59.0	714	41.0
BRISCOE	201	56.6	154	43.4*	786	67.5	378	32.5
BROOKS	596	70.0	255	30.0*	1374	56.8	1045	43.2
BROWN	1609	57.9	1171	42.1*	3293	59.6	2236	40.4
BURLESON	1021	74.9	343	25.1*	1942	67.3	942	32.7
BURNET	925	63.2	538	36.8*	1667	59.8	1119	40.2
CALDWELL	1168	66.1	599	33.9*	2101	61.8	1298	38.2
CALHOUN	674	54.3	567	45.7*	2107	59.2	1450	40.8
CALLAHAN	808	63.9	457	36.1*	1543	63.0	906	37.0
CAMERON	5020	49.6	5104	50.4*	7818	55.4	6304	44.6
CAMP	455	63.1	266	36.9*	1205	57.4	894	42.6
CARSON	406	47.2	455	52.8*	1112	66.5	560	33.5
CASS	1114	59.9	747	40.1*	1855	41.9	2573	58.1
CASTRO	592	66.9	293	33.1*	998	72.8	372	27.2
CHAMBERS	464	53.4	405	46.6*	1760	59.1	1219	40.9
CHEROKEE	1701	55.8	1349	44.2*	4886	58.2	3503	41.8
CHILDRESS	661	62.5	396	37.5*	1495	57.9	1086	42.1
CLAY	858	67.2	418	32.8*	1638	66.1	840	33.9
COCHRAN	503	61.6	313	38.4*	750	51.2	714	48.8
COKE	360	64.2	201	35.8*	413	59.5	281	40.5
COLEMAN	967	53.8	831	46.2*	1832	55.4	1473	44.6
COLLIN	2719	70.3	1150	29.7*	4501	54.9	3705	45.1
CLNGSWORTH	508	58.0	368	42.0*	917	55.6	731	44.4
COLORADO	955	49.2	988	50.8*	2743	56.9	2078	43.1
COMAL	812	37.3	1367	62.7*	1900	57.3	1417	42.7

```
              DEMOC.  RUNOFF    1961* DEMOC.  SENATOR    1964
                                    *
     COUNTY      BLAKLEY     TOWER      *   R. YARBRO   MCCLENDON
                 #     %     #     %*   #       %    #       %
     -----------------------------------------------------------------------------------------------------------
     COMANCHEE   978  61.1   622  38.9* 1939  56.4   1500  43.6
     CONCHO      362  65.1   194  34.9*  735  63.7    418  36.3
     COOKE      1192  51.3  1132  48.7* 2535  43.4   3307  56.6
     CORYELL    1224  71.9   478  28.1* 1600  56.4   1237  43.6
     COTTLE      464  77.5   135  22.5*  892  70.6    371  29.4
                                    *
     CRANE       261  51.4   247  48.6*  676  53.1    596  46.9
     CROCKETT    160  46.8   182  53.2*  500  51.0    480  49.0
     CROSBY      581  59.1   402  40.9* 1418  62.9    835  37.1
     CULBERSON   125  46.3   145  53.7*  331  45.1    403  54.9
     DALLAM      244  42.3   333  57.7*  592  52.6    533  47.4
                                    *
     DALLAS    44506  43.8 57044  56.2*56470 46.4  65288  53.6
     DAWSON      808  50.5   793  49.5* 2104  56.7   1604  43.3
     DEAFSMITH   474  40.0   712  60.0* 1395  56.6   1071  43.4
     DELTA       675  85.8   112  14.2*  969  54.6    805  45.4
     DENTON     2458  58.8  1724  41.2* 4712  56.4   3645  43.6
                                    *
     DEWITT      811  40.0  1214  60.0* 2165  47.6   2387  52.4
     DICKENS     462  68.1   216  31.9*  946  64.4    523  35.6
     DIMMIT      411  59.7   277  40.3*  418  28.8   1032  71.2
     DONLEY      314  52.3   286  47.7*  915  53.3    802  46.7
     DUVAL      2326  87.8   323  12.2* 3990  94.3    240   5.7
                                    *
     EASTLAND   1666  59.5  1132  40.5* 3150  56.1   2467  43.9
     ECTOR      2212  35.5  4027  64.5* 4179  48.1   4504  51.9
     EDWARDS      75  27.5   198  72.5*  240  33.1    485  66.9
     ELLIS      2498  71.1  1016  28.9* 3208  55.1   2618  44.9
     ELPASO     7119  38.6 11342  61.4*16131 63.5   9259  36.5
                                    *
     ERATH      1222  58.8   855  41.2* 2466  56.3   1911  43.7
     FALLS      1634  72.9   607  27.1* 2837  63.5   1634  36.5
     FANNIN     2019  81.6   456  18.4* 4074  62.4   2454  37.6
     FAYETTE    1551  58.8  1087  41.2* 2301  56.1   1804  43.9
     FISHER      713  75.5   231  24.5* 1502  65.3    797  34.7
                                    *
     FLOYD       633  53.7   545  46.3* 1282  54.7   1062  45.3
     FOARD       271  79.5    70  20.5*  361  72.9    134  27.1
     FORTBEND   1663  46.7  1896  53.3* 4338  54.2   3661  45.8
     FRANKLIN    500  76.8   151  23.2* 1109  61.3    700  38.7
     FREESTONE   894  66.2   456  33.8* 2035  54.7   1688  45.3
                                    *
     FRIO        528  60.8   340  39.2* 1047  50.7   1017  49.3
     GAINES      543  55.7   431  44.3* 1347  54.4   1128  45.6
     GALVESTON  6560  46.5  7534  53.5*14728 63.1   8622  36.9
     GARZA       286  50.0   286  50.0*  934  56.6    716  43.4
     GILLESPIE   279  19.3  1167  80.7*  310  42.0    428  58.0
                                    *
     GLASCOCK     96  52.2    88  47.8*  102  45.5    122  54.5
     GOLIAD      244  39.5   373  60.5*  642  63.3    373  36.7
     GONZALES   1030  65.3   547  34.7* 1725  51.8   1607  48.2
     GRAY       1044  32.7  2151  67.3* 1742  56.4   1348  43.6
     GRAYSON    3812  65.6  2003  34.4* 7807  58.5   5543  41.5
                                    *
     GREGG      2443  42.1  3359  57.9* 3885  34.8   7276  65.2
```

COUNTY	DEMOC. RUNOFF 1961*				DEMOC. SENATOR 1964			
	BLAKLEY		TOWER		R. YARBRO		MCCLENDON	
	#	%	#	%*	#	%	#	%
GRIMES	1041	64.3	577	35.7*	1946	62.3	1178	37.7
GUADALUPE	903	35.9	1613	64.1*	1694	57.5	1254	42.5
HALE	1446	48.1	1562	51.9*	3167	54.6	2632	45.4
HALL	593	74.0	208	26.0*	1323	63.5	759	36.5
HAMILTON	750	54.9	615	45.1*	1272	44.1	1614	55.9
HANSFORD	166	29.9	390	70.1*	207	44.2	261	55.8
HARDEMAN	431	52.8	385	47.2*	1444	59.9	967	40.1
HARDIN	1431	71.5	571	28.5*	4839	69.6	2118	30.4
HARRIS	40215	33.9	78479	66.1*	92805	57.8	67734	42.2
HARRISON	1634	57.9	1187	42.1*	3130	42.7	4192	57.3
HARTLEY	155	51.0	149	49.0*	264	52.5	239	47.5
HASKELL	1043	80.2	257	19.8*	2141	64.8	1164	35.2
HAYS	1212	60.3	798	39.7*	2750	64.2	1534	35.8
HEMPHILL	170	39.8	257	60.2*	569	56.1	445	43.9
HENDERSON	1519	58.9	1058	41.1*	4411	61.1	2810	38.9
HIDALGO	6483	45.7	7695	54.3*	10595	50.3	10484	49.7
HILL	2313	77.7	664	22.3*	3570	59.6	2416	40.4
HOCKLEY	1220	58.3	873	41.7*	2395	58.0	1735	42.0
HOOD	402	66.0	207	34.0*	999	57.2	746	42.8
HOPKINS	1593	72.9	592	27.1*	2558	50.2	2537	49.8
HOUSTON	920	59.8	619	40.2*	3311	61.2	2101	38.8
HOWARD	1414	54.1	1198	45.9*	4663	61.8	2882	38.2
HUDSPETH	165	55.7	131	44.3*	379	54.5	316	45.5
HUNT	1951	62.3	1182	37.7*	4492	52.1	4126	47.9
HUTCHISON	1119	36.0	1986	64.0*	3357	59.7	2262	40.3
IRION	199	64.0	112	36.0*	235	49.8	237	50.2
JACK	563	51.7	527	48.3*	1105	54.4	927	45.6
JACKSON	713	57.7	522	42.3*	1785	51.9	1656	48.1
JASPER	1026	59.6	695	40.4*	3474	64.0	1952	36.0
JEFFDAVIS	76	47.8	83	52.2*	132	59.7	89	40.3
JEFFERSON	12919	51.9	11984	48.1*	32092	60.4	21033	39.6
JIMHOGG	231	77.0	69	23.0*	1123	70.9	460	29.1
JIMWELLS	1383	56.8	1050	43.2*	4894	60.2	3235	39.8
JOHNSON	1964	57.1	1477	42.9*	4006	52.7	3602	47.3
JONES	1360	66.9	672	33.1*	2370	59.3	1624	40.7
KARNES	1161	65.5	611	34.5*	1950	56.6	1495	43.4
KAUFMAN	1602	69.6	699	30.4*	3175	53.8	2724	46.2
KENDALL	181	21.1	675	78.9*	174	48.5	185	51.5
KENEDY	51	45.9	60	54.1*	31	28.2	79	71.8
KENT	282	81.0	66	19.0*	458	66.4	232	33.6
KERR	697	31.5	1513	68.5*	1262	48.7	1328	51.3
KIMBLE	327	48.2	351	51.8*	633	49.2	653	50.8
KING	84	77.1	25	22.9*	129	58.1	93	41.9
KINNEY	89	44.7	110	55.3*	270	56.1	211	43.9
KLEBERG	1000	52.2	914	47.8*	3063	59.6	2075	40.4
KNOX	616	72.3	236	27.7*	953	66.0	491	34.0

```
              DEMOC.  RUNOFF    1961* DEMOC.  SENATOR    1964
                                    *
   COUNTY     BLAKLEY      TOWER         R. YARBRO    MCCLENDON
              #      %     #      %*     #      %      #      %
   ----------------------------------*-----------------------------------------------------------------
   LAMAR      2101 70.4    883 29.6*    4566 55.5    3668 44.5
   LAMB       1135 52.4   1032 47.6*    2102 56.9    1590 43.1
   LAMPASAS    612 55.9    483 44.1*    1242 55.3    1003 44.7
   LASALLE     294 70.2    125 29.8*     530 53.7     457 46.3
   LABACA     1892 72.4    720 27.6*    2773 60.6    1806 39.4
                                    *
   LEE         635 52.4    577 47.6*    1270 62.2     771 37.8
   LEON        714 75.3    234 24.7*    1549 59.7    1047 40.3
   LIBERTY    1509 54.2   1273 45.8*    3539 57.6    2600 42.4
   LIMESTONE  1389 71.7    548 28.3*    2512 53.3    2201 46.7
   LIPSCOMB    113 27.2    302 72.8*     470 49.7     475 50.3
                                    *
   LIVEOAK     362 41.9    502 58.1*     984 46.5    1134 53.5
   LLANO       587 62.6    351 37.4*    1050 56.3     815 43.7
   LOVING       16 44.4     20 55.6*      25 36.8      43 63.2
   LUBBOCK    5783 42.4   7867 57.6*   10441 52.8    9346 47.2
   LYNN        735 68.6    336 31.4*    1193 49.8    1201 50.2
                                    *
   MADISON     375 69.7    163 30.3*    1252 58.5     889 41.5
   MARION      279 56.1    218 43.9*     598 40.5     880 59.5
   MARTIN      359 75.7    115 24.3*     447 55.7     356 44.3
   MASON       291 37.6    483 62.4*     676 52.9     601 47.1
   MATAGORDA   983 44.3   1235 55.7*    2472 50.5    2426 49.5
                                    *
   MAVERICK    762 74.5    261 25.5*    1303 56.8     992 43.2
   MCCULLOCH   730 61.5    457 38.5*    1264 57.0     954 43.0
   MCLENNAN   9223 64.0   5195 36.0*   18919 68.2    8802 31.8
   MCMULLEN    115 49.6    117 50.4*     136 44.7     168 55.3
   MEDINA      714 42.0    985 58.0*    1308 57.5     966 42.5
                                    *
   MENARD      191 42.2    262 57.8*     219 54.5     183 45.5
   MIDLAND    2094 27.8   5440 72.2*    3433 43.3    4498 56.7
   MILAN      1624 69.5    714 30.5*    2945 63.8    1674 36.2
   MILLS       469 52.8    420 47.2*     998 52.6     901 47.4
   MITCHELL    924 70.6    384 29.4*    1260 65.4     668 34.6
                                    *
   MONTAGE    1190 62.8    705 37.2*    2594 60.6    1688 39.4
   MONTGOMRY   991 48.5   1052 51.5*    3892 51.3    3693 48.7
   MOORE       420 38.6    667 61.4*    1857 59.9    1243 40.1
   MORRIS      850 65.5    448 34.5*    1789 51.9    1655 48.1
   MOTLEY      251 64.4    139 35.6*     481 51.3     457 48.7
                                    *
   NACDOCHES  1352 63.9    763 36.1*    4112 49.2    4254 50.8
   NAVARRO    2338 69.1   1046 30.9*    3829 62.7    2277 37.3
   NEWTON      509 67.9    241 32.1*    1812 67.8     862 32.2
   NOLAN      1396 60.1    925 39.9*    2693 58.0    1947 42.0
   NUECES     8282 51.6   7766 48.4*   19867 65.2   10602 34.8
                                    *
   OCHILTREE   168 22.8    570 77.2*     333 37.1     565 62.9
   OLDHAM      144 50.0    144 50.0*     254 58.1     183 41.9
   ORANGE     2625 59.7   1774 40.3*    7698 60.3    5076 39.7
   PALOPINTO  1207 58.6    854 41.4*    2300 51.9    2134 48.1
   PANOLA     1022 69.3    453 30.7*    1744 35.0    3235 65.0
                                    *
   PARKER     1488 56.8   1131 43.2*    3233 56.0    2539 44.0
```

SOUTHERN ELECTIONS/308

```
            DEMOC.  RUNOFF    1961*  DEMOC.  SENATOR    1964
                               *
COUNTY      BLAKLEY      TOWER    *  R. YARBRO    MCCLENDON
            #      %     #      %* #      %     #      %
-----------------------------------*----------------------------------------------------------------------------------
PARMER      487  45.9   573  54.1*   835  57.2    626  42.8
PECOS       732  58.9   511  41.1*  1133  50.7   1101  49.3
POLK        655  65.4   346  34.6*  2549  61.1   1623  38.9
POTTER     2998  38.9  4705  61.1*  7710  64.7   4214  35.3
PRESIDIO    246  54.9   202  45.1*   777  58.6    549  41.4
                               *
RAINES      282  74.0    99  26.0*   602  59.3    413  40.7
RANDALL    1291  34.5  2456  65.5*  2930  56.1   2290  43.9
REAGAN      378  74.0   133  26.0*   520  52.4    473  47.6
REAL        129  46.6   148  53.4*   219  49.4    224  50.6
REDRIVER   1160  76.6   355  23.4*  2242  51.2   2133  48.8
                               *
REEVES      789  57.0   595  43.0*  1490  53.8   1278  46.2
REFUGIO     684  60.6   444  39.4*  1273  58.1    917  41.9
ROBERTS      85  37.1   144  62.9*    94  51.9     87  48.1
ROBERTSON  1054  78.8   284  21.2*  2348  67.8   1113  32.2
ROCKWALL    511  76.0   161  24.0*   887  53.4    773  46.6
                               *
RUNNELLS    863  50.3   853  49.7*  1600  51.6   1499  48.4
RUSK       1736  41.8  2413  58.2*  2866  38.3   4619  61.7
SABINE      406  69.5   178  30.5*  1509  64.2    843  35.8
SNAUGSTNE   399  55.2   324  44.8*  1290  54.2   1090  45.8
SNJACINTO   357  69.6   156  30.4*  1349  67.1    661  32.9
                               *
SNPATRICIO 1767  61.3  1115  38.7*  4582  61.8   2827  38.2
SANSABA     710  71.9   277  28.1*  1410  62.9    830  37.1
SCHLEICHER  216  46.6   248  53.4*   318  51.0    306  49.0
SCURRY     1111  60.5   724  39.5*  2471  53.7   2130  46.3
SHACKELFRD  360  61.4   226  38.6*   766  53.5    667  46.5
                               *
SHELBY      928  70.7   384  29.3*  3356  50.5   3291  49.5
SHERMAN     131  35.2   241  64.8*   295  47.9    321  52.1
SMITH      3352  38.5  5363  61.5*  8268  54.3   6958  45.7
SOMERVELL   195  60.9   125  39.1*   553  57.1    416  42.9
STARR      2087  95.4   101   4.6*  3707  89.5    434  10.5
                               *
STEPHENS    716  54.4   600  45.6*  1349  49.0   1405  51.0
STERLING    125  67.2    61  32.8*    71  41.3    101  58.7
STONEWALL   331  81.5    75  18.5*   803  61.0    514  39.0
SUTTON      179  47.0   202  53.0*   236  45.9    278  54.1
SWISHER     533  56.4   412  43.6*  1745  74.2    608  25.8
                               *
TARRANT   22702  46.0 26652  54.0* 44128  57.6  32549  42.4
TAYLOR     4093  50.2  4060  49.8*  7970  53.1   7041  46.9
TERRELL     123  51.5   116  48.5*   172  46.9    195  53.1
TERRY       820  51.8   763  48.2*  2060  54.8   1699  45.2
THRCKMORTN  313  68.6   143  31.4*   814  66.6    409  33.4
                               *
TITUS       996  68.0   468  32.0*  2095  50.1   2088  49.9
TOMGREEN   3436  49.0  3579  51.0*  5685  54.7   4714  45.3
TRAVIS    14224  54.2 12030  45.8* 26645  61.9  16396  38.1
TRINITY     426  58.3   305  41.7*  1573  60.8   1014  39.2
TYLER       565  49.3   582  50.7*  1540  56.0   1211  44.0
                               *
UPSHUR     1000  64.0   562  36.0*  3100  52.8   2774  47.2
```

TEXAS/309

```
              DEMOC.  RUNOFF    1961* DEMOC.  SENATOR    1964
                                    *
   COUNTY      BLAKLEY       TOWER      * R. YARBRO    MCCLENDON
              #       %      #      %*   #       %      #       %
-------------------------------------*----------------------------------------------------------------------------
UPTON         268  51.6     251  48.4*   552  47.9     600  52.1
UVALDE        522  34.4     997  65.6*  1553  42.6    2094  57.4
VALVERDE      581  48.8     609  51.2*  2427  69.2    1078  30.8
VANZANDT     1409  67.3     686  32.7*  2891  59.5    1968  40.5
VICTORIA     1898  48.7    2000  51.3*  4211  56.2    3277  43.8
                                    *
WALKER        590  48.6     623  51.4*  2419  59.1    1674  40.9
WALLER        522  50.5     511  49.5*  1340  62.4     806  37.6
WARD          716  50.4     705  49.6*  1399  53.7    1206  46.3
WASHINGTON    590  32.7    1215  67.3*  1105  58.6     781  41.4
WEBB         3881  82.1     848  17.9*  6528  85.7    1087  14.3
                                    *
WHARTON      2162  55.9    1708  44.1*  3582  61.7    2227  38.3
WHEELER       490  49.5     499  50.5*   775  56.1     607  43.9
WICHITA      5922  52.6    5334  47.4* 12468  71.3    5022  28.7
WILBARGER     846  57.7     621  42.3*  2487  59.0    1727  41.0
WILLACY      1107  58.4     790  41.6*  1445  50.5    1419  49.5
                                    *
WILLIAMSON   2778  70.4    1168  29.6*  4612  67.4    2228  32.6
WILSON       1146  69.4     505  30.6*  2360  64.6    1296  35.4
WINKLER       459  42.4     624  57.6*  1548  47.8    1692  52.2
WISE         1136  59.5     774  40.5*  2068  55.4    1668  44.6
WOOD         1253  59.0     872  41.0*  2509  56.1    1962  43.9
                                    *
YOAKUM        376  48.1     405  51.9*  1133  54.4     950  45.6
YOUNG        1180  60.1     785  39.9*  2356  59.1    1628  40.9
ZAPATA        137  53.7     118  46.3*   823  83.9     158  16.1
ZAVALA        253  45.1     308  54.9*  1357  45.9    1600  54.1
-------------------------------------*----------------------------------------------------------------------------
                                    *
TOTALS      437874        448217       * 905041       672573
% OF VOTE     49.4          50.6       *   57.4         42.6
                                    *
                                    *
GEOGRAPHIC CLASS                    *
                                    *
LOWLANDS    152451 48.    162868 52.* 353493 57.    263311 43.
BLACK BELT    3846 62.      2356 38.*   8765 53.      7652 47.
WEST TEXAS  240212 50.    244962 50.* 456920 57.    345438 43.
MEX. TEXAS   41365 52.     38031 48.*  85863 60.     56172 40.
                                    *
                                    *
DEMOGRAPHIC CLASS                   *
                                    *
METRO       232609 44.    295295 56.* 461186 58.    330809 42.
TOWN         37468 53.     33864 47.*  77771 56.     62075 44.
RURAL       167797 58.    119058 42.* 366084 57.    279689 43.
```

	DEMOC. SENATOR 1970*		DEMOC. SENATOR 1972				
COUNTY	BENTSEN # %	R. YARBRO # %*	R. YARBRO # %	SANDERS # %	WILSON # %	CARTLIDGE # %	VELOZ # %
ANDERSON	3433 58.2	2468 41.8*	3679 46.4	2904 36.6	933 11.8	336 4.2	82 1.0
ANDREWS	1482 65.2	792 34.8*	1012 39.8	1208 47.5	187 7.4	102 4.0	34 1.3
ANGELINA	5995 54.5	5000 45.5*	7384 48.5	6156 40.5	1021 6.7	502 3.3	154 1.0
ARANSAS	852 53.6	738 46.4*	1161 47.0	970 39.3	170 6.9	63 2.6	104 4.2
ARCHER	902 51.0	866 49.0*	848 45.0	904 48.0	60 3.2	59 3.1	14 .7
ARMSTRONG	419 56.6	321 43.4*	307 37.1	442 53.4	46 5.6	28 3.4	5 .6
ATASCOSA	2386 51.6	2236 48.4*	2390 52.2	1427 31.2	301 6.6	173 3.8	290 6.3
AUSTIN	766 57.0	579 43.0*	1841 52.0	1375 38.8	205 5.8	83 2.3	38 1.1
BAILEY	549 57.1	413 42.9*	572 47.2	674 47.9	81 5.8	53 3.8	26 1.8
BANDERA	1159 70.0	496 30.0*	924 47.5	744 38.3	185 9.5	78 4.0	13 .7
BASTROP	1492 46.3	1730 53.7*	2269 57.3	1159 29.3	316 8.0	151 3.8	63 1.6
BAYLOR	1095 51.2	1043 48.8*	926 49.5	749 40.1	100 5.4	85 4.5	9 .5
BEE	2259 44.8	2789 55.2*	2294 49.7	1451 31.4	391 8.5	115 2.5	368 8.0
BELL	5498 54.1	4657 45.9*	7766 50.1	4967 32.0	1423 9.2	695 4.5	658 4.2
BEXAR	49624 53.3	43542 46.7*	57055 54.1	32214 30.5	7472 7.1	4546 4.3	4177 4.0
BLANCO	268 62.3	162 37.7*	306 40.8	338 45.1	76 10.1	23 3.1	7 .9
BORDEN	263 63.1	154 36.9*	141 21.7	183 28.2	314 48.3	5 .8	7 1.1
BOSQUE	1707 63.9	965 36.1*	1501 40.9	1772 48.3	215 5.9	142 3.9	38 1.0
BOWIE	4072 54.4	3420 45.6*	8615 60.8	4102 29.0	884 6.2	329 2.3	236 1.7
BRAZORIA	8567 51.7	7992 48.3*	11012 51.9	7262 34.2	1619 7.6	832 3.9	478 2.3
BRAZOS	4009 51.6	3760 48.4*	6239 49.7	4600 36.6	1089 8.7	366 2.9	263 2.1
BREWSTER	818 44.0	1041 56.0*	703 44.0	560 35.1	96 6.0	30 1.9	207 13.0
BRISCOE	298 38.1	484 61.9*	484 52.7	333 36.2	63 6.9	18 2.0	21 2.3
BROOKS	1099 37.8	1805 62.2*	1798 61.5	504 17.2	96 3.3	28 1.0	498 17.0
BROWN	1705 63.0	1002 37.0*	3672 48.1	3354 44.0	417 5.5	126 1.7	58 .8
BURLESON	790 41.3	1123 58.7*	2191 61.0	981 27.3	307 8.5	63 1.8	50 1.4
BURNET	1494 54.0	1274 46.0*	1858 47.8	1571 40.5	343 8.8	70 1.8	41 1.1
CALDWELL	1927 53.8	1653 46.2*	2072 49.1	1620 38.4	240 5.7	141 3.3	143 3.4
CALHOUN	1491 51.1	1428 48.9*	3098 57.5	1699 31.5	271 5.0	109 2.0	210 3.9
CALLAHAN	943 57.0	710 43.0*	949 36.7	1442 55.8	116 4.5	62 2.4	17 .7
CAMERON	11602 52.0	10694 48.0*	11384 53.3	7612 35.6	799 3.7	446 2.1	1121 5.2
CAMP	1307 52.5	1184 47.5*	1584 61.1	751 29.0	195 7.5	44 1.7	18 .7
CARSON	750 48.8	788 51.2*	843 52.4	645 40.1	78 4.8	32 2.0	11 .7
CASS	3044 61.5	1902 38.5*	3641 58.9	1744 28.2	531 8.6	200 3.2	62 1.0
CASTRO	653 46.8	742 53.2*	1084 54.2	722 36.1	97 4.8	29 1.4	69 3.4
CHAMBERS	1213 58.8	849 41.2*	1584 52.7	1058 35.2	241 8.0	100 3.3	21 .7
CHEROKEE	2765 54.9	2276 45.1*	3804 46.9	2943 36.3	924 11.4	388 4.8	55 .7
CHILDRESS	1100 55.6	877 44.4*	729 40.7	775 43.3	87 4.9	195 10.9	5 .3
CLAY	1324 51.5	1245 48.5*	764 30.7	662 26.6	102 4.1	943 37.9	15 .6
COCHRAN	956 67.3	465 32.7*	637 41.3	700 45.4	91 5.9	67 4.3	48 3.1
COKE	378 55.5	303 44.5*	422 39.6	536 50.3	79 7.4	20 1.9	9 .8
COLEMAN	1329 64.3	737 35.7*	1119 37.3	1639 54.6	122 4.1	87 2.9	37 1.2
COLLIN	5401 63.4	3115 36.6*	4913 39.9	6232 50.7	524 4.3	475 3.9	160 1.3
CLNGSWORTH	799 52.3	730 47.7*	852 52.2	673 41.3	45 2.8	52 3.2	9 .6
COLORADO	1222 53.6	1057 46.4*	2435 51.7	1451 30.8	630 13.4	144 3.1	47 1.0
COMAL	2493 70.1	1061 29.9*	2058 43.8	1946 41.4	276 5.9	284 6.0	139 3.0

COUNTY	BENTSEN #	%	R. YARBRO #	%*	R. YARBRO #	%	SANDERS #	%	WILSON #	%	CARTLIDGE #	%	VELOZ #	%
COMANCHEE	1771	64.0	997	36.0*	2151	50.4	1678	39.3	175	4.1	223	5.2	38	.9
CONCHO	350	57.5	259	42.5*	474	46.6	446	43.8	66	6.5	20	2.0	12	1.2
COOKE	3759	65.8	1953	34.2*	2673	44.9	2506	42.1	336	5.6	372	6.3	63	1.1
CORYELL	2701	63.4	1558	36.6*	2583	50.3	2113	41.1	227	4.4	167	3.3	47	.9
COTTLE	395	37.4	660	62.6*	678	58.5	415	35.8	43	3.7	9	.8	13	1.1
CRANE	749	64.6	410	35.4*	805	43.9	776	42.3	109	5.9	75	4.1	68	3.7
CROCKETT	677	66.4	343	33.6*	552	43.2	429	33.6	106	8.3	53	4.1	138	10.8
CROSBY	973	55.2	790	44.8*	1184	49.1	930	38.6	108	4.5	46	1.9	141	5.9
CULBERSON	356	51.9	330	48.1*	437	50.6	247	28.6	81	9.4	14	1.6	85	9.8
DALLAM	572	60.5	374	39.5*	334	47.6	280	39.9	56	8.0	27	3.8	5	.7
DALLAS	76614	60.3	50397	39.7*	62912	38.6	83088	51.0	10304	6.3	4338	2.7	2375	1.5
DAWSON	1932	65.6	1012	34.4*	1032	34.1	1745	57.7	131	4.3	62	2.0	55	1.8
DEAFSMITH	1394	60.7	904	39.3*	1021	39.5	1279	49.5	151	5.8	83	3.2	48	1.9
DELTA	771	54.6	641	45.4*	306	24.9	776	63.2	85	6.9	32	2.6	29	2.4
DENTON	5672	56.5	4372	43.5*	8136	49.0	7006	42.2	829	5.0	384	2.3	243	1.5
DEWITT	2337	71.0	954	29.0*	1993	49.0	1383	34.0	304	7.5	310	7.6	79	1.9
DICKENS	732	53.8	628	46.2*	783	57.1	457	33.3	53	3.9	47	3.4	31	2.3
DIMMIT	782	51.0	751	49.0*	686	34.8	598	30.4	209	10.6	128	6.5	348	17.7
DONLEY	661	56.4	511	43.6*	669	48.2	598	43.1	87	6.3	31	2.2	3	.2
DUVAL	264	6.2	3993	93.8*	4061	94.1	174	4.0	29	.7	21	.5	31	.7
EASTLAND	2375	54.0	2027	46.0*	2309	44.5	2448	47.2	240	4.6	147	2.8	46	.9
ECTOR	5233	66.8	2601	33.2*	4138	33.1	6682	53.4	920	7.4	376	3.0	396	3.2
EDWARDS	324	81.4	74	18.6*	189	34.9	261	48.2	41	7.6	41	7.6	10	1 8
ELLIS	3262	57.8	2382	42.2*	4638	49.6	3935	42.1	349	3.7	325	3.5	95	1.0
ELPASO	18546	45.7	22051	54.3*	29232	66.9	8922	20.4	2228	5.1	1045	2.4	2258	5.2
ERATH	2168	59.7	1465	40.3*	3153	52.5	2116	35.3	335	5.6	351	5.8	46	.8
FALLS	1771	48.8	1857	51.2*	2723	56.1	1676	34.5	266	5.5	106	2.2	87	1.8
FANNIN	2541	48.1	2746	51.9*	3558	53.2	2588	38.7	286	4.3	216	3.2	44	.7
FAYETTE	1984	57.7	1452	42.3*	3070	60.9	1227	24.4	597	11.9	102	2.0	41	.8
FISHER	740	39.6	1127	60.4*	1030	48.2	958	44.9	76	3.6	24	1.1	47	2.2
FLOYD	1201	58.0	869	42.0*	1210	45.4	1154	43.3	163	6.1	55	2.1	86	3.2
FOARD	272	45.0	333	55.0*	273	49.6	240	43.6	15	2.7	15	2.7	7	1.3
FORTBEND	3663	50.9	3534	49.1*	4304	51.0	3161	37.4	370	4.4	400	4.7	206	2.4
FRANKLIN	874	53.4	763	46.6*	769	47.9	682	42.5	84	5.2	57	3.5	14	.9
FREESTONE	1595	50.7	1554	49.3*	1633	48.6	1163	34.6	404	12.0	124	3.7	33	1.0
FRIO	1289	58.3	921	41.7*	918	37.4	757	30.9	146	6.0	112	4.6	519	21.2
GAINES	1173	67.3	571	32.7*	940	40.2	1087	46.5	151	6.5	100	4.3	60	2.6
GALVESTON	9217	40.1	13748	59.9*	19559	59.3	10175	30.9	1203	3.7	1013	3.1	1006	3.1
GARZA	914	63.1	535	36.9*	738	52.6	492	35.0	99	7.1	22	1.6	53	3.8
GILLESPIE	466	76.0	147	24.0*	451	33.4	803	59.4	54	4.0	36	2.7	7	.5
GLASCOCK	233	69.8	101	30.2*	147	41.5	166	46.9	20	5.6	21	5.9	0	.0
GOLIAD	819	50.5	802	49.5*	565	50.2	386	34.3	99	8.8	36	3.2	40	3.6
GONZALES	2285	60.7	1477	39.3*	1404	44.7	1073	34.2	449	14.3	112	3.6	103	3.3
GRAY	2146	63.3	1243	36.7*	1730	40.6	2064	48.5	357	8.4	61	1.4	47	1.1
GRAYSON	5164	56.5	3974	43.5*	7897	49.8	6442	40.6	550	3.5	842	5.3	135	.9
GREGG	6025	73.1	2216	26.9*	4654	31.6	7435	50.5	1866	12.7	472	3.2	292	2.0

COUNTY	BENTSEN #	%	R. YARBRO #	%*	R. YARBRO #	%	SANDERS #	%	WILSON #	%	CARTLIDGE #	%	VELOZ #	%
GRIMES	1129	55.0	922	45.0*	1650	49.3	1109	33.1	428	12.8	104	3.1	59	1.8
GUADALUPE	2389	62.2	1454	37.8*	2972	45.6	2681	41.2	311	4.8	243	3.7	306	4.7
HALE	3398	67.4	1642	32.6*	2612	43.1	2667	44.0	378	6.2	239	3.9	168	2.8
HALL	618	49.0	643	51.0*	868	51.6	726	43.2	37	2.2	21	1.2	30	1.8
HAMILTON	1503	63.1	878	36.9*	963	44.0	967	44.2	131	6.0	113	5.2	14	.6
HANSFORD	515	74.1	180	25.9*	449	36.2	634	51.2	65	5.2	75	6.1	16	1.3
HARDEMAN	619	56.0	486	44.0*	610	45.1	609	45.0	89	6.6	41	3.0	5	.4
HARDIN	3714	46.7	4232	53.3*	4814	54.4	2850	32.2	988	11.2	142	1.6	62	.7
HARRIS	76271	43.7	98416	56.3*	148889	55.4	97875	36.4	9120	3.4	6896	2.6	6144	2.3
HARRISON	4979	60.8	3216	39.2*	4402	50.8	3044	35.2	751	8.7	190	2.2	270	3.1
HARTLEY	286	61.0	183	39.0*	317	49.8	247	38.8	41	6.4	27	4.2	5	.8
HASKELL	1058	43.6	1367	56.4*	1374	47.5	1277	44.1	131	4.5	63	2.2	50	1.7
HAYS	2780	47.7	3050	52.3*	3574	56.5	1945	30.8	284	4.5	239	3.8	281	4.4
HEMPHILL	349	50.3	345	49.7*	338	44.3	338	44.3	61	8.0	17	2.2	9	1.2
HENDERSON	2969	43.8	3813	56.2*	5231	55.8	3172	33.8	589	6.3	319	3.4	70	.7
HIDALGO	15835	45.5	18983	54.5*	14770	53.3	8800	31.7	1691	6.1	1113	4.0	1348	4.9
HILL	2909	57.0	2198	43.0*	2959	48.7	2521	41.5	244	4.0	284	4.7	65	1.1
HOCKLEY	1923	62.2	1167	37.8*	1887	42.8	1921	43.6	287	6.5	174	4.0	135	3.1
HOOD	919	50.9	886	49.1*	1383	51.8	916	34.3	207	7.7	133	5.0	33	1.2
HOPKINS	3127	65.1	1674	34.9*	2177	40.1	2829	52.1	262	4.8	116	2.1	48	.9
HOUSTON	2470	45.6	2950	54.4*	2848	52.6	1723	31.8	595	11.0	200	3.7	45	.8
HOWARD	2938	51.0	2823	49.0*	2647	49.2	2253	41.9	187	3.5	167	3.1	124	2.3
HUDSPETH	401	56.2	313	43.8*	384	59.4	120	18.6	55	8.5	24	3.7	63	9.8
HUNT	4916	58.0	3556	42.0*	5053	51.9	3808	39.1	380	3.9	395	4.1	102	1.0
HUTCHISON	1992	63.0	1172	37.0*	1728	37.7	2560	55.9	144	3.1	107	2.3	39	.9
IRION	202	74.0	71	26.0*	190	39.2	205	42.3	50	10.3	24	4.9	16	3.3
JACK	1220	58.2	877	41.8*	1262	50.2	945	37.6	181	7.2	101	4.0	25	1.0
JACKSON	2230	55.5	1790	44.5*	2063	55.7	1186	32.0	264	7.1	130	3.5	59	1.6
JASPER	1769	54.3	1487	45.7*	3677	52.2	2387	33.9	766	10.9	170	2.4	50	.7
JEFFDAVIS	227	46.1	265	53.9*	205	43.1	149	31.3	40	8.4	8	1.7	74	15.5
JEFFERSON	17444	49.9	17485	50.1*	21540	48.8	13513	30.6	6047	13.7	1424	3.2	1656	3.7
JIMHOGG	499	27.8	1299	72.2*	1225	68.7	241	13.5	50	2.8	59	3.3	209	11.7
JIMWELLS	3334	37.1	5659	62.9*	5411	60.4	2096	23.4	405	4.5	276	3.1	772	8.6
JOHNSON	2918	56.5	2246	43.5*	5062	53.8	3474	36.9	441	4.7	309	3.3	126	1.3
JONES	1039	51.6	975	48.4*	1393	38.0	2008	54.7	172	4.7	58	1.6	37	1.0
KARNES	1702	51.3	1613	48.7*	1934	50.2	1232	32.0	334	8.7	126	3.3	224	5.8
KAUFMAN	3185	56.9	2410	43.1*	2601	44.4	2805	47.9	243	4.1	162	2.8	49	.8
KENDALL	243	73.4	88	26.6*	275	34.6	390	49.1	85	10.7	35	4.4	10	1.3
KENEDY	84	49.4	86	50.6*	58	31.7	105	57.4	13	7.1	0	.0	7	3.8
KENT	375	56.1	293	43.9*	336	49.6	253	37.3	43	6.3	24	3.5	22	3.2
KERR	1403	67.1	687	32.9*	1780	42.5	1689	40.4	414	9.9	238	5.7	64	1.5
KIMBLE	458	68.4	212	31.6*	414	36.9	479	42.7	124	11.0	67	6.0	39	3.5
KING	91	49.2	94	50.8*	97	52.4	67	36.2	8	4.3	4	2.2	9	4.9
KINNEY	369	59.0	256	41.0*	283	55.5	143	28.0	23	4.5	12	2.4	49	9.6
KLEBERG	2363	42.1	3253	57.9*	4034	55.2	2351	32.2	263	3.6	104	1.4	557	7.6
KNOX	739	50.2	732	49.8*	865	50.1	709	41.0	58	3.4	68	3.9	28	1.6

COUNTY	BENTSEN #	%	R. YARBRO #	%	R. YARBRO #	%	SANDERS #	%	WILSON #	%	CARTLIDGE #	%	VELOZ #	%
LAMAR	3769	56.3	2930	43.7*	4051	41.9	4923	50.9	460	4.8	159	1.6	72	.7
LAMB	1217	68.4	563	31.6*	1056	37.6	1468	52.2	178	6.3	69	2.5	39	1.4
LAMPASAS	1145	58.7	806	41.3*	1312	48.6	1071	39.7	222	8.2	62	2.3	33	1.2
LASALLE	790	64.2	441	35.8*	498	42.3	443	37.6	135	11.5	48	4.1	54	4.6
LABACA	3004	66.7	1503	33.3*	2412	54.4	1201	27.1	547	12.3	214	4.8	61	1.4
LEE	714	46.7	816	53.3*	1630	60.8	731	27.3	227	8.5	50	1.9	43	1.6
LEON	868	50.1	864	49.9*	1223	48.4	691	27.3	545	21.6	56	2.2	13	.5
LIBERTY	3147	55.4	2535	44.6*	3991	48.5	2978	36.2	1025	12.5	165	2.0	67	.8
LIMESTONE	2091	51.1	2001	48.9*	2271	50.4	1792	39.7	265	5.9	133	2.9	49	1.1
LIPSCOMB	482	65.6	253	34.4*	330	46.9	279	39.6	69	9.8	17	2.4	9	1.3
LIVEOAK	1485	57.6	1092	42.4*	954	37.3	1198	46.8	189	7.4	78	3.0	142	5.5
LLANO	957	58.7	674	41.3*	859	39.3	1073	49.1	197	9.0	36	1.6	20	.9
LOVING	37	56.1	29	43.9*	27	40.9	26	39.4	9	13.6	2	3.0	2	3.0
LUBBOCK	11669	63.7	6642	36.3*	13060	42.0	15400	49.5	1363	4.4	435	1.4	867	2.8
LYNN	965	65.5	508	34.5*	1027	43.0	1032	43.3	182	7.6	45	1.9	100	4.2
MADISON	1228	54.7	1018	45.3*	1201	50.1	855	35.7	244	10.2	85	3.5	11	.5
MARION	1156	55.7	919	44.3*	1025	53.2	568	29.5	272	14.1	43	2.2	18	.9
MARTIN	643	63.4	371	36.6*	369	40.4	461	50.5	39	4.3	33	3.6	11	1.2
MASON	860	61.6	536	38.4*	493	41.7	494	41.8	149	12.6	29	2.5	16	1.4
MATAGORDA	2588	55.5	2076	44.5*	3072	56.6	1859	34.2	237	4.4	149	2.7	111	2.0
MAVERICK	1327	47.7	1457	52.3*	1640	55.6	431	14.6	132	4.5	140	4.7	605	20.5
MCCULLOCH	1192	55.4	961	44.6*	1213	43.2	1254	44.6	225	8.0	57	2.0	60	2.1
MCLENNAN	11105	50.0	11114	50.0*	19968	55.5	12675	35.2	1966	5.5	957	2.7	395	1.1
MCMULLEN	211	65.3	112	34.7*	154	36.7	199	47.4	32	7.6	16	3.8	19	4.5
MEDINA	2151	57.1	1613	42.9*	2644	53.9	1487	30.3	266	5.4	271	5.5	236	4.8
MENARD	563	52.9	502	47.1*	436	44.2	368	37.3	75	7.6	59	6.0	48	4.9
MIDLAND	3687	67.6	1766	32.4*	2948	29.1	5742	56.7	622	6.1	502	5.0	319	3.1
MILAN	1866	45.9	2199	54.1*	3502	62.5	1615	28.8	268	4.8	151	2.7	64	1.1
MILLS	847	65.4	449	34.6*	670	39.9	717	42.7	227	13.5	51	3.0	13	.8
MITCHELL	1245	52.7	1117	47.3*	1153	44.7	1150	44.6	157	6.1	43	1.7	77	3.0
MONTAGE	2199	62.4	1323	37.6*	1510	42.3	1685	47.3	144	4.0	195	5.5	32	.9
MONTGOMRY	6342	58.2	4551	41.8*	5744	40.8	5528	39.3	2274	16.2	347	2.5	172	1.2
MOORE	2027	61.4	1274	38.6*	1013	42.8	1032	43.6	158	6.7	112	4.7	52	2.2
MORRIS	1662	53.7	1434	46.3*	2122	58.7	1063	29.4	209	5.8	182	5.0	36	1.0
MOTLEY	398	66.8	198	33.2*	370	43.0	398	46.2	55	6.4	27	3.1	11	1.3
NACDOCHES	4342	61.4	2731	38.6*	4246	43.6	4175	42.9	713	7.3	466	4.8	141	1.4
NAVARRO	3136	50.8	3033	49.2*	4400	51.6	3281	38.5	455	5.3	308	3.6	79	.9
NEWTON	1802	52.4	1637	47.6*	1924	55.6	972	28.1	440	12.7	89	2.6	36	1.0
NOLAN	1805	54.5	1508	45.5*	1782	69.1	198	7.7	189	7.3	347	13.5	62	2.4
NUECES	15223	40.0	22809	60.0*	25414	52.3	17762	36.5	2445	5.0	1175	2.4	1837	3.8
OCHILTREE	884	79.9	223	20.1*	733	39.5	888	47.8	140	7.5	72	3.9	24	1.3
OLDHAM	314	54.6	261	45.4*	245	45.0	238	43.8	28	5.1	26	4.8	7	1.3
ORANGE	6715	56.3	5219	43.7*	9581	50.8	6265	33.2	2343	12.4	485	2.6	202	1.1
PALOPINTO	2824	54.0	2402	46.0*	3272	53.9	2122	35.0	271	4.5	314	5.2	92	1.5
PANOLA	2994	71.4	1197	28.6*	2766	49.5	1717	30.7	623	11.1	427	7.6	55	1.0
PARKER	3965	57.7	2902	42.3*	4368	52.2	3133	37.4	491	5.9	275	3.3	107	1.3

		DEMOC. SENATOR 1970*					DEMOC. SENATOR 1972							
COUNTY	BENTSEN		R. YARBRO		R. YARBRO		SANDERS		WILSON		CARTLIDGE		VELOZ	
	#	%	#	%*	#	%	#	%	#	%	#	%	#	%
PARMER	932	63.0	548	37.0*	543	36.3	820	54.8	76	5.1	40	2.7	17	1.1
PECOS	1520	51.6	1428	48.4*	1200	39.6	1214	40.0	201	6.6	56	1.8	363	12.0
POLK	1903	50.4	1870	49.6*	2727	55.6	1428	29.1	508	10.4	193	3.9	48	1.0
POTTER	5508	55.7	4379	44.3*	5919	47.2	5407	43.1	693	5.5	255	2.0	269	2.1
PRESIDIO	472	37.4	790	62.6*	569	46.8	287	23.6	54	4.4	57	4.7	248	20.4
RAINES	584	44.5	729	55.5*	859	58.7	481	32.9	49	3.3	48	3.3	27	1.8
RANDALL	4096	64.8	2228	35.2*	3471	38.8	4669	52.2	428	4.8	253	2.8	124	1.4
REAGAN	639	63.6	365	36.4*	333	37.2	373	41.7	113	12.6	23	2.6	52	5.8
REAL	169	69.3	75	30.7*	234	40.5	263	45.5	38	6.6	32	5.5	11	1.9
REDRIVER	3112	67.8	1476	32.2*	2352	54.4	1562	36.1	263	6.1	107	2.5	38	.9
REEVES	1283	55.5	1029	44.5*	1428	39.2	1350	37.1	162	4.5	54	1.5	645	17.7
REFUGIO	1078	54.6	895	45.4*	1444	49.3	1074	36.7	203	6.9	48	1.6	159	5.4
ROBERTS	263	72.5	100	27.5*	122	35.0	199	57.0	16	4.6	9	2.6	3	.9
ROBERTSON	1569	38.2	2533	61.8*	2697	64.0	1121	26.6	233	5.5	120	2.8	46	1.1
ROCKWALL	923	63.8	523	36.2*	975	40.0	1257	51.6	128	5.3	48	2.0	29	1.2
RUNNELLS	1106	64.9	597	35.1*	1165	39.5	1465	49.6	194	6.6	93	3.2	34	1.2
RUSK	4689	68.1	2193	31.9*	3168	43.1	3062	41.7	631	8.6	342	4.7	146	2.0
SABINE	942	50.5	924	49.5*	1568	60.3	644	24.8	323	12.4	46	1.8	19	.7
SNAUGSTNE	819	57.3	611	42.7*	1271	49.7	802	31.4	372	14.5	70	2.7	42	1.6
SNJACINTO	787	38.6	1253	61.4*	1442	60.7	595	25.0	251	10.6	74	3.1	15	.6
SNPATRICIO	4090	40.9	5906	59.1*	5762	52.4	3779	34.4	398	3.6	157	1.4	897	8.2
SANSABA	737	54.9	605	45.1*	975	49.0	783	39.4	162	8.1	31	1.6	37	1.9
SCHLEICHER	545	63.3	316	36.7*	369	40.4	373	41.0	89	9.8	31	3.4	47	5.2
SCURRY	1993	59.4	1365	40.6*	1622	37.6	2139	49.5	286	6.6	188	4.4	82	1.9
SHACKELFRD	786	57.2	589	42.8*	549	38.3	778	54.3	70	4.9	23	1.6	14	1.0
SHELBY	2221	58.0	1606	42.0*	4419	63.2	1531	21.9	687	9.8	283	4.0	71	1.0
SHERMAN	219	71.8	86	28.2*	229	40.6	268	47.5	35	6.2	22	3.9	10	1.8
SMITH	10792	63.0	6342	37.0*	6487	34.5	8454	44.9	1879	10.0	1695	9.0	308	1.6
SOMERVELL	311	56.5	239	43.5*	545	45.7	392	32.9	206	17.3	38	3.2	11	.9
STARR	2409	46.5	2777	53.5*	2845	77.1	294	8.0	47	1.3	314	8.5	192	5.2
STEPHENS	1520	63.0	893	37.0*	1237	37.7	1634	49.8	239	7.3	133	4.1	36	1.1
STERLING	137	60.4	90	39.6*	88	35.3	128	51.4	27	10.8	4	1.6	2	.8
STONEWALL	568	46.2	662	53.8*	416	48.5	354	41.3	41	4.8	31	3.6	15	1.8
SUTTON	484	69.5	212	30.5*	229	37.4	276	45.0	52	8.5	20	3.3	36	5.9
SWISHER	724	31.5	1576	68.5*	1487	65.3	613	26.9	100	4.4	20	.9	57	2.5
TARRANT	35020	54.1	29704	45.9*	52143	46.9	46711	42.0	4490	4.0	4608	4.1	3185	2.9
TAYLOR	5900	59.9	3945	40.1*	5441	31.3	10829	62.3	643	3.7	294	1.7	185	1.1
TERRELL	267	57.2	200	42.8*	266	47.7	191	34.2	38	6.8	10	1.8	53	9.5
TERRY	1345	66.0	692	34.0*	968	33.8	1642	57.4	93	3.2	93	3.2	66	2.3
THRCKMORTN	587	56.9	444	43.1*	536	47.6	467	41.5	67	6.0	39	3.5	16	1.4
TITUS	1604	50.5	1573	49.5*	2153	48.6	1826	41.3	255	5.8	166	3.8	26	.6
TOMGREEN	5669	66.5	2853	33.5*	5396	42.6	5440	42.9	1195	9.4	299	2.4	341	2.7
TRAVIS	21505	45.0	26296	55.0*	53316	61.1	27141	31.1	3236	3.7	1616	1.9	1972	2.3
TRINITY	1345	48.5	1427	51.5*	1305	49.0	1042	39.1	241	9.0	66	2.5	10	.4
TYLER	1567	54.8	1291	45.2*	1948	49.5	1266	32.1	606	15.4	99	2.5	20	.5
UPSHUR	3331	57.1	2498	42.9*	2981	47.2	2477	39.2	511	8.1	300	4.8	44	.7

COUNTY	BENTSEN #	%	R. YARBRO #	%*	R. YARBRO #	%	SANDERS #	%	WILSON #	%	CARTLIDGE #	%	VELOZ #	%
UPTON	993	67.7	473	32.3*	453	33.9	643	48.1	102	7.6	69	5.2	69	5.2
UVALDE	2317	61.6	1442	38.4*	1618	35.4	1824	39.9	442	9.7	218	4.8	468	10.2
VALVERDE	2783	51.2	2655	48.8*	2265	52.5	1146	26.6	210	4.9	146	3.4	544	12.6
VANZANDT	2101	53.0	1866	47.0*	2620	46.0	2524	44.3	258	4.5	254	4.5	37	.6
VICTORIA	6461	60.4	4239	39.6*	6380	50.6	4507	35.8	840	6.7	453	3.6	425	3.4
WALKER	2093	53.8	1796	46.2*	3527	55.9	1937	30.7	669	10.6	101	1.6	76	1.2
WALLER	1107	45.3	1335	54.7*	2277	61.3	1129	30.4	175	4.7	81	2.2	50	1.3
WARD	1708	59.3	1171	40.7*	1052	39.3	1129	42.2	224	8.4	80	3.0	192	7.2
WASHINGTON	738	56.8	562	43.2*	2223	52.9	1573	37.4	198	4.7	177	4.2	34	.8
WEBB	4373	56.9	3309	43.1*	7098	67.8	2379	22.7	322	3.1	165	1.6	501	4.8
WHARTON	2515	48.4	2680	51.6*	3455	54.9	2219	35.2	352	5.6	143	2.3	128	2.0
WHEELER	806	59.2	556	40.8*	510	39.0	676	51.6	37	2.8	75	5.7	11	.8
WICHITA	5063	44.6	6294	55.4*	10492	50.3	8866	42.5	640	3.1	651	3.1	219	1.0
WILBARGER	2152	66.7	1075	33.3*	1050	38.3	1389	50.7	182	6.6	84	3.1	34	1.2
WILLACY	1715	56.2	1337	43.8*	1675	45.7	1274	34.7	229	6.2	53	1.4	438	11.9
WILLIAMSON	2870	48.3	3070	51.7*	4779	56.4	2735	32.3	630	7.4	221	2.6	113	1.3
WILSON	1404	51.3	1331	48.7*	2440	52.7	1501	32.4	266	5.7	215	4.6	212	4.6
WINKLER	1851	64.6	1015	35.4*	1315	38.7	1654	48.7	228	6.7	85	2.5	113	3.3
WISE	2340	60.6	1521	39.4*	2344	46.5	2090	41.5	231	4.6	310	6.2	62	1.2
WOOD	1742	40.8	2528	59.2*	1955	41.8	2030	43.4	382	8.2	264	5.6	44	.9
YOAKUM	1383	74.0	486	26.0*	844	38.7	1026	47.1	153	7.0	107	4.9	50	2.3
YOUNG	1223	58.7	862	41.3*	1903	44.1	2028	46.9	178	4.1	183	4.2	28	.6
ZAPATA	455	30.1	1056	69.9*	874	46.5	143	10.6	45	3.3	86	6.3	207	15.3
ZAVALA	981	49.9	984	50.1*	353	25.7	753	54.8	149	10.8	56	4.1	63	4.6
TOTALS	814226		726447		*1032606		787504		125468		66240		53943	
% OF VOTE	52.8		47.2		50.0		38.1		6.1		3.2		2.6	

GEOGRAPHIC CLASS

	BENTSEN #	%	R. YARBRO #	%*	R. YARBRO #	%	SANDERS #	%	WILSON #	%	CARTLIDGE #	%	VELOZ #	%
LOWLANDS	285687	51.	279774	49.*	417546	52.	289904	36.	54076	7.	25106	3.	14416	2.
BLACK BELT	9598	51.	9256	49.*	11843	57.	6457	31.	1682	8.	508	2.	399	2.
WEST TEXAS	429177	56.	334496	44.*	492272	47.	437983	42.	59941	6.	35030	3.	25068	2.
MEX. TEXAS	89764	47.	102921	53.*	110945	57.	53160	27.	9769	5.	5596	3.	14060	7.

DEMOGRAPHIC CLASS

	BENTSEN #	%	R. YARBRO #	%*	R. YARBRO #	%	SANDERS #	%	WILSON #	%	CARTLIDGE #	%	VELOZ #	%
METRO	410852	51.	393026	49.*	580587	51.	437254	38.	60814	5.	33550	3.	29969	3.
TOWN	77417	53.	67758	47.*	91243	48.	72935	39.	12407	7.	6051	3.	5524	3.
RURAL	325957	55.	265663	45.*	360776	49.	277315	38.	52247	7.	26639	4.	18450	3.

COUNTY	SANDERS #	%	YARBRO #	%*	FOR #	%	AGAINST #	%
ANDERSON	4119	54.4	3446	45.6*	549	25.1	1635	74.9
ANDREWS	1294	71.2	524	28.8*	138	32.4	288	67.6
ANGELINA	8804	58.4	6265	41.6*	960	39.9	1448	60.1
ARANSAS	1022	56.0	804	44.0*	126	46.5	145	53.5
ARCHER	1018	66.8	506	33.2*	246	34.5	468	65.5
ARMSTRONG	386	70.3	163	29.7*	44	14.8	254	85.2
ATASCOSA	2135	44.4	2672	55.6*	356	36.5	620	63.5
AUSTIN	1845	56.4	1428	43.6*	244	26.3	684	73.7
BAILEY	842	65.4	446	34.6*	91	14.3	544	85.7
BANDERA	1208	60.6	787	39.4*	185	30.5	421	69.5
BASTROP	1646	45.7	1956	54.3*	696	38.6	1107	61.4
BAYLOR	1029	59.9	688	40.1*	129	29.2	313	70.8
BEE	1917	52.5	1737	47.5*	335	36.0	595	64.0
BELL	8262	52.0	7621	48.0*	1045	42.8	1397	57.2
BEXAR	57708	47.9	62763	52.1*	18072	53.4	15764	46.6
BLANCO	470	61.4	296	38.6*	128	29.8	302	70.2
BORDEN	261	75.4	85	24.6*	45	21.7	162	78.3
BOSQUE	1957	63.5	1123	36.5*	273	28.6	683	71.4
BOWIE	6626	56.2	5158	43.8*	692	22.1	2440	77.9
BRAZORIA	10440	49.1	10828	50.9*	1521	43.7	1962	56.3
BRAZOS	6294	53.3	5514	46.7*	939	47.9	1022	52.1
BREWSTER	671	62.0	411	38.0*	97	36.3	170	63.7
BRISCOE	326	52.8	292	47.2*	55	15.2	307	84.8
BROOKS	858	27.5	2265	72.5*	428	72.3	164	27.7
BROWN	2957	58.2	2122	41.8*	446	32.4	932	67.6
BURLESON	1374	37.2	2320	62.8*	350	39.0	547	61.0
BURNET	1800	55.6	1437	44.4*	443	39.2	688	60.8
CALDWELL	1958	52.6	1764	47.4*	533	32.8	1091	67.2
CALHOUN	2403	46.1	2808	53.9*	565	57.7	415	42.3
CALLAHAN	1560	66.5	786	33.5*	201	28.3	508	71.7
CAMERON	8485	41.8	11799	58.2*	2488	46.5	2865	53.5
CAMP	1151	46.7	1316	53.3*	174	31.0	388	69.0
CARSON	742	55.1	604	44.9*	255	43.5	331	56.5
CASS	2356	56.9	1788	43.1*	255	20.6	980	79.4
CASTRO	802	52.5	727	47.5*	127	20.3	499	79.7
CHAMBERS	1618	55.9	1277	44.1*	135	36.2	238	63.8
CHEROKEE	3593	53.1	3179	46.9*	628	33.3	1258	66.7
CHILDRESS	864	67.4	417	32.6*	122	18.2	549	81.8
CLAY	1462	62.5	876	37.5*	295	40.0	442	60.0
COCHRAN	945	68.2	441	31.8*	54	17.2	260	82.8
COKE	584	66.2	298	33.8*	142	31.3	312	68.7
COLEMAN	1575	67.1	773	32.9*	243	23.7	782	76.3
COLLIN	6100	65.6	3203	34.4*	563	24.5	1732	75.5
CLNGSWORTH	844	58.0	611	42.0*	104	18.2	468	81.8
COLORADO	2589	52.0	2391	48.0*	336	35.0	623	65.0
COMAL	2107	60.0	1406	40.0*	391	32.1	828	67.9

TEXAS/317

```
                DEMOC.  RUNOFF    1972* SPECL.  REFERENDUM 1963
                                      *
      COUNTY,   SANDERS      YARBRO       FOR          AGAINST
                #      %     #      %*    #      %      #      %
--------------------------------------*-----------------------------------------------------------------------------------

COMANCHEE   2197 56.2    1713 43.8*    220 25.2     654 74.8
CONCHO       532 53.9     455 46.1*     67 20.7     256 79.3
COOKE       3304 65.3    1759 34.7*    395 26.4    1100 73.6
CORYELL     2228 58.0    1613 42.0*    433 32.9     884 67.1
COTTLE       352 48.4     376 51.6*     85 24.4     263 75.6
                                      *
CRANE        799 69.0     359 31.0*    103 34.7     194 65.3
CROCKETT     624 58.4     445 41.6*     47 28.7     117 71.3
CROSBY       851 52.3     777 47.7*     88 15.4     485 84.6
CULBERSON    280 63.3     162 36.7*     49 36.6      85 63.4
DALLAM       387 64.9     209 35.1*    105 32.2     221 67.8
                                      *
DALLAS    100283 60.3   66031 39.7*  25653 42.9   34204 57.1
DAWSON      1815 71.6     720 28.4*    163 17.4     773 82.6
DEAFSMITH   1467 66.7     734 33.3*    160 18.8     691 81.2
DELTA        838 57.7     615 42.3*    105 20.1     418 79.9
DENTON      8867 53.9    7588 46.1*   1011 39.8    1531 60.2
                                      *
DEWITT      1977 59.4    1353 40.6*    406 28.2    1032 71.8
DICKENS      421 48.4     449 51.6*     88 20.9     334 79.1
DIMMIT       959 53.5     834 46.5*    167 32.0     355 68.0
DONLEY       631 58.4     449 41.6*     92 17.7     428 82.3
DUVAL        295  6.8    4012 93.2*   2437 97.9      52  2.1
                                      *
EASTLAND    2490 57.1    1871 42.9*    630 31.2    1390 68.8
ECTOR       7989 74.6    2721 25.4*    919 32.5    1906 67.5
EDWARDS      372 77.7     107 22.3*     31 17.8     143 82.2
ELLIS       3815 56.7    2919 43.3*    619 28.5    1555 71.5
ELPASO     17094 38.0   27872 62.0*   6379 62.8    3772 37.2
                                      *
ERATH       2684 50.0    2683 50.0*    288 24.3     896 75.7
FALLS       1946 52.5    1764 47.5*    362 31.6     784 68.4
FANNIN      2619 52.2    2400 47.8*    491 30.8    1105 69.2
FAYETTE     2340 52.6    2112 47.4*    573 35.5    1039 64.5
FISHER       816 54.5     680 45.5*    178 27.3     473 72.7
                                      *
FLOYD       1410 62.4     848 37.6*    146 13.4     946 86.6
FOARD        227 60.5     148 39.5*     71 29.5     170 70.5
FORTBEND    4503 55.9    3553 44.1*   1040 44.5    1298 55.5
FRANKLIN     615 61.4     386 38.6*     99 26.5     274 73.5
FREESTONE   1641 48.5    1742 51.5*    167 24.6     512 75.4
                                      *
FRIO        1188 55.7     944 44.3*    164 28.4     414 71.6
GAINES      1352 64.8     736 35.2*    111 25.6     323 74.4
GALVESTON  13193 41.5   18569 58.5*   6007 60.7    3887 39.3
GARZA        654 55.7     521 44.3*     74 25.1     221 74.9
GILLESPIE   1004 72.1     389 27.9*    179 27.5     472 72.5
                                      *
GLASCOCK     183 77.5      53 22.5*     21 12.7     144 87.3
GOLIAD       560 57.4     415 42.6*    185 36.1     328 63.9
GONZALES    1641 60.5    1072 39.5*    243 20.8     927 79.2
GRAY        2110 66.8    1049 33.2*    450 29.3    1085 70.7
GRAYSON     6750 56.5    5205 43.5*   1062 39.7    1616 60.3
                                      *
GREGG       8793 72.7    3303 27.3*    856 22.6    2925 77.4
```

SOUTHERN ELECTIONS/318

```
                DEMOC.  RUNOFF     1972* SPECL.  REFERENDUM 1963
                                       *
COUNTY        SANDERS        YARBRO        FOR           AGAINST
               #      %       #      %*     #      %       #      %
---------------------------------------------*----------------------------------------------------------------
GRIMES        1845  55.8    1461  44.2*   192  24.3     598  75.7
GUADALUPE     3065  55.7    2440  44.3*   712  30.6    1612  69.4
HALE          3368  65.1    1807  34.9*   621  26.7    1708  73.3
HALL           830  56.4     641  43.6*   122  22.9     411  77.1
HAMILTON      1165  66.2     596  33.8*   183  22.1     645  77.9
                                       *
HANSFORD       737  69.7     321  30.3*   111  27.3     295  72.7
HARDEMAN       621  63.2     362  36.8*   144  28.2     366  71.8
HARDIN        4201  48.5    4468  51.5*   358  52.9     319  47.1
HARRIS      129369  47.3  144303  52.7* 46282  53.6   40035  46.4
HARRISON      4510  60.9    2896  39.1*   771  29.6    1837  70.4
                                       *
HARTLEY        342  60.2     226  39.8*    63  33.7     124  66.3
HASKELL       1114  57.4     828  42.6*   221  23.6     715  76.4
HAYS          2425  44.9    2980  55.1*   856  45.9    1007  54.1
HEMPHILL       292  60.5     191  39.5*   267  51.4     252  48.6
HENDERSON     3389  43.0    4492  57.0*   695  44.0     884  56.0
                                       *
HIDALGO      11642  38.9   18314  61.1*  4573  50.9    4411  49.1
HILL          3255  54.0    2777  46.0*   359  20.8    1369  79.2
HOCKLEY       2790  63.1    1630  36.9*   225  21.6     817  78.4
HOOD          1154  51.7    1078  48.3*    93  22.0     330  78.0
HOPKINS       3204  65.1    1720  34.9*   393  30.8     885  69.2
                                       *
HOUSTON       2439  57.2    1827  42.8*   412  32.4     860  67.6
HOWARD        2748  58.4    1959  41.6*   535  34.7    1005  65.3
HUDSPETH       203  46.2     236  53.8*    81  46.6      93  53.4
HUNT          4122  56.3    3193  43.7*   641  25.2    1903  74.8
HUTCHISON     2129  66.1    1094  33.9*   823  37.8    1355  62.2
                                       *
IRION          278  66.8     138  33.2*    43  30.7      97  69.3
JACK          1478  59.3    1014  40.7*   162  22.6     555  77.4
JACKSON       1854  55.3    1497  44.7*   278  35.4     508  64.6
JASPER        3614  50.2    3590  49.8*   352  48.0     381  52.0
JEFFDAVIS      172  56.6     132  43.4*    40  42.6      54  57.4
                                       *
JEFFERSON    20181  47.9   21949  52.1*  7363  59.3    5062  40.7
JIMHOGG        359  22.2    1256  77.8*   217  85.4      37  14.6
JIMWELLS      2936  36.1    5186  63.9*  1263  66.8     628  33.2
JOHNSON       4796  54.1    4074  45.9*   493  20.6    1906  79.4
JONES         2164  65.5    1142  34.5*   268  29.2     650  70.8
                                       *
KARNES        1799  50.1    1790  49.9*   225  22.5     776  77.5
KAUFMAN       2427  59.8    1632  40.2*   325  19.7    1325  80.3
KENDALL        589  68.9     266  31.1*   137  22.1     484  77.9
KENEDY         104  60.1      69  39.9*    39  47.6      43  52.4
KENT           338  50.4     333  49.6*    55  27.9     142  72.1
                                       *
KERR          2205  67.4    1067  32.6*   619  37.4    1034  62.6
KIMBLE         758  63.8     431  36.2*    89  23.9     284  76.1
KING            61  56.0      48  44.0*    24  24.2      75  75.8
KINNEY         218  46.0     256  54.0*    33  33.0      67  67.0
KLEBERG       2698  40.5    3961  59.5*   848  47.0     956  53.0
                                       *
KNOX           772  53.8     663  46.2*   189  31.1     418  68.9
```

```
              DEMOC.   RUNOFF    1972*  SPECL.  REFERENDUM 1963
                                     *
  COUNTY     SANDERS      YARBRO       FOR          AGAINST
               #     %      #     %*     #     %       #     %
--------------------------------------------------------------------------------------------
LAMAR        5653 60.1   3753 39.9*   680 43.7      876 56.3
LAMB         1680 66.1    861 33.9*   224 14.3     1338 85.7
LAMPASAS     1249 58.5    886 41.5*   130 22.1      459 77.9
LASALLE       586 55.2    475 44.8*   107 36.4      187 63.6
LABACA       2129 61.7   1319 38.3*   502 39.0      785 61.0
                                *
LEE           939 43.7   1212 56.3*   388 37.2      654 62.8
LEON          955 51.8    888 48.2*   210 33.3      421 66.7
LIBERTY      4442 52.1   4084 47.9*   466 39.1      726 60.9
LIMESTONE    2259 55.0   1848 45.0*   233 24.3      724 75.7
LIPSCOMB      226 55.5    181 44.5*   102 37.5      170 62.5
                                *
LIVEOAK      1373 64.7    748 35.3*   115 22.0      408 78.0
LLANO        1252 61.9    769 38.1*   128 36.7      221 63.3
LOVING         30 71.4     12 28.6*    14 37.8       23 62.2
LUBBOCK     16993 61.0  10853 39.0*  1321 31.9     2820 68.1
LYNN         1219 62.9    718 37.1*    85 13.0      569 87.0
                                *
MADISON       969 53.7    836 46.3*   111 25.0      333 75.0
MARION       1051 49.1   1090 50.9*   174 31.7      375 68.3
MARTIN        461 69.5    202 30.5*    77 19.3      321 80.7
MASON         715 64.4    396 35.6*   106 26.2      299 73.8
MATAGORDA    2515 54.2   2122 45.8*   379 39.3      585 60.7
                                *
MAVERICK     1028 35.8   1847 64.2*   149 48.2      160 51.8
MCCULLOCH    1421 60.1    945 39.9*   144 26.1      408 73.9
MCLENNAN    17216 48.9  18024 51.1*  3658 48.6     3875 51.4
MCMULLEN      209 66.1    107 33.9*    27 21.8       97 78.2
MEDINA       1892 49.9   1903 50.1*   384 27.3     1023 72.7
                                *
MENARD        465 68.8    211 31.2*    79 28.4      199 71.6
MIDLAND      6420 73.4   2325 26.6*  1491 42.0     2058 58.0
MILAN        2384 46.0   2796 54.0*   427 30.2      985 69.8
MILLS         790 64.6    433 35.4*    97 20.8      370 79.2
MITCHELL     1059 67.3    515 32.7*   192 26.4      534 73.6
                                *
MONTAGE      1744 66.8    866 33.2*   302 27.6      792 72.4
MONTGOMRY    7156 59.6   4852 40.4*   757 44.0      963 56.0
MOORE        1137 60.4    744 39.6*   291 35.3      534 64.7
MORRIS       1817 46.9   2059 53.1*   196 26.0      558 74.0
MOTLEY        402 69.7    175 30.3*    47 14.2      284 85.8
                                *
NACDOCHES    5328 62.4   3209 37.6*   480 28.1     1230 71.9
NAVARRO      4133 52.6   3723 47.4*   651 33.9     1269 66.1
NEWTON       1681 42.8   2245 57.2*   205 48.0      222 52.0
NOLAN        2185 61.2   1388 38.8*   290 25.5      849 74.5
NUECES      21611 43.9  27653 56.1*  5511 55.0     4510 45.0
                                *
OCHILTREE     808 72.3    310 27.7*   100 23.0      334 77.0
OLDHAM        253 62.3    153 37.7*    22 16.3      113 83.7
ORANGE       8517 49.8   8584 50.2*  1854 57.0     1401 43.0
PALOPINTO    2439 50.8   2359 49.2*   328 26.6      905 73.4
PANOLA       2877 64.7   1570 35.3*   226 16.8     1117 83.2
                                *
PARKER       4067 50.6   3970 49.4*   397 24.6     1218 75.4
```

```
              DEMOC.   RUNOFF      1972*  SPECL.   REFERENDUM 1963
                                       *
  COUNTY       SANDERS        YARBRO       FOR           AGAINST
               #       %      #      %*    #       %     #       %
-------------------------------------*-----------------------------------------------------------------------------
PARMER         816   66.1    418   33.9*   117   18.3    522   81.7
PECOS         1344   64.7    734   35.3*   206   37.2    348   62.8
POLK          2342   51.7   2188   48.3*   240   33.6    475   66.4
POTTER        6006   57.5   4437   42.5*  1734   37.5   2889   62.5
PRESIDIO       385   62.6    230   37.4*   141   52.2    129   47.8
                                       *
RAINES         399   46.4    460   53.6*   102   32.4    213   67.6
RANDALL       4958   66.1   2547   33.9*   793   32.2   1666   67.8
REAGAN         426   73.6    153   26.4*    61   32.4    127   67.6
REAL           319   61.6    199   38.4*    42   18.6    184   81.4
REDRIVER      2374   59.5   1617   40.5*   221   21.4    811   78.6
                                       *
REEVES        1292   67.9    612   32.1*   156   28.6    390   71.4
REFUGIO       1634   51.9   1512   48.1*   194   41.5    274   58.5
ROBERTS        186   75.3     61   24.7*    23   13.2    151   86.8
ROBERTSON     1375   39.7   2086   60.3*   334   39.4    514   60.6
ROCKWALL       941   66.4    477   33.6*    87   23.4    285   76.6
                                       *
RUNNELLS      1568   66.8    780   33.2*   189   17.8    871   82.2
RUSK          4949   66.7   2469   33.3*   463   20.6   1789   79.4
SABINE         746   46.0    876   54.0*    98   27.0    265   73.0
SNAUGSTNE     1379   59.3    945   40.7*    84   17.4    398   82.6
SNJACINTO      648   44.1    823   55.9*   430   45.9    506   54.1
                                       *
SNPATRICIO    4528   44.4   5663   55.6*   693   38.4   1112   61.6
SANSABA        865   57.3    645   42.7*   149   30.3    343   69.7
SCHLEICHER     507   63.9    286   36.1*    71   31.0    158   69.0
SCURRY        2602   68.3   1207   31.7*   244   24.5    750   75.5
SHACKELFRD     688   71.2    278   28.8*    84   26.7    231   73.3
                                       *
SHELBY        3160   49.1   3271   50.9*   283   18.3   1261   81.7
SHERMAN        290   70.7    120   29.3*    44   20.0    176   80.0
SMITH        12612   65.6   6628   34.4*  1504   28.7   3736   71.3
SOMERVELL      451   51.8    420   48.2*    61   34.5    116   65.5
STARR          821   16.9   4051   83.1*  1658   97.6     41    2.4
                                       *
STEPHENS      2195   67.5   1059   32.5*   188   31.9    401   68.1
STERLING       158   71.2     64   28.8*    23   22.1     81   77.9
STONEWALL      373   51.8    347   48.2*    53   18.9    228   81.1
SUTTON         353   69.5    155   30.5*    51   31.3    112   68.7
SWISHER        760   41.0   1095   59.0*   164   24.2    515   75.8
                                       *
TARRANT      53898   53.0  47749   47.0* 12866   43.3  16832   56.7
TAYLOR        9901   67.4   4780   32.6*  1375   35.7   2479   64.3
TERRELL        245   66.8    122   33.2*   115   38.5    184   61.5
TERRY         1613   69.5    707   30.5*   134   22.5    461   77.5
THRCKMORTN     423   66.4    214   33.6*    54   20.9    204   79.1
                                       *
TITUS         1870   57.4   1387   42.6*   289   29.9    677   70.1
TOMGREEN      7168   62.6   4285   37.4*  1395   39.5   2137   60.5
TRAVIS       33958   39.7  51586   60.3* 14913   55.4  12030   44.6
TRINITY       1075   53.3    940   46.7*   212   46.7    242   53.3
TYLER         1864   50.2   1846   49.8*   179   27.2    480   72.8
                                       *
UPSHUR        2438   58.8   1705   41.2*   534   37.2    903   62.8
```

COUNTY	DEMOC. RUNOFF 1972* SANDERS #	%	YARBRO #	%*	SPECL. REFERENDUM 1963 FOR #	%	AGAINST #	%
UPTON	687	76.0	217	24.0*	92	28.0	236	72.0
UVALDE	2951	64.8	1602	35.2*	248	20.2	979	79.8
VALVERDE	1642	43.0	2173	57.0*	386	39.9	581	60.1
VANZANDT	2719	58.0	1971	42.0*	315	23.8	1009	76.2
VICTORIA	5944	57.8	4335	42.2*	861	51.2	822	48.8
WALKER	2820	51.9	2616	48.1*	564	52.4	513	47.6
WALLER	1337	47.9	1455	52.1*	195	30.4	447	69.6
WARD	1172	73.0	434	27.0*	321	38.2	519	61.8
WASHINGTON	2627	55.3	2125	44.7*	731	40.6	1071	59.4
WEBB	2714	25.4	7963	74.6*	2042	93.5	142	6.5
WHARTON	2990	48.7	3155	51.3*	994	41.2	1417	58.8
WHEELER	680	65.7	355	34.3*	158	23.4	516	76.6
WICHITA	8729	56.2	6793	43.8*	2122	56.3	1644	43.7
WILBARGER	1682	68.5	774	31.5*	215	25.0	644	75.0
WILLACY	1570	45.9	1854	54.1*	1000	49.6	1018	50.4
WILLIAMSON	3421	45.4	4114	54.6*	1348	42.1	1854	57.9
WILSON	2108	49.0	2190	51.0*	340	39.4	524	60.6
WINKLER	2186	75.1	724	24.9*	221	36.5	385	63.5
WISE	2238	60.0	1495	40.0*	346	27.4	916	72.6
WOOD	2509	60.6	1629	39.4*	291	21.0	1095	79.0
YOAKUM	1278	69.6	557	30.4*	117	33.1	236	66.9
YOUNG	1957	64.1	1095	35.9*	286	24.2	895	75.8
ZAPATA	157	20.5	609	79.5*	262	93.2	19	6.8
ZAVALA	880	79.4	229	20.6*	499	42.9	663	57.1
TOTALS	1008499		928087	*	243120		316775	
% OF VOTE	52.1		47.9	*	43.4		56.6	

GEOGRAPHIC CLASS

				*				
LOWLANDS	387119	51.	371639	49.*	92709	45.	113290	55.
BLACK BELT	8921	52.	8350	48.*	1904	34.	3679	66.
WEST TEXAS	538060	55.	435863	45.*	120379	40.	177117	60.
MEX. TEXAS	74399	40.	112235	60.*	28128	55.	22689	45.

DEMOGRAPHIC CLASS

				*				
METRO	566671	50.	562825	50.*	165641	50.	166488	50.
TOWN	91247	53.	80664	47.*	17161	41.	24401	59.
RURAL	350581	55.	284598	45.*	60318	32.	125886	68.

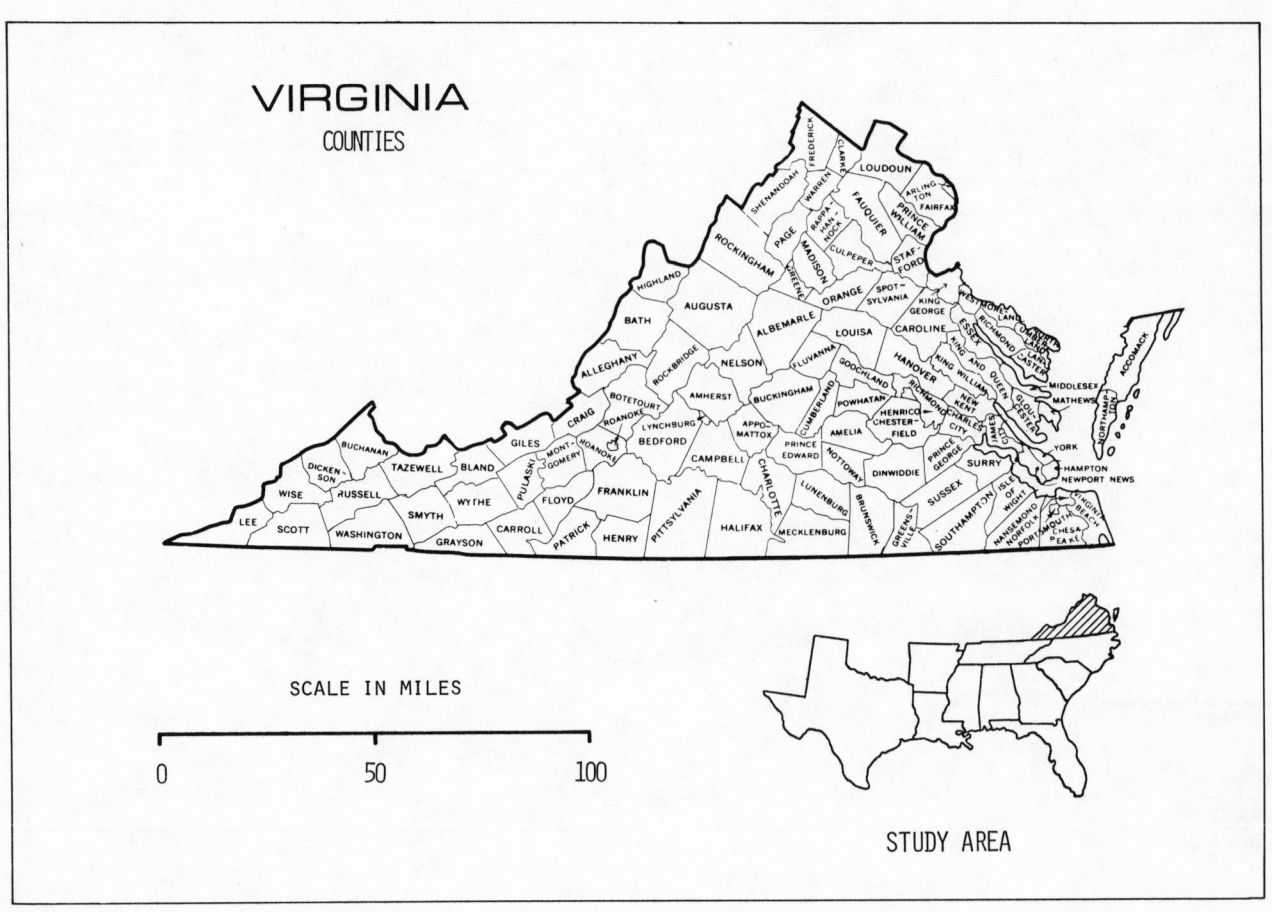

VIRGINIA

COUNTIES

SCALE IN MILES

0   50   100

STUDY AREA

VIRGINIA

A $1.50 poll tax, payable at least six months prior to election day and cumulative for three previous years, and a literacy test kept the Virginia electorate "purified." When the Twenty-Fourth Amendment declared the poll tax unconstitutional in federal elections, Virginia, like Texas, retained the tax as a requirement for voting for nonfederal elective officials. The 1965 Voting Rights Act banned the literacy test as a prerequisite for registration, however, and the Supreme Court in 1966 ruled the poll tax unconstitutional in state elections.

In 1960 an estimated 867,000 whites and 100,000 blacks were registered, which was approximately 46 percent of the white voting-age population and 23 percent of black adults. By 1970 there were almost 1.5 million white and 270,000 black registrants, or 64.5 percent of whites and 57 percent of blacks of voting-age population registered.

The following table summarizes the behavior of the Virginia electorate in presidential elections from 1948 to 1972. Turnout figures are expressed both in number of ballots counted and in the percentage of citizens of voting age who participated.

Reprinted below are 8 Democratic primary elections, 4 for the governor's office and 4 for the senate. The 1966 senatorial contest between A. Willis Robertson and William B. Spong, Jr., was for a regular six-year term; the simultaneous race between Harry F. Byrd, Jr., and Armistead L. Boothe was for the unexpired term of the seat made vacant by the retirement of Senator Harry Flood Byrd, who was in failing health. When the latter seat came up for the regular six-year term in 1970, incumbent Harry Byrd, Jr., chose to run as an Independent and did not compete in the Democratic primary.

Gubernatorial Primaries

1. July 14, 1953: Thomas B. Stanley 150,459 (65.9%), Charles R. Fenwick 77,715 (34.1%). Total vote was 228,174; turnout of voting-age citizens was 10.8%.
* (July 9, 1957: J. Lindsay Almond, Jr., won 79.5% against 1 opponent. Total vote was 150,101; turnout was 6.8%.)
2. July 11, 1961: A. E. S. Stephens 152,639 (43.3%), Albertis S. Harrison, Jr., 199,519 (56.7%). Total vote was 352,158; turnout was 14.9%.
* (Mills E. Godwin, Jr., was unopposed in 1965).
3. July 15, 1969: William C. Battle 158,956 (38.9%), Henry E. Howell 154,617 (37.8%), Fred G. Pollard 95,067 (23.3%). Total vote was 408,640; turnout was 14.9%.
4. August 19, 1969: William C. Battle 226,108 (52.1%), Henry E. Howell 207,505 (47.9%). Total vote was 433,613; turnout was 15.8%.

Senatorial Primaries

1. July 15, 1952: Harry Flood Byrd 216,438 (62.7%), Francis Pickens Miller 128,869 (37.3%). Total vote was 345,307.
* (A. Willis Robertson was unopposed in 1954.)
* (Harry Flood Byrd was unopposed in 1958.)
* (A. Willis Robertson was unopposed in 1960.)

* (Harry Flood Byrd was unopposed in 1964.)

2. July 12, 1966: A. Willis Robertson 216,274 (49.9%), William B. Spong, Jr., 216,885 (50.1%). Total vote was 433,159.

3. July 12, 1966: Harry F. Byrd, Jr., 221,221 (50.9%), Armistead L. Boothe 212,996 (49.1%). Total vote was 434,217.

4. July 14, 1970: George C. Rawlings 58,874 (45.7%), Clive L. DuVal II 58,174 (45.1%), Milton Colvin 11,911 (9.2%). Total vote was 128,959. (DuVal did not file for a runoff election.)

* (William B. Spong, Jr., was unopposed in 1972.)

RETURNS FROM PRESIDENTIAL ELECTIONS

Year	Turnout		Partisan Vote*
1948	419,256	(21.8%)[+]	Democrat 47.9%, Republican 41.0%, Dixiecrat 10.4%
1952	619,689	(29.9%)	Republican 56.3%, Democrat 43.4%
1956	697,978	(31.8%)	Republican 55.4%, Democrat 38.4%
1960	771,449	(33.4%)	Republican 52.4%, Democrat 47.0%
1964	1,042,267	(41.6%)	Democrat 53.5%, Republican 46.2%
1968	1,361,491	(50.5%)	Republican 43.1%, Democrat 32.5%, American Independent 23.6%
1972	1,457,019	(45.9%)	Republican 67.8%, Democrat 30.1%

*Totals do not necessarily equal 100%, since minor party percentages are excluded.

[+]Percentages of citizens of voting age who voted is calculated on the basis of a straight-line interpolation of citizen population between census years.

```
              DEMOC.  GOVERNOR   1953* DEMOC.  GOVERNOR   1961
                                      *
   COUNTY      FENWICK      STANLEY     STEPHENS     HARRISON
               #      %     #     %*    #      %     #      %
--------------------------------------*------------------------------------------------------------------
ACCOMACK      619  24.4  1920  75.6*  1473  33.2  2968  66.8
ALBEMARLE     578  37.3   970  62.7*   798  34.3  1529  65.7
ALLEGHANY     129  33.2   259  66.8*   271  38.3   436  61.7
AMELIA         98  19.8   397  80.2*   235  21.8   841  78.2
AMHERST       838  39.8  1265  60.2*   702  30.4  1611  69.6
                                      *
APPOMATTX     131  10.1  1170  89.9*   218  11.9  1608  88.1
ARLINGTON    7911  82.4  1686  17.6*  9004  66.0  4641  34.0
AUGUSTA       216  19.1   916  80.9*   431  25.1  1283  74.9
BATH           95  28.8   235  71.2*    79  26.0   225  74.0
BEDFORD       917  28.3  2322  71.7*  1550  38.1  2520  61.9
                                      *
BLAND          94  21.2   349  78.8*   284  47.5   314  52.5
BOTETOURT     190  29.0   466  71.0*   552  56.2   430  43.8
BRUNSWICK     442  26.8  1210  73.2*   393  13.4  2537  86.6
BUCHANAN      273  21.0  1029  79.0*  1276  79.0   340  21.0
BUCKINGHM     131  17.6   614  82.4*   258  19.2  1085  80.8
                                      *
CAMPBELL      599  34.3  1147  65.7*   604  28.5  1518  71.5
CAROLINE      104  18.3   464  81.7*   284  29.2   688  70.8
CARROLL       135  15.3   749  84.7*   778  78.2   217  21.8
CHAS CITY      52  10.6   439  89.4*   266  66.0   137  34.0
CHARLOTTE     173  12.5  1214  87.5*   251  15.7  1344  84.3
                                      *
CHESTRFLD     637  30.6  1445  69.4*  1660  25.9  4751  74.1
CLARKE        254  42.6   342  57.4*   444  34.3   850  65.7
CRAIG          51  29.5   122  70.5*   171  60.6   111  39.4
CULPEPER      282  32.7   581  67.3*   603  29.9  1417  70.1
CUMBERLND     550  50.2   545  49.8*   191  25.4   562  74.6
                                      *
DICKENSON     890  58.1   642  41.9*  1277  94.9    69   5.1
DINWIDDIE     213  20.4   832  79.6*   386  21.7  1390  78.3
ELIZ CITY       0    .0     0    .0*     0    .0     0    .0
ESSEX         151  30.4   346  69.6*   184  28.8   454  71.2
FAIRFAX      4617  70.6  1924  29.4* 11427  69.9  4932  30.1
                                      *
FAUQUIER      495  36.7   853  63.3*  1083  37.2  1827  62.8
FLOYD          51  24.8   155  75.2*   309  84.7    56  15.3
FLUVANNA      190  35.7   342  64.3*   131  25.7   378  74.3
FRANKLIN      336  20.1  1337  79.9*  1285  51.2  1224  48.8
FREDERICK     141  15.7   759  84.3*   609  30.6  1378  69.4
                                      *
GILES         190  21.6   688  78.4*   645  52.7   579  47.3
GLOUCESTR     103  15.1   581  84.9*   434  36.5   756  63.5
GOOCHLAND     270  34.0   525  66.0*   229  21.4   841  78.6
GRAYSON       204  13.0  1368  87.0*   922  75.0   307  25.0
GREENE        111  38.3   179  61.7*    90  50.8    87  49.2
                                      *
GREENSVLE     185  25.1   553  74.9*   448  19.6  1843  80.4
HALIFAX       847  23.0  2843  77.0*   370  15.0  2091  85.0
HANOVER       743  32.0  1578  68.0*   842  23.2  2784  76.8
HENRICO      1113  33.3  2227  66.7*  3318  23.4 10861  76.6
HENRY         513  20.1  2037  79.9*   838  42.9  1114  57.1
                                      *
HIGHLAND       29  12.8   198  87.2*    51  24.5   157  75.5
```

COUNTY	DEMOC. GOVERNOR 1953*				DEMOC. GOVERNOR 1961			
	FENWICK		STANLEY		STEPHENS		HARRISON	
	#	%	#	%*	#	%	#	%
ISLE WIGT	202	19.8	820	80.2*	1775	67.4	859	32.6
JAMES CTY	147	32.7	302	67.3*	376	51.4	355	48.6
KING GEO	110	34.9	205	65.1*	160	33.8	314	66.2
KING+QUN	59	36.9	101	63.1*	140	34.2	269	65.8
KING WM	101	23.3	333	76.7*	267	27.4	706	72.6
LANCASTER	436	40.3	645	59.7*	541	39.8	820	60.2
LEE	313	19.2	1319	80.8*	1278	84.5	234	15.5
LOUDON	1229	44.9	1509	55.1*	759	34.6	1434	65.4
LOUISA	529	40.3	783	59.7*	243	18.2	1089	81.8
LUNENBURG	341	23.5	1110	76.5*	252	13.4	1635	86.6
MADISON	127	33.3	254	66.7*	101	20.3	396	79.7
MATHEWS	86	22.2	301	77.8*	189	26.5	525	73.5
MECKLENBG	237	18.9	1020	81.1*	339	10.4	2926	89.6
MIDDLESEX	140	36.0	249	64.0*	272	34.2	524	65.8
MONTGOMRY	309	26.9	838	73.1*	1161	68.3	539	31.7
NANSEMOND	251	18.0	1141	82.0*	2073	49.5	2112	50.5
NELSON	258	39.2	401	60.8*	474	33.4	946	66.6
NEW KENT	69	22.5	238	77.5*	130	32.3	272	67.7
NORFOLK	2303	39.2	3566	60.8*	1724	41.0	2480	59.0
NORTHAMTN	158	16.3	812	83.7*	271	17.2	1309	82.8
NORTHUMLD	284	34.5	539	65.5*	383	36.5	666	63.5
NOTTOWAY	194	17.2	932	82.8*	493	22.4	1703	77.6
ORANGE	271	29.5	648	70.5*	313	29.4	752	70.6
PAGE	614	40.0	920	60.0*	297	25.4	873	74.6
PATRICK	44	2.6	1666	97.4*	623	42.4	848	57.6
PITTSLVNA	735	16.5	3723	83.5*	1196	21.3	4414	78.7
POWHATAN	69	18.8	299	81.3*	212	32.0	450	68.0
PRINCE ED	194	18.8	838	81.2*	558	20.8	2129	79.2
PRIN GEO	289	32.4	604	67.6*	231	23.4	756	76.6
PRINCE WM	457	39.5	700	60.5*	827	39.0	1294	61.0
PRIN ANNE	925	28.3	2339	71.7*	1437	26.3	4019	73.7
PULASKI	585	24.6	1795	75.4*	878	50.3	866	49.7
RAPPAHANK	75	17.4	357	82.6*	137	24.0	435	76.0
RICHMOND	288	37.0	490	63.0*	194	28.3	492	71.7
ROANOKE	608	32.4	1271	67.6*	1303	46.0	1529	54.0
ROCKBRIDG	253	29.6	603	70.4*	578	32.7	1189	67.3
ROCKINGHM	168	18.9	722	81.1*	426	35.4	776	64.6
RUSSELL	479	25.1	1433	74.9*	1270	75.8	406	24.2
SCOTT	224	21.7	808	78.3*	1022	69.4	450	30.6
SHENANDOH	335	28.3	847	71.7*	347	24.5	1070	75.5
SMYTH	136	12.7	939	87.3*	963	65.9	498	34.1
SOUTHMPTN	507	27.4	1340	72.6*	885	32.5	1834	67.5
SPOTSYLVN	258	34.0	500	66.0*	691	57.6	508	42.4
STAFFORD	297	62.3	180	37.7*	801	65.3	426	34.7
SURRY	149	25.5	435	74.5*	476	43.4	620	56.6
SUSSEX	166	15.7	888	84.3*	259	15.3	1429	84.7

```
           DEMOC.  GOVERNOR   1953* DEMOC.  GOVERNOR   1961
                                   *
   COUNTY     FENWICK       STANLEY      STEPHENS     HARRISON
              #    %       #     %*     #     %       #     %
-----------------------------------------*----------------------------------------------------------------
TAZEWELL     305  22.0    1079  78.0*   1667  71.1    677  28.9
WARREN       288  35.8     516  64.2*    622  31.0   1383  69.0
WARWICK      680  43.3     889  56.7*      0   .0       0   .0
WASHINGTN    228  22.7     775  77.3*   1395  68.3    648  31.7
WESTMRLND    779  61.9     480  38.1*    594  43.3    777  56.7
                                   *
WISE         606  21.0    2281  79.0*   2343  87.0    349  13.0
WYTHE        149   8.3    1657  91.7*    628  50.9    607  49.1
YORK         545  35.2    1004  64.8*    951  46.9   1078  53.1
ALEXANDRA   3559  62.5    2139  37.5*   5678  62.5   3400  37.5
BEDFORD        0   .0        0   .0*      0   .0       0   .0
                                   *
BRISTOL      390  22.0    1380  78.0*    628  46.3    729  53.7
BUENA VTA     77  25.4     226  74.6*    150  25.1    447  74.9
CHARLSTVL   1439  49.5    1469  50.5*   1841  46.9   2088  53.1
CHESAPKE       0   .0        0   .0*      0   .0       0   .0
CLIFTN FG    188  49.7     190  50.3*    269  44.0    343  56.0
                                   *
COL HGHTS    141  24.6     432  75.4*    262  16.4   1334  83.6
COVINGTON    198  33.3     397  66.7*    487  44.3    613  55.7
DANVILLE     981  17.8    4543  82.2*   1664  26.5   4611  73.5
EMPORIA        0   .0        0   .0*      0   .0       0   .0
FAIRFAX        0   .0        0   .0*    544  59.3    373  40.7
                                   *
FALLS CH     783  83.7     153  16.3*    619  62.5    371  37.5
FRANKLIN       0   .0        0   .0*      0   .0       0   .0
FREDRKSBG    329  37.4     551  62.6*    872  51.1    833  48.9
GALAX          0   .0        0   .0*    272  59.9    182  40.1
HAMPTON     1004  39.7    1522  60.3*   4373  56.5   3365  43.5
                                   *
HARRISNBG    178  31.0     396  69.0*    239  29.3    576  70.7
HOPEWELL     765  36.8    1311  63.2*    769  30.2   1778  69.8
LEXINGTON      0   .0        0   .0*      0   .0       0   .0
LYNCHBURG   2620  42.4    3565  57.6*   2563  37.3   4311  62.7
MARTINSVL    246  17.8    1134  82.2*    571  38.9    896  61.1
                                   *
NEWPRT NS   1256  36.4    2191  63.6*   4705  50.9   4536  49.1
NORFOLK     2965  35.9    5305  64.1*  13085  53.1  11556  46.9
NORTON         0   .0        0   .0*    251  67.1    123  32.9
PETERSBRG    632  23.8    2026  76.2*   1373  36.1   2433  63.9
PORTSMTH    2640  37.2    4457  62.8*   6203  57.7   4542  42.3
                                   *
RADFORD       92  25.4     270  74.6*    564  75.2    186  24.8
RICHMOND    5083  27.6   13330  72.4*  11804  42.3  16082  57.7
ROANOKE     2363  33.8    4624  66.2*   4253  54.5   3556  45.5
SALEM          0   .0        0   .0*      0   .0       0   .0
S BOSTON       0   .0        0   .0*    147  20.6    567  79.4
                                   *
S NORFOLK    526  40.9     761  59.1*    526  36.1    931  63.9
STAUNTON     645  33.4    1287  66.6*    426  26.1   1205  73.9
SUFFOLK      501  42.6     675  57.4*    895  39.7   1358  60.3
VA BEACH     357  29.6     850  70.4*    286  26.5    794  73.5
WANESBORO    581  36.9     995  63.1*    310  28.7    772  71.3
                                   *
WILLMSBRG    197  35.6     357  64.4*    294  49.3    302  50.7
```

```
           DEMOC.  GOVERNOR   1953* DEMOC.  GOVERNOR   1961
                                 *
 COUNTY      FENWICK       STANLEY     STEPHENS      HARRISON
            #      %      #      %*    #      %      #      %
-------------------------------------*------------------------------------------------------------------------
 WINCHESTR   499  23.2  1656  76.8*   537  25.9   1540  74.1
-------------------------------------*------------------------------------------------------------------------
                                 *
 TOTALS     77715       150459    *  152639        199519
 % OF VOTE   34.1         65.9    *    43.3          56.7
                                 *
                                 *
 GEOGRAPHIC CLASS                *
                                 *
 LOWLANDS   42346  42.  58673  58.*  85371  47.   97368  53.
 BLACK BELT  7382  27.  19736  73.*  13797  29.   33477  71.
 PIEDMONT   12557  28.  32647  72.*  19048  34.   37167  66.
 MOUNTAIN   15430  28.  39403  72.*  34423  52.   31507  48.
                                 *
                                 *
 DEMOGRAPHIC CLASS               *
                                 *
 METRO      42632  42.  58324  58.*  84748  48.   90042  52.
 TOWN        6825  27.  18073  73.*   9489  30.   21887  70.
 RURAL      28258  28.  74062  72.*  58402  40.   87590  60.
```

                                        VIRGINIA

```
            DEMOC.  GOVERNOR   1969    * DEMOC.  RUNOFF    1969
                                      *
 COUNTY     BATTLE      HOWELL      POLLARD     BATTLE      HOWELL
            #     %     #     %     #     %*    #     %     #     %
---------------------------------------------*--------------------------------------------------------
 ACCOMACK   2039 50.3   831 20.5  1185 29.2*  2387 60.8  1542 39.2
 ALBEMARLE  1699 57.8   557 18.9   685 23.3*  2098 67.7   999 32.3
 ALLEGHANY   394 43.5   367 40.6   144 15.9*   469 40.5   689 59.5
 AMELIA      152 14.8   427 41.5   451 43.8*   514 51.7   481 48.3
 AMHERST     520 38.2   451 33.1   391 28.7*   827 54.0   705 46.0
                                          *
 APPOMATTX   314 21.6   397 27.3   742 51.1*  1254 71.5   499 28.5
 ARLINGTON  4521 37.6  5151 42.9  2344 19.5*  7101 54.3  5980 45.7
 AUGUSTA     710 49.9   392 27.6   320 22.5*  1082 57.5   800 42.5
 BATH        209 56.9    62 16.9    96 26.2*   321 71.5   128 28.5
 BEDFORD     424 40.8   392 37.7   223 21.5*   640 48.7   674 51.3
                                          *
 BLAND       170 41.2    40  9.7   203 49.2*   316 76.5    97 23.5
 BOTETOURT   490 57.9   246 29.1   110 13.0*   590 55.5   473 44.5
 BRUNSWICK   473 19.9  1139 47.9   766 32.2*  1129 47.1  1266 52.9
 BUCHANAN    864 59.2    80  5.5   516 35.3*  1623 87.7   228 12.3
 BUCKINGHM   323 19.3   530 31.6   823 49.1*   840 56.1   657 43.9
                                          *
 CAMPBELL    642 34.1   460 24.5   778 41.4*  1196 62.4   721 37.6
 CAROLINE    431 27.6   859 55.0   273 17.5*   726 37.1  1233 62.9
 CARROLL     716 83.3   111 12.9    33  3.8*   966 84.0   184 16.0
```

```
              DEMOC.  GOVERNOR   1969    * DEMOC.  RUNOFF    1969
                                          *
COUNTY      BATTLE      HOWELL      POLLARD      BATTLE      HOWELL
            #     %     #     %     #     %*    #     %     #     %
------------------------------------------------*---------------------------------------------------------------
CHAS CITY    60   9.0   530  79.5    77  11.5*   123  12.0   903  88.0
CHARLOTTE  1228  40.6   818  27.0   979  32.4*   880  57.6   648  42.4
CHESTRFLD  3812  43.6  2898  33.2  2029  23.2*  5843  56.5  4491  43.5
CLARKE      210  32.2   138  21.2   304  46.6*   616  70.7   255  29.3
CRAIG       169  63.3    52  19.5    46  17.2*   229  69.2   102  30.8
                                          *
CULPEPER    512  45.0   225  19.8   400  35.2*   930  67.3   452  32.7
CUMBERLND   282  20.7   707  51.9   373  27.4*   489  39.7   742  60.3
DICKENSON  1006  51.5   324  16.6   625  32.0*  1755  77.2   519  22.8
DINWIDDIE  1223  42.4   925  32.1   738  25.6*  1443  56.3  1122  43.7
ELIZ CITY     0   .0      0   .0      0   .0*     0   .0      0   .0
                                          *
ESSEX       319  35.3   373  41.3   211  23.4*   635  54.4   533  45.6
FAIRFAX    7843  36.8  8854  41.6  4592  21.6* 12224  50.5 12002  49.5
FAUQUIER    834  43.5   497  25.9   586  30.6*  1275  59.7   859  40.3
FLOYD       251  69.5    88  24.4    22   6.1*   343  65.2   183  34.8
FLUVANNA    221  54.8    94  23.3    88  21.8*   295  63.7   168  36.3
                                          *
FRANKLIN   1634  72.2   350  15.5   279  12.3*  1785  76.9   537  23.1
FREDERICK   594  37.4   647  40.8   346  21.8*  1000  49.1  1035  50.9
GILES      1031  71.6   238  16.5   170  11.8*  1341  71.7   529  28.3
GLOUCESTR   894  50.2   541  30.4   346  19.4*   814  54.4   682  45.6
GOOCHLAND   367  25.2   657  45.2   431  29.6*   920  49.8   928  50.2
                                          *
GRAYSON     857  85.4    74   7.4    72   7.2*  1186  88.2   158  11.8
GREENE      166  61.5    67  24.8    37  13.7*   206  65.4   109  34.6
GREENSVLE   435  24.6   796  45.1   535  30.3*   552  35.7   996  64.3
HALIFAX    1572  47.5   583  17.6  1157  34.9*  2421  77.0   724  23.0
HANOVER    1189  37.2  1006  31.4  1005  31.4*  1965  56.2  1531  43.8
                                          *
HENRICO    8242  45.5  4657  25.7  5213  28.8* 11769  66.2  6009  33.8
HENRY      1185  46.8   766  30.3   581  22.9*  1849  53.7  1596  46.3
HIGHLAND     90  60.8    18  12.2    40  27.0*   148  79.1    39  20.9
ISLE WIGT   892  34.8  1172  45.8   496  19.4*  1186  45.3  1430  54.7
JAMES CTY   466  39.4   499  42.2   218  18.4*   656  43.8   842  56.2
                                          *
KING GEO    125  34.0   146  39.7    97  26.4*   222  45.9   262  54.1
KING+QUN    208  28.0   379  51.1   155  20.9*   338  41.7   472  58.3
KING WM     239  25.5   434  46.3   265  28.3*   552  50.2   548  49.8
LANCASTER   502  35.2   488  34.2   438  30.7*   924  56.0   727  44.0
LEE        1462  93.5    46   2.9    55   3.5*  2000  96.9    65   3.1
                                          *
LOUDON     1122  41.5   614  22.7   966  35.8*  1738  63.8   988  36.2
LOUISA      460  38.8   422  35.6   303  25.6*   703  52.8   629  47.2
LUNENBURG   415  34.0   462  37.9   343  28.1*   768  55.1   625  44.9
MADISON     394  47.9   101  12.3   328  39.9*   479  67.8   228  32.2
MATHEWS     303  44.8   230  34.0   144  21.3*   404  53.4   352  46.6
                                          *
MECKLENBG   921  32.5  1020  36.0   889  31.4*  1628  54.3  1369  45.7
MIDDLESEX   346  40.0   213  24.7   305  35.3*   485  64.9   262  35.1
MONTGOMRY  1051  54.8   550  28.7   317  16.5*  1436  64.4   795  35.6
NANSEMOND  1553  38.0  2016  49.3   523  12.8*  1638  40.0  2458  60.0
NELSON      657  58.5   235  20.9   231  20.6*   677  60.4   443  39.6
                                          *
NEW KENT    136  30.8   216  49.0    89  20.2*   245  43.3   321  56.7
```

```
              DEMOC.  GOVERNOR    1969    * DEMOC.  RUNOFF    1969
                                          *
COUNTY      BATTLE        HOWELL        POLLARD      BATTLE        HOWELL
            #     %       #     %       #     %*     #     %       #     %
----------------------------------------------------------*----------------------------------------------------------
NORFOLK        0    .0       0    .0       0    .0*      0    .0       0    .0
NORTHAMTN    565  34.3     640  38.8     443  26.9*    908  55.2     738  44.8
NORTHUMLD    247  30.5     373  46.0     191  23.6*    505  45.3     609  54.7
NOTTOWAY     852  46.4     627  34.2     357  19.4*   1168  56.9     883  43.1
ORANGE       389  38.2     184  18.1     445  43.7*    767  62.6     459  37.4
                                          *
PAGE         555  47.4     276  23.6     340  29.0*   1263  75.1     418  24.9
PATRICK      763  72.2     108  10.2     186  17.6*   1587  88.1     215  11.9
PITTSLVNA   3614  40.3    1712  19.1    3647  40.6*   3495  64.7    1905  35.3
POWHATAN     170  20.7     471  57.3     181  22.0*    359  35.8     645  64.2
PRINCE ED   1535  54.1     491  17.3     811  28.6*   1671  68.4     771  31.6
                                          *
PRIN GEO     569  34.3     754  45.4     336  20.3*    771  44.7     954  55.3
PRINCE WM   1289  37.3    1059  30.6    1108  32.1*   2029  57.1    1524  42.9
PRIN ANNE      0    .0       0    .0       0    .0*      0    .0       0    .0
PULASKI     1056  50.9     730  35.2     287  13.8*   1628  60.6    1057  39.4
RAPPAHANK    156  36.3     100  23.3     174  40.5*    240  57.0     181  43.0
                                          *
RICHMOND     203  38.0     109  20.4     222  41.6*    444  61.8     275  38.2
ROANOKE     1817  48.3    1311  34.8     636  16.9*   2059  52.3    1880  47.7
ROCKBRIDG    404  58.6     149  21.6     136  19.7*    511  65.5     269  34.5
ROCKINGHM    829  58.5     316  22.3     271  19.1*   1294  65.9     671  34.1
RUSSELL     1349  82.3     129   7.9     162   9.9*   1943  88.8     246  11.2
                                          *
SCOTT        768  84.9      97  10.7      40   4.4*   1043  83.8     202  16.2
SHENANDOH    611  58.0     226  21.4     217  20.6*   1010  72.8     378  27.2
SMYTH        687  61.6     237  21.3     191  17.1*    971  66.6     488  33.4
SOUTHMPTN    902  42.3     700  32.8     529  24.8*   1282  54.1    1088  45.9
SPOTSYLVN    758  28.0    1600  59.1     348  12.9*    681  28.9    1676  71.1
                                          *
STAFFORD     916  34.7    1318  50.0     403  15.3*    737  33.1    1491  66.9
SURRY        351  24.4     712  49.5     374  26.0*    505  42.8     676  57.2
SUSSEX       783  29.5    1042  39.2     830  31.3*   1132  50.2    1125  49.8
TAZEWELL    1174  36.3     989  30.6    1073  32.2*   1001  47.2    1119  52.8
WARREN       720  40.5     763  42.9     296  16.6*   1066  48.9    1114  51.1
                                          *
WARWICK        0    .0       0    .0       0    .0*      0    .0       0    .0
WASHINGTN    984  57.4     322  18.8     409  23.8*   1652  75.7     531  24.3
WESTMRLND    341  36.0     339  35.8     266  28.1*    528  48.1     569  51.9
WISE        1835  80.7     186   8.2     252  11.1*   3047  87.0     455  13.0
WYTHE        604  45.6     191  14.4     529  40.0*   1239  78.2     345  21.8
                                          *
YORK         980  39.4    1064  42.8     441  17.7*   1298  44.4    1624  55.6
ALEXANDRA   2791  32.7    3599  42.1    2152  25.2*   3841  45.5    4609  54.5
BEDFORD      191  44.9     132  31.1     102  24.0*    320  61.4     201  38.6
BRISTOL      893  69.9     145  11.4     239  18.7*   1125  82.9     232  17.1
BUENA VTA    142  49.3      70  24.3      76  26.4*    213  63.2     124  36.8
                                          *
CHARLSTVL   2544  52.5    1432  29.5     872  18.0*   2911  56.8    2215  43.2
CHESAPKE    2155  24.9    4713  54.4    1798  20.7*   3979  36.6    6881  63.4
CLIFTN FG    272  52.3     166  31.9      82  15.8*    357  56.7     273  43.3
COL HGHTS    869  50.9     303  17.8     535  31.3*   1210  67.2     591  32.8
COVINGTON    444  39.1     495  43.6     196  17.3*    503  37.6     834  62.4
                                          *
DANVILLE    3318  38.5    2191  25.4    3106  36.1*   4756  64.9    2577  35.1
```

```
                    DEMOC.  GOVERNOR   1969      * DEMOC.  RUNOFF     1969
                                                 *
      COUNTY      BATTLE       HOWELL         POLLARD      BATTLE       HOWELL
                  #      %     #      %       #      %*    #      %     #      %
      ------------------------------------------------------*-------------------------------------------------
      EMPORIA      414  29.3   423  29.9      577  40.8*   624  52.9    555  47.1
      FAIRFAX      393  29.8   535  40.6      391  29.6*   830  54.6    690  45.4
      FALLS CH     322  32.1   428  42.7      252  25.1*   565  50.0    565  50.0
      FRANKLIN     308  33.7   315  34.4      292  31.9*   590  58.4    421  41.6
      FREDRKSBG    957  35.5  1171  43.5      564  21.0*  1084  44.9   1329  55.1
                                                 *
      GALAX        285  72.0    35   8.8       76  19.2*   525  88.1     71  11.9
      HAMPTON     3843  31.3  6704  54.5     1748  14.2*  4897  36.4   8558  63.6
      HARRISNBG    433  56.6    80  10.5      252  32.9*   717  76.7    218  23.3
      HOPEWELL     926  44.2   654  31.2      513  24.5*  1240  51.3   1178  48.7
      LEXINGTON    309  54.0   122  21.3      141  24.7*   384  68.9    173  31.1
                                                 *
      LYNCHBURG    952  27.9  1300  38.1     1160  34.0*  2160  54.7   1791  45.3
      MARTINSVL    935  43.7   691  32.3      512  23.9*  1453  55.8   1153  44.2
      NEWPRT NS   4492  37.3  5587  46.4     1971  16.4*  5886  44.9   7223  55.1
      NORFOLK    10206  32.5 17030  54.2     4201  13.4* 11113  34.8  20789  65.2
      NORTON       219  68.4    28   8.7       73  22.8*   292  87.4     42  12.6
                                                 *
      PETERSBRG   1689  28.0  3030  50.2     1312  21.8*  2684  42.2   3677  57.8
      PORTSMTH    5509  33.7  8840  54.0     2017  12.3*  7058  38.8  11118  61.2
      RADFORD      512  59.1   285  32.9       69   8.0*   665  60.5    435  39.5
      RICHMOND    8906  26.3 16206  47.9     8724  25.8* 13524  42.0  18680  58.0
      ROANOKE     2825  44.3  2396  37.5     1160  18.2*  4094  50.0   4088  50.0
                                                 *
      SALEM        473  38.8   421  34.5      325  26.7*   738  50.9    713  49.1
      S BOSTON     647  53.9   117   9.7      436  36.3*   946  79.7    241  20.3
      S NORFOLK      0   .0      0   .0        0   .0*      0   .0       0   .0
      STAUNTON     656  46.8   322  23.0      425  30.3*  1184  65.5    624  34.5
      SUFFOLK      980  49.0   553  27.7      466  23.3*  1123  65.4    594  34.6
                                                 *
      VA BEACH    5351  37.1  5332  37.0     3728  25.9*  7207  46.9   8173  53.1
      WANESBORO    450  56.4   169  21.2      179  22.4*   661  63.1    387  36.9
      WILLMSBRG    465  48.6   266  27.8      226  23.6*   632  60.8    407  39.2
      WINCHESTR    535  39.8   348  25.9      461  34.3*   989  67.8    470  32.2
      ------------------------------------------------------*-------------------------------------------------
                                                 *
      TOTALS     158956       154617         95067   * 226108        207505
      % OF VOTE     38.9         37.8          23.3   *    52.1          47.9
```

```
              DEMOC.  GOVERNOR   1969    * DEMOC.  RUNOFF     1969
                                         *
COUNTY    BATTLE       HOWELL        POLLARD    BATTLE       HOWELL
          #      %     #      %      #      %*  #      %     #      %
-----------------------------------------------------------------------------------------------------------------
GEOGRAPHIC CLASS                         *
                                         *
LOWLANDS    83407 35.  101152 43.    50575 22.* 115941 47.  131372 53.
BLACK BELT  17129 34.   20166 39.    13813 27.*  25710 50.   25711 50.
PIEDMONT    23295 40.   17125 30.    17404 30.*  33471 59.   23604 41.
MOUNTAIN    35125 54.   16174 25.    13275 21.*  50986 66.   26818 34.
                                         *
                                         *
DEMOGRAPHIC CLASS                        *
                                         *
METRO       76459 35.   96685 44.    45849 21.* 107670 46.  125341 54.
TOWN        17061 42.   11698 29.    12039 30.*  21952 58.   15938 42.
RURAL       65436 44.   46234 31.    37179 25.*  96486 59.   66226 41.
```

VIRGINIA

```
              DEMOC.  SENATOR   1952* DEMOC.  SENATOR   1966
                                    *
COUNTY    BYRD         MILLER        ROBERTSON    SPONG
          #      %     #      %*     #      %     #      %
-----------------------------------------------------------------------------------------------------------------
ACCOMACK   2368 73.7    847 26.3*   1790 51.7   1672 48.3
ALBEMARLE  2063 76.8    624 23.2*   1599 55.8   1266 44.2
ALLEGHANY  1340 47.2   1496 52.8*    442 62.9    261 37.1
AMELIA      838 68.4    388 31.6*    909 66.1    466 33.9
AMHERST    1260 51.6   1184 48.4*   1291 70.2    548 29.8
                              *
APPOMATTX  1636 85.9    269 14.1*   2556 85.3    439 14.7
ARLINGTON  7377 52.3   6725 47.7*   6113 34.5  11591 65.5
AUGUSTA    2038 76.7    619 23.3*   1415 69.2    631 30.8
BATH        471 81.6    106 18.4*    262 81.6     59 18.4
BEDFORD    2277 65.6   1192 34.4*   1615 73.8    572 26.2
                              *
BLAND       552 65.2    294 34.8*    254 60.0    169 40.0
BOTETOURT   912 62.7    542 37.3*    588 59.8    396 40.2
BRUNSWICK  1642 72.1    634 27.9*   1776 61.0   1134 39.0
BUCHANAN    813 33.8   1590 66.2*    499 31.4   1092 68.6
BUCKINGHM   981 71.2    397 28.8*   1578 77.8    450 22.2
                              *
CAMPBELL   1981 61.8   1222 38.2*   1730 74.7    586 25.3
CAROLINE    908 73.6    326 26.4*    873 49.9    875 50.1
CARROLL     504 38.8    796 61.2*    166 20.7    635 79.3
CHAS CITY   286 48.1    308 51.9*    222 23.2    735 76.8
CHARLOTTE  1538 70.9    631 29.1*   1323 77.0    395 23.0
                              *
CHESTRFLD  2904 61.0   1857 39.0*   4837 64.0   2718 36.0
CLARKE      967 84.8    174 15.2*    911 65.5    480 34.5
CRAIG       221 58.5    157 41.5*    133 53.8    114 46.2
```

	DEMOC. SENATOR 1952*				DEMOC. SENATOR 1966			
COUNTY	BYRD		MILLER		ROBERTSON		SPONG	
	#	%	#	%*	#	%	#	%
CULPEPER	1418	84.3	264	15.7*	1430	69.4	631	30.6
CUMBERLND	792	81.2	183	18.8*	943	58.3	674	41.7
DICKENSON	531	26.8	1448	73.2*	688	45.6	822	54.4
DINWIDDIE	1337	69.2	595	30.8*	1887	67.1	924	32.9
ELIZ CITY	2744	47.8	2997	52.2*	0	.0	0	.0
ESSEX	578	78.9	155	21.1*	594	63.5	342	36.5
FAIRFAX	4968	51.7	4645	48.3*	8531	30.1	19848	69.9
FAUQUIER	1934	83.8	375	16.2*	2076	63.7	1183	36.3
FLOYD	174	47.8	190	52.2*	144	50.0	144	50.0
FLUVANNA	689	80.5	167	19.5*	453	76.8	137	23.2
FRANKLIN	1543	55.5	1237	44.5*	1174	59.3	807	40.7
FREDERICK	1745	84.3	325	15.7*	1647	68.0	774	32.0
GILES	920	60.6	597	39.4*	517	47.6	569	52.4
GLOUCESTR	1034	74.3	358	25.7*	798	60.0	533	40.0
GOOCHLAND	807	66.4	408	33.6*	1265	60.2	838	39.8
GRAYSON	768	37.4	1285	62.6*	381	38.7	603	61.3
GREENE	180	77.6	52	22.4*	126	61.2	80	38.8
GREENSVLE	1081	71.4	433	28.6*	1595	54.8	1316	45.2
HALIFAX	3111	75.8	995	24.2*	2163	77.2	638	22.8
HANOVER	1679	68.7	764	31.3*	2348	66.7	1171	33.3
HENRICO	4974	63.5	2858	36.5*	11288	66.4	5701	33.6
HENRY	1293	46.0	1515	54.0*	928	51.8	862	48.2
HIGHLAND	489	90.1	54	9.9*	203	89.0	25	11.0
ISLE WIGT	1035	66.7	517	33.3*	909	45.0	1109	55.0
JAMES CTY	321	74.1	112	25.9*	555	52.0	512	48.0
KING GEO	488	76.0	154	24.0*	452	55.4	364	44.6
KING+QUN	451	78.6	123	21.4*	446	51.4	421	48.6
KING WM	637	74.0	224	26.0*	718	60.4	471	39.6
LANCASTER	951	75.9	302	24.1*	1525	74.8	513	25.2
LEE	818	30.2	1890	69.8*	200	10.3	1738	89.7
LOUDON	2130	80.3	521	19.7*	1949	59.8	1312	40.2
LOUISA	1080	71.0	442	29.0*	1410	67.5	678	32.5
LUNENBURG	1177	66.2	600	33.8*	1178	63.5	677	36.5
MADISON	653	88.5	85	11.5*	496	71.7	196	28.3
MATHEWS	681	72.2	262	27.8*	575	64.1	322	35.9
MECKLENBG	2471	77.1	733	22.9*	2189	68.3	1016	31.7
MIDDLESEX	628	75.4	205	24.6*	428	69.0	192	31.0
MONTGOMRY	1589	70.5	664	29.5*	882	56.7	673	43.3
NANSEMOND	1262	59.4	861	40.6*	1512	39.6	2310	60.4
NELSON	828	51.3	787	48.7*	705	71.5	281	28.5
NEW KENT	243	56.4	188	43.6*	328	44.9	403	55.1
NORFOLK	3107	43.9	3972	56.1*	993	68.1	466	31.9
NORTHAMTN	1556	77.5	453	22.5*	0	.0	0	.0
NORTHUMLD	650	73.1	239	26.9*	759	55.0	622	45.0
NOTTOWAY	1551	70.7	643	29.3*	1695	66.5	854	33.5
ORANGE	1323	79.6	339	20.4*	1017	66.7	507	33.3

```
          DEMOC.  SENATOR   1952* DEMOC.  SENATOR    1966
                                 *
  COUNTY     BYRD       MILLER      ROBERTSON   SPONG
              #     %     #     %*    #     %     #     %
------------------------------------------+-----------------------------------------------------------
PAGE       1450 80.5   351 19.5* 1261 79.6    323 20.4
PATRICK    1632 87.4   235 12.6*  612 44.8    754 55.2
PITTSLVNA  3757 68.8  1702 31.2* 3411 62.9   2011 37.1
POWHATAN    470 66.2   240 33.8*  583 54.2    493 45.8
PRINCE ED  1426 80.3   350 19.7* 2127 63.7   1210 36.3
                                 *
PRIN GEO    523 61.2   331 38.8*  980 55.7    781 44.3
PRINCE WM  1385 74.3   479 25.7* 2505 55.2   2035 44.8
PRIN ANNE  2491 63.4  1439 36.6*    0   .0      0   .0
PULASKI    1768 69.4   781 30.6*  763 41.4   1080 58.6
RAPPAHANK   827 90.3    89  9.7*  816 79.8    207 20.2
                                 *
RICHMOND    573 79.7   146 20.3*  589 66.3    300 33.7
ROANOKE    3032 65.5  1597 34.5* 2213 59.5   1507 40.5
ROCKBRIDG  1377 72.7   517 27.3*  906 78.2    252 21.8
ROCKINGHM  2462 88.2   328 11.8* 1138 67.1    557 32.9
RUSSELL    1537 61.7   954 38.3*  523 30.0   1221 70.0
                                 *
SCOTT       688 34.4  1314 65.6*  284 21.9   1011 78.1
SHENANDOH  2356 86.8   357 13.2* 1430 77.7    410 22.3
SMYTH      1149 57.3   857 42.7*  539 37.7    889 62.3
SOUTHMPTN  1521 65.4   803 34.6* 1272 55.4   1024 44.6
SPOTSYLVN   929 58.8   652 41.2* 1130 46.7   1290 53.3
                                 *
STAFFORD    747 55.7   594 44.3* 1187 44.0   1508 56.0
SURRY       562 74.1   196 25.9*  843 52.5    764 47.5
SUSSEX     1287 77.7   370 22.3* 1686 66.9    835 33.1
TAZEWELL   1385 56.5  1067 43.5*  770 47.7    844 52.3
WARREN     1545 74.0   544 26.0* 1246 58.6    882 41.4
                                 *
WARWICK    2008 59.4  1370 40.6*    0   .0      0   .0
WASHINGTN   864 42.3  1180 57.7*  929 42.2   1272 57.8
WESTMRLND   852 78.1   239 21.9*  868 56.0    683 44.0
WISE       1389 38.0  2263 62.0* 1471 50.2   1457 49.8
WYTHE      1543 79.1   407 20.9*  650 46.3    755 53.7
                                 *
YORK        865 53.7   746 46.3* 1206 53.1   1065 46.9
ALEXANDRA  4340 54.0  3699 46.0* 3870 35.0   7180 65.0
BEDFORD       0   .0     0   .0*    0   .0      0   .0
BRISTOL     783 50.4   772 49.6*  556 38.4    892 61.6
BUENA VTA   398 65.6   209 34.4*  416 79.2    109 20.8
                                 *
CHARLSTVL  2186 66.6  1095 33.4* 2123 46.5   2444 53.5
CHESAPKE      0   .0     0   .0* 4820 43.4   6277 56.6
CLIFTN FG   533 47.0   600 53.0*  401 69.3    178 30.7
COL HGHTS   660 62.0   405 38.0* 1478 80.0    369 20.0
COVINGTON     0   .0     0   .0*  575 59.3    395 40.7
                                 *
DANVILLE   3853 69.0  1733 31.0* 2691 60.0   1793 40.0
EMPORIA       0   .0     0   .0*    0   .0      0   .0
FAIRFAX       0   .0     0   .0*  773 36.4   1351 63.6
FALLS CH    576 51.7   539 48.3*  441 31.3    966 68.7
FRANKLIN      0   .0     0   .0*  536 55.7    427 44.3
                                 *
FREDRKSBG  1142 69.0   513 31.0* 1406 45.2   1707 54.8
```

VIRGINIA/337

```
           DEMOC.  SENATOR    1952* DEMOC.  SENATOR    1966
                                 *
    COUNTY     BYRD        MILLER        ROBERTSON    SPONG
               #     %     #     %*      #      %     #     %
    --------------------------------*--------------------------------
    GALAX         0   .0      0   .0*    182  40.3    270  59.7
    HAMPTON     565  50.7    550  49.3*  5335  50.5   5229  49.5
    HARRISNBG  1527  90.3    164   9.7*   844  70.2    358  29.8
    HOPEWELL   1047  51.0   1007  49.0*  1376  56.0   1079  44.0
    LEXINGTON     0   .0      0   .0*    662  68.3    307  31.7
                                 *
    LYNCHBURG  4079  68.4   1881  31.6*  3188  59.3   2188  40.7
    MARTINSVL  1422  64.5    783  35.5*   811  49.7    820  50.3
    NEWPRT NS  2034  48.6   2152  51.4*  6313  49.3   6484  50.7
    NORFOLK    8774  55.4   7060  44.6*  9773  33.8  19175  66.2
    NORTON        0   .0      0   .0*    151  34.8    283  65.2
                                 *
    PETERSBRG  2532  67.8   1205  32.2*  2723  46.6   3126  53.4
    PORTSMTH   3120  47.9   3390  52.1*  4460  26.8  12187  73.2
    RADFORD     524  46.4    605  53.6*   334  50.8    324  49.2
    RICHMOND  19088  63.2  11098  36.8* 14628  46.9  16579  53.1
    ROANOKE    8189  62.1   4995  37.9*  4135  55.0   3388  45.0
                                 *
    SALEM         0   .0      0   .0*      0   .0      0   .0
    S BOSTON      0   .0      0   .0*    599  79.7    153  20.3
    S NORFOLK   547  35.8    982  64.2*     0   .0      0   .0
    STAUNTON   1762  77.5    511  22.5*  1356  66.5    684  33.5
    SUFFOLK    1422  75.1    472  24.9*   997  54.7    826  45.3
                                 *
    VA BEACH   1068  70.8    440  29.2*  6396  42.8   8560  57.2
    WANESBORO  1040  69.2    463  30.8*   740  59.1    513  40.9
    WILLMSBRG   440  67.4    213  32.6*   470  45.8    557  54.2
    WINCHESTR  2091  89.7    241  10.3*  1795  70.7    744  29.3
    --------------------------------*--------------------------------
                                 *
    TOTALS   216438       128869      * 216274      216885
    % OF VOTE   62.7         37.3      *  49.9        50.1
                                 *
                                 *
    GEOGRAPHIC CLASS             *
                                 *
    LOWLANDS  77921  59.   54983  41.* 109957  44.  138487  56.
    BLACK BELT 33091  65.   17465  35.*  32841  59.   22831  41.
    PIEDMONT  38024  69.   16823  31.*  35311  61.   23027  39.
    MOUNTAIN  67402  63.   39598  37.*  38165  54.   32540  46.
                                 *
                                 *
    DEMOGRAPHIC CLASS            *
                                 *
    METRO     78669  59.   53784  41.* 101992  44.  131367  56.
    TOWN      29906  61.   19200  39.*  19973  57.   15307  43.
    RURAL    107863  66.   55885  34.*  94309  57.   70211  43.
```

| | DEMOC. SENATOR 1966* | | | DEMOC. SENATOR 1970 | | |
| COUNTY | BYRD | BOOTHE | RAWLINGS | DUVAL | COLVIN |
	# %	# %*	# %	# %	# %
ACCOMACK	1850 53.4	1616 46.6*	363 47.0	231 29.9	179 23.2
ALBEMARLE	1635 56.9	1237 43.1*	201 26.3	469 61.5	93 12.2
ALLEGHANY	420 59.9	281 40.1*	109 46.8	85 36.5	39 16.7
AMELIA	916 66.3	465 33.7*	225 83.3	31 11.5	14 5.2
AMHERST	1224 66.3	622 33.7*	91 30.7	127 42.9	78 26.4
APPOMATTX	2559 85.1	447 14.9*	220 69.8	60 19.0	35 11.1
ARLINGTON	6658 37.0	11333 63.0*	1989 30.3	4121 62.8	456 6.9
AUGUSTA	1338 65.6	703 34.4*	164 43.4	151 39.9	63 16.7
BATH	226 71.3	91 28.7*	30 21.4	76 54.3	34 24.3
BEDFORD	1603 72.3	615 27.7*	91 37.8	98 40.7	52 21.6
BLAND	298 68.8	135 31.2*	58 36.7	74 46.8	26 16.5
BOTETOURT	521 52.8	465 47.2*	120 32.3	184 49.6	67 18.1
BRUNSWICK	1793 60.3	1180 39.7*	668 83.0	96 11.9	41 5.1
BUCHANAN	430 27.2	1152 72.8*	399 45.6	456 52.1	20 2.3
BUCKINGHM	1583 77.9	450 22.1*	514 80.7	58 9.1	65 10.2
CAMPBELL	1734 73.4	628 26.6*	101 41.7	81 33.5	60 24.8
CAROLINE	848 48.1	916 51.9*	622 74.4	166 19.9	48 5.7
CARROLL	218 27.2	582 72.7*	61 19.2	245 77.0	12 3.8
CHAS CITY	210 21.9	748 78.1*	171 81.0	24 11.4	16 7.6
CHARLOTTE	1361 77.9	385 22.1*	280 74.3	71 18.8	26 6.9
CHESTRFLD	5041 66.2	2571 33.8*	476 49.0	333 34.3	163 16.8
CLARKE	1135 77.7	326 22.3*	51 42.1	50 41.3	20 16.5
CRAIG	116 47.0	131 53.0*	24 19.4	85 68.5	15 12.1
CULPEPER	1336 62.8	791 37.2*	103 27.3	214 56.8	60 15.9
CUMBERLND	955 58.7	673 41.3*	556 92.1	33 5.5	15 2.5
DICKENSON	652 42.6	879 57.4*	333 35.3	575 61.0	35 3.7
DINWIDDIE	1915 67.3	929 32.7*	280 66.0	90 21.2	54 12.7
ELIZ CITY	0 .0	0 .0*	0 .0	0 .0	0 .0
ESSEX	583 61.9	359 38.1*	200 65.6	78 25.6	27 8.9
FAIRFAX	9148 32.0	19443 68.0*	3965 26.1	10211 67.3	988 6.5
FAUQUIER	1943 58.1	1399 41.9*	391 40.5	374 38.8	200 20.7
FLOYD	135 45.9	159 54.1*	94 43.9	96 44.9	24 11.2
FLUVANNA	463 77.6	134 22.4*	25 21.6	67 57.8	24 20.7
FRANKLIN	1116 55.7	887 44.3*	82 12.7	518 80.1	47 7.3
FREDERICK	1978 76.9	594 23.1*	113 34.3	160 48.6	56 17.0
GILES	592 54.5	495 45.5*	76 13.3	455 79.8	39 6.8
GLOUCESTR	870 66.3	442 33.7*	146 52.7	96 34.7	35 12.6
GOOCHLAND	1280 60.2	846 39.8*	486 71.7	140 20.6	52 7.7
GRAYSON	360 36.9	615 63.1*	212 42.5	265 53.1	22 4.4
GREENE	135 64.3	75 35.7*	34 33.3	56 54.9	12 11.8
GREENSVLE	1626 55.6	1300 44.4*	412 86.6	38 8.0	26 5.5
HALIFAX	2181 77.7	625 22.3*	415 53.8	185 24.0	172 22.3
HANOVER	2430 68.0	1144 32.0*	385 44.9	315 36.7	158 18.4
HENRICO	11744 68.3	5443 31.7*	850 31.3	1355 49.9	510 18.8
HENRY	928 52.9	825 47.1*	319 55.0	218 37.6	43 7.4
HIGHLAND	192 85.7	32 14.3*	20 27.4	35 47.9	18 24.7

```
            DEMOC.  SENATOR   1966*        DEMOC.  SENATOR   1970
                                  *
COUNTY      BYRD          BOOTHE       RAWLINGS      DUVAL         COLVIN
            #      %      #      %*     #      %     #      %      #      %
------------------------------------*-----------------------------------------------------------
ISLE WIGT   1006 50.0    1006 50.0*    565 77.0    116 15.8      53   7.2
JAMES CTY    520 46.3     604 53.7*    252 64.8    101 26.0      36   9.3
KING GEO     427 51.5     402 48.5*    115 61.5     49 26.2      23  12.3
KING+QUN     449 51.0     432 49.0*    210 75.5     53 19.1      15   5.4
KING WM      725 60.5     474 39.5*    189 60.0     86 27.3      40  12.7
                                  *
LANCASTER   1518 74.5     519 25.5*    349 63.9    142 26.0      55  10.1
LEE          257 13.2    1695 86.8*    456 53.5    388 45.5       9   1.1
LOUDON      1931 58.3    1383 41.7*    509 40.7    602 48.1     140  11.2
LOUISA      1424 67.0     701 33.0*    227 50.3    156 34.6      68  15.1
LUNENBURG   1201 64.2     671 35.8*    311 66.3    102 21.7      56  11.9
                                  *
MADISON      502 70.5     210 29.5*     65 39.4     67 40.6      33  20.0
MATHEWS      589 65.3     313 34.7*    110 56.1     45 23.0      41  20.9
MECKLENBG   2309 71.2     933 28.8*    689 73.8    144 15.4     101  10.8
MIDDLESEX    443 71.0     181 29.0*     42 40.0     35 33.3      28  26.7
MONTGOMRY    875 56.1     685 43.9*    195 29.7    383 58.3      79  12.0
                                  *
NANSEMOND   1690 44.9    2076 55.1*    549 67.4    193 23.7      72   8.8
NELSON       630 64.2     352 35.8*     68 23.9    164 57.7      52  18.3
NEW KENT     322 43.9     411 56.1*    112 76.2     24 16.3      11   7.5
NORFOLK        0   .0       0   .0*      0   .0      0   .0       0    .0
NORTHAMTN   1026 69.6     449 30.4*     88 40.4     82 37.6      48  22.0
                                  *
NORTHUMLD    746 53.2     655 46.8*    299 79.5     57 15.2      20   5.3
NOTTOWAY    1743 68.2     814 31.8*    218 59.2     94 25.5      56  15.2
ORANGE      1048 68.2     489 31.8*    135 37.9    151 42.4      70  19.7
PAGE        1246 78.3     346 21.7*    243 63.3    103 26.8      38   9.9
PATRICK      595 43.1     787 56.9*     45  7.7    501 86.1      36   6.2
                                  *
PITTSLVNA   3711 67.9    1756 32.1*    527 54.2    219 22.5     227  23.3
POWHATAN     591 54.2     499 45.8*    297 90.3     23  7.0       9   2.7
PRINCE ED   2169 64.5    1194 35.5*    502 76.4    112 17.0      43   6.5
PRIN GEO     975 55.4     785 44.6*    480 79.3     93 15.4      32   5.3
PRINCE WM   2532 55.2    2051 44.8*    677 45.7    524 35.4     281  19.0
                                  *
PRIN ANNE      0   .0       0   .0*      0   .0      0   .0       0    .0
PULASKI      961 51.5     904 48.5*    140 21.6    472 72.8      36   5.6
RAPPAHANK    811 77.6     234 22.4*     45 47.9     25 26.6      24  25.5
RICHMOND     598 66.5     301 33.5*    112 53.1     68 32.2      31  14.7
ROANOKE     2117 57.2    1585 42.8*    454 46.3    416 42.4     110  11.2
                                  *
ROCKBRIDG    720 62.2     438 37.8*     59 22.4     83 31.6     121  46.0
ROCKINGHM   1112 65.1     596 34.9*    130 25.7    287 56.7      89  17.6
RUSSELL      504 28.8    1243 71.2*    287 37.0    466 60.1      22   2.8
SCOTT        275 21.1    1028 78.9*    303 57.8    148 28.2      73  13.9
SHENANDOH   1413 75.5     459 24.5*    152 35.7    218 51.2      56  13.1
                                  *
SMYTH        540 37.7     892 62.3*     88 19.2    351 76.5      20   4.4
SOUTHMPTN   1422 61.4     895 38.6*    230 57.9    120 30.2      47  11.8
SPOTSYLVN   1057 42.5    1428 57.5*   1214 81.9    204 13.8      64   4.3
STAFFORD    1182 43.0    1566 57.0*    698 67.1    292 28.0      51   4.9
SURRY        891 54.7     739 45.3*    298 76.0     63 16.1      31   7.9
                                  *
SUSSEX      1774 70.3     749 29.7*    436 78.0     70 12.5      53   9.5
```

```
            DEMOC.  SENATOR    1966*      DEMOC.  SENATOR   1970
                                    *
   COUNTY     BYRD       BOOTHE      RAWLINGS    DUVAL        COLVIN
              #    %     #     %*    #     %     #    %       #     %
-----------------------------------------------*-------------------------------------------------------------------------
TAZEWELL     775  47.1   870  52.9*  830  77.6   191  17.9    49   4.6
WARREN      1196  55.6   957  44.4*  235  40.2   307  52.5    43   7.4
WARWICK        0   .0      0    .0*    0   .0      0   .0      0    .0
WASHINGTN   1037  45.2  1255  54.8*  155  26.8   393  68.0    30   5.2
WESTMRLND    853  53.9   729  46.1*  282  64.5   108  24.7    47  10.8
                                *
WISE        1440  49.2  1485  50.8*  201  16.4   974  79.6    48   3.9
WYTHE        699  49.6   711  50.4*   93  18.5   387  77.1    22   4.4
YORK        1154  50.3  1138  49.7*  200  47.1   150  35.3    75  17.6
ALEXANDRA   3821  33.6  7541  66.4* 1387  39.3  1869  53.0   270   7.7
BEDFORD        0   .0      0    .0*   28  23.0    88  72.1     6   4.9
                                *
BRISTOL      632  43.3   827  56.7*   27   6.0   400  89.1    22   4.9
BUENA VTA    403  77.1   120  22.9*   25  27.5    19  20.9    47  51.6
CHARLSTVL   2148  46.0  2523  54.0*  544  39.7   722  52.7   103   7.5
CHESAPKE    5352  48.6  5663  51.4* 1121  48.3  1016  43.8   185   8.0
CLIFTN FG    406  70.6   169  29.4*   42  27.6    79  52.0    31  20.4
                                *
COL HGHTS   1456  78.4   401  21.6*   72  43.9    60  36.6    32  19.5
COVINGTON    529  54.4   443  45.6*  113  43.5    86  33.1    61  23.5
DANVILLE    2873  64.2  1602  35.8*  721  80.5   115  12.8    60   6.7
EMPORIA        0   .0      0    .0*  227  69.0    67  20.4    35  10.6
FAIRFAX      896  41.4  1268  58.6*  177  31.4   361  64.0    26   4.6
                                *
FALLS CH     510  36.0   907  64.0*   98  15.5   493  77.9    42   6.6
FRANKLIN     589  62.7   350  37.3*   81  53.3    53  34.9    18  11.8
FREDRKSBG   1432  45.5  1715  54.5* 1038  71.0   333  22.8    92   6.3
GALAX        173  38.5   276  61.5*   35   9.6   306  83.8    24   6.6
HAMPTON     4742  44.8  5839  55.2* 1144  37.7  1538  50.7   349  11.5
                                *
HARRISNBG    888  73.6   318  26.4*   49  35.5    71  51.4    18  13.0
HOPEWELL    1471  61.1   937  38.9*  295  56.1   179  34.0    52   9.9
LEXINGTON    451  46.7   515  53.3*   33  11.2    63  21.4   199  67.5
LYNCHBURG   3294  60.7  2131  39.3*  116  11.9   774  79.4    85   8.7
MARTINSVL    873  54.8   721  45.2*  225  60.2   117  31.3    32   8.6
                                *
NEWPRT NS   5621  44.4  7047  55.6* 1436  51.3  1025  36.6   337  12.0
NORFOLK     9759  34.1 18845  65.9* 6277  53.8  4723  40.5   658   5.6
NORTON       194  44.6   241  55.4*   59  57.8    35  34.3     8   7.8
PETERSBRG   2813  48.1  3033  51.9* 1014  73.4   260  18.8   107   7.7
PORTSMTH    5535  35.7  9983  64.3* 2338  46.5  2388  47.5   301   6.0
                                *
RADFORD      309  47.3   344  52.7*   73  34.3   120  56.3    20   9.4
RICHMOND   14713  47.2 16483  52.8* 5037  49.7  4299  42.4   804   7.9
ROANOKE     3713  49.7  3760  50.3*  983  46.7   914  43.5   206   9.8
SALEM          0   .0      0    .0*  165  38.6   212  49.6    50  11.7
S BOSTON     609  80.4   148  19.6*   43  29.1    80  54.1    25  16.9
                                *
S NORFOLK      0   .0      0    .0*    0   .0      0   .0      0    .0
STAUNTON    1269  61.4   799  38.6*  150  46.2   131  40.3    44  13.5
SUFFOLK     1121  62.2   680  37.8*  145  46.9   118  38.2    46  14.9
VA BEACH    7193  48.9  7531  51.1* 1525  51.1  1198  40.2   259   8.7
WANESBORO    719  56.9   544  43.1*   80  37.6   103  48.4    30  14.1
                                *
WILLMSBRG    435  40.2   648  59.8*  176  50.7   145  41.8    26   7.5
```

```
            DEMOC.  SENATOR    1966*     DEMOC.  SENATOR    1970
                                  *
 COUNTY      BYRD      %     BOOTHE      %*   RAWLINGS    %    DUVAL    %    COLVIN    %
              #      %       #        %*      #       %      #      %      #      %
-------------------------------------------*-----------------------------------------------------------------------------
 WINCHESTR   2269 85.0     401 15.0*      84 42.4      66 33.3      48 24.2
                                  *                                                       -------------------------------
------------------------------------------*-------------------------------------------------
                                  *
 TOTALS     221221       212996      *  58874        58174        11911
 % OF VOTE    50.9         49.1      *   45.7         45.1          9.2
                                  *
                                  *
 GEOGRAPHIC CLASS                 *
                                  *
 LOWLANDS   112227 46.   134286 54.* 32891 43.    37721 49.    6694  9.
 BLACK BELT  33422 61.    21693 39.* 10263 71.     2971 20.    1263  9.
 PIEDMONT    37453 61.    23863 39.*  7281 50.     5691 39.    1681 11.
 MOUNTAIN    38119 53.    33154 47.*  8439 38.    11791 52.    2273 10.
                                  *
                                  *
 DEMOGRAPHIC CLASS                *
                                  *
 METRO      104546 45.   128038 55.* 29814 41.    36596 51.    5988  8.
 TOWN        18379 58.    13188 42.*  4091 54.     2624 35.     887 12.
 RURAL       98296 58.    71770 42.* 24290 51.    18481 39.    4967 10.
```

II Precinct Election Data

The following section contains a substantial
sampling of precinct election data from 24
cities in the 11 southern states. All candidates in the state elections are Democrats,
unless otherwise identified as Republican (R),
Independent (I), etc. For full names of
candidates and other information about the
Democratic primary contests, the reader may
consult the state introductions in the preceding section. For further information
about general elections, the most convenient
source is Richard M. Scammon's <u>America</u> <u>Votes</u>
series.

Preceding the precinct data for each
state is a list of the elections reported.
As described in the introduction to this
volume, the precinct data are presented in
socioeconomic and racial categories.

ALABAMA PRECINCT ELECTIONS

Montgomery (Montgomery County)

General President	1948	Thurmond-Dewey
Civil Service Amendment	1951	For-1, Against-1
Voter Qualifications		
Amendment	1951	For-2, Against-2
General President	1952	Stevenson-Eisenhower
Primary Governor	1954	Allen-Faulkner-Folsom-Henderson-Owen
Primary Senate	1954	Battle-Crommelin-Irby-Sparkman
General Governor	1954	Folsom-Tom Abernethy (R)
Primary Senate	1956	Crommelin-Hill
General President	1956	Stevenson-Eisenhower-States' Rights
Primary Governor	1958	Faulkner-Patterson-Todd-Wallace-Other
Runoff Governor	1958	Patterson-Wallace
General President	1960	Democrat (5 electors pledged to Kennedy, 6 pledged to Harry F. Byrd)-Nixon
General Senate	1960	Sparkman-Julian Elgin (R)
Primary Governor	1962	Connor-deGraffenried-Folsom-Gallion-Wallace
Runoff Governor	1962	deGraffenried-Wallace
Primary Senate	1962	Crommelin-Hallmark-Hill
General Senate	1962	Hill-James D. Martin (R)
General President	1964	Democrat (unpledged)-Goldwater
Primary Senate	1966	Crommelin-Dixon-Sparkman-Stewart
Primary Governor	1966	Elliott-Flowers-Gilchrist-Wallace-Other
General Governor	1966	Wallace-Robinson (I)-James D. Martin (R)
General Senate	1966	Sparkman-John Grenier (R)-Elgin (I)
Runoff Senate	1968	Allen-Selden
General Senate	1968	Allen-Perry Hooper (R)-Schwenn (NDPA)
General President	1968	Alabama Independent Democrats (pledged to Humphrey)-Democrat (pledged to Wallace)-Republican (pledged to Nixon)-National Democratic Party of Alabama (pledged to Humphrey)
Primary Governor	1970	Brewer-Wallace-Woods-Other
Runoff Governor	1970	Brewer-Wallace
General Governor	1970	Wallace-Cashin (NDPA)-Other

Birmingham (Jefferson County)

General President	1948	Thurmond-Dewey
General Senate	1950	Hill-John G. Crommelin (I)
Civil Service Amendment	1951	For-1, Against-1
Voter Qualifications Amendment	1951	For-2, Against-2
General President	1952	Stevenson-Eisenhower
General Governor	1954	Folsom-Tom Abernethy (R)
Freedom of Choice Amendment	1956	For-Against
General President	1956	Stevenson-Eisenhower-States' Rights
Runoff Governor	1958	Patterson-Wallace
General President	1960	Democrat (5 electors pledged to Kennedy, 6 pledged to Harry F. Byrd)-Nixon
General Senate	1960	Sparkman-Julian Elgin (R)
Primary Governor	1962	Connor-deGraffenried-Folsom-Gallion-Wallace
Primary Senate	1962	Crommelin-Hallmark-Hill
Runoff Governor	1962	deGraffenried-Wallace
General Senate	1962	Hill-James D. Martin (R)
General President	1964	Democrat (unpledged)-Goldwater
Primary Senate	1966	Crommelin-Dixon-Sparkman-Stewart
Primary Governor	1966	Elliott-Flowers-Gilchrist-Wallace-Other
General Governor	1966	Wallace-Robinson (I)-James D. Martin (R)
General Senate	1966	Sparkman-John Grenier (R)-Elgin (I)
Runoff Senate	1968	Allen-Selden
General President	1968	Alabama Independent Democrats (pledged to Humphrey)-Democrat (pledged to Wallace)-Republican (pledged to Nixon)-National Democratic Party of Alabama (pledged to Humphrey)
General Senate	1968	Allen-Perry Hooper (R)-Schwenn (NDPA)
Primary Governor	1970	Brewer-Wallace-Woods-Other
Runoff Governor	1970	Brewer-Wallace
General Governor	1970	Wallace-Cashin (NDPA)-Other

CANDIDATE	LOWER # %	LOWER-MIDDLE # %	UPPER-MIDDLE # %	UPPER # %	BLACK # %	*	CANDIDATE	LOWER # %	LOWER-MIDDLE # %	UPPER-MIDDLE # %	UPPER # %	BLACK # %

GENERAL PRESIDENT 1948 * · **SPECIAL REFERENDM 1951**

CANDIDATE	LOWER	LOWER-MIDDLE	UPPER-MIDDLE	UPPER	BLACK	CANDIDATE	LOWER	LOWER-MIDDLE	UPPER-MIDDLE	UPPER	BLACK
THURMOND	1244 .91	890 .88	638 .87	1621 .83	520 .90	FOR-1	641 .49	558 .69	494 .65	1464 .75	366 .64
DEWEY	121 .09	120 .12	98 .13	328 .17	55 .10	AGAINST-1	664 .51	246 .31	262 .35	497 .25	210 .36

SPECIAL REFERENDM 1951 · **GENERAL PRESIDENT 1952**

CANDIDATE	LOWER	LOWER-MIDDLE	UPPER-MIDDLE	UPPER	BLACK	CANDIDATE	LOWER	LOWER-MIDDLE	UPPER-MIDDLE	UPPER	BLACK
FOR-2	461 .40	333 .43	272 .38	945 .50	233 .47	STEVENSON	1804 .63	1054 .55	1202 .51	2040 .42	1062 .59
AGAINST-2	705 .60	447 .57	452 .62	927 .50	261 .53	EISENHOWE	1040 .37	852 .45	1135 .49	2861 .58	724 .41

PRIMARY GOVERNOR 1954 · **PRIMARY SENATOR 1954**

CANDIDATE	LOWER	LOWER-MIDDLE	UPPER-MIDDLE	UPPER	BLACK	CANDIDATE	LOWER	LOWER-MIDDLE	UPPER-MIDDLE	UPPER	BLACK
ALLEN	260 .08	308 .10	247 .09	966 .19	174 .08	BATTLE	1226 .42	1217 .46	1257 .49	2534 .50	695 .35
FAULKNER	875 .27	904 .31	1068 .39	2096 .40	492 .23	CROMMELIN	225 .08	234 .09	161 .06	461 .09	142 .07
FOLSOM	1849 .58	1337 .46	1059 .39	1252 .24	1337 .61	IRBY	14 .00	9 .00	6 .00	39 .01	14 .01
HENDERSON	199 .06	352 .12	331 .12	814 .16	158 .07	SPARKMAN	1421 .49	1205 .45	1121 .44	1995 .40	1109 .57
OWEN	23 .01	36 .01	34 .01	89 .02	21 .01		0 .00	0 .00	0 .00	0 .00	0 .00

GENERAL GOVERNOR 1954 · **PRIMARY SENATOR 1956**

CANDIDATE	LOWER	LOWER-MIDDLE	UPPER-MIDDLE	UPPER	BLACK	CANDIDATE	LOWER	LOWER-MIDDLE	UPPER-MIDDLE	UPPER	BLACK
FOLSOM	871 .80	1055 .67	1145 .64	1865 .64	936 .73	CROMMELIN	789 .54	177 .34	224 .23	140 .27	113 .28
ABERNETHY	215 .20	509 .33	637 .36	1071 .36	343 .27	HILL	666 .46	350 .66	730 .77	385 .73	289 .72

GENERAL PRESIDENT 1956 · **PRIMARY GOVERNOR 1958**

CANDIDATE	LOWER	LOWER-MIDDLE	UPPER-MIDDLE	UPPER	BLACK	CANDIDATE	LOWER	LOWER-MIDDLE	UPPER-MIDDLE	UPPER	BLACK
STEVENSON	649 .41	455 .35	882 .38	441 .34	362 .35	FAULKNER	490 .16	1051 .18	623 .21	769 .22	168 .14
EISENHOWR	640 .40	583 .44	1018 .44	713 .55	533 .52	PATTERSON	789 .26	1593 .27	759 .26	768 .22	257 .21
STATS RTS	300 .19	279 .21	429 .18	131 .10	135 .13	TODD	262 .09	225 .04	22 .01	31 .01	325 .26
	0 .00	0 .00	0 .00	0 .00	0 .00	WALLACE	1168 .39	2308 .40	1118 .38	1313 .38	375 .30
	0 .00	0 .00	0 .00	0 .00	0 .00	OTHER	304 .10	648 .11	441 .15	591 .17	110 .09

PRIMARY RUN-OFF 1958 · **GENERAL PRESIDENT 1960**

CANDIDATE	LOWER	LOWER-MIDDLE	UPPER-MIDDLE	UPPER	BLACK	CANDIDATE	LOWER	LOWER-MIDDLE	UPPER-MIDDLE	UPPER	BLACK
PATTERSON	1283 .48	2738 .51	1295 .47	1454 .48	382 .34	DEMOCRAT	1416 .55	2321 .43	1324 .39	1219 .34	652 .59
WALLACE	1402 .52	2659 .49	1454 .53	1580 .52	739 .66	NIXON	1163 .45	3097 .57	2042 .61	2320 .66	451 .41

GENERAL SENATOR 1960 · **PRIMARY GOVERNOR 1962**

CANDIDATE	LOWER	LOWER-MIDDLE	UPPER-MIDDLE	UPPER	BLACK	CANDIDATE	LOWER	LOWER-MIDDLE	UPPER-MIDDLE	UPPER	BLACK
SPARKMAN	1698 .67	3332 .61	1996 .59	1979 .56	769 .69	CONNOR	19 .01	46 .01	15 .00	23 .01	21 .02
ELGIN	855 .33	2139 .39	1402 .41	1570 .44	339 .31	DEGRAFFND	393 .15	1082 .17	1001 .25	1339 .33	103 .08
	0 .00	0 .00	0 .00	0 .00	0 .00	FOLSOM	522 .20	697 .11	422 .10	415 .10	598 .47
	0 .00	0 .00	0 .00	0 .00	0 .00	GALLION	443 .17	1134 .18	733 .18	643 .16	139 .11
	0 .00	0 .00	0 .00	0 .00	0 .00	WALLACE	1291 .48	3298 .53	1902 .47	1628 .40	423 .33

PRIMARY RUN-OFF 1962 · **PRIMARY SENATOR 1962**

CANDIDATE	LOWER	LOWER-MIDDLE	UPPER-MIDDLE	UPPER	BLACK	CANDIDATE	LOWER	LOWER-MIDDLE	UPPER-MIDDLE	UPPER	BLACK
DEGRAFFND	756 .30	1452 .24	1247 .32	1554 .40	623 .51	CROMMELIN	526 .24	1223 .25	575 .18	450 .14	187 .18
WALLACE	1774 .70	4524 .76	2653 .68	2327 .60	590 .49	HALLMARK	462 .21	1307 .26	904 .28	746 .23	154 .15
	0 .00	0 .00	0 .00	0 .00	0 .00	HILL	1194 .55	2431 .49	1744 .54	2017 .63	675 .66

GENERAL SENATOR 1962 · **GENERAL PRESIDENT 1964**

CANDIDATE	LOWER	LOWER-MIDDLE	UPPER-MIDDLE	UPPER	BLACK	CANDIDATE	LOWER	LOWER-MIDDLE	UPPER-MIDDLE	UPPER	BLACK
HILL	909 .49	1697 .37	1114 .35	1342 .39	542 .63	DEMOCRAT	810 .27	978 .14	635 .12	774 .16	997 .63
MARTIN	946 .51	2868 .63	2091 .65	2114 .61	325 .37	GOLDWATER	2233 .73	6083 .86	4546 .88	4033 .84	594 .37

MONTGOMERY   ALABAMA
****

CANDIDATE	LOWER #	%	LOWER-MIDDLE #	%	UPPER-MIDDLE #	%	UPPER #	%	BLACK #	%
PRIMARY SENATOR 1966										
CROMMELIN	560	.41	2068	.35	1595	.31	969	.23	246	.15
DIXON	253	.18	913	.15	627	.12	460	.11	981	.60
SPARKMAN	491	.36	2521	.43	2616	.50	2479	.60	352	.22
STEWART	73	.05	420	.07	361	.07	232	.06	53	.03
	0	.00	0	.00	0	.00	0	.00	0	.00
GENERAL GOVERNOR 1966										
WALLACE	1993	.74	5762	.72	4004	.57	2699	.45	2518	.65
ROBINSON	32	.01	102	.01	88	.01	117	.02	489	.13
MARTIN	663	.25	2185	.27	2971	.42	3219	.53	887	.23
PRIMARY RUN-OFF 1968										
ALLEN	1025	.69	1896	.68	1496	.55	987	.38	920	.67
SELDEN	465	.31	880	.32	1207	.45	1588	.62	461	.33
	0	.00	0	.00	0	.00	0	.00	0	.00
GENERAL PRESIDENT 1968										
ALAINDEM	145	.03	447	.06	256	.03	438	.06	1130	.19
DEMOCRAT	3982	.80	5822	.77	5889	.74	4005	.59	860	.14
REPUBLICN	500	.10	923	.12	1670	.21	2335	.34	233	.04
NDEMOFALA	339	.07	410	.05	124	.02	60	.01	3778	.63
PRIMARY RUN-OFF 1970										
BREWER	2023	.35	3350	.44	4313	.50	4604	.66	5417	.89
WALLACE	3813	.65	4324	.56	4271	.50	2326	.34	656	.11
	0	.00	0	.00	0	.00	0	.00	0	.00

CANDIDATE	LOWER #	%	LOWER-MIDDLE #	%	UPPER-MIDDLE #	%	UPPER #	%	BLACK #	%
PRIMARY GOVERNOR 1966										
ELLIOTT	34	.02	239	.03	294	.04	438	.08	46	.01
FLOWERS	413	.21	978	.12	325	.05	265	.05	2842	.78
GILCHRIST	39	.02	348	.04	616	.09	852	.16	33	.01
WALLACE	1188	.62	5608	.68	4292	.64	2846	.53	551	.15
OTHER	252	.13	1125	.14	1148	.17	993	.18	192	.05
GENERAL SENATOR 1966										
SPARKMAN	1711	.51	3975	.51	3457	.49	3096	.53	2850	.81
GRENIER	1566	.46	3618	.46	3362	.48	2722	.46	602	.17
ELGIN	108	.03	212	.03	187	.03	70	.01	48	.01
GENERAL SENATOR 1968										
ALLEN	2231	.49	3278	.46	3013	.40	2111	.32	762	.15
HOOPER	1962	.43	3407	.48	4364	.58	4372	.66	580	.11
SCHWENN	340	.08	430	.06	149	.02	101	.02	3835	.74
PRIMARY GOVERNOR 1970										
BREWER	1587	.32			3866	.49	4192	.63	3170	.58
WALLACE	2517	.51	3262	.45	3180	.40	1863	.28	437	.08
WOODS	660	.13	687	.10	722	.09	470	.07	1655	.30
OTHER	190	.04	265	.04	193	.02	180	.03	206	.04
GENERAL GOVERNOR 1970										
WALLACE	4305	.84	5351	.81	5730	.77	3739	.64	740	.17
CASHIN	459	.09	366	.06	195	.03	145	.02	3549	.79
OTHER	384	.07	899	.14	1474	.20	1984	.34	193	.04

```
                  GENERAL  PRESIDENT 1948              *              GENERAL  SENATOR   1950
                  ***************************                         ***************************
THURMOND  1750 .85  1258 .84  1170 .79  1828 .73   73 .40 * HILL       1236 .74   748 .67   778 .63   949 .41   410 .93
DEWEY      317 .15   238 .16   304 .21   680 .27  111 .60 * CROMMELIN   437 .26   372 .33   453 .37  1351 .59    31 .07

                  SPECIAL  REFERENDM 1951              *              SPECIAL  REFERENDM 1951
                  ***************************                         ***************************
FOR-1      909 .63   571 .65   805 .74  1761 .86  358 .91 * FOR-2       509 .37   365 .44   521 .49  1063 .55    40 .10
AGAINST-1  524 .37   304 .35   281 .26   275 .14   34 .09 * AGAINST-2   855 .63   467 .56   532 .51   875 .45   341 .90

                  GENERAL  PRESIDENT 1952              *              GENERAL  GOVERNOR  1954
                  ***************************                         ***************************
STEVENSON 2206 .67  1425 .60  1288 .48  1152 .30  513 .81 * FOLSOM     3720 .69  2313 .61  2960 .51  2640 .32   732 .75
EISENHOWR 1081 .33   948 .40  1416 .52  2716 .70  120 .19 * ABERNETHY  1672 .31  1494 .39  2898 .49  5589 .68   246 .25

                  SPECIAL  REFERENDM 1956              *              GENERAL  PRESIDENT 1956
                  ***************************                         ***************************
FOR       2439 .64  2142 .62  2557 .63  4681 .76  256 .31 * STEVENSN   2604 .54  2246 .50  2072 .42  1965 .28   352 .33
AGAINST   1348 .36  1286 .38  1472 .37  1450 .24  573 .69 * EISENHOWR  1808 .38  1955 .44  2523 .51  4851 .68   658 .62
             0 .00     0 .00     0 .00     0 .00    0 .00 * STATESRTS   409 .08   278 .06   352 .07   299 .04    50 .05

                       RUN-OFF   1958                  *              GENERAL  PRESIDENT 1960
                  ***************************                         ***************************
PATTERSN  2839 .61  2850 .64  3404 .66  4500 .73  297 .32 * DEMOCRAT   2533 .51  2015 .43  1879 .39  1927 .26   492 .46
WALLACE   1849 .39  1637 .36  1746 .34  1691 .27  623 .68 * NIXON      2440 .49  2641 .57  2897 .61  5460 .74   585 .54

                  GENERAL  SENATOR   1960              *              PRIMARY  GOVERNOR  1962
                  ***************************                         ***************************
SPARKMAN  3605 .72  3242 .68  3256 .68  4015 .57  565 .53 * CONNOR      334 .12   510 .14   447 .14   359 .07    15 .02
ELGIN     1418 .28  1531 .32  1563 .32  3072 .43  507 .47 * DEGRAFNRD   797 .28  1333 .36  1309 .41  2612 .53    93 .11
             0 .00     0 .00     0 .00     0 .00    0 .00 * FOLSOM      421 .15   343 .09   269 .08   310 .06   667 .81
             0 .00     0 .00     0 .00     0 .00    0 .00 * GALLION     414 .14   514 .14   434 .14   917 .19    27 .03
                                                           * WALLACE     922 .32   966 .26   731 .23   696 .14    24 .03

                  PRIMARY  SENATOR   1962              *              PRIMARY  RUN-OFF   1962
                  ***************************                         ***************************
CROMMELIN  269 .10   279 .10   287 .10   309 .07   10 .01 * DEGRAFFND  2188 .44  2311 .49  2545 .52  5426 .69   982 .91
HALLMARK   516 .20   578 .21   547 .19  1142 .27   62 .09 * WALLACE    2788 .56  2387 .51  2360 .48  2409 .31   103 .09
HILL      1801 .70  1896 .69  2067 .71  2853 .66  622 .90 *              0 .00     0 .00     0 .00     0 .00     0 .00

                  GENERAL  SENATOR   1962              *              GENERAL  PRESIDENT 1964
                  ***************************                         ***************************
HILL      1545 .44  1486 .41  1411 .37  1725 .29  765 .86 * DEMOCRAT   3217 .24  2794 .19  2370 .16  3890 .16  3779 .99
MARTIN    1984 .56  2122 .59  2361 .63  4268 .71  125 .14 * GOLDWATER 10343 .76 11817 .81 12670 .84 19845 .84    34 .01

                  PRIMARY  SENATOR   1966              *              PRIMARY  GOVERNOR  1966
                  ***************************                         ***************************
CROMMELIN 3418 .36  4255 .36  4106 .38  3797 .23  346 .06 * ELLIOTT     813 .07  1163 .08  1066 .08  3110 .17   429 .05
DIXON     2062 .21  2127 .18  1504 .14  2273 .14 4255 .76 * FLOWERS    2285 .19  1765 .13  1255 .10  1339 .07  8252 .88
SPARKMAN  3903 .41  5068 .43  4943 .46  9942 .60  933 .17 * GILCHRIST   363 .03   692 .05   755 .06  3206 .18    56 .01
STEWART    216 .02   298 .03   222 .02   494 .03   36 .01 * WALLACE    7309 .61  8802 .63  7910 .63  5365 .30   393 .04
             0 .00     0 .00     0 .00     0 .00    0 .00 * OTHER      1194 .10  1619 .12  1589 .13  4937 .27   246 .03

                  GENERAL  GOVERNOR  1966              *              GENERAL  SENATOR   1966
                  ***************************                         ***************************
WALLACE   9064 .64  8879 .57  7449 .57  6158 .27  876 .31 * SPARKMAN   7069 .52  7115 .47  5635 .44  9866 .44  2319 .88
ROBINSON   751 .05   808 .05   472 .04  1120 .05  962 .34 * GRENIER    6444 .47  7882 .52  6830 .54 12583 .56   270 .10
MARTIN    4340 .31  5891 .38  5055 .39 15704 .68  984 .35 * ELGIN       202 .01   174 .01   199 .02   156 .01    42 .02
```

PRECINCT DATA/349

BIRMINGHAM ALABAMA

CANDIDATE	LOWER #	%	LOWER-MIDDLE #	%	UPPER-MIDDLE #	%	UPPER #	%	BLACK #	%	*	CANDIDATE	LOWER #	%	LOWER-MIDDLE #	%	UPPER-MIDDLE #	%	UPPER #	%	BLACK #	%
RUN-OFF 1968											*	**GENERAL PRESIDENT 1968**										
ALLEN	2456	.67	3417	.63	2937	.57	975	.24	584	.14	*	ALAINDEM	590	.06	663	.05	622	.05	1020	.08	8969	.83
SELDEN	1198	.33	2046	.37	2255	.43	3024	.76	3726	.86	*	DEMOCRAT	7367	.77	10424	.77	7217	.63	3841	.32	312	.03
	0	.00	0	.00	0	.00	0	.00	0	.00	*	REPUBLICN	1433	.15	2350	.17	3480	.31	7114	.59	167	.02
	0	.00	0	.00	0	.00	0	.00	0	.00	*	NDEMOFALA	137	.01	86	.01	47	.00	58	.00	1331	.12
GENERAL SENATOR 1968											*	**PRIMARY GOVERNOR 1970**										
ALLEN	6908	.70	9062	.70	6054	.56	3396	.28	366	.11	*	BREWER	2825	.33	4173	.37	6026	.54	8282	.80	7882	.82
HOOPER	2699	.27	3773	.29	4624	.43	8285	.69	350	.10	*	WALLACE	4626	.54	5618	.50	3949	.35	1554	.15	138	.01
SCHWENN	216	.02	132	.01	147	.01	286	.02	2734	.79	*	WOODS	1043	.12	1366	.12	1126	.10	465	.04	1418	.15
	0	.00	0	.00	0	.00	0	.00	0	.00	*	OTHER	86	.01	128	.01	90	.01	40	.00	164	.02
PRIMARY RUN-OFF 1970											*	**GENERAL GOVERNOR 1970**										
BREWER	3552	.36	5050	.40	7367	.58	9826	.82	10408	.98	*	WALLACE	6744	.85	8229	.80	6857	.68	3643	.40	243	.04
WALLACE	6322	.64	7427	.60	5441	.42	2203	.18	205	.02	*	CASHIN	221	.03	229	.02	395	.04	459	.05	4644	.84
	0	.00	0	.00	0	.00	0	.00	0	.00	*	OTHER	978	.12	1818	.18	2784	.28	5041	.55	611	.11

ARKANSAS PRECINCT ELECTIONS

Little Rock (Pulaski County)

General President	1948	Truman-Dewey-Thurmond
Primary Governor	1950	Harris-McMath-Laney
General Governor	1950	McMath-Jefferson W. Speck (R)
Primary Governor	1952	Murry-Tackett-McMath-Holt-Cherry
Runoff Governor	1952	McMath-Cherry
General President	1952	Stevenson-Eisenhower
Primary Governor	1954	Jones-McMillan-Cherry-Faubus
Runoff Governor	1954	Cherry-Faubus
Primary Governor	1956	Faubus-Johnson-Snoddy
General President	1956	Stevenson-Eisenhower-Other (States' Rights)
Primary Governor	1958	Faubus-Finkbeiner-Ward
Primary Governor	1960	Faubus-Millsap-Bennett-Williams-Hardin
General President	1960	Nixon-States' Rights-Kennedy
Primary Governor	1962	Whitten-Alford-Faubus-Coffelt-McMath-Cox
Primary Governor	1964	Hubbard-Dorsey-Faubus-Burrow
General President	1964	Johnson-Goldwater
General Governor	1964	Faubus-Winthrop Rockefeller (R)
Primary Governor	1966	Boyce-Johnson-Alford-Hays-Holt-Rebsamen
Runoff Governor	1966	Johnson-Holt
General Governor	1966	Winthrop Rockefeller (R)-Johnson
Primary Governor	1968	Whitbeck-Bennett-Crank-Boswell-Johnson
General Governor	1968	Crank-Winthrop Rockefeller (R)
General President	1968	Humphrey-Nixon-Wallace
Runoff Governor	1970	Faubus-Bumpers
General Governor	1970	Bumpers-Winthrop Rockefeller (R)
Primary Senate	1972	Johnson-Pryor-McClellan-Boswell

CANDIDATE	LOWER # %	LOWER-MIDDLE # %	UPPER-MIDDLE # %	UPPER # %	BLACK # %	CANDIDATE	LOWER # %	LOWER-MIDDLE # %	UPPER-MIDDLE # %	UPPER # %	BLACK # %
GENERAL PRESIDENT 1948						**PRIMARY GOVERNOR 1950**					
TRUMAN	130 .37	251 .61	1602 .48	618 .34	776 .59	HARRIS	8 .02	7 .01	15 .00	7 .00	8 .00
DEWEY	131 .37	51 .12	935 .28	723 .40	274 .21	MCMATH	275 .59	289 .58	2160 .59	1191 .54	1234 .70
THURMOND	89 .25	109 .27	791 .24	458 .25	266 .20	LANEY	186 .40	202 .41	1457 .40	1012 .46	530 .30
GENERAL GOVERNOR 1950						**PRIMARY GOVERNOR 1952**					
MCMATH	466 .85	387 .81	3434 .82	1613 .78	1409 .85	MURRY	50 .09	37 .09	496 .15	454 .23	128 .10
SPECK	82 .15	89 .19	756 .18	454 .22	249 .15	TACKETT	74 .13	33 .08	246 .07	120 .06	97 .07
	0 .00	0 .00	0 .00	0 .00	0 .00	MCMATH	81 .14	111 .28	701 .21	250 .13	471 .36
	0 .00	0 .00	0 .00	0 .00	0 .00	HOLT	86 .15	90 .23	385 .11	222 .11	153 .12
	0 .00	0 .00	0 .00	0 .00	0 .00	CHERRY	270 .48	125 .32	1542 .46	936 .47	450 .35
PRIMARY RUN-OFF 1952						**GENERAL PRESIDENT 1952**					
MCMATH	119 .19	137 .25	1014 .25	291 .15	640 .45	STEVENSON	360 .50	348 .54	2579 .42	909 .32	717 .55
CHERRY	511 .81	403 .75	3058 .75	1699 .85	798 .55	EISENHOWE	365 .50	296 .46	3525 .58	1952 .68	585 .45
PRIMARY GOVERNOR 1954						**PRIMARY RUN-OFF 1954**					
JONES	77 .13	53 .12	243 .05	67 .03	136 .10	CHERRY	448 .70	308 .62	3362 .71	2307 .90	951 .68
MCMILLAN	12 .02	8 .02	29 .01	5 .00	34 .02	FAUBUS	193 .30	185 .38	1391 .29	251 .10	453 .32
CHERRY	397 .66	268 .61	3570 .79	2218 .90	920 .67		0 .00	0 .00	0 .00	0 .00	0 .00
FAUBUS	114 .19	111 .25	654 .15	166 .07	293 .21		0 .00	0 .00	0 .00	0 .00	0 .00
PRIMARY GOVERNOR 1956						**GENERAL PRESIDENT 1956**					
FAUBUS	198 .43	206 .52	2265 .56	2286 .59	668 .60	STEVENSON	305 .48	309 .55	3102 .42	1471 .31	1062 .50
JOHNSON	182 .40	124 .31	860 .21	518 .13	284 .26	EISENHOWR	311 .48	233 .41	4003 .54	3214 .67	983 .46
SNODDY	79 .17	66 .17	936 .23	1069 .28	159 .14	OTHER	26 .04	22 .04	325 .04	103 .02	83 .04
PRIMARY GOVERNOR 1958						**PRIMARY GOVERNOR 1960**					
FAUBUS	605 .78	414 .80	2702 .55	1721 .38	471 .27	FAUBUS	605 .78	348 .76	2363 .44	2036 .37	711 .29
FINKBEINR	110 .14	81 .16	1431 .29	2233 .49	270 .15	MILLSAP	7 .01	4 .01	53 .01	53 .01	7 .00
WARD	59 .08	24 .05	813 .16	592 .13	1002 .57	BENNETT	57 .07	34 .07	500 .09	384 .07	107 .04
	0 .00	0 .00	0 .00	0 .00	0 .00	WILLIAMS	31 .04	6 .01	355 .07	323 .06	171 .07
	0 .00	0 .00	0 .00	0 .00	0 .00	HARDIN	71 .09	63 .14	2084 .39	2643 .49	1474 .60
GENERAL PRESIDENT 1960						**PRIMARY GOVERNOR 1962**					
NIXON	244 .33	151 .33	1605 .40	3349 .55	627 .38	WHITTEN	35 .06	29 .04	584 .11	1028 .18	84 .05
STATESRTS	218 .29	82 .18	470 .12	343 .06	213 .13	ALFORD	121 .21	67 .10	1190 .22	1087 .19	157 .10
KENNEDY	283 .38	231 .50	1972 .49	2413 .40	800 .49	FAUBUS	355 .61	212 .33	2216 .41	1739 .30	380 .25
	0 .00	0 .00	0 .00	0 .00	0 .00	COFFELT	5 .01	0 .00	27 .01	24 .00	10 .01
	0 .00	0 .00	0 .00	0 .00	0 .00	MCMATH	64 .11	340 .52	1341 .25	1863 .32	899 .59
						COX	3 .01	2 .00	22 .00	25 .00	5 .00
PRIMARY GOVERNOR 1964						**GENERAL PRESIDENT 1964**					
HUBBARD	21 .05	28 .11	477 .14	620 .18	291 .30	JOHNSON	365 .49	2013 .45	3559 .43	3886 .40	1455 .70
DORSEY	72 .18	49 .19	890 .26	973 .29	198 .20	GOLDWATER	381 .51	2491 .55	4648 .57	5737 .60	628 .30
FAUBUS	314 .76	174 .69	2034 .59	1761 .52	333 .34		0 .00	0 .00	0 .00	0 .00	0 .00
BURROW	4 .01	3 .01	55 .02	59 .02	161 .16		0 .00	0 .00	0 .00	0 .00	0 .00

CANDIDATE	LOWER #	%	LOWER-MIDDLE #	%	UPPER-MIDDLE #	%	UPPER #	%	BLACK #	%

GENERAL GOVERNOR 1964

CANDIDATE	LOWER #	%	LOWER-MIDDLE #	%	UPPER-MIDDLE #	%	UPPER #	%	BLACK #	%
FAUBUS	1177	.68	2568	.62	4152	.46	3661	.36	773	.35
ROCKFELLR	559	.32	1596	.38	4870	.54	6631	.64	1438	.65
	0	.00	0	.00	0	.00	0	.00	0	.00
	0	.00	0	.00	0	.00	0	.00	0	.00
	0	.00	0	.00	0	.00	0	.00	0	.00
	0	.00	0	.00	0	.00	0	.00	0	.00

PRIMARY GOVERNOR 1966

CANDIDATE	LOWER #	%	LOWER-MIDDLE #	%	UPPER-MIDDLE #	%	UPPER #	%	BLACK #	%
BOYCE	396	.18	497	.18	1051	.18	420	.13	221	.14
JOHNSON	409	.18	556	.21	655	.11	189	.06	155	.10
ALFORD	449	.20	529	.20	804	.14	309	.09	132	.08
HAYS	243	.11	231	.09	759	.13	549	.17	660	.42
HOLT	499	.23	601	.22	1386	.24	779	.24	296	.19
REBSAMEN	217	.10	295	.11	1144	.20	1020	.31	103	.07

PRIMARY RUN-OFF 1966

CANDIDATE	LOWER #	%	LOWER-MIDDLE #	%	UPPER-MIDDLE #	%	UPPER #	%	BLACK #	%
JOHNSON	1217	.54	1510	.57	2253	.41	790	.24	313	.22
HOLT	1026	.46	1144	.43	3181	.59	2453	.76	1096	.78

GENERAL GOVERNOR 1966

CANDIDATE	LOWER #	%	LOWER-MIDDLE #	%	UPPER-MIDDLE #	%	UPPER #	%	BLACK #	%
ROCKEFLLR	1392	.46	2204	.54	5134	.68	3807	.79	1856	.81
JOHNSON	1633	.54	1907	.46	2459	.32	1021	.21	435	.19

PRIMARY GOVERNOR 1968

CANDIDATE	LOWER #	%	LOWER-MIDDLE #	%	UPPER-MIDDLE #	%	UPPER #	%	BLACK #	%
WHITBECK	177	.09	204	.09	793	.16	790	.26	107	.12
BENNETT	314	.17	262	.12	447	.09	166	.06	105	.11
CRANK	289	.15	426	.19	856	.17	534	.18	132	.14
BOSWELL	637	.34	848	.38	2100	.43	1322	.44	468	.51
JOHNSON	466	.25	502	.22	718	.15	183	.06	102	.11

GENERAL GOVERNOR 1968

CANDIDATE	LOWER #	%	LOWER-MIDDLE #	%	UPPER-MIDDLE #	%	UPPER #	%	BLACK #	%
CRANK	1710	.54	1762	.57	2302	.36	969	.29	166	.14
ROCKEFLLR	1450	.46	1340	.43	4096	.64	2372	.71	1029	.86
	0	.00	0	.00	0	.00	0	.00	0	.00
	0	.00	0	.00	0	.00	0	.00	0	.00

GENERAL PRESIDENT 1968

CANDIDATE	LOWER #	%	LOWER-MIDDLE #	%	UPPER-MIDDLE #	%	UPPER #	%	BLACK #	%
HUMPHREY	823	.28	684	.20	1715	.28	862	.32	1223	.77
NIXON	779	.27	1062	.31	2709	.44	1377	.52	175	.11
WALLACE	1310	.45	1659	.49	1702	.28	417	.16	192	.12

PRIMARY RUN-OFF 1970

CANDIDATE	LOWER #	%	LOWER-MIDDLE #	%	UPPER-MIDDLE #	%	UPPER #	%	BLACK #	%
FAUBUS	1015	.49	1221	.43	1154	.28	586	.28	683	.40
BUMPERS	1045	.51	1537	.57	2903	.72	1517	.72	1042	.60
	0	.00	0	.00	0	.00	0	.00	0	.00

GENERAL GOVERNOR 1970

CANDIDATE	LOWER #	%	LOWER-MIDDLE #	%	UPPER-MIDDLE #	%	UPPER #	%	BLACK #	%
BUMPERS	2051	.74	2742	.80	3301	.62	2239	.50	941	.54
ROCKFELLR	727	.26	688	.20	2065	.38	2215	.50	807	.46
	0	.00	0	.00	0	.00	0	.00	0	.00
	0	.00	0	.00	0	.00	0	.00	0	.00

PRIMARY SENATOR 1972

CANDIDATE	LOWER #	%	LOWER-MIDDLE #	%	UPPER-MIDDLE #	%	UPPER #	%	BLACK #	%
JOHNSON	28	.01	37	.01	29	.01	30	.01	39	.03
PRYOR	952	.40	1367	.40	1081	.33	1422	.34	651	.42
MCCLELLAN	970	.41	1405	.41	1627	.50	1842	.44	436	.28
BOSWELL	419	.18	594	.17	548	.17	913	.22	433	.28

Miami (Dade County)

General President	1948	Truman-Dewey-Thurmond
Primary Senate	1950	Pepper-Smathers
Primary Governor	1952	Adams-McCarty-Odham-Other
Runoff Governor	1952	McCarty-Odham
General President	1952	Stevenson-Eisenhower
Primary Governor	1954	Collins-Johns-Odham
Runoff Governor	1954	Collins-Johns
Primary Governor	1956	Bryant-Collins-Lowry-Warren-Other
General President	1956	Stevenson-Eisenhower
Primary Senate	1958	Holland-Pepper
General Senate	1958	Holland-Leland Hyzer (R)
Primary Governor	1960	Bryant-Burns-Carlton-David-Dickinson-McCarty
Runoff Governor	1960	Bryant-Carlton
General Governor	1960	Bryant-George C. Peterson (R)
General President	1960	Kennedy-Nixon
General Senate	1962	Smathers-Emerson H. Rupert (R)
Primary Governor	1964	Burns-Dickinson-High-Kelly-Other
Runoff Governor	1964	Burns-High
General Governor	1964	Burns-Charles R. Holley (R)
General President	1964	Johnson-Goldwater
General Senate	1964	Holland-Claude R. Kirk (R)
Primary Governor	1966	Burns-High-Kelly-Foor
Runoff Governor	1966	Burns-High
General Governor	1966	High-Claude R. Kirk (R)
Primary Senate	1968	Collins-Faircloth-Other
Runoff Senate	1968	Collins-Faircloth
General President	1968	Nixon-Humphrey-Wallace
General Senate	1968	Collins-Edward J. Gurney (R)
Runoff Governor	1970	Askew-Faircloth
Runoff Senate	1970	Bryant-Chiles
General Governor	1970	Claude R. Kirk (R)-Askew
General Senate	1970	William C. Cramer (R)-Chiles
Eighteen-Year-Old- Vote Amendment	1970	For-Against

Income Tax on
  Corporations Amendment   1971   For-Against
General President   1972   McGovern-Nixon

Jacksonville (Duval County)

Primary Senate	1950	Pepper-Smathers
Primary Governor	1952	Adams-McCarty-Odham-Other
Runoff Governor	1952	McCarty-Odham
General President	1952	Stevenson-Eisenhower
Primary Governor	1954	Collins-Johns-Odham
Runoff Governor	1954	Collins-Johns
Primary Governor	1956	Bryant-Collins-Lowry-Warren-Other
General President	1956	Stevenson-Eisenhower
Primary Senate	1958	Holland-Pepper
Primary Governor	1960	Bryant-Burns-Carlton-David-Dickinson-McCarty
Runoff Governor	1960	Bryant-Carlton
General President	1960	Kennedy-Nixon
General Governor	1960	Bryant-George C. Petersen (R)
General Senate	1962	Smathers-Emerson H. Rupert (R)
Primary Governor	1964	Burns-Dickinson-High-Karl-Kelly-Mathews
Runoff Governor	1964	Burns-High
General President	1964	Johnson-Goldwater
General Senate	1964	Holland-Claude R. Kirk (R)
General Governor	1964	Burns-Charles R. Holley (R)
Primary Governor	1966	Burns-High-Kelly-Other
Runoff Governor	1966	Burns-High
General Governor	1966	High-Claude R. Kirk (R)
Primary Senate	1968	Collins-Faircloth-Other
Runoff Senate	1968	Collins-Faircloth
General President	1968	Nixon-Humphrey-Wallace
General Senate	1968	Edward J. Gurney (R)-Collins
Primary Senate	1970	Bryant-Chiles-Daves-Hastings-Schultz
Runoff Senate	1970	Bryant-Chiles
Runoff Governor	1970	Askew-Faircloth
General Senate	1970	William C. Cramer (R)-Chiles
General Governor	1970	Claude R. Kirk (R)-Askew
Income Tax on		
Corporations Amendment	1971	For-Against

| Primary President | 1972 | Humphrey-Jackson-Muskie-Wallace-Other |
| General President | 1972 | McGovern-Nixon |

GENERAL PRESIDENT 1948 | PRIMARY SENATOR 1950

CANDIDATE	LOWER #	%	LOWER-MIDDLE #	%	UPPER-MIDDLE #	%	UPPER #	%	BLACK #	%	*	CANDIDATE	LOWER #	%	LOWER-MIDDLE #	%	UPPER-MIDDLE #	%	UPPER #	%	BLACK #	%
TRUMAN	7550	.61	6523	.59	4891	.49	1964	.34	1649	.65	*	PEPPER	7171	.52	7586	.52	5691	.42	2098	.28	2519	.70
DEWEY	4166	.33	3901	.35	4497	.45	3241	.56	741	.29	*	SMATHERS	6611	.48	7016	.48	7870	.58	5450	.72	1071	.30
THURMOND	763	.06	704	.06	683	.07	543	.09	151	.06	*		0	.00	0	.00	0	.00	0	.00	0	.00

PRIMARY GOVERNOR 1952 | PRIMARY RUN-OFF 1952

CANDIDATE	LOWER #	%	LOWER-MIDDLE #	%	UPPER-MIDDLE #	%	UPPER #	%	BLACK #	%	*	CANDIDATE	LOWER #	%	LOWER-MIDDLE #	%	UPPER-MIDDLE #	%	UPPER #	%	BLACK #	%
ADAMS	1434	.15	1193	.15	1031	.14	1016	.13	282	.16	*	MCCARTY	5598	.51	4770	.50	3616	.49	4060	.58	946	.54
MCCARTY	4480	.48	4078	.50	3879	.52	3867	.50	830	.48	*	ODHAM	5375	.49	4742	.50	3792	.51	2911	.42	819	.46
ODHAM	3096	.33	2775	.34	2368	.32	2719	.35	564	.33	*		0	.00	0	.00	0	.00	0	.00	0	.00
OTHER	246	.03	148	.02	181	.02	140	.02	56	.03	*		0	.00	0	.00	0	.00	0	.00	0	.00

GENERAL PRESIDENT 1952 | PRIMARY GOVERNOR 1954

CANDIDATE	LOWER #	%	LOWER-MIDDLE #	%	UPPER-MIDDLE #	%	UPPER #	%	BLACK #	%	*	CANDIDATE	LOWER #	%	LOWER-MIDDLE #	%	UPPER-MIDDLE #	%	UPPER #	%	BLACK #	%
STEVENSON	7366	.46	5993	.47	4334	.37	2867	.27	1446	.52	*	COLLINS	3627	.39	3516	.41	3131	.43	3947	.55	498	.38
EISENHOWER	8508	.54	6884	.53	7399	.63	7869	.73	1342	.48	*	JOHNS	2493	.27	1957	.23	1306	.18	1041	.14	393	.30
	0	.00	0	.00	0	.00	0	.00	0	.00	*	ODHAM	3222	.34	3030	.36	2862	.39	2212	.31	432	.33

PRIMARY RUN-OFF 1954 | PRIMARY GOVERNOR 1956

CANDIDATE	LOWER #	%	LOWER-MIDDLE #	%	UPPER-MIDDLE #	%	UPPER #	%	BLACK #	%	*	CANDIDATE	LOWER #	%	LOWER-MIDDLE #	%	UPPER-MIDDLE #	%	UPPER #	%	BLACK #	%
COLLINS	6574	.64	6717	.70	6166	.75	6392	.81	905	.60	*	BRYANT	593	.06	516	.05	412	.05	214	.06	50	.04
JOHNS	3745	.36	2935	.30	2018	.25	1477	.19	594	.40	*	COLLINS	6488	.65	6829	.71	6242	.78	3138	.81	956	.69
	0	.00	0	.00	0	.00	0	.00	0	.00	*	LOWRY	1694	.17	1152	.12	758	.09	313	.08	173	.13
	0	.00	0	.00	0	.00	0	.00	0	.00	*	WARREN	947	.09	901	.09	507	.06	172	.04	74	.05
	0	.00	0	.00	0	.00	0	.00	0	.00	*	OTHER	253	.03	197	.02	89	.01	46	.01	123	.09

GENERAL PRESIDENT 1956 | PRIMARY SENATOR 1958

CANDIDATE	LOWER #	%	LOWER-MIDDLE #	%	UPPER-MIDDLE #	%	UPPER #	%	BLACK #	%	*	CANDIDATE	LOWER #	%	LOWER-MIDDLE #	%	UPPER-MIDDLE #	%	UPPER #	%	BLACK #	%
STEVENSON	6912	.49	6535	.49	4907	.39	2624	.30	914	.49	*	HOLLAND	3279	.41	3419	.41	3485	.49	2869	.63	260	.20
EISENHOWR	7304	.51	6679	.51	7565	.61	6081	.70	942	.51	*	PEPPER	4677	.59	4876	.59	3693	.51	1694	.37	1051	.80

GENERAL SENATOR 1958 | PRIMARY GOVERNOR 1960

CANDIDATE	LOWER #	%	LOWER-MIDDLE #	%	UPPER-MIDDLE #	%	UPPER #	%	BLACK #	%	*	CANDIDATE	LOWER #	%	LOWER-MIDDLE #	%	UPPER-MIDDLE #	%	UPPER #	%	BLACK #	%
HOLLAND	3583	.72	3297	.71	2881	.63	2629	.56	327	.67	*	BRYANT	1065	.15	742	.11	686	.12	921	.13	106	.07
HYZER	1379	.28	1375	.29	1702	.37	2026	.44	160	.33	*	BURNS	1286	.18	1124	.17	873	.15	730	.10	62	.04
	0	.00	0	.00	0	.00	0	.00	0	.00	*	CARLTON	1786	.24	1686	.25	1446	.26	2187	.30	355	.23
	0	.00	0	.00	0	.00	0	.00	0	.00	*	DAVID	737	.10	831	.13	671	.12	1080	.15	856	.55
	0	.00	0	.00	0	.00	0	.00	0	.00	*	DICKINSON	583	.08	480	.07	458	.08	615	.08	31	.02
											*	MCCARTY	1884	.26	1774	.27	1504	.27	1738	.24	136	.09

PRIMARY RUN-OFF 1960 | GENERAL GOVERNOR 1960

CANDIDATE	LOWER #	%	LOWER-MIDDLE #	%	UPPER-MIDDLE #	%	UPPER #	%	BLACK #	%	*	CANDIDATE	LOWER #	%	LOWER-MIDDLE #	%	UPPER-MIDDLE #	%	UPPER #	%	BLACK #	%
BRYANT	3443	.40	2669	.35	2278	.35	2408	.31	192	.09	*	BRYANT	8459	.59	7204	.58	5183	.50	5383	.41	1401	.62
CARLTON	5168	.60	5014	.65	4285	.65	5359	.69	1931	.91	*	PETERSON	5766	.41	5311	.42	5143	.50	7622	.59	854	.38

GENERAL PRESIDENT 1960 | GENERAL SENATOR 1962

CANDIDATE	LOWER #	%	LOWER-MIDDLE #	%	UPPER-MIDDLE #	%	UPPER #	%	BLACK #	%	*	CANDIDATE	LOWER #	%	LOWER-MIDDLE #	%	UPPER-MIDDLE #	%	UPPER #	%	BLACK #	%
KENNEDY	8994	.59	7722	.56	5304	.49	5447	.40	2903	.78	*	SMATHERS	6478	.74	6065	.74	5260	.73	7198	.68	1223	.85
NIXON	6146	.41	6005	.44	5416	.51	8286	.60	799	.22	*	RUPERT	2309	.26	2078	.26	1993	.27	3461	.32	217	.15

PRIMARY GOVERNOR 1964 | RUN-OFF 1964

CANDIDATE	LOWER #	%	LOWER-MIDDLE #	%	UPPER-MIDDLE #	%	UPPER #	%	BLACK #	%	*	CANDIDATE	LOWER #	%	LOWER-MIDDLE #	%	UPPER-MIDDLE #	%	UPPER #	%	BLACK #	%
BURNS	2504	.31	1653	.26	1412	.25	1343	.18	92	.03	*	BURNS	3452	.37	2324	.31	2186	.34	2646	.33	122	.03
DICKINSON	1222	.15	905	.14	854	.15	1179	.16	139	.05	*	HIGH	5880	.63	5161	.69	4334	.66	5481	.67	3968	.97
HIGH	2964	.36	2716	.42	2084	.36	2441	.33	2421	.82	*		0	.00	0	.00	0	.00	0	.00	0	.00
KELLY	590	.07	405	.06	407	.07	369	.05	72	.02	*		0	.00	0	.00	0	.00	0	.00	0	.00
OTHER	882	.11	728	.11	972	.17	2017	.27	212	.07	*		0	.00	0	.00	0	.00	0	.00	0	.00

MIAMI   FLORIDA

Left side

CANDIDATE	LOWER #	%	LOWER-MIDDLE #	%	UPPER-MIDDLE #	%	UPPER #	%	BLACK #	%
GENERAL GOVERNOR 1964										
BURNS	6927	.61	5061	.58	4087	.51	4071	.41	1319	.78
HOLLEY	4427	.39	3716	.42	3851	.49	5906	.59	366	.22
GENERAL SENATOR 1964										
HOLLAND	7344	.64	5946	.64	5172	.60	6426	.57	1553	.83
KIRK	4141	.36	3333	.36	3383	.40	4904	.43	310	.17
	0	.00	0	.00	0	.00	0	.00	0	.00
	0	.00	0	.00	0	.00	0	.00	0	.00
PRIMARY RUN-OFF 1966										
BURNS	2323	.38	2138	.34	1831	.35	1813	.38	542	.24
HIGH	3820	.62	4082	.66	3363	.65	2932	.62	1743	.76
PRIMARY SENATOR 1968										
COLLINS	2134	.59	2454	.65	2274	.64	2450	.67	975	.76
FAIRCLOTH	1335	.37	1229	.32	1180	.33	1152	.31	263	.21
OTHER	131	.04	100	.03	101	.03	78	.02	43	.03
GENERAL PRESIDENT 1968										
NIXON	3624	.39	3803	.41	4158	.49	5497	.63	141	.05
HUMPHREY	3459	.38	3829	.41	2839	.33	2546	.29	2831	.91
WALLACE	2109	.23	1653	.18	1486	.18	666	.08	138	.04
PRIMARY RUN-OFF 1970										
ASKEW	1685	.47	1963	.51	2197	.57	2248	.65	394	.27
FAIRCLOTH	1867	.53	1881	.49	1641	.43	1186	.35	1056	.73
GENERAL GOVERNOR 1970										
KIRK	2538	.35	2396	.32	2679	.38	3225	.44	119	.06
ASKEW	4626	.65	5033	.68	4318	.62	4109	.56	1971	.94
SPECIAL REFERENDM 1970										
FOR	2118	.41	2481	.43	2427	.42	2912	.45	333	.67
AGAINST	3061	.59	3227	.57	3351	.58	3596	.55	163	.33
GENERAL PRESIDENT 1972										
MCGOVERN	2815	.32	2991	.32	2838	.29	2972	.27	1843	.87
NIXON	6042	.68	6495	.68	6875	.71	8070	.73	266	.13

Right side

CANDIDATE	LOWER #	%	LOWER-MIDDLE #	%	UPPER-MIDDLE #	%	UPPER #	%	BLACK #	%
GENERAL PRESIDENT 1964										
JOHNSON	8286	.61	6427	.60	4947	.52	5518	.44	5219	.96
GOLDWATER	5244	.39	4329	.40	4482	.48	6987	.56	239	.04
PRIMARY GOVERNOR 1966										
BURNS	1950	.38	1793	.33	1512	.32	1577	.37	581	.29
HIGH	2256	.43	2837	.52	2236	.48	1976	.46	1148	.58
KELLY	899	.17	797	.14	869	.19	688	.16	202	.10
FOOR	94	.02	76	.01	52	.01	49	.01	65	.03
GENERAL GOVERNOR 1966										
HIGH	4022	.56	4190	.59	3281	.55	2888	.46	2065	.85
KIRK	3213	.44	2953	.41	2714	.45	3441	.54	373	.15
PRIMARY RUN-OFF 1968										
COLLINS	2401	.58	2694	.62	2466	.62	2782	.68	1559	.87
FAIRCLOTH	1733	.42	1658	.38	1540	.38	1292	.32	236	.13
	0	.00	0	.00	0	.00	0	.00	0	.00
GENERAL SENATOR 1968										
COLLINS	4724	.55	5049	.58	4286	.52	4156	.49	2732	.95
GURNEY	3920	.45	3692	.42	3879	.48	4393	.51	136	.05
	0	.00	0	.00	0	.00	0	.00	0	.00
PRIMARY RUN-OFF 1970										
BRYANT	952	.31	991	.29	933	.26	772	.24	363	.38
CHILES	2150	.69	2452	.71	2590	.74	2508	.76	595	.62
GENERAL SENATOR 1970										
CRAMER	2661	.39	2657	.37	2973	.44	3886	.53	150	.08
CHILES	4162	.61	4581	.63	3784	.56	3381	.47	1720	.92
SPECIAL REFERENDM 1971										
FOR	3380	.83	4085	.84	3980	.82	3610	.69	719	.81
AGAINST	805	.17	727	.16	889	.18	1599	.31	166	.19
	0	.00	0	.00	0	.00	0	.00	0	.00
	0	.00	0	.00	0	.00	0	.00	0	.00

JACKSONVILLE   FLORIDA
****

PRIMARY SENATOR 1950 / PRIMARY GOVERNOR 1952

PEPPER	1770 .35	1394 .29	1715 .26	1003 .17	3339 .86	* ADAMS	508 .10	483 .10	590 .10	396 .08	218 .15
SMATHERS	3273 .65	3466 .71	4900 .74	4775 .83	556 .14	* MCCARTY	2255 .43	2032 .41	2887 .47	2749 .56	932 .64
	0 .00	0 .00	0 .00	0 .00	0 .00	* ODHAM	2371 .45	2237 .45	2629 .43	1759 .36	233 .16
	0 .00	0 .00	0 .00	0 .00	0 .00	* OTHER	104 .02	171 .03	59 .01	32 .01	69 .05

PRIMARY RUN-OFF 1952 / GENERAL PRESIDENT 1952

MCCARTY	2363 .43	2054 .41	3073 .47	3081 .59	3051 .83	* STEVENSON	3735 .53	2976 .49	3164 .38	1589 .25	4837 .91
ODHAM	3173 .57	2943 .59	3420 .53	2162 .41	623 .17	* EISENHOWE	3354 .47	3143 .51	5115 .62	4751 .75	493 .09

PRIMARY GOVERNOR 1954 / PRIMARY RUN-OFF 1954

COLLINS	606 .21	773 .21	1499 .35	2056 .46	614 .19	* COLLINS	1233 .44	1620 .46	2466 .57	2839 .63	916 .27
JOHNS	1231 .42	1345 .36	1342 .31	1260 .28	2150 .66	* JOHNS	1570 .56	1899 .54	1841 .43	1674 .37	2419 .73
ODHAM	1076 .37	1594 .43	1467 .34	1148 .26	479 .15	*	0 .00	0 .00	0 .00	0 .00	0 .00

PRIMARY GOVERNOR 1956 / GENERAL PRESIDENT 1956

BRYANT	780 .24	1151 .27	1239 .26	1103 .23	73 .02	* STEVENSON	2410 .62	2655 .56	2477 .43	1900 .33	2599 .53
COLLINS	528 .16	751 .18	1534 .33	2037 .42	3795 .93	* EISENHOWE	1463 .38	2070 .44	3275 .57	3813 .67	2346 .47
LOWRY	1104 .34	1106 .26	909 .19	787 .16	36 .01	*	0 .00	0 .00	0 .00	0 .00	0 .00
WARREN	792 .25	1186 .28	987 .21	886 .18	48 .01	*	0 .00	0 .00	0 .00	0 .00	0 .00
OTHER	11 .00	17 .00	14 .00	11 .00	132 .03	*	0 .00	0 .00	0 .00	0 .00	0 .00

PRIMARY SENATOR 1958 / PRIMARY GOVERNOR 1960

HOLLAND	1546 .59	2424 .66	2744 .71	3477 .79	283 .08	* BRYANT	615 .22	717 .18	841 .24	1149 .25	404 .11
PEPPER	1067 .41	1246 .34	1139 .29	927 .21	3272 .92	* BURNS	1403 .50	2341 .57	1596 .46	2009 .43	708 .20
	0 .00	0 .00	0 .00	0 .00	0 .00	* CARLTON	185 .07	242 .06	270 .08	456 .10	1834 .52
	0 .00	0 .00	0 .00	0 .00	0 .00	* DAVID	48 .02	56 .01	84 .02	91 .02	356 .10
	0 .00	0 .00	0 .00	0 .00	0 .00	* DICKERSON	361 .13	488 .12	424 .12	515 .11	91 .03
	0 .00	0 .00	0 .00	0 .00	0 .00	* MCCARTY	180 .06	250 .06	292 .08	414 .09	154 .04

PRIMARY RUN-OFF 1960 / GENERAL PRESIDENT 1960

BRYANT	2421 .87	3460 .88	2695 .80	3385 .75	245 .06	* KENNEDY	2186 .62	2505 .53	2065 .45	2042 .36	4434 .78
CARLTON	370 .13	479 .12	677 .20	1102 .25	3786 .94	* NIXON	1367 .38	2215 .47	2520 .55	3607 .64	1281 .22

GENERAL GOVERNOR 1960 / GENERAL SENATOR 1962

BRYANT	2857 .86	3862 .86	3060 .74	3777 .70	2268 .65	* SMATHERS	1484 .84	1754 .87	1441 .77	2428 .77	943 .80
PETERSEN	448 .14	654 .14	1080 .26	1623 .30	1248 .35	* RUPERT	292 .16	253 .13	421 .23	735 .23	229 .20

PRIMARY GOVERNOR 1964 / PRIMARY RUN-OFF 1964

BURNS	2716 .70	3143 .72	2347 .58	2840 .58	236 .05	* BURNS	3275 .89	3762 .92	2986 .88	3864 .86	277 .06
DICKENSON	226 .06	219 .05	583 .14	213 .04	155 .03	* HIGH	419 .11	333 .08	401 .12	652 .14	4563 .94
HIGH	115 .03	51 .01	87 .02	88 .02	3054 .65	*	0 .00	0 .00	0 .00	0 .00	0 .00
KARL	51 .01	39 .01	62 .02	78 .02	77 .02	*	0 .00	0 .00	0 .00	0 .00	0 .00
KELLY	371 .10	600 .14	343 .08	344 .07	77 .02	*	0 .00	0 .00	0 .00	0 .00	0 .00
MATHEWS	389 .10	291 .07	632 .16	1311 .27	1124 .24	*	0 .00	0 .00	0 .00	0 .00	0 .00

JACKSONVILLE FLORIDA
****

CANDIDATE	LOWER # %	LOWER-MIDDLE # %	UPPER-MIDDLE # %	UPPER # %	BLACK # %	*	CANDIDATE	LOWER # %	LOWER-MIDDLE # %	UPPER-MIDDLE # %	UPPER # %	BLACK # %

GENERAL PRESIDENT 1964 | GENERAL SENATOR 1964

CANDIDATE	LOWER	LOWER-MIDDLE	UPPER-MIDDLE	UPPER	BLACK	CANDIDATE	LOWER	LOWER-MIDDLE	UPPER-MIDDLE	UPPER	BLACK
JOHNSON	1976 .43	1653 .35	1582 .36	1699 .30	6864 .98	HOLLAND	2787 .71	2936 .71	2707 .68	3365 .64	3143 .92
GOLDWATER	2639 .57	3095 .65	2849 .64	3953 .70	157 .02	KIRK	1128 .29	1216 .29	1259 .32	1914 .36	290 .08

GENERAL GOVERNOR 1964 | PRIMARY GOVERNOR 1966

CANDIDATE	LOWER	LOWER-MIDDLE	UPPER-MIDDLE	UPPER	BLACK	CANDIDATE	LOWER	LOWER-MIDDLE	UPPER-MIDDLE	UPPER	BLACK
BURNS	3240 .72	3351 .72	2840 .67	3385 .61	3380 .80	BURNS	1702 .51	2447 .56	1759 .52	2195 .56	763 .23
HOLLEY	1258 .28	1312 .28	1413 .33	2175 .39	834 .20	HIGH	647 .20	392 .09	443 .13	582 .15	2289 .70
	0 .00	0 .00	0 .00	0 .00	0 .00	KELLY	930 .28	1508 .35	1131 .34	1102 .28	130 .04
	0 .00	0 .00	0 .00	0 .00	0 .00	OTHER	31 .01	19 .00	18 .01	23 .01	76 .02

PRIMARY RUN-OFF 1966 | GENERAL GOVERNOR 1966

CANDIDATE	LOWER	LOWER-MIDDLE	UPPER-MIDDLE	UPPER	BLACK	CANDIDATE	LOWER	LOWER-MIDDLE	UPPER-MIDDLE	UPPER	BLACK
BURNS	2562 .72	3500 .74	2425 .70	2820 .68	522 .15	HIGH	1115 .32	1258 .28	1061 .30	1169 .27	3082 .94
HIGH	1009 .28	1256 .26	1047 .30	1315 .32	2846 .85	KIRK	2338 .68	3208 .72	2437 .70	3132 .73	206 .06

PRIMARY SENATOR 1968 | PRIMARY RUN-OFF 1968

CANDIDATE	LOWER	LOWER-MIDDLE	UPPER-MIDDLE	UPPER	BLACK	CANDIDATE	LOWER	LOWER-MIDDLE	UPPER-MIDDLE	UPPER	BLACK
COLLINS	470 .26	574 .21	612 .29	800 .37	1116 .73	COLLINS	526 .23	367 .14	367 .18	628 .30	1560 .88
FAIRCLOTH	1227 .69	2015 .74	1422 .67	1310 .60	322 .21	FAIRCLOTH	1756 .77	2207 .86	1622 .82	1438 .70	221 .12
OTHER	86 .05	128 .05	94 .04	78 .04	92 .06		0 .00	0 .00	0 .00	0 .00	0 .00

GENERAL PRESIDENT 1968 | GENERAL SENATOR 1968

CANDIDATE	LOWER	LOWER-MIDDLE	UPPER-MIDDLE	UPPER	BLACK	CANDIDATE	LOWER	LOWER-MIDDLE	UPPER-MIDDLE	UPPER	BLACK
NIXON	935 .23	1057 .24	1465 .34	2792 .49	90 .02	GURNEY	2263 .63	3438 .69	2661 .67	3153 .68	85 .03
HUMPHREY	914 .23	692 .16	818 .19	1215 .21	3441 .95	COLLINS	1304 .37	1512 .31	1313 .33	1478 .32	3038 .97
WALLACE	2165 .54	2661 .60	2004 .47	1711 .30	102 .03		0 .00	0 .00	0 .00	0 .00	0 .00

PRIMARY SENATOR 1970 | RUN-OFF 1970

CANDIDATE	LOWER	LOWER-MIDDLE	UPPER-MIDDLE	UPPER	BLACK	CANDIDATE	LOWER	LOWER-MIDDLE	UPPER-MIDDLE	UPPER	BLACK
BRYANT	502 .29	662 .27	629 .30	864 .32	224 .16	BRYANT	646 .37	866 .32	870 .40	1209 .45	934 .66
CHILES	273 .16	416 .17	342 .17	417 .15	36 .03	CHILES	1099 .63	1829 .68	1283 .60	1492 .55	480 .34
DAVES	42 .02	71 .03	53 .03	64 .02	49 .03		0 .00	0 .00	0 .00	0 .00	0 .00
HASTINGS	158 .09	141 .06	127 .06	136 .05	982 .69		0 .00	0 .00	0 .00	0 .00	0 .00
SCHULTZ	776 .44	1139 .47	914 .44	1250 .46	137 .10		0 .00	0 .00	0 .00	0 .00	0 .00

PRIMARY RUN-OFF 1970 | GENERAL SENATOR 1970

CANDIDATE	LOWER	LOWER-MIDDLE	UPPER-MIDDLE	UPPER	BLACK	CANDIDATE	LOWER	LOWER-MIDDLE	UPPER-MIDDLE	UPPER	BLACK
ASKEW	839 .51	1358 .51	1062 .50	1251 .47	544 .34	CRAMER	880 .34	1553 .42	1368 .44	2008 .55	75 .04
FAIRCLOTH	810 .49	1300 .49	1057 .50	1404 .53	1033 .66	CHILES	1689 .66	2189 .58	1741 .56	1621 .45	1645 .96

GENERAL GOVERNOR 1970 | SPECIAL REFERENDM 1971

CANDIDATE	LOWER	LOWER-MIDDLE	UPPER-MIDDLE	UPPER	BLACK	CANDIDATE	LOWER	LOWER-MIDDLE	UPPER-MIDDLE	UPPER	BLACK
KIRK	1406 .49	2290 .54	1856 .55	2406 .60	121 .06	FOR	1135 .64	1774 .61	1295 .56	1391 .46	427 .69
ASKEW	1460 .51	1956 .46	1522 .45	1588 .40	1912 .94	AGAINST	625 .36	1141 .39	1003 .44	1654 .54	190 .31

PRIMARY PRESIDENT 1972 | GENERAL PRESIDENT 1972

CANDIDATE	LOWER	LOWER-MIDDLE	UPPER-MIDDLE	UPPER	BLACK	CANDIDATE	LOWER	LOWER-MIDDLE	UPPER-MIDDLE	UPPER	BLACK
HUMPHREY	425 .14	310 .08	283 .10	274 .08	1536 .62	MCGOVERN	666 .16	790 .17	476 .17	544 .14	2260 .84
JACKSON	380 .12	468 .12	464 .16	821 .24	20 .01	NIXON	3378 .84	3768 .83	2250 .83	3330 .86	440 .16
MUSKIE	117 .04	134 .04	275 .09	163 .05	68 .03		0 .00	0 .00	0 .00	0 .00	0 .00
WALLACE	1864 .60	2680 .70	1611 .55	1882 .54	7 .00		0 .00	0 .00	0 .00	0 .00	0 .00
OTHER	285 .09	206 .05	237 .08	298 .09	835 .34		0 .00	0 .00	0 .00	0 .00	0 .00

GEORGIA PRECINCT ELECTIONS

Atlanta (Fulton County)

County-Unit Amendment	1952	For-Against
General President	1952	Eisenhower-Stevenson
Private Schools Amendment	1954	For-Against
General President	1956	Eisenhower-Stevenson
General President	1960	Kennedy-Nixon
Primary Governor	1962	Griffin-Sanders
General President	1964	Johnson-Goldwater
Primary Governor	1966	Arnall-Byrd-Carter-Gray-Maddox
Runoff Governor	1966	Arnall-Maddox
General Governor	1966	Howard H. Callaway (R)-Maddox-Arnall (write-in)
General President	1968	Nixon-Humphrey-Wallace
Primary Senate	1968	Jackson-Talmadge
General Senate	1968	E. Earl Patton (R)-Talmadge
Primary Governor	1970	Carter-King-Sanders-Stoner-Other
Runoff Governor	1970	Carter-Sanders
General Governor	1970	Hal Suit (R)-Carter
General President	1972	McGovern-Nixon
General Senate	1972	Nunn-Fletcher Thompson (R)

Macon (Bibb County)

General President	1948	Thurmond-Truman-Dewey
Primary Governor	1950	Talmadge-Thompson-Other
County-Unit Amendment	1952	For-Against
General President	1952	Eisenhower-Stevenson
Private Schools Amendment	1954	For-Against
Primary Governor	1954	Griffin-Linder-Gowan-Thompson-Other
General President	1956	Eisenhower-Stevenson
Primary Governor	1958	William T. Bodenhamer-Vandiver-Other
General President	1960	Nixon-Kennedy
Primary Governor	1962	Griffin-Sanders-Other
General President	1964	Goldwater-Johnson

Primary Governor	1966	Arnall-Byrd-Carter-Gray-Maddox
Runoff Governor	1966	Maddox-Arnall
General Governor	1966	Maddox-Howard H. Callaway (R)
Primary Senate	1968	Talmadge-Jackson
General Senate	1968	Talmadge-E. Earl Patton (R)
General President	1968	Nixon-Humphrey-Wallace
Primary Governor	1970	Carter-King-Sanders-Stoner-Other
Runoff Governor	1970	Carter-Sanders
General Governor	1970	Hal Suit (R)-Carter
Primary Senate	1972	Gambrell-Nunn-Vandiver-Williams-Other
Runoff Senate	1972	Gambrell-Nunn
General Senate	1972	Nunn-Fletcher Thompson (R)
General President	1972	McGovern-Nixon

ATLANTA GEORGIA
****

CANDIDATE	LOWER # %	LOWER-MIDDLE # %	UPPER-MIDDLE # %	UPPER # %	BLACK # %	*	CANDIDATE	LOWER # %	LOWER-MIDDLE # %	UPPER-MIDDLE # %	UPPER # %	BLACK # %

SPECIAL REFERENDM 1952 | **GENERAL PRESIDENT 1952**

CANDIDATE	LOWER	LOWER-MIDDLE	UPPER-MIDDLE	UPPER	BLACK	*	CANDIDATE	LOWER	LOWER-MIDDLE	UPPER-MIDDLE	UPPER	BLACK
FOR	448 .38	475 .25	1314 .19	1387 .18	52 .03	*	EISENHOWR	327 .24	789 .34	2578 .35	6045 .64	704 .26
AGAINST	733 .62	1420 .75	5702 .81	6360 .82	2016 .97	*	STEVENSON	1037 .76	1510 .66	4832 .65	3358 .36	2038 .74

SPECIAL REFERENDM 1954 | **GENERAL PRESIDENT 1956**

CANDIDATE	LOWER	LOWER-MIDDLE	UPPER-MIDDLE	UPPER	BLACK	*	CANDIDATE	LOWER	LOWER-MIDDLE	UPPER-MIDDLE	UPPER	BLACK
FOR	1811 .61	1260 .50	1599 .39	2972 .34	312 .07	*	EISENHOWR	1716 .24	2572 .25	3990 .27	9724 .54	8037 .85
AGAINST	1138 .39	1265 .50	2521 .61	5808 .66	4060 .93	*	STEVENSON	5384 .76	7614 .75	10645 .73	8277 .46	1380 .15

GENERAL PRESIDENT 1960 | **PRIMARY GOVERNOR 1962**

CANDIDATE	LOWER	LOWER-MIDDLE	UPPER-MIDDLE	UPPER	BLACK	*	CANDIDATE	LOWER	LOWER-MIDDLE	UPPER-MIDDLE	UPPER	BLACK
KENNEDY	4578 .64	6181 .58	11319 .61	7273 .40	6277 .42	*	GRIFFIN	3117 .42	3821 .35	5168 .30	3412 .16	79 .00
NIXON	2520 .36	4538 .42	7302 .39	10761 .60	8808 .58	*	SANDERS	4294 .58	7186 .65	11901 .70	17307 .84	17628 ***

GENERAL PRESIDENT 1964 | **PRIMARY GOVERNOR 1966**

CANDIDATE	LOWER	LOWER-MIDDLE	UPPER-MIDDLE	UPPER	BLACK	*	CANDIDATE	LOWER	LOWER-MIDDLE	UPPER-MIDDLE	UPPER	BLACK
JOHNSON	4159 .42	3540 .39	8952 .37	11551 .45	24147 .99	*	ARNALL	1521 .21	2397 .23	3049 .30	4704 .41	9839 .92
GOLDWATER	5705 .58	5569 .61	15306 .63	14146 .55	185 .01	*	BYRD	228 .03	392 .04	398 .04	256 .02	322 .03
	0 .00	0 .00	0 .00	0 .00	0 .00	*	CARTER	1611 .22	2792 .27	2981 .29	3728 .33	457 .04
	0 .00	0 .00	0 .00	0 .00	0 .00	*	GRAY	853 .12	1363 .13	1199 .12	1305 .11	71 .01
	0 .00	0 .00	0 .00	0 .00	0 .00	*	MADDOX	3026 .42	3365 .33	2687 .26	1423 .12	23 .00

PRIMARY RUN-OFF 1966 | **GENERAL GOVERNOR 1966**

CANDIDATE	LOWER	LOWER-MIDDLE	UPPER-MIDDLE	UPPER	BLACK	*	CANDIDATE	LOWER	LOWER-MIDDLE	UPPER-MIDDLE	UPPER	BLACK
ARNALL	2732 .31	4695 .38	5177 .43	9308 .72	17091 ***	*	CALLAWAY	3345 .32	6703 .46	7773 .57	13654 .82	7019 .52
MADDOX	6076 .69	7572 .62	6734 .57	3669 .28	48 .00	*	MADDOX	6657 .64	7175 .49	5210 .39	1700 .10	360 .03
	0 .00	0 .00	0 .00	0 .00	0 .00	*	ARNALL	464 .04	687 .05	540 .04	1372 .08	6177 .46

GENERAL PRESIDENT 1968 | **PRIMARY SENATOR 1968**

CANDIDATE	LOWER	LOWER-MIDDLE	UPPER-MIDDLE	UPPER	BLACK	*	CANDIDATE	LOWER	LOWER-MIDDLE	UPPER-MIDDLE	UPPER	BLACK
NIXON	3046 .33	4639 .38	5983 .46	9033 .58	256 .02	*	JACKSON	703 .14	1111 .15	1275 .17	2810 .33	8912 .99
HUMPHREY	1709 .19	2792 .23	2883 .22	4925 .32	12457 .98	*	TALMADGE	4239 .86	6198 .85	6438 .83	5748 .67	133 .01
WALLACE	4371 .48	4851 .39	4220 .32	1564 .10	34 .00	*		0 .00	0 .00	0 .00	0 .00	0 .00

GENERAL SENATOR 1968 | **PRIMARY GOVERNOR 1970**

CANDIDATE	LOWER	LOWER-MIDDLE	UPPER-MIDDLE	UPPER	BLACK	*	CANDIDATE	LOWER	LOWER-MIDDLE	UPPER-MIDDLE	UPPER	BLACK
PATTON	1928 .22	2723 .24	3888 .30	7098 .46	3812 .35	*	CARTER	3263 .61	3590 .56	4147 .50	3541 .32	372 .02
TALMADGE	6890 .78	8842 .76	9215 .70	8363 .54	7031 .65	*	KING	135 .03	120 .02	434 .05	326 .03	5860 .35
	0 .00	0 .00	0 .00	0 .00	0 .00	*	SANDERS	1619 .30	2396 .37	3343 .40	6992 .63	10300 .62
	0 .00	0 .00	0 .00	0 .00	0 .00	*	STONER	204 .04	190 .03	216 .03	101 .01	29 .00
	0 .00	0 .00	0 .00	0 .00	0 .00	*	OTHER	156 .03	169 .03	157 .02	157 .01	53 .00

PRIMARY RUN-OFF 1970 | **GENERAL GOVERNOR 1970**

CANDIDATE	LOWER	LOWER-MIDDLE	UPPER-MIDDLE	UPPER	BLACK	*	CANDIDATE	LOWER	LOWER-MIDDLE	UPPER-MIDDLE	UPPER	BLACK
CARTER	3793 .71	5025 .68	4713 .62	3246 .38	713 .06	*	SUIT	3636 .47	5732 .52	6961 .59	10580 .73	4625 .42
SANDERS	1514 .29	2405 .32	2879 .38	5212 .62	10310 .94	*	CARTER	4050 .53	5257 .48	4876 .41	3963 .27	6396 .58

GENERAL PRESIDENT 1972 | **GENERAL SENATOR 1972**

CANDIDATE	LOWER	LOWER-MIDDLE	UPPER-MIDDLE	UPPER	BLACK	*	CANDIDATE	LOWER	LOWER-MIDDLE	UPPER-MIDDLE	UPPER	BLACK
MCGOVERN	623 .17	994 .19	1250 .23	1201 .19	5748 .92	*	NUNN	1302 .33	2093 .37	2190 .39	2285 .35	5439 .90
NIXON	3104 .83	4333 .81	4252 .77	4977 .81	509 .08	*	THOMPSON	2674 .67	3529 .63	3495 .61	4257 .65	587 .10

MACON GEORGIA

****

GENERAL PRESIDENT 1948

THURMOND	588	.34	1486	.35	201	.31	1086	.32	8	.00
TRUMAN	829	.48	2209	.52	223	.35	1330	.40	1828	.65
DEWEY	310	.18	591	.14	216	.34	934	.28	958	.34

PRIMARY GOVERNOR 1950

TALMADGE	820	.56	2312	.47	379	.42	1569	.35	31	.01
THOMPSON	594	.41	2490	.51	494	.55	2875	.63	2314	.98
OTHER	51	.03	116	.02	21	.02	90	.02	9	.00

SPECIAL REFERENDM 1952

FOR	979	.56	3010	.47	530	.37	2150	.35	113	.04
AGAINST	769	.44	3432	.53	901	.63	4072	.65	2878	.96

GENERAL PRESIDENT 1952

EISENHWR	320	.19	1415	.22	614	.47	2425	.39	296	.14
STEVENSO	1404	.81	4938	.78	706	.53	3834	.61	1754	.86

SPECIAL REFERENDM 1954

FOR	579	.64	1893	.57	414	.48	1688	.47	192	.12
AGAINST	323	.36	1422	.43	445	.52	1938	.53	1378	.88
	0	.00	0	.00	0	.00	0	.00	0	.00
	0	.00	0	.00	0	.00	0	.00	0	.00
	0	.00	0	.00	0	.00	0	.00	0	.00

PRIMARY GOVERNOR 1954

GRIFFIN	792	.54	2448	.50	425	.38	1870	.38	50	.02
LINDER	124	.08	338	.07	79	.07	162	.03	24	.01
GOWAN	167	.11	724	.15	281	.25	1210	.25	254	.09
THOMPSON	328	.22	1209	.24	269	.24	1323	.27	2220	.79
OTHER	55	.04	225	.05	73	.06	318	.07	265	.09

GENERAL PRESIDENT 1956

EISENHWR	911	.20	450	.18	939	.31	1741	.43	2148	.64
STEVENSON	3697	.80	2090	.82	2062	.69	2336	.57	1224	.36
	0	.00	0	.00	0	.00	0	.00	0	.00

PRIMARY GOVERNOR 1958

BODENHMR	820	.21	630	.26	306	.27	422	.08	86	.03
VANDIVER	3059	.77	1638	.69	758	.68	4900	.90	2701	.93
OTHER	111	.03	110	.05	51	.05	106	.02	124	.04

GENERAL PRESIDENT 1960

NIXON	1328	.36	970	.35	762	.40	3818	.53	1355	.37
KENNEDY	2359	.64	1806	.65	1159	.60	3352	.47	2351	.63
	0	.00	0	.00	0	.00	0	.00	0	.00

PRIMARY GOVERNOR 1962

GRIFFIN	1772	.52	1983	.54	1711	.54	2761	.31	51	.01
SANDERS	1524	.45	1581	.43	1356	.43	5863	.67	5146	.97
OTHER	99	.03	105	.03	96	.03	161	.02	114	.02

GENERAL PRESIDENT 1964

GOLDWATR	3809	.71	4998	.69	3866	.71	4682	.70	311	.11
JOHNSON	1527	.29	2235	.31	1569	.29	2050	.30	2478	.89
	0	.00	0	.00	0	.00	0	.00	0	.00
	0	.00	0	.00	0	.00	0	.00	0	.00
	0	.00	0	.00	0	.00	0	.00	0	.00

PRIMARY GOVERNOR 1966

ARNALL	484	.16	791	.19	613	.20	1180	.27	1583	.84
BYRD	346	.12	478	.12	295	.10	370	.08	46	.02
CARTER	590	.20	760	.18	707	.23	1333	.31	124	.07
GRAY	813	.27	1108	.27	815	.27	935	.21	79	.04
MADDOX	757	.25	1001	.24	638	.21	535	.12	54	.03

PRIMARY RUN-OFF 1966

MADDOX	2186	.71	2989	.68	1859	.59	1798	.43	154	.07
ARNALL	873	.29	1388	.32	1282	.41	2361	.57	1972	.93

GENERAL GOVERNOR 1966

MADDOX	2205	.50	3118	.52	1764	.38	1262	.22	237	.13
CALLAWAY	2192	.50	2912	.48	2918	.62	4600	.78	1647	.87

PRIMARY SENATOR 1968

TALMADGE	2724	.91	3516	.86	2957	.90	3765	.90	227	.14
JACKSON	265	.09	567	.14	316	.10	419	.10	1405	.86

GENERAL SENATOR 1968

TALMADGE	3701	.80	5250	.81	3839	.76	4676	.73	1890	.93
PATTON	917	.20	1237	.19	1212	.24	1699	.27	152	.07

GENERAL PRESIDENT 1968

NIXON	1394	.29	1849	.27	1979	.36	3614	.56	134	.06
HUMPHREY	558	.11	1038	.15	723	.13	1002	.16	2004	.87
WALLACE	2917	.60	3952	.58	2862	.51	1831	.28	175	.08
	0	.00	0	.00	0	.00	0	.00	0	.00
	0	.00	0	.00	0	.00	0	.00	0	.00

PRIMARY GOVERNOR 1970

CARTER	1552	.61	2141	.56	1597	.56	1555	.43	134	.07
KING	86	.03	243	.06	86	.03	68	.02	681	.37
SANDERS	612	.24	1032	.27	946	.33	1800	.50	948	.52
STONER	160	.06	209	.05	123	.04	80	.02	9	.00
OTHER	141	.06	191	.05	121	.04	108	.03	49	.03

MACON   GEORGIA
****

PRIMARY RUN-OFF 1970

CANDIDATE	LOWER #	%	LOWER-MIDDLE #	%	UPPER-MIDDLE #	%	UPPER #	%	BLACK #	%
CARTER	2176	.76	2968	.72	2198	.68	2070	.55	193	.10
SANDERS	692	.24	1183	.28	1024	.32	1691	.45	1745	.90

GENERAL GOVERNOR 1970

CANDIDATE	LOWER #	%	LOWER-MIDDLE #	%	UPPER-MIDDLE #	%	UPPER #	%	BLACK #	%
SUIT	1771	.41	2232	.38	2550	.50	4192	.65	281	.15
CARTER	2574	.59	3658	.62	2594	.50	2250	.35	1639	.85

PRIMARY SENATOR 1972

CANDIDATE	LOWER #	%	LOWER-MIDDLE #	%	UPPER-MIDDLE #	%	UPPER #	%	BLACK #	%
GAMBRELL	449	.28	605	.27	798	.33	773	.30	251	.31
NUNN	724	.45	1057	.47	1102	.45	1230	.48	109	.13
VANDIVER	155	.10	258	.11	300	.12	321	.13	49	.06
WILLIAMS	24	.01	47	.02	42	.02	27	.01	235	.29
OTHER	259	.16	287	.13	210	.09	206	.08	177	.22

PRIMARY RUN-OFF 1972

CANDIDATE	LOWER #	%	LOWER-MIDDLE #	%	UPPER-MIDDLE #	%	UPPER #	%	BLACK #	%
GAMBRELL	479	.23	710	.26	1042	.37	1031	.35	593	.61
NUNN	1608	.77	2015	.74	1785	.63	1881	.65	378	.39
	0	.00	0	.00	0	.00	0	.00	0	.00
	0	.00	0	.00	0	.00	0	.00	0	.00
	0	.00	0	.00	0	.00	0	.00	0	.00

GENERAL SENATOR 1972

CANDIDATE	LOWER #	%	LOWER-MIDDLE #	%	UPPER-MIDDLE #	%	UPPER #	%	BLACK #	%
NUNN	2534	.65	3316	.61	3232	.62	2684	.55	1557	.87
THOMPSON	1367	.35	2100	.39	2023	.38	2173	.45	232	.13

GENERAL PRESIDENT 1972

CANDIDATE	LOWER #	%	LOWER-MIDDLE #	%	UPPER-MIDDLE #	%	UPPER #	%	BLACK #	%
MCGOVERN	500	.13	606	.12	878	.17	644	.13	1747	.84
NIXON	3328	.87	4567	.88	4150	.83	4304	.87	342	.16

LOUISIANA PRECINCT ELECTIONS

New Orleans (Orleans Parish)

Primary Governor	1952	Boggs-Dodd-Kennon-McLemore-Parker-Spaht
Runoff Governor	1952	Kennon-Spaht
General President	1952	Stevenson-Eisenhower
Primary Governor	1956	Grevemberg-Long-McLemore-Morrison-Preaus
General President	1956	Stevenson-Eisenhower-States'Rights (pledged to T. Coleman Andrews)
Primary Governor	1959	Davis-Dodd-Morrison-Noe-Rainach
Runoff Governor	1960	Davis-Morrison
General President	1960	Kennedy-Nixon-Independent (unpledged)
Primary Governor	1963	Jackson-Kennon-Long-McKeithen-Morrison
Runoff Governor	1964	McKeithen-Morrison
General President	1964	Johnson-Goldwater
General Governor	1964	McKeithen-C. H. Lyons (R)
General President	1968	Wallace-Humphrey-Nixon
Primary Governor	1971	Davis-Edwards-Johnston-Long-Schwegmann-Other
Runoff Governor	1971	Edwards-Johnston
General Governor	1972	Edwards-David C. Treen (R)
General President	1972	McGovern-Nixon-Schmitz
General Senate	1972	Johnston-Ben C. Toledano (R)-McKeithen (I)-Lyons (American)

Baton Rouge (East Baton Rouge Parish)

Primary Governor	1952	Boggs-Dodd-Kennon-McLemore-Parker-Spaht
Runoff Governor	1952	Kennon-Spaht
Runoff Lt. Governor	1952	Barham-McKeithen
General President	1952	Stevenson-Eisenhower
Primary Governor	1956	Grevemberg-Long-McLemore-Morrison-Preaus
Primary Lt. Governor	1956	Alexander-Barham-Clanton-Frazar-Moore
General President	1956	Stevenson-Eisenhower-States' Rights (pledged to T. Coleman Andrews)
Primary Governor	1959	Davis-Dodd-Morrison-Noe-Rainach
Runoff Governor	1960	Davis-Morrison
General President	1960	Kennedy-Nixon-Independent (unpledged)

Primary Governor	1963	Jackson-Kennon-Long-McKeithen-Morrison-Other
Runoff Governor	1964	McKeithen-Morrison
General Governor	1964	McKeithen-C. H. Lyons (R)
General President	1964	Johnson-Goldwater
General President	1968	Wallace-Humphrey-Nixon
Primary Governor	1971	Davis-Edwards-Johnston-Long-Schwegmann-Other
Runoff Governor	1971	Edwards-Johnston
General Governor	1972	Edwards-David C. Treen (R)
General President	1972	McGovern-Nixon-Schmitz
General Senate	1972	Johnston-Ben C. Toledano (R)-McKeithen (I)-Lyons (American)

Shreveport (Caddo Parish)

Primary Governor	1952	Boggs-Dodd-Kennon-McLemore-Spaht-Parker
Runoff Governor	1952	Kennon-Spaht
Runoff Lt. Governor	1952	Barham-McKeithen
General President	1952	Stevenson-Eisenhower
Primary Senate	1954	Ellender-Ellis-Other
Primary Governor	1956	Grevemberg-Long-McLemore-Morrison-Preaus
Primary Lt. Governor	1956	Alexander-Barham-Clanton-Frazar-Moore
General President	1956	Stevenson-Eisenhower-Independent (pledged to T. Coleman Andrews)
Primary Governor	1959	Davis-Dodd-Morrison-Noe-Rainach
Runoff Governor	1960	Davis-Morrison
General President	1960	Kennedy-Nixon-Independent (unpledged)
Primary Governor	1963	Jackson-Kennon-Long-McKeithen-Morrison
General Governor	1964	McKeithen-C. H. Lyons (R)
General President	1964	Johnson-Goldwater
General President	1968	Wallace-Humphrey-Nixon
Primary Governor	1971	Davis-Edwards-Johnston-Long-Schwegmann-Other
Runoff Governor	1971	Edwards-Johnston
General Governor	1972	Edwards-David C. Treen (R)
General President	1972	McGovern-Nixon-Schmitz
General Senate	1972	Johnston-Ben C. Toledano (R)-McKeithen (I)-Lyons (American)

CANDIDATE	LOWER #	%	LOWER-MIDDLE #	%	UPPER-MIDDLE #	%	UPPER #	%	BLACK #	%

PRIMARY GOVERNOR 1952

CANDIDATE	LOWER #	%	LOWER-MIDDLE #	%	UPPER-MIDDLE #	%	UPPER #	%	BLACK #	%
BOGGS	1466	.22	1839	.35	1976	.34	1720	.32	1535	.53
DODD	483	.07	267	.05	267	.05	284	.05	361	.12
KENNON	1365	.21	1314	.25	1464	.25	1424	.27	170	.06
MCLEMORE	433	.07	866	.16	957	.16	911	.17	66	.02
PARKER	6	.00	19	.00	11	.00	24	.00	172	.06
SPAHT	2767	.42	1021	.19	1208	.21	985	.18	612	.21

PRIMARY RUN-OFF 1952

CANDIDATE	LOWER #	%	LOWER-MIDDLE #	%	UPPER-MIDDLE #	%	UPPER #	%	BLACK #	%
KENNON	3543	.53	4218	.74	4539	.75	4354	.79	1107	.39
SPAHT	3176	.47	1452	.26	1507	.25	1187	.21	1709	.61
	0	.00	0	.00	0	.00	0	.00	0	.00
	0	.00	0	.00	0	.00	0	.00	0	.00
	0	.00	0	.00	0	.00	0	.00	0	.00
	0	.00	0	.00	0	.00	0	.00	0	.00

GENERAL PRESIDENT 1952

CANDIDATE	LOWER #	%	LOWER-MIDDLE #	%	UPPER-MIDDLE #	%	UPPER #	%	BLACK #	%
STEVENSON	2480	.51	2120	.40	967	.32	414	.27	2886	.87
EISENHOWR	2354	.49	3240	.60	2094	.68	1143	.73	432	.13
	0	.00	0	.00	0	.00	0	.00	0	.00
	0	.00	0	.00	0	.00	0	.00	0	.00

PRIMARY GOVERNOR 1956

CANDIDATE	LOWER #	%	LOWER-MIDDLE #	%	UPPER-MIDDLE #	%	UPPER #	%	BLACK #	%
GREVEMBRG	320	.05	426	.06	481	.08	518	.08	60	.02
LONG	3251	.48	2077	.31	1678	.27	1600	.25	1641	.46
MCLEMORE	604	.09	684	.10	528	.08	500	.08	51	.01
MORRISON	2241	.33	2923	.43	3025	.48	3054	.47	1771	.50
PREAUS	374	.06	618	.09	596	.09	768	.12	18	.01

GENERAL PRESIDENT 1956

CANDIDATE	LOWER #	%	LOWER-MIDDLE #	%	UPPER-MIDDLE #	%	UPPER #	%	BLACK #	%
STEVENSON	2833	.45	1896	.31	843	.29	1839	.27	1442	.44
EISENHOWR	3290	.52	3915	.65	1930	.66	4699	.69	1762	.54
STATESRTS	228	.04	256	.04	131	.05	235	.03	58	.02
	0	.00	0	.00	0	.00	0	.00	0	.00
	0	.00	0	.00	0	.00	0	.00	0	.00

PRIMARY GOVERNOR 1959

CANDIDATE	LOWER #	%	LOWER-MIDDLE #	%	UPPER-MIDDLE #	%	UPPER #	%	BLACK #	%
DAVIS	2369	.39	1846	.28	1592	.27	1502	.26	134	.04
DODD	354	.06	362	.06	284	.05	181	.03	126	.03
MORRISON	2201	.36	3154	.48	3045	.51	3355	.57	2933	.81
NOE	397	.07	249	.04	240	.04	131	.02	391	.11
RAINACH	766	.13	898	.14	755	.13	679	.12	43	.01

PRIMARY GOVERNOR 1960

CANDIDATE	LOWER #	%	LOWER-MIDDLE #	%	UPPER-MIDDLE #	%	UPPER #	%	BLACK #	%
DAVIS	3597	.57	3011	.45	2457	.41	2329	.38	211	.06
MORRISON	2691	.43	3727	.55	3602	.59	3805	.62	3608	.94
	0	.00	0	.00	0	.00	0	.00	0	.00

GENERAL PRESIDENT 1960

CANDIDATE	LOWER #	%	LOWER-MIDDLE #	%	UPPER-MIDDLE #	%	UPPER #	%	BLACK #	%
KENNEDY	3109	.50	1982	.42	1543	.47	1066	.39	1018	.75
NIXON	1079	.17	1299	.27	948	.29	1077	.39	322	.24
INDEPENDN	2006	.32	1487	.31	823	.25	623	.23	17	.01

PRIMARY GOVERNOR 1963

CANDIDATE	LOWER #	%	LOWER-MIDDLE #	%	UPPER-MIDDLE #	%	UPPER #	%	BLACK #	%
JACKSON	241	.05	260	.04	180	.03	165	.03	33	.01
KENNON	708	.14	1061	.18	813	.15	969	.18	22	.01
LONG	1397	.27	832	.14	588	.11	426	.08	167	.05
MCKEITHEN	764	.15	835	.14	804	.14	645	.12	115	.03
MORRISON	2111	.40	3015	.50	3166	.57	3140	.59	3247	.91

PRIMARY RUN-OFF 1964

CANDIDATE	LOWER #	%	LOWER-MIDDLE #	%	UPPER-MIDDLE #	%	UPPER #	%	BLACK #	%
MCKEITHE	2433	.45	2466	.39	1849	.31	1547	.28	108	.03
MORRISON	2928	.55	3808	.61	4030	.69	4042	.72	3570	.97
	0	.00	0	.00	0	.00	0	.00	0	.00
	0	.00	0	.00	0	.00	0	.00	0	.00
	0	.00	0	.00	0	.00	0	.00	0	.00

GENERAL PRESIDENT 1964

CANDIDATE	LOWER #	%	LOWER-MIDDLE #	%	UPPER-MIDDLE #	%	UPPER #	%	BLACK #	%
JOHNSON	2330	.43	2000	.33	2219	.38	1858	.33	3587	.97
GOLDWATER	3039	.57	4133	.67	3671	.62	3839	.67	105	.03

GENERAL GOVERNOR 1964

CANDIDATE	LOWER #	%	LOWER-MIDDLE #	%	UPPER-MIDDLE #	%	UPPER #	%	BLACK #	%
MCKEITHEN	2819	.66	2377	.48	2018	.44	1629	.34	1259	.67
LYONS	1426	.34	2559	.52	2598	.56	3136	.66	628	.33

GENERAL PRESIDENT 1968

CANDIDATE	LOWER #	%	LOWER-MIDDLE #	%	UPPER-MIDDLE #	%	UPPER #	%	BLACK #	%
WALLACE	2648	.53	2528	.43	1358	.34	1418	.29	180	.06
HUMPHREY	1062	.21	999	.17	862	.21	850	.17	3057	.93
NIXON	1266	.25	2335	.40	1800	.45	2696	.54	35	.01
	0	.00	0	.00	0	.00	0	.00	0	.00
	0	.00	0	.00	0	.00	0	.00	0	.00
	0	.00	0	.00	0	.00	0	.00	0	.00

PRIMARY GOVERNOR 1971

CANDIDATE	LOWER #	%	LOWER-MIDDLE #	%	UPPER-MIDDLE #	%	UPPER #	%	BLACK #	%
DAVIS	444	.10	426	.08	213	.05	266	.06	20	.01
EDWARDS	1018	.23	1413	.26	1145	.29	1234	.26	376	.14
JOHNSTON	491	.11	1055	.20	986	.25	1407	.29	61	.02
LONG	815	.19	502	.09	506	.13	561	.12	1377	.50
SCHWEGMNN	1008	.23	1196	.22	624	.16	724	.15	69	.03
OTHER	620	.14	816	.15	507	.13	604	.13	836	.31

PRIMARY RUN-OFF 1971

CANDIDATE	LOWER #	%	LOWER-MIDDLE #	%	UPPER-MIDDLE #	%	UPPER #	%	BLACK #	%
EDWARDS	1942	.44	1900	.37	1317	.36	1504	.31	1757	.76
JOHNSTON	2448	.56	3267	.63	2350	.64	3279	.69	556	.24

GENERAL GOVERNOR 1972

CANDIDATE	LOWER #	%	LOWER-MIDDLE #	%	UPPER-MIDDLE #	%	UPPER #	%	BLACK #	%
EDWARDS	2120	.51	2096	.39	1538	.41	1385	.35	3409	.91
TREEN	2036	.49	3241	.61	2171	.59	2581	.65	322	.09

CANDIDATE	LOWER #	%	LOWER-MIDDLE #	%	UPPER-MIDDLE #	%	UPPER #	%	BLACK #	%	* CANDIDATE	LOWER #	%	LOWER-MIDDLE #	%	UPPER-MIDDLE #	%	UPPER #	%	BLACK #	%
			GENERAL PRESIDENT 1972								*			GENERAL SENATOR 1972							
MCGOVERN	714	.19	832	.16	785	.22	843	.17	2880	.68	* JOHNSTON	1765	.41	2621	.44	1777	.45	2767	.52	2992	.77
NIXON	2972	.77	4110	.81	2732	.76	3904	.79	545	.13	* TOLEDANO	1393	.32	1875	.31	1261	.32	1706	.32	88	.02
SCHMITZ	169	.04	135	.03	101	.03	214	.04	829	.19	* MCKEITHEN	1036	.24	1348	.23	836	.21	767	.15	690	.18
	0	.00	0	.00	0	.00	0	.00	0	.00	* LYONS	101	.02	136	.02	63	.02	42	.01	115	.03

```
                              BATON ROUGE      LOUISIANA
                       ****************************

              PRIMARY  GOVERNOR  1952              *        PRIMARY   RUN-OFF   1952
              ****************************                  ****************************
BOGGS      707 .17    506 .15    349 .15    328 .17    321 .18  * KENNON   3461 .73   2887 .75   1802 .73   1492 .75   223 .11
DODD       457 .11    394 .12    155 .07    137 .07    517 .30  * SPAHT    1266 .27    950 .25    679 .27    498 .25  1778 .89
KENNON    2125 .50   1797 .53    842 .37    759 .40    104 .06  *            0 .00      0 .00      0 .00      0 .00     0 .00
MCLEMORE   312 .07    257 .08    525 .23    372 .20     10 .01  *            0 .00      0 .00      0 .00      0 .00     0 .00
PARKER       4 .00      0 .00      2 .00      1 .00     76 .04  *            0 .00      0 .00      0 .00      0 .00     0 .00
SPAHT      667 .16    416 .12    429 .19    305 .16    723 .41  *            0 .00      0 .00      0 .00      0 .00     0 .00

              PRIMARY  RUN-OFF  1952               *        GENERAL   PRESIDENT 1952
              ****************************                  ****************************
BARHAM    3182 .68   2588 .68   1762 .71   1505 .76    275 .14 * STEVENSON 2585 .58   2172 .58    829 .32    647 .30  1440 .77
MCKEITHEN 1497 .32   1202 .32    706 .29    474 .24   1641 .86 * EISENHOWE 1864 .42   1550 .42   1800 .68   1493 .70   425 .23

              PRIMARY  GOVERNOR  1956              *        PRIMARY   LT-GOVNR  1956
              ****************************                  ****************************
GREVEMBRG  755 .15    728 .16    555 .15    402 .19     57 .02 * ALEXANDER  780 .17    704 .16    423 .12    223 .11   139 .04
LONG      1899 .38   1634 .36    891 .24    412 .20   2692 .76 * BARHAM     877 .19    701 .16   1068 .30    619 .31   744 .23
MCLEMORE   523 .11    546 .12    157 .04    115 .06     20 .01 * CLANTON    470 .10    477 .11    306 .09    274 .14    27 .01
MORRISON   739 .15    596 .13   1024 .28    569 .27    734 .21 * FRAZAR    1508 .32   1333 .31    718 .20    316 .16  2242 .70
PREAUS    1039 .21   1012 .22   1026 .28    579 .28     18 .01 * MOORE     1036 .22   1063 .25   1010 .29    567 .28    42 .01

              GENERAL  PRESIDENT 1956             *        PRIMARY   GOVERNOR  1959
              ****************************                  ****************************
STEVENSON 2063 .52   1943 .52    960 .28    573 .28    602 .35 * DAVIS     1766 .36   2022 .36   1567 .30    982 .33    77 .02
EISENHOWR 1772 .45   1673 .45   2351 .69   1408 .70   1057 .62 * DODD      1141 .23   1161 .21    662 .13    297 .10   227 .07
STATESRTS  147 .04    138 .04    115 .03     35 .02     40 .02 * MORRISON  1075 .22   1231 .22   2121 .41   1235 .62  2594 .76
             0 .00      0 .00      0 .00      0 .00      0 .00 * NOE        237 .05    271 .05    182 .04     70 .02   481 .14
             0 .00      0 .00      0 .00      0 .00      0 .00 * RAINACH    702 .14    892 .16    635 .12    363 .12    16 .00

                       RUN-OFF  1960              *        GENERAL   PRESIDENT 1960
              ****************************                  ****************************
DAVIS     3905 .70   4473 .70   2703 .50   1573 .50    109 .03 * KENNEDY   2632 .51   2812 .47   1913 .43    871 .35  1814 .66
MORRISON  1693 .30   1929 .30   2730 .50   1565 .50   3832 .97 * NIXON      994 .19   1447 .24   1807 .40   1253 .50   892 .32
             0 .00      0 .00      0 .00      0 .00      0 .00 * INDEPENDN 1513 .29   1759 .29    754 .17    358 .14    44 .02

              PRIMARY  GOVERNOR  1963             *        PRIMARY   RUN-OFF   1964
              ****************************                  ****************************
JACKSON    755 .16    986 .16    436 .08    317 .09     58 .01 * MCKEITHEN 3239 .62   4114 .61   2023 .37    930 .35    40 .01
KENNON     641 .14    936 .16    908 .17    676 .19     17 .00 * MORRISON  1984 .38   2634 .39   3510 .63   1749 .65  4574 .99
LONG       726 .15    744 .12    474 .09    299 .08    284 .07 *             0 .00      0 .00      0 .00      0 .00     0 .00
MCKEITHEN  968 .21   1052 .18    567 .11    332 .09     81 .02 *             0 .00      0 .00      0 .00      0 .00     0 .00
MORRISON  1152 .24   1567 .26   2067 .40   1333 .38   3378 .87 *             0 .00      0 .00      0 .00      0 .00     0 .00
OTHER      467 .10    708 .12    766 .15    584 .16     60 .02 *             0 .00      0 .00      0 .00      0 .00     0 .00

              GENERAL  GOVERNOR  1964             *        GENERAL   PRESIDENT 1964
              ****************************                  ****************************
MCKEITHEN 2998 .68   3658 .63   1831 .36   1151 .31   1336 .49 * JOHNSON   1764 .37   2169 .34   1732 .31   1069 .27  4765 .99
LYONS     1429 .32   2137 .37   3310 .64   2511 .69   1410 .51 * GOLDWATER 2994 .63   4153 .66   3843 .69   2962 .73    53 .01

              GENERAL  PRESIDENT 1968            *        PRIMARY   GOVERNOR  1971
              ****************************                  ****************************
WALLACE   4133 .71   4155 .64   1697 .35   2008 .32    110 .03 * DAVIS      882 .20   1353 .20    503 .11    495 .09    47 .01
HUMPHREY   629 .11    791 .12    687 .14    726 .11   3655 .96 * EDWARDS    779 .18   1205 .18    551 .12    780 .14  1317 .36
NIXON     1089 .19   1555 .24   2503 .51   3614 .57     34 .01 * JOHNSTON  1503 .35   2464 .37   2457 .56   3332 .58   258 .07
             0 .00      0 .00      0 .00      0 .00      0 .00 * LONG       258 .06    423 .06    278 .06    355 .06  1119 .31
             0 .00      0 .00      0 .00      0 .00      0 .00 * SCHWEGMNN  278 .06    384 .06    245 .06    338 .06    23 .01
             0 .00      0 .00      0 .00      0 .00      0 .00 * OTHER      629 .15    864 .13    385 .09    402 .07   892 .24
```

BATON ROUGE   LOUISIANA
****

CANDIDATE	LOWER # %	LOWER-MIDDLE # %	UPPER-MIDDLE # %	UPPER # %	BLACK # %	*	CANDIDATE	LOWER # %	LOWER-MIDDLE # %	UPPER-MIDDLE # %	UPPER # %	BLACK # %

PRIMARY RUN-OFF 1971   **GENERAL GOVERNOR 1972**

CANDIDATE	LOWER # %	LOWER-MIDDLE # %	UPPER-MIDDLE # %	UPPER # %	BLACK # %	CANDIDATE	LOWER # %	LOWER-MIDDLE # %	UPPER-MIDDLE # %	UPPER # %	BLACK # %
EDWARDS	1707 .39	2405 .36	1122 .23	1275 .21	3210 .81	EDWARDS	2433 .45	3238 .40	1535 .29	1709 .23	3853 .97
JOHNSTON	2636 .61	4191 .64	3719 .77	4656 .79	746 .19	TREEN	2926 .55	4850 .60	3837 .71	5593 .77	116 .03

GENERAL PRESIDENT 1972   **GENERAL SENATOR 1972**

CANDIDATE	LOWER # %	LOWER-MIDDLE # %	UPPER-MIDDLE # %	UPPER # %	BLACK # %	CANDIDATE	LOWER # %	LOWER-MIDDLE # %	UPPER-MIDDLE # %	UPPER # %	BLACK # %
MCGOVERN	724 .20	1138 .18	774 .17	856 .12	2960 .90	JOHNSTON	2224 .52	3830 .56	3244 .64	4722 .63	2519 .70
NIXON	2835 .77	4877 .78	3789 .81	5825 .85	122 .04	TOLEDANO	708 .16	1088 .16	998 .20	1677 .22	52 .01
SCHMITZ	127 .03	267 .04	96 .02	193 .03	215 .07	MCKEITHEN	1237 .29	1766 .26	783 .15	1007 .13	921 .26
	0 .00	0 .00	0 .00	0 .00	0 .00	LYONS	144 .03	176 .03	68 .01	89 .01	103 .03

```
                    PRIMARY  GOVERNOR  1952                    *              PRIMARY  RUN-OFF  1952
                    *****************************                             *****************************
BOGGS       698 .16   556 .17   569 .19   419 .16   318 .35 * KENNON    4061 .74  3606 .81  2990 .88  2991 .91  705 .55
DODD        332 .07   221 .07   116 .04   100 .04    98 .11 * SPAHT     1406 .26   854 .19   396 .12   305 .09  585 .45
KENNON     1400 .31  1061 .32   836 .29   656 .25    93 .10 *             0 .00     0 .00     0 .00     0 .00    0 .00
MCLEMORE   1559 .35  1256 .38  1255 .43  1339 .51    89 .10 *             0 .00     0 .00     0 .00     0 .00    0 .00
SPAHT       432 .10   227 .07   146 .05    93 .04   160 .18 *             0 .00     0 .00     0 .00     0 .00    0 .00
PARKER       24 .01     7 .00    10 .00     9 .00   143 .16 *             0 .00     0 .00     0 .00     0 .00    0 .00

                    PRIMARY  RUN-OFF  1952                     *              GENERAL  PRESIDENT 1952
                    *****************************                             *****************************
BARHAM     3907 .72  3492 .79  2963 .88  2931 .90   323 .30 * STEVENSON 2330 .37  1706 .31   744 .18   554 .14 1034 .75
MCKEITHEN  1489 .28   935 .21   403 .12   342 .10   742 .70 * EISENHOWE 4013 .63  3808 .69  3372 .82  3408 .86  343 .25

                    PRIMARY  SENATOR  1954                     *              PRIMARY  GOVERNOR  1956
                    *****************************                             *****************************
ELLENDER   3013 .59  2555 .61  2008 .71  2498 .70   597 .48 * GREVEMBRG  352 .06   423 .07   172 .04   154 .04   66 .04
ELLIS      1769 .34  1305 .31   561 .20   708 .20   606 .49 * LONG      2523 .45  2045 .34   753 .18   494 .13 1459 .78
OTHER       356 .07   300 .07   268 .09   359 .10    34 .03 * MCLEMORE   234 .04   228 .04   130 .03    97 .03   33 .02
              0 .00     0 .00     0 .00     0 .00     0 .00 * MORRISON   909 .16  1206 .20  1386 .33  1492 .39  192 .10
              0 .00     0 .00     0 .00     0 .00     0 .00 * PREAUS    1603 .29  2064 .35  1700 .41  1591 .42  109 .06

                    PRIMARY  LT-GOVNR  1956                    *              GENERAL  PRESIDENT 1956
                    *****************************                             *****************************
ALEXANDER   253 .05   223 .04    86 .02    83 .02    39 .02 * STEVENSON 1868 .31  1805 .25   700 .15   556 .12 1133 .56
BARHAM     1364 .26  1518 .26  1631 .40  1626 .44   311 .20 * EISENHOWR 3353 .55  4374 .61  3442 .76  3639 .79  771 .38
CLANTON     249 .05   297 .05   113 .03    93 .03    55 .04 * INDEPENDN  871 .14   939 .13   391 .09   402 .09  121 .06
FRAZAR     1863 .35  1822 .31   651 .16   457 .12  1042 .67 *             0 .00     0 .00     0 .00     0 .00    0 .00
MOORE      1581 .30  2061 .35  1574 .39  1439 .39   113 .07 *             0 .00     0 .00     0 .00     0 .00    0 .00

                    PRIMARY  GOVERNOR  1959                    *              PRIMARY  RUN-OFF  1960
                    *****************************                             *****************************
DAVIS      1720 .33  1949 .31  1694 .29  1104 .29   225 .16 * DAVIS     5182 .82  5651 .80  3798 .64  2559 .65  473 .28
DODD        485 .09   511 .09   198 .03    80 .02    48 .03 * MORRISON  1124 .18  1394 .20  2183 .36  1391 .35 1235 .72
MORRISON    569 .11   869 .14  1419 .24   987 .26   293 .20 *             0 .00     0 .00     0 .00     0 .00    0 .00
NOE         266 .05   176 .03    81 .01    41 .01   719 .50 *             0 .00     0 .00     0 .00     0 .00    0 .00
RAINACH    2099 .41  2775 .44  2438 .42  1550 .41   154 .11 *             0 .00     0 .00     0 .00     0 .00    0 .00

                    GENERAL  PRESIDENT 1960                    *              PRIMARY  GOVERNOR  1963
                    *****************************                             *****************************
KENNEDY    1685 .25  1795 .23  1193 .17   675 .14  1140 .64 * JACKSON   1619 .31  1761 .28   876 .17   596 .16  122 .07
NIXON      3030 .45  4164 .52  5037 .71  3680 .75   473 .27 * KENNON    1575 .30  2189 .35  2422 .46  1818 .49  117 .07
INDEPENDNT 2003 .30  1992 .25   874 .12   538 .11   162 .09 * LONG       628 .12   600 .10   297 .06   164 .04  480 .29
              0 .00     0 .00     0 .00     0 .00     0 .00 * MCKEITHEN  965 .18   964 .16   579 .11   335 .09   97 .06
              0 .00     0 .00     0 .00     0 .00     0 .00 * MORRISON   466 .09   667 .11  1035 .20   785 .21  851 .51

                    GENERAL  GOVERNOR  1964                    *              GENERAL  PRESIDENT 1964
                    *****************************                             *****************************
MCKEITHEN  2052 .34  2333 .30  1063 .16   571 .11   650 .49 * JOHNSON   1005 .14  1157 .13   974 .13   657 .12 1636 .74
LYONS      3905 .66  5352 .70  5633 .84  4517 .89   683 .51 * GOLDWATER 6269 .86  7712 .87  6394 .87  4885 .88  569 .26

                    GENERAL  PRESIDENT 1968                    *              PRIMARY  GOVERNOR  1971
                    *****************************                             *****************************
WALLACE    5247 .71  3493 .56  1610 .35  1256 .25   126 .03 * DAVIS      534 .12   410 .09   205 .06   171 .04   52 .02
HUMPHREY    327 .04   412 .07   430 .09   494 .10  4317 .96 * EDWARDS    315 .07   348 .08   312 .09   278 .07  130 .04
NIXON      1841 .25  2279 .37  2520 .55  3315 .65    68 .02 * JOHNSTON  2145 .49  2374 .54  2165 .59  2654 .65  680 .20
              0 .00     0 .00     0 .00     0 .00     0 .00 * LONG       395 .09   239 .05   142 .04   197 .05 1237 .37
              0 .00     0 .00     0 .00     0 .00     0 .00 * SCHWEGMNN  399 .09   557 .13   553 .15   518 .13   20 .01
              0 .00     0 .00     0 .00     0 .00     0 .00 * OTHER      585 .13   450 .10   271 .07   257 .06 1266 .37
```

SHREVEPORT   LOUISIANA

****

CANDIDATE	LOWER # %	LOWER-MIDDLE # %	UPPER-MIDDLE # %	UPPER # %	BLACK # %

PRIMARY RUN-OFF 1971

CANDIDATE	LOWER # %	LOWER-MIDDLE # %	UPPER-MIDDLE # %	UPPER # %	BLACK # %
EDWARDS	1374 .28	1193 .25	697 .18	683 .16	1767 .55
JOHNSTON	3480 .72	3524 .75	3241 .82	3723 .84	1438 .45

GENERAL GOVERNOR 1972

CANDIDATE	LOWER # %	LOWER-MIDDLE # %	UPPER-MIDDLE # %	UPPER # %	BLACK # %
EDWARDS	1711 .30	1341 .24	881 .20	958 .18	3234 .96
TREEN	3959 .70	4179 .76	3625 .80	4384 .82	126 .04

GENERAL PRESIDENT 1972

CANDIDATE	LOWER # %	LOWER-MIDDLE # %	UPPER-MIDDLE # %	UPPER # %	BLACK # %
MCGOVERN-	599 .11	446 .08	393 .08	477 .09	3253 .89
NIXON	4834 .86	4828 .88	4160 .89	4898 .90	140 .04
SCHMITZ	202 .04	200 .04	96 .02	96 .02	268 .07
	0 .00	0 .00	0 .00	0 .00	0 .00

GENERAL SENATOR 1972

CANDIDATE	LOWER # %	LOWER-MIDDLE # %	UPPER-MIDDLE # %	UPPER # %	BLACK # %
JOHNSTON	2769 .50	3029 .53	2928 .59	3589 .63	2468 .77
TOLEDANO	1308 .23	1472 .26	1341 .27	1482 .26	49 .02
MCKEITHEN	1311 .23	1120 .19	584 .12	562 .10	579 .18
LYONS	202 .04	144 .02	91 .02	77 .01	95 .03

Jackson (Hinds County)

Primary Senate	1954	Eastland-Gartin
Primary Governor	1955	Barnett-Coleman-Johnson-Wright-Cain
Runoff Governor	1955	Coleman-Johnson
General President	1956	Stevenson-Eisenhower (Mississippi Republican Party)-Eisenhower (Black and Tan Republicans)-Independent
Primary Governor	1959	Barnett-Gartin-Sullivan
Runoff Governor	1959	Barnett-Gartin
General President	1960	Kennedy-Independent Democrat (unpledged)-Nixon
Right-To-Work Amendment	1960	For-Against
Primary Governor	1963	Coleman-Johnson-Sullivan
Runoff Governor	1963	Coleman-Johnson
General Governor	1963	Johnson-Rubel L. Phillips (R)
General President	1964	Johnson-Goldwater
General Senate	1966	Eastland-Prentiss Walker (R)
Primary Governor	1967	Barnett-Swan-Waller-Williams-Winter
Runoff Governor	1967	Williams-Winter
General Governor	1967	Williams-Rubel L. Phillips (R)
General President	1968	Wallace-Humphrey-Nixon
Primary Governor	1971	Sullivan-Swan-Waller-Other
Runoff Governor	1971	Sullivan-Waller
General Governor	1971	Waller-Evers (I)

CANDIDATE	LOWER # %	LOWER-MIDDLE # %	UPPER-MIDDLE # %	UPPER # %	BLACK # %	* CANDIDATE	LOWER # %	LOWER-MIDDLE # %	UPPER-MIDDLE # %	UPPER # %	BLACK # %

PRIMARY SENATOR 1954 ************************ / **PRIMARY GOVERNOR 1955** ***************************

CANDIDATE	LOWER	LOWER-MIDDLE	UPPER-MIDDLE	UPPER	BLACK	* CANDIDATE	LOWER	LOWER-MIDDLE	UPPER-MIDDLE	UPPER	BLACK
EASTLAND	1011 .65	1269 .65	1402 .66	1275 .71	396 .43	* BARNETT	635 .36	835 .33	770 .27	498 .22	416 .32
GARTIN	543 .35	675 .35	731 .34	511 .29	523 .57	* COLEMAN	170 .10	254 .10	319 .11	169 .07	73 .06
	0 .00	0 .00	0 .00	0 .00	0 .00	* JOHNSON	228 .13	253 .10	244 .09	133 .06	430 .34
	0 .00	0 .00	0 .00	0 .00	0 .00	* WRIGHT	663 .38	1107 .44	1440 .51	1427 .62	309 .24
	0 .00	0 .00	0 .00	0 .00	0 .00	* CAIN	48 .03	63 .03	73 .03	70 .03	53 .04

PRIMARY RUN-OFF 1955 ************************ / **GENERAL PRESIDENT 1956** ***************************

CANDIDATE	LOWER	LOWER-MIDDLE	UPPER-MIDDLE	UPPER	BLACK	* CANDIDATE	LOWER	LOWER-MIDDLE	UPPER-MIDDLE	UPPER	BLACK
COLEMAN	1113 .57	1552 .63	1776 .65	1448 .67	470 .36	* STEVENSON	777 .42	709 .36	750 .29	540 .22	290 .28
JOHNSON	823 .43	908 .37	976 .35	726 .33	821 .64	* EISENHOWR	559 .30	673 .34	1008 .39	1140 .46	235 .23
	0 .00	0 .00	0 .00	0 .00	0 .00	* EISENHOWR	10 .01	9 .00	16 .01	7 .00	327 .32
	0 .00	0 .00	0 .00	0 .00	0 .00	* INDEPENDN	525 .28	589 .30	831 .32	813 .33	174 .17

PRIMARY GOVERNOR 1959 ************************ / **PRIMARY RUN-OFF 1959** ***************************

CANDIDATE	LOWER	LOWER-MIDDLE	UPPER-MIDDLE	UPPER	BLACK	* CANDIDATE	LOWER	LOWER-MIDDLE	UPPER-MIDDLE	UPPER	BLACK
BARNETT	1245 .52	1153 .48	1388 .40	943 .33	419 .37	* BARNETT	1497 .63	1409 .59	1731 .51	1256 .45	505 .44
GARTIN	707 .29	740 .31	1203 .34	1122 .39	541 .48	* GARTIN	881 .37	978 .41	1654 .49	1509 .55	635 .56
SULLIVAN	462 .19	525 .22	896 .26	797 .28	170 .15	*	0 .00	0 .00	0 .00	0 .00	0 .00

GENERAL PRESIDENT 1960 ************************ / **SPECIAL REFERENDM 1960** ***************************

CANDIDATE	LOWER	LOWER-MIDDLE	UPPER-MIDDLE	UPPER	BLACK	* CANDIDATE	LOWER	LOWER-MIDDLE	UPPER-MIDDLE	UPPER	BLACK
KENNEDY	468 .20	402 .17	606 .17	436 .14	402 .36	* FOR	937 .72	1003 .74	1651 .83	1717 .94	268 .47
IDEMOCRAT	1028 .45	1053 .45	1347 .37	836 .27	295 .27	* AGAINST	372 .28	348 .26	334 .17	104 .06	308 .53
NIXON	802 .35	865 .37	1672 .46	1831 .59	412 .37	*	0 .00	0 .00	0 .00	0 .00	0 .00

PRIMARY GOVERNOR 1963 ************************ / **PRIMARY RUN-OFF 1963** ***************************

CANDIDATE	LOWER	LOWER-MIDDLE	UPPER-MIDDLE	UPPER	BLACK	* CANDIDATE	LOWER	LOWER-MIDDLE	UPPER-MIDDLE	UPPER	BLACK
COLEMAN	1245 .31	2003 .37	1531 .46	2237 .50	620 .58	* COLEMAN	1642 .42	2607 .49	1859 .59	2860 .65	752 .62
JOHNSON	1690 .42	1803 .33	843 .25	924 .21	266 .25	* JOHNSON	2273 .58	2749 .51	1318 .41	1568 .35	459 .38
SULLIVAN	1136 .28	1679 .31	946 .28	1323 .30	186 .17	*	0 .00	0 .00	0 .00	0 .00	0 .00

GENERAL GOVERNOR 1963 ************************ / **GENERAL PRESIDENT 1964** ***************************

CANDIDATE	LOWER	LOWER-MIDDLE	UPPER-MIDDLE	UPPER	BLACK	* CANDIDATE	LOWER	LOWER-MIDDLE	UPPER-MIDDLE	UPPER	BLACK
JOHNSON	2391 .67	2695 .54	1384 .43	1515 .34	415 .48	* JOHNSON	265 .06	266 .04	258 .07	460 .09	862 .57
PHILLIPS	1190 .33	2332 .46	1823 .57	2919 .66	455 .52	* GOLDWATER	3963 .94	5845 .96	3693 .93	4710 .91	646 .43

GENERAL SENATOR 1966 ************************ / **PRIMARY GOVERNOR 1967** ***************************

CANDIDATE	LOWER	LOWER-MIDDLE	UPPER-MIDDLE	UPPER	BLACK	* CANDIDATE	LOWER	LOWER-MIDDLE	UPPER-MIDDLE	UPPER	BLACK
EASTLAND	2627 .77	3894 .73	2399 .76	3331 .69	833 .47	* BARNETT	677 .16	876 .12	495 .12	588 .09	319 .10
WALKER	790 .23	1464 .27	770 .24	1504 .31	951 .53	* SWAN	554 .13	771 .10	185 .05	139 .02	144 .04
	0 .00	0 .00	0 .00	0 .00	0 .00	* WALLER	455 .10	916 .12	471 .12	808 .13	407 .12
	0 .00	0 .00	0 .00	0 .00	0 .00	* WILLIAMS	1726 .40	3008 .40	1293 .33	1656 .27	437 .13
	0 .00	0 .00	0 .00	0 .00	0 .00	* WINTER	940 .22	1931 .26	1531 .39	3033 .49	2035 .61

PRIMARY RUN-OFF 1967 ************************ / **GENERAL GOVERNOR 1967** ***************************

CANDIDATE	LOWER	LOWER-MIDDLE	UPPER-MIDDLE	UPPER	BLACK	* CANDIDATE	LOWER	LOWER-MIDDLE	UPPER-MIDDLE	UPPER	BLACK
WILLIAMS	3105 .71	4826 .65	2123 .53	2999 .46	827 .22	* WILLIAMS	2768 .77	4230 .70	1936 .58	2450 .45	811 .29
WINTER	1274 .29	2614 .35	1916 .47	3524 .54	3000 .78	* PHILLIPS	839 .23	1842 .30	1391 .42	2944 .55	2022 .71

GENERAL PRESIDENT 1968 ************************ / **PRIMARY GOVERNOR 1971** ***************************

CANDIDATE	LOWER	LOWER-MIDDLE	UPPER-MIDDLE	UPPER	BLACK	* CANDIDATE	LOWER	LOWER-MIDDLE	UPPER-MIDDLE	UPPER	BLACK
WALLACE	3645 .81	5703 .72	2253 .55	2625 .39	831 .17	* SULLIVAN	1764 .31	1162 .30	2065 .42	1259 .44	600 .25
HUMPHREY	105 .02	191 .02	181 .04	385 .06	3953 .79	* SWAN	670 .12	296 .08	117 .02	57 .02	494 .21
NIXON	770 .17	2053 .26	1660 .41	3796 .56	219 .04	* WALLER	2531 .45	1904 .50	2259 .46	1365 .47	1105 .47
	0 .00	0 .00	0 .00	0 .00	0 .00	* OTHER	648 .12	448 .12	421 .09	204 .07	166 .07

JACKSON   MISSISSIPPI
****

CANDIDATE	LOWER # %	LOWER-MIDDLE # %	UPPER-MIDDLE # %	UPPER # %	BLACK # %	*	CANDIDATE	LOWER # %	LOWER-MIDDLE # %	UPPER-MIDDLE # %	UPPER # %	BLACK # %
		PRIMARY	RUN-OFF	1971		*			GENERAL	GOVERNOR	1971	
		**************************				*			**************************			
SULLIVAN	1938 .36	1292 .34	2186 .45	1645 .47	1242 .46	*	WALLER	5899 .98	2572 .98	3143 .96	3490 .96	92 .02
WALLER	3434 .64	2516 .66	2675 .55	1891 .53	1481 .54	*	EVERS	97 .02	57 .02	147 .04	153 .04	4836 .98

NORTH CAROLINA PRECINCT ELECTIONS

Raleigh (Wake County)

Primary Governor	1952	Olive-Umstead
General President	1952	Stevenson-Eisenhower
Primary Senate	1954	Scott-Lennon
General President	1956	Stevenson-Eisenhower
Primary Governor	1960	Sanford-Larkins-Seawell-Lake
Runoff Governor	1960	Sanford-Lake
General President	1960	Kennedy-Nixon
General Governor	1960	Sanford-Robert L. Gavin (R)
General President	1964	Johnson-Goldwater
Primary Governor	1964	Lake-Preyer-Moore
General Governor	1964	Moore-Robert L. Gavin (R)
Primary Governor	1968	Scott-Broughton-Hawkins
General President	1968	Humphrey-Nixon-Wallace
General Governor	1968	Scott-James C. Gardner (R)

Greensboro (Guilford County)

Primary Senate	1950	Smith-Graham-Reynolds
General President	1952	Stevenson-Eisenhower
General Governor	1952	Umstead-H. F. Seawell (R)
Primary Senate	1954	Scott-Lennon
General Senate	1954	Scott-Paul C. West (R)
Primary Governor	1956	Hodges-Sawyer
Primary Senator	1956	Ervin-Kurfees
General President	1956	Stevenson-Eisenhower
General Governor	1956	Hodges-Kyle Hayes (R)
General Senate	1958	Jordan-Richard C. Clarke (R)
Primary Senate	1960	Jordan-Hewlett
Primary Governor	1960	Sanford-Larkins-Seawell-Lake
Runoff Governor	1960	Sanford-Lake
General President	1960	Kennedy-Nixon
General Governor	1960	Sanford-Robert L. Gavin (R)
General Senate	1960	Jordan-Kyle Hayes (R)
General Senate	1962	Ervin-Claude L. Greene (R)

Primary Governor	1964	Lake-Preyer-Moore
Runoff Governor	1964	Preyer-Moore
General President	1964	Johnson-Goldwater
General Governor	1964	Moore-Robert L. Gavin (R)
General Senate	1966	Jordan-John S. Shallcross (R)
Primary Governor	1968	Scott-Broughton-Hawkins
General President	1968	Humphrey-Nixon-Wallace
General Governor	1968	Scott-James C. Gardner (R)
General Senator	1968	Ervin-Robert V. Somers (R)
Primary Governor	1972	Bowles-Hawkins-Hobby-Taylor
Primary Senate	1972	Brown-Galifianakis-Grace-Jordan
General Senate	1972	Galifianakis-Jesse Helms (R)
General Governor	1972	Bowles-James E. Holshouser (R)
Primary President	1972	Wallace-Sanford-Chisholm

Charlotte (Mecklenburg County)

Primary Governor	1960	Sanford-Larkins-Lake-Seawell
Runoff Governor	1960	Sanford-Lake
General Governor	1960	Sanford-Robert L. Gavin (R)
General President	1960	Kennedy-Nixon
Primary Governor	1964	Lake-Preyer-Moore
Runoff Governor	1964	Moore-Preyer
General Governor	1964	Moore-Robert L. Gavin (R)
General President	1964	Johnson-Goldwater
Primary Governor	1968	Scott-Broughton-Hawkins
General Governor	1968	Scott-James C. Gardner (R)
General President	1968	Humphrey-Nixon-Wallace
General Governor	1972	Bowles-James E. Holshouser (R)
General Senate	1972	Galifianakis-Jesse Helms (R)
General President	1972	McGovern-Nixon-Schmitz

RALEIGH   N.CAROLINA
****

CANDIDATE	LOWER # %	LOWER-MIDDLE # %	UPPER-MIDDLE # %	UPPER # %	BLACK # %	*	CANDIDATE	LOWER # %	LOWER-MIDDLE # %	UPPER-MIDDLE # %	UPPER # %	BLACK # %
PRIMARY GOVERNOR 1952						*	**GENERAL PRESIDENT 1952**					
OLIVE	508 .49	661 .47	492 .43	774 .41	669 .50	*	STEVENSON	1302 .88	539 .64	729 .52	2128 .43	290 .41
UMSTEAD	531 .51	758 .53	641 .57	1119 .59	667 .50	*	EISENHOWE	179 .12	300 .36	673 .48	2839 .57	414 .59
PRIMARY SENATOR 1954						*	**GENERAL PRESIDENT 1956**					
SCOTT	114 .48	741 .57	541 .64	1483 .45	594 .92	*	STEVENSON	360 .35	645 .62	580 .54	2211 .47	481 .47
LENNON	123 .52	567 .43	309 .36	1803 .55	50 .08	*	EISENHOWE	677 .65	391 .38	499 .46	2498 .53	535 .53
PRIMARY GOVERNOR 1960						*	**PRIMARY RUN-OFF 1960**					
SANFORD	168 .32	398 .36	510 .42	1485 .34	2209 .95	*	SANFORD	242 .48	602 .53	745 .59	2531 .64	2449 .98
LARKINS	63 .12	123 .11	147 .12	509 .12	44 .02	*	LAKE	261 .52	533 .47	518 .41	1412 .36	42 .02
SEAWELL	119 .23	256 .23	248 .21	1661 .38	63 .03	*		0 .00	0 .00	0 .00	0 .00	0 .00
LAKE	168 .32	331 .30	304 .25	719 .16	20 .01	*		0 .00	0 .00	0 .00	0 .00	0 .00
GENERAL PRESIDENT 1960						*	**GENERAL GOVERNOR 1960**					
KENNEDY	605 .43	1334 .59	1263 .57	3109 .49	2258 .81	*	SANFORD	672 .50	1239 .56	1221 .57	3333 .54	1411 .88
NIXON	792 .57	944 .41	945 .43	3199 .51	541 .19	*	GAVIN	664 .50	979 .44	921 .43	2833 .46	196 .12
GENERAL PRESIDENT 1964						*	**PRIMARY GOVERNOR 1964**					
JOHNSON	556 .49	1173 .50	1414 .48	3455 .53	2744 .98	*	LAKE	407 .57	787 .50	915 .49	1556 .35	11 .01
GOLDWATER	565 .51	1195 .50	1554 .52	3027 .47	60 .02	*	PREYER	106 .15	282 .18	328 .17	1423 .32	1953 .98
	0 .00	0 .00	0 .00	0 .00	0 .00	*	MOORE	200 .28	507 .32	640 .34	1510 .34	23 .01
GENERAL GOVERNOR 1964						*	**PRIMARY GOVERNOR 1968**					
MOORE	548 .51	1181 .52	1505 .52	3606 .57	2031 .88	*	SCOTT	252 .45	553 .45	618 .43	1695 .39	173 .10
GAVIN	520 .49	1102 .48	1389 .48	2675 .43	268 .12	*	BROUGHTON	286 .51	654 .53	793 .55	2438 .56	30 .02
	0 .00	0 .00	0 .00	0 .00	0 .00	*	HAWKINS	19 .03	32 .03	43 .03	251 .06	1575 .89
GENERAL PRESIDENT 1968						*	**GENERAL GOVERNOR 1968**					
HUMPHREY	195 .15	476 .19	623 .17	2469 .34	2323 .98	*	SCOTT	477 .36	1015 .42	1467 .41	4088 .59	1934 .98
NIXON	567 .43	1230 .50	1716 .48	3877 .54	52 .02	*	GARDNER	343 .64	1386 .58	2133 .59	2844 .41	46 .02
WALLACE	569 .43	743 .30	1263 .35	836 .12	7 .00	*		0 .00	0 .00	0 .00	0 .00	0 .00

```
                 PRIMARY  SENATOR  1950                  *              GENERAL  PRESIDENT 1952
                 ****************************                           *****************************
SMITH      473 .43   506 .33  1162 .39   931 .41    12 .01 * STEVENSON   887 .43    2063 .66  2296 .41  1925 .45   2227 .93
GRAHAM     567 .51   892 .57  1649 .56  1158 .51  1231 .98 * EISENHOWE  1180 .57    1006 .34  3310 .59  2354 .55    179 .07
REYNOLDS    64 .06   155 .10   148 .05   175 .08    15 .01 *              0 .00       0 .00     0 .00     0 .00      0 .00

                 GENERAL  GOVERNOR  1952                 *              PRIMARY  SENATOR  1954
                 ****************************                           *****************************
UMSTEAD   1442 .70  1987 .65  3788 .70   983 .64  1947 .92 * SCOTT       218 .35     464 .50   797 .40   384 .71    591 .96
SEAWELL    632 .30  1071 .35  1657 .30   553 .36   178 .08 * LENNON      407 .65     466 .50  1176 .60   157 .29     26 .04

                 GENERAL  SENATOR  1954                  *              PRIMARY  GOVERNOR  1956
                 ****************************                           *****************************
SCOTT      515 .68   832 .73  1777 .72   377 .75   442 .89 * HODGES      399 .97     589 .90  1163 .94   307 .81     55 .19
WEST       243 .32   300 .27   691 .28   124 .25    54 .11 * SAWYER       13 .03      65 .10    68 .06    74 .19    234 .81

                 PRIMARY  SENATOR  1956                  *              GENERAL  PRESIDENT 1956
                 ****************************                           *****************************
ERVIN      362 .90   501 .81  1084 .89   234 .71   103 .24 * STEVENSON   618 .43    1118 .50  1907 .44   634 .54    534 .34
KURFEES     42 .10   115 .19   138 .11    96 .29   328 .76 * EISENHOWE   806 .57    1114 .50  2473 .56   542 .46   1046 .66

                 GENERAL  GOVERNOR  1956                 *              GENERAL  SENATOR  1958
                 ****************************                           *****************************
HODGES    1061 .76  1744 .73  3400 .78  2807 .75   333 .22 * JORDAN      640 .80     588 .81  1583 .82   912 .84    460 .64
HAYES      343 .24   640 .27   949 .22   912 .25  1214 .78 * CLARKE      160 .20     139 .19   356 .18   177 .16    254 .36

                 PRIMARY  SENATOR  1960                  *              PRIMARY  GOVERNOR  1960
                 ****************************                           *****************************
JORDAN     169 .67   496 .64  1321 .66  2354 .73   423 .21 * SANFORD     111 .37     247 .31   739 .34  1028 .30   2067 .92
HEWLETT     84 .33   279 .36   667 .34   867 .27  1555 .79 * LARKINS      35 .12     145 .15   259 .12   449 .13     37 .02
             0 .00     0 .00     0 .00     0 .00     0 .00 * SEAWELL      47 .16     196 .21   731 .33  1502 .43    125 .06
             0 .00     0 .00     0 .00     0 .00     0 .00 * LAKE        108 .36     317 .33   455 .21   479 .14     12 .01

                 PRIMARY  RUN-OFF  1960                  *              GENERAL  PRESIDENT 1960
                 ****************************                           *****************************
SANFORD    148 .46   436 .45  1179 .60  2078 .67  2228 *** * KENNEDY     460 .39    1225 .45  1960 .45  2366 .35   1449 .67
LAKE       173 .54   524 .55   779 .40  1018 .33     6 .00 * NIXON       710 .61    1516 .55  2378 .55  4309 .65    717 .33

                 GENERAL  GOVERNOR  1960                 *              GENERAL  SENATOR  1960
                 ****************************                           *****************************
SANFORD    401 .35  1048 .40  1933 .45  2540 .39  2592 .85 * JORDAN      675 .45    1018 .49  2359 .58  3435 .54   2365 .84
GAVIN      759 .65  1592 .60  2317 .55  4010 .61   450 .15 * HAYES       837 .55    1058 .51  1730 .42  2881 .46    464 .16

                 GENERAL  SENATOR  1962                  *              PRIMARY  GOVERNOR  1964
                 ****************************                           *****************************
ERVIN      267 .45   646 .48  1276 .59  2046 .51   568 .65 * LAKE         95 .23     234 .22   274 .14   485 .11     11 .00
GREENE     331 .55   686 .52   878 .41  1977 .49   312 .35 * PREYER      210 .50     521 .49  1347 .67  3301 .72   2580 .97
             0 .00     0 .00     0 .00     0 .00     0 .00 * MOORE       104 .25     292 .28   371 .19   775 .17     22 .01

                 PRIMARY  RUN-OFF  1964                  *              GENERAL  PRESIDENT 1964
                 ****************************                           *****************************
PREYER     396 .35  1012 .41  1584 .47  2872 .38  2969 .91 * JOHNSON     460 .39    1248 .48  1929 .54  3515 .46   3950 .99
MOORE      721 .65  1455 .59  1776 .53  4663 .62   311 .09 * GOLDWATER   721 .61    1356 .52  1616 .46  4166 .54     23 .01
```

CANDIDATE	LOWER # %	LOWER-MIDDLE # %	UPPER-MIDDLE # %	UPPER # %	BLACK # %	*	CANDIDATE	LOWER # %	LOWER-MIDDLE # %	UPPER-MIDDLE # %	UPPER # %	BLACK # %
			GENERAL GOVERNOR 1964			*			GENERAL SENATOR 1966			
MOORE	396 .35	1012 .41	1584 .47	2862 .38	2969 .91	*	JORDAN	261 .57	801 .57	1378 .66	4407 .62	518 .82
GAVIN	721 .65	1455 .59	1776 .53	4663 .62	311 .09	*	SHALLCROS	195 .43	602 .43	714 .34	2717 .38	115 .18
			PRIMARY GOVERNOR 1968			*			GENERAL PRESIDENT 1968			
SCOTT	192 .57	645 .55	970 .58	2752 .52	111 .06	*	HUMPHREY	190 .19	735 .23	1188 .33	1842 .24	2736 .98
BROUGHTON	116 .34	465 .40	590 .36	2283 .43	24 .01	*	NIXON	420 .42	1323 .41	1807 .51	5018 .66	44 .02
HAWKINS	29 .09	67 .06	101 .06	220 .04	1579 .92	*	WALLACE	389 .39	1166 .36	555 .16	794 .10	3 .00
			GENERAL GOVERNOR 1968			*			GENERAL SENATOR 1968			
SCOTT	483 .47	1321 .52	2113 .60	4959 .59	2586 .99	*	ERVIN	995 .59	1157 .58	2159 .67	8189 .64	334 .33
GARDNER	537 .53	1234 .48	1392 .40	3425 .41	34 .01	*	SOMERS	696 .41	848 .42	1065 .33	4611 .36	683 .67
			PRIMARY GOVERNOR 1972			*			PRIMARY SENATOR 1972			
BOWLES	963 .56	1269 .63	1074 .58	2697 .61	1377 .46	*	BROWN	227 .14	131 .07	55 .03	142 .03	61 .02
HAWKINS	40 .02	59 .03	40 .02	38 .01	1391 .46	*	GALFANAKS	1012 .61	1209 .63	1185 .66	2904 .66	2104 .86
HOBBY	274 .16	229 .11	222 .12	261 .06	94 .03	*	GRACE	16 .01	20 .01	20 .01	50 .01	22 .01
TAYLOR	444 .26	473 .23	528 .28	1456 .33	162 .05	*	JORDAN	411 .25	564 .29	549 .30	1314 .30	261 .11
			GENERAL SENATOR 1972			*			GENERAL GOVERNOR 1972			
GALFANAKS	2370 .51	1720 .59	2797 .56	3405 .51	2271 .98	*	BOWLES	2323 .49	1494 .50	3209 .62	3261 .47	2603 .96
HELMS	2267 .49	1188 .41	2185 .44	3308 .49	47 .02	*	HOLSHOUSE	2445 .51	1494 .50	1982 .38	3654 .53	113 .04
			PRIMARY PRESIDENT 1972			*						
CHISHOLM	59 .03	102 .05	96 .05	81 .02	1772 .58	*		0 .00	0 .00	0 .00	0 .00	0 .00
JACKSON	7 .00	19 .01	18 .01	71 .02	17 .01	*		0 .00	0 .00	0 .00	0 .00	0 .00
MUSKIE	42 .02	70 .03	60 .03	119 .03	91 .03	*		0 .00	0 .00	0 .00	0 .00	0 .00
SANFORD	338 .19	619 .30	923 .50	2082 .47	1146 .38	*		0 .00	0 .00	0 .00	0 .00	0 .00
WALLACE	1324 .75	1260 .61	761 .41	2112 .47	14 .00	*		0 .00	0 .00	0 .00	0 .00	0 .00

PRIMARY GOVERNOR 1960
****

SANFORD	664 .36	337 .36	522 .37	1087 .31	1490 .73	* SANFORD	1017 .55
LARKINS	130 .07	46 .05	78 .06	248 .07	270 .13	* LAKE	826 .45
LAKE	452 .24	130 .14	172 .12	374 .11	25 .01	*	0 .00
SEAWELL	613 .33	418 .45	632 .65	1839 .52	266 .13	*	0 .00

PRIMARY RUN-OFF 1960
****

541 .70	1000 .76	2239 .72	1689 .99
228 .30	314 .24	866 .28	15 .01
0 .00	0 .00	0 .00	0 .00
0 .00	0 .00	0 .00	0 .00

GENERAL GOVERNOR 1960
****

SANFORD	2728 .51	1170 .50	1641 .38	2529 .35	4345 .92	* KENNEDY	1839 .49
GAVIN	2578 .49	1158 .50	2650 .62	4717 .65	389 .08	* NIXON	1893 .51

GENERAL PRESIDENT 1960
****

1024 .43	1399 .32	1777 .24	12485 .96
1358 .57	3032 .68	5617 .76	584 .04

PRIMARY GOVERNOR 1964
****

LAKE	496 .26	475 .22	312 .19	411 .13	37 .01	* MOORE	1451 .68
PREYER	670 .36	868 .41	640 .40	1290 .40	3662 .95	* PREYER	692 .32
MOORE	714 .38	800 .37	648 .40	1541 .48	140 .04	*	0 .00

PRIMARY RUN-OFF 1964
****

1370 .63	1025 .62	1943 .63	211 .05
807 .37	640 .38	1120 .37	4273 .95
0 .00	0 .00	0 .00	0 .00

GENERAL GOVERNOR 1964
****

MOORE	2299 .51	2594 .47	1415 .33	2356 .36	6067 .89	* JOHNSON	2233 .49
GAVIN	2236 .49	2979 .53	2855 .67	4126 .64	774 .11	* GOLDWATER	2310 .51

GENERAL PRESIDENT 1964
****

2622 .47	1694 .39	2110 .32	8181 ***
2986 .53	2615 .61	4430 .68	32 .00

PRIMARY GOVERNOR 1968
****

SCOTT	1014 .66	1321 .62	1242 .55	1336 .47	95 .02	* SCOTT	2118 .52
BROUGHTON	486 .31	694 .33	893 .40	1380 .49	27 .01	* GARDNER	1983 .48
HAWKINS	45 .03	106 .05	113 .05	126 .04	4237 .97	*	0 .00

GENERAL GOVERNOR 1968
****

3438 .49	3613 .47	3755 .51	6719 .98
3642 .51	4081 .53	3635 .49	120 .02
0 .00	0 .00	0 .00	0 .00

GENERAL PRESIDENT 1968
****

HUMPHREY	921 .22	1665 .19	1357 .17	1423 .18	7320 .99	* BOWLES	1724 .44
NIXON	2095 .50	5069 .59	5773 .72	5920 .76	94 .01	* HOLSHOUSR	2207 .56
WALLACE	1199 .28	1880 .22	909 .11	476 .06	4 .00	*	0 .00

GENERAL GOVERNOR 1972
****

2956 .38	3425 .35	2881 .35	3575 .88
4761 .62	6366 .65	5407 .65	465 .12
0 .00	0 .00	0 .00	0 .00

GENERAL SENATOR 1972
****

GALIFNAKS	5713 .43	3259 .43	0 .00	3200 .39	3185 .90	* MCGOVERN	1148 .27
HELMS	7709 .57	4289 .57	0 .00	4914 .61	363 .10	* NIXON	2975 .71
	0 .00	0 .00	0 .00	0 .00	0 .00	* SCHMITZ	92 .02

GENERAL PRESIDENT 1972
****

1720 .21	1918 .19	1642 .19	4938 .93
6317 .77	8113 .79	6902 .80	325 .06
136 .02	186 .02	118 .01	21 .00

SOUTH CAROLINA PRECINCT ELECTIONS

Charleston (Charleston County)

General President	1948	Dewey-Thurmond-Truman
Primary Senate	1950	Johnston-Thurmond
Primary Governor	1950	Bates-Byrnes-Pope
Private Schools		
Amendment	1952	For-Against
General President	1952	Stevenson-Eisenhower (Republican Electors)-Eisenhower (Independent Electors)
Primary Governor	1954	Bates-Timmerman
General Senate	1954	Edgar A. Brown (official Democratic nominee)-J. Strom Thurmond (Democratic write-in candidate)
General President	1956	Stevenson-Eisenhower-Independent (pledged to Harry F. Byrd)
Primary Governor	1958	Johnston-Hollings-Russell
Runoff Governor	1958	Hollings-Russell
General President	1960	Kennedy-Nixon
Primary Senate	1962	Hollings-Johnston
Primary Governor	1962	Russell-Maybank-Other
Primary Lt. Governor	1962	McNair-Parker
General Senate	1962	Johnston-William D. Workman (R)
General President	1964	Johnson-Goldwater
Primary Senate	1966	Hollings-Russell
Primary Senate	1966	Culbertson-Morrah
General Senate	1966	Hollings-Marshall Parker (R)
General Senate	1966	Morrah-J. Strom Thurmond (R)
General Governor	1966	McNair-Joseph O. Rogers (R)
Primary Senate	1968	Culbertson-Hollings
General President	1968	Humphrey-Nixon-Wallace
General Senate	1968	Hollings-Marshall Parker (R)
General Governor	1970	West-Albert W. Watson (R)-Other
General President	1972	McGovern-Nixon-Schmitz
General Senate	1972	Zeigler-J. Strom Thurmond (R)

Columbia (Richland County)
===

Office	Year	Candidates
General President	1948	Dewey-Thurmond-Truman
Primary Senate	1950	Johnston-Thurmond
Primary Governor	1950	Bates-Byrnes-Pope
Private Schools Amendment	1952	For-Against
General President	1952	Stevenson-Eisenhower (Republican Electors)-Eisenhower (Independent Electors)
Primary Governor	1954	Bates-Timmerman
General Senate	1954	Edgar A. Brown (official Democratic nominee)-J. Strom Thurmond (Democratic write-in candidate)
General President	1956	Stevenson-Eisenhower-Independent (pledged to Harry F. Byrd)
Primary Governor	1958	Johnston-Hollings-Russell
Runoff Governor	1958	Hollings-Russell
General President	1960	Kennedy-Nixon
Primary Senate	1962	Hollings-Johnston
Primary Governor	1962	Russell-Maybank-Other
Primary Lt. Governor	1962	McNair-Parker
General Senate	1962	Johnston-William D. Workman (R)
General President	1964	Johnson-Goldwater
Primary Senate	1966	Hollings-Russell
Primary Senate	1966	Culbertson-Morrah
General Senate	1966	Hollings-Marshall Parker (R)
General Senate	1966	Morrah-J. Strom Thurmond (R)
General Governor	1966	McNair-Joseph O. Rogers (R)
Sale of Alcoholic Beverages Amendment	1966	For-Against
Primary Senate	1968	Culbertson-Hollings
General President	1968	Humphrey-Nixon-Wallace
General Senate	1968	Hollings-Marshall Parker (R)
General Governor	1970	West-Albert W. Watson (R)-Other
Primary Senate	1972	Culbertson-Zeigler
General Senate	1972	J. Strom Thurmond (R)-Zeigler
General President	1972	Nixon-McGovern-Schmitz

CHARLESTON   S.CAROLINA

CANDIDATE	LOWER #	%	LOWER-MIDDLE #	%	UPPER-MIDDLE #	%	UPPER #	%	BLACK #	%

GENERAL PRESIDENT 1948

CANDIDATE	LOWER #	%	LOWER-MIDDLE #	%	UPPER-MIDDLE #	%	UPPER #	%	BLACK #	%
DEWEY	55	.04	23	.05	75	.05	47	.07	14	.03
THURMOND	1204	.86	376	.78	1225	.87	621	.87	267	.56
TRUMAN	146	.10	81	.17	103	.07	47	.07	195	.41

PRIMARY SENATOR 1950

CANDIDATE	LOWER #	%	LOWER-MIDDLE #	%	UPPER-MIDDLE #	%	UPPER #	%	BLACK #	%
JOHNSTON	825	.43	287	.38	555	.26	126	.14	411	.67
THURMOND	1102	.57	473	.62	1599	.74	782	.86	205	.33
	0	.00	0	.00	0	.00	0	.00	0	.00

PRIMARY GOVERNOR 1950

CANDIDATE	LOWER #	%	LOWER-MIDDLE #	%	UPPER-MIDDLE #	%	UPPER #	%	BLACK #	%
BATES	372	.20	130	.17	169	.08	40	.04	270	.46
BYRNES	1371	.72	566	.75	1705	.80	769	.86	252	.43
POPE	156	.08	58	.08	251	.12	89	.10	66	.11

SPECIAL REFERENDM 1952

CANDIDATE	LOWER #	%	LOWER-MIDDLE #	%	UPPER-MIDDLE #	%	UPPER #	%	BLACK #	%
FOR	857	.68	362	.71	1416	.78	652	.77	200	.43
AGAINST	405	.32	147	.29	399	.22	197	.23	270	.57
	0	.00	0	.00	0	.00	0	.00	0	.00

GENERAL PRESIDENT 1952

CANDIDATE	LOWER #	%	LOWER-MIDDLE #	%	UPPER-MIDDLE #	%	UPPER #	%	BLACK #	%
STEVENSON	671	.33	189	.24	404	.16	93	.08	440	.61
EISENHOWR	49	.02	16	.02	42	.02	8	.01	24	.03
EISENHOWER	1324	.65	569	.74	2112	.83	1032	.91	253	.35

PRIMARY GOVERNOR 1954

CANDIDATE	LOWER #	%	LOWER-MIDDLE #	%	UPPER-MIDDLE #	%	UPPER #	%	BLACK #	%
BATES	562	.46	166	.37	439	.29	136	.17	237	.65
TIMMERMAN	662	.54	284	.63	1060	.71	658	.83	129	.35
	0	.00	0	.00	0	.00	0	.00	0	.00

GENERAL SENATOR 1954

CANDIDATE	LOWER #	%	LOWER-MIDDLE #	%	UPPER-MIDDLE #	%	UPPER #	%	BLACK #	%
BROWN	414	.36	147	.34	315	.19	143	.17	279	.75
THURMOND	748	.64	280	.66	1314	.81	694	.83	93	.25
	0	.00	0	.00	0	.00	0	.00	0	.00

GENERAL PRESIDENT 1956

CANDIDATE	LOWER #	%	LOWER-MIDDLE #	%	UPPER-MIDDLE #	%	UPPER #	%	BLACK #	%
STEVENSON	280	.19	80	.16	218	.11	61	.06	234	.44
EISENHOWR	398	.27	134	.26	450	.24	206	.21	254	.48
INDEPENDE	799	.54	294	.58	1242	.65	696	.72	43	.08

PRIMARY GOVERNOR 1958

CANDIDATE	LOWER #	%	LOWER-MIDDLE #	%	UPPER-MIDDLE #	%	UPPER #	%	BLACK #	%
JOHNSTON	235	.16	67	.11	71	.05	19	.02	148	.32
HOLLINGS	1047	.72	414	.68	1043	.69	634	.52	274	.59
RUSSELL	179	.12	132	.22	392	.26	567	.46	41	.09

PRIMARY RUN-OFF 1958

CANDIDATE	LOWER #	%	LOWER-MIDDLE #	%	UPPER-MIDDLE #	%	UPPER #	%	BLACK #	%
HOLLINGS	1153	.85	446	.78	1105	.77	711	.62	312	.75
RUSSELL	204	.15	123	.22	339	.23	438	.38	102	.25
	0	.00	0	.00	0	.00	0	.00	0	.00

GENERAL PRESIDENT 1960

CANDIDATE	LOWER #	%	LOWER-MIDDLE #	%	UPPER-MIDDLE #	%	UPPER #	%	BLACK #	%
KENNEDY	750	.43	436	.31	310	.17	414	.21	412	.79
NIXON	1013	.57	961	.69	1473	.83	1601	.79	111	.21

PRIMARY SENATOR 1962

CANDIDATE	LOWER #	%	LOWER-MIDDLE #	%	UPPER-MIDDLE #	%	UPPER #	%	BLACK #	%
HOLLINGS	480	.58	442	.57	987	.66	517	.71	178	.21
JOHNSTON	354	.42	339	.43	503	.34	216	.29	683	.79

PRIMARY GOVERNOR 1962

CANDIDATE	LOWER #	%	LOWER-MIDDLE #	%	UPPER-MIDDLE #	%	UPPER #	%	BLACK #	%
RUSSELL	470	.55	482	.60	958	.60	409	.51	562	.66
MAYBANK	324	.38	266	.33	565	.36	364	.45	208	.24
OTHER	64	.07	52	.06	66	.04	35	.04	82	.10

PRIMARY LT-GOVNR 1962

CANDIDATE	LOWER #	%	LOWER-MIDDLE #	%	UPPER-MIDDLE #	%	UPPER #	%	BLACK #	%
MCNAIR	546	.66	524	.67	1072	.68	540	.68	356	.45
PARKER	281	.34	254	.33	497	.32	254	.32	428	.55
	0	.00	0	.00	0	.00	0	.00	0	.00

GENERAL SENATOR 1962

CANDIDATE	LOWER #	%	LOWER-MIDDLE #	%	UPPER-MIDDLE #	%	UPPER #	%	BLACK #	%
JOHNSTON	408	.33	380	.35	502	.25	171	.15	946	.90
WORKMAN	832	.67	702	.65	1508	.75	962	.85	107	.10

GENERAL PRESIDENT 1964

CANDIDATE	LOWER #	%	LOWER-MIDDLE #	%	UPPER-MIDDLE #	%	UPPER #	%	BLACK #	%
JOHNSON	296	.18	251	.16	439	.18	142	.11	1874	.93
GOLDWATER	1375	.82	1304	.84	1955	.82	1199	.89	150	.07

PRIMARY SENATOR 1966

CANDIDATE	LOWER #	%	LOWER-MIDDLE #	%	UPPER-MIDDLE #	%	UPPER #	%	BLACK #	%
HOLLINGS	565	.78	552	.80	930	.79	461	.79	690	.66
RUSSELL	161	.22	141	.20	254	.21	123	.21	352	.34

PRIMARY SENATOR 1966

CANDIDATE	LOWER #	%	LOWER-MIDDLE #	%	UPPER-MIDDLE #	%	UPPER #	%	BLACK #	%
CULBERTSN	251	.38	204	.32	258	.24	123	.23	773	.84
MORRAH	409	.62	427	.68	822	.76	414	.77	147	.16

GENERAL SENATOR 1966

CANDIDATE	LOWER #	%	LOWER-MIDDLE #	%	UPPER-MIDDLE #	%	UPPER #	%	BLACK #	%
HOLLINGS	640	.46	578	.42	914	.45	391	.35	1663	.96
PARKER	760	.54	806	.58	1118	.55	714	.65	66	.04

GENERAL SENATOR 1966

CANDIDATE	LOWER #	%	LOWER-MIDDLE #	%	UPPER-MIDDLE #	%	UPPER #	%	BLACK #	%
MORRAH	325	.24	277	.19	460	.23	154	.14	1629	.95
THURMOND	1006	.76	1197	.81	1557	.77	941	.86	81	.05

CANDIDATE	LOWER # %	LOWER-MIDDLE # %	UPPER-MIDDLE # %	UPPER # %	BLACK # %	*	CANDIDATE	LOWER # %	LOWER-MIDDLE # %	UPPER-MIDDLE # %	UPPER # %	BLACK # %
		GENERAL GOVERNOR 1966				*			PRIMARY SENATOR 1968			
MCNAIR	734 .52	660 .48	1080 .53	484 .44	1671 .96	*	CULBERTSN	172 .14	158 .12	270 .11	90 .08	876 .48
ROGERS	674 .48	720 .52	956 .47	618 .56	64 .04	*	HOLLINGS	1065 .86	812 .88	2079 .89	1054 .92	941 .52
		GENERAL PRESIDENT 1968				*			GENERAL SENATOR 1968			
HUMPHREY	264 .13	224 .15	572 .15	179 .09	2234 .96	*	HOLLINGS	1098 .55	903 .59	2282 .59	1121 .57	2422 .95
NIXON	1250 .63	1021 .68	2501 .67	1455 .76	63 .03	*	PARKER	899 .45	617 .41	1568 .41	833 .43	116 .05
WALLACE	482 .24	250 .17	637 .17	290 .15	32 .01	*		0 .00	0 .00	0 .00	0 .00	0 .00
		GENERAL GOVERNOR 1970				*			GENERAL PRESIDENT 1972			
WEST	507 .33	498 .41	1227 .41	581 .36	2609 .95	*	MCGOVERN	283 .13	258 .17	480 .11	182 .09	1526 .86
WATSON	1010 .65	693 .57	1753 .58	995 .62	118 .04	*	NIXON	1836 .86	1261 .82	3671 .87	1816 .88	239 .13
OTHER	27 .02	16 .01	43 .01	29 .02	12 .00	*	SCHMITZ	24 .01	27 .02	84 .02	73 .04	16 .01
		GENERAL SENATOR 1972				*						
ZEIGLER	468 .21	424 .26	865 .20	348 .16	2101 .88	*		0 .00	0 .00	0 .00	0 .00	0 .00
THURMOND	1773 .79	1219 .74	3480 .80	1827 .84	278 .12	*		0 .00	0 .00	0 .00	0 .00	0 .00

COLUMBIA   S.CAROLINA
****

GENERAL PRESIDENT 1948 / PRIMARY SENATOR 1950

DEWEY	41 .05	59 .07	57 .06	61 .09	129 .16	* JOHNSTON 1184 .62	1450 .59	1078 .51	831 .49	1249 .95
THURMOND	678 .76	676 .76	783 .80	485 .75	107 .13	* THURMOND 715 .38	1018 .41	1018 .49	863 .51	72 .05
TRUMAN	168 .19	153 .17	142 .14	104 .16	567 .71	* 0 .00	0 .00	0 .00	0 .00	0 .00

PRIMARY GOVERNOR 1950 / SPECIAL REFERENDM 1952

BATES	578 .30	523 .21	350 .17	264 .15	1176 .90	* FOR 931 .82	1499 .83	1490 .72	1699 .80	213 .18
BYRNES	1207 .63	1722 .70	1603 .76	1241 .73	108 .08	* AGAINST 210 .18	309 .17	575 .28	422 .20	976 .82
POPE	127 .07	223 .09	164 .08	201 .12	23 .02	* 0 .00	0 .00	0 .00	0 .00	0 .00

GENERAL PRESIDENT 1952 / PRIMARY GOVERNOR 1954

STEVENSON	580 .34	647 .26	792 .23	484 .17	1247 .90	* BATES 584 .42	663 .33	803 .31	679 .30	932 .92
EISENHOWR	58 .03	72 .03	82 .02	42 .01	35 .03	* TIMMERMAN 816 .58	1363 .67	1804 .69	1589 .70	84 .08
EISENHOWER	1047 .62	1805 .72	2534 .74	2319 .82	110 .08	* 0 .00	0 .00	0 .00	0 .00	0 .00

GENERAL SENATOR 1954 / GENERAL PRESIDENT 1956

BROWN	244 .22	354 .18	641 .27	444 .19	619 .91	* STEVENSON 362 .30	520 .24	591 .22	519 .18	551 .50
THURMOND	886 .78	1632 .82	1746 .73	1919 .81	58 .09	* EISENHOWR 280 .23	577 .26	726 .27	874 .30	504 .45
	0 .00	0 .00	0 .00	0 .00	0 .00	* INDEPENDN 567 .47	1083 .50	1383 .51	1504 .52	56 .05

PRIMARY GOVERNOR 1958 / PRIMARY RUN-OFF 1958

JOHNSTON	349 .18	461 .15	241 .09	180 .06	515 .52	* HOLLINGS 1043 .51	1504 .44	833 .31	1054 .31	147 .16
HOLLINGS	679 .35	1099 .35	642 .25	684 .22	82 .08	* RUSSELL 1000 .49	1885 .56	1875 .69	2382 .69	757 .84
RUSSELL	909 .47	1593 .51	1727 .66	2316 .73	385 .39	* 0 .00	0 .00	0 .00	0 .00	0 .00

GENERAL PRESIDENT 1960 / PRIMARY SENATOR 1962

KENNEDY	660 .32	1198 .31	764 .26	765 .19	1112 .80	* HOLLINGS 351 .26	740 .29	728 .39	1512 .51	62 .07
NIXON	1413 .68	2676 .69	2169 .74	3333 .81	280 .20	* JOHNSTON 1024 .74	1793 .71	1154 .61	1427 .49	820 .93

PRIMARY GOVERNOR 1962 / PRIMARY LT-GOVNR 1962

RUSSELL	977 .67	2001 .74	1704 .80	2492 .79	777 .85	* MCNAIR 918 .64	1674 .63	1197 .58	1815 .58	688 .82
MAYBANK	358 .25	514 .19	324 .15	534 .17	85 .09	* PARKER 515 .36	975 .37	862 .42	1328 .42	148 .18
OTHER	113 .08	196 .07	105 .05	129 .04	48 .05	* 0 .00	0 .00	0 .00	0 .00	0 .00

GENERAL SENATOR 1962 / GENERAL PRESIDENT 1964

JOHNSTON	1025 .53	1926 .50	1012 .38	1027 .27	1093 .94	* JOHNSON 617 .24	1235 .28	938 .29	936 .19	2203 .98
WORKMAN	892 .47	1896 .50	1642 .62	2794 .73	74 .06	* GOLDWATER 1923 .76	3253 .72	2270 .71	3888 .81	55 .02

PRIMARY SENATOR 1966 / PRIMARY SENATOR 1966

HOLLINGS	954 .67	1541 .61	911 .48	1724 .57	218 .19	* CULBERTSN 393 .33	706 .33	387 .24	457 .17	841 .84
RUSSELL	474 .33	1000 .39	995 .52	1291 .43	934 .81	* MORRAH 783 .67	1418 .67	1214 .76	2208 .83	166 .16

GENERAL SENATOR 1966 / GENERAL SENATOR 1966

HOLLINGS	841 .41	1596 .44	1204 .45	1650 .39	1409 .97	* MORRAH 529 .26	1029 .28	890 .34	987 .23	1408 .97
PARKER	1232 .59	2051 .56	1467 .55	2570 .61	46 .03	* THURMOND 1545 .74	2622 .72	1724 .66	3252 .77	45 .03

COLUMBIA   S.CAROLINA
****

CANDIDATE	LOWER #	%	LOWER-MIDDLE #	%	UPPER-MIDDLE #	%	UPPER #	%	BLACK #	%	*	CANDIDATE	LOWER #	%	LOWER-MIDDLE #	%	UPPER-MIDDLE #	%	UPPER #	%	BLACK #	%
											*											

GENERAL GOVERNOR 1966   *   SPECIAL REFERENDM 1966
****************************   ****************************

| MCNAIR | 841 | .43 | 1753 | .48 | 1496 | .57 | 2244 | .53 | 1441 | .97 | * FOR | 763 | .42 | 1499 | .48 | 1212 | .61 | 2475 | .66 | 467 | .63 |
| ROGERS | 1098 | .57 | 1894 | .52 | 1131 | .43 | 1985 | .47 | 47 | .03 | * AGAINST | 1050 | .58 | 1624 | .52 | 789 | .39 | 1284 | .34 | 270 | .37 |

PRIMARY SENATOR 1968   *   GENERAL PRESIDENT 1968
****************************   ****************************

CULBERTSN	380	.28	326	.23	431	.22	285	.14	885	.68	* HUMPHREY	686	.20	477	.16	1020	.25	597	.13	3444	.99
HOLLINGS	998	.72	1077	.77	1518	.78	1773	.86	419	.32	* NIXON	1956	.56	1640	.56	2648	.65	3546	.80	39	.01
	0	.00	0	.00	0	.00	0	.00	0	.00	* WALLACE	849	.24	786	.27	435	.11	301	.07	12	.00

GENERAL SENATOR 1968   *   GENERAL GOVERNOR 1970
****************************   ****************************

HOLLINGS	1693	.58	1535	.43	2119	.47	2195	.46	3549	.97	* WEST	1558	.40	1185	.41	1720	.48	2009	.49	2725	.94
PARKER	1233	.42	2003	.57	2363	.53	2549	.54	118	.03	* WATSON	2190	.56	1640	.56	1795	.50	2031	.49	33	.01
	0	.00	0	.00	0	.00	0	.00	0	.00	* OTHER	149	.04	81	.03	106	.03	65	.02	144	.05

PRIMARY SENATOR 1972   *   GENERAL SENATOR 1972
****************************   ****************************

| CULBERTSN | 697 | .44 | 505 | .39 | 770 | .40 | 708 | .31 | 717 | .50 | * THURMOND | 3014 | .64 | 2388 | .73 | 3144 | .70 | 3857 | .80 | 140 | .05 |
| ZEIGLER | 882 | .56 | 776 | .61 | 1152 | .60 | 1589 | .69 | 719 | .50 | * ZEIGLER | 1716 | .36 | 866 | .27 | 1332 | .30 | 967 | .20 | 2697 | .95 |

GENERAL PRESIDENT 1972   *
****************************   ****************************

NIXON	2041	.72	2280	.75	3169	.75	4142	.86	129	.06	*	0	.00	0	.00	0	.00	0	.00	0	.00
MCGOVERN	763	.27	707	.23	1029	.24	604	.13	2155	.94	*	0	.00	0	.00	0	.00	0	.00	0	.00
SCHMITZ	46	.02	52	.02	53	.01	45	.01	5	.00	*	0	.00	0	.00	0	.00	0	.00	0	.00

TENNESSEE PRECINCT ELECTIONS

Nashville (Davidson County)

Primary Governor	1954	Browning-Clement-Schoolfield
Primary Senate	1954	Kefauver-Sutton
General President	1956	Stevenson-Eisenhower-T. Coleman Andrews (States' Rights)
Primary Governor	1958	Allen-Ellington-Orgill-Taylor
Primary Senate	1958	Cooper-Gore
Primary Senate	1960	Kefauver-Taylor
General President	1960	Kennedy-Nixon
Primary Governor	1962	Clement-Farris-Olgiati
Primary Senate	1964	Bass-Bullard-Clement
General Senate	1964	Gore-Dan H. Kuykendall (R)
General President	1964	Goldwater-Johnson
General Senate	1964	Howard H. Baker (R)-Bass
Primary Governor	1966	Ellington-Hooker
Primary Senate	1966	Bass-Clement
General Senate	1966	Clement-Howard H. Baker (R)
General President	1968	Humphrey-Nixon-Wallace
General Governor	1970	Hooker-Winfield Dunn (R)-Heinsohn (American)
General Senate	1970	Gore-William E. Brock (R)
General President	1972	McGovern-Nixon-Schmitz
General Senate	1972	Blanton-Howard H. Baker (R)

Memphis (Shelby County)

General President	1960	Kennedy-Nixon
General President	1964	Johnson-Goldwater
General Senate	1964	Gore-Dan H. Kuykendall (R)
General Senate	1964	Bass-Howard H. Baker (R)
Primary Governor	1966	Ellington-Hooker
Primary Senate	1966	Bass-Clement
General Senate	1966	Clement-Howard H. Baker (R)
General President	1968	Humphrey-Nixon-Wallace
General Governor	1970	Winfield Dunn (R)-Heinsohn
General Senate	1970	William E. Brock (R)-Gore

General President   1972   McGovern-Nixon-Schmitz
General Senate   1972   Blanton-Howard H. Baker (R)

Column key for all tables: Candidate | LOWER (# / %) | LOWER-MIDDLE (# / %) | UPPER-MIDDLE (# / %) | UPPER (# / %) | BLACK (# / %)

PRIMARY GOVERNOR 1954

Candidate	LOWER #	%	LOWER-MIDDLE #	%	UPPER-MIDDLE #	%	UPPER #	%	BLACK #	%
BROWNING	1213	.31	1595	.32	1014	.29	1861	.35	185	.17
CLEMENT	2392	.61	3064	.62	2277	.65	3227	.60	855	.80
SCHLFIELD	330	.08	282	.06	234	.07	247	.05	28	.03

PRIMARY SENATOR 1954

Candidate	LOWER #	%	LOWER-MIDDLE #	%	UPPER-MIDDLE #	%	UPPER #	%	BLACK #	%
KEFAUVER	2832	.81	1655	.76	2989	.75	2597	.57	763	.93
SUTTON	655	.19	517	.24	1003	.25	1921	.43	61	.07
	0	.00	0	.00	0	.00	0	.00	0	.00

GENERAL PRESIDENT 1956

Candidate	LOWER #	%	LOWER-MIDDLE #	%	UPPER-MIDDLE #	%	UPPER #	%	BLACK #	%
STEVENSON	4523	.76	4870	.70	3621	.62	3646	.38	776	.52
EISENHOWR	1381	.23	2001	.29	2161	.37	5840	.61	693	.47
ANDREWS	44	.01	76	.01	63	.01	109	.01	10	.01
	0	.00	0	.00	0	.00	0	.00	0	.00

PRIMARY GOVERNOR 1958

Candidate	LOWER #	%	LOWER-MIDDLE #	%	UPPER-MIDDLE #	%	UPPER #	%	BLACK #	%
ALLEN	1728	.43	1801	.36	1047	.30	754	.11	432	.50
ELLINGTON	996	.25	1454	.29	1090	.31	2248	.33	100	.12
ORGILL	951	.24	1204	.24	918	.26	2385	.35	307	.36
TAYLOR	344	.09	551	.11	476	.13	1465	.21	17	.02

PRIMARY SENATOR 1958

Candidate	LOWER #	%	LOWER-MIDDLE #	%	UPPER-MIDDLE #	%	UPPER #	%	BLACK #	%
COOPER	844	.26	1157	.26	796	.25	2418	.35	117	.19
GORE	2443	.74	3333	.74	2386	.75	4494	.65	483	.80

PRIMARY SENATOR 1960

Candidate	LOWER #	%	LOWER-MIDDLE #	%	UPPER-MIDDLE #	%	UPPER #	%	BLACK #	%
KEFAUVER	3382	.79	4167	.76	2885	.72	4236	.52	1171	.93
TAYLOR	882	.21	1325	.24	1135	.28	3968	.48	83	.07

GENERAL PRESIDENT 1960

Candidate	LOWER #	%	LOWER-MIDDLE #	%	UPPER-MIDDLE #	%	UPPER #	%	BLACK #	%
KENNEDY	3801	.60	5569	.54	3005	.50	4123	.34	1283	.68
NIXON	2587	.40	4734	.46	3039	.50	8024	.66	604	.32
	0	.00	0	.00	0	.00	0	.00	0	.00

PRIMARY GOVERNOR 1962

Candidate	LOWER #	%	LOWER-MIDDLE #	%	UPPER-MIDDLE #	%	UPPER #	%	BLACK #	%
CLEMENT	1568	.37	2096	.38	1359	.40	3455	.43	781	.78
FARRIS	1269	.30	1903	.35	1116	.33	3463	.43	124	.12
OLGIATI	1384	.33	1450	.27	912	.27	1063	.13	94	.09

PRIMARY SENATOR 1964

Candidate	LOWER #	%	LOWER-MIDDLE #	%	UPPER-MIDDLE #	%	UPPER #	%	BLACK #	%
BASS	2907	.65	2469	.65	5522	.60	3724	.42	5389	.88
BULLARD	369	.08	340	.09	965	.10	876	.10	79	.01
CLEMENT	1229	.27	997	.26	2763	.30	4341	.49	644	.11

GENERAL SENATOR 1964

Candidate	LOWER #	%	LOWER-MIDDLE #	%	UPPER-MIDDLE #	%	UPPER #	%	BLACK #	%
GORE	4599	.68	4107	.67	8339	.61	6424	.26	10274	.97
KUYKENDAL	2143	.32	1987	.33	5406	.39	18697	.74	326	.03
	0	.00	0	.00	0	.00	0	.00	0	.00

GENERAL PPESIDENT 1964

Candidate	LOWER #	%	LOWER-MIDDLE #	%	UPPER-MIDDLE #	%	UPPER #	%	BLACK #	%
GOLDWATER	2228	.33	2190	.35	5979	.43	9783	.64	196	.02
JOHNSON	4451	.67	4077	.65	8064	.57	5507	.36	8299	.98

GENERAL SENATOR 1964

Candidate	LOWER #	%	LOWER-MIDDLE #	%	UPPER-MIDDLE #	%	UPPER #	%	BLACK #	%
BAKER	2451	.36	1713	.36	6081	.44	10409	.68	264	.02
BASS	4417	.64	3104	.64	7612	.56	4819	.32	10913	.98

PRIMARY GOVERNOR 1966

Candidate	LOWER #	%	LOWER-MIDDLE #	%	UPPER-MIDDLE #	%	UPPER #	%	BLACK #	%
ELLINGTON	3670	.63	3271	.64	7823	.70	9626	.80	1088	.11
HOOKER	2201	.37	1850	.36	3405	.30	2457	.20	8435	.89

PRIMARY SENATOR 1966

Candidate	LOWER #	%	LOWER-MIDDLE #	%	UPPER-MIDDLE #	%	UPPER #	%	BLACK #	%
BASS	2739	.48	1891	.46	4422	.40	2585	.22	5678	.84
CLEMENT	2944	.52	2180	.54	6501	.60	9129	.78	1049	.16

GENERAL SENATOR 1966

Candidate	LOWER #	%	LOWER-MIDDLE #	%	UPPER-MIDDLE #	%	UPPER #	%	BLACK #	%
CLEMENT	2918	.58	2204	.61	5726	.54	4847	.38	4454	.87
BAKER	2106	.42	1428	.39	4878	.46	7954	.62	650	.13
	0	.00	0	.00	0	.00	0	.00	0	.00

GENERAL PRESIDENT 1968

Candidate	LOWER #	%	LOWER-MIDDLE #	%	UPPER-MIDDLE #	%	UPPER #	%	BLACK #	%
HUMPHREY	2287	.22	1544	.21	3214	.22	3506	.21	5061	.94
NIXON	2312	.22	1696	.23	5051	.34	10397	.62	216	.04
WALLACE	5929	.56	4089	.56	6638	.45	2778	.17	81	.02

GENERAL GOVERNOR 1970

Candidate	LOWER #	%	LOWER-MIDDLE #	%	UPPER-MIDDLE #	%	UPPER #	%	BLACK #	%
HOOKER	3898	.53	2946	.52	6150	.45	4359	.21	4998	.97
DUNN	3229	.44	2535	.45	7231	.52	15928	.78	158	.03
HEINSOHN	276	.04	197	.03	433	.03	159	.01	9	.00

GENERAL SENATOR 1970

Candidate	LOWER #	%	LOWER-MIDDLE #	%	UPPER-MIDDLE #	%	UPPER #	%	BLACK #	%
GORE	4364	.60	3554	.60	6692	.50	5702	.31	4861	.97
BROCK	2923	.40	2326	.40	6629	.50	12507	.69	127	.03
	0	.00	0	.00	0	.00	0	.00	0	.00

GENERAL PRESIDENT 1972

Candidate	LOWER #	%	LOWER-MIDDLE #	%	UPPER-MIDDLE #	%	UPPER #	%	BLACK #	%
MCGOVERN	708	.32	1184	.25	1188	.23	1326	.20	2567	.92
NIXON	1437	.64	3356	.72	3743	.73	5314	.79	200	.07
SCHMITZ	93	.04	115	.02	164	.03	115	.02	15	.01

GENERAL SENATOR 1972

Candidate	LOWER #	%	LOWER-MIDDLE #	%	UPPER-MIDDLE #	%	UPPER #	%	BLACK #	%
BLANTON	1174	.54	1733	.38	2257	.44	1196	.18	1318	.64
BAKER	1018	.46	2835	.62	2816	.56	5500	.82	729	.36
	0	.00	0	.00	0	.00	0	.00	0	.00

```
                      GENERAL  PRESIDENT 1960              *              GENERAL  PRESIDENT 1964
                      ****************************                        ****************************
KENNEDY     2702 .50  4844 .41  4052 .44  2790 .30  7516 .66 * JOHNSON    2062 .34  4033 .33  3191 .32  3814 .30 12661 .99
NIXON       2675 .50  7001 .59  5227 .56  6571 .70  3936 .34 * GOLDWATER  3962 .66  8335 .67  6778 .68  8991 .70   140 .01

                      GENERAL  SENATOR  1964               *              GENERAL  SENATOR  1964
                      ****************************                        ****************************
GORE        2041 .35  4139 .34  3704 .36  3771 .30 11805 .98 * BASS       2122 .37  4314 .36  3348 .35  3764 .30 12001 .99
KUYKENDALL  3793 .65  7934 .66  6531 .64  8836 .70   181 .02 * BAKER      3627 .63  7599 .64  6265 .65  8728 .70   124 .01

                      PRIMARY  GOVERNOR 1966               *              PRIMARY  SENATOR  1966
                      ****************************                        ****************************
ELLINGTON   1743 .53  3463 .62  3183 .62  4066 .70  1423 .20 * BASS       1942 .48  2318 .46  2277 .46  1755 .32  4286 .60
HOOKER      1528 .47  2113 .38  1967 .38  1762 .30  5757 .80 * CLEMENT    2099 .52  2745 .54  2702 .54  3696 .68  2847 .40

                      GENERAL  SENATOR  1966               *              GENERAL  PRESIDENT 1968
                      ****************************                        ****************************
CLEMENT     1360 .32  2805 .31  2304 .30  2644 .25  8255 .96 * HUMPHREY    636 .09  1706 .13  1091 .10  2011 .16  9624 .98
BAKER       2914 .68  6304 .69  5504 .70  7795 .75   340 .04 * NIXON      1787 .24  4735 .36  3762 .33  8038 .62   205 .02
               0 .00     0 .00     0 .00     0 .00     0 .00 * WALLACE    4975 .67  6692 .51  6512 .57  2831 .22    28 .00

                      GENERAL  GOVERNOR 1970               *              GENERAL  SENATOR  1970
                      ****************************                        ****************************
DUNN        4144 .67  7303 .68  5099 .79  9255 .85   183 .02 * BROCK      3951 .73  4537 .64  5953 .76  8751 .79   137 .02
HEINSOHN     230 .04   417 .04   152 .02   116 .01    17 .00 * GORE       1487 .27  2575 .36  1851 .24  2262 .21  8136 .98
HOOKER      1790 .29  3046 .28  1233 .19  1570 .14  9699 .98 *
                      GENERAL  PRESIDENT 1972              *              GENERAL  SENATOR  1972
                      ****************************                        ****************************
MCGOVERN    1079 .24   364 .10   503 .10   674 .10  9303 .88 * BLANTON    1326 .32   981 .29  1234 .26  1147 .18  3361 .60
NIXON       3370 .74  3085 .87  4315 .87  5710 .88  1242 .12 * BAKER      2844 .68  2411 .71  3483 .74  5192 .82  2249 .40
SCHMITZ      102 .02   107 .03   135 .03   140 .02    29 .00 *              0 .00     0 .00     0 .00     0 .00     0 .00
```

TEXAS PRECINCT ELECTIONS

Fort Worth (Tarrant County)

General President	1952	Stevenson-Eisenhower
Primary Governor	1954	Yarborough-Shivers
Runoff Governor	1954	Yarborough-Shivers
Primary Governor	1956	Haley-O'Daniel-Daniel-Yarborough-Other
Runoff Governor	1956	Daniel-Yarborough
General President	1956	Stevenson-Eisenhower
Special Senate	1957	Dies-Hutcheson-Yarborough
Primary Governor	1958	Daniel-Gonzalez-Irwin-O'Daniel
Primary Senate	1958	Blakley-Yarborough
General Senate	1960	Johnson-John G. Tower (R)
General President	1960	Kennedy-Nixon
Special Senate	1961	Blakley-Gonzalez-Maverick-Tower-Wilson
Runoff Senate	1961	Blakley-Tower
Runoff Governor	1962	Connally-Yarborough
General Governor	1962	Connally-Jack Cox (R)
Poll Tax Repeal Amendment	1963	For-Against
Primary Senate	1964	Yarborough-McLendon
Primary Governor	1964	Connally-Yarborough
General President	1964	Johnson-Goldwater
General Senate	1964	Yarborough-George Bush (R)
Primary Governor	1966	Woods-Connally
Primary Senate	1966	Willoughby-Carr
General Senate	1966	Carr-John G. Tower (R)
Runoff Governor	1968	Smith-Yarborough
General President	1968	Humphrey-Nixon-Wallace
General Governor	1968	Smith-Paul W. Eggers (R)
General Governor	1970	Smith-Paul W. Eggers (R)
Primary Senate	1970	Yarborough-Bentsen
General Senate	1970	Bentsen-George Bush (R)
Primary Senate	1972	Yarborough-Sanders
Primary Governor	1972	Barnes-Smith-Farenthold-Briscoe
General President	1972	McGovern-Nixon
General Senate	1972	Sanders-John G. Tower (R)
General Governor	1972	Briscoe-Henry C. Grover (R)

Houston (Harris County)

General Senate	1960	John G. Tower (R)-Johnson-Logar (Constitution)
General President	1960	Nixon-Kennedy
Special Senate	1961	Blakley-Gonzalez-Maverick-Tower-Wilson Wright
Runoff Senate	1961	Blakley-Tower
Primary Governor	1962	Yarborough-Wilson-Walker-Daniel-Connally-Other
Runoff Governor	1962	Connally-Yarborough
General Governor	1962	Connally-Jack Cox (R)
Poll Tax Repeal Amendment	1963	For-Against
Primary Senate	1964	McLendon-Yarborough
Primary Governor	1964	Yarborough-Connally-Other
General President	1964	Johnson-Goldwater
General Senate	1964	Yarborough-George Bush (R)
Primary Senate	1966	Carr-Willoughby
Primary Governor	1966	Woods-Connally-Other
General Senate	1966	Carr-John G. Tower (R)
Runoff Governor	1968	Yarborough-Smith
General Governor	1968	Smith-Paul W. Eggers (R)
General President	1968	Humphrey-Nixon-Wallace
Primary Senate	1970	Bentsen-Yarborough
General Senate	1970	Bentsen-George Bush (R)
General Governor	1970	Smith-Paul W. Eggers (R)
Runoff Governor	1972	Briscoe-Farenthold
Runoff Senate	1972	Yarborough-Sanders

Waco (McLennan County)

General President	1948	Truman-Dewey-Thurmond
Primary Governor	1950	Shivers-March-Other
Primary Governor	1952	Yarborough-Shivers-Other
Primary Senate	1952	Daniel-Other-Beckworth
General President	1952	Stevenson-Eisenhower
Primary Governor	1954	Yarborough-Shivers-Other
Runoff Governor	1954	Yarborough-Shivers
Primary Governor	1956	O'Daniel-Daniel-Yarborough-Other
Runoff Governor	1956	Daniel-Yarborough
General President	1956	Stevenson-Eisenhower

Special Senate	1957	Dies-Hutcheson-Yarborough
Primary Senate	1958	Blakley-Yarborough
Primary Governor	1958	Daniel-Other-O'Daniel-Gonzalez
Primary Governor	1958	Daniel-Cox
General President	1960	Kennedy-Nixon
General Senate	1960	Johnson-John G. Tower (R)
Special Senate	1961	Maverick-Gonzalez-Blakley-Wilson-Wright-Tower
Runoff Senate	1961	Blakley-Tower
Primary Governor	1962	Walker-Connally-Daniel-Formby-Wilson-Yarborough
Runoff Governor	1962	Connally-Yarborough
General Governor	1962	Connally-Jack Cox (R)
Poll Tax Repeal		
Amendment	1963	For-Against
Primary Senate	1964	McLendon-Yarborough
Primary Governor	1964	Connally-Yarborough
General Senate	1964	Yarborough-George Bush (R)
General President	1964	Johnson-Goldwater
Primary Senate	1966	Carr-Willoughby
Primary Governor	1966	Woods-Connally
General Senate	1966	Carr-John G. Tower (R)
Runoff Governor	1968	Yarborough-Smith
General President	1968	Humphrey-Nixon-Wallace
General Governor	1968	Smith-Paul W. Eggers (R)
Primary Senate	1970	Yarborough-Bentsen
General Senate	1970	Bentsen-George Bush (R)
General Governor	1970	Smith-Paul W. Eggers (R)
Runoff Governor	1972	Briscoe-Farenthold
Runoff Senate	1972	Sanders-Yarborough
General President	1972	McGovern-Nixon
General Senate	1972	Sanders-John G. Towers (R)-Amaya (Raza Unida)
General Governor	1972	Briscoe-Henry C. Grover (R)-Muniz (Raza Unida)

FORT WORTH TEXAS

CANDIDATE	LOWER #	%	LOWER-MIDDLE #	%	UPPER-MIDDLE #	%	UPPER #	%	BLACK #	%	* CANDIDATE	LOWER #	%	LOWER-MIDDLE #	%	UPPER-MIDDLE #	%	UPPER #	%	BLACK #	%
GENERAL PRESIDENT 1952											**PRIMARY GOVERNOR 1954**										
STEVENSON	4480	.57	4422	.45	2662	.28	2040	.25	1915	.89	YARBOROUGH	1062	.58	791	.59	677	.34	294	.23	359	.83
EISENHOWER	3411	.43	5377	.55	7005	.72	6234	.75	244	.11	SHIVERS	779	.42	554	.41	1314	.66	977	.77	71	.17
PRIMARY RUN-OFF 1954											**PRIMARY GOVERNOR 1956**										
YARBOROUGH	2651	.60	2671	.52	1662	.29	657	.19	1223	.94	HALEY	1097	.23	1465	.22	1229	.21	880	.16	19	.01
SHIVERS	1763	.40	2459	.48	3985	.71	2833	.81	79	.06	ODANIEL	977	.20	1006	.15	407	.07	320	.06	29	.02
	0	.00	0	.00	0	.00	0	.00	0	.00	DANIEL	1155	.24	1922	.29	2879	.50	3290	.62	44	.03
	0	.00	0	.00	0	.00	0	.00	0	.00	YARBOROUGH	1563	.32	2079	.31	1080	.19	724	.14	1370	.92
	0	.00	0	.00	0	.00	0	.00	0	.00	OTHER	54	.01	138	.02	124	.02	123	.02	20	.01
PRIMARY RUN-OFF 1956											**GENERAL PRESIDENT 1956**										
DANIEL	1804	.40	2675	.45	3843	.72	3858	.80	57	.03	STEVENSON	4432	.50	4261	.46	2801	.29	1736	.22	1495	.70
YARBOROUGH	2668	.60	3270	.55	1479	.28	958	.20	1573	.97	EISENHOWE	4454	.50	4939	.54	6723	.71	6309	.78	650	.30
SPECIAL SENATOR 1957											**PRIMARY GOVERNOR 1958**										
DIES	1242	.37	1630	.39	2243	.48	1967	.47	22	.02	DANIEL	1926	.62	2636	.63	3315	.78	3634	.80	54	.05
HUTCHESON	531	.16	692	.17	1421	.31	1561	.37	120	.12	GONZALEZ	468	.15	640	.15	501	.12	487	.11	909	.90
YARBOROUGH	1622	.48	1855	.44	990	.21	657	.16	896	.86	IRWIN	149	.05	161	.04	95	.02	77	.02	19	.02
	0	.00	0	.00	0	.00	0	.00	0	.00	ODANIEL	586	.19	763	.18	351	.08	354	.08	28	.03
PRIMARY SENATOR 1958											**GENERAL SENATOR 1960**										
BLAKLEY	1009	.32	1346	.32	2479	.58	3058	.67	64	.07	JOHNSON	6080	.66	5814	.62	4665	.46	4337	.40	837	.85
YARBOROUGH	2139	.68	2830	.68	1798	.42	1540	.33	836	.93	TOWER	3130	.34	3534	.38	5498	.54	6444	.60	142	.15
GENERAL PRESIDENT 1960											**SPECIAL SENATOR 1961**										
KENNEDY	5144	.55	4730	.50	3461	.34	3102	.29	1744	.87	BLAKLEY	236	.06	262	.05	500	.09	610	.09	8	.01
NIXON	4165	.45	4718	.50	6696	.66	7723	.71	260	.13	GONZALEZ	150	.04	36	.01	43	.01	43	.01	173	.28
	0	.00	0	.00	0	.00	0	.00	0	.00	MAVERICK	275	.07	268	.05	220	.04	93	.01	89	.14
	0	.00	0	.00	0	.00	0	.00	0	.00	TOWER	803	.20	1086	.21	2150	.37	3113	.44	28	.05
											WILSON	87	.02	110	.02	120	.02	175	.02	18	.03
RUN-OFF 1961											**GENERAL GOVERNOR 1962**										
BLAKLEY	1750	.59	1807	.55	1760	.38	1744	.30	285	.65	CONNALLY	3139	.62	3296	.58	2935	.41	3428	.37	1099	.93
TOWER	1234	.41	1466	.45	2823	.62	4020	.70	155	.35	COX	1919	.38	2435	.42	4298	.59	5719	.63	89	.07
PRIMARY RUN-OFF 1962											**SPECIAL REFERENDM 1963**										
CONNALLY	1327	.51	1993	.54	2553	.70	3540	.77	449	.43	FOR	648	.38	664	.36	702	.30	996	.36	1064	.95
YARBOROUGH	1271	.49	1665	.46	1102	.30	1037	.23	590	.57	AGAINST	1080	.63	1165	.64	1670	.70	1737	.64	56	.05
PRIMARY GOVERNOR 1964											**PRIMARY SENATOR 1964**										
CONNALLY	3022	.78	3900	.82	4399	.90	6239	.91	490	.31	YARBOROUG	2587	.67	2939	.63	2199	.46	3104	.43	1550	.95
YARBOROUGH	835	.22	839	.18	498	.10	645	.09	1067	.69	MCLENDON	1288	.33	1757	.37	2571	.54	4117	.57	77	.05
GENERAL PRESIDENT 1964											**GENERAL SENATOR 1964**										
JOHNSON	7236	.75	6574	.70	5232	.52	6483	.46	2712	.99	YARBOROUGH	6717	.70	5926	.64	4209	.42	4586	.33	2658	.98
GOLDWATER	2447	.25	2783	.30	4888	.48	7571	.54	35	.01	BUSH	2878	.30	3376	.36	5895	.58	9448	.67	42	.02

FORT WORTH　　　TEXAS
****

Left panel

CANDIDATE	LOWER #	%	LOWER-MIDDLE #	%	UPPER-MIDDLE #	%	UPPER #	%	BLACK #	%
PRIMARY GOVERNOR 1966										
WOODS	829	.31	878	.30	598	.17	700	.13	706	.57
CONNALLY	1814	.69	2088	.70	2851	.83	4705	.87	526	.43
GENERAL SENATOR 1966										
CARR	1402	.54	1820	.46	1452	.28	2046	.23	1396	.94
TOWER	1177	.46	2140	.54	3662	.72	6898	.77	89	.06
PRIMARY RUN-OFF 1968										
SMITH	1174	.44	1670	.49	2819	.76	4857	.78	52	.03
YARBOROUGH	1521	.56	1762	.51	879	.24	1380	.22	1539	.97
	0	.00	0	.00	0	.00	0	.00	0	.00
GENERAL GOVERNOR 1970										
SMITH	3062	.57	3643	.55	3155	.42	3273	.29	2147	.89
EGGERS	2313	.43	3019	.45	4386	.58	7948	.71	255	.11
GENERAL SENATOR 1970										
BENTSEN	3718	.66	3980	.60	3430	.42	3470	.31	2179	.92
BUSH	1956	.34	2618	.40	4673	.58	7708	.69	189	.08
PRIMARY GOVERNOR 1972										
BARNES	968	.24	1219	.23	720	.20	1508	.16	1243	.58
SMITH	216	.05	317	.06	179	.05	360	.04	132	.06
FARENTHLD	1256	.31	1514	.28	1118	.30	2810	.30	607	.28
BRISCOE	1625	.40	2270	.43	1664	.45	4824	.51	173	.08
GENERAL SENATOR 1972										
SANDERS	3618	.51	4109	.48	2058	.31	4513	.26	3315	.96
TOWER	3434	.49	4455	.52	4595	.69	12559	.74	131	.04

Right panel

CANDIDATE	LOWER #	%	LOWER-MIDDLE #	%	UPPER-MIDDLE #	%	UPPER #	%	BLACK #	%
PRIMARY SENATOR 1966										
WILLOGHBY	719	.29	783	.27	706	.21	995	.21	496	.52
CARR	1725	.71	2067	.73	2662	.79	3644	.79	459	.48
GENERAL GOVERNOR 1968										
SMITH	4721	.61	6087	.59	4203	.43	6216	.36	2374	.68
EGGERS	2965	.39	4254	.41	5601	.57	11258	.64	1109	.32
GENERAL PRESIDENT 1968										
HUMPHREY	4044	.50	5214	.48	3254	.32	4739	.27	3698	.99
NIXON	2395	.30	3577	.33	5519	.55	11422	.64	41	.01
WALLACE	1652	.20	2055	.19	1349	.13	1718	.10	12	.00
PRIMARY SENATOR 1970										
YARBOROUGH	1724	.62	1855	.52	1011	.28	1390	.24	1574	.97
BENTSEN	1065	.38	1698	.48	2640	.72	4385	.76	55	.03
PRIMARY SENATOR 1972										
YARBOROUGH	2285	.63	2749	.59	1463	.41	3122	.37	1861	.97
SANDERS	1358	.37	1887	.41	2141	.59	5218	.63	67	.03
GENERAL PRESIDENT 1972										
MCGOVERN	3001	.40	3163	.36	1514	.22	3077	.18	3455	.97
NIXON	4412	.60	5579	.64	5244	.78	14210	.82	122	.03
	0	.00	0	.00	0	.00	0	.00	0	.00
	0	.00	0	.00	0	.00	0	.00	0	.00
GENERAL GOVERNOR 1972										
BRISCOE	3708	.55	4278	.51	2316	.36	5254	.32	3068	.95
GROVER	3001	.45	4029	.49	4077	.64	11140	.68	164	.05

GENERAL   SENATOR   1960
****

								GENERAL PRESIDENT 1960							

TOWER   2342 .39   2318 .44   4210 .60   4704 .78   604 .10 * NIXON   2913 .48   3051 .51   4666 .66   5034 .83   736 .11
JOHNSON   3426 .57   2778 .53   2646 .38   1254 .21   5365 .87 * KENNEDY   3219 .52   2981 .49   2430 .34   1022 .17   5922 .89
LOGAN   236 .04   146 .03   184 .03   63 .01   210 .03 *   0 .00   0 .00   0 .00   0 .00   0 .00

SPECIAL   SENATOR   1961
****************************   SPECIAL   RUN-OFF   1961

BLAKLEY   270 .13   260 .11   334 .11   570 .14   22 .01 * BLAKLEY   1018 .50   855 .41   797 .25   736 .17   600 .73
GONZALEZ   66 .03   51 .02   84 .03   54 .01   787 .46 * TOWER   1010 .50   1209 .59   2390 .75   3609 .83   227 .27
MAVERICK   563 .27   746 .31   319 .11   140 .03   134 .08 *   0 .00   0 .00   0 .00   0 .00   0 .00
TOWER   718 .34   970 .41   1766 .58   2777 .68   35 .02 *   0 .00   0 .00   0 .00   0 .00   0 .00
WILSON   314 .15   201 .08   278 .09   415 .10   628 .36 *   0 .00   0 .00   0 .00   0 .00   0 .00
WRIGHT   179 .08   160 .07   250 .08   138 .03   118 .07 *   0 .00   0 .00   0 .00   0 .00   0 .00

PRIMARY   GOVERNOR   1962
****************************   PRIMARY   RUN-OFF   1962

YARBOROUGH 1198 .42   1191 .39   724 .22   238 .07   2695 .68 * CONNALLY   707 .30   856 .35   1045 .47   2076 .81   1024 .34
WILSON   192 .07   196 .06   235 .07   203 .06   187 .05 * YARBOROUGH 1664 .70   1622 .65   1160 .53   488 .19   2010 .66
WALKER   395 .14   374 .12   577 .18   569 .18   49 .01 *   0 .00   0 .00   0 .00   0 .00   0 .00
DANIEL   601 .21   681 .23   898 .28   1152 .36   152 .04 *   0 .00   0 .00   0 .00   0 .00   0 .00
CONNALLY   453 .16   503 .17   717 .22   946 .30   857 .22 *   0 .00   0 .00   0 .00   0 .00   0 .00
OTHER   38 .01   73 .02   69 .02   84 .03   20 .01 *   0 .00   0 .00   0 .00   0 .00   0 .00

GENERAL   GOVERNOR   1962
****************************   SPECIAL   REFERENDM 1963

CONNALLY   2036 .54   2110 .53   1739 .35   1141 .21   4949 .96 * FOR   655 .43   739 .46   835 .43   784 .36   2685 .90
COX   1728 .46   1907 .47   3175 .65   4233 .79   227 .04 * AGAINST   872 .57   856 .54   1087 .57   1421 .64   285 .10

PRIMARY   SENATOR   1964
****************************   PRIMARY   GOVERNOR   1964

MCLENDON   1170 .38   1254 .40   1773 .55   2291 .73   393 .10 * YARBOROUGH 1297 .41   1345 .42   794 .24   551 .16   2734 .63
YARBOROUGH 1885 .62   1885 .60   1465 .45   840 .27   3513 .90 * CONNALLY   1836 .58   1809 .57   2531 .75   2787 .83   1534 .35
              0 .00   0 .00   0 .00   0 .00   0 .00 * OTHER   28 .01   40 .01   32 .01   21 .01   100 .02

GENERAL   PRESIDENT 1964
****************************   GENERAL   SENATOR   1964

JOHNSON   4106 .63   4081 .61   3450 .46   1939 .30   9138 .99 * YARBOROUGH 3713 .58   3569 .53   2761 .37   1201 .19   8874 .99
GOLDWATER 2369 .37   2635 .39   4063 .54   4470 .70   57 .01 * BUSH   2685 .42   3104 .47   4722 .63   5185 .81   72 .01

PRIMARY   SENATOR   1966
****************************   PRIMARY   GOVERNOR   1966

CARR   1284 .74   1455 .73   1799 .74   2183 .85   1033 .73 * WOODS   832 .37   964 .37   553 .20   229 .08   1981 .57
WILLOUGHBY 441 .26   525 .27   627 .26   372 .15   384 .27 * CONNALLY   1386 .61   1618 .62   2126 .78   2680 .92   1390 .40
              0 .00   0 .00   0 .00   0 .00   0 .00 * OTHER   38 .02   32 .01   40 .01   12 .00   125 .04

GENERAL   SENATOR   1966
****************************   PRIMARY   RUN-OFF   1968

CARR   1557 .45   1453 .39   1496 .28   1144 .19   3898 .94 * YARBOROUGH 1389 .58   1597 .60   1121 .36   681 .17   3407 .98
TOWER   1927 .55   2272 .61   3766 .72   4900 .81   244 .06 * SMITH   995 .42   1060 .40   1983 .64   3326 .83   65 .02

GENERAL   GOVERNOR   1968
****************************   GENERAL   PRESIDENT 1968

SMITH   3860 .58   3668 .51   3895 .46   2590 .32   4049 .71 * HUMPHREY   2218 .31   2416 .32   2191 .25   1503 .18   6356 .98
EGGERS   2781 .42   3505 .49   4504 .54   5453 .68   1620 .29 * NIXON   2130 .30   2676 .35   4634 .53   6056 .74   99 .02
              0 .00   0 .00   0 .00   0 .00   0 .00 * WALLACE   2856 .40   2518 .33   1858 .21   635 .08   22 .00

HOUSTON   TEXAS
****

CANDIDATE	LOWER # %	LOWER-MIDDLE # %	UPPER-MIDDLE # %	UPPER # %	BLACK # %	* CANDIDATE	LOWER # %	LOWER-MIDDLE # %	UPPER-MIDDLE # %	UPPER # %	BLACK # %
		PRIMARY SENATOR 1970 ************************				*		GENERAL SENATOR 1970 ************************			
BENTSON	1036 .45	1218 .48	1820 .62	2553 .77	97 .03	* BENTSON	2621 .53	2502 .46	2266 .32	1797 .22	3623 .83
YARBOROUGH	1254 .55	1321 .52	1104 .38	775 .23	3481 .97	* BUSH	2360 .47	2934 .54	4823 .68	6294 .78	744 .17
		GENERAL GOVERNOR 1970 ************************				*		PRIMARY RUN-OFF 1972 ************************			
SMITH	2740 .55	2848 .53	2644 .37	2209 .27	3461 .80	* BRISCOE	1579 .46	905 .42	3050 .52	3097 .54	289 .10
EGGERS	2233 .45	2534 .47	4432 .63	5827 .73	875 .20	* FARENTHO	1869 .54	1258 .58	2812 .48	2607 .46	2701 .90
		PRIMARY RUN-OFF 1972 ************************				*		************************			
YARBOROUGH	1783 .54	1498 .50	2304 .41	1745 .32	2445 .94	*	0 .00	0 .00	0 .00	0 .00	0 .00
SANDERS	1494 .46	1527 .50	3337 .59	3734 .68	158 .06	*	0 .00	0 .00	0 .00	0 .00	0 .00

WACO   TEXAS
****

<pre>
                  GENERAL PRESIDENT 1948   *   PRIMARY GOVERNOR 1950
                  *****************************   *****************************
TRUMAN   1604 .82 1823 .80 1761 .72 1598 .68   740 .88 * SHIVERS   829 .49 1114 .57 1469 .71 1687 .70 220 .31
DEWEY   250 .13   356 .16   533 .22   615 .26   85 .10 * MARCH   811 .48   811 .41   556 .27   691 .29 459 .66
THURMOND   97 .05   90 .04   142 .06   134 .06   17 .02 * OTHER   37 .02   36 .02   32 .02   32 .01   20 .03

                  PRIMARY GOVERNOR 1952   *   PRIMARY SENATOR 1952
                  *****************************   *****************************
YARBOROUGH 1060 .49   958 .41   732 .34 1161 .34   514 .68 * DANIEL   1462 .69 1677 .73 1627 .75 2595 .76 412 .57
SHIVERS   1074 .50 1324 .57 1408 .65 2250 .65   206 .27 * OTHER   89 .04   64 .03   53 .02   56 .02   69 .09
OTHER   32 .01   35 .02   20 .01   29 .01   38 .05 * BECKWORTH 567 .27   565 .25   475 .22   771 .23 246 .34

                  GENERAL PRESIDENT 1952   *   PRIMARY GOVERNOR 1954
                  *****************************   *****************************
STEVENSON 1907 .58 1673 .50 1353 .41 1911 .37 1084 .82 * YARBOROUGH 1614 .68 1271 .58   917 .44   824 .41 760 .85
EISENHOWER 1405 .42 1676 .50 1932 .59 3227 .63   237 .18 * SHIVERS   709 .30   891 .41 1133 .54 1150 .58 109 .12
              0 .00   0 .00   0 .00   0 .00   0 .00 * OTHER   47 .02   28 .01   40 .02   19 .01   21 .02

                  PRIMARY RUN-OFF 1954   *   PRIMARY GOVERNOR 1956
                  *****************************   *****************************
YARBOROUGH 1521 .61 1142 .49   773 .34   661 .31   935 .87 * ODANIEL   941 .23   634 .18   453 .12   209 .09 200 .24
SHIVERS   993 .39 1204 .51 1473 .66 1483 .69   144 .13 * DANIEL   1345 .33 1639 .46 2121 .54 1530 .64   89 .10
              0 .00   0 .00   0 .00   0 .00   0 .00 * YARBOROUGH 1591 .39 1092 .30 1068 .27   475 .20 532 .63
              0 .00   0 .00   0 .00   0 .00   0 .00 * OTHER   225 .05   216 .06   255 .07   162 .07   30 .04

                  PRIMARY RUN-OFF 1956   *   GENERAL PRESIDENT 1956
                  *****************************   *****************************
DANIEL   1546 .40 1717 .51 2210 .59 1612 .71   123 .15 * STEVENSON 2765 .56 2041 .47 2202 .43 1116 .34 763 .61
YARBOROUGH 2310 .60 1640 .49 1544 .41   662 .29   695 .85 * EISENHOWE 2173 .44 2320 .53 2875 .57 2152 .66 488 .39

                  SPECIAL SENATOR 1957   *   PRIMARY SENATOR 1958
                  *****************************   *****************************
DIES   533 .25   596 .32   787 .35   622 .39   51 .12 * BLAKLEY   1125 .28   693 .34 1554 .49   864 .55   82 .08
HUTCHESON   282 .13   341 .18   526 .23   470 .29   51 .12 * YARBOROUGH 2879 .72 1331 .66 1636 .51   699 .45 892 .92
YARBOROUGH 1320 .62   949 .50   952 .42   505 .32   316 .76 *   0 .00   0 .00   0 .00   0 .00   0 .00

                  PRIMARY GOVERNOR 1958   *   PRIMARY GOVERNOR 1960
                  *****************************   *****************************
DANIEL   2075 .62 1993 .71 2496 .76 2088 .84   172 .18 * DANIEL   2844 .68 2836 .73 2909 .69 2666 .71 678 .55
OTHER   95 .03   54 .02   71 .02   27 .01   20 .02 * COX   1327 .32 1064 .27 1311 .31 1073 .29 565 .45
ODANIEL   793 .24   506 .18   406 .12   198 .08   106 .11 *   0 .00   0 .00   0 .00   0 .00   0 .00
GONZALEZ   387 .12   252 .09   297 .09   171 .07   676 .69 *   0 .00   0 .00   0 .00   0 .00   0 .00

                  GENERAL PRESIDENT 1960   *   GENERAL SENATOR 1960
                  *****************************   *****************************
KENNEDY   2950 .61 2387 .53 2501 .48 1869 .40 1249 .80 * JOHNSON   3427 .71 2946 .65 3120 .62 2490 .53 1314 .82
NIXON   1921 .39 2153 .47 2665 .52 2836 .60   307 .20 * TOWER   1430 .29 1602 .35 1899 .38 2192 .47 282 .18

                  SPECIAL SENATOR 1961   *   SPECIAL RUN-OFF 1961
                  *****************************   *****************************
MAVERICK   389 .21   313 .17   339 .13   204 .09   114 .08 * BLAKLEY   1217 .69 1114 .63 1460 .56 1117 .52 235 .59
GONZALEZ   38 .02   40 .02   43 .02   35 .02 1047 .73 * TOWER   550 .31   663 .37 1159 .44 1011 .48 161 .41
BLAKLEY   569 .31   632 .34   964 .36   762 .35   76 .05 *   0 .00   0 .00   0 .00   0 .00   0 .00
WILSON   310 .17   285 .16   351 .13   221 .10   127 .09 *   0 .00   0 .00   0 .00   0 .00   0 .00
WRIGHT   232 .13   218 .12   359 .13   301 .14   18 .01 *   0 .00   0 .00   0 .00   0 .00   0 .00
TOWER   288 .16   346 .19   652 .24   659 .30   51 .04 *   0 .00   0 .00   0 .00   0 .00   0 .00
</pre>

WACO TEXAS

****

CANDIDATE	LOWER # %	LOWER-MIDDLE # %	UPPER-MIDDLE # %	UPPER # %	BLACK # %	* CANDIDATE	LOWER # %	LOWER-MIDDLE # %	UPPER-MIDDLE # %	UPPER # %	BLACK # %

PRIMARY GOVERNOR 1962 / PRIMARY RUN-OFF 1962

CANDIDATE	LOWER	LOWER-MIDDLE	UPPER-MIDDLE	UPPER	BLACK	CANDIDATE	LOWER	LOWER-MIDDLE	UPPER-MIDDLE	UPPER	BLACK
WALKER	219 .07	197 .06	224 .05	160 .05	32 .02	CONNALLY	1018 .38	1054 .45	1720 .53	1657 .67	741 .52
CONNALLY	928 .28	885 .29	1305 .31	947 .29	734 .50	YARBOROUGH	1664 .62	1290 .55	1526 .47	806 .33	678 .48
DANIEL	695 .21	737 .24	1068 .26	983 .30	119 .08		0 .00	0 .00	0 .00	0 .00	0 .00
FORMBY	176 .05	180 .06	415 .10	366 .11	60 .04		0 .00	0 .00	0 .00	0 .00	0 .00
WILSON	356 .11	312 .10	388 .09	296 .09	114 .08		0 .00	0 .00	0 .00	0 .00	0 .00
YARBOROUGH	929 .28	783 .25	774 .19	477 .15	418 .28		0 .00	0 .00	0 .00	0 .00	0 .00

GENERAL GOVERNOR 1962 / SPECIAL REFERENDM 1963

CANDIDATE	LOWER	LOWER-MIDDLE	UPPER-MIDDLE	UPPER	BLACK	CANDIDATE	LOWER	LOWER-MIDDLE	UPPER-MIDDLE	UPPER	BLACK
CONNALLY	1840 .64	1639 .57	2312 .54	1520 .46	1119 .88	FOR	389 .45	347 .46	465 .42	404 .45	813 .92
COX	1052 .36	1237 .43	1995 .46	1772 .54	157 .12	AGAINST	466 .55	401 .54	641 .58	494 .55	75 .08

PRIMARY SENATOR 1964 / PRIMARY GOVERNOR 1964

CANDIDATE	LOWER	LOWER-MIDDLE	UPPER-MIDDLE	UPPER	BLACK	CANDIDATE	LOWER	LOWER-MIDDLE	UPPER-MIDDLE	UPPER	BLACK
MCLENDON	890 .27	991 .31	1661 .38	1519 .47	224 .11	CONNALLY	2195 .65	2310 .70	3427 .78	2811 .85	837 .44
YARBOROUGH	2458 .73	2221 .69	2693 .62	1711 .53	1858 .89	YARBOROUGH	1183 .35	980 .30	960 .22	492 .15	1083 .56

GENERAL SENATOR 1964 / GENERAL PRESIDENT 1964

CANDIDATE	LOWER	LOWER-MIDDLE	UPPER-MIDDLE	UPPER	BLACK	CANDIDATE	LOWER	LOWER-MIDDLE	UPPER-MIDDLE	UPPER	BLACK
YARBOROUGH	3476 .72	2861 .64	3384 .54	1936 .41	2825 .93	JOHNSON	3683 .76	3119 .71	3969 .64	2544 .54	2643 .97
BUSH	1345 .28	1643 .36	2882 .46	2771 .59	197 .07	GOLDWATER	1132 .24	1287 .29	2275 .36	2153 .46	69 .03

PRIMARY SENATOR 1966 / PRIMARY GOVERNOR 1966

CANDIDATE	LOWER	LOWER-MIDDLE	UPPER-MIDDLE	UPPER	BLACK	CANDIDATE	LOWER	LOWER-MIDDLE	UPPER-MIDDLE	UPPER	BLACK
CARR	1188 .81	1134 .81	1896 .85	1733 .86	895 .85	WOODS	512 .35	456 .32	537 .24	272 .13	433 .41
WILLOUGHBY	275 .19	260 .19	334 .15	276 .14	155 .15	CONNALLY	972 .65	956 .68	1707 .76	1773 .87	633 .59

GENERAL SENATOR 1966 / PRIMARY RUN-OFF 1968

CANDIDATE	LOWER	LOWER-MIDDLE	UPPER-MIDDLE	UPPER	BLACK	CANDIDATE	LOWER	LOWER-MIDDLE	UPPER-MIDDLE	UPPER	BLACK
CARR	1279 .58	1076 .49	1631 .42	1151 .32	1184 .88	YARBOROU	2319 .59	1241 .54	1030 .33	834 .25	1927 .89
TOWER	910 .42	1140 .51	2229 .58	2395 .68	158 .12	SMITH	1423 .41	1078 .46	2071 .67	2472 .75	235 .11

GENERAL PRESIDENT 1968 / GENERAL GOVERNOR 1968

CANDIDATE	LOWER	LOWER-MIDDLE	UPPER-MIDDLE	UPPER	BLACK	CANDIDATE	LOWER	LOWER-MIDDLE	UPPER-MIDDLE	UPPER	BLACK
HUMPHREY	3272 .48	1863 .44	2244 .39	1901 .32	3392 .90	SMITH	4508 .69	2709 .65	3338 .59	3172 .54	2956 .82
NIXON	1819 .27	1393 .33	2656 .46	3414 .58	208 .06	EGGERS	1987 .31	1434 .35	2305 .41	2669 .46	628 .18
WALLACE	1693 .25	1021 .24	890 .15	561 .10	163 .04		0 .00	0 .00	0 .00	0 .00	0 .00

PRIMARY SENATOR 1970 / GENERAL SENATOR 1970

CANDIDATE	LOWER	LOWER-MIDDLE	UPPER-MIDDLE	UPPER	BLACK	CANDIDATE	LOWER	LOWER-MIDDLE	UPPER-MIDDLE	UPPER	BLACK
YARBOROUGH	1897 .61	902 .54	1162 .37	949 .24	1687 .86	BENTSON	2918 .69	1670 .64	2780 .57	2274 .44	2139 .91
BENTSON	1229 .39	770 .46	2000 .63	2938 .76	278 .14	BUSH	1282 .31	928 .36	2070 .43	2838 .56	217 .09

GENERAL GOVERNOR 1970 / PRIMARY RUN-OFF 1972

CANDIDATE	LOWER	LOWER-MIDDLE	UPPER-MIDDLE	UPPER	BLACK	CANDIDATE	LOWER	LOWER-MIDDLE	UPPER-MIDDLE	UPPER	BLACK
SMITH	2793 .66	1574 .62	2690 .54	2378 .46	2112 .86	BRISCOE	2521 .57	1882 .61	3223 .67	3615 .73	510 .23
EGGERS	1423 .34	978 .38	2251 .46	2743 .54	353 .14	FARENTHOL	1866 .43	1180 .39	1581 .33	1361 .27	1753 .77

PRIMARY RUN-OFF 1972 / GENERAL GOVERNOR 1972

CANDIDATE	LOWER	LOWER-MIDDLE	UPPER-MIDDLE	UPPER	BLACK	CANDIDATE	LOWER	LOWER-MIDDLE	UPPER-MIDDLE	UPPER	BLACK
SANDERS	1902 .44	1478 .46	2663 .55	3350 .67	345 .16	BRISCOE	3071 .53	2151 .53	3452 .53	3298 .47	2532 .74
YARBOROUGH	2459 .56	1751 .54	2130 .45	1631 .33	1873 .84	GROVER	2132 .37	1584 .39	2863 .44	3565 .50	465 .14
	0 .00	0 .00	0 .00	0 .00	0 .00	MUNIZ	591 .10	343 .08	257 .04	188 .03	443 .13

```
                                        WACO          TEXAS
                                        ***************************
                                                      *
CANDIDATE       LOWER      LOWER-     UPPER-               *
                           MIDDLE     MIDDLE     UPPER         BLACK  * CANDIDATE      LOWER      LOWER-     UPPER-               
                # %        # %        # %        # %           # %    *                # %        MIDDLE     MIDDLE     UPPER         BLACK
                                                                      *                           # %        # %        # %           # %
***********************************************************************************************************************************************

                           GENERAL  SENATOR   1972                 *                              GENERAL   PRESIDENT 1972
                           **************************                *                             **************************
SANDERS       3201 .52    1989 .50   2700 .40   2158 .30    2894 .83 * MCGOVERN     2286 .37    1209 .29   1562 .24   1109 .16    2904 .81
TOWER         2771 .45    1891 .47   3940 .59   4899 .69     544 .16 * NIXON        3838 .63    2992 .71   5051 .76   5877 .84     669 .19
AMAYA          200 .03     126 .03     53 .01     27 .00      48 .01 *                 0 .00       0 .00      0 .00      0 .00       0 .00
```

VIRGINIA PRECINCT ELECTIONS

Norfolk

General President	1952	Stevenson-Eisenhower
Primary Governor	1953	Stanley-Fenwick
General Governor	1953	Stanley-Ted Dalton (R)
General President	1956	Stevenson-Eisenhower
Primary Governor	1957	Almond-Carwile
General Governor	1957	Almond-Ted Dalton (R)
General Senate	1958	Byrd-Robb (Social Democrat)-Wensel (I)
General President	1960	Kennedy-Nixon
Primary Governor	1961	Harrison-Stephens
Primary Lt. Governor	1961	Godwin-Boothe
General Governor	1961	Harrison-H. Clyde Pearson (R)
General President	1964	Johnson-Goldwater
General Governor	1965	Godwin-Linwood Holton (R)
Primary Senate	1966	Byrd-Boothe
Primary Senate	1966	Spong-Robertson
General Senate	1966	Byrd-Lawrence M. Traylor (R)
General Senate	1966	Spong-James P. Ould (R)
General President	1968	Humphrey-Nixon-Wallace
Primary Governor	1969	Pollard-Howell-Battle
General Governor	1969	Battle-Linwood Holton (R)

Richmond

General President	1948	Truman-Dewey-Thurmond
General President	1952	Stevenson-Eisenhower
Primary Governor	1953	Fenwick-Stanley
General Governor	1953	Stanley-Ted Dalton (R)
General President	1956	Stevenson-Eisenhower
Primary Governor	1957	Almond-Carwile
General Governor	1957	Almond-Ted Dalton (R)
General President	1960	Kennedy-Nixon
Primary Governor	1961	Harrison-Stephens
General Governor	1961	Harrison-H. Clyde Pearson (R)
General President	1964	Johnson-Goldwater

PRECINCT DATA/403

General Senate	1964	Byrd-Respess (I)
General Governor	1965	Godwin-Linwood Holton (R)-Story (Conservative)
Primary Senate	1966	Byrd-Boothe
Primary Senate	1966	Spong-Robertson
General Senate	1966	Byrd-Lawrence M. Traylor (R)
General President	1968	Humphrey-Nixon-Wallace
Primary Governor	1969	Battle-Howell-Pollard
Runoff Governor	1969	Battle-Howell
General Governor	1969	Battle-Linwood Holton (R)
Primary Senate	1970	DuVal-Rawlings
General Senate	1970	Ray Garland (R)-Rawlings-Byrd (I)

Roanoke

General President	1948	Truman-Dewey-Thurmond
Primary Senate	1952	Byrd-Miller
General President	1952	Stevenson-Eisenhower
Primary Governor	1953	Fenwick-Stanley
General Governor	1953	Stanley-Ted Dalton (R)
General President	1956	Stevenson-Eisenhower
General Governor	1957	Almond-Ted Dalton (R)
General President	1960	Kennedy-Nixon
General Governor	1961	Harrison-H. Clyde Pearson (R)
General President	1964	Johnson-Goldwater
General Governor	1965	Godwin-Linwood Holton (R)
General Senate	1966	Byrd-Lawrence M. Traylor (R)
General Senate	1966	Spong-James P. Ould (R)
General President	1968	Humphrey-Nixon-Wallace
Primary Governor	1969	Battle-Howell-Pollard
Runoff Governor	1969	Battle-Howell
General Governor	1969	Battle-Linwood Holton (R)
General Senate	1970	Ray Garland (R)-Rawlings-Byrd (I)

NORFOLK   VIRGINIA
****

CANDIDATE	LOWER #	%	LOWER-MIDDLE #	%	UPPER-MIDDLE #	%	UPPER #	%	BLACK #	%	*	CANDIDATE	LOWER #	%	LOWER-MIDDLE #	%	UPPER-MIDDLE #	%	UPPER #	%	BLACK #	%
GENERAL PRESIDENT 1952											*	**PRIMARY GOVERNOR 1953**										
STEVENSON	1500	.75	1719	.43	518	.37	1107	.35	547	.84	*	STANLEY	220	.56	571	.59	292	.64	802	.61	164	.73
EISENHOWER	501	.25	2258	.57	879	.63	2015	.65	106	.16	*	FENWICK	171	.44	394	.41	165	.36	515	.39	62	.27
GENERAL GOVERNOR 1953											*	**GENERAL PRESIDENT 1956**										
STANLEY	326	.55	584	.42	388	.49	1356	.43	195	.52	*	STEVENSON	1160	.60	1138	.52	1302	.44	2433	.43	148	.22
DALTON	269	.45	800	.58	397	.51	1782	.57	179	.48	*	EISENHOWE	775	.40	1037	.48	1682	.56	3265	.57	515	.78
PRIMARY GOVERNOR 1957											*	**GENERAL GOVERNOR 1957**										
ALMOND	267	.54	800	.89	542	.86	1047	.87	22	.06	*	ALMOND	425	.68	2128	.78	1129	.73	2610	.69	21	.03
CARWILE	226	.46	94	.11	89	.14	156	.13	338	.94	*	DALTON	203	.32	607	.22	413	.27	1174	.31	667	.97
GENERAL SENATOR 1958											*	**GENERAL PRESIDENT 1960**										
BYRD	948	.97	1719	.98	1124	.97	1456	.99	17	.38	*	KENNEDY	1475	.70	2414	.55	1656	.57	3149	.50	608	.78
ROBB	25	.03	33	.02	38	.03	20	.01	28	.62	*	NIXON	620	.30	1936	.45	1258	.43	3212	.50	176	.22
WENSEL	0	.00	0	.00	0	.00	0	.00	0	.00	*		0	.00	0	.00	0	.00	0	.00	0	.00
PRIMARY GOVERNOR 1961											*	**PRIMARY LT-GOVNR 1961**										
HARRISON	955	.59	1209	.56	673	.62	1335	.63	44	.03	*	GODWIN	771	.49	1192	.56	594	.56	1257	.60	48	.04
STEPHENS	659	.41	954	.44	419	.38	785	.37	1243	.97	*	BOOTHE	809	.51	927	.44	475	.44	835	.40	1215	.96
GENERAL GOVERNOR 1961											*	**GENERAL PRESIDENT 1964**										
HARRISON	999	.81	1322	.71	667	.75	1284	.75	170	.25	*	JOHNSON	1638	.51	1879	.56	1412	.51	2756	.57	6859	.99
PEARSON	237	.19	544	.29	217	.25	422	.25	511	.75	*	GOLDWATER	1597	.49	1503	.44	1336	.49	2102	.43	75	.01
GENERAL GOVERNOR 1965											*	**PRIMARY SENATOR 1966**										
GODWIN	724	.60	775	.61	583	.54	5508	.87	1551	.74	*	BYRD	875	.47	830	.45	550	.36	1246	.39	42	.02
HOLTON	489	.40	486	.39	491	.46	828	.13	538	.26	*	BOOTHE	996	.53	1027	.55	958	.64	1909	.61	2521	.98
PRIMARY SENATOR 1966											*	**GENERAL SENATOR 1966**										
SPONG	818	.61	901	.51	946	.62	1540	.60	3911	.92	*	BYRD	655	.55	1207	.64	851	.56	1885	.62	178	.13
ROBERTSON	531	.39	850	.49	580	.38	1045	.40	342	.08	*	TRAYLOR	541	.45	606	.36	677	.44	1169	.38	1151	.87
GENERAL SENATOR 1966											*	**GENERAL PRESIDENT 1968**										
SPONG	1054	.66	1314	.67	1022	.64	2403	.72	3331	.98	*	HUMPHREY	1856	.58	1739	.34	991	.24	2484	.35	7385	.94
OULD	554	.34	652	.33	575	.36	916	.28	83	.02	*	NIXON	680	.21	1689	.33	1598	.39	3613	.51	434	.06
	0	.00	0	.00	0	.00	0	.00	0	.00	*	WALLACE	637	.20	1735	.34	1458	.36	1024	.14	37	.00
PRIMARY GOVERNOR 1969											*	**GENERAL GOVERNOR 1969**										
POLLARD	137	.11	243	.15	242	.14	569	.16	84	.03	*	BATTLE	964	.60	1357	.45	857	.42	2036	.46	2591	.80
HOWELL	776	.62	862	.52	878	.52	1441	.41	2565	.83	*	HOLTON	653	.40	1664	.55	1189	.58	2377	.54	644	.20
BATTLE	332	.27	552	.33	570	.34	1486	.43	443	.14	*		0	.00	0	.00	0	.00	0	.00	0	.00

```
                    GENERAL   PRESIDENT 1948              *                    GENERAL   PRESIDENT 1952
                    ****************************          *                    ****************************
TRUMAN      1156 .71  1330 .61  2614 .42  1210 .32   473 .77 * STEVENSON   1233 .44    901 .36  1475 .22   490 .16  1963 .88
DEWEY        412 .25   651 .30  2857 .46  2168 .56   133 .22 * EISENHOWE   1573 .56   1611 .64  5218 .78  2600 .84   256 .12
THURMOND      57 .04   201 .09   692 .11   461 .12     9 .01 *              0 .00      0 .00     0 .00     0 .00     0 .00

                    PRIMARY   GOVERNOR  1953              *                    GENERAL   GOVERNOR  1953
                    ****************************          *                    ****************************
FENWICK      349 .38   302 .33   650 .26   274 .20   212 .21 * STANLEY      627 .52    943 .56  2126 .49  1222 .57   760 .54
STANLEY      572 .62   625 .67  1864 .74  1080 .80   810 .79 * DALTON       571 .47    743 .44  2166 .50   907 .43   548 .39

                    GENERAL   PRESIDENT 1956              *                    PRIMARY   GOVERNOR  1957
                    ****************************          *                    ****************************
STEVENSON    828 .41   568 .34  1383 .25   403 .15   564 .25 * ALMOND       653 .92    596 .93  1717 .93   836 .96   323 .19
EISENHOWER  1182 .59  1126 .66  4178 .75  2337 .85  1686 .75 * CARWILE       54 .08     47 .07   127 .07    31 .04  1389 .81

                    GENERAL   GOVERNOR  1957              *                    GENERAL   PRESIDENT 1960
                    ****************************          *                    ****************************
ALMOND      1583 .86  1390 .86  3518 .75  1795 .78   574 .28 * KENNEDY     1086 .43    806 .37  1865 .26   642 .19  1538 .62
DALTON       265 .14   235 .14  1150 .25   512 .22  1487 .72 * NIXON       1469 .57   1354 .63  5339 .74  2756 .81   924 .38

                    PRIMARY   GOVERNOR  1961              *                    GENERAL   GOVERNOR  1961
                    ****************************          *                    ****************************
HARRISON     870 .72   846 .78  3467 .81  1969 .87   107 .06 * HARRISON     972 .80    970 .85  3501 .80  1409 .83   155 .10
STEPHENS     333 .28   245 .22   833 .19   307 .13  1801 .94 * PEARSON      236 .20    167 .15   875 .20   297 .17  1344 .90

                    GENERAL   PRESIDENT 1964              *                    GENERAL   SENATOR   1964
                    ****************************          *                    ****************************
JOHNSON     1212 .38   842 .33  2474 .29   795 .21  4967 .99 * BYRD        2852 .95   1383 .98  6670 .97  3233 .98   238 .07
GOLDWATER   1992 .62  1690 .67  6033 .71  3041 .79    38 .01 * RESPESS      135 .05     34 .02   211 .03    54 .02  3093 .93

                    GENERAL   GOVERNOR  1965              *                    PRIMARY   SENATOR   1966
                    ****************************          *                    ****************************
GODWIN       646 .42   649 .45  2413 .44  1229 .44  1632 .81 * BYRD         841 .70    862 .73  3415 .74  2019 .83    52 .02
HOLTON       311 .20   410 .28  1972 .36   976 .35   359 .18 * BOOTHE       357 .30    315 .27  1214 .26   412 .17  2334 .98
STORY        578 .38   390 .27  1078 .20   571 .21    22 .01 *              0 .00      0 .00     0 .00     0 .00     0 .00

                    PRIMARY   SENATOR   1966              *                    GENERAL   SENATOR   1966
                    ****************************          *                    ****************************
SPONG        367 .31   329 .28  1342 .29   472 .19  2268 .95 * BYRD        1067 .54   1029 .55  4345 .55  2182 .57   130 .04
ROBERTSON    824 .69   841 .72  3302 .71  1963 .81   114 .05 * TRAYLOR      925 .46    852 .45  3492 .45  1651 .43  2903 .96

                    GENERAL   PRESIDENT 1968              *                    PRIMARY   GOVERNOR  1969
                    ****************************          *                    ****************************
HUMPHREY     879 .20   675 .26  1815 .20   446 .12  4497 .98 * BATTLE       417 .31    430 .41  1925 .43   722 .38   289 .10
NIXON       1874 .43  1446 .55  6367 .71  2817 .78    69 .02 * HOWELL       645 .48    319 .27   406 .09   148 .08  2205 .79
WALLACE     1583 .37   501 .19   791 .09   340 .09     7 .00 * POLLARD      274 .21    372 .32  2128 .48  1040 .54   302 .11

                    PRIMARY   RUN-OFF   1969              *                    GENERAL   GOVERNOR  1969
                    ****************************          *                    ****************************
BATTLE       773 .40  1371 .79  3371 .83  1544 .88   174 .07 * BATTLE       708 .38    788 .42  2762 .39  1092 .36   969 .37
HOWELL      1178 .60   361 .21   699 .17   216 .12  2477 .93 * HOLTON      1153 .62   1089 .58  4282 .61  1929 .64  1682 .63

                    PRIMARY   SENATOR   1970              *                    GENERAL   SENATOR   1970
                    ****************************          *                    ****************************
DUVAL        115 .39    91 .52   419 .70   158 .76   369 .34 * GARLAND      158 .06    120 .06   410 .06   169 .07   169 .06
RAWLINGS     180 .61    85 .48   178 .30    49 .24   724 .66 * RAWLINGS     645 .26    299 .16   151 .02   151 .06  2687 .92
               0 .00     0 .00     0 .00     0 .00     0 .00 * BYRD        1664 .67   1492 .78  6232 .92  2247 .88    63 .02
```

ROANOKE VIRGINIA

		GENERAL PRESIDENT 1948			
TRUMAN	732 .57	585 .33	506 .28	334 .21	174 .65
DEWEY	508 .39	1032 .58	1071 .60	1023 .64	90 .33
THURMOND	55 .04	169 .09	206 .12	235 .15	5 .02
		GENERAL PRESIDENT 1952			
STEVENSON	1242 .47	410 .57	1310 .25	401 .17	983 .82
EISENHOWER	1405 .53	306 .43	3915 .75	2024 .83	218 .18
		GENERAL GOVERNOR 1953			
STANLEY	731 .43	181 .33	1481 .40	853 .46	251 .33
DALTON	987 .57	361 .67	2210 .60	996 .54	519 .67
		GENERAL GOVERNOR 1957			
ALMOND	1124 .67	387 .62	2778 .57	1257 .60	26 .02
DALTON	555 .33	240 .38	2066 .43	844 .40	1060 .98
		GENERAL GOVERNOR 1961			
HARRISON	708 .56	279 .49	2094 .50	1309 .61	64 .11
PEARSON	560 .44	285 .51	2078 .50	821 .39	493 .89
		GENERAL GOVERNOR 1965			
GODWIN	580 .48	264 .39	1588 .36	816 .30	398 .51
HOLTON	618 .52	414 .61	2811 .64	1876 .70	381 .49
		GENERAL SENATOR 1966			
SPONG	563 .49	329 .50	2173 .44	1106 .46	719 .93
OULD	594 .51	326 .50	2765 .56	1322 .54	50 .07
	0 .00	0 .00	0 .00	0 .00	0 .00
		PRIMARY GOVERNOR 1969			
BATTLE	164 .42	143 .44	900 .54	593 .58	60 .15
HOWELL	175 .45	153 .47	460 .28	105 .10	309 .80
POLLARD	47 .12	28 .09	309 .19	320 .31	19 .05
		GENERAL GOVERNOR 1969			
BATTLE	731 .48	563 .48	2858 .40	1164 .36	563 .61
HOLTON	805 .52	605 .52	4349 .60	2093 .64	363 .39
	0 .00	0 .00	0 .00	0 .00	0 .00

		PRIMARY SENATOR 1952			
BYRD	546 .39	111 .25	2258 .77	1460 .88	39 .05
MILLER	855 .61	328 .75	686 .23	199 .12	755 .95
	0 .00	0 .00	0 .00	0 .00	0 .00
		PRIMARY GOVERNOR 1953			
FENWICK	267 .44	74 .37	582 .34	233 .22	156 .51
STANLEY	343 .56	126 .63	1140 .66	843 .78	148 .49
		GENERAL PRESIDENT 1956			
STEVENSON	1063 .44	416 .48	1531 .24	468 .19	255 .21
EISENHOWE	1342 .56	447 .52	4867 .76	2054 .81	959 .79
		GENERAL PRESIDENT 1960			
KENNEDY	1056 .49	536 .55	2199 .31	681 .24	771 .68
NIXON	1103 .51	445 .45	4994 .69	2181 .76	359 .32
		GENERAL PRESIDENT 1964			
JOHNSON	1414 .58	856 .61	3668 .46	1022 .32	2101 ***
GOLDWATER	1034 .42	522 .39	4230 .54	2156 .68	10 .00
		GENERAL SENATOR 1966			
BYRD	630 .57	317 .51	2740 .57	1607 .66	109 .15
TRAYLOR	482 .43	299 .49	2108 .43	830 .34	619 .85
		GENERAL PRESIDENT 1968			
HUMPHREY	894 .31	336 .23	1949 .22	606 .16	1248 .97
NIXON	1284 .45	618 .42	5466 .61	2788 .75	38 .03
WALLACE	669 .23	524 .35	1486 .17	310 .08	2 .00
		PRIMARY RUN-OFF 1969			
BATTLE	208 .40	192 .47	1342 .63	1031 .87	50 .09
HOWELL	311 .60	217 .53	791 .37	159 .13	527 .91
	0 .00	0 .00	0 .00	0 .00	0 .00
		GENERAL SENATOR 1970			
GARLAND	203 .15	160 .18	1292 .21	462 .16	272 .34
RAWLINGS	323 .25	216 .24	863 .14	214 .07	514 .64
BYRD	786 .60	515 .58	3963 .65	2287 .77	19 .02